Mergers and Acquisitions

ASPEN CASEBOOK SERIES

Mergers and Acquisitions Cases, Materials, and Problems

Third Edition

Therese H. Maynard
Professor of Law and Leo J. O'Brien Fellow
Loyola Law School, Los Angeles

Wolters Kluwer
Law & Business

Copyright © 2013 CCH Incorporated.

Published by Wolters Kluwer Law & Business in New York.

Wolters Kluwer Law & Business serves customers worldwide with CCH, Aspen Publishers, and Kluwer Law International products. (www.wolterskluwerlb.com)

No part of this publication may be reproduced or transmitted in any form or by any means, electronic or mechanical, including photocopy, recording, or utilized by any information storage or retrieval system, without written permission from the publisher. For information about permissions or to request permissions online, visit us at www.wolterskluwerlb.com, or a written request may be faxed to our permissions department at 212-771-0803.

To contact Customer Service, e-mail customer.service@wolterskluwer.com, call 1-800-234-1660, fax 1-800-901-9075, or mail correspondence to:

> Wolters Kluwer Law & Business
> Attn: Order Department
> PO Box 990
> Frederick, MD 21705

Printed in the United States of America.

1 2 3 4 5 6 7 8 9 0

ISBN 978-1-4548-2502-9

Library of Congress Cataloging-in-Publication Data
Maynard, Therese H.
  Mergers and acquisitions : cases, materials, and problems / Therese H. Maynard, Professor of Law and Leo J. O'Brien Fellow Loyola Law School, Los Angeles.—Third edition.
      pages cm.
  Includes bibliographical references and index.
  ISBN 978-1-4548-2502-9 (casebound : alk. paper)
  1. Consolidation and merger of corporations—United States. I. Title.
  KF1477.M329 2013
  346.73'06626—dc23

                                           2013005742

SUSTAINABLE FORESTRY INITIATIVE

Certified Sourcing
www.sfiprogram.org
SFI-01234

SFI label applies to the text stock

About Wolters Kluwer Law & Business

Wolters Kluwer Law & Business is a leading global provider of intelligent information and digital solutions for legal and business professionals in key specialty areas, and respected educational resources for professors and law students. Wolters Kluwer Law & Business connects legal and business professionals as well as those in the education market with timely, specialized authoritative content and information-enabled solutions to support success through productivity, accuracy and mobility.

Serving customers worldwide, Wolters Kluwer Law & Business products include those under the Aspen Publishers, CCH, Kluwer Law International, Loislaw, Best Case, ftwilliam.com and MediRegs family of products.

CCH products have been a trusted resource since 1913, and are highly regarded resources for legal, securities, antitrust and trade regulation, government contracting, banking, pension, payroll, employment and labor, and healthcare reimbursement and compliance professionals.

Aspen Publishers products provide essential information to attorneys, business professionals and law students. Written by preeminent authorities, the product line offers analytical and practical information in a range of specialty practice areas from securities law and intellectual property to mergers and acquisitions and pension/benefits. Aspen's trusted legal education resources provide professors and students with high-quality, up-to-date and effective resources for successful instruction and study in all areas of the law.

Kluwer Law International products provide the global business community with reliable international legal information in English. Legal practitioners, corporate counsel and business executives around the world rely on Kluwer Law journals, looseleafs, books, and electronic products for comprehensive information in many areas of international legal practice.

Loislaw is a comprehensive online legal research product providing legal content to law firm practitioners of various specializations. Loislaw provides attorneys with the ability to quickly and efficiently find the necessary legal information they need, when and where they need it, by facilitating access to primary law as well as state-specific law, records, forms and treatises.

Best Case Solutions is the leading bankruptcy software product to the bankruptcy industry. It provides software and workflow tools to flawlessly streamline petition preparation and the electronic filing process, while timely incorporating ever-changing court requirements.

ftwilliam.com offers employee benefits professionals the highest quality plan documents (retirement, welfare and non-qualified) and government forms (5500/PBGC, 1099 and IRS) software at highly competitive prices.

MediRegs products provide integrated health care compliance content and software solutions for professionals in healthcare, higher education and life sciences, including professionals in accounting, law and consulting.

Wolters Kluwer Law & Business, a division of Wolters Kluwer, is headquartered in New York. Wolters Kluwer is a market-leading global information services company focused on professionals.

To my Mom and Dad, Anne and Bill Huber,
for always believing in me

and

to my four daughters, who are the source of all inspiration
in my life—Catherine, Hayley Del, Annie, and Remington

Summary of Contents

Contents

‖ 2 ‖

Corporate Formalities: The Mechanics of Structuring
Acquisition Transactions   49

‖ 3 ‖

Scope of Successor Liability: Transferring the Assets (and Liabilities) of Target Co. to Bidder Co.   219

|| 4 ||

Selected Federal Securities Law Provisions that Apply to Negotiated Business Combinations   251

|| 5 ||

Negotiating and Documenting the Transaction   293

▌▌ 6 ▌▌

Federal Regulation of Stock Purchases: Tender Offers and the Williams Act — 399

▌ 7 ▌

Fiduciary Duty Law: The Responsibilities of Boards of Directors, Senior Executive Officers, and Controlling Shareholders 481

▌ 8 ▌

Tax, Accounting, and Antitrust Considerations Related to Mergers and Acquisition Transactions   845

Appendices:

Preface

The third edition of this casebook was written in the wake of the meltdown within the financial industry and the ensuing Great Recession. These events have only served to intensify interest in, and attention on, the topic of this book: the *law of mergers and acquisitions*. While in the past, this subject may not have been offered on a regular basis, law schools today are facing increasing pressure to provide comprehensive treatment of this important area of modern corporate transactional law practice. Recognizing the increasing importance of this subject within the modern law school curriculum, this casebook is designed to meet the needs of the upper-division law student who seeks to master the basic principles that form the framework of the ever-evolving body of law related to mergers and acquisitions (M&A).

Toward that end, the third edition of this casebook continues to be organized based on the fundamental precept that the law student who takes this course is curious about this subject, but generally has limited familiarity with the business world of mergers and acquisitions. Therefore, the third edition of this casebook carries forward the essential goal of the earlier editions, which is to introduce the topics traditionally covered in the study of M&A law in terms that are accessible to the uninitiated law student, and further, to stimulate the student's curiosity in this subject by demystifying what is often an intimidating and overwhelmingly jargon-laden body of law. As such, this third edition continues to eschew string citations to the ever-growing body of literature in this area of the law, in favor of a more accessible style that breaks the law of mergers and acquisitions down into manageable chunks. In both the selection and editing of the cases and other materials to be included in this edition of this casebook, the guiding principle has been to present the material in a manner that will enable the law student to master the fundamental principles of M&A and to appreciate the public policies that underlie this legal framework.

The other, closely related objective of my casebook is to present the relevant legal principles of mergers and acquisitions in a manner that will allow law students to hit the ground running when they graduate and enter the practice of business law, which I presume will include M&A transactions. To this end, the third edition of this casebook continues to be designed so that the law student will appreciate the inherent dynamics of M&A transactions and will be able to become an effective junior member of a law firm whose practice includes representing businesses involved in M&A transactions. As part of this effort, this casebook endeavors to instill in the law student a sense of what it takes to be a good business lawyer in the modern practice of law in a transactional setting.[1]

A big part of the modern practice of business law involves analyzing statutes and advising business clients about how to structure their business and financial affairs in order to comply with the mandate of the relevant statute(s). As was the case when I wrote the earlier editions, I (regrettably) continue to believe that, for many law students today, their law school education does not provide them with rigorous and systematic exposure to statutory analysis. This casebook attempts to address this void, primarily by requiring students to analyze problems in light of the relevant state and/or federal statutes. In particular, the problems in Chapter 2, which I consider to be the very heart of the casebook, require the students to work through the terms of various statutes in order to understand what must be done in order to validly consummate the transaction and also to understand why the law imposes these requirements. In so doing, the law student will develop a framework for understanding the materials to be covered in *all* of the remaining chapters, as well as a perspective that allows the student to better appreciate how to *integrate* all of these materials as part of planning an M&A transaction.

Along these same lines, another common complaint (made, most often in my experience, by experienced lawyers who work with recent law school graduates) is that students fail to appreciate the important role that statutes play in the modern practice of business law. The most common complaint is that today's law students tend to view statutes as prescriptive, whose literal terms are to be mechanically complicd with — almost like following the steps in a recipe. As a result, students often fail to appreciate that literal or strict compliance with statutory requirements may yield a harsh or anomalous result. In these cases, students are ill equipped to analyze the proper course in order to avoid inequitable results. Like the first and second editions, the problems and other materials in this edition of my casebook are designed to fill in this gap. Most importantly, I require my students to buy a statutory supplement that includes relevant provisions of the Delaware and California corporations codes as well as the full text of the ABA's Model Business Corporation Act (along with selected provisions of the federal securities laws that are relevant to M&A transactions). Like the earlier editions, the third edition includes numerous problems that require the students to work through the various requirements imposed by these statutes. In the process, students analyze the differences (if any) in the results obtained under these statutes. Where there are differences, the materials in the casebook are designed to promote class discussion that explores the public policy premise(s) that lead the legislature (or other state or federal regulators, as the case may be) to opt for a particular statutory treatment.

For all of these reasons, the third edition continues to be reflective of the modern practice of M&A law, both from a transactional perspective as well as from the litigator's perspective. Like many other areas of business law, M&A law comes from the courts, legislatures, regulatory agencies, and the ever-changing

---

1. As for my understanding of the qualities that I consider important to being a good business lawyer, *see* Therese Maynard, *Teaching Professionalism: The Lawyer as a Professional,* 34 GEORGIA LAW REVIEW 895, 909-920 (2000).

practices of the modern business world. While the book includes many cases, the third edition of this casebook continues to be designed for use in conjunction with a supplemental text that includes the statutes and regulations. The cases included in the casebook then serve to illustrate how the judges endeavor to interpret (and apply) the statutes and regulations to further shape our understanding of M&A law.

In addition to a heavy emphasis on the use of problems to illustrate the planning of modern M&A transactions, this third edition also incorporates a heavy emphasis on the following themes in its presentation of the law of mergers and acquisitions. First, unlike the focus of many other casebooks dealing with mergers and acquisitions, the third edition of this casebook continues to emphasize the role of the lawyer as transaction planner. Second, as part of this focus on transaction planning, my casebook emphasizes the increasing importance of fiduciary duty law over the past twenty-five years and its all-important role in guiding the transaction planner in structuring M&A deals. Starting with the problems in Chapter 2 and continuing throughout the remaining chapters, as part of our analysis of the role of fiduciary duty law in M&A deals, this casebook is constantly asking the law student to consider the corporate governance implications of M&A transactions. Most notably, the third edition asks the students to critically assess the relative balance of power among the shareholders, the board of directors, and the senior executive officers—most importantly, the role of the modern chief executive officer— a balance that has been sorely tested in the years since the first edition was published. Indeed, Chapter 7 of the third edition (dealing with fiduciary duty obligations) was expanded considerably to address corporate governance concerns that have emerged in the wake of the Great Recession, as well as to include a new unit on "going private" transactions.

Finally, and most importantly, these themes are developed in the context of M&A activity that occurs on *both* Wall Street *and* on Main Street. That is to say, this book emphasizes not only the type of high-profile M&A transactions that the law student is likely to read about on the front pages of the Wall Street Journal, but also provides comprehensive treatment of the sale of a closely held business, the type of transaction that continues to form the basis of M&A practice for many of today's transactional lawyers.

As was the case with the earlier editions, the general convention followed in this edition is to omit case and statute citations from the principal cases as well as quoted excerpts from other materials. In addition, most footnotes have been omitted without indication in the original case or other text, but those footnotes that remain do retain their original numbering.

December 2012

Therese H. Maynard
Loyola Law School,
Los Angeles, California

Acknowledgments

I am indebted to many persons for helping me give birth to this labor of love. This project never would have been conceived without many generations of my students who impressed on me the need to write a casebook that facilitated the law student's ability to understand and master the law of mergers and acquisitions. To those many students of mine at Loyola Law School who suffered through various iterations of teaching materials as I worked my way through various drafts of this casebook to produce the first edition and to those who suffered through the various ideas that I experimented with in writing both the second edition and third editions, I am eternally grateful for your patience, understanding and feedback. This project is truly the better for having the benefit of your suggestions and guidance.

This book was inspired not only by my students and others in the academy, but also by the many fine business lawyers who practice in the area of M&A law. While there are many who gave me the benefit of their sage counsel over the years, there are several who were instrumental in guiding me toward the goal of educating the law student to be prepared to hit the ground running on graduating law school and embarking on the practice of M&A law. I am particularly grateful to Greg Noell, Mark Bonenfant, Keith Bishop, Jennifer Guzee, Jeff Sklar, and most importantly, my husband, Philip Maynard, who is the best corporate lawyer I know.

Over the years, many research assistants have made valuable contributions to the development and refinement of this casebook, which I consider to still be a "work-in-progress." I want to express particular thanks to Alex Shukman, Ann Carey Camacho, Gregory Ezor, Arif Sikora, April Ho and Clint Stiffler for their invaluable help in writing the first and second editions. With respect to this third edition, words can never express my appreciation and gratitude for the extraordinary efforts of my research assistant, Sean Montgomery. His research and editorial contributions to the third edition were extremely valuable.

This casebook has required a lot of help, but a special word of appreciation goes out to my administrative assistants, Ruth Busch and Elisa Gonzalez, without whose friendship, unfailing support, and amazing secretarial skills this project never would have come to fruition. Finally, I had invaluable support at Aspen Publishers from Lynn Churchill, Darren Kelly, and Lisa Connery (and, I am sure, many others unknown to me).

I also want to gratefully acknowledge the permission of the following publishers, authors, and periodicals to reprint excerpts from their publications:

Afsharipour, Afra, *Transforming the Allocation of Deal Risk Through Reverse Termination Fees*, 63 Vand. L. Rev. 1161 (2010). Reprinted with author's permission.

American Bar Association's Subcommittee on Federal Regulation of Securities of the Securities Regulation Committee of the Business Law Section, *Annual Review of Federal Securities Regulation: Significant 1999 Legislative and Regulatory Developments*, 55 Bus. Law. 1505 (2000). © Copyright 2000 by the American Bar Association. Reprinted with permission. This information or any or portion thereof may not be copied or disseminated in any form or by any means or stored in an electronic database or retrieval system without the express written consent of the American Bar Association.

American Bar Association's Committee on Corporate Laws, ABA Section of Business Law, *Changes in the MBCA*, 65 Bus. Law. 1121, 1138 (2010). © Copyright 2010 by the American Bar Association. Reprinted with permission. This information or any or portion thereof may not be copied or disseminated in any form or by any means or stored in an electronic database or retrieval system without the express written consent of the American Bar Association.

Bainbridge, Stephen M., *Exclusive Merger Agreements and Lock-Ups in Negotiated Corporate Acquisitions*, 75 Minn. L. Rev. 239, 241-243 (1990). Copyright © 1990. Reprinted with author's permission.

Bishop, Gregory, *Changed Circumstances or Buyer's Remorse?* Published in Business Law Today, Volume 11, Number 4, March/April 2002. © Copyright 2002 by the American Bar Association. Reprinted with permission. This information or any or portion thereof may not be copied or disseminated in any form or by any means or stored in an electronic database or retrieval system without the express written consent of the American Bar Association.

Bishop, Keith Paul, *The War Between the States—Delaware's Supreme Court Ignores California's "Outreach" Statute.* Copyright © 2005 Wolters Kluwer. All Rights Reserved. Reprinted from Insights July 2005, Volume 19, with permission from Wolters Kluwer.

Blomberg, Jeffrey, *Private Equity Transactions: Understanding Some Fundamental Principles*, published in Business Law Today, Volume 17, Number 3, January/February 2008. © Copyright 2008 by the American Bar Association. Reprinted with permission. This information or any or portion thereof may not be copied or disseminated in any form or by any means or stored in an electronic database or retrieval system without the express written consent of the American Bar Association.

Borgogni, Lorenzo and James J. Moloney, *Resales of Stock Acquired in Merger Transactions.* © Copyright 2003 Wolters Kluwer. All Rights Reserved. Reprinted from Insights February 2003, Volume 16-17, with permission from Wolters Kluwer.

Bryd, Francis H., *Dual Class Share Structures: The Next Campaign*, Harvard Law School Forum on Corporate Governance and Financial Regulation (Sep. 16, 2012 10:18 AM), http://blogs.law.harvard.edu/corpgov/2012/09/16/dual-class-share-structures-the-next-campaign/. Reprinted with author's permission.

Campbell, Rutherford B., Jr., *Fair Value at Fair Price in Corporate Acquisitions*, 78 N.C.L. Rev. 101, 110-11 (1999). Copyright © 1999. Reprinted with permission of North Carolina Law Review, vol. 78, pp. 110-111.

Campbell, Rutherford B., *The Impact of Modern Finance Theory in Acquisition Cases*, 53 Syracuse L. Rev. 1, 2-3, 5-6, 9-11, 14-16 (2003). Copyright © 2003. Reprinted with permission of Syracuse Law Review.

Cowles, Julia, Julie Ryan, and Charles Ortmeyer, *Selected 2011 Developments in Corporate Law*, 2012 Annual Review, State Bar of California, Business Law News, 7, 9-10. Reprinted with authors' permission.

Emmerich, Adam O., Theodore Mirvis, et. al., *Fair Markets and Fair Disclosure: Some Thoughts on the Law and Economics of Blockholder Disclosure, and the Use and Abuse of Shareholder Power*, 3 Harv. Bus. L. Rev. (forthcoming 2013). Columbia Law & Econ., Working Paper No. 428, 2012, available at http://ssrn.com/abstract=2138945. Reprinted with authors' permission.

Gilson, Ronald J., Unocal *Fifteen Years Later (and What We Can Do About It)*, 26 Del. J. Corp. L. 491-492, 513 (2001). Copyright © Delaware Journal of Corporation Law 2001. Reprinted with permission.

Grant, M. Duncan and Phillip T. Mellett, *Delaware Supreme Court Upholds Caremark Standard for Director Oversight Liability; Clarifies Duty of Good Faith*. Originally published in Pepper Hamilton LLP law firm memo, dated November 21, 2006. Reprinted with authors' permission.

Grinberg, David and Gordon Bava, *A Comeback for Tender Offers?* Mergers and Acquisitions 73-77 (March 2007). Reprinted with permission of Source Media.

Hamilton, Robert and Richard Booth, BUSINESS BASICS FOR LAW STUDENTS 172-73 (4th ed. 2006). Copyright © 2006 CCH Incorporated, reprinted with permission of Wolters Kluwer Law & Business.

Hu, Henry T.C. and Bernard Black, *Empty Voting and Hidden (Morphable) Ownership: Taxonomy, Implications, and Reforms*, 61 Bus. Law. 1011 (2006). © Copyright 2006 by the American Bar Association. Reprinted with permission. This information or any or portion thereof may not be copied or disseminated in any form or by any means or stored in an electronic database or retrieval system without the express written consent of the American Bar Association.

Kim, Suneela, et al., *Examining Data Points in Minority Buy-Outs: A Practitioners' Report*, 36 Del J. Corp. Law 939, 940-46 (2011). Copyright © Delaware Journal of Corporation Law. Reprinted with permission.

Kirkland & Ellis, LLP, *M&A Update: Break-Up Fees – Picking Your Number* (law firm memo, Sept. 6, 2012). Reprinted with permission.

Klein, Spencer D. & Michael G. O'Bryan, Partners, Morrison & Foerster, LLP, *Recent Cases Remind M&A Participants of When Disclosure of Merger Negotiations is Required* (law firm memo, July 14, 2010). Reprinted with authors' permission.

Lehot, Louis, et. al. *The Return of the Poison Pill – Lessons Learned in 2010 From the* Selectica *and* Barnes & Noble *Cases.* Copyright © 2010 Wolters Kluwer. All Rights Reserved. Reprinted from Insights December 2010, Volume 24, with permission from Wolters Kluwer.

Manne, Henry, Mergers and the Market for Corporate Control, 73 Journal of Political Economy 110, 112-113 (1965). Originally published in 73 Journal of Political Economy 110 (University of Chicago Press, 1965).

Mirvis, Theodore N., et. al., Wachtell, Lipton, Rosen & Katz, LLP, *Buyout and Deal Protections Enjoined Due to Conflicted Advisor to Clients* (law firm memo, Feb. 15, 2011). Reprinted with authors' permission.

Muller, Kenneth, Andrew Thorpe, Sean Byrne and Seth Chertole, *A Revised Net Worth Standard for Accredited Investors.* Copyright © 2011 Wolters Kluwer. All Rights Reserved. Reprinted from Insights March 2011, Volume 25, with permission from Wolters Kluwer.

Nixon Peabody, *2012 MAC Survey.* Reprinted with permission.

Pell, Owen and Paul Carberry, Partners, White & Case, LLP, *Delaware Court Interprets Material Adverse Effect Clause to Bar Hexion and Apollo from Abandoning Huntsman Deal,* (law firm memo, October 2008). Copyright © White & Case, LLP 2008. Reprinted with permission.

Silk, David, and David Katz, *Takeover Law and Practice* (PLI Program, Doing Deals 2003 at 327-329). Copyright © 2003 by David Silk and David Katz. Reprinted with permission of the authors.

Small, Marshall L., *Corporate Combinations under the New California General Corporation Law,* 23 UCLA L. Rev. 1190, 1190-1193 (1976). Originally published in 23 UCLA L. Rev. 1190 (1976).

Strine, Jr., Leo E., *One Fundamental Corporate Governance Question We Face: Can Corporations Be Managed for the Long Term Unless Their Power Electorates Also Act and Think Long Term?* 66 Bus. Law. 1, 19 (2010). © Copyright 2010 by the American Bar Association. Reprinted with permission. This information or any or portion thereof may not be copied or disseminated in any form or by any means or stored in an electronic database or retrieval system without the express written consent of the American Bar Association.

Subramanian, Guhan, *Go-Shops vs. No-Shops in Private Equity Deals: Evidence and Implications,* 63 Bus. Law. 729, 730 (2008). © Copyright 2008 by the American Bar Association. Reprinted with permission. This information or any or portion thereof may not be copied or disseminated in any form or by any means or stored in an electronic database or retrieval system without the express written consent of the American Bar Association.

Sullivan & Cromwell, LLP, *The JOBS Act – "General Solicitation" in Private Offerings* (law firm memo, Aug. 30, 2012). Copyright © Sullivan & Cromwell LLP 2012. Reprinted with permission.

Wachtell Lipton Rosen & Katz, *M&A in 2012.* Copyright © Wachtell, Lipton, Rosen & Katz 2012. Reprinted with permission.

Wachtell, Lipton, Rosen & Katz, *The Share Purchase Rights Plan* (1996). Copyright © Wachtell, Lipton, Rosen & Katz 1996. Reprinted with permission.

Wertheimer, Barry M., *The Purpose of the Shareholders' Appraisal Remedy*, 65 Tenn. L. Rev. 661, 662-664 (1998). Copyright © 1998 by Tennessee Law Review Association, Inc. Excerpt reprinted with permission of the Tennessee Law Review Association.

Wertheimer, Barry M., *The Shareholders' Appraisal Remedy and How Courts Determine Fair Value*, 1998 Duke L.J. 613, 616-617, 626-632, 643-645, 696-701. Copyright © 1998 by the Duke Law Journal. Reprinted with the permission of the Duke Law Journal.

Mergers and Acquisitions

‖ 1 ‖

Introduction to Business Acquisitions

A.   *What Business Activity Is Covered by M&A Law?*

Mergers and acquisitions (M&A) law is *not* a discrete body of law. Rather, M&A law refers to a particular kind of business activity whereby one business decides to take control of—that is, to purchase, to acquire—the income-producing operations of some other business entity. Hence, M&A is largely about combining previously independent, freestanding businesses into one business organization.

For reasons that are described in more detail in Chapter 2 regarding *interspecies mergers*, this casebook will generally assume that the two businesses that decide to combine together are organized as corporations, although business combinations involving other types of business entities (such as combining two limited liability companies) are also possible. In order to keep things simple and allow us to master the basic principles, our study of M&A law will generally be limited to business combinations involving corporations organized under modern state corporation codes.

In the terminology of these modern corporation codes, the companies that plan to combine are usually referred to as the *constituent corporations*. As we shall see, typically one of these constituent corporations plans to acquire control over the business operations of the other when the transaction is consummated. In our study of these transactions, we will usually refer to the acquiring corporation as the Bidder Company (Bidder Co. or Bidder), and the corporation to be acquired will generally be referred to as the Target Company (Target Co. or Target).

M&A is an important recurring part of the business world. Although each deal is unique, there are certain kinds of business combinations that are staples in the daily work of lawyers who practice M&A law. In order to give you a sense of the range of the deals that we will analyze in our study of M&A law, as well as a sense of the problems that M&A lawyers are asked to address in their daily practice, the next section tells the story of two deals that grabbed headlines in the financial press.

As we go through the materials in the following chapters, we will return to analyze the various legal issues raised by these acquisition transactions. These two stories are important because, for the most part, they include facts that raise the legal issues that we will study in the remaining chapters. These stories provide a real-world anchor in which to address the more abstract principles and legal rules that are the core focus of this casebook. These stories also reflect the time frame that is inherent in doing any M&A deal. The reason that this time frame has grown to be the convention in M&A deals will only become apparent as we address the topics in the remaining chapters. The legal rules and doctrines we will study have clearly shaped the process of—and timetable for—doing the deals that are described in these two stories, a point that can truly be appreciated only at the end of our study of M&A law.

B. *Two Different Stories—Two Different Deals*

1. The Story of Pfizer Corporation's Acquisition of Pharmacia, Inc.

In what turned out to be the largest deal of its kind in calendar year 2002, Pfizer Inc. acquired Pharmacia Corp. The deal was announced in July 2002 and was completed in March 2003. When announced in July 2002, the deal was valued at $60 billion, with Pharmacia shareholders to receive 1.4 shares of Pfizer stock for each share of Pharmacia stock they owned. *See* WALL STREET JOURNAL, July 15, 2002 at A1. This exchange ratio represented a 36 percent premium over the then-trading price of Pharmacia's common stock. The size of the acquisition would capture public attention in any environment, but it was all the more striking given the turmoil of the summer of 2002. At the time, Congress was still putting the final touches on major reform legislation, which came to be known as the Sarbanes-Oxley Act. Moreover, the capital markets were still reeling from a rash of accounting scandals that had significantly dampened activity in the M&A market.

Pfizer's acquisition of Pharmacia was all the more striking because it was reminiscent of the type of bold transformational transaction that came to symbolize M&A activity during the 1990s, as typified by the high-profile merger of AOL-Time-Warner in 2000, a business combination that has since engendered harsh investor criticism. Shareholder criticism of the AOL-Time-Warner deal has centered primarily on investor disappointment in the dismal financial performance of the entertainment behemoth following this mega-merger. Consequently, shareholders of all corporations have since taken a more probing, critical view of managers' decisions to grow the company's business through acquisitions, a fact of life that was not lost on the corporate managers who proposed the merger of Pfizer and Pharmacia.

Given the turmoil that prevailed in the capital markets at the time, why would Pfizer proceed with such an ambitious, large-scale acquisition? The press release accompanying the deal indicated that the goal of the merger was to create a global powerhouse in the pharmaceutical industry. Not the least among the strategic business incentives that formed the basis for Pfizer's offer for Pharmacia was Celebrex, the blockbuster arthritis drug that represented the crown jewel of Pharmacia's business. Indeed, Celebrex was widely regarded as key to the financial turnaround of Pharmacia under the leadership of its chief executive officer (CEO), Fred Hassan. Since taking the helm of Pharmacia in 1997, Hassan was widely credited with engineering a dramatic financial turn-around, making good on his promise to build Pharmacia into a world leader in the pharmaceutical industry. As for Pharmacia's business decision to sell itself to Pfizer, the CEO of Pharmacia claimed that merging with Pfizer presented Pharmacia and its shareholders with the opportunity to participate in a fast-growing company that should have the resources to bring new pharmaceutical products to the market quickly.

As originally structured, Hassan, Pharmacia's CEO, was to become vice-chairman of Pfizer, the surviving company, and a member of Pfizer's board of directors, the only Pharmacia board member to sit on Pfizer's board. Henry McKinnell, the CEO of Pfizer, was to become the CEO and chairman of the board of directors of the combined firm. Although the proposed deal was widely touted by the companies' respective CEOs, the announcement that Hassan was to become vice-chairman of the combined firm took many by surprise, as it meant that Hassan had agreed to relinquish control over his company to Pfizer's Henry McKinnell. As it turned out, however, Hassan's tenure as vice-chairman of the combined business was quite short-lived. Soon after the Pfizer-Pharmacia merger was consummated in March 2003, Hassan announced that he would be leaving Pfizer to take the top job at Schering-Plough Corp., another pharmaceutical company.

Once the deal was consummated, Pfizer's shareholders ended up holding approximately 77 percent of the combined company. Pharmacia's shareholders owned the remaining 23 percent of Pfizer's outstanding common stock. There was some concern as to the market's reaction to the public announcement of this mega-deal, the first of its kind in the more difficult M&A climate that prevailed for most of 2002. Although widely viewed among industry experts as a good strategic fit, it was not clear how investors would react to the announce-ment of such a large deal.

As originally contemplated, the acquisition was expected to close by Decem-ber 31, 2002, subject to obtaining approval from antitrust regulators and the shareholders of both companies. As it turned out, the shareholders of both companies approved the deal at their respective special meetings in December 2002. Nonetheless, the deal did not close until March 2003.

As reported at the time the deal was announced, many observers thought the Pfizer-Pharmacia combination was likely to receive tough scrutiny by anti-trust regulators. Many speculated that the deal would be reviewed by the Fed-eral Trade Commission (FTC) rather than the Justice Department because of that agency's experience and expertise in the area of mergers within the drug industry. Some observers went so far as to predict that the antitrust regulators were likely to engage in a market-by-market investigation of the two companies. These same observers cautioned that such analysis could result in requiring divestitures in those areas where the FTC concluded that the two companies have a combined dominant market share. Other observers, however, anticipated that the deal would encounter minimal antitrust problems, primarily because the two companies had few overlapping products. These observers predicted that Pfizer's global share of total pharmaceutical sales—currently estimated to be about 8 percent—would rise to only approximately 11 percent of global sales once the acquisition was completed, thereby lessening the regulators' concern and allowing the merger to be completed without any divestitures.

The two CEOs who orchestrated this $60 billion deal were certainly not strangers to the world of M&A activity. McKinnell, who joined Pfizer in 1971, was widely credited with executing Pfizer's hostile takeover of Warner-Lambert, an acquisition that continues to be regarded as one of the success stories to emerge from the "go-go" years of M&A activity that prevailed in the late 1990s. In May 2000, following the Warner-Lambert acquisition, Pfizer took over the number one ranking among pharmaceuticals makers. Once the acquisition closed, Pfizer moved swiftly to cut operations and staff within Warner-Lambert in order to integrate the business operations of the two companies. Indeed, as but one measure of Pfizer's successful integration of Warner-Lambert's business operations and product sales, drug sales were higher across the board for the combined companies than when they were separate. This quick and successful integration of Warner-Lambert certainly enhanced the reputation of Pfizer's management team and ultimately led to McKinnell being appointed CEO of Pfizer in January 2001, thereby cementing his reputation as a visionary executive in the pharmaceutical industry. His success is particularly noteworthy given the dismal failures of other recent business combinations in the drug industry, such as Bristol-Myers Squibb Co. and GlaxoSmithKline PLC. Both of these companies failed to thrive following their respective business combinations, leading many investors to disfavor such mergers as a business strategy.

Like McKinnell, Hassan was no stranger to deal making. In the late 1990s, as CEO of Pharmacia, he orchestrated the acquisition of Monsanto, Inc. It was in this merger with Monsanto that Pharmacia acquired the celebrated arthritis drug, Celebrex, which substantially contributed to the financial success of Pharmacia. In fact, when Hassan took over as CEO of Pharmacia in 1997, following a long stint at American Home Products Corp. (now Wyeth), the company was widely regarded as floundering. Hassan immediately moved to restructure Pharmacia's business, easing out executives, consolidating its far-flung business operations, and streamlining its product lines and drug development. With the sale of his company to Pfizer, Hassan cemented his reputation as a successful turnaround artist within the drug industry.

Even before the decision to sell its business to Pfizer, Pharmacia had publicly announced its intention to divest the 83 percent stake it still owned in Monsanto, following the 1999 merger of the two companies. The terms of Pfizer's acquisition of Pharmacia contemplated that Pharmacia would complete the divestiture of Monsanto to Pharmacia's shareholders before Pfizer closed on its acquisition of Pharmacia.

Given the extraordinary success of these two CEOs, what would prompt them to agree to combine their two companies into a single business, especially from the perspective of Hassan, who would be relinquishing the helm of the ship to a competitor in the industry, McKinnell, the CEO of Pfizer? According to press reports, each had his own separate and—as is usually the case in business acquisitions—highly individualized set of concerns. In the case of

Pharmacia, from the seller's perspective, the offer from Pfizer provided the company with the opportunity to grow its business quickly, thereby allowing it to compete more effectively in the global marketplace. From Pfizer's perspective, the acquisition of Pharmacia presented the opportunity to acquire a strong drug company with a sizable stable of premier drugs capable of producing billions in sales revenue to augment Pfizer's already impressive product lineup. Just as important from Pfizer's perspective, the deal allowed Pfizer to obtain the talent and leadership of Pharmacia's CEO, Fred Hassan—human capital that is very hard to come by. On the financial side, the deal was expected to allow the new Pfizer to cut costs substantially—perhaps as much as $1.4 billion in 2003 alone—thereby creating some breathing room to facilitate the company's efforts to develop new drugs.

As it turned out, however, Pfizer's acquisition of Pharmacia did not yield the positive returns that Pfizer had anticipated. One of the primary business incentives for the Pfizer-Pharmacia business combination was to allow Pfizer to take advantage of Pharmacia's profitable pain reliever, Celebrex. However, just a year after the merger was announced, a competing product was pulled from the market for safety reasons. As a result of the growing fear among consumers regarding the safety of other pain-relieving drugs, Pfizer saw sales of Celebrex sharply decline, leading many analysts to criticize Pfizer's purchase of Pharmacia. Not surprisingly, these developments led to a significant financial decline in Pfizer stock. Furthermore, much to the chagrin of pharmaceutical industry professionals, the deal was accompanied by severe cost-cutting measures, including employee layoffs and factory closures. These developments ultimately led to the departure of Hank McKinnell, one of the masterminds behind the Pfizer-Pharmacia deal, who formally resigned as CEO of Pfizer in 2006. His departure was fueled, in large part, by the company's lackluster revenue growth and 40 percent stock price decline since the consummation of the mega-merger with Pharmacia. Investors were further angered by McKinnell's "generous" $180 million retirement package, which included $82.3 million in pension benefits, $77.9 million in deferred compensation, and $20.9 million in cash and stock. Fearful of having to make a similar payment to the successor CEO, Jeffrey Kindler, the company negotiated an employment agreement with Kindler in which the new CEO's compensation was tied to the performance of Pfizer's stock price.

The deal between Pfizer and Pharmacia typifies the kind of mega-deal that top-tier Wall Street bankers specialize in, as it combines two large, well-known, widely followed, and publicly traded companies. This is the type of deal that is also sure to be closely followed by investors and the financial press. At the other end of the spectrum is the type of deal described in the next section, which reflects another very common but very different type of deal that M&A lawyers routinely work on for their corporate clients.

2.   The Story of Nestlé's Acquisition of Chef America, Inc.

In the fall of 2002, Nestlé SA, a Swiss-based (multinational) conglomerate, offered to buy Chef America, Inc., a closely held company based in Englewood, Colorado. Since Chef America was a privately held family business, little information was publicly available about its financial affairs and stock owner-ship. Moreover, Nestlé, a foreign company organized under Swiss law, was sub-ject to limited disclosure obligations under U.S. law. Piecing together details from press coverage of Nestlé's announcement of its intent to acquire Chef America (based primarily on articles published in the *Wall Street Journal*), a plausible story of Nestlé's acquisition of Chef America, Inc. would go something like this—admittedly embellished a little in order to fill in certain gaps in the reported coverage of the terms of the parties' deal.

Nestlé's acquisition of Chef America, Inc. marked the latest deal in a string of acquisitions that Nestlé had completed in the United States. Nestlé, the world's largest food company, had previously bought a 67 percent con-trolling stake in Dreyer's Grand Ice Cream, Inc. and took over full control of the U.S. operations of Häagen-Dazs, another premium ice cream brand. In addition, in 2000, Nestlé completed its $10.3 billion purchase of Ralston-Purina, Inc., thereby combining Ralston-Purina's popular Dog Chow brand with Nestlé's Friskies and Alpo brands. These previous acquisitions, along with Nestlé's decision to acquire Chef America's line of frozen sandwiches, was consistent with its announced restructuring of its business operations in order to refocus its efforts on certain core brands. *See* WALL STREET JOUR-NAL, August 6, 2002, at A3. Although not entirely clear from press accounts, we will assume that Nestlé paid cash for its $2.5 billion purchase of Chef America, Inc.

As for Chef America, Inc., it appears that this Colorado company was founded in the late 1970s by two brothers, one of whom, Paul Merage, con-tinued to serve as the company's CEO. The other brother, David Merage, was the company's chief operating officer (COO). Chef America was a well-known, family-owned business that made the best-selling frozen sandwiches sold under the label "Hot Pockets." In fact, sales of its Hot Pockets sandwiches alone were reported to be up 32 percent during the first six months of 2002, immediately prior to the announcement that negotiations were underway between Nestlé and Chef America. Moreover, in a continuing effort to capitalize on its exper-tise in the frozen food product area, Chef America had also introduced Quick Bakes, a new line of chicken-based frozen dinners. Quick Bakes had been mar-keted by the company exclusively in Wal-Mart Stores, Inc.'s discount warehouse chain of stores, Sam's Club. By combining with Nestlé, Chef America could achieve greater distribution of, and a much broader marketing base for, its products by accessing Nestlé's well-established, worldwide delivery and product distribution system.

Although we do not know much about the capital structure of Chef Amer-ica, we will assume that the founding brothers each owned one-half of the vot-ing common stock, giving each brother a 50 percent stake in the business. In addition, we will assume that Chef America had a two-person board, consist-ing of just the two brothers, a situation not uncommon in a family-owned and -operated business. The $2.5 billion all-cash purchase price to be paid by Nestlé represented a substantial premium for Chef America, whose sales topped $700 million for 2001 and were up approximately 18 percent for the first six months of 2002, immediately prior to the announcement that acquisition negotiations were underway between the two companies. *See* WALL STREET JOURNAL, August 6, 2002, at A3. Indeed, the purchase price illustrated the increased attractiveness of up-and-coming food businesses like Chef America to major players like Nestlé and the substantial premiums that the Nestlés of the world were willing to pay, a premium that presumably was to be divided between the two brothers as co-owners of the business. Moreover, this "fat premium" offered by Nestlé must have met with approval by the two shareholders of Chef America, unlike the result back in the late 1990s when they had previously put Chef America up for sale. Ultimately, the two brothers took their company off the auction block when they were apparently unable to obtain their asking price for Chef America's business.

On Nestlé's part, the acquisition of Chef America appears to have generated positive returns. By adding the successful "Hot Pocket" frozen food brand to its product line, Nestlé gained a competitive edge in the frozen food industry. Nestlé also continued its practice of "serial acquisitions" subsequent to its purchase of Chef America. Notably, in April 2007, Nestle agreed to acquire the Gerber baby food brand from the Swiss drugmaker Novartis for $5.5 billion in cash. *See* Hugo Miller & Eva Von Schaper, *Nestle Buys Gerber for $5.5 Billion,* April 12, 2007, WASHINGTON POST (Bloomberg News Link: http://www.bloomberg.com/apps/news?pid=newsarchive&sid=ax11ACn9U57s&refer=home). At the time, analysts generally applauded Nestlé's decision, which would give Nestle (still the world's biggest food company) 82 percent of the U.S. baby food market. Moreover, analysts welcomed the deal as it presented a "win-win situation [since] baby food isn't part of Novartis' core business and is a key part of Nestlé's [business operations]." *Id.* More recently, as part of its continuing business strategy of focusing on well-known consumer food brands, Nestle acquired Kraft Foods' frozen pizza business in 2010 for $3.7 billion in another all-cash deal. *See Nestle Pays $3.7 Billion for Kraft Pizzas, available at* http://www.industryweek.com/companies-amp-executives/nestle-pays-37-billion-kraft-pizzas.

3. Wall Street M&A *vs.* Main Street M&A.

Nestlé's acquisition of Chef America, Inc. grabbed headlines in the financial press, both because of the size of the deal (with its $2.5 billion purchase price) and the high profile of the acquiring company (the widely followed global firm Nestlé SA). It bears emphasizing, however, that many more closely held companies get acquired each year without garnering this kind of banner headline in the financial press. Some of these acquisitions are sizable deals, often involving purchase prices totaling several hundred million dollars, whereas many other deals involve the sale of very small, closely held firms with just a few owners (like Chef America, Inc.) but where the purchase price is much more modest. Such a deal—what is often referred to as *Main Street M&A*—is an important part of the daily practice of M&A law. Indeed, for many practicing lawyers, the purchase and sale of closely held businesses (often family-owned and -managed) are the very lifeblood of their practice. This book will address the planning considerations inherent in both types of deals—high-profile *Wall Street M&A* deals (such as Pfizer's acquisition of Pharmacia) and the generally much-less-publicized Main Street M&A deals.

If you have not already formed the habit, I would strongly encourage you to read the financial pages (the business section) of a newspaper on a daily basis. I make this recommendation for a number of reasons. First, M&A law is about *business* activity and many law students have no prior exposure to the real-world activity that is the focus of M&A law. In order to fully grasp why the law worries about regulating this set of business transactions, it is important to develop a sense as to what the business side of M&A activity is all about. Reading about current deals in your daily newspaper will help you to understand the rules and legal concepts that we will study in this course. In addition, M&A law, like most other areas of the law, is full of jargon peculiar to this area of business activity. I have found that one of the best ways to acquaint yourself with the lexicon of doing deals is to read about ongoing deals in the daily paper. In this way, you, the law student, will develop a better appreciation and understanding of the range of business activity that is addressed by M&A law.

Equally important, the law student who reads the daily business section will develop a fuller appreciation that doing deals is not stagnant; that the way deals get done continues to evolve as business practices change; and that business practices change as the economic environment for doing deals continues to shift—as we have seen most recently in the dramatic shift from the speculative "dot-com" bubble of the 1990s to the currently much more difficult environment in the wake of the recent Great Recession of 2008-2009, where deals frequently struggle to get done. Indeed, "Wall Street is a profoundly cyclical place that has a way of changing just as journalists try to pin it down. A mid-[1990s] bust in the . . . market [gave] way to a tech boom [peaking in the early 2000, to be] followed eventually by a real estate bubble [that led to the Great Recession of 2008-2009, from which the markets are continuing to struggle to bounce back]." Yvette Kantrow, *Goodbye to All That, Wall Street*, THE DEAL, Feb. 24, 2012, *available at* http://www.pipeline.thedeal.com/tdd/ViewArticle .dl?id=10006673193.

Thus, deal making in the M&A markets continues to evolve, responding to ever-changing economic conditions and pressures—and M&A lawyers need to be well informed regarding the current business environment in order to be able to provide effective legal counsel. In sum, reading the daily business news will serve to reinforce a fundamental tenet of this casebook: each deal is different since the business incentives and client objectives vary widely from deal to deal. Moreover, the legal advice must be tailored to the business considerations that animate and are specific to the particular deal the M&A lawyer is currently working on.

QUESTIONS

In considering these two very different stories of M&A deals (Pfizer's acquisition of publicly traded Pharmacia and Nestlé's purchase of privately held Chef America), and in reading through the note material that follows, ask yourself the following questions with respect to each of these two deals and consider if there is any variation in your answer as to each deal:

1. Who is the Target? Who is the Bidder?

2. Does this deal present any antitrust concerns? Will this deal require any other regulatory approvals?

3. How will investors in Bidder Co. learn of the proposed acquisition of Target Co.? How will investors in Target Co. learn of the proposed sale of their company?

4. In the case of the Pfizer-Pharmacia deal, what is the nature of management's concern as to the market's reaction to the public announcement of this proposed transaction between Pfizer and Pharmacia? How will management gauge the market's reaction? Why is management worried about the market's reaction to the deal when it gets announced? Why is this concern not mentioned in the press coverage of Nestlé's acquisition of Chef America?

5. What is the acquisition consideration? In other words, what is Bidder offering to pay to acquire Target?

6. Why does Bidder want to buy Target? What business objective is to be served by making this acquisition? Is Bidder a strategic or financial buyer?

7. What is the business incentive for Target to engage in this deal? Why is Target willing to let itself be acquired?

8. What does each company hope to accomplish in the due diligence process? What will (actually) be done during the course of this due diligence process?

9. What will happen when Pharmacia "spins off"—that is, divests itself of—the stake it holds in Monsanto?

10. In describing the deal between Pfizer and Pharmacia, the financial press referred to Hassan as selling "his company." In what sense is Hassan selling "his company"? In what sense is Hassan not selling "his company"? Along these same lines, in what sense is Paul Merage selling "*his* company"?

NOTES

1. Sale of Venture Capital–Backed Companies.   There is one other type of deal that has become so common in the modern business world that it deserves special mention. Many closely held firms (such as Chef America) may seek investment funds from venture capital (VC) or private equity (PE) firms in order to establish and/or grow their business. For these VC investors, the time horizon for use of their capital varies, but is usually somewhere between three to seven years. This means that when the VC firm invests its capital and buys stock in the start-up company, the VC firm usually considers its *exit strategy* as part of its overall investment decision. The goal of these financial investors is usually to obtain the return of their invested capital along with a certain rate of return on their investment. The VC (or PE) investor's goal, however, often may be at odds with the founding shareholder(s) of the company, who frequently are entrepreneur(s) who closely identify with the business of the company.

Often, these entrepreneurs will find themselves unwilling to separate from the company's business. Other entrepreneurs, however, have a very different set of business objectives, often intending only to grow the young business until it is mature enough to be sold off to another (usually more established) business.

Among the exit strategies typically considered by a VC or PE investor is the sale of the business to another company. When the start-up company is acquired, these financial investors will usually get cashed out along with all the other shareholders, including the founding shareholders. Often, though, the acquiring corporation will purchase the start-up company in order to acquire the talent and expertise (human capital) of its founding shareholders and/or managers. In that case, the consideration offered to those founding shareholder(s) and/or manager(s) that the acquiring corporation would like to retain is likely to be different than the consideration offered to the other shareholders, including the financial investors. This disparate treatment of shareholders raises obvious fiduciary duty concerns, which we will examine as we go through the materials in the later chapters.

As of this writing (Fall 2012), the M&A markets continue to provide the preferred exit strategy for VC and PE investors to obtain their financial objectives. Indeed, following the bursting of the "tech bubble" in the early years of the twenty-first century, venture capitalists and other institutional investors (such as hedge funds) became increasingly reliant on the M&A market as the preferred exit strategy, a trend that only intensified in the wake of the Great Recession of 2008-2009—particularly in light of the continuing moribund market for initial public offerings (IPOs). "For venture capitalists and other prominent investors in young companies, an initial public offering is supposed to be the big pay-off for years of patience. It's not working out that way [for many investors, especially for backers of new Internet companies]." Scott Thurm and Pei-Wing Tam, *Prominent Investors Miss Web IPO Payoff*, WALL STREET JOURNAL, June 19, 2012, at A1.

2. Sale of Closely Held Company to Another Closely Held Company.   Another common variation of the Main Street M&A deal is where one small business is acquired by another small, closely held business. These transactions will not make the headlines of the *Wall Street Journal* (or even the *Smallville Tribune*), but are the lifeblood for many corporate lawyers and their small business clients. As an example, an established plumbing business is put up for sale when its founder decides to retire from the business. In its simplest form, we will assume that the founder and manager of the business is the sole shareholder of this thriving business that has added a couple of employees over the years. There are a number of different ways that this founder may go about finding a buyer for his plumbing business. For example, he may offer the business to existing employees or transfer ownership to the next generation of family members. Alternatively, the founder may decide to list the business for sale with a business broker. The broker will actively search for a buyer for the business, usually in exchange for a commission if the broker is successful in finding a buyer and closing on the sale of the business.

Deals involving businesses owned and operated as small closely held corporations are not usually going to make headlines in the *Wall Street Journal*. However, for the founding shareholder(s), these deals represent an important

and defining milestone, often culminating a long career in the business. More
to the point in our study of M&A law, exactly the same legal structures are
available to both the small Main Street M&A deal as are available to structure
the large-scale M&A deal that gets done on Wall Street. Further, the essential
sequence of steps necessary to complete any such deal follows a similar chronology, which is described in the next section. However, the dynamics of a deal
done on Wall Street will vary considerably from Main Street M&A deals, as we
will see when we analyze the problems in Chapter 2.

3. Divestitures vs. Acquisitions.   In the case of Pfizer's acquisition of Pharmacia, the decision to sell off Monsanto's business operations had already been
made by Pharmacia's management before entering into the agreement to be
acquired by Pfizer. This type of transaction is generally referred to as a "divestiture" and is largely beyond the scope of this casebook, since this casebook
focuses on "acquisitive" transactions. That is, this casebook focuses on the business decision to acquire another company. However, very often a company will
decide that certain assets are no longer core to its business model, in which
case it will usually undertake to *divest* itself of these assets, either by selling off
the assets or by spinning off the business to its shareholders, as in the case of
Pharmacia's decision to divest itself of Monsanto. We will briefly examine the
mechanics of a "spin-off" transaction as part of our discussion of the problem
sets in the next chapter.

4. Strategic vs. Financial Buyers.   Since 2004, the M&A market has seen an
explosive growth of private equity firms, which have increasingly become active
as deal players in the M&A market in the United States. Indeed, statistics show
that by the mid-2000s buyout (i.e., private equity) firms accounted for more
than a quarter of all M&A activity, by deal value, in the U.S., and "accounted for
40% of all deals involving public targets in the first quarter [of 2007]." John E.
Morris, *Going Private, Mostly*, THE DEAL, May 2007, at 20.
    How do private equity buyers differ from strategic buyers?

> . . . This article provides a brief review of some basic elements of a private
> equity transaction and some key considerations that distinguish private equity
> deals from more traditional M&A.
>   Private equity sponsors (also referred to as financial sponsors) seek to ac-
> quire companies that they can grow or improve (or both) with a view toward
> eventual sale or public offering. In terms of growth, the financial sponsor will
> usually acquire a platform company in a particular industry and then seek to add
> additional companies to the platform through acquisition. . . .
>   Strategic buyers, on the other hand, are companies that are already in the
> target company's industry or in a similar industry. While strategic buyers use ac-
> quisitions for growth, they may have different goals than a financial sponsor. For
> example, a strategic buyer may not be concerned about an exit strategy for an
> acquired business because it expects a seamless integration of the target into its
> own operations.
>   . . . Private equity investors generally acquire new companies through lever-
> aged buyouts. The use of leverage distinguishes financial sponsors from strategic
> buyers engaged in more traditional merger and acquisition transactions. A pri-
> vate equity sponsor needs the assets of the target company as collateral to borrow

the funds necessary to acquire the company. Therefore, private equity investors seek target companies that can generate sufficient cash to service the debt that is incurred to acquire them. . . .

In contrast, because strategic buyers often can fund acquisitions from cash on hand, they generally do not need to incur debt and can consummate transactions more quickly. . . .

Private equity investors also are looking for a particular type of seller (references to "seller" refer to the owners/operators of the target company). Since the private equity sponsor will not run the target company's day-to-day operations following the closing, it is imperative that the seller be willing and desirous of continuing to run the company. Ideally, the target must have a founder or principal who will remain with the business . . . to implement its strategy for growth and eventual exit. This is in stark contrast with the desire of strategic buyers who often do not want members of the target's management to continue with the business following the closing. More traditional merger and acquisition transactions usually lead to job eliminations to maximize efficiency. Strategic buyers in the same industry as the target usually have personnel in their organization who can run the target's business.

Jeffrey Blomberg, *Private Equity Transactions: Understanding Some Fundamental Principles*, 17 BUSINESS LAW TODAY 51, at 51-52 (January/February 2008). As we go through the remaining chapters, we will study transactions involving both financial buyers and strategic bidders and we will study in more detail the different set of incentives and business considerations that guide these different types of prospective Bidders.

    5. What is an "LBO"?   The excerpt in the preceding note refers to "leveraged buyouts," or "LBOs" as they are more popularly known. An LBO employs the extensive use of debt to finance Bidder's purchase of Target and contemplates that the cash flow generated by Target's business and/or the disposition of Target assets will be used to secure and repay the debt that Bidder incurs. Particularly in the current environment of historically low interest rates, debt financing usually has a lower cost of capital than does equity financing. For reasons to be explored in more detail as part of use of the problem sets in Chapter 2 (where we describe LBOs in more detail), debt financing effectively serves as a "lever," if you will, to increase the returns to the equity investors (i.e., the shareholders), which helps to explain the origin of the term "LBO."

> Usually, the business being purchased becomes the ultimate debtor whose cash flow is expected to discharge the debts incurred in the takeover. This type of acquisition is called . . . a leveraged buyout (if incumbent management and outside financiers end up as the ultimate owners of the business). . . . The decision as to whether such a transaction is feasible may be based on (1) a cash-flow analysis indicating the maximum amount of debt the business can possibly carry [i.e., the amount of interest that the business can pay to its lenders as the cost of the borrowed capital], and (2) estimates of the amounts for which nonessential assets or peripheral lines of business can be sold for. In the most extreme case, most of the business's assets may be sold off to raise funds to reduce the outstanding indebtedness incurred to finance the [original] purchase price [a transaction that is often referred to on Wall Street as a "bust up" bid].

Robert W. Hamilton and Richard A Booth, BUSINESS BASICS FOR LAW STUDENTS, 173 (4th Ed. 2006). We will examine LBOs in more detail in analyzing the problem sets in Chapter 2.

6. Payment of a "Premium."   In both of the deal stories described at the beginning of this chapter, the Bidder offered to pay a "premium" in order to acquire Target's business. Indeed, M&A transactions are usually characterized by Bidder's payment of a "premium" in order to gain ownership (control) of Target's business. Why? In the case of the sale of Target, Target will no longer remain a freestanding, independent business. Instead, managerial control of Target's business assets and operations will shift to Bidder, as the buyer of Target's business. In the usual case, Target's owners will demand payment of a "premium" to reflect the "true value" (or "inherent value") of Target's business in order to entice Target's shareholders to "sell" (that is, to transfer managerial control and/or ownership of Target as a freestanding business) to the Bidder. As we shall see in the problem sets and other materials in Chapter 2, the "true value" of Target's business is typically a matter that is heavily negotiated between the parties, and the parties' assessment of "true value" can vary considerably, such variance often depending on the assumptions that the parties make as to the future financial potential of Target's business. We will explore this issue (and the nature of the assumptions to be made in determining what is a "fair price" to be paid by Bidder in order to acquire Target's business) as part of the valuation materials included at the end of Chapter 2. By way of summary, the following excerpt provides an explanation for the observed phenomenon that Bidders inevitably pay a premium in a takeover transaction—an explanation that is widely accepted by many knowledgeable participants in the M&A market:

> When the common stock of a company is publicly traded on an exchange or in the over-the-counter market, the market price is often considered to be a reliable measure of value. But it is clearly not always so.
>
> * * *
>
> Even when a publicly traded stock has a broad market with numerous [daily trading] transactions, it does not necessarily follow that the total value of the business, if it were sold as a single entity, equals the current market price per share multiplied by the total number of shares outstanding [or what is often referred to on Wall Street as the "*market capitalization*" or "*float*" of a publicly traded company.]. If this conclusion were correct, valuation of publicly held corporations would be relatively easy, because one could obtain the current value of the entire business simply by adding up the current market values of all outstanding shares. But the premiums typically paid to shareholders in corporate takeovers demonstrate that the value placed on a business by the securities markets is often significantly lower than the amount that a purchaser is willing to pay for the *entire business* (or *all* the outstanding stock). In other words, the market often appears to understate the value of the entire company. This phenomenon has been the subject of considerable speculation.
>
> One plausible explanation for [the payment of a premium in a takeover transaction] . . . is that the trading markets for securities are primarily markets for *investments*, not markets for *controlling interests* in companies. Almost all transactions on public securities markets involve minute fractions of the total outstanding

shares of companies, and these transactions individually do not carry with them any meaningful opportunity to affect the company's business policies. If the transactions increase in size so that control of the company may be involved, the purchasers are willing to pay more—usually significantly more—than the prices for smaller blocks of shares that are traded [on the open market] solely as investments. . . . The result is that the market for the whole corporation—the takeover market— . . . is different from the market for investment securities.

Robert Hamilton and Richard Booth, BUSINESS BASICS FOR LAW STUDENTS (4th Ed. 2006) at pp. 172-173 (*emphasis added*).

At this point, it bears emphasizing that the public announcement of a deal (or, as we shall see in subsequent chapters, even rumors/speculation that a company may be the target of a proposed acquisition) will have a dramatic impact on the trading price of the common stock of the putative Target in the open market. The fundamental reason for this impact on Target's trading price, once the company is "put in play,"* is that the pricing of Target stock in the open market shifts from traders pricing Target stock based on what a willing buyer would be willing to pay to a willing seller for a fungible share of Target's common stock—to traders pricing Target's stock based on the assumption Target Co. is being sold—with the trading price being discounted, of course, for the possibility that the deal with Bidder might not close. This shift in perspective among traders in the open market has the inevitable effect of putting upward pressure on the price of Target's stock, as was described in the case of Pfizer's acquisition of Pharmacia's business.

As another example of this shift in traders' perspective once a company is "put in play," the *Los Angeles Times* reported in August 2011, that shares of the ever popular discount retailer, 99¢ Only Stores Inc., traded up following reports that the company would receive a new buyout offer. *See* Andrea Chang, *99 Cent Only Stock Jumps on Expectations of New Buyout Offer,* LOS ANGELES TIMES, August 23, 2011, at B3. Earlier in the year, 99¢ Only had received a buyout proposal that "[i]nvestors viewed as too low . . . [and so traders] quickly pushed the stock price [above] the $19.09" price per share that had been offered in March 2011 by the Schiffer/Gold family (the company's controlling shareholder) and Leonard Green and Partners, a (buyout/private equity) firm. *Id.* Indeed, after the initial buyout proposal was announced in March 2011, "several industry analysts said they expected a higher offer to emerge for the company. . . ." *Id.* Eventually, 99¢ Only Stores was acquired by another buyout fund for $22 per share, representing a 32 percent premium over the company's trading price in March 2011, the day before the company announced the terms of the initial acquisition proposal that it had received from a different private equity firm. *See 99 Cents Only to be Sold for $1.6 B,* THE ASSOCIATED PRESS, Oct. 11, 2011, *available at* http://finance.yahoo.com/news/Retailer-99-Cents-Only-to-be-apf -2517412550.html. *Query:* Why would the trading price of the company's stock rise above the price offered by the original Bidder?

---

*What does it mean to "put a company in play"? In Wall Street parlance, this colloquial phrase is generally used to refer to a company that has become (or is rumored to become) the subject of a takeover bid and thus whose stock has become the subject of speculation by traders in the stock markets.

7. The Problem of "Bidder Overpayment." We have noted that M&A transactions generally involve the payment of a "premium" to acquire Target, thus typically generating considerable extra value for Target shareholders. Indeed, "[o]ne important, and undisputed, datum about acquisitive transactions should be noted: acquisitions generate substantial gains to target company shareholders. . . . Without question, the announcement of a [takeover bid or merger agreement] is good news for target shareholders." Roberta Romano, *A Guide to Takeovers: Theory, Evidence & Regulation,* 9 YALE J. ON REG. 119, 122 (1992). With respect to Bidder and its shareholders, there is considerable more controversy as to the benefits achieved through M&A transactions:

> Whether shareholders of acquirers [Bidders] gain from acquisitions, however, is substantially more heavily debated with results from numerous studies finding much more complexity than with respect to target shareholders. Scholars continue to generate extensive empirical research on the effects of acquisitions on acquirer shareholders and on how the interests of acquirer management affect these transactions. While several early studies reported that [Bidder] shareholders benefit from acquisitions, others reported losses to them. A significant body of more recent finance literature finds evidence that many, although clearly not all, acquisitions destroy value for long-term [Bidder] shareholders. This is particularly true in the case of takeovers of publicly traded targets by publicly traded acquirers.

Afra Afsharipour, *A Shareholders' Put Option: Counteracting the Acquirer Overpayment Problem,* 96 MINN. L. REV. 1018, 1028 (2012). In thinking about this issue, consider the following observation made by an experienced M&A lawyer:

> A major merger or acquisition can be a company-defining moment. The right business combination at the right price, with good execution, can reposition the company, accelerate profitable growth and shareholder return, and even change the game for an industry as a whole. But a bad deal—whether the failure is rooted in the concept [i.e., the "logic of the deal," that is, the business justification for the proposed acquisition], the price, or the execution—is probably the fastest legal means of destroying shareholder value.

Ken Smith, *The M&A Buck Stops at the Board,* 41 *Mergers and Acquisitions* 48, at 49 (April 2006).

8. Hostile Takeover vs. Friendly Acquisition. Pfizer's friendly $60 billion acquisition of Pharmacia in 2002 was not an isolated M&A event for Pfizer. As previously mentioned, Pfizer made another blockbuster acquisition in 2000 in the form of its hostile takeover of Warner-Lambert Co. What is a hostile takeover? A takeover is deemed "hostile" when the management of Target Co. is opposed to the proposed transaction, as was the case with Pfizer's bid for Warner-Lambert. Management of Warner-Lambert objected to Pfizer's acquisition because Warner-Lambert's management had already agreed to be acquired by another pharmaceutical giant—American Home Products Corp. (AHP)—for $71.1 billion. If Warner-Lambert consummated the deal with AHP, the impact of this deal on Pfizer would have been serious because AHP ultimately would have been able to reduce Pfizer's access to Lipitor—Warner-Lambert's blockbuster cholesterol drug that reportedly accounted for approximately

$4 billion of Pfizer's total revenue of $13.5 billion in 1998. In response to the public announcement of Warner-Lambert's deal with AHP, "Pfizer rushed in the same day . . . with a competing $74.6 billion bid, which it eventually sweetened to $90 billion. . . . [and] which ultimately became the largest hostile takeover in U.S. history and produced the No. 2 drug maker in the world, with $29.6 billion in revenue, the top animal health business, the leading marketer in over-the-counter healthcare and the largest R&D budget: $4.7 billion." Sara Behunek, *Postmortem: The Weight,* THE DEAL, Deals of the Year 2012, at p. 54; February 4, 2011, www.thedeal.com/magazine/JD/038258/2011/theweight.php. In the case of a friendly acquisition, such as Pfizer's deal with Pharmacia, the terms of the transaction are fully negotiated by the respective management teams of Bidder and Target and are also approved by each company's board of directors. As part of the materials in Chapter 6 and 7, we will discuss "hostile takeovers" in more detail and we will examine in more detail how the deal-making process in the case of hostile takeovers varies from the type of fully negotiated deal that is described in the next section.

C. The Flow of a Deal: Introducing Timing, Pricing, and Other Structural Considerations

Every acquisition—whether done on Wall Street or Main Street—tends to follow the same timeline. The reason for this convention is that all acquisitions face the same threshold issues, although the way the issues get resolved varies widely depending on a number of variables, not the least of which is the size of the acquisition. As we study the materials in the remaining chapters, we will explore the nature of these threshold issues and the legal rules that must be taken into account in addressing these issues. Since these legal and business issues create a time frame that is fairly typical of any M&A deal, it is worth sketching out the basic steps of any business acquisition, even though the precise reasons for this chronology will not be made clear until we analyze the materials in the remaining chapters.

   With some slight variations that reflect inherent differences between Wall Street and Main Street M&A activity, the essential sequence of an M&A transaction follows a similar pattern that will be referred to as the "flow of a deal." As an illustration of a fairly typical deal flow, this section starts off by describing the process by which Pfizer made its offer to acquire Pharmacia. The remainder of this section then breaks this timeline down into the various steps involved in a typical acquisition that will culminate in Bidder getting control over Target's business operations.

Deal Flow: How Did the Pfizer-Pharmacia Deal Get Done?

According to the Pfizer/Pharmacia joint proxy statement, on which this account of the deal flow of Pfizer's acquisition of Pharmacia is based, Pfizer's

CEO, Henry McKinnell, began floating various acquisition proposals to his counterpart at Pharmacia, Fred Hassan, more than a year and a half before the deal was announced. The two CEOs were well acquainted with each other, and would frequently run into each other at meetings of the drug industry's main trade group, generally known as PhRMA (the Pharmaceutical Research & Manufacturers of America). Indeed, in 2002, Hassan replaced McKinnell as the chairman and chief executive of this trade group.

In the three years preceding the merger, the management of Pfizer periodically considered the possibility of a business combination or other strategic transaction with Pharmacia and its predecessor companies. Accordingly, whenever the two CEOs met professionally, McKinnell invited Hassan to entertain a more permanent and lasting business relationship between the two companies. All of these overtures by McKinnell were politely rebuffed by Hassan.

However, a turning point in the relationship came in April 2002, when McKinnell met briefly with Hassan and suggested that it would be productive to discuss the state of the pharmaceutical industry and the possibility of a more meaningful business relationship between Pfizer and Pharmacia. Hassan agreed to meet. On May 9, 2002, McKinnell and Hassan met in New York, at which time McKinnell informed Hassan of his belief in the benefits of combining with Pharmacia. On May 13, 2002, Hassan, in a telephone conference call, informed the Pharmacia board of McKinnell's interest in a business combination. Around this time, both companies decided to retain financial advisors to assist in valuation issues.

On June 7, 2002, at a special meeting of the Pharmacia board, Hassan described McKinnell's interest in the business combination. The board reviewed Pharmacia's financial data with its advisors and further authorized Hassan to meet with McKinnell and inquire into his proposal. On June 11, 2002, the two CEOs met and McKinnell proposed a merger transaction that would result in the Pharmacia shareholders receiving 1.3 shares of Pfizer common stock in exchange for each share of Pharmacia common stock. Hassan, believing that the exchange ratio was unacceptable, nevertheless informed his board of the offer. On June 18, 2002, the board rejected the initial offer as inadequate but authorized Hassan and members of senior management to continue discussions with Pfizer. Hassan informed McKinnell that the Pharmacia board remained open to further discussions, but it believed that the 1.3 exchange ratio offered by Pfizer did not accurately reflect Pharmacia's intrinsic value.

In order for discussions to proceed, the two companies needed to undertake their due diligence process, which would necessitate the exchange of highly sensitive proprietary information. To accommodate this process, the two companies entered into a confidentiality agreement on June 27, 2002. Recognizing the prevailing climate of fear as to hidden accounting problems and other potential finance-related issues, the parties wanted to do an exhaustive review of each other's business, with a heavy emphasis on the books and financial records, as well as research and development of new drugs in the pipeline. So from July 2 until July 13, 2002, the respective teams of legal and financial advisors conducted extensive due diligence of the other company. During that same time period, Pfizer and Pharmacia, together with their respective legal and financial advisors, negotiated the terms for a definitive merger agreement.

The breakthrough in negotiations came when McKinnell suggested an increase in the exchange ratio to 1.4 shares of Pfizer stock for each share of Pharmacia common stock was realistic—provided, however, that each company expedited its due diligence and entered into a mutually agreed-upon definitive merger agreement, and further, that such merger agreement was approved by the respective boards. Although some of Pharmacia's board members still harbored reservations about the 1.4 exchange ratio, believing it to be too low, Hassan was able to persuade the board that the deal was a good one since Pfizer was using its stock as the acquisition and the value of the combined company would likely appreciate. *See* WALL STREET JOURNAL, July 15, 2002, at A1.

On July 13, 2002, both boards convened independently at special meetings to discuss and vote on the definitive merger agreement. After detailed financial, strategic, and legal presentations, both the Pfizer board and the Pharmacia board approved the merger agreement by unanimous votes. Thus, before the opening for trading on July 15, 2002, which was only approximately three months since the initial discussions began, Pfizer and Pharmacia issued a joint press release announcing the execution of the merger agreement.

Although the deal seemed to originate with the CEOs of the two companies, both firms retained outside advisors to help with the acquisition process. In particular, these advisors helped negotiate the terms and the structure of the deal, document the transaction, and conduct the required due diligence. Pfizer relied on its team of investment bankers, Lazard LLC and Bear Stearns & Co., and the law firm of Cadwalader, Wickersham, & Taft for legal advice. For its part, Pharmacia retained the investment banking firm of Goldman Sachs & Co. and for legal advice, it turned to the law firm of Sullivan & Cromwell.

After the deal has been approved by the boards of both companies, much legal work remains to be done, no matter what method is used to structure the acquisition. As we will see in the next chapter, there are essentially three methods by which business acquisitions get done. These three consist of statutory mergers, asset purchases, and stock purchases. Much of the focus of the required legal work in this regard consists of assuring compliance with the corporate formalities required to validly complete a transaction using any of these different methods, including the process for obtaining any required shareholder approvals. We will examine the nature of the requirements imposed by state and federal law in the next chapter, where we analyze in more detail these different methods for combining corporations. Before we examine this substantive detail, let's conceptually break down the process described above into its essential components, each of which will be examined in more detail as we go through the remaining chapters.

D.   *"Deal Flow": Conceptualizing the Deal Process*

As we shall see when we analyze the problem sets in Chapter 2, there are differences in the timing as well as certain other aspects of the deal-making process that vary depending on whether the acquisition involves publicly traded companies or privately held companies. Nonetheless, there is a certain convention with respect to the deal-making process that M&A transactions tend to follow—regardless of whether the deal is getting done on Wall Street or Main Street. The legal and business considerations that shape the conventional deal-making process for M&A transactions are the subject matter of the remaining chapters. However, it is helpful to begin our study of M&A law by providing a broad overview of the steps generally involved in any given M&A transaction, which is the topic of the next section.

1.   The Start of Negotiations

Deals get started in a variety of different ways. Acquisitions, for example, often get started because a financial advisor (frequently an investment banking firm) will identify a particular business as a potential acquisition candidate. The potential acquisition candidate may be a client of the investment banking firm, who has retained this financial advisor to help the corporate client find a buyer for the company's business. Alternatively, the investment banker may be scouting for potential acquisition candidates for one of its established corporate clients, either at the request of its client or, alternatively, as part of the banker's ongoing professional relationship with that particular corporate client. Yet another way for a deal to get launched is for the Bidder's existing management to contact management of a company that the Bidder itself has identified as a potential acquisition target based on its own internal assessment of the industry and the Bidder's business goals and objectives. In cases where existing management identifies the potential acquisition target, early discussions between Bidder and Target may initially proceed without the assistance of outside advisors. Eventually, though, financial and legal advisors will get involved in the deal-making process.

2.   The Role of Financial Advisors

As negotiations are launched in earnest, the assistance of financial and legal advisors becomes important in addressing two issues that are common to all acquisitions: how should the deal be structured, and how much will the Bidder pay to acquire Target? In Chapter 2, we will analyze the different types of deal structures available to complete the acquisition. As we shall see, the legal rules that must be satisfied for each type of deal structure will often influence the decision as to which type of structure is most appropriate for a particular deal. In addition, financial advisors will be assisting Bidder in its decision as to how much to pay to acquire Target, which necessarily requires Bidder to value Target's business. On the other side, Target will engage its own set of financial advisors to help it determine whether Bidder is offering a fair price to acquire Target's business. Since Target only gets one chance to sell its business and relinquish control over its income-producing operations, Target has a strong vested interest in making sure that it obtains the best price available. Although Target's management may have a strong sense of what it thinks its business is worth, there are other variables that influence the price that it can obtain for its business, not the least of which is the general condition of the market at the time of sale and the general business environment within Target's specific industry. These variables, as well as the financial well-being of Target's own business, will heavily influence the bargaining process between Bidder and Target as to the purchase price.

Even though Target may have strong convictions as to the true value of its business, there are many variables to be juggled in reaching a consensus with Bidder as to the purchase price. In dealing with the confluence of all these variables in the context of a particular deal, most buyers and sellers — regardless of the size of the deal — understand the need to bring in the expertise of outside advisors. All of which illustrates the fundamental truism that valuation is an art, not a science. And, just as beauty is in the eye of the beholder, judgments as to valuation can vary widely between buyers and sellers. Outside advisors can often provide the experience and expertise that will result in closing the gap between Bidder and Target, thereby facilitating the ability of the parties to reach an agreement as to the terms of the acquisition purchase price and the nature of the consideration to be paid. As part of these negotiations, Bidder may require that Target share information about its business and financial affairs so that Bidder can more accurately determine what it is willing to pay to acquire Target.

Use of Confidentiality Agreements.   This exchange of information between Bidder and Target may require the parties to share with each other highly sensitive, confidential, and proprietary information about their businesses. Obviously, each side will be concerned about maintaining the confidentiality of this information. This concern usually will lead to the use of confidentiality agreements to protect against misuse of the business and financial information that Bidder and Target will exchange with each other. Accordingly, early in the deal process, the parties will usually enter into a confidentiality agreement (commonly referred to as a *non-disclosure agreement* or *NDA*) to assure each other that confidential and proprietary business information shared during the acquisition process will be carefully protected and not used for any purpose other than evaluating the proposed transaction. We will discuss the use of NDAs in detail in Chapter 5.

Who Are the Deal Players?   In mega-deals, such as Pfizer's acquisition of Pharmacia, each side will generally rely on its own Wall Street investment banker, such as the well-known firms of Goldman Sachs, Morgan Stanley, or Merrill Lynch. In smaller deals involving closely held companies, mid-size investment bankers may get involved, firms whose names are not as well known. And, in even smaller deals involving the sale of closely held, often family-owned businesses, no investment banker is used. Instead, the company is listed for sale with a business broker, much in the same way that homeowners list their homes for sale with a real estate broker, who will typically receive a commission when the deal closes. Likewise, the financial advisor will receive a fee for its services as a business broker, which is often framed in terms of a commission to be paid when the deal between Bidder and Target closes. For reasons that we explore in the remaining chapters, M&A transactions are "complex affairs":

[typically] involving a large number of parties that may—or may not—be prepared to bid higher . . . [Completing an acquisition] may sprawl over weeks and months. The [financial advisors] at the center of these often freewheeling [deals] take on a number of [different] roles: information gatherer and valuation analyst; matchmaker who tries to bring together the right buyer for the right seller; psychologist who can detect subtle shifts in sentiment. He—and they are mostly men—must work discretely, even secretly; he must be seen to be operating even-handedly, and yet also in the best interests of the client. He must pit bidders against each other [in order] to extract the highest price [for Target Co.]. He must keep the client informed while nudging the [deal-making process] forward, fanning interest at opportune moments, moving [the deal participants forward] from stage to stage. [Finally,] [h]e must be able to close the deal when the time comes.

Vyvyan Tenorio, *Investment Bankers as Auction Stars,* THE DEAL, May 29, 2012 at pp. 6-7. As we shall see in the remaining chapters, the role of the legal advisor often overlaps with that of the financial advisor, with the lawyer sharing important responsibilities for keeping the deal-making process moving forward while also being sensitive to shifts in sentiment among the participants on the deal and simultaneously keeping the client informed.

"Delayed Closing." As with the financial advisor, the lawyer also bears important responsibility for moving the deal from "signing to closing," since virtually all M&A transactions involve a "delayed closing." That is to say, the parties negotiate the transaction and then sign the definitive acquisition agreement reflecting the terms as bargained for by the parties to the transaction. However, the actual transfer of the business typically will not occur until some later date as specified in the parties' acquisition agreement (i.e., the closing date). This is similar to the process involved when a willing seller agrees to sell a parcel of real property to a willing buyer. Once the land sale contract is signed, the parties move into the escrow period, during which time both buyer and seller typically are contractually obligated to complete certain responsibilities before closing the deal. Likewise, in an M&A transaction, the acquisition agreement will typically specify responsibilities that the parties to the transaction must complete before closing on the acquisition. The nature of these obligations is explored in more detail in Chapter 5, as part of a more extensive discussion of the steps involved in documenting and completing an M&A transaction.

Meeting the Client's Business Objectives: Speed, Certainty, and Price. In the situation where Target Co. decides to sell its business (often referred to colloquially as "putting itself on the auction block"), Target's managers will usually retain legal and financial advisors who will be responsible for designing a sale process that allows Target to meet its business objectives, which generally consist of speed, certainty, and price. Let me elaborate. "Speed" refers to the risk that the deal process will disrupt the seller's business; that is, Target's management is often concerned that the sale process will disrupt the orderly management of Target's business operations by resulting in the loss of employees (who fear that their jobs may be at risk if the company is sold); the loss of customers; the loss of vendors; and the like. "Certainty" refers to minimizing execution risk; that is, minimizing the risk that Target's deal with Bidder will not close, given that the typical M&A transaction contemplates a delayed closing (as described above). Finally, and probably the most important objective from Target's point of view, is "price," in that Target usually seeks to obtain the best price available for Target's business. For reasons that were described earlier in this chapter, the determination of best price for Target's business generally focuses on the adequacy of the premium being offered by the Bidder.

3. Use of Non-Cash Consideration to Finance the Purchase Price

Often Bidder will seek to acquire Target for non-cash consideration. As we will see when we analyze the diagrams in Appendix A at the end of this book, this will result in a very different treatment of Target Co.'s shareholders after the acquisition is completed. When Bidder issues its stock in exchange for Target's business, Target Co. shareholders will end up owning Bidder Co. stock. This presents a very different investment decision for Target's shareholders. Now they must decide whether they want to invest in Bidder Co., which means that Target Co. shareholders face a separate and often rather complicated valuation decision of their own. In addition to deciding the amount for which they are willing to sell Target's business, Target's shareholders now must determine what value they place on Bidder's business on a going forward basis. This decision usually will require Bidder to provide to Target's shareholders information about Bidder's business and its plans for the future after acquiring Target's business.

4. The Due Diligence Process

"Due diligence" is a term of art used to describe the process of information gathering and analysis, which will usually be undertaken by each party to the business acquisition. The focus is on gathering all relevant information necessary to a thorough evaluation of the other company's business and financial affairs. From the perspective of Bidder, the goal of its due diligence investigation of Target is to gain all the information it needs—good and bad—to be sure that it does not overpay to acquire Target, an inherent possibility associated with any M&A transaction. For reasons to be explored in more detail in Chapter 5, Bidder's risk of overpayment is substantially mitigated through adequate due diligence, among other protective provisions, although this risk can never be completely eliminated.

From Target's perspective, the scope of its due diligence will depend in large part on the nature of the acquisition consideration offered by the Bidder. In the case of an all-cash deal, Target's primary concern is the adequacy of the price offered. Since Target gets only one chance to sell its business operations, it has a vested interest in making sure that it obtains the largest premium possible—in other words, the best price it can negotiate. In making this determination, however, Target needs minimal, if any, information about Bidder and its plans for the future since Target shareholders will have no further equity participation in the case of an all-cash purchase price.

On the other hand, if Bidder is offering to acquire Target in exchange for Bidder's stock, Target's due diligence process will be broader in scope. In this situation, Target shareholders need information about Bidder's plans to integrate Target's assets into Bidder's business operations. This information from Bidder Co. will be an important factor in the Target Co. shareholders' decision whether to remain independent and continue as the equity owners of Target Co., or alternatively, to combine with Bidder Co. and rely on Bidder Co.'s leadership and business model to maximize their financial return. We will talk at greater length in Chapter 4 about the process for disseminating this information to Target Co. shareholders and the manner in which the federal securities laws regulate this disclosure process in the case of constituent corporation(s) that is/are publicly traded.

5. Board Approval of an Acquisition

In the case of most acquisitions, approval by the board of directors of both Bidder and Target will be required in order for the transaction to proceed. Generally speaking, the acquisition proposal does not originate with the company's board. Rather, the CEO, supported by his or her senior executive officers, initiates the process and is usually responsible for negotiating the terms of the transaction. Ultimately, the deal will be made binding on the company only if the board approves the terms of the negotiated agreement. In our modern world of corporate governance, and particularly in this post-financial-crisis business environment, there is an interesting tension at work. This tension has always been present, but has been receiving increased attention in light of the recent spate of financial scandals. The origins of this tension stem from the fundamental tenet that the board manages the business affairs of the company; however, it is the company's officers, most importantly the company's CEO, who are responsible for implementing these policy decisions as the agents of the corporation. The board members act collectively (generally by way of a duly noticed board meeting); consequently, no single board member has the individual authority to bind the corporation. Officers, on the other hand, have authority by virtue of their position to bind the company. So, the CEO may enter into contracts that are binding on the company, provided that they are in the ordinary course of business and are not extraordinary.

In the case of an acquisition, there is an interesting threshold question as to whether the CEO has the authority to initiate discussions with another company's CEO about a proposed business combination. If so, at what point is the CEO required to bring these discussions to the attention of the company's board of directors? What level of involvement is the board required to exercise in the process of negotiating the terms of a business acquisition in order to fulfill its fiduciary obligations to the company, as well as any other statutory requirements that may be imposed under the terms of modern corporation codes? The nature of these requirements under state and federal law will be introduced when we analyze the problems in Chapter 2.

As a preliminary matter, it is worth noting that the relative balance of power between the board and the company's CEO is a topic of renewed interest in the wake of the crisis in investor confidence spawned by the numerous financial scandals dating back to the turn of the twenty-first century. In the wake of these scandals, legislators, institutional investors, and other observers have demanded greater oversight of management and greater accountability of managers and directors with respect to the decision-making process. After all, one of the most important decisions to be made in today's corporate boardrooms is the decision to pursue a business combination. As we go through the problems in Chapter 2, we will examine this question of the board's involvement in the deal-making process in more detail, along with the corporate governance implications triggered by this issue.

6. Shareholder Approval of an Acquisition

As we will learn when we analyze the problems in the next chapter, state law will often require shareholder approval of the terms of the proposed acquisition in order for the transaction to be validly completed. In those cases where shareholder approval is required, there will be an inevitable delay associated with noticing and conducting a meeting of the shareholders in compliance with the requirements imposed by the law of the state where the company is organized. Further delay may result if the company is publicly traded because the company may be required to prepare and disseminate the disclosure required by the federal proxy rules whenever a publicly traded company solicits a vote by proxy from its shareholders. In Chapter 4, we will examine the nature of the disclosure required under the federal proxy rules of the Securities and Exchange Commission (SEC), along with certain other provisions of the federal securities laws. At this juncture, however, the point to be emphasized is that compliance with these requirements imposed by state and federal law will definitely impact the time frame for completing a proposed acquisition.

7. Regulatory Approval of an Acquisition

Many acquisitions will require approval from federal and/or state regulators in order for the transaction to be validly consummated. This requirement may be imposed contractually (as a condition included in the terms of the parties' acquisition agreement) or alternatively may be imposed by statute. The approval most often required is clearance from antitrust regulators. This casebook will not dwell on the criteria used by the antitrust regulators to decide whether to approve — or clear — an acquisition, thereby allowing the business combination transaction to be completed. I assume that the criteria used by the regulators to decide whether a particular acquisition poses a threat to consumer welfare in violation of the terms of antitrust law is covered as part of a separate course on antitrust law offered in the curriculum of most law schools. Therefore, in Chapter 8, we will mention only a few details of antitrust law that directly and regularly affect M&A activity and of which M&A lawyers need to be aware. For transactions that may present antitrust issues, antitrust counsel typically will be brought in to advise respective companies. For example, in the failed AT&T-T-Mobile merger, antitrust counsel likely advised the two companies of the negative stance that antitrust regulators were likely to take if two of the four largest cell phone providers within the United States merged. Sure enough, once the deal was announced, U.S. antitrust regulators filed a lawsuit to block the impending merger, citing the likelihood of decreased competition within the cell phone market and, in turn, higher prices for cell phone services as causes for concern. Michael J. De La Merced, *AT&T Ends $39 Billion Bid for T-Mobile*, DEALBOOK N.Y. TIMES (Dec. 19, 2011), *available at* http://dealbook.nytimes.com/2011/12/19/att-withdraws-39-bid-for-t-mobile/. In the end, AT&T succumbed to pressure from the antitrust regulators and abandoned its $39 billion bid to acquire T-Mobile, ultimately paying a $4 billion "break-up" fee to Deutsche Telekom, the parent company of T-Mobile. *Id.* We will examine the use of "break-up fees" in more detail in Chapter 7 as part of our discussion of deal protection devices.

In the case of companies operating within regulated industries—such as telecommunications, banking, or the airlines—separate approvals may be required from other government regulators (either at the state or federal level) in order to validly complete the transaction. As was the case with antitrust clearance, the requirement for these other regulatory approvals is often imposed contractually or may be required as a matter of law. In the case of regulated industries, government officials intervene to impose some form of regulatory review and approval in order to protect some interest not adequately represented in the process of negotiating and completing a business acquisition, or to promote some other public policy goal that may be undermined by a proposed business combination. The public policy considerations that motivate policymakers at the federal or state level to intervene in the deal-making process through legislative action is not the focus of this class on M&A law. Further, specialized bodies of law—such as labor law, environmental law, pension law, products liability law, telecommunications law, and intellectual property law—may be implicated in the context of a particular M&A deal. In those deals, the M&A lawyer may be required to seek specialized counsel to ensure compliance with the requirements imposed by the terms of these respective laws.

8. Closing on the Acquisition Transaction

As previously mentioned, the parties' agreement will usually fix a date for closing on the acquisition. At this time, the Bidder will be obligated to pay the agreed-upon consideration and the Target will be obligated to surrender control over its business operations. Until then, Target continues to run the business, much in the same way that the seller continues to be in possession of a house until the close of escrow in a real estate transaction, at which time title and possession of the house are transferred from the seller to the buyer. As in the case of a real estate transaction, there is also the possibility that the deal may never close, even though the parties have a signed acquisition agreement in place. In many cases, the acquisition agreement will include certain conditions that must be satisfied in order for the deal to close. Most notably, the acquisition agreement will usually require that all necessary approvals (including antitrust clearance) be obtained before the closing can occur. If these conditions are not satisfied, the acquisition will not close and Target will remain independent. The nature of these *conditions to closing*, and the consequences that flow from failure to satisfy such conditions, are explored in detail in Chapter 5, as part of our discussion of documenting the transaction.

E.   Business Incentives for M&A Transactions

The following excerpt provides further insight into the business incentives that generally motivate corporate managers to propose "business combinations," which the author (an economist, not an M&A lawyer) generally refers to as "mergers."

> **Senate Judiciary Committee Hearings on Mergers and Corporate Consolidation in the New Economy, Senate Hearing 105-934 (Serial No. J-105-106 at 38)**
> June 16, 1998, *Testimony of Dr. Janet Yellin, Chair, Council of Economic Advisers**

Mr. Chairman and members of the Committee, it is a pleasure to be here this morning to talk about some of the economic issues raised by the current merger wave. . . . [Among other things, my testimony] looks at the causes and consequences of mergers. Here there is no simple conclusion. Many, if not most mergers are motivated by the desire to achieve greater operating efficiencies and lower costs. But it is impossible to rule out anticompetitive motives or simple managerial hubris as explanations for mergers. . . .

. . . [L]et me now turn to the causes and consequences of mergers. The main reason managers give for undertaking mergers is to increase efficiency. And studies show that, on average, the combined equity value of the acquired company and the purchasing company rises as a result of the merger. However, an increase in shareholder value can arise for reasons other than greater efficiency—such as increased market power and the resulting ability to increase profits by raising prices. And the separation of ownership from control in the modern corporation means that mergers may serve the interests of managers more than shareholders (e.g., empire building, increased salary associated with

---

*In April 2010, President Barack Obama nominated Dr. Yellin to serve as the vice-chair of the Board of Governors of the Federal Reserve system, and she was sworn in for a 4-year term in October 2010 following Senate confirmation. Dr. Yellin simultaneously began a 14-year term as a member of the Federal Reserve Board that will expire on January 31, 2024. Previously, Dr. Yellin chaired the Council of Economic Advisors in the Clinton administration from February 1997 through August 1999 and, before assuming that position, she served as the Eugene E. & Catherine M. Trefethen Professor of Business and Economics at the University of California, Berkeley's Haas School of Business, where she is now Emeritus Professor.

running a larger firm). Finally, even if mergers are designed to enhance efficiency, they often don't work and can instead create inefficiencies (some see the merger of the Union Pacific and Southern Pacific railroads in 1995 as a notable example of such an outcome).

There are numerous ways that mergers can contribute to economic efficiency. One is by reducing excess capacity (this justification has been invoked in hospital, defense, and banking mergers). Another is by achieving economies of scale or network externalities (the hub and spoke system that emerged following the deregulation of the airline industry is one example, though it is one that raises questions of increased concentration as well) or economies of scope ("synergy") as in the case of investment/commercial banking, where similar risk management techniques and credit evaluation skills are utilized in a wide variety of financial services. Mergers may also improve management (studies suggest large differences in efficiency among seemingly similar firms like banks).

Most mergers probably are undertaken with the expectation of achieving efficiencies, though the outcomes may sometimes be disappointing and divorces are not uncommon (such as the unraveling of AT&T's 1991 acquisition of NCR). Studies of bank mergers suggest that, in spite of the potential for improved efficiency, in general, they have not improved the efficiency or profitability of banks.

Mergers can also be undertaken to increase market power and reduce competition. In this event consumers could be harmed through higher prices, lower service, reduced variety, and, in the view of some, a reduced pace of innovation, although some argue that increased market power should raise innovation due to the increased ability to appropriate the benefits of R&D. Mergers can also work to decrease the potential for future competition. There is abundant evidence that, when one compares markets of a given type, such as local banking markets, the degree of concentration in a market is correlated with such measures of economic performance as prices and profits. And there is some evidence that mergers have raised prices, as in the case of the mid-1980s airline mergers. Other things equal, higher concentration leads to worsened performance, which is why the Merger Guidelines, [promulgated by U.S. antitrust regulators] after assessing what the appropriate definition of the market is from a product and geographical perspective, look at the impact of a merger on the level of concentration. However, statistical evidence suggests this is not the main motive for most mergers, perhaps reflecting the presence of antitrust monitoring and enforcement.

Thus far, I have been discussing motives for mergers generally. A natural question is why so many firms are merging now. There is no single reason. The following are some of the prevailing explanations:

1. *Adjusting to falling regulatory barriers.* Mergers have followed the removal of branching restrictions in banking and ownership restrictions in radio. . . . Mergers in the telecommunications industry are also tied to the breakup of AT&T and to the deregulation and market opening steps that followed the Telecommunications Act of 1996.

2. *Technological change.* Innovation can change the size and type of firm that is seen as most profitable. Some mergers today may be motivated

by the widely touted, but still nascent, phenomenon of "convergence" in the information technology industry. For instance, as textbook publishers begin to supplement their materials with multimedia software, they may acquire small software companies. . . .

3. *Globalization.* The emergent global economy may demand large scale to participate. A European and American firm may combine to take advantage of the distribution networks that each has on its own continent. . . .

4. *High stock market.* Price-earnings ratios have increased to near-record levels during the current merger wave, and some analysts feel that the market may be overvalued. Such high stock market values may make it seem attractive to fund an acquisition with stock (this is the dominant funding source in the current merger wave). But an overvalued stock market should not necessarily lead to more mergers, because if other firms are also overvalued then there are fewer attractive targets to acquire.

As I mentioned earlier, in evaluating the consequences of mergers we should focus on particular well-defined markets. In this regard, it is important to recognize that mergers do not necessarily increase concentration in any well-defined market. Merging firms may be in different businesses, noncompeting regions, or in supplier-buyer relationships. In banking, for example, national concentration has increased dramatically due to mergers, but concentration measures for local banking deposits have been extremely stable because most mergers have been between banks serving different regions. Even when the merger is among competitors, increasing global competition or domestic entry could be simultaneously reducing concentration. In addition, the entry of new firms or the threat of entry can offset the potentially anticompetitive impact of a merger. And finally, the structural characteristics of markets, and not just the number of firms, influence the nature of competition in a given market. We cannot automatically conclude that markets with 2 or 3 competitors will be less competitive than those with 20 or 30. . . .

F. Historical Perspective and Current Status of M&A Activity

1. Historical Perspective on M&A Activity

Historically, the U.S. economy has been marked by what observers of the financial markets generally agree can be characterized as five different "waves" of merger activity. The following excerpt provides a historical overview that briefly summarizes these "waves" of merger activity, again as seen from the perspective of a well-known economist.

Senate Judiciary Committee Hearings on Mergers and Corporate Consolidation in the New Economy, Senate Hearing 105-934 (Serial No. J-105-106 at 38)

June 16, 1998, *Testimony of Dr. Janet Yellin, Chair, Council of Economic Advisers*

. . . The United States is in the midst of its fifth major merger wave in a hundred years. The previous four merger waves provide background and perspective for assessing today's merger activity.

- *The Great Merger Wave of the 1890s.* The first great merger wave at the turn of the last century was the culmination of the trust movement, when numerous small and mid-sized firms were consolidated into single dominant firms in a number of industries. Examples include Standard Oil and U.S. Steel. One estimate is that this merger wave encompassed at least 15 percent of all plants and employees in manufacturing at the turn of the century. An estimated 75 percent of merger-related firm disappearances occurred as a result of mergers involving at least five firms, and about a quarter involved ten or more firms at a time. The sharp decline in merger activity during 1903 and 1904 was probably related to the onset of a severe recession and the legal precedent for prohibiting market-dominating mergers under the antitrust laws that was established by the Northern Securities Case.
- *The Roaring Twenties.* The merger movement of the 1920s saw the consolidation of many electric and gas utilities as well as manufacturing and minerals mergers. Some of the most prominent manufacturing mergers (such as the one that produced Bethlehem Steel) created relatively large number-two firms in industries previously dominated by one giant.
- *The "Go-Go" Sixties.* The 1960s conglomerate wave represented a deflection of the "urge to merge" away from horizontal (same-industry) mergers, perhaps due to stronger antitrust enforcement. The constant dollar value of mergers in manufacturing and minerals surpassed the prior peak attained in 1899 (though it remained much smaller as a share of the economy). The 1960s boom was also fueled by a strong stock market and financial innovation (such as convertible preferred stocks and debentures). This merger wave ended with a decline in stock prices that was especially severe for companies that had aggressively pursued conglomerate mergers.
- *The Deal Decade of the 1980s.* Unlike other merger booms, this one began in a depressed stock market. With stock prices low relative to the cost of building new capacity, it appeared cheaper to expand by takeover. The 1980s boom was marked by an explosion of hostile takeovers and financial innovation (such as junk bonds and leveraged buyouts). The 1980s wave was unique in the prevalence of cash purchases (as opposed to acquisition through stock). Efforts to dismantle conglomerate firms put together in the previous wave and redeploy their assets more efficiently may have been an important driving force. Finally, the antitrust environment was more permissive and companies were more willing to attempt horizontal mergers.

Qualitatively, the current merger wave [of the late 1990s] appears to be a reversion to pre-1980s form in some ways: It is taking place in a strong stock market, and stock rather than cash is the preferred medium. But many mergers are neither purely horizontal (in general large horizontal mergers would raise antitrust issues) nor purely conglomerate. Rather they represent market extension mergers (companies in the same industry that serve different and currently non-competing markets) or mergers seeking "synergy," in which companies in related markets expect to take advantage of "economies of scope."

By almost any quantitative measure, the current merger boom is substantial . . . . The total value of all deals announced in 1992—a year of especially low activity—was only $150 billion. The value of all deals announced in 1997 ($957 billion) was equivalent to about 12 percent of GDP, and activity so far in 1998 suggests another record year by this measure. . . . The last time merger activity was this large a share of GDP was during the Great Merger Wave at the turn of the last century.

One reason current merger activity is so large relative to the size of the economy is the run up in stock prices in the past few years. When merger activity is expressed relative to the market value of U.S. companies, its level remains lower than it was in the 1980s. . . .

---

2.   Current Status of M&A Activity

By the 1990s, the hostile takeovers that had characterized the deal-making craze of the 1980s had largely disappeared. Indeed, M&A activity all but dried up following the collapse of the junk bond market and the ensuing recessionary environment of the early 1990s. The junk bond market had provided much of the financing for the hostile bids of the 1980s. In addition to the demise of the junk bond market, there were other forces that contributed to the decline of hostile takeovers. As we will discuss in detail in Chapter 7, many publicly traded companies have adopted some form of defensive measures that are designed to insulate the company from an unsolicited (i.e., hostile) bid. Probably the most popular of these defensive tactics is what is known as the *poison pill*, which we will analyze in detail in Chapter 7. Another effective barrier to the unwanted bid is the development of antitakeover statutes under state law that operate to further insulate the company from a hostile takeover. We will analyze these state antitakeover statutes (of which Delaware's business combination statute is perhaps the best known) in Chapter 6.

As noted in the preceding excerpt, merger activity increased dramatically by the end of the 1990s, peaking in 2000—just before the burst of the "dot-com bubble." In 2002, the total volume of M&A transactions stood at 26,531 deals, with a reported dollar value of approximately $1.2 trillion. This level of deal activity stands in stark contrast to the reported volume of 38,744 deals in the year 2000, with a reported dollar value of just under $3.4 trillion. *See* VyVyan Tenorio, *Anatomy of a Cycle: How Big Was It?* THE DEAL, Jan. 2008, at 44. Indeed, the largest acquisition announced in 2002 was Pfizer's acquisition of Pharmacia, which, as previously noted, closed in March 2003 after receiving approval from the antitrust regulators as required by the terms of the acquisition agreement entered into between Pfizer and Pharmacia. However, by 2004, the pace of M&A activity had rebounded and the M&A market had moved beyond the difficult environment that prevailed in 2002, when Pfizer and Pharmacia negotiated their M&A deal.

Calendar year 2005 proved to be the best year for M&A activity out of the previous five years, ushering in a new cycle of M&A activity of unprecedented proportions. Indeed, new high-water marks for the M&A market were reached in both 2006 and 2007, with a total of 42,921 deals reported in 2007 for a total value of almost $4.5 trillion, eclipsing the previous record set in 2006 of approximately $3.6 trillion in reported total value of M&A deals announced that year. The M&A market of calendar year 2007, however, was characterized by extraordinary volatility.

> The feverish pace of M&A activity continued unabated during the first two quarters of 2007, as mega-LBO transactions dominated the news headlines. The M&A market then seemed to hit a brick wall over the summer with the tightening of financing [credit] markets. The deterioration in [the credit markets] . . . and concerns about aggressive lending terms finally caused investors to pause— quickly slowing deal flow.

Jeff Rosenkranz, et al., *M&A Activity: A Macro Look — 2008*, 12 THE M&A LAW-YER 14, 14 (Jan. 2008).

The LBO boom of 2005-2007 came to a screeching halt as the U.S. economy entered the Great Recession of 2008-2009. Indeed, "the first quarter of 2008 featured the biggest quarterly decline, in terms of dollar value of M&A deals announced, of the past six years." Chris O'Leary, *From the Editor: M&A in the Face of Recession*, 12 The M&A LAWYER, April 2008 at 3. The first quarter of 2008 also witnessed the collapse of Bear Stearns, a well-known Wall Street investment banking firm. Amidst the collapse of Bear Stearns and talk of an economic recession, "[m]any would-be acquirers . . . parked themselves on the sidelines, hoping that the credit crisis [that began in summer 2007 and reportedly led to the collapse of Bear Stearns] will finally get under control (though no one really knows what that will take . . .). [Many other would-be Bidders are] waiting until the markets stabilize before agreeing to commit to transactions, even if the [Bidder] has a solid balance sheet and the [T]arget looks attractive. The result is, again, no surprise [to the experienced M&A lawyer]: a great many stalled deals, . . . and a general wariness about how to proceed." *Id.* But, that wariness yielded as

> The market for acquisition financing for leveraged buyouts rebounded strongly in 2010 and [the] first-quarter [of] 2011. Improved market sentiment and dramatically improved [deal] volume have had a profound effect not only on the process for securing financing commitments, but also on commitment terms.
>
> The process for securing financing commitments has begun to exhibit some of the same competitive, precedent-driven and time-compressed characteristics seen during the last LBO boom . . . [of 2005 to 2007]. . . .
>
> The long-awaited increase in LBO activity is upon us. If first quarter 2011 activity levels are any guide, this will continue to have a significant impact on [the M&A deal-making] process. . . .

Jason Kyrwood, *Industry Insight: Return of the Froth*, THE DEAL, April 25, 2011 at p. 28. As we entered 2012, some of that optimism continued to hold sway, although there was still a strong undercurrent of concern about what the future holds for M&A activity specifically and the capital markets more generally, as described more fully below by seasoned and very experienced M&A lawyers:

Wachtel, Lipton, Rosen & Katz
Mergers and Acquisitions — 2012

As we enter 2012 and as the U.S. economy continues to stabilize, there appears to be a growing sense of optimism about further recovery in the M&A market. During the first half of 2011, the M&A market continued a resurgence that began in the latter part of 2010, with higher aggregate deal value than had been seen since before the financial crisis. Though worldwide M&A activity declined in the second half of 2011, reflecting uncertainties regarding the volatile global financial climate, it has continued at a relatively strong pace, and a number of significant transactions have recently been announced, including Kinder Morgan's $38 billion acquisition of El Paso, United Technologies' $18 billion acquisition of Goodrich, and Gilead's $11 billion acquisition of Pharmasset.

Though current conditions make it difficult to gauge the size and nature of the M&A market in 2012, a number of factors suggest the possibility of increased deal activity in the coming year. The continuing, post-recession/post-financial-crisis emphasis on deleveraging and strengthening of corporate balance sheets makes cost-saving M&A synergies particularly valuable, especially as many companies have already exhausted their own cost-cutting opportunities. Global market pressures, economic volatility and industry-specific factors across a wide array of industries put pressure on corporations to increase scale, diversify their asset base and/or spread R&D costs across larger platforms. These trends were particularly apparent — and can be expected to continue — in the technology, health care and energy sectors, [as reflected in] Google's announced $12.5 billion acquisition of Motorola Mobility, . . . In addition, although debt markets have been volatile, financing has been and continues to be available for strategic acquirers with strong credit and for well-established private equity firms. LBO activity was high in 2011 compared to 2008-2010. . . .

Heightened economic, tax and regulatory uncertainties have, however, caused players in the M&A market to approach transactions with greater care and caution. The implications of the European financial crisis for the U.S. economy and financing markets remain unclear. Stock market volatility, uncertainty about changes to the U.S. corporate tax rate, increasingly aggressive U.S. antitrust enforcement, and the looming U.S. presidential election [in November 2012] also contribute to a lack of forecasting visibility, which in turn significantly impacts the willingness of CEOs and boards of directors to engage in M&A activity. Facing these uncertainties and risks, but also anticipating greater incentives or greater industry-imperatives to merge and acquire, M&A participants are approaching transactions with greater determination and creativity, and M&A transaction structures have trended toward greater complexity and sophistication. Most deals today are taking longer to incubate and execute than in the 2004-2007 period. But some deals that would have died on the drawing board during 2008-2010 are now getting done, due largely to the greater perseverance and problem-solving attitude of transaction participants.

Law firm memo, dated January 9, 2012 (copy on file with author). As of this writing (Fall 2012), an environment of uncertainty continues to prevail in the global economy, with the result — once again, that there is "general wariness about how to proceed"—an observation that should come as no surprise to an experienced M&A lawyer.

G.   Treatment of Fundamental Changes Under Modern Corporation Codes

1.   Historical Perspective

The law has long recognized that corporations grow and change, both from within and by acquisition. As they grow from within, modern statutes recognize that this process is largely controlled by the company's board of directors since they are statutorily mandated to manage the business affairs of the corporation without any direct intervention by the shareholders. (*See, e.g.*, MBCA §8.01, Delaware §141.) However, when it comes to major organic changes in the nature of the company's business, or alternatively in its financial structure, the law typically has required that the board obtain shareholder approval for these types of "fundamental changes." The board, therefore, cannot implement such fundamental changes unilaterally. So, for example, the board of directors cannot unilaterally amend the company's charter (articles of incorporation) without first obtaining consent from the company's shareholders. In this way, the owners of the corporation—that is, the shareholders—retain some residual control over fundamental changes in the company. Equally important, by requiring the board to persuade shareholders to approve a fundamental change in the company's business affairs, the shareholders retain some direct control over the company's managers and thus can hold management accountable by requiring management to explain and justify the major, organic changes they propose.

Early on, corporate law struggled with the threshold question of which types of organic change in a company's business and/or financial affairs qualified as a *fundamental change* that required shareholder approval, as well as the question of how many shareholders must approve a proposed fundamental change in order for it to be validly consummated. With the promulgation of modern corporation codes, and the development of the view that the modern corporation is entirely a creature of statute, these threshold issues are largely addressed today by the provisions of modern corporation statutes.

2.   Modern Perspective

For the most part, today's corporation statutes allow a business broad freedom to choose to organize itself as a corporation by satisfying the prerequisites imposed by the law of the state where the business chooses to incorporate itself. Delaware is the most popular state for incorporation, with most of the publicly traded corporations choosing to incorporate under Delaware's General Corporation Law (DGCL or Del.). Many small, closely held companies, however, choose to incorporate locally rather than in Delaware. This free-dom to choose is important because of the rule of law known as the *internal affairs doctrine*. Under this well-recognized choice of law principle, the law of the state where the business has decided to incorporate will govern the internal affairs of the corporation. Accordingly, under this doctrine, the law of the state where a constituent company is organized will apply to determine the prerequisites that must be satisfied in order for that company to validly consummate a particular method of business combination. Incorporators of a new business may be well advised to take into account the statutory pre-requisites for completing an M&A deal in making their decision where to incorporate.

Early on, state corporation codes usually required unanimous share-holder approval for proposed fundamental changes such as business combi-nations that were subject to a vote of the shareholders. This view was largely premised on the notion that stock ownership was in the nature of personal property, and therefore, no shareholder should be deprived of his/her/its property interests (here, his/her/its share ownership) without first obtaining his/her/its consent. Not surprisingly, the law quickly recognized the problem of the holdout shareholder and the consequent ability of a minority interest to hold hostage a deal that was otherwise favored by a majority of shareholders. Consequently, all modern statutes have scaled back the shareholder voting requirement to something less than unanimity, with a few imposing some type of supermajority shareholder vote (typically requiring approval by two-thirds or three-fourths of the outstanding shares entitled to vote). As we will see in Chapter 2 when we analyze in detail the statutory prerequisites imposed by modern codes, the dominant approach today, reflected in Delaware's statute, is to further relax the voting requirement to a standard known as the *absolute majority vote* (i.e., requiring approval by a majority of the outstanding shares entitled to vote). By relaxing the voting standard in this manner, Delaware and other modern corporation codes allow the majority of voting shares to overrule the minority of shares who object to a proposed business combina-tion, notwithstanding how strenuous or cogent the objections of the minority may be.

At this point, it is worth emphasizing that the bottom line of modern cor-poration codes is that minority shareholders may be deprived of their shares (and all the rights, preferences, privileges, and financial interests those shares originally carried) by the simple expedient of convincing a majority of the shares entitled to vote to approve the terms of a business combination as pro-posed by the company's management. It should come as no surprise that a big part of the study of M&A law, as we shall see in the remaining chapters, involves analyzing the scope and effectiveness of protections offered by state and federal law to prevent abusive treatment of minority shareholders at the hands of the corporate managers who propose a business combination and/or the majority shareholders who approve these proposals of management. Although we will examine the nature of these protections in more detail as we go through the next chapter, it is helpful to describe at the outset the general nature of these protections and the public policy concerns that form the basis for a particular set of protective provisions.

H.   An Introduction to Relevant Public Policy Concerns

1.   The Role of Modern Appraisal Rights

As modern corporation statutes were amended to allow the vote of the majority to eliminate the interest of any minority shareholders who objected to a
proposed business combination, the state legislatures generally felt compelled
to address the plight of this disenfranchised minority interest. The most widely
adopted form of statutory relief is the modern right of appraisal made available
to those shares who object to — that is, dissent from — certain types of proposed
business combinations. The essential nature of this statutory right of appraisal
is that it allows the objecting shareholders to compel the corporation to pay
them the fair value of their shares in cash. In this way, dissenting shareholders
are not locked into continued investment in a corporation that undertakes a
fundamental change that they oppose. Instead, these objecting shareholders
will receive cash, which they are then free to invest elsewhere as they see fit.

As we go through the problems in the next chapter, we will see that the
terms of modern appraisal statutes vary widely. In general, there are four basic
issues to consider:

1. *Availability of Appraisal Rights.* What transactions trigger the dissenting
    shareholder's right to demand payment in cash for his/her/its shares;
2. *Perfecting the Right to an Appraisal.* What procedures must be followed
    for dissenting shareholders to obtain cash payment from the company
    for their shares and how burdensome (i.e., time-consuming and costly)
    these procedures are;
3. *Valuation Issues.* What happens if the dissenting shareholder and the
    company cannot agree on fair value; and
4. *Exclusivity of the Appraisal Remedy.* Does the modern appraisal provide
    the *only* remedy the unhappy shareholder may pursue?

These conceptual issues are raised here at the outset so that you can give some
critical thought to the adequacy (and effectiveness) of the modern appraisal
remedy as you work through the problems in the next chapter and analyze the
differing treatment of dissenting shareholders under the modern corporation
codes.

2.   The Modern Importance of Fiduciary Duty Law

The other major source of protection for those shareholders who object to a proposed business combination is the law of fiduciary duty. A fundamental premise of modern state corporate law is that the company's senior executive officers
(and, more importantly, its board of directors) owe fiduciary obligations to the
company itself. Since management's fiduciary duty obligations run directly to
the corporation, as a matter of law, the board does not owe a duty to act as the
controlling shareholder directs even though the controlling shareholder may

elect the entire board. Instead, the board's duties run directly to the entity itself—that is, to an intangible legal construct that serves the interests of many constituencies, which in the usual case will include, at a minimum, minority shareholders, senior security holders (such as nonvoting preferred stock), debt holders, other business creditors (such as landlords, vendors, etc.), and employees. The relevance of these other interests in the decision-making process of the board as it contemplates a proposed business combination is an important theme of this book.

Duty of Care.   As a matter of law, the board owes a *duty of care* to the company, obligating the board to manage the company's business affairs in a manner that they reasonably believe to be in the company's best interests. The board's duty of care raises obvious questions as to whose interests are to be considered by the board when deciding what is in the company's "best interests." Although this is a matter of considerable disagreement among scholars of corporate law, it would seem that today, the dominant paradigm of board decision making is the *shareholder primacy model*. Under this approach, the board is required to exercise its decision-making responsibilities to maximize the wealth of the company's shareholders. In the case where there is more than one class of stock outstanding (as where there is an outstanding class of preferred stock), the conventional view is that the board is to maximize the wealth of the residual owners of the company, the common stockholders. This view has been subject to considerable criticism, as we shall explore in detail in Chapter 7 when we analyze the scope of these fiduciary duty obligations in more detail. Moreover, there is increasing pressure in recent years to compel the board to include the interests of "other constituencies" (such as the company's employees, suppliers, etc.) in making decisions about corporate acquisitions, among other things. We will discuss this development in more detail in Chapter 6, when we analyze the recent proliferation of *state antitakeover statutes*.

Even more important (for the study of M&A law), the process of deciding whether to engage in a business combination tests the very limits of business discretion conferred on modern corporate managers in a manner that is unlike any other business decision routinely made by a company's board of directors. Modern corporate law extends great deference to the board's business decisions with respect to managing the company's business affairs. Thus, the business judgment rule generally presumes that the board acts in the company's best interests in the absence of fraud, illegality, or self-dealing. However, the recent waves of merger activity (most notably the Deal Decade of the 1980s), along with the bursting of the speculative stock market bubble of the 1990s, have led to renewed concern as to what the board must demonstrate in order to obtain the benefit of the protection of the Business Judgment Rule. More specifically, what level of monitoring, oversight, analysis, and deliberation is required in order for the board to demonstrate that it has exercised informed decision making in good faith and in a manner not tainted by any conflict of interest? In the economic downturn of the early 2000s, the courts revisited this question in cases challenging failed business acquisitions. In these cases, very often the shareholders questioned the adequacy of the decision-making process that led the company's managers to propose a particular business combination that ultimately proved to be financially disastrous for the company.

As we shall see in the remaining chapters, the Great Recession of 2008-2009 and its aftermath have only served to intensify investor scrutiny of the role of the CEO and the conduct of the company's board of directors in the context of an M&A transaction. "Reviewing the merits and disadvantages of an M&A transaction constitutes an important area of board decision-making. In terms of the corporate governance environment, these are turbulent times indeed and never before have the actions of the board been subject to such strict scrutiny, given the lessons from the global financial crisis and a fair share of corporate governance scandals. . . . " Uma Kanth Varottil, *Corporate Governance in M&A Transactions: The Indian Story in Global Mergers and Acquisitions*, Luncheon Address, International Bar Association Conference, March 9, 2012 (copy on file with author). Consequently, today's transaction planners must give renewed consideration as to the conduct required of the board so that it may fulfill its fiduciary duty of care. We will consider this decision-making process in more detail in Chapter 5, as part of our discussion of negotiating and documenting the deal, and again in Chapter 7, when we analyze the scope of management's fiduciary duty obligations.

Duty of Loyalty.   The board's fiduciary obligations also include the separate duty of loyalty, which, like the duty of care, runs directly to the corporation itself. Today, this duty of loyalty requires the board to make business decisions that are not tainted by any conflict of interest—and increasingly, this includes avoiding even the appearance of a conflict of interest. In the wake of recent financial scandals, public policymakers (at both the state and federal level) have focused their attention and investigative resources on the threshold question: Who qualifies as a *truly* independent director? Which board members are free of *any* conflict of interest— direct or indirect? In other words, *whom* do we trust to make decisions that are *truly* in the best interests of the company? The fallout from the financial scandals surrounding Enron and others in the early years of the twenty-first century, and then the subsequent financial crisis in the banking industry, has resurrected serious corporate governance concerns reminiscent of the post-Watergate era of the 1970s. In the immediate aftermath of Watergate, introspective reform efforts were launched that ultimately led to increasing reliance on the use of outside directors. Specifically, boards were increasingly populated with nonmanagement directors; that is, directors who were not employed either directly (as company officers or managers), or indirectly (such as serving as the company's management consultant or investment banker).

Sarbanes-Oxley Act.   In the aftermath of Enron, Tyco, WorldCom, Rite-Aid, Adelphia, and other financial scandals on a scale not seen since the Great Depression, Congress, the SEC and other regulators of our financial markets responded by investigating, among other things, the decision-making process of the modern corporate boardroom. Congress's investigation culminated in 2002 with the enactment of a package of far-ranging reform measures commonly referred to as the Sarbanes-Oxley Act, and more affectionately known as "SOX."* The reforms legislated into place by SOX were the product of

---

*Sarbanes-Oxley Act of 2002, Pub. L. No. 107-204, 116 Stat. 745 (2002). Most of the provisions of this new law are codified in various provisions of the Securities Exchange Act of 1934, 15 U.S.C. §78 (2000).—Ed.

highly publicized hearings, conducted by both houses of Congress in the aftermath of the scandals involving fraud and mismanagement at such major U.S.
companies as Enron, Tyco, Adelphia and Worldcom. Hailed as a landmark and
comprehensive legislation scheme, SOX was intended to reform corporate governance and behavior, increase the standards of accountability for the accounting
profession, and ensure the reliability of financial statements of public companies.
[SOX established an] independent accounting oversight board [the PCAOB,
Public Company Accounting Oversight Board, which now polices the accounting profession and sets auditing standards], [mandated] auditor independence,
strengthened corporate governance and responsibility standards, and [imposed]
financial accuracy obligations . . . on senior management. [In adopting SOX],
Congress addressed what it perceived to be the corporate governance and auditing shortcomings that had contributed to the scandals culminating in the bankruptcy of Enron.

James M. Lyons, *Representing Independent Directors After Sarbanes-Oxley: The
Growing Role of Independent Counsel,* BUSINESS LAW TODAY, January-February
2010 at p. 53. As we celebrate the tenth anniversary of the enactment of SOX,
commentators are beginning to take stock (no pun intended) of the efficacy of
the various reforms introduced by what is widely regarded "as the [most] sweeping [set of] financial [regulatory reforms] since the Securities Act of 1934."
Paul Sweeney, *Sarbanes-Oxley—A Decade Later,* FINANCIAL EXECUTIVE, July-August
2012; *see also* Lixiong Guo and Ronald Masulis, *Board Structure and Monitoring:
New Evidence from CEO Turnover, available at* http://ssrn.com/abstract=2021468
(last modified Oct. 8, 2012) ("This paper uses the mandatory changes in board
composition brought about by the new exchange listing rules following the passage of [SOX in order] to estimate the effect of overall board independence . . .
on forced CEO turnover.").

One of the issues addressed in this reform legislation is the basic question
of *who* should decide what is in the company's best interests. As a result of the
reform measures introduced by SOX, the SEC (and other market regulators)
are addressing the related public policy questions: How much decision-making
discretion should be delegated to corporate managers? Which kind of business
decisions should be subject to shareholder approval? These same questions are
cornerstone issues in our study of M&A law.

Dodd-Frank Act.   Many Wall Street observers have questioned the strength
and effectiveness of SOX's reforms, and some have faulted SOX for not preventing the most recent financial crisis within the banking industry that ultimately
led to the Great Recession of 2008-2009, from which (as of this writing in Fall
2012) the U.S. economy—indeed, the global economy—has yet to fully recover.
Not surprisingly, Congress once again responded by enacting the Dodd-Frank
Wall Street Reform and Consumer Protection Act, Pub. L. No. 111-203, 124 Stat.
1376 (2010) ("Dodd-Frank"), which was signed into law by President Barack
Obama on July 21, 2010, almost eight years to the day following enactment of
SOX (which was signed into law by President George W. Bush on July 30, 2002).
The primary purpose of Dodd-Frank "is to identify and manage threats to the
stability of the nation's financial system, such as those that contributed to the
economic downturn commencing in 2008. [Among other matters of financial
industry regulation, Dodd-Frank addresses consumer protection, derivatives,

and hedge fund regulation.] Many [of Dodd-Frank's] provisions require various regulatory bodies to draft, adopt and implement regulations, and these will have a significant effect on the impact [and efficacy of Dodd-Frank's reform measures]." Peter Menard, *The Dodd-Frank Act: A Guide to the Corporate Governance, Executive Compensation, and Disclosure Provisions,* BUSINESS LAW NEWS, (State Bar of California, Issue 1, 2011) at p. 1.

In addition, and more important for our study of M&A law, Dodd-Frank "addresses corporate governance and executive compensation matters that will be relevant for most U.S. public companies." Stuart N. Alperin, et al., *Dodd-Frank Act Mandates Say-on-Pay Votes and Other Corporate Governance Changes,* 14 THE M&A LAWYER (Issue 7, July/August 2010). Of the various Dodd-Frank provisions that apply to U.S. public companies, most notable for our purposes are the following provisions, which mandate:

- Shareholder advisory votes on executive compensation—more popularly referred to as "say-on-pay" votes;
- "Clawbacks" of incentive compensation, when public companies are required to restate their financial statements (which go beyond the "clawback" requirements imposed on a company's CEO or CFO by SOX);
- Enhanced independence for board compensation committees and their advisors; and
- Enhanced proxy disclosures as to a number of matters, particularly with respect to disclosure of executive compensation arrangements (including "golden parachute" arrangements of the type we will discuss in Chapter 7, as part of our examination of "hostile takeovers").

See Peter Menard, *The Dodd-Frank Act: What Public Companies Should Do Now,* THE CORPORATE COUNSELOR, (Winter 2011) at p. 1; and *see also* Alperin, et al., *supra.* In addition, Dodd-Frank authorizes the SEC to adopt what is popularly known as "proxy access"; i.e., Dodd-Frank authorizes the SEC to promulgate rules that would allow shareholders of publicly traded companies to nominate candidates for election to the company's board of directors and to then have their nominees included in the company's annual proxy materials. The SEC is still in the process of adopting its proxy access rules. While a comprehensive examination of Dodd-Frank's reform measures is beyond the scope of this casebook, we will address several of Dodd-Frank's executive compensation provisions as part of the materials in Chapters 4 and 7.

The Impact of Modern Fiduciary Duty Law. In the most recent wave of merger activity in the 1980s and 1990s, the primary legal constraint on managerial discretion was the limitations imposed by the fiduciary obligations of a company's board of directors. The nature of these constraints, as developed primarily by the jurisprudence of the Delaware courts, will be the focus of the materials in Chapter 7. As we shall see, though, when we analyze the problems in Chapter 2, no matter what form the business acquisition takes, fiduciary duty law is implicated at every stage in the board's decision-making process. The problems in the next chapter serve to illustrate the importance of modern fiduciary duty law and to highlight the various pressure points in the deal-making process where fiduciary duty obligations intervene to constrain and guide managerial discretion. Later, in Chapter 7, we will study in more detail the case law that further refines and describes the nature and scope of management's fiduciary obligations in the context of M&A transactions.

The reason for this organizational approach is that you cannot fully appreciate the important constraints imposed by modern fiduciary law until *after* you have finished studying the various state and federal law requirements that regulate M&A activity in the modern financial markets. By introducing principles of fiduciary duty law early in the course, however, you are encouraged to think critically about the terms of these state and federal rules that regulate M&A transactions as we go through each of the topics that build up to Chapter 7, where we will study modern fiduciary duty obligations in considerable detail.

Specifically, you should think critically about whether the legal rules we will analyze in the next few chapters are sufficient from a public policy perspective to protect the competing interests in M&A transactions. In addition, you should consider whether, as a matter of public policy, these legal rules should be made mandatory, or alternatively, whether business persons should be allowed the freedom to customize the legal rules in order to accommodate their specific business objectives. If you decide that certain legal rules should be made mandatory, then you must consider the justification that supports this legal conclusion. In other words, you need to consider what arguments you would make to persuade the policymakers (whether they be legislators or regulators at either the state or federal level) to adopt the legal rule you advocate and to make that rule mandatory (i.e., nonwaivable).

These issues raise large and important questions for which no easy answers exist. These are the public policy issues that now dominate public debate in the wake of the recent financial crisis and the ensuing Great Recession as business leaders, legislators, regulators, and other policymakers consider how best to regulate our modern financial markets. Since the business environment most certainly will only continue to evolve and grow ever more complex, these issues certainly will not go away. Just as assuredly, though, the nature of the legal response that is appropriate is a matter that will require diligent attention so that the legal rules and regulatory environment adequately evolve so as to appropriately accommodate the ever-changing nature of business practices in the world of M&A transactions. The goal of this casebook is to introduce you to the principles that currently guide M&A law and to encourage you to think critically about the adequacy and legitimacy of the current legal framework. This is a large and important task because, after all, that is what you will be called upon to do as a practicing M&A lawyer.

I. *Overview of Different Methods for Structuring Business Acquisitions*

Before we launch into our analysis of the substantive detail of M&A law in the next chapter, it is helpful to get a sense of the forest before encountering very many of the trees. This section introduces the three basic methods for one corporation to acquire another: the asset purchase, the stock purchase, and the direct (or statutory) merger. In the process of introducing these basic methods, we will refer to the diagrams that are included in Appendix A. The diagrams are critical for two reasons. First, the diagrams are useful for conceptualizing, and ultimately understanding, the differences in legal consequences of each of the different methods available for structuring a proposed acquisition. Second, the diagrams are crucial to understanding the relationship between Bidder and Target and the financial terms of their acquisition agreement. As we go through the problems and cases in the next chapter, it is important to refer to these diagrams so that you fully appreciate the differences in the mechanics of each type of acquisition transaction.

Finally, the brief overview that follows will serve to highlight the fundamental observation that, as a practical matter, *any* of these three methods can be used today to reach an economic result that is virtually *identical* in each case, although the three different methods have very different legal consequences. In analyzing the problems in the next chapter, we will examine in detail the prerequisites imposed by modern statutes in order to validly consummate each of these three basic methods of business combinations. However, let's begin our study of M&A law by briefly comparing each of the three basic methods for structuring a business acquisition: the merger, the asset purchase, and the stock purchase.

1.   Traditional Form: Direct Merger (Diagram 1)

Under the traditional form of direct merger (or "statutory merger," as it is often called in the M&A literature), the boards of both Bidder Co. and Target Co. initiate a transaction in which, as a practical matter, Bidder will swallow up Target, who will then cease to exist as a separate entity when the transaction is consummated. Hence, the terminology of mergers generally refers to Bidder as the *surviving* corporation and to Target as the *disappearing* corporation.

In order to validly consummate a merger, modern state corporation codes typically require approval of the merger agreement (or the plan of merger as it is sometimes called) by the boards of both constituent corporations. The merger agreement then must be submitted to the shareholders for their approval. Historically, approval required a supermajority vote (most often two-thirds of the outstanding voting stock). Today, however, most states have relaxed the voting standard to an absolute majority of the outstanding shares entitled to vote. The plan of merger is required to set forth certain items. Specifically, the plan of merger must indicate which company is to survive and which company is to disappear, and must identify the nature and amount of the consideration to be exchanged in the merger (generally referred to as the "merger consideration"). In the traditional form of direct merger, the Target Co. shareholders would receive Bidder Co. stock in exchange for their Target shares. When the dust settles and the transaction is consummated, the former Target Co. shareholders end up as shareholders of Bidder Co., the surviving corporation.

Knowing which company is to survive is crucial in the law of mergers because of the rule of successor liability imposed under modern corporation codes. Under this rule, the surviving corporation succeeds by operation of law to all the rights and liabilities of *both* Bidder Co. and Target Co. as the constituent corporations. Briefly stated, the legal significance of this rule of successor liability lies in the transaction cost savings to the parties, which is often quite substantial because the individual assets and liabilities of Target do not have to be separately transferred to Bidder. As a practical matter, this cost savings may be the most efficient way to transfer certain (particularly large and complex) businesses, and often will be the big advantage of the merger over other available forms for structuring a business acquisition. As a final matter, appraisal rights traditionally have been made available (under modern state corporation statutes) to dissenting shareholders of both constituent corporations.

2.   Traditional Form: Asset Purchase for Cash (Diagram 4)

At early common law, the asset purchase was often used in those situations where state law did not permit Bidder to acquire Target using the merger procedures. Most often, this situation would arise where Bidder and Target were incorporated in different jurisdictions, and the law of the state of incorporation of either the Bidder or the Target did not authorize one or the other to merge with a foreign corporation. As a practical matter, the only option legally available to the determined Bidder was to purchase all of Target's assets directly from the company. Since Target continues to exist, this method of acquisition had the added advantage of allowing Bidder to take on only those debts of Target Co. that Bidder Co. had specifically agreed to assume (in the language of contract law, an *express assumption*).

 This rule of successor liability means that Target Co. continues to be obligated on all those claims not specifically transferred to the Bidder in the case of an asset acquisition. The direct consequence of this rule is that acquisitions structured as a sale of all of Target's assets will usually contemplate a second step involving the voluntary dissolution and orderly winding up of Target Co.'s business affairs. In dissolution, the proceeds from the sale of Target's assets are used to satisfy the claims of Target Co.'s creditors. Any funds left after paying off Target Co.'s creditors are then distributed in liquidation to Target's shareholders, with priority being given to those shares carrying a liquidation preference (*preferred shares*), as set forth in Target Co.'s Articles of Incorporation.

 In order to validly consummate the sale of all of its assets, most state corporation statutes require that the board of the selling corporation (Target Co.) must approve the transaction. Target's board then must obtain approval from Target's shareholders in order to complete the transaction, on the grounds that the sale of all of the company's assets constitutes a fundamental change for Target Co.

 As for Bidder, state corporation codes usually impose no board or shareholder voting requirements, largely on the grounds that this transaction does not involve a fundamental change for Bidder. Once Bidder consummates the transaction with Target, Bidder remains in place, having used its cash resources to acquire the business operations of Target Co. The state corporation statutes generally view this decision to use Bidder's cash resources to acquire Target's assets as a matter left to the business discretion of the board of directors of

Bidder Co. Under the traditional view of the corporate norm, this decision is generally entitled to protection under the Business Judgment Rule, and consequently, no vote of Bidder's shareholders is required.

Another advantage that further increased the popularity of the sale of assets method for business acquisitions is that many states deny the right of appraisal to Target's shareholders. These states limit this right of appraisal to *merger* transactions *only*. Moreover, Bidder Co. shareholders are denied appraisal rights since the transaction does not involve a fundamental change for Bidder Co. Consequently, the flexibility offered by the sale of assets method often proves quite attractive to Target's management, especially in those situations where Target's management anticipates a large number of shares (albeit less than a majority) to object.

3.   Traditional Form: Stock Purchase for Cash (Diagram 6)

As a final alternative, Bidder can acquire control over Target by the simple expedient of approaching Target shareholders individually and offering to buy Target shares directly from individual shareholders. Unlike the other two methods for acquiring Target, this transaction does not involve Target. Hence, the stock purchase agreement will be entered into directly between the Bidder and the individual shareholders of Target. So long as the relevant state corporation statute authorizes Bidder to own shares of another company and assuming that Bidder's powers are not otherwise limited by an appropriate provision in the company's articles of incorporation, there are usually no other specific statutory prerequisites to be satisfied in order for the parties to validly complete this type of transaction.

Most significantly for purposes of this discussion, Target's board is not required to approve the transaction since Target itself is *not* a party to the transaction. This will prove to be vitally important in those cases where Target's board refuses to make a deal with Bidder. As a practical matter, the only alternative left to the Bidder who remained determined to acquire control over Target (notwithstanding the failure of Target's management to negotiate with Bidder) would be for Bidder to buy Target shares directly from Target shareholders. By structuring the transaction this way, Bidder eliminates any need to obtain approval from Target's board in order to complete the acquisition. In certain situations, this will prove to be a major advantage over the alternative methods of acquiring Target—that is, the statutory merger or the purchase of all of Target's assets—both of which require approval by Target's board in order to be validly consummated. This is probably the key distinguishing feature of using the stock purchase to acquire control of Target. Here, no vote of either Target's board or its shareholders is required. Rather, Target shareholders simply express their objections to Bidder's proposal to acquire Target—that is, their dissent—by refusing to tender their shares. By holding on to their shares in Target, they effectively reject the contract offer made by Bidder. If enough Target shareholders refuse to sell to Bidder, then generally the acquisition fails. Recognizing this possibility, Bidder typically would condition its obligation to purchase Target shares (that is, to close on the stock purchase agreement) on Bidder's ability to get a sufficient number of Target shareholders to accept Bidder's offer. As a general proposition, Bidder usually would require that enough Target shareholders accept (by tendering their shares to Bidder) in order to give Bidder control over Target, even if it owns less than 100 percent of Target's outstanding voting shares. In this way, the determined Bidder can acquire effective *control* over Target even in the face of strenuous objections from Target's management. This has led to what has come to be known as the *market for corporate control*, a topic that will be introduced in analyzing the problem sets in Chapter 2 and then discussed at greater length later in Chapter 7 as part of our examination of fiduciary duty law.

One of the best-known hallmarks of the market for corporate control is the *hostile takeover*. While a detailed examination of the hostile takeover will be undertaken in Chapter 7, when we examine the landmark fiduciary duty cases that were decided by the Delaware Supreme Court in the 1980s, a brief description is in order at this point. The hostile takeover (which came to dominate the "Deal Decade of the 1980s," as pointed out in the testimony of Dr. Janet Yellin, see *supra* at p. 26-28), typically involves a two-step acquisition. First, the hostile bidder (often more popularly referred to as a "raider") makes an unsolicited offer to buy Target shares at a (usually rather substantial) premium over the current trading price in the open market. The raider's (Bidder's) obligation to close on this stock purchase is usually conditioned on the raider's ability to get a sufficient number of shares to obtain voting control of Target. Once the first step is completed, the raider will generally undertake the second step, which involves a back-end merger that eliminates ("squeezes out") the remaining minority shareholder interest in Target. In Chapter 2, we will study the corporate formalities that must be satisfied in order to validly complete this type of two-step acquisition under modern state corporation statutes. However, it bears emphasizing (at the outset) that these hostile takeovers are also subject to regulation under federal securities laws (which we will study in Chapter 6 as part of our discussion of the Williams Act). In addition, we will examine many of the better-known cases involving hostile takeovers as part of our discussion of fiduciary duty law in Chapter 7.

In the case of a stock purchase, Target remains intact, as does Bidder. By purchasing all of (or at least a controlling interest in) Target stock, this type of acquisition transaction will leave Target's business in place, to be operated as a wholly owned (or at least a controlled) subsidiary of Bidder. Hence, this method of acquisition is often referred to as a "change of control transaction" because there has been a change in ownership of all of—or at least a controlling interest in—Target's stock. Since Target remains in place, all of Target's assets remain available to satisfy the claims of Target's creditors, unlike the rule of successor liability that operates in the case of a merger. For reasons that we explore in Chapter 3 (regarding successor liability and the impact of M&A transactions on third-party creditors), it will often be advantageous to leave Target in place, making this method of structuring an acquisition the preferred approach over the other two methods.

As a final advantage, there are *no* appraisal rights available to the shareholders of *either* Bidder or Target in the case of a stock purchase. From the perspective of Target, those shareholders who object to Bidder's acquisition proposal simply hold onto their shares. Since the Target shareholders cannot be deprived of their share ownership without their consent in the case of a stock purchase, the law has never perceived the need to extend appraisal rights to this type of acquisition. As for Bidder shareholders, this transaction does not present a fundamental change; consequently, there generally is no requirement for a shareholder vote and therefore no appraisal rights.

NOTES

1. (*Getting Fancy by*) *Varying the Type of Consideration.*   As we shall see when we analyze the problems in the next chapter, modern statutes afford corporate managers considerable flexibility in the type of consideration that Bidder can use to acquire Target. Modern statutes generally provide this flexibility in one of two ways. First, today's state corporation codes generally authorize broad powers for the modern corporation unless the company's articles of incorporation limit the scope of its powers. Thus, modern corporations have all the powers of a natural person (unless specifically limited by a provision in their articles or charter), which includes the power to hold stock in another corporation (domestic or foreign) as well as the power to issue debt in the name of the company on any terms that the board decides are consistent with the company's best interests. *See*, e.g., MBCA §3.03 (describing powers conferred on modern corporation in the absence of a limiting provision in the company's articles of incorporation).

The other way in which modern statutes confer considerable flexibility on corporate managers lies in the specific provisions authorizing corporate acquisitions. Most important, today's merger statutes specify a broad range of consideration that Bidder may use to acquire Target shares, including cash, tangible or intangible property, or stock (or other securities) of Bidder or of some other corporation. In similar fashion, the modern corporation codes have liberalized the nature of the consideration that can be used to acquire substantially all of Target's assets.

By authorizing Bidder to use the shares of some *other* corporation, the law moved beyond two-party mergers (involving only the disappearing company and the surviving company) to authorize three-party mergers. These are more commonly known as *triangular mergers*. This topic is introduced in the next section.

2. *An Introduction to Three-Party Transactions.*   In the case of a three-party transaction, Bidder will generally create a wholly owned subsidiary for purposes of completing the acquisition. Acting as the incorporator, Bidder organizes a new corporation (referred to as "NewCo" in the diagrams of Appendix A). At the organizational meeting of NewCo's board of directors, all of NewCo's outstanding voting common stock is then issued to Bidder generally in exchange for the consideration that will be used to acquire Target—which will usually be either Bidder's stock (or other securities) or its cash. As a result, Bidder is the sole shareholder of NewCo, and as such, will appoint the entire board of directors of NewCo, thereby creating a parent-subsidiary relationship between Bidder and NewCo.

After incorporating NewCo, Bidder will then cause NewCo to complete the acquisition of Target. So, for example, in the case of an acquisition structured as a sale of assets, NewCo would acquire all of Target's assets, leaving Target's business operations to be held in a wholly owned subsidiary of Bidder once the transaction is completed. This may prove advantageous in those situations where Bidder desires (for either legal or business reasons) to segregate its assets from those of Target. We will explore these considerations in Chapter 3, when we analyze the rules of successor liability in more detail.

By far, however, the most popular form of a three-party acquisition transaction is the *triangular merger*. Triangular mergers are a fairly recent development in corporate law, having really gained popularity only in the last 25 years or so. Although the mechanics are too complicated to summarize here, the major advantage of a three-party (triangular) merger over the well-established two-party (direct) merger is easy to grasp. By using its wholly owned subsidiary (NewCo) to merge with Target, Bidder shields its assets from the business debts of Target. By operating Target as a wholly owned subsidiary, and assuming there is no reason for Target's creditors to pierce the subsidiary's corporate veil to reach the assets of the parent company, Bidder will be able to protect its asset base from the claims of Target's creditors.

Another significant advantage of the triangular merger is that it usually allows Bidder to eliminate the need to obtain approval from its shareholders and, generally speaking, will also eliminate any right of appraisal for Bidder's dissenting shares. This may prove to be advantageous to Bidder by allowing it to avoid the cost and delay associated with obtaining a vote of its shareholders and the availability of a dissenting right of appraisal, which may be particularly helpful in the case of a publicly traded Bidder. For all of these reasons, the triangular merger is probably the most widely used method for structuring business combinations in today's M&A market.

3. Cross-Border Transactions. Nestlé's acquisition of Chef America reflects a cross-border transaction that involves a Swiss-based conglomerate's takeover of a U.S.-based company. However, it is often the case that U.S.-based companies seek to expand their businesses beyond their own domestic markets by acquiring companies that are based in other countries. A recent, high-profile example of such a transaction is Kraft Foods Inc.'s 2010 bid for Cadbury plc, a business organized under United Kingdom law, which was ultimately successful. *See* Dana Climillica & Ilan Brat, *Kraft Wins a Reluctant Cadbury,* WALL STREET JOURNAL, Jan. 20, 2010, at B1.

Regulation of cross-border transactions (such as Kraft's takeover of Cadbury) is beyond the scope of this text. However, it is interesting to note that this acquisition in the *global* M&A market raises all of the same important corporate governance concerns that are an inherent attribute of *domestic* M&A transactions, and which are also an important theme of this casebook. As originally structured, 60 percent of Kraft's offer to acquire Cadbury consisted of Kraft stock, and the balance of Kraft's $16.7 billion bid was to be paid in cash. However, Warren Buffett, one of Kraft's largest stockholders, publicly objected to this aspect of the deal. In response to this very public criticism coming from a well-known and well-regarded investor, Kraft's management (led by its CEO, Irene Rosenfeld) revised the terms of its offer for Cadbury to include more cash in its bid and thereby significantly reduce the number of Kraft shares to be issued as part of the acquisition consideration. The nature of the corporate governance concerns that are implicated in the structure of Kraft's acquisition of Cadbury are to be explored further, starting with the problem sets in the next chapter.

‖2‖

Corporate Formalities: The Mechanics of Structuring Acquisition Transactions

A. An Introduction to Corporate Law Statutes: The Statutory Scheme of Delaware, Model Act, and California

In this chapter, we sketch out the regulatory framework that applies to the acquisition process. This includes a detailed review of the relevant provisions of state corporate law, focusing primarily on the corporation statutes of Delaware and California with references to the Model Act as well. The reason we focus on Delaware law is that Delaware is the most popular state for incorporation, particularly for large, publicly traded corporations. Accordingly, Delaware is the most important source of jurisprudence in the area of mergers and acquisitions (M&A) transactions. The reason to study California law, aside from the fact that it is an important commercial state much like Illinois, New York, and Texas, is because California has adopted a regulatory approach to M&A activity that is very different from any other jurisdiction. Since the regulatory philosophy adopted in California's Corporation Code (CCC) stands in stark contrast to Delaware's statute, the Delaware General Corporation Law (DGCL), detailed analysis of the provisions of these two jurisdictions allows for critical examination of the public policy considerations that are relevant to regulating the market for M&A transactions.

On a more practical note, the problems in this chapter require you to work through various provisions of each state's corporation code. In doing these problems, you will be exposed to the kind of statutory analysis that is part of the M&A lawyer's daily work. In addition, these problems will allow you to hone your skills involving statutory analysis, as you will be required to read statutory provisions to understand the meaning of the language of a particular statute and to determine how the various provisions of the statute work together to create a comprehensive regulatory framework. Finally, you will be asked to compare the results obtained under Delaware law with those reached in applying the provisions of the California law and examine the public policy implications of each state's regulatory approach.

In addition, we will introduce the role of the federal securities laws in regulating M&A activity. Although we will not study the relevant provisions of the federal securities law in detail until we get to Chapter 4, the problems are useful in illustrating the interaction between federal and state law. M&A lawyers must understand this interaction in order to structure the M&A transaction in compliance with both.

Since many states have adopted corporation statutes that are based in some measure on the Model Business Corporation Act (MBCA), references will be made throughout the materials in this chapter to the MBCA provision that corresponds to the particular Delaware provision at issue. Analyzing the problem under the relevant MBCA provision first, before turning to the relevant Delaware statute, may be helpful in mastering what is often the much more convoluted provisions of the DGCL. More important, the MBCA has undergone major revisions over the years, resulting in a substantial restructuring (and rewording) of its provisions. The statutory language of the MBCA provisions thus reflects a deliberate effort to make the MBCA provisions clearer and easier to understand.

A word of caution, though, is still in order. Notwithstanding these recent efforts to clarify the statutory language of the MBCA, there will still be times when the language of these statutes, including the MBCA, is ambiguous as applied to the facts of a particular problem. Alternatively, the statutory language may be clear enough, but as applied to the facts of a particular case, the result may be unjust or unreasonable. In these cases, as with other statutes that lawyers must grapple with as part of their daily practice, you will be called upon to consider how to interpret the statutory language in order to reach a fair result. As part of this analytical process, you will be required to consider the public policy concerns that underlie the relevant statute's regulatory approach. The problems in this chapter are intended to flesh out important public policy considerations—matters of particular concern today in light of the recent financial scandals that ultimately led to congressional enactment of the Sarbanes-Oxley Act in 2002 and then later the Dodd-Frank Act in 2010.

1.　The Requirement of Board and/or Shareholder Approval Under State Law

In the problems in this chapter, you will be asked to consider the relevant statutory prerequisites (generally referred to as the "corporate formalities") that must be satisfied for the M&A transaction to be validly consummated. As reflected in the cases to be analyzed in this chapter, the failure to satisfy the statutory prerequisites imposed by the law of the state where the company is organized may create the basis for a shareholder challenge to the validity of the transaction. Most often, this challenge will be an equitable action, usually seeking to enjoin completion of the transaction unless and until the relevant corporate formalities have been satisfied.

Where the transaction is challenged for failure to satisfy the required formalities imposed by state corporate law, the challenge will often focus on shareholder voting rights and/or the availability of appraisal rights. Accordingly, as part of each problem in this chapter, we will analyze whether the transaction requires approval by the shareholders and whether the transaction triggers a right of appraisal for those shareholders who object to the acquisition. In addition, we will consider the threshold requirement of board authorization of an acquisition and the statutory source of this obligation. One of the valuable contributions of the lawyer as a transaction planner is structuring the acquisition in compliance with all relevant statutory requirements on a cost-effective basis so that the transaction will proceed to close in a timely manner.

As an alternative to an injunctive action, which is generally intended to prevent consummation of an acquisition, the shareholder may bring an action for damages, or for rescission of the acquisition, *after* the transaction has been completed. The equitable action for rescission is generally doomed to fail, as most courts are reluctant to unwind completed transactions in order to restore the parties to the status quo ante, as called for under the remedy of rescission. For that reason, among others, it is incumbent on the shareholder who strongly opposes a proposed acquisition to bring an action prior to consummation of the deal if the shareholder's primary goal is to preserve the independence of the company by preventing completion of the transaction.

If, on the other hand, the shareholder's primary objection concerns the adequacy of the acquisition consideration, the shareholder may bring an action for damages. In these cases, the modern appraisal remedy may prove adequate to address the shareholder's grievances. In cases involving management's breach of fiduciary duty, however, there will be a threshold question as to the adequacy of the appraisal remedy to address the public policy concerns raised by this kind of shareholder complaint. At the end of this chapter, we will explore the scope of the appraisal remedy and examine cases that address the adequacy and the exclusivity of this remedy.

2.   Federal Securities Laws and the Stock Exchange Rules

In addition to a thorough understanding of the relevant default rules of state corporate law, the transaction planner must consider the application of the federal securities laws and the rules of self-regulatory organizations, such as the New York Stock Exchange (NYSE). Although we will discuss the federal securities laws in more detail in later chapters, it is useful at this point to summarize the provisions that are relevant to the process of obtaining (shareholder) approval of the proposed acquisition.

a.   The Federal Proxy Rules

In the case of acquisitions involving *reporting companies* under the 1934 Act, the federal proxy rules will apply. As you will recall, reporting companies fall into one of two categories: (i) companies whose shares are listed for trading on a national exchange (which includes the NYSE); or (ii) companies that meet both of the following criteria—they have a class of shareholders numbering 500 or more *and* they have assets totaling $10 million or more.

When management solicits votes from shareholders of a reporting company, the proxy rules of the Securities and Exchange Commission (SEC) require that the company's managers file a proxy statement with the SEC and distribute the proxy statement to the company's shareholders. The goal of the SEC's proxy rules is to provide the shareholders of a publicly traded company with the information they need to make an informed decision on whether to approve the terms of an acquisition negotiated by company managers. Hence, the SEC's proxy rules generally obligate company managers to provide full and adequate disclosure of all material facts about the proposed acquisition. We will analyze the appropriate standard of *materiality* in Chapter 4, as part of a more detailed review of the provisions of the federal securities laws that are relevant in the context of M&A transactions.

b. The Securities Act of 1933

Whenever Bidder Co. proposes to use its stock as the acquisition consideration, Bidder needs to comply with the requirements of the Securities Act of 1933 (the 1933 Act). Briefly summarized, the 1933 Act regulates the distribution (i.e., the issuance) of shares by requiring the issuer (here, Bidder) to register the distribution (i.e., the offer and sale) of Bidder's shares unless an exemption from registration is available. The goal of the registration requirements of the 1933 Act is to protect the purchaser of securities by requiring the issuer to disclose all material facts regarding the proposed offering (issuance) of its securities so that the prospective investor (purchaser) can make an informed investment decision. The issuer may avoid (or reduce) the delay and expense associated with preparing a registration statement by establishing that one of the SEC's exemptions from registration is available. In this way, the 1933 Act regulates the process of capital formation whereby companies sell their stock (or other securities) to the investing public in order to raise the capital they need to finance their business operations.

In the context of M&A transactions, the 1933 Act applies where Bidder proposes to use its stock as the acquisition consideration. In this situation, the SEC views Bidder's issuance of its stock (or other securities) to acquire Target as a distribution that is subject to the regulatory scheme of the 1933 Act. Thus, the issuer (Bidder Co.) must register or find an exemption in order to use its stock to acquire Target. This registration obligation is imposed on all issuers, whether publicly traded or privately held, who propose to sell their stock. Those rules promulgated by the SEC under the 1933 Act that are most pertinent to M&A transactions are discussed in more detail in Chapter 4.

c. Shareholder Approval Requirements of the NYSE

The NYSE is a secondary trading market where persons who already own outstanding shares of a company and wish to sell them deal with other investors who want to buy shares. Thus, the NYSE is *not* where a company goes to raise new capital by issuing (selling) securities to the public, and therefore, the provisions of the 1933 Act generally do not apply to the trading activity that occurs on the floor of the NYSE. Rather, the provisions of the Securities Exchange Act of 1934 (the 1934 Act) apply to regulate the trading practices of sellers, buyers, broker-dealer firms, and other securities professionals who participate in the trading activity of secondary markets such as the NYSE.

The NYSE and other secondary trading markets, most notably the NASDAQ Stock Market (NASDAQ), are heavily regulated by the SEC. Under provisions of the 1934 Act, the NYSE qualifies as a self-regulatory organization (SRO). As such, it has its own set of operating rules and procedures, and it regulates its membership by way of these rules and procedures. As an SRO, the rules and procedures adopted and enforced by the NYSE are subject to oversight by the SEC. Accordingly, any changes to a particular NYSE rule require approval of the SEC.

Very important for our study of M&A law are those NYSE rules that apply to companies whose securities are listed for trading on the NYSE. To be listed, a company must satisfy certain NYSE criteria as to size and share ownership, known as the *listing standards*. Further, each company must enter into a listing agreement with the NYSE, which obligates the *listed company* to comply with the rules and procedures contained in the NYSE's Listed Company Manual. Among the most important of these obligations, at least for our purposes, are the disclosure obligations and the shareholder voting rules that are imposed on all NYSE-listed companies. With respect to disclosure requirements, the NYSE obligates listed companies to make information about developments affecting the company publicly available on a timely basis. We will describe how this obligation comes into play later in Chapter 4, when we describe the obligation of publicly traded constituent corporations to disclose pending negotiations for mergers or other types of business combinations.

More important for purposes of the topic at hand are the shareholder voting rights imposed by the rules of the NYSE. The shareholder voting requirements that are most relevant are set forth in Rule 312 of the NYSE Listed Company Manual. Generally speaking, this NYSE provision grants to shareholders of NYSE-traded companies voting rights that are more rigorous than those required by most state corporation statutes, such as the Delaware statute.* For purposes of analyzing the problems in this chapter, the relevant portions of NYSE Rule 312 provide:

> Shareholder approval is a prerequisite to listing in four situations:
> . . . (c) Shareholder approval is required prior to the issuance of common stock, or of securities convertible into or exercisable for common stock, in any transaction or series of related transactions if:
>> (1) the common stock has, or will have upon issuance, voting power equal to or in excess of 20 percent of the voting power outstanding before the issuance of such stock or of securities convertible into or exercisable for common stock; or
>> (2) the number of shares of common stock to be issued is, or will be upon issuance, equal to or in excess of 20 percent of the number of shares

---

*The NASDAQ has similar shareholder voting rules, NASDAQ Stock Market Rule 4350(i), although this chapter and its problem sets will focus on the shareholder voting requirements of NYSE Rule 312.

of common stock outstanding before the issuance of the common stock or of securities convertible into or exercisable for common stock.

However, shareholder approval will not be required for any such issuance involving:

- Any public offering for cash;
- Any bona fide private financing, if such financing involves a sale of: common stock, for cash, at a price at least as great as each of the book and market value of the issuer's common stock; or securities convertible into or exercisable for common stock, for cash, if the conversion or exercise price is at least as great as each of the book and market value of the issuer's common stock. . . .

Where shareholder approval is a prerequisite to the listing of any additional or new securities of a listed company, the minimum vote which will constitute shareholder approval for listing purposes is defined as approval by a majority of votes cast on a proposal in a proxy bearing on the particular matter, provided that the total vote cast on the proposal represents over 50% in interest of all securities entitled to vote on the proposal.

New York Stock Exchange Listed Company Manual, Section 312.00, Shareholder Approval Policy, Sections 312.03 and 312.07.

Recent revisions to Section 6.21 of the MBCA were generally patterned on this NYSE shareholder voting requirement. Like Rule 312, MBCA §6.21 is not confined to merger transactions, but rather is part of the MBCA provisions dealing generally with the issuance of shares. Thus, these MBCA rules on issuance of shares apply to *any* M&A transaction where the Bidder proposes to use its own stock as the acquisition consideration. In the case of certain acquisitions, the provisions of MBCA §6.21(f) may require shareholder approval in order for the Bidder to validly issue its shares in exchange for consideration other than cash (or cash equivalent, such as a personal check). The operation of the NYSE's shareholder voting rule and the scope of the protection offered by Rule 312 to shareholders of a listed company are best appreciated by analyzing the problem sets in this chapter. In addition, the problem sets will analyze the requirement of a shareholder vote under the terms of MBCA §6.21(f).

From a public policy perspective, why would the NYSE want to impose a shareholder voting rule, especially one that grants more extensive shareholder voting rights than required by most states, such as Delaware's corporation statute? The reason for this type of NYSE rule is pretty basic: the NYSE is a trading market that provides essential *liquidity* to those persons who invest in publicly traded securities. Accordingly, the rules of the NYSE are intended to instill confidence in those investors that the trading market provided by the NYSE is efficient and fair—that trading expenses on the NYSE are minimized and the NYSE's market is free of manipulation and fraud. If investors lose confidence in the NYSE's ability to operate a trading market that is liquid, efficient, and honest, then the entire capital market system suffers.

NOTES

1. How Many Shareholders Must Approve the Acquisition? In the case of a plain vanilla capital structure consisting of a single class of common stock outstanding, the question of *who* gets to vote is easy to resolve. In these situations, the only really tough questions are *how many* shares must approve the proposed acquisition under the terms of the relevant statute (i.e., absolute majority vote standard vs. some supermajority voting standard), and separately, whether there is any basis for *eliminating* the statutory requirement of shareholder approval. As we will see when we analyze the problems, the statutes vary as to the situations where a shareholder vote is not required and the modern codes likewise vary as to the criteria that must be satisfied in order to eliminate the need to obtain shareholder approval. Later in this chapter, we will examine the *VantagePoint* case, where the company has a more complicated capital structure authorizing more than one class of stock, and there, we will analyze the more complex question of how many of these outstanding shares must approve the transaction and whether there is a right to vote separately as a class (i.e., right to a class vote).

2. Business Combinations in Which One Party Is Not a Corporation: "Interspecies" Transactions.   Many times, a corporation will decide to acquire a business that is *not* organized as a corporation—in what is known as an "interspecies" business combination. For example, a corporation may decide to merge with a business organized as a limited liability company (LLC) in a transaction often referred to as an *interspecies merger.* Until quite recently, this transaction was problematic, as most state corporation codes authorized mergers only between corporations, whether they were foreign or domestic. As we will see, most states have amended their codes to authorize "interspecies" business combinations— that is, to allow a corporation to merge with some other type of business entity such as an LLC. *See, e.g.,* MBCA § 11.02(a) and § 1.40(7D) and (24A) (which is typical of the statutory language that provides this kind of flexibility to modern corporations).

3. Are the Modern Corporations Statutes Enabling or Regulatory in Nature? The dominant view today, particularly in the case of Delaware jurisprudence, is to treat the corporation as (entirely) a creature of statute. Because corporations may engage *only* in business combinations authorized by statute and then *only* if done in compliance with *all* the requirements imposed by the relevant corporation statute, the modern statutes are said to be *enabling.* (Remember, the choice of law principle known as the *internal affairs doctrine* governs the company's ability to enter into a proposed acquisition transaction.)

As we analyze the cases later in this chapter, we will see how this view of modern corporation statutes influences judicial decision making and, in particular, how it influences the manner in which the courts (particularly the Delaware judiciary) go about interpreting the language of a specific corporation statute. The problem sets in this chapter are intended to focus attention on the important public policy question of how to balance responsibility and power between the courts, the legislature, and the parties themselves in structuring transactions, especially with regard to the scope of protection to be extended to minority shareholders, creditors, and other interests that are regularly implicated in any given M&A transaction.

B. Corporate Formalities Required for Statutory Mergers Under Delaware Law and the MBCA

1. General Background—Delaware Law of Direct Mergers

Section 251 is the basic merger statute in Delaware, which has been amended several times in the last quarter-century in order to further liberalize the procedures for effecting mergers. These piecemeal amendments have resulted in a rather long and often convoluted statutory provision containing many subparts that address different aspects of the merger process. This note material summarizes certain aspects of Delaware §251 but (most certainly) is not a substitute for reading the statutory language itself. The problem sets are intended to help you master the relevant statutory provisions by focusing on discrete issues one at a time. By the end of our analysis of these problem sets, you should have developed a sense of the merger process as a whole, particularly as regulated by Delaware law.

As part of this introduction to the merger process, references to corresponding provisions of the MBCA will be included. Chapter 11 contains the basic merger procedures under the MBCA. Significant differences between the MBCA and Delaware law will be noted where appropriate.

Board Approval.   Reflecting the enabling nature of modern corporation codes, Delaware §251 authorizes the merger of any two domestic corporations. In addition, Delaware §252 authorizes a domestic corporation to merge with a foreign corporation, and further authorizes that either the domestic or the foreign corporation may be designated as the surviving corporation. *See also* MBCA §11.02. Under Delaware §251, the board of directors of each *constituent corporation* that is a Delaware corporation must approve the merger agreement, reflecting the corporate norm that the board manages the business affairs of the corporation. Del. §141(a); *see also* MBCA §11.04 and §8.01. Delaware §251(b) describes the terms that must be set forth in the parties' merger agreement. *See also* MBCA §11.02.

Shareholder Approval.   Generally speaking, Delaware §251(c) requires that the merger agreement must be submitted to the shareholders for their approval in order for the merger to become effective. *See also* MBCA §11.04. Until revisions were made in 1967, mergers under Delaware law required the affirmative vote of two-thirds of all outstanding shares. Today, though, Delaware §251(c) has relaxed the voting standard to require approval by "a majority of the outstanding shares entitled to vote thereon," thereby making the statutory merger a more attractive means of accomplishing an acquisition. Prior to 1967, the shareholders of *each* constituent corporation were required to approve the terms of the merger. Subsequent amendments to Delaware §251(c), however, have further liberalized the merger process by eliminating the requirement of a shareholder vote in certain situations. Today, the vote of the surviving corporation shareholders may be eliminated if the three conditions of Delaware §251(f) are satisfied. *See also* MBCA §11.04(h).

Moreover, Delaware §251 requires approval by the vote of only an absolute majority of the outstanding common stock, although the certificate of incorporation of a constituent corporation may require a higher percentage. A provision for such a *supermajority vote* will generally be included at the insistence of those minority shareholders who, but for this type of supermajority voting requirement, would be vulnerable to the will of the majority, who could otherwise use their votes to force a merger onto the corporation. Since this requirement for a supermajority vote must be contained in the company's articles of incorporation (or *certificate of incorporation,* as it is called in Delaware), this type of protection is most likely to be bargained for at the time the shares are purchased from the corporation as part of the minority shareholder's original investment decision. (*See* Delaware §102(b)(4) and MBCA §11.04(e).)

Merger Consideration.   As a result of a series of revisions made to Delaware §251, a broad range of consideration may be used today to effect a merger. *See* Delaware §251(b); and MBCA §11.02(c)(3). "As far as Delaware law is concerned, virtually any type of consideration is now permissible in a merger." FOLK ON THE DELAWARE GENERAL CORPORATION LAW (2001 ed.) at §251.2. Thus, today, merger consideration may consist of cash or Bidder's stock (or other securities, such as debentures or other types of debt instruments). Where cash is used, the Bidder will acquire all of Target's business operations while simultaneously eliminating Target's shareholders from any continuing equity ownership in the combined firm. This liberalization of the modern corporation statutes has led to widespread use of the *cash merger* (sometimes referred to as the *cash out merger*), which is illustrated in Diagram 2 of Appendix A.

The great beauty—or, as I like to think of it, the "magic" of the merger procedure—is that the merger "effects *by operation of law* a transmutation of the stock interest in a constituent corporation" into whatever consideration is specified in the terms of the parties' agreement of merger. *Shields v. Shields,* 498 A.2d 161, 167 (Del. Ch. 1985) (*emphasis added*). As a result, significant transaction costs are avoided by the constituent corporations (and their shareholders). "At the moment a stock for stock merger [becomes] effective, the stock in a constituent corporation (other than the surviving corporation) ceases to exist legally." *Id.* at 168. This conversion occurs by operation of law, without the need for any action on the part of the shareholder and notwithstanding any objections or reservations that any individual (minority) shareholders may have.

Successor Liability.   In the case of a direct merger, the result is clear. The surviving corporation succeeds to *all* the rights and *all* the liabilities of *both* constituent corporations by operation of law once the merger takes effect. *See* Del. GCL §259; MBCA §11.07.

Abandonment of Merger.   Delaware's §251(d) also allows the board of directors of any constituent corporation to abandon a merger without the approval of the shareholders—even if the plan of merger has already been approved by the shareholders—so long as the merger agreement expressly reserves that power to the board. *See also* MBCA §11.08. If the directors reserve this power, however, Delaware case law makes clear that the board must exercise this power in a manner that is consistent with its fiduciary duties. Accordingly, it may be desirable for the merger agreement to specify the circumstances under which the board may decide to abandon a merger.

In 1983, Delaware §251 was amended to permit a board of directors to amend a merger agreement at any time before it is filed with the Secretary of State's office, provided the agreement expressly reserves this power to the board. *See also* MBCA §11.02. Although the board may reserve the right to amend the agreement either before or after obtaining shareholder approval of the merger, "any amendment made *after* adoption of the agreement by the stockholders may *not* change the consideration to be received in the merger, change any term of the certificate of incorporation of the surviving corporation, or change the agreement in such a way as to adversely affect any class or series of stock of any constituent corporation." *See* FOLK, *supra* at §251.2.4 (*emphasis added*).

2. Introduction to Dissenter's Right of Appraisal

General Background. As was noted in the materials at the end of Chapter 1, the modern evolution of appraisal rights was intended to address the fundamental tension inherent in any proposed acquisition, whether the deal is done on Main Street or Wall Street. In other words,

> [modern appraisal rights deal] with the tension between the desire of the corporate leadership to be able to enter new fields, acquire new enterprises, and rearrange investor rights, and the desire of investors to adhere to the rights and the risks on the basis of which they invested. Contemporary corporation statutes in the United States attempt to resolve this tension through a combination of two devices. On the one hand, through their approval of an amendment to the articles of incorporation, a merger, share exchange or disposition of assets, the majority may change the nature and shape of the enterprise and the rights of *all* its shareholders. On the other hand, shareholders who object to these changes may withdraw the fair value of their investment in cash through their exercise of appraisal rights.
>
> The traditional accommodation has been sharply criticized from two directions. From the viewpoint of investors who object to the transaction, the appraisal process is criticized for providing little help to the ordinary investor because its technicalities make its use difficult, expensive, and risky. From the viewpoint of the corporate leadership, the appraisal process is criticized because it fails to protect the corporation from demands that are motivated by the hope of a nuisance settlement or by fanciful conceptions of value. *See generally* Bayless Manning, *The Shareholders' Appraisal Remedy: An Essay for Frank Coker,* 72 YALE L.J. 223 (1962).
>
> [MBCA's] Chapter 13 is a compromise between these opposing points of view. It is designed to increase the frequency with which assertion of appraisal rights leads to economical and satisfying solutions, and to decrease the frequency with which such assertion leads to delay, expense, and dissatisfaction. It seeks to achieve these goals primarily by simplifying and clarifying the appraisal process, as well as by motivating the parties to settle their differences in private negotiations without resort to judicial appraisal proceedings.

Committee on Corporate Laws, ABA Section of Business Law, *Changes in the MBCA,* 65 BUS. LAW. 1121, 1138 (2010) (*emphasis added*).

Although appraisal rights—as both a matter of Delaware law and the MBCA—are designed to balance the competing interests described in the quoted passage above, there are significant differences in the *availability* of appraisal rights under Delaware law as compared to the MBCA. The problem sets in this chapter are intended to focus your attention on the transactions that will trigger appraisal rights for the "dissenting shareholder"; i.e., the shareholder who objects to a proposed acquisition. As was mentioned in Chapter 1, this is an important threshold issue to be taken into account in planning the structure of an acquisition transaction. However, once it is determined that appraisal rights are available to minority shareholders, there are several other issues that then need to be addressed, namely:

- the *procedures* that must be followed to perfect the right to an appraisal;
- the *valuation* issues that must be addressed in the context of a judicially surprised appraisal proceeding; and
- the *exclusivity* of the appraisal remedy, i.e., whether modern appraisal statutes provide the only remedy to the objecting shareholder.

After we analyze the transactions that trigger appraisal rights as part of our discussion of the various problem sets in the next few sections, then we will turn our attention to the issues described above as part of the appraisal materials included at the end of this chapter.

Scope of Appraisal Rights Under Delaware Law. The availability and scope of the dissenting shareholder's right of appraisal is set out in Delaware §262; moreover, Delaware case law makes clear that the sharcholder's right to an appraisal is "*entirely* a creature of statute." *Kaye v. Pantone, Inc.,* 395 A.2d 369, 375 (Del. Ch. 1978) (*emphasis added*). Delaware §262(b) grants a right of appraisal to the "shares of any class or series of stock of a constituent corporation in a merger" to be effected pursuant to Delaware §252. Although the Delaware statute does not define the term "constituent corporation," it is generally understood to refer to all of the corporations that are merging, whether they survive or disappear in the transaction. (*See* FOLK, *supra* at §262.2.2.) Accordingly, under Delaware law, there is *no* right of appraisal in the case of a sale of assets or an amendment to the company's certificate of incorporation (known in other states as the *articles of incorporation*).

Delaware's Market Out Exception.   As do many states, Delaware §262(b)(1) eliminates the right of appraisal as to any shares that are listed on a national exchange (such as the NYSE) or that are traded on the NASDAQ. Even if not so listed, the right of appraisal will still be eliminated as to those shares that meet certain criteria set forth in the Delaware statute, which are intended to show that the shares are so widely held as to imply a liquid and substantial trading market. The premise for this exception—customarily referred to as the *market out exception*—is that the right to be cashed out is not necessary where there is a liquid and accessible trading market for the dissenter's shares. Rather than compel the company to cash out the dissenting shareholder, the theory underlying this exception is that the objecting shareholder should simply sell his or her shares into the open market.

The second part of Delaware §262(b)(1) eliminates the right of appraisal as to shares of the *surviving* corporation, but *only* in those situations where the merger is effected without a vote of the shareholders pursuant to the terms of Delaware §251(f).

The "Exception to the Exception"—Restoring the Right of Appraisal Under Delaware Law.   Even in those cases where the market out exception operates to eliminate the dissenting shareholders' right of appraisal, their right to an appraisal may be restored if the tests of Delaware §262(b)(2) are satisfied. Whether appraisal rights are to be restored under Delaware §262(b)(2)—in what is customarily referred to as the *exception to the exception*—depends largely on the *type* of consideration that the dissenting shareholders are required to accept under the terms of the merger agreement. In a rather convoluted manner of drafting, the Delaware statute provides that where the market out exception is triggered and the dissenting shares are required to take any consideration other than stock (such as bonds, debentures, cash, or property), then an "exception to the (market out) exception" of Delaware §262(b)(1) is triggered, which operates to restore the dissenters' right to an appraisal.

So, while today's merger statute in Delaware authorizes use of a broad range of merger consideration (including cash), Delaware's appraisal statute preserves the right of appraisal—even if the dissenting shares are publicly traded—where the shareholders are required to accept merger consideration that consists of anything other than stock (plus cash for any fractional shares). Delaware §262(b)(2)(a) and (b) further specify that the stock that the dissenting shareholder is to receive must consist of *either* shares of the surviving corporation *or* stock of some other corporation which shares are publicly traded.

As a result of this rather convoluted style of drafting, Delaware's appraisal statute frequently is difficult to comprehend in the abstract. The problem sets that follow are intended to help you master the rather backhanded manner in which the Delaware appraisal statute is cobbled together. On another level, the problems will serve—much better than any mere narrative description—to illustrate the *availability* of the dissenter's right of appraisal.

Appraisal Rights Under the MBCA.   In contrast to Delaware law, the availability of appraisal rights is framed very differently under the equivalent provisions of the MBCA, which are found in Chapter 13. Recent revisions to Chapter 13 have made significant changes to the scope of appraisal rights available under the MBCA. Many of these changes work to bring the MBCA closer to Delaware law, but some of the modifications to the MBCA represent a dramatic departure from Delaware's approach to appraisal rights.

As a general proposition, the availability of appraisal rights under the MBCA proceeds from:

> the premise that judicial appraisal should be provided by statute only when two conditions co-exist. First, the proposed corporate action as approved by the majority will result in a fundamental change in the shares to be affected by the action. Second, uncertainty concerning the fair value of the affected shares may cause reasonable persons to differ about the fairness of the terms of the corporate action. Uncertainty is greatly reduced, however, in the case of publicly-traded

shares. This explains both the market exception [under §13.02(b)] . . . and the limits provided to [this] exception.

Appraisal rights in connection with . . . mergers and share exchanges under chapter 11, and dispositions of assets requiring shareholder approval under chapter 12 are provided when these two conditions co-exist. Each of these actions will result in a fundamental change in the shares that a disapproving shareholder may feel was not adequately compensated by the terms approved by the majority.

Committee on Corporate Laws, ABA Section of Business Law, *Changes in the MBCA*, 65 Bus. Law. 1121, 1138 (2010).

MCBA §13.02(a) sets forth the events that will trigger the right of appraisal. More specifically, MBCA §13.02(a) grants appraisal rights more broadly than Delaware law since appraisal rights under the MBCA are *not* limited to merger transactions only. With respect to merger transactions, appraisal rights are available in the case of those mergers that require shareholder approval, although appraisal rights are denied as to any shares of the *surviving* corporation that remain outstanding after the merger is completed. See MCBA §13.02(a). In addition, appraisal rights are granted under the MBCA in the case of (i) certain share exchanges effected pursuant to MBCA §11.03 (an acquisition procedure that we will discuss later in this chapter); (ii) certain sales of assets effected pursuant to MBCA §12.02; and (iii) certain amendments to the company's articles of incorporation.

Like Delaware, the MBCA includes a *market out exception*, which eliminates the right of appraisal in certain cases where the dissenter's shares are publicly traded. *See* MBCA §13.02(b)(1). Under MBCA §13.02(b), however, the appraisal right is *restored*—even if the dissenter's shares are publicly traded—in those situations where the dissenting shareholder is required to accept any consideration other than cash or some other publicly traded security. While expanding the availability of appraisal rights beyond that provided by Delaware law, the MBCA framed its market out exception very differently than Delaware. The manner in which the MBCA's market out exception operates, however, actually results in narrowing the availability of appraisal rights as compared to the Delaware approach. Although this difference in approach is a little difficult to appreciate in the abstract, the problem sets that follow are designed to illustrate the differences in the operation of the market out exception under Delaware §262 as compared to the approach adopted by the MBCA.

3. Perfecting the Statutory Right of Appraisal

Broadly speaking, the procedures set forth in Delaware §262, which are fairly typical of most states' appraisal statutes, require dissenting shareholders to take the following steps in order to perfect their right to an appraisal:

- First, before the shareholders vote on the proposed merger, the objecting shareholders must notify the company of their intent to demand an appraisal. This requirement essentially places the company on notice of the number of shareholders' complaints as to the terms of the proposed merger and the extent to which the company's cash resources may be called upon to fulfill this demand.

- At the time of the shareholder meeting, dissenting shareholders must either abstain or vote against the proposed merger. Within a relatively short period of time following shareholder approval of the proposed merger, dissenting shareholders must notify the company in writing of their intent to demand payment in cash for their shares.
- As a final matter, dissenting shareholders must continue to hold their shares through the effective date of the merger.

In order to appreciate the costs and delay associated with shareholders exercising their statutory right of appraisal, we will briefly examine the mechanics involved in perfecting this right as part of the materials at the end of this chapter. We will also examine the nature of the judicially supervised appraisal proceeding that will be instituted to resolve any disputes between the company and the dissenting shareholder over the valuation of the dissenter's shares.

PROBLEM SET NO. 1—STATUTORY (OR DIRECT) MERGERS UNDER DELAWARE LAW AND THE MBCA

A. Stock for Stock Mergers

1.   Merger Consideration Comprising 30 Percent of Bidder's Stock—(Plain Vanilla) Stock for Stock Merger (See Diagram 1—Appendix A).   Target Co., a closely held concern, plans to merge into Bidder Co., another closely held firm. The plan of merger calls for Target shareholders to receive shares of Bidder common stock comprising 30 percent of the voting power of Bidder shares that were outstanding immediately before closing on the proposed merger with Target. In addition, Target and Bidder each have a plain vanilla capital structure, consisting of only one class of voting common stock outstanding. Moreover, Bidder has sufficient authorized and unissued shares to complete the transaction.

    a.   Which corporation is to survive?

    b.   What action is required by the boards of Bidder and Target:

        (1)   Under Delaware law?
        (2)   Under the MBCA?

    c.   Do the shareholders of Bidder and Target have the right to vote:

        (1)   Under Delaware law?
        (2)   Under the MBCA?

    d.   Do the shareholders of Bidder and Target have the right to dissent:

        (1)   Under Delaware law?
        (2)   Under the MBCA?

    e.   What action would be required (under either Delaware law or the MBCA) if Bidder did *not* have a sufficient number of authorized shares to complete the proposed merger with Target?

2.   Assume that Pfizer, Inc., a NYSE-listed, Delaware company, and Pharmacia Co., another NYSE-listed, Delaware company, plan to combine into a single firm, with Pfizer designated as the surviving corporation. The plan of merger calls for Pharmacia shareholders to receive shares of Pfizer common stock comprising 27 percent of the voting power of Pfizer's common stock that was outstanding immediately before the proposed merger with Pharmacia.

   a.   What action is required of the boards of Pfizer and Pharmacia in order to complete this type of direct merger?
   b.   Do the shareholders of Pfizer and/or Pharmacia have the right to vote:

   (1)   Under Delaware law?
   (2)   Under the rules of the NYSE?

   c.   Do the shareholders of Pfizer and/or Pharmacia have the right to dissent?
   d.   What action would be required under Delaware law and/or the federal securities laws if Pfizer did *not* have a sufficient number of authorized but unissued common shares to complete the transaction?
   e.   Assume that Pfizer has 1 million common shares outstanding entitled to vote. How many shares must vote in favor of the transaction in order for it to be validly approved under the terms of:

   (1)   Delaware law?
   (2)   The rules of the NYSE? (*Hint*: Consider the text of NYSE 312, excerpted earlier in the text of this chapter.)
   (3)   The MBCA (assuming for purposes of this question only that the MBCA applies to determine the voting requirements for Pfizer shareholders)?

   f.   Will this merger automatically become effective once the requisite shareholder approval is obtained? *See* Delaware §251(c) and §259; and MBCA §11.06 and §11.07.

3.   Merger Consideration Consisting of 15 Percent of Bidder's Stock—Another Plain Vanilla Stock for Stock Direct Merger (See Diagram 1—Appendix A). Assume once again that Target plans to merge into Bidder, as set out in Problem 1, except that the shareholders of the privately held Target will receive stock in the privately held Bidder comprising only 15 percent of the voting power of Bidder's outstanding stock that was outstanding immediately before the proposed merger is completed.

   a.   What action is required by the boards of Bidder and Target:

   (1)   Under Delaware law?
   (2)   Under the MBCA?

   b.   Do the shareholders of Bidder and Target have the right to vote:

   (1)   Under Delaware law?
   (2)   Under the MBCA?

   c. Do the shareholders of Bidder and Target have the right to dissent:

      (1)   Under Delaware law?
      (2)   Under the MBCA?

4. Assume that Pharmacia, a publicly traded company, plans to merge with Pfizer, another publicly traded company, in exchange for shares comprising only 13 percent of the voting power of Pfizer's outstanding common stock before the merger is completed.

   a. What action is required of the boards of Pfizer and Pharmacia in order to validly consummate this merger:

      (1)   Under Delaware law?
      (2)   Under the MBCA?

   b. Do the shareholders of Pfizer and/or Pharmacia have the right to vote:

      (1)   Under Delaware law?
      (2)   Under the rules of the NYSE?
      (3)   Under the MBCA?

   c. Do the shareholders of Pfizer and/or Pharmacia have the right to dissent:

      (1)   Under Delaware law?
      (2)   Under the MBCA?

B. Cash Mergers: Merger Consideration Consists of All Cash (See Diagram 2—Appendix A)

1. Target Co., a closely held concern, plans to merge into Bidder Co., another closely held concern. The plan of merger calls for the three shareholders of Target to receive all cash. Target and Bidder each have a plain vanilla capital structure, consisting of only one class of voting common stock outstanding.

   a. What action is required by the boards of Bidder and Target:

      (1)   Under Delaware law?
      (2)   Under the MBCA?

   b. Do the shareholders of Bidder and Target have the right to vote:

      (1)   Under Delaware law?
      (2)   Under the MBCA?

   c. Do the shareholders of Bidder and Target have the right to dissent:

      (1)   Under Delaware law?
      (2)   Under the MBCA?

2. Assume that Chef America, Inc., a company incorporated under the MBCA, has decided to merge into Nestlé, Inc., an NYSE-listed, Delaware corporation, in exchange for $2 billion in cash.

a.   What action is required of the boards of Nestlé and Chef America in order to complete this cash merger?

b.   Do the shareholders of either Nestlé or Chef America have the right to vote?

c.   Do the shareholders of either Nestlé or Chef America have the right to dissent?

3. Assume that Pfizer, Inc., a publicly traded company, plans to acquire Pharmacia Co., another publicly traded company, in an all-cash statutory merger. Further assume that Pfizer can fund the $60 billion purchase through its own cash resources (and by borrowing any necessary funds).

a.   What action is required of the boards of Pfizer and Pharmacia in order to complete this cash merger:

(1)   Under Delaware law?
(2)   Under the MBCA?

b.   Do the shareholders of either Pfizer or Pharmacia have the right to vote:

(1)   Under Delaware law?
(2)   Under the MBCA?
(3)   Under the rules of the NYSE?

c.   Do the shareholders of either Pharmacia or Pfizer have the right to dissent:

(1)   Under Delaware law?
(2)   Under the MBCA?

C.   *Corporate Formalities Required for Short Form Mergers—Under Delaware Law and the MBCA*

Generally speaking, the short form merger procedure operates to allow a parent corporation to absorb a subsidiary without a vote of either the parent or the subsidiary's shareholders so long as the parent owns at least 90 percent of the subsidiary's stock. *See* Del. §253; MBCA §11.05. The theory is that the outcome of any vote of the subsidiary's shareholders in this situation is a foregone conclusion. Consequently, there is no need for the law to impose the delay and expense associated with obtaining a vote of the shareholders. Rather, modern corporation statutes allow the parent board to effect this type of merger unilaterally if the parent company's board of directors duly adopts a resolution approving the transaction. Since the law assumes that the parent board controls the subsidiary's board of directors by virtue of its share ownership, no action is required to be taken by the subsidiary's board.

While no vote of the shareholders is required to effect a short form merger, the parent corporation's dealings with the minority shareholders generally will be controlled by fiduciary duty law and therefore subjected to the *entire fairness test.* According to the landmark decision of the Delaware Supreme Court,

Weinberger v. UOP, Inc., 457 A.2d 701 (Del. 1983), the parent corporation is obligated to deal fairly with the minority shareholders of the subsidiary and to pay a fair price for the minority shares. As a general proposition, the Delaware courts are more willing to scrutinize this type of transaction to assure that the parent company does not use its position of control to take advantage of the minority shareholders. We will analyze the entire fairness standard in more detail as part of our discussion of the *Weinberger* case later in this chapter.

PROBLEM SET NO. 2—SHORT FORM MERGER

1. Assume that Parent Co. owns 92 percent of the outstanding voting common stock of Target Co. Parent Co. now proposes to acquire the remaining 8 percent of Target Co. common stock that it does not own by cashing out the minority shareholders of Target in a short form merger in which Parent survives. Target and Parent each have only one class of voting common stock outstanding, and each is closely held. (*See Diagram 3—Appendix A.*)

    a.   What action is required by the boards of Parent and Target:

        (1)   Under Delaware law?
        (2)   Under the MBCA?

    b.   Do the shareholders of either Parent or Target have the right to vote:

        (1)   Under Delaware law?
        (2)   Under the MBCA?

    c.   Do the shareholders of Parent and Target have the right to dissent:

        (1)   Under Delaware law?
        (2)   Under the MBCA?

    d.   Assume—for purposes of this question only—that the shares of both Parent and Target are listed for trading on the NYSE. Do the shareholders of either Parent or Target have the right to dissent:

        (1)   Under Delaware law?
        (2)   Under the MBCA?

    e.   Is this short form merger accomplished on a downstream basis or an upstream basis? (*Hint:* Which corporation is to survive and which is to disappear?)

D.   *Corporate Formalities Required for Asset Acquisitions—Under Delaware Law and the MBCA*

1.   General Background—Asset Acquisitions

In cases involving the sale of a company's assets, a threshold determination must be made in each case as to whether the company proposes to sell *all* or *substantially all* of its assets, as such a transaction is considered a fundamental change. Delaware §271, in turn, sets forth the corporate formalities that must be observed if an asset sale constitutes a fundamental change. Conversely, the sale of *less* than all or substantially all of the company's assets is not a fundamental change, and therefore does not require shareholder approval. As such, these transactions are committed to the business judgment of the company's board of directors. *See* Delaware §141(a); *see also* MBCA §§12.01, 12.02, and 8.01.

In many cases, the threshold determination of whether the transaction presents the sale of *all* the company's assets will be easy to ascertain. But in many cases where *less* than all of the company's assets are to be disposed, a (typically more complex) determination must be made as to whether the transaction involves the sale of "substantially all" of the company's assets. As we will see later in this chapter when we analyze the leading Delaware cases in this area (*Katz* and *Gimbel*), this determination "does not lend itself to a strict mathematical standard to be applied in every case." *Gimbel,* 316 A.2d at 605.

This threshold determination is of vital importance because the corporate formalities that must be observed in order to validly consummate the sale of "all or substantially all" of a company's assets differs from the formalities that must be observed if a company sells *less than substantially all* of its assets. At common law, the rule "was that neither the directors nor the stockholders of a prosperous going concern could sell all or substantially all of the corporation's property if a *single* stockholder objected." *See* Edward P. Welch & Andrew J. Turezyn, FOLK ON THE DELAWARE GENERAL CORPORATION LAW at §271.1 (Fundamentals 2004 ed.) (*emphasis added*). Today, all states' corporation statutes (including Delaware §271) recognize that a corporation may sell all or substantially all of the company's assets with the approval of *less* than all of the shareholders, usually based on the vote of an absolute majority of shares entitled to vote. Some states, though, may impose some form of supermajority vote, or alternatively, a supermajority vote may be imposed by private ordering, which is usually done by way of a provision in the company's articles of incorporation.

At common law, there was some confusion as to whether a company could sell all or substantially all of its assets for something other than cash, such as stock in the Bidder, the purchaser. Today, Delaware §271, like the statutes of most states, resolves this issue by authorizing the sale of Target's assets in exchange for Bidder's shares or other securities. (*See Diagram 5 in Appendix A.*) By varying the nature of the acquisition consideration, the substantive result of an acquisition structured as a sale of assets can bear a striking resemblance to a merger transaction. The problems to be analyzed in this section illustrate this point.

Since Target Co. is selling its assets, it will be a party to the asset purchase agreement, along with the acquiring corporation, Bidder Co. As such, Delaware §271 requires authorization of the transaction by the board of directors of the selling corporation, which most often will occur at a meeting of Target's board, although it is possible for the board to approve the sale without a meeting if all directors consent in writing. *See* Delaware §141(f) and MBCA §8.21 (regarding the requirements for board action by written consent). "The terms of Delaware §271(a) specifically require the Board of Directors to make a judgment that the terms of an asset sale 'are expedient and for the best interests of the corporation.'" FOLK, *supra,* DELAWARE CORPORATE LAW at §271.3.2.

As to shareholder approval, Delaware §271 specifically requires that the shareholders receive at least 20 days' notice of the meeting to vote on the company's proposed sale of assets. As to the shareholder voting standard, Delaware §271(a) requires approval by a vote of a majority of the outstanding shares entitled to vote, unless the written consent procedures of Delaware §228 are used to dispense with the need for a shareholder meeting.

After the dust settles on a sale of all or substantially all of Target Co.'s assets, the entity is left intact, but the company is very different than before the transaction. Now, Target holds all of the consideration received from the sale of its assets (typically, cash or Bidder's stock), in addition to whatever liabilities were not transferred to the Bidder as part of the sale of Target's assets. At this point, Target has several different options. First, it may decide to continue in existence as a holding company, holding the consideration received from Bidder on behalf of Target's shareholders. Alternatively, Target may distribute the consideration received from Bidder to its shareholders, usually in the form of an extraordinary dividend, leaving Target to continue in existence as a bare shell of a company. As a third option, Target may distribute the consideration received from Bidder and dissolve the company (a proceeding known as "voluntary dissolution").

With respect to the first two alternatives, Delaware case law generally assumes that the shareholders, by approving the transaction, have (implicitly) consented to one of these alternatives. Indeed, as described in greater detail in Chapter 4, the federal proxy rules require full and adequate disclosure of all material facts so that Target's shareholders, at least where Target is publicly traded, may make an informed decision as to whether to approve the proposed sale of assets transaction. By extension, Delaware case law has held that Target's proxy statement must adequately inform the shareholders as to matters that are relevant to the decision whether to approve the proposed sale of assets, including the consequences of the plan of sale and any plan for liquidation of Target Co. following the sale.

Very often, the company's future plans for distribution of the consideration received from Bidder will influence Target shareholders in their decision whether to approve the proposed sale of Target's assets. Thus, complete liquidation of Target is *not* the "inevitable legal result" of Target's decision to sell off all of its assets. (*See* FOLK, *supra* at §271.7.) Most often, though, Target's proposed sale of all of its assets will contemplate the second step of voluntary dissolution of Target and the orderly winding up of its business affairs.

For reasons discussed at length in Chapter 3, regarding the rules of successor liability, the sale of assets transaction has a very different impact on the creditors of Target. Since Target Co. remains intact following the sale of all of its assets, the general rule is that Target creditors should bring their claims to Target, which will generally be paid out of the proceeds that Target received from Bidder on the sale of all of its assets. Accordingly, the general rule is that Bidder Co. has no direct liability to the creditors of Target, *unless* the Bidder (expressly or impliedly) assumed such an obligation as part of its agreement to purchase Target's assets. As we will see in Chapter 3, this rule of successor liability creates the potential for opportunistic behavior on the part of Target and/or Bidder, which may work to the (financial) detriment of Target's creditors. In the materials in Chapter 3, we will examine in more detail the protections developed by the courts and state legislatures to protect Target creditors—both contract (voluntary) creditors and tort (involuntary) creditors—from overreaching on the part of Bidder and/or Target, including the judicially developed doctrine known as *de facto mergers*.

Recent amendments to MBCA Chapter 13 reflect that the typical sale of assets involves a two-step transaction, unlike the direct merger. As was just noted, however, the dissolution of Target Co. following the sale of all (or substantially all) of its assets is not the inevitable result. After the sale of its assets, Target remains in place, holding whatever liabilities were not assumed by Bidder, along with the proceeds from the sale of its assets. As we will explore in more detail in Chapter 3, this leaves Target's owners and managers with several choices, one of which is to dissolve Target. Until quite recently, the MBCA extended appraisal rights to any disposition of assets pursuant to §12.02 that required a shareholder vote. However, recent revisions to §13.02(a)(3) eliminate the shareholder's right to an appraisal if:

(i)   under the terms of the corporate action approved by the shareholders there is to be distributed to shareholders in cash its net assets, in excess of a reasonable amount reserved to meet claims of the type described in §14.06 and 14.07, (A) within one year after the shareholders' approval of the action and (B) in accordance with their respective interests determined at the time of distribution [i.e., in accordance with the stated liquidation rights of the shares, if any]; *and*

(ii) the disposition of assets is not an interested transaction.[*]

So, by way of summary, this new exception to the availability of appraisal rights in connection with the sale of assets pursuant to MBCA §12.02 is limited to those situations where liquidation of Target must take place within one year of the shareholder vote *and* Target's shareholders are to receive cash in accordance with their respective interests (i.e., in accordance with their liquidation preferences as set forth in the company's articles of incorporation), so long as the transaction does not present a conflict of interest as defined in MBCA §13.01. The premise for this recent amendment to the MBCA is that in the situation where Target "shareholders are being treated on a proportionate basis in accordance with the corporation's governing documents [i.e., the company's articles of incorporation] in an arms' length transaction (akin to a distribution in dissolution), there is no need for the added protection of appraisal rights." *Changes in the MBCA, supra,* 65 Bus. Law. at 1144.

NOTES

1. Non-Acquisitive Restructurings of a Single Firm: Reorganizations and Recapitalizations.   Companies will often decide to change the focus of their business operations, such as where conglomerates decide to strip down and concentrate their business operations within a single industry. In the process, the

---

[*]"Interested transaction" is a defined term in MBCA §13.01(5.1) that essentially refers to a transaction presenting one of two types of conflict of interests.

conglomerate will usually sell off (divest itself of) unwanted assets and business operations. These transactions do not involve combining two previously independent businesses into a single firm. Rather, these divestitures result in separating a single firm into different, freestanding business entities.

Divestitures are not the focus of this class since this course concentrates on business combinations. However, we will discuss a few cases that involve restructurings of a single company, often as an alternative to a business combination. Therefore, it will be useful to understand the mechanics and terminology of these deals. This note briefly summarizes the basic mechanics of divestitures and defines relevant terms customarily used in these deals. However, a more thorough analysis of the rules that regulate these recapitalization transactions is left to other law school courses.

In cases where company management has decided, as a business matter, to eliminate certain operations, management may dispose of those assets (which may even consist of entire divisions or operating subsidiaries) in one of several different ways.

First, the company may decide to sell off certain assets. Where the company disposes of unwanted assets that constitute *less* than substantially *all* of its assets, then the disposition does not involve a fundamental change. As such, the sale of these assets is a matter left to the business judgment of the company's board of directors. In this case, the company will find a buyer (often a leveraged buyout firm of the type described in the note material below) who will then enter into a contract for the purchase and sale of the company's unwanted assets. In the case of a management buyout (MBO), it will often be the managers of a particular division or subsidiary (i.e., the managers who are responsible for the assets to be sold off) who will take the initiative to find a buyout firm that will finance the purchase of the company's unwanted assets.

2. Spin-offs.   Alternatively, the company may dispose of assets that are held in a subsidiary by way of a transaction that is known on Wall Street as a *spin-off.* In the case of a spin-off, the assets and business operations to be disposed will be assembled in a subsidiary corporation; the shares of the subsidiary are then distributed out as a non-cash dividend to the shareholders of the parent company. When the dust settles, the shareholders of the parent company will own the subsidiary while still retaining ownership of their shares in the parent company. Henceforth, the former subsidiary will operate as a freestanding business with no continuing equity ownership or control on the part of the parent company, which likewise continues in place as a separate business entity. This type of reorganization of a single firm's business operations is not the focus of this casebook, although restructurings of this type are very common.

Another type of reorganization, which was quite common in the depressed capital markets of the early 2000s, is often referred to as *distressed M&A*. Here, a financially troubled company decides to sell off certain assets or business operations, usually in order to raise cash (and remain financially viable). This type of transaction is often undertaken as a last-ditch effort to remain solvent and avoid filing for bankruptcy. Reorganizations undertaken as part of bankruptcy court proceedings is a specialized area of M&A activity, which is typically covered in most law schools as part of a course on bankruptcy law, and as such, lie outside the scope of M&A law.

3. Recapitalization.   One final type of single-firm restructuring is worth noting. In the case of a *recapitalization,* the company decides to change its capital structure by amending its articles of incorporation. This is considered to be a fundamental change that cannot be implemented unilaterally by board action alone. Rather, any amendment of the company's articles—including an amendment to change the rights, preferences, or privileges of outstanding shares, or alternatively, to increase the number of authorized shares or to create a new class of authorized shares—will require board approval, along with approval by the requisite number of shares entitled to vote. *See, e.g.,* Del. §242; MCBA §10.03.

Today, most states require that an articles amendment receive approval by an absolute majority of outstanding shares of each class entitled to vote. In addition, many states provide for a right to class voting even if the shares are not otherwise entitled to vote. Under the terms of modern corporation statutes, this right to a class vote will most often be granted in situations where the proposed articles amendment would effect a change in the rights, preferences, and privileges of a class of outstanding shares that otherwise carry no voting rights. *See, e.g.,* Calif. §9.03. The public policy premise underlying this right to a class vote is that the articles represent a contract between the issuer (the company) and the investor (the shareholder), which cannot be unilaterally amended by the company and thus can be amended only if the company obtains the consent of the requisite number of the holders of those nonvoting shares affected by the terms of the proposed articles amendment.

4. Leveraging the Company's Balance Sheet.   As a final observation with respect to single firm restructurings, many recapitalizations are effected without any vote of the company's shareholders. For example, the company's board of directors may decide to leverage the company's balance sheet by borrowing a large amount of money, often granting a security interest in the company's assets to the lender. So long as there is no limitation on the company's issuance of debt (usually effected by way of a provision in the articles of incorporation), the company's board of directors may implement this decision by issuing, for example, new subordinated debentures (an unsecured form of corporate indebtedness) and then using the proceeds of this debt offering to distribute an extraordinary dividend in cash to the company's shareholders. When the dust settles, the shareholders hold the cash dividend, along with exactly the same shares they had *before* the transaction was completed. In the process, the company becomes highly leveraged, with a much higher debt-equity ratio. Although the shareholders remain as equity owners of the company, the nature of their investment is vastly different than before this type of recapitalization transaction was undertaken. In fact, their shares are usually worth much less than before the transaction. In spite of this typical dilution in value, no shareholder vote, generally speaking, is required to effect this type of *leveraged recapitalization.*

5. Blank Check Preferred Stock.   The widespread use today of *blank check preferred stock* offers yet another example of a recapitalization (in the sense of a substantial change in the company's financial structure) that does *not* require shareholder approval. Where blank check preferred shares are authorized, the rights, preferences, and privileges of these shares are not defined in the company's articles of incorporation or in any amendment approved by the shareholders. Rather, the rights, preferences, and privileges will be established later by the company's board of directors, usually at the time of issuance. As we will see in Chapter 7, blank check preferred forms the basis for the distribution of the *poison pill*, a strategy commonly used to block hostile takeovers.

6. An Introduction to Leveraged Buyouts.   Any acquisition can be structured as a *leveraged buyout* (LBO), although quite often, the LBO transaction will take the form of an asset purchase. The essential feature of an LBO is the use of borrowed funds to finance Bidder's acquisition of Target. In a typical scenario, Bidder will be an LBO firm, such as the well-known firm of Kohlberg Kravis & Roberts (KKR). When LBOs first became fashionable in the 1980s, this type of financial buyer would usually team up with Target managers to purchase assets, or even entire divisions, typically from a large conglomerate seeking to divest itself of underperforming businesses. Financial buyers such as KKR would finance the acquisition of these assets using a sliver of equity provided by the investment of its own funds coupled with substantial amounts of borrowed funds that would have to be repaid. This debt financing was usually raised by soliciting money from other investors (often institutional investors) who were looking to be repaid (with interest) out of the income stream generated from the purchased assets.

The leveraged acquisition is designed to allow the financial buyer to purchase the *greatest* amount of income-producing assets with the *least* amount of equity investment on the part of the financial buyer. By borrowing against the assets of Target Co., the typical LBO firm can invest a small amount of its own money (say, 10 percent to 20 percent of the purchase price) and borrow the balance of the purchase price, earning a substantial return on its invested equity after paying the carrying cost of the debt. In the typical case, the borrowed funds would be repaid out of the income stream generated by the assets purchased from Target, which hopefully would grow using the business strategies to be implemented by the new management team installed by the LBO firm. The financial buyer would typically plan to improve the financial performance by cutting costs and introducing new measures to streamline and improve business operations. In addition, the LBO firm typically gives the new management team stock options (or other equity participation) in order to tightly align management's financial interests with those of the new stockholders.

Given the heavy debt load usually taken on by the LBO firm in order to finance the acquisition, there will usually be intense pressure on the (sometimes newly installed) team of managers to streamline the business and increase its profitability in order to generate the revenue needed to finance the cost of the borrowed funds. Many financial buyers believe that the heavy debt burden carried on the company's balance sheet following an LBO exerts a disciplining influence on the managers, who must perform optimally in order to generate the income stream needed to provide the resources to pay the interest and principal on the borrowed capital. Of course, carrying this heavy debt load on its balance sheet also leads to an increased risk of default if the company does not generate the revenue stream required to pay the carrying cost of this debt. This heavy debt load also may serve to impair the company's ability to finance new business projects necessary to grow the company's business. In the jargon of Wall Street, this situation is often referred to as *leveraging the company's balance sheet.*

If things went as planned, the leveraged acquisition would usually be followed by a period of debt reduction, thereby reducing (or even eliminating) the borrowed capital from the company's balance sheet. As a direct result of this type of *leveraging,* the increase in value of the business remaining after paying off the debt would belong to the LBO firm. The ultimate goal of many financial buyers is to sell the cleaned-up company to another buyer within a few years for a substantial gain, or alternatively, to take the company public. In the most successful of LBOs, the financial buyer could earn a substantial return on the sliver of equity that it had originally invested.

One of the most well-known (indeed almost legendary) LBO deals involved Gibson Greeting Cards. In 1981, Wesray, which was an investment partnership established by William Simon, former secretary of the treasury in the Ford administration, purchased Gibson Greetings from RCA, a large well-known conglomerate that was shedding its assets in order to slim down and focus on its core business operations. At that time, RCA, an extremely motivated seller as it was anxious to eliminate underperforming assets, sold Gibson Greetings to Wesray for $80 million. Debt financing provided $79 million of the purchase price, with Wesray investing only $1 million of its own funds. This LBO also involved the equity participation of the existing managers of Gibson Greetings, who held a 20 percent interest in the company's common stock and stayed on to run the company. (This type of deal would come to be known on Wall Street as an MBO, a *management buyout.*) In 1983, less than two years later,

> Wesray took Gibson Greetings public by selling 30% of the company's [stock] for just over $96 million. The IPO valued the whole company at $330 million. Wesray had earned a $250 million pretax paper profit on its $1 million equity investment. [What's more,] Bill Simon looked like a genius.

Bruce Wasserstein, BIG DEAL, at 104-105 (2000). This same experienced M&A advisor went on to comment:

> Some observers wrote off Wesray's success as a fluke, a case of sophisticated investors who outwitted an unusually dense conglomerate. Others attributed Wesray's phenomenal profit to opportune timing. A strong economy, a booming stock market—a confluence of unpredictable events—allowed the partners to cash out quickly.
>
> However, other LBO's proved equally remarkable, and the vitality of this transaction structure soon became widely recognized.

Id.

7. The Era of the "Mega-Buyout."   For a remarkably long period of almost 20 years, there had been no bigger LBO deal than KKR's purchase of RJR Nabisco, Inc., the tobacco and food conglomerate, for the eye-popping price of $25.1 billion. This LBO deal—valued in today's dollars at $41.9 billion—was characterized by a "legendary, ego-driven bidding war" that ultimately came to be viewed as representing everything that was "grand and grotesque" about the

Wall Street money machine.* But, as the M&A market started to heat up in calendar year 2006, many experienced deal-makers began to speculate that the RJR record might finally be broken. *See* Dennis K. Berman and Henry Sender, *Big Deal: Records Were Made to Be Broken*, WALL STREET JOURNAL, January 9, 2006, at C1. Indeed, the first half of calendar year 2007 proved to be a watershed year for private equity firms as the M&A market witnessed an explosive growth of activity by private equity buyers. The extraordinary pace of activity in the first half of 2007 was fueled in substantial part by the extraordinary liquidity of the credit markets, leading to some of the largest LBO deals on record. Indeed, Blackstone Group, led by its CEO, Steven Schwarzman, signed up their LBO of Equity Office Properties Trust for the eye-popping amount of $39 billion— ranking it as the largest LBO in history—only to be "knocked off its perch" shortly thereafter by yet another private equity firm. *See* Gregg Wirth, *From the Editor: The Biggest LBO of All Time! (This Month's Contender)*, THE M&A LAW- YER at 2 (March 2007). "The *NEW* largest LBO in history—at least as of this writing—is the proposed $40 billion purchase of TXU," the large Texas utility conglomerate. *Id.* This "mega-deal" is being sponsored by two well-known private equity firms, Texas Pacific Group and KKR. This "mega-deal" for TXU puts LBO master Henry Kravis and his firm back on top of the "private equity mountain—although the competition to remain there is [currently] fierce." *Id.* In fact, the list of the top ten largest LBO deals in history looks more like a list of the top deals announced over the past two years of watershed activity in the M&A market. Indeed, the *only* deal that appears on this top ten list that was *not* announced since 2005 is the legendary 1988 buyout of RJR Nabisco by the iconic KKR firm. *Id.*

The feverish pace of LBO activity that led to the relatively brief "era of the mega-buyout" in the first half of 2007 came to an abrupt halt as the credit markets deteriorated. As the credit markets increasingly seized up over the summer months, many of those mega-buyouts collapsed and deal making in the M&A market generally came to a screeching halt in the latter half of 2007. However, by mid-2008, David Rubenstein, co-founder of Carlyle Group, a well-known buyout firm, was quoted as saying that he saw "light at the end of the tunnel," and was therefore expecting the flow of private equity deals to accelerate in the second half of 2008 as the participants in the M&A market learned to adapt to life beyond the era of the mega-buyout deals. See Rick Carew, *Deal-Making: It Shall Return*, WALL STREET JOURNAL, May 20, 2008, at C3. As it turned out, private equity dropped precipitously through the last half of 2008. Chris O'Leary, *From the Editor: Taking Stock, Looking for Opportunities*, 14 THE M&A LAWYER, at p. 3 (January 2010).

8. The LBO Market in the Wake of the Great Recession. Although private equity sponsors entered the year hopeful, "[t]he M&A market continued to face numerous challenges in 2009. Global mergers and acquisitions activity for 2009 was $2.3 trillion, down 22% from $2.94 trillion in 2008." Sherrie Nackman, *Readying for Resurgence: M&A Prospects for the Next 12 Months*, KPMG and

---

*All you movie buffs will recall that this is the deal made famous in the movie *Barbarians at the Gate.*

THE DEAL, Jan. 2010 at p. 2. While there were some positive signs for deal makers by the end of the fourth quarter of 2009, in the end, 2010 proved to be a fickle year for private equity deals. At the outset, "2010 seemed to present all of the predicates for a strong and broad M&A resurgence," but ultimately proved to be a disappointing year. Frank Aquila and Melissa Sawyer, *Diary of a Wary Market: 2010 in Review & What to Expect in 2011*, 14 THE M&A LAWYER, at p. 1 (November, December 2010). "2010 opened with seemingly all the elements in place. The market chaos of 2008-2009 seemed to have abated, the financing freeze looked to be thawing, low interest rates had made financing cheap, [particularly encouraging signs for private equity investors], and many companies were now in much stronger health." Chris O'Leary, *From the Editor*, 14 THE M&A LAWYER, at p. 3 (November/December 2010). In fact,

> 2010 global M&A volumes were up from 2009 levels based on both the size of the deals and the number of the deals. However, the number of deals discussed still vastly exceeded the number of deals [publicly] announced. So what happened? . . . On the buy-side, CEOs and lenders alike remained concerned about the risk of a double-dip recession, . . . continued weakness in the housing markets and the uncertain impact of regulatory reforms. GDP growth has slowed and unemployment remains high. Recent positive earnings announcements reflect, in part, expense cuts and inventory adjustments rather than revenue growth. . . . On the sell-side, boards were worried that they could be engaging in the wrong deals and were reluctant to foreclose any options. Financing risk remained a major concern.

Aquila and Sawyer, *supra, Diary of a Wary Market*, at p. 4.

Proving once again that hope springs eternal, by the end of 2010, Wall Street observers were anticipating that there would be a "steady increase in M&A activity" during calendar year 2011. *Id.* at p. 8. As it turned out though, 2011 bestowed "mixed blessings" on private equity.

> If they had their druthers, financial sponsors [i.e., private equity investors] would have preferred a longer first half of 2011—a time of bountiful realizations amid strong credit flows and a recovering market for initial public offerings. And they would have dispensed with the second half [of 2011] altogether, as worries deepened over the euro zone [debt crisis] and the U.S. debt-ceiling debate, casting a pall over private equity . . . [Private equity investors] may have put some distance between now and [the depth of the Great Recession in] 2008, but aftershocks continue, particularly for business burdened by debt obligations or maturities.
>
> In short, private equity remains a grind-it-out-struggle.

Vyvyan Tenorio, *Private Equity Deals of the Year: Introduction* THE DEAL at p. 26 (April 13, 2012). So, as we entered 2012, prospects for private equity deals remained "clouded." *See* David Carey, *2011 Review: Private Equity—The No Normal*, THE DEAL, at p. 52 (Dec. 12, 2011, to Jan. 15, 2012) ("Buyout shops have made some progress recovering from the boom [of 2006-2007] and subsequent bust [of 2008-2009]. But panic and volatility continue to cloud their prospects [for 2012]."). All of which only proves the truth of the earlier observation, to wit: the market for M&A activity is constantly changing.

PROBLEM SET NO. 3—ASSET ACQUISITIONS UNDER
DELAWARE LAW AND THE MBCA

1. Sale of Assets for Cash (See Diagram 4—Appendix A).   Target Co., is a bicycle store founded 20 years ago by Lance, who continues to own one-third of the outstanding common stock. The remaining shares are evenly divided between his two grown sons, Abe and Biff. Lance has decided to sell all of Target's assets and transfer certain of the company's liabilities to Bidder Co., another closely held firm, in exchange for cash. Immediately after the transfer, Target will be dissolved and liquidate its business affairs, with Target transferring to its shareholders any cash remaining after paying off its creditors.

   a.   What action is required to be taken by the boards of Bidder and Target:

   (1)   Under Delaware law?
   (2)   Under the MBCA?

   b.   Do the shareholders of Bidder and Target have the right to vote on the transaction:

   (1)   Under Delaware law?
   (2)   Under the MBCA?

   c.   Do the shareholders of Bidder or Target have the right to dissent:

   (1)   Under Delaware law?
   (2)   Under the MBCA?

2.   Assume that Chef America, Inc., a privately held corporation, has decided to sell all of its assets to Nestlé, Inc., a company whose stock is traded on the NYSE, in exchange for $2 billion in cash. Immediately following this sale, the Merage brothers, Paul and David, as equal owners of Chef America, plan to dissolve the company and distribute out to themselves (as the sole shareholders) any cash remaining after paying off the company's creditors.

   a.   What action is required to be taken by the boards of Chef America and Nestlé:

   (1)   Under Delaware law?
   (2)   Under the MBCA?

   b.   Do the shareholders of Chef America and/or Nestlé have the right to vote on the transaction:

   (1)   Under Delaware law?
   (2)   Under the rules of the NYSE?
   (3)   Under the MBCA?

   c.   Do the shareholders of Chef America and/or Nestlé have the right to dissent:

   (1)   Under Delaware law?
   (2)   Under the MBCA?

3. Sale of Assets in Exchange for 30 Percent of Bidder's Stock (See Diagram 5— Appendix A).   Assume that Chef America has agreed to sell all of its assets and transfer certain of its liabilities to Nestlé in exchange for shares of Nestlé common stock comprising 30 percent of the voting power of Nestlé's outstanding stock immediately before the proposed asset purchase. Immediately after the transfer of its assets, Chef America plans to dissolve and liquidate its business affairs, transferring the Nestlé shares to the company shareholders in exchange for all of Chef America's outstanding stock, which will then be canceled. Assume that Nestlé, Inc. has sufficient authorized and unissued shares to complete the transaction.

a.   What action is required to be taken by the boards of Nestlé and Chef America:

    (1)   Under Delaware law?
    (2)   Under the MBCA?

b.   Do the shareholders of either Nestlé or Chef America have the right to vote on the transaction:

    (1)   Under Delaware law?
    (2)   Under the MBCA?
    (3)   Under the rules of the NYSE?

c.   Do the shareholders of either Nestlé or Chef America have the right to dissent:

    (1)   Under Delaware law?
    (2)   Under the MBCA?

4. Sale of Assets in Exchange for 15 Percent of Bidder's Stock (See Diagram 5— Appendix A).   Assume that the facts are the same as set out in Problem 3, except that Nestlé will complete its acquisition of Chef America by issuing Nestlé shares to the two Merage brothers in an amount equal to 15 percent of the voting power of Nestlé's outstanding common stock immediately before the asset purchase is completed.

a.   What action is required to be taken by the boards of Nestlé and Chef America:

    (1)   Under Delaware law?
    (2)   Under the MBCA?

b.   Do the shareholders of either Nestlé or Chef America have the right to vote on the transaction:

    (1)   Under Delaware law?
    (2)   Under the rules of the NYSE?
    (3)   Under the MBCA?

c.   Do the shareholders of either Nestlé or Chef America have the right to dissent:

    (1)   Under Delaware law?
    (2)   Under the MBCA?

2.   What Qualifies as "Sale (or Transfer) of Substantially All the Assets"?

In the problems we just finished analyzing, we assumed that Target was selling *all* of its assets so it was easy for the transaction planner to conclude that this transaction involved a fundamental change requiring shareholder approval under state corporation law. However, in cases where the company proposes to sell *less* than all of its assets, the lawyer planning the transaction must analyze the proposed sale in order to determine if the proposed disposition of Target's assets falls under Delaware §271. The reason that this is an important threshold question is that if the sale is challenged by the shareholders and the court later determines that the transaction involved a sale of "substantially" all of Target's assets but did not receive shareholder approval, then the court may enjoin the transaction unless and until the requisite shareholder approval is obtained.

The following two decisions are generally viewed as the leading cases under Delaware law regarding the appropriate standard for deciding whether a particular disposition of corporate assets involves the sale of "substantially all" of the company's assets and thus cannot be effected unilaterally by the company's board of directors. The last case in this section, *Hollinger Inc. v. Hollinger International, Inc.*, is a more recent (and noteworthy) pronouncement by the Delaware Chancery Court regarding this important threshold determination.

Gimbel v. The Signal Companies, Inc.
316 A.2d 599 (Del. Ch. 1974)

QUILLEN, Chancellor:

This action was commenced on December 24, 1973 by plaintiff, a stockholder of the Signal Companies, Inc. ("Signal"). The complaint seeks, among other things, injunctive relief to prevent the consummation of the pending sale by Signal to Burmah Oil Incorporated ("Burmah") of all of the outstanding capital stock of Signal Oil and Gas Company ("Signal Oil"), a wholly-owned subsidiary of Signal. The effective sale price exceeds 480 million dollars. The sale was approved at a special meeting of the Board of Directors of Signal held on December 21, 1973.

The agreement provides that the transaction will be consummated on January 15, 1974 or upon the obtaining of the necessary governmental consents, whichever occurs later, but, in no event, after February 15, 1974 unless mutually agreed. The consents evidently have been obtained. On Monday, December 24, 1973, on the occasion of the plaintiff's application for a temporary restraining order, counsel for Signal and Signal Oil reported to this Court that the parties would not consummate this transaction prior to this Court's decision on the plaintiff's application for a preliminary injunction or January 15, 1974, whichever should occur first.

In light of that representation, no temporary restraining order was entered and the matter was set down for a hearing on plaintiff's application for a preliminary injunction. Affidavits and depositions were submitted. The matter was briefed and a hearing was held on January 4, 1974. By agreement, additional affidavits were filed on January 7th and January 9th. This is the Court's decision on plaintiff's application for a preliminary injunction to prevent the sale of Signal Oil to Burmah pending trial on the merits of plaintiff's contentions. . . .

. . . I regret that time has not permitted needed editing and that this opinion is therefore longer than desirable. In applying the law to the transaction in question, the Court believes it is first desirable to review the standards for a preliminary injunction.

An application for a preliminary injunction "is addressed to the sound discretion of the court. . . . "

In exercising its discretion, the Court must ask itself two familiar questions, which have long constituted the backdrop for evaluating the merits of any plaintiff's plea for a preliminary injunction.

Stated briefly, the first question is: "Has the plaintiff satisfied the Court that there is a reasonable probability of his ultimate success on final hearing?" . . .

The second question can be stated as follows: "Has the plaintiff satisfied the Court that he will suffer irreparable injury if the Court fails to issue the requested preliminary injunction?"

Moreover, this second question of irreparable injury to the plaintiff should injunctive relief be denied has a corollary which requires the Court to consider potential hardship to the defendant. . . .

. . . In order for the plaintiff here to "earn" his preliminary injunction against the sale of Signal Oil to Burmah, the Court must be satisfied, on the present record, that the plaintiff has a reasonable probability of succeeding on the merits of his claim. Further, the Court must also be satisfied that a preliminary injunction is necessary to protect the plaintiff from irreparable injury and that the plaintiff's need for such protection outweighs any harm that the Court can reasonably expect to befall the defendants if the injunction were granted.

Partly because of the enormous amount of money involved in this case, it is easy to discuss the irreparable injury aspect. From the plaintiff's point of view, the imminent threat of the closing of the sale does present a situation where it may be impossible to "unscramble the eggs." While the remedy of rescission is available [citation omitted], it is not difficult to imagine the various obstacles to such a remedy including, tax consequences, accounting practices, business reorganizations, management decisions concerning capital investments, dividends, etc. and a host of other problems which as a practical matter will make rescission very difficult indeed. Moreover, when the plaintiff claims with expert support, a potential damage in the neighborhood of $300,000,000, it is doubtful that any damage claim against the directors can reasonably be a meaningful alternative. In short, if the plaintiff can sustain his legal position, it seems to me that he has established he will suffer irreparable harm if the consummation of the sale is not enjoined.

On the other hand, the harm to Signal of entering an injunction is also massive. Under the contract, if the transaction is delayed by litigation, Burmah has a right to withdraw and the Court has no legal power to prevent such withdrawal.[2] The loss of Signal's legal right to enforce the contract is itself irreparable harm. . . .

In summary on the question of irreparable harm, it appears to me that there is irreparable harm to the losing side on this preliminary injunction application in the event the loser should ultimately prevail on the merits. Thus, in this case, the Court feels that the emphasis in analysis on this application for a preliminary injunction should focus on whether the plaintiff has a reasonable probability of success in this lawsuit. . . .

Turning specifically to the pleadings in this case, the complaint . . . alleges a class action on behalf of all Signal stockholders who, according to the complaint, were entitled to vote upon the proposed sale. . . .

Thus, in my judgment, the factual and legal issues are basically reduced to [the question:] does the sale require authorization by a majority of the outstanding stock of Signal pursuant to 8 Del. C. §271(a)? . . .

I turn first to the question of 8 Del. C. §271(a) which requires majority stockholder approval for the sale of "all or substantially all" of the assets of a Delaware corporation. A sale of less than all or substantially all assets is not covered by negative implication from the statute. Folk, The Delaware General Corporation Law, Section 271, p. 400, ftnt. 3; 8 Del. C. §141(a).

It is important to note in the first instance that the statute does not speak of a requirement of shareholder approval simply because an independent, important branch of a corporate business is being sold. The plaintiff cites several non-Delaware cases for the proposition that shareholder approval of such a sale is required. But that is not the language of our statute. Similarly, it is not our law that shareholder approval is required upon every "major" restructuring of the corporation. Again, it is not necessary to go beyond the statute. The statute requires shareholder approval upon the sale of "all or substantially all" of the corporation's assets. That is the sole test to be applied. While it is true that test does not lend itself to a strict mathematical standard to be applied in every case, the qualitative factor can be defined to some degree notwithstanding the limited Delaware authority. But the definition must begin with and ultimately necessarily relate to our statutory language.

In interpreting the statute the plaintiff relies on Philadelphia National Bank v. B.S.F. Co., 41 Del. Ch. 509, 199 A.2d 557 (Ch. 1964), rev'd on other grounds, 42 Del. Ch. 106, 204 A.2d 746 (Sup. Ct. 1964). In that case, B.S.F. Company owned stock in two corporations. It sold its stock in one of the corporations, and retained the stock in the other corporation. The Court found that the stock sold was the principal asset B.S.F. Company had available for sale and that the value of the stock retained was declining. The Court rejected the defendant's contention that the stock sold represented only 47.4% of consoli-

---

2. The purchaser has the option not to consummate the transaction if the following condition (paragraph 8.07 of the agreement) has not been met.

"8.07 No suit or action, investigation, inquiry, or request for information by an administrative agency, governmental body of private party, and no legal or administrative proceeding shall have been instituted or threatened which questions or reasonably appears to portend subsequent questioning of the validity or legality of this Agreement or the transactions provided for herein."

dated assets, and looked to the actual value of the stock sold. On this basis, the Court held that the stock constituted at least 75% of the total assets and the sale of the stock was a sale of substantially all assets.

But two things must be noted about the *Philadelphia National Bank* case. First, even though shareholder approval was obtained under §271, the case did not arise under §271 but under an Indenture limiting the activities of B.S.F. for creditor financial security purposes. On appeal, Chief Justice Wolcott was careful to state the following:

> "We are of the opinion that this question is not necessarily to be answered by references to the general law concerning the sale of assets by a corporation. The question before us is the narrow one of what particular language of a contract means and is to be answered in terms of what the parties were intending to guard against or to insure."

42 Del. Ch. at 111-112, 204 A.2d at 750.

Secondly, the *Philadelphia National Bank* case dealt with the sale of the company's only substantial income producing asset.

The key language in the Court of Chancery opinion in *Philadelphia National Bank* is the suggestion that "the critical factor in determining the character of a sale of assets is generally considered not the amount of property sold but whether the sale is in fact an unusual transaction or one made in the regular course of business of the seller." (41 Del. Ch. at 515, 199 A.2d at 561). Professor Folk suggests from the opinion that "the statute would be inapplicable if the assets sale is 'one made in furtherance of express corporate objects in the ordinary and regular course of the business'" (referring to language in 41 Del. Ch. at 516, 199 A.2d at 561). *Folk, supra,* Section 271, p. 401.

But any "ordinary and regular course of the business" test in this context obviously is not intended to limit the directors to customary daily business activities. Indeed, a question concerning the statute would not arise unless the transaction was somewhat out of the ordinary. While it is true that a transaction in the ordinary course of business does not require shareholder approval, the converse is not true. Every transaction out of normal routine does not necessarily require shareholder approval. The unusual nature of the transaction must strike at the heart of the corporate existence and purpose. As it is written at 6A Fletcher, Cyclopedia Corporations (Perm. Ed. 1968 Rev.) §2949.2, p. 648:

> "The purpose of the consent statutes is to protect the shareholders from fundamental change, or more specifically to protect the shareholders from the destruction of the means to accomplish the purposes or objects for which the corporation was incorporated and actually performs."

It is in this sense that the "unusual transaction" judgment is to be made and the statute's applicability determined. If the sale is of assets quantitatively vital to the operation of the corporation and is out of the ordinary and substantially affects the existence and purpose of the corporation, then it is beyond the power of the board of directors. With these guidelines, I turn to Signal and the transaction in this case.

Signal or its predecessor was incorporated in the oil business in 1922. But, beginning in 1952, Signal diversified its interests. In 1952, Signal acquired a substantial stock interest in American President lines. From 1957 to 1962 Signal was the sole owner of Laura Scudders, a nationwide snack food business. In 1964, Signal acquired Garrett Corporation which is engaged in the aircraft, aerospace, and uranium enrichment business. In 1967, Signal acquired Mack Trucks, Inc., which is engaged in the manufacture and sale of trucks and related equipment. Also in 1968, the oil and gas business was transferred to a separate division and later in 1970 to the Signal Oil subsidiary. Since 1967, Signal has made acquisition of or formed substantial companies none of which are involved or related with the oil and gas industry. *See* Walkup affidavit, docket number 34. As indicated previously, the oil and gas production development of Signal's business is now carried on by Signal Oil, the sale of the stock of which is an issue in this lawsuit.

According to figures published in Signal's last annual report (1972) and the latest quarterly report (September 30, 1973) and certain other internal financial information, the following tables can be constructed:

SIGNAL'S REVENUES (in millions)

	9 Mons. Ended September 30, 1973	December 31, 1972	December 31, 1971
Truck Manufacturing	$655.9	$712.7	$552.5
Aerospace and Industrial	407.1	478.2	448.0
Oil and Gas	185.8	267.2	314.1
Other	16.4	14.4	14.0

SIGNAL'S PRE-TAX EARNINGS (in millions)

	9 Mons. Ended September 30, 1973	December 31, 1972	December 31, 1971
Truck Manufacturing	$55.8	$65.5	$36.4
Aerospace and Industrial	20.7	21.5	19.5
Oil and Gas	10.1	12.8	9.9

SIGNAL'S ASSETS (in millions)

	9 Mons. Ended September 30, 1973	December 31, 1972	December 31, 1971
Truck Manufacturing	$581.4	$506.5	$450.4
Aerospace and Industrial	365.2	351.1	331.5
Oil and Gas	376.2	368.3	369.9
Other	113.1	102.0	121.6

SIGNAL'S NET WORTH (in millions)

	9 Mons. Ended September 30, 1973	December 31, 1972	December 31, 1971
Truck Manufacturing	$295.0	$269.7	$234.6
Aerospace and Industrial	163.5	152.2	139.6
Oil and Gas	280.5	273.2	254.4
Other	(55.4)	(42.1)	(2.0)

Based on the company's figures, Signal Oil represents only about 26% of the total assets of Signal. While Signal Oil represents 41% of Signal's total net worth, it produces only about 15% of Signal's revenues and earnings. Moreover, the additional tables shown in Signal's brief from the Chitiea affidavit are also interesting in demonstrating the low rate of return which has been realized recently from the oil and gas operations.

PRE-TAX DOLLAR RETURN ON VALUE OF ASSETS

	9 Mons. Ended September 30, 1973	December 31, 1972	December 31, 1971
Truck Manufacturing	12.8%	12.9%	8.1%
Aerospace and Industrial	7.5%	6.1%	5.9%
Oil and Gas	3.6%	3.5%	2.7%

PRE-TAX DOLLAR RETURN ON NET WORTH

	9 Mons. Ended September 30, 1973	December 31, 1972	December 31, 1971
Truck Manufacturing	25.1%	24.2%	15.5%
Aerospace and Industrial	16.8%	14.1%	14.0%
Oil and Gas	4.8%	4.7%	3.9%

While it is true, based on the experience of the Signal-Burmah transaction and the record in this lawsuit, that Signal Oil is more valuable than shown by the company's books, even if, as plaintiff suggests in his brief, the $761,000,000 value attached to Signal Oil's properties by the plaintiff's expert Paul V. Keyser, Jr., were substituted as the asset figure, the oil and gas properties would still constitute less than half the value of Signal's total assets. Thus, from a straight quantitative approach, I agree with Signal's position that the sale to Burmah does not constitute a sale of "all or substantially all" of Signal's assets.

In addition, if the character of the transaction is examined, the plaintiff's position is also weak. While it is true that Signal's original purpose was oil and gas and while oil and gas is still listed first in the certificate of incorporation, the simple fact is that Signal is now a conglomerate engaged in the aircraft and aerospace business, the manufacture and sale of trucks and related equipment, and other businesses besides oil and gas. The very nature of its business, as it now in fact exists, contemplates the acquisition and disposal of independent branches of its corporate business. Indeed, given the operations since 1952, it can be said that such acquisitions and dispositions have become part of the ordinary course of business. The facts that the oil and gas business was historically first and that authorization for such operations are listed first in the certificate do not prohibit disposal of such interest. As Director Harold M. Williams testified, business history is not "compelling" and "many companies go down the drain because they try to be historic." Williams' deposition, docket number 301, p. 28.

It is perhaps true, as plaintiff has argued, that the advent of multi-business corporations has in one sense emasculated §271 since one business may be sold without shareholder approval when other substantial businesses are retained. But it is one thing for a corporation to evolve over a period of years into a multi-business corporation, the operations of which include the purchase and sale of whole businesses, and another for a single business corporation by a one transaction revolution to sell the entire means of operating its business in exchange for money or a separate business. In the former situation, the processes of corporate democracy customarily have had the opportunity to restrain or otherwise control over a period of years. Thus, there is a chance for some shareholder participation. The Signal development illustrates the difference. For example, when Signal, itself formerly called Signal Oil and Gas Company, changed its name in 1968, it was for the announced "need for a new name appropriate to the broadly diversified activities of Signal's multi-industry complex." Walkup affidavit, docket number 34.

The situation is also dramatically illustrated financially in this very case. Independent of the contract with Burmah, the affidavit of Signal's Board Chairman shows that over $200,000,000 of Signal Oil's refining and marketing assets have been sold in the past five years. Walkup affidavit, docket number 34. This activity, prior to the sale at issue here, in itself constitutes a major restructuring of the corporate structure.

I conclude that measured quantitatively and qualitatively, the sale of the stock of Signal Oil by Signal to Burmah does not constitute a sale of "all or substantially all" of Signal's assets. This conclusion is supported by the closest case involving Delaware law which has been cited to the Court. Wingate v. Bercut, 146 F.2d 725 (9th Cir. 1944). Accordingly, insofar as the complaint rests on 8 Del. C. §271(a), in my judgment, it has no reasonable probability of ultimate success.

QUESTIONS

1. What is the focus of the inquiry under the quantitative approach to determining whether a sale of assets falls under Delaware §271? What criteria are to be taken into account under the qualitative approach to analyzing the scope of transactions covered by Delaware §271? Is this analysis consistent with the statutory language of Delaware §271?

2. As a matter of modern corporate governance, does this bifurcated approach make sense from a public policy perspective?

3. Along these lines, consider the court's reference to "the processes of corporate democracy" at work in the evolution of Signal's business. In what way does the change in corporate name effected in 1968 reflect on the "process of corporate democracy"?

Katz v. Bregman
431 A.2d 1274 (Del. Ch. 1981)

. . . MARVEL, Chancellor:

The complaint herein seeks the entry of an order preliminarily enjoining the proposed sale of the Canadian assets of Plant Industries, Inc. to Vulcan Industrial Packaging, Ltd., the plaintiff Hyman Katz allegedly being the owner of approximately 170,000 shares of common stock of the defendant Plant Industries, Inc., on whose behalf he has brought this action, suing not only for his own benefit as a stockholder but for the alleged benefit of all other record owners of common stock of the defendant Plant Industries, Inc. . . . Significantly, at common law, a sale of all or substantially all of the assets of a corporation required the unanimous vote of the stockholders, Folk, The Delaware General Corporation Law, p. 400.

The complaint alleges that during the last six months of 1980 the board of directors of Plant Industries, Inc., under the guidance of the individual defendant Robert B. Bregman, the present chief executive officer of such corporation, embarked on a course of action which resulted in the disposal of several unprofitable subsidiaries of the corporate defendant located in the United States, namely Louisiana Foliage Inc., a horticultural business, Sunaid Food Products, Inc., a Florida packaging business, and Plant Industries (Texas), Inc., a business concerned with the manufacture of woven synthetic cloth. As a result of these sales Plant Industries, Inc. by the end of 1980 had disposed of a significant part of its unprofitable assets.

According to the complaint, Mr. Bregman thereupon proceeded on a course of action designed to dispose of a subsidiary of the corporate defendant known as Plant National (Quebec) Ltd., a business which constitutes Plant Industries, Inc.'s entire business operation in Canada and has allegedly constituted Plant's only income producing facility during the past four years. The professed principal purpose of such proposed sale is to raise needed cash and thus improve Plant's balance sheets. And while interest in purchasing the corporate defendant's Canadian plant was thereafter evinced not only by Vulcan Industrial Packaging, Ltd. but also by Universal Drum Reconditioning Co., which latter corporation originally undertook to match or approximate and recently to top Vulcan's bid, a formal contract was entered into between Plant Industries, Inc. and Vulcan on April 2, 1981 for the purchase and sale of Plant National (Quebec) despite the constantly increasing bids for the same property being made by Universal. . . .

In seeking injunctive relief, as prayed for, plaintiff relies on two principles, one that [is] found in 8 Del. C. §271 to the effect that a decision of a Delaware

corporation to sell " . . . all or substantially all of its property and assets . . . "
requires not only the approval of such corporation's board of directors but also
a resolution adopted by a majority of the outstanding stockholders of the corporation entitled to vote thereon at a meeting duly called upon at least twenty
days' notice.

Support for the other principle relied on by plaintiff for the relief sought,
namely an alleged breach of fiduciary duty on the part of the board of directors of Plant Industries, Inc., is allegedly found in such board's studied refusal
to consider a potentially higher bid for the assets in question which is being
advanced by Universal.

Turning to the possible application of 8 Del. C. §271 to the proposed sale
of substantial corporate assets of National to Vulcan, it is stated in Gimbel v.
Signal Companies, Inc., Del. Ch., 316 A.2d 599 (1974) as follows:

> "If the sale is of assets quantitatively vital to the operation of the corporation and
> is out of the ordinary and substantially affects the existence and purpose of the
> corporation then it is beyond the power of the Board of Directors."

According to Plant's 1980 10K form, it appears that at the end of 1980,
Plant's Canadian operations represented 51% of Plant's remaining assets.
Defendants also concede that National represents 44.9% of Plant's sales' revenues and 52.4% of its pre-tax net operating income. Furthermore, such report
by Plant discloses, in rough figures, that while National made a profit in 1978
of $2,900,000, the profit from the United States businesses in that year was
only $770,000. In 1979, the Canadian business profit was $3,500,000 while the
loss of the United States businesses was $344,000. Furthermore, in 1980, while
the Canadian business profit was $5,300,000, the corporate loss in the United
States was $4,500,000. And while these figures may be somewhat distorted
by the allocation of overhead expenses and taxes, they are significant. In any
event, defendants concede that ". . . National accounted for 34.9% of Plant's
pre-tax income in 1976, 36.9% in 1977, 42% in 1978, 51% in 1979 and 52.4% in
1980." . . .

. . . I am first of all satisfied that historically the principal business of Plant
Industries, Inc. has not been to buy and sell industrial facilities but rather to
manufacture steel drums for use in bulk shipping as well as for the storage of
petroleum products, chemicals, food, paint, adhesives and cleaning agents, a
business which has been profitably performed by National of Quebec. Furthermore, the proposal, after the sale of National, to embark on the manufacture of
plastic drums represents a radical departure from Plant's historically successful
line of business, namely steel drums. I therefore conclude that the proposed sale
of Plant's Canadian operations, which constitute over 51% of Plant's total assets
and in which are generated approximately 45% of Plant's 1980 net sales, would,
if consummated, constitute a sale of substantially all of Plant's assets. By way of
contrast, the proposed sale of Signal Oil in Gimbel v. Signal Companies, Inc.,
supra, represented only about 26% of the total assets of Signal Companies, Inc.
And while Signal Oil represented 41% of Signal Companies, Inc. total net worth,
it generated only about 15% of Signal Companies, Inc. revenue and earnings.

I conclude that because the proposed sale of Plant National (Quebec) Ltd.
would, if consummated, constitute a sale of substantially all of the assets of

Plant Industries, Inc., as presently constituted, that an injunction should issue preventing the consummation of such sale at least until it has been approved by a majority of the outstanding stockholders of Plant Industries, Inc., entitled to vote at a meeting duly called on at least twenty days' notice.

In light of this conclusion it will be unnecessary to consider whether or not the sale here under attack, as proposed to be made, is for such an inadequate consideration, viewed in light of the competing bid of Universal, as to constitute a breach of trust on the part of the directors of Plant Industries, Inc.

QUESTIONS

1. What result on the facts of these two principal cases under the terms of the safe harbor approach of MBCA §12.02? Would the outcome be different than that reached by the Delaware courts?

2. As a public policy matter, what prompted the MBCA draftsmen to develop the safe harbor standard of MBCA §12.02? Whose interests are protected by the terms of MBCA §12.02—management or shareholders?

3. In what sense, if any, do these facts suggest a viable claim of breach of fiduciary duty on the part of the Board of Directors of Plant Industries, Inc.?

The following case provides a more recent application (and interpretation) of Delaware Section 271:

Hollinger Inc. v. Hollinger Intl., Inc.
858 A.2d 342 (Del. Ch. 2004)
Appeal Denied, 871 A.2d 1128 (Del. 2004)

STRINE, Vice Chancellor.

If the question[] [to be] resolved in this . . . opinion could be distilled to [its essence, it] . . . would be as follows: *Has the judiciary transmogrified the words "substantially all" in §271 of the Delaware General Corporation Law into the words "approximately half"?* . . . This opinion answers [that] question in [the negative].

Hollinger Inc. ("Inc.") seeks a preliminary injunction preventing Hollinger International, Inc. ("International") [a newspaper holding company] from selling the *Telegraph* Group Ltd. to Press Holdings International, an entity controlled by Frederick and David Barclay (the "Barclays"). The *Telegraph* Group is an indirect, wholly owned subsidiary of International and publishes the *Telegraph* newspaper and the *Spectator* magazine. The *Telegraph* newspaper is a leading one in the United Kingdom both in terms of its circulation and its journalistic reputation.

The key question addressed in this decision is whether Inc. [the controlling shareholder of International] and the other International stockholders must be provided with the opportunity to vote on the sale of the *Telegraph* Group because that sale involves "substantially all" the assets of International within the meaning of 8 *Del.* C. §271. The sale of the *Telegraph* followed a lengthy auction process whereby International and all of [its] operating assets were widely shopped to potential bidders. As a practical matter, Inc.'s vote would be the only one that matters because . . . [it] . . . controls 68% of the voting power [of International]. The controlling shareholder of Inc. is Lord Conrad Black. [However, Inc. cannot exercise control over International's management as a result of an agreement that was reached earlier in this case in order to settle charges of misconduct brought against Lord Conrad Black, the controlling shareholder of Inc.]

Inc. argues that a preliminary injunction should issue because it is clear that the sale of the *Telegraph* satisfies the quantitative and qualitative test used to determine whether an asset sale involves substantially all of a corporation's assets. . . .

. . .

[International, however,] contends that the sale of the *Telegraph* Group does not trigger §271.

. . .

In this opinion, I conclude that Inc.'s motion for a . . . preliminary injunction . . . should be denied as . . . its §271 [claim does not] . . . have a reasonable probability of success.

. . .

I. FACTUAL BACKGROUND

Because of the subject matter of this motion, it is important to understand what kind of company Hollinger International was, what kind of company it now is, and what kind of company it will become if the *Telegraph* sale is consummated. . . . Put simply, International regularly acquired and disposed of sizable publishing assets.

During the years 1995 to 2000, for example, International engaged in the following large transactions:

- The 1996 and 1997 sales of the company's Australian newspapers for more than $400 million.
- The 1998 acquisition of the *Post-Tribune* in Gary, Indiana and the sale of approximately 80 community newspapers, for gross cash proceeds of approximately $310 million.
- The 1998 acquisitions of *The Financial Post* (now *The National Post*), the *Victoria Times Colonist,* and other Canadian newspapers for a total cost of more than $208 million.
- The 1999 sale of 78 community newspapers in the United States, for more than $500 million.
- The 2000 sale of other United States community newspapers for $215 million.
- The 2000 acquisition of newspapers in and around Chicago, for more than $230 million.
- The 2000 sale of the bulk of the company's Canadian newspaper holdings to CanWest for over $2 billion.

The last of the cited transactions is particularly notable for present purposes. As of the year 2000, the so-called "Canadian Newspaper Group"—most of its metropolitan and community newspapers were in Canada—accounted for over 50 percent of International's revenues and EBITDA.[6] The EBITDA measure is significant because it is a measure of free cash flow that is commonly used by investors in valuing newspaper companies.

Notably, International sold the bulk of the Canadian Newspaper Group to CanWest for $2 billion without a stockholder vote (the "CanWest sale"). And Inc.—then controlled by the same person who controls it now . . . —never demanded one. . . .

INTERNATIONAL OPERATING UNITS AFTER THE CANWEST SALE

The CanWest sale left International with the set of operating assets it now controls. These operating assets fall into four basic groups, which I label in a reader-friendly manner as: the Canada Group; the Chicago Group, the Jerusalem Group, and the *Telegraph* Group. . . . The Groups operate with great autonomy and there appear to be negligible, if any, synergies generated by their operation under common ownership.

The Jerusalem Group

The Jerusalem Group owns four newspapers that are all editions of the *Jerusalem Post,* which is the most widely read English-language newspaper published in the Middle East and is considered a high-quality, internationally well-regarded source of news about Israel. The Jerusalem Group also owns the *Jerusalem Report,* a magazine, and Internet assets associated with its newspapers and magazine.

The Jerusalem Group makes only a very small contribution to International's revenues. In 2003, it had revenues of approximately $10.4 million, a figure amounting to only around 1% of International's total revenues, and its EBITDA was nearly $3 million in the red. . . .

The Canada Group

The Canada Group is the last of the Canadian publishing assets of International. It operates through three main businesses: 1) 29 daily and community newspapers in British Columbia and Quebec; 2) dozens of trade magazines, directories and websites in 17 different markets, addressed to various industries . . . ; and 3) 17 community newspapers and shopping guides in Alberta. . . .

The Canada Group is expected to generate over $80 million in revenues this year, a figure similar to last year. . . .

The Chicago Group

The Chicago Group is one of the two major operating asset groups that International controls. The Chicago Group owns more than 100 newspapers

---

6. That is, earnings before interest, taxes, depreciation and amortization.

in the greater Chicago metropolitan area. Its most prominent newspaper is the *Chicago Sun-Times,* a daily tabloid newspaper that might be thought of as the "Second Newspaper in the Second City." That moniker would not be a slight, however, when viewed from a national or even international perspective.

Even though it ranks behind the *Chicago Tribune* in terms of overall circulation and readership, the *Sun-Times* has traditionally been and remains one of the top ten newspapers in the United States in terms of circulation and readership. Even though it is a tabloid, the *Sun-Times* is not an undistinguished paper. Its sports coverage is considered to be excellent, its film critic Roger Ebert is nationally prominent, and its pages include the work of many well-regarded journalists.

That said, the *Sun-Times* is not the *New York Times* and it fills a niche within the Chicago area similar to the niche filled by tabloids in other areas. Tabloids are useful for commuters, sports fans, and for readers who are interested in a quicker portrayal of news than broadsheets, as well as for folks who care about what's going on in City Hall. For these reasons, the *Sun-Times* actually has a greater weekday readership within the City of Chicago itself than the *Tribune.*

. . .

Regardless of whether it lags the *Tribune,* the *Sun-Times* has generated very healthy EBITDA for International on a consistent basis during the recent past, producing $40 million in EBITDA in 2003, out of a total of nearly $80 million for the entire Chicago Group.

. . .

The *Sun-Times* is only one aspect of the Chicago Group, however. The Chicago Group also owns a valuable group of community newspapers that are published in the greater Chicago metropolitan area. . . .

These community papers have important economic value to the Chicago Group and to International. Their revenues and EBITDA, taken together, are roughly equal to that of the *Sun-Times.* . . .

In recent years, the Chicago Group as a whole has run neck-and-neck with the *Telegraph* Group in terms of generating EBITDA for International. . . .

The *Telegraph* Group

The *Telegraph* Group includes the Internet site and various newspapers associated with the *Daily Telegraph,* including the *Sunday Telegraph,* as well as the magazines *The Spectator* and *Apollo.* The *Spectator* is the oldest continually published English-language magazine in the world and has an impressive reputation as a journal of opinion for the British intelligentsia, but it is not an economically significant asset. Rather, the *Telegraph* newspaper is the flagship of the *Telegraph* Group economically.

The *Telegraph* is a London-based newspaper but it is international in importance and readership, with a reputation of the kind that U.S. papers like the *New York Times,* the *Washington Post,* and the *Wall Street Journal* enjoy. It is a high-quality, broadsheet newspaper that is noted for its journalistic excellence, with a conservative, establishment-oriented bent. Its daily circulation of over 900,000 is the largest among English broadsheets but it trails the *London Sunday Times* in Sunday circulation by a sizable margin. Several London tabloids also outsell the *Telegraph* by very large margins. London may be the most competitive newspaper market in the world and that market continues to involve a vigorous struggle for market share that has existed since the early 1990s, when the *Times'* owner, Rupert Murdoch, initiated a price war.

. . .

On balance, however, there is no question that the *Telegraph* Group is a profitable and valuable one. In the year 2003, it had over a half billion dollars in revenues and produced over $57 million in EBITDA. . . .

II.   LEGAL ANALYSIS . . .

A.   THE PRELIMINARY INJUNCTION STANDARD

The standard that a party seeking a preliminary injunction must satisfy is a well-known one. "On a motion for preliminary injunctive relief, the moving party must demonstrate a reasonable probability of success on the merits, that absent injunctive relief irreparable harm will occur, and that the harm the moving party will suffer if the requested relief is denied outweighs the harm the opponents will suffer if relief is granted." The resolution of Inc.'s motion in this case turns largely on the merits of its claims, which I now discuss. . . .

. . .

C.   AS A MATTER OF ECONOMIC SUBSTANCE, DOES THE *TELEGRAPH* GROUP COMPRISE SUBSTANTIALLY ALL OF INTERNATIONAL'S ASSETS?

I now discuss the major question presented by this motion: whether the *Telegraph* Group comprises "substantially all" of International's assets, such that its sale requires a vote under §271.

1.   The Legal Standards to Measure Whether the Telegraph Group Comprises Substantially All of International's Assets

Section 271 of the Delaware General Corporation Law authorizes a board of directors of a Delaware corporation to sell "all or substantially all of its property and assets, including goodwill and corporate franchises" only with the approval of a stockholder vote. The origins of §271 did not rest primarily in a desire by the General Assembly to protect stockholders by affording them a vote on transactions previously not requiring their assent. Rather, §271's predecessors were enacted to address the common law rule that invalidated any attempt to sell all or substantially all of a corporation's assets without unanimous stockholder approval.[42] . . . According to leading commentators, the addition of the words "substantially all" was "intended merely to codify the interpretation generally accorded to the language of the pre-1967 statute that the word 'all' meant

---

42. *See, e.g., Gimbel v. Signal Cos.,* 316 A.2d 599, 605 n. 3 (Del. Ch.) (indicating that this was the purpose of the predecessor to §271), *aff'd,* 316 A.2d 619 (Del. 1974); 1 R. Franklin Balotti & Jesse A. Finkelstein, DELAWARE LAW OF CORPORATIONS & BUSINESS ORGANIZATIONS §10.1, at 10-3 (3d ed. Supp. 2004) (same).

'substantially all,' so that the statute could not be evaded by retaining a small amount of property not vital to the operation of the business."[44]

As I will note, our courts arguably have not always viewed cases involving the interpretation of §271 through a lens focused by the statute's plain words. Nonetheless, it remains a fundamental principle of Delaware law that the courts of this state should apply a statute in accordance with its plain meaning, as the words that our legislature has used to express its will are the best evidence of its intent. To analyze whether the vote requirement set forth in §271 applies to a particular asset sale without anchoring that analysis to the statute's own words involves an unavoidable risk that normative preferences of the judiciary will replace those of the General Assembly.

Therefore, I begin my articulation of the applicable legal principles with the words of the statute itself. There are two key words here: "substantially" and "all." Although neither word is particularly difficult to understand, let's start with the easier one. "All" means "all," or if that is not clear, all, when used before a plural noun such as "assets," means "[t]he entire or unabated amount or quantity of; the whole extent, substance, or compass of; the whole."[46] "Substantially" is the adverb form of "substantial." Among other things, substantial means "being largely but not wholly that which is specified."[47] Substantially conveys the same meaning as "considerably" and "essentially"[48] because it means "to a great extent or degree" and communicates that it is very nearly the same thing as the noun it acts upon.[49] In all their relevant meanings, substantial and substantially convey the idea of amplitude, of something that is "[c]onsiderable in importance, value, degree, amount, or extent."[50] A fair and succinct equivalent to the term "substantially all" would therefore be "essentially everything."

. . . There are various metrics that can be used to determine how important particular assets are in the scheme of things. Should a court look to the percentage of the corporation's potential value as a sales target to measure the statute's application? Or measures of income-generating potential, such as contributions to revenues or operating income? To what extent should the flagship nature of certain assets be taken into account?

For all these reasons,

> The Supreme Court has long held that a determination of whether there is a sale of substantially all assets so as to trigger section 271 depends upon the particular qualitative and quantitative characteristics of the transaction at issue. Thus, the transaction must be viewed in terms of its overall effect on the corporation, and there is no necessary qualifying percentage.[51]

---

44. Balotti & Finkelstein, §10.1, at 10-4 (quoting *Cottrell v. Pawcatuck Co.*, 128 A.2d 225 (Del.1956)); *see also* . . . Ernest L. Folk, III, The Delaware General Corporation Law: A Commentary & Analysis 400 (1967 amendment adding "substantially all" explicitly codified "general consensus" that the existing statute "applied in that situation as well"). . . .

46. Oxford English Dictionary Online (2d ed. 1989), http://dictionary.oed.com.

47. Merriam-Webster On-line Dictionary, http://www.m-w.com.

48. MSN Encarta Dictionary, http://encarta.msn.com/encnet/features/dictionary/dictionaryhome.aspx.

49. http://www.dictionary.reference.com

50. American Heritage Dictionary 1727 (4th ed. 2000).

51. *Winston v. Mandor,* 710 A.2d 835, 843 (Del. Ch. 1997) (footnotes omitted).

In other words,

> Our jurisprudence eschewed a definitional approach to §271 focusing on the interpretation of the words "substantially all," in favor of a contextual approach focusing upon whether a transaction involves the sale "of assets quantitatively vital to the operation of the corporation and is out of the ordinary and substantially affects the existence and purpose of the corporation." *Gimbel v. Signal Cos., Inc.,* Del. Ch., 316 A.2d 599, 606, *aff'd,* Del.Supr., 316 A.2d 619 (1974). This interpretative choice necessarily involved a policy preference for doing equity in specific cases over the value of providing clear guidelines for transactional lawyers structuring transactions for the corporations they advise. *See* 1 David A. Drexler, et al., *Delaware Corporation Law and Practice* §37.03 (1999) ("[*Gimbel*] and its progeny represent a clear-cut rejection of the former conventional view that 'substantially all' in Section 271 meant only significantly more than one-half of the corporation's assets.").[52]

It would be less than candid to fail to acknowledge that the §271 case law provides less than ideal certainty about the application of the statute to particular circumstances. This may result from certain decisions that appear to deviate from the statutory language in a marked way[53] and from others that have dilated perhaps longer than they should in evaluating asset sales that do not seem to come at all close to meeting the statutory trigger for a required stockholder vote.[54] In this latter respect, the seminal §271 decision, *Gimbel v. Signal Cos.*, may have contributed to the lack of clarity. In the heat of an expedited injunction proceeding, the Chancellor examined in some detail whether the sale of assets comprising only 26% and 41% of the Signal Companies' total and net assets was subject to stockholder approval. Although the assets involved the oldest business line of the Signal Companies, the magnitude involved does not seem to approach §271's gray zone.

In the morass of particular percentages in the cases, however, remain the key principles articulated in *Gimbel*, which were firmly rooted in the statutory language of §271 and the statute's history. As has been noted, *Gimbel* set forth a quantitative and qualitative test designed to help determine whether a particular sale of assets involved substantially all of the corporation's assets. That test has been adopted by our Supreme Court as a good metric for determining whether an asset sale triggers the vote requirement of §271.[55]

. . .

The test that *Gimbel* articulated—requiring a stockholder vote if the assets to be sold "are quantitatively vital to the operation of the corporation" and

---

52. *In re General Motors Class H S'holders Litig.,* 734 A.2d 611, 623 (Del. Ch. 1999).

53. The case of *Katz v. Bregman,* 431 A.2d 1274 (Del. Ch. 1981), in particular, represents a striking one. In that case, a sale of assets constituting 51 percent of asset value, 44.9 percent of sales, and 52.4 percent of pre-tax net operating income was held to be subject to stockholder approval as a sale of "substantially all" the corporation's assets.

54. In a prior decision, a number of the Delaware opinions are summarized in terms of their treatment of assets sales involving certain percentages and factors. *See In re General Motors Class H S'holders Litig.,* 734 A.2d at 623 n. 10.

55. *Oberly v. Kirby,* 592 A.2d 445, 464 (Del.1991); *see also Thorpe v. CERBCO, Inc.,* 676 A.2d 436, 444 (Del.1996).

"substantially affect[ ] the existence and purpose of the corporation"—must therefore be read as an attempt to give practical life to the words "substantially all." It is for that reason that *Gimbel* emphasized that a vote would never be required for a transaction in the ordinary course of business and that the mere fact that an asset sale was out of the ordinary had little bearing on whether a vote was required.

. . .

And it is in that sense that I apply the *Gimbel* test in this case.

2. Is the *Telegraph* Group Quantitatively Vital to the Operations of International?

The first question under the *Gimbel* test is whether the *Telegraph* Group is quantitatively vital to the operations of International. The short answer to that question is no, it is not quantitatively vital within the meaning of *Gimbel*.

Why?

Because it is clear that International will retain economic vitality even after a sale of the *Telegraph* because it is retaining other significant assets, one of which, the Chicago Group, has a strong record of past profitability and expectations of healthy profit growth.

Now, it is of course clear that the *Telegraph* Group is a major quantitative part of International's economic value and an important contributor to its profits. I am even prepared to decide this motion on the assumption that the *Telegraph* Group is the single most valuable asset that International possesses, even more valuable than the Chicago Group.

. . .

Let's consider the relative contribution to International's revenues of the *Telegraph* Group and the Chicago Group. When considering this and other factors the reader must bear in mind that the contribution of the Canada Group dropped steeply after the 2000 CanWest sale. Before that sale, the Canada Group was a larger contributor to the economic value of International in many respects than the *Telegraph* and Chicago Groups combined and it was sold without a stockholder vote. Bearing that fact in mind, a look at the revenue picture at International since 2000 reveals the following:

Revenue (\$MM)								
Operating Unit	2000	%	2001	%	2002	%	Unaudited 2003	%
Telegraph Group	\$562.1	26.8	486.4	42.4	481.5	47.9	519.5	49.0
Chicago Group	401.4	19.2	442.9	38.6	441.8	43.9	450.8	42.5
Canada Group	1,065.2	50.8	197.9	17.3	69.6	6.9	80.5	7.6
Jerusalem Group	67.3	3.2	19.1	1.7	13.2	1.3	10.4	1.0
Other	0.0	0.0	0.0	0.0	0.0	0.0	0.0	0.0
Total	2,096.0	100.0	1,146.3	100.0	1,006.2	100.0	1,061.2	100.0

Put simply, the *Telegraph* Group has accounted for less than half of International's revenues during the last three years and the Chicago Group's contribution has been in the same ballpark.

In book value terms, neither the *Telegraph* Group nor the Chicago Group approach 50% of International's asset value because the company's other operating groups and non-operating assets have value:

Book Value of Assets ($MM)								
Operating Unit	2000	%	2001	%	2002	%	Unaudited 2003	%
Telegraph Group	$542.0	19.8	533.2	25.9	568.3	26.0	629.8	35.7
Chicago Group	613.7	22.4	595.9	29.0	557.9	25.5	537.9	30.5
Canada Group	551.6	20.2	448.7	21.8	214.0	9.8	262.0	14.9
Jerusalem Group	61.2	2.2	69.6	3.4	28.9	1.3	30.1	1.7
Other	968.8	35.4	410.5	19.9	819.1	37.4	302.8	17.2
Total	**2,737.2**	**100.0**	**2,058.0**	**100.0**	**2,188.1**	**100.0**	**1,762.6**	**100.0**

In terms of vitality, however, a more important measure is EBITDA contribution, as that factor focuses on the free cash flow that assets generate for the firm, a key component of economic value. As to that important factor, the Chicago Group is arguably more quantitatively nutritious to International than the *Telegraph* Group. Here is the picture considering all of International's operating groups:

EBITDA—All Operating Units ($MM)								
Operating Unit	2000	%	2001	%	2002	%	Unaudited 2003	%
Telegraph Group	$106.7	30.3	50.7	85.3	61.4	54.7	57.4	57.4
Chicago Group	59.8	17.0	47.6	80.1	72.1	64.2	79.5	79.4
Canada Group	190.5	54.1	(21.1)	(2.5)	(0.8)	(0.7)	(3.3)	(3.3)
Jerusalem Group	9.6	2.7	(1.5)	(2.5)	(2.8)	(2.5)	(5.3)	(5.3)
Other	(14.3)	(4.1)	(16.3)	(27.4)	(17.5)	(15.6)	(28.3)	(28.3)
Total	**352.3**	**100.0**	**59.5**	**100.0**	**112.4**	**100.0**	**100.0**	**100.0**

The picture that emerges is one of rough equality between the two Groups—with any edge tilting in the Chicago Group's direction. . . .

. . .

The evidence therefore reveals that neither the *Telegraph* Group nor the Chicago Group is quantitatively vital in the sense used in the *Gimbel* test. Although both Groups are profitable, [have] valuable economic assets and although the *Telegraph* Group is somewhat more valuable than the Chicago Group, International can continue as a profitable entity without either one of them. International is not a human body and the *Telegraph* and the Chicago Group are not its heart and liver. International is a business. Neither one of the two groups is "vital"—i.e., "necessary to the continuation of [International's] life" or "necessary to [its] continued existence or effectiveness."[72] Rather, a sale of either Group leaves International as a profitable entity, even if it chooses to distribute a good deal of the cash it receives from the *Telegraph* sale to its stockholders through a dividend or share repurchase.

---

72. AMERICAN HERITAGE DICTIONARY 1924 (4th ed. 2000).

3. Does the *Telegraph* Sale Substantially Affect the Existence and
    Purpose of International?

The relationship of the qualitative element of the *Gimbel* test to the quantitative element is more than a tad unclear. If the assets to be sold are not quantitatively vital to the corporation's life, it is not altogether apparent how they can
"substantially affect the existence and purpose of" the corporation within the
meaning of *Gimbel,* suggesting either that the two elements of the test are actually not distinct or that they are redundant. In other words, if quantitative vitality takes into account factors such as the cash-flow generating value of assets
and not merely book value, then it necessarily captures qualitative considerations as well. Simply put, the supposedly bifurcated *Gimbel* test . . . may simply
involve a look at quantitative and qualitative considerations in order to come up
with the answer to the single statutory question, which is whether a sale involves
substantially all of a corporation's assets. Rather than endeavor to explore the
relationship between these factors, however, I will just dive into my analysis of
the qualitative importance of the *Telegraph* Group to International.

Inc.'s demand for a vote places great weight on the qualitative element of
Gimbel. In its papers, Inc. stresses the journalistic superiority of the *Telegraph*
over the *Sun-Times* and the social cachet the *Telegraph* has. If you own the *Telegraph,* Inc. notes, "you can have dinner with the Queen."[73] To sell one of the
world's most highly regarded newspapers and leave International owning as its
flagship the Second Paper in the Second City is to fundamentally, qualitatively
transform International. Moreover, after the *Telegraph* sale, International's
name will even ring hollow, as it will own only publications in the U.S., Canada,
and Israel, and it will own only one paper of top-flight journalistic reputation,
the *Jerusalem Post,* which has only a modest readership compared to the *Telegraph.*

The argument that Inc. makes in its papers misconceives the qualitative
element of *Gimbel.* That element is not satisfied if the court merely believes
that the economic assets being sold are aesthetically superior to those being
retained; rather, the qualitative element of *Gimbel* focuses on economic quality and, at most, on whether the transaction leaves the stockholders with an
investment that in economic terms is qualitatively different than the one that
they now possess. Even with that focus, it must be remembered that the qualitative element is a gloss on the statutory language "substantially all" and not an
attempt to identify qualitatively important transactions but ones that "strike at
the heart of the corporate existence."[74]

The *Telegraph* sale does not strike at International's heart or soul, if that
corporation can be thought to have either one. When International went public, it did not own the *Telegraph.* During the course of its existence, International has frequently bought and sold a wide variety of publications. In the
CanWest sale, it disposed of a number of major newspapers in Canada—and
diminished its assets by half—all without a stockholder vote. That sale came on
the heels of its departure from Australia and an American downsizing. Thus,

---

73. Healy Dep. at 206.
74. *Gimbel,* 316 A.2d at 606.

no investor in International would assume that any of its assets were sacrosanct. In the words of *Gimbel,* it "can be said that . . . acquisitions and dispositions [of independent branches of International's business] have become part of the [company's] ordinary course of business."[75]

Even more importantly, investors in public companies do not invest their money because they derive social status from owning shares in a corporation whose controlling manager can have dinner with the Queen. Whatever the social importance of the *Telegraph* in Great Britain, the economic value of that importance to International as an entity is what matters for the *Gimbel* test, not how cool it would be to be the *Telegraph's* publisher. The expected cash flows from the *Telegraph* Group take that into account, as do the bids that were received for the *Telegraph* Group. The "trophy" nature of the *Telegraph* Group means that there are some buyers—including I discern, the Barclays, who run a private, not public, company—who are willing to pay a higher price than expected cash flows suggest is prudent, in purely economic terms, in order to own the *Telegraph* and to enjoy the prestige and access to the intelligentsia, the literary and social elite, and high government officials that comes with that control.

Although stockholders would expect that International would capitalize on the fact that some potential buyers of the *Telegraph* would be willing to pay money to receive some of the non-economic benefits that came with control of that newspaper, it is not reasonable to assume that they invested with the expectation that International would retain the *Telegraph* Group even if it could receive a price that was attractive in light of the projected future cash flow of that Group. Certainly, given the active involvement of International in the M & A market, there was no reason to invest based on that unusual basis. It may be that there exists somewhere an International stockholder (other than Mrs. Black or perhaps some personal friends of the Blacks) who values the opportunities that Conrad Black had to dine with the Queen and other eminent members of British society because he was the *Telegraph's* publisher. But the qualitative element of the *Gimbel* test addresses the rational economic expectations of reasonable investors, and not the aberrational sentiments of the peculiar (if not, more likely, the non-existent) persons who invest money to help fulfill the social ambitions of inside managers and to thereby enjoy (through the ownership of common stock) vicariously extraordinary lives themselves.

After the *Telegraph* Sale, International's stockholders will remain investors in a publication company with profitable operating assets, a well-regarded tabloid newspaper of good reputation and large circulation, a prestigious newspaper in Israel, and other valuable assets. While important, the sale of the *Telegraph* does not strike a blow to International's heart.

4.   Summary of §271 Analysis

When considered quantitatively and qualitatively, the *Telegraph* sale does not amount to a sale of substantially all of International's assets. This conclusion is consistent with the bulk of our case law under §271. Although by no

---

75. *Id.* at 608.

means wholly consistent, that case law has, by and large, refused to find that a disposition involved substantially all the assets of a corporation when the assets that would remain after the sale were, in themselves, substantial and profitable. As *Gimbel* noted, §271 permits a board to sell "one business . . . without shareholder approval when other substantial businesses are retained." In the cases when asset sales were deemed to involve substantially all of a corporation's assets, the record always revealed great doubt about the viability of the business that would remain, primarily because the remaining operating assets were not profitable. But, "if the portion of the business not sold constitutes a substantial, viable, ongoing component of the corporation, the sale is not subject to Section 271."[78]

To conclude that the sale of the *Telegraph* Group was a sale of substantially all of International's assets would involve a determination that International possesses two operating assets, the sale of either of which would trigger a stockholder vote under §271. That is, because there is no significant distinction between the economic importance of the Chicago and *Telegraph* Groups to International, a conclusion that the *Telegraph* Group was substantially all of International's assets would (impliedly but undeniably) supplant the plain language and intended meaning of the General Assembly with an "approximately half" test.[79] I decline Inc.'s invitation for me to depart so markedly from our

---

78. 1 R. Franklin Balotti & Jesse A. Finkelstein, DELAWARE LAW OF CORPORATIONS & BUSINESS ORGANIZATIONS §10.2, at 10-7 (3d ed. Supp. 2004).

79. As International points out, the MBCA now includes a safe harbor provision that is intended to provide a "greater measure of certainty than is provided by interpretations of the current case law." MODEL BUS. CORP. ACT §12.02 cmt. 1 (2002). The safe harbor is an objective test involving two factors:

> If a corporation retains a business activity that represented at least 25 percent of total assets at the end of the most recently completed fiscal year, and 25 percent of either income from continuing operations before taxes or revenues from continuing operations for that fiscal year, in each case of the corporation and its subsidiaries on a consolidated basis, the corporation will conclusively be deemed to have retained a significant continuing business activity.

Id. §12.02(a).

Moreover, both the MBCA and the ALI Principles of Corporate Governance usefully turn the "substantially all" inquiry on its head by focusing, as *Gimbel* does in a more oblique way, on what remains after a sale. *See* MODEL BUS. CORP. ACT §12.02 cmt. 1 (2002) (stockholder vote required if asset sale would "leave the corporation without a significant continuing business activity"); PRINCIPLES OF CORP. GOVERNANCE §§1.38(a)(2), 6.01(b) (text requiring stockholder approval when asset sale "would leave the corporation without a significant continuing business"); *id.*§1.38 cmt. 3 (commentary indicating that if a company has two principal operating divisions and one will remain following the asset sale, "there should normally be no doubt concerning the significance of the remaining division, even if the division to be sold represented a majority of the corporation's operating assets"). The MBCA, in particular, recognizes that while the "significant continuing business activity" test differs verbally from the "substantially all" language employed in many state corporation statutes, adoption of the MBCA provision would not entail a substantive change from existing law, because "[i]n practice, . . . courts interpreting these statutes [using the phrase 'substantially

legislature's mandate. By any reasonable interpretation, the *Telegraph* sale does not involve substantially all of International's assets as substantial operating (and non-operating) assets will be retained, and International will remain a profitable publishing concern. . . .

IV. CONCLUSION

Inc.'s motion for a preliminary injunction is DENIED. IT IS SO ORDERED.

NOTES

1. The Downfall of Lord Conrad Black. Following the attempted sale of the Telegraph Group to Barclays, Lord Conrad Black, Hollinger International's extravagant CEO, was charged and convicted of defrauding investors. As the trial records revealed, the sale of Hollinger International's various subsidiaries between 1998 and 2001 financed Lord Black's luxurious lifestyle to the tune of over $6 million. Ultimately, Lord Black was sentenced to 6 ½ years in prison and ordered to pay $125,000 in fines. Five years later, thanks to the Supreme Court's determination in *Skilling v. United States*, 130 S. Ct. 2896 (2010), that the honest services law (which was the law used to convict executive officers such as Enron's CEO, Jeffrey Skilling, of corporate fraud) was unconstitutionally vague, Lord Black was released from prison in May 2012. *See Conrad Black Is Freed*, N.Y. TIMES DEAL BOOK, May 4, 2012.

2. Clarifying Delaware Precedent? In the wake of Vice Chancellor Strine's opinion in *Hollinger*, one set of experienced practitioners made the following observation:

> Section 271 has been a thorn in the sides of practitioners for a long time. Although Delaware rightly prides itself on having the pre-eminent corporate law in the

---

all'] have commonly employed a test comparable to that embodied in 12.02(a)." MODEL BUS. CORP. ACT §12.02 cmt. 1 (2002). The commentary specifically cites several Delaware judicial decisions as examples of cases employing such a test. *Id.* These approaches support the conclusion I reach. Although not binding on me, these interpretative approaches provide a valuable perspective on §271 because they are rooted, as is *Gimbel*, in the intent behind the statute (and statutes like it in other jurisdictions). Indeed, taken together, a reading of §271 that: 1) required a stockholder vote for any sales contract to which a parent was a party that involved a sale by a wholly owned subsidiary that, in economic substance, amounted to a disposition of substantially all the parent's assets; combined with 2) a strict adherence to the words "substantially all" (á la the MBCA), could be viewed as the most faithful way to give life to the General Assembly's intended use of §271. That is, §271 would have substantive force but only with regard to transactions that genuinely involved substantially all of the corporation's assets.

U.S., with an extensive body of judicial decisions offering guidance and, in most cases, a relatively high degree of predictability for lawyers and their clients, the cases under Section 271 leave an uncomfortably wide range of transactions in a "grey area." Vice Chancellor Leo E. Strine, Jr. clearly saw in [the excerpted opinion above in] the *Hollinger* dispute an opportunity to clarify the precedents.

Elliot V. Stein and Ophir Nave, *Hollinger—Round Two: "Substantially All" Means "Substantially All,"* 8 THE M&A LAWYER 7 (Sept. 2004). Do you agree? Do you think Vice Chancellor Strine's opinion "clarifies the precedents"—resulting in a narrowing of the "grey area"?

E.   Corporate Formalities Required for Stock Acquisitions

1.   General Background

In Chapter 1, we learned that, under the terms of modern state corporation statutes, Bidder Co. has the power to hold and to vote shares of another corporation. This allows Bidder to negotiate directly with Target Co. shareholders for the purchase of their shares in Target. Assuming that Bidder acquires all (or at least a controlling interest in) Target shares, Bidder may then exercise its voting rights to remove the incumbent board of directors and replace them with Bidder's own slate of nominees. Consider the situation where Bidder is lucky enough to purchase all of Target's shares for cash, as reflected in Diagram 6 in Appendix A. After the parties close on their stock purchase agreement and this change of control transaction has been consummated, Target Co. will be left as a wholly owned subsidiary of Bidder.

Consider, though, the economic result where Bidder issues its shares in exchange for all of the shares of Target (as reflected in Diagram 7 in Appendix A), rather than paying cash to purchase Target shares. This transaction, commonly referred to as a "stock exchange offer," raises some interesting questions. Where do the former Target Co. shareholders end up? What is the economic decision that faces Target shareholders in a stock exchange offer? How does a stock exchange offer differ from the decision Target shareholders face when they receive an all-cash offer from Bidder? Finally, consider the situation that confronts the shareholders of Bidder Co. As a general proposition, does it make any difference to Bidder's shareholders whether Bidder uses its cash or its stock to acquire Target shares?

The next problem set is intended to flesh out the concerns that must be addressed in analyzing these issues. Before we analyze these problems, one further consideration deserves mention—the agency cost problem inherent in modern share ownership. This problem is most acute in the case of those investors who own shares in publicly traded companies. Briefly summarized, the agency cost problem is inherent in the corporate form of business organization because of the separation of ownership from control over the company's business operations. When the owners of a company (the shareholders) delegate managerial authority over the company's business affairs to agents (the board of directors and the company's senior executive officers), the resulting separation of ownership and managerial control creates divergent incentives. For example, corporate managers may be tempted to use their authority to load up on executive perks (such as company jets and club memberships), which allow the corporate managers to reap almost all of the benefits while bearing only a fraction of the costs. This is generally referred to as the *agency cost problem.*

The agency cost problem surfaces in M&A transactions, although it is not unique to this setting. (Indeed, the agency cost problem has been reflected most prominently in the ongoing, highly publicized controversy over the use of stock options as part of the executive compensation for corporate CEOs.) In the case of M&A deals, however, the agency cost problem is central to the legal rules imposed on this method of corporation acquisition. The next problem set is designed to flesh out the nature of the agency cost problem in the case of acquisitions structured as stock purchases and the nature of the law's response to this recurring problem. In addition, the problems are further designed to separate out the nature of the agency cost problem in the context of publicly traded companies versus privately held corporations.

PROBLEM SET NO. 4—STOCK PURCHASES UNDER DELAWARE LAW AND THE MBCA

1. Stock Purchase for Cash (See Diagram 6—Appendix A).   Assume that two brothers, Paul and David Merage, each own half of the outstanding common stock of Chef America, Inc., which is the only class of stock outstanding. The two brothers have signed a stock purchase agreement with Nestlé, Inc., a NYSE-listed U.S. company. Nestlé has agreed to pay $2 billion cash on closing of the parties' stock purchase agreement.

    a.   Who are the parties to the stock purchase agreement?

    b.   What board action is required of Chef America if the company is organized under Delaware law? Under the MBCA?

    c.   What board action is required of Nestlé, Inc. if Nestlé is organized under Delaware law? Under the MBCA?

    d.   Do the shareholders of Chef America have the right to vote:

        (1)   Under Delaware law?
        (2)   Under the MBCA?

    e.   Do the shareholders of Nestlé have the right to vote:

        (1)   Under Delaware law?
        (2)   Under the MBCA?

    f.   What options are available to the shareholders of Chef America (under either Delaware law or the MBCA) if they object to the terms of Nestlé's offer?

    g.   What options are available to the shareholders of Nestlé, Inc. (under either Delaware law or the MBCA) if they object to Nestlé's proposal to acquire Chef America?

2. Stock Purchase—in Exchange for 24 Percent of Bidder's Stock (See Diagram 7—Appendix A).   Assume the same facts as described in Problem 1, *except* that the parties' stock purchase agreement calls for Nestlé to pay at closing a portion of the $2 billion purchase price in cash, and the balance of the purchase price is to be paid by issuing shares of Nestlé common stock comprising 24 percent of the voting power of Nestlé's outstanding common stock immediately before the issuance is completed.

   a.   Who are the parties to the stock purchase agreement?
   b.   What board action is required of Chef America if the company is organized under Delaware law? Under the MBCA?
   c.   What board action is required of Nestlé, Inc. if Nestlé is organized under Delaware law? Under the MBCA?
   d.   Do the shareholders of Chef America have the right to vote:

   (1)   Under Delaware law?
   (2)   Under the MBCA?

   e.   Do the shareholders of Nestlé have the right to vote:

   (1)   Under Delaware law?
   (2)   Under the MBCA?

   f.   How does your analysis of these issues change if shares comprising only 14 percent of the voting power of Nestlé's outstanding stock immediately before the issuance are to be used as the acquisition consideration, and the balance of the purchase price is to be paid in cash?

3. Stock Purchase—in Exchange for 14 Percent of Bidder's Stock (See Diagram 7—Appendix A).   The three shareholders of Target Co. plan to sell all of their stock to Bidder Co. in exchange for shares of common stock of Bidder Co., a closely held corporation, comprising only 14 percent of the voting power of Bidder's outstanding common stock immediately before the transaction is completed.

   a.   What action is required by the boards of Bidder and Target:

   (1)   Under Delaware law?
   (2)   Under the MBCA?

   b.   Do the shareholders of Bidder and Target have the right to vote:

   (1)   Under Delaware law?
   (2)   Under the MBCA?

   c.   Do the shareholders of either Bidder or Target have the right to dissent:

   (1)   Under Delaware law?
   (2)   Under the MBCA?

NOTES

1. An Introduction to Hostile Takeovers.   Where management of Bidder Co. directly negotiates with management of Target Co., and these negotiations result in an acquisition proposal whereby Bidder offers to buy Target shares directly from Target shareholders, and further, Target's board recommends that its shareholders accept Bidder's offer, then this transaction is generally referred to on Wall Street as a *friendly takeover.* However, in those cases where Target's board refuses to negotiate and reach a deal with Bidder, then Bidder may bypass Target's management altogether and may take its offer to buy Target shares directly to Target's shareholders. In the jargon of Wall Street, this type of acquisition will be referred to as a *hostile takeover.* The ability of the determined Bidder to engage in this type of end run around existing management of Target Co. is the core tool of determined Bidders who seek to wrest control from incumbent managers in the *market for corporate control,* a term of art on Wall Street and in the M&A literature.

According to the market for corporate control, the potential for this type of hostile takeover operates as a disciplining influence on incumbent management, who know that if they underperform, and the stock price declines far enough in the trading market, the company may become an attractive candidate for a takeover. In the usual case, prospective Bidders will identify an underperforming Target and make an unsolicited offer directly to Target's shareholders for the purpose of getting control over Target and its business operations. Once in control, Bidder will usually move swiftly to replace incumbent management with a more effective business team.

The market for corporate control, therefore, rests in part on the premise that if incumbent management knows that it is vulnerable to this kind of market pressure, then management will be motivated to perform well to keep control over Target's business—and ultimately, their jobs. One of the major public policy debates growing out of the merger wave of the 1980s focused on the appropriate manner of regulating the market for corporate control. The nature of this public policy debate, vestiges of which linger even today, are explored in detail in Chapter 6, where we discuss federal regulation of takeovers under the terms of the Williams Act, and in Chapter 7, where we analyze the nature of directors' fiduciary duty obligations under state law, the limits of which are most acutely tested in the case of unsolicited (hostile) tender offers.

2. An Introduction to Two-Step Transactions.   As we saw in analyzing Problem Set No. 4, very often Bidder Co. will be in a financial position to purchase all of the outstanding shares of Target Co., as in the case of Nestlé's purchase of all of the outstanding shares of Chef America from the two Merage brothers. As a result, once the stock purchase is consummated, Chef America becomes a wholly owned subsidiary of Nestlé. Very often, though, Bidder will not be able to acquire 100 percent of the stock of Target. This problem is particularly acute in those cases where Target Co. is publicly traded. In these cases, Bidder will usually condition its obligation to purchase Target shares from the selling shareholders on its ability to obtain a sufficient number of Target shares to give Bidder a majority of the voting stock of Target. In many cases, this will leave a (perhaps substantial) minority interest in Target, which is now operated as a controlled subsidiary of Bidder Co.

For legal and business reasons which are developed in more detail in later chapters of this casebook, Bidder may then desire to eliminate the outstanding minority shares of the subsidiary by acquiring the remaining shares of Target that the parent company (Bidder) does not own. This second step is often referred to as a *squeeze-out* transaction (i.e., "squeezing out" the minority interest from any continued equity ownership of the subsidiary). Very often, the minority shares will be squeezed out in a second step transaction structured as a cash-out merger. (*See Diagram 12 in Appendix A.*) For reasons that are developed in the problem set in the next section, this back-end, second-step, cash-out merger will often be accomplished as a triangular merger (as reflected in Diagram 12 of Appendix A).

3. Distinguish the "Bust-up Bid" and the "Merger of Equals." In the case of certain LBO deals of the type described earlier in this chapter (*see supra*, pp. 72-75), the financial buyer's plan of acquisition often calls for the buyout firm to acquire Target in order to sell off the pieces. This LBO model reflects the financial buyer's determination that, in effect, Target is worth *more* if the pieces are sold off. The proceeds raised from the sale of Target's assets would then be used to reduce the debt that had been borrowed in order to finance the purchase price for Target.

The staff of many LBO firms invest much of their time searching for companies where the trading price reflects that management is underutilizing the present combination of business assets. In these cases, the financial buyer can afford to borrow the funds necessary to pay a premium in order to purchase enough Target Co. shares to give the buyout firm control of Target. In the case of a publicly traded Target Co., this purchase will usually take the form of a tender offer regulated by the federal securities laws, a topic that is addressed in Chapter 6. After obtaining control of Target, the buyout firm would then proceed to dismantle Target by selling off its assets in piecemeal fashion. This type of LBO deal became popular in the 1980s and was widely used to dismantle the large, diversified conglomerates that were established through acquisitions made during the M&A wave of the 1960s. As the dominant business paradigm shifted in the 1980s and 1990s to focus on core business activity, LBO firms and other financial buyers helped accelerate the process of deconglomeration.

In contrast to "bust-up" bids, deals known as "mergers of equals" became quite popular in the M&A market of the 1990s. Perhaps the best known of these *mergers-of-equals* is the AOL-Time-Warner deal. Billed as two firms combining together to be managed under the leadership of *both* companies' CEOs, the deal was deliberately structured to avoid the perception that one firm was acquiring (swallowing up) another company. In very short order, however, critics claimed that this kind of power-sharing arrangement between co-CEOs was doomed to fail. The story of the merger of AOL and Time-Warner validates the truth of this observation, as we shall see when we study this deal and its aftermath in Chapter 7. At this point, suffice it to say that the financial return of this combination proved dismal for the shareholders and, as it turns out, the power-sharing arrangement at AOL-Time-Warner was doomed almost from the very start.

F. Corporate Formalities Required for Triangular Mergers Under Delaware Law and the MBCA

1. General Background on Triangular (Three-Party) Mergers

Until the 1970s, the advantages (and convenience) of the merger was limited to direct mergers of the type studied in Problem Set No. 1 earlier in this chapter. In these transactions, Bidder would swallow up Target by operation of law and Target would cease to exist. However, this usually could be accomplished *only* by the vote of the shareholders of *both* constituent corporations.

Consider, though, the situation where Nestlé, Inc., a large NYSE-listed company, decides to buy Trixie's Delites, Inc., a small, gourmet chocolate manufacturer located in Denver, Colorado, in order to obtain Trixie's secret recipe for a unique white chocolate nut confection. The parties (Nestlé and Trixie, the sole shareholder and CEO of Trixie's Delites) agree to a $1 million purchase price. If the acquisition is structured as a direct merger, then the shareholders of *both* constituent corporations must approve the deal. As for the Target, the outcome of this shareholder vote is a foregone conclusion since Trixie is the only shareholder. As for Bidder, on the other hand, matters are much more cumbersome. The business decision to use Nestlé's resources (either the company's cash or a small number of the company's shares or a combination of both) to merge with this small company, Trixie Delites, Inc., must be put to a vote of Nestlé's shareholders, a time-consuming and expensive procedure. Over time, the law came to recognize that there are not sufficient benefits to justify the delay and expense associated with obtaining approval of Nestlé's public shareholders for this kind of small acquisition that does not present a fundamental change for the surviving corporation (Nestlé). However, the merger statute left no other alternative if this method was used to structure Nestlé's acquisition of Trixie's Delites.

It bears emphasizing that, in the context of a direct merger of Minnow (Target) into the Whale (Bidder), these transactions are greatly facilitated today by virtue of provisions such as Delaware §251(f), which eliminates the need for Bidder to obtain approval of its shareholders (assuming that the acquisition of Minnow is truly a *de minimis* transaction for Bidder and thus involves cash consideration or, alternatively, a sufficiently small number of shares of Bidder's stock so that Bidder avoids the need to obtain a vote of its shareholders by virtue of §251(f)). Of course, this transaction continues to constitute a fundamental change for Target and thus will require approval by Target's shareholders.

However, there will often be compelling business reasons for leaving Target in place rather than having it disappear by merging into the surviving corporation, Bidder, as called for by the direct merger. For example, Trixie's Delites, Inc., may have certain valuable rights, such as an established trademark, intellectual property license or a very attractive lease arrangement, that are nontransferable.* As a result, it may be advantageous to leave the corporation, Trixie's Delites, Inc., in place. In such a case, the direct merger would not be a viable acquisition structure since it would call for the Target (Trixie's Delites) to disappear, merging into the surviving corporation (Nestlé). To address this limitation in the merger procedure, and thereby allow the Bidder to acquire Target and operate it as a wholly owned subsidiary rather than disappear, the law authorized three-party mergers, also called *triangular mergers.*

In a triangular merger, the merger consideration will be provided by Bidder Co. Pursuant to the terms of their agreement, Target Co. will be merged with a wholly owned subsidiary of Bidder. In order to consummate this plan of merger, Bidder will incorporate a new, wholly owned subsidiary (NewCo) that will then merge with Target. The merger agreement will usually provide that Target shareholders will receive Bidder shares—*not* shares of NewCo—in exchange for their Target shares. *See* DGCL §251(b); MBCA §11.02(c). In the case of a *forward* triangular merger, NewCo will be the surviving corporation and Target Co. will disappear once the merger is consummated. In the case of a *reverse* triangular merger, NewCo will merge into Target, leaving Target Co. as the surviving company once the merger is consummated. "By preserving [Target] in the form of a subsidiary [of Bidder], the parties can [very often] preserve any valuable rights possessed by the acquired corporation without the necessity of transferring any patents, licenses, leases, or other rights of the acquired corporation and can in many cases avoid the necessity of securing the consent of a third party to such a transfer or the payment of sales or other transfer taxes." Marshall L. Small, *Corporate Combinations Under the New California General Corporation Law,* 23 UCLA L. Rev. 1190, 1193 n. 10 (1976).

As originally conceived, the triangular merger eliminated the need to obtain approval from Bidder's shareholders because the subsidiary, NewCo,— and *not* Bidder itself—was to be the acquiring corporation. As a constituent corporation, the merger statute would generally require the consent of NewCo's shareholders; however, this approval was a foregone conclusion since Bidder was the sole shareholder of NewCo.

So, for example, Nestlé (the Whale) could acquire the much smaller Trixie's Delites (the Minnow) using the triangular merger procedure, and in the process avoid the requirement of approval of the acquisition by Nestlé's shareholders. Since Nestlé (Bidder) is not a constituent corporation in a triangular merger, no vote of Nestlé's shareholders is required. Over time, transaction planners capitalized on the convenience of the triangular merger, extending it well beyond this rather simplistic Whale-Minnow type of business combination:

> To avoid the cost and delay of obtaining shareholder approval (and to avoid paying [any] dissenters), in recent years the use of triangular mergers has become popular, combining the acquired corporation [Target Co.] with a wholly-owned subsidiary of the acquiring corporation [Bidder Co.]. The use of a wholly-owned subsidiary [. . .] obviate[s] the need for one of the two shareholder votes—the subsidiary [can] merely obtain the written consent of its parent, and the shareholders of the parent would not get to vote—unless the

---

*We will explore these issues in more detail in Chapter 3, where we examine the impact of an acquisition transaction on creditors of Target Co.

number of shares issued by the parent was sufficient to require such vote under stock exchange listing requirements applicable to the parent.

Small, *supra,* at 1192-1193.

Triangular mergers have become increasingly popular over the last 30 years or so for essentially the reasons described in the quoted excerpt above. Triangular mergers are a variation on the direct merger, and therefore, are not a separate type or method of merger, unlike the short-form merger. In particular, triangular mergers are authorized under state corporate law by the simple expedient of amending the state's merger statute to expand on the type of consideration that may be used in a merger to include not only stock (or other securities) of the *surviving* corporation but to also authorize use of stock (or other securities) of *any* corporation. *See, e.g.,* MBCA § 11.02(c)(3) and DGCL § 251(b)(5). So, in a triangular merger, Bidder (for example, Nestlé) and Target (for example, Trixie) negotiate the terms of the merger agreement but the constituent corporations in the merger consist of NewCo (Nestlé's wholly owned subsidiary formed for purposes of completing this acquisition) and Target (Trixie). Moreover, since Bidder, the parent corporation, is not a party to the merger, no vote of Bidder's shareholders is required to complete the transaction, assuming that Bidder already has sufficient authorized but unissued shares to complete the transaction. Since the right of appraisal generally follows the right to vote under the provisions of most states' corporation statutes, Bidder shareholders customarily will have no right of appraisal either. "Thus, the triangular merger is a straightforward mechanism to avoid the acquiring [i.e., Bidder] corporation's shareholders having a direct vote, and, for that matter, an appraisal remedy, in an acquisition of another company." James D. Cox and Thomas Lee Hazen, Treatise on the Law of Corporations 613 (2d ed. 2003).

In the abstract, triangular mergers are a little difficult to grasp, although the end result may seem clear enough. The problem set that follows is designed to familiarize you with the mechanics of triangular mergers in general, and more specifically, will distinguish the results obtained in structuring the acquisition as either a *forward* or a *reverse* triangular merger.

PROBLEM SET NO. 5—FORWARD AND REVERSE TRIANGULAR MERGERS UNDER DELAWARE LAW AND THE MBCA

1. Forward Triangular Merger—Merger Consideration Consists of 30 Percent of Stock of Bidder Corporation (See Diagram 8—Appendix A).   Following extensive negotiations between representatives of closely held Bidder Co. and Target Co., Bidder forms New Company (NewCo), a wholly owned subsidiary, for the purpose of acquiring Target, another closely held corporation. Bidder funds NewCo, the acquisition subsidiary, with the merger consideration in exchange for all of the outstanding voting stock of NewCo. The parties plan to structure the acquisition as a forward triangular (or subsidiary) merger. The terms of the parties' merger agreement call for Target to merge into NewCo, with Target shareholders receiving shares of Bidder common stock comprising 30 percent of the voting power of Bidder's common shares that were outstanding immediately before closing on the proposed merger with Target. Assume further that Bidder has sufficient authorized but unissued common shares to complete the proposed transaction. The parties' merger agreement provides for a forward triangular merger. So when the dust settles and the transaction is consummated, the business of Target will be held in NewCo, to be operated as a wholly owned subsidiary of Bidder.

    a.   Which corporation is to survive? Which corporation is to disappear?

    b.   What action is required by the boards of Bidder, Target, and NewCo:

        (1)   Under Delaware law?

        (2)   Under the MBCA?

    c.   Do the shareholders of Bidder, NewCo, and/or Target have the right to vote:

        (1)   Under Delaware law?

        (2)   Under the MBCA?

    d.   Do the shareholders of Bidder, NewCo, and/or Target have the right to dissent:

        (1)   Under Delaware law?

        (2)   Under the MBCA?

    e.   What action would be required under either Delaware law or the MBCA if Bidder did not have sufficient authorized but unissued shares to complete the proposed acquisition of Target? *See* MBCA §11.07(a)(6); Delaware §251(c) and (e).

    f.   What is the effect of a *forward* triangular merger? How does this transaction differ from the *direct* merger illustrated in Diagram 1?

    2. Reverse Triangular Merger—Merger Consideration Consists of 23 Percent of Bidder Stock (See Diagram 10—Appendix A).   Pfizer, Inc. forms New Company (NewCo), a wholly owned subsidiary, for the purpose of acquiring Pharmacia Corp., a NYSE-listed corporation, in a triangular merger. The parties' merger agreement calls for the transaction to be structured as a reverse triangular (or subsidiary) merger, with the Pharmacia shareholders to receive (in exchange for all of their Pharmacia stock) shares of Pfizer's common stock comprising 23 percent of the voting power of Pfizer's common shares that were outstanding immediately before closing on the proposed transaction with Pharmacia. In addition, all of Pfizer's stock in NewCo will be converted (by operation of law) into stock of Pharmacia when the merger is consummated. So, in the case of a reverse triangular merger, when the dust settles and the transaction is consummated, the business of Pharmacia Corp. will be operated as a wholly owned subsidiary of Pfizer, Inc., a NYSE-listed corporation. Assume further that Pfizer has a sufficient number of authorized but unissued voting common shares to complete the proposed transaction. In considering the following questions, you will need to refer to Articles I and II of the Pfizer/Pharmacia Merger Agreement (which is included as Appendix B at the end of the casebook).

    a.   Who are the parties to the merger agreement?

    b.   What is the acquisition consideration?

c. Which company is to disappear and which is to survive?

d. What is the effect of a *reverse* triangular merger? How does this transaction differ from the *forward* triangular merger described above in Problem 1?

e. What action is required by the boards of Pfizer Inc., Pharmacia Corp., and NewCo:

(1) Under Delaware law?
(2) Under the MBCA?

f. Do the shareholders of Pfizer Inc., Pharmacia Corp., or NewCo have the right to vote:

(1) Under Delaware law?
(2) Under the rules of the NYSE?
(3) Under the MBCA?

g. Will the merger automatically become effective once the requisite shareholder approvals have been obtained? (*Hint:* Read §1.3 of the Pfizer/Pharmacia merger agreement and refer to Delaware §251(c) and MBCA §11.06.)

h. In considering Section 1.8 of the Pfizer/Pharmacia merger agreement in Appendix B, what happens to the shares of:

(1) Pharmacia Corp.?
(2) Merger Sub?
(3) Pfizer, Inc.?

i. Assume that an individual shareholder owns 151 shares of Pharmacia common stock, how many Pfizer shares will she receive when the merger is consummated?

j. Do the shareholders of Pfizer Inc. and/or Pharmacia Corp. have the right to dissent:

(1) Under Delaware law?
(2) Under the MBCA?

3. Reverse Triangular Merger—Merger Consideration Consists of 4.8 Percent of Bidder's Stock.   Assume that Bidder Co., a NYSE-listed company, intends to acquire closely held Hi-Tech Co. in a transaction structured as a *reverse* triangular merger. The terms of the parties' merger agreement call for the shareholders of Hi-Tech Co. to receive shares of Bidder's common stock comprising only 4.8 percent of the voting power of Bidder's common shares that were outstanding before the acquisition is completed. Hi-Tech Co. has four equal shareholders consisting of the founder and three venture capital firms. Assume further that Bidder has sufficient authorized but unissued shares to complete the proposed transaction and that Bidder has formed NewCo for the purposing of completing the acquisition of Hi-Tech Co.

a. Who should be made parties to the merger agreement?
b. Which corporation is to survive and which is to disappear?
c. What is the acquisition consideration?

d. What is the effect of this reverse triangular merger? In other words, when the dust settles and the transaction is consummated, what will happen to the shares of:

(1) Bidder Co.?
(2) High Tech Co.?
(3) NewCo?

e. What action is required by the boards of Bidder Co., Hi-Tech Co., and NewCo in order to consummate this acquisition as a *reverse* triangular merger:

(1) Under Delaware law?
(2) Under the MBCA?

f. Do the shareholders of Bidder Co., Hi-Tech Co., or NewCo have the right to vote:

(1) Under Delaware law?
(2) Under the rules of the NYSE?
(3) Under the MBCA?

g. Do the shareholders of Bidder Co. or Hi-Tech Co. have the right to dissent:

(1) Under Delaware law?
(2) Under the MBCA?

h. Assume that Founder does not want to sell her shares of Hi-Tech Co. What advice do you give Founder as to the options available to her under either the MBCA or Delaware law?

4. Reverse Triangular Merger—Merger Consideration Consists of Cash (See Diagram 11—Appendix A).   Assume that Pfizer, Inc., a NYSE-listed company, plans to acquire Pharmacia Co., another NYSE-listed company, in a transaction structured as a reverse triangular merger. The plan of merger calls for Pharmacia's shareholders to receive $60 billion in cash when the transaction closes. Pfizer has formed NewCo, a wholly owned subsidiary, for the purpose of acquiring Pharmacia in this *reverse* triangular merger. Further assume that Pfizer can fund the $60 billion purchase price through its own cash resources (and by borrowing any necessary funds).

a. What action is required by the boards of Pfizer, NewCo, and Pharmacia:

(1) Under Delaware law?
(2) Under the MBCA?

b. Do the shareholders of either Pfizer, Pharmacia, or NewCo have the right to vote:

(1) Under Delaware law?
(2) Under the rules of the NYSE?
(3) Under the MBCA?

c. Do the shareholders of either Pfizer or Pharmacia have the right to dissent:

(1)   Under Delaware law?
(2)   Under the MBCA?

5. Hewlett-Packard's Acquisition of Compaq.   On September 3, 2001, Hewlett-Packard Company (HP) announced that it had signed a deal to acquire Compaq Computer Corporation (Compaq) using HP's stock as the acquisition consideration. The parties' agreement described the acquisition as follows: (i) Under the terms of the merger agreement, a wholly owned subsidiary of HP will merge with and into Compaq and Compaq will survive the merger as a wholly owned subsidiary of HP. (ii) As of the signing of the merger agreement, the authorized capital stock of HP consisted of 9,600,000,000 common shares and there were 1,939,159,231 shares of HP common stock issued and outstanding. (iii) The exchange ratio negotiated by the parties provided that Compaq shareholders would receive 0.6325 share of HP common stock for each Compaq share outstanding. Compaq had 1.8 billion shares outstanding as of the signing of the merger agreement.

a.   What type of merger is this? Which company will survive? Which company will disappear?
b.   Do the shareholders of Compaq have the right to vote:

(1)   Under Delaware law?
(2)   Under the MBCA?
(3)   Under the rules of the NYSE?

c.   Do the shareholders of HP have the right to vote:

(1)   Under Delaware law?
(2)   Under the MBCA?
(3)   Under the rules of the NYSE?

d.   Assume that, as part of the parties' acquisition agreement, HP represented that "all shares of capital stock of HP which may be issued as contemplated or permitted by this agreement will be, when issued, duly authorized." Does HP have sufficient authorized and unissued shares to complete the transaction? If not, what must be done in order for HP to fulfill the commitment it made as part of the parties' agreement:

(1)   Under Delaware law? (*Hint*: You may want to refer to Delaware §242.)
(2)   Under the MBCA? (*Hint*: You may want to refer to MBCA §10.03.)

e.   Assume that HP's management reported the following results with respect to the vote of its shareholders on the transaction with Compaq: (i) there were 838,401,376 shares of HP common stock voted for the proposed transaction; (ii) there were 793,094,105 shares voted against the proposed transaction; and (iii) there were 13,950,651 HP common shares that abstained from voting. Did the proposed transaction receive shareholder approval under the terms of:

(1)   Delaware law?
(2)   The rules of the NYSE?
(3)   The MBCA?

2. A Recent MBCA Innovation: The Binding Share Exchange

The *binding share exchange,* an innovation of the MBCA that has been adopted in numerous states, is another method that can be used to accomplish essentially the same result as a *reverse triangular merger.* The binding share exchange is authorized under the terms of MBCA §11.03, which has no counterpart under Delaware law. Using this method of corporate combination, Bidder Co. obtains ownership of *all* of Target Co.'s shares in exchange for either cash or shares (or other securities) of Bidder. Like the merger, the plan (or agreement) of share exchange *must* be approved in accordance with the terms of MBCA §11.04, including the requisite shareholder vote. The mechanics and result of the share exchange procedure are reflected in the following diagram and are best understood by analyzing the problems that follow.

DIAGRAM — SHARE EXCHANGE

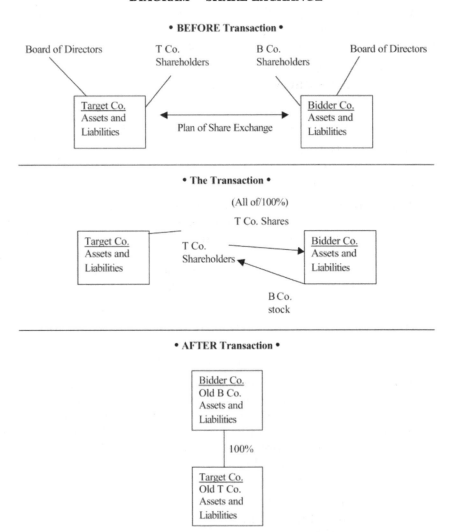

PROBLEM SET NO. 6—MBCA §11.03: THE BINDING
(OR COMPULSORY) SHARE EXCHANGE

1. Assume that Target (T) is going to be acquired by Bidder (B) in a compulsory share exchange authorized by MBCA §11.03. Both T and B are closely held, and each has only one class of voting common stock outstanding. Both companies are incorporated under the provisions of the MBCA. The plan of share exchange calls for T shareholders to receive shares of Bidder common stock comprising 30 percent of the voting power of Bidder's outstanding common stock immediately before the acquisition is completed. Assume further that B has a sufficient number of authorized but unissued shares to complete the proposed transaction.

   a. What action is required by the boards of B and T?
   b. Do the shareholders of B and/or T have the right to vote?
   c. Do the shareholders of B and/or T have the right to dissent?
   d. How does this analysis vary if the plan of share exchange consists of shares of Bidder common stock comprising only 15 percent of the voting power of Bidder's common stock that is outstanding immediately before the acquisition is complete?
   e. How does this method of acquisition differ from the direct merger illustrated in Diagram 1 in Appendix A? How does this method of acquisition differ from the stock exchange offer illustrated in Diagram 7 in Appendix A?

2. Assume that Pfizer Inc., a NYSE-listed company organized under the MBCA, has agreed to acquire Pharmacia Corp., another NYSE-listed company that is also incorporated under the MBCA, in a compulsory share exchange authorized by MBCA §11.03. The plan of share exchange provides that Pharmacia shareholders are to receive shares of Pfizer's common stock comprising 23 percent of the voting power of Pfizer's common stock that is outstanding immediately before the acquisition is completed. Assume further that Pfizer has sufficient authorized but unissued shares to complete the proposed transaction.

   a. What action is required by the boards of Pfizer Inc. and Pharmacia Corp.?
   b. Do the shareholders of Pfizer Inc. and/or Pharmacia Corp. have the right to vote?
   c. Do the shareholders of Pfizer Inc. and/or Pharmacia Corp. have the right to dissent?
   d. How does this method of acquisition differ from the reverse triangular merger illustrated in Diagram 10 in Appendix A? How does this method of acquisition differ from the stock exchange offer illustrated in Diagram 7 in Appendix A?

G. De Facto Merger Doctrine: Form vs. Substance Debate

As we have seen in analyzing the mechanics of triangular mergers, the share-holders of Bidder Co. are denied voting rights under the merger statutes of most states since Bidder is not a party to the transaction. Likewise, there is generally no right of appraisal available to those Bidder shareholders who object to the transaction. The transaction planner's decision to use a three-party merger structure may operate to deny Bidder shareholders protections granted by law in cases where the acquisition is structured as a direct merger.

For similar reasons, the transaction planner may decide to structure an acquisition as a sale of assets rather than a direct merger. If the transaction involves a sale of assets, then Bidder Co., as the buyer of all of Target Co.'s assets, does not have to obtain shareholder approval in order to validly consummate the purchase, nor will the right of appraisal be available to those Bidder shareholders who object to the proposed transaction. Generally speaking, the purchase of all of Target's assets does not involve a fundamental change for Bidder, and therefore no shareholder approval is required.

On occasion, however, shareholders may bring an action, claiming that a proposed acquisition has the same substantive result as a merger, even though the acquisition is structured in some other form (such as an asset sale). In these cases, the complaining shareholder will usually invoke the court's equity jurisdiction, asking the court to enjoin a proposed acquisition unless and until the statutory requirements for merger transactions are satisfied, including the requirement of shareholder approval and the satisfaction of any available appraisal rights. By invoking this equitable remedy, the complaining shareholder is asking the court to look through the form of the transaction and to recognize the substance of the transaction as a merger. These cases are known as *de facto mergers,* and this doctrine rests on a principle of equivalency, which simply says that transactions that have the same substantive effect ought to be entitled to the same legal safeguards. In other words, the courts should look through the form of the transaction to ensure that like transactions are treated alike. Of course, there is the threshold question of how the court should go about deciding whether a particular transaction is—in substance—a merger. The cases that follow illustrate the wide disagreement as to the viability of the de facto merger doctrine. Delaware courts, in particular, refuse to recognize the doctrine.

1. What Is the De Facto Merger Doctrine?

Applestein v. United Board & Carton Corporation
60 N.J. Super. 333, 159 A.2d 146 (Ch. Div. 1960)
Aff'd 33 N.J. 72, 161 A.2d 474 (1960) (per curiam)

. . . KILKENNY, J.S.C.
. . . [The] issue is whether the agreement of July 7, 1959 among United Board and Carton Corporation, hereinafter referred to as [United], Interstate

Container Corporation, [Interstate], and Saul L. Epstein, [Epstein], and the transaction set forth in the proxy solicitation statement, [proxy statement], dated September 22, 1959, amount to a merger, entitling dissenting stockholders of United to an appraisal of their stock, and is therefore invalid. . . .

United is [a] New Jersey [corporation primarily engaged] in the manufacture and sale of paper-board, folding boxes, corrugated containers and laminated board, . . . Its present authorized capital stock consists of 400,000 shares, of which 240,000 have already been issued and are held by a great number of stockholders, no one of whom holds in excess of 10% of the outstanding shares. There are 160,000 shares not yet issued. The United stock is publicly held, there being 1,086 shareholders of record as of September 22, 1959, and the stock is traded on the New York Stock Exchange. The book value of each share of stock, as indicated by the proxy statement, is approximately $31.97. The consolidated balance sheet of United and its wholly owned subsidiaries, as of May 31, 1958, shows total assets of $10,121,233, and total liabilities of $2,561,724, and a net total capital of $7,559,509. Its business is managed by the usual staff of officers and a board of directors consisting of seven directors.

Interstate [is a] New York [corporation that] owns several operating subsidiaries . . . engaged primarily in the manufacture and sale of corrugated shipping containers, . . . Interstate has issued and outstanding 1,250 shares, all of which are owned and controlled by a single stockholder, Epstein, . . . The consolidated balance sheet of Interstate and its subsidiaries, as of October 31, 1958, shows that its total assets are $7,956,424, and its total liabilities are $6,318,371, leaving a net total capital of $1,638,053. . . .

United entered into a written agreement with Interstate and Epstein on July 7, 1959. In its language, it is not designated or referred to as a merger agreement, *eo nomine*. In fact, the word "merger" nowhere appears in that agreement. On the contrary, the agreement recites that it is an "exchange of Interstate stock for United Stock." Epstein agrees to assign and deliver to United his 1,250 shares of the common stock of Interstate solely in exchange for 160,000 as yet unissued shares of voting common stock (par value $10) of United. Thus, by this so-called "exchange of stock" United would wholly own Interstate and its subsidiaries, and Epstein would thereupon own a 40% stock interest in United. Dollar-wise, on the basis of the book values of the two corporations hereinabove set forth, a combination of the assets and liabilities of United and Interstate would result in a net total capital of approximately $9,200,000, as against which there would be outstanding 400,000 shares, thereby reducing the present book value of each United share from about $31.97 to about $23, a shrinkage of about 28%. Epstein would contribute, book value-wise, the net total capital of Interstate in the amount of $1,638,053, for which he would receive a 40% interest in $9,200,000, the net total combined capital of United and Interstate, or about $3,680,000. The court is not basing its present decision upon the additional charge made by dissenting stockholders of United that the proposed agreement is basically unfair and inequitable. That is one of the reserved issues. The court recognizes that book values and real values are not necessarily the same thing, and, therefore, apparent inequities appearing from a comparison of the book values might be explained and justified.

The agreement of July 7, 1959 does not contemplate the continued future operation of Interstate, as a subsidiary corporation of United. Rather, it provides that United will take over all the outstanding stock of Interstate, that all of Interstate's "assets and liabilities will be recorded on the books of the Company (United)," and that Interstate will be dissolved. At the time of closing, Epstein has agreed to deliver the resignations of the officers and directors of Interstate and of its subsidiary corporations, so that, in effect, Interstate would have no officers, directors, or stockholders, other than United's. The agreement further stipulates that the by-laws of United shall be amended to increase the number of directors from 7 to 11. It provides for the filling of the additional director-ships, it pre-ordains who will be the officers and new directors of United in the combined enterprise, and even governs the salaries to be paid. Epstein would become the president and a director of United and, admittedly, would be in "effective control" of United. As stated in the proxy statement, "The transac-tion will be accounted for as a 'pooling of interests' of the two corporations."

The stipulation of the parties removed from the court's present consider-ation not only the issue of the basic equity or fairness of the agreement, but also the legal effect and validity of the pre-determination of directorships, officers, salaries, and other similar terms of the bargain between the parties. The fair-ness of a merger agreement generally presents a question of a factual nature, ordinarily reserved for final hearing. If the alleged injustice of the project were the sole objection, I would be hesitant to substitute *preliminarily* my judgment for that of a transcendent majority of the stockholders.

In notifying its stockholders of a meeting to be held on October 15, 1959, in its proxy statement United advised the stockholders that "the proposal to approve the issuance of the common stock of the company is being submitted to the vote of the stockholders solely because of the requirements of the New York Stock Exchange; and accordingly stockholders who vote against or who do not vote in favor of the proposal will not . . . be entitled to any [appraisal] rights . . . They were also advised that adoption of the proposal would require the affirmative vote of the holders of only a *majority* of the shares present at the meeting in person or by proxy, provided a majority of all shares outstanding and entitled to vote thereon was present at the meeting.

The attorneys for the respective parties herein have conceded in the record that the proposed corporate action would be invalid, if this court determines that it would constitute a merger of United and Interstate, entitling the dis-senting stockholders of United to an appraisal of their stock. The notice of the stockholders' meeting and the proxy statement did not indicate that the pur-pose of the meeting was to effect a *merger,* and failed to give notice to the share-holders of their right to dissent to the plan of merger, if it were one, and claim their appraisal rights under the statute, as inferentially required by R.S. 14:12-3, N.J.S.A. Obviously, the notice of the meeting and proxy statement stressed the contrary, by labeling the proposed corporate action "an exchange of Interstate stock for United stock" rather than a merger, by its emphasis upon the need for a *majority vote* only, instead of the required two-thirds vote for a merger under the statute, and by the express declaration that dissenting stockholders would not be entitled to any rights of appraisal of their stock. . . .

Despite the contrary representations by United to its stockholders in its proxy statement, United's present position is that the proposed corporate action in acquiring and absorbing Interstate is a merger. This is evidenced by its answer to the cross-claim of Interstate and Epstein against it for specific performance of the agreement of July 7, 1959. At the hearing of the motions United's attorney stated in the record that United now contended, in addition to its other asserted defenses, that the fulfillment of the agreement would constitute a merger. In fairness to United's attorney herein, it should be noted that this coincided with an earlier letter opinion furnished privately by him to United's officers substantially to the same effect, which letter he made part of the record, in his affidavit, when a question of good faith was raised.

Needless to say, if United, a New Jersey corporation, had followed that early advice given by its present New Jersey counsel herein and had followed the statutory procedure for corporate mergers, this litigation would have been avoided. Instead, it chose the opposite opinion of New York counsel that the plan would not be a merger, and so indicated to its stockholders in the proxy statement. It now finds itself ready and willing to agree with the plaintiff stockholders that the plan would be a merger of United and Interstate, and relies thereon, *inter alia*, in resisting the cross-claim for specific performance. . . .

The legal contention of Epstein and Interstate, and the four intervening United stockholders—Conway, Terry, McKenney, and Corsuti—is that the transaction constitutes a valid purchase by United of Epstein's shares in Interstate, and thereby the property of Interstate, pursuant to R.S. 14.3-9, N.J.S.A., to be followed by a merger of United, as the parent corporation, with its wholly-owned corporation, Interstate, pursuant to N.J.S.A. 14:12-10. Thus, it is claimed that United's dissenting stockholders have no appraisal rights under these two sections of the statutes, and especially since N.J.S.A. 14:12-10 expressly provides that N.J.S.A. 14:12-6 and R.S. 14:12-7, N.J.S.A., which grant appraisal rights in the usual merger, under R.S. 14:12-1, N.J.S.A., shall not apply to a merger under N.J.S.A. 14:12-10.

When a corporation *sells or exchanges* all, or substantially all of its property and assets, including its good will, as permitted by R.S. 14:3-5, N.J.S.A., the stockholders of the *selling* corporation must approve by a two-thirds vote, and objecting stockholders of the *selling* corporation are given appraisal rights, as provided in N.J.S.A. 14:12-6 in the case of a merger.

But when a corporation *buys* real or personal property, or the stock of another corporation, as permitted under R.S. 14:3-9, N.J.S.A., stockholder approval is not required, and objecting shareholders of the *purchasing* corporation are given no appraisal rights in such a case. Further, the *buying* corporation may pay for such property or stock acquired by it in cash or in the capital stock of the purchasing corporation.

It is true that our present corporation law, R.S. 14:3-5, N.J.S.A., sanctions a corporate *sale* of all or substantially all of the property and assets of the selling corporation, with stockholder approval and appraisal rights in favor of objecting shareholders of the selling corporation. Likewise, our statute, R.S. 14:3-9, N.J.S.A., allows a corporate *purchase* of the property and stock of another corporation to be paid for in cash or the stock of the purchasing corporation. There is no dispute as to the existence of these present statutory devices for the sale and acquisition of corporate property and shares of stock. Hence, if the purchase by United of Interstate and its shares represented a *bona fide* utilization of the corporate power conferred by R.S. 14:3-9, N.J.S.A., and if the intended dissolution of Interstate represented a *bona fide* merger of a parent corporation with a wholly-owned corporation under N.J.S.A. 14:12-10 without more,

United's dissenting shareholders would then have no right to an appraisal of their shares.

But when an authorized device, such as that provided for in a sale of [sic] purchase of assets, or a dissolution, is used to bring about a virtual consolidation or merger, minority stockholders may object on the ground that a direct method has been authorized for such a purpose. If consolidation or merger is permitted through a pretended sale of assets or dissolution, minority stockholders may be frozen out of their legal rights of appraisal. If the court is obliged to consider only the device employed, or the mere form of the transaction, a corporate merger in fact can be achieved without any compliance with the statutory requirements for a valid merger, and without any regard for the statutory rights of dissenting shareholders. It would be strange if the powers conferred by our Legislature upon corporations under R.S. 14:3-9, N.J.S.A. for a purchase of the property and shares of another corporation and, under N.J.S.A. 14:12-10, for the merger of a parent corporation with a wholly-owned corporation can effect a corporate merger *de facto*, with all the characteristics and consequences of a merger, without any of the legislative safeguards and rights afforded to a dissenting shareholder in a *de jure* merger under R.S. 14:12-1 et seq., N.J.S.A. If that were so, we obtain the anomalous result of one part of the corporation law rendering nugatory another part of the same law in accomplishing the same result.

That the proposed corporate action is more than an "exchange of Interstate stock for United stock," as it is labeled in the agreement of July 7, 1959, and more than a purchase by United of Epstein's Interstate stock and the corporate properties of Interstate, pursuant to R.S. 14:3-9, N.J.S.A., is demonstrated by the following facts.

1. The exchange of stock is made expressly contingent upon stockholder approval of Proposal No. 2 increasing the number of directors of United from 7 to 11.
2. United admits that by the exchange of stock Epstein will acquire 40% of United's outstanding stock "and effective control."
3. Epstein's "effective control" of United is made obvious, by the fact that two directors of United's present board of seven "will resign as directors." This would leave United with only five of its present directors on the new enlarged board of 11 directors, which Proposal No. 2 insures as a contingent part of the deal. Thus, Epstein and the five new directors, presumably his associates and friends from Interstate, are assured a majority vote of six and control of the new 11-man board. It is clear that he who controls a majority of the board of directors generally controls the management and destiny of the corporation . . .
5. While the proposed issuance by United to Epstein of 160,000 shares of United's total authorized 400,000 shares seems to give Epstein only a 40% stock interest in United, which by itself is substantial enough to control United as against the 1,086 other stockholders, but still less than the combined 60% of those 1,086 present United shareholders, 8 of those 1,086 present United shareholders, who would become directors on the enlarged board, already own 49,200 shares of United. Therefore, Epstein's new 160,000 shares plus those 49,200 shares would add up to 209,200 shares of the total 400,000, or better than 50%. . . . Combined with his real control of the board of

directors, the conclusion is inescapable that control of the affairs of United would pass out of the present board of directors and out of the present majority of United's stockholders to Epstein and those associated with him in Interstate.

6. The proxy statement expressly recites: "The transaction will be accounted for as a *'pooling of interests'* of the two corporations." Such a characterization is descriptive of a merger or consolidation of two corporations, rather than a mere exchange of stock or purchase of corporate assets.

7. It is intended that Interstate will be dissolved. Dissolution is always an element of merger or consolidation and it is not a necessary concomitant of a mere exchange of stock or purchase of corporate assets.

8. United expressly represents that Interstate's "*assets and liabilities will be recorded on the books of the Company* [United] as set forth in the pro forma balance sheet." This is indicative of the fact that United is *assuming* Interstate's liabilities, a necessary legal consequence of a merger or consolidation, as contrasted with the normal non-assumption of the debts of the selling corporation, in the absence of special agreement, upon a mere "sale-of-assets" transaction. While one might argue that the language, "its assets and liabilities will be recorded on the books of the Company," is equivocal and not a clearly expressed intention on United's part to *assume* Interstate's liabilities, the intent to assume liabilities is made crystal clear, at least as to Interstate's almost million dollar debt to Mr. Jno. F. McKenney, an intervening defendant stockholder of United, and a former president of Interstate, who favors United's purported acquisition of Interstate.

9. Also, as a further evidence of Interstate's control and intervention in United's management,

> "It is contemplated that the present executive and operating personnel of Interstate will be retained in the employ of the Company [United]."

Thus, every factor present in a corporate merger is found in this corporate plan, except, perhaps, a formal designation of the transaction as a "merger." There is proposed: (1) a transfer of all the shares and all the assets of Interstate to United; (2) an assumption by United of Interstate's liabilities; (3) a "pooling of interests" of the two corporations; (4) the absorption of Interstate by United, and the dissolution of Interstate; (5) a joinder of officers and directors from both corporations on an enlarged board of directors; (6) the present executive and operating personnel of Interstate will be retained in the employ of United; and (7) the shareholders of the absorbed corporation, Interstate, as represented by the sole stockholder, Epstein, will surrender his 1,250 shares in Interstate for 160,000 newly issued shares in United, the amalgamated enterprise.

If, in truth and in substance the proposed plan in this case is a "merger," why should the interested parties not frankly and honestly recognize it as such and pursue the statutory procedure under R.S. 14:12-1 et seq., N.J.S.A. for validating the proposal? It is a fundamental maxim of equity that "Equity looks to the substance rather than the form." . . . The courts of equity in New Jersey, and elsewhere, have never hesitated to look behind the form of a particular corporate transaction and find that it constituted a corporate merger, if in fact and in substance it was a merger, regardless of its deceptive outward appearance. . . .

The courts of this State and of other jurisdictions have never hesitated in the past in finding that a particular corporate combination was in fact and in legal effect a merger or a consolidation, even though the transaction might have been otherwise labeled by the parties. This is not a new legal philosophy, but is grounded upon the common sense observation that judges, as well as laymen, have the right, and often the duty, to call a spade a spade, and to follow the long established equitable maxim of looking to the substance rather than the form, whenever justice requires. . . .

Furthermore, in this case, if it were necessary to make the determination, it seems clear to this court that while United appears to be acquiring Interstate, the converse is more probably true in practical effect. We cannot blind ourselves to the realities of the situation in this case, as shown by the facts. Even United in its proxy statement concedes that Epstein and Interstate are taking over United, by their reference to the fact that Epstein and Interstate will be in "effective control" of United. While technically Interstate, as a corporate entity, is being dissolved, and the name Interstate will disappear from this corporate combination, the control and management passes out of United and its 1,086 present shareholders to Epstein and his associates in Interstate. In substance, therefore, United is being sold to Epstein and Interstate, and the present board of directors and management of United are abdicating to Epstein and his corporate *alter ego*, Interstate. There is no good reason why the proposal should not have been submitted to the stockholders of United for their approval as a merger. The dissenting stockholders then would have the statutory right to object to the plan and obtain an appraisal of their respective shares. The majority, no matter however overwhelming it may turn out to be, may not trample upon the property and appraisal rights of the minority shareholders of United, no matter how few they may be in number.

CONCLUSION

This court holds that the corporate combination of United and Interstate, contemplated by their executory contract of July 7, 1959, and explained in United's proxy solicitation statement of September 22, 1959, would be a practical or *de facto* merger, in substance and in legal effect, within the protective purview of N.J.S.A. 14:12-7. Accordingly, the shareholders of United are and were entitled to be notified and advised of their statutory rights of dissent and appraisal. The failure of the corporate officers of United to take these steps and to obtain stockholder approval of the agreement by the statutory two-thirds vote under R.S. 14:12-3, N.J.S.A. at a properly convened meeting of the stockholders would render the proposed corporate action invalid.

Therefore, there will be partial summary judgment on the single, limited issue submitted in accordance with this holding.

NOTES

1. Successor Liability and the De Facto Merger Doctrine.   The de facto merger doctrine also arises in another, quite different context. As we'll see in the materials on successor liability in Chapter 3, creditors of Target Co. will often claim that Target's sale of substantially all of its assets is, in substance, a merger. By claiming that the transaction between Bidder and Target is in substance a merger, the creditor of Target is seeking to invoke the rule of successor liability that is part of the law of mergers. If the creditor is successful in showing that the transaction constitutes a de facto merger, then the Target creditor generally will be able to collect from Bidder as the successor in interest to Target. As we will see in Chapter 3, the public policy considerations involved in these cases are very different than the considerations that dominated the court's reasoning in *Applestein,* and accordingly, the courts will often be persuaded to take a different view of the de facto merger doctrine in this context.

2. Attorney Professional Responsibility Rules Under Sarbanes-Oxley Act. In July 2002, Congress passed the Sarbanes-Oxley Act (more commonly referred to as SOX), enacting a major package of legislative reforms that addressed, among other things, the structure and function of audit committees of 1934 Act reporting companies, the regulation of the accounting profession, and the accountability of CEOS and CFOs. We will examine various aspects of SOX in the remaining chapters. In connection with the facts of the *Applestein* case, however, it is worth mentioning that, as part of SOX, Congress directed the SEC to adopt regulations intended to strengthen the professional obligations of those attorneys who represent public companies, such as Enron and Tyco. The legislative history of SOX makes clear that Congress intended to impose on lawyers some measure of responsibility to take steps in order to prevent financial scandals (such as those that engulfed Enron and Tyco) from occurring in the future.

Pursuant to this legislative mandate, the SEC adopted the attorney professional responsibility rules in January 2003, *see* SEC Release No. 33-8185, Implementation of Standards of Professional Conduct for Attorneys (Jan. 29, 2003). These rules became effective in August 2003; *see* 17 C.F.R. Part 205. Briefly summarized, the key principle to be implemented by the detailed, and somewhat complex, provisions of the SEC's new professional responsibility rules is widely referred to as the "up-the-ladder" rule. Under the SEC's new rules, if a lawyer for a publicly traded company becomes aware of "evidence of a material violation" of the federal securities laws (or a material violation of state law, including evidence of a material breach of fiduciary duty), the lawyer *must* disclose the matter to the company's chief legal officer (CLO) or to the CLO and the company's CEO.[*] The CLO then *must* conduct an investigation into the matter forming the basis for the "evidence of a material violation" of the federal securities laws. If the attorney who originally reported the violation fails to obtain an appropriate response, then he or she *must* go up the chain—taking the matter all the way "up the ladder" to the board of directors, if necessary. The more controversial aspect of the SEC rules as originally proposed—known as the "noisy withdrawal rule"—was not adopted as part of the SEC's newly enacted professional responsibility rules; instead, this rule was reproposed by

---

*As another alternative, the lawyer may refer the matter to a Qualified Legal Compliance Committee (QLCC). If the lawyer opts to refer the matter to a QLCC, the obligations under the SEC's new rules are very different.

the SEC and put out for further comment. *See* SEC Release No. 33-8186 (Proposed Rule, Feb. 6, 2003). As of this writing (Fall 2012), no final action has been taken on the proposed "noisy withdrawal rule."

As adopted, the SEC's new rule clearly is designed to implement the congressional mandate of SOX, which had its impetus in the widely held sentiment that corporate advisors, including company counsel, who become aware of misconduct within the corporation should be held accountable. Only time will tell whether these congressional reform measures will evoke the desired result of rehabilitating the corporate governance practices of public companies and restoring investor confidence in our markets. However, it should come as no surprise that Congress should react to the spate of corporate financial scandals (such as Enron and Tyco) by legislating mandates that hold company managers and their legal advisors responsible for their conduct.

3. California Law.   California, in effect, has legislated into place the de facto merger doctrine. The mechanics of the California statute are analyzed in more detail later in this chapter. Suffice it to say, at this point, that California accepts the fundamental premise of the de facto merger doctrine, which says that like transactions should be treated alike.

QUESTIONS

1.   What is the public policy premise for the de facto merger doctrine? Where did the court get the authority to decide the case the way it did?

2.   What facts must be present in order to invoke the de facto merger doctrine?

3.   What is the professional responsibility of the lawyers advising the parties as to the structure of the acquisition in *Applestein*? What would be the obligation of the transactional lawyers working on this deal under the professional responsibility rules that were adopted by the SEC pursuant to the congressional mandate of the Sarbanes-Oxley Act of 2002?

4.   Even if the court had refused to recognize the de facto merger doctrine in the *Applestein* case, the court hints that plaintiff's lawsuit might still proceed on the basis of other causes of action challenging the validity of the transaction at issue in that case. What other claims does the *Applestein* court hint at, but which it indicates are not presented for decision at this time?

5.   As a matter of public policy, does the de facto merger doctrine make sense?

6.   As a matter of modern corporate governance, who should decide whether United should issue 40 percent of its stock to acquire the business of Interstate Corp.?

2.   De Facto Merger Doctrine Under Delaware Law

The Delaware courts have flatly rejected the de facto merger doctrine. The basis for this rejection is grounded in the *doctrine of independent legal significance*, the origins of which date back to *Federal United Corp. v. Havender*, 11 A.2d 331 (Del. 1940), a Depression-era case decided by the Delaware Supreme Court. As explained by leading Delaware corporate law practitioners:

> The doctrine of independent legal significance ("ILS") is one of the "bedrock" doctrines of Delaware corporate law. The Delaware Supreme Court has defined ILS as providing that "action taken under one section of that law is legally independent, and its validity is not dependent upon, nor to be tested by the requirements of other unrelated sections under which the same final result might be attained by different means."[2] That is, so long as a transaction is effected in compliance with the requirements of one section of the Delaware General Corporation Law ("DGCL"), Delaware courts will not invalidate it for failing to comply with the requirements of a different section of the DGCL—even if the substance of the transaction is such that it could have been structured under the other section. . . .
>
> [The doctrine of independent legal significance] provides a benefit to Delaware corporations and their counsel by allowing certainty. If corporate lawyers structure a transaction in a certain way, in a way compliant with one section of the DGCL, they can have comfort that the courts will not invalidate the transaction for its failure to comply with a different section.[5] As the Court of Chancery noted in *Speiser v. Baker*:
>
>> As a general matter, those who must shape their conduct to conform to the dictates of statutory law should be able to satisfy such requirements by satisfying the literal demands of the law rather than being required to guess about the nature and extent of some broader or different restriction at the risk of an *ex post facto* determination of error. The utility of a literal approach to statutory construction is particularly apparent in the interpretation of the requirements of our corporation law—where both the statute itself and most transactions governed by it are carefully planned and result from a thoughtful and highly rational process.
>>
>> Thus, Delaware courts, when called upon to construe the technical and carefully drafted provisions of our statutory corporation law, do so with a sensitivity to the importance of the predictability of that law. That sensitivity causes our law, in that setting, to reflect an enhanced respect for the literal statutory language.[6]

---

2. *Orzeck v. Englehart*, 195 A.2d 375, 378 (Del. 1963).

5. *See* 1 R. FRANKLIN BALOTTI & JESSE A. FINKELSTEIN, THE DELAWARE LAW OF CORPORATIONS AND BUSINESS ORGANIZATIONS §9.4, at 9-9 (3d ed. 2007) ("The doctrine [of independent legal significance] has become a keystone of Delaware corporate law and is continually relied upon by practitioners to assure that transactions can be structured under one section of the General Corporation Law without having to comply with other sections which could lead to the same result.").

6. *Speiser v. Baker*, 525 A.2d 1001, 1008 (Del. Ch.), *appeal refused*, 525 A.2d 582 (Del. 1987) (unpublished table decision); *see also Uni-Marts, Inc. v. Stein*, C.A. Nos. 14713 & 14893, 1996 WL 466961, at *9 (Del. Ch. Aug. 12, 1996) ("Formality in the analysis of intellectual problems has been largely out of fashion for much of this century, and Delaware corporation law has sometimes been criticized for its reliance on formality. But the entire field of corporation law has largely to do with formality. Corporations come into existence and are accorded their characteristics, including most importantly limited liability, because of formal acts. Formality has significant utility for business planners and investors. While the essential fiduciary analysis component of corporation law is not formal but substantive, the utility offered by formality in the analysis of our statutes has been a central feature of Delaware corporation law.").

Thus, [the doctrine of independent legal significance] allows Delaware corporations and their counsel to plan transactions secure in the advance knowledge of the legal requirements for, and legal consequences of, those transactions.

C. Stephen Bigler & Blake Rohrbacher, *Form or Substance? The Past Present and Future of the Doctrine of Independent Legal Significance*, 63 Bus. Law. 1, at 1-2 (Nov. 2007).

Hariton v. Arco Electronics, Inc.
188 A.2d 123 (Del. 1963)

. . . SOUTHERLAND, Chief Justice.

This case involves a sale of assets under §271 of the corporation law, 8 Del. C. It presents for decision the question presented, but not decided, in Heilbrunn v. Sun Chemical Corporation, Del., 150 A.2d 755. It may be stated as follows:

A sale of assets is effected under §271 in consideration of shares of stock of the purchasing corporation. The agreement of sale embodies also a plan to dissolve the selling corporation and distribute the shares so received to the stockholders of the seller, so as to accomplish the same result as would be accomplished by a merger of the seller into the purchaser. Is the sale legal?

The facts are these:

The defendant Arco [Electronics, Inc. (Arco)] and Loral Electronics Corporation [(Loral)], a New York corporation, are both engaged, in somewhat different forms, in the electronic equipment business. In the summer of 1961 they negotiated for an amalgamation of the companies. As of October 27, 1961, they entered into a "Reorganization Agreement and Plan." The provisions of this Plan pertinent here are in substance as follows:

1. Arco agrees to sell all its assets to Loral in consideration (inter alia) of the issuance to it of 283,000 shares of Loral.
2. Arco agrees to call a stockholders meeting for the purpose of approving the Plan and the voluntary dissolution.
3. Arco agrees to distribute to its stockholders all the Loral shares received by it as a part of the complete liquidation of Arco.

At the Arco meeting all the stockholders voting (about 80%) approved the Plan. It was thereafter consummated.

Plaintiff, a stockholder who did not vote at the meeting, sued to enjoin the consummation of the Plan on the grounds (1) that it was illegal, and (2) that it was unfair. The second ground was abandoned. Affidavits and documentary evidence were filed, and defendant moved for summary judgment and dismissal of the complaint. The Vice Chancellor granted the motion and plaintiff appeals.

The question before us we have stated above. Plaintiff's argument that the sale is illegal runs as follows:

The several steps taken here accomplish the same result as a merger of Arco into Loral. In a "true" sale of assets, the stockholder of the seller retains the right to elect whether the selling company shall continue as a holding company. Moreover, the stockholder of the selling company is forced to accept an investment in a new enterprise without the right of appraisal granted under the merger statute. §271 cannot therefore be legally combined with a dissolution proceeding under §275 and a consequent distribution of the purchaser's stock. Such a proceeding is a misuse of the power granted under §271, and a *de facto* merger results.

The foregoing is a brief summary of plaintiff's contention.

Plaintiff's contention that this sale has achieved the same result as a merger is plainly correct. The same contention was made to us in Heilbrunn v. Sun Chemical Corporation, Del., 150 A.2d 755. Accepting it as correct, we noted that this result is made possible by the overlapping scope of the merger statute and section 271, mentioned in Sterling v. Mayflower Hotel Corporation, 33 Del. Ch. 293, 93 A.2d 107, 38 A.L.R.2d 425. We also adverted to the increased use, in connection with corporate reorganization plans, of §271 instead of the merger statute. Further, we observed that no Delaware case has held such procedure to be improper, and that two cases appear to assume its legality. Finch v. Warrior Cement Corporation, 16 Del. Ch. 44, 141 A. 54, and Argenbright v. Phoenix Finance Co., 21 Del. Ch. 288, 187 A. 124. But we were not required in the Heilbrunn case to decide the point.

We now hold that the reorganization here accomplished through §271 and a mandatory plan of dissolution and distribution is legal. This is so because the sale-of-assets statute and the merger statute are independent of each other. They are, so to speak, of equal dignity, and the framers of a reorganization plan may resort to either type of corporate mechanics to achieve the desired end. This is not an anomalous result in our corporation law. As the Vice Chancellor pointed out, the elimination of accrued dividends, though forbidden under a charter amendment (Keller v. Wilson & Co., 21 Del. Ch. 391, 190 A. 115) may be accomplished by a merger. Federal United Corporation v. Havender, 24 Del. Ch. 318, 11 A.2d 331.

In Langfelder v. Universal Laboratories, D.C., 68 F.Supp. 209, Judge Leahy commented upon "the general theory of the Delaware Corporation Law that action taken pursuant to the authority of the various sections of that law constitute acts of independent legal significance and their validity is not dependent on other sections of the Act." 68 F.Supp. 211, footnote.

In support of his contentions of a *de facto* merger plaintiff cites Finch v. Warrior Cement Corporation, 16 Del. Ch. 44, 141 A. 54, and Drug Inc. v. Hunt, 5 W.W.Harr. 339, 35 Del. 339, 168 A. 87. They are patently inapplicable. Each involved a disregard of the statutory provisions governing sales of assets. Here it is admitted that the provisions of the statute were fully complied with.

Plaintiff concedes, as we read his brief, that if the several steps taken in this case had been taken separately they would have been legal. That is, he concedes that a sale of assets, followed by a separate proceeding to dissolve and distribute, would be legal, even though the same result would follow. This concession exposes the weakness of his contention. To attempt to make any such distinction between sales under §271 would be to create uncertainty in the law and invite litigation.

We are in accord with the Vice Chancellor's ruling, and the judgment below is affirmed.

QUESTIONS

1. How is the proposed business combination between Arco Electronics, Inc. and Loral Electronics Corp. to be structured? What diagram in Appendix A does this proposed transaction between Arco and Loral look like? What is the acquisition consideration?

2. What corporate formalities must be satisfied in order for this acquisition to be validly consummated under Delaware law?

3. How did the Delaware court dispose of plaintiff's claim?

4. How would the transaction at issue in *Hariton* be treated under the terms of the modern MBCA?

NOTES

1. Before deciding *Hariton*, the Delaware Supreme Court had addressed the applicability of the de facto merger doctrine in the context of asset sales in the well-known case *Heilbrunn v. Sun Chemical Corp.*, 150 A.2d 755 (Del. 1959). The plaintiffs in that case were shareholders of Sun Chemical Corp. and were upset with the terms of the asset purchase agreement that Sun had entered into with Ansbacher-Siegle Corp. This agreement provided, in effect, that Sun Chemical would acquire Ansbacher's assets and assume all of its liabilities in exchange for 225,000 shares of Sun Chemical common stock. Although the court recognized the "overlapping scope of the merger statute and the statute authorizing the sale of all the corporate assets," *id.* at 757, it rejected the de facto merger doctrine and did not grant the disgruntled plaintiffs appraisal rights. Accordingly, the only source of relief available to the plaintiffs was under fiduciary duty law. How do the facts of *Heilbrunn* differ from those presented in the principal case?

2. Unlike Delaware law, California has accepted the principle of equivalency that led the common law courts to develop the de facto merger doctrine in the first place. In fact, California has codified the substance of the de facto merger doctrine. In other words, California's statute is predicated on the basic premise that the legal safeguards granted by statute to shareholders of a constituent corporation in the context of a (direct) merger should be extended to any transaction that has the same effect as a merger. For reasons that are described in detail later in this chapter, these legal safeguards cannot be avoided by structuring the transaction either as a sale of assets or as a triangular merger. The operation of California's statute is described at length later in this chapter, along with a more detailed examination of the public policy premise that underlies California's approach.

3.   The Modern Importance of Clear Default Rules

‖ **Pasternak v. Glazer**
‖ Civil Action No. 15026, 1996 WL 549960 (Del. Ch. Sept. 24, 1996)

. . . JACOBS, Vice Chancellor

On May 31, 1996, the plaintiffs commenced this action challenging a proposed merger (the "Merger") between Zapata Corporation ("Zapata") and Houlihan's Restaurant Group, Inc. ("Houlihan's"). On July 11, 1996, the plaintiffs amended their complaint to allege that the proposed merger is invalid because the June 4, 1996 Agreement and Plan of Merger (the "Merger Agreement") requires approval by only a simple majority of Zapata's shareholders, whereas Article SEVENTH of Zapata's Restated Certificate of Incorporation (the "Supermajority Provision") requires approval by 80% of Zapata's shareholders.

The plaintiffs moved to enjoin the proposed Merger, and a final hearing on their injunction application was held on September 6, 1996. For the reasons next discussed, the application to enjoin the proposed Merger will be granted.

I.   FACTS

A.   THE MERGER AGREEMENT

The defendant, Zapata, is a Delaware corporation. Defendant Malcolm Glazer ("Glazer") is the Chairman of Zapata's board of directors, and owns or beneficially controls approximately 35% of Zapata's stock. Glazer also owns or controls 73.3% of the outstanding shares of Houlihan's.

On June 4, 1996, Zapata, Houlihan's and Zapata Acquisition Corp., a wholly owned subsidiary of Zapata specially created to effect the Merger ("Zapata Sub"), entered into the Merger Agreement. Under that Agreement, Houlihan's will merge with and into Zapata Sub, and Houlihan's stockholders will receive shares of Zapata in exchange for their Houlihan's stock.

The Merger Agreement provides that only the approval of a simple majority of Zapata's outstanding shares is required to approve the Merger:

> Section 4.14. Vote Required. The affirmative vote of the holders of a majority of the outstanding shares of [Zapata] Common Stock and Preference Stock, voting together as a class, on the issuance of the shares of [Zapata] Common Stock in the Merger, as required by the NYSE, is the only vote of the holders of any class or series of [Zapata's] capital stock necessary to approve the Merger and the transactions contemplated thereby.

Pl. Cert. Ex. B, at A-23.

The shareholders meeting to vote on the proposed merger was originally scheduled for August 22, 1996, but it has been postponed pending the outcome of this litigation.

B.   ARTICLE SEVENTH OF ZAPATA'S RESTATED CERTIFICATE

The charter provision critical to this motion is Article SEVENTH, Subsection (A)(i) of Zapata's Restated Certificate of Incorporation. Article SEVENTH, which was adopted in 1971, states in relevant part as follows:

> . . . the affirmative vote or consent of the holders of 80% of all stock of this corporation entitled to vote in elections of directors, considered for the purposes of this Articles SEVENTH as one class, shall be required:
>
> > (i) *for a merger or consolidation with or into any other corporation,* or
> > (ii) for any sale or lease of all or any substantial part of the assets of this corporation to any other corporation, person or other entity, or
> > (iii) any sale or lease to this corporation or any subsidiary thereof of any assets . . . in exchange for voting securities . . . of this corporation or any subsidiary by any corporation, person or entity. . . .

Pl. Cert. Ex. C, at 31-32 (*emphasis added*). . . .

II.   THE PARTIES' CONTENTIONS

The plaintiffs claim that Article SEVENTH unambiguously requires an 80% shareholder approval of the proposed Merger. Specifically, plaintiffs contend that Subsection (A)(i), which governs "a merger or consolidation with or into any other corporation," applies not only to a merger with or into Zapata itself, but also to a merger with or into a wholly owned Zapata subsidiary. That is because, plaintiffs argue, Subsection (A)(i) is broadly worded and contains no language that explicitly limits its application to mergers involving only Zapata itself.[2]

Defendants disagree. They contend that Article SEVENTH is unambiguously inapplicable to mergers with or into a Zapata subsidiary, because Subsection (A)(i) has no language that explicitly encompasses subsidiary merger transactions. Therefore, defendants conclude, Subsection (A)(i), by its own terms and when viewed in the larger context of Article SEVENTH, applies only to a merger where Zapata itself is a constituent corporation.

---

2. In addition to their contract interpretation argument, Plaintiffs claim that the defendants' decision to structure the transaction as a three-party merger (i.e., into a Zapata-owned subsidiary) was specifically intended to circumvent the supermajority voting provision. That, according to plaintiffs, constitutes an inequitable manipulation of the corporate machinery which creates an independent basis to enjoin the Merger. Defendants respond that the current merger structure was contemplated before the supermajority vote issue was even considered. Therefore, defendants say, there is no evidence that the transaction was structured to avoid the Supermajority Provision, or that any inequitable manipulation occurred. Because the Court finds that supermajority approval of the proposed Merger is required by the plain meaning of the Article SEVENTH, Subsection (A)(i), it does not reach the inequitable manipulation claim.

III.   ANALYSIS

A.   APPLICABLE PRINCIPLES OF INTERPRETATION

Because a certificate of incorporation is a contract between the corporation and its shareholders, it is interpreted according to the rules of contract construction. . . . Accordingly, this Court must give effect to the intent of the contracting parties as evidenced by "the language of the certificate and the circumstances surrounding its creation and adoption." . . .

Except in the case where a charter provision is found ambiguous, this Court must give effect to its clear language. "'A contract is not rendered ambiguous simply because the parties do not agree upon its proper construction. Rather, . . . [it] is ambiguous only when the provisions in controversy are reasonably or fairly susceptible of different interpretations or may have two or more different meanings.'" In determining whether a charter provision is ambiguous, the intent of the stockholders in enacting the provision is instructive. . . .

Having set forth the applicable principles of construction, I turn to the parties' respective arguments.

B.   THE STRUCTURE AND PLAIN LANGUAGE OF ARTICLE SEVENTH

The defendants contend that this Court must read the Supermajority provision as applying solely to a merger "of this corporation," i.e., a merger involving Zapata itself. Although the defendants concede that these words are not explicitly found in Subsection (A)(i), they argue that that meaning is implicit, because the phrase "this corporation" is found in the paragraph that immediately precedes the enumeration, in the subparts immediately following, of the three categories of transactions requiring supermajority approval.[3] In this Court's view, nothing in Article SEVENTH supports the position that Subsection (A)(i) is or was intended to be so limited.

Unlike the broad language of Subsection (A)(i) (which covers "a merger with or into another corporation"), the language of Subsections (A)(ii) and (A)(iii) explicitly and precisely limits the scope of those two latter Subsections. Thus, Subsection (A)(ii) covers a sale or lease of "all or any substantial part of the assets *of this corporation* to any other corporation, person or other entity . . . " Pl. Cert. Ex. C, at 31 (*emphasis added*). Subsection (A)(iii) refers to a sale or lease "to *this corporation or any subsidiary thereof* . . . " *Id.,* at 32 (*emphasis added*). No such language appears in Subsection A(i). If the defendants' argued-for limitation is added to the three Subsections by implication, the explicit limitations in Subsections (A)(ii) and (A)(iii) would become surplusage. An interpretation of a contract that renders one or more terms redundant is not preferred over a construction that gives effect to each of the agreement's terms. See Warner Commun. v. Chris-Craft Industries, Del. Ch., 583 A.2d 962, 971 (1989), aff'd Del. Supr., 567 A.2d 419 (1989).

---

3. Specifically, a merger [Subsection (A)(i)], a sale of all or substantially all of Zapata's assets [Subsection (A)(ii)], and a sale of assets of $2 million or more to Zapata or its subsidiary in exchange for voting securities of Zapata or its subsidiary [Subsection (A)(iii)].

The use of the phrase "of this corporation" in Subsections (A)(ii) and (A)(iii) demonstrates that had the drafters of Article SEVENTH intended to limit the scope of Subsection A(i) to mergers involving only Zapata, they knew fully well how to accomplish that. The total absence in Subsection A(i) of the limitation expressly contained in Subsections (A)(ii) and (A)(iii), shows that the drafters intended no such limitation. . . .

In contrast to the defendants' interpretation, the plaintiffs' construction of Subsection (A)(i) as encompassing subsidiary mergers requires no implication or importation of any language from other sections of Article SEVENTH. Nor does the plaintiffs' interpretation render any term of that Article redundant. Rather, the plaintiffs' interpretation flows directly from the clear, explicit language requiring a supermajority vote for "any merger with or into any other corporation." . . .

IV. CONCLUSION

For the reasons stated above, the defendants have failed to persuade this Court that their interpretation of Subsection (A)(i) of Article SEVENTH is reasonable or fair, or (as a consequence) that that provision is ambiguous. Clearly and on its face the Supermajority Provision of Article SEVENTH applies to mergers involving a wholly owned subsidiary of Zapata, as well as mergers involving Zapata itself.

To the extent that the Merger Agreement requires only a simple majority stockholder approval of the proposed Merger, it contravenes Article SEVENTH of Zapata's Certificate of Incorporation. On that basis, an injunction prohibiting the consummation of the proposed Merger will issue. Counsel shall submit an implementing form of order.

QUESTIONS

1. How is the proposed business combination between Zapata Corp. and Houlihan's Restaurant Group, Inc. to be structured? What requirements must be satisfied in order to validly consummate this proposed acquisition transaction?

2. Who is suing, and what relief does plaintiff seek?

3. What is the basis for the decision of the Delaware court in this case? In other words, is this a de facto merger case?

H. California Law

1. General Background—California's Approach

As we learned from the problems and cases analyzed earlier in this chapter, Delaware law places a premium on the form used to structure an acquisition. Since each method of acquisition carries independent legal significance, transaction planners—that is, Delaware lawyers and their business clients (the corporate managers)—have a great deal of flexibility in deciding how to structure an acquisition under Delaware law. Indeed, Delaware has often been referred to as the leader in corporate law's modern day "race of the lax." One of the big reasons that critics of Delaware law refer to it as the leader in this race of the lax is Delaware's willingness to elevate form over substance, seen most prominently in Delaware's M&A law.

By contrast, the M&A provisions of California's corporation statute reflect a willingness to look through the form of the transaction to its economic substance. California's approach is designed to ensure that shareholders receive essentially the same legal protections when their corporation is involved in an acquisition that represents a fundamental change in the company's business—regardless of the method the transaction planner uses to complete the acquisition. In other words, California has legislated into place the basic premise of the judicially developed doctrine of de facto mergers.

Under California law, the same basic methods are available to structure an acquisition: mergers (both direct and triangular), sales of assets, and stock purchases. However, in order to assure that shareholders receive the protections commonly associated with mergers—namely, shareholder voting rights and the right to an appraisal—California introduces new terminology to the law of M&A by referring to certain types of business combinations as *reorganizations,* a term that is defined in Section 181 of the California statute. The concept of reorganization becomes key to understanding California's statutory scheme and the legal requirements that must be satisfied in planning a business combination under California law. The essential elements of California's statutory scheme are laid out in the following law review excerpt:

Marshall L. Small
Corporate Combinations Under the New California General Corporation Law
23 UCLA L. Rev. 1190 (1976)

INTRODUCTION

California's new Corporation Law retains the three basic forms of corporate combination with which the bar is familiar: the statutory merger (including the currently popular triangular or reverse triangular merger), the sale of assets, and the stock-for-stock exchange. Shareholder approval requirements, dissenter appraisal rights, and other provisions, however, have been altered in an attempt to achieve two basic objectives:[3] (1) to permit shareholders to vote on a

---

3. The basic purpose of those provisions of the new law dealing with corporate combinations, as explained in the Assembly Select Committee's report, commenting on the new law, is as follows: Report of the Assembly Select Committee on the Revision of the Corporations Code 93-95 (1975) (footnotes omitted).

§1200. Reorganizations-Board Approval.
SOURCE: New. Under the new law, various methods of corporate fusion are treated as different means to the same end for the purpose of codifying the "de facto merger" doctrine. . . .

Report of the Assembly Select Committee on the Revision of the Corporations Code 93-95 1975) (footnotes omitted).

transaction and to provide dissenters with compensation, but only if the transaction will significantly dilute their control of the enterprise or change their
rights; and (2) to create a statutory framework under which both the form of
the transaction and the entity chosen to be the acquiring or surviving corporation are determined by considerations other than avoidance of stockholders'
voting and appraisal rights. Whether this ambitious undertaking has resulted
in a promise spoken to the ear but broken to the hope[5] will be left for the reader
to judge after analysis of the new law. . . .

II.   CORPORATE COMBINATIONS UNDER THE REVISED CALIFORNIA CORPORATIONS CODE

Under the new law, reorganization is defined [in Section 181] as:

> (a) A merger pursuant to Chapter 11 . . . other than a short-form merger (a
> "merger reorganization");
> (b) The acquisition by one corporation in exchange in whole or in part for
> its equity securities (or the equity securities of a corporation which is in control of
> the acquiring corporation) of shares of another corporation if, immediately after
> the acquisition, the acquiring corporation has control of such other corporation
> (an "exchange reorganization"); or
> (c) The acquisition by one corporation in exchange in whole or in part for
> its equity securities (or the equity securities of a corporation which is in control of
> the acquiring corporation) or for its debt securities (or debt securities of a corpo-
> ration which is in control of the acquiring corporation) which are not adequately
> secured and which have a maturity date in excess of five years after the consum-
> mation of the reorganization, or both, of all or substantially all of the assets of
> another corporation (a "sale-of-assets reorganization").

Chapter 12 of the new law applies to all reorganizations. Mergers are additionally regulated by chapter 11. Sale-of-assets and exchange reorganizations
are dealt with only in chapter 12. Certain sales of assets for cash or for a form
of consideration which was thought not to subject the recipient to the risk of
long term investment in the acquiring corporation (herein referred to as "cash
equivalent") are not treated as "reorganizations" at all and are dealt with separately in chapter 10. Dissenters' appraisal rights are dealt with in chapter 13.
This Part will consider the application of the reorganization provisions generally to mergers, sales of assets and exchanges which qualify as "reorganizations" under the new law's definitions.

A.   BOARD OF DIRECTORS' AUTHORIZATION

Section 1200 of the new law requires that a reorganization be approved by
the board of directors of:

(a)   Each constituent corporation in a merger reorganization;
(b)   The acquiring corporation in an exchange reorganization;

---

5. W. SHAKESPEARE. MACBETH, Act v scene viii, II. 21-22.

(c)   The acquiring corporation and the corporation whose property and assets are acquired in a sale-of-assets reorganization; . . . and

(e)   The corporation in control of any constituent or acquiring corporation
under subdivision (a), (b) or (c) and whose equity securities are issued
or transferred in the reorganization (a "parent party").[19]

In effect section 1200 requires approval of the board of each corporation which
is a party to the reorganization. The only board approval not needed is that of
the acquired corporation in an exchange reorganization because individual
shareholders must decide whether or not to sell their stock in such a reorganization.

Subsections (a), (b) and (c) of section 1200 do not represent a significant
change in the law. In the old law, board approval was expressly required for both
parties in a merger, but only for the acquired corporation in a sale of assets,
and for neither in an exchange. Since all powers of a corporation are generally exercised by its board of directors, however, the acquiring corporation in
an exchange or sale-of-assets reorganization was also required to act pursuant
to board approval under the old law. In addition, subsection (d) merely recognizes existing practice by requiring that the board of the corporation in control
approve reorganizations carried out through subsidiaries such as, for example,
triangular mergers.

B.   SHAREHOLDERS' AUTHORIZATION

Subsection 1201(a) provides that the principal terms of a reorganization
must be approved by the outstanding shares of each class of each corporation
where the board of directors is required by section 1200 to approve the reorganization, unless one of two exceptions discussed below applies. A majority vote,
or a higher proportion if mandated by the articles or a shareholders' agreement, is required by the shares of each class, regardless of any limitations on
the voting power of a class. . . .

The first exception to the requirement of shareholder approval is fairly
simple. Preferred shares in the surviving or acquiring corporation or its parent
need not assent to the reorganization if the "rights, preferences, privileges, and
restrictions granted to or imposed upon" such shares remain unchanged by
the reorganization. This exception does not apply if the articles require shareholder approval or if in a merger reorganization the articles of the surviving
corporation are amended in a way which would otherwise require the approval
of preferred shareholders.[29]

The second exception to the requirement of shareholder consent is more
complex. Neither preferred nor common shareholder approval is needed if
the corporation, or its shareholders immediately before the reorganization, or

---

19. Control is defined for the purposes of sections 181, 1001 and 1200 as "ownership
directly or indirectly of shares possessing more than 50 percent of the total voting power."
[*See* §160(b).]

29. *Id.* §1201(c). . . .

both, will own immediately after the reorganization equity securities of the surviving or acquiring corporation or its parent possessing more than five-sixths of the voting power of the surviving or acquiring corporation or its parent. This exception, however, does not apply under two circumstances:

(1) Shareholder approval is needed despite retention of five-sixths of the voting power for the surviving or acquiring corporation or its parent if any amendment which would otherwise require shareholder approval is made to the articles of the surviving corporation in connection with a merger reorganization. [*See* Cal. Corp. Code §1201(c).] In such event, the reorganization must be approved by the "outstanding shares" where the articles expressly provide for such approval or where such approval is required by sections 902 (a) or 903 of the new law. The qualification for contemplated amendments to the articles of the surviving corporation is limited to merger reorganizations for a very simple reason: Of all reorganizations, only mergers permit amendments to the articles as part of the reorganization document. If amendments are contemplated in connection with exchange or sale-of-assets reorganizations,[36] they must be adopted in the usual fashion by amendment of the articles pursuant to chapter 9 with shareholder consent. If shareholder approval were not statutorily required in connection with mergers, however, it could be avoided by inserting amendments to the articles into the merger agreement. Thus, the special qualification for merger reorganizations merely insures voting rights to the shareholders by recognizing the unique method of effecting amendments in mergers.

(2) Under section 1201(d) of the new law the outstanding shares of a class in a disappearing corporation must give their consent to a merger reorganization even though the five-sixths rule applies if the holders of such class receive shares of the surviving corporation that have different rights than those surrendered. . . . [42]

III. MERGER REORGANIZATIONS

In addition to the reorganization provisions of chapter 12, merger reorganizations and short-form mergers are regulated by the provisions of chapter 11. Section 1100 states the general proposition that any two or more corporations may be merged into one under chapter 11. Although "corporation" is defined to include only domestic corporations, section 1108 makes clear that mergers are authorized between domestic and foreign corporations and that the surviving corporation may be either domestic or foreign. The new law eliminates as unnecessary the provision of the old law permitting the little used technique

---

36. An example of this would be an amendment under section 903(a)(1) of the new law in the case of an increase in authorized shares.

42. Although the new law breaks new ground in many respects, it does not go as far as the proposed addition of section 72-A [the predecessor provision to current Section 11.03] to the Model Business Corporation Act, which would permit a majority of the shareholders of a selling corporation to bind all shareholders in an exchange reorganization and accord dissenters' rights to those who do not approve the transaction. *See* ABA, *Report of Committee on Corporate Laws: Changes in the Model Business Corporation Act*, 30 Bus. Law. 991 (1975). . . .

of "consolidation" whereby two corporations could agree to be consolidated into a new corporation which would come into being and absorb the existing corporations upon the filing of a consolidation agreement.

A.   THE MERGER AGREEMENT

As explained above, a merger reorganization must be approved by the board of each constituent corporation. Section 1101 requires that the merger agreement also be approved by each board. . . .

The reorganization provisions clearly contemplate that shareholders of a constituent corporation may, in a triangular merger, receive *equity* securities of a parent corporation. These provisions should not be construed to limit the type and source of securities to be issued in a merger to equity securities of a constituent corporation or parent, or to securities of a corporation which is technically in "control" of one of the constituent corporations within the meaning of section 160(b). Section 1101(d) certainly suggests a broader range of alternatives.[56] . . .

B.   SHORT-FORM MERGERS

If a domestic corporation owns all the outstanding shares of a domestic or foreign corporation, the merger of the subsidiary into the parent may, as under the old law, be effected by a resolution adopted by the board of the parent and the filing of a certificate of ownership with the Secretary of State. [*See* Cal. Corp. Code §1110(a).] Under the new law, a domestic corporation which owns at least 90 percent of the outstanding shares of each class of a corporation may merge the subsidiary into the parent by resolutions adopted by the boards of the parent and subsidiary and by filing a certificate of ownership with the Secretary of State. The resolution of the parent's board must set forth the consideration to be granted by the parent for each share of the subsidiary not owned by the parent, and the resolution of the board of the subsidiary must approve the fairness of the consideration to be received for each share of the subsidiary not owned by the parent, which may include securities, cash, property, or rights. . . .

---

56. One question that was occasionally raised about triangular mergers under the old law was whether a subsidiary's, rather than a parent's, receipt of the assets of the acquired business was adequate consideration to the parent for direct issuance of the parent's securities to the disappearing corporation or its shareholders. Section 409(a) of the new law now establishes that shares may be issued in exchange for property actually received either by the issuing corporation or by a wholly-owned subsidiary. However, under section 409(a), it appears that a parent corporation may not use a *partly-owned* subsidiary to effect a triangular merger involving the direct issuance of the parent's shares to shareholders of the disappearing corporation.

C.　DISSENTERS' APPRAISAL RIGHTS

If the approval of outstanding shares of a corporation is required for a merger reorganization under section 1201(a) and (b) . . . , each shareholder of that corporation may require it to pay, in cash, the fair market value of all "dissenting shares." [*See* Cal. Corp. Code §1300(a).] A similar right is accorded to each shareholder of a disappearing corporation in a short-form merger. [*Id.*] Certain shares, including shares listed on a national securities exchange certified by the Commissioner of Corporations to be exempt securities . . . are not "dissenting shares" subject to the appraisal procedures. [*See* Cal. Corp. Code §1300(b)(1). Thus California also includes a "market out exception" for those dissenting shares that are publicly traded, but restores the right of appraisal to these shares if "demands for payment are filed with respect to 5% or more of the outstanding shares of that class." *Id.*]

IV.　SALE-OF-ASSETS TRANSACTIONS

Unlike statutory mergers under chapter 11, all of which (except for short form mergers) constitute reorganizations under chapter 12, sale-of-assets transactions are divided into two distinct categories, depending upon the types of consideration issued in the transaction. Chapters 12 (reorganizations) and 13 (dissenters' rights) govern "sale-of-assets reorganizations." [*See* Cal. Corp. Code §181 (c).] Such a sale will occur if the acquiring corporation issues any of its equity securities, any equity securities of a corporation which controls the acquiring corporation, any debt securities of the acquiring corporation which are not "adequately secured" and which have a maturity date more than five years after completion of the reorganization, or a combination of equity securities and such debt securities, in exchange for all or substantially all of the property and assets of the selling corporation. If none of these securities is issued as a part of the consideration for transfer of all or substantially all of the assets, then chapters 12 and 13 are inapplicable; instead, the provisions of chapter 10 (sale of assets) apply to the transaction. Chapter 10 governs only sales of assets which are not "sale-of-assets reorganizations" . . . [.]

The original exposure draft of the State Bar Committee on Corporations limited a sale-of-assets reorganization under the new law to one in which the acquiring corporation or its parent issued only equity securities. Since debt securities might be issued in a merger reorganization, after further consideration the Committee extended the provisions of chapters 12 and 13 to sale-of-assets transactions where the consideration issued by the acquiring corporation included debt securities which forced the shareholders of the selling corporation to rely on the long-term prospects of the acquiring corporation for payment. Where the acquiring corporation issues only "adequately secured" long-term debt securities, whose repayment is presumably assured, or short-term debt securities, the drafters concluded that the provisions of chapters 12 and 13 should not apply. . . .

One may question whether a debt security with a maturity date deferred as much as five years is indeed the equivalent of cash, eliminating the investment risk for one who receives the security. Furthermore, the absence of a definition of "adequately secured" in the new law may cause many practitioners to be extremely cautious in concluding that any sale of assets not solely for cash or debt securities of less than five years maturity is anything other than a sale-of-assets reorganization subject to chapters 12 and 13. Where consideration other than cash is given, many practitioners will resolve the matter by using the merger vehicle. In those cases where a limited assumption of liabilities of the selling corporation is desired, they will make sure that some of the securities received constitute equity securities or debt securities with a maturity of more than five years so that the transaction is clearly a sale-of-assets reorganization or else they will consider voluntarily extending to the shareholders of the selling corporation those voting and dissenters' rights to which the shareholders would otherwise be entitled if the transaction were a sale-of-assets reorganization. However, because the new law does attempt to draw a distinction between sales of assets which are reorganizations and those which are for cash or "cash equivalents," and because some sale-of-assets transactions will clearly be for cash, it is useful to consider how the new law treats each type of sale-of-assets transaction.

A.   SALES OF ASSETS FOR CASH OR CASH EQUIVALENTS

Chapter 10 of the new law contains provisions substantially similar to those appearing in the old law. Section 1000 continues the rule of section 3900 of the old law that unless the articles otherwise provide, the board of directors may, without shareholder approval, mortgage or hypothecate any part of the corporation's property for the purpose of securing performance of any contract or obligation. . . .

Section 1001 sets forth the general rule that a corporation may sell or otherwise dispose of all of its assets if its board of directors approves the principal terms of the transaction. The principal terms of the transaction must also be approved by the holders of a majority of the outstanding shares entitled to vote unless the transaction is in the usual course of business. . . .

One may question why a shareholder who receives debt securities with a maturity of five years or less should be denied dissenters' rights or, for that matter, why a shareholder who receives only cash should be denied the right to question the fairness of the sale through dissenters' proceedings. Under section 1312(b) of the new law, a shareholder in a *reorganization* transaction may decline to assert dissenters' rights and may attack the fairness of the transaction if one of the parties to the transaction is controlled by or under common control with another party to the reorganization. No similar right to either assert dissenters' rights or attack the fairness of the transaction is expressly extended or denied to a shareholder in a cash or cash equivalent sale.[113] . . .

---

113. A shareholder in a cash or cash equivalent sale may have the right to attack the fairness of the transaction whether or not there is common control since such a shareholder is not expressly precluded from such an attack. *Id.*§1312(a). This is a dubious result, since, in the absence of common control, it may be better social policy to extend dissenters' rights to aggrieved shareholders in cash or cash equivalent transactions, and, as a quid pro quo, preclude such shareholders from collaterally attacking the transaction under section 1312(a), as in the case of reorganization transactions.

A proposal to sell "substantially all" the assets of a corporation must be approved by the shareholders, but the new law does not define this term. . . .

B.   SALE-OF-ASSETS REORGANIZATIONS

Unlike statutory mergers, which are subject to the detailed procedural provisions of chapter 11, there is no separate chapter in the new law setting forth procedural provisions governing sale-of-assets reorganizations. These transactions are governed by chapter 12 and, to a limited extent, by section 1002, which set forth certification provisions to establish compliance with the applicable law for the benefit of third parties.

V.   EXCHANGE REORGANIZATIONS

As in the case of sale-of-assets reorganizations, no separate chapter in the new law sets forth the procedural provisions governing exchange reorganizations subject to chapter 12. The basic requirements are set forth solely in chapter 12.

An "exchange reorganization" is defined [in California Corporation Code §181(b)] as:

> The acquisition by one corporation in exchange in whole or in part for its equity securities (or the equity securities of a corporation which is in control of the acquiring corporation) of shares of another corporation if, immediately after the acquisition, the acquiring corporation has control of such other corporation. . . .

Section 160(b) provides that control in section 181 means the ownership directly or indirectly of shares possessing more than 50 percent of the voting power.

Although the new law regulates exchange reorganizations in the limited manner described above, no attempt has been made to regulate contested tender offers in the manner undertaken by a growing number of states. [We will consider the modern proliferation of state antitakeover statutes later, in Chapter 6.] Aside from the absence of a takeover bid statute, which absence may be viewed as less than helpful to those defending against tender offers, the new law discloses no marked bias in favor of, or opposition to, hostile tender offers. . . .

PROBLEM SET NO. 7—CALIFORNIA LAW

The following problems are based on problems that we previously analyzed under the terms of Delaware law and the MBCA. For ease of reference, I have noted the problem number where this problem was previously considered in order to facilitate comparison of results obtained applying the reorganization provisions of California law. In analyzing the following problems, you will need to refer to the relevant provisions of the California Corporations Code.

Direct Mergers—California Law

1. Merger—Consideration Consists of 30 Percent of Bidder's Stock (Same as Problem 1 at p. 62).   Target Co., a closely held California corporation, plans to merge into Bidder Co., another closely held California corporation. The plan of merger calls for Target shareholders to receive shares of Bidder common stock comprising 30 percent of the voting power of Bidder's common stock that was outstanding immediately prior to completion of the acquisition. Target and Bidder each have only one class of voting common stock outstanding. Bidder has sufficient authorized and unissued shares to complete the transaction.

    a.   What action is required by the boards of Bidder and Target under California law?

    b.   Do the shareholders of either Bidder or Target have the right to vote under California law?

    c.   Do the shareholders of either Bidder or Target have the right to dissent under California law?

    d.   How would this analysis of shareholder voting rights and the availability of the appraisal remedy change if both Bidder Corp. and Target Corp. are publicly traded?

2. Merger—Consideration Consists of 15 Percent of Bidder's Stock (Same as Problem 3 at p. 63).   Assume that the facts are the same as set out in Problem 1—*except* that the shareholders of Target will receive shares comprising 15 percent of the voting power of Bidder's common stock that was outstanding immediately prior to the completion of the acquisition.

    a.   What action is required by the boards of Bidder and Target under California law?

    b.   Do the shareholders of either Bidder or Target have the right to vote under California law?

    c.   Do the shareholders of either Bidder or Target have the right to dissent under California law?

3. Merger—Consideration Consists of All Cash (Same as Problem 1 at p. 64).   Assume that the facts are the same as set out in Problem 1—*except* that the merger agreement provides that shareholders of Target will receive all *cash* in exchange for their Target shares.

    a.   What action is required by the boards of Target and Bidder under California law?

    b.   Do the shareholders of either Bidder or Target have the right to vote under California law?

    c.   Do the shareholders of Bidder and/or Target have the right to dissent under California law?

    d.   How would the analysis of shareholder voting rights and the availability of the appraisal remedy change if both Bidder and Target were publicly traded?

Asset Purchases—California Law

4. Sale of Assets for Cash (Same as Problem 2 at p. 76). Chef America, Inc., a closely held California corporation, plans to sell all of its assets and transfer certain of its liabilities to Nestlé, Inc., a NYSE-listed California corporation, in exchange for cash. Immediately after the transfer, Chef America will dissolve and liquidate itself, with the company distributing out to its shareholders any cash remaining after paying off its creditors.

    a.   What action is required by the boards of Chef America, Inc., and Nestlé, Inc., under California law?

    b.   Do the shareholders of Chef America, Inc., and Nestlé, Inc., have the right to vote under California law?

    c.   Do the shareholders of Chef America, Inc., and/or Nestlé, Inc., have the right to dissent under California law?

5. Asset Acquisition—Using 30 Percent of Bidder's Stock (Same as Problem 3 at p. 77). Assume that Chef America, a closely held California company, plans to sell all of its assets and transfer certain of its liabilities to Nestlé, Inc., another California company that is publicly traded on the NYSE, in exchange for shares comprising 30 percent of the voting power of Nestlé's common stock that was outstanding immediately prior to the completion of the acquisition. Immediately after the transfer, Chef America will dissolve and liquidate itself, with Chef America transferring to its shareholders the Nestlé shares in exchange for the Chef America stock, which will then be canceled in dissolution of the company. Assume further that Nestlé has sufficient authorized and unissued shares to complete the transaction.

    a.   What action is required by the boards of Chef America and Nestlé under California law?

    b.   Do the shareholders of either Chef America or Nestlé have the right to vote under California law?

    c.   Do the shareholders of Chef America and/or Nestlé have the right to dissent under California law?

6. Asset Acquisition—Using 15 Percent of Bidder's Stock (Same as Problem 4 at p. 77). Assume that the facts are the same as set out in Problem 5—*except* that Nestlé completes the acquisition by issuing its stock in an amount equal to 15 percent of the voting power of Nestlé's common stock that was outstanding immediately prior to the completion of the acquisition.

    a.   What action is required by the boards of Chef America and Nestlé under California law?

    b.   Do the shareholders of either Chef America and Nestlé have the right to vote under California law?

    c.   Do the shareholders of Chef America and/or Nestlé have the right to dissent under California law?

Stock Purchases—California Law

   7. Stock Purchase—for Cash (Same as Problem 1 at p. 101).   Two brothers, Paul and David Merage, each own 50 percent of the outstanding common stock of Chef America, Inc., a California corporation with only one class of authorized shares. The two brothers have signed a stock purchase agreement with Nestlé, Inc., a NYSE-listed California company. Nestlé has agreed to pay $2 billion cash on closing of the parties' stock purchase agreement.

   a.   What action is required by the boards of Chef America, Inc., and Nestlé, Inc., under California law?
   b.   Do the shareholders of either Chef America, Inc., or Nestlé, Inc., have the right to vote under California law?
   c.   Do the shareholders of Chef America, Inc., or Nestlé, Inc., have the right to dissent under California law?

   8. Stock Purchase—Using 24 Percent of Bidder's Stock (Same as Problem 2 at p. 102—also known as Stock Exchange Offer).   Assume the same facts as described in Problem 7, *except* that the parties' stock purchase agreement calls for Nestlé to pay at closing a portion of the $2 billion purchase price in cash and the balance of the purchase price to be paid immediately in shares of Nestlé common stock comprising 24 percent of the voting power of Nestlé's common stock that was outstanding before the transaction is completed.

   a.   What action is required by the boards of Chef America and Nestlé under California law?
   b.   Do the shareholders of Chef America and Nestlé have the right to vote under California law?
   c.   Do the shareholders of Chef America and/or Nestlé have the right to dissent under California law?

   9. Stock Purchase—Using 14 Percent of Bidder's Stock (Similar to Problem 3 at p. 102).   Assume that the facts are the same as set out in Problem 8—*except* that Nestlé plans to complete the acquisition of Chef America by issuing shares of its stock in an amount comprising 14 percent of the voting power of its common stock that was outstanding immediately before the acquisition is completed.

   a.   What action is required by the boards of Chef America and Nestlé under California law?
   b.   Do the shareholders of Nestlé and/or Chef America have the right to vote under California law?
   c.   Do the shareholders of Nestlé and/or Chef America have the right to dissent under California law?

Triangular Merger Problems—California Law

   10. Triangular Merger—Consideration Consisting of 23 Percent of Stock of Bidder Corporation (Same as Problem 2 at p. 108).   Pfizer Corp., a NYSE-listed California company, forms New Company (NewCo), a wholly owned subsidiary, for the purpose of acquiring Pharmacia Co., another NYSE-listed California company, in a triangular merger. The parties' merger agreement calls for Pfizer to issue shares of its common stock in an amount equal to 23 percent of the voting power of Pfizer's common stock that was outstanding immediately prior to the completion of the transaction. Although California law allows for the transaction to be structured either as a *forward* triangular (subsidiary) merger or a *reverse* triangular (subsidiary) merger, the parties have decided to use a *reverse* triangular merger, thereby preserving Pharmacia Co. as a wholly owned subsidiary of Pfizer Corp. Assume further that Pfizer Corp. has sufficient authorized but unissued shares to complete the transaction.

    a.   What action is required by the boards of Pfizer Corp., Pharmacia Co., and NewCo under California law?

    b.   Do the shareholders of either Pfizer Corp. or Pharmacia Co. have the right to vote under California law?

    c.   Do the shareholders of Pfizer Corp. and/or Pharmacia Co. have the right to dissent under California law?

11. Triangular Merger—Consideration Consisting of 15 Percent of Bidder's Stock (Similar to Problem 3 at p. 109).   Assume that the facts are the same as set out in Problem 10—*except* that the shareholders of Pharmacia Co. will receive shares of common stock in Pfizer Corp. amounting to 15 percent of the voting power of its common stock that was outstanding immediately before the acquisition is completed.

    a.   What action is required by the boards of Pfizer Corp., Pharmacia Co., and NewCo under California law?

    b.   Do the shareholders of either Pfizer Corp. or Pharmacia Co. have the right to vote under California law?

    c.   Do the shareholders of Pfizer Corp. and/or Pharmacia Co. have the right to dissent under California law?

12. Triangular Merger—Consideration Consists of Cash (Same as Problem 4 at p. 110).   Assume that the facts are the same as set out above in Problem 10—*except* that the terms of the merger agreement call for the Pharmacia shareholders to receive *all cash* for their Pharmacia shares.

    a.   What action is required by the boards of Pfizer Corp., Pharmacia Co., and NewCo under California law?

    b.   Do the shareholders of either Pfizer Corp. or Pharmacia Co. have the right to vote under California law?

    c.   Do the shareholders of Pfizer Corp. and/or Pharmacia Co. have the right to dissent under California law?

QUESTIONS

1.   From a public policy perspective, which approach do you prefer: California or Delaware? In considering this issue of "form over substance," does it matter whether Target or Bidder is publicly traded?

2. As to dissenters' rights, what do you think of California's approach to the market out exception? Do you prefer this approach to that of Delaware or the MBCA? If so, why?

I.   Is There a Right to Vote as a Class?

In the case of a corporation with multiple classes of outstanding voting stock (i.e., Class A common stock, Class B common stock, and Class C common stock), the issue of whether each class of shares must vote separately to approve a transaction involving a "fundamental change" may arise. As a threshold matter, we must determine the shareholders' rights by looking to both the provisions of the respective state's corporation code and the corporation's articles of incorporation. Assuming that a right to a class vote is mandated, what is the effect of class voting? In a class vote, *each class* of shares entitled to vote on such transaction must approve it by the requisite majority. Thus, shareholder approval votes are not tallied in the aggregate for all outstanding shares, but instead, the requisite approval must be obtained separately within each distinct class.

By way of example, assume that Corporation X has three classes of outstanding shares common stock—Class A (1,000 shares), Class B (500 shares), and Class C (250 shares). Further assume that the voting standard required to effectuate the "fundamental change" under the terms of relevant state law is an absolute majority. If a right to vote as a class is available, then any proposed merger must be approved by at least 501 shares of Class A, 251 shares of Class B, and 126 shares of Class C. Obviously, the right to vote as a class provides an additional layer of protection for each class of shares even if that class represents a minority interest within the corporation.

The following case provides a nice illustration of how the right to vote as a class creates the potential for a veto power. The case also reflects on the continued importance of the internal affairs doctrine in determining which corporate laws must be satisfied in order to validly complete corporate transactions such as mergers, sale of assets, and distributions to shareholders, among others.

▌▌ **VantagePoint Venture Partners 1996 v. Examen, Inc.**
871 A.2d 1108 (Del. 2005)

HOLLAND, Justice:
This is an expedited appeal from the Court of Chancery following the entry of a final judgment on the pleadings. We have concluded that the judgment must be affirmed.

DELAWARE ACTION

On March 3, 2005, the plaintiff-appellee, Examen, Inc. ("Examen"), filed a Complaint in the Court of Chancery against VantagePoint Venture Partners,

Inc. ("VantagePoint"), a Delaware Limited Partnership and an Examen Series A Preferred shareholder, seeking a judicial declaration that pursuant to the controlling Delaware law and under the Company's Certificate of Designations of Series A Preferred Stock ("Certificate of Designations"), VantagePoint was not entitled to a class vote of the Series A Preferred Stock on the proposed merger between Examen and a Delaware subsidiary of Reed Elsevier Inc.

CALIFORNIA ACTION

On March 8, 2005, VantagePoint filed an action in the California Superior Court seeking: (1) a declaration that Examen was required to identify whether it was a "quasi-California corporation" under section 2115 of the California Corporations Code[1]; (2) a declaration that Examen was a quasi-California corporation pursuant to California Corporations Code section 2115 and therefore subject to California Corporations Code section 1201(a), and that, as a Series A Preferred shareholder, VantagePoint was entitled to vote its shares as a separate class in connection with the proposed merger; (3) injunctive relief; and (4) damages incurred as the result of alleged violations of California Corporations Code sections 2111(f) and 1201.

DELAWARE ACTION DECIDED

On March 10, 2005, the Court of Chancery granted Examen's request for an expedited hearing on its motion for judgment on the pleadings. On March 21, 2005, the California Superior Court stayed its action pending the ruling of the Court of Chancery. On March 29, 2005, the Court of Chancery ruled that the case was governed by the internal affairs doctrine as explicated by this Court in *McDermott v. Lewis*, 531 A.2d 206 (Del.1987). In applying that doctrine, the Court of Chancery held that Delaware law governed the vote that was required to approve a merger between two Delaware corporate entities.

---

1. Section 2115 of the California Corporations Code purportedly applies to corporations that have contacts with the State of California, but are incorporated in other states. *See* Cal. Corp. Code §§171 (defining "foreign corporation"); and Cal. Corp. Code §§2115(a), (b). Section 2115 of the California Corporations Code provides that, irrespective of the state of incorporation, **foreign corporations' articles of incorporation are deemed amended** to comply with California law and are subject to the laws of California if certain criteria are met. *See* Cal. Corp. Code §2115 (*emphasis added*). To qualify under the statute: (1) the average of the property factor, the payroll factor and the sales factor as defined in the California Revenue and Taxation Code must be more than 50 percent during its last full income year; and (2) more than one-half of its outstanding voting securities must be held by persons having addresses in California. *Id.* If a corporation qualifies under this provision, California corporate laws apply "to the exclusion of the law of the jurisdiction where [the company] is incorporated." *Id.* Included among the California corporate law provisions that would govern is California Corporations Code section 1201, which states that the principal terms of a reorganization shall be approved by the outstanding shares of each class of each corporation the approval of whose board is required. *See* Cal. Corp. Code §§2115, 1201 [emphasis in original].

On April 1, 2005, VantagePoint filed a notice of appeal with this Court. On April 4, 2005, VantagePoint sought to enjoin the merger from closing pending its appeal. On April 5, 2005, this Court denied VantagePoint's request to enjoin the merger from closing, but granted its request for an expedited appeal.

MERGER WITHOUT MOOTNESS

Following this Court's ruling on April 5, 2005, Examen and the Delaware subsidiary of Reed Elsevier consummated the merger that same day. This Court directed the parties to address the issue of mootness, simultaneously with the expedited briefing that was completed on April 13, 2005. VantagePoint argues that if we agree with its position "that a class vote was required, then Vantage-Point could pursue remedies for loss of this right, including rescission of the Merger, rescissory damages or monetary damages." Examen submits that "the need for final resolution of the validity of the merger vote remains important to the parties and to the public interest" because a decision from this Court will conclusively determine the parties' rights with regard to the law that applies to the merger vote. We have concluded that this appeal is not moot.

FACTS

Examen was a Delaware corporation engaged in the business of providing web-based legal expense management solutions to a growing list of Fortune 1000 customers throughout the United States. Following consummation of the merger on April 5, 2005, LexisNexis Examen, also a Delaware corporation, became the surviving entity. VantagePoint is a Delaware Limited Partnership organized and existing under the laws of Delaware. VantagePoint, a major venture capital firm that purchased Examen Series A Preferred Stock in a negotiated transaction, owned eighty-three percent of Examen's outstanding Series A Preferred Stock (909,091 shares) and no shares of Common Stock.

On February 17, 2005, Examen and Reed Elsevier executed the Merger Agreement, which was set to expire on April 15, 2005, if the merger had not closed by that date. Under the Delaware General Corporation Law and Examen's Certificate of Incorporation, including the Certificate of Designations for the Series A Preferred Stock, adoption of the Merger Agreement required the affirmative vote of the holders of a majority of the issued and outstanding shares of the Common Stock and Series A Preferred Stock, *voting together as a single class.* Holders of Series A Preferred Stock had the number of votes equal to the number of shares of Common Stock they would have held if their Preferred Stock was converted. Thus, VantagePoint, which owned 909,091 shares of Series A Preferred Stock and no shares of Common Stock, was entitled to vote based on a converted number of 1,392,727 shares of stock.

There were 9,717,415 total outstanding shares of the Company's capital stock (8,626,826 shares of Common Stock and 1,090,589 shares of Series A Preferred Stock), representing 10,297,608 votes on an as-converted basis. An affirmative vote of at least 5,148,805 shares, constituting a majority of the outstanding voting power on an as-converted basis, was required to approve the merger. If the stockholders were to vote by class, VantagePoint would have controlled

83.4 percent of the Series A Preferred Stock, which would have permitted VantagePoint to block the merger. VantagePoint acknowledges that, if Delaware law applied, it would not have a class vote.

Chancery Court Decision

The Court of Chancery determined that the question of whether VantagePoint, as a holder of Examen's Series A Preferred Stock, was entitled to a separate class vote on the merger with a Delaware subsidiary of Reed Elsevier, was governed by the internal affairs doctrine because the issue implicated "the relationship between a corporation and its stockholders." The Court of Chancery rejected VantagePoint's argument that section 2115 of the California Corporation Code did not conflict with Delaware law and operated only in addition to rights granted under Delaware corporate law. In doing so, the Court of Chancery noted that section 2115 "expressly states that it operates 'to the exclusion of the law of the jurisdiction in which [the company] is incorporated.'"

Specifically, the Court of Chancery determined that section 2115's requirement that stockholders vote as a separate class conflicts with Delaware law, which, together with Examen's Certificate of Incorporation, mandates that the merger be authorized by a majority of all Examen stockholders voting together as a single class. The Court of Chancery concluded that it could not enforce both Delaware and California law. Consequently, the Court of Chancery decided that the issue presented was solely one of choice-of-law, and that it need not determine the constitutionality of section 2115.

VantagePoint's Argument

According to VantagePoint, "the issue presented by this case is not a choice of law question, but rather the constitutional issue of whether California may promulgate a narrowly-tailored exception to the internal affairs doctrine that is designed to protect important state interests." VantagePoint submits that "Section 2115 was designed to provide an additional layer of investor protection by mandating that California's heightened voting requirements apply to those few foreign corporations that have chosen to conduct a majority of their business in California and meet the other factual prerequisite of Section 2115." Therefore, VantagePoint argues that "Delaware either must apply the statute if California can validly enact it, or hold the statute unconstitutional if California cannot." We note, however, that when an issue or claim is properly before a tribunal, "the court is not limited to the particular legal theories advanced by the parties, but rather retains the independent power to identify and apply the proper construction of governing law." *Kamen v. Kemper Fin. Serv.*, 500 U.S. 90, 111 S.Ct. 1711, 114 L.Ed.2d 152 (1991).

Standard of Review

In granting Examen's Motion for Judgment on the Pleadings, the Court of Chancery held that, as a matter of law, the rights of stockholders to vote on the proposed merger were governed by the law of Delaware—Examen's state of incorporation—and that an application of Delaware law resulted in the Class A Preferred shareholders having no right to a separate class vote. The issue of whether VantagePoint was entitled to a separate class vote of the Series A Preferred Stock on the merger is a question of law that this Court reviews *de novo*.

INTERNAL AFFAIRS DOCTRINE

In *CTS Corp. v. Dynamics Corp. of Am.,* the United States Supreme Court stated that it is "an accepted part of the business landscape in this country for States to create corporations, to prescribe their powers, and to define the rights that are acquired by purchasing their shares." 481 U.S. 69, 91, 107 (1987). In *CTS*, it was also recognized that "[a] State has an interest in promoting stable relationships among parties involved in the corporations it charters, as well as in ensuring that investors in such corporations have an effective voice in corporate affairs." *Id.* The internal affairs doctrine is a long-standing choice of law principle which recognizes that only one state should have the authority to regulate a corporation's internal affairs—the state of incorporation.

The internal affairs doctrine developed on the premise that, in order to prevent corporations from being subjected to inconsistent legal standards, the authority to regulate a corporation's internal affairs should not rest with multiple jurisdictions. It is now well established that only the law of the state of incorporation governs and determines issues relating to a corporation's internal affairs. By providing certainty and predictability, the internal affairs doctrine protects the justified expectations of the parties with interests in the corporation.

The internal affairs doctrine applies to those matters that pertain to the relationships among or between the corporation and its officers, directors, and shareholders. . . . Accordingly, the conflicts practice of both state and federal courts has consistently been to apply the law of the state of incorporation to "the entire gamut of internal corporate affairs."[14]

The internal affairs doctrine is not, however, only a conflicts of law principle. Pursuant to the Fourteenth Amendment Due Process Clause, directors and officers of corporations "have a significant right . . . to know what law will be applied to their actions" and "[s]tockholders . . . have a right to know by what standards of accountability they may hold those managing the corporation's business and affairs." Under the Commerce Clause, a state "has no interest in regulating the internal affairs of foreign corporations." Therefore, this Court has held that an "application of the internal affairs doctrine is mandated by constitutional principles, except in the 'rarest situations,'" *e.g.,* when "the law of the state of incorporation is inconsistent with a national policy on foreign or interstate commerce."

---

14. *McDermott Inc. v. Lewis,* 531 A.2d [206, 216 (Del. 1987)] (quoting John Kozyris, *Corporate Wars and Choice of Law,* 1985 Duke L.J. 1, 98 (1985)). The internal affairs doctrine does not apply where the rights of third parties external to the corporation are at issue, *e.g.,* contracts and torts. *Id. See also Rogers v. Guaranty Trust of N.Y.,* 288 U.S. 123, 130-31, 53 S.Ct. 295, 77 L.Ed. 652 (1933).

CALIFORNIA SECTION 2115

VantagePoint contends that section 2115 of the California Corporations Code is a limited exception to the internal affairs doctrine. Section 2115 is characterized as an outreach statute because it requires certain foreign corporations to conform to a broad range of internal affairs provisions. Section 2115 defines the foreign corporations for which the California statute has an outreach effect as those foreign corporations, half of whose voting securities are held of record by persons with California addresses, that also conduct half of their business in California as measured by a formula weighing assets, sales and payroll factors.

VantagePoint argues that section 2115 "mandates application of certain enumerated provisions of California's corporation law to the internal affairs of 'foreign' corporations if certain narrow factual prerequisites [set forth in section 2115] are met." Under the California statute, if more than one half of a foreign corporation's outstanding voting securities are held of record by persons having addresses in California (as disclosed on the books of the corporation) on the record date, *and* the property, payroll and sales factor tests are satisfied, then on the first day of the income year, one hundred and thirty five days after the above tests are satisfied, *the foreign corporation's articles of incorporation are deemed amended to the exclusion of the law of the state of incorporation*. If the factual conditions precedent for triggering section 2115 are established, many aspects of a corporation's internal affairs are purportedly governed by California corporate law to the exclusion of the law of the state of incorporation.[22]

In her comprehensive analysis of the internal affairs doctrine, Professor Deborah A. DeMott examined section 2115. As she astutely points out:

> In contrast to the certainty with which the state of incorporation may be determined, the criteria upon which the applicability of section 2115 hinges are not constants. For example, whether half of a corporation's business is derived from California and whether half of its voting securities have record holders with California addresses may well vary from year to year (and indeed throughout any given year). Thus, a corporation might be subject to section 2115 one year but not the next, depending on its situation at the time of filing the annual statement required by section 2108.[23]

---

22. If Section 2115 applies, California law is deemed to control the following: the annual election of directors; removal of directors without cause; removal of directors by court proceedings; the filing [sic] of director vacancies where less than a majority in office are elected by shareholders; the director's standard of care; the liability of directors for unlawful distributions; indemnification of directors, officers, and others; limitations on corporate distributions in cash or property; the liability of shareholders who receive unlawful distributions; the requirement for annual shareholders' meetings and remedies for the same if not timely held; shareholder's entitlement to cumulative voting; the conditions when a supermajority vote is required; limitations on the sale of assets; limitations on mergers; limitations on conversions; requirements on conversions; the limitations and conditions for reorganization (including the requirement for class voting); dissenter's rights; records and reports; actions by the Attorney General and inspection rights. *See* Cal. Corp. Code §2115(b) (1977 & Supp. 1984).

23. Deborah A. DeMott, *Perspectives on Choice of Law for Corporate Internal Affairs,* 48 Law & Contemp. Probs. 161, 166 (1985).

INTERNAL AFFAIRS REQUIRE UNIFORMITY

In *McDermott,* this Court noted that application of local internal affairs law (here California's section 2115) to a foreign corporation (here Delaware) is "apt to produce inequalities, intolerable confusion, and uncertainty, and intrude into the domain of other states that have a superior claim to regulate the same subject matter . . . " Professor DeMott's review of the differences and conflicts between the Delaware and California corporate statutes with regard to internal affairs, illustrates why it is imperative that only the law of the state of incorporation regulate the relationships among a corporation and its officers, directors, and shareholders. To require a factual determination to decide which of two conflicting state laws governs the internal affairs of a corporation at any point in time, completely contravenes the importance of stability within inter-corporate relationships that the United States Supreme Court recognized in *CTS.* . . .

STATE LAW OF INCORPORATION GOVERNS INTERNAL AFFAIRS

In *McDermott,* this Court held that the "internal affairs doctrine is a major tenet of Delaware corporation law having important federal constitutional underpinnings." Applying Delaware's well-established choice-of-law rule—the internal affairs doctrine—the Court of Chancery recognized that Delaware courts must apply the law of the state of incorporation to issues involving corporate internal affairs, and that disputes concerning a shareholder's right to vote fall squarely within the purview of the internal affairs doctrine.

Examen is a Delaware corporation. The legal issue in this case—whether a preferred shareholder of a Delaware corporation had the right, under the corporation's Certificate of Designations, to a Series A Preferred Stock class vote on a merger—clearly involves the relationship among a corporation and its shareholders. As the United States Supreme Court held in *CTS,* "[n]o principle of corporation law and practice is more firmly established than a *State's authority* to regulate domestic corporations, including the authority to *define the voting rights of shareholders.*"[34]

In *CTS,* the Supreme Court held that the Commerce Clause "prohibits States from regulating subjects that 'are in their nature national, or admit only of one uniform system, or plan of regulation,'" and acknowledged that the internal affairs of a corporation are subjects that require one uniform system of regulation. In *CTS,* the Supreme Court concluded that "[s]o long as each State regulates voting rights *only in the corporations it has created,* each corporation will be subject to the law of only one State." Accordingly, we hold Delaware's well-established choice of law rules and the federal constitution mandated that Examen's internal affairs, and in particular, VantagePoint's voting rights, be

---

34. *CTS Corp. v. Dynamics Corp. of Am.,* 481 U.S. 69, 89, 107 S.Ct. 1637, 95 L.Ed.2d 67 (1987) *(emphasis added). See* Restatement (Second) of Conflict of Laws §304 (1971) (concluding that the law of the incorporating State generally should "determine the right of a shareholder to participate in the administration of the affairs of the corporation").

adjudicated exclusively in accordance with the law of its state of incorporation, in this case, the law of Delaware.

ANY FORUM—INTERNAL AFFAIRS—SAME LAW

VantagePoint acknowledges that the courts of Delaware, as the forum state, may apply Delaware's own substantive choice of law rules. VantagePoint argues, however, that Delaware's "choice" to apply the law of the state of incorporation to internal affairs issues—notwithstanding California's enactment of section 2115—will result in future forum shopping races to the courthouse. VantagePoint submits that, if the California action in these proceedings had been decided first, the California Superior Court would have enjoined the merger until it was factually determined whether section 2115 is applicable. If the statutory prerequisites were found to be factually satisfied, VantagePoint submits that the California Superior Court would have applied the internal affairs law reflected in section 2115, "to the exclusion" of the law of Delaware—the state where Examen is incorporated.

In support of those assertions, VantagePoint relies primarily upon a 1982 decision by the California Court of Appeals in *Wilson v. Louisiana-Pacific Resources, Inc.* [138 Cal.App.3d 216, 187 Cal.Rptr. 852 (1982).] In *Wilson v. Louisiana-Pacific Resources, Inc.*, a panel of the California Court of Appeals held that section 2115 did not violate the federal constitution by applying the California Code's mandatory cumulative voting provision to a Utah corporation that had not provided for cumulative voting but instead had elected the straight voting structure set forth in the Utah corporation statute. The court in *Wilson* did not address the implications of the differences between the Utah and California corporate statutes upon the expectations of parties who chose to incorporate in Utah rather than California. As Professor DeMott points out, "[a]lthough it is possible under the Utah statute for the corporation's charter to be amended by the shareholders and the directors, that mechanical fact does not establish California's right to coerce such an amendment" whenever the factual prerequisites of section 2115 exist.

Wilson was decided before the United States Supreme Court's decision in *CTS* and before this Court's decision in *McDermott.* Ten years after *Wilson,* the California Supreme Court cited with approval this Court's analysis of the internal affairs doctrine in *McDermott,* in particular, our holding that corporate voting rights disputes are governed by the law of the state of incorporation. Two years ago, in *State Farm v. Superior Court,* a different panel of the California Court of Appeals questioned the validity of the holding in *Wilson* following the broad acceptance of the internal affairs doctrine over the two decades after *Wilson* was decided.[46] In *State Farm,* the court cited with approval the United States Supreme Court decision in *CTS Corp. v. Dynamics* and our decision in *McDermott.* In *State Farm,* the court also quoted at length that portion of our decision in *McDermott* relating to the constitutional imperatives of the internal affairs doctrine.

---

46. *State Farm Mut. Auto. Ins. v. Superior Court,* 114 Cal.App.4th 434 (2d Dist.2003).

Since *Wilson* was decided, the United States Supreme Court has recognized the constitutional imperatives of the internal affairs doctrine.[50] In *Draper v. Gardner,* this Court acknowledged the *Wilson* opinion in a footnote[51] and nevertheless permitted the dismissal of a Delaware action in favor of a California action in which a California court would be called upon to decide the internal affairs "demand" issue involving a Delaware corporation. As stated in *Draper,* we had no doubt that after the *Kamen* and *CTS* holdings by the United States Supreme Court, the California courts would "apply Delaware [demand] law [to the internal affairs of a Delaware corporation], given the vitality and constitutional underpinnings of the internal affairs doctrine." We adhere to that view in this case.

CONCLUSION

The judgment of the Court of Chancery is affirmed.

QUESTIONS

1.   What is the public policy premise behind §2115? In other words, why did the California legislature decide to adopt §2115?

2.   How does Delaware law treat the right to a class vote? How is Delaware's default rule on class voting different from California's statutory provision?

3.   How did the Delaware Supreme Court interpret the internal affairs doctrine in deciding this case?

4.   The decision of the Delaware Supreme Court in the *VantagePoint* case prompted one experienced California corporate lawyer to make the following observation:

> California is a huge state in terms of geography, population and the size of its economy. It is no surprise, therefore, that it serves as headquarters to more public companies than any other state. One recent study found that California serves as headquarters to more than 1200 public companies while Delaware is headquarters to only 27.[26] These numbers are reversed when the relative numbers of corporations incorporated in the two states but headquartered elsewhere are compared. In this comparison, Delaware accounts for over 3700 corporations while California accounts for only 10.[27] Clearly, California has to a large extent ceded to Delaware (and other states) the ability to charter and thereby govern the corporations that call California home. Viewed in this context, it is not surprising that California would attempt to regain some measure of authority over

---

50. *E.g., Edgar v. MITE Corp.* 457 U.S. 624, 102 S.Ct. 2629, 73 L.Ed.2d 269 (1982); *CTS Corp. v. Dynamics Corp. of Am.,* 481 U.S. 69, 107 S.Ct. 1637, 95 L.Ed.2d 67 (1987). . . .

51. *Draper v. Gardner,* 625 A.2d 859, 867 n. 10 (Del.1993).

26. Bebchuk & Cohen, "Firms Decisions Where to Incorporate," 46 J. LAW & ECON. 383, 395 (2003).

27. *Id.* California does slightly better with respect to corporations headquartered in this state. It counts 273 corporations incorporated in the state.

these corporations through the enactment of outreach statutes such as Section 2115. These data also illustrate why Delaware has a strong interest in knocking out corporate outreach statutes such as Section 2115. If they are allowed to stand, Delaware's ability to compete is reduced by the possible override of headquarters state legislation. On the other hand, if it is ultimately determined that California cannot apply its laws to foreign corporations, it is likely that the exodus of corporations from California will accelerate.

Keith Paul Bishop, *The War Between the States—Delaware's Supreme Court Ignores California's "Outreach" Statute*, 19 INSIGHTS at 19 (July 2005). The author of this article (who previously served as California's Commissioner of Corporations) sounds a rather ominous tone in referring to the "exodus of corporations from California." Do you agree with the author's observation? If so, is this troubling as a public policy matter?

J. Appraisal Rights

1. Introduction

When the topic of appraisal rights was first introduced earlier in this chapter, we laid out four issues that generally must be considered in analyzing this topic. The first issue, the availability of appraisal rights, has been thoroughly examined as part of our discussion of the various problem sets earlier in this chapter, where we analyzed each of the different types of acquisition structures. In this section, we will examine the other three issues:

- Procedural requirements to perfect dissenters' appraisal rights
- Valuation of dissenters' shares
- Exclusivity of the appraisal remedy

Each of these issues has generated a substantial body of case law and scholarly literature, and so no attempt is made here to canvass these other issues in any sort of exhaustive manner. Rather, the materials that follow sketch out the fundamental nature of the public policy concerns presented by each of these issues regarding the scope of the modern appraisal remedy.

As part of our analysis of the problems earlier in this chapter, we observed a wide disparity as to which transactions involving a fundamental corporate change will trigger the right of appraisal for the dissenting (minority) shareholder. In analyzing these problems, we noted the different public policy considerations that underlie the legislative decision to grant a mandatory right of appraisal without delving into any extended analysis of the scope, purpose, and efficacy of this remedy. Now that we have developed a better sense of the potentially conflicting interests that are implicated whenever a corporation proposes to enter into a transaction resulting in a fundamental change, it is time to turn our attention to the role of appraisal rights as a matter of modern corporate law.

Although this area of law has generated considerable academic commentary, a clear consensus as to the exact purpose to be served by legislatively granting an appraisal remedy for dissenting shares has yet to emerge. The following excerpt offers some perspective on this topic and serves as an excellent overview of the disparate threads of analysis reflected in the various appraisal statutes that we have studied so far in this chapter.

Barry Wertheimer
The Purpose of the Shareholders' Appraisal Remedy
65 Tenn. L. Rev. 661, 662-664 (1998)

At one time, unanimous shareholder approval was required before a corporation could engage in a fundamental corporate transaction. Eventually, corporate statutes were amended to permit such transactions to proceed upon receipt of approval by a majority of shareholders. As a result, individual shareholders no longer had the ability to veto fundamental corporate changes.

There is general agreement that when corporate statutes were amended to allow majority approval of fundamental changes, appraisal rights were granted to shareholders to compensate them for their loss of the power to veto corporate changes. The standard explanation for the existence of the appraisal remedy, therefore, is that it serves as quid pro quo for the loss of shareholders' right to veto fundamental corporate changes.

The other oft-cited justification for the appraisal remedy is that it serves a liquidity rationale. Once shareholders lost the right to veto fundamental changes, it was possible for shareholders to find themselves involuntarily holding an investment in an entity vastly different from the one originally contemplated. For example, if a majority of a corporation's shareholders approved a merger with another entity, a shareholder voting against that transaction would, in the absence of an appraisal remedy, have no choice but to remain a shareholder in the merged entity.[7] The appraisal remedy allows the shareholder a "way out" of an investment involuntarily altered by a fundamental corporation change.

At the time that appraisal rights became part of corporate statutes, merger transactions typically were engaged in by unrelated corporations and structured so that stock in the acquiring corporation was issued to shareholders of the acquired corporation. Cash generally was not used as merger consideration, and the use of a merger or fundamental transaction as a way to eliminate or "cash out" minority shareholders certainly was not contemplated.

---

7. This assumes, of course, that the corporation's shares are not publicly traded. If a market exists for the shares of the corporation, the shareholder voting against the merger could sell its shares in the market, rather than be forced to remain an investor in the newly merged corporation. Thus, the liquidity rationale for the appraisal remedy loses force with respect to publicly traded corporations. As a result, a number of states, relying on the liquidity rationale for the appraisal remedy, have created "market exceptions" to their appraisal statutes. . . . These "market exceptions" provide that no appraisal remedy will be available for shareholders of publicly traded corporations. *E.g. Del. Code Ann. tit. 8, 262(b);* . . .

Financial practices and legal requirements have changed, however, and today mergers often are used solely to eliminate minority shareholders. This change in the use of fundamental corporate transactions requires a change in thinking about the purpose served by the appraisal remedy. The historic liquidity function of the remedy has diminished, and the remedy now serves a minority shareholder protection rationale, primarily in the context of cash out merger transactions. Although commentators are beginning to recognize that changes in the nature of fundamental transactions have implications for the appraisal remedy,[9] courts and legislators have been more slow to do so.

As you read through the materials that follow and examine the rules that have been adopted as part of the modern appraisal statutes, you should consider the purpose of this remedy and the efficacy of appraisal rights in light of the public policy to be served by this modern remedy.

2. Procedural Requirements to Perfect Appraisal Rights

The steps that the dissenting shareholder generally must follow under the terms of the appraisal statutes of most states were described earlier in this chapter (*see supra,* at p. 61-62), albeit in a general manner. It bears emphasizing that the law of the particular state must be consulted because local statutes will often modify the nature and timing of these procedural requirements, if only slightly. Compliance with the specific requirements of local statutes is of vital importance, as most courts construe appraisal statutes very strictly. Accordingly, any failure to comply with the requirements of the relevant appraisal statute will usually deprive the dissenting shareholders of their appraisal remedy.

In considering the procedural requirements that dissenting shareholders must satisfy in order to obtain cash payment for their shares, a few observations are in order. There are several affirmative steps that the dissenting shareholder must satisfy in a timely manner. First, the dissenting shareholder must file—*before* the date of the shareholder vote on the proposed transaction—the shareholder's notice of intent to dissent. Later, and separately, the dissenting shareholder must file the shareholder's written demand for payment, which is to be filed *after* the transaction has received the requisite approval of the shareholders. Modern case law makes clear that these detailed requirements as to the content and timing of these filing obligations must be followed carefully;

---

9. Professor Thomson's excellent article in the *Georgetown Law Journal* is the best example. [*See* Robert B. Thompson, *Exit, Liquidity, and Majority Rule: Appraisal's Role in Corporate Law,* 84 Geo. L.J. 1, 3-4, 9-11 (1995); *see also* Daniel R. Fischel, *The Appraisal Remedy in Corporate Law,* 1983 Am. B. Found. Res. J. 875, 877-884; Hideki Kanda & Saul Levmore, *The Appraisal Remedy and the Goals of Corporate Law,* 32 UCLA L. Rev. 429 (1985); Mary Siegel, *Back to the Future: Appraisal Rights in the Twenty-First Century,* 32 Harv. J. on Legis. 79, 93-111 (1995); Melvin Eisenberg, THE STRUCTURE OF THE CORPORATION: A LEGAL ANALYSIS, 77-79 (1976); Bayless Manning, *The Shareholder's Appraisal Remedy: An Essay for Frank Coker,* 72 Yale L.J. 223, 246 (1962).]

the dissenting shareholder who fails to do so runs the risk of losing this remedy. *Query:* Why does the law impose these filing obligations on the dissenting shareholder? What purpose is served by imposing a filing obligation *before* the date of the shareholder vote?

Perhaps the best way to appreciate the complexity of modern appraisal procedures is to review the description of the process as contained in a recent proxy filing. Below is an excerpt from the proxy statement of Motorola Mobility Holdings, Inc., a publicly traded Delaware corporation, seeking shareholder approval to sell its business to Google, Inc., another well-known Delaware corporation headquartered in Silicon Valley, California. In order to understand the basic terms of the transaction and the process employed for obtaining shareholder approval of this transaction as required by Delaware law, the complete text of the "Notice of Special Meeting of Stockholders" that accompanied Motorola Mobility's proxy statement is also reproduced below. This Notice refers to "Appraisal Rights," which is a particular section of the company's proxy statement; the full text of this section of Motorola Mobility's proxy statement is also reproduced below.

By way of general background, Motorola Inc. completed a spin-off of its mobile devices and home businesses in January 2011.* Following the spin-off, the mobile device business operated under the new name of Motorola Mobility and Motorola, the parent company, rebranded itself as Motorola Solutions. Grant Goss, *Motorola Completes Spinoff from Parent Company*, COMPUTER WORLD (Jan. 4, 2011), *available at* http://www.computerworld.com/s/article/9203142/Motorola_Mobility_completes_spinoff_from_parent_ company. Following the spinoff, Motorola Mobility, which was then listed for trading on the NYSE, began using its approximately 20,000 employees and 24,500 patents to develop the next generation of smartphones, including the Droid. *Id.* In addition, Dr. Sanjay Jha was appointed to serve as CEO of Motorola Mobility. By contrast, Motorola Solutions began to focus on "providing next-generation communication solutions to its government, public safety, and enterprise customers." *Motorola's Separation/Reverse Stock Split, Frequently Asked Questions*, Motorola Solutions (Dec. 27, 2010), *available at* http://files.sharcholder.com/downloads/ABEA-2FO3VV/0x0x424776/31F725Bf-E0BD-45B3-8F89-84E564FC3542/11-30-2010_-_Motorola_Separation_Reverse_Stock_Split_FAQs.pdf.

On August 15, 2011, seven months after the spinoff became effective, Google announced its intention to acquire all of the outstanding shares of Motorola Mobility for $40 per share, in cash, which valued the deal at $12.5 billion. Google's decision to acquire Motorola Mobility, using only its cash reserves, stemmed from Motorola Mobility's large cadre of patents and came on the heels of the company's failed efforts to acquire Nortel Networks. The acquisition price, a victory for Motorola Mobility shareholders, was due in large part to the financial advisory services of Frank Quattrone, a Silicon Valley investment banker who had established himself as "*the* advisor" to Silicon Valley's

---

*The spin-off of Motorola Mobility followed a long period of urging by the activist investor, Carl Icahn. We will describe in more detail the role of activist investors (including a review of the Schedule 13D filing that Carl Icahn made to reflect his ownership stake in Motorola) as part of our discussion in Chapter 6 of the scope of the requirements imposed by the Williams Act.

notable technology firms. In particular, Quattrone has been credited with convincing Google to substantially increase its offer from the initial $20 to $30 range. Clearly ecstatic over the high offer price, 99 percent of the shareholders who voted at Motorola Mobility's special meeting, which comprised 74 percent of the company's outstanding common stock, voted to approve the transaction. The deal, which makes Google a viable competitor in the smartphone market, cleared regulatory approval in various countries between February and May 2012, and finally closed on May 22, 2012.

As you read through this excerpt from Motorola Mobility's proxy statement, consider the time and expense involved on the part of the minority shareholder who should decide to assert his/her/its right of appraisal. Although this remedy is available to the Motorola Mobility shareholder objecting to the transaction, consider also the scope of protection this remedy offers to the minority shareholder as a practical matter, particularly in light of the costs imposed on any Motorola Mobility shareholder who asserts this right of appraisal.

Motorola Mobility Holdings, Inc.
600 N. U.S. Highway 45
Libertyville, Il 60048
October 14, 2011

NOTICE OF SPECIAL MEETING OF STOCKHOLDERS

To Our Stockholders:

A Special Meeting of stockholders of Motorola Mobility Holdings, Inc., a Delaware corporation (which we refer to as "Motorola Mobility"), will be held on Thursday, November 17, 2011, starting at 10:00 A.M., local time, at the Hyatt Regency, La Jolla at Aventine, located at 3777 La Jolla Village Drive, San Diego, California 92122 for the following purposes:

1. to consider and vote on a proposal to adopt the Agreement and Plan of Merger, dated as of August 15, 2011, by and among Google Inc., a Delaware corporation, RB98 Inc., a Delaware corporation and a wholly owned subsidiary of Google Inc., and Motorola Mobility, as it may be amended from time to time, pursuant to which RB98 Inc. will merge with and into Motorola Mobility;

2. to consider and vote on a proposal to adjourn the Special Meeting to a later date or time, if necessary or appropriate, to solicit additional proxies in the event there are insufficient votes at the time of such adjournment to adopt the merger agreement; and

3. to consider and vote, on an advisory (non-binding) basis, on a proposal to approve the compensation that may be paid or become payable to Motorola Mobility's named executive officers in connection with the merger, including the agreements and understandings pursuant to which such compensation may be paid or become payable.[1]

---

1. [By the author] You will recall from Chapter 1 (see pp. 38-39) that Congress enacted the Dodd-Frank Act in 2010. Among the many reforms introduced by this legislation,

The Motorola Mobility Board of Directors has set the close of business on October 11, 2011 as the record date for the purpose of determining the stockholders who are entitled to receive notice of, and to vote at, the Special Meeting and at any adjournment or postponement thereof. Only stockholders of record at the close of business on the record date are entitled to notice of and to vote at the Special Meeting and at any adjournment or postponement thereof. Each stockholder is entitled to one vote for each share of Motorola Mobility common stock held by such stockholder on the record date. Please vote in one of the following ways:

- visit the website shown on your proxy card to vote via the Internet;
- use the toll-free telephone number listed on your proxy card;
- mark, sign, date and return the enclosed proxy card using the postage-paid envelope provided; or
- in person at the Special Meeting.

YOUR VOTE IS VERY IMPORTANT TO THE COMPLETION OF THE MERGER. Regardless of whether you plan to attend the Special Meeting in person, we request that you complete, sign, date and return the enclosed proxy or submit your proxy via Internet or by telephone prior to the Special Meeting to ensure that your shares will be represented at the Special Meeting. If you have Internet access, we encourage you to submit your proxy via the Internet. Properly executed proxy cards with no instructions indicated on the proxy card will be voted "FOR" the adoption of the merger agreement, "FOR" the adjournment of the Special Meeting, if necessary or appropriate, to solicit additional proxies and "FOR" the approval, on an advisory (non-binding) basis, of the compensation that may be paid or become payable to Motorola Mobility's named executive officers in connection with the merger, including the agreements and understandings pursuant to which such compensation may be paid or become payable. If you are a record holder of Motorola Mobility common stock and you attend the Special Meeting, you may revoke your proxy and vote in person if you wish, even if you have previously returned your proxy card or submitted your proxy via Internet or by telephone.

Under Delaware law, Motorola Mobility stockholders who do not vote in favor of the proposal to adopt the merger agreement will have the right to seek appraisal of the fair value of their shares as determined by the Delaware

---

Congress addressed the topic of executive compensation. As part of Dodd-Frank's provisions, Congress mandated what has come to be known as the "say-on-pay" vote, a topic to be addressed in more detail in Chapter 4 as part of our discussion of various aspects of the federal securities laws that relate to M&A transactions. At this point, it bears mentioning that Motorola Mobility was required by the Dodd-Frank Act to solicit shareholder approval of compensation to be paid to the company's senior executives (including its CEO, Dr. Sanjay Jha) as part of Google's proposed acquisition of Motorola Mobility. More specifically, Section 951 of Dodd-Frank (and the SEC rules implementing these provisions of the Dodd-Frank Act) mandate an advisory vote of Motorola Mobility's shareholders with respect to any severance payments (i.e., "golden parachute" compensation) that would be triggered by the acquisition and which payment had not previously been approved by an appropriate "say-on-pay" vote of Motorola Mobility's shareholders.

Court of Chancery if the merger is completed, but only if they submit a written demand for such an appraisal prior to the vote on the proposal to adopt the merger agreement and comply with the other Delaware law procedures explained in the [section titled "Appraisal Rights," which is part of the] accompanying proxy statement.

THE MOTOROLA MOBILITY BOARD OF DIRECTORS UNANIMOUSLY RECOMMENDS THAT YOU VOTE "FOR" THE ADOPTION OF THE MERGER AGREEMENT.

> By order of the Motorola Mobility Board of Directors,
> Carol H. Forsyte
> Secretary

SPECIAL MEETING OF STOCKHOLDERS TO BE HELD ON NOVEMBER 17, 2011

October 14, 2011

Dear Motorola Mobility Holdings, Inc. Stockholders:

You are cordially invited to attend a Special Meeting of Motorola Mobility Holdings, Inc. (which we refer to as "Motorola Mobility") stockholders to be held on Thursday, November 17, 2011, starting at 10:00 a.m., local time, at the Hyatt Regency La Jolla at Aventine, located at 3777 La Jolla Village Drive, San Diego, California 92122.

At the Special Meeting, you will be asked to consider and vote upon a proposal to adopt the merger agreement under which Motorola Mobility would be acquired by Google Inc., and related matters. We entered into this merger agreement on August 15, 2011. If the merger agreement is adopted and the merger is completed, Motorola Mobility will become a wholly owned subsidiary of Google and you, as a holder of Motorola Mobility common stock, will be entitled to receive $40.00 in cash, without interest and less any applicable tax withholdings, for each share of Motorola Mobility common stock owned by you at the consummation of the merger.

After careful consideration, the Motorola Mobility Board of Directors has unanimously determined that the merger and the other transactions contemplated by the merger agreement are advisable and fair to, and in the best interests of, Motorola Mobility stockholders and unanimously recommends that you vote "FOR" the adoption of the merger agreement, "FOR" the adjournment of the Special Meeting, if necessary or appropriate, to solicit additional proxies and "FOR" the approval, on an advisory (non-binding) basis, of the compensation that may be paid or become payable to Motorola Mobility's named executive officers in connection with the merger, including the agreements and understandings pursuant to which such compensation may be paid or become payable.

YOUR VOTE IS VERY IMPORTANT TO THE COMPLETION OF THE MERGER. We cannot consummate the merger unless the merger agreement is approved by at least a majority of the outstanding shares of our common stock. **Therefore, the failure of any Motorola Mobility stockholder to vote and**

abstentions from voting will have the same effect as a vote by that Motorola Mobility stockholder "AGAINST" the adoption of the merger agreement.

Only stockholders of record at the close of business on October 11, 2011 are entitled to notice of and to vote at the special meeting and at any adjournment or postponement thereof.

The attached proxy statement provides you with detailed information about the Special Meeting, the merger agreement and the merger. A copy of the merger agreement is attached as Annex A to this document.[2] We encourage you to read the attached proxy statement and the merger agreement carefully and in their entirety. You may also obtain more information about Motorola Mobility from documents we have filed with the U.S. Securities and Exchange Commission.

Thank you in advance for your continued support and your consideration of this matter.

Sincerely,

Sanjay K. Jha
Chairman and CEO
Motorola Mobility Holdings, Inc.

Neither the Securities and Exchange Commission nor any state securities regulatory agency has approved or disapproved the merger, passed upon the merits or fairness of the merger or passed upon the adequacy or accuracy of the disclosure in this document. Any representation to the contrary is a criminal offense.

This proxy statement is dated October 14, 2011 and is first being mailed to Motorola Mobility stockholders on or about that date.

APPRAISAL RIGHTS

***

Under the DGCL, you have the right to dissent from the merger and to receive payment in cash for the "fair value" of your shares of Motorola Mobil-

---

2. [By the author] The proxy statement (soliciting shareholder approval of this acquisition transaction) and Annex A thereto (the merger agreement) have been omitted. As a reporting company under the 1934 Act, Motorola Mobility was required to prepare a proxy statement in compliance with the federal proxy rules promulgated by the SEC. In Chapter 4, we will describe the scope of disclosure that Motorola Mobility was required to include in this proxy statement soliciting shareholder approval of the company's proposed transaction with Google. In addition, we will consider what information the Motorola Mobility shareholders would need in order to make an informed decision to approve the sale of the company's business to Google on the terms negotiated and agreed to by the boards of Motorola Mobility and Google. In connection with our discussion of the adequacy of the modern appraisal remedy, it bears emphasizing that the SEC's proxy disclosure rules specifically call for disclosure of certain items regarding the availability and procedural requirements of any appraisal rights granted by state law. *See* Regulation M-A, Item 1004.

ity common stock as determined by the Delaware Court of Chancery, together with interest, if any, as determined by the court, but exclusive of any element of value arising from the accomplishment or expectation of the merger, in lieu of the consideration you would otherwise be entitled to pursuant to the merger agreement. These rights are known as appraisal rights. Motorola Mobility stockholders electing to exercise appraisal rights must comply with the provisions of Section 262 of the DGCL in order to perfect their rights. We will require strict compliance with the statutory procedures.

The following is intended as a brief summary of the material provisions of the Delaware statutory procedures required to be followed properly and in a timely manner by a Motorola Mobility stockholder in order to dissent from the merger and perfect appraisal rights.

This summary, however, is not a complete statement of all applicable requirements and is qualified in its entirety by reference to Section 262 of the DGCL, the full text of which appears in Annex D to this proxy statement.[3] Failure to precisely follow any of the statutory procedures set forth in Section 262 of the DGCL may result in a termination or waiver of your appraisal rights. All references in Section 262 of the DGCL and in this summary to a "stockholder" are to the record holder of shares of Motorola Mobility common stock immediately prior to the effective time of the merger as to which appraisal rights are asserted, unless otherwise indicated.

Section 262 of the DGCL requires that stockholders for whom appraisal rights are available be notified not less than 20 days before the stockholders' meeting where the merger will be voted that appraisal rights will be available. A copy of Section 262 of the DGCL must be included with such notice. This proxy statement constitutes our notice to Motorola Mobility stockholders of the availability of appraisal rights in connection with the merger in compliance with the requirements of Section 262 of the DGCL. If you wish to consider exercising your appraisal rights, you should carefully review the text of Section 262 of the DGCL contained in Annex D to this proxy statement, since failure to timely and properly comply with the requirements of Section 262 of the DGCL will result in the loss of your appraisal rights under the DGCL.

If you elect to demand appraisal of your shares, you must satisfy each of the following conditions:

- You must deliver to us a written demand for appraisal of your shares before the vote with respect to the merger agreement is taken. This written demand for appraisal must be in addition to and separate from any proxy or vote abstaining from or voting against the adoption of the merger agreement. Voting against or failing to vote for the adoption of the merger agreement by itself does not constitute a demand for appraisal within the meaning of Section 262 of the DGCL.
- You must not vote in favor of, or consent in writing to, the adoption of the merger agreement. A vote in favor of the adoption of the merger agreement, by proxy, over the Internet, by telephone or in person, will con-

---

3. [By the author] Annex D (containing the full text of Delaware Section 262) has been omitted.

stitute a waiver of your appraisal rights in respect of the shares so voted and will nullify any previously filed written demands for appraisal. A proxy which does not contain voting instructions will, unless revoked, be voted in favor of the adoption of the merger agreement. Therefore, a Motorola Mobility stockholder who votes by proxy and who wishes to exercise and perfect appraisal rights must vote against the merger agreement and the merger or abstain from voting on the merger agreement and the merger.

- You must continue to hold your shares of Motorola Mobility common stock through the effective date of the merger. Therefore, a Motorola Mobility stockholder who is the record holder of shares of Motorola Mobility common stock on the date the written demand for appraisal is made but who thereafter transfers the shares prior to the effective date of the merger will lose any right to appraisal with respect to such shares.

If you fail to comply with any of these conditions and the merger is completed, you will be entitled to receive the per share merger consideration, but you will have no appraisal rights with respect to your shares of Motorola Mobility common stock.

All demands for appraisal should be addressed to Motorola Mobility, 600 N. U.S. Highway 45, Libertyville, Illinois 60048, Attn: Secretary [which is the address of the company's principal executive offices], and must be delivered before the vote on the merger agreement is taken at the Special Meeting and should be executed by, or on behalf of, the record holder of the shares of Motorola Mobility common stock. The demand must reasonably inform us of the identity of the Motorola Mobility stockholder and the intention of the Motorola Mobility stockholder to demand appraisal of his, her, or its shares of Motorola Mobility common stock.

To be effective, a demand for appraisal by a Motorola Mobility stockholder must be made by, or in the name of, such registered Motorola Mobility stockholder, fully and correctly, as the Motorola Mobility stockholder's name appears on his, her or its stock certificate(s). Beneficial owners [such as Motorola Mobility shareholders who hold their shares in "street name"] and thus are not the record owner of these shares of Motorola Mobility common stock . . . may not directly make appraisal demands to us. The beneficial holder must, in such cases, have the registered owner, such as a bank, broker or other nominee, submit the required demand in respect of those shares. . . .

If you hold your shares of Motorola Mobility common stock in an account with a bank, broker, or other nominee and you wish to exercise appraisal rights, you are urged to consult with your bank, broker, or the other nominee to determine the appropriate procedures for the making of a demand for appraisal.

Within ten days after the effective time of the merger, the surviving corporation must give written notice that the merger has become effective to each Motorola Mobility stockholder who has properly filed a written demand for appraisal and who did not vote in favor of the adoption of the merger agreement. At any time within 60 days after the effective time of the merger, any Motorola Mobility stockholder who has demanded an appraisal, and who has not commenced an appraisal proceeding or joined that proceeding as a named party, will have the right to withdraw the demand and to accept the cash payment specified by the merger agreement for his, her, or its shares of common stock; after this period, the Motorola Mobility stockholder may withdraw such demand for appraisal only with the written consent of the surviving corporation. Within 120 days after the effective date of the merger, any Motorola Mobility stockholder who has complied with Section 262 of the DGCL will, upon written request to the surviving corporation, be entitled to receive a written statement setting forth the aggregate number of shares not voted in favor of the adoption of the merger agreement and with respect to which demands for appraisal rights have been received and the aggregate number of holders of such shares. . . . Within 120 days after the effective time of the merger, but not thereafter, either the surviving corporation or any Motorola Mobility stockholder who has complied with the requirements of Section 262 of the DGCL and who is otherwise entitled to appraisal rights may commence an appraisal proceeding by filing a petition in the Delaware Court of Chancery demanding a determination of the fair value of the shares of Motorola Mobility common stock held by such stockholder. . . . Upon the filing of the petition by a Motorola Mobility stockholder, service of a copy of such petition must be made upon Motorola Mobility, as the surviving corporation. The surviving corporation has no obligation to file such a petition if there are dissenting Motorola Mobility stockholders. Accordingly, the failure of a Motorola Mobility stockholder to file such a petition within the period specified could nullify the Motorola Mobility stockholder's previously written demand for appraisal. There is no present intent on the part of Motorola Mobility to file an appraisal petition, and Motorola Mobility stockholders seeking to exercise appraisal rights should not assume that Motorola Mobility will file such a petition or that Motorola Mobility will initiate any negotiations with respect to the fair value of such shares. Accordingly, Motorola Mobility stockholders who desire to have their shares appraised should initiate any petitions necessary for the perfection of their appraisal rights within the time periods and in the manner prescribed in Section 262 of the DGCL.

If a petition for appraisal is timely filed by a Motorola Mobility stockholder and a copy of the petition is delivered to the surviving corporation, the surviving corporation will then be obligated, within 20 days after receiving service of a copy of the petition, to file with the Delaware Register in Chancery with a duly verified list containing the names and addresses of all Motorola Mobility stockholders who have demanded an appraisal of their shares and with whom agreements as to the value of their shares have not been reached by the surviving corporation. After notice is made to dissenting Motorola Mobility stockholders who demanded appraisal of their shares as required by the Delaware Court of Chancery, the Delaware Court of Chancery is empowered to conduct a hearing upon the petition to determine those Motorola Mobility stockholders who have complied with Section 262 of the DGCL and who have become entitled to the appraisal rights thereunder. The Delaware Court of Chancery may require Motorola Mobility stockholders who have demanded appraisal of their shares to submit their stock certificates to the Register in Chancery for notation thereon of the pendency of the appraisal proceedings; and if any Motorola Mobility stockholder fails to comply with that direction, the Delaware Court of Chancery may dismiss the proceedings as to that Motorola Mobility stockholder.

After the Delaware Court of Chancery determines which Motorola Mobility stockholders are entitled to appraisal of their shares of Motorola Mobility common stock, the appraisal proceeding will be conducted in accordance with the rules of the Delaware Court of Chancery, including any rules specifically governing appraisal proceedings. Through such proceeding, the Delaware Court of Chancery will appraise the shares of Motorola Mobility common stock, determining the fair value of the shares exclusive of any element of value arising from the accomplishment or expectation of the merger, together with interest, if any, to be paid upon the amount determined to be the fair value.[4] Unless the Delaware Court of Chancery in its discretion determines otherwise for good cause shown, interest from the effective date of the merger through the date of payment of the judgment will be compounded quarterly and will accrue at 5% over the Federal Reserve discount rate (including any surcharge) as established from time to time during the period between the effective date of the merger and the date of payment of the judgment. When the value is determined, the Delaware Court of Chancery will direct the payment of such value, with interest thereon accrued during the pendency of the proceeding, if the Delaware Court of Chancery so determines, to the Motorola Mobility stockholders entitled to receive the same, upon surrender by such holders of the certificates representing those shares.

In determining fair value, and, if applicable, interest, the Delaware Court of Chancery is required to take into account all relevant factors. . . .

***

You should be aware that the fair value of your shares of Motorola Mobility common stock as determined under Section 262 of the DGCL could be more than, the same as, or less than the value that you are entitled to receive under the terms of the merger agreement if you did not seek appraisal of your shares. Investment banking opinions as to the fairness from a financial point of view of the per share merger consideration payable in the merger are not necessarily opinions as to fair value under Section 262 of the DGCL.

Costs of the appraisal proceeding may be imposed upon the surviving corporation and the Motorola Mobility stockholders participating in the appraisal proceeding by the Delaware Court of Chancery as the Court deems equitable in the circumstances. Upon the application of a Motorola Mobility stockholder, the Delaware Court of Chancery may order all or a portion of the expenses incurred by any Motorola Mobility stockholder in connection with the appraisal proceeding, including, without limitation, reasonable attorneys' fees and the fees and expenses of experts, to be charged pro rata against the value of all shares entitled to appraisal. Any Motorola Mobility stockholder who had demanded appraisal rights will not, after the effective time of the merger, be entitled to vote shares subject to that demand for any purpose or to receive payments of dividends or any other distribution with respect to those shares, other than with respect to payment as of a record date prior to the effective time of

---

4. [By the author] Determining the "fair value" of the dissenter's shares will be the focus of a judiciary supervised appraisal proceeding in the event that the dissenting shareholder and the company cannot reach agreement as to fair value. Cases and other materials later in this section explore the difficult factual issues that are inherent in determining what is "fair value," particularly in light of the statutory mandate to ignore "any element of value arising from the accomplishment or expectation of the proposed merger." See *infra* at pp. 165-207.

the merger; however, if no petition for appraisal is filed within 120 days after the effective time of the merger, or if the Motorola Mobility stockholder delivers a written withdrawal of his or her demand for appraisal and an acceptance of the terms of the merger within 60 days after the effective time of the merger, then the right of that Motorola Mobility stockholder to appraisal will cease and that Motorola Mobility stockholder will be entitled to receive the cash payment for shares of his, her or its shares of Motorola Mobility common stock pursuant to the merger agreement.[5] No appraisal proceeding in the Delaware Court of Chancery will be dismissed as to any Motorola Mobility stockholder without the prior approval of the Court, and such approval may be conditioned upon such terms as the Delaware Court of Chancery deems just; provided, however, that any Motorola Mobility stockholder who has not commenced an appraisal proceeding or joined that proceeding as a named party will maintain the right to withdraw its demand for appraisal and to accept the cash that such holder would have received pursuant to the merger agreement within 60 days after the effective date of the merger.

In view of the complexity of Section 262 of the DGCL, Motorola Mobility stockholders who may wish to dissent from the merger and pursue appraisal rights should consult their legal advisors.

QUESTIONS

1. In view of the disclosure contained in Motorola Mobility's proxy statement, do you think lay investors holding shares of Motorola Mobility common stock could competently decide on their own whether to exercise their right of appraisal?

2. Why does the law require shareholders to follow these procedures? What are the competing interests to be balanced in designing the procedures for perfecting the statutorily mandated appraisal remedy? How do the recent reforms adopted by the MBCA address these competing interests? *See generally* MBCA Chapter 13, Subchapter B (Procedure for Exercise of Appraisal Rights). More specifically, consider the provisions of MBCA §13.24 and the following commentary to that section:

> Section 13.24 changes the relative balance [of power] between the corporation and [those] shareholders demanding an appraisal by requiring the corporation to pay in cash within 30 days after the required form [of demand for payment has been submitted by the dissenting shareholder pursuant to MBCA §§13.22 and 13.23] is due the corporation's estimate of the fair value of the stock plus interest. . . . [Consequently, the dissenting shareholders should have] immediate use of such money. A difference of opinion over the total amount to be paid should not delay payment of the amount that is undisputed. Thus, the corporation must pay its estimate of fair value, plus interest from the effective date of the corporate action, without waiting for the conclusion of the appraisal proceeding.

---

5. [By the author] Generally speaking, the failure to perfect as the right of appraisal will result in the dissenting shares being converted into the right to receive the consideration set forth under the terms of the merger agreement.

Since the former shareholder must decide whether or not to accept the payment in full satisfaction, the corporation must at this time furnish the former shareholder with the information specified in section 13.24(b), with a reminder of the former shareholder's further rights and liabilities [including the right to contest the corporation's estimate of fair value in a judicially supervised appraisal proceeding]. Even though the specified information was previously furnished under section 13.20(d) at the time notice of appraisal rights was given, it must still be furnished under section 13.24(b) at the time of payment.

With respect to the *costs* incurred in bringing an appraisal action, consider the provisions of MBCA §13.31 and the following commentary to that section:

Section 13.31(a) provides a general rule that the court costs of the appraisal proceeding should be assessed against the corporation. Nevertheless, the court is authorized to assess these court costs, in whole or in part, against all or some of the shareholders demanding appraisal if it concludes they acted arbitrarily, vexatiously, or not in good faith regarding the rights provided by this chapter. Under section 13.31(b), the court may assess expenses against the corporation or against all or some of the shareholders demanding appraisal for the reasons stated in this subsection. Under section 13.31(c), if the corporation is not required to pay the expenses incurred by any shareholder demanding appraisal, the court may require all shareholders who benefitted to share in the payment of such expenses. The purpose of all these grants of discretion with respect to expenses is to increase the incentives of both sides to proceed in good faith under this chapter to attempt to resolve their disagreement without the need of a formal judicial appraisal of the value of shares.

3. As a general proposition, management usually tries to structure the transaction to avoid appraisal rights altogether. Why such hostility to the appraisal remedy? Alternatively, management may condition the company's obligation to close on the M&A transaction on receiving no more than a *de minimis* number of demands, typically expressed as a percentage of the company's outstanding shares (e.g., the company's obligation to close is conditioned on no more than 3 percent of the company's outstanding shares exercising the statutory right to an appraisal).

3. Determining Fair Value in an Appraisal Proceeding

In its seminal decision in *Weinberger v. UOP, Inc.*, the Delaware Supreme Court touches on two important issues in considering the modern appraisal remedy: *valuation* of dissenters' shares and the *exclusivity* of the appraisal remedy. Rather than disrupt the flow of the court's analysis by trying to parse the opinion to separate out the court's discussion of these two related issues, the text of this landmark opinion dealing with these two issues is set forth below. In the last section of this chapter, we will consider whether the appraisal proceeding has, in fact, turned out to be the *exclusive remedy* available to the dissenting shareholder as part of our analysis of the Delaware Supreme Court's subsequent decision in *Rabkin v. Philip A. Hunt Chemical Corp.* In the materials that immediately follow the *Weinberger* opinion, we will consider the *valuation* issues that arise from the court's holding.

Weinberger v. UOP, Inc.
457 A.2d 701 (Del. 1983)

MOORE, Justice:

This post-trial appeal was reheard en banc from a decision of the Court of Chancery. It was brought by the class action plaintiff below, a former shareholder of UOP, Inc., who challenged the elimination of UOP's minority shareholders by a cash-out merger between UOP and its majority owner, The Signal Companies, Inc. Originally, the defendants in this action were Signal, UOP, certain officers and directors of those companies, and UOP's investment banker, Lehman Brothers Kuhn Loeb, Inc. The present Chancellor held that the terms of the merger were fair to the plaintiff and the other minority shareholders of UOP. Accordingly, he entered judgment in favor of the defendants.

Numerous points were raised by the parties, but we address only the following questions presented by the trial court's opinion:

1. The plaintiff's duty to plead sufficient facts demonstrating the unfairness of the challenged merger;
2. The burden of proof upon the parties where the merger has been approved by the purportedly informed vote of a majority of the minority shareholders;
3. The fairness of the merger in terms of adequacy of the defendants' disclosures to the minority shareholders;
4. The fairness of the merger in terms of adequacy of the price paid for the minority shares and the remedy appropriate to that issue; . . .

. . . In ruling for the defendants, the Chancellor re-stated his earlier conclusion that the plaintiff in a suit challenging a cash-out merger must allege specific acts of fraud, misrepresentation, or other items of misconduct to demonstrate the unfairness of the merger terms to the minority. We approve this rule and affirm it.

The Chancellor also held that even though the ultimate burden of proof is on the majority shareholder to show by a preponderance of the evidence that the transaction is fair, it is first the burden of the plaintiff attacking the merger to demonstrate some basis for invoking the fairness obligation. We agree with that principle. However, where corporate action has been approved by an informed vote of a majority of the minority shareholders, we conclude that the burden entirely shifts to the plaintiff to show that the transaction was unfair to the minority. But in all this, the burden clearly remains on those relying on the vote to show that they completely disclosed all material facts relevant to the transaction

Here, the record does not support a conclusion that the minority stockholder vote was an informed one. Material information, necessary to acquaint those shareholders with the bargaining positions of Signal and UOP, was withheld under circumstances amounting to a breach of fiduciary duty. We therefore conclude that this merger does not meet the test of fairness, at least as we address that concept, and no burden thus shifted to the plaintiff by reason of the minority shareholder vote. Accordingly, we reverse and remand for further proceedings consistent herewith.

In considering the nature of the remedy available under our law to minority shareholders in a cash-out merger, we believe that it is, and hereafter should be, an appraisal under 8 Del. C. §262 as hereinafter construed. . . . But to give full effect to section 262 within the framework of the General Corporation Law we adopt a more liberal, less rigid and stylized, approach to the valuation process than has heretofore been permitted by our courts. While the present state of these proceedings does not admit the plaintiff to the appraisal remedy per se, the practical effect of the remedy we do grant him will be co-extensive with the liberalized valuation and appraisal methods we herein approve for cases coming after this decision. . . .

Our treatment of these matters has necessarily led us to a reconsideration of the business purpose rule announced in the trilogy of *Singer v. Magnavox Co.*, [380 A.2d 969 (Del 1977)]; *Tanzer v. International General Industries, Inc.*, Del.Supr., 379 A.2d 1121 (1977); and *Roland International Corp. v. Najjar*, Del. Supr., 407 A.2d 1032 (1979). For the reasons hereafter set forth we consider that the business purpose requirement of these cases is no longer the law of Delaware.

I

The facts found by the trial court, pertinent to the issues before us, are supported by the record, and we draw from them as set out in the Chancellor's opinion.

Signal is a diversified, technically based company operating through various subsidiaries. Its stock is publicly traded on the New York, Philadelphia and Pacific Stock Exchanges. UOP, formerly known as Universal Oil Products Company, was a diversified industrial company engaged in various lines of business, including petroleum and petro-chemical services and related products, construction, fabricated metal products, transportation equipment products, chemicals and plastics, and other products and services including land development, lumber products and waste disposal. Its stock was publicly held and listed on the New York Stock Exchange.

In 1974 Signal sold one of its wholly-owned subsidiaries for $420,000,000 in cash. *See Gimbel v. Signal Companies, Inc.*, Del. Ch., 316 A.2d 599, *aff'd*, Del. Supr., 316 A.2d 619 (1974).* While looking to invest this cash surplus, Signal became interested in UOP as a possible acquisition. Friendly negotiations ensued, and Signal proposed to acquire a controlling interest in UOP at a price of $19 per share. UOP's representatives sought $25 per share. In the arm's length bargaining that followed, an understanding was reached whereby Signal agreed to purchase from UOP 1,500,000 shares of UOP's authorized but unissued stock at $21 per share.

This purchase was contingent upon Signal making a successful cash tender offer for 4,300,000 publicly held shares of UOP, also at a price of $21 per share. This combined method of acquisition permitted Signal to acquire 5,800,000 shares of stock, representing 50.5% of UOP's outstanding shares. The UOP

---

*[By the author] The text of this opinion appears at p. 78.

board of directors advised the company's shareholders that it had no objection to Signal's tender offer at that price. Immediately before the announcement of the tender offer, UOP's common stock had been trading on the New York Stock Exchange at a fraction under $14 per share.

The negotiations between Signal and UOP occurred during April 1975, and the resulting tender offer was greatly oversubscribed. However, Signal limited its total purchase of the tendered shares so that, when coupled with the stock bought from UOP, it had achieved its goal of becoming a 50.5% shareholder of UOP.

Although UOP's board consisted of thirteen directors, Signal nominated and elected only six. Of these, five were either directors or employees of Signal. The sixth, a partner in the banking firm of Lazard Freres & Co., had been one of Signal's representatives in the negotiations and bargaining with UOP concerning the tender offer and purchase price of the UOP shares.

However, the president and chief executive officer of UOP retired during 1975, and Signal caused him to be replaced by James V. Crawford, a long-time employee and senior executive vice president of one of Signal's wholly-owned subsidiaries. Crawford succeeded his predecessor on UOP's board of directors and also was made a director of Signal.

By the end of 1977 Signal basically was unsuccessful in finding other suitable investment candidates for its excess cash, and by February 1978 considered that it had no other realistic acquisitions available to it on a friendly basis. Once again its attention turned to UOP.

The trial court found that at the instigation of certain Signal management personnel, including William W. Walkup, its board chairman, and Forrest N. Shumway, its president, a feasibility study was made concerning the possible acquisition of the balance of UOP's outstanding shares. This study was performed by two Signal officers, Charles S. Arledge, vice president (director of planning), and Andrew J. Chitiea, senior vice president (chief financial officer). Messrs. Walkup, Shumway, Arledge, and Chitiea were all directors of UOP in addition to their membership on the Signal board.

Arledge and Chitiea concluded that it would be a good investment for Signal to acquire the remaining 49.5% of UOP shares at any price up to $24 each. Their report was discussed between Walkup and Shumway who, along with Arledge, Chitiea and Brewster L. Arms, internal counsel for Signal, constituted Signal's senior management. In particular, they talked about the proper price to be paid if the acquisition was pursued, purportedly keeping in mind that as UOP's majority shareholder, Signal owed a fiduciary responsibility to both its own stockholders as well as to UOP's minority. It was ultimately agreed that a meeting of Signal's Executive Committee would be called to propose that Signal acquire the remaining outstanding stock of UOP through a cash-out merger in the range of $20 to $21 per share.

The Executive Committee meeting was set for February 28, 1978. As a courtesy, UOP's president, Crawford, was invited to attend, although he was not a member of Signal's executive committee. On his arrival, and prior to the meeting, Crawford was asked to meet privately with Walkup and Shumway. He was then told of Signal's plan to acquire full ownership of UOP and was asked for his reaction to the proposed price range of $20 to $21 per share. Crawford said he thought such a price would be "generous," and that it was certainly one which should be submitted to UOP's minority shareholders for their ultimate consideration. He stated, however, that Signal's 100% ownership could cause internal problems at UOP. He believed that employees would have to be given some assurance of their future place in a fully-owned Signal subsidiary. Otherwise, he feared the departure of essential personnel. Also, many of UOP's key employees had stock option incentive programs which would be wiped out by a merger. Crawford therefore urged that some adjustment would have to be made, such as providing a comparable incentive in Signal's shares, if after the merger he was to maintain his quality of personnel and efficiency at UOP.

Thus, Crawford voiced no objection to the $20 to $21 price range, nor did he suggest that Signal should consider paying more than $21 per share for the minority interests. Later, at the Executive Committee meeting the same factors were discussed, with Crawford repeating the position he earlier took with Walkup and Shumway. Also considered was the 1975 tender offer and the fact that it had been greatly oversubscribed at $21 per share. For many reasons, Signal's management concluded that the acquisition of UOP's minority shares provided the solution to a number of its business problems.

Thus, it was the consensus that a price of $20 to $21 per share would be fair to both Signal and the minority shareholders of UOP. Signal's executive committee authorized its management "to negotiate" with UOP "for a cash acquisition of the minority ownership in UOP, Inc., with the intention of presenting a proposal to [Signal's] board of directors . . . on March 6, 1978." Immediately after this February 28, 1978 meeting, Signal issued a press release stating:

> The Signal Companies, Inc. and UOP, Inc. are conducting negotiations for the acquisition for cash by Signal of the 49.5 per cent of UOP which it does not presently own, announced Forrest N. Shumway, president and chief executive officer of Signal, and James V. Crawford, UOP president.
>
> Price and other terms of the proposed transaction have not yet been finalized and would be subject to approval of the boards of directors of Signal and UOP, scheduled to meet early next week, the stockholders of UOP and certain federal agencies.

The announcement also referred to the fact that the closing price of UOP's common stock on that day was $14.50 per share.

Two days later, on March 2, 1978, Signal issued a second press release stating that its management would recommend a price in the range of $20 to $21 per share for UOP's 49.5% minority interest. This announcement referred to Signal's earlier statement that "negotiations" were being conducted for the acquisition of the minority shares.

Between Tuesday, February 28, 1978 and Monday, March 6, 1978, a total of four business days, Crawford spoke by telephone with all of UOP's non-Signal, i.e., outside, directors. Also during that period, Crawford retained Lehman Brothers to render a fairness opinion as to the price offered the minority for its stock. He gave two reasons for this choice. First, the time schedule between the announcement and the board meetings was short (by then only three business days) and since Lehman Brothers had been acting as UOP's investment banker for many years, Crawford felt that it would be in the best position to respond on such brief notice. Second, James W. Glanville, a long-time director of UOP and a partner in Lehman Brothers, had acted as a financial advisor to UOP for many years. Crawford believed that Glanville's familiarity with UOP, as a member of its board, would also be of assistance in enabling Lehman Brothers to render a fairness opinion within the existing time constraints.

Crawford telephoned Glanville, who gave his assurance that Lehman Brothers had no conflicts that would prevent it from accepting the task. Glanville's immediate personal reaction was that a price of $20 to $21 would certainly be fair, since it represented almost a 50% premium over UOP's market price. Glanville sought a $250,000 fee for Lehman Brothers' services, but Crawford thought this too much. After further discussions Glanville finally agreed that Lehman Brothers would render its fairness opinion for $150,000.

During this period Crawford also had several telephone contacts with Signal officials. In only one of them, however, was the price of the shares discussed. In a conversation with Walkup, Crawford advised that as a result of his communications with UOP's non-Signal directors, it was his feeling that the price would have to be the top of the proposed range, or $21 per share, if the approval of UOP's outside directors was to be obtained. But again, he did not seek any price higher than $21.

Glanville assembled a three-man Lehman Brothers team to do the work on the fairness opinion. These persons examined relevant documents and information concerning UOP, including its annual reports and its Securities and Exchange Commission filings from 1973 through 1976, as well as its audited financial statements for 1977, its interim reports to shareholders, and its recent and historical market prices and trading volumes. In addition, on Friday, March 3, 1978, two members of the Lehman Brothers team flew to UOP's headquarters in Des Plaines, Illinois, to perform a "due diligence" visit, during the course of which they interviewed Crawford as well as UOP's general counsel, its chief financial officer, and other key executives and personnel.

As a result, the Lehman Brothers team concluded that "the price of either $20 or $21 would be a fair price for the remaining shares of UOP." They telephoned this impression to Glanville, who was spending the weekend in Vermont.

On Monday morning, March 6, 1978, Glanville and the senior member of the Lehman Brothers team flew to Des Plaines to attend the scheduled UOP directors meeting. Glanville looked over the assembled information during the flight. The two had with them the draft of a "fairness opinion letter" in which the price had been left blank. Either during or immediately prior to the directors' meeting, the two-page "fairness opinion letter" was typed in final form and the price of $21 per share was inserted.

On March 6, 1978, both the Signal and UOP boards were convened to consider the proposed merger. Telephone communications were maintained between the two meetings. Walkup, Signal's board chairman, and also a UOP director, attended UOP's meeting with Crawford in order to present Signal's position and answer any questions that UOP's non-Signal directors might have. Arledge and Chitiea, along with Signal's other designees on UOP's board, participated by conference telephone. All of UOP's outside directors attended the meeting either in person or by conference telephone.

First, Signal's board unanimously adopted a resolution authorizing Signal to propose to UOP a cash merger of $21 per share as outlined in a certain merger agreement and other supporting documents. This proposal required that the merger be approved by a majority of UOP's outstanding minority shares voting at the stockholders meeting at which the merger would be considered, and that the minority shares voting in favor of the merger, when coupled with Signal's 50.5% interest would have to comprise at least two-thirds of all UOP shares. Otherwise the proposed merger would be deemed disapproved.

UOP's board then considered the proposal. Copies of the agreement were delivered to the directors in attendance, and other copies had been forwarded earlier to the directors participating by telephone. They also had before them UOP financial data for 1974-1977, UOP's most recent financial statements, market price information, and budget projections for 1978. In addition they had Lehman Brothers' hurriedly prepared fairness opinion letter finding the price of $21 to be fair. Glanville, the Lehman Brothers partner, and UOP director, commented on the information that had gone into preparation of the letter.

Signal also suggests that the Arledge-Chitiea feasibility study, indicating that a price of up to $24 per share would be a "good investment" for Signal, was discussed at the UOP directors' meeting. The Chancellor made no such finding, and our independent review of the record, detailed infra, satisfies us by a preponderance of the evidence that there was no discussion of this document at UOP's board meeting. Furthermore, it is clear beyond peradventure that nothing in that report was ever disclosed to UOP's minority shareholders prior to their approval of the merger.

After consideration of Signal's proposal, Walkup and Crawford left the meeting to permit a free and uninhibited exchange between UOP's non-Signal directors. Upon their return a resolution to accept Signal's offer was then proposed and adopted. While Signal's men on UOP's board participated in various aspects of the meeting, they abstained from voting. However, the minutes show that each of them "if voting would have voted yes."

On March 7, 1978, UOP sent a letter to its shareholders advising them of the action taken by UOP's board with respect to Signal's offer. This document pointed out, among other things, that on February 28, 1978 "both companies had announced negotiations were being conducted."

Despite the swift board action of the two companies, the merger was not submitted to UOP's shareholders until their annual meeting on May 26, 1978. In the notice of that meeting and proxy statement sent to shareholders in May, UOP's management and board urged that the merger be approved. The proxy statement also advised:

> The price was determined after *discussions* between James V. Crawford, a director of Signal and Chief Executive Officer of UOP, and officers of Signal which took place during meetings on February 28, 1978, and in the course of several subsequent telephone conversations. (*Emphasis added.*)

In the original draft of the proxy statement the word "negotiations" had been used rather than "discussions." However, when the Securities and Exchange Commission sought details of the "negotiations" as part of its review of these materials, the term was deleted and the word "discussions" was substituted. The proxy statement indicated that the vote of UOP's board in approving the merger had been unanimous. It also advised the shareholders that Lehman

Brothers had given its opinion that the merger price of $21 per share was fair to UOP's minority. However, it did not disclose the hurried method by which this conclusion was reached.

As of the record date of UOP's annual meeting, there were 11,488,302 shares of UOP common stock outstanding, 5,688,302 of which were owned by the minority. At the meeting only 56%, or 3,208,652, of the minority shares were voted. Of these, 2,953,812, or 51.9% of the total minority, voted for the merger, and 254,840 voted against it. When Signal's stock was added to the minority shares voting in favor, a total of 76.2% of UOP's outstanding shares approved the merger while only 2.2% opposed it.

By its terms the merger became effective on May 26, 1978, and each share of UOP's stock held by the minority was automatically converted into a right to receive $21 cash.

II

A

A primary issue mandating reversal is the preparation by two UOP directors, Arledge and Chitiea, of their feasibility study for the exclusive use and benefit of Signal. This document was of obvious significance to both Signal and UOP. Using UOP data, it described the advantages to Signal of ousting the minority at a price range of $21-$24 per share. Mr. Arledge, one of the authors, outlined the benefits to Signal:[6]

Purpose of the Merger

1) Provides an outstanding investment opportunity for Signal—(Better than any recent acquisition we have seen.)
2) Increases Signal's earnings.
3) Facilitates the flow of resources between Signal and its subsidiaries—(Big factor—works both ways.)
4) Provides cost savings potential for Signal and UOP.
5) Improves the percentage of Signal's "operating earnings" as opposed to "holding company earnings."
6) Simplifies the understanding of Signal.
7) Facilitates technological exchange among Signal's subsidiaries.
8) Eliminates potential conflicts of interest.

Having written those words, solely for the use of Signal, it is clear from the record that neither Arledge nor Chitiea shared this report with their fellow directors of UOP. We are satisfied that no one else did either. This conduct hardly meets the fiduciary standards applicable to such a transaction. . . .

. . . The Arledge-Chitiea report speaks for itself in supporting the Chancellor's finding that a price of up to $24 was a "good investment" for Signal. It

---

6. The parentheses indicate certain handwritten comments of Mr. Arledge.

shows that a return on the investment at $21 would be 15.7% versus 15.5% at $24 per share. This was a difference of only two-tenths of one percent, while it meant over $17,000,000 to the minority. Under such circumstances, paying UOP's minority shareholders $24 would have had relatively little long-term effect on Signal, and the Chancellor's findings concerning the benefit to Signal, even at a price of $24, were obviously correct. *Levitt v. Bouvier*, Del. Supr., 287 A.2d 671, 673 (1972).

Certainly, this was a matter of material significance to UOP and its shareholders. Since the study was prepared by two UOP directors, using UOP information for the exclusive benefit of Signal, and nothing whatever was done to disclose it to the outside UOP directors or the minority shareholders, a question of breach of fiduciary duty arises. This problem occurs because there were common Signal-UOP directors participating, at least to some extent, in the UOP board's decision-making processes without full disclosure of the conflicts they faced.[7]

B

In assessing this situation, the Court of Chancery was required to:

> examine what information defendants had and to measure it against what they gave to the minority stockholders, in a context in which "complete candor" is required. In other words, the limited function of the Court was to determine whether defendants had disclosed all information in their possession germane to the transaction in issue. And by "germane" we mean, for present purposes, information such as a reasonable shareholder would consider important in deciding whether to sell or retain stock. . . . Completeness, not adequacy, is both the norm and the mandate under present circumstances.

Lynch v. Vickers Energy Corp., Del. Supr., 383 A.2d 278, 281 (1977) (*Lynch I*). This is merely stating in another way the long-existing principle of Delaware law that these Signal designated directors on UOP's board still owed UOP and its shareholders an uncompromising duty of loyalty. The classic language of *Guth v. Loft, Inc.*, Del. Supr., 23 Del. Ch. 255, 5 A.2d 503, 510 (1939), requires no embellishment:

---

7. Although perfection is not possible, or expected, the result here could have been entirely different if UOP had appointed an independent negotiating committee of its outside directors to deal with Signal at arm's length. *See, e.g., Harriman v. E.I. duPont de Nemours & Co.*, 411 F. Supp. 133 (D. Del. 1975). Since fairness in this context can be equated to conduct by a theoretical, wholly independent, board of directors acting upon the matter before them, it is unfortunate that this course apparently was neither considered nor pursued. *Johnston v. Greene*, Del. Supr., 35 Del. Ch. 479, 121 A.2d 919, 925 (1956). Particularly in a parent-subsidiary context, a showing that the action taken was as though each of the contending parties had in fact exerted its bargaining power against the other at arm's length is strong evidence that the transaction meets the test of fairness. *Getty Oil Co. v. Skelly Oil Co.*, Del. Supr., 267 A.2d 883, 886 (1970); *Puma v. Marriott*, Del. Ch., 283 A.2d 693, 696 (1971).

A public policy, existing through the years, and derived from a profound knowledge of human characteristics and motives, has established a rule that demands of a corporate officer or director, peremptorily and inexorably, the most scrupulous observance of his duty, not only affirmatively to protect the interests of the corporation committed to his charge, but also to refrain from doing anything that would work injury to the corporation, or to deprive it of profit or advantage which his skill and ability might properly bring to it, or to enable it to make in the reasonable and lawful exercise of its powers. The rule that requires an undivided and unselfish loyalty to the corporation demands that there shall be no conflict between duty and self-interest.

Given the absence of any attempt to structure this transaction on an arm's length basis, Signal cannot escape the effects of the conflicts it faced, particularly when its designees on UOP's board did not totally abstain from participation in the matter. There is no "safe harbor" for such divided loyalties in Delaware. When directors of a Delaware corporation are on both sides of a transaction, they are required to demonstrate their utmost good faith and the most scrupulous inherent fairness of the bargain. The requirement of fairness is unflinching in its demand that where one stands on both sides of a transaction, he has the burden of establishing its entire fairness, sufficient to pass the test of careful scrutiny by the courts. *Sterling v. Mayflower Hotel Corp.,* Del. Supr., 33 Del. Ch. 293, 93 A.2d 107, 110 (1952); *Bastian v. Bourns, Inc.,* Del. Ch., 256 A.2d 680, 681 (1969), aff'd, Del. Supr., 278 A.2d 467 (1970); *David J. Greene & Co. v. Dunhill International Inc.,* Del. Ch., 249 A.2d 427, 431 (1968).

There is no dilution of this obligation where one holds dual or multiple directorships, as in a parent-subsidiary context. *Levien v. Sinclair Oil Corp.,* Del. Ch., 261 A.2d 911, 915 (1969). Thus, individuals who act in a dual capacity as directors of two corporations, one of whom is parent and the other subsidiary, owe the same duty of good management to both corporations, and in the absence of an independent negotiating structure (*see* note 7, *supra*), or the directors' total abstention from any participation in the matter, this duty is to be exercised in light of what is best for both companies. The record demonstrates that Signal has not met this obligation.

C

The concept of fairness has two basic aspects: fair dealing and fair price. The former embraces questions of when the transaction was timed, how it was initiated, structured, negotiated, disclosed to the directors, and how the approvals of the directors and the stockholders were obtained. The latter aspect of fairness relates to the economic and financial considerations of the proposed merger, including all relevant factors: assets, market value, earnings, future prospects, and any other elements that affect the intrinsic or inherent value of a company's stock. Moore, *The "Interested" Director or Officer Transaction,* 4 Del. J. Corp. L. 674, 676 (1979); Nathan & Shapiro, *Legal Standard of Fairness of Merger Terms Under Delaware Law,* 2 Del. J. Corp. L. 44, 46-47 (1977). *See Tri-Continental Corp. v. Battye,* Del. Supr., 31 Del. Ch. 523, 74 A.2d 71, 72 (1950); 8 Del. C. §262(h). However, the test for fairness is not a bifurcated one as between fair dealing and price. All aspects of the issue must be examined as a whole since the question is one of entire fairness. However, in a nonfraudulent transaction we recognize that price may be the preponderant consideration outweighing other features of the merger. Here, we address the two basic aspects of fairness separately because we find reversible error as to both.

D

Part of fair dealing is the obvious duty of candor required by *Lynch I, supra.* Moreover, one possessing superior knowledge may not mislead any stockholder by use of corporate information to which the latter is not privy. Delaware has long imposed this duty even upon persons who are not corporate officers or directors, but who nonetheless are privy to matters of interest or significance to their company. *Brophy v. Cities Service Co.,* Del. Ch., 31 Del. Ch. 241, 70 A.2d 5, 7 (1949). With the well-established Delaware law on the subject, and the Court of Chancery's findings of fact here, it is inevitable that the obvious conflicts posed by Arledge and Chitiea's preparation of their "feasibility study," derived from UOP information, for the sole use and benefit of Signal, cannot pass muster.

The Arledge-Chitiea report is but one aspect of the element of fair dealing. How did this merger evolve? It is clear that it was entirely initiated by Signal. The serious time constraints under which the principals acted were all set by Signal. It had not found a suitable outlet for its excess cash and considered UOP a desirable investment, particularly since it was now in a position to acquire the whole company for itself. For whatever reasons, and they were only Signal's, the entire transaction was presented to and approved by UOP's board within four business days. Standing alone, this is not necessarily indicative of any lack of fairness by a majority shareholder. It was what occurred, or more properly, what did not occur, during this brief period that makes the time constraints imposed by Signal relevant to the issue of fairness.

The structure of the transaction, again, was Signal's doing. So far as negotiations were concerned, it is clear that they were modest at best. Crawford, Signal's man at UOP, never really talked price with Signal, except to accede to its management's statements on the subject, and to convey to Signal the UOP outside directors' view that as between the $20-$21 range under consideration, it would have to be $21. The latter is not a surprising outcome, but hardly arm's length negotiations. Only the protection of benefits for UOP's key employees and the issue of Lehman Brothers' fee approached any concept of bargaining.

As we have noted, the matter of disclosure to the UOP directors was wholly flawed by the conflicts of interest raised by the Arledge-Chitiea report. All of those conflicts were resolved by Signal in its own favor without divulging any aspect of them to UOP.

This cannot but undermine a conclusion that this merger meets any reasonable test of fairness. The outside UOP directors lacked one material piece of information generated by two of their colleagues, but shared only with Signal. True, the UOP board had the Lehman Brothers' fairness opinion, but that firm has been blamed by the plaintiff for the hurried task it performed, when more properly the responsibility for this lies with Signal. There was no disclosure of the circumstances surrounding the rather cursory preparation of the Lehman Brothers' fairness opinion. Instead, the impression was given UOP's minority that a careful study had been made, when in fact speed was the hallmark, and Mr. Glanville, Lehman's partner in charge of the matter, and also a UOP director, having spent the weekend in Vermont, brought a draft of the "fairness opinion letter" to the UOP directors' meeting on March 6, 1978 with the price left blank. We can only conclude from the record that the rush imposed on Lehman Brothers by Signal's timetable contributed to the difficulties under which this investment banking firm attempted to perform its responsibilities. Yet, none of this was disclosed to UOP's minority.

Finally, the minority stockholders were denied the critical information that Signal considered a price of $24 to be a good investment. Since this would have meant over $17,000,000 more to the minority, we cannot conclude that the shareholder vote was an informed one. Under the circumstances, an approval by a majority of the minority was meaningless. *Lynch I,* 383 A.2d at 279, 281; *Cahall v. Lofland,* Del. Ch., 12 Del. Ch. 299, 114 A. 224 (1921).

Given these particulars and the Delaware law on the subject, the record does not establish that this transaction satisfies any reasonable concept of fair dealing, and the Chancellor's findings in that regard must be reversed.

E

Turning to the matter of price, plaintiff also challenges its fairness. His evidence was that on the date the merger was approved the stock was worth at least $26 per share. In support, he offered the testimony of a chartered investment analyst who used two basic approaches to valuation: a comparative analysis of the premium paid over market in ten other tender offer-merger combinations, and a discounted cash flow analysis.

In this breach of fiduciary duty case, the Chancellor perceived that the approach to valuation was the same as that in an appraisal proceeding. Consistent with precedent, he rejected plaintiff's method of proof and accepted defendants' evidence of value as being in accord with practice under prior case law. This means that the so-called "Delaware block" or weighted average method was employed wherein the elements of value, i.e., assets, market price, earnings, etc., were assigned a particular weight and the resulting amounts added to determine the value per share. This procedure has been in use for decades. *See In re General Realty & Utilities Corp.,* Del. Ch., 29 Del. Ch. 480, 52 A.2d 6, 14-15 (1947). However, to the extent it excludes other generally accepted techniques used in the financial community and the courts, it is now clearly outmoded. It is time we recognize this in appraisal and other stock valuation proceedings and bring our law current on the subject.

While the Chancellor rejected plaintiff's discounted cash flow method of valuing UOP's stock, as not corresponding with "either logic or the existing law" (426 A.2d at 1360), it is significant that this was essentially the focus, i.e., earnings potential of UOP, of Messrs. Arledge and Chitiea in their evaluation of the merger. Accordingly, the standard "Delaware block" or weighted average method of valuation, formerly employed in appraisal and other stock valuation cases, shall no longer exclusively control such proceedings. We believe that a more liberal approach must include proof of value by any techniques or methods which are generally considered acceptable in the financial community and otherwise admissible in court, subject only to our interpretation of 8 Del. C. §262(h), *infra*. This will obviate the very structured and mechanistic procedure that has heretofore governed such matters.

Fair price obviously requires consideration of all relevant factors involving the value of a company. This has long been the law of Delaware as stated in *Tri-Continental Corp.*, 74 A.2d at 72:

> The basic concept of value under the appraisal statute is that the stockholder is entitled to be paid for that which has been taken from him, viz., his proportionate interest in a going concern. By value of the stockholder's proportionate interest in the corporate enterprise is meant the true or intrinsic value of his stock which has been taken by the merger. In determining what figure represents this true or intrinsic value, the appraiser and the courts must take into consideration all factors and elements which reasonably might enter into the fixing of value. Thus, market value, asset value, dividends, earning prospects, the nature of the enterprise and any other facts which were known or which could be ascertained as of the date of merger and which throw any light on *future prospects* of the merged corporation are not only pertinent to an inquiry as to the value of the dissenting stockholders' interest, but *must be considered* by the agency fixing the value. (*Emphasis added.*)

This is not only in accord with the realities of present day affairs, but it is thoroughly consonant with the purpose and intent of our statutory law. Under 8 Del. C. §262(h), the Court of Chancery:

> shall appraise the shares, determining their *fair* value exclusive of any element of value arising from the accomplishment or expectation of the merger, together with a fair rate of interest, if any, to be paid upon the amount determined to be the fair value. In determining such fair value, the Court shall take into account *all relevant factors* . . . (*Emphasis added.*)

See also Bell v. Kirby Lumber Corp., Del. Supr., 413 A.2d 137, 150-51 (1980) (Quillen, J., concurring).

It is significant that section 262 now mandates the determination of "fair" value based upon "all relevant factors." Only the speculative elements of value that may arise from the "accomplishment or expectation" of the merger are excluded. We take this to be a very narrow exception to the appraisal process, designed to eliminate use of pro forma data and projections of a speculative variety relating to the completion of a merger. But elements of future value, including the nature of the enterprise, which are known or susceptible of proof as of the date of the merger and not the product of speculation, may be considered. When the trial court deems it appropriate, fair value also includes any damages, resulting from the taking, which the stockholders sustain as a class. If that was not the case, then the obligation to consider "all relevant factors" in the valuation process would be eroded. . . .

. . . Although the Chancellor received the plaintiff's evidence, his opinion indicates that the use of it was precluded because of past Delaware practice. While we do not suggest a monetary result one way or the other, we do think the plaintiff's evidence should be part of the factual mix and weighed as such. Until the $21 price is measured on remand by the valuation standards mandated by Delaware law, there can be no finding at the present stage of these proceedings that the price is fair. Given the lack of any candid disclosure of the material facts surrounding establishment of the $21 price, the majority of the minority vote, approving the merger, is meaningless.

The plaintiff has not sought an appraisal, but rescissory damages of the type contemplated by *Lynch v. Vickers Energy Corp.,* Del. Supr., 429 A.2d 497, 505-06 (1981) (*Lynch II*). In view of the approach to valuation that we announce today, we see no basis in our law for *Lynch II*'s exclusive monetary formula for relief. On remand the plaintiff will be permitted to test the fairness of the $21 price by the standards we herein establish, in conformity with the principle applicable to an appraisal—that fair value be determined by taking "into account all relevant factors" [*see* 8 Del. C. §262(h), *supra*]. In our view this includes the elements of rescissory damages if the Chancellor considers them susceptible of proof and a remedy appropriate to all the issues of fairness before him. To the extent that *Lynch II,* 429 A.2d at 505-06, purports to limit the Chancellor's discretion to a single remedial formula for monetary damages in a cash-out merger, it is overruled.

While a plaintiff's monetary remedy ordinarily should be confined to the more liberalized appraisal proceeding herein established, we do not intend any limitation on the historic powers of the Chancellor to grant such other relief as the facts of a particular case may dictate. The appraisal remedy we approve may not be adequate in certain cases, particularly where fraud, misrepresentation, self-dealing, deliberate waste of corporate assets, or gross and palpable overreaching are involved. Under such circumstances, the Chancellor's powers are complete to fashion any form of equitable and monetary relief as may be appropriate, including rescissory damages. Since it is apparent that this long completed transaction is too involved to undo, and in view of the Chancellor's discretion, the award, if any, should be in the form of monetary damages based upon entire fairness standards, *i.e.,* fair dealing and fair price.

Obviously, there are other litigants, like the plaintiff, who abjured an appraisal and whose rights to challenge the element of fair value must be preserved.[8] Accordingly, the quasi-appraisal remedy we grant the plaintiff here will apply only to: (1) this case; (2) any case now pending on appeal to this Court; (3) any case now pending in the Court of Chancery which has not yet been appealed but which may be eligible for direct appeal to this Court; (4) any case challenging a cash-out merger, the effective date of which is on or before February 1, 1983; and (5) any proposed merger to be presented at a shareholders' meeting, the notification of which is mailed to the stockholders on or before February 23, 1983. Thereafter, the provisions of 8 Del. C. §262, as herein construed, respecting the scope of an appraisal and the means for perfecting the same, shall govern the financial remedy available to minority shareholders in a cash-out merger. Thus, we return to the well established principles of *Stauffer v. Standard Brands, Inc.,* Del. Supr., 41 Del. Ch. 7, 187 A.2d 78 (1962) and *David J. Greene & Co. v. Schenley Industries, Inc.,* Del. Ch., 281 A.2d 30 (1971), mandating a stockholder's recourse to the basic remedy of an appraisal. . . .

---

8. Under 8 Del. C. §262(a), (d) & (e), a stockholder is required to act within certain time periods to perfect the right to an appraisal.

III.

Finally, we address the matter of business purpose. The defendants contend that the purpose of this merger was not a proper subject of inquiry by the trial court. The plaintiff says that no valid purpose existed—the entire transaction was a mere subterfuge designed to eliminate the minority. The Chancellor ruled otherwise, but in so doing he clearly circumscribed the thrust and effect of *Singer. Weinberger v. UOP*, 426 A.2d at 1342-43, 1348-50. This has led to the thoroughly sound observation that the business purpose test "may be . . . virtually interpreted out of existence, as it was in *Weinberger*".[9]

The requirement of a business purpose is new to our law of mergers and was a departure from prior case law. *See Stauffer v. Standard Brands, Inc.,* [187 A.2d 78 (Del. 1962)]*; David J. Greene & Co. v. Schenley Industries, Inc.,*[281 A.2d 30 (Del. ch 1971)].

In view of the fairness test which has long been applicable to parent-subsidiary mergers, *Sterling v. Mayflower Hotel Corp.,* Del.Supr., 93 A.2d 107, 109–10 (1952), the expanded appraisal remedy now available to shareholders, and the broad discretion of the Chancellor to fashion such relief as the facts of a given case may dictate, we do not believe that any additional meaningful protection is afforded minority shareholders by the business purpose requirement of the trilogy of *Singer, Tanzer,*[10] *Najjar,*[11] and their progeny. Accordingly, such requirement shall no longer be of any force or effect.

The judgment of the Court of Chancery, finding both the circumstances of the merger and the price paid the minority shareholders to be fair, is reversed. The matter is remanded for further proceedings consistent herewith. Upon remand the plaintiff's post-trial motion to enlarge the class should be granted.

REVERSED AND REMANDED.

QUESTIONS

1. In determining fair value in *Weinberger*, the Delaware Supreme Court interprets §262(h) to exclude any consideration of "pro forma data and projections of a speculative variety relating to the completion of a merger." If the statute mandates consideration of "all relevant factors," why does the Delaware Supreme Court conclude that this information must be excluded? In considering this question, *see Cede & Co. v. Technicolor, Inc., infra,* at p. 199, which further expands on the court's holding in *Weinberger*.

2. This case involves a two-step transaction of the type illustrated in Diagram 12 of Appendix A. Following Signal's purchase of 50.1 percent of UOP's

---

9. Weiss, *The Law of Take Out Mergers: A Historical Perspective,* 56 N.Y.U.L.Rev. 624, 671, n. 300 (1981).

10. *Tanzer v. International General Industries, Inc.,* Del.Supr., 379 A.2d 1121, 1124–25 (1977).

11. *Roland International Corp. v. Najjar,* Del.Supr., 407 A.2d 1032, 1036 (1979).

stock, what are the legitimate expectations of the remaining 49.9 percent minority interest in UOP that is publicly traded? In other words, if you were an owner of one of the minority shares of UOP, what could you reasonably expect out of this investment?

3. In *Weinberger*, the Delaware Supreme Court established the entire fairness test, which generally requires the parent to carry the burden of proving both procedural fairness ("fair dealing") and substantive fairness ("fair price") in order for a transaction between the parent and its partially owned subsidiary to withstand judicial scrutiny if challenged by a minority shareholder of the subsidiary. Why did the Delaware Supreme Court decide to impose this obligation on the parent corporation? What public policy supports this result?

4. In fn. 7 of its opinion, the Delaware Supreme Court pointed out that one way in which the parent corporation might avoid, or at least lessen, its burden of proving entire fairness would be to rely on an independent committee of the board of directors of the subsidiary to negotiate the terms of the transaction with representatives of the parent company. What standard will the courts use to review the decision-making process of the committee of the board in this context? In light of the numerous recent financial scandals that ultimately led Congress to enact the Dodd-Frank reform legislation, do you feel confident that an independent board committee will provide adequate protection for the interests of the minority shareholders of the subsidiary?

5. Why did the *Weinberger* court not rely on the principles of Delaware §144 (the cleansing procedures invoked in cases presenting a conflict of interest) to decide this case involving a related party transaction?

6. After *Weinberger*, we know that the entire fairness test requires the controlling shareholder to satisfy a two-pronged test. From a public policy perspective, does this mean that a cash-out merger transaction can satisfy the entire fairness test if the controlling shareholder can establish the fairness of the price, even though the procedures used do not satisfy the "fair dealing" prong of *Weinberger*?

NOTES

1. Importance of the Weinberger Decision.   The significance of the Delaware Supreme Court's *Weinberger* decision lies in the judicial willingness to rely on the appraisal proceeding to efficiently and expeditiously resolve minority shareholder challenges to the terms of a proposed merger transaction. In reaching this decision, the court has sanctioned the use of merger procedures for the sole purpose of eliminating the minority interest, thereby extending considerable flexibility to the board in discharging its statutory responsibility to "manage the company's business affairs." One commentator has summarized the significance of the Delaware Supreme Court's *Weinberger* decision as follows:

Weinberger apparently was intended to revamp the appraisal remedy so that shareholder challenges to merger transactions would be efficiently resolved in an appraisal proceeding, rather than some other form of legal challenge to the transaction.[19] Toward that end, the court in *Weinberger* did three things. First, it eliminated the ability of shareholders to challenge a merger on the ground that it was not undertaken for a valid business purpose.[20] Second, the court stated that the appraisal remedy should ordinarily be the exclusive remedy available to a shareholder objecting to a merger.[21] Finally, and perhaps most importantly, in order to make this now generally exclusive appraisal remedy workable and fair, the court abandoned the inflexible "Delaware block" method of valuation as the exclusive means of establishing fair value. Instead, courts were directed to take a "more liberal approach [that] must include proof of value by any techniques or methods which are generally considered acceptable in the financial community and otherwise admissible in court."

Barry M. Wertheimer, *The Shareholders' Appraisal Remedy and How Courts Determine Fair Value*, 47 DUKE L.J. 613, 616-617 (1998). Until Weinberger, "Delaware (and many other states) followed the Delaware block method of valuing a [Target] company. This was a mechanistic formula that required a judge to determine separate values of the company—e.g., asset value, market value, and earnings value; to assign a percentage to each of the three methods (so that their sum added up to 100 percent); and then to do a weighted average calculation to come up with the valuation number." Robert B. Thompson, MERGERS AND ACQUISITIONS: LAW AND FINANCE at p. 287 (2010). In the next section, we will examine the range of valuation methods that are now available in the post-*Weinberger* era.

---

19. The most common way to object to a merger transaction, outside of an appraisal proceeding, is to allege that the officers, directors, or shareholders of the corporation breached a fiduciary duty in approving or recommending the transaction. See, e.g., *Smith v. Van Gorkom*, 488 A.2d 858, 872-73 (Del. 1985) (alleging directors breached fiduciary duty by failing to exercise due care in approving cash-out merger). A shareholder making such an allegation might seek injunctive relief, thus preventing the merger from going forward (*see, e.g., Sealy Mattress Co. v. Sealy, Inc.*, 532 A.2d 1324, 1326 (Del. Ch. 1987)), or damages (*see, e.g., Cede & Co. v. Technicolor, Inc.*, No. CIV.A.7129, 1990 Del. Ch. LEXIS 171, at *2-3 (Oct. 19, 1990), rev'd, 684 A.2d 289 (Del. 1996)).

20. See *Weinberger*, 457 A.2d at 715. In 1977, the Delaware Supreme Court had concluded that a majority shareholder could not "cause a merger to be made for the sole purpose of eliminating a minority on a cash-out basis." *Singer v. Magnavox Co.*, 380 A.2d 969, 978-79 (Del. 1977), overruled by *Weinberger v. UOP, Inc.*, 457 A.2d 701 (Del. 1983); cf. *Tanzer v. International General Indus., Inc.*, 379 A.2d 1121, 1123-25 (Del. 1977) (holding that a parent corporation can engage in a cash-out merger of a subsidiary corporation, if the real purpose of the transaction is not to "rid itself of unwanted minority shareholders in the subsidiary," and the transaction satisfies the "entire fairness" test), overruled by *Weinberger v. UOP, Inc.*, 457 A.2d 701 (Del. 1983).

21. See *Weinberger*, 457 A.2d at 714. The court noted that the appraisal remedy may not be adequate in some instances, particularly situations involving "fraud, misrepresentation, self-dealing, deliberate waste of corporate assets, or gross and palpable overreaching," and left open the possibility that litigants may not be limited to the appraisal remedy in those circumstances. *Id.;* see also Model Bus. Corp. Act 13.02(b) (1991) (making the appraisal remedy the exclusive means of challenging corporate action creating an entitlement to appraisal unless such action is unlawful or fraudulent).

2. Business Purpose Test.   In Part III of its opinion, the *Weinberger* court overruled the business purpose test, which was established in prior Delaware case law. Before *Weinberger*, Delaware cases emphasized two factors when analyzing the proper treatment of "freeze-out" transactions:

> (1) the purpose of the transaction and (2) fairness to the minority shareholders. . . . The utility of the business purpose test appears to be its invitation to the court to review somewhat more widely the overall terms, objectives, and [the controlling shareholder's] motivations surrounding the acquisition. There is little evidence that the business purpose test otherwise provides strong and predictable protection to the minority [shareholders] or [that the test] ensures the majority [shareholders] against unnecessary [judicial] scrutiny of a fair transaction.

James D. Cox and Thomas Lee, Hazen, CORPORATIONS at p. 641 (2d Ed. 2003). Against the backdrop of these criticisms, the Delaware Supreme Court abandoned the business purpose test, thereby allowing the minority shareholders' continuing equity interest in the business to be "terminated, albeit at a *fair price*, by the will of the majority [shareholder]." *Id.* at p. 642 (*emphasis added*). In light of the court's holding in *Weinberger*, the remedy of an appraisal action, with its focus on determining "fair value," takes on heightened importance and also raises the separate question of "whether the appraisal remedy should [form the basis for] the minority's exclusive right to complain" about the fairness of a "freeze-out" transaction. *Id.* The question of the "exclusivity" of the appraisal remedy is to be taken up at the end of this chapter, when we discuss the Delaware Supreme Court's opinion in *Rabkin v. Philip A. Hunt Chemical Corp.* While Delaware has abandoned the business purpose test, it does bear mentioning that not all courts have followed suit, with several opting instead to impose some form of business purpose requirement in connection with "freeze-out" transactions. *See, e.g., M & W Inc. v. Pacific Guardian Life Ins. Co., Ltd.*, No. 19276, 1998 WL 32685 (Haw. Ct. App. 1998); *Alpert v. 28 Williams St. Corp.*, 473 N.E.2d 19 (N.Y. 1984).

3. Cleansing Procedures of Del. §144.   In *Weinberger*, the Delaware Supreme Court recognized that "squeeze-out" (or freeze-out) transactions—whereby the minority shareholder is "cashed out" and thus deprived of the opportunity to share in the future success of the surviving corporation—present an inherent conflict of interest since all of the future gains will accrue to the majority shareholder. This raises the possibility of using modern "cleansing statutes" (such as Del. §144) to "cleanse" the transaction of the taint of this conflict of interest. In footnote 7 of the *Weinberger* opinion, the court alluded to the possibility of a "cleansing" vote by relying on approval of a proposed "squeeze-out" transaction by "an independent negotiating committee" of the subsidiary's (i.e., UOP's) board of directors; an independent negotiating committee should consist of truly independent outside directors who would then bargain at arm's length with the controlling shareholder/the parent company (i.e., Signal). Use of independent negotiating committees in the post-*Weinberger* era is described in the following note and will be analyzed further as part of the fiduciary duty materials in Chapter 7.

4. Entire Fairness and the Use of Independent Negotiating Committees. In addition to the statutorily mandated appraisal remedy, the *Weinberger* decision also recognizes common law fiduciary duty obligations as a further line of protection for shareholders of the Target Co. by imposing an "entire fairness" requirement in connection with freeze-out transactions in order to be sure that the minority interest receives adequate consideration for its interest. In the words of one leading commentator:

> Shareholders of acquired corporations are also protected by fiduciary duty principles. Fiduciary duty claims by disgruntled shareholders of corporations that are acquired in arm's length acquisitions typically are evaluated under the business judgment standard.[28] The standard requires corporate managers to perform their tasks, including the facilitation of acquisitions, in good faith and without any significant conflict and reasonably to investigate the proposed action. If these criteria are met, the ultimate decision of an acquired corporation's managers to pursue a particular acquisition of their company under particular terms violates their fiduciary duty only if that judgment is so bad as to amount to something similar to gross negligence.
>
> On the other hand, an acquisition undertaken in a conflict of interest setting, such as a corporate parent's acquisition through a statutory merger of a public minority's interest in its subsidiary [*i.e.* a "freeze-out" transaction], is evaluated under the intrinsic fairness test.[31] Under the intrinsic fairness test, the decisions of the acquired (subsidiary) corporation's managers and its controlling stockholder (parent) to facilitate or undertake the acquisition are evaluated against a more general concept of fairness. In considering whether the acquisition is fair, courts look at two elements, fair price and fair dealing. . . .
>
> In all cases, whether or not a conflict is present, managers' conduct in acquisitions is measured against some fair price criterion. In cases without a conflict, corporate managers' facilitation of an acquisition of their company at an unfair price will violate their fiduciary duty under the business judgment standard. . . . Cases involving a conflict apply the intrinsic fairness doctrine, and the fair price obligation is even more direct. In these cases, unless managers of the acquired corporation obtain a fair price for the stock of the acquired corporation, the managers risk a determination that the transaction was not intrinsically fair.[33]

Rutherford B. Campbell, Jr., *Fair Value at Fair Price in Corporate Acquisitions,* 78 N.C. L. Rev. 101, 110-111 (1999).

Following *Weinberger,* the Delaware courts consistently applied the entire fairness standard to review transactions such as the takeout (squeeze-out) merger at issue in *Weinberger,* where the transaction is structured as a long-form

---

28. *Smith v. Van Gorkom,* 488 A.2d 858 (Del. 1985), is probably the most famous case applying the business judgment test to acquisitions.

31. *See, e.g., Weinberger v. UOP, Inc.,* 457 A.2d 701, 710 (Del. 1983).

33. Although the fiduciary standard by which managers' conduct is evaluated appropriately changes, depending on whether such managers are acting in a conflict or a non-conflict setting, the constancy of the fair price requirement across all such decisions makes sense. Fundamentally, the fair price requirement is based on the managers' broad obligation to maximize shareholder wealth, and that obligation of managers is ubiquitous. Thus, managers' approval of any acquisition of their company, irrespective of the existence of conflict, always must maximize shareholder wealth in order to meet the managers' fiduciary obligation. In other words, managers must always ensure that shareholders receive a fair price for their shares. . . .

merger effectuated pursuant to Delaware section 251. Thus, following *Weinberger,*

> majority shareholders wishing to eliminate minority shareholders [typically used a long-form merger, short-form merger, or a tender offer followed by either a long- or short-form merger]. In light of the general belief that short-form mergers, like long-form mergers, were subject to entire fairness review, controlling shareholders sought in the first step tender offer to acquire as many shares as possible so as to reduce the size of the class of potential challengers to the second step merger. The general belief that entire fairness would apply to all mergers spurred majority shareholders to use independent committees or majority of the minority votes to achieve burden shifting.[66]

Bradley R. Aronstam, et al., *Delaware's Going Private Dilemma: Fostering Protections for Minority Shareholders in the Wake of* Siliconix *and* Unocal Exploration, 58 Bus. Law. 519 (Feb. 2003).

Though Delaware caselaw is (widely) credited with developing protection for minority interests eliminated via a "squeeze-out" merger, more recently the Delaware courts have qualified the scope of the entire fairness standard originally established in *Weinberger*:

> In *Glassman v. Unocal Exploration Corporation,* [777 A.2d 242 (Del. 2001)], the court held that the parent company that exercises its right under the short-form merger provision to rid itself of the minority shareholders in the subsidiary does not have to establish the entire fairness for its actions. In such a case the exclusive remedy to the minority, absent fraud or illegality, is the appraisal remedy. The court believed that the legislative intent in providing a short-form merger procedure would be frustrated if the parent company [that is, the controlling shareholder] were subject to the entire fairness [standard of judicial review. In addition, in *In re Siliconix, Inc. Shareholder Litigation,* 2000 De. Ch. LEXIS 1583 (Del. Ch. 2001)], the Delaware courts further decided that] the entire fairness standard does not apply to a controlling stockholder's [*i.e.,* parent company's] tender offer for the minority shares . . . because the decision to accept a tender offer is an individual one [that is, the decision whether to tender their shares into the offer submitted by the controlling shareholder is left to the discretion of each individual minority shareholder].

James D. Cox and Thomas Lee Hazen, Corporations at p. 640 (2d Ed. 2003). As part of the fiduciary duty materials in Chapter 7, we will analyze the *Glassman* and *Siliconix* decisions in connection with our examination of the modern regulation of "going private" transactions.

5. Fairness Opinions. In the wake of *Weinberger* and its progeny, it became increasingly common for boards of directors (of both Bidders and Targets) to obtain "fairness opinions" from their respective investment bankers, and each

---

66. *See* Dennis J. Friedman & Scott A. Kislin, *Going-Private Transactions: Are Special Committees an Endangered Species?* M & A Lawyer, Apr. 2002, at 10. Because entire fairness was believed to apply regardless of the transaction's form, there was no significant benefit to choosing one transactional alternative over another.

board relied on the banker's fairness opinion as one of the factors that it took into account in reaching its determination that the price offered was "fair." However, as *Weinberger* and its progeny make clear, the board of directors cannot abdicate its ultimate responsibility for determining the fair price for Target to the company's bankers. This point is articulated at greater length in the Delaware Supreme Court decision in *Smith v. Van Gorkom,* which we will study as part of our discussion of fiduciary duty law in Chapter 7. In the course of preparing their fairness opinions, the range of valuation methods commonly used by the company's investment bankers is described in the materials in the next section.

4. Valuation Techniques and Fair Price

As was emphasized in the last section, the Delaware Supreme Court's *Weinberger* decision liberalized the methods available for assessing the *fair value* of the dissenter's shares in the context of an appraisal proceeding. Although it is easy to frame the objective of an appraisal proceeding—to find the "fair value" of the dissenting shares—this is not nearly so easy to accomplish in practice. The following excerpt, from an article that thoroughly examines the procedural and valuation issues that often arise in the context of a modern appraisal proceeding, elaborates on the reasons why the appraisal proceeding reflects that well-established truism: "valuation is an art rather than a science."

Barry M. Wertheimer
The Shareholders' Appraisal Remedy
and How the Courts Determine Fair Value
47 Duke L.J. 613, 626-632 (1998)

The statutory command in an appraisal proceeding is to find the "fair value" of the dissenting shares, or sometimes the "fair market value" or "fair cash value." Fair value is typically defined by statute as "the value of the shares immediately before the effectuation of the corporate action to which the dissenter objects, excluding any appreciation or depreciation in anticipation of the corporate action."[74] Statutes generally provide no further guidance with respect to ascertaining fair value in an appraisal proceeding.[75]

---

74. Model Bus. Corp. Act 13.01(3). The Model Act further provides that appreciation or depreciation resulting from the corporate action does not have to be excluded from consideration if it would be fair and equitable to take account of such effects. *See id.* The Delaware statute directs the court to determine fair value of the dissenting shares "exclusive of any element of value arising from the accomplishment or expectation of the merger or consolidation," Del. Code Ann. tit. 8, 262(h) (1991), and goes on to state that in determining fair value, "the Court shall take into account all relevant factors." *Id.*

75. *See* Model Bus. Corp. Act 13.01 cmt. (3) ("The definition of 'fair value' . . . leaves to the parties (and ultimately to the courts) the details by which 'fair value' is to be determined. . . . ").

Before *Weinberger,* the traditional means of determining fair value was the Delaware block method of valuation. After *Weinberger* opened up the valuation process to "any techniques or methods which are generally considered acceptable in the financial community," the most prominent method of valuation in Delaware has been the discounted cash flow (DCF) method. This valuation technique operates on the premise that the value of a company is determined by the present value of its projected future cash flows. The DCF method has been described by the Delaware courts as "the preeminent valuation methodology" and "in many situations . . . [theoretically] the single best technique to estimate the value of an economic asset."[80] As described by the Delaware Court of Chancery:

> The DCF model entails three basic components: an estimation of net cash flows that the firm will generate and when, over some period; a terminal or residual value equal to the future value, as of the end of the projection period, of the firm's cash flows beyond the projection period; and finally a cost of capital with which to discount to a present value both the projected net cash flows and the estimated terminal or residual value.[81]

The DCF method, although probably the most prominent and frequently used *post-Weinberger* method of appraisal, has not been the exclusive valuation method employed. The Delaware courts have continued to use a variety of valuation techniques, depending on the facts and circumstances of the particular case, including the Delaware block method,[82] valuation based on a comparison to other companies (the "comparable company approach"), valuation based on net asset value, valuation based on earnings and book value, and valuation based on combinations of these techniques.

---

80. *Cede & Co. v. Technicolor, Inc.,* No. CIV.A.7129, 1990 Del. Ch. LEXIS 259, at 23 (Oct. 19, 1990) (stating that DCF technique has "become prominent"), *rev'd* on other grounds, 684 A.2d 289 (Del. 1996).

81. *Id.* Dean Samuel C. Thompson, Jr., recognizing the importance of the DCF method in appraisal proceedings (as well as for purposes of fairness opinions, disclosure documents, etc.), has written a "lawyer's guide" explaining the nuts and bolts of this valuation technique. *See generally* Samuel C. Thompson, Jr., *A Lawyer's Guide to Modern Valuation Techniques in Mergers and Acquisitions,* 21 J. Corp. L. 457 (1996).

82. *Weinberger* did not prohibit use of the Delaware block method, and this method has continued to be used in Delaware and elsewhere. *See, e.g., Rosenblatt v. Getty Oil Co.,* 493 A.2d 929, 940 (Del. 1985) (noting that "*Weinberger* did not abolish the block formula, only its exclusivity"); *Gonsalves v. Straight Arrow Publishers, Inc.,* No. CIV.A.8474, 1996 WL 696936, at 4-8 (Del. Ch. Nov. 27, 1996) (noting that *Weinberger* "did not invalidate the Delaware Block Method," and ultimately adopting the valuation calculated by the corporation's expert using that method), *rev'd* on other grounds, 701 A.2d 357 (Del. 1997); *Elk Yarn Mills v. 514 Shares of Common Stock of Elk Yarn Mills,* 742 S.W.2d 638, 640-44 (Tenn. Ct. App. 1987) (applying the Delaware block method); *cf. Oakridge Energy, Inc. v. Clifton,* 937 P.2d 130, 135 (Utah 1997) (suggesting that the appraisal valuation should consider each of three measures of value used in the Delaware block method); *Hernando Bank v. Huff,* 609 F. Supp. 1124, 1126-27 (N.D. Miss. 1985) (considering each of the three Delaware block measures of value, but not employing a weighted average approach), *aff'd,* 796 F.2d 803 (5th Cir. 1986) . . .

The valuation technique used by a court is highly dependent on the valuation evidence presented by the parties. "The parties, not the court, establish the record and the court is limited by the record created."[87] Thus, if both parties present evidence of fair value utilizing the DCF method, the court's resolution of the dispute will likely employ a DCF analysis. Similarly, if the parties agree that a net asset value approach is called for, the court typically will adopt such an approach.

There are problems endemic to an appraisal proceeding that cannot be eliminated by the choice of appraisal methodology. Each appraisal technique is but a way of estimating the "fair value" or "true value" or "intrinsic value" of a company, and undeniably, "valuation is an art rather than a science."[90] The valuation "answer" given by each of these techniques is very dependent on the assumptions underlying the calculations employed. For example, even though the DCF approach is highly regarded, it relies heavily on a guess as to the future cash flows of the enterprise. This "guess" may be informed by looking at historical data, operating trends, and other relevant factors, but it is still nothing more than a prediction of future events. Once these future cash flows are predicted, they must be discounted to a present value. What discount rate should be employed? Again, there is much room for guesswork and subjectivity.[92] The DCF technique also requires that a terminal value be established and then discounted to a present value; both are further exercises in guesswork and subjectivity.[93]

As a practical matter, this means that both parties to the appraisal proceeding will present expert testimony of valuation. Because of the inherent

---

87. *Cede & Co. v. Technicolor, Inc.*, No. CIV.A.7129, 1990 Del. Ch. LEXIS 259, at 26 (Oct. 19, 1990), *rev'd* on other grounds, 684 A.2d 289 (Del. 1996).

90. *In re Appraisal of Shell Oil Co.*, No. CIV.A.8080, 1990 Del. Ch. LEXIS 199, at 16 (Dec. 11, 1990) (quoting testimony of expert witness), *aff'd*, 607 A.2d 1213 (Del. 1992).

92. Factors courts have looked at to determine the discount rate include the firm's cost of equity capital, the risk-free rate of return as reflected in United States treasury bill rates, and the riskiness of the firm's business. *See, e.g., Technicolor*, 1990 Del. Ch. LEXIS 259, at 9093 (using the cost of capital to supply the discount rate); *Neal v. Alabama By-Products Corp.*, No. CIV.A.8282, 1990 WL 109243, at 20 (Del. Ch. Aug. 1, 1990) (accepting capital asset pricing model to determine the discount rate), *aff'd*, 588 A.2d 255 (Del. 1991).

93. These criticisms are not unique to the DCF method. The Delaware block method and other valuation techniques are susceptible to similar criticisms. Under the Delaware block method, it is necessary to determine a company's asset value on a going concern basis. This requires estimation and guesswork. Determining earnings value requires the selection of a price/earnings multiplier, an inherently imprecise and subjective endeavor. After these tasks are accomplished, and a market value is selected, the various valuation factors must be weighted. The selection of the appropriate weight to be accorded each type of valuation is almost wholly arbitrary. *See* [Joel Seligman, *Reappraising the Appraisal Remedy*, 52 GEO. WASH. L. REV. 829, 854-856 (1984)]. As a result, huge discrepancies in the value of companies, as determined by each party's expert, are common under the Delaware block method. *See Francis I. duPont & Co. v. Universal City Studios, Inc.*, 312 A.2d 344, 346 (Del. Ch. 1973) (illustrating how two parties, each employing the Delaware block method, obtained substantially different values: the plaintiff argued for a per share value of $131.89, while the defendant argued for a $52.36 per share value), *aff'd*, 334 A.2d 216 (Del. 1975).

subjectivity and estimation involved, the parties' experts can compute dramatically different valuations, even if they utilize the same methodology.[94] Of course, each expert is "handsomely paid by one side or the other"[95] such that, "whether consciously or unconsciously, the opinions expressed by the expert witnesses significantly reflect[ ] the desires of their clients."[96] Thus, the expert retained by the dissenting shareholder invariably concludes that the corporation has a very high fair value, while the corporation's expert determines that the fair value of the corporation is much lower. It is not unusual for the opinions of the experts to differ by a factor of ten. It is, therefore, not surprising that courts have evidenced frustration with this process.

NOTES

1. The Problem of "Dueling Experts."   In the post-*Weinberg* era, the courts are becoming increasingly frustrated (and often overwhelmed) by the technical nature of the financial information introduced into evidence as part of the valuation decision to be made in the context of an appraisal proceeding. Professor Wertheimer has explained the nature of this problem as follows:

> The primary institutional issue in appraisal proceedings involves the court's task of sorting through the testimony of dueling experts to arrive at the fair value of a corporation. The experts' valuation opinions tend to be partisan, and highly divergent. Accordingly, while recognizing that these problems are "to be expected in an adversarial system," courts have expressed frustration with the use of competing experts to resolve appraisal proceedings.
>
> The Delaware courts have gingerly explored two mechanisms to alleviate some of the problems associated with the inevitable battle of partisan experts. Although these mechanisms have some appeal in reducing the courts' task of resolving conflicting expert testimony, they unfortunately import the risk that they will operate to frustrate the achievement of equitable results in appraisal proceedings.
>
> a. Choosing One Party's Valuation. The first mechanism that has been employed in appraisal cases to deal with the "dueling experts" problem is a "rule," adopted in two Delaware Court of Chancery decisions, stating that a court should decide which of the experts' opinions is the more credible, and then accept that expert's model, rather than attempt judicially to create a valuation model composed of the more credible portions of each expert's model. In other words, after each party presents its case, the court should choose the more credible of the two

---

94. For example, differences in future cash flow assumptions can yield very different valuations under the DCF method. For illustrations of the variance in expert valuations, *see Technicolor,* 1990 Del. Ch. LEXIS 259, at 4; *Neal,* 1990 WL 109243, at 7-8; *Cavalier Oil Corp. v. Harnett,* Nos. CIV.A.7959, 7960, 7967, 7968, 1988 Del. Ch. LEXIS 28, at 32-36, 70-72 (Feb. 22, 1988), *aff'd,* 564 A.2d 1137 (Del. 1989). Sometimes the respective experts use different valuation methodologies, which also can lead to significant variance in their valuation conclusions.

95. *In re Appraisal of Shell Oil Co.,* 1990 Del. Ch. LEXIS 199, at 16.

96. *Id., see also Salomon Bros., Inc. v. Interstate Bakeries Corp.,* No. CIV.A.10054, 1992 Del. Ch. LEXIS 100, at 20 (May 1, 1992) ("It appeared to me, both from the experts' reports and their testimony, that their assumptions and choices of multiples were colored by their respective clients' interests.").

and not attempt to craft a compromise valuation (referred to as a rule requiring a court to "choose one party's valuation"). . . .

b. *Court-Appointed Neutral Experts.* The second mechanism courts have explored in appraisal cases to address the dueling experts problem is the use of a court-appointed neutral expert. . . .

. . . The use of a neutral expert can, in proper circumstances, be useful to a court conducting an appraisal proceeding. There are, however, two points of caution. First, the use of an additional expert imposes additional costs to the proceeding and probably increases the time involved to reach a final result. It also adds a host of procedural issues associated with the appointment of the expert and how the expert will function in the process. The court must be careful to insure that the benefits of appointing a neutral expert justify the added time and expense and the additional layer of procedure.

The second point of caution involves the potential for excessive reliance by the court on the neutral expert. The court is charged with the statutory responsibility of conducting the appraisal, and should not excessively delegate that responsibility to the neutral expert. . . .

Barry M. Wertheimer, *The Shareholders' Appraisal Remedy and How Courts Determine Fair Value*, 47 DUKE L.J. 613, 696-701 (1998).

2. Methods of Valuation. Since the *Weinberger* decision liberalized Delaware's approach to valuation, perhaps the most dominant method for valuing Target's business is to rely on discounted cash flow (DCF). The following excerpt provides a brief overview of this method of valuation, as well as a brief introduction to the other relevant methods of valuation commonly relied on by the parties for determining the value of a company's shares in an appraisal proceeding:

Rutherford B. Campbell, Jr.
The Impact of Modern Finance Theory in Acquisition Cases
53 Syracuse L. Rev. 1, 2-3, 5-6, 9-11, 14-16 (2003)

In February of 1983, the Supreme Court of Delaware decided *Weinberger v. UOP, Inc.* The case holds that, in determining the present value of a corporation involved in an acquisition, courts are free to use "any techniques or methods [of valuation] which are generally considered acceptable in the financial community. . . . "

The rule in Delaware prior to *Weinberger* required courts to determine the present value of a corporation by use of the Delaware block method of valuation[3] exclusively. The Delaware block method, however, is a poor way to determine the present value of a corporation. As a result, even before the *Weinberger*

---

3. See, e.g., Note, *Valuation of Dissenters' Stock Under Appraisal Statutes,* 79 HARV. L. REV. 1453, 1468-71 (1966) (discussing Delaware's use of the weighted average or Delaware block approach). Under the Delaware Block valuation methodology, up to four factors are considered. *Id.* The factors are earnings value, asset value, market value and dividend value. *Id.* Each value is determined and then weighted to arrive at the final value for the company. *Id.; see also, e.g.,* Steven Rogers, *Note, The Dissenting Shareholder's Appraisal Remedy,* 30 OKLA. L. REV. 629, 632-643 (1977) (discussing the use by courts of the weighted average approach).

decision, commentators had sharply criticized the methodology, and Delaware courts occasionally had strayed from a rigid application of this mandated valuation method. The *Weinberger* opinion, therefore, offered a welcome opportunity to move away from this tired and unsound valuation methodology. Courts, it seemed, were encouraged to develop a new common law of valuation, one that was informed by sensible, modern finance theory. . . . This section describes the fundamentals of modern present value theory and offers a series of relatively simple rules or concepts about which there is broad agreement among financial economists. [The remainder of this section provides a brief description of other widely used valuation methodologies.]

A. VALUATION BASED ON DISCOUNTED CASH FLOWS

To the financial economist, present value of an asset, including a company or a partial ownership interest in the company, is determined by projected cash flows discounted by an appropriate factor. This approach is broadly agreed upon by financial economists and thus, for example, is the basis for a major portion of modern corporate finance books, such as Professors Brealey and Myers's standard text, *Principles of Corporate Finance.* For an evaluator, including a court, to arrive at a sound estimate of present value, therefore, the evaluator must make a sound estimate of cash flows and determine a sound discount rate.

1. FUTURE—NOT HISTORIC CASH FLOWS

Present value of an asset, including a company or share of stock, is determined by the person's (or the market's) expectations regarding the future value that the asset will generate. A corollary of this is that historical performance is per se irrelevant to present value.

Consider, for example, an apartment building. Assume that last year an apartment generated total cash flows (e.g., revenues less expenses) of $100,000. Due to a dramatic decrease in demand for the apartments in the building (one may assume, for example, that the major employer in the area moved recently), the best estimate of the cash flows from the apartment building for the foreseeable future is $10,000 per year. A rational purchaser determines the price she or he is willing to pay by reference to the future cash flows ($10,000 in this case). It is irrelevant to today's price that last year, in very different conditions from those anticipated in the future, the cash flows from the apartment building were ten times the amount anticipated for next year. . . .

[2.] DISCOUNTING TO REFLECT THE TIME VALUE OF MONEY AND RISK

A stream of payments to be received over a period of time is worth less than the sum of the payments. For example, in our apartment building example above, if one predicts that the apartment building will generate cash flows of $100 per year for ten years and will at that point have no further earning capacity and no salvage, then a rational investor will not pay $1,000 (the sum of the cash flows) for the building.

One reason the investor will not give up $1,000 today for a promise to repay an equal amount of dollars at some future time is because the investor is giving up the use of her or his money for a period of time, which means that the investor must defer consumption or forego a return on the invested sum during the period of time before the investment is repaid. The investor, therefore, demands a return, because money has a "time value." The amount the investor demands as compensation for the time value of money is referred to as the riskless rate of return, since it represents the return demanded for investment that has no risk respecting the future return.

In addition to the riskless rate, the rational investor will demand an additional amount for any risk that is present in an investment. Risk is generally understood as volatility or variability of possible outcomes. Thus, the more volatile an investment or, stated differently, the wider the dispersion of possible outcomes from the investment, the more risk in the investment and the more return an investor demands. The additional return over and above the riskless rate of return that an investor demands for such volatility is referred to as the risk premium.

Financial economists, therefore, will essentially build a discount rate by first determining the appropriate riskless rate of return and then adding to that rate an appropriate risk premium. The first part of this—determining the riskless rate of return—is typically done by reference to government securities, such as treasury bills. It is in the determination of the appropriate risk premium, however, where financial economists begin to disagree with one another.

During the last three decades, the theory of the risk premium that has most dominated the discussion among financial economists has been the capital asset pricing model. Under this theory, the risk premium required for an investment in a particular stock is generally considered to involve only a premium for the systematic or market risk, which is the risk that cannot be eliminated by diversification. The risk premium under the capital asset pricing model is calculated by multiplying the average marketwide risk premium by the company's beta. Beta is a measure of the sensitivity of an individual security to market movements.

The capital asset pricing model is also an integral part of the weighted average cost of capital method for determining a discount rate. Under this method, one first determines the company's cost of equity capital, normally by using the capital asset pricing model. Then, the company's cost of debt is determined, typically by estimating what the company is required to pay for its borrowed money. The cost of the company's equity and its debt are then weighted by the percentages of the company's total capitalization represented by each of the two components, and this weighted average cost of capital is used to discount the company's cash flows before any deduction for interest payments. The result is a present value for the entire stream of earnings or cash flows that are available to service the company's debt and for shareholders. In essence, one ends up with a present value for the company's debt and equity. Finally, in the typical situation in which the issue is the value of the junior equity, the value of the company's debt is subtracted out, which leaves the value of the shareholders' interest in the company.

In more recent times, the capital asset pricing model has been challenged by a number of economists, and alternative theories have been proposed.

Nonetheless, the capital asset pricing model continues to have its defenders and continues to draw significant coverage in standard corporate finance treatises. . . .

B. ASSET VALUE

"Asset value" amounts to the market value of the net assets of the company. In this valuation method, therefore, the evaluator calculates the fair market value that the assets of the company would bring in the event of liquidation and subtracts from that figure the liabilities of the company.

A couple of points should be made in order to establish the distinct nature of this methodology. First, asset value is determined by the liquidation value of the assets and not by the going concern value of the assets as presently deployed by the company and its managers. In other words, asset value is essentially an opportunity cost measure of the value of the company's assets and thus amounts to the most valuable alternate use of the assets. It is possible, therefore, that the asset value of a company could exceed the company's going concern value.

The second point is that an asset value methodology does not involve applying any multiple or discount to the net liquidation value of the company's assets. Asset value is merely the amount that the company would bring, if all the assets were sold and all the debts were paid. . . .

C. DEAL VALUE

In this methodology, a company's value is established by reference to the price at which similar companies were acquired. So, for example, if Petroleum Company A were recently acquired at a price of 1.8 times its book value, Petroleum Company B might be valued at 1.8 times its book value. Or, if the acquisition price for Company A were fifteen times its most recently reported earnings, a claim may be made that Company B should be valued at fifteen times its most recent earnings. . . .

D. COMPARATIVE RATIO VALUE

An evaluator using the comparative ratio valuation methodology bases its valuation on certain key ratios derived from comparable companies that are actively traded in the market and that are not being acquired. Significant trading activity in the comparable stock is necessary to ensure that the pricing of the comparable stock is efficient and that data about the comparable stock is readily available.

The ratios from the comparable company are constructed using the market price of the comparable's stock over various financial data from the comparable company. These financial data may include: (a) total revenues, (b) book value, (c) earnings, (d) earnings before deducting certain expenses, such as interest and taxes (EBIT) or interest, taxes, depreciation and amortization (EBITDA).

For example, if the present trading price of a computer manufacturer, C Co., is two times its total revenues, then under this methodology one might claim that the fair value of another computer manufacturer, D Co., should be two times D Co.'s total revenues. . . .

E. WEIGHTED AVERAGE VALUE

The old Delaware block method is the most commonly used weighted average valuation technique. There, for example, the evaluator considers up to four separate factors of value and then arrives at a final valuation by weighting each of the factors. The factors typically found in a Delaware block evaluation are: (1) asset value, (2) market value, (3) earnings value, and (4) dividend value. The weights assigned to the factors vary from case to case, and, indeed, not all of the four factors are accorded weight in all cases. Dividend value, for example, is the particular element of value that is omitted from consideration most often. . . .

NOTE

The valuation methods described in the preceding excerpt are not limited to use in the appraisal context. Indeed, it bears emphasizing that these valuation methods are routinely used by investment bankers (and other valuation specialists) as part of the financial advisory services they render in connection with an M&A transaction. "The starting point for both the buyer [i.e., Bidder] and the seller [i.e., Target] in any merger or acquisition transaction is to determine the *value* of the target corporation. For the buyer (i.e., the acquiring corporation), this is a capital budgeting decision similar to any other investment decision, such as the decision to build a new plant. For the seller (i.e., either the target corporation in a sale of assets or its shareholders in a sale of stock), the determination of the target's [intrinsic] value sets the reservation price at which the seller [can be expected to] stop holding and sell [his/hers/it's shares] . . . In many situations it may be appropriate to use multiple techniques in valuing a target." Samuel C. Thompson, *A Lawyer's Guide to Modern Valuation Techniques in Mergers & Acquisitions*, 21 J. CORP. LAW 457, 460-462 (1996) (*emphasis added*).

This next set of Delaware cases focuses on the fundamental question of just exactly *what* it is that the investment banker (or other valuation expert) is supposed to value in connection with the modern appraisal remedy. In other words, is the purpose of the appraisal remedy to value the *corporation*? Or, is the goal to value the *shares* of the corporation held by a particular shareholder? Also, how should the court go about determining the relevant elements of value—especially in light of the statutory language in Del §262(h) that directs the court to exclude "any element of value arising from the accomplishment or expectation of this merger?"

Cavalier Oil Corp. v. Harnett
564 A.2d 1137 (Del. 1989)

. . . WALSH, Justice:

This is an appeal by Cavalier Oil Corporation ("Cavalier") and a cross-appeal by William J. Harnett ("Harnett") from a final judgment of the Court of Chancery determining the fair value of 1,250 shares of stock owned by Harnett in EPIC Mortgage Servicing, Inc. ("EMSI"), a closely-held Delaware corporation. The appraisal action followed a short form merger, pursuant to 8 Del. C. §253, of EMSI into Cavalier on November 20, 1984.

Harnett rejected Cavalier's offer of $93,950 for his EMSI shares, electing instead to assert his appraisal rights under 8 Del. C. §262. Consolidated appraisal proceedings were tried in the Court of Chancery which, after extensive post-trial briefing, entered judgment fixing the value of Harnett's EMSI stock at $347,000. This appeal and cross-appeal resulted. . . .

We conclude that the Court of Chancery, in both its findings and methodology, correctly applied the standards which govern an appraisal proceeding under Delaware law. Accordingly, we affirm the judgment in all respects.

I

The Court of Chancery appraisal action was the culmination of a complex and litigious business relationship between Harnett and the two majority shareholders of Cavalier, Tom J. Billman ("Billman") and Clayton C. McCuistion ("McCuistion"). All three individuals were original investors in Equity Programs Investment Corporation ("EPIC"), a Virginia corporation established in 1975. EPIC's principal business activity was the purchasing of model homes from builders for lease-back purposes. Directly and through subsidiaries, EPIC later expanded into other types of real estate management and mortgage servicing. By 1983, Billman and McCuistion together owned over ninety percent of EPIC's shares while Harnett held the balance of shares. . . .

III

Having concluded that Harnett's corporate opportunity claim was not subject to the bar of *res judicata,* we next consider the related question of whether such a claim may be asserted by a shareholder incident to a section 262 appraisal proceeding. We agree with the Court of Chancery that, under the circumstances in which such a claim evolved here and in light of the consent of the parties to accord recognition to derivative-like claims for future valuation purposes, the claim was cognizable in an appraisal action.

A shareholder who dissents from a cash-out merger is nonetheless entitled to receive the fair or intrinsic value of his shares. Under Delaware law the sole remedy available to minority shareholders in a cash-out merger, absent a challenge to the merger itself, is an appraisal under 8 Del. C. §262. *Weinberger v. UOP, Inc.,* Del. Supr., 457 A.2d 701, 703 (1983). An action seeking appraisal is intended to provide shareholders who dissent from a merger, on the basis of the inadequacy of the offering price, with a judicial determination of the fair value of their shares. *Cede and Co. v. Technicolor, Inc.*, Del. Supr., 542 A.2d 1182, 1186 (1988); *Weinberger v. UOP, Inc.*, 457 A.2d at 714.

The standard for determining the "fair value" of the company's outstanding shares was liberalized in *Weinberger*, which broadened the process from the exclusive use of the "Delaware Block" method to include all generally accepted techniques of valuation used in the financial community. *See Cede and Co. v. Technicolor, Inc.*, 542 A.2d at 1186-87; *Weinberger v. UOP, Inc.*, 457 A.2d at 71213. The scope of the appraisal action is limited, with the only litigable issue being the determination of the value of petitioner's shares on the date of the merger. *Cede and Co. v. Technicolor, Inc.*, 542 A.2d at 1187. Although the justiciable issue in an appraisal action is a limited one, as this Court held in *Weinberger* "all relevant factors" are to be considered in determining fair value of shares subject to appraisal. *Weinberger v. UOP, Inc.*, 457 A.2d at 713; *see also* 8 Del. C. §262(h). . . .

Cavalier argues that the Court of Chancery's decision to extend the scope of valuation to embrace Harnett's corporate opportunity claim impermissibly expands the appraisal remedy to include questions of breaches of fiduciary duty, contrary to this Court's holding in *Rabkin. See Rabkin v. Philip A. Hunt Chemical Corp.*, 498 A.2d at 1106. Fiduciary duty/common law fraud claims have been disallowed in appraisal actions under both *Rabkin v. Phillip A. Hunt Chemical Corp., id.* (unfair dealing claims, based on breaches of the duties of loyalty and care, raise "issues which an appraisal cannot address") and *Weinberger v. UOP, Inc.*, 457 A.2d at 714 (the appraisal remedy may not be adequate in cases involving fraud, misrepresentation, self-dealing, waste of corporate assets, or gross and palpable overreaching). We believe, however, that our previous rulings do not control this case.

While ordinarily a section 262 appraisal proceeding does not lend itself to any claims other than those incident to the appraisal proceeding itself, the unusual facts of this case, particularly the consent of the parties as reflected in the *Harnett I* settlement order providing that the derivative-like claims are viable for appraisal purposes, require that Harnett's corporate opportunity claim be considered in valuing his shares.

Nor is our decision, upholding the viability of a fraud-based claim on the present facts on the appraisal action, to be viewed as undercutting the holding in *Cede*, that derivative claims are lost in subsequent appraisal proceedings because the derivative plaintiff loses his standing to assert these claims on behalf of the corporation. It is true that this Court in *Cede* held that where allegations of fraud and breaches of fiduciary duty exist in connection with a merger, an action separate and distinct from an appraisal proceeding may and indeed must be maintained. *Cede and Co. v. Technicolor Inc.*, 542 A.2d at 1189. *See also Kramer v. Western Pacific Industries, Inc.*, Del. Supr., 546 A.2d 348, 354 (1988). In *Cede* this Court permitted a separate action for fraud in the merger itself because " . . . an appraisal action may not provide a complete remedy for unfair dealing or fraud . . . " in the merger. *Cede and Co. v. Technicolor, Inc.*, 542 A.2d at 1187. The Court in *Cede* also noted that "[a] determination of fair value does not involve an inquiry into claims of wrongdoing in the merger." *Id.* at 1189. Further, this Court held in *Kramer* that " . . . direct attacks against a given corporate transaction (attacks involving fair dealing or fair price) give complaining shareholders standing to pursue individual actions even after they are cashed out through the effectuation of a merger." *Kramer v. Western Pacific Industries, Inc.,* 546 A.2d at 354.

The wrongdoing alleged by Harnett relates directly to the fair value of his stock, not to the validity of the merger itself. Harnett does not dispute that there was a legitimate business purpose to be served by the merger. His claim relates strictly to the value of his shares, and is the one issue that all of the parties had agreed to preserve. His claim is thus viewed as more personal than derivative and appropriately so, in view of his status as the sole minority shareholder whose claims of fraud are directed against the two controlling shareholders. The EMSI corporate opportunity claim, if considered on its derivative merits, would inure almost entirely to the benefit of the alleged wrongdoers, an inequitable result at variance with the fair value quest of the appraisal proceeding. In the present case a fair value determination in an appraisal action will satisfactorily redress the claimed wrongdoing. Additionally, the Vice Chancellor found that Harnett did not have knowledge of the basis for the corporate opportunity claim prior to the institution of the appraisal proceeding and that, as a matter of credibility, those claims were based on misrepresentations by the principal shareholders. We conclude that, under the unusual configuration of facts present here, the corporate opportunity claim was assertable in the section 262 proceeding.

On the merits of the corporate opportunity claim, the Court of Chancery, in valuing EMSI, viewed the combined EMSI/EMI mortgage servicing portfolio in light of a finding that the business was a corporate opportunity belonging to EMSI and unlawfully diverted to EMI. The Court ruled that, had this business not been transferred to EMI, EMSI's earnings would have increased, resulting in a higher per share valuation at the time of the merger. This finding was based upon the minutes of EPIC's Directors' meetings, which reflected the purpose for which EMSI was created and representations made to Harnett by Billman and McCuistion. Since Harnett testified before the Vice Chancellor concerning those representations while the other principals declined to do so, the findings supporting the diversion of business from EMSI turns, in large part, on matters of credibility. Under our standard of review, we perceive no basis to disturb those findings. *Levitt v. Bouvier,* 287 A.2d at 673.

IV

Cavalier's final claim of error is directed to the Vice Chancellor's refusal to apply a minority discount in valuing Harnett's EMSI stock. Cavalier contends that Harnett's "de minimis" (1.5%) interest in EMSI is one of the "relevant factors" which must be considered under *Weinberger*'s expanded valuation standard. In rejecting a minority or marketability discount, the Vice Chancellor concluded that the objective of a section 262 appraisal is "to value the *corporation* itself, as distinguished from a specific fraction of its *shares* as they may exist in the hands of a particular shareholder" [emphasis in original]. We believe this to be a valid distinction.

A proceeding under Delaware's appraisal statute, 8 Del. C. §262, requires that the Court of Chancery determine the "fair value" of the dissenting stockholders' shares. The fairness concept has been said to implicate two consider-ations: fair dealing and fair price. *Weinberger v. UOP, Inc.*, 457 A.2d at 711. Since the fairness of the merger process is not in dispute, the Court of Chancery's task here was to value what has been taken from the shareholder: "viz. his propor-tionate interest in a going concern." *Tri-Continental Corp. v. Battye*, Del. Supr., 74 A.2d 71, 72 (1950). To this end the company must be first valued as an oper-ating entity by application of traditional value factors, weighted as required, but without regard to post-merger events or other possible business combinations. *See Bell v. Kirby Lumber Corp.*, Del. Supr., 413 A.2d 137 (1980). The dissenting shareholder's proportionate interest is determined only after the company as an entity has been valued. In that determination the Court of Chancery is not required to apply further weighting factors at the shareholder level, such as dis-counts to minority shares for asserted lack of marketability. . . .

The application of a discount to a minority shareholder is contrary to the requirement that the company be viewed as a "going concern." Cavalier's argu-ment, that the only way Harnett would have received value for his 1.5% stock interest was to sell his stock, subject to market treatment of its minority status, misperceives the nature of the appraisal remedy. Where there is no objective market data available, the appraisal process is not intended to reconstruct a *pro forma* sale but to assume that the shareholder was willing to maintain his investment position, however slight, had the merger not occurred. Discounting individual shareholdings injects into the appraisal process speculation on the various factors which may dictate the marketability of minority shareholdings. More important, to fail to accord to a minority shareholder the full proportion-ate value of his shares imposes a penalty for lack of control, and unfairly enriches the majority shareholders who may reap a windfall from the appraisal process by cashing out a dissenting shareholder, a clearly undesirable result. . . .

The judgment of the Court of Chancery is affirmed in all respects.

QUESTIONS

1. What is the decision to be made in a judicially supervised appraisal proceed-ing? In considering this question, does it matter whether the dissenting shareholder owns stock in a publicly traded or a privately held company?

2. Why should a minority shareholder get more in an appraisal proceeding than if he/she/it sold his/her/its shares in a secondary, open-market trans-action?

NOTES

1. Use of Minority Discounts.   One of the more perplexing questions that a court must decide in determining the *fair value* of the minority's dissenting shares is whether to apply a minority discount in order to reflect that the dis-senters' shares are illiquid or otherwise worth less per share than a controlling block of shares in the company. In *Cavalier Oil*, the Delaware Supreme Court rejected the use of a minority discount, focusing instead on valuing the corporation itself and then awarding the dissenter his/her/its proportion of the corporation's value as a going concern by dividing the value of the business by the number of outstanding shares. This approach seems to reflect the view of a majority of courts, although a few have applied a minority discount largely on the grounds that the purpose of an appraisal proceeding is to value the dissenters' *minority shares* and not to award the dissenter a pro rata share of the value of the corporation *as a whole*. If the statutorily mandated appraisal proceeding must include a minority discount in calculating the fair value of the dissenters' shares, then what behavior on the part of the controlling shareholder is encouraged by framing the default rule in this manner? Consider the following reasoning on this question:

> Courts that have declined to apply a minority discount in the appraisal context have correctly focused on the purpose of the appraisal remedy to justify their conclusion. The primary purpose of the appraisal remedy today is to protect minority shareholders from wrongful conduct. If this purpose is to be fulfilled, the dissenting shareholder must receive a pro rata share of the value of the corporation. . . .
>
> . . . Imposing a minority discount in the appraisal process encourages controlling shareholders to take advantage of minority shareholders, and allows them to appropriate a portion of the value of the corporation from the minority shareholders.[146] This problem is exacerbated when the corporation's value as a whole is initially determined by reference to market price. Because market price reflects the value of a small quantity of stock, market price already reflects a minority discount. If a court values a corporation by reference to market price, and then imposes a minority discount, it in effect discounts the stock twice to reflect its minority status, and confers a further windfall on the majority shareholder.

Barry M. Wertheimer, *The Shareholders' Appraisal Remedy and How Courts Determine Fair Value*, 47 DUKE L.J. 613, 643-645 (1998).

2. *Statutory Mandate.* Appraisal statutes commonly mandate that the focus of the appraisal proceeding is to determine *the fair value* of the dissent-

---

146. It might be argued that if a dissenting shareholder acquired his stock taking advantage of a minority discount, for example by purchasing the stock at a market price, the shareholder should similarly be saddled with a minority discount at the time of exit via an appraisal proceeding. This argument is misguided for several reasons. First, as noted above, if minority shareholders receive less than their pro rata share of the value of the corporation, those engaging in the cash-out merger would necessarily receive more than their pro rata share. This would violate tenets of fundamental fairness, and encourage wrongful conduct. Second, shareholders willing to invest their capital and purchase a minority position in a corporation do so with the expectation that if the corporation is acquired or taken private, they will realize their pro rata share of the corporation's value. If such shareholders can be involuntarily removed from their investment through a cash-out merger without receiving a pro rata share of the corporation's value, they will be less willing to make such investments. This would result in an increase in the cost of capital for corporations. Finally, shareholders who are able to acquire corporate stock at a minority discount "pay" for that discount by virtue of their inability to control or influence corporate decision making. They should not have to pay again by virtue of a discount in connection with a forced exit from the corporation.

ers' shares "exclusive of any element of value arising from the accomplishment or expectation of the merger . . . together with a fair rate of interest. . . . " Del. §262(h). Or, as expressed in the language of the predecessor provision to MBCA §13.01(4), *fair value* excludes "any appreciation . . . [in the value of dissenting shares] in anticipation of the [acquisition] . . . unless [such] exclusion would be inequitable." MBCA §13.01(3) (1984). Considerable controversy exists as to the meaning of this statutory language, however. Does this statutory language dictate that the courts ignore any control premium in determining fair value? In other words, does this language require the court to exclude the dissenting shares from participating in any of the synergistic gains from the acquisition? If so, how should the court go about measuring those gains? As a broader issue of public policy, how should the gains generated by a merger be divided as between Bidder Co. and Target's shareholders since the acquisition involves a change of control of Target? Consider the guidance given on this difficult question of public policy by the Delaware Supreme Court in the case that follows.

Cede & Co. v. Technicolor, Inc.
684 A.2d 289 (Del. 1996)

. . . HOLLAND, Justice:

This appeal is from a final judgment of the Court of Chancery in an appraisal action. The proceeding arises from a cash-out merger of the minority shareholders of Technicolor Incorporated ("Technicolor"), a Delaware corporation. With the approval from a majority of Technicolor's shareholders, MacAndrews & Forbes Group Incorporated ("MAF") merged its wholly-owned subsidiary, Macanfor Corporation ("Macanfor"), into Technicolor. The only defendant-appellee in this appraisal action is Technicolor, the surviving corporation of the merger. The plaintiffs-appellants are Cinerama, Incorporated, the beneficial owner of 201,200 shares of Technicolor common stock, and Cede & Company, the record owner of those shares (collectively "Cinerama").

Cinerama contends, *inter alia*, that the Court of Chancery erred, as a matter of law, in appraising the fair value of its Technicolor shares. According to Cinerama, that legal error was a refusal to include in the valuation calculus "MAF's new business plans and strategies for Technicolor, which the [C]ourt [of Chancery] *found* were not speculative but had been developed, adopted and implemented" between the date of the merger agreement and the date of the merger. That contention is correct and dispositive of this appeal. *Weinberger v. UOP, Inc.*, Del. Supr., 457 A.2d 701 (1983). Accordingly, the appraisal action will be remanded for further proceedings in accordance with this opinion. . . .

FACTS

. . . Technicolor was a corporation with a long and prominent history in the film/audio-visual industries. By the early eighties, Technicolor's increase in market share had leveled off. The company's core business earnings had stagnated.

Technicolor engaged in a number of distinct businesses through separate operating units. Technicolor's Professional Services Group was its main source of revenue and profit. The Videocassette Duplicating Division operated one of the largest duplicating facilities in the world. The Consumer Services Group operated film processing laboratories ("Consumer Photo Processing Division" or "CPPD"), which provided film processing services to other photofinishers. CPPD also operated the Standard Manufacturing Company ("Standard"), which manufactured film splicers and associated equipment. The Government Services Group ("Government Services") provided photographic and nonphotographic support and management services under contract to governmental agencies. Technicolor's Gold Key Entertainment Division ("Gold Key"), licensed motion pictures and other programs for television exhibition. The Audio Visual Division ("Audio Visual") distributed film and video equipment.

Morton Kamerman ("Kamerman"), Technicolor's Chief Executive Officer and Board Chairman, concluded that Technicolor's principal business, theatrical film processing, did not offer sufficient long-term growth for Technicolor. Kamerman proposed that Technicolor enter the field of rapid processing of consumer film by establishing a network of stores across the country offering one-hour development of film. The business, named One Hour Photo ("OHP"), would require Technicolor to open approximately 1,000 stores over five years and to invest about $150 million.

In May 1981, Technicolor's Board of Directors approved Kamerman's plan. The following month, Technicolor announced its ambitious venture with considerable fanfare. On the date of its OHP announcement, Technicolor's stock had risen to a high of $22.13.

In the months that followed, Technicolor fell behind on its schedule for OHP store openings. The few stores that did open reported operating losses. At the same time, Technicolor's other major divisions were experiencing mixed, if not disappointing, results.

As of August 1982, Technicolor had opened only twenty-one of a planned fifty OHP retail stores. Its Board was anticipating a $5.2 million operating loss for OHP in fiscal 1983. On August 25, 1982, the Technicolor Board "authorized the company's officers to seek a buyer for Gold Key." During 1982, Technicolor also decided to terminate the Audio Visual Division. Nevertheless, Kamerman remained committed to OHP. In Technicolor's Annual Report, issued September 7, 1982, Kamerman stated, "We remain optimistic that the One Hour Photo business represents a significant growth opportunity for the Company."

Technicolor's September 1982 financial statements, for the fiscal year ending June 1982, reported an eighty percent decline of consolidated net income—from $17.073 million in fiscal 1981 to $3.445 million in 1982. Profits had declined in Technicolor's core business, film processing. Technicolor's management also attributed the decline in profits to write-offs for losses in its Gold Key and Audio Visual divisions, which had already been targeted for sale. By September 1982, Technicolor's stock had reached a new low of $8.37 after falling by the end of June to $10.37 a share.

In the late summer of 1982, Ronald O. Perelman ("Perelman"), MAF's controlling stockholder, concluded that Technicolor would be an attractive candidate for a takeover or acquisition by MAF. Kamerman and Perelman met for the first time on October 4, 1982 at Technicolor's offices in Los Angeles.

Perelman informed Kamerman that MAF would be willing to pay $20 per share to acquire Technicolor. Kamerman replied that he would not consider submitting the matter to Technicolor's Board at a price below $25 a share.

Perelman met with Kamerman in Los Angeles for a second time on October 12, 1982. MAF's Chief Financial Officer also attended the meeting. The meeting's principal purposes were: (1) to allow MAF's Chief Financial Officer to review Technicolor financial data; and (2) to give Perelman a tour of Technicolor's Los Angeles facilities.

On October 27, Kamerman and Perelman reached an agreement by telephone. Perelman initially offered $22.50 per share for Technicolor's stock. Kamerman countered with a figure of $23 per share. He also stated that he would recommend its acceptance to the Technicolor Board. Perelman agreed to the $23 per share price.

The Technicolor Board convened on October 29, 1982 to consider MAF's proposal. All nine directors of Technicolor attended the meeting. Kamerman outlined the history of his negotiations with Perelman. Kamerman explained the basic structure of the transaction: a tender offer by MAF at $23 per share for all the outstanding shares of common stock of Technicolor; and a second-step merger with the remaining outstanding shares converted into $23 per share, with Technicolor becoming a wholly owned subsidiary of MAF. Kamerman recommended that MAF's $23 per share offer be accepted in view of the present market value of Technicolor's shares. Kamerman stated that accepting $23 a share was "advisable rather than shooting dice" on the prospects of Technicolor's OHP venture.

On October 29, 1982, the Technicolor Board agreed to the acquisition proposal by MAF. The Technicolor Board approved the Agreement and Plan of Merger with MAF; recommended to the stockholders of Technicolor the acceptance of the offer of $23 per share; [and]. . . . Technicolor filed forms 14D-9 and 13D with the Securities and Exchange Commission which reflected those Board actions and recommendations.

In November 1982, MAF commenced an all-cash tender offer of $23 per share to the shareholders of Technicolor. When the tender offer closed on November 30, 1982, MAF had gained control of Technicolor. By December 3, 1982, MAF had acquired 3,754,181 shares, or 82.19%, of Technicolor's shares. Thereafter, MAF and Technicolor were consolidated for tax and financial reporting purposes.

The Court of Chancery made a factual finding that, "upon acquiring control" of Technicolor, Perelman and his associates "began to dismember what they saw as a badly conceived mélange of businesses." Perelman testified: "Presumably we made the evaluation of the business of Technicolor before we made the purchase, not after." That evaluation assumed the retention of the Professional and Government Services Groups and the disposition of OHP, CPPD, Gold Key and Audio Visual.

Consequently, immediately after becoming Technicolor's controlling shareholder, MAF "started looking for buyers for several of the [Technicolor] divisions." Bear Stearns & Co. was also retained by MAF in December 1982 to assist it in disposing of Technicolor assets. A target date of June 30, 1983 was set for liquidating all of Technicolor's excess assets. As of December 31, 1982, MAF was projecting that $54 million would be realized from asset sales.

In December 1982, the Board of Technicolor notified its stockholders of a special shareholders meeting on January 24, 1983. At the meeting, the Technicolor shareholders voted to repeal the supermajority amendment and in favor of the proposed merger. MAF and Technicolor completed the merger.

VALUATION OF TECHNICOLOR
PERELMAN PLAN OR KAMERMAN PLAN

The merger was accomplished on January 24, 1983. The parties agree that the appraised value of Technicolor must be fixed as of that date. *See Alabama By-Products Corp. v. Neal*, Del. Supr., 588 A.2d 255, 256-57 (1991). There is a fundamental disagreement between the litigants, however, concerning the nature of the enterprise to be appraised.

Cinerama argues that the Court of Chancery should have valued Technicolor as it existed on the date of the merger and, in particular, with due regard for the strategies that had been conceived and implemented following the merger agreement by MAF's controlling shareholder, Ronald O. Perelman ("Perelman Plan"). Technicolor argues that the Court of Chancery properly considered Technicolor without regard to the Perelman Plan and only as it existed on or before October 29, 1982, with the then extant strategies that had been conceived and implemented by Technicolor's Chairman, Morton Kamerman ("Kamerman Plan"). According to Cinerama:

> Reduced to its simplest form, the dispute was whether the trial court should value Perelman's Technicolor—a company whose business plans and strategies focused on the processing and duplication of film and videotape and the provision of services to the United States Government and which planned and expected to generate $50 million in cash during 1983 from the sale of unwanted and/or unsuccessful businesses, namely, OHP, CPPD, Gold Key and Audio Visual; or Kamerman's Technicolor—a company whose business plans and strategies assumed diversification away from a concentration on film processing and videotape duplication for the professional market toward consumer oriented businesses, especially OHP.

The economic experts for both parties used a form of discounted cash flow methodology to value Technicolor. Cinerama's expert was John Torkelsen ("Torkelsen"), a financial analyst with Princeton Venture Research, Inc. Technicolor's primary expert witness was Alfred Rappaport ("Rappaport"), a professor at Northwestern University Graduate Business School and a consultant with The Alcar Group ("Alcar"). The fundamental nature of the disagreement between the parties about the Perelman Plan and the Kamerman Plan, however, resulted in different factual assumptions by their respective experts.

QUESTION OF LAW
PERELMAN PLAN OR KAMERMAN PLAN

Court of Chancery recognized that the parties' disagreement about valuing Technicolor based upon either the Perelman Plan or the Kamerman Plan presented a question of law with regard to the proper interpretation of the appraisal statute. *See* 8 Del. C. §262(h). According to the Court of Chancery, that legal issue is whether in valuing Technicolor as of January 24, 1983, the court should assume the business plan for Technicolor that MAF is said by [Cinerama] to have had in place at that time [Perelman Plan], or whether a proper valuation is premised upon ignoring such changes as Mr. Perelman had in mind because to the extent they create value they are "elements of value arising from the accomplishment or expectation of the merger." 8 Del. C. §262(h). . . .

COURT OF CHANCERY'S HOLDING
MAJORITY ACQUIROR PRINCIPLE PROXIMATE CAUSE EXCEPTION

The Court of Chancery acknowledged that, based upon the quoted language from *Weinberger,* Cinerama's legal argument appeared to be persuasive. The Court of Chancery concluded, however, "that reading [of *Weinberger*] is too difficult to square with the plain words of the statute to permit the conclusion that that is what was intended." The Court of Chancery then stated "in order to understand the quoted passage [from *Weinberger*] when read together with the statutory language, I assume an unexpressed phrase to the effect 'unless, but for the merger, such elements of future value would not exist.'" According to the Court of Chancery, the language in *Weinberger* would read: "But elements of future value, including the nature of the enterprise, which are known or susceptible of proof as of the date of the merger and not the product of speculation, may be considered [unless, but for the merger, such elements of future value would not exist]." *Weinberger v. UOP, Inc.,* Del. Supr., 457 A.2d 701, 713 (1983).

In explaining the "but for" caveat that it had superimposed upon this Court's holding in *Weinberger,* the Court of Chancery reasoned that, as a matter of policy, the valuation process in a statutory appraisal proceeding should be the same irrespective of whether a merger is accomplished in one or two steps:

> Delaware law traditionally and today accords to a dissenting shareholder "his proportionate interest in a going concern" and that going concern is the corporation in question, with its asset deployment, business plan and management unaffected by the plans or strategies of the acquiror. When value is created by substituting new management or by redeploying assets "in connection with the accomplishment or expectation" of a merger, that value is not, in my opinion, a part of the "going concern" in which a dissenting shareholder has a legal (or equitable) right to participate.
>
> If one accepts this principle, the question arises how is it to be applied in a two-step arms'-length acquisition transaction. In such a transaction there will be a period following close [to] the first-step tender offer in which the [majority] acquiror may, as a practical matter, be in a position to influence or change the nature of the corporate business, or to freeze controversial programs until they are reviewed following the second-step merger.

Accordingly, the Court of Chancery concluded that "[f]uture value that would not exist *but for* the merger . . . even if it is capable of being proven on the date of the merger," is irrelevant in a Delaware statutory appraisal proceeding.

(*Emphasis added.*) Consequently, the Court of Chancery held "that value added to [Technicolor] by the implementation or the expectation of the implementation of Mr. Perelman's new business plan for [Technicolor] is not value to which, in an appraisal action, [Cinerama] is entitled to a *pro rata* share, but is value that is excluded from consideration by the statutory exclusion for value arising from the merger or its expectation."

Legal scholars have written extensively with regard to the economic desirability of including or excluding certain valuation elements in an appraisal proceeding,[5] especially with regard to cash-out two-step mergers. *See, e.g.,* John C. Coffee, Jr., *Transfers of Control and the Quest for Efficiency: Can Delaware Law Encourage Efficient Transactions While Chilling Inefficient Ones?* 21 Del. J. Corp. L. 359 (1996); Robert B. Thompson *Exit, Liquidity, and Majority Rule: Appraisal's Role in Corporate Law,* 84 Geo. L.J. 1 (1995).[6] The Court of Chancery's construction of "fair value" followed logically from its concept of what was economically desirable and efficient. However, the majority acquiror principle and correlative proximate cause exception for two-step mergers, upon which the Court of Chancery premised its holding, are inconsistent with this Court's interpretation of the appraisal statute in *Weinberger.*

ALL RELEVANT FACTORS
ONLY SPECULATION EXCLUDED

An appraisal proceeding is a limited statutory remedy. *Technicolor I,* 542 A.2d at 1186. Its legislative purpose is to provide equitable relief for shareholders dissenting from a merger on grounds of inadequacy of the offering price. *Id.* The appraisal statute affords the dissenters the right to a judicial determination of the fair value of their shareholdings. *Id.* (citing *Weinberger v. UOP, Inc.* Del. Supr., 457 A.2d 701, 714 (1983)); *accord Cavalier Oil Corp. v. Harnett,* Del. Supr., 564 A.2d 1137, 1142 (1989). We summarized the nature of the proceeding in *Technicolor I,* as follows:

> in a section 262 appraisal action the only litigable issue is the determination of the value of the appraisal petitioners' shares on the date of the merger, the only party defendant is the surviving corporation and the only relief available is a judgment against the surviving corporation for the fair value of the dissenters' shares.

Technicolor I, 542 A.2d at 1187.

---

5. *See, e.g.,* FRANK H. EASTERBROOK & DANIEL R. FISCHEL, THE ECONOMIC STRUCTURE OF CORPORATE LAW (Harvard Univ. Press 1991); Benjamin Hermalin & Alan Schwartz, *Buyouts in Large Companies,* 25 J. Legal Stud. 351 (1996); Lynn A. Stout, *Are Takeover Premiums Really Premiums? Market Price, Fair Value, and Corporate Law,* 99 Yale L.J. 1235 (1990); Angie Woo, Note, *Appraisal Rights in Mergers of Publicly-Held Delaware Corporations: Something Old, Something New, Something Borrowed, and Something B.L.U.E.,* 68 S. Cal. L. Rev. 719 (1995).

6. *See also* Bate C. Toms, III, *Compensating Shareholders Frozen Out in Two-Step Mergers,* 78 Colum. L. Rev. 548 (1978).

The seminal decision by this Court regarding an appraisal proceeding is *Weinberger v. UOP, Inc.,* Del. Supr., 457 A.2d 701 (1983). In *Weinberger,* this Court broadened the process for determining the "fair value" of the company's outstanding shares by including all generally accepted techniques of valuation used in the financial community. *Weinberger v. UOP, Inc.,* 457 A.2d at 712-13; *see Technicolor I,* 542 A.2d at 1186-87. The result of that expansion was the holding in *Weinberger* that "the standard 'Delaware block' or weighted average method of valuation, formerly employed in appraisal and other stock valuation cases, shall no longer exclusively control such proceedings." *Weinberger v. UOP, Inc.,* 457 A.2d at 712-13.

The Delaware appraisal statute provides that the Court of Chancery:

> shall appraise the shares, determining their fair value exclusive of any element of value arising from the accomplishment or expectation of the merger or consolidation, together with a fair rate of interest, if any, to be paid upon the amount determined to be the fair value. In determining such fair value, the Court shall take into account all relevant factors.

8 Del. C. §262(h). In *Weinberger,* this Court construed the appraisal statute. That construction required this Court to reconcile the dual mandates of Section 262(h) which direct the Court of Chancery to: determine "fair" value based upon "all relevant factors;" but, to exclude "any element of value arising from the accomplishment or expectation of the merger." In making that reconciliation, the *ratio decidendi* of this Court was, as follows:

> *Only the speculative elements of value that may arise from the "accomplishment or expectation" of the merger are excluded. We take this to be a very narrow exception to the appraisal process,* designed to eliminate use of *pro forma* data and projections of a speculative variety relating to the completion of a merger. But elements of future value, including the *nature of the enterprise,* which are known or susceptible of proof as of the date of the merger and not the product of speculation, may be considered. . . .

Weinberger v. UOP, Inc., 457 A.2d at 713 (*emphasis added*).

After examining the evolution of the statutory text in Section 262(h), this Court concluded "there is a legislative intent to fully compensate shareholders for whatever their loss may be, *subject only to the narrow limitation that one can not take speculative effects of the merger into account.*" *Id.* at 714 (*emphasis added*). . . .

PERELMAN PLAN
SUSCEPTIBLE OF PROOF/NON-SPECULATIVE

The underlying assumption in an appraisal valuation is that the dissenting shareholders would be willing to maintain their investment position had the merger not occurred. *Cavalier Oil Corp. v. Harnett,* Del. Supr., 564 A.2d 1137, 1145 (1989). Accordingly, the Court of Chancery's task in an appraisal proceeding is to value what has been taken from the shareholder, *i.e.,* the proportionate interest in the going concern. *Id.* at 1144 (citing *Tri-Continental Corp. v. Battye,*

Del. Supr., 74 A.2d 71, 72 (1950)). To that end, this Court has held that the corporation must be valued as an operating entity. *Id.* We conclude that the Court of Chancery did not adhere to this principle.

The Court of Chancery determined that Perelman "had a fixed view of how [Technicolor's] assets would be sold before the merger and had begun to implement it" prior to January 24, 1983. Consequently, the Court of Chancery found that the Perelman Plan for Technicolor was the operative reality on the date of the merger. Nevertheless, the Court of Chancery held that Cinerama was not entitled to an appraisal of Technicolor as it was actually functioning on the date of the merger pursuant to the Perelman Plan.

The Court of Chancery reached that holding by applying its majority acquiror principle and correlative proximate cause exception. The Court of Chancery excluded any value that was admittedly part of Technicolor as a going concern on the date of the merger, if that value was created by substituting new management or redeploying assets during the transient period between the first and second steps of this two-step merger, *i.e.,* Perelman's Plan. The Court of Chancery reasoned that valuing Technicolor as a going concern, under the Perelman Plan, on the date of the merger, would be tantamount to awarding Cinerama a proportionate share of a control premium, which the Court of Chancery deemed to be both economically undesirable and contrary to this Court's holding in *Bell v. Kirby Lumber Corp.,* Del. Supr., 413 A.2d 137, 140-42 (1980). *See also Rapid-American Corp. v. Harris,* Del. Supr., 603 A.2d 796, 805-07 (1992). Thus, the Court of Chancery concluded "that value [added by a majority acquiror] is not . . . a part of the 'going concern' in which a dissenting shareholder has a legal (or equitable) right to participate." . . .

In a two-step merger, to the extent that value has been added following a change in majority control before cash-out, it is still value attributable to the going concern, *i.e.,* the extant "nature of the enterprise," on the date of the merger. *See Rapid-American Corp. v. Harris,* 603 A.2d at 805. The dissenting shareholder's proportionate interest is determined only after the company has been valued as an operating entity on the date of the merger. *Cavalier Oil Corp. v. Harnett,* 564 A.2d at 1144; *cf. Walter W.B. v. Elizabeth P.B.,* Del. Supr., 462 A.2d 414, 415 (1983). Consequently, value added to the going concern by the "majority acquiror," during the transient period of a two-step merger, accrues to the benefit of all shareholders and must be included in the appraisal process on the date of the merger. *See Rapid-American Corp. v. Harris,* 603 A.2d 796; *Cavalier Oil Corp. v. Harnett,* 564 A.2d 1137; *cf. Walter W.B. v. Elizabeth P.B.,* 462 A.2d at 415.

In this case, the question in the appraisal action was the fair value of Technicolor stock on the date of the merger, January 24, 1983, as Technicolor was operating pursuant to the Perelman Plan. The Court of Chancery erred, as a matter of law, by determining the fair value of Technicolor on the date of the merger "but for" the Perelman Plan; or, in other words, by valuing Technicolor as it was operating on October 29, 1982, pursuant to the Kamerman Plan. By failing to accord Cinerama the *full proportionate value of its shares in the going concern on the date of the merger,* the Court of Chancery imposed a penalty upon Cinerama for lack of control. *Cavalier Oil Corp. v. Harnett,* 564 A.2d at 1145; *accord Rapid-American Corp. v. Harris,* 603 A.2d at 805-07; *Bell v. Kirby Lumber Corp.,* 413 A.2d at 140-42.

The "accomplishment or expectation" of the merger exception in Section 262 is very narrow, "designed to eliminate use of *pro forma* data and projections of a speculative variety relating to the completion of a merger." *Weinberger v. UOP, Inc.*, 457 A.2d at 713. That narrow exclusion does not encompass known elements of value, including those which exist on the date of the merger because of a majority acquiror's interim action in a two-step cash-out transaction. "[O]nly the *speculative* elements of value that may arise from the 'accomplishment or expectation' of the merger" should have been excluded from the Court of Chancery's calculation of fair value on the date of the merger. *Weinberger v. UOP, Inc.*, 457 A.2d at 713 (*emphasis added*).

The Court of Chancery's determination not to value Technicolor as a going concern on the date of the merger under the Perelman Plan, resulted in an understatement of Technicolor's fair value in the appraisal action. . . . .

CONCLUSION

The judgment of the Court of Chancery in the appraisal action is reversed. This matter is remanded for further proceedings in accordance with this opinion.

QUESTIONS

1. What is the structure of the acquisition at issue in this case? What is the effective date of this acquisition?

2. What is the enterprise to be valued here? As of what date?

3. Is there any other method available for the transaction planner to use to structure Perelman's acquisition of Technicolor? If so, what corporate formalities must be satisfied in using such an alternative method to structure Perelman's acquisition?

4. Does the court's ruling discourage Bidder's use of a two-step transaction to acquire Target? Could Perelman have used a one-step transaction to acquire Technicolor?

5. On the facts of this case, would you reach a different result under the present MBCA standard set forth in §13.01(4), which focuses on the value of the shares "immediately before the effectuation of the corporate action"?

6. Would Perelman have made an offer for Technicolor if he did not believe that he could complete the merger? In other words, does the rule of this case reduce the incentives for prospective bidders to make offers to acquire financially troubled target companies?

7. How does the court address the problem of dueling experts on the facts of this case?

5.   Appraisal Rights as Exclusive Remedy

As was noted earlier in this section, *Weinberger* involved a transaction popularly referred to as a "freeze-out" transaction, where the controlling shareholder buys out the minority shareholders' interest, even if the minority shareholder(s) object to being eliminated. Until *Weinberger* was decided, Delaware caselaw imposed a business purpose requirement, which acted as a limitation on the controlling shareholder's ability to "freeze out" the minority shareholder. Under this business purpose test, a merger could not be effected for the "sole purpose of freezing out minority shareholders." *Singer v. Magnovox*, 380 A.2d 969, 980 (Del. 1977). Subsequent Delaware caselaw, however, "effectively eviscerated the business purpose test by requiring only that the merger serve some bona fide purpose of the parent corporation [i.e., the controlling shareholder].[22] Because competent transaction planners easily could create a paper trail showing [that] the merger promoted some business interest of the parent, the test was left as mere formalism." Stephen M. Bainbridge, Corporate Law at p. 181 (2d Ed. 2009). Recognizing that the business purpose test provided the minority interest with no meaningful protections, the Delaware Supreme Court overruled the business purpose requirement in *Weinberger*. In doing so, the court explained that "a plaintiff's monetary remedy ordinarily should be confined to the more liberalized appraisal proceeding herein established," *Weinberger, supra,* at p. 714, but at the same time, the court went on to say that "we do not intend any limitation on the historic powers of the Chancellor to grant such other relief as the facts of a particular case may dictate." So the *Weinberger* court recognized that the appraisal remedy "may not be adequate in certain cases, particularly where fraud, misrepresentation, self-dealing, deliberate waste of corporate assets, or gross and palpable overreaching are involved." *Id.*

From this, many commentators concluded that "*Weinberger* appeared to unequivocally leave appraisal as the exclusive remedy in freeze-out mergers. If a minority shareholder thought a merger was unfair, [his/her/its sole] remedy was to bring an appraisal proceeding, which meant there would be no class action and the shareholder would have to perfect [his/her/its] appraisal rights." Bainbridge, *supra,* at p. 184. As you read the next case, ask yourself whether the appraisal action is, in fact, the shareholder/plaintiff's *exclusive remedy*. Or, did the Delaware Supreme Court "take it all back," *id.,*—and thus allow shareholders to bring a class action for money damages—even if these same shareholders had *not* perfected their right to an appraisal remedy?

▌ Rabkin v. Philip A. Hunt Chemical Corp.
▌ 498 A.2d 1099 (Del. 1985)

Moore, Justice.

These consolidated class actions were filed in the Court of Chancery on behalf of the minority stockholders of Philip A. Hunt Chemical Corporation

---

22. See, e.g., Tanzer v International General Industries, Inc., 379 A2d 1121 (Del. 1977).

(Hunt), challenging the merger of Hunt with its majority stockholder, Olin Corporation (Olin). For the first time since our decision in *Weinberger v. UOP, Inc.*, Del. Supr., 457 A.2d 701 (1983), we examine the exclusivity of the appraisal remedy in a cash-out merger where questions of procedural unfairness having a reasonable bearing on substantial issues affecting the price being offered are the essential bases of the suit. The Vice Chancellor ordered these cases dismissed on the ground that absent deception *Weinberger* mandated appraisal as the only remedy available to the minority. The plaintiffs sought and were denied leave to amend their complaints. They appeal these rulings.

In our view, the holding in *Weinberger* is broader than the scope accorded it by the trial court. The plaintiffs have charged, and by their proposed amended complaints contend, that the merger does not meet the entire fairness standard required by *Weinberger*. They aver specific acts of unfair dealing constituting breaches of fiduciary duties which if true may have substantially affected the offering price. These allegations, unrelated to judgmental factors of valuation, should survive a motion to dismiss. Accordingly, the decision of the Court of Chancery is reversed, and the matter is remanded with instructions that the plaintiffs be permitted to amend their complaints.

I

The factual background of the merger is critical to the issues before us and will be set forth in substantial detail. On July 5, 1984, Hunt merged into Olin pursuant to a merger agreement that was recommended by the Hunt board of directors.[2] Hunt was a Delaware corporation, while Olin is incorporated in Virginia. On March 1, 1983, Olin bought 63.4% of the outstanding shares of Hunt's common stock from Turner and Newall Industries, Inc. (Turner & Newall) at $25 per share pursuant to a Stock Purchase Agreement (the agreement).

At Turner & Newall's insistence, the agreement also required Olin to pay $25 per share if Olin acquired the remaining Hunt stock within one year thereafter (the one year commitment). It provided:

SUBSEQUENT ACQUISITIONS OF COMMON STOCK

Should [Olin] or an affiliate of [Olin] acquire, through a merger, consolidation, tender offer, or similar transaction, all or substantially all of the remaining outstanding shares of common stock within one year of the closing date [March 1, 1983], [Olin] agrees that the per share consideration to be paid in any such transaction shall, in the opinion of a reputable investment banking firm, be substantially equivalent in value to at least the net purchase price per share paid pursuant to this agreement. . . .

On March 1, 1983, concurrently with the closing of the agreement, the two Hunt directors affiliated with Turner & Newall resigned. They were replaced

---

2. Under Delaware law an agreement of merger or consolidation must first be approved by the board of the merging Delaware company before it is submitted to the stockholders. See 8 Del. C. §§251(b), (c) and 252(c).

by John M. Henske, chairman of the board and chief executive officer of Olin, and Ray R. Irani, then president and chief operating officer of Olin. In June 1983, Dr. Irani resigned as a director of both Olin and Hunt. At that time the Hunt board was expanded to nine members, and the resulting vacancies were filled by Richard R. Berry and John W. Johnstone, Jr., executive vice presidents and directors of Olin.

When Olin acquired its 63.4% interest in Hunt, Olin stated in a press release that while it was "considering the acquisition of the remaining public shares of Hunt, it [had] no present intention to do so." Apparently, there were no discussions or negotiations between the boards of Hunt and Olin regarding any purchase of Hunt stock during the one year commitment period.

However, it is clear that Olin always anticipated owning 100% of Hunt. Several Olin interoffice memoranda referred to the eventual merger of the two companies. One document dated September 16, 1983 sent by Peter A. Danna to Johnstone, then a director of both Olin and Hunt, spoke of Olin's long-term strategy which would be relevant "when the rest of Hunt is acquired." Another communication from R.N. Clark to Johnstone and Berry concluded as follows:

> In any event, *until Hunt is all Olin* and we are in the position to have their leadership participate in a centralization decision, any activity to bring Hunt to a new central location must be in abeyance. (*Emphasis added.*)

Finally, on September 19, 1983, Thomas Berardino, then an Olin staff vice-president in Planning and Corporate Development, sent a confidential memorandum to four of the Olin directors, three of whom, Berry, Henske and Johnstone, were also Hunt directors. That document catalogued the "pros and cons of doing a backend of Hunt acquisition this year." Nine "pros" were listed for acquiring Hunt stock prior to March 1, 1984. On the "con" side the following three [sic] considerations were detailed:

- Immediate control will cost approximately $7.3M more in purchase payments than waiting until mid-1984 (e.g. $25 vs 21 1/2 share)
- Can recoup $1.2-$1.4M (after tax) of this amount within 12 months through savings noted above
- Since Hunt's performance is currently not covering Olin's goodwill and borrowing costs, additional ownership will increase the dilution of Olin's reported earnings from the current projected 3 cents to 5 cents/share.
- Potential negative reaction of Hunt personnel
- Will be risk whenever Olin buys backend

The Court of Chancery found that it was "apparent that, from the outset, Olin anticipated that it would eventually acquire the minority interest in Hunt." *Rabkin v. Philip A. Hunt Chemical Corp.*, Del. Ch., 480 A.2d 655, 657-58 (1984). This observation is consistent with the Olin board's authorization, a week before the one year commitment period expired, for its Finance Committee to acquire the rest of Hunt should the Committee conclude on the advice of management that such an acquisition would be appropriate.

On Friday, March 23, 1984, the senior management of Olin met with a representative of the investment banking firm of Morgan, Lewis, Githens & Ahn,

Inc. (Morgan Lewis) to discuss the possible acquisition and valuation of the Hunt minority stock. Olin proposed to pay $20 per share and asked Morgan Lewis to render a fairness opinion on that price. Four days later, on Tuesday, March 27, Morgan Lewis delivered its opinion to Olin that $20 per share was fair to the minority. That opinion also contained the following statement:

> We have conducted such investigations as we deemed appropriate including, but not limited to, a review of current financial statements, projections, business activities of Hunt (which information has been supplied to us by Olin) as well as comparative information on other companies. We have not had an appraisal of the assets of Hunt made in connection with our evaluation. We have also regularly monitored the activity of the Hunt stock on the New York Stock Exchange during 1983 and to date. However, we have not met directly with the management of Hunt because of the requirement that Olin maintain total confidentiality prior to you making this merger proposal.

In reaching its conclusion Morgan Lewis evidently gave no consideration to Olin's obligation, including the bases thereof, to pay $25 per share if the stock had been acquired prior to March 1, 1984.

The same day, March 27, 1984, Olin's management presented the Morgan Lewis fairness opinion to the Olin Finance Committee with the recommendation that the remaining Hunt stock be acquired for $20 per share. At that meeting it was stated that management had determined the price based on the following factors: the Morgan Lewis analysis, Hunt's net worth, Hunt's earnings history, including current prospects for 1984, Hunt's failures to achieve the earnings projections set forth in its business plans, and the current and historical market value of Hunt stock from 1982 to 1983. The Finance Committee unanimously voted to acquire the remaining Hunt stock for $20 per share. Later that same evening Henske, Olin's chief executive officer, called Hunt President Alfred Blomquist to inform him that the Finance Committee, acting for Olin's board, had approved Olin's acquisition of the Hunt minority. The following morning, March 28, Olin and Hunt issued a joint press release announcing the cash-out merger.

Later that day the Hunt Board appointed a Special Committee, consisting of the four Hunt outside directors, to review and determine the fairness of Olin's merger proposal. These directors met on April 4, 1984, and retained Merrill Lynch as their financial advisor and the law firm of Shea and Gould as legal counsel. This committee met again on three other occasions. At the May 10, 1984 meeting the Special Committee heard a presentation by the lawyers for several plaintiffs who had filed class actions on behalf of the minority shareholders to enjoin the proposed merger. A representative of Merrill Lynch advised the meeting that $20 per share was fair to the minority from a financial standpoint, but that the range of values for the common stock was probably $19 to $25 per share.

The outside directors subsequently notified the Hunt board that they had unanimously found $20 per share to be fair but not generous. They therefore recommended that Olin consider increasing the price above $20. The next day, May 11, 1984, Olin informed the Hunt Special Committee that it had considered its recommendation but declined to raise the price. The Hunt outside directors then met again on May 14, 1984, by teleconference call, and at a meeting of the Hunt board on May 15, also held by teleconference, the Special Committee announced that it had unanimously found the $20 per share price fair and recommended approval of the merger.

On June 7, 1984, Hunt issued its proxy statement favoring the merger. That document also made clear Olin's intention to vote its 64% of the Hunt shares in favor of the proposal, thereby guaranteeing its passage. There was no requirement of approval by a majority of the minority stockholders.

The proxy statement also described in substantial detail most of the facts related above. Specifically, it disclosed the existence of the one year commitment, the Merrill Lynch conclusion that a fair range for the Hunt common stock was between $19 and $25, and the pendency of these class actions opposing the merger.

II

Taken together, the plaintiffs' complaints challenge the proposed Olin-Hunt merger on the grounds that the price offered was grossly inadequate because Olin unfairly manipulated the timing of the merger to avoid the one year commitment, and that specific language in Olin's Schedule 13D, filed when it purchased the Hunt stock, constituted a price commitment by which Olin failed to abide, contrary to its fiduciary obligations.

The Vice Chancellor granted the defendants' motion to dismiss on the ground that the plaintiffs' complaints failed to state claims upon which relief could be granted. The court's rationale was that absent claims of fraud or deception a minority stockholder's rights in a cash-out merger were limited to an appraisal. *Rabkin v. Philip A. Hunt Chemical Corp.*, Del. Ch., 480 A.2d 655, 660-62 (1984). . . .

A

The issue we address is whether the trial court erred, as a matter of law, in dismissing these claims on the ground that absent deception the plaintiffs' sole remedy under *Weinberger* is an appraisal. The plaintiffs' position is that in cases of procedural unfairness the standard of entire fairness entitles them to relief that is broader than an appraisal. Indeed, the thrust of plaintiffs' contentions is that they eschew an appraisal, since they consider Olin's manipulative conduct a breach of its fiduciary duty to pay the $25 per share guaranteed by the one year commitment. . . .

B

On a motion to dismiss for failure to state a claim it must appear with a reasonable certainty that a plaintiff would not be entitled to the relief sought under any set of facts which could be proven to support the action. . . .

In ordering the complaints dismissed the Vice Chancellor reasoned that:

Where, . . . there are no allegations of non-disclosures or misrepresentations, *Weinberger* mandates that plaintiffs' entire fairness claims be determined in an appraisal proceeding.

Rabkin, 480 A.2d at 660.

We consider that an erroneous interpretation of *Weinberger,* because it fails to take account of the entire context of the holding.

The Court of Chancery seems to have limited its focus to our statement in *Weinberger* that:

[T]he provisions of 8 Del. C. §262, as herein construed, respecting the scope of an appraisal and the means for perfecting the same, shall govern the financial remedy available to minority shareholders in a cash-out merger. Thus, we return to the well established principles of *Stauffer v. Standard Brands, Inc.,* Del. Supr., 187 A.2d 78 (1962) and *David J. Greene & Co. v. Schenley Industries, Inc.,* Del. Ch., 281 A.2d 30 (1971), mandating a stockholder's recourse to the basic remedy of an appraisal.

Weinberger, 457 A.2d at 715.

However, *Weinberger* makes clear that appraisal is not necessarily a stockholder's sole remedy. We specifically noted that:

[W]hile a plaintiff's monetary remedy ordinarily should be confined to the more liberalized appraisal proceeding herein established, we do not intend any limitation on the historic powers of the Chancellor to grant such other relief as the facts of a particular case may dictate. The appraisal remedy we approve may not be adequate in certain cases, particularly where fraud, misrepresentation, self-dealing, deliberate waste of corporate assets, or gross and palpable overreaching are involved. *Cole v. National Cash Credit Association,* Del. Ch., 156 A. 183, 187 (1931).

Id. at 714.

Thus, the trial court's narrow interpretation of *Weinberger* would render meaningless our extensive discussion of fair dealing found in that opinion. In *Weinberger* we defined fair dealing as embracing "questions of when the transaction was timed, how it was initiated, structured, negotiated, disclosed to the directors, and how the approvals of the directors and the stockholders were obtained." 457 A.2d at 711. While this duty of fairness certainly incorporates the principle that a cash-out merger must be free of fraud or misrepresentation, *Weinberger*'s mandate of fair dealing does not turn solely on issues of deception. We particularly noted broader concerns respecting the matter of procedural fairness. *Weinberger,* 457 A.2d at 711, 714. Thus, while "in a nonfraudulent transaction . . . price *may* be the preponderant consideration," *id.* at 711 (*emphasis added*), it is not necessarily so.[6]

Although the Vice Chancellor correctly understood *Weinberger* as limiting collateral attacks on cash-out mergers, her analysis narrowed the procedural protections which we still intended *Weinberger* to guarantee. Here, plaintiffs

6. For a thoughtful analysis of this issue of when stockholders have standing to sue after *Weinberger,* see Weiss, *Balancing Interests in Cash-Out Mergers: The Promise of Weinberger v. UOP, Inc.,* 8 Del. J. Corp. L. 1, 54-56 (1983).

are not arguing questions of valuation which are the traditional subjects of an appraisal. Rather, they seek to enforce a contractual right to receive $25 per share, which they claim was unfairly destroyed by Olin's manipulative conduct.

While a plaintiff's mere allegation of "unfair dealing," without more, cannot survive a motion to dismiss, averments containing "specific acts of fraud, misrepresentation, or other items of misconduct" must be carefully examined in accord with our views expressed both here and in *Weinberger. See* 457 A.2d at 703, 711, 714.

III

A

Having outlined the facts and applicable principles, we turn to the details of the Hunt-Olin merger and the plaintiffs' complaints to determine whether the specific acts of misconduct alleged are sufficient to withstand a motion to dismiss.

The Court of Chancery stated that "[t]he gravamen of all the complaints appears to be that the cash-out price is unfair." *Rabkin,* 480 A.2d at 658. However, this conclusion, which seems to be more directed to issues of valuation, is neither supported by the pleadings themselves nor the extensive discussion of unfair dealing found in the trial court's opinion. There is no challenge to any method of valuation or to the components of value upon which Olin's $20 price was based. The plaintiffs want the $25 per share guaranteed by the one year commitment, which they claim was unfairly denied them by Olin's manipulations.

According to the Vice Chancellor's analysis, the plaintiffs' complaints alleged three claims—"breach of the fiduciary duty of entire fairness, breach of fiduciary duty under *Schnell v. Chris-Craft Industries,* Del. Supr., 285 A.2d 437 (1971) and promissory estoppel." *Id.* at 659. The entire fairness claim was rejected on the ground that the plaintiffs' exclusive remedy was an appraisal. *Id.* at 660. The *Schnell* analogy was repudiated on the theory that Olin had not impinged on any rights of the minority shareholders by letting the one-year commitment expire before consummating the merger. *Id.* at 661. The court also rejected what it categorized as the promissory estoppel claim on the grounds that the language allegedly forming the promise was too vague to constitute such an undertaking, and that estoppel cannot be predicated upon a promise to do that which the promisor is already obliged to do. *Id.*

B

In *Weinberger* we observed that the timing, structure, negotiation and disclosure of a cash-out merger all had a bearing on the issue of procedural fairness. 457 A.2d at 711. The plaintiffs contend *inter alia* that Olin breached its fiduciary duty of fair dealing by purposely timing the merger, and thereby unfairly manipulating it, to avoid the one year commitment. In support of that contention plaintiffs have averred specific facts indicating that Olin knew it would eventually acquire Hunt, but delayed doing so to avoid paying $25 per share. Significantly, the trial court's opinion seems to accept that point:

> It is apparent that, from the outset, Olin anticipated that it would eventually acquire the minority interest in Hunt. Olin's chief executive officer expected as much when the Agreement was executed and, in evaluating the Agreement, Olin prepared computations based upon the assumption that it would acquire 100% of Hunt.

Rabkin, 480 A.2d at 657-58.

Consistent with this observation are the confidential Berardino memo to the three Olin and Hunt directors, Henske, Johnstone and Berry, about the disadvantages of paying a higher price during the one year commitment; the deposition testimony of Olin's chief executive officer, Mr. Henske, that the one year commitment "meant nothing"; and what could be considered a quick surrender by the Special Committee of Hunt directors in the face of Olin's proposal to squeeze out the minority at $20 per share.[7] While we do not pass on the merits of such questions, Olin's alleged attitude toward the minority, at least as it appears on the face of the complaints and their proposed amendments, coupled with the apparent absence of any meaningful negotiations as to price, all have an air reminiscent of the dealings between Signal and UOP in *Weinberger.* See 457 A.2d at 711. Certainly the Berardino memorandum, although not unusual as an Olin planning document, raises unanswered questions about the recognition by three of its recipients, all Hunt directors, of their undiminished duty of loyalty to Hunt. See *Rosenblatt v. Getty Oil Company,* Del. Supr., 493 A.2d 929, 938-39 (1985). . . . These are issues which an appraisal cannot address, and at this juncture are matters that cannot be resolved by a motion to dismiss.

In our opinion the facts alleged by the plaintiffs regarding Olin's avoidance of the one year commitment support a claim of unfair dealing sufficient to defeat dismissal at this stage of the proceedings. The defendants answer that they had no legal obligation to effect the cash-out merger during the one year period. While that may be so, the principle announced in *Schnell v. Chris-Craft Industries*[8] establishes that inequitable conduct will not be protected merely because it is legal. 285 A.2d at 439. *See also Unocal Corp. v. Mesa Petroleum Co.,*

---

7. As we noted in *Weinberger,* the use of an independent negotiating committee of outside directors may have significant advantages to the majority stockholder in defending suits of this type. See 457 A.2d at 709-711; 709 n. 7. The efficacy of that procedure was recently indicated by our opinion in *Rosenblatt v. Getty Oil Company,* Del. Supr., 493 A.2d 929, 937-939 (1985). However, we recognize that there can be serious practical problems in the use of such a committee as even *Rosenblatt* demonstrated. See 493 A.2d at 933-936; Herzel & Colling, *Establishing Procedural Fairness in Squeeze-Out Mergers after Weinberger v. UOP,* 39 Business Law. 1525, 1534-37 (1984); Weiss, *Balancing Interests in Cash-Out Mergers: The Promise of Weinberger v. UOP, Inc.,* 8 Del. J. Corp. Law 1, 50-53 (1983). Thus, we do not announce any rule, even in the context of a motion to dismiss, that the absence of such a bargaining structure will preclude dismissal in cases bottomed on claims of unfair dealing.

8. The trial court's narrow interpretation of this principle misconceives the thrust of *Schnell. See Rabkin,* 480 A.2d at 661.

493 A.2d 946, 955 (1985); *Giuricich v. Emtrol Corp.*, Del. Supr., 449 A.2d 232, 239 (1982); *Lynch v. Vickers Energy Corp.*, Del. Ch., 351 A.2d 570, 575 (1976); *Petty v. Penntech Papers, Inc.*, Del. Ch., 347 A.2d 140, 143 (1975). At the very least the facts alleged import a form of overreaching, and in the context of entire fairness they deserve more considered analysis than can be accorded them on a motion to dismiss.

Similarly, the plaintiffs' pleas arising from the language in Olin's Schedule 13D (referred to by the trial court as the claim for promissory estoppel) should not have been dismissed on the ground that appraisal was the only remedy available to the plaintiffs challenging the entire fairness of the merger.[9]

IV

In conclusion we find that the trial court erred in dismissing the plaintiffs' actions for failure to state a claim upon which relief could be granted. As we read the complaints and the proposed amendments, they assert a conscious intent by Olin, as the majority shareholder of Hunt, to deprive the Hunt minority of the same bargain that Olin made with Hunt's former majority shareholder, Turner and Newall. But for Olin's allegedly unfair manipulation, the plaintiffs contend, this bargain also was due them. In short, the defendants are charged with bad faith which goes beyond issues of "mere inadequacy of price." *Cole v. National Cash Credit Association*, Del. Ch., 156 A. 183, 187-88 (1931). In *Weinberger* we specifically relied upon this aspect of *Cole* in acknowledging the imperfections of an appraisal where circumstances of this sort are present. See 457 A.2d at 714.

Necessarily, this will require the Court of Chancery to closely focus upon *Weinberger*'s mandate of entire fairness based on a careful analysis of both the fair price and fair dealing aspects of a transaction. See 457 A.2d at 711, 714. We recognize that this can present certain practical problems, since stockholders may invariably claim that the price being offered is the result of unfair dealings. However, we think that plaintiffs will be tempered in this approach by the prospect that an ultimate judgment in defendants' favor may have cost plaintiffs their unperfected appraisal rights. Moreover, our courts are not without a degree of sophistication in such matters. A balance must be struck between sustaining complaints averring faithless acts, which taken as true would constitute breaches of fiduciary duties that are reasonably related to and have a substantial impact upon the price offered, and properly dismissing those allegations questioning judgmental factors of valuation. *Cole v. National Cash Credit Association*, 156 A. at 187-88. Otherwise, we face the anomalous result that stockholders who are eliminated without appraisal rights can bring class actions, while in other cases a squeezed-out minority is limited to an appraisal, provided there

---

9. Again, we emphasize that we are not reaching the merits of the plaintiffs' claims. Our holding today is to make clear the scope of *Weinberger* when the Court of Chancery addresses a motion to dismiss a minority stockholder's suit attacking a cash-out merger. However, it is important to bear in mind that *Weinberger* was a case decided after trial on the merits. Here we address those issues solely in a pre-trial context. We neither express nor imply any views as to the outcome of these matters after they have had a fuller exploration at a later stage of the proceedings.

was no deception, regardless of the degree of procedural unfairness employed to take their shares. Without that balance, *Weinberger*'s concern for entire fairness loses all force.

Accordingly, the decision of the Court of Chancery dismissing these consolidated class actions is REVERSED. The matter is REMANDED with directions that the plaintiffs be permitted to file their proposed amendments to the pleadings.

QUESTIONS

1. What is the purpose of the modern appraisal remedy? Is the *sole* purpose to provide the dissatisfied minority shareholder with the opportunity to challenge the price offered by Bidder (i.e., the adequacy of the premium offered)? In other words, in what way does the *mandatory* right to an appraisal serve to hold management accountable for its decision to enter into the proposed transaction?

2. What does "fair dealing" require? Who has the burden to establish fair dealing?

3. Why isn't approval by a majority of outstanding shares sufficient protection against shareholders receiving inadequate acquisition consideration? In other words, if management obtains the requisite shareholder approval, what interests are to be protected by granting the remedy of an appraisal?

4. Delaware §262(c) and MBCA §13.02(a)(5) both allow a corporation's articles to extend the right of appraisal to transactions beyond those described in the statute as a matter of private ordering. Conversely, should the corporation be allowed to amend its articles of incorporation to eliminate the right of appraisal granted by statute, assuming the requisite shareholder approval is obtained for such an articles amendment? In analyzing this issue, does it matter whether the corporation is publicly traded or privately held?

||3||

Scope of Successor
Liability: Transferring
the Assets (and Liabilities)
of Target Co. to Bidder Co.

In Chapter 2, we analyzed the requirements imposed by state corporate law in connection with each of the different methods for structuring an acquisition. In the process, we examined the substantive differences among the regulatory approaches taken by Delaware, California, and the Model Business Corporation Act (MBCA) as to the requirement of board and/or shareholder approval, as well as the availability of appraisal rights in connection with each of the different methods of effecting an acquisition. In this chapter, we examine the rules of successor liability, another important set of considerations that influence the transaction planner's decision as to the most appropriate method to use to structure a proposed acquisition.

When considering the rules of successor liability, the focus of analysis shifts away from the analysis we conducted in Chapter 2, where we examined who *within* the company should decide whether the company should be acquired. In the process of analyzing the problem sets in Chapter 2, we largely ignored the impact of the proposed transaction on constituencies *outside* the company. In this chapter, we examine the mechanics of transferring ownership of the business of Target (the acquired company) to its new owner, Bidder (the acquiring corporation). As part of our analysis, we will observe how the various forms of business combinations affect constituents *outside* the company. Not surprisingly, the impact of this transfer of ownership on the *creditors* of Target will depend on the method used to complete the acquisition; that is, whether the transaction is structured as a merger, stock purchase, or asset purchase. For reasons that we will analyze later in this chapter, the most problematic form of business combination from a public policy perspective is the acquisition structured as an asset purchase.

A.   Successor Liability in Merger Transactions and Stock Purchases

1.   Introductory Note

In most states, a merger takes effect once the articles of merger are accepted for filing by the secretary of state's office. *See, e.g.,* DGCL §251(c). The articles of merger must specify, among other things, the company that is to survive the merger and the company whose shares are to be cancelled (by operation of law) once the merger takes effect. As we learned in Chapter 2, the merger agreement must specify the manner of converting the shares of Target that are to be cancelled. *See, e.g.,* MBCA §11.02(c). Once the merger is effective, the holder of any Target shares has no further ownership interest in the business assets of Target and instead will be entitled to receive only the consideration specified in the merger agreement, which may consist of cash or stock (or other securities) of the surviving corporation or stock of some other corporation (or some combination of the foregoing).

As reflected in Diagram 1 in Appendix A, once the merger takes effect, the assets and liabilities of the disappearing corporation, Target, are pooled together with the assets and liabilities of the surviving corporation, Bidder. In effect, once the articles of merger are filed with the secretary of state's office, Bidder succeeds — by operation of law—to *all* of the rights and *all* of the liabilities of Target. No individual transfer of ownership is required. Therein lies the beauty—the magic, if you will—of the merger procedure. Once the merger takes effect, Target disappears in the sense that its separate legal existence is extinguished. At the same time, Target's business operations are transferred by operation of law to the surviving corporation, Bidder. The convenience of the merger procedure lies in the fact that this transfer of control over Target's business takes place by operation of law and without the need for any further action on the part of either Target or Bidder. *See, e.g.,* MBCA §11.07. This is known as the *rule of successor liability,* which is part of the statutorily authorized merger procedure.

From the perspective of a creditor of Target, the economic existence of Target continues as part of the surviving corporation, even though Target as a legal entity disappears by operation of law once the *merger* takes effect. Under this rule of successor liability, *all* of the assets of the surviving company are available to satisfy creditors of *both* constituent corporations in a direct merger—that is, the creditors of both Target and Bidder—regardless of whether the third party's claim arises under contract or tort.

By contrast, an acquisition structured as a *stock purchase* leaves the entity, Target, in place. *See* Diagram 7 in Appendix A. Consequently, *all* of Target's assets remain in place to satisfy the claims of Target's creditors, which also remain in place. Even though the ownership of all Target stock has been transferred to Bidder, the assets of Bidder are insulated from liability on the claims of Target's creditors. This is the direct result of the well-established corporate law principle that the corporation is a separate legal entity. As such, the company's owners (the shareholders) are typically shielded from any personal liability on the business debts incurred by the corporation, in the absence of some factual basis that persuades a court to pierce the corporate veil.[1] Particularly in the case of a business operated as a small, closely held corporation, the independent existence of the corporation may get blurred, which may result in the judicial decision to pierce the corporate veil and hold the company's shareholders (and/or managers) personally liable on the business debt. In the case of a publicly traded corporation, however, the existence of the corporation as a separate legal entity that provides the shield of limited liability to its owners (and managers) is of crucial importance, as we shall see in the cases that follow.

Since the corporate entity remains intact after the stock purchase is completed, the assets of Target remain available to satisfy the claims of Target's creditors. On the other hand, whether the assets of Bidder will become subject to the claims of Target's creditors will depend in large part on whether Bidder, as the new controlling shareholder of Target, operates its subsidiary in such a way as to create the basis for liability on a "piercing the corporate veil" cause of action.

2. Commercial Leases

Consider the classic example of a contract creditor: the landlord who has entered into a commercial lease with the tenant, Target Co. This type of contract claim is routinely part of the world of mergers and acquisitions (M&A) transactions because many businesses operate out of some type of office, or storefront, or manufacturing facility, any of which may involve the leasing of commercial space. If Target has entered into a long-term commercial lease with the landlord, the majority view (as you learned in your first-year property and/or contracts courses) is that leases are freely assignable (transferable) unless the lease expressly includes a clause prohibiting assignments (transfers). This default rule is grounded in the strong public policy prevalent throughout the law of real property favoring the free alienability (transferability) of interests in real property. The modern view, however, allows restraints on alienation (i.e., restrictions on the right to assign or otherwise transfer leasehold interests), so long as the terms of the restriction satisfy a standard of reasonableness. This modern view allowing reasonable restraints on alienation has led to widespread use of clauses that allow the landlord to prevent assignment of the tenant's interest under the terms of a commercial lease. In cases where the lease includes a nonassignment clause, the tenant generally will not be able to assign the lease without first obtaining the consent of a third party, usually the landlord. If the tenant, Target, later proposes to enter into a business combination structured as either a merger or a stock purchase, the question arises whether the acquisition qualifies as the type of *transfer* that triggers the nonassignment clause contained in Target's lease with the landlord. The cases that follow address this chronic problem.

---

1. As you learned in your introductory Business Associations or Corporations class, a company's shareholders may be held personally liable for the business debts of their corporation if the plaintiff/creditor establishes a factual basis sufficient to persuade the court to exercise its equity powers and disregard the corporation's shield of limited liability.

3.   Intellectual Property Licensing Agreements

The issue of transferability also arises frequently in the case of licenses of intellectual property rights, such as agreements that grant rights to use patented technology or copyrighted material. Whereas the transfer of rights under commercial leases is usually governed by state law, the analysis of the transfer of rights to intellectual property is further complicated by federal law that protects certain intellectual property rights, particularly patents and copyrights. Accordingly, in an acquisition, the transaction planner must first analyze the threshold question of whether federal or state law applies to determine the transferability of rights to intellectual property.

Although this threshold question can be an issue for any business that licenses intellectual property to, or from, third parties, this issue presents itself most acutely in the case of technology companies. The high-tech company often becomes an attractive acquisition candidate because of its portfolio of intellectual property rights. The portfolio may include intellectual property licensed from third parties ("in-licensed I.P.") as well as licenses of intellectual property to customers and other third parties ("out-licensed I.P."). For many privately held technology companies, the value of the company lies in these license agreements. In these cases, Bidder's willingness to acquire Target is often driven by the ability of Target to transfer its rights under these licensing agreements.

4.   Tort Liability

In the case of tort claims, the same rule of successor liability applies regardless of whether the acquisition is structured as either a merger or a stock purchase. Consequently, the assets of Target will generally be available to satisfy prior tort claims. During the course of its due diligence investigation of Target's financial affairs and business operations, Bidder will generally be able to identify the known, current claims pending against Target, including both contractual and tort claims. Obviously, the information disclosed during the course of Bidder's due diligence investigation as to the number and dollar value of known claimants against Target will affect Bidder's valuation of Target's business and accordingly the purchase price that Bidder is willing to pay to acquire Target. The manner, scope, and dynamics of the due diligence process will be covered in Chapter 5 as part of our discussion of negotiating and preparing the acquisition agreement.

From Bidder's perspective, an area of primary concern in negotiating the terms of the acquisition of Target will usually center on *long-tail* claimants; that is, those claims that may not arise until *long after* the acquisition is completed. Among the most prominent of these long-tail claimants are product liability and environmental claimants. In the case of these types of long-tail claimants, Bidder's primary concern is that, as the successor-in-interest to Target, it will unwittingly absorb liabilities that are not reflected in the purchase price that Bidder paid to acquire Target.

In Chapter 5, where we discuss documenting the acquisition transaction, we will examine strategies that can be used to minimize the potentially disastrous consequences presented by these types of long-tail claims that may surface long after Bidder has closed on its acquisition of Target. As we will see, these strategies typically include the use of due diligence procedures in advance of closing on the acquisition, representation and warranties included in the acquisition agreement itself, and indemnification provisions, all of which are described in more detail in Chapter 5.

Another option that can be used to minimize Bidder's liability exposure to claims of Target's creditors is to structure the acquisition as an asset purchase. By using this method to acquire Target, Bidder can decide which of Target's liabilities it wants to assume expressly, thereby leaving behind all other business debts of Target, whether in tort or in contract. The public policy concerns inherent in using this method of acquisition will be examined later in this chapter. *See Ruiz v. Blentech Corp., infra.*

5.   Successor Liability in Direct (Statutory) Mergers vs. Triangular Mergers

In this section, we look at the scope of successor liability imposed "by operation of law" under the terms of modern merger statutes such as MBCA §11.07. The following case is notable because it addresses the intersection of federal law on patents *and* state law on the effect of mergers.

PPG Industries, Inc. v. Guardian Industries Corporation
597 F.2d 1090 (6th Cir. 1979)

LIVELY, Circuit Judge.

The question in this case is whether the surviving or resultant corporation in a statutory merger acquires patent license rights of the constituent corporations. The plaintiff, PPG Industries, Inc. (PPG), appeals from a judgment of the district court dismissing its patent infringement action on the ground that the defendant, Guardian Industries, Corp. (Guardian), as licensee of the patents in suit, was not an infringer. Guardian cross-appeals from a holding by the district court that its alternate defense based on an equipment license agreement was ineffective. The district court opinion is reported at 428 F. Supp. 789 (N.D. Ohio 1977).

I

Prior to 1964 both PPG and Permaglass, Inc., were engaged in fabrication of glass products, which required that sheets of glass be shaped for particular uses. Independently of each other the two fabricators developed similar processes, which involved "floating glass on a bed of gas, while it was being heated and bent." This process is known in the industry as "gas hearth technology" and "air float technology"; the two terms are interchangeable. After a period of negotiations PPG and Permaglass entered into an agreement on January 1,

1964 whereby each granted rights to the other under "gas hearth system" patents already issued and in the process of prosecution. The purpose of the agreement was set forth in the preamble as follows:

> WHEREAS, PPG is desirous of acquiring from PERMAGLASS a world-wide exclusive license with right to sublicense others under PERMAGLASS Technical Data and PERMAGLASS Patent Rights, subject only to reservation by PERMA-GLASS of non-exclusive rights thereunder; and
>
> WHEREAS, PERMAGLASS is desirous of obtaining a nonexclusive license to use Gas Hearth Systems under PPG Patent Rights, excepting in the Dominion of Canada.

This purpose was accomplished in the two sections of the agreement quoted below:

SECTION 3. GRANT FROM PERMAGLASS TO PPG

> 3.1 Subject to the reservation set forth in Subsection 3.3 below, PERMA-GLASS hereby grants to PPG an exclusive license, with right of sub-license, to use PERMAGLASS Technical Data in Gas Hearth Systems throughout the United States of America, its territories and possessions, and all countries of the world foreign thereto.
>
> 3.2 Subject to the reservation set forth in Subsection 3.3 below, PERMA-GLASS hereby grants to PPG an unlimited exclusive license, with right of sublicense, under PERMAGLASS Patent Rights.
>
> 3.3 The licenses granted to PPG under Subsections 3.1 and 3.2 above shall be subject to the reservation of a non-exclusive, non-transferable, royalty-free, world-wide right and license for the benefit and use of PERMAGLASS.

SECTION 4. GRANT FROM PPG TO PERMAGLASS

> 4.1 PPG hereby grants to PERMAGLASS a non-exclusive, non-transferable, royalty-free right and license to heat, bend, thermally temper and/or anneal glass using Gas Hearth Systems under PPG Patent Rights, excepting in the Dominion of Canada, and to use or sell glass articles produced thereby, but no license, express or implied, is hereby granted to PERMAGLASS under any claim of any PPG patent expressly covering any coating method, coating composition, or coated article.

Assignability of the agreement and of the license granted to Permaglass and termination of the license granted to Permaglass were covered in the following language:

SECTION 9. ASSIGNABILITY

> 9.1 This Agreement shall be assignable by PPG to any successor of the entire flat glass business of PPG but shall otherwise be non-assignable except with the consent of PERMAGLASS first obtained in writing.
>
> 9.2 This Agreement and the license granted by PPG to PERMAGLASS hereunder shall be personal to PERMAGLASS and non-assignable except with the consent of PPG first obtained in writing.

SECTION 11. TERMINATION

11.2 In the event that a majority of the voting stock of PERMAGLASS shall at any time become owned or controlled directly or indirectly by a manufacturer of automobiles or a manufacturer or fabricator of glass other than the present owners, the license granted to PERMAGLASS under Subsection 4.1 shall terminate forthwith.

Eleven patents are involved in this suit. Nine of them originated with Permaglass and were licensed to PPG as exclusive licensee under Section 3.2, *supra,* subject to the non-exclusive, non-transferable reservation to Permaglass set forth in Section 3.3. Two of the patents originated with PPG. Section 4.1 granted a non-exclusive, non-transferable license to Permaglass with respect to the two PPG patents. In Section 9.1 and 9.2 assignability was treated somewhat differently as between the parties, and the Section 11.2 provisions with regard to termination apply only to the license granted to Permaglass.

As of December 1969 Permaglass was merged into Guardian pursuant to applicable statutes of Ohio and Delaware. Guardian was engaged primarily in the business of fabricating and distributing windshields for automobiles and trucks. It had decided to construct a facility to manufacture raw glass and the capacity of that facility would be greater than its own requirements. Permaglass had no glass manufacturing capability and it was contemplated that its operations would utilize a large part of the excess output of the proposed Guardian facility.

The "Agreement of Merger" between Permaglass and Guardian did not refer specifically to the 1964 agreement between PPG and Permaglass. However, among Permaglass' representations in the agreement was the following:

(g) Permaglass is the owner, assignee or licensee of such patents, trademarks, trade names and copyrights as are listed and described in Exhibit "C" attached hereto. None of such patents, trademarks, trade names or copyrights is in litigation and Permaglass has not received any notice of conflict with the asserted rights of third parties relative to the use thereof.

Listed on Exhibit "C" to the merger agreement are the nine patents originally developed by Permaglass and licensed to PPG under the 1964 agreement which is involved in this infringement action.

Shortly after the merger was consummated PPG filed the present action, claiming infringement by Guardian in the use of apparatus and processes described and claimed in eleven patents, which were identified by number and origin. The eleven patents were covered by the terms of the 1964 agreement. PPG asserted that it became the exclusive licensee of the nine patents which originated with Permaglass under the 1964 agreement and that the rights reserved by Permaglass were personal to it and non-transferable and non-assignable. PPG also claimed that Guardian had no rights with respect to the two patents, which had originated with PPG because the license under these patents was personal to Permaglass and non-transferable and non-assignable except with the permission of PPG. In addition it claimed that the license with respect to these two patents had terminated under the provisions of Section 11.2, *supra,* by reason of the merger.

One of the defenses pled by Guardian in its answer was that it was a licensee of the patents in suit. It described the merger with Permaglass and claimed it "had succeeded to all rights, powers, ownerships, etc., of Permaglass, and as Permaglass' successor, defendant is legally entitled to operate in place of Permaglass under the January 1, 1964 agreement between Permaglass and plaintiff, free of any claim of infringement of the patents. . . . "

After holding an evidentiary hearing the district court concluded that the parties to the 1964 agreement did not intend that the rights reserved by Permaglass in its nine patents or the rights assigned to Permaglass in the two PPG patents would not pass to a successor corporation by way of merger. The court held that there had been no assignment or transfer of the rights by Permaglass, but rather that Guardian acquired these rights by operation of law under the merger statutes of Ohio and Delaware. The provisions of the 1964 agreement making the license rights of Permaglass non-assignable and non-transferable were held not to apply because of the "continuity of interest inherent in a statutory merger that distinguishes it from the ordinary assignment or transfer case." 428 F. Supp. at 796.

With respect to the termination provision in Section 11.2 of the 1964 agreement, the district court again relied on "the nature of a statutory merger in contrast to an outright sale or acquisition of stock" in holding that a majority of the voting stock of Permaglass did not become owned or controlled by Guardian. 428 F. Supp. at 796.

II

Questions with respect to the assignability of a patent license are controlled by federal law. It has long been held by federal courts that agreements granting patent licenses are personal and not assignable unless expressly made so. . . . This has been the rule at least since 1852 when the Supreme Court decided *Troy Iron & Nail v. Corning*, 55 U.S. (14 How.) 193, 14 L. Ed. 383 (1852). . . . The district court recognized this rule in the present case, but concluded that where patent licenses are claimed to pass by operation of law to the resultant or surviving corporation in a statutory merger there has been no assignment or transfer.

There appear to be no reported cases where the precise issue in this case has been decided. At least two treatises contain the statement that rights under a patent license owned by a constituent corporation pass to the consolidated corporation in the case of a consolidation, W. Fletcher, *Cyclopedia of the Law of Corporations* §7089 (revised ed. 1973); and to the new or resultant corporation in the case of a merger, A. Deller, Walker on Patents §409 (2d ed. 1965). . . .

Guardian relies on two classes of cases where rights of a constituent corporation have been held to pass by merger to the resultant corporation even though such rights are not otherwise assignable or transferable. It points out that the courts have consistently held that "shop rights" does pass in a statutory merger. See e.g., *Papazian v. American Steel & Wire Co.*, 155 F. Supp. 111 (N.D. Ohio 1957); *Neon Signal Devices, Inc. v. Alpha-Claude Neon Corp.*, 54 F.2d 793 (W.D. Pa.1931); *Wilson v. J.G. Wilson Corp.*, 241 F. 494 (E.D. Va.1917). A shop right is an implied license, which accrues to an employer in cases where an employee has perfected a patentable device while working for the employer. Though the employee is the owner of the patent he is estopped from claiming infringement by the employer. This estoppel arises from the fact that the patent work has been done on the employer's time and that the employer has furnished materials for the experiments and financial backing to the employee.

The rule that prevents an employee-inventor from claiming infringement against a successor to the entire business and good will of his employer is but one feature of the broad doctrine of estoppel, which underlies the shop right cases. No element of estoppel exists in the present case. The license rights of Permaglass did not arise by implication. They were bargained for at arms length and the agreement, which defines the rights of the parties, provides that Permaglass received non-transferable, non-assignable personal licenses. We do not believe that the express prohibition against assignment and transfer in a written instrument may be held ineffective by analogy to a rule based on estoppel in situations where there is no written contract and the rights of the parties have arisen by implication because of their past relationship.

The other group of cases, which the district court and Guardian found to be analogous, holds that the resultant corporation in a merger succeeds to the rights of the constituent corporations under real estate leases. . . . The most obvious difficulty in drawing an analogy between the lease cases and those concerning patent licenses is that a lease is an interest in real property. As such, it is subject to the deep-rooted policy against restraints on alienation. Applying this policy, courts have construed provisions against assignability in leases strictly and have concluded that they do not prevent the passage of interests by operation of law. . . . There is no similar policy, which is offended by the decision of a patent owner to make a license under his patent personal to the licensee, and non-assignable and non-transferable. In fact the law treats a license as if it contained these restrictions in the absence of express provisions to the contrary.

We conclude that the district court misconceived the intent of the parties to the 1964 agreement. We believe the district court put the burden on the wrong party in stating:

> Because the parties failed to provide that Permaglass' rights under the 1964 license agreement would not pass to the corporation surviving a merger, the Court finds that Guardian succeeded to Permaglass' license pursuant to 8 Del. C. s 259, and Ohio Revised Code §§1701.81 and 1701.83.

The agreement provides with respect to the license, which Permaglass granted to PPG that Permaglass reserved "a non-exclusive, non-transferable, royalty-free, world-wide right and license for *the benefit and use of Permaglass*." (*emphasis added*). Similarly, with respect to its own two patents, PPG granted to Permaglass "a non-exclusive, non-transferable, royalty-free right and license. . . . " Further, the agreement provides that both it and the license granted to Permaglass "shall be personal to PERMAGLASS and non-assignable except with the consent of PPG first obtained in writing."

The quoted language from Sections 3, 4, and 9 of the 1964 agreement evinces an intent that only Permaglass was to enjoy the privileges of licensee. If the parties had intended an exception in the event of a merger, it would have been a simple matter to have so provided in the agreement. Guardian contends such an exception is not necessary since it is universally recognized that patent licenses pass from a licensee to the resultant corporation in case of a merger. This does not appear to be the case. In *Packard Instrument Co. v. ANS, Inc.,* 416 F.2d 943 (2d Cir. 1969), a license agreement provided that rights thereunder could not be transferred or assigned "except . . . (b) if the entire ownership and business of ANS is transferred by sale, merger, or consolidation, . . . " 416 F.2d at 944 n. 1. Similarly, the agreement construed in *Freeman v. Seiberling Rubber Co.,* 72 F.2d 124 (6th Cir. 1934), provided that the license was not assignable except with the entire business and goodwill of the licensee. We conclude that if the parties had intended an exception in case of a merger to the provisions against assignment and transfer they would have included it in the agreement. It should be noted also that the district court in *Packard, supra,* held that an assignment had taken place when the licensee was merged into another corporation.

The district court also held that the patent licenses in the present case were not transferred because they passed by operation of law from Permaglass to Guardian. This conclusion is based on the theory of continuity, which underlies a true merger. However, the theory of continuity relates to the fact that there is no dissolution of the constituent corporations and, even though they cease to exist, their essential corporate attributes are vested by operation of law in the surviving or resultant corporation. . . . It does not mean that there is no transfer of particular assets from a constituent corporation to the surviving or resultant one.

The Ohio merger statute provides that following a merger all property of a constituent corporation shall be "deemed to be *transferred* to and vested in the surviving or new corporation without further act or deed, . . . " (*emphasis added*). Ohio Revised Code, [former] §1701.81(A)(4). This indicates that the transfer is by operation of law, not that there is no transfer of assets in a merger situation. The Delaware statute, which was also involved in the Permaglass-Guardian merger, provides that the property of the constituent corporations "shall be vested in the corporation surviving or resulting from such merger or consolidation, . . . " 8 Del. C. s 259(a). The Third Circuit has construed the "shall be vested" language of the Delaware statute as follows:

> In short, the underlying property of the constituent corporations is *transferred* to the resultant corporation upon the carrying out of the consolidation or merger. . . . *Koppers Coal & Transportation Co. v. United States,* 107 F.2d 706, 708 (3d Cir. 1939). (*emphasis added*).

In his opinion in *Koppers,* Judge Biggs disposed of arguments very similar to those of Guardian in the present case, based on the theory of continuity. Terming such arguments "metaphysical" he found them completely at odds with the language of the Delaware statute. *Id.* Finally, on this point, the parties themselves provided in the merger agreement that all property of Permaglass "shall be deemed transferred to and shall vest in Guardian without further act or deed. . . . " A transfer is no less a transfer because it takes place by operation of law rather than by a particular act of the parties. The merger was effected by the parties and the transfer was a result of their act of merging.

Thus, Sections 3, 4, and 9 of the 1964 agreement between PPG and Permaglass show an intent that the licenses held by Permaglass in the eleven patents in suit not be transferable. While this conclusion disposes of the license defense as to all eleven patents, it should be noted that Guardian's claim to licenses under the two patents, which originated with PPG is also defeated by Section 11.2 of the 1964 agreement. This section addresses a different concern from that addressed in Sections 3, 4, and 9. The restrictions on transferability and assignability in those sections prevent the patent licenses from becoming the property of third parties. The termination clause, however, provides that Permaglass' license with respect to the two PPG patents will terminate if the ownership of a majority of the voting stock of Permaglass passes from the 1964 stockholders to designated classes of persons, even though the licenses themselves might never have changed hands.

Apparently PPG was willing for Permaglass to continue as licensee under the nine patents even though ownership of its stock might change. These patents originated with Permaglass and so long as Permaglass continued to use the licenses for its own benefit a mere change in ownership of Permaglass stock would not nullify the licenses. Only a transfer or assignment would cause a termination. However, the agreement provides for termination with respect to the two original PPG patents in the event of an indirect takeover of Permaglass by a change in the ownership of a majority of its stock. The fact that PPG sought and obtained a stricter provision with respect to the two patents which it originally owned in no way indicates an intention to permit transfer of licenses under the other nine in case of a merger. None of the eleven licenses was transferable; but two of them, those involving PPG's own development in the field of gas hearth technology, were not to continue even for the benefit of the licensee if it came under the control of a manufacturer of automobiles or a competitor of PPG in the glass industry "other than the present owners" of Permaglass. A consistency among the provisions of the agreement is discernible when the different origins of the various patents are considered. . . .

NOTES

1. Form Matters.   This case illustrates, once again, that the default rules associated with the different methods for structuring an acquisition *do* influence the choice of structure to be used for a particular deal. It also demonstrates the importance of mastering the default rules so that the transaction planner can responsibly and competently anticipate potential problems and address them in the process of negotiating and documenting the acquisition. Finally, this case illustrates the manner in which the default rules serve to allocate the economic risks associated with completing a particular acquisition, as well as allocating the costs associated with bargaining around the default rule in order to obtain a different economic result that is desired by the parties.

2. Due Diligence.   Consider the provision quoted by the court at page 225 from the merger agreement entered into by Permaglass and Guardian. Although the language of this provision does not specifically refer to the licenses at issue in the principal case, the language used in this provision clearly seems to anticipate the possibility of an infringement action of the type presented in this case. The language of the representation quoted by the court from the parties' agreement is carefully worded. This wording is likely a direct outgrowth of the *due diligence* process undertaken by the parties prior to signing this merger agreement. As we shall see in Chapter 5, *representations* are a customary provision in the acquisition agreement. One of the most important purposes served by these representations is to allocate business and financial risks between the parties to the agreement. *Query:* What business risk is being allocated to each party by the language of the representation quoted by the court in the principal case? How did the parties learn of this risk inherent in Permaglass's business so that they could negotiate the allocation of this business risk as part of the acquisition agreement?

QUESTIONS

1. Who are the parties to this acquisition? Who is the Bidder? Who is the Target?

2. What is the structure used to make this acquisition?

3. What is the impact of this acquisition on the creditors of Target?

4. What was the business incentive for Bidder to propose to acquire Target?

5. Who is the plaintiff? What relief does plaintiff seek?

6. What is the issue that the court must decide? Does state or federal law control on this issue?

7. What is the major difference between the reasoning used in the district court's decision and that of the appellate court in this case? Based on this difference, what is the lesson that the transaction planner should take away from reading this case, which will then inform this M&A lawyer in considering how to advise future clients as to the best way to structure future transactions?

8. What was the scope of the representation that Target gave to Bidder in this case? See subpart (g) of the acquisition agreement, quoted at page 225.

9. Based on the reasoning of the appellate court, what result if the parties had structured the transaction as a triangular merger, leaving Permaglass as the surviving corporation? What result if Guardian had purchased all the stock of Permaglass?

B.   Use of Change of Control Clauses

Branmar Theatre Co. v. Branmar, Inc.
264 A.2d 526 (Del. Ch. 1970)

SHORT, Vice Chancellor.

This is an action for a declaratory judgment in which plaintiff seeks to enjoin defendant from cancelling a lease agreement previously executed by the parties. Defendant, by its answer, prays the court to find that it was entitled to treat the lease agreement as terminated because of a violation of a covenant therein prohibiting assignment by the lessee. This is the decision after final hearing.

Plaintiff was incorporated under the laws of Delaware on June 7, 1967. The owners of its outstanding capital stock were the Robert Rappaport family of Cleveland, Ohio. On June 9, 1967 plaintiff and defendant entered into a lease agreement for a motion picture theatre in the Branmar Shopping Center, New Castle County, Delaware. The lease, sixteen pages in length, recites that the lessor is to erect a theatre building in the shopping center. It provides for the payment of rent by the lessee to the lessor of $27,500 per year plus a percentage of gross admissions receipts, plus five per cent of any amounts paid to the lessee by refreshment concessionaires. The percentage of admissions figure is regulated by the type of attractions in the theatre, the minimum being five per cent and the maximum ten. The lease provides for a twenty year term with an option in the lessee to renew for an additional ten years. The lessee is to provide the lessor with a loan of $60,000, payable in installments, to be used for construction. The lessee is to provide, at its cost, whatever fixtures and equipment are necessary to operate the theatre. Paragraph 12 of the lease, the focal point of this lawsuit, provides:

> "Lessee shall not sublet, assign, transfer, or in any manner dispose of the said premises or any part thereof, for all or any part of the term hereby granted, without the prior written consent of the Lessor, such consent shall not be unreasonably withheld."

Joseph Luria, the principal for Branmar Shopping Center testified at trial that he negotiated the lease agreement with Isador Rappaport; that he made inquiries about Rappaport's ability to manage a theatre and satisfied himself that Rappaport had the competence and the important industry connections to successfully operate the theatre. It appears that Rappaport and his son operate a successful theatre in Cleveland, Ohio and have owned and operated theatres elsewhere.

Following execution of the lease the Rappaports were approached by Muriel Schwartz and Reba Schwartz, operators of ten theatres in the Delaware and neighboring Maryland area, with an offer to manage the theatre for the Rappaports who had no other business interests in the Wilmington area. This offer was not accepted but the Schwartzes subsequently agreed with the Rappaports to purchase the lease from plaintiff and have it assigned to them. An assignment was executed by plaintiff to the Schwartzes. Defendant rejected the assignment under the power reserved in Paragraph 12 of the lease. On May 29, 1969 the Schwartzes purchased the outstanding shares of plaintiff from the Rappaports. Upon receipt of notice of the sale defendant advised plaintiff that it considered the sale of the shares to the Schwartzes to be a breach of Paragraph 12 of the lease and the lease to be null and void.

The theatre building is now substantially completed and ready for occupancy. The Schwartzes are ready and willing to perform under the lease agreement. Defendant intends to substitute a new tenant, Sameric Theatres, for the corporate plaintiff, contending that Sameric is a better qualified operator than the Schwartzes.

Defendant argues that the sale of stock was in legal effect an assignment of the lease by the Rappaports to the Schwartzes, was in breach of Paragraph 12 of the lease, and that it was, therefore, justified in terminating plaintiff's leasehold interest. That in the absence of fraud, and none is charged here, transfer of stock of a corporate lessee is ordinarily not a violation of a clause prohibiting assignment is clear from the authorities. . . . Defendant contends, however, that this is not the ordinary case. Here, it says, due to the nature of the motion picture business, the performance required was by the Rappaports personally. But while defendant's negotiations were with a member of the Rappaport family when the lease was executed it chose to let the theatre to a corporation whose stock might foreseeably be transferred by the then stockholders. In the preparation of the lease, a document of sixteen pages, defendant was careful to spell out in detail the rights and duties of the parties. It did not, however, see fit to provide for forfeiture in the event the stockholders sold their shares. Had this been the intent it would have been a simple matter to have so provided. . . .

Defendant contends that the evidence clearly shows that the Schwartzes do not have the connections in the industry to obtain first quality motion pictures which is of prime importance to a landlord under "a percentage rental agreement." If these were the facts defendant's theory that the lease called for personal performance by the Rappaports might have some merit. . . . But the evidence on which defendant relies is a comparison of connections by the Schwartzes with those of defendant's proposed new lessee. This is wholly immaterial. If the question of ability to perform to defendant's best advantage is material at all it is as between the Schwartzes and the Rappaports and there is simply no competent evidence in the record to answer this question. Moreover, defendant's characterization of the lease as "a percentage rental agreement" is not justified. The rental terms are not based solely on percentages but on a substantial stipulated annual rent plus percentages. What difference in dollars the percentages would amount to depending upon the identity of the theatre's management does not appear. . . .

Defendant suggests that since "the Rappaports" could not assign the lease without its consent they should not be permitted to accomplish the same result by transfer of their stock. But the rule that precludes a person from doing indirectly what he cannot do directly has no application to the present case. The attempted assignment was not by the Rappaports but by plaintiff corporation, the sale of stock by its stockholders. Since defendant has failed to show circumstances to justify ignoring the corporation's separate existence reliance upon the cited rule is misplaced.

I find that the sale of stock by the Rappaports to the Schwartzes was not an assignment within the terms of Paragraph 12 of the lease and that the same remains in full force and effect. Order on notice.

QUESTIONS

1.   What method was used to structure the acquisition at issue in this case?

2.   What is a *change of control* clause? On the facts of this case, who would want to include a change of control clause? In which agreement involved in the facts of the principal case? Why?

PROBLEMS

1. Assume that Target has ten years left on the commercial lease for its primary manufacturing facility. What will happen to Target's rights and liabilities under the lease if Bidder should acquire Target by way of:
    a. A direct merger?
    b. A stock purchase?
    c. A reverse triangular merger?
    d. A forward triangular merger?
    e. A sale of assets?
2. Assume that Target has ten years left on the commercial lease for its primary manufacturing facility. Assume further that this lease includes a nonassignment clause that requires the consent of the landlord in order for Target to assign its interest under the lease. What will happen to Target's rights and obligations under the lease if Bidder should acquire Target by way of:
    a. A direct merger?
    b. A stock purchase?
    c. A reverse triangular merger?
    d. A forward triangular merger?
    e. A sale of assets?

C. Successor Liability in Asset Acquisitions

1. Introductory Note

The key characteristic of an asset purchase is that Target remains in place, even though it has sold all (or substantially all) of its assets to Bidder. In many deals, Bidder and Target may negotiate for certain (or even all) of Target's liabilities to be transferred to Bidder as well. This obligation is usually accomplished, as a matter of contract law, by including Bidder's express written assumption of certain designated liabilities of Target as part of the asset purchase agreement entered into by Bidder and Target.

Once the parties close on this asset acquisition, Target remains intact and is generally left holding all of the liabilities that were not expressly assumed by Bidder, along with the consideration paid by Bidder to acquire all or substantially all of Target's assets. As reflected in Diagram 4 (of Appendix A), the asset purchase customarily contemplates a two-step transaction in order to distribute the acquisition consideration (usually consisting of either cash or Bidder's stock) into the hands of Target shareholders. To accomplish this, Target will often dissolve following the sale of all of its assets and distribute out the remaining proceeds in liquidation to Target shareholders *after* satisfying the claims of Target's creditors.

Dissolution is another type of fundamental change that requires shareholder approval. *See, e.g.,* MBCA §14.02. Often, the board of Target will solicit Target shareholders to approve the dissolution of the company as part of the process of soliciting shareholder approval for the sale of all of Target's assets to

Bidder. Indeed, Bidder may insist, as a condition to its obligation to close on the agreement to purchase all of Target's assets, that Target shareholders vote to dissolve Target and distribute the acquisition consideration to Target share-holders in liquidation of the company. *Query:* Why might Bidder insist that Target be contractually obligated to proceed with dissolution of the company following closing on the sale of assets to Bidder, particularly in cases where the acquisition consideration consists entirely of Bidder stock?

At closing on the parties' asset purchase agreement, Bidder will deliver the agreed-upon consideration to Target and, generally speaking, Target will be obligated to transfer ownership of Target's assets to Bidder. This is a more cumbersome procedure than closing an acquisition structured as a merger (regardless whether it is a direct or triangular merger) because Target typically must prepare deeds or bills of sale for each of Target's assets (real and personal). In most cases involving an asset purchase, this method of transferring ownership of Target's business results in substantial transaction costs incurred in connection with preparing the necessary documentation (such as deeds) and the cost and delay associated with making any necessary filings with appropriate state and/or local authorities.

By contrast, in a merger, this transfer of ownership is effected by operation of law, avoiding the necessity of preparing evidence of transfer of ownership of individual assets of Target's business. Consequently, in certain types of businesses, the merger may offer significant advantages over other methods of structuring an acquisition since title to *all* assets owned by each constituent corporation is *automatically* vested in the surviving corporation. This transfer takes effect *by operation of law* once the articles of merger are filed with the secretary of state's office. Thus, the only document required to effectuate the transfer of Target's business to Bidder consists of the articles of merger, which will be filed with the secretary of state. Furthermore, in a direct merger, the issue of a second-step dissolution of Target is rendered moot, as Target Co. ceases to exist by operation of law once the merger becomes effective.

2. Dissolution of Target

The second step in an asset acquisition usually involves the orderly winding up and liquidation of Target's business in a voluntary dissolution that has been approved by the shareholders. In most states, voluntary dissolution of a corporation involves the following steps:

1. Gather all of the company's assets.
2. Convert the company's assets to cash.
3. Use the cash to pay off the company's creditors (in their order of priority).
4. Distribute the remaining cash (or other non-cash assets) to the company's shareholders (giving priority to those shares carrying a liquidation preference).

In the case of a dissolution that follows the sale of all of Target's assets, the first two steps have essentially been accomplished by closing on the sale of all of

Target's assets to Bidder. At that point, dissolution of Target primarily involves notifying Target Co.'s creditors that Target is winding up its business affairs and providing them with the opportunity to submit their claims to be paid before anything is distributed to Target shareholders in a final, liquidating distribution. The dissolution proceeding extinguishes the separate existence of Target Co. once the articles of dissolution are filed (which, generally speaking, are to be filed with the secretary of state's office).

In most states, the corporation statute sets forth detailed procedures for Target to use to notify its creditors that Target is winding up its business affairs in a voluntary dissolution of the company. The purpose of these detailed procedural requirements is to protect the legitimate interests of the company's business creditors. It is imperative for directors and shareholders to carefully follow these requirements in the manner prescribed by statute because, in most states, the failure to follow these statutory requirements may result in personal liability to the company's directors and/or shareholders (usually based on the theory that the liquidating distribution to Target shareholders constitutes the unauthorized return of capital). Generally speaking, the detailed notice and other steps prescribed by statutory law for dissolution and winding up are there to protect the rights of creditors against the possibility of opportunistic behavior on the part of Target insiders—a possibility that is inherent in the very process of winding up and dissolving Target. The concern is that Target insiders may be tempted to take advantage of the company's creditors by distributing the proceeds from the sale of all its assets to Target shareholders rather than first applying the acquisition consideration to satisfy the claims of Target creditors. As for contract creditors, these fixed and therefore knowable claims against Target will generally be satisfied in a dissolution proceeding out of the consideration that Bidder paid to acquire all of Target's assets if the statutory procedures for an orderly liquidation are carefully followed.

The traditional approach to voluntary dissolution, followed by most state corporation codes, allows the company to distribute any surplus from a sale of the company's assets to its shareholders after the company has paid off its known creditors. In language that is typical of these modern statutes, MBCA §14.06 provides that Target must notify *all known claimants* in writing of the pending dissolution proceeding. These claimants then have 120 days to present their claims. If a claim is rejected, the statute provides that the claimant must sue on its claim within 90 days of the rejection. Most state statutes then bar claims of Target's creditors who come forward after the expiration of the notice and claims period provided by local law. *See, e.g.,* MBCA §14.06 and §14.07. This statutory scheme does not unfairly prejudice *contract creditors* because Target's creditors are no worse off than if Target were still in existence, assuming that Target received fair value for its assets. More specifically, their claims can be satisfied against Target itself, which remains in place, or alternatively, Target's contract creditors will have an opportunity to present their claim for payment as part of the orderly dissolution of Target, and these claims will be paid ahead of any distributions to Target's shareholders.

More problematic, however, are the claims of *involuntary creditors,* particularly those tort claims that do not arise until sometime *after* the dissolution of Target. These are often referred to as *long-tail* (or contingent) *claims.* As to those tort claims pending at the time of Bidder's acquisition of Target, these are known claims, to be handled in the orderly liquidation of Target Co. in exactly the same manner as the contract claims discussed above.

From a public policy perspective, the most troubling of these long-tail claims in today's M&A market are those product liability claims and environmental claims that arise *long after* Target has sold all of its assets to Bidder and distributed the acquisition consideration to Target shareholders in the process of an orderly winding up and dissolution of Target. As for these long-tail claims, the public policy concerns presented by this two-step method of acquiring Target are reflected in the *Ruiz* case, *infra.*

3. Contract Creditors

American Paper Recycling Corp. v. IHC Corp.
707 F. Supp. 2d 114 (D. Mass. 2010)

STEARNS, District Judge.

American Paper Recycling Corporation (APR), brought this action in Bristol Superior Court seeking to compel performance by defendants IHC Corporation (IHC)* and MPS/IH, LLC (MPS) of a waste paper sales contract. APR also seeks to enjoin the sale of waste paper by MPS to a competitor, Wilmington Paper Corporation (Wilmington). Defendants removed the case to the federal court on diversity grounds, and then moved to dismiss the Complaint.

* * *

BACKGROUND

The following material facts are not in dispute or where disputed are viewed in the light most favorable to the relevant non-moving party. APR is an Illinois corporation engaged in the business of purchasing waste paper and other paper products for recycling. APR is registered as a foreign corporation in Massachusetts and has its principal office in Mansfield, Massachusetts. IHC is a subsidiary of Cinram (U.S.) Holdings, Inc. (Cinram). Cinram is the sole shareholder of IHC. Prior to the events giving rise to this litigation, Ivy (now IHC) was engaged in the business of manufacturing paper packaging for use in the media industry. Ivy operated plants in Terre Haute, Indiana, and Louisville, Kentucky. As a by-product of its manufacturing business, Ivy generated significant quantities of recyclable waste paper. APR paid Ivy an agreed rate based on the volume and quality of the waste paper.

On November 6, 1990, Ivy and APR entered into a Waste Paper Sales Contract (Sales Contract), under which Ivy agreed to sell all of its waste paper to

---

*[By the author] After this litigation commenced, the seller, who was known as Ivy Hill Corporation (Ivy) at the time that the original sales contract was signed on Nov. 6, 1990, changed its corporate name to IHC Corporation (IHC).

APR. In return, APR provided Ivy with manufacturing equipment on generous terms. The Sales Contract, in relevant part, provided that:

E. It is mutually agreed that the quantities, classification, price periods during which the Agreement shall be effective, packing, shipping and other provisions shall be as follows:

1. Entire accumulation of saleable waste paper stock generated at [Ivy] plants.

* * *

3. This Agreement shall continue throughout December 31, 2004, and shall be automatically renewed at the same terms unless written cancellation is given by either party 90 days prior to the expiration of this contract period.

Beginning in February of 1991, Ivy and APR executed the first of ten amendments to the Sales Contract dealing with the provision by APR of additional processing equipment and financing to Ivy. In conjunction with several of these amendments, Ivy agreed to extensions of the Sales Contract . . . The final relevant amendment to the Sales Contract occurred on May 1, 2006. Under Amendment #10, APR agreed to finance [a repair project at one of Ivy's plants] and Ivy agreed to an extension of the sales contract. The final version of the Sales Contract, as modified by the series of amendments, was set to expire on December 31, 2020.

* * *

On April 9, 2009, pursuant to an Asset Purchase Agreement (APA), Cinram sold substantially all of Ivy's assets to MPS in a cash-and-stock deal.[5] Under the terms of the APA, Cinram received $23,250,000 in cash and 7,750 shares of Series C Preferred Stock in Multi Packaging Solutions, Inc., the parent company of MPS.[6] The APA provided that:

Buyer hereby purchases and acquires from the Company [Ivy], all of the right, title and interest in and to the Company's Assets, rights, properties and interest in properties of the Company of every kind, nature and description, whether real, personal or mixed, tangible and intangible, whether or not used in, held for usage in or otherwise relating to the Business (other than Excluded assets) . . .

Additionally, as part of the transaction, MPS agreed to assume substantially all of Ivy's liabilities.

Assumed Liabilities. On the terms and subject to the conditions contained in this Agreement, simultaneously with the sale, transfer, conveyance and assignment

---

5. Prior to its sale to MPS, Ivy had undergone two prior acquisitions. Ivy was first purchased by Time Warner Company, which then sold Ivy to Cinram. In both of these transactions, the Sales Contract was included among the transferred assets. Neither acquisition impacted on APR's ability to continue to purchase Ivy's waste paper.

6. Multi Packaging Solutions, Inc., is a Delaware corporation and the sole owner of a second Delaware corporation, John Henry Holdings, Inc., which in turns owns MPS.

to Buyer of Purchased Assets, Buyer hereby assumes all of the Liabilities of the Company [Ivy] relating to the Business other than the Excluded Liabilities.

APA ¶ 2.1.[7]

The APA then identified certain assets that would not be transferred including cash, pre-paid expenses, insurance policies, pre-paid taxes, corporate documents, bank accounts, certain employee benefit plans, and all real estate owned in fee simple. *See id.* In addition, Schedule 1.2(m) of the APA identified specific assets excluded from the sale, including:

> Waste Paper Sales Contract dated November 6, 1990, as amended, . . . between American Paper Recycling Corporation and [Ivy].

On April 16, 2009, Ray Wheelan, a MPS Vice–President, notified Kenneth Golden, APR's President, that MPS intended to consolidate the recycling business at the [Terre Haute and Louisville plants acquired pursuant to the APA] with MPS's existing contract with Wilmington. Wheelan told Golden that APR's recycling services at these facilities were being terminated effective May 10, 2009. On April 24, 2009, Wheelan wrote to APR warning that "[y]ou need to stop scheduling pick ups at the Terre Haute and Louisville plants effective immediately. All pick ups have been discontinued." APR then filed this lawsuit.

DISCUSSION

* * *

THE DE FACTO MERGER EXCEPTION

[In order to hold MPS liable on a breach of contract theory, the federal district court concluded that APR must first establish that the asset purchase constituted a de facto merger between MPS and Ivy Hill (now named IHC).] "Under generally accepted corporate law principles, the purchaser of the assets of another corporation does not assume the debts and liabilities of the transferor. The traditional rule is subject to four generally recognized exceptions: (1) the purchasing corporation expressly or impliedly agrees to assume the selling corporation's liabilities; (2) the transaction is a merger of the two entities; (3) the purchaser is a mere continuation of the seller corporation; and (4) the transaction is a fraudulent attempt to evade the seller's liabilities." *Devine & Devine Food Brokers, Inc. v. Wampler Foods, Inc.*, 313 F.3d 616, 618 (1st Cir.2002), citing *Dayton v. Peck, Stow & Wilcox Co.*, 739 F.2d 690, 692 (1st Cir.1984). *See also* 15 W. Fletcher, *Cyclopedia of Law of Private Corporations* § 7122, at 227–243 (1999). Massachusetts law adheres "to traditional corporate

---

7. The excluded obligations listed at APA ¶ 2.2 are standard exclusions, including tax liabilities, employee benefit plans, environmental contamination, and liabilities covered by existing insurance contracts.

law principles that the liabilities of a selling predecessor corporation are not imposed on the successor corporation which purchases its assets unless [one of these four exceptions is met]." *Cargill, Inc. v. Beaver Coal & Oil Co.*, 424 Mass. 356, 359 (1997). . . . In this instance, there is no dispute that the Sales Contract was expressly excluded from the transferred assets. Nor is there any contention that the transaction involved a fraudulent conveyance to MPS. Thus, the first and fourth exceptions do not apply. APR relies instead on the de facto merger and "mere continuation" exceptions.

In determining whether to characterize an asset sale as a de facto merger, courts are to consider whether:

> (1) there is a continuation of the enterprise of the seller corporation so that there is continuity of management, personnel, physical location, assets, and general business operations; whether (2) there is a continuity of shareholders which results from the purchasing corporation paying for the acquired assets with shares of its own stock, this stock ultimately coming to be held by the shareholders of the seller corporation so that they become a constituent part of the purchasing corporation; whether (3) the seller corporation ceases its ordinary business operations, liquidates, and dissolves as soon as legally and practically possible; and whether (4) the purchasing corporation assumes those obligations of the seller ordinarily necessary for the uninterrupted continuation of normal business operations of the seller corporation.

Goguen v. Textron, Inc., 476 F.Supp.2d 5, 12–13 (D.Mass.2007) (quoting *Cargill*, 424 Mass. at 360), . . . Of the four factors, "no single [one] is necessary or sufficient to establish a de facto merger." *Goguen*, 476 F.Supp.2d at 13 (citing *Cargill*, 424 Mass. at 360). "When a *de facto* merger is alleged, the court must determine 'the substance of the agreement [regardless of] the title put on it by the parties.'" Here, APR argues that none of the four *Cargill* factors emblematic of a de facto merger applies. The court will consider each factor in turn.

CONTINUITY OF THE ENTERPRISE

MPS absorbed the bulk of Ivy's workforce, two of its physical plants, and its core business. However, "[i]n determining whether a de facto merger has occurred, courts pay particular attention to the continuation of management, officers, directors and shareholders." *Cargill*, 424 Mass. at 360. MPS did not retain key members of Ivy's management team, including Ivy's Chief Operating Officer, the Vice President of Finance, the Chief Engineer, the Plant Manager, the Controller, and the IT Director. It had none of the same officers or directors, and as noted below, the exchange involved an arms-length exchange of good and fair consideration, namely a substantial sum of cash and only a nominal interest in the shares of Multi Packaging Solutions, MPS's parent company. MPS discontinued a number of Ivy's previous vendors, including vendors who had supplied the plants with paper, paper board, and corrugate. Finally, MPS chose to exclude the real property at the Louisville plant from the list of purchased assets, and instead chose to lease the property from Ivy–IHC.

Cargill provides an instructive contrast. In that case, not only did the work force remain the same, the key manager stayed in place, and all of the other employees and key people (with one exception) remained the same, "maintaining their same positions and responsibilities." *Cargill*, 424 Mass. at 360. The owner of the former company became a director of the new company and its largest individual shareholder. *Id.* The new company "used the same telephone numbers [as the old company], the same trucks and the same equipment. [The old company's] customer lists and contracts were transferred to [the new company] all of whom were serviced just as they had been. . . . " *Id.* at 361. In short, the new became the old. Similarly, in [*In re Acushet River & New Bradford Proceedings*, 712 F.Supp. 1010 (D. Mass 1989)], the new company continued all of the old company's product lines, the president, vice-president and treasurer of the old company took the same titles and functions in the new company (as well as being made directors), the middle management remained intact, and even the banking and insurance facilities remained the same. "For all the world could tell from outward appearance, [the new company] had simply shortened its name." 712 F.Supp. at 1016. This factor weighs heavily against a de facto merger.

CONTINUITY OF SHAREHOLDERS

The First Circuit, consistent with other courts and learned treatises, has observed that continuity of shareholders is one of the "key requirements" for application of the de facto merger doctrine. *Dayton*, 739 F.2d at 693. Continuity of the shareholders "is found where the purchaser corporation exchanges its own stock as consideration for the seller corporation's assets so that the shareholders of the seller corporation become a constituent part of the purchaser corporation." *Id.* In this case, as consideration for the sale, Cinram received $23,250,000 in cash and 7,750 shares of Series C Preferred Stock in Multi Packaging Solutions. The shares, however, represent less than 3.2 percent of Multi Packaging Solutions' stock. Moreover, as the only Series C stockholder, Cinram has no voting rights, cannot transfer its shares, and holds the shares subject to a right of unilateral redemption by Multi Packaging Solutions. [While in] *Cargill*, a twelve and one-half percent voting interest was sufficient to tip the balance, this was so because the sale was between two closely-held corporations and left the owner of the predecessor entity with a seat on the successor corporation's board of directors and the largest personal holding of shares of stock. No members of Cinram's board of directors or any of its officers hold a similar position with MPS or were given individual shares of voting stock. This factor weighs decidedly against a de facto merger.

SELLER CORPORATION CEASES ITS FORMER BUSINESS OPERATIONS

A third emblematic factor is the immediate liquidation of the predecessor entity. The rationale underlying this exception is the protection of third parties, for example, consumers harmed by a product defect. "[W]hatever the reach of successor liability under the law of Massachusetts, the doctrine has no applicability where . . . the original manufacturer remains in existence to respond in tort for its alleged negligence and breach of warranty." *Roy v. Bolens Corp.*, 629 F.Supp. 1070, 1073 (D. Mass. 1986). Here, Ivy did not dissolve after the sale and liquidate its assets so as to put them out of the reach of creditors, but remains in existence as IHC. It retained ownership of the real estate where the Louisville plant is located. It collects rents from MPS, and otherwise functions as a commercial landlord with assets, profits, and employees. As in *Roy*, because Ivy "is alive and well and able to respond in damages," *id.*, a finding of a de facto merger is virtually precluded.

ASSUMPTION OF OBLIGATIONS NECESSARY TO CONTINUE NORMAL BUSINESS OPERATIONS

While MPS has continued Ivy's core business, operational changes since acquiring Ivy's manufacturing plants have replaced most of the management. MPS has discontinued or changed vendors, and did not take ownership of Ivy's real property where the Louisville plant is situated. On balance, this factor too weighs against the argument that MPS has simply continued Ivy's business without interruption or notice.

Taking the four factors as a whole, and particularly the "key requirement" of continuity of management, officers, directors, and shareholders, it is clear that no de facto merger occurred.

THE MERE CONTINUATION EXCEPTION

Under the mere continuation exception, "the imposition of liability on the purchaser is justified on the theory that, in substance if not in form, the purchasing corporation is the same company as the selling corporation." *McCarthy v. Litton Indus., Inc.*, 410 Mass. 15, 22, 570 N.E.2d 1008 (1991). Accordingly, "the indices of 'continuation' are, at a minimum: continuity of directors, officers, and stockholders; and the continued existence of only one corporation after the sale of assets." *Goguen*, 476 F. Supp. 2d at 14–15 (citing *McCarthy*, 410 Mass. at 23, 570 N. E. 2d 1008). As the minimum threshold is not met—there is no continuity of directors, officers, or shareholders, or for that matter senior management—this exception has no applicability.

* * *

QUESTIONS

1. What is the general rule on transfer of a corporation's liabilities when it sells all of its assets to Bidder?

2. Who is the plaintiff? What relief does plaintiff seek?

3. What does it take for a creditor of Target to impose liability on Bidder, as the successor-in-interest to Target, in reliance on the de facto merger doctrine?

4. From a public policy perspective, do you think the court reached the right result on the facts of this case? If the plaintiff had prevailed, do you think that would have resulted in a windfall to the plaintiff?

4.   Tort Creditors

Ruiz v. Blentech Corporation
89 F.3d 320 (7th Cir. 1996)

CUDAHY, Circuit Judge.

Felipe Ruiz's case turns on a rather mystifying choice-of-law problem. Ruiz, a citizen of Illinois, suffered an injury in his home state from an allegedly defective product manufactured in California by a California corporation. The manufacturer has dissolved, but another California corporation has followed in its footsteps by purchasing its principal assets and continuing its business. Ruiz seeks to make the successor corporation answer for his tort claims against the manufacturer. Illinois and California have different rules for determining when one corporation is responsible, as a successor, for the tort liabilities of its predecessors. The district court concluded that Illinois' rules, which are less favorable to Ruiz, should apply. As a consequence of this conclusion, it entered summary judgment against him. Ruiz appeals this judgment, arguing that the district court incorrectly resolved the conflict between the rules adopted, respectively, by Illinois and California. We affirm.

I

Felipe Ruiz operated a screw conveyor in a food processing plant in Schiller Park, Illinois. On June 16, 1992, he somehow became entangled in the conveyor's machinery and sustained several grievous injuries, the most severe of which left him paralyzed. He soon filed a lawsuit in an Illinois state court, bringing claims of strict products liability and negligence, among others. The case was removed to the district court on the basis of diversity jurisdiction.

Ruiz eventually directed his case at five defendants, all of whom had some legally significant connection with the screw conveyor. Three of the five had been involved in the sale of the conveyor to Ruiz's employer. These defendants were Weiler and Company, a Wisconsin corporation, Weiler East, a New Jersey corporation, and Dan Schwerdtfeger, an agent for those two companies. Another defendant was Custom Stainless Equipment, the California corporation that had manufactured the conveyor in 1983 and had dissolved in 1986. The last defendant was an entity that Ruiz identified as the successor to Custom Stainless' liabilities in tort. When Custom Stainless dissolved, it sold all of its assets for cash to Blentech, another California corporation. Blentech continued to manufacture Custom Stainless' product lines under its own name, using the same product designs, the same factory, the same management and the same employees. Ruiz contended in the district court that California law defined the relationship between Custom Stainless and Blentech and, therefore, between Blentech and himself. According to Ruiz's interpretation of that law, Blentech's assimilation of Custom Stainless included an assumption of strict liability for any defective products that Custom Stainless had manufactured.

Schwerdtfeger and the two Weilers settled with Ruiz, and Ruiz won a default judgment against the defunct Custom Stainless. The fifth defendant, Blentech, resisted Ruiz's claim by arguing that it did not belong in the case at all. Blentech maintained that its purchase of Custom Stainless' assets had not involved a conveyance of Custom Stainless' tort liabilities, and it made this argument the basis for a motion for summary judgment. The district court held that Illinois law defined the relationship between Custom Stainless, Blentech and Ruiz, and that Illinois law would not permit Ruiz to sustain an action against Blentech. Therefore, the court granted summary judgment to Blentech. *See Ruiz v. Weiler,* 860 F. Supp. 602, 604-06 (N.D. Ill. 1994).

II

Ruiz appeals the entry of summary judgment in Blentech's favor. When considering a summary judgment, our review of matters both factual and legal is *de novo.* Of course there are not issues of fact; Ruiz only contests the district court's legal rulings. He contends that the district court erred by holding that Illinois tort law determined the nature of Blentech's liabilities as a successor to Custom Stainless. He believes that California corporate law should inform this determination and that it prescribes a result favorable to him. He also argues that, even if Illinois law applies, the district court misinterpreted its prescriptions regarding the products liability of successor corporations. . . .

Ruiz's challenge to the summary judgment for Blentech relies on his argument that the choice of state law governing the crucial issues in the case was in error. In a diversity case, of course, state law governs, and the district court determines what state law to apply in accordance with the choice-of-law principles of the state in which it sits. . . . The district court here was bound by the choice-of-law method defined by the Restatement (Second) of Conflicts of Law, which Illinois has adopted. . . .

The Second Restatement method is constructed around the principle that the state with the most significant contacts to an issue provides the law governing that issue. A court therefore conducts a separate choice-of-law analysis for each issue in a case, attempting to determine which state has the most significant contacts with that issue. . . . The Second Restatement enumerates specific factors that identify the state with the most significant contacts to an issue, and the relevant factors differ according to the area of substantive law governing the issue and according to the nature of the issue itself. *See, e.g.,* Restatement (Second) at §§6, 145, 188. To properly apply the Second Restatement method, a court must begin its choice-of-law analysis with a characterization of the issue at hand in terms of substantive law. By prescribing this analytical approach, the Second Restatement follows the principle of *depecage,*[1] which has been long applied in connection with various methods for choice of law. *See* Willis L.M. Reese, *Depecage: A Common Phenomenon in Choice of Law,* 73 Colum. L. Rev. 58 (1973).

With respect to Ruiz's claim against Blentech, the choice-of-law analysis had crucial importance. Only two states have significant contacts with the issues

---

1. When roughly translated, depecage refers to the process of cutting something into pieces. Here it refers to the process of cutting up a case into individual issues, each subject to a separate choice-of-law analysis.

raised. California was the place of the legal relationship between Custom Stainless and Blentech; and Illinois was the place of Ruiz's residence and his injury. The decisive issue in the case was whether Blentech had succeeded to Custom Stainless' liabilities by virtue of its purchase of Custom Stainless' assets and its business. Illinois and California shared a basic rule about corporate successor liability, but California provided an exception to that rule that was not available in Illinois.

Illinois mandates that, as a general rule of corporate law, a corporation that purchases the principal assets of another corporation does not assume the seller's liabilities arising from tort claims or from any other kind of claims. . . . Illinois does recognize four exceptions to this rule. The purchasing corporation assumes the seller's liabilities when: (1) it expressly agrees to assume them; (2) the asset sale amounts to a *de facto* merger; (3) the purchaser is a mere continuation of the seller; (4) the sale is for the fraudulent purpose of escaping liability for the seller's obligations. *Hernandez*, 26 Ill. Dec. at 778-79, 388 N.E.2d at 779-80. California's corporate law establishes the same general rule and the same four exceptions. *Ray v. Alad Corp.*, 19 Cal. 3d 22, 136 Cal. Rptr. 574, 578, 560 P.2d 3, 7 (1977).

California departs from the Illinois rules, however, by adopting a fifth exception. That exception provides that a corporation that purchases a manufacturing business and continues to produce the seller's line of products assumes strict liability in tort for defects in units of the same product line previously manufactured and distributed by the seller. *Ray*, 136 Cal. Rptr. at 582, 560 P.2d at 11. This "products line" exception applies in cases involving tort claims where: (1) the plaintiff lacks an adequate remedy against the seller/manufacturer; (2) the purchaser knows about product risks associated with the line of products that it continues; and (3) the seller transfers good will associated with the product line.

The difference between Illinois' and California's rules is decisive here because Ruiz's case against Blentech depends entirely upon whether the "products line" exception applies. Although Ruiz does argue that he can maintain a cause of action against Blentech even without this exception, it is clear that he cannot do so under the basic rule of successor liability, which both Illinois and California share. Blentech did not acquire Custom Stainless' obligations to Ruiz under one of the four standard exceptions to the general rule of successor liability. Blentech has not agreed to assume that obligation. It did expressly agree to assume all of Custom Stainless' tort liabilities arising before the date of the asset sale in 1986, but it emphatically disclaimed all liabilities arising after that date, and Ruiz was not injured until 1992. Neither did Blentech and Custom Stainless combine their corporate identities, either through a *de facto* merger or through some other means. In either Illinois or California, a court will conclude that an asset sale merges two corporations or makes the buyer the continuation of the seller only if it finds an identity of ownership between the two. In effect, the *de facto* merger and continuation exceptions are identical; each exception depends upon an identity of ownership between the seller and purchaser. . . . When Custom Stainless sold its assets to Blentech, Custom Stainless' owners received cash, not stock, and they have not participated in the ownership of Blentech in any way. Finally, Ruiz makes no allegation that the asset sale between Blentech and Custom Stainless was an occasion for fraud; moreover, nothing in the record even remotely supports such an allegation. Thus, Blentech can be liable to Ruiz only if the "products line" exception applies.

The "products line" exception can apply in Illinois courts only through the choice of foreign law. On numerous occasions, Illinois courts have specifically declined to make the "product line" exception part of Illinois law, and they have therefore declined to apply it to tort claims governed by Illinois law. . . . Illinois courts have not, however, specifically decided whether they would apply the "products line" exception to an issue governed by the law of a state which accepted that exception. Our research of Illinois law suggests that the crucial issue in this case is a matter of first impression in Illinois.

As it must, Ruiz's challenge to the district court's decision depends upon the contention that an Illinois court would choose California's "products line" exception as part of the law governing his claim against Blentech. In deciding whether to apply Illinois or California law, the district court considered whether Illinois or California had the most significant contacts with the tort that Ruiz alleged. *Ruiz v. Weiler & Co., Inc.*, 860 F. Supp. 602, 604 (N.D. Ill. 1994). It found that the two states had essentially equal contacts with Ruiz's action, but it concluded that the balance tipped towards Illinois because there is a presumption in favor of applying the laws of the state where the alleged tort occurred. . . . On the basis of this conclusion, the district court applied Illinois law to all of the issues in the case, including both of the issues relevant to Ruiz's claim against Blentech.

Ruiz argues that the district court's choice-of-law analysis was fundamentally flawed because it failed to follow the principles of *depecage*. As we have noted, these principles prescribe that the rules of different states can determine different issues in a single case. In Ruiz's view, the issue of Blentech's assumption of Custom Stainless' tort liabilities is separate and distinct from other issues in the case; and he believes it requires an analysis of significant contacts different from the one that the district court performed. When he applies the principles of *depecage* to this issue, Ruiz concludes that the district court should have determined the legal relationship between Custom Stainless and Blentech according to California law with its "products line" exception.

Ruiz correctly invokes the principle of *depecage* and persuasively criticizes the district court's choice-of-law analysis. The district court threw a single analytical blanket over all of the issues in the case, and this is, of course, a departure from the prescriptions of the Second Restatement. The district court should have conducted one analysis for issues of successor liability and a separate analysis for issues of tort liability. As a matter of corporate law, the issue of successor liability pertains to different significant contacts than does the tort law issue of liability for Ruiz's injury. California clearly has the most significant contacts with a sale of corporate assets by one California corporation to another. Here both corporations have their principal places of business in California. Consequently, California corporate law should determine what liabilities, if any, were conveyed when Custom Stainless sold its business to Blentech. It is equally clear that Illinois has the most significant relationship to an alleged tort befalling one of its citizens within its borders. The district court erred when, ignoring *depecage,* it applied Illinois law to all the issues in the case.

The question we now encounter is whether that error makes any difference here. Ruiz certainly believes that it does. He characterizes California's "product

line" exception as a rule of corporate law—a relative of the other four exceptions to the rule determining corporate successor liability. Unlike his argument
about the flaws in the district court's choice-of-law analysis, this contention is
not so clearly correct. The area of substantive law to which the "product line"
exception belongs is a difficult question, and the courts of several states have
struggled to decide whether it is a part of corporate law or of tort law.

This struggle has been especially evident in Illinois. As we have noted, Illinois courts have often considered whether to make the "products line" exception a part of Illinois law. In opinions addressing this issue, they have advanced
various explanations of the nature of this exception. Consequently, the Illinois precedents contain conflicting characterizations of the exception. Many
of these cases insist that there is one and only one way to characterize this rule
in terms of substantive law, but these same courts do not agree about what that
interpretation would be. . . .

. . . Part of the uncertainty over the nature of the "products line" exception
comes from the fact that the exception has a variety of sources each of which
articulates a different rationale for the exception and each of which places it
within a different realm of substantive law. The way in which the exception is
characterized may depend upon the source from which it comes. Michigan
law has apparently established the "products line" exception as a means of
making it easier to prove that the predecessor and successor corporations have
effected a *de facto* merger, although the reasoning behind this conclusion is
not entirely clear. *See Turner v. Bituminous Casualty Co.,* 397 Mich. 406, 244
N.W.2d 873, 879-80 (1976). Therefore, in Michigan, the exception seems to
be an instrument of corporate law that defines what must pass through an
asset sale. In New Jersey, on the other hand, the supreme court has held that
the exception has nothing to do with determining whether a *de facto* merger
occurred. Instead, the court there held that the exception is an instrument for
preserving the system of strict liability for products liability claims by imposing
duties on manufacturers. *See Ramirez v. Amsted Indus., Inc.,* 86 N.J. 332, 431
A.2d 811, 819-20 (1981).

For our purposes, California's understanding of the nature of the "products line" exception is what matters. *See* Restatement (Second) at §7(3). At least
with respect to this argument, Ruiz does not ask us to generate an abstract
version of the exception out of the air and make it a part of Illinois law. In any
event, this would be a futile effort because Illinois courts have so emphatically
rejected this request when other claimants have made it. . . . Ruiz does, however,
ask us to apply a California rule to his case through choice of law. Because the
only California rules that we can apply here are the rules of corporate law, we
must see whether California characterizes the "products line" exception as a
matter of corporate law.

California courts have quite clearly established that the exception is a matter of products liability law, not corporate law. The California Supreme Court
derived the exception from its line of cases prescribing strict liability in tort
for injuries resulting from defective products. *See Ray,* 136 Cal. Rptr. at 579-80,
560 P.2d at 8-9 (discussing the landmark products liability cases of *Greenman v.
Yuba Power Prods., Inc.,* 59 Cal. 2d 57, 27 Cal. Rptr. 697, 377 P.2d 897 (1963) and
Escola v. Coca Cola Bottling Co. of Fresno, 24 Cal. 2d 453, 150 P.2d 436 (1944)).
Moreover, California has limited the application of the exception to cases in

which it preserves a plaintiff's ability to collect on a valid strict liability claim. *See Lundell,* 190 Cal. App. 3d at 1556, 236 Cal. Rptr. at 78. In this way, California has established the "products line" exception as a means of advancing the cost-shifting purposes behind its regime of strict liability for injuries caused by defective products. Unlike Michigan, California has not employed the exception generally as a means to limit efforts by corporations to erase corporate identity in the course of asset sales. Instead, California uses the exception to insure that manufacturers generally will bear the costs of defective products.

As we have noted, Ruiz could maintain his case against Blentech only if the "products line" exception applied. Because the exception is a matter of California tort law, not California corporate law, it does not apply to this case. The judgment of the district court is, therefore,

AFFIRMED.

QUESTIONS

1. How would Mr. Ruiz's claim (a product liability claimant) be treated if the acquisition of Custom Stainless Equipment Corp. (Target Co.) had been structured as
    a. A direct merger?
    b. A stock purchase?
    c. A triangular merger? Does it matter to your analysis of this question if the merger is structured as a *reverse* vs. a *forward* triangular merger?

2. What happened to the company's assets when Custom Stainless Equipment Corp. was dissolved?

3. In the principal case, Mr. Ruiz did not sue the shareholders of Custom Stainless Equipment to recover from them. Why not?

4. What is the choice of law problem that confronts the court in this case?

5. What is the public policy concern raised by long-tail claimants such as Mr. Ruiz?

6. How should the law address this public policy concern? What is the role of the courts in this area of the law?

7. How can a Bidder in an asset acquisition—or for that matter, in structuring any acquisition, regardless of the method used to complete the transaction—minimize Bidder's risk of unexpected liabilities (such as the claim presented by Mr. Ruiz)?

NOTES

1. Statute of Limitations. The dissolution proceeding allows Target Co. to distribute to its shareholders the assets remaining *after* satisfying the known claims of Target's creditors. What happens to those claims that are not ascertainable at the time that Target commences the statutorily authorized dissolution process? These long-tail claims—such as tort claims that are based on injuries that occur or are discovered (knowable) only after dissolution—present difficult questions of fairness. By distributing out Target's assets in liquidation of the company's business affairs, the shareholders of Target have been able to appropriate for themselves funds that should have been available to satisfy long-tail claimants, such as Mr. Ruiz.

This externality—the opportunity to shift foreseeable risks of Target's business operations to third parties who are not represented in the process of negotiating Bidder's acquisition of Target—is an inherent attribute of this method of acquisition. One obvious solution is to allow long-tail claimants to recover from Target's shareholders the amounts paid as liquidating distributions in the dissolution of Target. Indeed, many state statutes continue to follow the traditional approach and allow those long-tail claimants whose claims mature shortly after payment of the liquidating distribution to Target shareholders to recover directly from the shareholders on their claim. Typically, these state statutes provide that the claim must be brought within two or three years after the dissolution proceeding has concluded, and further provide that each shareholder of Target will be liable only to the extent of the shareholder's personal distribution received in liquidation of Target (or a pro rata share of the claim, whichever is less). Some states have even extended this limitations period to five years, following the lead of prior versions of the MBCA, although the current MBCA provision establishes a limitations period of three years after publication of notice. *See* MBCA §14.07. Although this enhances the possibility of the long-tail claimant to recover for harm suffered, this remedy is not without its costs. The tort victim, such as Mr. Ruiz, is left with the often expensive (and therefore, rather unappealing) prospect of chasing down a diffuse group of shareholders in order to recover for his injuries.

2. Delaware's (Innovative) Procedures for Dissolution.

The externalities presented by long-tail claimants in the context of asset acquisitions are a problem that has long vexed public policy makers. On the one hand, business managers (and shareholder investors) need the certainty provided by statutes of limitations, which operate to cut off claims of potential creditors, so that they may proceed confidently to invest in and manage the newly acquired assets and business operations of its predecessor, Target Co. On the other hand, the long-tail claims presented by plaintiffs such as Mr. Ruiz are compelling and present difficult questions of fairness that often result in liability being imposed on Bidder, contrary to the agreement it originally made with the seller, Target.

In 1987, the Delaware legislature responded to this long-standing public policy dilemma by adopting an innovative set of procedures as part of its dissolution provisions. Like the traditional approach followed by most states, Delaware section 281(a) requires Target Co. to use the acquisition proceeds from the sale of all its assets to satisfy all claims known to the corporation at the time of its dissolution. However, the provisions of Delaware sections 280-282 go further and establish two distinct, alternative procedures that allow Delaware corporations to dissolve *and* eliminate potential director and shareholder liability with respect to the amounts distributed in a liquidating distribution. The mandatory default rule of Delaware section 281(b) specifies that the board of directors of the dissolving corporation must adopt a plan of distribution that includes "such provision as will be reasonably likely to be sufficient to provide compensation for claims that have not been made known, or that have not arisen, but that, based on facts known to the corporation, . . . are likely to arise or to become known to the corporation . . . within *ten years* after the date of dissolution." (*emphasis added*). Such claims are not limited to contract creditors but also include long-tail claimants such as product liability claims of the type at issue in *Ruiz*.

> Although section 281(c) provides that directors of the corporation "shall not be personally liable to the claimants of the dissolved corporation" if subsections (a) or (b) are complied with, compliance with subsection (b)'s "reasonably likely to be sufficient" standard will, in principle, always be litigable. Reliance upon the section 281(b) mechanism may present a risky situation for corporate directors regardless of their good faith and due care.

Edward P. Welch, et al., FOLK ON THE DELAWARE GENERAL CORPORATION LAW at p. 877 (Fundamentals 2012 Edition). Moreover, if the amount provided in the plan of distribution is ultimately found to be insufficient, Delaware section 282(a) still allows claimants to pursue shareholders for amounts received in the liquidating distribution or their pro rata share of the claim, whichever is less, subject to the statute of limitations on the underlying claim itself.

For those shareholders and directors of dissolving corporations who want greater certainty as to their ability to avoid personal liability on long-tail claims, the Delaware legislature adopted an optional safe harbor procedure, which is set forth in section 280(c)(3). It bears emphasizing that compliance with the detailed notice provisions of Delaware section 280(a) is required in order to take advantage of this optional safe harbor. As part of the dissolution proceeding conducted pursuant to section 280, Target Co. may petition the court to determine the amount and form of security that is "reasonably likely to be sufficient to provide compensation for claims that have not been made known to the corporation or that have not risen but that, based on facts known to the corporation or successor entity, are likely to arise or to become known to the corporation or successor entity within 5 years after the date of dissolution or such longer period of time as the Court of Chancery may determine not to exceed 10 years after the date of dissolution." Del. Gen. Corp. L. §280(c)(3). The Delaware statute also allows the court to appoint a guardian *ad litem* to represent the long-tail claimants. *Id.* Assuming compliance with the court's orders as well as the detailed statutory notice requirements of Delaware section 280(a), Target Co. shareholders will not be liable for any claims initiated after the three-year winding-up period established by §278. *See* Del. Gen. Corp. L. §282(b). Likewise, Target Co. directors will not be personally liable to any long-tail claimants either. *See* Del. Gen. Corp. L. §281(c).

Recently, the MBCA was amended to add a new provision that is similar to the innovation of Delaware §280(c)(3). MBCA §14.08 authorizes a safe harbor procedure to protect directors and shareholders of a dissolving corporation against personal liability on long-tail claims (contingent claims that are not barred by publication) by providing security for claims that are reasonably estimated to arise within three years of the effective date of Target's dissolution. This three-year period is considerably shorter than the potential ten-year period provided for in Delaware §280(c)(3), raising anew the public policy dilemma presented by these various long-tail claims.

Notwithstanding the appeal of Delaware's new procedure, there are some practical problems in administering this new safe harbor. Most prominently, the courts have had some difficulty in determining what qualifies as an adequate security arrangement in satisfaction of the terms of Delaware §280(c)(3). *See, e.g., In re Rego Co.,* 623 A.2d 92 (Del. Ch. 1992); *see also In re Transamerica Airlines, Inc.,* 2006 WL 587846 (Del. Ch. 2006); *In re Via Networks Inc.,* C.A. No. 2053-N, slip op. at 3 (Del. Ch. June 14, 2006); *In re Kraft-Murphy Co.,* No. 6049-VCP, 2011 WL 5420808 (Del. Ch. Nov. 9, 2011).

‖4‖

Selected Federal Securities Law Provisions that Apply to Negotiated Business Combinations

In Chapter 2, we analyzed the state law provisions that regulate the different methods for structuring an acquisition. In the process, we noted that if either Bidder Co. or Target Co. is publicly traded, then the rules of the New York Stock Exchange (NYSE) apply (or the corresponding provisions of other organized trading markets, such as the NASDAQ Stock Market). We also noted certain differences in the legal rules that apply depending on the type of consideration used to complete the acquisition of Target Co. (i.e., cash vs. Bidder Co. stock).

As part of our discussion of the problems in Chapter 2, we referred to various aspects of the federal securities laws that may also apply depending on (i) how the transaction is structured; (ii) whether the companies involved are publicly traded or privately held; and, finally (iii) whether the acquisition consideration consists of cash or Bidder stock (or, perhaps, a combination of both). Although we noted, in analyzing the problems in Chapter 2, how a transaction may implicate various provisions of the federal securities laws, we deferred any discussion of these federal rules until after we finished our analysis of the requirements imposed by state law. In this chapter, we take up the various provisions of the federal securities laws that must be considered by the mergers and acquisitions (M&A) lawyer in the context of planning an acquisition transaction.

As a preliminary word of caution, this chapter presents only a cursory overview of the various provisions of the Securities Act of 1933 (1933 Act) and the Securities Exchange Act of 1934 (1934 Act) that must be considered as a threshold matter in planning any business combination. In no way, however, is this a substitute for taking an introductory law school course on securities regulation. Indeed, the M&A lawyer must be well informed about the topics covered in this chapter, regardless of whether the M&A lawyer represents publicly traded companies or privately held corporations. As we will see in this chapter, the provisions of the federal securities laws that get triggered are substantially different depending on whether your client is publicly traded or privately held. So, the modern M&A lawyer, practicing on either Wall Street or Main Street, is typically knowledgeable about *both* corporate and securities laws.

Briefly summarized, this chapter focuses on certain aspects of the 1933 Act and the 1934 Act. Whenever Bidder proposes to use its own stock (or other securities) as the acquisition consideration, Bidder Co., as the issuer, must comply with the registration requirements of the 1933 Act or find an exemption. This obligation to register the transaction or establish an exemption is imposed on *all* issuers, regardless of whether the company is privately held or publicly traded. On the other hand, whenever Bidder or Target is publicly traded *and* must obtain shareholder approval for a proposed transaction, then the company *must* comply with the federal proxy rules in connection with its solicitation of shareholder votes to approve a proposed acquisition.

Finally, both Bidders and Targets must be mindful of the antifraud provisions of the federal securities laws in the context of any communications (oral or written) regarding a proposed acquisition transaction. Most notably, the M&A lawyer must be aware of the implications of Rule 10b-5 in the context of either a negotiated or a hostile acquisition. Although issues surrounding potential liability for Rule 10b-5 violations may surface in a number of different (and often quite novel) ways during the course of negotiating and documenting a particular business combination, M&A lawyers routinely face problems involving potential Rule 10b-5 violations in two contexts when planning an acquisition. The first involves the issue of what triggers the company's duty to disclose ongoing negotiations for a merger or some other type of business combination. The second recurring area of concern under Rule 10b-5 for the transaction planner involves the potential for insider trading in anticipation of a business combination, such as the potential merger of two companies. The possibility of insider trading in the face of a pending merger implicates not only a potential violation of Rule 10b-5, but may lead to liability under §16(b) of the 1934 Act as well, both of which we will briefly consider at the end of this chapter.

A.   *Securities Act of 1933: Issuance of Shares (or Other Securities) to Complete the Acquisition*

At the risk of oversimplifying the rules covered in the introductory law school course on securities regulation, all of the 1933 Act can be effectively summarized in the following sentence:

> Any time a corporation, regardless whether it is a large, publicly traded or a small, privately held company, proposes to use an instrumentality of interstate commerce in order to issue its stock (or any other securities such as convertible debentures), the corporation (as the issuer of the securities) *must* register the offering *or* find an exemption for the transaction.

In a situation where Bidder offers all cash to acquire Target, the requirements of the 1933 Act do not apply since Bidder does not propose to *issue* (*sell*) any of its *securities* as part of the acquisition transaction. However, if either Bidder or Target is publicly traded, then the federal proxy rules may still apply, regardless of the type of acquisition consideration used in the deal. The requirements imposed by the federal proxy rules are described below.

1.   Registered Transactions

If Bidder Co. issues its stock as the acquisition consideration, then it must either register or find an exemption for this distribution of its securities. Thus, the 1933 Act is transaction oriented; that is to say, the 1933 Act registers transactions, not securities. This is an important distinction. Since only the transaction in which the issuer sells the security to the investor is registered, this means that any subsequent resale of the security is a *separate transaction*. As such, the resale either must be registered or an exemption must be available to the selling shareholder.

In those cases where the investor seeks to dispose of a security purchased from the issuer in a registered transaction, the provision most often relied on by the seller to exempt this resale is the §4(a)(1) exemption. This workhorse exemption is important because most of the trading activity in the U.S. public markets (such as the trading activity on the NYSE) is exempt under §4(a)(1) as transactions "not involving an issuer, underwriter, or dealer." Consequently, those resales by persons who fall under the statutory definition of an "underwriter" or a "dealer" are not entitled to the §4(a)(1) exemption. The scope of the 1933 Act definitions of these terms is an important component of the study of federal securities regulation.

If the distribution transaction is *registered*, the issuer must file a registration statement (usually using a Form S-4 in the context of an M&A transaction) with the Securities and Exchange Commission (SEC), which will be reviewed by the staff of the Division of Corporate Finance of the SEC. Once the SEC review process is complete and the SEC declares the registration statement effective, Bidder may issue (that is, sell) its securities in order to complete its acquisition of Target. Before the SEC will declare the registration effective, however, Target shareholders must have received the *prospectus* (which is typically Part I of the registration statement filed by the issuer with the SEC). The process of preparing and filing the registration statement, as well as completing the SEC's review of the required disclosures contained therein, is obviously time-consuming and expensive. Moreover, in those cases where Bidder proposes to use its stock as the acquisition consideration, the closing date for the transaction will be dependent on the timing of the SEC staff's review of the adequacy and completeness of the registration statement—which adds further delay in completing Bidder's acquisition of Target. Finally, as we will discuss below, certain insiders of Target, referred to as *affiliates* (or *control persons*), may be subject to restrictions on the resale of the stock (or other securities) of Bidder that they receive in the acquisition transaction. *See* Securities Act Rules 145(c) and (d).

In cases where a publicly traded Bidder Co. proposes to issue additional shares in order to acquire a publicly traded Target Co. (such as the case of Pfizer's acquisition of Pharmacia using Pfizer common stock as the acquisition consideration), the 1933 Act must be satisfied (since Pfizer is issuing additional common shares to complete the acquisition). Historically, there was some confusion as to whether this type of "exchange offer" qualified as a "sale of securities" sufficient to trigger the requirements of the 1933 Act. Today, however, it is clear that this transaction involves a distribution of the issuer's (Pfizer's) securities in exchange for valuable consideration (the surrender of Pharmacia shares). Since Pharmacia is publicly traded, this distribution involves a public offering of Pfizer stock for which no exemption is available and therefore the transaction must be registered. In certain other types of acquisitions, however, an exemption may be available to eliminate the need to register the issuance of Bidder's stock.

The fundamental premise underlying the issuer's registration obligation under §5, which is the very heart of the 1933 Act, is that prospective investors must be provided with adequate information about the issuer and the terms of the proposed offering. By doing so, the prospective investor can make an informed decision on whether to purchase the issuer's securities. The prospectus filed by the issuer (generally as Part I of its registration statement) must set forth detailed disclosures including information about the issuer, its business and financial affairs, and the proposed use of the proceeds received from the offer and sale of the company's stock. The specific items of information that issuers must include in their registration statements are set forth as items of required disclosure; the requirements differ slightly depending on the form of registration statement used by the issuer (known as the *registrant*). The SEC has promulgated a number of different forms of registration statements, (e.g., Form S-1, Form S-3, Form S-4), and detailed instructions for completing these required items of disclosure are set forth in Regulation S-K (also promulgated by the SEC). The form of registration statement most often used in an acquisition transaction is Form S-4, which is the form of registration statement used in business combination transactions in which securities (i.e., Bidder's stock) are being used as the acquisition consideration. Indeed, in connection with Pfizer's acquisition of Pharmacia, the parties prepared a Form S-4 in satisfaction of their obligations under the 1933 Act. The scope of disclosure required to be provided under the terms of Form S-4 is described in more detail later in this chapter, as part of our examination of the SEC's federal proxy rules promulgated pursuant to the 1934 Act.

2.   Exempt Transactions

Compliance with the registration obligation imposed by §5 of the 1933 Act very often imposes greater costs than the public benefits to be obtained from the issuer's preparation of the detailed disclosures that are required to be part of a registration statement. Congress provided for this possibility by adopting various provisions to exempt the issuer from the §5 registration obligation. These exemptions are set forth in sections 3 and 4 of the 1933 Act. For our purposes, the most important of these exemptions are (i) the statutory private placement authorized by §4(a)(2) of the 1933 Act; and (ii) the limited offering exemptions made available by the rules of Regulation D, originally promulgated by the SEC in 1982 and further refined by subsequent SEC rulemaking.

The proposed transaction between Nestlé, Inc. and Chef America, Inc. illustrates the need for some type of exemption from the delay and expense associated with filing a registration statement to satisfy the obligations imposed on the issuer by the 1933 Act. Although the deal involved an all-cash purchase price (and thus no issuance of securities that would trigger the requirements of the 1933 Act), very different considerations are presented if the purchase price were to involve the issuance of Bidder's stock. Assume that, instead of using cash, Nestlé proposed to issue 2 percent of its stock as the acquisition consideration to acquire Chef America, with the terms of the acquisition calling for the two brothers, Paul and David Merage, to each receive 1 percent of Nestlé stock in exchange for all of their stock in Chef America, Inc. The federal proxy rules do not apply to this transaction because (i) Chef America is not a 1934 Act reporting company (even though the transaction may be structured so as to grant the shareholders a right to vote); and further, (ii) Nestlé (even though a reporting company) is not required to solicit shareholder approval for the transaction as a matter of state law (assuming, of course, that Nestlé has sufficient authorized but unissued shares). But what about the requirements of the 1933 Act?

Private Placements.   In cases where Bidder (Nestlé) issues shares in an acquisition transaction, the 1933 Act will apply. However, where the terms of the acquisition call for the securities (Nestlé shares) to be issued to a limited number of investors (the two shareholders of Chef America, Inc.), the expense and delay associated with preparing a registration statement will not produce sufficient public benefits to justify these transaction costs. Therefore, the issuer (Nestlé) will try to qualify the issuance of its stock under one of the available exemptions, most often using the *private placement exemption* available under §4(a)(2) of the 1933 Act.*

Under the terms of the §4(a)(2) private placement, the issuer must show that the proposed transaction does not involve a public offering of its securities; i.e., the issuer must show that it is a nonpublic offering. In *SEC v. Ralston Purina, Inc.*, 346 U.S. 119, 125-126 (1953), the seminal case analyzing whether an offering of the issuer's securities was public or private, the Supreme Court defined a nonpublic offering for purposes of §4(a)(2) as a transaction where the proposed offer and sale of the issuer's securities was limited to those who could "fend for themselves," and thus did need not the protections provided by the 1933 Act. In the context of Nestlé's acquisition of Chef America, assuming that Nestlé's stock is used as the acquisition consideration, then the Supreme Court's decision in *Ralston Purina* requires the issuer (Nestlé) to establish that all the offerees and purchasers (the two shareholders of Chef America) had "access to the same kind of information that the [1933 Act] would make available in the form of a registration statement." *Id.*

The standards that must be satisfied in order to qualify an offeree as a "self-fending" type have been further developed by subsequent case law in the lower courts, often producing a hodgepodge of confusing (sometimes even conflicting) set of requirements. The SEC subsequently stepped in to provide a safe harbor in response to pressure (from both the issuer community and the practicing bar) to provide more objective criteria as to what qualifies as a private placement for purposes of §4(a)(2) of the 1933 Act.

---

* When the Supreme Court decision in *Ralston-Purina* was handed down in 1953, the statutory private placement exemption was found in §4(2) of the 1933 Act. Congressional enactment of the Jumpstart Our Business Startups (JOBS) Act in 2012 resulted in the renumbering of the provisions of §4 of the 1933 Act and now the private placement exemption is found in §4(a)(2).

Regulation D. Today, the SEC's safe harbor standard for §4(a)(2) is set forth as Rule 506 of Regulation D. This regulation, promulgated in 1982, is composed of Rules 501 through 508. The substantive exemptions consist of Rules 504, 505, and 506. Consistent with Supreme Court precedent, there is no dollar limit on the private offering exemption available under Rule 506, so long as the offering is made only to "accredited purchasers" and there are no more than 35 "nonaccredited purchasers" who must also satisfy a Regulation D standard of "financial sophistication."

The requirement of financial sophistication has led to a rather substantial body of case law and academic commentary interpreting the standards that the issuer must satisfy to demonstrate sophistication of investors. This is a substantial burden to impose on the issuer because the SEC has interpreted the scope of the Regulation D exemption to mean that a *single* purchaser who fails to satisfy the financial sophistication standard may destroy the basis of the exemption as to the *entire* offering. If the issuer loses the exemption, it will face liability under §12(a)(1) of the 1933 Act, which in effect allows *all* purchasers in the failed offering to rescind the transaction and recover from the issuer the purchase price they paid to acquire shares of issuer's stock.

By contrast, the other two substantive exemptions (Rules 504 and 505) are known as the *limited offering* exemptions. These two exemptions are promulgated by the SEC pursuant to §3(b) of the 1933 Act, which delegates rulemaking authority to the SEC to exempt offerings up to $5 million. These small offering exemptions are often used in the acquisition of small private companies. Where Bidder proposes to issue more than $5 million of its securities to acquire Target, these small offering exemptions will not be available, and generally the issuer will be forced to rely on the private placement exemption to eliminate the need to file a registration statement for the transaction. There is no dollar limit on either the statutory private placement under §4(a)(2) or the safe harbor exemption under Rule 506. Although when it was originally adopted, Regulation D was intended to facilitate capital formation by small business, today companies of all sizes rely on its exemptions to avoid the burdens of registration under the 1933 Act.

Historically, offerings conducted pursuant to a Regulation D exemption must be done on a nonpublic basis. In one of the more controversial aspects of Regulation D, since its adoption the SEC has consistently prohibited the use of *any* general advertising or general solicitation. This prohibition has often proven to be quite troubling for small businesses that do not have the services of financial advisors readily available to them. In these situations, small businesses generally have found it to be quite difficult—in some cases, virtually impossible—to recruit investors. In recent years, the SEC has attempted to soften this prohibition through a series of no-action letters that allow broker-dealer firms, in effect, to screen investors. These brokers in turn then match investors up with small business issuers seeking investment capital.

At the urging of many commentators and businesses, "the SEC issued a series of proposed revisions to Regulation D in August 2007. *See* Securities Act Release No. 33-8828. These proposals included changes to the definition of 'accredited investor,' a new exemption from the registration requirements of the 1933 Act for offers and sales to 'large accredited investors,' a new rule to restrict certain 'bad actors' from relying on Regulation D, and other general changes." Morgan, Lewis & Bockius, LLP, *SEC Issues Proposed Revisions of Limited Offering Exemptions in Regulation D* (law firm memo, August 10, 2007) (copy on file with author). The SEC's proposed amendments to Regulation D were prompted in part by recommendations that had been made to the SEC for a comprehensive overhaul of its regulatory framework for exempt offerings, including proposed changes to Regulation D. However, it is worth noting that "the SEC's [2007] proposals do not eliminate the broad restrictions on general advertising and general solicitation in Regulation D offerings. . . . " Sullivan & Cromwell, LLP, *Private Offering Reform* (law firm memo, August 14, 2007) (copy on file with author). This led many commentators to question whether the SEC's proposed revisions, if adopted, would result in any significant improvements in the capital formation process, especially for small businesses.

SEC Amendments to Definition of "Accredited Investor." Although the SEC never adopted its proposed 2007 amendments to Regulation D, the reforms adopted by Congress, as part of the Dodd-Frank Act,[*] spurred the SEC into action because of the statute's mandate that the SEC:

> update the decades-old "accredited investor" standard appearing in Regulation D . . . in the manner described below. In general, prior to the Dodd-Frank Act, an "accredited investor" was defined in Rule 501 (with respect to Regulation D) . . . as (1) any natural person whose individual net worth, or joint net worth with that person's spouse, at the time of his purchase exceeds $1 million, (2) any natural person who had an individual income in excess of $200,000 in each of the two most recent years or joint income with that person's spouse in excess of $300,000 in each of those years and has a reasonable expectation of reaching the same income level in the current year; or (3) any entity not formed for the specific purpose of acquiring the securities offered, with total assets in excess of $5 million.
>
> [Section 413 of the] Dodd-Frank Act requires the [SEC] to adjust any net worth standard for an "accredited investor" so that the individual net worth of any natural person, or joint net worth with the spouse of that person, at the time of purchase, is more than $1,000,000 (as such amount is adjusted periodically by rule of the [SEC] *excluding* the value of the primary residence of such natural person. Furthermore, until July 21, 2014, any net worth standard will be $1,000,000, excluding the value of the primary residence of such natural person.
>
> The Dodd-Frank Act gives the [SEC] the authority to determine whether the requirements of the term "accredited investor" as such term applies to natural persons, excluding the exclusion of the primary residence requirement relating to the net worth requirement, should be adjusted for the protection of investors, in the public interest and in light of the economy. . . .
>
> Moreover, under the Dodd-Frank Act, the [SEC] has the obligation to conduct subsequent reviews every four years of the term "accredited investors" as such term applies to natural persons in order to determine whether the requirements of the definition should be adjusted or modified for the protection of investors, in the public interest, and in light of the economy.
>
> . . .

---

[*] On July 21, 2010, Congress enacted the Dodd-Frank Wall Street Reform and Consumer Protection Act, commonly referred to as the Dodd-Frank Act. *See* Public Law 111-203, 124 Stat. 1376.

On January 25, 2011, in Securities Act Release No. 33-9177, (Jan. 25, 2011) [76 Fed. Reg. 5307] (Release), the [SEC] proposed amendments to the accredited investor standards in its rules under [Regulation D] to reflect the requirements of Section 413(a) of the Dodd-Frank Act. The [SEC] also proposed technical amendments to Form D and a number of rules thereunder to conform them to the language of Section 413(a) and to correct cross-references to former Section 4(6) of the Securities Act, which was renumbered Section 4(5) by Section 944 of the Dodd-Frank Act.

"ACCREDITED INVESTOR" PROPOSED CHANGES

Calculation of Accredited Investor "Net Worth"

In calculating accredited investor net worth, the [SEC] first noted that the term "net worth" was undefined [in the Dodd-Frank Act]. The [SEC] first proposed to define "net worth" under Rule 501 and . . . to give effect to its conventional meaning, *i.e.*, [that net worth reflects] the difference between the value of a person's assets and the value of the person's liabilities. Note that in this article we use the term accredited investor net worth differently from net worth, since the [SEC] has proposed using a modified net worth standard when calculating net worth for purposes of determining if a person is an "accredited investor" [under Regulation D] . . .

Prior to the Dodd-Frank Act, accredited investor net worth was defined [under Regulation D] as individual net worth, or joint net worth with that person's spouse, at the time of purchase exceeding $1 million. . . . Pursuant to the mandate of Dodd-Frank Act, [the SEC's proposed definition of] accredited investor net worth would be defined as individual net worth, or joint net worth with that person's spouse, at the time of purchase, exceeding $1,000,000, *excluding* the value of the primary residence of such natural person, [which is to be] calculated by subtracting from the estimated fair market value of the property the amount of debt secured by the property, up to the estimated fair market value of the property.*

The [SEC] stated in the Release that its purpose was to ensure that net worth is calculated by excluding *only* the investor's net equity in the primary residence,

---

* Thus, in calculating the investor's net worth,

The amended rule directs that indebtedness up to the value of the personal residence and secured by the residence (*i.e.*, a standard home mortgage) is not treated as a liability unless the borrowing occurred within sixty days prior to the purchase of securities in the Regulation D offering and is not in connection with the acquisition of the residence (*i.e.*, is a refinancing). The sixty-day exception is designed to prevent a homeowner from manipulating net worth on the eve of purchasing securities by borrowing against home equity and inflating net worth with the proceeds of the borrowing. As the [SEC] noted in the adopting release, "If the rule does not address that issue, the population Congress intended to protect—individuals whose net worth is below $1 million unless their home equity is taken into account—may be incentivized (or urged by unscrupulous salespeople) to take on debt secured by their homes for the purpose of qualifying as accredited investors and participating in investments without the protection to which they are entitled."

that is, the amount by which the fair market value of the home exceeds the mortgage. Thus, under the [SEC]'s proposal, accredited investor net worth would effectively be calculated [using] the following formula:

> Accredited Investor Net Worth = Net Worth (Total Assets—Total Liabilities) — Primary Residence Net Equity (Value of Residence—Debt Secured by Residence up to Value of Residence)

The [SEC] endorsed the above proposed approach because it believed that such approach will reduce the accredited investor net worth measure by the amount that the primary residence contributed to the investor's net worth before enactment of Section 413(a) of the Dodd-Frank Act. . . .

DEFINITION OF "PRIMARY RESIDENCE"

The [SEC] did not propose explicitly to define "primary residence." The [SEC] stated that issuers and investors should be able to use the commonly understood meaning of "primary residence"—the home where a person lives most of the time. The [SEC] noted that if additional analysis is needed under complex or unusual circumstances, helpful guidance may be found in rules that apply in other contexts, such as income tax rules and rules that apply when acquiring a mortgage loan for a primary residence, which often bears a lower interest rate than other mortgage loans.

Kenneth Muller, Andrew Thorpe, Sean Byrne and Seth Chertole, *A Revised Net Worth Standard for Accredited Investors*, 25 Insights 17-21 (March 2011) (*emphasis added*). On December 21, 2011, the SEC issued its Final Release adopting these proposed amendments to Regulation D's definition of "accredited investor." *See Net Worth Standard for Accredited Investors*, 76 Fed. Reg. 81,793 (Dec. 29, 2011) (codified at 17 C.F.R. pt. 230.501); *see also* SEC Release No. 33-9297 (Dec. 21, 2011).

An Exception to the Ban on General Advertising.   In April 2012, Congress passed the Jumpstart Our Business Startups (JOBS) Act.* In Section 201(a) of the JOBS Act, Congress directed the SEC to amend Rule 502(c) of Regulation D to provide that the ban on general advertising and general solicitation does *not* apply to offers and sales under the safe harbor of Rule 506, provided that *all* purchasers qualify as accredited investors. This represents a significant departure from the rather strict limitations that the SEC historically has imposed on the manner and scope of a Rule 506 offering. Notably, though, the Dodd Frank Act "does not mention the applicability of [the] Rule 502(c) [ban on general

---

For underwater mortgages where mortgage debt exceeds the value of the home, the amount of the excess is considered a liability for purposes of the net worth calculation, without regard to whether the loan is nonrecourse.

James D. Cox, et al., 2012 Supplement, Securities Regulation, Cases & Materials (6th Ed. 2012) at pp. 78-79.

* Pub. L. No. 112-106, 126 Stat. 306 (2012).

advertising] to the [small offering] exemptions provided under Rules 504 and 505 [of Regulation D]. Congress directed the [SEC] to revise Regulation D within 270 days." Cox et al., 2012 SUPPLEMENT, *supra*, at p. 79. Pursuant to this statutory mandate, on August 29, 2012, the SEC proposed amendments to Regulation D to eliminate the ban on general solicitation in transactions effected under Rule 506. The scope of these proposed reforms has been summarized as follows:

> Under proposed Rule 506(c), an issuer (and any selling agents) would be permitted to use general solicitation and general advertising to offer and sell securities, provided that the following conditions are satisfied:
>
> * The issuer must take reasonable steps to verify that all purchasers of the securities are accredited investors.
> * All purchasers of the securities must be accredited investors, either because they come within one of the enumerated categories of persons that qualify as accredited investors or because the issuer reasonably believes that they do, at the time of the sale of the securities, in each case as defined under existing Rule 501 of Regulation D.
> * All terms and conditions of existing Rules 501 (definitions), 502(a) (integration restriction) and 502(d) (resale limitations) of Regulation D must be satisfied. Existing Rule 502(c), prohibiting general solicitation and general advertising, would not apply.

The SEC did not propose specific verification methods that the issuer must use to verify the accredited investor status of the purchasers that would be deemed "reasonable" for the purposes of proposed Rule 506(c). Rather, the SEC proposed an objective test for determining the reasonableness of the steps that an issuer has taken, under which the issuer must consider the facts and circumstances of the transaction, including, among other things:

* The nature of the purchaser and the type of accredited investor that the purchaser claims to be.
* The amount and type of information that the issuer has about the purchaser.
* The nature of the offering, such as the manner in which the purchaser was solicited to participate in the offering, and the terms of the offering, such as a minimum investment amount.

This new verification requirement, which is discussed further below, would only apply to offerings of securities conducted pursuant to the new Rule 506(c). Other offerings conducted pursuant to existing Rule 506(b) that do not involve general solicitation or general advertising will not be subject to the verification requirements.

VERIFICATION—NATURE OF THE PURCHASER

Under this factor, the SEC recognized that taking reasonable steps to verify the accredited investor status of natural persons poses greater practical difficulties as compared to other categories enumerated in the definition of "accredited investor" in Rule 501(a), such as a registered broker-dealer or a registered investment company. Natural persons may be accredited investors based on either the "net worth test" or the "income test." As between the two tests, the SEC recognized that it may be more difficult for an issuer to obtain information about a person's assets and liabilities than it would be to obtain information about a person's income, although the SEC noted there could be privacy concerns with respect to either test.

Sullivan & Cromwell, LLP, *The* JOBS *Act — "General Solicitation" in Private Offerings* (law firm memo, August 30, 2012) at p. 3 (copy on file with author). As of this writing, (Fall 2012) these proposed rules have yet to be adopted by the SEC. Accordingly, the impact of these developments on future M&A transactions is yet to be fully understood.

Restricted Securities and Rule 144.   Shares that are issued by Bidder under any of the Regulation D exemptions, as well as securities that are sold in reliance on the §4(a)(2) private placement exemption, are treated as *restricted securities*. This means that there are significant restrictions on the resale of these shares, even if Bidder's stock is listed for trading on the NYSE or is otherwise publicly traded. The basis for imposing these limitations on resale is rooted in the fundamental tenet of the 1933 Act, which is to register (or exempt) *transactions* — not classes of securities. In order to protect the important 1933 Act concept of registering those *transactions* that qualify as a *distribution,* the SEC historically has imposed rather stringent limitations on the ability of the holder of restricted stock to dispose of these shares. Today, resales of restricted stock are largely governed by SEC's Rule 144.

Until recently, restricted stock could be resold by its owner pursuant to the terms of SEC Rule 144 only after the purchaser held the stock for one year. After satisfying this one-year holding period, owners of restricted stock were permitted to dispose of their shares in open-market transactions, but only in amounts that did not exceed the quantity limitations of Rule 144. After holding the restricted shares for two years, the shares were then freely tradable in open-market transactions without regard to the quantity limitations of Rule 144.

Historically, the limitations on resale imposed by the terms of Rule 144 were an important consideration for Target shareholders to take into account in deciding whether to accept Bidder stock as acquisition consideration. If the issuance of Bidder shares was not registered, and therefore Target shareholders received restricted stock of Bidder at closing on the acquisition, it was important for Target shareholders to be aware of the economic risk that they were being asked to assume. Since these former Target shareholders received restricted stock of Bidder, as a practical matter, this meant that they were locked into an investment in Bidder for at least a year before they could rely on the protections of Rule 144 to permit resale of their Bidder shares. However, effective February 2008, the SEC amended Rule 144 to substantially shorten the holding period imposed by the Rule. *See* Release No. 34-56914 (December 6, 2007). The amendments to Rule 144 reduce the holding period from one year to six months for resales of restricted securities of reporting companies. Thus, under the amended rules, if the issuer is a reporting company that is current in its filing obligations under the 1934 Act. (i.e., the "current public information requirement"), then non-affiliates may sell their restricted securities without any further limitations. (Broadly speaking, a "non-affiliate" is a person who is not in control of the issuer of the securities, which, for our purposes, refers to the Bidder who uses its shares as the acquisition consideration; it bears emphasizing that the concept of "control" is an important one under the federal securities laws and has been the subject of intense scrutiny both by the courts and the commentators.) Furthermore, after one year, the requirement that the issuer meet the "current public information" requirement is eliminated. These reforms should work to substantially reduce the economic risk associated with the decision to take restricted shares of Bidder's stock under the predecessor provisions of Rule 144 by enhancing the liquidity of Bidder's shares in the hands of the former Target shareholders. *See* Keith F. Higgins, Thomas Holden & Paul M. Kinsella, *SEC Adopts Amendments to Rules 144 and 145*, 22 INSIGHTS 8 (January 2008).

Registration Rights. Another common way for Target shareholders to address the financial risk inherent in holding restricted stock of Bidder is to bargain for resale registration rights as part of the acquisition agreement. If Bidder is subject to a resale registration obligation, then after closing, Bidder must register the shares that were issued to Target shareholders. On registration, these shares of Bidder's stock will be freely tradable and thereby provide liquidity for the Target shareholders' investment in Bidder.

QUESTIONS

1. Assume that you are counsel to Nestlé in connection with its acquisition of all the stock of Chef America, for cash. How would you advise Nestlé as to the application of the federal securities law provisions described above?

2. How would your analysis of these federal securities law provisions change if Nestlé proposed to acquire Chef America by paying half the purchase price in Nestlé common stock and the balance of the agreed-upon purchase price was to be paid in cash? If the shares issued to the two Merage brothers are not registered, who has the burden to establish that all the terms of an exemption have been satisfied?

3. From a public policy perspective, does it make sense to eliminate the need to register Nestlé's stock in connection with its acquisition of Chef America? What about the shareholders of Nestlé, the issuer? Do they need to know about the transaction? Does the 1933 Act address the information needs of Nestlé's shareholders?

3. Rule 145: Resales by Control Persons

A further problem is presented where the resale of Bidder's stock is made by an affiliate of Target Co., a constituent corporation in the merger transaction with Bidder Co. Here, some background is necessary in order to understand the nature of the problem presented by these resales. The following excerpt succinctly summarizes the regulatory framework that existed until certain reform measures were adopted by the SEC (and became effective in February 2008):

> A recurring issue in mergers and similar transactions in which all or part of the consideration consists of stock of the acquiring company is the ability of the target company's stockholders to freely resell those securities after the transaction is completed. In 1972, the SEC reversed its long-standing position that no

"sale," . . . occurs when securities are issued in a business combination transaction subject to stockholder vote. In so doing, the SEC adopted Rule 145 under the Securities Act, which requires registration of securities issued in a merger or similar transaction, unless an exemption is available. Form S-4 . . . is the SEC form typically used for the registration of securities issued in business combination transactions. If the acquiror [i.e., Bidder] registers its stock in compliance with Rule 145, target stockholders generally will receive freely tradable stock in the merger and [thus will] not have to worry about registering resales of such stock after the merger is completed.

However, Rule 145 also provides that any party to a merger or other transaction subject to the rule (other than the acquiror issuing stock in the transaction) and any person who at the time the transaction is submitted for stockholder vote . . . is an affiliate of that party, and who publicly offers or sells securities acquired in the transaction, is deemed to be engaged in a distribution of the securities and therefore an "underwriter," unless the resale limitations of [Rule 145] are satisfied. As a presumptive underwriter, a target affiliate who resells acquiror stock [will not be able to rely on the exemption found in [§4(a)(1)] of the 1933 Act]. Therefore, with respect to target affiliates, resales of stock acquired in merger transactions can give rise to significant registration issues, whether or not the acquiror's stock is registered under the Securities Act.[4] . . .

Almost invariably, target company stockholders receiving acquiror stock in a merger transaction will be concerned with their ability to liquidate their investment in the acquiror, either immediately or at some future date after the transaction is completed. If a merger is completed privately in reliance on an exemption from registration, all target stockholders will face potential registration issues because the stock received in the transaction is typically restricted. As noted, when the acquiror stock issued in the merger is registered under the Securities Act, those stockholders who are affiliated with the target company will face potential resale restrictions under Rule 145, while most other stockholders will be able to resell their stock without registration concerns, immediately after completion of the merger.[9]

In order to avoid the issues associated with underwriter status under Rule 145 described previously, target affiliates should either have their resales registered under the Securities Act or comply with the Rule 145(d) safe harbor. Under Rule 145(d), a target affiliate will not be deemed an underwriter, and therefore may resell acquiror stock without need for registration under the Securities Act, so long as:

- The amount limitations, public information, and manner of sale requirements of Rule 144 are met;
- The person is not an affiliate of the acquiror, a period of at least one year has passed since the securities were acquired in the merger and the acquiror satisfies the public information requirements of Rule 144 (i.e., generally, has

4. The practice has developed in public company mergers to require directors, officers, and principal stockholders of the target company to deliver "affiliate letters" to the acquiror, essentially acknowledging that they are subject to, and will comply with, the provisions of Rule 145.

9. Target stockholders who are not initially affiliates of the target but who, as a result of the merger, become affiliates of the acquiror, are subject to the Rule 144 limitations customarily applied to sales by affiliates. *See* Release No. 33-6099 (August 2, 1979), Question & Answer No. 85.

been subject to the reporting requirements of the Securities Exchange Act of 1934 for at least 90 days immediately prior to the sale of the securities and has filed all the reports required to be filed under such Act during the 12 months preceding the sale or for such shorter period that the acquiror was required to file such reports); or

- The person is not, and has not been for at least three months, an affiliate of the acquiror and two years have passed since the securities were acquired in the merger.

    In some cases, the acquiror's capitalization and trading volume is sufficient to permit resales by target affiliates immediately after the close of the merger with little or no restrictions imposed by Rule 145(d).[12] In all other cases, target affiliates likely will seek resale registration of their stock. . . . The terms of the agreement usually provide for registration within an agreed-on time or as soon as practicable after closing.

Lorenzo Borgogni & James J. Moloney, *Resales of Stock Acquired in Merger Transactions*, 17 INSIGHTS 16-17 (February 2003).

As part of the reform measures recently adopted by the SEC to Rule 144, which became effective in February 2008, the SEC also amended Rule 145. Under revised Rule 145, securities of Bidder that are held by affiliates of the acquired company, Target, are now freely tradable, *provided* that these holders are *not* affiliates of the Bidder (i.e., the acquiring company). However, as to those transactions that are subject to Rule 145 but which are effected pursuant to an exemption from registration (such as the private placement exemption under §4(a)(2) or its safe harbor provision, Rule 506), any securities issued in these transactions will result in the issuance of restricted securities and therefore may be resold only pursuant to an effective registration statement or an available exemption, which most often will be Rule 144. *See* Cooley, LLP, *SEC Approves Major Changes to Rule 144 and Rule 145* (law firm memo, January 2008) (copy on file with author). These changes in Rules 144 and 145 should serve to reduce the costs and burdens associated with using Bidder's stock as the acquisition currency.

B.   Scope of Federal Proxy Rules

If shareholder approval is required for a particular acquisition and the company has a class of securities registered under §12 of the 1934 Act ("reporting companies"), then any solicitation of shareholder votes will trigger the provisions of §14 of the 1934 Act and the SEC rules promulgated thereunder (collectively referred to as the "federal proxy rules").

---

12. The amount limitations are set forth in Rule 144(e)(1) under the Securities Act, which limits aggregate sales to the greater of: (1) one percent of the relevant class of (acquiror) securities outstanding; (2) the average weekly reported trading volume in the relevant class of (acquiror) securities on all exchanges and/or automated quotation systems during the four calendar weeks preceding the sale; and (3) the average weekly trading volume in the relevant class of (acquiror) securities reported through the consolidated transaction reporting system during the same four-week period.

SEC's Proxy Rules.   Section 14(a) of the 1934 Act prohibits solicitation of proxies from shareholders of reporting companies unless made in compliance with the federal proxy rules. The process of soliciting proxies is governed by Regulation 14A, promulgated by the SEC pursuant to the authority delegated to it by Congress under the terms of §14(a) of the 1934 Act. Regulation 14A is a complex set of rules that govern the timing and the process of soliciting share-holder votes to approve an M&A transaction. In addition, the SEC has promul-gated Schedule 14A, which sets forth the required items of information that must be included in the proxy statement pursuant to which proxies are solic-ited. Subject to certain limited exceptions, no solicitation of shareholder votes may be made unless the shareholder being solicited is provided with a written proxy statement that contains the items of information required by Schedule 14A. In the alternative, where Bidder Co. proposes to use its securities as the acquisition consideration and therefore must file a registration statement in order to satisfy the 1933 Act, then Form S-4 is to be used in lieu of Schedule 14A under the proxy rules. Not surprisingly, the information required by Form S-4 and Schedule 14A are very similar, at least insofar as the information required to be disclosed about the proposed acquisition transaction is concerned.

Proxy Statement.   Like other required forms of disclosure, proxy state-ments have developed a conventional form of presentation for the various dif-ferent types of acquisition transaction. For example, in the case of a proxy state-ment soliciting shareholder approval of a stock for stock merger in which only the vote of Target shareholders is required, the proxy statement will typically consist of: (i) a cover page that usually takes the form of a short letter to Tar-get shareholders that briefly describes the proposed acquisition; (ii) a formal notice of the meeting, which is usually one page; (iii) a table of contents that lists the different items of disclosure contained in the proxy statement; and (iv) the proxy statement itself. Under the detailed terms of Regulation 14A, and as a result of the SEC's disclosure initiative known as the plain English rules, the typical proxy statement will consist of the following components (all of which should be referenced in the table of contents):

- A question-and-answer section
- A summary section, typically consisting of a few pages (usually three to five pages in length) of narrative text and a few pages of financial and stock price information
- A section describing the risk factors related to the proposed transaction and/or the companies involved
- A section containing cautionary statements concerning any forward-looking information (such as sales projections, earnings forecasts, etc.) included in the proxy statement
- A section containing basic information about the details for conducting the shareholder meeting, addressing such things as the vote required, how to vote, how to change or withdraw a vote, and the effect of abstentions
- A section that provides a narrative description of the events and negotia-tions leading up to the parties' agreement
- A section setting forth the reasons that support the Target board's deci-sion to approve the transaction and recommend shareholder approval as well

- A section detailing the analytical basis for the conclusion of the company's investment banker as to the fairness of the transaction — generally known as the *fairness opinion*
- A section that sets forth any interests that individual officers or directors might have in the transaction, with a particular focus on those interests that present a conflict of interest
- A section that describes the federal income tax consequences to the company and its shareholders
- A section setting forth required financial information disclosures, including pro forma financial information regarding the transaction
- A detailed summary of the terms of the merger agreement, which is a bit of an oxymoron since this "summary" often runs to ten pages or more
- At the very end of the proxy statement are the exhibits, which typically consist of a copy of the merger agreement itself and a copy of the investment banker's fairness opinion

"Say-on-Pay" Votes and "Golden Parachute" Arrangements. Section 951 of the Dodd-Frank Act is popularly referred to as the "say-on-pay" requirement. "Say-on-pay" refers to the process by which shareholders of publicly traded companies are asked to give a nonbinding advisory vote on compensation arrangements for the companies' senior executive officers. The Dodd-Frank Act also includes provisions that relate to compensation paid to senior executives as part of an M&A transaction. On January 25, 2011, the SEC adopted its final rules, implementing the Congressional mandate of Section 951 of the Dodd-Frank Act. *See* SEC Release Nos. 33-9178, 34-63768 (Jan. 25, 2011).

> Under the new rules, public companies subject to the federal proxy rules must provide their shareholders with an advisory vote on executive compensation — generally known as a "say-on-pay" vote — at least once every three calendar years, and an advisory vote on the desired frequency of say-on-pay votes at least once every six calendar years.
>
> They must also provide additional proxy statement disclosure regarding the general nature and effect of the "say-on-pay" and frequency votes, including whether the votes are binding. In addition, the Compensation Discussion and Analysis disclosure ("CD&A") must address whether and how the company has responded to the most recent say-on-pay vote, and, to the extent material in determining compensation policies and decisions, include disclosure concerning the results of previous say-on-pay votes.
>
> The "say-on-pay" and frequency votes apply to annual meetings of shareholders at which directors will be elected or special meetings in lieu thereof taking place on or after January 21, 2011. Smaller reporting companies — those with a public float of less than $75 million — are not required to conduct say-on-pay or frequency votes until annual meetings occurring on or after January 21, 2013.

GOLDEN PARACHUTES

The new rules also require disclosure, in connection with M&A transactions, of "golden parachute" arrangements. "Golden parachutes" are broadly defined to include all agreements and understandings between the target or the acquirer and each named executive officer of the target or the acquirer [i.e., Bidder Co.] that relate to an M&A transaction. Certain types of compensation deemed unrelated to the M&A transaction are excluded from the definition of "golden parachute" payments.

The disclosure requirements apply to solicitation materials for all types of M&A transactions involving a company subject to the SEC's proxy rules (whether involving a tender offer, merger or sale of all or substantially all of a company's assets). Exceptions are provided for third party bidders' tender offer statements in transactions that are not subject to Rule 13e-3, and for foreign private issuers. For an M&A transaction requiring shareholder approval under the SEC's proxy rules, the soliciting company must also include an advisory shareholder vote regarding golden parachute arrangements, known as "say-on-golden parachute" vote.

A company may, but is not required to, address golden parachute arrangements as part of the say-on-pay vote taken at its annual meeting. A company will not be required to include an advisory vote on golden parachutes in a subsequent proxy statement for an M&A transaction if the golden parachute arrangements have already been voted upon in an annual say-on-pay vote and have not been modified to increase total compensation.

These new golden parachute rules are effective for proxy statements and other schedules and forms relating to M&A transactions initially filed on or after April 25, 2011.

Julia Cowles, et al., *Selected 2011 Developments in Corporate Law*, 2012 Annual Review, State Bar of California, Business Law News, 7, 9-10.

As a general proposition,

> The theory behind "Say on Pay" is that giving shareholders a periodic referendum on executive compensation will decrease the likelihood that overly generous compensation packages will be paid to senior executives. The vote may also motivate companies to align manager compensation with manager performance more closely, in the belief that shareholders respond most negatively to large compensation packages when stock performance is poor. Additionally, although the vote is non-binding, it might nonetheless powerfully influence the behavior of compensation committees [of publicly traded companies] who may wish to avoid the public opprobrium associated with a negative vote.

Jeffery D. Bauman, 2012 SUPPLEMENT to CORPORATIONS: LAW & POLICY (7th Ed. 2010) at p. 53.

Fairness Opinions.   Although there is no requirement under the federal proxy rules that a company obtain a fairness opinion, it has become customary for boards of directors to obtain opinions from their investment bankers as to the fairness of the price offered in an M&A transaction. However, almost as soon as it became commonplace to obtain a *fairness opinion*, criticism as to the practice surfaced. First, critics complained that quite often, the fairness opinion was rendered by the very same investment banking firm that brought the deal to the company—and the very same firm that will typically collect a fee when the transaction closes—which, for many commentators, hardly seems to be a completely objective appraiser. While some fairness opinions are written by independent firms that have no connection to the deal, the vast majority of such opinions are written by investment banking firms who stand to make substantial sums of money if the deal closes, thereby creating inherent conflicts of interest that have long troubled many observers of the M&A markets. Critics have raised other concerns as well. "The opinions are loaded with legal disclaimers. [Although the SEC's proxy rules do require disclosure of the fairness opinion obtained by the company as part of its proxy statement, the opinion is] often out of date by the time shareholders vote on the deal. Furthermore, the opinions tend to be so narrowly focused on the specifics of the agreement being evaluated that they do not even address whether directors could have secured a better deal." David Henry, *A Fair Deal—But for Whom?*, BUSINESS WEEK November 24, 2003, at 108.

This same 2003 news article went on to report that Eliot Spitzer, then the attorney general of New York, was expected to investigate Wall Street's practice of preparing fairness opinions, although he had not yet taken any action. Shortly thereafter, however, in November 2004, the National Association of Securities Dealers (NASD) announced that it was requesting comment on whether the NASD should propose a rule that would address conflicts of interest that inevitably arise when its members prepare fairness opinions in M&A transactions. After receiving 20 comment letters, the NASD in June 2005 proposed a new rule, NASD Rule 2290, to address procedures used by its members to prepare fairness opinions, as well as disclosure practices surrounding the disclosure of fairness opinions. As a self-regulatory organization (SRO), the NASD's rulemaking was subject to SEC approval before the rule could be made effective.* However, the road to final adoption of this rule was quite complicated, entailing several amendments by the NASD that culminated in final SEC approval of Rule 2290 in October 2007. FINRA Rule 2290 establishes "(1) certain required disclosures in fairness opinions issued by its members that are disclosed to public shareholders; and (2) certain required procedures in connection with its member firms' fairness opinions practice." Anne L. Benedict, *New FINRA Fairness Opinion Requirements*, 21 INSIGHTS 22 (December 2007).

Specifically, Rule 2290 lists certain disclosures "that must be included in the fairness opinion if, at the time the fairness opinion is issued to the board of directors of a company, the member firm issuing the fairness opinion *knows or has reason to know* that the fairness opinion will be provided or described to the public shareholders of the company . . . ." *Id.* (*emphasis in original*). In its adopting release, the SEC made clear that if stockholder approval of the transaction is required (thereby triggering the preparation of a proxy statement in compliance with the SEC's proxy rules), the member firm will be "deemed to have reason to know that the fairness opinion will be shared with the public." *Id.* at n. 3. Most notable, at least for our purposes, is that one of the required items of disclosure calls for disclosure of the fact that the compensation that a member firm will receive for rendering a fairness opinion is *contingent* upon

---

* The Financial Industry Regulatory Authority (FINRA) combined NASD's regulatory functions with the regulatory arm of the NYSE effective as of July 30, 2007. All registered broker-dealers that had been members of NASD automatically became members of FINRA. NASD (and now FINRA) serves as the primary regulator for broker-dealer firms, whose investment banking departments are the key providers of fairness opinions. FINRA combines the regulatory, enforcement and arbitration functions of the NYSE with those of NASD, and the resulting SRO is now known as FINRA.

successful completion of the M&A transaction. *See* FINRA Rule 2290(a)(1). It bears emphasizing, however, that the rule, as finally adopted, neither requires quantitative disclosure (as to the amount of the banker's fee), nor does it ban contingent fee arrangements despite recommendations to the contrary that were submitted by several commentators. Indeed, no less than the likes of "institutional investing heavyweights CALPERS and the AFL-CIO [argued] that a flat prohibition on contingent fee arrangements would be appropriate. . . . [However, securities industry professionals] took the opposite point of view arguing that . . . boards of directors [acting on behalf of the company in making the fee arrangement with the investment banking firm] are quite capable of taking into account any impact that a contingent fee arrangement might have on the [banker's] fairness analysis." Stephen I. Glover & William J. Robers, *The NASD's Proposed Rule Governing Fairness Opinion Practice*, THE M&A LAWYER, September 2005, at pp. 22-23.

In the end, the SEC indicated, in its Adopting Release, that it believes "that a descriptive disclosure that alerts shareholders to the existence of a contingent compensation arrangement is sufficient to serve the basic purpose of highlighting for investors that the [member firm] stands to benefit financially from the successful completion of the transaction, and therefore, that a conflict of interests may exist." *See* SEC Release No. 34-56645 (October 11, 2007), 72 FR 59317, 59319 (October 19, 2007). *Query:* Do you find the SEC's reasoning on this issue persuasive?

Recent Delaware Caselaw Regarding Fairness Opinions. In addition to the disclosure requirements of FINRA Rule 2290, the Delaware judiciary has weighed in on this issue. Delaware caselaw is clear that

> Directors of Delaware corporations owe to their stockholders a duty of disclosure derived from their ordinary fiduciary duties of care and loyalty. A common disclosure claim [in connection with an M&A transaction] is that the target company's disclosure document . . . was materially misleading or incomplete with respect to the fairness opinion relied on by the target's board in evaluating the transaction. The Delaware courts have decided numerous cases involving claims that disclosure as to some element of a fairness opinion—projections, analysis, assumptions—is defective.

Blake Rohrbacher and John Mark Zeberkiewicz, *Fair Summary: Delaware Framework for Disclosing Fairness Opinions*, 63 BUSINESS LAWYER 881, 881 (2008). As a direct outgrowth of this fiduciary duty obligation, there are legions of Delaware cases addressing disclosure claims relating to investment bankers' fairness opinions in M&A transactions. These cases supplement the disclosures otherwise required under the federal securities laws and provide an additional source of merger-related litigation. While the issues described above regarding fairness opinions continued to be litigated,

> the Court of Chancery has noted that financial disclosures in recent years have been far more robust than they had been in the past—undoubtedly due largely to the court's rulings. In response, plaintiffs have sought new lines of attack, and the Delaware courts have therefore begun to focus not only on the disclosure of underlying financial analyses broadly, but also on specific and discrete

issues involving fairness opinions and projections as well as on issues beyond the fairness opinion itself,[1] most notably the financial advisors potential conflicts and incentives.

Blake Rohrbacher and John Mark Zeberkiewicz, *Fair Summary II: An Update on Delaware's Disclosure Regime Regarding Fairness Opinions*, 66 BUSINESS LAWYER 943, 943-944 (August 2011). One can only expect that Delaware caselaw on this topic will continue to evolve in the coming years, presumably prompting yet another update.

Rule 14a-9.   By way of general summary, you can readily see that the preparation of the proxy statement is a labor-intensive, costly, and time-consuming process. Careful attention to detail is required lest any material information is omitted. Liability for false and/or misleading disclosures in the proxy statement is imposed by the terms of Rule 14a-9, which bears a strong family resemblance to the terms of Rule 10b-5. Specifically, liability under Rule 14a-9 extends to materially misleading disclosures contained in a proxy statement filed pursuant to Regulation 14A. In this regard, it is important to emphasize that Schedule 14A establishes only a minimum level of required disclosure. The standard to avoid liability for false and misleading proxy disclosure requires full and adequate disclosure of all material facts, which may require disclosure beyond that mandated by the specific items set forth in Schedule 14A. The relevant standard of materiality is analyzed in detail in the Supreme Court's landmark decision, *Basic Inc. v. Levinson*, set forth below.

C.   Rule 10b-5 and the Timing of Disclosure of Acquisition Negotiations

Basic Incorporated v. Levinson
485 U.S. 224 (1988)

Justice BLACKMUN delivered the opinion of the Court.

This case requires us to apply the materiality requirement of §10(b) of the Securities Exchange Act of 1934, (1934 Act), 48 Stat. 881, as amended, 15 U.S.C. §78a *et seq.* and the Securities and Exchange Commission's Rule 10b-5, 17 CFR §240.10b-5 (1987), promulgated thereunder, in the context of preliminary corporate merger discussions. . . .

Prior to December 20, 1978, Basic Incorporated was a publicly traded company primarily engaged in the business of manufacturing chemical refractories

---

1. *Fair Summary, supra* note 1 [63 Bus. Law 881], at 882-883 ("Fairness opinions are typically produced at the request of the target's board (or special committee of the board) by investment bankers who value the target company and come up with a range of values. The bankers then opine on whether the consideration to be received by the target company's stockholders in the business combination is fair . . . ." (footnote omitted)).

for the steel industry. As early as 1965 or 1966, Combustion Engineering, Inc., a company producing mostly alumina-based refractories, expressed some interest in acquiring Basic, but was deterred from pursuing this inclination seriously because of antitrust concerns it then entertained. In 1976, however, regulatory action opened the way to a renewal of Combustion's interest. The "Strategic Plan," dated October 25, 1976, for Combustion's Industrial Products Group included the objective: "Acquire Basic Inc. $30 million."

Beginning in September 1976, Combustion representatives had meetings and telephone conversations with Basic officers and directors, including petitioners here, concerning the possibility of a merger. During 1977 and 1978, Basic made three public statements denying that it was engaged in merger negotiations On December 18, 1978, Basic asked the New York Stock Exchange to suspend trading in its shares and issued a release stating that it had been "approached" by another company concerning a merger. On December 19, Basic's board endorsed Combustion's offer of $46 per share for its common stock, and on the following day publicly announced its approval of Combustion's tender offer for all outstanding shares.

Respondents are former Basic shareholders who sold their stock after Basic's first public statement of October 21, 1977, and before the suspension of trading in December 1978. Respondents brought a class action against Basic and its directors, asserting that the defendants issued three false or misleading public statements and thereby were in violation of §10(b) of the 1934 Act and of Rule 10b-5. Respondents alleged that they were injured by selling Basic shares at artificially depressed prices in a market affected by petitioners' misleading statements and in reliance thereon.

The District Court adopted a presumption of reliance by members of the plaintiff class upon petitioners' public statements that enabled the court to conclude that common questions of fact or law predominated over particular questions pertaining to individual plaintiffs. See Fed. Rule Civ. Proc. 23(b)(3). The District Court therefore certified respondents' class. On the merits, however, the District Court granted summary judgment for the defendants. It held that, as a matter of law, any misstatements were immaterial: there were no negotiations ongoing at the time of the first statement, and although negotiations were taking place when the second and third statements were issued, those negotiations were not "destined, with reasonable certainty, to become a merger agreement in principle."

The United States Court of Appeals for the Sixth Circuit affirmed the class certification, but reversed the District Court's summary judgment, and remanded the case. 786 F.2d 741 (1986). The court reasoned that while petitioners were under no general duty to disclose their discussions with Combustion, any statement the company voluntarily released could not be "'so incomplete as to mislead.'" In the Court of Appeals' view, Basic's statements that no negotiations were taking place, and that it knew of no corporate developments to account for the heavy trading activity, were misleading. With respect to materiality, the court rejected the argument that preliminary merger discussions are immaterial as a matter of law, and held that "once a statement is made denying the existence of any discussions, even discussions that might not have been material in absence of the denial are material because they make the statement made untrue."

The Court of Appeals joined a number of other Circuits in accepting the "fraud-on-the-market theory" to create a rebuttable presumption that respondents relied on petitioners' material misrepresentations, noting that without the presumption it would be impractical to certify a class under Federal Rule of Civil Procedure 23(b)(3).

We granted certiorari to resolve the split, see Part III, *infra,* among the Courts of Appeals as to the standard of materiality applicable to preliminary merger discussions, and to determine whether the courts below properly applied a presumption of reliance in certifying the class, rather than requiring each class member to show direct reliance on Basic's statements.

II

. . . The Court previously has addressed various positive and common-law requirements for a violation of §10(b) or of Rule 10b-5. See, *e.g., Santa Fe Industries, Inc. v. Green, supra* ("manipulative or deceptive" requirement of the statute); *Blue Chip Stamps v. Manor Drug Stores, supra* ("in connection with the purchase or sale" requirement of the Rule); *Dirks v. SEC,* 463 U.S. 646, 103 S. Ct. 3255, 77 L. Ed. 2d 911 (1983) (duty to disclose); *Chiarella v. United States,* 445 U.S. 222, 100 S. Ct. 1108, 63 L. Ed. 2d 348 (1980) (same); *Ernst & Ernst v. Hochfelder,* [425 U.S. 185 (1976)] (scienter). The Court also explicitly has defined a standard of materiality under the securities laws, see *TSC Industries, Inc. v. Northway, Inc.,* 426 U.S. 438, 96 S. Ct. 2126, 48 L. Ed. 2d 757 (1976), concluding in the proxy-solicitation context that "[a]n omitted fact is material if there is a substantial likelihood that a reasonable shareholder would consider it important in deciding how to vote." Acknowledging that certain information concerning corporate developments could well be of "dubious significance," the Court was careful not to set too low a standard of materiality; it was concerned that a minimal standard might bring an overabundance of information within its reach, and lead management "simply to bury the shareholders in an avalanche of trivial information—a result that is hardly conducive to informed decisionmaking." It further explained that to fulfill the materiality requirement "there must be a substantial likelihood that the disclosure of the omitted fact would have been viewed by the reasonable investor as having significantly altered the 'total mix' of information made available." We now expressly adopt the *TSC Industries* standard of materiality for the §10(b) and Rule 10b-5 context.

III

The application of this materiality standard to preliminary merger discussions is not self-evident. Where the impact of the corporate development on the target's fortune is certain and clear, the *TSC Industries* materiality definition admits straightforward application. Where, on the other hand, the event is contingent or speculative in nature, it is difficult to ascertain whether the "reasonable investor" would have considered the omitted information significant at the time. Merger negotiations, because of the ever-present possibility that the contemplated transaction will not be effectuated, fall into the latter category.

A

Petitioners urge upon us a Third Circuit test for resolving this difficulty. Under this approach, preliminary merger discussions do not become material until "agreement-in-principle" as to the price and structure of the transaction has been reached between the would-be merger partners. See *Greenfield v. Heublein, Inc.,* 742 F.2d 751, 757 (CA3 1984), cert. denied, 469 U.S. 1215, 105 S. Ct. 1189, 84 L. Ed. 2d 336 (1985). By definition, then, information concerning any negotiations not yet at the agreement-in-principle stage could be withheld or even misrepresented without a violation of Rule 10b-5.

Three rationales have been offered in support of the "agreement-in principle" test. The first derives from the concern expressed in *TSC Industries* that an investor not be overwhelmed by excessively detailed and trivial information, and focuses on the substantial risk that preliminary merger discussions may collapse: because such discussions are inherently tentative, disclosure of their existence itself could mislead investors and foster false optimism. The other two justifications for the agreement-in-principle standard are based on management concerns: because the requirement of "agreement-in-principle" limits the scope of disclosure obligations, it helps preserve the confidentiality of merger discussions where earlier disclosure might prejudice the negotiations; and the test also provides a usable, bright-line rule for determining when disclosure must be made.

None of these policy-based rationales, however, purports to explain why drawing the line at agreement-in-principle reflects the significance of the information upon the investor's decision. The first rationale, and the only one connected to the concerns expressed in *TSC Industries,* stands soundly rejected, even by a Court of Appeals that otherwise has accepted the wisdom of the agreement-in-principle test. "It assumes that investors are nitwits, unable to appreciate—even when told—that mergers are risky propositions up until the closing." *Flamm v. Eberstadt,* 814 F.2d [1169, 1175 (7th Cir.) *cert. denied,* 484 U.S. 853 (1987)]. Disclosure, and not paternalistic withholding of accurate information, is the policy chosen and expressed by Congress. We have recognized time and again, a "fundamental purpose" of the various Securities Acts, "was to substitute a philosophy of full disclosure for the philosophy of *caveat emptor* and thus to achieve a high standard of business ethics in the securities industry." The role of the materiality requirement is not to "attribute to investors a child-like simplicity, an inability to grasp the probabilistic significance of negotiations," *Flamm v. Eberstadt,* 814 F.2d, at 1175, but to filter out essentially useless information that a reasonable investor would not consider significant, even as part of a larger "mix" of factors to consider in making his investment decision.

The second rationale, the importance of secrecy during the early stages of merger discussions, also seems irrelevant to an assessment whether their existence is significant to the trading decision of a reasonable investor. To avoid a "bidding war" over its target, an acquiring firm often will insist that negotiations remain confidential, see, *e.g., In re Carnation Co.,* Exchange Act Release No.

22214, 33 S.E.C. Docket 1025 (1985), and at least one Court of Appeals has stated that "silence pending settlement of the price and structure of a deal is beneficial to most investors, most of the time." *Flamm v. Eberstadt,* 814 F.2d, at 1177.[11]

We need not ascertain, however, whether secrecy necessarily maximizes shareholder wealth—although we note that the proposition is at least disputed as a matter of theory and empirical research—for this case does not concern the *timing* of a disclosure; it concerns only its accuracy and completeness.[13] We face here the narrow question whether information concerning the existence and status of preliminary merger discussions is significant to the reasonable investor's trading decision. Arguments based on the premise that some disclosure would be "premature" in a sense are more properly considered under the rubric of an issuer's duty to disclose. The "secrecy" rationale is simply inapposite to the definition of materiality.

The final justification offered in support of the agreement-in-principle test seems to be directed solely at the comfort of corporate managers. A bright-line rule indeed is easier to follow than a standard that requires the exercise of judgment in the light of all the circumstances. But ease of application alone is not an excuse for ignoring the purposes of the Securities Acts and Congress' policy decisions. Any approach that designates a single fact or occurrence as always determinative of an inherently fact-specific finding such as materiality, must necessarily be overinclusive or underinclusive. In *TSC Industries* this Court explained: "The determination [of materiality] requires delicate assessments of the inferences a 'reasonable shareholder' would draw from a given set of facts and the significance of those inferences to him. . . . " 426 U.S., at 450, 96 S. Ct., at 2133. After much study, the Advisory Committee on Corporate Disclosure cautioned the SEC against administratively confining materiality to a rigid formula.[14] Courts also would do well to heed this advice.

We therefore find no valid justification for artificially excluding from the definition of materiality information concerning merger discussions, which would otherwise be considered significant to the trading decision of a reasonable investor, merely because agreement-in-principle as to price and structure has not yet been reached by the parties or their representatives. . . .

---

11. Reasoning backwards from a goal of economic efficiency, that Court of Appeals stated: "Rule 10b-5 is about *fraud,* after all, and it is not fraudulent to conduct business in a way that makes investors better off. . . . " 814 F.2d, at 1177.

13. See *SEC v. Texas Gulf Sulphur Co.,* 401 F.2d 833, 862 (CA2 1968) (en banc) ("Rule 10b-5 is violated whenever assertions are made, as here, in a manner reasonably calculated to influence the investing public . . . if such assertions are false or misleading or are so incomplete as to mislead . . . "), cert. denied *sub nom. Coates v. SEC,* 394 U.S. 976, 89 S. Ct. 1454, 22 L. Ed. 2d 756 (1969).

14. "Although the Committee believes that ideally it would be desirable to have absolute certainty in the application of the materiality concept, it is its view that such a goal is illusory and unrealistic. The materiality concept is judgmental in nature and it is not possible to translate this into a numerical formula. The Committee's advice to the [SEC] is to avoid this quest for certainty and to continue consideration of materiality on a case-by-case basis as disclosure problems are identified." House Committee on Interstate and Foreign Commerce, Report of the Advisory Committee on Corporate Disclosure to the Securities and Exchange [SEC], 95th Cong., 1st Sess., 327 (Comm. Print 1977).

C

Even before this Court's decision in *TSC Industries,* the Second Circuit had explained the role of the materiality requirement of Rule 10b-5, with respect to contingent or speculative information or events, in a manner that gave that term meaning that is independent of the other provisions of the Rule. Under such circumstances, materiality "will depend at any given time upon a balancing of both the indicated probability that the event will occur and the anticipated magnitude of the event in light of the totality of the company activity." *SEC v. Texas Gulf Sulphur Co.,* 401 F.2d [833, 849 (2d Cir. 1968) (en banc), *cert. denied sub nom. Coates v. SEC,* 394 U.S. 976 (1969)]. Interestingly, neither the Third Circuit decision adopting the agreement-in-principle test nor petitioners here take issue with this general standard. Rather, they suggest that with respect to preliminary merger discussions, there are good reasons to draw a line at agreement on price and structure.

In a subsequent decision, the late Judge Friendly, writing for a Second Circuit panel, applied the *Texas Gulf Sulphur* probability/magnitude approach in the specific context of preliminary merger negotiations. After acknowledging that materiality is something to be determined on the basis of the particular facts of each case, he stated:

> "Since a merger in which it is bought out is the most important event that can occur in a small corporation's life, to wit, its death, we think that inside information, as regards a merger of this sort, can become material at an earlier stage than would be the case as regards lesser transactions — and this even though the mortality rate of mergers in such formative stages is doubtless high."

SEC v. Geon Industries, Inc., 531 F.2d 39, 47-48 (1976). We agree with that analysis.

Whether merger discussions in any particular case are material therefore depends on the facts. Generally, in order to assess the probability that the event will occur, a factfinder will need to look to indicia of interest in the transaction at the highest corporate levels. Without attempting to catalog all such possible factors, we note by way of example that board resolutions, instructions to investment bankers, and actual negotiations between principals or their intermediaries may serve as indicia of interest. To assess the magnitude of the transaction to the issuer of the securities allegedly manipulated, a factfinder will need to consider such facts as the size of the two corporate entities and of the potential premiums over market value. No particular event or factor short of closing the transaction need be either necessary or sufficient by itself to render merger discussions material.[17]

---

17. To be actionable, of course, a statement must also be misleading. Silence, absent a duty to disclose, is not misleading under Rule 10b-5. "No comment" statements are generally the functional equivalent of silence. See *In re Carnation Co.,* Exchange Act Release No. 22214, 33 S.E.C. Docket 1025 (1985). See also New York Stock Exchange Listed Company Manual §202.01, reprinted in 3 CCH Fed. Sec. L. Rep. ¶ 23,515 (1987) (premature public announcement may properly be delayed for valid business purpose and where adequate security can be maintained); American Stock Exchange Company Guide §§401-405, reprinted in 3 CCH

As we clarify today, materiality depends on the significance the reasonable investor would place on the withheld or misrepresented information. The fact-specific inquiry we endorse here is consistent with the approach a number of courts have taken in assessing the materiality of merger negotiations. Because the standard of materiality we have adopted differs from that used by both courts below, we remand the case for reconsideration of the question whether a grant of summary judgment is appropriate on this record. . . .

V

In summary:

1. We specifically adopt, for the §10(b) and Rule 10b-5 context, the standard of materiality set forth in *TSC Industries, Inc. v. Northway, Inc.*, 426 U.S., at 449, 96 S. Ct., at 2132.
2. We reject "agreement-in-principle as to price and structure" as the bright-line rule for materiality.
3. We also reject the proposition that "information becomes material by virtue of a public statement denying it."
4. Materiality in the merger context depends on the probability that the transaction will be consummated, and its significance to the issuer of the securities. Materiality depends on the facts and thus is to be determined on a case-by-case basis. . . .

The judgment of the Court of Appeals is vacated, and the case is remanded to that court for further proceedings consistent with this opinion.
It is so ordered. . . .

NOTES

1. NYSE Guidelines.   The policies of the NYSE provide an important source of disclosure obligation for publicly traded companies, as reflected in the following excerpt.

Fed. Sec. L. Rep. ¶¶ 23, 124A-23, 124E (1985) (similar provisions). It has been suggested that given current market practices, a "no comment" statement is tantamount to an admission that merger discussions are underway. See *Flamm v. Eberstadt*, 814 F.2d, at 1178. That may well hold true to the extent that issuers adopt a policy of truthfully denying merger rumors when no discussions are underway, and of issuing "no comment" statements when they are in the midst of negotiations. There are, of course, other statement policies firms could adopt; we need not now advise issuers as to what kind of practice to follow, within the range permitted by law. Perhaps more importantly, we think that creating an exception to a regulatory scheme founded on a prodisclosure legislative philosophy, because complying with the regulation might be "bad for business," is a role for Congress, not this Court. See also *id.*, at 1182 (opinion concurring in judgment and concurring in part).

‖ NYSE Listed Company Manual

202.05   TIMELY DISCLOSURE OF MATERIAL NEWS DEVELOPMENTS

A listed company is expected to release quickly to the public any news or information which might reasonably be expected to materially affect the market for its securities. This is one of the most important and fundamental purposes of the listing agreement which the company enters into with the Exchange.

A listed company should also act promptly to dispel unfounded rumors which result in unusual market activity or price variations. . . .

202.01   INTERNAL HANDLING OF CONFIDENTIAL CORPORATE MATTERS

Unusual market activity or a substantial price change has on occasion occurred in a company's securities shortly before the announcement of an important corporate action or development. Such incidents are extremely embarrassing and damaging to both the company and the Exchange since the public may quickly conclude that someone acted on the basis of inside information.

Negotiations leading to mergers and acquisitions, . . . [or] the making of arrangements preparatory to an exchange or tender offer, . . . are the type of developments where the risk of untimely and inadvertent disclosure of corporate plans are most likely to occur. Frequently, these matters require extensive discussion and study by corporate officials before final decisions can be made. Accordingly, extreme care must be used in order to keep the information on a confidential basis.

Where it is possible to confine formal or informal discussions to a small group of the top management of the company or companies involved, and their individual confidential advisors where adequate security can be maintained, premature public announcement may properly be avoided. In this regard, the market action of a company's securities should be closely watched at a time when consideration is being given to important corporate matters. If unusual market activity should arise, the company should be prepared to make an immediate public announcement of the matter.

At some point it usually becomes necessary to involve other persons to conduct preliminary studies or assist in other preparations for contemplated transactions, e.g., business appraisals, tentative financing arrangements, attitude of large outside holders, availability of major blocks of stock, engineering studies and market analyses and surveys. Experience has shown that maintaining security at this point is virtually impossible. Accordingly, fairness requires that the company make an immediate public announcement as soon as disclosures relating to such important matters are made to outsiders.

2. Form 8-K Disclosure Requirements.   The 1934 Act imposes periodic disclosure obligations on reporting companies. Historically, publicly traded companies generally made disclosure by filing three quarterly reports on Form 10-Q and an annual report on Form 10-K, along with an annual proxy statement.

In addition, reporting companies historically have been required to file a current report on Form 8-K, although traditionally the events that would trigger a Form 8-K filing obligation have been limited to a handful of significant events. However, as noted earlier in this casebook, in the wake of financial scandals involving Enron and WorldCom, Congress enacted the Sarbanes-Oxley Act. Under Section 409 of the Sarbanes Oxley Act of 2002, Congress mandated that the SEC move to a "real-time disclosure" model. Proposed even before the provisions of the Sarbanes-Oxley Act became final, the SEC adopted new Form 8-K rules that became effective in August 2004, and which were later amended in 2006. These new rules "represent the SEC's decision to implement 'real time disclosure' by overlaying enhanced current reporting requirements through Form 8-K [filing obligations] on the traditional periodic reporting system. The new rules are designed to provide investors with greater and more timely disclosure of significant and material corporate events . . . . " Wilmer, Cutler, Pickering, Hall & Dorr, LLP, *Keeping Current with Form 8-K: A Practical Guide* (law firm memo, December 2004) at 2 (copy on file with author).

The SEC's new rules significantly expanded the range of events that must be reported, and further, significantly shortened the time period for filing the Form 8-K disclosure to four business days after a triggering event occurs. The SEC's expanded Form 8-K disclosure requirements accelerate a trend that predates enactment of the Sarbanes-Oxley Act. Even before the SEC's new Form 8-K rules became effective, "many public companies [had established] practices of communicating with their investors and the market outside of their [periodic] Exchange Act reports through a variety of means, including press releases, analyst calls, discussions with financial press and other media, participation in conferences, and website postings. While less formal than Exchange Act reporting, these communications served to provide material information to the market on a relatively current basis. As a result, investors and analysts now generally expect to receive material information in 'real time.' In addition, stock markets have required and encouraged current disclosure of material developments through press releases by companies with listed securities." *Id.* at 1.

For our purposes, among the most important of the expanded disclosures now required by Form 8-K is new Item 1.01, which calls for the company to disclose that it has entered into a "material definitive agreement" not made in the ordinary course of business, the definition of which would include agreements relating to a *material* merger, acquisition, or divestiture. Of course, compliance with this new disclosure obligation still entails the determination that the acquisition agreement at issue is "material," which as we have seen in the principal case is often a complex matter requiring difficult judgment calls to be made. It also bears emphasizing that the Form 8-K must be filed within four business days after entering into any such material agreement.

3. Duty to Disclose. By itself, Rule 10b-5 does not impose a duty to disclose. Where does this duty come from? The most important source of a duty to disclose for publicly traded companies is the periodic reporting obligations imposed by the terms of the 1934 Act. However, once you speak—whether you are volunteering information in a periodic filing *or* by way of a press release announcing a proposed acquisition *or* in response to an inquiry from a regulator—then

Rule 10b-5 requires that you speak truthfully, providing full and adequate disclosure of *all material* facts. This is the very clear message of *Basic Inc. v. Levinson,* a point that was recently emphasized by the Supreme Court in its opinion in *Matrixx Initiatives, Inc. v. Siracusano,* 131 S.Ct. 1309 (2011). During the course of its opinion, the Supreme Court observed:

> §10(b) and Rule 10b-5(b) do not create an affirmative duty to disclose any and all material information. Disclosure is required under these provisions only when necessary "to make . . . statements made, in the light of the circumstances under which they were made, not misleading." . . . Even with respect to information that a reasonable investor might consider material, companies can control what they have to disclose under these provisions *by controlling what they say to the market.*

Matrixx, 131 S.Ct. at 1321 (*emphasis added*). The Court's express statement that public companies can control what they *must* disclose "by controlling what they say to the market" has led many M&A lawyers to recommend that their clients keep merger negotiations strictly confidential in order to avoid triggering an obligation to disclose ongoing merger negotiations. The importance of this strategy has been highlighted in several recent cases. *See, e.g. Thesling v. Bioenvision, Inc.* 374 F. App'x 141 (2d Cir. 2010); and *Levie v. Sears Roebuck & Co.,* 676 F. Supp. 2d 680, 686-688 (D. Ill. 2009). Notably, the courts have reiterated the following guidelines, which were drawn from the Supreme Court's decision in *Basic, Inc. v. Levinson* and which (as made clear in the following commentary) are helpful to any public company in considering the scope of its disclosure obligations with respect to ongoing merger negotiations:

- A corporation is not required to disclose a fact merely because a reasonable investor would very much like to know that fact. Disclosure is required only when the corporation is subject to a duty to disclose.
- There are three circumstances in which a duty to disclose arises:

  (1)   when the rules of the SEC affirmatively require disclosure;
  (2)   when a corporation or corporate insider trades on the basis of material, non-public information; and
  (3)   when disclosure is required to make prior statements not misleading.

- No SEC rule requires disclosure of merger negotiations until they ripen into a definitive agreement, in which case a Current Report on Form 8-K is required.
- If, however, a company speaks about mergers or acquisitions or related topics, it must speak truthfully. So it could be materially misleading for a company to deny merger negotiations while negotiations are ongoing. But general statements about a company's business, financial projections, or strategy do not give rise to a duty to disclose merger negotiations that might materially impact its business, projections, or strategy. On the other hand, a statement that the company's business, projections, or strategy will not change could result in a disclosure obligation.
- In the absence of a duty to disclose, silence (or a "no comment" statement) is an acceptable response to questions about merger discussions.

The opinions underscore the fact-specific nature of their conclusions. Decisions regarding when to disclose merger negotiations (or other steps preceding an acquisition) should be made in light of all the relevant circumstances, including other statements [that] the company has made or intends to make and other actions [that] the company may be taking (such as where the company itself is trading in its stock through a repurchase program or otherwise). Disclosure obligations also may arise from other sources, such as stock exchange rules or state law. Finally, we note that there are sometimes tactical reasons for a company to make disclosure even when it has no legal obligation to do so.

Spencer D. Klein & Michael G. O'Bryan, Morrison & Foerster, LLP, *Recent Cases Remind M&A Participants of When Disclosure of Merger Negotiations is Required,* (law firm memo, July 14, 2010) (copy on file with author).

D.   Insider Trading in Anticipation of Acquisitions

1.   Liability Under Rule 14e-3

United States v. O'Hagan
521 U.S. 642, 117 S. Ct. 2199 (1997)

Justice GINSBURG delivered the opinion of the Court.

This case concerns the interpretation and enforcement of §10(b) and §14(e) of the Securities Exchange Act of 1934, and rules made by the Securities and Exchange Commission pursuant to these provisions, Rule 10b-5 and Rule 14e-3(a). Two prime questions are presented. The first relates to the misappropriation of material, nonpublic information for securities trading; the second concerns fraudulent practices in the tender setting. In particular, we address and resolve these issues: (1) Is a person who trades in securities for personal profit, using confidential information misappropriated in breach of a fiduciary duty to the source of the information, guilty of violating §10(b) and Rule 10b-5? (2) Did the Commission exceed its rulemaking authority by adopting Rule 14e-3(a), which proscribes trading on undisclosed information in the tender offer setting, even in the absence of a duty to disclose? Our answer to the first question is yes, and to the second question, viewed in the context of this case, no.

I

Respondent James Herman O'Hagan was a partner in the law firm of Dorsey & Whitney in Minneapolis, Minnesota. In July 1988, Grand Metropolitan PLC (Grand Met), a company based in London, England, retained Dorsey & Whitney as local counsel to represent Grand Met regarding a potential tender offer for the common stock of the Pillsbury Company, headquartered in Minneapolis. Both Grand Met and Dorsey & Whitney took precautions to protect the confidentiality of Grand Met's tender offer plans. O'Hagan did no work on the Grand Met representation. Dorsey & Whitney withdrew from representing Grand Met on September 9, 1988. Less than a month later, on October 4, 1988, Grand Met publicly announced its tender offer for Pillsbury stock.

On August 18, 1988, while Dorsey & Whitney was still representing Grand Met, O'Hagan began purchasing call options for Pillsbury stock. Each option gave him the right to purchase 100 shares of Pillsbury stock by a specified date in September 1988. Later in August and in September, O'Hagan made additional purchases of Pillsbury call options. By the end of September, he owned 2,500 unexpired Pillsbury options, apparently more than any other individual investor. O'Hagan also purchased, in September 1988, some 5,000 shares of Pillsbury common stock, at a price just under $39 per share. When Grand Met announced its tender offer in October, the price of Pillsbury stock rose to nearly $60 per share. O'Hagan then sold his Pillsbury call options and common stock, making a profit of more than $4.3 million.

The Securities and Exchange Commission (SEC or Commission) initiated an investigation into O'Hagan's transactions, culminating in a 57-count indictment. The indictment alleged that O'Hagan defrauded his law firm and its client, Grand Met, by using for his own trading purposes material, nonpublic information regarding Grand Met's planned tender offer.[1] According to the indictment, O'Hagan used the profits he gained through this trading to conceal his previous embezzlement and conversion of unrelated client trust funds.[2] O'Hagan was charged with 20 counts of mail fraud, in violation of 18 U.S.C. §1341; 17 counts of securities fraud, in violation of §10(b) of the Securities Exchange Act of 1934 (Exchange Act), and SEC Rule 10b-5; 17 counts of fraudulent trading in connection with a tender offer, in violation of §14(e) of the Exchange Act, 15 U.S.C. §78n(e), and SEC Rule 14e-3(a); and 3 counts of violating federal money laundering statutes. A jury convicted O'Hagan on all 57 counts, and he was sentenced to a 41-month term of imprisonment.

A divided panel of the Court of Appeals for the Eighth Circuit reversed all of O'Hagan's convictions. 92 F.3d 612 (1996). Liability under §10(b) and Rule 10b-5, the Eighth Circuit held, may not be grounded on the "misappropriation theory" of securities fraud on which the prosecution relied. *Id.*, at 622. The Court of Appeals also held that Rule 14e-3(a) — which prohibits trading while in possession of material, nonpublic information relating to a tender

---

1. As evidence that O'Hagan traded on the basis of nonpublic information misappropriated from his law firm, the Government relied on a conversation between O'Hagan and the Dorsey & Whitney partner heading the firm's Grand Met representation. That conversation allegedly took place shortly before August 26, 1988. O'Hagan urges that the Government's evidence does not show he traded on the basis of nonpublic information. O'Hagan points to news reports on August 18 and 22, 1988, that Grand Met was interested in acquiring Pillsbury, and to an earlier, August 12, 1988, news report that Grand Met had put up its hotel chain for auction to raise funds for an acquisition. O'Hagan's challenge to the sufficiency of the evidence remains open for consideration on remand.

2. O'Hagan was convicted of theft in state court, sentenced to 30 months' imprisonment, and fined. See *State v. O'Hagan*, 474 N.W.2d 613, 615, 623 (Minn. App. 1991). The Supreme Court of Minnesota disbarred O'Hagan from the practice of law. See *In re O'Hagan*, 450 N.W.2d 571 (Minn. 1990).

offer—exceeds the SEC's §14(e) rulemaking authority because the Rule contains no breach of fiduciary duty requirement . . . .

Decisions of the Courts of Appeals are in conflict on the propriety of the misappropriation theory under §10(b) and Rule 10b-5, . . . and on the legitimacy of Rule 14e-3(a) under §14(e). We granted certiorari, 519 U.S. 1087, (1997), and now reverse the Eighth Circuit's judgment.

II

We address first the Court of Appeals' reversal of O'Hagan's convictions under §10(b) and Rule 10b-5. Following the Fourth Circuit's lead, see *United States v. Bryan*, 58 F.3d 933, 943-959 (1995), the Eighth Circuit rejected the misappropriation theory as a basis for §10(b) liability. We hold, in accord with several other Courts of Appeals,[3] that criminal liability under §10(b) may be predicated on the misappropriation theory.[4] . . .

III

We consider next the ground on which the Court of Appeals reversed O'Hagan's convictions for fraudulent trading in connection with a tender offer, in violation of §14(e) of the Exchange Act and SEC Rule 14e-3(a). A sole question is before us as to these convictions: Did the [SEC], as the Court of Appeals held, exceed its rulemaking authority under §14(e) when it adopted Rule 14e-3(a) without requiring a showing that the trading at issue entailed a breach of fiduciary duty? We hold that the Commission, in this regard and to the extent relevant to this case, did not exceed its authority.

The governing statutory provision, §14(e) of the Exchange Act, reads in relevant part:

> "It shall be unlawful for any person . . . to engage in any fraudulent, deceptive, or manipulative acts or practices, in connection with any tender offer . . . . The [SEC] shall, for the purposes of this subsection, by rules and regulations

---

3. See, *e.g., United States v. Chestman,* 947 F.2d 551, 566 (C.A.2 1991) (en banc), cert. denied, 503 U.S. 1004, 112 S. Ct. 1759, 118 L. Ed. 2d 422 (1992); *SEC v. Cherif,* 933 F.2d 403, 410 (C.A.7 1991), cert. denied, 502 U.S. 1071, 112 S. Ct. 966, 117 L. Ed. 2d 131 (1992); *SEC v. Clark,* 915 F.2d 439, 453 (C.A.9 1990).

4. Twice before we have been presented with the question whether criminal liability for violation of §10(b) may be based on a misappropriation theory. In *Chiarella v. United States,* 445 U.S. 222, 235-237, 100 S. Ct. 1108, 1118-1119, 63 L. Ed. 2d 348 (1980), the jury had received no misappropriation theory instructions, so we declined to address the question. See *infra,* at 2211. In *Carpenter v. United States,* 484 U.S. 19, 24, 108 S. Ct. 316, 319-320, 98 L. Ed. 2d 275 (1987), the Court divided evenly on whether, under the circumstances of that case, convictions resting on the misappropriation theory should be affirmed. See Aldave, The Misappropriation Theory: *Carpenter* and Its Aftermath, 49 Ohio St. L.J. 373, 375 (1988) (observing that "*Carpenter* was, by any reckoning, an unusual case," for the information there misappropriated belonged not to a company preparing to engage in securities transactions, *e.g.,* a bidder in a corporate acquisition, but to the Wall Street Journal).

define, and prescribe means reasonably designed to prevent, such acts and practices as are fraudulent, deceptive, or manipulative." 15 U.S.C. §78n(e).

Section 14(e)'s first sentence prohibits fraudulent acts in connection with a tender offer. This self-operating proscription was one of several provisions added to the Exchange Act in 1968 by the Williams Act, ... The section's second sentence delegates definitional and prophylactic rulemaking authority to the Commission. Congress added this rulemaking delegation to §14(e) in 1970 amendments to the Williams Act. . . .

Through §14(e) and other provisions on disclosure in the Williams Act, Congress sought to ensure that shareholders "confronted by a cash tender offer for their stock [would] not be required to respond without adequate information." *Rondeau v. Mosinee Paper Corp.,* 422 U.S. 49, 58 (1975); see *Lewis v. McGraw,* 619 F.2d 192, 195 (C.A.2 1980) (*per curiam*) ("very purpose" of Williams Act was "informed decisionmaking by shareholders"). As we recognized in *Schreiber v. Burlington Northern, Inc.,* 472 U.S. 1 (1985), Congress designed the Williams Act to make "disclosure, rather than court imposed principles of 'fairness' or 'artificiality,' . . . the preferred method of market regulation." Section 14(e), we explained, "supplements the more precise disclosure provisions found elsewhere in the Williams Act, while requiring disclosure more explicitly addressed to the tender offer context than that required by §10(b)."

Relying on §14(e)'s rulemaking authorization, the Commission, in 1980, promulgated Rule 14e-3(a). That measure provides:

> "(a) If any person has taken a substantial step or steps to commence, or has commenced, a tender offer (the 'offering person'), it shall constitute a fraudulent, deceptive or manipulative act or practice within the meaning of section 14(e) of the [Exchange] Act for any other person who is in possession of material information relating to such tender offer which information he knows or has reason to know is nonpublic and which he knows or has reason to know has been acquired directly or indirectly from:
> "(1) The offering person,
> "(2) The issuer of the securities sought or to be sought by such tender offer, or
> "(3) Any officer, director, partner or employee or any other person acting on behalf of the offering person or such issuer, to purchase or sell or cause to be purchased or sold any of such securities or any securities convertible into or exchangeable for any such securities or any option or right to obtain or to dispose of any of the foregoing securities, unless within a reasonable time prior to any purchase or sale such information and its source are publicly disclosed by press release or otherwise." 17 CFR §240.14e-3(a) (1996).

As characterized by the Commission, Rule 14e-3(a) is a "disclose or abstain from trading" requirement. 45 Fed. Reg. 60410 (1980).[15] The Second Circuit concisely described the Rule's thrust:

> "One violates Rule 14e-3(a) if he trades on the basis of material nonpublic information concerning a pending tender offer that he knows or has reason to

---

15. The Rule thus adopts for the tender offer context a requirement resembling the one Chief Justice Burger would have adopted in *Chiarella* for misappropriators under § 10(b).

know has been acquired 'directly or indirectly' from an insider of the offeror or issuer, or someone working on their behalf. Rule 14e-3(a) is a disclosure provision. It creates a duty in those traders who fall within its ambit to abstain or disclose, *without regard to whether the trader owes a pre-existing fiduciary duty* to respect the confidentiality of the information."

United States v. Chestman, 947 F.2d 551, 557 (1991) (en banc) (*emphasis added*), cert. denied, 503 U.S. 1004 (1992) . . . .

In the Eighth Circuit's view, because Rule 14e-3(a) applies whether or not the trading in question breaches a fiduciary duty, the regulation exceeds the SEC's §14(e) rulemaking authority . . . . In support of its holding, the Eighth Circuit relied on the text of §14(e) and our decisions in *Schreiber* and *Chiarella*. See 92 F.3d, at 624-627.

* * *

For the meaning of "fraudulent" under §10(b), the Eighth Circuit looked to *Chiarella*. . . . In that case, the Eighth Circuit recounted, this Court held that a failure to disclose information could be "fraudulent" under §10(b) only when there was a duty to speak arising out of "'a fiduciary or other similar relation of trust and confidence.'" *Chiarella*, 445 U.S., at 228, 100 S. Ct., at 1114 (quoting Restatement (Second) of Torts §551(2)(a) (1976)). Just as §10(b) demands a showing of a breach of fiduciary duty, so such a breach is necessary to make out a §14(e) violation, the Eighth Circuit concluded. . . .

We need not resolve in this case whether the Commission's authority under §14(e) to "define . . . such acts and practices as are fraudulent" is broader than the [SEC]'s fraud-defining authority under §10(b), for we agree with the United States that Rule 14e-3(a), as applied to cases of this genre, qualifies under §14(e) as a "means reasonably designed to prevent" fraudulent trading on material, nonpublic information in the tender offer context.[17] A prophylactic measure, because its mission is to prevent, typically encompasses more than the core activity prohibited. . . . We hold, accordingly, that under §14(e), the Commission may prohibit acts not themselves fraudulent under the common law or §10(b), if the prohibition is "reasonably designed to prevent . . . acts and practices [that] are fraudulent." . . .

The United States emphasizes that Rule 14e-3(a) reaches trading in which "a breach of duty is likely but difficult to prove." "Particularly in the context of a tender offer," as the Tenth Circuit recognized, "there is a fairly wide circle of

_____

17. We leave for another day, when the issue requires decision, the legitimacy of Rule 14e-3(a) as applied to "warehousing," which the Government describes as "the practice by which bidders leak advance information of a tender offer to allies and encourage them to purchase the target company's stock before the bid is announced." As we observed in *Chiarella*, one of the Commission's purposes in proposing Rule 14e-3(a) was "to bar warehousing under its authority to regulate tender offers." 445 U.S., at 234, 100 S. Ct., at 1117-1118. The Government acknowledges that trading authorized by a principal breaches no fiduciary duty. The instant case, however, does not involve trading authorized by a principal; therefore, we need not here decide whether the Commission's proscription of warehousing falls within its §14(e) authority to define or prevent fraud.

people with confidential information," notably, the attorneys, investment bankers, and accountants involved in structuring the transaction [*SEC v. Peters*, 978 F.2d 1162, 1167 (10th Cir. 1992)]. The availability of that information may lead to abuse, for "even a hint of an upcoming tender offer may send the price of the target company's stock soaring." *SEC v. Materia*, 745 F.2d 197, 199 (2d Cir. 1984). Individuals entrusted with nonpublic information, particularly if they have no long-term loyalty to the issuer, may find the temptation to trade on that information hard to resist in view of "the very large short-term profits potentially available [to them]." *Peters*, 978 F.2d, at 1167.

"[I]t may be possible to prove circumstantially that a person [traded on the basis of material, nonpublic information], but almost impossible to prove that the trader obtained such information in breach of a fiduciary duty owed either by the trader or by the ultimate insider source of the information." *Ibid*. The example of a "tippee" who trades on information received from an insider illustrates the problem. Under Rule 10b-5, "a tippee assumes a fiduciary duty to the shareholders of a corporation not to trade on material nonpublic information only when the insider has breached his fiduciary duty to the shareholders by disclosing the information to the tippee and the tippee knows or should know that there has been a breach." [*Dirks v. SEC*, 463, U.S. 646, 660 (1983)]. To show that a tippee who traded on nonpublic information about a tender offer had breached a fiduciary duty would require proof not only that the insider source breached a fiduciary duty, but that the tippee knew or should have known of that breach. "Yet, in most cases, the only parties to the [information transfer] will be the insider and the alleged tippee." *Peters*, 978 F.2d, at 1167.

In sum, it is a fair assumption that trading on the basis of material, nonpublic information will often involve a breach of a duty of confidentiality to the bidder or target company or their representatives. The SEC, cognizant of the proof problem that could enable sophisticated traders to escape responsibility, placed "disclose or abstain from trading" command within the text of Rule 14e-3(a), which does not require specific proof of a breach of fiduciary duty. That prescription, we are satisfied, applied to this case, is a "means reasonably designed to prevent" fraudulent trading on material, nonpublic information in the tender offer context. [*See U.S. v. Chestman*, 947 F.2d 551, 560 (2d. Cir. 1990)] ("While dispensing with the subtle problems of proof associated with demonstrating fiduciary breach in the problematic area of tender offer insider trading, [Rule 14e-3(a)] retains a close nexus between the prohibited conduct and the statutory aims."); accord, *SEC v. Malo*, 51 F.3d 623, 635 n. 14 (7th Cir. 1994); *Peters*, 978 F.2d, at 1167. Therefore, insofar as it serves to prevent the type of misappropriation charged against O'Hagan, Rule 14e-3(a) is a proper exercise of the [SEC]'s prophylactic power under §14(e) . . . .

The judgment of the Court of Appeals for the Eighth Circuit is reversed, and the case is remanded for further proceedings consistent with this opinion.

It is so ordered.

NOTES

1. The SEC's Response to Chiarella. The practical impact of the Supreme Court's holding as to the validity of Rule 14e-3 is to prohibit insider trading surrounding tender offers regulated by §14 of the 1934 Act. In its release adopting Rule 14e-3, the SEC explained why it felt compelled to adopt Rule 14e-3 in reaction to the Supreme Court's earlier decision in *Chiarella v. United States,* 445 U.S. 222 (1980):

> The *Chiarella* case arose from a series of securities transactions by an employee of a financial printer. On the basis of confidential information obtained in the course of his employment, Mr. Chiarella deducted the identities of various companies that were to be the subject of tender offers that had not yet been publicly announced. Without disclosing the fact of the impending tender offers, Mr. Chiarella purchased target securities and then sold them at a profit immediately after the tender offers were made public.
>
> In the U.S. District Court for the Southern District of New York, Mr. Chiarella was convicted of a criminal violation of Section 10(b) and Rule 10b-5. The U.S. Court of Appeals for the Second Circuit affirmed the conviction and held that he was a "market insider" because of his regular access to market information, and, therefore, was barred from trading on the basis of material, nonpublic information obtained in that capacity.
>
> The Supreme Court reversed the Second Circuit's decision and held "that a duty to disclose under Section 10b does not arise from the mere possession of nonpublic market information." [By adopting Rule 14e-3, the SEC established] a "disclose or abstain from trading" rule under the Williams Act . . . .
>
> The Commission has previously expressed and continues to have serious concerns about trading by persons in possession of material, nonpublic information relating to a tender offer. This practice results in unfair disparities in market information and market disruption.[2] Security holders who purchase from or sell to such persons are effectively denied the benefits of disclosure and the substantive protections of the Williams Act . . . . Moreover, the Williams Act was designed to avert a "stampede effect" in the context of tender offers[3] and the trading on material, nonpublic information and the dissemination of leaks and rumors in connection with such trading tends to promote this detrimental effect.
>
> In view of the continued trading and potential for trading by persons while in possession of material, nonpublic information relating to tender offers and the detrimental impact which such trading has on tender offer practice, shareholder protection and the securities markets, the Commission has determined that Rule 14e-3 is necessary and appropriate in the public interest and for the protection of investors. As adopted, Rule 14e-3 pertains to both the person who receives the information, the tippee, and the person who transmits the information, the tipper.

SEC Release No. 17120 (Sept. 4, 1980) 1980 SEC LEXIS 775.

   2. Recent Insider Trading Cases.   In an interesting development, the most recent wave of activity in the M&A market, which seemed to peak in mid-2007, also saw "a spike in prosecutions for insider trading," reminiscent of what has been described as the "Deal Decade of the 1980s" (*see* p. 29 of Chapter 1). In the 1980s, the SEC pursued some of its highest-profile insider trading scandals, including

---

2. Such purchases may result in rapid and unexplained price and volume movements in the subject company's and the bidder's securities.

3. *Rondeau v. Mosinee Paper Co.,* 422 U.S. 49, 58 N.8 (1975).

its case against Ivan Boesky, which ultimately led to the prosecution of "junk bond king" Michael Milken and the downfall of his firm, Drexel Burnham. Interestingly enough, four of the five largest M&A transactions announced in 2007 "have been linked to suspicious trading patterns, including proposed deals for TXU Corp., Alcan Inc., First Data Corp., and SLM Corp., . . . [Indeed,] a recent study . . . concluded that 49% of all public M&A transactions displayed evidence of suspicious trading activity preceding the public deal announcements." Brent Shearer, *Forbidden Fruit*, MERGERS AND ACQUISITIONS (October 2007) at 66-67. This phenomenon has not escaped notice by the market regulators, including the SEC, which reports an increase in prosecutions for insider trading. *Id.* at 69.

Even more interesting, recent SEC cases involving charges of insider trading have tended to focus on peripheral deal players, unlike the "Deal Decade of the 1980s," where the SEC's insider trading cases tended to focus on high-profile names (such as Ivan Boesky and Michael Milken) who were often at the center of the M&A deals in the 1980s. Today, however, "perpetrators [do not] require direct access to the transactions. The network from the deal in question to the ultimate illegal trader can be extensive and convoluted. And deals today involve more advisers, lawyers, and accountants than ever before, meaning that before merger agreements are announced, hundreds of people . . . are kept abreast of the [deal] negotiations." *Id.* at 68. *Query:* What are the (practical) implications of these developments for the lawyer representing either Bidder or Target in an acquisition transaction?

2. Liability Under Section 16(b)

Texas International Airlines v. National Airlines, Inc.
714 F.2d 533 (5th Cir. 1983)

JOHNSON, Circuit Judge:

Texas International (TI) appeals the grant of summary judgment for National Airlines (National) holding TI liable to National under section 16(b) of the Securities Exchange Act of 1934 (the Exchange Act) for the "short swing profits" made on the sale of 121,000 shares of National common stock. Section 16(b) . . . provides, in pertinent part:

> For the purpose of preventing the unfair use of information which may have been obtained by such beneficial owner, director, or officer by reason of his relationship to the issuer, any profit realized by him from any purchase and sale, or any sale and purchase, of any equity security of such issuer (other than an exempted security) within any period of less than six months, unless such security was acquired in good faith in connection with a debt previously contracted, shall inure to and be recoverable by the issuer, irrespective of any intention on the part of such beneficial owner, director, or officer in entering into such transaction of holding the security purchased or of not repurchasing the security sold for a period exceeding six months.

The three factors which trigger section 16(b) liability were all present—TI was a ten percent beneficial owner of National that purchased and sold National stock within a six-month period. The district court, therefore, found TI subject to automatic section 16(b) liability to National for the short swing profits TI made on the sale.[1] On appeal, TI argues that equity bars any recovery by National and, in the alternative, that proof of "nonaccess" to inside information should be decisive in a section 16(b) inquiry. This Court affirms the grant of summary judgment for National.

FACTS

On March 14, 1979, during an attempt by TI to gain control of National, TI purchased 121,000 shares of National common stock in open-market brokerage transactions. On March 14, the date of the purchase, TI was a beneficial owner of more than ten percent of National's common stock. On July 28, 1979, within six months of the March 14 purchase, TI and Pan American World Airways, Inc. (Pan Am) entered into a stock purchase agreement whereby TI agreed to sell 790,700 shares of National common stock to Pan Am at $50 per share. The closing was held on July 30, 1979. Under the matching rules of section 16(b) the 790,700 shares sold by TI on July 28, 1979 are deemed to include the 121,000 shares purchased by TI in March.

On September 6, 1978, National and Pan Am had entered into a merger agreement which provided for the merger of National into Pan Am contingent upon certain conditions and, in connection with the merger, for the exchange by Pan Am of not less than $50 in cash for each share of National common stock, other than the shares held by Pan Am. On May 16, 1979, National stockholders approved the merger agreement dated September 6, 1978, as amended. TI, as a National stockholder, stood to receive $50 per share for its National stock if and when the merger closed. For whatever reason, TI decided not to wait until the merger went through to negotiate for the disposition of its holdings to Pan Am. It was not until after the July 28, 1979 sale by TI of its National stock to Pan Am that the National-Pan Am merger was effectuated.

On August 2, 1979, only five days after TI sold its National stock to Pan Am, TI sought declaratory relief that it was not liable to National under section 16(b) for profits realized on the purchase and sale of National common stock. In the alternative, TI sought to reduce its short swing profits by deducting expenses it allegedly incurred in connection with the purchase and sale of its National stock. On September 26, 1979, National counterclaimed, seeking recovery of TI's short swing profits under section 16(b). National moved for summary judgment on November 24, 1980.[6]

On May 11, 1981, the district court granted National's motion in part, finding that TI's purchase and sale of the 121,000 shares of National stock constituted a violation of section 16(b). The district court squarely rejected TI's contention that the control contest situation rendered the transaction at issue "unorthodox" within the meaning of *Kern County Land Co. v. Occidental*

---

1. The district court recognized the narrow "unorthodox" transaction exception to §16(b) but held that TI's purchase and sale did not fit within this exception.

6. By early January 1980, the merger of Pan Am and National had been effectuated. Pan Am became the surviving corporation.

Petroleum Corp., 411 U.S. 582, 93 S.Ct. 1736, 36 L.Ed.2d 503 (1973). In reaching its conclusion that TI was liable under section 16(b), the district court stated that no court has exempted the type of transaction at issue here—a cash-for-stock transaction—from the automatic application of section 16(b) . . . .

EQUITABLE ESTOPPEL

In making its argument that equitable estoppel should be allowed as a defense in a section 16(b) action, TI first states the purpose of section 16(b): the evil Congress sought to curb was market speculation by corporate insiders based on abuse of their positions of trust and access to confidential information. TI urges that section 16(b) embodies the equitable remedy of restitution traditionally imposed on fiduciaries. If a fiduciary profits by inside information concerning the affairs of his principal, the fiduciary's profits go to the principal. Given that the section is merely an application of an equitable doctrine, equitable defenses must be allowed, according to TI. TI eschews the section 16(b) cases disallowing equitable defenses as a matter of law by claiming that the instant case is factually distinguishable from those cases. Here, TI urges, there are no innocent outside stockholders of the issuer who need protection. Rather, Pan Am, the only party that would benefit from a recovery, is the very party that has engaged in conduct giving rise to an estoppel. This conduct, according to TI, consisted of Pan Am's involvement in the transaction that created section 16(b) liability at a time when Pan Am was the controlling stockholder of National and had an agreement in place requiring the shareholders to accept $50 for their shares.

The case law uniformly rejects equitable defenses in section 16(b) cases . . . . The facts of this case do not warrant an aberration from the principle that holds equitable defenses in section 16(b) cases insufficient as a matter of law. . . . This Court is not disposed to create an exception to the disallowance of equitable defenses in section 16(b) cases based on the mere difference that in this instance Pan Am, who participated in the section 16(b) transaction, was a shareholder of the issuer (National) who subsequently merged into its shareholder (Pan Am). Allowance of equitable defenses in section 16(b) cases would only serve to thwart the remedial purpose of the statute . . . .

A STANDARD OF NONACCESS TO INSIDE INFORMATION

TI urges this Court to create an exception to automatic section 16(b) liability in cases where a defendant can prove that, notwithstanding its ownership of over ten percent of the stock of the issuer, the defendant had no access to inside information concerning the issuer. According to TI, the classic example of such a case is a sale of stock in the hostile takeover context. Application of section 16(b) in this type of case, argues TI, does not serve congressional goals—Congress intended short-swing profits to be disgorged only when the particular transaction serves as a vehicle for the realization of these profits based upon access to inside information.

TI's argument is unsupported by the legislative history of section 16(b). Although the abuse Congress sought to curb was speculation by stockholders with inside information, "the only method Congress deemed effective to curb the evils of insider trading was a *flat rule* taking the profits out of a *class of transactions* in which the possibility of abuse was believed to be intolerably great." *Kern County [Land Co. v. Occidental Petroleum Corp.,* 411 U.S. 582, 93 S. Ct. 173 (1973)] (*emphasis added*). In explaining the necessity for a "crude rule of thumb" to Congress, Thomas Corcoran, a principal draftsman of the Act, stated: "You have to have a general rule. In particular transactions it might work a hardship, but those transactions that are a hardship represent the sacrifice to the necessity of having a general rule." Hearings on Stock Exchange Practices before the Senate Committee on Banking and Currency, 73d Cong., 2d Sess., 6557 and 6558 (1934). The Supreme Court explained the necessity for the flat rule or "objective approach" of the statute in *Reliance Electric Company v. Emerson Electric Company,* 404 U.S. 418, 92 S. Ct. 596, 599, 30 L. Ed. 2d 575 (1972) *quoting Bershad v. McDonough,* 428 F.2d 693, 696 (7th Cir. 1970):

> In order to achieve its goals, Congress chose a relatively arbitrary rule capable of easy administration. The objective standard of Section 16(b) imposes strict liability upon substantially all transactions occurring within the statutory time period, regardless of the intent of the insider or the existence of actual speculation. This approach maximized the ability of the rule to eradicate speculative abuses by reducing difficulties in proof. Such arbitrary and sweeping coverage was deemed necessary to insure the optimum prophylactic effect. . . .

This Court is in agreement with the statements of legislative purpose as expressed . . . by the Supreme Court in *Emerson Electric* and *Kern County*—the mechanical application of section 16(b) to the specified class of transactions is necessary in order to guarantee that the abuse at which the statute is aimed will be effectively curbed.

In *Kern County*, the Supreme Court approved an extremely narrow exception to the objective standard of section 16(b). The Court held that when a transaction is "unorthodox" or "borderline," the courts should adopt a pragmatic approach in imposing section 16(b) liability which considers the opportunity for speculative abuse, i.e., whether the statutory "insider" had or was likely to have access to inside information.

TI engages in an analogy between the hostile and adversary situation that existed between the target company and the putative insider in *Kern County* and the adversary relationship between TI and National in the instant case. Even assuming the alleged parallelism between the adversary situations in the two cases and assuming that TI could prove that it neither had nor was likely to have access to inside information by virtue of its statutory "insider" status, no valid basis for an exception to section 16(b) liability on these facts is perceived. The Supreme Court in *Kern County* inquired into whether the transaction had the potential for abuse of inside information only because the transaction fell under the rubric of "unorthodox" or "borderline."[9] *In Kern County,* Occidental, a shareholder in Kern County Land Company (Old Kern) converted its shares in Old Kern into shares of the acquiring corporation pursuant to a merger. The Supreme Court clearly distinguished the unorthodox transaction—a conver-

---

9. The Court, in a nonexhaustive list, enumerated certain transactions which are unorthodox: stock conversions, exchanges pursuant to mergers and other corporate reorganizations, stock reclassifications, and dealings in options, rights, and warrants. *Kern County,* 93 S. Ct. at 1744 n. 24.

sion of securities—before it from the traditional cash-for-stock transaction in the instant case: "traditional cash-for-stock transactions . . . are clearly within the purview of §16(b)." *Kern County*, 411 U.S. at 593.

TI lays frontal attack on the unorthodox transaction test as fundamentally flawed, principally because the form of consideration received—cash or stock—has nothing to do with whether inside information was or might have been used. What this attack fails to consider, however, is the significance of the factor of voluntariness in the Supreme Court's decision. The Court's sole concern was not that cash-for-stock sales present a greater opportunity for abuse of inside information than do stock-for-stock sales. Rather, language in the Supreme Court's opinion indicates that traditional cash-for-stock sales were excluded from the concept of unorthodox transactions because of their voluntary nature:

> The critical fact is that the exchange took place and was required pursuant to a merger . . . .
> Occidental could, of course, have disposed of its shares of Old Kern for cash before the merger was closed. Such an act would have been a section 16(b) sale and would have left Occidental with a prima facie section 16(b) liability . . . . But the *involuntary nature* of Occidental's exchange, when coupled with the absence of the possibility of speculative abuse of inside information, convinces us that section 16(b) should not apply to transactions such as this one.

Id. at 1747 (*emphasis added*). In the instant case, TI voluntarily entered into the stock purchase agreement with Pan Am before the National-Pan Am merger was effectuated. Despite the alleged lack of access to inside information and therefore the possibility of speculative abuse, the volitional character of the exchange is sufficient reason to trigger applicability of the language of section 16(b). For whatever reason, after the National-Pan Am merger had been approved, TI decided to take the initiative for the course of subsequent events into its own hands rather than wait for the merger to become accomplished. These circumstances do not warrant the creation of an exception to automatic section 16(b) liability . . . .

CONCLUSION

This Court finds no valid justification for deviation from the express terms of section 16(b) or the case law interpreting it. The judgment of the district court is affirmed.

AFFIRMED.

QUESTIONS

1. Who has standing to sue for violations of §16(b)?

2. Who is a potential defendant in a §16(b) lawsuit?

3. What is the remedy for §16(b) violations?

4. What is the lesson to be learned from this case? (*Hint:* Is there any planning that could have been done in the principal case so as to avoid a §16(b) violation?)

║5║

Negotiating and Documenting the Transaction

In considering the process of negotiating, documenting, and closing on a business acquisition, the parties typically will be required to prepare and sign various documents. While each deal is unique, and the facts of any particular deal may require a wide array of documents not specifically mentioned in this discussion, mergers and acquisitions (M&A) transactions generally follow a certain convention as to the documents required to effect the transaction. In this chapter, we consider the nature and terms of the agreements that are customarily drafted as part of an acquisition transaction, regardless of the method used to structure the deal.

We begin our discussion by considering the use of a LOI and/or confidentiality agreement early in the deal process. Next, we consider certain mechanisms that are commonly used to close the gap between Bidder and Target in negotiating the terms of the purchase price to be paid by Bidder to acquire Target's business. The devices most commonly used in the acquisition of a privately held company are earn-outs and escrows, both of which are discussed below. In the case of a public company deal where Bidder's stock is to be used as the acquisition consideration, we need to examine the difficult valuation issues that arise in fixing the terms of the exchange ratio and the use of collars to address certain risks inherent in the parties' negotiation over price.

Once the parties have reached consensus on the essential terms of the deal—price and structure—the lawyer turns his or her attention to the preparation of the acquisition agreement, which will generally take the form of either an asset purchase agreement, a stock purchase agreement, or a plan of merger (merger agreement), depending on the deal structure used in that particular acquisition. In Part C of this chapter, we will look at the provisions commonly included in the basic agreement regardless of the method used to structure the acquisition. As part of this discussion, we will examine the dynamic relationship among the key provisions of any acquisition agreement: *representations and warranties, covenants,* and *conditions to closing.* As part of our examination of the process of drafting the acquisition agreement, we will also consider the scope and purpose of the all-important investigative process known as "due diligence" and the role that due diligence plays in determining the scope of the other provisions commonly included in the acquisition agreement. The last component of the acquisition agreement that we need to consider is what rights the parties might have after closing on the acquisition, the most important of which are rights of *indemnification.*

A. Planning Problem: Negotiating and Documenting the Acquisition of a Privately Held Company

A New York–based shoe manufacturer, Galaxy International, Inc., plans to acquire Trekker Marketing Co., which is based in San Diego, California. As proposed, the transaction involves the purchase of all the outstanding capital stock of Trekker in exchange for $35 million of cash, notes, and Galaxy stock, plus the ability for Trekker shareholders to earn up to an additional $7 million if certain performance targets are achieved.

Trekker, a privately held company, was founded ten years ago by two professional skateboarders, Stanley Rockledge and Randy Moses, and started making high-quality, high-priced skateboards and related accessories. Today, Trekker still makes top-end skateboards but also makes snowboards, surfboards, and several lines of apparel that are very popular with California skateboarders and surfers. Trekker's irreverent attitude and edgy, bad-boy designs appeal to the rebellious teen skaters and boarders, often to the ire of their customers' parents. In 1998, some parents organized a letter writing campaign to stop a Trekker product promotion that offered a free skateboard to those willing to "relinquish their souls."

As the popularity of skateboarding and snowboarding grew rapidly, so did Trekker's business. The rapid growth sometimes created problems as Trekker experienced product shortages, supply and delivery interruptions, and accompanying lost sales, particularly beyond the southern California market. Nevertheless, Trekker did grow its revenues at a compounded annual growth rate (CAGR) of 12 percent over the last five years, with net income of $4.5 million on revenues of $45 million in its most recently completed fiscal year.

Galaxy, a company traded on the New York Stock Exchange (NYSE), makes several lines of shoes that are popular with the youthful skateboard crowd. By buying Trekker, Galaxy is adding both skateboard hard goods and several top-brand apparel lines to its stable of youth brand products. By moving into skateboarding and related hard goods, Galaxy hopes to gain a competitive advantage over its skate-shoe rivals. Galaxy sees the acquisition of Trekker as a key part of its larger effort to push the edgy sport of skateboarding into the mainstream and grow the business by committing substantial capital resources to expand marketing, production, and distribution capabilities for Trekker product lines.

A sport born of youthful rebellion, skateboarding has grown into an industry that generated $1.4 billion in sales with an estimated target market of about 16 million skateboarders—and skateboard wannabes. Coupling Trekker's popular brands with Galaxy's capital resources and worldwide distribution network of direct and indirect channels, Galaxy intends to take the Trekker irreverence beyond the surf shops and specialty stores and penetrate deep into traditional distribution channels including large department stores such as J. C. Penney, Sears, Target, and Kohls Corp.

Galaxy intends to conduct an offering of its common stock to raise the estimated $30 million needed to close the transaction. Based on its most recent NYSE closing price, Galaxy will be issuing approximately 3 million shares, which is roughly a 6 percent increase in the number of Galaxy's outstanding common shares.

B. *Negotiating the Transaction*

1. Initial Negotiations and the Use of Letter of Intent

In negotiating the terms of a business acquisition, there will often come a point in the process where the parties may wish to commit to paper many of the deal points that they have been discussing. Reasons for doing so are many and quite varied. Sometimes the writing is intended to serve as a discussion outline for future negotiations. In other instances, the writing is intended to memorialize those key terms on which the parties feel they have reached agreement and to identify those items on which no consensus has been reached and on which they will continue to negotiate. Also, a writing may be used when one party faces certain other obligations, often disclosure requirements imposed by the federal securities laws or the rules of NYSE or other such self-regulatory organizations (SROs), and, before making any disclosures that may be required of the public company, either Bidder or Target (or both) wants the other side to demonstrate its commitment to the transaction by signing some writing.

In these situations, the parties will customarily sign a *letter of intent* (LOI). Generally speaking, this signed writing will expressly provide that the writing is *not* binding on either party. As a result of this almost schizophrenic nature of the LOI, there is a wide divergence of opinion among practicing M&A lawyers as to the usefulness and desirability of entering into an LOI. The potential pitfalls of signing an LOI, even where the writing expressly provides that it is nonbinding, are nicely illustrated in the following case.

‖ Turner Broadcasting System, Inc. v. McDavid
‖ 693 S.E.2d 873 (Ga. Ct. App. 2010)

This case involves Turner Broadcasting System, Inc.'s ("Turner") alleged breach of an oral agreement to sell the Atlanta Hawks and Atlanta Thrashers sports teams and the operating rights to Phillips Arena to appellee David McDavid. Following a jury trial, a $281 million verdict was entered in favor of McDavid on his breach of contract claim. Turner filed a motion for judgment notwithstanding the verdict ("j.n.o.v."), or in the alternative, for a new trial, which the trial court denied. Turner appeals, contending [among other things] that the evidence failed to show (a) [either] that the parties intended to be bound in the absence of an executed written agreement or (b) that the parties reached [an] agreement on all material terms of the sale; [and that] the damages were speculative, excessive, and decidedly against the weight of the evidence. We discern no error and affirm.

* * *

. . . [T]he evidence at trial showed that Turner is the former owner of the Hawks and the Thrashers, with operating rights to Philips Arena (the "assets"). In October 2002, Turner publicly announced its interest in selling the assets as part of a "deleveraging program" to reduce its mounting debts. In November 2002, McDavid expressed an interest in buying the assets and entered into negotiations with Turner.

On April 30, 2003, the parties executed a "Letter of Intent," outlining the proposed sale terms and establishing a 45-day exclusive negotiating period. On June 14, 2003, the Letter of Intent expired with no agreement, but the parties continued to negotiate. When McDavid inquired about extending the Letter of Intent, Turner's principal negotiator told him, "Don't worry about it. We're very, very close to a deal. You're our guy."

The parties scheduled a meeting for mid-July 2003, expecting that they would be able to resolve all of the outstanding issues and finalize their agreement. At the meeting, Turner raised a tax loss allocation issue, which the parties failed to resolve. Frustrated with the lack of progress being made during the negotiations, McDavid walked out of the meeting, while his advisors continued their efforts to resolve the tax issue.

On July 30, 2003, the parties engaged in a conference call. During the conference call, McDavid's advisors stated that McDavid would agree to Turner's proposed resolution of the tax issue on the condition that it would resolve all the issues and finalize the deal. Turner's CEO, Phil Kent, agreed and announced, "we have a deal."

* * *

On or about August 1, 2003, Turner drafted an internal memo to its employees and planned for a press conference to publicly announce the deal with McDavid. In August 2003, Turner consulted with McDavid and his advisor on team management decisions, including the hiring of a general manager and head coach for the Hawks. Turner also obtained McDavid's approval before hiring a trainer, assistants, and scouts.

On or about August 16, 2003, as the drafting process continued, Turner's executive and principal negotiator, James McCaffrey, approached McDavid about a simplified restructure for the transaction, assuring him that the restructure would "not change the deal," that the "deal was done," and that "they were ready to close on the deal that [they] made on July 30th." McDavid agreed to the simplified restructure, and the attorneys circulated revised draft agreements that reflected the restructured terms.

On August 19, 2003, the corporate board of directors of Time Warner, Turner's parent company, approved the sale of the assets to McDavid based upon the restructured terms. However, two of the board members, Ted Turner and Steve Case, opposed the deal, concerned that the assets had been undervalued and had resulted in a "fire sale."

On the day after the Turner board of directors meeting, Ted Turner's son-in-law, Rutherford Seydel, and the son of a member of the Hawks board of directors, Michael Gearon, Jr., approached Turner about purchasing the assets on behalf of their corporation, Atlanta Spirit, LLC. While Turner continued to exchange drafts of the purchase agreement with appellees, it also began negotiations with Atlanta Spirit.

On or about September 12, 2003, McDavid and Turner verbally reached a final agreement on each of the alleged open items for the written agreement and Turner's principal negotiator announced, "[t]he deal is done. Let's get documents we can sign and we'll meet in Atlanta for a press conference and a closing [early next week]." But later that same day, Turner's principal negotiator and its in-house counsel signed an agreement for the sale of the assets to Atlanta Spirit.

On September 15, 2003, as McDavid was preparing to travel to Atlanta for the closing and a press conference to announce the sale, he received a phone call informing him that Turner was "going in another direction" and had sold the assets to Atlanta Spirit. McDavid and his advisors, who had spent months finalizing the McDavid deal, were "stunned," "shocked," "disappointed," and felt "completely broadsided."

McDavid filed suit against Turner, alleging claims of breach of an oral contract to sell the assets, promissory estoppel, fraud, and breach of a confidentiality agreement. Turner denied the existence of any binding agreement, arguing that the parties had not executed a final written purchase agreement and had continued to negotiate the material terms of the transaction. Following an eight-week trial, the jury returned a verdict in favor of McDavid on the breach of oral contract claim and awarded $281 million in damages. Judgment was entered accordingly.

[On appeal,] Turner first argues that the trial court erred in denying its motion for j.n.o.v. or for a new trial on the breach of oral contract claim. Turner contends that the uncontroverted evidence established that the parties manifested an intent to be bound only in writing, and that the parties never reached agreement on all material terms of the sale. We disagree. The evidence on the issue of contract formation was highly controverted and presented genuine issues of fact for the jury's resolution. Because there was evidence supporting the jury's verdict, we must affirm. "To constitute a valid contract, there must be parties able to contract, a consideration moving to the contract, the assent of the parties to the terms of the contract, and a subject matter upon which the contract can operate."

As an initial matter, Georgia law recognizes that oral contracts falling outside the purview of the Statute of Frauds may be binding and enforceable. . . . Even complex or expensive contracts may be oral, as long as the evidence establishes the parties' mutual assent to all essential terms of the contract.

* * *

. . . In this case, the determination of whether an oral contract existed, notwithstanding the parties' failure to sign a written agreement, was a question of fact for the jury to decide.

(a)   Parties' Intent to be Bound.

(i) The Parties' Expressions and Conduct. The parties' objective manifestations of their mutual assent and intent to be bound to the McDavid acquisition deal

included testimony that Turner's CEO formally announced, "we have a deal" during the parties' July 30th conference call. On or about August 16, 2003, Turner's principal negotiator, further confirmed the existence of an agreement during discussions pertaining to the deal restructure by stating that the "deal was done," and that "they were ready to close on the deal that [they] made on July 30th." And yet again, on or about September 12, 2003, during the course of another conference call to confirm the parties' final agreement on the terms to be incorporated into the written agreements, Turner's principle negotiator announced, "[t]he deal is done. Let's get documents we can sign and we'll meet in Atlanta for a press conference and a closing [early next week]."

In addition, Turner engaged in conduct from which the jury could conclude that an agreement had been reached. On or about August 1, 2003, Turner drafted an internal memo to its employees and planned for a press conference to publicly announce the deal with McDavid. Furthermore, in August 2003, Turner consulted with McDavid and his advisor on team management decisions, including the hiring of a general manager and head coach for the Hawks. Turner also obtained McDavid's approval before hiring a trainer, assistants, and scouts. There was testimony that according to industry standards, a buyer typically would not be given such formal input on team decisions until after the parties were committed and had formed an agreement. This evidence authorized the jury to conclude that both parties intended to be bound to the McDavid acquisition deal.

(ii) The Letter of Intent. Turner nevertheless argues that no binding oral agreement could have been reached since the parties' April 30th Letter of Intent expressly provided that "neither party nor any of [their] affiliates [would] be bound unless and until such party (or affiliate) has executed the Definitive Agreements" and that "[n]o such binding agreement shall exist or arise unless and until the parties have negotiated, executed and delivered to each other Definitive Agreements." Undoubtedly, the express terms of the Letter of Intent reflect an intent that the parties would not be bound absent written, signed agreements. Significantly, however, it is undisputed that the terms of the Letter of Intent expired on June 14, 2003, and further that Turner declined to renew it.[7] The Letter of Intent provided that all of its terms, with the exception of the confidentiality terms, would "automatically terminate and be of no further force and effect at 5:00 p.m. (Atlanta time) on [June 14, 2003,] the date on which the Exclusive Negotiation Period expire[d]." Turner's general counsel affirmed that when the Letter of Intent expired, it "no longer ha[d] any meaning" and the only terms that survived related to confidentiality. The jury therefore was authorized to conclude that upon the expiration of the Letter of Intent, the terms imposing the written agreement requirement also expired and had no effect. And, as recognized by Turner's general counsel, if Turner intended for the writing requirement of the Letter of Intent to remain effective

---

7. After the Letter of Intent expired and McDavid inquired about extending it, Turner's principal negotiator told him that it was unnecessary since they were close to finalizing the deal and assured him, "You're our guy." Based upon this evidence, in addition to Turner's other assurances, the jury was authorized to infer that Turner intended to be bound to the McDavid deal.

after the expiration date, it could have set forth a survival provision in the same manner that it did for the confidentiality terms. Its failure to do so serves as some evidence contradicting Turner's claim that it maintained an objective manifestation to be bound only by a written agreement.

Turner's general counsel stated that the Letter of Intent was the only place where the parties had expressed their intent to be bound exclusively by executed, written agreements. McDavid and his advisors testified that after the Letter of Intent expired, no one expressed an intention that the parties would be bound only upon the execution of written contracts. When Turner's CEO and principal negotiator made their statements, "we have a deal" and the "deal was done," McDavid and his advisors believed that both parties intended to be bound to the agreement. Although Turner maintains that their intent to be bound only by written agreements never changed, its general counsel conceded that statements such as "we have a deal" may convey otherwise. The parties' failure to communicate an intent to be bound only in writing following the expiration of the Letter of Intent provided some evidence that an oral agreement was not precluded.

(iii) Contemplation of Written Instrument.   It is undisputed that the parties intended to sign written documents that memorialized the terms of their oral agreement. McDavid and his advisors testified that in accordance with the customary deal-making process, the parties first had to reach an oral agreement upon the material terms, and then the lawyers were expected to prepare the written documents that memorialized the parties' agreed upon terms. The evidence further established that the parties' respective lawyers exchanged multiple draft agreements purportedly attempting to ensure that the documents reflected the agreed upon terms. And, while the draft agreements contained a merger clause providing that the written agreement would "supersede all prior agreements, understandings and negotiations, both written and oral," such language could be construed as acknowledging the possibility of an oral agreement, particularly under these circumstances in which the merger clause did not become effective.

McDavid's witnesses further testified that all of the material issues for the written agreements had been resolved by mid-September, when they were planning to travel to Atlanta to formally sign the documents and publicly announce the deal. The evidence thus authorized a finding that the only reason for the failure to execute the written agreements was Turner's refusal to proceed with McDavid's deal and its decision to consummate a deal with Atlanta Spirit instead.

While circumstances indicating that the parties intended to prepare a subsequent writing is strong evidence that they did not intend to be bound by a preliminary agreement, contrary evidence bearing upon the parties' intent to be bound and reflecting the existence of a binding oral agreement presents a question of fact for the jury's determination. Moreover, "[a]lthough the parties contemplated the future execution of a written . . . agreement, the jury was authorized to find that a binding oral agreement was in effect, and the failure to sign the written instrument did not affect the validity of the oral agreement." [Citation omitted.]

* * *

(b) Agreement Upon All Material Terms.   To constitute a binding agreement, the evidence must establish that the parties agreed upon all essential terms.

Again, the evidence on this issue was hotly contested and presented a genuine issue for the jury's determination. While Turner points to evidence that several open issues remained for discussion, that evidence merely conflicted with McDavid's evidence that all the material issues had been resolved.

* * *

According to McDavid, all of the material deal terms had been resolved; but when Atlanta Spirit entered into negotiations, Turner suddenly tried to reopen the issues to derail McDavid's deal and to buy time to complete the deal with Atlanta Spirit. Atlanta Spirit's counsel testified that he assumed Turner was using documents from the McDavid deal for their transaction since the terms were already very detailed and the drafts were complete. Material terms of the Atlanta Spirit deal, including the percentage of ownership interest, purchase price value, working capital liabilities, employee severance terms, letter of credit terms for the arena, expansion fee terms, preferred vendor terms regarding naming rights, and television rights, were the same or substantially similar to those reached in the McDavid deal. While McDavid spent 8 to 10 months negotiating the terms of his deal, Atlanta Spirit obtained the same deal within a matter of weeks.

Despite the conflicts in the evidence, the evidence adduced at trial supports the jury's determination that the parties had reached an agreement on all material terms such that a binding oral agreement had been reached by September 12, 2003 when Turner announced, "[t]he deal is done," before Turner went "in another direction" with Atlanta Spirit. . . .

* * *

Lastly, Turner argues that the $281 million judgment entered upon the verdict must be reversed since the jury's damages award was speculative, excessive, and decidedly against the weight of the evidence.

Generally, the jury's award cannot be successfully attacked so as to warrant a new trial unless it is so flagrantly excessive or inadequate, in light of the evidence, as to create a clear implication of bias, prejudice or gross mistake on the part of the jurors. Even though the evidence is such as to authorize a greater or lesser award than that actually made, the appellate court will not disturb it unless it is so flagrant as to shock the conscience. Moreover, the trial court's approval of the verdict creates a presumption of correctness that will not be disturbed absent compelling evidence. . . .

The jury was instructed that the proper measure of damages in this case was "the difference between the contract price and the fair market value of the [assets] at the time the contract was breached." The trial court further defined fair market value as "the price that [the asset] will bring when it is offered for sale by one who desires but is not obliged to sell it and is bought by one who wishes to buy but is not under a necessity to do so." The parties raise no challenge to the propriety of the trial court's instructions in this regard.

The fair market value of the assets was a highly contested issue, and both parties presented experts who gave valuation opinions. Turner's expert, Donald Erickson, was an experienced business appraiser. Erickson opined that the fair market value was $255 million based upon 100% ownership of the assets, and that the contract price offered by McDavid was the determinative fair market value. Erickson's valuation was based upon the assumption of normal market conditions in which Turner was a willing seller, not under any compulsion, and in which McDavid was a knowledgeable buyer.

McDavid's experts were Roger Brinner, Ph.D., a renowned economist with experience in business valuations, and Robert Lieb, a consultant who specialized in sports economics. Dr. Brinner opined that the value of the assets was $516 million for 100% ownership interest, based upon a market approach method used to value the teams and an income approach method to value the arena. Dr. Brinner's opinion was based upon his finding that the contract price was low compared to comparable team assets and acquisition deals in the market.

Lieb opined that the value of the assets was approximately $647 million for 100% ownership interest. Lieb also opined that McDavid's contract price was "amazingly low" based upon market comparables and did not reflect the fair market value of the assets.

In addition to the expert's opinions, there was evidence that *Forbes*, a valuation source, had valued the team assets at $340 million, excluding the arena value and debt. There was also evidence that Turner had internally valued the assets at $400 million. . . .

* * *

As argued by McDavid, under Lieb's valuation, damages could be calculated at $335 million. McDavid further argued that under the *Forbes* value, adjusted to include the $140 million arena debt and Dr. Brinner's $106 million arena value, damages could be calculated at $283 million. Because the jury's $281 million verdict was within the range of the evidence, no basis for reversal has been shown.

* * *

Judgment affirmed.

QUESTIONS

1. What are the main advantages to entering into an LOI? What are the disadvantages of entering into this kind of written agreement, even if it specifies that it is nonbinding?

2. Would you recommend the use of an LOI in the context of our problem involving Galaxy's proposed acquisition of Trekker? If so, what provisions should be included? Does your recommendation depend on whether you are Bidder's counsel or the lawyer for Target?

3. Consider the LOI included in Appendix D. This is the first draft of an LOI that was prepared — not by lawyers — but rather by senior executives of Bidder (Galaxy International, Inc.) and Target (Trekker Marketing, Inc.), as no lawyers were involved in the early negotiations. This LOI followed a brief but intense period of negotiations between the two sides. In this deal, the lawyers became involved (as is often the case in the real world of M&A deals)

when the business clients (i.e., Target's CEO and Bidder's CEO) asked their respective lawyers to review this draft LOI before the parties signed it. As you read through this draft, consider the following:

a. If you were Target's counsel, what changes would you want to make to this first draft *before* the parties sign this LOI?

b. From Bidder's perspective, what changes would Bidder's lawyer want to make to this draft LOI *before* agreeing to have Bidder sign it?

c. Of these provisions, which should be made binding? Which provisions should be made expressly nonbinding?

d. Are there any provisions that are *not* contained in this draft that you think should be made part of the LOI? In considering this issue, does it matter whether you are Bidder's lawyer or counsel for Target? (*Hint:* You may want to consult the reading in the next section as part of your analysis of this question.)

2.　Use of Non-Disclosure/Confidentiality Agreements

Regardless whether a letter of intent is signed by the parties, generally speaking, Target Co. (and very often Bidder Co. as well) will insist on the use of a *confidentiality agreement,* or, as it is sometimes called, a *non-disclosure agreement* (NDA). In certain cases, the NDA may be made part of the LOI, in which case Target will want to make clear that this provision of the parties' LOI is binding even if the other provisions of the LOI are specifically made nonbinding. Alternatively, or in lieu of an LOI, the NDA may be the subject of a separate, freestanding written agreement between Bidder and Target.

　　Why does Target typically insist, fairly early in the bargaining process, that Bidder sign a NDA? In considering this question, you may want to reflect on the following matters, which are typically addressed in any NDA:

- Is Bidder a competitor (or potential competitor) of Target? Why does this make a difference in negotiating terms of the parties' NDA?
- What is the scope of Bidder's obligation under the terms of the NDA? Does it go beyond a simple non-disclosure obligation? Should there be a prohibition on Bidder's use of confidential information that it receives from Target during the course of the parties' negotiations and the due diligence process?
- Should the NDA include a restriction on the solicitation and/or hiring of Target's employees?
- Should the NDA include any restrictions on Bidder's right to contact or otherwise communicate with Target's customers or vendors?
- How long should the terms of the NDA be binding on the parties?
- Why does Bidder typically insist that Target sign an NDA?

In thinking about how to deal with these issues, which are an inherent part of drafting an NDA for any type of M&A transaction, consider the guidance offered by the Delaware Supreme Court in the following case.

Martin Marietta Materials, Inc. v. Vulcan Materials
2012 WL 2783101 (Del. July 12, 2012)

JACOBS, Justice:

On May 14, 2012, the Court of Chancery entered a final judgment and order after a trial in this action initially brought by Martin Marietta Materials, Inc. ("Martin") against Vulcan Materials Company ("Vulcan"). Granting judgment against Martin on Vulcan's counterclaims, the Court of Chancery enjoined Martin, for a four month period, from continuing to prosecute its pending Exchange Offer and Proxy Contest to acquire control of Vulcan. That injunctive relief was granted to remedy Martin's adjudicated violations of two contracts between Martin and Vulcan: a Non-Disclosure Letter Agreement (the "NDA") and a Common Interest, Joint Defense and Confidentiality Agreement (the "JDA").[1]

Martin appealed to this Court from that judgment. On May 16, 2012, this Court ordered that the case proceed on an expedited basis. Following briefing, oral argument was held on May 31, 2012. That same day, after deliberating, the Court entered an Order stating that the judgment would be affirmed for reasons that would be explicated in a formal Opinion to issue in due course. This is the Opinion contemplated by this Court's May 31, 2012 Order.

THE FACTS

A.   BACKGROUND LEADING TO THE CONFIDENTIALITY AGREEMENTS

Vulcan and Martin are the two largest participants in the United States construction aggregates industry. That industry engages in mining certain commodities and processing them into materials used to build and repair roads, buildings and other infrastructure. Vulcan, a New Jersey corporation headquartered in Birmingham, Alabama, is the country's largest aggregates business; and Martin, a North Carolina corporation headquartered in Raleigh, North Carolina, is the country's second-largest.

Since the early 2000s, Vulcan and Martin episodically discussed the possibility of a business combination, but the discussions were unproductive and no significant progress was made. In 2010, Ward Nye, who had served as Martin's Chief Operating Officer since 2006, was appointed Martin's Chief Executive Officer ("CEO"). After that, Nye and Vulcan's CEO, Don James, restarted merger talks. In early April 2010, Vulcan's investment banker at Goldman Sachs first "test[ed] out" the new Martin CEO's interest. Nye's positive response prompted a meeting with James later that month, which led to more formal discussions.

At the outset Nye was receptive to a combination with Vulcan, in part because he believed the timing was to Martin's advantage. Vulcan's relative

---

1. Both agreements expressly provided that they would be construed under Delaware law. Except where otherwise indicated, these two agreements are referred to collectively in this Opinion as the "Confidentiality Agreements."

strength in markets that had been hard hit by the financial crisis, such as Florida and California, had now become a short-term weakness. As a result, Vulcan's financial and stock price performance were unfavorable compared to Martin's, whose business was less concentrated in those beleaguered geographic regions. To Nye, therefore, a timely merger—before a full economic recovery and before Vulcan's financial results and stock price improved—was in Martin's interest. Moreover, Nye had only recently been installed as Martin's CEO, whereas James, Vulcan's CEO, was nearing retirement age with no clear successor. To Nye, that suggested that a timely merger would also create an opportunity for him to end up as CEO of the combined companies.

Relatedly, although Nye was willing to discuss a possible merger with his Vulcan counterpart, he was not willing to risk being supplanted as CEO. The risk of Nye being displaced would arise if Martin were put "in play" by a leak of its confidential discussions with Vulcan, followed by a hostile takeover bid by Vulcan or a third party. Nye's concern about a hostile deal was not fanciful: recently Martin had engaged in friendly talks with a European company that had turned hostile. The European company's hostile attempt to acquire Martin failed only because the financial crisis "cratered" the bidder's financing.

Understandably, therefore, when Nye first spoke to Vulcan's banker, Goldman Sachs, in April 2010, he stressed that Martin was not for sale, and that Martin was interested in discussing the prospect of a friendly merger, but not a hostile acquisition of Martin by Vulcan. As the Chancellor found, Nye's notes prepared for a conversion [sic] with Vulcan's banker made it clear that "(i) Martin . . . would talk and share information about a *consensual* deal only, and not for purposes of facilitating an *unwanted* acquisition of Martin . . . by Vulcan; and even then only if (ii) absolute confidentiality, even as to the fact of their discussions, was maintained." When James and Nye first met in April 2010, they agreed that their talks must remain completely confidential, and they operated from the "shared premise" that any information exchanged by the companies would be used only to facilitate a friendly deal.

To secure their understanding, Nye and James agreed that their respective companies would enter into confidentiality agreements. That led to the drafting and execution of the two Confidentiality Agreements at issue in this case: the NDA and the JDA.

B.   THE NDA

Nye related the substance of his conversations with James to Roselyn Bar, Esquire, Martin's General Counsel, and instructed Bar to prepare the NDA. In drafting the NDA, Bar used as a template an earlier agreement between Martin and Vulcan that had facilitated an asset swap transaction. Consistent with Nye's desire for strict confidentiality, Bar proposed changes to the earlier template agreement that were "unidirectional," *i.e.*, that enlarged the scope of the information subject to its restrictions and limited the permissible uses and disclosures of that covered information.

In its final form, the NDA prohibited both the "use" and the "disclosure" of "Evaluation Material," except where expressly allowed. Paragraph 2 permitted either party to *use* the other party's Evaluation Material, but "*solely for the purpose of evaluating a Transaction.*" Paragraph 2 also categorically prohibited either party from *disclosing* Evaluation Material to anyone except the receiving party's representatives. The NDA defined "Evaluation Material" as "any non-public information furnished or communicated by the disclosing party" as well as "all analyses, compilations, forecasts, studies, reports, interpretations, financial statements, summaries, notes, data, records or other documents and materials prepared by the receiving party . . . that contain, reflect, are based upon or are generated from any such nonpublic information. . . . " The NDA defined "Transaction" as "a possible business combination transaction . . . between [Martin] and [Vulcan] or one of their respective subsidiaries."

Paragraph 3 of the NDA also prohibited the disclosure of the merger negotiations between Martin and Vulcan, and certain other related information, except for disclosures that were "legally required." Paragraph 3 relevantly provided that:

> Subject to paragraph (4), each party agrees that, without the prior written consent of the other party, it . . . will not disclose to any other person, *other than as legally required*, the fact that any Evaluation Material has been made available hereunder, that discussions or negotiations have or are taking place concerning a Transaction or any of the terms, conditions or other facts with respect thereto (including the status thereof or that this letter agreement exists).

Paragraph 4 defined specific conditions under which "legally required" disclosure of Evaluation Material (and certain other information covered by Paragraph 3) would be permitted:

> In the event that a party . . . [is] requested or required (by oral questions, interrogatories, requests for information or documents in legal proceedings, subpoena, civil investigative demand or other similar process) to disclose any of the other party's Evaluation Material or any of the facts, the disclosure of which is prohibited under paragraph (3) of this letter agreement, the party requested or required to make the disclosure shall provide the other party with prompt notice of any such request or requirement so that the other party may seek a protective order or other appropriate remedy and/or waive compliance with the provisions of this letter agreement. If, in the absence of . . . the receipt of a waiver by such other party, the party requested or required to make the disclosure . . . should nonetheless, in the opinion of such party's . . . counsel be legally required to make the disclosure, such party . . . may, without liability hereunder, disclose only that portion of the other party's Evaluation Material which such counsel advises is legally required to be disclosed. . . .

As the Chancellor found, "Paragraph (4) establishes the Notice and Vetting Process for disclosing Evaluation Material and Transaction Information that would otherwise be confidential under the NDA in circumstances [where] a party is 'required' to do so in the sense that the party had received an External Demand." The Chancellor further concluded that Ms. Bar's addition of the words "Subject to paragraph (4)" at the beginning of NDA paragraph (3), is "most obviously read as being designed to prevent any reading of ¶ 3 that would permit escape from ¶ 4's narrow definition of legally required and ¶ 4's rigorous Notice and Vetting Process."

Vulcan shared Martin's confidentiality concerns. It therefore agreed to include in the NDA the changes that Ms. Bar proposed to the predecessor template agreement.

C. THE JDA

Because the parties were exploring a combination of the two largest companies in their industry, antitrust scrutiny appeared unavoidable. After the NDA was signed, the two companies' inside and outside counsel met to discuss that issue. The discussions implicated nonpublic, privileged information and attorney work-product, leading Martin and Vulcan also to execute the JDA (which was drafted by outside counsel) to govern those exchanges.

The JDA, like the NDA, prohibits and limits the use and the disclosure of information that the JDA describes as "Confidential Materials." The critical prohibitions and limitations are found in JDA Paragraphs 2 and 4. Paragraph 2 prohibits the disclosure of Confidential Materials without "the consent of all Parties who may be entitled to claim any privilege or confidential status with respect to such materials. . . . " JDA Paragraph 4 relevantly provides that "Confidential Materials will be used, consistent with the maintenance of the privileged and confidential status of those materials, solely for purposes of pursuing and completing *the Transaction*." The JDA defines "Transaction" as "a *potential transaction being discussed* by Vulcan and Martin[ ] . . . involving the combination or acquisition of all or certain of their assets or stock. . . . "

D. MARTIN'S USE AND DISCLOSURE OF VULCAN'S INFORMATION COVERED BY THE NDA AND JDA

After the JDA and the NDA were executed, Vulcan provided to Martin nonpublic information that gave Martin a window into Vulcan's organization, including detailed confidential information about Vulcan's business, revenues, and personnel. Those disclosures enabled Martin to project more reliably the value of synergistic cost-cutting measures that could be achieved from a combination of the two companies. Therefore, Martin needed Vulcan's nonpublic information to evaluate the two "gating issues" critical to any business combination transaction: possible antitrust-related divestitures and merger synergies.

The Court of Chancery found, and Martin does not dispute, that Martin used and disclosed Vulcan's nonpublic information in preparing its Exchange Offer and its Proxy Contest to oust some of Vulcan's board members (collectively, the "hostile takeover bid"). Martin's position is that its use and disclosure of that nonpublic information was not legally prohibited by the Confidentiality Agreements. We address that legal argument in the Analysis section of this Opinion. At this juncture, we merely complete the factual narrative and highlight the trial court's findings regarding Martin's use and disclosure of Vulcan's non-public information to evaluate, plan and promote its Exchange Offer and Proxy Contest.

It is undisputed that antitrust counsel and other representatives of both companies met on various occasions and exchanged non-public "Confidential

Materials" relating to antitrust divestiture risks and synergies. What resulted
was a joint antitrust analysis prepared by antitrust counsel for both sides in 2010.
Months later, a meeting between Martin's and Vulcan's CFOs and controllers
took place on March 8, 2011. The information exchanged at that meeting and
the nonpublic information Martin had previously received, caused Martin to
revise its estimated merger synergies upwards by as much as $100 million annu-
ally, from the $150–$200 million it previously estimated. That synergy jump,
plus the fact that Martin's stock price had increased in relation to Vulcan's, led
Martin to conclude that it "could offer Vulcan's shareholders a premium in a
stock-for-stock exchange, yet still justify the deal to Martin's stockholders" on
economic grounds. Martin knew, however, that if it wanted to use all of its projected synergistic gains to justify the transaction, time was of the essence. Not
only did current market conditions favor Martin, but also Vulcan already had
plans to obtain certain cost savings on its own, independent of any deal with
Martin.

   Accordingly, as the talks floundered soon after the March 8 meeting, Martin and its bankers began using Vulcan's confidential, nonpublic information
to consider alternatives to a friendly deal. By April 2011, Martin's bankers were
evaluating the constraints imposed by the NDA upon a non-consensual transaction. At a mid-August 2011 meeting, Martin's board formally authorized management to pursue alternatives to a friendly deal. Four months later, Martin
launched its unsolicited Exchange Offer.

   As a regulatory matter, an exchange offer carries a line-item requirement
under federal securities law to disclose past negotiations. Martin announced its
Exchange Offer on December 12, 2011, by sending Vulcan a public "bear hug"
letter* and filing a Form S-4 with the United States Securities and Exchange
Commission ("SEC"). On January 24, 2012, Martin announced its Proxy Contest and filed a proxy statement in connection therewith.[28]

   Both before and after Martin commenced its hostile takeover bid, Martin
disclosed Vulcan's nonpublic information, first to third party advisors (investment bankers, lawyers and public relations advisors), and later publicly. Martin
did that without Vulcan's prior consent and without adhering to the Notice

---

   * [By the author] On Wall Street, a "bear hug letter" typically refers to a Bidder's unsolicited offer to acquire Target at a substantial premium over the market price of Target's
shares in an effort to squeeze ("hug") the Target's board of directors into accepting the offer.
Bidder will often use a "bear hug letter" when Bidder's board believes that Target's board is
likely to resist Bidder's takeover attempt. We will discuss "bear hugs" in more detail as part of
our analysis of hostile takeover bids in Chapter 7.

   28. In the Exchange Offer, Martin sought to acquire all of Vulcan's outstanding shares,
based on an exchange ratio of .5 Martin share for each share of Vulcan. The exchange offer
was conditioned on the receipt of tenders from 80% of Vulcan's shareholders, and contained
a waivable condition that "Vulcan . . . have entered into a definitive merger agreement with
Martin[ ] with respect to the proposed transaction that is reasonably satisfactory to Martin[ ]
and Vulcan." In its Proxy Contest, Martin sought to elect four new members to Vulcan's classified board at Vulcan's upcoming annual meeting, which was scheduled to occur on June 1,
2012. The Chancellor found that the purpose of the Proxy Contest was "[t]o create a Vulcan
board more receptive of its offer." *Id.*, at *2.

and Vetting Process mandated by the NDA. Regarding Martin's public relations advisors, the Chancellor found:

> Despite the Confidentiality Agreements, no effort was made to shield these advisors from receiving Evaluation Material or information relating to James' and Nye's negotiations. To the contrary, it is plain that the public relations advisors were given a blow-by-blow of Nye's and [Martin's CFO's] view of the negotiations with Vulcan and access to other Evaluation Material, and they advised Martin['s] . . . management how the process and substance of information sharing and negotiation could be translated into a public communications strategy that would exert pressure on Vulcan to accept an unsolicited bid from Martin . . .

As for its public disclosures, Martin's Form S-4 disclosed not only the history of the negotiations, but also other detailed information that constituted "Evaluation Material" and "Confidential Materials" under the respective Confidentiality Agreements. Those details, as the Court of Chancery found, included:

- Martin's anticipated annual cost synergies of $200 million to $250 million resulting from a merger with Vulcan;
- James' estimates of "achievable synergies" from a merger at different stages of the discussions, "including his belief as of June 2010 that 'a combination of the companies would result in approximately $100 million in synergies,' and not 'synergies at the $175 million to $200 million levels that Mr. Nye believed were achievable'; and James' supposed belief at the time the merger discussions ended, that 'the cost synergies to be achieved in a combination would [not] be greater than $50 million;'"
- "James' view of alternative deal structures designed to minimize tax leakage;"
- "James' conclusion, based on the merger discussions, that the 'potential tax leakage (*i.e.*, taxes arising from the sale or other disposition of certain assets that may be required to obtain regulatory approvals) and the ability to divest overlap[ping] business were significant impediments to a transaction;'" and
- "The fact that 'the legal teams did not identify any significant impediments to a business combination transaction' at their antitrust meeting on May 19, 2010."

The disclosures by Martin to the SEC, the Chancellor found, "were . . . a tactical decision influenced by [Martin's] flacks," and "the influence of these public relations advisors is evident in the detailed, argumentative S-4 filed by Martin[ ]." Those disclosures, the trial court found, "exceeded the scope of what was legally required," and involved "selectively using that [Evaluation] Material and portraying it in a way designed to cast Vulcan's management and board in a bad light, to make Martin['s] own offer look attractive, and to put pressure on Vulcan's board to accept a deal on Martin ['s] terms."

Lastly, the Chancellor found that after it launched its hostile takeover bid, Martin disclosed Evaluation Material and other confidential information "in push pieces to investors, off the record and on the record communications to the media, and investor conference calls." Those disclosures "include[d] a detailed history of the discussions [and] negotiations that [had taken] place concerning 'the Transaction,' [and] references revealing the 'opinions,' 'analyses' and 'non-public information' of Vulcan" regarding issues such as required antitrust divestitures and synergies.

E.   THE COURT OF CHANCERY'S POST-TRIAL DETERMINATIONS

On December 12, 2011, the same day it launched its hostile takeover bid, Martin commenced this Court of Chancery action for a declaration that nothing in the NDA barred Martin from conducting its Exchange Offer and Proxy Contest. Vulcan counterclaimed for a mirror-image determination that Martin breached the NDA, and later amended its counterclaim to add claims that Martin had violated the JDA. Vulcan sought an injunction prohibiting Martin from proceeding with its hostile takeover bid. . . . On May 4, 2012 that court issued its post-trial Opinion. On May 14, 2012, the Chancellor entered a final order and judgment, enjoining Martin from (among other things) proceeding with its Exchange Offer and Proxy Contest for a four month period. Martin then terminated its Exchange Offer and Proxy Contest, and appealed to this Court from the trial court's final order and judgment.

In its Opinion, the Court of Chancery ultimately determined that Martin had breached the NDA and the JDA by impermissibly using and disclosing Evaluation Material under the NDA and Confidential Materials under the JDA. . . .

Specifically, the Court of Chancery found that, although the Confidentiality Agreements did not contain a "standstill" provision, they did bar Martin (and Vulcan) from:

- "Using the broad class of 'evaluation material' defined by the confidentiality agreements except for the consideration of a contractually negotiated business combination transaction between the parties, and not for a combination that was to be effected by hostile, unsolicited activity of one of the parties;"
- "Disclosing either the fact that the parties had merger discussions or any evaluation material shared under the confidentiality agreements unless the party was legally required to disclose because: (i) it had received 'oral questions, interrogatories, requests for information or documents in legal proceedings, subpoena, civil investigative demand or other similar process;' and (ii) its legal counsel had, after giving the other party notice and the chance for it to comment on the extent of disclosure required, limited disclosure to the minimum necessary to satisfy the requirements of law;" and
- "Disclosing information protected from disclosure by the confidentiality agreements through press releases, investor conference calls, and communications with journalists that were in no way required by law."

MARTIN'S CLAIMS OF ERROR

* * *

Martin advances four specific claims of error on this appeal. *First*, Martin contends that the trial court erred in going beyond the plain language of the NDA, which unambiguously permitted the use of Evaluation Material to conduct its hostile Exchange Offer and Proxy Contest. *Second*, Martin claims that the court erroneously held that the NDA prohibited Martin from disclosing Evaluation Material and information about the merger discussions without prior notice and vetting, because the disclosures it made were "legally required" to conduct its hostile takeover bid. *Third*, Martin argues that the trial court's determination that Martin breached the JDA was erroneous, because: (i) the JDA unambiguously makes itself "subservient" to the NDA, with the result that compliance with the NDA *ipso facto* constitutes compliance with the JDA, and (ii) alternatively, and in any event, the trial court erroneously found that Martin had breached the JDA's "use" restriction. *Fourth*, Martin claims that the Court of Chancery erred by improperly balancing the equities and granting injunctive relief without proof of actual injury.

Martin's first three claims of error involve judicial interpretation of a contract, which present questions of law that this Court reviews *de novo*. Martin's fourth claim, which challenges the grant of injunctive relief, is reviewed for abuse of discretion.

We conclude, for the reasons next discussed, that the Chancellor committed no legal error or abuse of discretion, and correctly concluded (*inter alia*) that: (i) the JDA prohibited Martin from using and disclosing Vulcan Confidential Materials to conduct its hostile bid; (ii) the NDA prohibited Martin from disclosing Vulcan Evaluation Material without affording Vulcan pre-disclosure notice and without engaging in a vetting process; (iii) Martin breached the use and disclosure restrictions of the JDA and the disclosure restrictions of the NDA; and (iv) injunctive relief in the form granted was the appropriate remedy for those adjudicated contractual violations. Because we affirm the Court of Chancery's judgment on these grounds, we do not reach or decide the other bases for the contractual violations adjudicated by the trial court.

ANALYSIS

* * *

B.   MARTIN'S VIOLATIONS OF THE JDA

The Chancellor determined that Martin, in making its hostile bid, both "used" and "disclosed" Vulcan Confidential Materials in violation of the JDA. That agreement (the trial court found) unambiguously prohibits the use of "Confidential Materials" without Vulcan's consent, except "for purposes of pursuing and completing the Transaction," which the JDA defines as "a potential transaction being discussed by Vulcan and Martin . . . . " The Court of Chancery found as fact that "the only transaction that was 'being discussed' at the time the parties entered into the JDA was a negotiated merger," and that "neither [the] Exchange Offer nor [the] Proxy Contest . . . was 'the' transaction that was 'being discussed' at the time that the JDA was negotiated."

Martin asserts that those determinations are reversibly erroneous, for three reasons. First, Martin claims, the court erred in concluding that the only transaction "being discussed" when the parties entered into the JDA was a negotiated merger. Second, Martin advances the related claim that, even if "Transaction" meant a negotiated transaction, Martin committed no contractual breach, because "the JDA expressly allows the use of [protected] information 'for purposes of *pursuing and completing* the Transaction,'" and Martin's hostile bid "ultimately will facilitate . . . a negotiated transaction." Third, Martin claims that the JDA, by its own terms, is "subservient" to the NDA, because JDA Paragraph 12 relieves Martin of liability for any breach of the JDA so long as Martin complies with the NDA. All these claims lack merit.

Martin portrays its first argument—that the Chancellor erroneously concluded that neither the Proxy Contest nor the Exchange Offer was the "potential transaction being discussed"—as presenting a purely legal question of contractual interpretation that is subject to de novo review. That portrayal is not accurate. The challenged determination presents a mixed question of fact and law. Although our review of its contract interpretation component is *de novo*, the challenged factual component will not be overturned unless it is found to be clearly wrong.

The trial court properly found that the relevant operative language of the JDA—"a potential transaction being discussed"—is unambiguous, and Martin does not seriously contend otherwise. The only remaining dispute, accordingly, is factual: what transaction was "being discussed?" The *only* transaction being discussed, the trial court found, was a negotiated merger. To say that that finding is not "clearly wrong" would be an understatement: the finding is amply supported by the evidence. Nye told Vulcan that Martin was not for sale. Nye told Vulcan that Martin was interested in discussing the prospect of a merger, not an acquisition, whether by Vulcan or otherwise. And, Nye described the transaction under discussion as a "modified merger of equals."

Equally unpersuasive is Martin's alternative contention that even if "Transaction" means a negotiated merger, Martin did not violate the JDA's use restriction, because the JDA expressly allowed Martin to use Confidential Materials "for purposes of pursuing and completing the Transaction," and Martin's hostile bid "ultimately will facilitate . . . a negotiated transaction." That claim fails because the Chancellor found as fact that the only transaction being discussed would be "friendly" or "negotiated." That finding expressly and categorically excluded Martin's "hostile bid or a business combination . . . effected by a pressure strategy." We uphold the Chancellor's factual finding that the transaction "being discussed" for purposes of the JDA's "use" restriction did not encompass a merger accomplished by means of hostile tactics. Martin's second claim of error, therefore, fails for the same reason as its first.

Martin's third claim is essentially that the JDA creates no restrictions independent of those already imposed by the NDA. Therefore (the argument runs), since Martin did not violate the NDA, it could not have violated the JDA. The sole foundation for this argument is language found in Paragraph 12 of the JDA, which provides that "[n]either the existence of nor any provision contained in this Agreement shall affect or limit any other confidentiality agreements, or rights or obligations created thereunder, between the Parties in connection with the Transaction."

The Chancellor was not persuaded by this argument, and neither are we. If adopted, Martin's reading would turn Paragraph 12's language on its head. That provision, in context, plainly says—and means—that neither the existence nor the contents of the JDA ("this Agreement") shall "affect or limit any other confidentiality agreements (the NDA) or rights or obligations created thereunder." Martin's reading would generate the opposite result, namely, that the rights and obligations created in the NDA would specify and limit when Vulcan and Martin could use and disclose Confidential Materials protected by the JDA. As Vulcan correctly argues, no reasonable reading of the JDA (or the NDA) "support[s] that absurd result, which would reduce the JDA to a nullity. . . . " That result would also violate the "cardinal rule . . . that, where possible, a court should give effect to *all* contract provisions." The Chancellor correctly declined to adopt an interpretation of Paragraph 12 that would rob the JDA of any independent legal significance.

Other than its claim based on Paragraph 12, which we reject, Martin suggests no basis to overturn the Court of Chancery's reading of the JDA's "disclosure" restrictions in JDA Paragraph 2. The court read the JDA to require Martin to obtain Vulcan's approval before disclosing any Confidential Materials covered by the JDA. We agree that the JDA unambiguously so required, and the Court of Chancery's factual finding—that Martin disclosed JDA-protected Confidential Materials without Vulcan's approval in the course of conducting its hostile bid—is uncontested.

For these reasons, we uphold the Chancellor's conclusion that Martin used and disclosed Vulcan Confidential Materials in violation of the JDA.

C.   MARTIN'S VIOLATIONS OF THE NDA

We next consider Martin's challenges to the Chancellor's determination that Martin violated the disclosure restrictions of the NDA. The Chancellor found as fact that Martin disclosed Vulcan confidential information, including Evaluation Material, in the course of pursuing its hostile bid, and Martin does not contest that finding. Rather, Martin's claim before us is that its disclosure of Vulcan confidential information was permitted by Paragraph 3 of the NDA, and that the Court of Chancery erred in holding otherwise. This claim rests upon a somewhat intricate (and fragile) structure of subsidiary arguments, which run as follows: (i) Martin was entitled to disclose Vulcan confidential information, including Evaluation Material, that was otherwise protected under the NDA without Vulcan's prior consent, if disclosure was "legally required;" (ii) the disclosure of Vulcan's confidential information in publicly filed documents was "legally required" by SEC Rules applicable to exchange offers; (iii) the Vulcan confidential information that Martin disclosed to investors was legally permitted because that disclosure was already "legally required" by SEC Rules; and (iv) Martin was not contractually obligated to give Vulcan prior notice of any intended disclosures, or to engage in a pre-disclosure vetting process, because those procedural requirements applied only to disclosures made in response to an "External Demand" arising in the course of a legal proceeding, and no such External Demand was ever made.

These arguments were presented to the Court of Chancery, which rejected them for a host of reasons that entailed a searching and intensive analysis of a multitude of factual and legal issues. To oversimplify, the Court of Chancery analyzed Martin's position under two separate, alternative approaches. First, the court held that Paragraphs 3 and 4 were ambiguous. After resorting to extrinsic evidence, the court determined that Paragraph 3, most reasonably interpreted, does not independently allow a contracting party to make legally required disclosures, unless the disclosures are preceded and triggered by an External Demand. In the alternative, the Chancellor also held that Paragraph 3, viewed alone, *unambiguously* did *not* permit the disclosure of one specifically defined information category—"Evaluation Material"—even if disclosure were otherwise "legally required." The right to disclose Evaluation Material, the trial court held, was conferred only by Paragraph 4, and could be exercised only if preceded and triggered by an External Demand, and after having engaged in the Notice and Vetting Process outlined in that paragraph.

In our review of the Court of Chancery's resolution of this question, we need not, and do not, reach or decide the merits of its ambiguity-based analysis. Instead, we uphold the result based on the trial court's alternative holding. More specifically, we conclude, as a matter of law based upon the NDA's unambiguous terms, that: (i) Paragraph 3, of itself, does not authorize the disclosure of "Evaluation Material," even if such disclosure is otherwise "legally required;" (ii) Paragraph 4 is the only NDA provision that authorizes the disclosure of Evaluation Material; (iii) any disclosure under Paragraph 4 is permitted only in response to an External Demand and after complying with the pre-disclosure Notice and Vetting Process mandated by that paragraph; and (iv) because no External Demand was made and Martin never engaged in the Notice and Vetting Process, its disclosure of Vulcan's Evaluation Material violated the disclosure restrictions of the NDA.

The contract provisions that relate to this issue are Paragraphs 2, 3, and 4 of the NDA. Paragraph 2, entitled "Use of Evaluation Material," categorically prohibits the disclosure of a party's Evaluation Material to anyone other than the receiving party's representatives. Paragraph 3, which is entitled "Non-Disclosure of Discussions; Communications," also prohibits the disclosure of certain information relating to merger "discussions or negotiations" between Martin and Vulcan. But, Paragraph 3 also carves out an exception that permits disclosure of that information where disclosure is "legally required":

> Subject to paragraph (4), each party agrees that, without the prior written consent of the other party, it and its Representatives will not disclose to any other person, other than as legally required, the fact that any Evaluation Material has been made available hereunder, that discussions or negotiations have or are taking place concerning a Transaction or any of the terms, conditions or other facts with respect thereto (including the status thereof or that this letter agreement exists).

At this point it is helpful to pause and identify which "legally required" disclosures Paragraph 3 does—and does not—permit. By its terms, Paragraph 3 covers only three categories of information: (a) the fact that any Evaluation Material has been made available; (b) the fact that discussions or negotiations concerning a Transaction have been taken or are taking place; and (c) any of the terms, conditions or other facts with respect thereto [*i.e.*, to the negotiations] including the status thereof [*i.e.*, the negotiations] or that the NDA exists. *Not included within those categories is the substance of a party's Evaluation Material*—as distinguished from "the fact that . . . Evaluation Material has been made available."

The omission of Evaluation Material from the coverage of Paragraph 3 is both intentional and logical. Although Paragraph 3 does not expressly prohibit the disclosure of Evaluation Material, it does not need to. Paragraph 2 accomplishes that. Evaluation Material does not fall with Paragraph 3's "legally required" carve-out exception, because that exception can *only* apply to the confidential information specifically identified in Paragraph 3. Moreover—and of critical importance—the permitted disclosure of Evaluation Material is explicitly and separately made the subject of Paragraph 4, which is entitled "Required Disclosure." Paragraph 4, by its terms, addresses the disclosure of "any of the other party's Evaluation Material or any of the facts, the disclosure of which is prohibited under paragraph (3) of [the NDA]."

Paragraph 4 also mandates a procedural framework within which legally required disclosure of Evaluation Material is permissible. That framework has two elements. The first is that Evaluation Material must be the subject of an External Demand. The second is that a party contemplating disclosure of that information must give pre-disclosure notice of any intended disclosure and (where applicable) engages in a vetting process.

To illustrate how these two elements operate structurally, we divide Paragraph 4 into two parts. The first creates a right to prior notice to enable the adversely affected party to seek appropriate judicial relief:

> In the event that a party or any of its Representatives are requested or required (by oral questions, interrogatories, requests for information or documents in legal proceedings, subpoena, civil investigative demand or other similar process) to disclose any of the other party's Evaluation Material or any of the facts, the disclosure of which is prohibited under paragraph (3) of this letter agreement, the party requested or required to make the disclosure shall provide the other party with prompt notice of any such request or requirement so that the other party may seek a protective order or other appropriate remedy and/or waive compliance with the provisions of this letter agreement.

The second part comes into play if a contracting party, for whatever reason, does not seek or obtain court protection. In those circumstances, Paragraph 4 mandates an extrajudicial "vetting" process:

> If, in the absence of a protective order or other remedy or the receipt of a waiver by such other party, the party requested or required to make the disclosure or any of its Representatives should nonetheless, in the opinion of such party's [or its Representative's] counsel, be legally required to make the disclosure, such party or its Representative may, without liability hereunder, disclose only that portion of the other party's Evaluation Material which such counsel advises is legally required to be disclosed; provided that the party requested or required to make the disclosure exercises its reasonable efforts to preserve the confidentiality of the other party's Evaluation Material, including, without limitation, by cooperating with the other party to obtain an appropriate protective order or

other reliable assurance that confidential treatment will be accorded the other party's Evaluation Material.

To recapitulate, Paragraphs 2, 3, and 4, both internally and when read together, unambiguously permit a party to the NDA to disclose "legally required" Evaluation Material. But, that may be done *only* if an External Demand for such information has first been made, and *only* if the non-disclosing party is then given prior notice of any intended disclosure and (where applicable) an opportunity to vet the information sought to be disclosed. The Court of Chancery properly so concluded. In our view, that interpretation is compelled by the text of these NDA provisions, their relationship to each other, and by the canon of construction that requires all contract provisions to be harmonized and given effect where possible. That also is the only interpretation that is consistent with the found facts relating to the NDA's overall purpose and import, and the parties' reasons for negotiating the specific language of the disputed NDA provisions.

Martin's contrary argument rests on the premise that Evaluation Material is textually included within the purview of Paragraph 3. Martin claims that the following italicized phrase in Paragraph 3 captures Evaluation Material: "[E]ach party agrees [not to disclose, other than as legally required,] . . . that discussions or negotiations have or are taking place concerning a Transaction or any of the terms, conditions, or *other facts with respect thereto* (including the status thereof or that this letter agreement exists)."

Martin's argued-for interpretation — that "other facts with respect thereto" must be read to cover Evaluation Material — finds no support in the specific language and structure of the NDA. It is also unreasonable. Any doubt about the scope of the phrase "other facts with respect thereto" is put to rest by considering the broader language of which that phrase is but one moving part. The context clarifies that the phrase, "other facts with respect *thereto*," means specific facts indicating that there were "discussions or negotiations . . . concerning a Transaction," including the fact that the NDA even exists. That peripheral species of information differs markedly from the substantive, company-specific internal information that the parties exchanged in order to facilitate their discussions or negotiations (*i.e.*, Evaluation Material).

Evaluation Material is a term that is central to, and defined in, the NDA. That term is specifically referred to by name throughout the agreement. Martin's interpretation of the NDA attempts to shoehorn "Evaluation Material" into language in Paragraph 3 that does not, and is not intended to, include "Evaluation Material." If the drafters of the NDA intended to include Evaluation Material within the category of information disclosable under Paragraph 3, they easily could have done that by referring directly to "Evaluation Material," as they did repeatedly elsewhere in the NDA.

The NDA also clearly distinguishes Evaluation Material from the disclosable information covered by Paragraph 3. Paragraph 4 addresses the disclosure of "any of the other party's Evaluation Material *or* any of the facts, the disclosure of which is prohibited under paragraph (3) of this letter agreement." The disjunctive "or" plainly contradicts Martin's claim that Evaluation Material falls within the purview of Paragraph 3. And, the basic logic and structure of the NDA makes the trial court's reading the only reasonable one, because Paragraph 2 (which precedes Paragraph 3) flatly prohibits the disclosure of

Evaluation Material, and Paragraph 4 expressly mandates the conditions and procedures that must be complied with before Evaluation Material may be disclosed (assuming disclosure is otherwise "legally required").

We conclude, for these reasons, that the only reasonable construction of the NDA is that Paragraph 4 alone permitted the disclosure of Evaluation Material, and even then only if triggered by an External Demand and preceded by compliance with Paragraph 4's Notice and Vetting Process. The Court of Chancery found as fact that Martin disclosed Evaluation Material in the course of conducting its hostile bid, without having received an External Demand and without having engaged in the Notice and Vetting Process. Martin has not challenged that finding. We therefore uphold the Court of Chancery's determination that Martin breached the NDA's disclosure restrictions.

D. THE REMEDY

Lastly, Martin claims that the Court of Chancery reversibly erred in balancing the equities and granting injunctive relief to Vulcan without any evidence that Vulcan was threatened with, or suffered, actual irreparable injury. The injunction prohibited Martin, for a four-month period, from going forward with its Exchange Offer and Proxy Contest, from otherwise taking steps to acquire control of Vulcan shares or assets, and from further violating the NDA and the JDA. As earlier noted, we review this claim for an abuse of discretion.

Martin's claim fails both legally and factually. It fails legally because, as the trial court noted, in Paragraph 9 of the NDA both parties stipulated that "money damages would not be [a] sufficient remedy for *any* breach . . . by either party," and that "the non-breaching party *shall be entitled to equitable relief*, including injunction and specific performance, as a remedy for any such breach." The JDA has a similar provision that obligates the parties to pursue "equitable or injunctive relief"—and *not* monetary damages—in the event of a breach of that agreement.

Our courts have long held that "contractual stipulations as to irreparable harm alone suffice to establish that element for the purpose of issuing . . . injunctive relief." Martin offers no persuasive reason why the parties' stipulation in the NDA that "money damages would not be [a] sufficient remedy for any breach" should not be regarded as a stipulation to irreparable injury, nor why the stipulation that "any breach . . . shall entitle[ ]" the non-breaching party "to equitable relief" should not be given effect in this case. Nor does Martin persuade us that, although the JDA expressly disclaims any right to a money damages remedy, the harm imposed by a breach of that contract is not "irreparable" for injunctive purposes.

Martin's assertions also fail factually, because the Chancellor did make a finding of "actual"—and irreparable—injury. The trial court found, as fact, that "Vulcan is now suffering from exactly the same kind of harm Nye demanded the Confidentiality Agreements shield Martin [ ] from[;]" that Vulcan was injured by Martin's "contractually improper selective revelation of nonpublic Vulcan information[;]" and that Vulcan suffered a loss of "negotiating leverage."

Unable to deny that the trial court so found, Martin shifts ground and asserts that any finding of harm was "speculative" and made "without any support." To the contrary, the adjudicated harm was not speculative and is supported by ample record evidence. For example, Vulcan's CEO James testified that when Martin revealed publicly the fact of the negotiations, "[i]t put us in play at a time that we would not have wanted to be put into play," because "this industry is in a recession." James also testified that "our employees were very concerned," and that "[o]ur executive team obviously is completely distracted from pursuing our internal strategic plan." That and other non-speculative record evidence solidly supports the Court of Chancery's finding of "actual" irreparable injury.

Martin also attacks the scope of the remedy itself, claiming that the injunction was unreasonable because it would delay Martin's Proxy Contest by one year, rather than four months. In different circumstances that kind of harm might be a legally cognizable factor that a court will take into account in balancing the equities for and against granting an injunction. Here, however, the "delay" is attributable to the NDA's May 3, 2012 expiration date, which—when combined with Vulcan's advance notice bylaw—precluded Martin from disclosing Vulcan confidential information to support its Proxy Contest in time for Vulcan's 2012 annual meeting. Because New Jersey law requires director elections to be held annually, the practical reality was that Martin's first opportunity to disclose that information lawfully to promote a Proxy Contest would not occur until 2013.

Given those facts, the Court of Chancery did not abuse its discretion by holding that the equities favored Vulcan, because "Martin's breaches prevented Vulcan from seeking injunctive relief before the confidential information was made public" and Vulcan "[had] been measured in its request for injunctive relief." The court properly balanced the need to "vindicat[e] Vulcan's reasonable [contractual] expectations" against the "delay" imposed on Martin as a "result of its own conduct." The Chancellor stated that although "an argument can be made that a longer injunction would be justified by the pervasiveness of Martin['s] breaches," an injunction lasting four months was "a responsible period" reflecting the time interval between when Martin launched its Exchange Offer on December 12, 2011, and the NDA's May 3, 2012 expiration date. That this measured form of relief also resulted in delaying Martin for a longer period from seeking to replace the Vulcan board, does not detract from the propriety of the relief the court granted.

CONCLUSION

For the foregoing reasons, the judgment of the Court of Chancery is affirmed.

QUESTIONS

1. In the context of a breach of an NDA, there is no possibility for suing to enjoin (i.e., prevent) disclosure or misuse of the company's information. As a result, there is only the possibility of an ex-post remedy. In light of that practical reality, just how valuable are these NDA provisions?

2. Should NDAs include agreed-upon remedies for breach? Is there any language that Vulcan could/should have included in the NDA that would have made it more watertight? In other words, does this case really involve an oversight in drafting the terms of the NDA?

3. In the context of our planning problem (involving Galaxy's acquisition of Trekker's business), would you recommend the use of an NDA? Does your analysis of this issue vary depending on whether you are Trekker's counsel or Galaxy's?

4. In considering the matters that are customarily included in an NDA, what advice would you give Trekker on these issues? What advice would you give to Galaxy on these matters?

C. Acquisition Consideration: Business Considerations and Legal Issues

The key factor in determining whether the parties' negotiations will ultimately result in a deal usually turns on price and price-related considerations. In negotiating the terms of the purchase price in the context of any particular acquisition, there are typically three issues that must be considered as a threshold matter:

> (i) Will the acquisition consideration consist of cash or Bidder's stock (or some combination of the two)?[1]
> (ii) Once the parties agree on the nature of the acquisition consideration, then they have to reach agreement on the crucial deal point— *how much?*
> (iii) Finally, the parties have to agree on *when* the acquisition consideration is to be paid, which generally will be at closing on the acquisition agreement— *unless* the parties agree that payment of some portion of the purchase paid is to be deferred until some time *after* closing.

Each of these issues will be examined in more detail in this section. It bears emphasizing at the outset, however, that resolution of these issues varies widely

---

1. As an alternative to using Bidder's stock, Bidder may ask Target to accept Bidder's note or other debt securities of Bidder. This raises a separate set of financing issues (including, most prominently, issues under the federal securities laws, among other things); the complexity created by the use of debt financing generally goes beyond the scope of the introductory materials presented in this chapter. As but one example of the additional legal considerations that counsel must address—where Bidder's debt is to be part of the acquisition consideration—is the threshold issue of whether the debt is a security under federal law and under relevant state blue sky laws. In addition, as a business matter, the parties will have to negotiate the terms of the debt instrument (interest rate, payment schedule, etc.), and further, analyze the impact of these obligations on the company's cash flow and other aspects of its business operations.

from deal to deal, and consequently, is not susceptible to generalizable conclusions. The terms reached in the context of any particular acquisition will generally depend on the relative bargaining power of each side, which can be influenced by a myriad of different factors.

1. Purchase Price: Cash vs. Stock as Acquisition Consideration

If Bidder's stock is to be used as the acquisition consideration, then Bidder will have to comply with the requirements of the Securities Act of 1933 (the "1933 Act"). The obligations imposed on Bidder by the terms of the 1933 Act generally require Bidder to either register the shares or find an exemption from the registration requirement for the issuance of its shares in connection with the acquisition of Target. Detailed examination of the nature of these obligations under the federal securities laws is covered in Chapter 4. Suffice it to say, the delay and cost that results from triggering the requirements of the 1933 Act will often be an important factor in determining whether to use cash or Bidder's securities as the acquisition consideration.

Another important factor that will influence the parties' negotiations regarding the use of cash vs. Bidder's stock as the acquisition consideration is the financial motivations of the parties to the transaction and the business objectives they hope to accomplish by engaging in the proposed transaction. For example, in connection with Nestlé's acquisition of Chef America, Inc., it is likely that the owners of Chef America, Inc. (Paul and David Merage), insisted on using cash as the acquisition consideration. As described in more detail in Chapter 1, it appears that the Merage brothers wanted to get out of Chef America's business completely. Their stock in the company constituted an illiquid asset that presumably represented a substantial portion (if not virtually all) of their personal wealth. Assuming that Paul and David were nearing retirement age, they probably faced the pressure of needing to diversify their investment portfolios and the desire to stop working to grow and manage Chef America's business. Therefore, if Nestlé had proposed financing its purchase using Nestlé's common stock, the Merage brothers likely would have broken off any further discussions with Nestlé. Why is this result likely in the context of this particular deal? In other words, why would the business objectives of the Merage brothers *not* be satisfied if Nestlé stock were to be used as the acquisition consideration?

2. Different Mechanisms for Making Purchase Price Adjustments

a. *Earn-Outs*

Earn-out provisions are a type of pricing formulation most commonly found in agreements for the acquisition of a privately held Target. Simply put, an earn-out is a pricing formulation that allows the financial performance of

Target's business on a post-closing basis to affect directly the amount of purchase price that Bidder will ultimately pay to acquire Target's business. Earn-out provisions may serve several purposes. Typically, earn-out clauses are used to address a big valuation gap in the purchase price expectations of Target's owners versus the price that Bidder is willing to pay to acquire Target's business. An earn-out provision may be used to bridge this valuation gap. In addition, earn-out provisions are often used to provide financial incentives—motivation to "keep their head in the game"—for those selling shareholders who Bidder desires to remain with Target as executives or management after the acquisition closes.

Consequently, an earn-out provision generally will result in a post-closing adjustment to the agreed-upon purchase price. What factors influence the parties' determination to use an earn-out? The decision to use an earn-out may be the product of the stubbornness of the ever-optimistic seller (Target) clinging to, say, a $50 million purchase price, and who cannot understand why Bidder cannot raise its valuation numbers to this $50 million level. On the other hand, the skeptical Bidder insists that it cannot responsibly pay more than $45 million to acquire Target's business. In such a case, Bidder may not believe the rosy forecasts proffered by Target to support its high valuation position. Under these circumstances, the parties might decide to bridge their differing perspectives on the proper valuation of Target's business by resorting to the use of an earn-out. Thus, if the Target executive team can actually achieve the rosy forecasts they have proffered to support the Target's high valuation, then Bidder will pay the additional purchase price. As such, the earn-out may be viewed as just another variation on that time-honored expression, "Put your money where your mouth is."

On the facts of the hypothetical scenario described above, where an earn-out is used in order to close the valuation gap between Bidder and Target, the parties might agree to frame the terms of the purchase price as follows: a base price of $45 million to be paid at closing (either in cash or Bidder's stock), subject to an earn-out component that would allow the purchase price to increase by as much as $5 million, with the exact amount of the post-closing price adjustment to be determined by a formula agreed to by the parties. The formula to be used to calculate this post-closing price adjustment may be based on the cumulative pre-tax income of the business operations that Bidder acquired from Target over a period of time (say, three years) following the closing on the acquisition agreement. In this hypothetical case, a three-year period is likely to be used in the parties' formula for the earn-out because—as is often the case in the real world—that was the period covered by the seller's (Target's) projections. If these projections are met over the three-year period following closing on the deal, then Target's owners will receive an additional payment of $5 million, thereby allowing the sellers to realize the $50 million purchase price that they (stubbornly) insisted on and thus avoiding a stalemate in the parties' negotiations. On its face, this might seem to be a simple resolution of the parties' differences. In truth, though, this is only the beginning, as the parties then must negotiate the complex terms that make up the formula for a typical earn-out provision.

In the context of our planning problem involving Galaxy's acquisition of Trekker's business, the initial draft of the acquisition agreement (see Appendix C) includes an earn-out provision. As you read through the following materials concerning earn-outs, consider whether the principals of Galaxy or Trekker proposed use of an earn-out and what purpose was to be served by including an earn-out provision in their agreement.

Negotiating the Terms of an Earn-Out. From the perspective of Bidder, drafting an earn-out is a fairly straightforward exercise. For Bidder, the crucial consideration centers on careful drafting of the key accounting terms that will be part of any earn-out provision (such as, in our example, the calculation of *pre-tax income*). However, things may quickly become complicated. The selling shareholders (who may or may not remain with the Target business as managers or executives) will want to maximize pre-tax profit, but the new owner, Bidder, may want to increase sales and marketing expenses, or research and development expenses, which will build for future growth but may reduce near-term profitability; and therein lies the risk.

Accordingly, the current owners of Target's business typically will want assurances that Target's business will be run as an isolated business unit (such as a separate subsidiary or division of Bidder) so that the financial revenues generated by Target's business can be measured in a reliable and accurate manner. In addition, and especially in those cases where the existing Target owners/managers are to stay on to run the business after closing, these managers can be expected to demand some measure of autonomy in operating the business during the period covered by the earn-out (which in our simple example above is a three-year post-closing period). Of course, Bidder is likely to resist these demands, insisting that the full value of the acquisition for Bidder can only be realized if Target's business is promptly integrated into Bidder's business operations. Notwithstanding the outcome of the parties' negotiations on this particular issue, there also is likely to be extended negotiations over other details regarding the financial terms of the earn-out (such as the amount of administrative overhead that Bidder—now the parent company—will be able to push down and require Target's business to absorb). Moreover, it is likely that counsel for Bidder will be equally concerned about the possibility for manipulation of business expenses and other items by the managers of Target's business, who Bidder fears may be tempted to act in an opportunistic manner in running the business operations on a post-closing basis in order to satisfy the terms of the parties' earn-out formula, possibly at the expense of the longer term best interests of the business.

Drafting the Formula for the Earn-Out. From both sides, negotiating and drafting the earn-out formula is likely to become exceedingly complex as each side tries to anticipate what *might* happen to the business *after* closing. Consequently, in the experience of many M&A lawyers, earn-outs frequently prove to be unworkable. Even though there may be an agreement in principle between the parties as to the use of an earn-out, the devil obviously is in the details. Even the simplest of earn-out formulas agreed to in the abstract by the parties quickly devolves into nightmarish drafting sessions as the parties begin focusing on the myriad variables that could affect making, or missing, the earn-out formula, and begin adding adjustments, restrictions, and covenants to address or offset the effect of those variables. For example, if the earn-out is based on achieving a certain amount of pre-tax income, the selling shareholders may seek to limit the new owner's ability to increase expenses, or alternatively, create an adjustment so that increased expenses are not counted against income for purposes of the earn-out formula. Faced with these complexities, it is not uncommon for the parties ultimately to decide to abandon the use of an earn-out, notwithstanding its initial appeal as a creative tool to bridge the valuation gap facing the parties at the outset of their negotiations. Of course, that still leaves a valuation gap to be addressed by the parties.

Even with all these time-consuming negotiating and drafting difficulties, earn-outs are used often in the real world of M&A transactions, particularly in those deals where the valuation differences between the parties are significant. In these cases, as a practical matter, the only way the deal will get done — the only way to close the big gap between the price sought by the optimistic owners of Target and the much lower price offered by the skeptical Bidder — is to use an earn-out to forge a compromise.

Dispute Resolution Mechanisms.   One final thing to mention in connection with the use of an earn-out is the perceived need to include some dispute resolution mechanism as part of the acquisition agreement. Although a dispute resolution provision may apply to the agreement as a whole, many lawyers believe that the parties should include a provision that separately and specifically addresses disputes over how to apply the terms of the earn-out formula in order to resolve any differences that may arise between the parties as to the amount of purchase price to be paid on a *post-closing* basis. For example, the parties may agree to appoint a particular accounting firm to resolve issues related to the application of the financial terms of the earn-out formula used in their agreement. Often, though, counsel for seller may resist including such a provision on the grounds that this kind of arbitration provision is an open invitation to the buyer to litigate the terms of the earn-out, which will inevitably result in an arbitration proceeding. In the event of arbitration, Bidder's ultimate concern usually is that the arbitrator is likely to just "split the difference," meaning that Bidder will likely be required to pay half of the maximum amount of the earn-out as set forth under the terms of the parties' acquisition agreement. Depending on the degree of Bidder's apprehension, Bidder may refuse to provide for any specific dispute resolution mechanism, even though it may ultimately agree to the use of an earn-out as part of the acquisition agreement.

NOTE

The other consideration that the parties need to keep in mind when negotiating the terms of the earn-out is that the use of an earn-out means that the parties will need to maintain some sort of business relationship *after* closing on the acquisition. In light of this, the parties have strong incentives to avoid contentious and protracted negotiations that might damage, or at least sour, the basis for such a continuing business relationship.

Indeed, the kind of polar disagreement that we have seen reflected in the parties' negotiations over the terms of the earn-out actually reflects a more fundamental tension inherent in the deal process as a whole: a natural suspicion of the other party, tempered by a business need to trust in the good faith of the other party. As the remaining materials in this chapter make abundantly clear, there is an inherent tension in M&A transactions between profit-maximizing Bidders on the one hand and equally profit-motivated Targets on the other. This tension typically surfaces in rather dramatic fashion in negotiating the specific terms of an earn-out formula. But even in the absence of an earn-out, this inherent tension between Bidder and Target will inevitably spill over to color their negotiations over the wording and terms of the other provisions that are typically made part of the parties' acquisition agreement. While at some level the two parties share a common interest in completing the transaction, their negotiations over the specific terms of the acquisition agreement invariably reflect the parties' divergent interests and desires. Yet the ability to get the deal done—to close on the agreement—depends on the parties' ability to get past these inherent differences and reach an acceptable compromise.

The give and take inherent in the deal process for any acquisition is reflected in the remaining materials in this chapter, most notably in Part D (at pp. 348-359), describing a hypothetical dialogue between Bidder's lawyer and Target's lawyer as they negotiate the terms of a specific provision to be made part of the parties' acquisition agreement. The dialogue in this hypothetical bargaining process reflects another important attribute of the good business lawyer when advising clients in an M&A transaction: the vital importance of the lawyer's strong negotiating and drafting skills. These important skills are acquired through experience and the lawyer's continued commitment to communicate effectively and represent his/her client's interest in a responsible and ethical manner. The remaining materials in this chapter are intended to emphasize this fundamental point about the important role of the good business lawyer in the context of *any* acquisition—whether the deal is done on Wall Street or Main Street.

b.   Escrows

In lieu of negotiating an earn-out, the parties may use an *escrow* as the tool of choice to resolve their fundamental differences over valuation. Under this alternative, Bidder will hold back a specified portion of the purchase price at closing. These funds will then be placed in escrow with an independent escrow agent for a specified period of time after closing. The escrow agreement, usually attached as an exhibit to the acquisition agreement and signed and delivered at the closing, will provide specific conditions (or triggers), which, when satisfied, authorize the escrow holder to disburse money to the appropriate party. An escrow, like an earn-out, may serve more than one purpose. An escrow can be used together with an earn-out formula, thereby giving Target's shareholders comfort that the additional purchase price will be paid as soon as the earn-out condition is met.

An escrow fund may also be established to facilitate Bidder's ability to recover on indemnification claims that may arise post-closing. When faced with a requirement by Bidder that a portion of the price be set aside in an escrow to serve as security for possible indemnity claims, Target may respond by insisting that the escrowed funds provide Bidder with its sole remedy for any post-closing claims that may arise. This is explored in more detail later in Part E of this chapter, in connection with the topic of indemnification rights that may be granted to Bidder on a post-closing basis under the terms of the parties' agreement.

c. *Post-Closing Purchase Price Adjustments*

This final type of purchase price provision, a post-closing purchase price adjustment, is used most often when the parties agree to the essential method for calculating the purchase price but either contemplate considerable delay between signing and closing on their acquisition agreement or certain factors that will affect the calculation cannot be known or finalized until after the closing. For example, the parties may use a purchase price adjustment provision to address the concern that there may be changes in the value of Target between the date of signing the agreement and the date of closing on the acquisition. This is of particular concern in those cases where antitrust review, or the need to obtain some other regulatory approvals, may lead to considerable delay between signing and closing on the parties' acquisition agreement. Likewise, if securities (such as Bidder's stock) must be registered with the SEC or a proxy statement must be filed with the SEC in order to obtain shareholder approval of the proposed transaction, considerable delay may ensue.

In these cases involving the potential for delay, the purchase price adjustment serves to allocate the financial risks associated with the delay. If a purchase price adjustment were not made, then the earnings generated by Target's business between signing and closing will typically accrue to the benefit of Bidder, since most acquisition agreements prohibit Target from making any distributions during the period between signing and closing. Similarly, losses sustained in Target's business would be absorbed by Bidder in the absence of a provision for a post-closing adjustment in the purchase price.

QUESTIONS

In reviewing the planning problem set forth at the beginning of the chapter, consider the following questions in light of the terms of the purchase price that Galaxy agreed to pay to acquire Trekker's business:

1. What is the purchase price? What is the acquisition consideration?

2. What factors do you suppose influenced the parties' determination to use an earn-out in this transaction? Why was an earn-out preferable to an escrow?

3. Why might Trekker not want an escrow? Why might Galaxy want to use an escrow?

4. Did the parties include any dispute resolution mechanism as part of the terms of their earn-out provision?

5. How do the parties treat the potential for existing management of Target to distribute the company's earnings before closing on the agreement?

3. Valuing Exchanges of Stock — Fixing the Exchange Ratio

In analyzing the problem sets in Chapter 2, we learned that difficult valuation decisions must be made as part of any acquisition, regardless of how the deal is structured. From the perspective of Target Co., the board must determine the inherent value of Target's business in order to decide at what price to sell the company. In situations where cash is the acquisition consideration, Bidder Co. faces the same business decision — determining what is a fair price for Target so that Bidder does not pay too much to acquire Target's business. If Bidder pays too great a premium to acquire Target, Bidder's management knows that it will face the ire of its own shareholders, whose equity interest will be diluted. On the other hand, from the perspective of Target, the business decision as to the amount of premium is even more compelling. Target's board faces a similar business valuation decision as Bidder's board — *exactly how much is Target worth?* As we have seen in analyzing the problems in Chapter 2, the decision as to price is vitally important since the acquisition is a fundamental change for Target. As such, the business decision as to the amount of premium that Target should receive in an all-cash purchase price is vitally important since an all-cash deal will eliminate the existing shareholders of Target from any further equity participation in the business. Consequently, the proposed sale of the company's business to Bidder for an all-cash purchase price presents Target shareholders with their *only* opportunity to receive a premium for their investment in Target's business.

As described earlier, determining the amount of this premium involves a complex valuation exercise. However, in those deals where Bidder's stock (or other securities) will be used as the acquisition consideration, the valuation decision is even more complicated. In this situation, Target's board faces a separate — but equally important — valuation determination. In addition to valuing Target in order to determine what is fair value for Target's business, the board of Target must also value the securities that Bidder proposes to issue in order to acquire Target to be sure that the exchange is fair to Target. The board of Bidder faces a similarly complex valuation decision whenever Bidder proposes to use its stock as the acquisition consideration, as it must be sure that it does not pay too much to acquire Target's business.

As the problems in Chapter 2 illustrated, the boards of both Bidder and Target generally will retain financial advisors to assist them in their respective valuation exercises. The ultimate decision-making responsibility, however, belongs to the board. The complexity of these valuation determinations is reflected in the following case, as is the scope of the board's fiduciary obligation to the company's shareholders in discharging this decision-making responsibility.

In re RJR Nabisco, Inc. Shareholders Litigation
1989 WL 7036 (Del. Ch. Jan. 31, 1989), 14 Del. J. Corp. L. 1132

ALLEN, Chancellor. . . .

I.

THE COMPANY

RJR is a Delaware corporation formed following the 1985 merger of RJ Reynolds Tobacco Company and Nabisco Brands, Inc. The Company's principal offices are now in Atlanta, Georgia. Through its subsidiaries, which include RJ Reynolds, Nabisco Brands, Inc., Del Monte Corporation and Planters Life Savers Company, the Company holds leading positions in the tobacco, food and consumer products industries. The Company has 225,519,911 shares of common stock and 1,251,904 shares of preferred stock issued and outstanding. Immediately prior to the events here in question, RJR's common stock was trading on the New York Stock Exchange in the mid 50's.

THE MANAGEMENT GROUP'S INITIAL PROPOSAL TO ACQUIRE THE COMPANY

At an October 19, 1988 RJR board of directors meeting, F. Ross Johnson, speaking on behalf of the Management Group, informed the board that that group was seeking to develop a transaction to take the Company private by means of a leveraged buyout. He suggested a price of $75 per share. Mr. Charles E. Hugel, the Chairman of RJR's board but not an officer of the Company, had had some advance notice that this subject would be brought up at the meeting and had prepared for it to the limited extent of having invited Peter Atkins, Esquire, an attorney with experience with transactions of the type proposed, present.

On October 20, 1988, the board issued a press release announcing the proposed transaction. It also announced the appointment of a special committee of the board comprising Charles E. Hugel as Chairman, John D. Macomber as Vice Chairman, Martin S. Davis, William S. Anderson and Albert L. Butler, Jr. The Special Committee immediately retained two financial advisors, Dillon, Read & Co. (the Company's regular investment banker) and Lazard Freres, Inc. The Committee also retained Mr. Atkins' firm, Skadden, Arps, Slate, Meagher & Flom, to render legal advice to the Committee and to the Company's outside directors. The Delaware firm of Young, Conaway, Stargatt & Taylor was retained as special legal counsel to the Company.

KKR'S INITIAL BID FOR THE COMPANY

On October 24, KKR, who had purportedly earlier been rebuffed in an effort to entice management to join it in a leveraged buyout, informed the Special Committee that it was planning to extend an offer to acquire the Company for $90 per share in cash and securities. On October 27, KKR commenced a tender offer at $90 per share cash for up to 87% of the Company's stock. The offer stated that the balance of RJR's shares were to be exchanged for new securities in a second step merger.

THE RESPONSE OF THE SPECIAL COMMITTEE TO THE CONTEST THAT HAD EMERGED

On November 2, the Special Committee issued a press release announcing that it was interested in receiving proposals to acquire the Company. On November 7, the Committee disseminated Rules and Procedures for Submission of Proposals. This provided, *inter alia,* for a deadline of 5:00 p.m. November 18, 1988 for the final submission of bids. The rules specified that "[t]he rules and procedures outlined above are intended to constitute a single round of bidding. Any Proposal should reflect the potential purchaser's highest offer." The Special Committee also stated that it "encourage[d] proposals that provided to current RJR shareholders a prospect for a substantial common stock related interest in the purchasing entity." *Id.*

BIDS RECEIVED BY THE SPECIAL COMMITTEE NOVEMBER 18

Three bids were in the hands of the Special Committee on the appointed deadline of November 18. The Management Group bid was valued by the Management Group at $100 per share, consisting of $90 in cash, $6 preferred stock and an equity interest of $4. KKR's bid came in at a claimed $94 per share ($75 in cash, $11 in preferred stock and $8 in convertible debt which would convert into 25% of the purchasing entity's equity). The third bidder was the First Boston Corporation. Its proposal, while not fully developed, was in some respects the most interesting. It contemplated an acquisition of the Company's tobacco business in 1989 for approximately $15.75 billion in cash and warrants, and an installment sale of the Company's food businesses immediately (by year end 1988), with the proceeds of such sale to be held for the account of the Company's shareholders. The total value of the First Boston Group proposal, if it could be realized, was estimated to be in the range of $98 to $110 in cash and cash equivalents, securities valued at $5, and warrants valued at $2–$3. The warrants would entitle RJR shareholders to acquire up to 20% of the Company's tobacco business.

The First Boston approach was innovative, appealing and problematic. Its primary appeal lay in the fact that the installment sale mechanism would provide tax advantages estimated to be as high as $3 billion. There were two difficulties, however, with this proposal. First, its terms were not fully worked out. Second, impending changes in the tax code created time constraints which placed the realization of those tax benefits at risk.

THE DECISION TO DEFER A DECISION AND INVITE FURTHER BIDDING

In view of the fact that the First Boston Group's proposal was at this point potentially the most attractive, and that more time was necessary to develop it further, the Committee decided to extend the bidding until November 29. In its press release announcing the terms of the extension, it also published the terms of the three bids it had received, including the percentage of potential equity participation each contemplated.

The Special Committee met with the three bidders at various times during the week of November 21. Bids were actively solicited by the Committee's investment bankers, and there is testimony that the bidders were reminded that the Committee was concerned that a significant equity component be provided to shareholders.

At 5:00 p.m. November 29, the Committee again received three bids. The Management Group raised its bid only minimally; it valued its new bid at $101 per share ($88 cash; $9 preferred stock; $4 convertible preferred). It was the lowest of the three bids. KKR's bid jumped appreciably to a claimed value of $106 ($80 cash; $17 preferred stock; $8 automatically converting debenture), the First Boston Group's bid was said to be in a range from $103 to $115.

CONSIDERATION OF THE NOVEMBER 29 BIDS

The Special Committee concluded early on that the First Boston Group's bid, while attractive, was subject to too much uncertainty to be practicable. Between the remaining bids, KKR's bid plainly appeared to be the higher if the securities included in the bids were worth what the bidders claimed. The Committee determined that before it would choose between these two bids it would seek to assure that KKR's higher bid was worth what it claimed. Accordingly, it directed its lawyers and investment bankers to negotiate concerning the terms of the securities and the details of a merger agreement. This was done during the course of the evening of the 29th and the morning of the 30th.

Some time late in the evening of November 29, the Management Group learned of these talks, apparently from a newspaper reporter. The Management Group apparently realized that it had made a tactical error in raising its bid only $1 when, as later events show, it was willing to pay substantially more. It attempted to recoup by advising the Committee that it had yet to submit its best bid. It requested an opportunity to do so. This request was not responded to before the Management Group pressed ahead late in the following morning to present another bid.

THE NOVEMBER 30 MEETINGS

The Special Committee reconvened at 7:45 a.m. on November 30, together with its financial advisors and six independent outside directors of RJR. Once convened, this group, with a few recesses, remained in session throughout the day.

The independent directors were first informed that the terms of the merger agreement with KKR were essentially complete, but that KKR had expressed displeasure because of its suspicion that its bid had been leaked to the press and from there to the Management Group. In light of its fears, KKR had requested, first informally and then by letter, that its bid be acted upon that day. The letter required action on the bid by 1:00 p.m. November 30. This assertedly created concern in the minds of some of the directors that the KKR bid might be withdrawn if not acted upon in a timely manner.

At some time early on in the meeting on November 30, before the Committee turned to its consideration of the competing bids, the meeting was informed that a letter had been hand-delivered from the Management Group protesting the board's negotiation the night before of the KKR bid as a final offer. The letter stated the Management Group's willingness to discuss all aspects of its proposal. The Committee agreed to waive the terms of the rules and procedures and consider new bids from both parties should such bids be forthcoming. It did not, however, invite or encourage further bidding. Further bidding did, however, eventuate; before describing it, I turn to a brief outline of the alternatives before the Committee on the morning of the 30th.

THE KKR OFFER OF $106

The KKR proposal of $106, made on the night of November 29, consisted of $80 in cash, $17 in cumulative exchangeable pay-in-kind preferred stock and $8 in face value senior converting debentures, which KKR valued at $9 because of the conversion feature.

The terms of the KKR PIK preferred eventually agreed to were designed to achieve the aim that the security would trade at par at some point following distribution.[5] The concern was that a massive public sale of securities, anticipated in order to refinance the bridge loans used to fund the purchase of RJR shares, would push down the value of the preferred stock. This problem was addressed by a provision to reset the rate after the market had absorbed the securities needed to pay off the bridge loans. The Committee also sought to achieve as brief an interval as possible in which the yield on the preferred would float. KKR eventually agreed to reset the rate at the earlier of one year following the refinancing of the bridge loan or two years after the tender offer closed. In light of these agreements, the Committee's investment advisors informed the Committee of their view that the securities should trade at close to their face value of $17 per share.

The senior converting debentures were to convert automatically into common stock of the Company at the end of three years unless the holder "opts out" during a two week option period which then arises. If none of the debenture

---

5. The terms of the pay-in-kind preferred are as follows: Initially, that is, for the first six years, the stock pays dividends "in kind." The dividend rate would initially be a floating rate set at 5-1/2% over a basket of interest rates (defined as the highest of (i) the three month Treasury bill rate, (ii) the 10-year Treasury bond rate, and (iii) the 30-year Treasury bond rate), subject to a ceiling of 16-5/8% and a floor of 12-5/8%. The dividend rate is subject to a reset mechanism that will reset the rate at a fixed rate within one year of any refinancing of the bridge loans used to finance the transaction or two years after consummation of the tender offer. The fixed rate is to be set in an arbitration proceeding among the advisors to KKR, the advisors to the Company, and, if necessary, a third-party investment banker. The hope is to permit the security to trade at par at the time the fixed rate is determined.

holders were to opt out, the debenture holders as a class would own 25% of the equity of the Company at the end of four years. These securities were to pay interest in kind for the first ten years following their issuance, and generate cash distributions thereafter. The interest rate was to float initially, subject to a reset identical to the preferred stock reset. The rate initially would be approximately 14.5%.

THE MANAGEMENT GROUP'S $101 BID

On the morning of the 30th, before the Management Group presented further proposals, the Special Committee also considered the apparently lower bid, the Management Group's November 29 bid of $101, consisting of $88 per share in cash, $9 cumulative PIK preferred stock, and $4 face amount 13% junior convertible exchangeable preferred stock.

At the time of submission, the terms of the cumulative PIK preferred stock were not final. The other security proposed—the 13% junior convertible exchangeable preferred stock—would initially accrue, but not pay, dividends calculated at a rate of 13%. By its terms, this stock could be converted at any time into a maximum of 15% of the fully diluted stock of the surviving tobacco entity. The stock, however, had a "call" feature that allowed the Company to redeem it at any time at par plus accrued and unpaid dividends. RJR's investment advisors were of the view that this unrestricted call provided the issuer with the ability to destroy the equity aspects of the security before it would make financial sense to exercise them. This was said to deprive Management's convertible preferred of any premium value in addition to its value as a straight debt instrument. This security remained unchanged in the final bid and was assigned a value of $2-$2.50.

THE RECAPITALIZATION ALTERNATIVE

In addition to the two bids before it on the morning of November 30, the Special Committee and the outside directors also analyzed the value of a recapitalization of the Company. They concluded that neither a breakup nor a recapitalization would yield value to shareholders in excess of the $106 being offered by KKR.

Having reviewed the three alternatives, the Special Committee invited Messrs. Kravis and Roberts to make a presentation to the meeting concerning their plans should they acquire the Company. Following the presentation, which took place around 11:00 a.m., Mr. Hugel asked Mr. Roberts to extend the 1:00 p.m. deadline for consideration of KKR's bid. Mr. Roberts gave no assurances that the deadline would be extended.

THE MANAGEMENT GROUP'S $108 BID

Following a brief recess, the meeting was reconvened at about 12:30 p.m. A representative of the Management Group then reported to the Committee orally that the Management Group was raising its bid to $108 per share consisting of $84 cash, $20 in PIK preferred stock, and $4 in convertible preferred (*i.e.*, $4 less cash and $11 more preferred stock than the bid of the prior evening). No terms for the component securities were given, but it was stated that the Management Group was willing to negotiate all terms, including price, with the Committee.

With this in mind, the Special Committee told KKR that another bid had been received and again requested an extension of the 1:00 p.m. deadline. This time an extension until 2:00 p.m. was granted.[7] The minutes of the November 30 board meeting reflect that the Management Group had been asked to make its highest and best bid shortly after 1:00 p.m. Mr. Hugel testified that the directors discussed the need to obtain their highest and best bid and agreed that this was to be relayed to the Management Group. James A. Stern, an officer of Shearson Lehman involved in the process, testified that the Management Group was told about 1:00 p.m. or 1:30 p.m. to "[s]harpen your pencils and put your best bid on the table." In response to which the Management Group "reached back and submitted a final proposal, final bid that again had $84 a share in cash, a $24 a share of PIK preferred and the same 15% equity interest via the convertible preferred." *Id.*

THE MANAGEMENT GROUP'S LAST OFFER

The Management Group's last proposal was submitted to the Committee shortly before 1:30 p.m. The Management Group asserted it to be worth $112; the additional $4 of value was all additional preferred stock, raising the face amount of the PIK preferred securities from $20 to $24. Like the previous bid, Management's $112 offer left open certain significant terms, including provisions of the PIK preferred stock and the convertible preferred. As it had done the previous evening with KKR's $106 bid, the Special Committee began negotiating with the Management Group to determine if it could achieve terms for the securities offered which would allow them to trade at their stated value.

KKR'S FINAL BID

In view of KKR's actions in extracting assurance of $.20 per share expense reimbursement provision before it agreed to an extension (*see* note 7 *supra*), the Special Committee and its advisors assert that they were concerned that KKR might simply withdraw its bid altogether at this point. This would, it is said, have left the Committee in a markedly worse negotiating position than the position it was in with competing bids on the table.

Assertedly in order to protect the shareholders from the risk of losing the bird in hand, after receiving the Management Group's face value $112 proposal,

---

7. In consideration, KKR got the Company to agree to reimburse KKR's expenses up to $.20 per share in the event that no merger agreement was signed between the Company and KKR. KKR agreed, on its part, to reduce the topping fee provision in its proposed merger agreement from $1 to $.75 per share.

the Committee offered to KKR to enter into the now fully negotiated merger agreement with it at $106 per share, subject to a $1 topping fee should the Company accept another offer within seven days, but with the agreement that no further expenses would be paid. It also offered KKR the opportunity to bid again prior to the acceptance of any other offer. In response to the Committee's offer to enter into a contract, KKR declined but delivered a revised bid which it claimed to be worth $108 per share. The new bid, which was not subject to a deadline, consisted of $80 per share in cash, $18 PIK preferred and converting debentures which KKR valued at $10. The terms of the PIK preferred remained the same as those of the previous bid, but the conversion period for the other security, the automatically converting debentures, was extended another year which was the basis for KKR's assertion that the same face amount of converting debt was now worth $1 per share more. The Committee's advisors gave their preliminary opinion that the revised KKR bid was worth between $107 and $108 per share.

THE FINAL REQUEST FOR BIDS

There were no on-going discussions with KKR for the remainder of the afternoon of November 30; during that time, the Special Committee's investment advisors negotiated with the Management Group in an attempt to improve the terms of the Management Group's securities. Specifically, there was an attempt to get the Management Group to agree to tie the length of the reset period on its PIKs to the refinancing of the bridge loans used to finance the stock acquisition. The Management Group declined to do so. Its PIK preferred had the potential, indeed the likelihood, of not being reset to the market for almost three years.

Attempts to increase the lower rate on Management's PIK were unavailing. The Management Group also declined to put a reset mechanism on its convertible preferred.

By about 6:00 p.m., when the Special Committee reconvened to confer concerning the discussions with the Management Group, it was reported to the Special Committee that no significant progress had been made with respect to the terms of the Management Group's securities. It was further reported by the Committee's investment advisors that in its view, the securities were unlikely to trade at the values assigned them by the Management Group. The Committee apparently decided to return to both bidders one last time. . . .

. . . KKR responded to this further invitation after receiving reassurances that the members of the Management Group would not be in attendance at any board meeting at which the offers were considered. It submitted a merger agreement with its final bid of $109; $1 more in cash. This final bid consisted of $81 in cash, $18 PIK preferred, and $10 converting debentures. KKR placed a 30-minute fuse on this offer when it was submitted.

The Management Group replied to a last communication from the Committee that "they had our final proposal." It is possible, however, that an imperfect communication occurred at this point. The Committee's advisors had been negotiating with the Management Group concerning the reset provision of the preferred stock. The communication at about 5:00 p.m. or 6:00 p.m. on

November 30 may have been thought to relate only to that subject or may have been thought to relate to all subjects concerning the bids. . . .

THE SPECIAL COMMITTEE'S INVESTMENT ADVISORS' PRESENTATIONS CONCERNING THE BIDS

The Special Committee's investment advisors, Lazard Freres and Dillon Read, met with the Special Committee after both "final" bids were received. It estimated the Management Group's proposal to be worth between $108.50 and $109 per share, based on its conclusions that (1) the Management Group's PIK preferred stock should be discounted approximately $2 per share because of the longer term of its reset provisions, its below market dividend rate, and its weaker yield curve protections;[9] and (2) that the Management Group's convertible preferred should be discounted from $4 to $2.50 because it had no reset mechanism, also carried a low dividend rate and was callable at any time.

The advisors only discounted the KKR PIK preferred stock between $.50 and $1. With respect to the KKR converting debentures, they advised the Special Committee that they should trade at their estimated value of $10 and determined as a result that the KKR bid was worth approximately $108 to $108.50 per share.

Based on these valuations, the unprecedented size of the debt offerings of high yield securities involved, and the inherent limitations of predicting future markets, the investment advisors concluded that the bids were substantially equivalent. Both investment bankers advised the Committee that, in their view, the Committee could exercise sound business judgment in recommending either offer, and that they were prepared to give fairness opinions on either transaction.

According to the minutes of the meeting (which are attacked as *post hoc* creations by lawyers for use in litigation), the Committee then reviewed the following factors:

1. the risk that further negotiating with either the management group or KKR could result in the withdrawal of either party from the bidding process;
2. the 15% equity interest in the management group proposal as contrasted with the 25% equity interest in the KKR proposal;
3. the fact that the KKR structure contemplated that the tobacco and a substantial part of the food businesses would remain going forward versus the tobacco only business contemplated by the management group proposal;
4. the greater amount of permanent equity in the KKR proposal;

---

9. The fluctuating rate on the Management Group security was pegged to LIBOR (London Inter-Bank Offering Rate) which is a short-term rate, as opposed to the "basket" of rates against which the KKR security was measured. By opting for the highest of several rates with different maturities to fix the current interest rate, as opposed to a single rate, an investor is offered greater protection against market changes with respect to different maturities.

5. the fact that the amount of PIK securities in both proposals was unprecedented and that there would be an additional $1.5 billion in PIK secu-
rities issued in the management group transaction;

6. the fact that the management group proposal provided for $84 in cash
per share of common stock while the KKR proposal provided for $81
in cash per share of common stock.

7. the potential issues arising under the Company's debt indentures in
connection with the management group's proposal but not in connection with the KKR proposal; and

8. that KKR (but not the management group) was willing to provide for
the presentation of benefits for employees whose jobs were terminated
as the result of business divestitures.

Based on these considerations, and without attempting to seek a higher bid
from either party, the Committee elected to recommend the KKR bid and the
board shortly thereafter authorized the execution of the KKR merger agreement that had been negotiated.

II.

The pending motion is for preliminary injunction. Such a remedy is dis-
cretionary in the sense that, in determining to issue it, a number of competing
factors, whose weight is not scientifically ascertainable, must be evaluated. The
factors themselves are not controversial. They include first, a preliminary determination that a reasonable likelihood exists that plaintiffs will be able to prove
their claims at trial. Secondly, plaintiffs must show that they are threatened with
irreparable injury before final relief may be afforded to them. Should the court
determine that both of these elements appear, it is necessary to consider what
sort of injury, if any, may be visited upon defendants by the improvident granting of the remedy, how great that injury might be in relation to the injury with
which plaintiffs are faced, and whether a bond may offer adequate protection
against that risk or whether it might be avoided by the shaping of relief. Lastly,
the court must be alert to the legitimate interests of the public or innocent third
parties whose property rights or other legitimate interests might be affected by
the issuance of the remedy. All of this, of course, is perfectly well settled.

III.

The requested preliminary relief importantly involves a preliminary injunction against KKR, although no claim is made that KKR has itself violated any
duty that it owed to the RJR shareholders. Nor does the amended complaint
contain any allegations that a conspiracy exists which joins KKR in a breach of
duties owed by the directors of the Company to the shareholders. The briefs of
plaintiffs, inspired no doubt by recent history, now claim that KKR was tipped
by the agents of the Special Committee concerning the Committee's desire for
an equity participation in the range of 25%-35%. But the record at this stage
makes any such claim appear far too flimsy to support provisional acceptance
of it for these purposes. Thus, I must treat this application as one in which no

reasonable probability has been shown that plaintiffs will be able to prove that KKR has itself committed or participated in a wrong.

A number of cases in this court have expressed the not surprising view that a preliminary injunction will not issue to restrain an innocent third party who has extended a tender offer. In none of these cases, however, did the court actually find that it was likely that a breach of fiduciary duty by corporate directors had occurred in connection with the board's negotiation or endorsement of the offer. Thus, in none of them was the court actually faced with the hard choice between two innocent parties, one of which will suffer by its decision: the innocent third party who would lose his bargain if the injunction issued or the innocent shareholders who would be injured by the denial of the relief and the consummation of the transaction. . . .

IV.

In assessing the probability of success of plaintiffs' various claims, I first note that this action constitutes an attack upon a decision made by an apparently disinterested board in the exercise of its statutory power to manage the business and affairs of the corporation. That being apparently the case, the appropriate format or structure for judicial review of the action under attack would be provided by the business judgment rule, *Pogostin v. Rice*, Del. Supr., 480 A.2d 619 (1984). . . .

The business judgment form of judicial review encompasses three elements: a threshold review of the objective financial interests of the board whose decision is under attack (i.e., independence), a review of the board's subjective motivation (i.e., good faith), and an objective review of the process by which it reached the decision under review (i.e., due care). *Polk v. Good*, Del. Supr., 507 A.2d 531 (1986); *Aronson v. Lewis*, Del. Supr., 473 A.2d 805 (1984); *Smith v. Van Gorkom*, Del. Supr., 488 A.2d 858 (1985); *Grobow v. Perot*, Del. Supr., 539 A.2d 180 (1988). . . .

. . . [As to the first of these factors, independence, the court concludes that the Special Committee] passes easily over the threshold for application of the business judgment form of judicial review in this instance.

2. GOOD FAITH: THE CLAIM THAT THE SPECIAL COMMITTEE WAS NOT MOTIVATED TO SEEK THE BEST AVAILABLE TRANSACTION FOR THE STOCKHOLDERS

. . . In reviewing, with respect to *bona fides*, the Special Committee's decision to accept one of the proposals in the early evening of November 30, two circumstances must be first noted. First, the consideration offered in both proposals contained complex securities not susceptible to intuitive evaluation. Sophisticated and effective business generalists of the type likely to be found on the board of such companies as RJR will seldom have the specialized skills useful to most accurately value such securities. Our law, of course, recognizes the appropriateness of directors relying upon the advice of experts when specialized judgment is necessary as part of a business judgment. *See* 8 Del. C. §141(e).

In this instance, the Committee did receive the advice of Lazard Freres and of Dillon Read that when the respective securities were appropriately valued, they regarded the bids as substantially equivalent.

Plaintiffs spend a good deal of effort in attacking this judgment. The effort (as it relates to this theory of liability) is to show that the opinion was not only incorrect but was implausible. From this plaintiffs would infer a motive to favor KKR (the unspoken link being the assumption that the bankers detected a preference by the Committee and fell in with it). I have reviewed the competing affidavits by the investment bankers. I cannot conclude that plaintiffs have shown the Lazard Freres or Dillon Read work to be flawed. . . .

Thus, the fact that the board was faced with what it could reasonably believe were bids that were essentially equivalent from a financial point of view is a relevant circumstance in assessing its good faith in acting as it did.

The second especially relevant circumstance with respect to the Committee's decision to act when it did relates to the fact that the Committee had been placed under severe time constraints by KKR in submitting its final proposal—the Committee was given thirty minutes to accept the bid on pain of its being withdrawn. Of course, this may have been an empty threat. I suppose that few thought the chances of such a withdrawal very high but no one, of course, was in a position to assure that it would not happen. Were it to have happened, it is plain that the recap option would have provided a poor substitute at the range of values the bidding had been driven to. Thus, the Committee would have been left with the Management Group's proposal of substantially equivalent value but with some important terms that were plainly less appealing. . . .

In the light of these circumstances, the decision not to attempt to break the tie but to accept one of the bids at that point and thus avoid the risk of the loss of that bid—no matter that my personal view might be that the risk was rather small—can in no event be seen as justifying an inference that those who made such a choice must have had some motivation other than the honest pursuit of the corporation's welfare.

Nor can the decision to prefer KKR's bid with $3 less cash and with less nominal or face value per share be seen as so beyond the bounds of reasonable judgment as to raise an inference of bad faith in my opinion. The larger equity stub, the different future business plans of the two bidders, and the superior reset provision of KKR's proposed converting debentures, all provide a basis to support the notion that the choice was a rational one. That KKR as an acquiror presented antitrust questions or offered a somewhat lower proportion of cash simply presents an occasion for the exercise of judgment; the judgment reached does not, as indicated, appear so far afield as to raise a question of the motivation of the board.

3. DUE CARE: THE CHARGE THAT THE SPECIAL COMMITTEE WAS GROSSLY NEGLIGENT IN CONDUCTING AND CONCLUDING THE AUCTION

I cannot conclude that plaintiffs have demonstrated a reasonable likelihood that this theory of liability will be sustained. In connection with it, their burden of course will be to establish at final hearing that in electing to sign the KKR proposed merger agreement, the directors were grossly negligent. *Aronson v. Lewis,* Del. Supr., 473 A.2d 805 (1984); *Smith v. Van Gorkom,* Del. Supr., 488 A.2d 858 (1985). . . . [T]here appears to have been no neglect of duty of any sort in this instance.

This would appear quite evident given the amount of attention the directors lavished upon this important transaction and the responsible steps they took to be competently advised concerning alternatives open to them. . . .

. . . Accordingly, I conclude that the Committee had at the time it made its decision "all material information reasonably available" to it. *Aronson, supra* at 812. Moreover, there is, in my opinion, no sufficient evidence that it then failed "to act with requisite care" thereafter in reaching the particular decision to prefer the KKR proposal. It is the case that that decision was made under extreme time pressure. But where an arm's-length negotiating adversary imposes time limits, a board is forced to contend with that circumstance. If it exercises informed judgment in the circumstances, considers the risks posed by the deadline imposed, and concludes that it is prudent to act and acts with care, it has satisfied its duty. . . .

. . . The pending motion will therefore be denied.

NOTES

1. Fiduciary Duty Law. The facts presented in the principal case, *RJR Nabisco Shareholders Litigation,* involved a situation commonly known as competitive bidding. In cases where Target is presented with multiple offers from competing Bidders, the board of Target Co. must act carefully in order to fulfill its fiduciary obligations to the company and its shareholders. The nature and scope of this fiduciary obligation is explored in more detail in Chapter 7, where we take up the all-important topic of fiduciary duty law.

2. Fixing the Terms of the Exchange Ratio in Public Company Deals. When stock is used as the acquisition consideration, the situation is more complicated for the transaction planner than the all-cash deal. As reflected in *RJR Nabisco,* much of this complexity arises from the need to fix the terms of the *exchange ratio.* The need to fix the exchange ratio is an inherent attribute of any stock for stock transaction—regardless of how the deal gets structured (i.e., direct merger, stock purchase, triangular merger, etc.). By contrast, in an all-cash transaction, the acquisition agreement simply specifies the amount of cash that Bidder is obligated to pay to Target shareholders at closing for each Target share they own. In the case of a stock for stock transaction, however, the acquisition agreement must specify the number of shares of Bidder that Target shareholders are to receive at closing in exchange for *each* of Target's outstanding shares.

As reflected in the facts of the principal case, there is a complicated valuation exercise inherent in the board's determination of the terms of any exchange ratio, a process that is quite complex from the perspective of *both* Bidder and Target. For starters, the board of Bidder must be confident in its determination of the inherent value of Target's business. The same is also true for Target's board with respect to the inherent value of Target's business. As we saw in analyzing the problems in Chapter 2, nothing less than a fully informed decision-making process will satisfy the directors' fiduciary obligations to their respective shareholders. Where Bidder proposes to pay the purchase price all in cash, valuation of Target's business is the principal focus of the valuation exercise undertaken by the boards of both Bidder and Target.

Determining Fair Value.   However, in cases where Bidder proposes to use its own shares as the acquisition consideration, the situation is far more complex for the boards of both Bidder and Target. Bidder's board needs to be sensitive to the potential for equity dilution of its existing shareholders because of the issuance of its own stock as the acquisition consideration. Therefore, Bidder's board must take care to document its determination as to the value of *both* Bidder Co. *and* Target Co. in order to be sure that Bidder is receiving fair value for the shares that it proposes to issue to acquire Target. As we saw in analyzing the problems in Chapter 2, the potential for equity dilution of Bidder's shareholders in these cases is often going to trigger their right to vote on the transaction. In general, the public policy justification for giving Bidder shareholders a voice in this transaction when the amount of new shares to be issued exceeds some particular percentage of Bidder's then-outstanding shares (which is 20 percent under NYSE Rule 312)—even though Bidder is going to survive with all of its outstanding shares in place—reflects the difficulties inherent in valuing the non-cash consideration to be received by Bidder in exchange for this large block of its shares. The potential for substantial disagreement as to the precise value that Bidder is to receive in this exchange justifies the delay and cost associated with imposing the requirement that Bidder's shareholders approve the issuance of Bidder's shares in exchange for non-cash consideration (here, in the form of Target's business). As a matter of corporate governance, the need for shareholder approval forces management to explain the basis of its decision to acquire Target, including its valuation determination, thereby allowing Bidder shareholders to hold management accountable for their boardroom decision making.

From Target's perspective, Target shareholders will generally get a right to vote on the transaction as a matter of corporate governance since it involves a fundamental change for the company. Regardless of whether cash or Bidder's stock serves as the acquisition consideration, Target's board owes a fiduciary duty to Target shareholders to obtain the best price available. In those cases where Target is publicly traded, this fiduciary obligation will require the board to negotiate with Bidder for a premium over the trading price of Target's stock. The amount of the premium is a matter of bargaining between Bidder and Target. In any case, however, the decision of the Target board whether to accept the price offered by Bidder will depend on the board's decision as to the inherent value (i.e., true value) of Target's business. Again, in all cash deals, this is the principal focus of the board's decision-making process.

By contrast, in those cases where Bidder is to acquire Target's business in exchange for shares of Bidder Co., the decision-making process of Target's board is more complicated. In such a case, Target's board must determine the value of Bidder and its prospects for the future. Only by engaging in this difficult valuation exercise—valuing Bidder, a business that Target's board is not as familiar with as it (hopefully) is with its own—can Target's board be sure that it is getting the best deal—*fair value*—for Target's shareholders under the terms of Bidder's exchange offer. This valuation exercise is at the very heart of negotiating the terms of the exchange ratio in those acquisitions where Bidder's stock is to be used as currency in the acquisition.

Once the exchange ratio is fixed based on the respective valuation determinations made by the boards of both Bidder and Target, the parties usually face another round of negotiations, at least in those cases where Bidder is publicly traded. In these cases, the parties must address the problem of changes in the price of Bidder's stock in the time interval between signing the acquisition agreement and closing on the deal, a period that can be quite lengthy (often many months or more) in the case of acquisitions involving publicly traded companies. For example, in the case of Pfizer's acquisition of Pharmacia (as described in detail in Chapter 1), the parties signed the acquisition agreement in July 2002, but the deal did not close until the spring of 2003 pending antitrust clearance of the transaction. Accordingly, the parties to the transaction must address the inevitable possibility that the price of Bidder's stock will fluctuate during this period and evaluate the impact (if any) that this fluctuation will have on the value of the transaction from the perspective of both Bidder and Target shareholders.

At the time of negotiating a stock for stock transaction, the parties must deal with the problem that there will be an inevitable delay between the time of signing the acquisition agreement and the time of closing on the agreement. This delay means that the transaction planner cannot determine precisely the number of shares that Target shareholders will receive at closing since the price of Bidder may change in the time interval between signing and closing. In practice, this leads to the use of one of two basic strategies for dealing with fluctuations in the price of Bidder's stock in the interval between signing and closing on the acquisition.

Use of Fixed Exchange Ratio. The simplest structure is conventionally known as a *fixed exchange ratio.* Here, the acquisition agreement simply says that at closing, every Target share has the right to receive a fixed number of Bidder shares. In the case of a fixed exchange ratio, the number of Bidder shares to be received by Target shareholders at closing will not vary, regardless of what happens to the price of Bidder's shares in the interval between signing and closing. At the other end of the spectrum, the parties to the transaction may agree that Target shareholders shall receive a certain value at the time of closing, which leads to the use of a *fixed dollar value exchange ratio.* Using this kind of ratio means that at closing, every Target share will be exchanged for Bidder shares with a specified dollar value as of the date of closing. Where this kind of ratio is used, the parties will also have to negotiate and agree as to the *method* to be used to determine the *value* of Bidder's shares.

In practice, the *fixed dollar value exchange ratio* is often quite difficult to draft because the parties may be reluctant to agree to a formula that calls for the value to be determined *solely* by reference to the price of Bidder's stock on the day of closing. One obvious concern with this method of determining the value that Target shares are to receive is that the price of Bidder's stock on that particular date (i.e., the day of closing) is hard to predict and may turn out to be an aberration from the historical price performance of Bidder's stock. Another concern is that this method of determining value (i.e., solely by reference to price of Bidder's stock on the day of closing) is potentially subject to manipulation. In order to address these concerns regarding use of a fixed dollar value exchange ratio, the parties will typically include a provision in the acquisition agreement that looks to fix the dollar value that Target shares will receive by taking an *average* of the price of Bidder's stock in the trading market over, say, a 10- to 20-day period *prior* to the date of closing on the parties' agreement. Of course, this leads to further negotiations over the number of days to be included in the trading period, and further, how to calculate the average of these trading prices. As a matter of drafting, there are numerous ways for the transaction planner to compute the average trading price of Bidder's stock: that is, whether to volume-weight the average, just take the arithmetic average, or other options.

Use of Fixed Dollar Value Exchange Ratio. When the parties agree to use a fixed dollar value exchange ratio, or as it is more often called today, a *pure floating exchange ratio*, the impact on Target shareholders is quite different. When a *pure floating exchange ratio* is used, the parties agree at the outset that Target shareholders are to receive a fixed value, say $40 for every Target share outstanding as of the signing of the acquisition agreement—no matter what price Bidder's stock is trading at as of the date of closing. For example, if Bidder's stock is trading at $20 as of closing, then under the terms of this particular floating exchange ratio, Target shareholders would receive *two* shares of Bidder stock for every one share of Target stock. On the other hand, if Bidder's stock is trading at $40 at the time of closing, then Target shareholders will receive only *one* share of Bidder stock in exchange for each of their Target shares. Here, the Target shareholders are assured of receiving a fixed value ($40) no matter how many Bidder shares it takes to provide that value. Hence the name is *pure floating exchange ratio*. Moreover, in the case of floating exchange ratios, the price fluctuations in Bidder's stock during the time period between signing and closing on the acquisition agreement are of no concern to Target shareholders.

Caps, Floors, and the Use of Collars. In between these two polar extremes, there are several permutations that result from the use of *collars*, the term of art used to refer to the practice of placing limitations (i.e., an upper and lower limit) on the range within which the price of Bidder's stock may vary for purposes of fixing the terms of the exchange ratio. The collar, which may be used in connection with either the fixed exchange ratio or the fixed dollar value ratio, is, in effect, the floor and the cap on valuation resulting from price fluctuations in the trading of Bidder's stock, and may be expressed in terms of either share price, or alternatively, the number of shares to be issued in the transaction. For example, the terms of the collar may be expressed in our example as a share price of no greater than $40 (known as a *cap*) but no less than $20 (referred to as the *floor*); or alternatively, the collar could be expressed in terms of no more than 1.5 million Bidder shares to be issued, but no fewer than 1.25 million.

When using a collar to fix the terms of the exchange ratio, the parties' agreement will typically provide for a right to terminate the transaction if the price extends beyond the limits imposed by the collar. So, for example, the agreement might provide that in the event that Bidder's stock trading price falls below the lower limit (the floor)—say, $20—then Bidder may, but is not required to, provide additional cash consideration to bring the purchase price up to $20, which is the floor established by the terms of the parties' exchange ratio. In the event that Bidder is unwilling to provide the additional consideration, the acquisition agreement will generally provide that Target has the right to terminate the agreement if Target is unwilling to accept the lower price. This simple example illustrates how the use of a collar to establish a floor and a cap on the terms of the agreed-upon exchange ratio operates to protect the parties against extreme fluctuations in the price of Bidder's stock — both on the upside and the downside.

In addition to the use of collars, the investment banking firm working on any particular deal can engineer further variations on these themes as the economics of any particular business acquisition may demand. And therein lays the creative drafting exercise that routinely faces the M&A lawyer as transaction planner: to reduce to writing, in an understandable fashion, the specific terms of whatever novel exchange ratio the parties may negotiate in the context of a particular acquisition.

QUESTIONS

To be clear on the conceptual differences between these two different types of exchange ratios, consider the terms of Pfizer's acquisition of Pharmacia as set forth in the parties' merger agreement (see Appendix B):

1. What type of exchange ratio did the parties agree to use in this transaction?

2. Under the terms of the agreed-upon exchange ratio, what risks were the Pharmacia shareholders being asked to assume?

3. Shifting to Pfizer's shareholders, what financial risks were they assuming once the parties signed their agreement of merger?

D.   Negotiating and Drafting the Acquisition Agreement

1.   The Basic Agreement

At this point, it is useful to look at the organizational structure of the merger agreement included in Appendix B and compare it to the structure of the stock purchase agreement included in Appendix D. This stock purchase agreement is fairly typical of the kind of stock purchase agreement that may be used in a deal involving the acquisition of all of the stock of a closely held Target Co. by a single buyer, a publicly traded Bidder Co.

As can be readily discerned from this cursory review of these two different agreements, the basic architecture of any acquisition agreement follows a certain convention regardless of the deal structure. For reasons that are described in more detail in the remaining sections of this chapter, the acquisition agreement will usually include the following provisions, which are customarily ordered in the sequence set forth below:

1. *Introductory provisions*—which typically consist of the names of the parties, recitals, and definitions; often, though, the definitions are made in the very first section of the body of the agreement
2. *Description of the structure of the transaction*—asset, stock, or merger; in an asset acquisition, it is very important for the terms of the agreement to describe exactly what is being sold
3. *Terms of the purchase price* and the payment
4. Target's *representations and warranties*
5. Bidder's *representations and warranties*
6. Target's *pre-closing covenants*
7. Bidder's *pre-closing covenants*
8. *Closing on the transaction:*

   a.   When and where.
   b.   Conditions to Target's obligation to close
   c.   Conditions to Bidder's obligation to close
   d.   Deliveries at closing

   - By Target (and/or its shareholders)
   - By Bidder

9. *Termination* of the acquisition agreement
10. *Indemnification*

    a.   In favor of Bidder
    b.   In favor of Target (and/or its selling shareholders)
    c.   Time limitations on bringing claims for indemnification under the terms of the agreement
    d.   Limitations on indemnification claims (generally involving use of *caps* and *baskets)*
    e.   Procedural issues with respect to the assertion of claims of indemnification
11. Other post-closing covenants of the parties
12. General ("*Miscellaneous*") provisions

a.   *Preparation of the First Draft*

The custom among practicing M&A lawyers generally calls for Bidder's lawyer to prepare the initial draft of the acquisition agreement. This is not surprising, given that most of the provisions exist for the protection of the buyer, Bidder; and therefore, the length and complexity of the agreement generally will be driven by the scope of protection that Bidder seeks. Accordingly, the convention has grown up for Bidder's lawyer to prepare the initial draft of the parties' agreement.

The practical wisdom among M&A lawyers is that, if given the chance, the lawyer should *always* seize the opportunity to prepare the initial draft. Most lawyers seize this opportunity to control the draft because they believe that they are in a better negotiating position when their role is evaluating and granting or rejecting requests for changes made by the other party, rather than being the party requesting the changes. In addition, by seizing control of the initial draft, Bidder's lawyers take advantage of the opportunity to slant the agreement to Bidder's advantage, thereby shifting the burden to Target and its lawyer to neutralize these effects through the comment process.

In any acquisition, the purchase price and the terms for the payment of the purchase price (i.e., use cash or Bidder's stock; payment in full at closing or do the parties contemplate deferral of some portion of the purchase price) will be the threshold issue. Typically, the most heavily negotiated section of the acquisition agreement is the set of representations and warranties to be made by Target (and/or its owners) regarding Target's business and financial affairs. Finally, the terms of the indemnification section will usually be another heavily negotiated aspect of the acquisition agreement in a transaction involving the acquisition of a privately held Target, as it is a central tool for allocating and limiting the risks of the transaction.

b. Circulating First Draft for Comment

As recently as fifteen years ago, the initial draft of the acquisition agreement was typically circulated in print form, leaving Target's lawyer to review and make comments in the margin of the agreement and then generally communicate any limiting language orally or by way of a comment letter that summarized Target's objections to the provisions of Bidder's initial draft. Today, however, initial drafts are often circulated electronically, usually delivered as e-mail file attachments. This development has resulted in somewhat cannibalizing the conventional practice for circulating and reviewing drafts of acquisition agreements since e-mail delivery allows the recipient to download the entire file. In these cases, rather than making suggestions for changes, either orally or by a comment letter, Target's lawyer now has greater freedom to essentially rewrite the provisions of Bidder's initial draft. Typically, though, Target's lawyer will track any changes made to Bidder's draft by utilizing the "redlining" function available with most word processing programs.

This ability to essentially rewrite the draft agreement as part of the review and comment process raises the separate question of what professional etiquette should be followed when making changes to drafts circulated by the other side. Best practices are presently in a state of evolution, as the commenting lawyers are now empowered to make more substantial and extensive changes to the provisions of the original draft than the prior practice of circulating drafts only in print form may have allowed. Consequently, electronic delivery of drafts may make it more difficult for the initial draftsperson to assert control over the preparation of the document and the process of making revisions to the agreement. Therefore, many lawyers for Bidders continue to distribute drafts in print form and avoid using electronic delivery in an effort to keep greater control over the document drafting process.

2. Representations and Warranties vs. Covenants vs. Conditions to Closing

a. *Representations and Warranties*

The parties' *representations and warranties* serve several important functions that are interrelated. First, they are disclosure tools; as such, they are an extension of the due diligence review undertaken by the parties as part of the deal process, a process described in more detail later in this chapter. As part of its ongoing diligence process, Bidder is gaining detailed knowledge of Target's business operations and financial well-being. Bidder's understanding of Target's business and financial affairs is then confirmed by a set of representations and warranties[2] made by Target that are Target's way of telling the Bidder, "This is what the company's business is all about, as of this particular moment in time," which is usually the date the acquisition agreement is signed by the parties.

Representations and warranties serve another important purpose in that they are used as risk allocation tools. Most importantly, Target's representations will usually serve as the basis for a *condition to closing* on the acquisition. At the closing—which typically is a date fixed in the agreement for the acquisition of a privately held Target, usually 30 to 60 days after signing the agreement—the truth of Target's representations will be tested again. To clarify, Target's representations in the acquisition agreement regarding the state of its business and financial affairs must be true and accurate not only as of the date that the parties signed the agreement, but also must be true and accurate as of the date of closing on the agreement. This is vitally important to Bidder because it tells Bidder that Target's description of its business and financial affairs, as reflected in its representations and warranties, is true and accurate, not only on the date the parties made their agreement, but continues to remain so as of the date of closing on the agreement. This way, Bidder is assured that there have been no material changes in Target's business and financial affairs in the time period between signing and closing on the agreement. In the event that there has been a material change in Target's business or financial affairs in between signing and closing on the agreement, Bidder will typically be excused from performing on the agreement. As described in more detail later in this section, Target's representations form the basis for Bidder's right to walk away from the

---

2. Some practicing M&A lawyers will draw a distinction between *representations* on the one hand, and *warranties* on the other, pointing out that *representations* are usually limited to statements as to existing circumstances or historical facts, whereas "warranties may also cover future situations." James C. Freund, ANATOMY OF A MERGER 153 n. 33 (Law Journal Press 1975). More recently, however, this distinction has faded away into obscurity. *See* Comment to *§3. Representations and Warranties of Seller and Shareholders,* MODEL ASSET PURCHASE AGREEMENT WITH COMMENTARY, prepared by the American Bar Association, Business Law Section, Committee on Negotiated Acquisitions (2001). Consequently, "representations" and "warranties" have become virtually indistinguishable from each other, and the terms are used interchangeably in this discussion.

deal, thereby relieving Bidder of its obligation under the agreement to pay the purchase price to Target.

Finally, in some acquisitions, most often those involving the acquisition of a privately held Target, the parties' agreement will provide that certain of the representations are to survive closing. In such a case, the representations and warranties will also serve as the basis for contractual liability on a post-closing basis, commonly giving rise to a claim for *indemnification*. Rights of indemnification are discussed in more detail at the end of this chapter.

In sum, the most important purposes served by the parties' representations and warranties in the context of negotiating and documenting any acquisition are disclosure, termination rights, and indemnification rights. The overriding importance served by the representations section of the agreement and its dynamic relationship with other aspects of the acquisition agreement and deal-making process can be conceptualized in the time line set forth below:

The dynamic relationship among these various provisions is explored in detail in the remaining materials in this chapter.

Disclosure Schedules.   Generally speaking, the representations will refer to information contained in other documents known as "disclosure schedules." For example, the terms of a particular representation will refer to patents owned by Target Co., but to determine exactly which patents Target owns, the reader must refer to a separate disclosure schedule that lists all of Target's patents. This schedule (listing all the patents) is then incorporated by reference into the terms of Target's representation and warranty. Through the use of these disclosure schedules, Bidder learns about Target's business and financial affairs. Often, these disclosures reveal information that results in the parties changing the terms of their business deal (and, consequently, the terms of their acquisition agreement) in order to reflect the impact of the information revealed during the course of the due diligence process.

Bring-Down.   Second, in the typical acquisition agreement, the representations and warranties will serve as the basis for a closing condition. Since Target's representations and warranties speak as of a particular moment in time—generally the date the acquisition agreement is signed—the parties will customarily include in their agreement a provision known as a "bring-down." The use of a bring-down provision reflects the inevitable delay that typically occurs between the date the parties sign the acquisition agreement and the date of closing on the agreement. In most cases, therefore, the buyer (Bidder Co.) will be allowed to test the accuracy of the representations made by the seller (Target Co. and/or its shareholders) at the time of *signing* the acquisition agreement, and again at the time of *closing.* If the conditions vary to some degree of *materiality,* this difference will operate to excuse Bidder from performance under the agreement and thereby relieve Bidder of the obligation to pay the purchase price.

This bring-down condition forms the basis for what is known as a "walkaway right." The degree of variance that will trigger Bidder's right to walk away from the deal is usually hotly negotiated by the parties. The terms of this variance are reflected in a clause typically referred to as the "material adverse change" clause (a MAC) or the "material adverse effect" clause (a MAE). The importance of materiality qualifiers is specifically addressed later in this chapter in connection with the *IBP* decision.

Basis for Indemnification. Finally, the last contractual purpose generally served by Target's representations and warranties is that these provisions usually provide the basis for Bidder's rights of indemnification *after* closing on the acquisition agreement. The typical agreement for the acquisition of a privately held company will provide that to the extent the representations and warranties were not accurate and the buyer (Bidder) suffers damages following closing as a result of these inaccuracies, Bidder will have a financial remedy based on the parties' contract. The scope and customary terms of Bidder's right of indemnification are described in more detail later in this chapter.

Once again, Target does not want to be financially responsible for just *any* amount (no matter how slight or trivial), so typically this post-closing right of indemnification will also include some form of materiality qualifier. To implement this qualification on the scope of indemnification, the parties will typically negotiate some form of dollar *basket* (or deductible) that must be satisfied before triggering rights of indemnification. The concept of *baskets* (and the related concept of *caps*) is discussed in more detail later in this chapter, as part of a more fulsome discussion of rights of indemnification.

b. Covenants

By contrast to representations and warranties, a *covenant* does not relate to a particular point in time. Rather, a covenant is the promise of a party to the agreement that relates to the future, obligating the party to do something (or a promise *not* to do something) during the time period between signing and closing on the agreement. As such, covenants typically deal with matters pending the closing on the parties' agreement and therefore usually expire at closing. In certain cases, though, the parties may specify in their agreement that a particular covenant will extend beyond closing on the acquisition. In the vernacular of the M&A lawyer, these provisions are said to "survive closing." A typical example would be Bidder's covenant to register stock that it is issuing to Target as part of the acquisition consideration. Another example would be Target's covenant to proceed with dissolution following closing on the sale of all of the company's assets to Bidder.

To illustrate the difference between a *representation* and a *covenant,* consider the treatment of Target's balance sheet under the terms of a typical acquisition agreement. In most cases, Target Co.'s last balance sheet will be prepared as of a date that *precedes* the date the parties sign the acquisition agreement. In this situation, Target will give Bidder a *representation* to the effect that, from the date that the balance sheet was prepared to the date that the agreement was signed, Target has not taken certain specific actions (most commonly, these would include paying dividends or making significant capital expenditures). Virtually the same terms will appear as a separate provision in the *covenants* portion of the parties' acquisition agreement, where they constitute seller's promise that Target will not pay a dividend or make a significant capital expenditure in the time period between the date the agreement is signed and the date of closing on the acquisition. *Query:* In considering the stock purchase agreement included in Appendix C, can you find any example(s) of representation(s) that are repeated as covenants in the parties' agreement?

Negative vs. Affirmative Covenants. The acquisition agreement will typically include both negative and affirmative covenants. The negative covenants restrict the party from taking certain actions, such as the prohibition (described above) against Target paying any dividends between signing and closing of the acquisition agreement. Very often, these negative covenants are phrased in terms of actions that cannot be taken "without the consent of the other party." In these cases, Target may be able to take a particular action—such as making an otherwise prohibited capital expenditure—prior to closing if Target can adequately justify the action and thereby obtain Bidder's consent to the expenditure. As another alternative, Target will often negotiate for a middle ground with respect to these negative covenants by phrasing the covenant in terms of actions that cannot be taken "without the consent of the other party, such consent not to be unreasonably withheld." Why does Target generally find this formulation of the covenant more appealing? Obviously, if Target knows, in advance of signing the acquisition agreement, that it plans to take a certain action *prior* to closing that would otherwise violate the terms of a particular covenant, Target should disclose its plans to Bidder and negotiate an exception to the covenant allowing Target to take such action. *Query:* In considering the terms of the Pfizer/Pharmacia merger agreement in Appendix B, can you find an example of a provision that allows Target to proceed with certain action(s) that would otherwise violate the terms of the parties' merger agreement?

Generally speaking, the burdens imposed by the covenants contained in the typical acquisition agreement will fall on the seller of the business, Target. Occasionally, covenants may impose obligations on Bidder, such as the obligation to list any shares that are to be issued as part of the acquisition consideration. In the usual case of the acquisition of a privately held Target by a large, publicly traded Bidder, it is highly unlikely that Bidder would consent to any type of negative covenant that restricts Bidder in the operation of its business during the time between signing and closing on the acquisition of Target.

c. Conditions to Closing

The *conditions* section of the parties' agreement creates obligations that must be satisfied by the parties at (or before) the closing on the acquisition. If these conditions are not satisfied, the deal will not close, and the parties can walk away from the transaction. As an example, a typical condition of Bidder's obligation to close on the acquisition and pay the purchase price is the receipt of certain written assurances from Target's auditors. If Target cannot satisfy this *condition* at (or before) the date set for closing, then Bidder can *walk away* from the deal without any recourse on the part of Target. As such, *conditions to closing* give rise to what M&A lawyers customarily refer to as *walk-away rights*.

Bring-Down Condition. Among the most important of the conditions to closing—one typically made a part of any acquisition agreement—is the provision that all representations and warranties made by the other party to the transaction will be true at the closing as if they had been made as of that date. This kind of provision is commonly referred to as the *bring-down condition*. This provision is typically included in order to allocate risks that something might happen in the time period between signing and closing that render the earlier representation untrue. In effect, by including a bring-down, the other side has contracted for the right to refuse to close on the deal. Since one side is usually not willing to let the other side off the hook for just a slight discrepancy in the terms of a representation included in the acquisition agreement, it is not uncommon for the parties to agree to qualify a condition to closing by the express use of a materiality standard. *Materiality qualifiers*—known as MACs and MAEs—are discussed in more detail later in this chapter in connection with the *IBP* decision.

3.　Closing: Post-Closing Covenants and Closing Documents

The acquisition agreement will usually contain a description of what happens at closing. This description will vary depending on deal structure (i.e., merger vs. asset purchase vs. stock purchase) and also will vary depending on the nature of the acquisition consideration. For example, in a stock purchase for cash, the stock purchase agreement would typically provide, at a minimum, that Target's shareholders deliver at closing duly endorsed certificates representing the shares to be transferred to Bidder. In exchange, Bidder typically would be required at closing to deliver a specified cash amount to the selling shareholders of Target, usually by way of a bank cashier's check, or perhaps by a wire transfer to certain bank accounts specified by the selling shareholders. This assumes an all-cash purchase price, and that all the conditions to closing have been satisfied so that the parties are obligated to perform under the terms of the acquisition agreement. *Query:* In the case of the stock purchase agreement in Appendix C, involving the acquisition of a privately held company (Trekker) by a publicly traded Bidder (Galaxy), what do the parties contemplate will happen at closing on their agreement?

In addition to the exchange of shares for cash described above, the parties' stock purchase agreement may list other documents that will be exchanged at closing. This obligation often leads to the practice of preparing a *closing checklist* of all the documents that must be prepared for delivery at closing. A representative form of a closing checklist—crafted for purposes of our planning problem involving Galaxy's acquisition of Trekker's business—is included as Appendix F. This checklist serves to illustrate once again the high transaction costs associated with transferring ownership of Target's business, a point originally made in the analysis of the problems in Chapter 2.

4.　A Mock Negotiation Over the Terms of Target's Representations and Warranties

Target's representations and warranties operate in two different time frames. First, they give *pre-closing* walk-away rights to Bidder. Second, they serve as the basis for Bidder's *post-closing* indemnification rights. This raises a predictable tension between the position of Bidder and that of Target during the course of negotiating and documenting the terms of the parties' representations and warranties.

Bidder typically seeks to maximize its protection by obtaining from Target a detailed set of representations and warranties that carefully describe Target's business so that Bidder actually gets the business that it thinks it is buying. Moreover, the level of detail Bidder seeks to obtain in these representations is designed to give Bidder comfort that, if there are *any* discrepancies, Bidder will have one of the two remedies just described: either pre-closing walk-away rights *or* post-closing indemnification rights. From Bidder's perspective, therefore, the goal in these negotiations over the terms of Target's representations is to describe as accurately as possible the business that Bidder is buying, including (but not limited to) the property rights that come with Target's business, the historical performance of Target's business operations, and, finally, that Target's business is free from claims of other third parties. In this way, Target's representations and warranties provide Bidder with assurance that it is getting what it agreed to pay for when the parties agreed to the purchase price that Bidder is to pay Target for its business. In addition, Bidder's negotiations seek assurance that Bidder will have an effective remedy—such as a mechanism to adjust the purchase price or to walk away from the deal—*if* the facts represented by Target should later turn out *not* to be true. In sum, the parties' negotiations over the scope of the representations and warranties to be included in their acquisition agreement serve to allocate financial risk between the seller, Target Co., and the buyer, Bidder Co.

Not surprisingly, Target's perspective in these negotiations is dramatically different from that of Bidder. As the seller of an ongoing business, Target is likely to take the position that it is selling the business as a going concern—that is, the business is being sold to Bidder as is, warts and all. Target is usually going to be willing to protect Bidder against fraud on the part of Target as well as against anything truly extraordinary that might arise between the time of signing and closing on the acquisition agreement. In the typical negotiation, therefore, Target will usually try to resist many of the detailed representations and warranties that Bidder is likely to demand that Target make.

And so the battle lines get drawn between the parties. Ultimately, where the line falls—in other words, just how much risk Bidder can require Target to absorb on a pre-closing and on a post-closing basis—will ultimately depend on the relative negotiating power of the two parties, which usually depends on which side wants to get the deal done the most.

In this section, I present a hypothetical negotiation between Bidder's lawyer and Target's lawyer that is designed to illustrate how this tension between Bidder and Target influences the negotiating process between the parties and their counsel.[3] Let us assume that the Bidder has presented a first draft of the

---

3. This section was inspired by various mock negotiation panels presented as part of several professional education programs that I have attended over the past few years. Most prominently, the continuing education programs sponsored by both Practicing Law Institute (PLI) and the American Bar Association (ABA) provided the basis for the description in the text of a hypothetical bargaining process between Bidder's counsel and Target's lawyer over the terms of just one aspect of the parties' acquisition agreement—the financial statements representation. *See, e.g., Acquiring or Selling Privately Held Company*, 1313 PLI/CORP (June 2002) (David W. Pollack & John F. Seegal, Chairs); and *Negotiating Business Acquisitions* (ABA-CLE Nov. 2003).

stock purchase agreement that includes the following financial statements representation:

§3.4 FINANCIAL STATEMENTS

Sellers have delivered to Buyer: (a) audited consolidated balance sheets of the Acquired Companies as at December 31 in each of the years 2001 through 2002, and the related consolidated statements of income, changes in stockholders' equity, and cash flow for each of the fiscal years then ended, (b) an audited consolidated balance sheet of the Acquired Companies as at December 31, 2003 (including the notes thereto, the "Balance Sheet"), and the related consolidated statements of income, changes in stockholders' equity, and cash flow for the fiscal year then ended, together with the report thereon of Ernst & Young, independent certified public accountants, and (c) an unaudited consolidated balance sheet of the Acquired Companies as at April 1, 2004 (the "Interim Balance Sheet") and the related unaudited consolidated statements of income, changes in stockholders' equity, and cash flow for the 3 months then ended, including in each case the notes thereto. Such financial statements and notes fairly present the financial condition and the results of operations, changes in stockholders' equity, and cash flow of the Acquired Companies as at the respective dates of and for the periods referred to in such financial statements, all in accordance with GAAP[, subject, in the case of interim financial statements, to normal recurring year-end adjustments (the effect of which will not, individually or in the aggregate, be materially adverse) and the absence of notes (that, if presented, would not differ materially from those included in the Balance Sheet)]; the financial statements referred to in this Section 3.4 reflect the consistent application of such accounting principles throughout the periods involved[, except as disclosed in the notes to such financial statements]. No financial statements of any Person other than the Acquired Companies are required by GAAP to be included in the consolidated financial statements of the company.[4]

Why include this particular representation? By including this representation, Bidder seeks Target's assurance as to the integrity of the company's consolidated financial statements. Accordingly, as part of this representation, Target confirms that its financial statements have been prepared in accordance with generally accepted accounting principles (GAAP), and that they fairly present the financial condition of Target and its results of operations. This representation will usually cover several years of audited financial statements (here, the years 2001-2003), including the most recently concluded fiscal year (2003), and will also typically cover Target's unaudited ("stub period") financial statements relating to some interim period following the end of the most recent fiscal year (here, the stub period is January 1 to April 1, 2004).

To understand why Bidders and Targets haggle so intensely over the terms of the representations and warranties sections of their agreements, consider

---

4. Section 3.4 of the MODEL STOCK PURCHASE AGREEMENT WITH COMMENTARY, prepared by the Committee on Negotiated Acquisitions of the American Bar Association's Business Law Section (1995). By way of general background, this ABA Model Agreement was deliberately drafted to reflect the form of agreement that Target's lawyer could typically expect to receive as Bidder's initial draft circulated for Target's lawyer to review and comment on.

whether Bidder would ever be willing to forego this type of representation regarding Target's financial statements and therefore agree to *eliminate* this representation *completely* from the terms of the parties' acquisition agreement. For example, Target might try to persuade Bidder that Bidder ought to be able to get the comfort it needs from Target's *audited* financial statements, as prepared by the company's outside, independent auditing firm, and thus dispense with the need for a separate representation from Target itself. Target will try to persuade Bidder that the truthfulness and completeness of Target's financial statements can be assured solely by relying on the accountant's/auditor's certification; that is, by relying on the auditor's opinion with respect to its audit of Target's financials (and for the sake of argument here, we will further assume that the auditing firm was one of the remaining Big Four firms (here, Ernst & Young) and that the auditor issued an unqualified ("clean") opinion on Target's audited financials).

In the face of this kind of argument, one can expect Bidder's counsel to flat out reject Target's request to completely eliminate the financial statement representation based on two different, albeit related, reasons. It bears emphasizing that from Bidder's perspective, this representation serves two purposes. This representation forms the basis for Bidder's financial protection *and* its walk-away rights if Target's statements prove inaccurate.[5] In light of these purposes, Bidder can be expected to argue that the auditor's certification of Target's financials does *not* provide Bidder with sufficient comfort. Why not? Because if Bidder were to rely *only* on the auditor's opinion, Bidder would fail to obtain any walk-away right if Bidder should learn—before closing—that Target's audited financials are wrong. If Target makes *no* representation in the stock purchase agreement as to the accuracy of its own audited financials—because it has convinced Bidder to rely solely on the auditor's certification—then there will be no condition to closing that allows Bidder the right to walk away from the deal at closing if Bidder learned that Target's audited financials are inaccurate. In other words, if Bidder is persuaded to accept the audited financials in lieu of a representation from Target itself, then Bidder will deprive itself of the ability to test the accuracy of this representation by relying on it as a condition to closing. In effect, Bidder would eliminate a potential basis for a right to walk away from the deal. In such a case, the only basis that Bidder might have to refuse to close and thereby walk away from the deal would be some sort of fraud claim, rather than a contractual right to walk away from the deal. Generally speaking, fraud is very tough to establish, and thus Bidder is likely to view the contractual remedy as a far more attractive alternative.

The other reason we can expect Bidder to flat out refuse any request to eliminate the financial statement covenant is that, in fact, Bidder *wants* to impose a measure of responsibility and accountability on Target itself, even as

---

5. Indeed, as we have previously mentioned in this chapter, the influence of the twofold purposes for these representations and warranties will guide and dominate Bidder's thinking and decision making throughout the parties' negotiation as to specific terms of the parties' representations and warranties. As such, this influence is not limited to the context of the parties' negotiations for the terms of the financial statement representations.

to its *audited* financial statements. Realizing the limitations inherent in the audit process, Bidder's counsel will be quick to point out that the auditor's certification is *not* a guarantee of the accuracy of Target's audited financial statements. Rather, this opinion is simply the auditor's representation—based on its auditing (i.e., accepted testing) procedures and applying GAAP—that these financial statements fairly represent Target's business. However, as the now infamous financial scandals at Adelphia, WorldCom, Tyco, and other companies more than amply demonstrate, the auditor's opinion may be *wrong* even though the auditor may have done nothing wrong during the course of its audit. Rather, the insiders may have "cooked the books"—committed financial fraud—so cleverly that the auditors failed to detect it during the course of their audit of Target. In this extreme case, where Target's financial statements are the product of management's fraud, an auditor would not catch the fraud since generally accepted auditing standards (GAAS) are not designed to detect fraud.

Moreover, in these situations involving financial fraud, there generally would be no basis for Bidder to claim malpractice (professional negligence) against the accounting firm. It is entirely possible that the audit firm could completely fail to detect the fraud and still have conducted the audit nonnegligently by strictly following GAAS. Conversely, in those (rather infrequent) cases involving some factual basis for a claim of professional negligence against the auditor, the ability of Bidder to bring this malpractice claim is often hampered in many jurisdictions by privity requirements imposed by local law. These privity requirements limit the ability of a third party (such as Bidder) to bring a cause of action against the auditor based on a defective audit report of Target, a client of the audit firm. In the absence of privity between Bidder and Target's audit firm, Bidder generally will have no claim for negligence against the audit firm. Consequently, Bidder will generally be left with only a fraud claim, a much harder case for Bidder to prevail on (as we all know well from our first-year torts class).

In negotiating with Target's lawyer over whether to exclude any form of financial statement representation, Bidder's lawyer can be expected to engage in this type of reasoning process to conclude that it is not in Bidder's best interests to exclude a financial statement representation from Target itself.[6] As a result, with respect to negotiating whether to omit any form of a financial statement covenant from their agreement, this issue is most likely to be resolved in favor of Bidder as Bidder is likely to have the more persuasive argument on this point.

Deciding Which Issues* Not *to Negotiate Over.   In the "give and take" inherent in negotiating an acquisition, many Targets will decide *not* to spend any

---

6. This summary of the respective positions of Bidder Co. and Target Co. in negotiating the exclusion of the financial statement representation only serves to illustrate the tension inherent in virtually all aspects of the parties' negotiations over the terms of the acquisition agreement. The acquisition agreement, the initial draft of which is customarily prepared by Bidder's counsel, will quite predictably contain the usual provisions, all of which are drafted in terms designed to give as much protection as possible to Bidder. Just as predictably, counsel for Target can be expected to object to the breadth of these provisions—and thus the negotiations begin.

time trying to negotiate this financial covenant out of the parties' agreement. Recognizing that it would take considerable effort to convince Bidder to omit a financial statement representation *entirely,* why is the prudent Target (and its lawyer) likely to decide *not* to expend any such effort to negotiate this covenant out of the agreement? As a practical matter, Target's lawyer is likely to advise his/her client that the very act of trying to disassociate Target and its management from their own audited financial statements would cause such apprehension and nervousness on the part of Bidder (and its lawyer) that the whole effort may ultimately backfire and jeopardize the entire deal. What is the moral of the story? As a negotiating strategy, Bidders and Targets are often well advised *not* to negotiate over every point that the parties could potentially argue about.

Assuming that Bidder has carried the day on this issue, the parties will turn their attention to haggling over the specific terms of the Target's financial statement representation and warranty ("rep"). The next section of this hypothetical bargaining process addresses the tension that inevitably results as Target's lawyer seeks to limit the scope of the representation demanded by Bidder in the first draft of the acquisition agreement. Target's lawyer can be expected to resist the terms of Bidder's formulation of the financial statement covenant for two principal reasons: first, to curtail the availability of a walk-away right for Bidder at closing; and second, to limit the scope of Bidder's financial remedy on a post-closing basis. In the process of negotiating the terms of the financial statement representation, the general goal of Target's lawyer is to minimize the chance that the deal will "fall out of bed" (fail to close) or otherwise deprive Target of the benefit of the bargain (payment of the full purchase price) that it made with Bidder.

Now that we have concluded that the financial statement covenant will cover *both* audited and unaudited financial statements of Target, let us consider how the negotiations between Bidder and Target might play themselves out as to the specific terms of this representation. The language of the financial statement covenant is typically tied into GAAP, although Bidder may insist on other language. For example, Bidder's first draft of the acquisition agreement may request that Target represent that its "financial statements are true, correct, and complete." How is Target's lawyer likely to respond to this language? Target will probably strongly object to this formulation because, from Target's perspective, the financial statement representation is an essential building block of the parties' acquisition agreement. Many other provisions of the acquisition agreement are keyed to the terms of this financial statement representation. Consequently, the terms of this representation are likely to be quite important to Target as the lawyer for Target anticipates further negotiating difficulties down the road in negotiating the terms of *other* representations and warranties in the agreement.[7]

---

7. As a matter of negotiating strategy, it is worth pointing out that it is vitally important for the lawyer to thoroughly understand the terms of the acquisition agreement, and further, to understand how the various provisions work together. In this way, the lawyer can prioritize with the client which terms are most important to the client. Understanding the client's business objectives in doing the deal allows the lawyer to, in effect, horse-trade with opposing counsel. In other words, the lawyer may concede less important points in order to best preserve Target's bargaining position on those points that are of greater importance to Target's lawyer and business client.

Target, therefore, is likely to respond that the GAAP standard, used to prepare the company's audited financials, is fundamentally inconsistent with a representation that Target's financials are "true, correct, and complete." At this point, Target's counsel may point out that the GAAP standard has many instances requiring the auditor's exercise of professional judgment to make estimates *or* to determine if a standard of materiality has been triggered. Target is likely to contend that these kinds of professional judgments are fundamentally at odds with Target making a representation as to 100 percent accuracy and completeness of its financial statements. Although Bidder often seeks this type of financial statement representation by including it in the first draft of the acquisition agreement, Bidder is likely to be persuaded by Target's reasoning and thus will usually settle for a financial statement covenant that is tied to compliance with GAAP.

The Impact of Sarbanes-Oxley Reforms on Negotiations for Financial Statement Covenant. All of this raises the basic question: is there any danger to Bidder in agreeing to eliminate this more aggressive form of financial statement covenant from the acquisition agreement? In the future, we may see Bidders increasingly insist on this more aggressive formulation of the financial statement covenant in order to ensure that Target's financial statements do not contain any surprises giving rise to problems for Bidder (on a post-acquisition basis) in its efforts to comply with the requirements of the Sarbanes-Oxley Act ("SOX"). Specifically, SOX requires the managers of a publicly traded company to certify that the company's financial statements are a fair representation of the company and its financial affairs. Since Bidder must start making these representations as to Target's business once the acquisition is completed (at least where Bidder is publicly traded), Bidder will naturally worry about the integrity of Target's financial statements. M&A lawyers increasingly report that Bidders are insisting on a financial statement covenant more congruent with the language of the certification that Bidder's officers are required to use under the terms of SOX. If Bidder makes this argument to convince Target to accept the more aggressive form of financial statement representation proposed by the Bidder, Target is likely to respond that SOX compliance is not Target's problem since Target is privately held. Indeed, Target may claim that avoiding this type of SOX-related issue is one of the main reasons that Target decided to sell the business rather than do an initial public offering (IPO), which would force the company to comply with all of the many detailed requirements imposed by SOX (including the mandatory officer certification requirements). Moreover, Target will likely suggest that the purchase price that it agreed to accept from Bidder has already been discounted to reflect that Target is avoiding the costs associated with doing an IPO and complying with SOX.

Introduction of a "Materiality Qualifier." Assuming the parties agree to use a GAAP-based financial statement representation (of the type quoted above—as taken from §3.4 of the ABA's Model Stock Purchase Agreement), Target's lawyer is likely to object to the breadth of this representation unless it is modified to include a provision known as a "materiality qualifier." Target is likely to insist that the financial statement covenant be modified to read that the company's "financial statements fairly present in all *material* respects the financial condition of Target and its results from operation." Target will point out that this language is entirely consistent with the language used in the opinion letter of the company's auditor, which typically reads: "In our [the auditor's] opinion, the [audited] financial statements fairly present, in all *material* respects, the financial condition of Target."[8]

When faced with this kind of requested limitation, Bidder's counsel is likely to object on the grounds that, by including a materiality qualifier in the representation itself, Target is in effect including a *double* materiality qualifier. The basis for this argument is that GAAP's provisions already include a materiality standard that requires the auditor to make certain judgment calls or estimates based on a standard of materiality. By including a separate materiality qualifier in the language of Target's financial statement representation, Target is further limiting the scope of the protection offered to Bidder by this representation. In essence, Bidder claims that Target is "double-dipping" on the materiality qualifier. From Bidder's perspective, the language of this representation is designed to allocate risk between Bidder and Target, and this qualifying language is objectionable because it requires Bidder to absorb more than a "material" measure of financial risk.

A reasonable response by Target's counsel is to agree with Bidder's lawyer that a materiality qualifier may be inappropriate as to the company's *audited* financials but that the materiality qualifier should be left in the representation as to the company's interim, *unaudited* ("stub") financials. Target's lawyer will likely point out that the unaudited, interim financials are not likely to fully comply with GAAP, so a materiality qualifier is appropriate (i.e., as modified, there is no concern of double-dipping on the part of Target). Bidder's lawyer is likely to object on the grounds that Target's concern (regarding the use of *unaudited* interim financial statements) has already been addressed through other provisions in the agreement. For example, Bidder will point out that it has already agreed to several exceptions to GAAP in the preparation of Target's interim financial statements by agreeing, among other things, to the omission of footnotes and normal year-end adjustments. From Bidder's perspective, these accommodations should adequately address Target's concerns and therefore eliminate the need for any further qualification to the terms of this representation. Thus, Bidder is likely to object strongly to using a materiality standard to qualify the terms of Target's representation as to its *interim* financials.

Although superficially appealing, Target may dig a little deeper into these exceptions that Bidder has proposed in order to further explicate the nature of Target's concerns if the materiality qualifier is omitted with respect to its unaudited ("stub") financials. For example, the terms of one of the exceptions that Bidder has just pointed to as an accommodation to Target reads:

> The footnotes to Target Co.'s financial statements [which are to be omitted with respect to Target's stub financials] if presented, would not differ materially from the footnotes presented in the last audited financial statements of Target Co.

---

8. In order to help clarify the dynamic of this negotiation, in most cases today, the auditor's opinion letter will expressly include a "materiality" qualification. This practice is being adopted so that the auditor's opinion letter better reflects the fact that auditing is not a science of precise measurement, but rather an exercise in professional judgment by the outside auditor.

However, it is often the case that considerable time has elapsed since the date of the Target's last audited financials; consequently, Target is likely to contend that it is quite possible that the footnotes *will differ* considerably from the footnotes that were part of Target's last audited financials. To address this concern, Target is likely to insist that the financial statement covenant be modified to read: "The adjustments to Target's unaudited financials will not individually or in the aggregate be materially adverse." In other words, Target Co. continues to propose using a materiality qualifier to ameliorate its concern over the scope of its representation as to its interim (stub) financials. Why? Target may be concerned about the post-closing risk that Bidder will manipulate the numbers in an opportunistic manner. In other words, Target will point out that Bidder will be responsible for preparing the next set of year-end financial statements for Target's business. Thus, Bidder will decide the footnotes to be made part of the year-end audited financials for Target's business. Target will point out that GAAP is *not* a precise science but rather requires many judgment calls in preparing the company's audited financials, all of which inevitably results in considerable elasticity in reporting the numbers in the company's year-end financials. Unless the limiting language that Target proposes is made part of the terms of Target's representation, then Target will argue that Bidder is left in the enviable position of being able to make year-end adjustments in an opportunistic manner—which works to Bidder's financial advantage and to Target's financial detriment. Consequently, Target's lawyer is likely to insist on this modification to the financial statement covenant, at least with respect to the company's interim (unaudited) financials in order to adequately protect Target's financial interest in getting a fair price for its business. Target's lawyer will also point out that Target's interim unaudited financials may not comply with GAAP in a number of other respects, all of which are unknowable without an audit and which therefore cannot be anticipated at the time of signing and closing on the parties' agreement. Without a materiality qualifier to address the uncertainty inherent in stub financials, Target is likely to insist on obtaining an audit prior to closing to remove this uncertainty, which will delay the closing and incur additional expense to get the deal done.

Bidder's counsel is likely to respond that Target's concern regarding year-end adjustments is a red herring. By insisting on a financial statement representation that omits any materiality qualifier, Bidder merely wants assurance that Target's interim numbers are accurate—subject, of course, to normal year-end GAAP adjustments. This means that if Bidder, in connection with its preparation of audited financials for Target's business on a post-closing basis, proposes to make a year-end adjustment that is *not* normal (or alternatively, *refuses* to make an adjustment that *is* normal), then Target has no grounds for concern under the terms of the representation as Bidder originally drafted it (i.e., without a materiality qualifier). In sum, Bidder is merely asking that Target examine its interim financials to determine the extent to which they are not prepared in accordance with GAAP and provide this information to Bidder by way of a disclosure letter. Bidder is likely to insist that it needs to analyze this information thoroughly in order to be sure that Bidder understands Target's financial statements and thus fully understands exactly what Bidder is buying. Even though they are not audited, these interim financial statements are of crucial importance to Bidder since they reflect the *current* state of affairs as to

Target's business. Not surprisingly, Target's stub financials are likely to be an important factor to Bidder in determining the price that it is willing to pay for Target's business. Seen from this perspective, it is likely that Bidder will insist that Target provide a form of financial statement representation that omits *any* use of a materiality qualifier.

And so the negotiations will continue. This kind of back-and-forth between the lawyers for Target and Bidder will persist until they reach some acceptable solution regarding specific terms of the financial statement representation. What form that solution will take depends on many factors, not the least of which is the relative bargaining strength of the parties. This will generally be a function of which party (Bidder or Target) wants (or needs) to get the deal done the most.

In the end, Target will likely provide Bidder with a fairly comprehensive set of representations as to Target's financial statements, both audited and unaudited. The reason for this result is that, from Bidder's perspective, the uncertainty that results if it *cannot* obtain this representation from Target means that Bidder will be required to absorb too great a risk as to the true state of financial affairs currently existing in Target's business. Indeed, Bidder is likely to view Target's unwillingness to provide a fairly comprehensive representation as a red flag that trouble lies ahead. At this point, negotiations over the terms of the all-important financial statement representation may become a "deal-breaker." Unless Target concedes and gives Bidder the scope of protection that Bidder demands, then Bidder is likely to refuse to do the deal (i.e., Bidder is likely to refuse to sign the acquisition agreement because it does not afford Bidder the comfort it needs as to the true state of Target's financial affairs and therefore the deal presents too great a financial risk to Bidder).

Horse Trading Between Bidder and Target.   As part of its willingness to acquiesce to Bidder's demand for a comprehensive financial statement representation, Target's lawyer may then seek to "horse-trade" with Bidder for concessions on the terms of other representations (or, perhaps, the indemnity provisions) contained in the acquisition agreement.[9]

---

9. In order for the lawyer to function as an effective negotiator and obtain the best result for his/her business client, it is obvious that the lawyer must understand the client's business objectives and the terms that are most important to the client. In addition, the lawyer must be thoroughly familiar with the terms of the document and understand how the acquisition agreement is put together as an organic whole. Only by thoroughly preparing in this way will the lawyer be able to identify and anticipate those issues that are likely to be the points of serious contention between the parties. The lawyer, together with his/her business client, can then prioritize these items of potential disagreement so that the lawyer is prepared to deal with them appropriately as they arise during the course of the parties' negotiations. *See generally,* James C. Freund, ANATOMY OF A MERGER: STRATEGIES AND TECHNIQUES FOR NEGOTIATING CORPORATE ACQUISITIONS (Law Journal Seminars-Press 1975); Robert Mnookin, et al., BEYOND WINNING: NEGOTIATING TO CREATE VALUE IN DEALS AND DISPUTES (Harvard University Press 2000); Roger Fisher, William Ury, and Bruce Patton, GETTING TO YES: NEGOTIATING AGREEMENT WITHOUT GIVING IN (Houghton Mifflin Company 1991).

As an example of the kind of horse trading that may result (and which can only be done effectively if the lawyer is adequately informed as to the client's priorities), let us assume that Target is prepared to provide Bidder with a comprehensive representation of its financial statements, in the form originally demanded by Bidder. Target may then try to use this concession as a bargaining chip to get Bidder to compromise on the terms of some other representation in the agreement, such as the provision regarding specific line items of Target's financial statements. For example, Target may seek to limit the scope of the representation regarding its accounts receivable (§3.8 of ABA's Model Stock Purchase Agreement) or its inventory (§3.9 of ABA Agreement).

Regarding these specific line items of Target's balance sheet (e.g., inventory and accounts receivable), Target is likely to object to these provisions on the grounds that these additional representations are essentially redundant to the financial statement covenant that has already been agreed to by the parties and pursuant to which Target has already represented that its balance sheet is accurate. Under the terms of the fairly comprehensive financial statement representation (and the accompanying *bring-down* provision),[10] Target will argue that it has, in effect, already agreed to make an adjustment in the purchase price to reflect any changes in value of the business. In other words, Target has already agreed to make any necessary adjustments to the shareholders' equity (as reflected on the company's balance sheet) to address anything that may arise in the interim between signing and closing on the acquisition agreement. By virtue of agreeing to the terms that Bidder originally sought as part of the financial statement representation, Target has already agreed to take into account (on its balance sheet) any adjustments that may be required due to changes in its inventory or its accounts receivable that may arise after signing the agreement but before closing. Therefore, Target's lawyer is likely to regard Bidder's demand for separate representations as to certain line items of Target's balance sheet as onerous (and inappropriate) and thus unfair to Target because of the protection that Bidder has already been granted by the terms of Target's financial statement representation that the parties just finished negotiating, which now covers *both* audited and unaudited (interim) financials of Target. Given the scope of the financial statement representation that Target has already agreed to include in the agreement, coupled with the customary use of a bring-down condition, Target is likely to claim that Bidder is adequately protected.

Bidder, on the other hand, may argue that these supplemental line-item representations are not superfluous. Rather, they are geared specifically toward certain attributes of Target's business that are of particular concern to Bidder. As such, they are intended to give Bidder a clearer understanding of the financial condition of Target's business in areas that Bidder deems important, such as inventory levels or collectability of accounts receivable. From a due diligence

---

10. In connection with the terms of the financial statement representation just negotiated, it would be entirely appropriate for Bidder to insist on a bring-down of this representation as a condition to closing. Thus, in this context, use of a bring-down condition (of the type described earlier in this chapter, see *supra*, at page 347) would be a customary term included in the conditions section of the parties' acquisition agreement.

perspective, Bidder may have legitimate business reasons for demanding certain line-item representations in order to give Bidder the comfort it needs over and above that provided by Target's balance sheet (financial statements) prepared in accordance with GAAP. In these areas, Bidder may seek the additional comfort it needs as a business matter by demanding specific representations from Target as to certain line-items of its balance sheet.

Target may try to avoid including these line-item representations in the acquisition agreement by arguing that Target's obligation is to deliver to Bidder at closing a company that has a certain financial condition as a whole. As such, Target did not contemplate that it would have to take on the burden of digging into all this minutiae as part of the deal it made with Bidder. By insisting on these specific line-item representations, Bidder is forcing Target to go far beyond what is required by GAAP because these line-item representations are in effect allocating (certain economic) risks to Target that are inappropriate. For example, by including a line-item representation as to Target's accounts receivable, Bidder is in effect allocating the risk of the collectability of the company's accounts receivable to the sellers of Target. From Target's perspective, this is tantamount to asking it to guarantee the collection of the company's accounts receivable. In many cases, that is simply going to be a business risk that Target's sellers will be unwilling to take on, believing that this is a risk inherent in operating Target's business and as such goes with the business.

NOTE

Impact of Sarbanes-Oxley Act on Acquisition Negotiations.   In July 2002, Congress enacted the Sarbanes-Oxley Act (SOX), legislating a far-reaching set of reforms addressing the boardroom practices of directors of publicly traded companies, as well as their senior executive officers, lawyers, auditors, and other financial advisors. While the impact of these federal reform measures is most pronounced in the case of publicly traded corporations, SOX is also having an impact on acquisitions in the M&A market for private companies, such as the kind of deal involved in the hypothetical bargaining described above (between lawyers negotiating the terms of the financial statement covenant to be given by a closely held Target Co. to a publicly traded Bidder Co.). As such, the impact of SOX is being felt beyond the context of public company M&A transactions.

From Bidder's perspective, it is likely that the financial results of Target's business will have to be made part of Bidder's financial statements and thus subject to the requirements of SOX (such as the officer and director certifications required by §303 of SOX) after Bidder closes on the acquisition. Moreover, in the wake of recent financial scandals, the current business climate leads to a great deal of skepticism about accepting financial statements at face value and relying on them without any further inquiry or probing and without the benefit of any additional contractual protections. Many Bidders are simply not willing in today's environment to accept Target's proffer of its financial statements, even though they have been audited by one of the reputable Big Four audit firms. Faced with such a proffer, most Bidders respond by simply rejecting such a proposal and point to WorldCom, Enron, Tyco, and other high-profile financial/accounting scandals as the basis for its rejection.

5. Use of Materiality Qualifier — Herein of MACs and MAEs

To illustrate the use of a *materiality qualifier,* consider the typical provision in Bidder's original draft of the acquisition agreement calling for Target to represent that its business is in compliance with *all laws.* Target is likely to insist that this representation be qualified to limit its scope to refer to *material compliance with all laws.* In this way, Target is informing Bidder that its business is generally in compliance with all laws, without going so far as to represent that it is in 100 percent compliance with *every* provision of federal, state, and local law. Alternatively, the materiality qualifier might be framed slightly differently to provide that Target's business is in *compliance with all material laws.* When the representation is framed in this way, Target is essentially representing that out of the whole universe of laws that might apply to Target's business and focusing only on those that are most relevant to Target's business, Target represents that it is in compliance with all of those laws that really affect the company's business in a meaningful way.

To further illustrate how this materiality qualifier can be used to tailor the scope of Target's representation, consider yet another alternative — a third formulation of the materiality qualifier in the context of this same representation. Target could insist that this representation be framed to read that the company is in *compliance with all laws except as to those laws where the failure to comply would not materially and adversely affect the company's business.* Many M&A lawyers prefer this third formulation of the materiality qualifier. Why? In what way does this provision differ from the prior two formulations of the materiality qualifier? Why is this third alternative an improvement over the other two? In thinking about this question, consider the scope of the representation that Target is making to Bidder under this third formulation of the materiality qualifier.

These different formulations of the materiality qualifier in the context of this particular representation reflect yet another important point about the process of negotiating the terms of the representations to be included in any acquisition agreement. As part of the bargaining process, it is important that the lawyers fully understand the business terms of the parties' deal. In that way, the lawyer for each side will be well informed as to which formulation of the materiality qualifier will be most appropriate for use in the context of that particular transaction.

This point was made in dramatic fashion in a well-known, high-profile M&A case that required the court to construe the use of a *materiality qualifier* as part of a particular representation contained in the parties' acquisition agreement:

In re IBP, Inc. Shareholders Litigation
IBP, Inc. v. Tyson Foods, Inc.
789 A.2d 14 (Del. Ch. 2001)

STRINE, Vice Chancellor.

This post-trial opinion addresses a demand for specific performance of a "Merger Agreement" by IBP, Inc., the nation's number one beef and number two pork distributor. By this action, IBP seeks to compel the "Merger" between itself and Tyson Foods, Inc., the nation's leading chicken distributor, in a trans-action in which IBP stockholders will receive their choice of $30 a share in cash or Tyson stock, or a combination of the two.

The IBP-Tyson Merger Agreement resulted from a vigorous auction pro-cess that pitted Tyson against the nation's number one pork producer, Smith-field Foods. To say that Tyson was eager to win the auction is to slight its ardent desire to possess IBP. During the bidding process, Tyson was anxious to ensure that it would acquire IBP, and to make sure Smithfield did not. By succeed-ing, Tyson hoped to create the world's preeminent meat products company — a company that would dominate the meat cases of supermarkets in the United States and eventually throughout the globe.

During the auction process, Tyson was given a great deal of information that suggested that IBP was heading into a trough in the beef business. Even more, Tyson was alerted to serious problems at an IBP subsidiary, DFG, which had been victimized by accounting fraud to the tune of over $30 million in charges to earnings and which was the active subject of an asset impairment study. Not only that, Tyson knew that IBP was projected to fall seriously short of the fiscal year 2000 earnings predicted in projections prepared by IBP's Chief Financial Officer in August, 2000.

By the end of the auction process, Tyson had come to have great doubts about IBP's ability to project its future earnings, the credibility of IBP's man-agement, and thought that the important business unit in which DFG was located — Foodbrands — was broken.

Yet, Tyson's ardor for IBP was such that Tyson raised its bid by a total of $4.00 a share after learning of these problems. Tyson also signed the Merger Agreement, which permitted IBP to recognize unlimited additional liabilities on account of the accounting improprieties at DFG. It did so without demand-ing any representation that IBP meet its projections for future earnings, or any escrow tied to those projections.

After the Merger Agreement was signed on January 1, 2001, Tyson trum-peted the value of the merger to its stockholders and the financial commu-nity, and indicated that it was fully aware of the risks that attended the cyclical nature of IBP's business. In early January, Tyson's stockholders ratified the merger agreement and authorized its management to take whatever action was needed to effectuate it.

During the winter and spring of 2001, Tyson's own business performance was dismal. Meanwhile, IBP was struggling through a poor first quarter. Both companies' problems were due in large measure to a severe winter, which adversely affected livestock supplies and vitality. As these struggles deepened, Tyson's desire to buy IBP weakened.

This cooling of affections first resulted in a slow-down by Tyson in the pro-cess of consummating a transaction, a slow-down that was attributed to IBP's on-going efforts to resolve issues that had been raised about its financial state-ments by the Securities and Exchange Commission ("SEC"). The most impor-tant of these issues was how to report the problems at DFG, which Tyson had been aware of at the time it signed the Merger Agreement. Indeed, all the key issues that the SEC raised with IBP were known by Tyson at the time it signed the Merger Agreement. The SEC first raised these issues in a faxed letter on December 29, 2000 to IBP's outside counsel. Neither IBP management nor

Tyson learned of the letter until the second week of January, 2001. After learning of the letter, Tyson management put the Merger Agreement to a successful board and stockholder vote.

But the most important reason that Tyson slowed down the Merger process was different: it was having buyer's regret. Tyson wished it had paid less especially in view of its own compromised 2001 performance and IBP's slow 2001 results.

By March, Tyson's founder and controlling stockholder, Don Tyson, no longer wanted to go through with the Merger Agreement. He made the decision to abandon the Merger. His son, John Tyson, Tyson's Chief Executive Officer, and the other Tyson managers followed his instructions. Don Tyson abandoned the Merger because of IBP's and Tyson's poor results in 2001, and not because of DFG or the SEC issues IBP was dealing with. Indeed, Don Tyson told IBP management that he would blow DFG up if he were them.

After the business decision was made to terminate, Tyson's legal team swung into action. They fired off a letter terminating the Agreement at the same time as they filed suit accusing IBP of fraudulently inducing the Merger that Tyson had once so desperately desired.

This expedited litigation ensued, which involved massive amounts of discovery and two weeks of trial.

In this opinion, I address IBP's claim that Tyson had no legal basis to avoid its obligation to consummate the Merger Agreement, as well as Tyson's contrary arguments. The parties' extensive claims are too numerous to summarize adequately, as are the court's rulings.

At bottom, however, I conclude as follows:

- The Merger Agreement and related contracts were valid and enforceable contracts that were not induced by any material misrepresentation or omission;
- The Merger Agreement specifically allocated certain risks to Tyson, including the risk of any losses or financial effects from the accounting improprieties at DFG, and these risks cannot serve as a basis for Tyson to terminate the Agreement;
- None of the non-DFG related issues that the SEC raised constitute a contractually permissible basis for Tyson to walk away from the Merger;
- IBP has not suffered a Material Adverse Effect within the meaning of the Agreement that excused Tyson's failure to close the Merger; and
- Specific performance is the decisively preferable remedy for Tyson's breach, as it is the only method by which to adequately redress the harm threatened to IBP and its stockholders.

I.   FACTUAL BACKGROUND

IBP's KEY MANAGERS

IBP was first incorporated in 1960. Its current Chairman of the Board and Chief Executive Officer, Robert Peterson, has been with the company from the beginning. . . .

Peterson is a strong and committed CEO, who loves the business he has helped build and the people who work for it. By the late 1990s, however,

Peterson was in his late sixties and cognizant that it would soon be time to turn the reins over to a new CEO. Peterson's heir apparent was IBP's President and Chief Operating Officer, Richard "Dick" Bond. . . .

IBP'S BUSINESS

The traditional business of IBP is being a meat processor that acts as the middleman between ranchers and retail supermarkets and food processors. This is the so-called "fresh meats" business of IBP. . . .

. . . IBP was endeavoring to build up its food processing businesses. These are the businesses that take raw food products and turn them into something canned or packaged for supermarket or restaurant sale. Because these processing activities "add value," they tend to have higher profit margins and generate more stable earnings than middleman meat slaughtering.

To carry out this strategy, IBP had recently made a series of acquisitions, including the purchase of Corporate Food Brands America, Inc. ("CFBA") in February 2000. These purchased entities were being put together within IBP under the larger heading of Foodbrands. . . .

IBP hoped that these processed food investments would provide a vehicle for growth and reduce the year-to-year volatility of IBP's earnings. . . .

Moreover, while Foodbrands was a central part of IBP's strategy for the future, it remained at that time a much smaller contributor to the bottom line than IBP's' fresh meats business. . . . Thus, while Foodbrands had a higher profit margin, fresh meats remained by far the most substantial part of IBP's business.

IBP MANAGEMENT PROPOSES AN LBO

During 1999 and early 2000, IBP's management was frustrated by the stock market's valuation of the company's stock. As earnings-less dot.coms traded at huge multiples to eyeball hits, IBP's stock traded at a relatively small multiple to actual earnings. In response to this problem, Peterson, Bond, and [Larry] Shipley [IBP's chief financial officer] were receptive when the investment bank of Donaldson, Lufkin & Jenrette, Inc. ("DLJ") expressed interest in a leveraged-buyout ("LBO") of the company.

In July, management informed the IBP board that it would like to pursue an LBO seriously. With the help of DLJ, a syndicate of investors who called themselves "Rawhide" was prepared to take the company private if a deal could be negotiated with the IBP board. The board formed a special committee comprised of outside directors, who then selected Wachtell, Lipton, Rosen, & Katz as its legal advisor and J.P. Morgan Securities, Inc. as its financial advisor. . . .

THE IBP BOARD ACCEPTS A BID FROM THE RAWHIDE GROUP

After several months of negotiations, the Rawhide Group and the special committee struck a deal on October 1, 2000 whereby the Rawhide Group would purchase all of IBP's shares at $22.25 per IBP share. . . .

The Rawhide deal was publicly announced the next day. By this time, rumors had been circulating within the financial community about the possibility of such a deal.

The announcement of the transaction inspired class action lawsuits in this court, alleging that the transaction was unfair. . . .

PROBLEMS AT DFG FOODS BEGIN TO SURFACE

In 1998, as part of its strategy to grow IBP's higher-margin food processing business, IBP management purchased a specialty hors d'oeuvres, kosher foods, and "airline food" business for $91 million, including assumed debt. IBP bought this business from its managers, including its President, Andrew Zahn. Within IBP, the business became known as DFG Foods, Inc. or "DFG." In late 1999, IBP purchased a competitor of DFG named Wilton Foods, and combined its operations with DFG. Zahn stayed on board after the purchase of DFG and continued to run the business, with a right to certain earn-out payments upon his departure that were tied to the unit's performance.

Although IBP hoped that DFG would become a useful part of its overall strategy to move into higher-margin businesses, as of the year 2000, DFG was an insignificant portion of IBP's overall business. . . .

On September 30, 2000, Andrew Zahn left DFG and took a sizable earn-out payment with him. On October 16, 2000, IBP issued a press release announcing earnings for the third quarter of FY 2000 of $83.9 million and year-to-date earnings of $203 million. Soon after this announcement, Dick Bond learned that there were problems with the integrity of DFG's books and records, and that it was possible that DFG's inventory value was overstated. . . .

When IBP top management learned of the problems at DFG, a full inventory audit was ordered. The audit concluded that DFG's inventory was overvalued by $9 million. On November 7, 2000, IBP therefore announced that it would take a $9 million reduction over pre-tax earnings from the amounts previously reported for third quarter of FY 2000. These amounts were reported to the SEC in IBP's third quarter 10-Q. As of that time, Peterson and Bond were led to believe that the $9 million overstatement was the extent of the problem at DFG, although efforts to get control of DFG's financials continued.

THE AUCTION FOR IBP BEGINS

The rumors about IBP's possible sale had not gone unnoticed among meat industry leaders. Two industry participants had toyed with the idea of making a play for IBP for years.

One was Smithfield Foods, the nation's number one pork processing firm. When combined with IBP, Smithfield would be the number one producer of beef and pork products. The strength of the Smithfield-IBP combination was also its weakness. Because of IBP's own strength in pork, anti-trust and political concerns were bound to be raised about a merger. Nonetheless, those concerns did not impede Smithfield from making an unsolicited bid for IBP on November 12, 2000. The Smithfield bid offered $25 in Smithfield stock for each share of IBP stock. This was not the best of news for IBP management, whose relationship with Smithfield management was not warm.

Meanwhile, Tyson Foods had been pondering a deal with IBP for several years. Bob Peterson and Tyson founder and controlling stockholder, Don Tyson, were old industry friends with great respect for one another. In the preceding year or so, Peterson had bantered with Don Tyson about the idea of putting Tyson and IBP together. This would create a company that was number one in beef and chicken, number two in pork, and that would have a diverse processed food business. Put mildly, Peterson's ardor for a combination with Tyson was much stronger than for a deal with Smithfield. . . .

TYSON MAKES ITS OPENING BID

In early December, the Tyson board of directors met to consider making a bid for IBP. John Tyson's vision for the deal was fundamental: he wanted to dominate the meat case of America's supermarkets and be the "premier protein center-of-the-plate provider" in the world. Tyson/IBP would be number one in beef and chicken, and number two in pork. It would therefore be able to provide supermarkets with nearly all the meat they needed.

Not only that, John Tyson saw the potential to bring Tyson Foods' own experience and unique expertise to bear outside of the poultry realm. As all parties agree, Tyson was an innovator in the meat industry, which had been the leader in demonstrating that a meat processor could produce value-added meat products of a ready-to-eat and ready-to-heat nature. In the past, meat processors sold large portions of meat to supermarkets and other processors, who butchered them and cooked them into higher priced serving sizes. Tyson began to do much of that work itself, thus preserving more of the profit for itself.

IBP was acknowledged to have a great fresh beefs business with an excellent, long-term track record. While it was beginning to embark on value-added strategies in the beef and pork industry, IBP was by all accounts not as far along in that corporate strategy and could most benefit from Tyson's expertise in that particular area. John Tyson saw the potential for Tyson's expertise to help IBP do in beef and pork what Tyson had done in poultry. His vision of the companies, however, had little to do with DFG specifically, a small subpart of Foodbrands that he knew little, if anything, about.

Tyson's board supported management's recommendation to make a bid. On December 4, 2000, Tyson proposed to acquire IBP in a two-step transaction valued at $26 (half cash, half stock) per share. Tyson trumpeted the fact that its offer was preferable to Smithfield's, in no small measure because Tyson did not face the same degree of anti-trust complications that Smithfield did and could thus deliver on its offer more quickly. To emphasize this point, Tyson said that its offer was "subject to completion of a quick, confirmatory due diligence review and negotiation of a definitive merger agreement."

To that end, Tyson sent IBP an executed "Confidentiality Agreement," modeled on one signed by Smithfield, which would permit it to have access to non-public, due diligence information about IBP. That Agreement contains a broad definition of "Evaluation Material" that states:

> For purposes of this Agreement, Evaluation Material shall mean *all* information, data, reports, analyses, compilations, studies, interpretations, projections, forecasts, records, and other *materials (whether prepared by the Company, its agent*

or advisors or otherwise), regardless of the form of communication, that contain or other-wise reflect information concerning the Company that we or our Representatives may be provided by or on behalf of the Company or its agents or advisors in the course of our evaluation of a possible Transaction.

The agreement carves out from the definition the following:

> This Agreement shall be inoperative as to those particular portions of the Evaluation Material that (i) become available to the public other than as a result of a disclosure by us or any of our Representatives, (ii) were available to us on a non-confidential basis prior to the disclosure of such Evaluation Material to us pursuant to this Agreement, or (iii) becomes available to us or our Representatives on a non-confidential basis from a source other than the Company or its agents or advisors provided that the source of such information was not known by us to be contractually prohibited from making such disclosure to us or such Representative.

As plainly written, the Confidentiality Agreement thus defines Evaluation Material to include essentially all non-public information in IBP's possession, regardless of whether the company's employees or agents prepared it. The terms of the Confidentiality Agreement also emphasize to an objective reader that the merger negotiation process would not be one during which Tyson could reasonably rely on oral assurances. Instead, if Tyson wished to protect itself, it would have to ensure that any oral promises were converted into con-tractual representations and warranties. The Confidentiality Agreement does so by providing:

> We understand and agree that none of the Company, its advisors or any of their affiliates, agents, advisors or representatives (i) have made or make any rep-resentation or warranty, expressed or implied, as to the accuracy or completeness of the Evaluation Material or (ii) shall have any liability whatsoever to us or our Representatives relating to or resulting from the use of the Evaluation Material or any errors therein or omissions therefrom, except in the case of (i) and (ii), to the extent provided in any definitive agreement relating to a Transaction.

THE DUE DILIGENCE PROCESS BEGINS

Tyson did not enter into the due diligence process alone. It retained Mill-bank, Tweed, Hadley & McCoy as its primary legal advisor, Merrill Lynch & Co. as its primary financial advisor, and Ernst & Young as its accountants.

The bidding process was being run by IBP's special committee. . . .

On December 5 and 6, 2000, Tyson's due diligence team reviewed informa-tion in the data room at Wachtell, Lipton. Tyson soon learned that the data room did not contain certain information about Foodbrands and the reason why that was so: IBP was reluctant to share competitively sensitive information with Smithfield. The special committee's approach to this sales process was to treat the bidders with parity. As a result, Tyson was told that any information it wanted that was not in the data room could be provided, but that if Tyson received that information, so would Smithfield.

As a result of its due diligence, Tyson flagged certain items including:

- Possible asset impairments at DFG and certain other Foodbrands companies.
- Discrepancies in the way that IBP reported its business segments.
- Concerns regarding whether the CFBA acquisition qualified as a pooling.
- IBP's policy of recognizing revenue upon invoicing, which was going to have to change on a going-forward basis because of new SEC guidance.
- IBP's possible over-confidence about the outcome of certain environmental cases.
- IBP's decision to treat its stock option plan as involving the issuance of "fixed" rather than "variable" options, and whether the accounting treatment for the plan, which was disclosed in the company's financial statements, was proper.

IBP AND TYSON HOLD A DECEMBER 8, 2000 DUE DILIGENCE MEETING

On December 8, 2000, due diligence teams from Tyson and IBP met in Sioux City, Iowa. The meeting was attended by the top managers from each side. . . .

Tyson came to the meeting expecting the now *de rigeur* PowerPoint presentation. IBP came expecting to answer Tyson's questions. As a result, the meeting became a question and answer session that covered IBP's business, segment by segment.

At least two important issues were discussed at the meeting. I will start with the DFG issue. Going into the December 8, 2000 meeting, the chairwoman of the IBP special committee, Joann Smith, specifically told John Tyson to ask about DFG at the meeting.

According to IBP witnesses, the DFG situation had gotten more serious by December 8. IBP's top management was concerned that the accounting problems at DFG were deeper than they had recognized and that additional charges to earnings might be necessary. The IBP employee-witnesses all remember Peterson saying that the DFG problem had gotten worse by at least $20 million. Peterson himself remembers speaking in angry and vehement terms about Andy Zahn, labeling him as a "thief in the hen house," and the progeny of a female dog who should be hanged on main street in front of a crowd. He also recalls saying that DFG was a "black hole." His colleagues at IBP have far less specific recollections, but do recall Peterson being quite upset.

The Tyson witnesses have a different recollection. They recall being told that DFG was a $9 million problem. Leatherby's notes of the meeting note that there had been a "$9 mm writedown here (guy fired) fudged earnout," that DFG was "not doing well," but that IBP "believe[d] in bus." Hankins's notes about DFG tersely state: "DFG—At bottom of problem." None of the Tyson witnesses heard Peterson describe Zahn—at that meeting—in such unforgettable terms. They do admit, however, that Peterson appeared agitated and upset by the issue, that the problem was attributed to fraud by Zahn, that Zahn had been the head of the business, that Zahn was now gone, and that IBP was looking into his activities. . . .

I cannot conclude with any certainty exactly what was said at the December 8, 2000 meeting. I find it unlikely that Peterson spoke as vividly as he now recalls at that meeting; rather I believe that Peterson is recalling later comments he made to Tyson representatives. But the parties were then engaged in very intensive efforts on several fronts at once. The DFG discussion on December 8, 2000 then had little of the significance that it has now. . . .

TYSON ASKS FOR ADDITIONAL DUE DILIGENCE REGARDING FOODBRANDS

After the December 8, 2000 meeting, Tyson quickly commenced its tender offer. As due diligence continued, Tyson requested access to additional accounting information involving Foodbrands. IBP management responded with this basic and consistent theme: "if you want to look at it, we have to show it to Smithfield, too. But if you want Smithfield to see it, you can have it."

This line of reasoning was frustrating to certain members of Tyson's due diligence team. Nonetheless, Tyson was never denied access to documents, it was simply told to make a tactical decision. Because Tyson wanted to buy IBP and wanted to compete with Smithfield after doing so, Tyson did not wish Smithfield to see the information. Nor did IBP management, who preferred that Tyson come out on top in the bidding.

Tyson also never chose to narrow its due diligence requests to deal only with the fraud at DFG. It did so even though its own accountants were concerned about the issue and whether IBP had really gotten to the bottom of the problem. While Tyson says it did not dig deeper because IBP management told it there was nothing bad at Foodbrands and Tyson relied upon those assurances, I do not find that testimony credible. While IBP management may have said that there were no problems at Foodbrands other than DFG, there is no credible evidence that any such statements were untrue when made, or, as we shall see, that Tyson placed any trust in those statements. Most important, IBP never denied Tyson access and had already told Tyson that there had been fraud at DFG. As a result, it is more probable that Tyson simply wanted to keep Smithfield from having knowledge about a business unit Tyson hoped to soon own. What is certain is that Tyson never demanded access to additional due diligence as a condition to going forward with a merger. . . .

By mid to late December, the IBP special committee was preparing to conduct an auction between Tyson and Smithfield. By this point, the Rawhide group was out of the running and happy to receive a termination fee courtesy of the winning bidder. . . .

On December 21, J.P. Morgan sent Tyson and Smithfield bid instructions which called for them to submit best and final bids, along with proposed merger contracts, by 5:00 p.m. on December 29, 2000. The instructions informed the bidders that the special committee was free to change the rules of the process and that no agreement would be binding until reduced to a signed contract. . . .

TYSON PROCEEDS TO RAISE ITS BID IN THE FACE OF WAVING RED FLAGS

In keeping with its skepticism about IBP's assurances, Tyson was receiving advice from its investment bankers that allowed it to examine whether an acquisition of IBP would make sense if Foodbrands performed at much lower levels than were projected in the Rawhide Projections. . . .

TYSON WINS THE AUCTION — TWICE

On December 30, 2000, Smithfield advised the special committee that $30 was its best and final offer. Special committee chair Smith called John Tyson and told him that if Tyson bid $28.50 in cash it would have a deal. John Tyson agreed and Smith said they had a deal. Later, the IBP special committee met to consider the Tyson and Smithfield bids. With the advice of J. P. Morgan, the special committee considered Tyson's $28.50 cash and stock bid to exceed the value of Smithfield's all stock $30 bid. The special committee decided to accept Tyson's bid, subject to negotiation of a definitive merger agreement.

As a courtesy, the special committee and its counsel informed Smithfield that it had lost the auction. On December 31, Smithfield increased its all stock bid to $32.00. With deep chagrin, Smith went back to John Tyson and explained what had happened and the committee's duty to consider the higher bid. John Tyson was justifiably angry, but understood the realities of the situation.

Tyson Foods went to the well again and drew out another $1.50 a share, increasing its bid to $30 per share. IBP agreed and this time the price stuck.

THE MERGER AGREEMENT NEGOTIATIONS

While the auction was on, the lawyers for IBP's special committee had been negotiating possible merger agreements with Tyson and Smithfield. By December 30, the IBP lawyers were mostly focused on Tyson because it appeared they had prevailed in the auction.

The document that was used as a template for what became the final Merger Agreement was initially prepared by Millbank Tweed, whose team was led by Lawrence Lederman. . . .

Late on December 30, IBP sent Tyson's negotiators the disclosure schedules to the Merger Agreement, which had been drafted by IBP's General Counsel Hagen. These schedules included a Schedule 5.11 that expressly qualified Section 5.11 of the Merger Agreement, which reads as follows:

> Section 5.11. *No Undisclosed Material Liabilities.* Except as set forth in *Schedule 5.11* the Company 10-K or the Company 10-Qs, there are no liabilities of the Company of [sic] any Subsidiary of any kind whatsoever, whether accrued, contingent, absolute, determined, determinable or otherwise, and there is no existing condition, situation or set of circumstances which could reasonably be expected to result in such a liability, other than:
>
> (a) liabilities disclosed or provided for in the Balance Sheet;
> (b) liabilities incurred in the ordinary course of business consistent with past practice since the Balance Sheet Date or as otherwise specifically contemplated by this Agreement;
> (c) liabilities under this agreement;

(d) other liabilities which individually or in the aggregate do not and could not reasonably be expected to have a Material Adverse Effect.

Schedule 5.11 itself states:

No Undisclosed Material Liabilities
Except as to those potential liabilities disclosed in Schedule 5.12, 5.13, 5.16 and 5.19, the Injunction against IBP in the Department of Labor Wage and Hour litigation (requiring compliance with the Wage and Hour laws), and *any further liabilities (in addition to IBP's restatement of earnings in its 3rd Quarter 2000) associ- ated with certain improper accounting practices at DFG Foods, a subsidiary of IBP, there are none. . . .* [emphasis in original]

THE MERGER AGREEMENT'S BASIC TERMS AND STRUCTURE

The Merger Agreement contemplated that:

- Tyson would amend its existing cash tender offer (the "Cash Offer") to increase the price to $30 per share.
- Tyson would couple the cash tender offer with an "Exchange Offer" in which it would offer $30 of Tyson stock (subject to a collar) for each share of IBP stock. This would permit IBP stockholders who wished to partici- pate in the potential benefits of the Tyson/IBP combination to do so.
- The Cash Offer would close no later than February 28, 2001 unless the closing conditions set forth in Annex I of the Merger Agreement were not satisfied.
- If the conditions to the Cash Offer were not met by February 28, 2001, Tyson would proceed with a "Cash Election Merger" to close on or be- fore May 15, 2001 unless the closing conditions set forth in Annex III of the Merger Agreement were not satisfied. In the cash election merger, IBP stockholders would be able to receive $30 in cash, $30 in Tyson stock (subject to a collar), or a combination of the two.

TYSON'S BOARD AND SHAREHOLDERS VOTE FOR THE MERGER AGREEMENT

On January 12, 2001, Tyson's board of directors met and ratified manage- ment's decision to enter into the Merger Agreement. . . .

The same day the Tyson shareholders meeting was held. The Merger Agree- ment was put to a vote of the Tyson stockholders. . . . The Tyson's stockholders approved the Merger Agreement and authorized management to consummate the transactions it contemplated.

TYSON GETS NERVOUS AND WANTS TO REPRICE THE DEAL

During February, Tyson Foods became increasingly nervous about the IBP deal and began to stall for time. While Tyson still believed that the deal made strategic sense, it was keen on finding a way to consummate the deal at a lower price. The negotiations with the SEC [over the accounting problems at DMG] were a pressure point that Tyson could use for that purpose and it did.

Tyson's anxiety was heightened by problems it and IBP were experiencing in the first part of 2001. A severe winter had hurt both beef and chicken supplies, with chickens suffering more than cows.

. . . Tyson's performance was way down from previous levels. Eventually, Tyson would have to reduce its earnings estimate for this period, only to find out its reduction was not sufficient. Eventually, Tyson reported a loss of $6 million for the pertinent quarter, compared to a profit of $35.7 million for the prior year's period. . . .

By mid-February, these factors led the Tyson and IBP factions to approach each other warily. IBP sensed that Tyson wanted to renegotiate. Hagen prepared for an even worse possibility: that Tyson would walk away and IBP would have to enforce the deal. Bond tried to deal with the problem by being responsive to John Tyson's calls for help in reassuring his father, Don Tyson, that the deal still made sense.

On the Tyson side, its key managers began to slow down the merger implementation process to buy time for John and Don Tyson. While Tyson and IBP continued to do all the merger integration planning that precedes a large combination, Tyson was also bent on using its leverage to extract concessions from IBP. . . .

On March 7, 2001, John Tyson sent all the Tyson employees a memorandum stating that Tyson Foods was still committed to the transaction. But on March 13, 2001, he expressed concern to Bond about IBP's first quarter performance and wanted Bond's best estimates for the rest of the year. . . .

IBP FILED ITS RESTATED FINANCIALS AND TYSON CONTINUES ITS
STRATEGY TO PUT PRESSURE ON IBP TO RENEGOTIATE

On March 13, 2001, IBP also formally filed its restatements to the Warranted Financials. The formal restatements were in line with the previous release regarding DFG, as was the $60.4 million DFG "Impairment Charge" took in its year 2000 10-K. None of the other issues covered had any impact on IBP's prospects. Tyson reacted in print in a March 14 press release that indicated that Tyson was pleased IBP had resolved most of its issues with the SEC. The press release also indicated that Tyson was continuing to look at IBP's business and noted its weak first quarter results. Behind the scenes, Tyson's investor relations officer, Louis Gottsponer, was turning up the heat on IBP through comments to analysts. . . .

Sure enough, the next day analysts began reporting that IBP's earnings outlook would possibly lead to a renegotiation of the deal.

On March 15, 2001, Tyson in-house counsel Read Hudson sent a letter to Hagen at Baledge's instruction. The letter reads:

> Congratulations on getting your restated SEC filings behind you. I know they involved a lot of hard work on your part.
>
> Now that all you have left to file is the 2000 10-K, it seems that we should begin preparation of documentation, filings, etc. as we move forward with the cash election merger. . . .

TYSON TERMINATES AND SUES IBP

. . . On March 28, 2001, Don Tyson called a meeting of the "old guard" and Tyson's current top management. The agenda's first two items were the state of the economy in general, and the state of Tyson's business. As of that day, Tyson's own performance for the year was very disappointing and it had been forced to admit so publicly only days earlier. Only after discussing the first two items on the agenda did the participants discuss the IBP deal. Don Tyson expressed continued concerns about IBP's current year performance and about mad cow disease. When it came time to make the decision how to proceed, Don Tyson left to caucus with the old guard. The new guard was excluded, including John Tyson. Don Tyson returned to the meeting and announced that Tyson should find a way to withdraw. The problems at DFG apparently played no part in his decision, nor did the comments from the SEC. Indeed, DFG was so unimportant that neither John nor Don Tyson knew about Schedule 5.11 of the Agreement until this litigation was underway.

After the old guard had decided that the Merger should not proceed, Tyson's legal team swung into action. Late on March 29, 2001, Baledge sent a letter stating:

> Tyson Foods . . . will issue a press release today announcing discontinuation of the transactions contemplated by the Agreement and Plan of Merger dated as of January 1, 2001 among IBP, Inc. ("IBP") and Tyson (the "Merger Agreement"). We intend to include this letter with our press release.
>
> On December 29, 2000, the Friday before final competitive negotiations resulting in the Merger Agreement, your counsel received comments from the Securities and Exchange Commission ("SEC") raising important issues concerning IBP's financial statements and reports filed with the SEC. As you know, we learned of the undisclosed SEC comments on January 10, 2001. Ultimately, IBP restated its financials and filings to address the SEC's issues and correct earlier misstatements. Unfortunately, we relied on that misleading information in determining to enter into the Merger Agreement. In addition, the delays and restatements resulting from these matters have created numerous breaches by IBP of representations, warranties, covenants and agreements contained in the Merger Agreement which cannot be cured.
>
> Consequently, whether intended or not, we believe Tyson Foods, Inc. was inappropriately induced to enter into the Merger Agreement. Further, we believe IBP cannot perform under the Merger Agreement. Under these facts, Tyson has a right to rescind or terminate the Merger Agreement and to receive compensation from IBP. We have commenced legal action in Arkansas seeking such relief. We hope to resolve these matters outside litigation in an expeditious and business-like manner. However, our duties dictate that we preserve Tyson's rights and protect the interests of our shareholders.
>
> If our belief is proven wrong and the Merger Agreement is not rescinded, this letter will serve as Tyson's notice, pursuant to sections 11.01 (f) and 12.01 of the Merger Agreement, of termination.

Notably, the letter does not indicate that IBP had suffered a Material Adverse Effect as a result of its first-quarter performance.

But as indicated in the letter, Tyson had sued IBP in Arkansas that evening, shortly before the close of the business day. The next day IBP filed this suit to enforce the Merger Agreement.

II.   THE BASIC CONTENTIONS OF THE PARTIES

The parties have each made numerous arguments that bear on the central question of whether Tyson properly terminated the Merger Agreement, which is understandable in view of the high stakes. The plethora of theories and nuanced arguments is somewhat daunting and difficult to summarize. But the fundamental contentions are as follows.

IBP argues that Tyson had no valid reason to terminate the contract on March 29, 2001 and that the Merger Agreement should be specifically enforced. In support of that position, IBP argues that it has not breached any of the contractual representations and warranties. . . .

Tyson argues that its decision to terminate was proper for several reasons. First, Tyson contends that IBP breached its contractual representations regarding the Warranted Financials, as evidenced by the Restatements. Second, Tyson contends that the DFG Impairment Charge as well as IBP's disappointing first quarter 2001 performance are evidence of a Material Adverse Effect, which gave Tyson the right to terminate. . . .

Before turning to the resolution of the parties' various arguments, it is necessary to pause to discuss certain choice of law issues. The parties are in accord that New York law governs the substantive aspects of the contractual and misrepresentation claims before the court. This accord is in keeping with the parties' choice to have New York contract law govern the interpretation of the Merger Agreement.[87] But they part company on certain issues with respect to the precise burden of proof governing these claims.[88] For the sake of clarity, I will outline the approach I take up front.

Under either New York or Delaware law, IBP bears the burden of persuasion to justify its entitlement to specific performance. Under New York law, IBP must show that: (1) the Merger Agreement is a valid contract between the parties; (2) IBP has substantially performed under the contract and is willing and able to perform its remaining obligations; (3) Tyson is able to perform its obligations; and (4) IBP has no adequate remedy at law. . . .

III.   RESOLUTION OF THE PARTIES' MERITS ARGUMENTS

In the pages that follow, I first address whether IBP breached a representation and warranty that justified Tyson's termination of the Merger Agreement. I then analyze the merits of Tyson's rescission claims. I conclude with the question of whether Tyson was entitled to terminate its Cash Offer on February 28, 2001.

---

87. I have not quibbled with this rare area of agreement, although I note that the Confidentiality Agreement and the agreement giving rise to Tyson's payment of the Rawhide termination fee are governed by the contract law of Delaware.

88. It is fair to say that this is one of the more tersely argued disputes in the briefs.

A.   GENERAL PRINCIPLES OF NEW YORK CONTRACT LAW

The Merger Agreement's terms are to be interpreted under New York law. Like Delaware, New York follows traditional contract law principles that give great weight to the parties' objective manifestations of their intent in the written language of their agreement. If a contract's meaning is plain and unambiguous, it will be given effect. . . .

In reading a contract, "the [court's] aim is a practical interpretation of the expressions of the parties to the end that there be a realization of [their] reasonable expectations." . . .

D.   WAS TYSON'S TERMINATION JUSTIFIED BECAUSE IBP HAS
SUFFERED A MATERIAL ADVERSE EFFECT?

Tyson argues that it was also permitted to terminate because IBP had breached §5.10 of the Agreement, which is a representation and warranty that IBP had not suffered a material adverse effect since the "Balance Sheet Date" of December 25, 1999, except as set forth in the Warranted Financials or Schedule 5.10 of the Agreement. Under the contract, a material adverse effect (or "MAE") is defined as "any event, occurrence, or development of a state of circumstances or facts which has had or reasonably could be expected to have a Material Adverse Effect" . . . "on the condition (financial or otherwise), business, assets, liabilities or results of operations of [IBP] and [its] Subsidiaries taken as a whole. . . ."[146]

Tyson asserts that the decline in IBP's performance in the last quarter of 2000 and the first quarter of 2001 evidences the existence of a Material Adverse Effect. It also contends that the DFG Impairment Charge constitutes a Material Adverse Effect. And taken together, Tyson claims that it is virtually indisputable that the combination of these factors amounts to a Material Adverse Effect.

In addressing these arguments, it is useful to be mindful that Tyson's publicly expressed reasons for terminating the Merger did not include an assertion that IBP had suffered a Material Adverse Effect. The post-hoc nature of Tyson's arguments bear on what it felt the contract meant when contracting, and suggests that a short-term drop in IBP's performance would not be sufficient to cause a MAE. To the extent the facts matter, it is also relevant that Tyson gave no weight to DFG in contracting.

The resolution of Tyson's Material Adverse Effect argument requires the court to engage in an exercise that is quite imprecise. The simplicity of §5.10's words is deceptive, because the application of those words is dauntingly complex. On its face, §5.10 is a capacious clause that puts IBP at risk for a variety of uncontrollable factors that might materially affect its overall business or results of operation as a whole. Although many merger contracts contain specific exclusions from MAE clauses that cover declines in the overall economy or

---

146. Agreement §5.10(a) (specific warranty dealing generally with MAE); §5.01 (defining MAE for entire agreement).

the relevant industry sector, or adverse weather or market conditions,[147] §5.10 is unqualified by such express exclusions.

IBP argues, however, that statements in the Warranted Financials that emphasize the risks IBP faces from swings in livestock supply act as an implicit carve-out, because a Material Adverse Effect under that section cannot include an Effect that is set forth in the Warranted Financials. I agree with Tyson, however, that these disclaimers were far too general to preclude industrywide or general factors from constituting a Material Adverse Effect. Had IBP wished such an exclusion from the broad language of §5.10, IBP should have bargained for it. At the same time, the notion that §5.10 gave Tyson a right to walk away simply because of a downturn in cattle supply is equally untenable. Instead, Tyson would have to show that the event had the required materiality of effect.[148]

The difficulty of addressing that question is considerable, however, because §5.10 is fraught with temporal ambiguity. By its own terms, it refers to any Material Adverse Effect that has occurred to IBP since December 25, 1999 unless that Effect is covered by the Warranted Financials or Schedule 5.10. Moreover, Tyson's right to refuse to close because a Material Adverse Effect has occurred is also qualified by the other express disclosures in the Schedule, by virtue of (i) the language of the Annexes that permits Tyson to refuse to close for breach of a warranty unless that breach results from "actions specifically permitted" by the Agreement; and (ii) the language of the Agreement that makes all disclosure schedules apply to Schedule 5.10 where that is the reasonably apparent intent of the drafters. Taken together, these provisions can be read to require the court to examine whether a MAE has occurred against the December 25, 1999 condition of IBP as adjusted by the specific disclosures of the Warranted Financials and the Agreement itself. This approach makes commercial sense because it establishes a baseline that roughly reflects the status of IBP as Tyson indisputably knew it at the time of signing the Merger Agreement.

But describing this basic contractual approach is somewhat easier than applying it. For example, the original IBP 10-K for FY 1999 revealed the following five-year earnings from operations and earnings per share before extraordinary items:

	1999	1998	1997	1996	1995
Earnings from Operations (in Thousands)	$528,473	$373,735	$226,716	$322,908	$480,096
Net Earnings Per Share	$3.39	$2.21	$1.26	$2.10	$2.96

---

147. *See generally* Rod J. Howard, *Deal Risk, Announcement Rick, and Interim Changes—Allocating Risks in Recent Technology M&A Agreements,* 1219 PLI/Corp. 217 (Dec. 2000); Joel I. Greenberg & A. Julia Haddad, *The Material Adverse Change Clause,* N.Y.L.J. 55 (Apr. 23, 2001).

148. *But see Pittsburgh Coke & Chem. Co. v. Bollo,* 421 F. Supp. 908, 930 (E.D.N.Y. 1976) (where Material Adverse Condition ("MAC") clause applied to a company's "financial condition," "business," or "operations," court read that clause narrowly to exclude "technological and economic changes in the aviation industry which undoubtedly affected the business of all who had dealings with that industry").

The picture that is revealed from this data is of a company that is consistently profitable, but subject to strong swings in annual EBIT and net earnings. The averages that emerge from this data are of EBIT of approximately $386 million per year and net earnings of $2.38 per share. If this average is seen as weighting the past too much, a three-year average generates EBIT of $376 million and net earnings of $2.29 per share.

The original Warranted Financials in FY 2000 also emphasize that swings in IBP's performance were a part of its business reality. For example, the trailing last twelve month's earnings from operations as of the end of third quarter of FY 2000 were $462 million, as compared to $528 million for full year 1999, as originally reported. In addition, the third quarter 10-Q showed that IBP's earnings from operations for the first 39 weeks of 2000 were lagging earnings from operations for the comparable period in 1999 by $40 million, after adjusting for the CFBA Charges.

The financial statements also indicate that Foodbrands was hardly a stable source of earnings, and was still much smaller in importance than IBP's fresh meat operations. Not only that, FY 2000 Foodbrands performance was lagging 1999, even accounting for the unusual, disclosed items.

The Rawhide Projections add another dimension to the meaning of §5.10. These Projections indicated that IBP would not reach the same level of profitability as originally reported *until FY 2004*. In FY 2001, IBP was expected to have earnings from operations of $446 and net profits of $ 1.93 a share, down from what was expected in FY 2000. This diminishment in expectations resulted from concern over an anticipated trough in the cattle cycle that would occur during years 2001 to 2003. Moreover, the performance projected for FY 2001 was a drop even from the reduced FY 2000 earnings that Tyson expected as of the time it signed the Merger Agreement.

These negotiating realities bear on the interpretation of §5.10 and suggest that the contractual language must be read in the larger context in which the parties were transacting. To a short-term speculator, the failure of a company to meet analysts' projected earnings for a quarter could be highly material. Such a failure is less important to an acquiror who seeks to purchase the company as part of a long-term strategy.[151] To such an acquiror, the important thing is whether the company has suffered a Material Adverse Effect in its business or results of operations that is consequential to the company's earnings power over a commercially reasonable period, which one would think would be measured in years rather than months. It is odd to think that a strategic buyer would view a short-term blip in earnings as material, so long as the target's earnings-generating potential is not materially affected by that blip or the blip's cause.[152]

---

151. James C. Freund, *Anatomy of a Merger: Strategies and Techniques for Negotiating Corporate Acquisitions* 246 (Law Journals Seminars-Press 1975) ("[W]hatever the concept of materiality may mean, at the very least it is always relative to the situation.").

152. *Pine State Creamery Co. v. Land-O-Sun Dairies, Inc.*, 201 F.3d 437, 1999 WL 1082539, at *6 (4th Cir. 1999) (*per curiam*) (whether severe losses during a two month period evidenced a MAC was a jury question where there was evidence that the business was seasonal and that such downturns were expected as part of the earnings cycle of the business).

In large measure, the resolution of the parties' arguments turns on a difficult policy question. In what direction does the burden of this sort of uncertainty fall: on an acquiror or on the seller? What little New York authority exists is not particularly helpful, and cuts in both directions. One New York case held a buyer to its bargain even when the seller suffered a very severe shock from an extraordinary event, reasoning that the seller realized that it was buying the stock of a sound company that was, however, susceptible to market swings.[153] Another case held that a Material Adverse Effect was evidenced by a short-term drop in sales, but in a commercial context where such a drop was arguably quite critical.[154] The non–New York authorities cited by the parties provide no firmer guidance.

Practical reasons lead me to conclude that a New York court would incline toward the view that a buyer ought to have to make a strong showing to invoke a Material Adverse Effect exception to its obligation to close. Merger contracts are heavily negotiated and cover a large number of specific risks explicitly. As a result, even where a Material Adverse Effect condition is as broadly written as the one in the Merger Agreement, that provision is best read as a backstop protecting the acquiror from the occurrence of unknown events that substantially threaten the overall earnings potential of the target in a durationally significant manner.[155] A short-term hiccup in earnings should not suffice; rather the Material Adverse Effect should be material when viewed from the longer-term perspective of a reasonable acquiror. In this regard, it is worth noting that IBP never provided Tyson with *quarterly* projections.

When examined from this seller-friendly perspective, the question of whether IBP has suffered a Material Adverse Effect remains a close one. IBP had a very sub-par first quarter. The earnings per share of $.19 it reported exaggerate IBP's success, because part of those earnings were generated from

---

153. *Bear Stearns Co. v. Jardine Strategic Holdings,* No. 31371187, slip. op. (N.Y. Supr. June 17, 1988), *aff'd mem.,* 143 A.D. 2d 1073, 533 N.Y.S. 2d 167 (1988) (Tender offeror who was to purchase 20% of Bear Stearns could not rely on the MAC clause to avoid contract despite $100 million loss suffered by Bear Stearns on Black Monday, October 19, 1987, and the fact that Bear Stearns suffered a $48 million quarterly loss, its first in history. The buyer knew that Bear Stearns was in a volatile cyclical business.).

154. *In Pan Am Corp. v. Delta Air Lines,* 175 B.R. 438, 492-493 (S.D.N.Y. 1994), Pan Am airlines suffered sharp decline in bookings over a three-month period that was shocking to its management. The court held that a MAC had occurred. It did so, however, in a context where the party relying on the MAC clause was providing funding in a work-out situation, making any further deterioration of Pan Am's already compromised condition quite important.

In another New York case, *Katz v. NVF,* 100 A.D. 2d 470, 473 N.Y.S. 2d 786 (1984), two merger partners agreed that one partner has suffered a material adverse change when its full year results showed a *net loss* of over $6.3 million, compared to a $2.1 million profit a year before, and steep operating losses due to plant closure. *Id.* at 788. The *Katz* case thus presents a negative change of much greater magnitude and duration than exists in this case.

155. A contrary rule will encourage the negotiation of extremely detailed "MAC" clauses with numerous carve-outs or qualifiers. An approach that reads broad clauses as addressing fundamental events that would materially affect the value of a target to a reasonable acquiror eliminates the need for drafting of that sort.

a windfall generated by accounting for its stock option plan, a type of gain that is not likely to recur. On a normalized basis, IBP's first quarter of 2001 earnings from operations ran 64% behind the comparable period in 2000. If IBP had continued to perform on a straight-line basis using its first quarter 2001 performance, it would generate earnings from operations of around $200 million. This sort of annual performance would be consequential to a reasonable acquiror and would deviate materially from the range in which IBP had performed during the recent past.[156]

Tyson says that this impact must also be coupled with the DFG Impairment Charge of $60.4 million. That Charge represents an indication that DFG is likely to generate far less cash flow than IBP had previously anticipated. At the very least, the Charge is worth between $.50 and $.60 cents per IBP share, which is not trivial. It is worth even more, says Tyson, if one realizes that the Rawhide Projections portrayed Foodbrands as the driver of increased profitability in an era of flat fresh meats profits. This deficiency must be considered in view of the overall poor performance of Foodbrands so far in FY 2001. The Rawhide Projections had targeted Foodbrands to earn $137 million in 2001. In a January 30, 2001 presentation to Tyson, Bond had presented an operating plan that hoped to achieve $145 million from Foodbrands. As of the end of the first quarter, Foodbrands had earned only $2 million, and thus needed another $135 million in the succeeding three quarters to reach its Rawhide Projection. IBP's overall trailing last twelve month's earnings had declined from $488 million as of the end of the third quarter of 2000 to $330 million.

As a result of these problems, analysts following IBP issued sharply reduced earnings estimates for FY 2001. Originally, analysts were predicting that IBP would exceed the Rawhide Projections in 2001 by a wide margin. After IBP's poor first quarter, some analysts had reduced their estimate from $2.38 per share to $1.44 a share. *Even accounting for Tyson's attempts to manipulate the analyst community's perception of IBP,* this was a sharp drop.

Tyson contends that the logical inference to be drawn from the record evidence that is available is that IBP will likely have its worst year since 1997, a year which will be well below the company's average performance for all relevant periods. As important, the company's principal driver of growth is performing at markedly diminished levels, thus compromising the company's future results as it enters what is expected to be a tough few years in the fresh meats business.

IBP has several responses to Tyson's evidence. IBP initially notes that Tyson's arguments are unaccompanied by expert evidence that identifies the diminution in IBP's value or earnings potential as a result of its first quarter performance.[160] The absence of such proof is significant. Even after Hankins

---

156. *See Raskin v. Birmingham Steel Corp.,* Del. Ch., 1990 WL 193326, at *5, Allen, C. (Dec. 4, 1990) (while "a reported 50% decline in earnings over two consecutive quarters might not be held to be a material adverse development, it is, I believe unlikely to think that might happen").

160. It has admittedly taken its own payment multiples based on the Rawhide Projections and simply "valued" the effect that way. But IBP never warranted that it would meet those Projections.

generated extremely pessimistic projections for IBP in order to justify a lower deal price, Merrill Lynch still concluded that a purchase of IBP at $30 per share was still within the range of fairness and a great long-term value for Tyson. The Merrill Lynch analysis casts great doubt on Tyson's assertion that IBP has suffered a Material Adverse Effect.[161]

IBP also emphasizes the cyclical nature of its businesses. It attributes its poor first quarter to an unexpectedly severe winter. This led ranchers to hold livestock back from market, causing a sharp increase in prices that hurt both the fresh meats business and Foodbrands. Once April was concluded, IBP began to perform more in line with its recent year results, because supplies were increasing and Foodbrands was able to begin to make up its winter margins. Bond testified at trial that he expects IBP to meet or exceed the Rawhide Projection of $1.93 a share in 2001, and the company has publicly indicated that it expects earnings of $1.80 to $2.20 a share. Peterson expressed the same view.

IBP also notes that any cyclical fall is subject to cure by the Agreement's termination date, which was May 15, 2001. By May 15, IBP had two weeks of strong earnings that signaled a strong quarter ahead. Moreover, by that time, cattle that had been held back from market were being sold, leading to plentiful supplies that were expected to last for most of the year.

Not only that, IBP notes that not all analyst reporting services had been as pessimistic as Tyson portrays. In March, Morningstar was reporting a mean analyst prediction of $1.70 per share for IBP in 2001. By May, this had grown to a mean of $1.74 a share. Throughout the same period, Morningstar's consensus prediction was an FY 2002 performance of $2.33 range in March, and $2.38 in May. Therefore, according to Morningstar, the analyst community was predicting that IBP would return to historically healthy earnings next year, and that earnings for this year would fall short of the Rawhide Projections by less than $.20 per share.

IBP also argues that the Impairment Charge does not approach materiality as a big picture item. That Charge is a one-time, non-cash charge, and IBP has taken large charges of that kind as recently as 1999. While IBP does not deny that its decision to buy DFG turned out disastrously, it reminds me that DFG is but a tiny fraction of IBP's overall business and that a total shut-down of DFG would likely have little effect on the future results of a combined Tyson/IBP. And as a narrow asset issue, the charge is insignificant to IBP as a whole.

I am confessedly torn about the correct outcome. As Tyson points out, IBP has only pointed to two weeks of truly healthy results in 2001 before the contract termination date of May 15. Even these results are suspect, Tyson contends, due to the fact that IBP expected markedly better results for the second week just days before the actual results come out. In view of IBP's demonstrated incapacity to accurately predict near-term results, Tyson says with some justification that I should be hesitant to give much weight to IBP's assurances that it will perform well for the rest of the year.

---

161. Tyson's only expert on this subject testified that a MAE would have occurred in his view even if IBP met the Rawhide Projections, because those Projections were more bearish than the analysts. This academic theory is of somewhat dubious practical utility, as it leaves the enforceability of contracts dependent on whether predictions by third-parties come true.

In the end, however, Tyson has not persuaded me that IBP has suffered a Material Adverse Effect. By its own arguments, Tyson has evinced more confidence in stock market analysts than I personally harbor. But its embrace of the analysts is illustrative of why I conclude that Tyson has not met its burden.

As of May 2001, analysts were predicting that IBP would earn between $1.50 to around $1.74 per share in 2001. The analysts were also predicting that IBP would earn between $2.33 and $2.42 per share in 2002. These members are based on reported "mean" or "consensus" analyst numbers. Even at the low end of this *consensus* range, IBP's earnings for the next two years would not be out of line with its historical performance during troughs in the beef cycle. As recently as years 1996-1998, IBP went through a period with a three year average earnings of $1.85 per share. At the high end of the analysts' consensus range, IBP's results would exceed this figure by $.21 per year.

This predicted range of performance from the source that Tyson vouches for suggests that no Material Adverse Effect has occurred.[170] Rather, the analyst views support the conclusion that IBP remains what the baseline evidence suggests it was—a consistently but erratically profitable company struggling to implement a strategy that will reduce the cyclicality of its earnings. Although IBP may not be performing as well as it and Tyson had hoped, IBP's business appears to be in sound enough shape to deliver results of operations in line with the company's recent historical performance. Tyson's own investment banker still believes IBP is fairly priced at $30 per share. The fact that Foodbrands is not yet delivering on the promise of even better performance for IBP during beef troughs is unavailing to Tyson, since §5.10 focuses on IBP as a whole and IBP's performance as an entire company is in keeping with its baseline condition.

Therefore, I conclude that Tyson has not demonstrated a breach of §5.10. I admit to reaching this conclusion with less than the optimal amount of confidence.[171] The record evidence is not of the type that permits certainty. . . .

. . . [My conclusion] is that Tyson is in breach of the Merger Agreement because it improperly terminated in late March, 2001. That is, it is in breach of its obligation to close the Cash Election Merger on or before May 15, 2001.[200]

---

170. Again, I emphasize that my conclusion is heavily influenced by my temporal perspective, which recognizes that even good businesses do not invariably perform at consistent levels of profitability. If a different policy decision is the correct one, a contrary conclusion could be reached. That different, more short-term approach will, I fear, make merger agreements more difficult to negotiate and lead to Material Adverse Effect clauses of great prolixity.

171. Tyson has tried to suggest that other factors exist that contribute to the conclusion that IBP has suffered a Material Adverse Effect. These include unsubstantiated charges that other Foodbrands units suffer the same type of serious accounting problems as DFG and that other IBP assets are impaired, as well as the effects of DFG-related lawsuits that Tyson admits were covered by Schedule 5.11. I find none of Tyson's other Material Adverse Effect arguments meritorious.

200. Throughout the course of this case, IBP has urged upon me another proposition that it believes compels a ruling in its favor. IBP asserts that under New York law, a party cannot refuse to close on a contract in reliance upon a breached contractual representation if that party knew that the representation was false at the time of contracting. Put directly,

IV.   IBP Is Entitled to an Award of Specific Performance

Having determined that the Merger Agreement is a valid and enforceable contract that Tyson had no right to terminate, I now turn to the question of whether the Merger Agreement should be enforced by an order of specific performance. Although Tyson's voluminous post-trial briefs argue the merits fully, its briefs fail to argue that a remedy of specific performance is unwarranted in the event that its position on the merits is rejected.

This gap in the briefing is troubling. A compulsory order will require a merger of two public companies with thousands of employees working at facilities that are important to the communities in which they operate. The impact of a forced merger on constituencies beyond the stockholders and top managers of IBP and Tyson weighs heavily on my mind. The prosperity of IBP and Tyson means a great deal to these constituencies. I therefore approach this remedial issue quite cautiously and mindful of the interests of those who will be affected by my decision.

I start with a fundamental question: is this is a truly unique opportunity that cannot be adequately monetized? If the tables were turned and Tyson was seeking to enforce the contract, a great deal of precedent would indicate that the contract should be specifically enforced. In the more typical situation, an acquiror argues that it cannot be made whole unless it can specifically enforce the acquisition agreement, because the target company is unique and will yield value of an unquantifiable nature, once combined with the acquiring

---

IBP says it can win this case even if there was a breach of a representation in the Merger Agreement so long as it can prove that it informed Tyson of facts that demonstrate that the representation was untrue and thus that Tyson did not in fact rely upon the representation in deciding to sign the Merger Agreement. IBP's arguments find some support in some cases applying New York law. *See, e.g., Rogath v. Siebenmann,* 129 F.3d 261, 264-65 (2d Cir. 1997) ("Where the seller discloses up front the inaccuracy of certain of his warranties, it cannot be said that the buyer—absent the express preservation of his rights—believed he was purchasing the seller's promise as to the truth of the warranties."). There is, however, no definitive authority from the New York Court of Appeals to this effect, and the leading case can be read as being at odds with IBP's position. *See CBS v. Ziff-Davis Publishing Co.,* 75 N.Y. 2d 496, 554 N.Y.S. 2d 449, 553 N.E. 2d 997, 1000-01 (1990). Most of IBP's cases also deal with a distinct context, namely situations where a buyer signed the contract on day one, learned that a representation is false from the seller on day three, closed the contract on day five, and sued for damages for breach of warranty on day 10. The public policy reasons for denying relief to the buyer in those circumstances are arguably much different than are implicated by a decision whether to permit a buyer simply to walk away before closing in reliance on a specific contractual representation that it had reason to suspect was untrue as of the time of signing. In any event, my more traditional contract analysis applies settled principles of New York contract law and eliminates any need to delve into these novel issues of another state's law. Likewise, there is no present need to address IBP's other arguments, which are grounded in equitable doctrines such as estoppel, acquiescence, and waiver and ratification. Nor do I address IBP's argument that Tyson breached the Agreement's implied covenant of good faith and fair dealing by terminating for pretextual reasons (i.e., DFG and the Comment Letter) that had no relationship to Tyson's actual motives (i.e., Tyson's alleged desire to renegotiate the deal to a much lower price or terminate because of its own poor performance).

company. In this case, the sell-side of the transaction is able to make the same argument, because the Merger Agreement provides the IBP stockholders with a choice of cash or Tyson stock, or a combination of both. Through this choice, the IBP stockholders were offered a chance to share in the upside of what was touted by Tyson as a unique, synergistic combination. This court has not found, and Tyson has not advanced, any compelling reason why sellers in mergers and acquisitions transactions should have less of a right to demand specific performance than buyers, and none has independently come to my mind.

In addition, the determination of a cash damages award will be very difficult in this case. And the amount of any award could be staggeringly large. No doubt the parties would haggle over huge valuation questions, which (Tyson no doubt would argue) must take into account the possibility of a further auction for IBP or other business developments. A damages award can, of course, be shaped; it simply will lack any pretense to precision. An award of specific performance will, I anticipate, entirely eliminate the need for a speculative determination of damages.

Finally, there is no doubt that a remedy of specific performance is practicable. Tyson itself admits that the combination still makes strategic sense. At trial, John Tyson was asked by his own counsel to testify about whether it was fair that Tyson should enter any later auction for IBP hampered by its payment of the Rawhide Termination Fee. This testimony indicates that Tyson Foods is still interested in purchasing IBP, but wants to get its original purchase price back and then buy IBP off the day-old goods table. I consider John Tyson's testimony an admission of the feasibility of specific performance.

Probably the concern that weighs heaviest on my mind is whether specific performance is the right remedy in view of the harsh words that have been said in the course of this litigation. Can these management teams work together? The answer is that I do not know. Peterson and Bond say they can. I am not convinced, although Tyson's top executives continue to respect the managerial acumen of Peterson and Bond, if not that of their financial subordinates.

What persuades me that specific performance is a workable remedy is that Tyson will have the power to decide all the key management questions itself. It can therefore hand-pick its own management team. While this may be unpleasant for the top level IBP managers who might be replaced, it was a possible risk of the Merger from the get-go and a reality of today's M&A market.

The impact on other constituencies of this ruling also seems tolerable. Tyson's own investment banker thinks the transaction makes sense for Tyson, and is still fairly priced at $30 per share. One would think the Tyson constituencies would be better served on the whole by a specific performance remedy, rather than a large damages award that did nothing but cost Tyson a large amount of money.

In view of these factors, I am persuaded that an award of specific performance is appropriate, regardless of what level of showing was required by IBP. That is, there is clear and convincing evidence to support this award. Such an award is decisively preferable to a vague and imprecise damages remedy that cannot adequately remedy the injury to IBP's stockholders. . . .

NOTES

1. Litigation vs. Renegotiation.   The use of MAC provisions creates the potential for renegotiating the terms of a deal when one of the parties decides to invoke a MAC provision. Even though the other side may disagree whether the MAC provision has been triggered under the circumstances, renegotiation may often be preferable to the alternative — *litigation*. Moreover, litigation over MACs and MAEs is inherently a fact-intensive proceeding that will turn on both the specific language of the MAC or MAE at issue, as well as the facts of the particular transaction. This is reflected in Vice-Chancellor Strine's detailed (and quite lengthy) opinion in the principal case, *IBP*.

2. What Triggers "Walk-Away Rights"?   Be careful not to confuse a purchase price adjustment provision of the type described earlier in this chapter at pages 319-324 with a "material adverse change" clause of the type at issue in the principal case. Only the MAC gives rise to a walk-away right, which will allow Bidder to walk away from the deal and refuse to close *if* Target's financial results have materially deteriorated in the time period between signing and closing on the acquisition agreement. *Query:* Given this function of a MAC, how broadly do you think courts should construe MACs and MAEs?

3. The Lessons of **IBP.**   What lessons can be learned from the result (and the court's reasoning) in *IBP*? The *IBP* decision led one commentator to offer the following practical guidance:

> Unlike most prior case law interpreting MAC clauses that provides little practical precedential assistance, the *[IBP]* court seems to be sending a clear message. Merger agreements, by their nature, are heavily negotiated documents, and public policy is in favor of making sure the parties honor the spirit of such agreements.
>
> Therefore, any party wishing to terminate a deal on the basis of the broad language of a MAC clause must be able to demonstrate that the "adverse change" is of such a quality and magnitude to overcome a strong presumption in favor of closing the transaction. That will be particularly difficult if the court suspects that the true reason for the termination is buyer's remorse.
>
> The following provides some helpful advice to consider when drafting MAC clauses in purchase or merger agreements. . . .
>
> [Bidder] should specifically address risks of which [Bidder] is aware. Ratios, performance benchmarks and other financial tests (objective criteria) are common methods used to determine thresholds for such specifically identified risks. Care should be taken, however, to not be "overly" specific (as courts could find that such a high level of specificity rules out other risks not otherwise specified).
>
> [Bidder] should also include potential adverse events not within the seller's control. Courts often find the following events to fall outside the scope of a MAC (unless specifically included):
>
> - events from the announcement or consummation of the transaction;
> - business turndowns (generally or industry wide);
> - enactment of legislation;
> - cancellation of a significant contract; and
> - future prospects of the seller.

Therefore, if the buyer wishes such events to trigger the MAC clause, they should be specifically included. After the buyer includes those risks that can be reasonably identified, the most comprehensive, general language should be included to cover unknown risks (both within and outside the seller's control).

Remember the lesson from the *[IBP]* case — courts are not likely to allow a buyer to back out of a transaction due to buyer's remorse. If a buyer is concerned about something specific, it should include that concern in the agreement. The broad language of a general MAC clause should only be triggered by a "durationally significant" event.

The "seller" [Target] should attempt to limit all of the specific carveouts proposed by the buyer [Bidder] — especially those over which it has no control (that is, general or industry economic conditions and adverse effects resulting from the performance of the purchase agreement). The seller should seek to eliminate the remaining specific carve-outs, such as financial benchmarks (over which it *does* have control), or at least negotiate the benchmarks so that the risks of such benchmarks triggering a MAC are low.

The seller will likely encounter heavy resistance to eliminate (or limit) these financial benchmarks. The seller might also propose specific carve-outs that *do not* trigger a MAC. Finally, the seller should attempt to limit the scope of the MAC clause by a qualification requiring "knowledge" of material adverse events.

Gregory Bishop, *Changed Circumstances or Buyer's Remorse?* BUSINESS LAW TODAY at 49-52 (March/April 2002).

4. Recent "MAC" Clause Litigation.   Since then-Vice Chancellor Strine handed down his opinion in *IBP*, there have been several subsequent cases further reinforcing the principles enunciated in *IBP*. *See, e.g., Genesco, Inc. v. Finish Line, Inc.,* No. 07-2137-II (Tenn. Ch. Dec. 27, 2007); *United Rentals, Inc. v. Ram Holdings, Inc.,* 937 A.2d 810 (Del. Ch. 2007); and *Hexicon Specialty Chemicals, Inc. v. Huntsman Corp.,* 965 A.2d 715 (Del. Ch. 2008). Vice Chancellor Stephen Lamb's decision in *Hexion* is widely regarded as an important development in the law relating to MAC/MAE clauses, which are an important part of acquisition agreements in today's M&A market — both in the context of public company M&A deals as well as in acquisitions of privately held companies. Briefly summarized:

> Hexion, a producer of adhesives used in plywood, agreed to purchase Huntsman, the world's largest producer of epoxy additives, in July 2007. Apollo filed suit in June 2008, claiming both that it had no obligation to close the deal as the post-merger entity would be insolvent, and because Huntsman had suffered a MAE. The MAE language in the merger agreement provided that Apollo's obligation to close was conditioned on the absence of "any event, change or development that has had or is reasonably expected to have, individually or in the aggregate" a MAE. "MAE" was in turn defined as "any occurrence . . . that is materially adverse to the financial condition . . . of the Company . . . ," *excluding* changes in "general economic or financial market conditions" or occurrences "affect[ing] the chemical industry generally." . . .
>
> In finding that Huntsman has not suffered a MAE, the Court relied heavily on *In re IBP*, a leading Delaware case (applying New York law) on the interpretation of MAE clauses. Noting that, "absent clear language to the contrary" the party seeking to invoke an MAE clause bears the burden of proving that an MAE has occurred, the Court cited *In re IBP* for the proposition that "a buyer faces a

heavy burden when it attempts to invoke a material adverse effect clause in order to avoid its obligation to close," and noted that "Delaware courts have never found a material adverse effect to have occurred in the context of a merger agreement." Elaborating on the oft-cited reasoning from *In re IBP* that "[a] short-term hiccup in earnings should not suffice" to succeed on a MAE claim, the Court explained that "a significant decline in earnings by the target corporation during the period after signing but prior . . . to closing" could constitute a MAE if those poor results can be "expected to persist significantly into the future."

* * *

Having found that no MAE had occurred as to Huntsman as a whole, the Court rejected Apollo's claim that (i) a five percent increase in Huntsman's post-closing debt was not material to Apollo's valuation of the transaction and (ii) problems with two Huntsman divisions amounted to a MAE, given that "Huntsman as a whole is not materially impaired by their results."

* * *

Hexion is consistent with prior rulings in showing that purchasers face a heavy burden in attempting to use MAE clauses to avoid merger agreements. The case also highlights the importance of carve-outs often used in MAE clauses—as the parties here had excepted general economic or financial market changes, which language figured prominently in the Court's ruling. *Hexion* suggests that parties negotiating MAE clauses seriously consider terms that might (i) shift the burden of proof regarding use of the clause and (ii) provide greater specificity in the types of changes that may constitute a MAE, *including* changes in general market or macroeconomic conditions.

White & Case, LLP, *Delaware Court Interprets Material Adverse Effect Clause to Bar Hexion and Apollo from Abandoning Huntsman Deal,* (law firm memo, October 2008) (copy on file with author).

5. "MAC" Clause Surveys. Over the past decade or so, a trend has emerged: several firms and organizations (most notably the ABA Business Law Section's Committee on Mergers and Acquisitions) publish annual surveys of the use and terms of MACs and MAEs. As a general proposition, the purpose of such surveys is to observe and track year to year

> . . . the impact of . . . market, economic, and societal conditions on the negotiation of material adverse change provisions in M&A deals. Acquisition agreements typically contain material adverse change or material adverse effect provisions, which are commonly referred to as MAC or MAE clauses, to assist the parties in allocating risks in the transaction that relate to adverse changes or events occurring over time, usually between signing and closing of a transaction, and typically impacting the target company but sometimes also with regard to the acquisition bidder.
> [Since the time that our first survey was] published in 2002, following the tragic event of September 11, 2001, . . . we witnessed a trend [in 2003] toward pro-bidder MAC clauses accompanied, however, with an expansion in the specific exclusions that are focused on acts of war and terrorism and on broad-based market volatility. As time passed and the business environment improved during the 2004-2007 period, our surveys reported increasingly pro-target formulations with a far more robust list of exclusions. That pro-target trend ceased between our 2008 and 2009 results when our surveys showed an increase in the negotiating

strength of bidders with a declining list of exclusions to MAC provisions. The results for 2010 and 2011 showed slight increases in the use of exclusions over 2008-2009, signaling increased negotiating strength of targets over the prior period.

Results from our [2012] survey show the average number of exceptions per deal remained about the same year-over-year, but with both marked increases and decreases in specific elements and exclusions as further discussed herein, signaling continued robust negotiation to the overall formulation of MAC provisions without a clear year-over-year shift in overall negotiating strength between bidders and targets. Given the overall decline in M&A deal activity during the fourth quarter of 2011 and in 2012 . . . , we expected to see a greater degree of change in MAC clauses toward formulations favoring bidders. However, this year's [2012's] mixed bag may simply reflect a general shift in attention to certain risks over others rather than an overall shift in bargaining power.

As further background on the risk allocation uses of MAC clauses, the MAC provision generally serves two functions. First of all, the MAC definition is used in qualifications to various representations, warranties, and covenants, establishing a threshold for determining the scope of disclosure or compliance relating to risks associated with changes in the target's business. For instance, a representation may provide that the target has complied with all environmental laws "except as would not have a Material Adverse Effect." Use of the MAC qualification in representations and warranties in this manner causes minor breaches to become irrelevant. As a second function, the MAC definition is used to delineate the circumstances under which a bidder would be permitted to abandon the transaction without liability. This walkaway right is frequently referred to as a "MAC out" and appears in the conditions precedent to the bidder's obligation to close. A typical condition precedent MAC out provision would state as a condition to closing that "there shall not have occurred a Material Adverse Change in the Company." While negotiating the delineated changes or events that constitute a MAC, the bidder and target also often agree to dilute the definition by listing more specific changes or events, commonly referred to as the "MAC exceptions," that do not constitute a MAC and the occurrence of which will not permit a bidder from backing out of a deal or seeking a renegotiation of pricing or other material terms on the basis that a MAC has occurred. The delineated events defining a MAC together with the MAC exceptions allocate carefully calibrated risks of loss between the bidder and the target that may arise out of adverse circumstances occurring in the target's business between signing and closing.

The specifics of MAC clauses are heavily negotiated between the parties, with targets seeking to narrow the MAC definitional elements and to expand the exceptions in order to shift more risk to the bidder. In this way, the target enhances its ability to preserve the deal pricing and certainty of closing. Bidders, on the other hand, attempt to shift the risk to the target by expanding the elements and narrowing the exceptions, and thereby providing more room to untie the knot in the event of adverse circumstances.

2012 Nixon Peabody MAC Survey at 1-2, (law firm memo, October 22, 2012) (copy on file with author).

6. The Implications of IBP and Its Progeny.   In considering the terms of the representations and conditions to closing included in Galaxy's original draft of the stock purchase agreement delivered to Trekker's lawyer for review and comment (see Appendix C), what are the implications of the *IBP* decision for the lawyers engaged to prepare the agreement for Galaxy's proposed acquisition of Trekker?

PROBLEM — USE OF MATERIALITY QUALIFIERS

For purposes of the following problem, assume that the parties' acquisition agreement contains a materiality qualifier framed as a MAE which is framed in terms substantially the same as the MAE clause at issue in the *IBP* case:

> a MAE is defined as "any event, occurrence or development of a state of circumstances or facts which has had or reasonably could be expected to have a Material Adverse Effect" . . . "on the condition (financial or otherwise), business, assets, liabilities or results of operations of [IBP] and [its] Subsidiaries taken as whole." . . .

As a drafting exercise, consider the following situations and analyze whether the language of this MAE clause would offer your client, Bidder, the right to walk away from the deal. Or, is there a better way to draft/frame the MAC/MAE clause in order to better protect your client's interests?

a. Bidder has agreed to purchase a broadcast station in Texas. In the period between signing and closing on the acquisition agreement, the broadcast station loses half of its subscribers (i.e., viewers and/or listeners), although all of its assets remain in place.

b. Target has two key employees that are critical to Bidder's decision to buy Target's business. Before closing, these two employees either quit, or alternatively, have advised Target's current management that they plan to quit.

Planning Problem
Preparing the Stock Purchase Agreement
for Galaxy's Acquisition of Trekker

The first draft of the acquisition agreement for Galaxy's (Bidder's) purchase of Trekker's (Target's) business is set forth in Appendix C. As you read through this draft agreement, please consider the following:

QUESTIONS

1. What are the corporate formalities to be followed if the parties had decided to structure this acquisitions as (i) a direct merger; (ii) a triangular merger; (iii) or a sale of assets? To what extent do these structural considerations influence the advice you would give the parties as to the choice of deal structure for Galaxy's proposed acquisition of Trekker?

2. During the course of conducting its due diligence investigation and before signing the definitive agreement, Galaxy Corp. learns that Trekker's manufacturing plant located in a border town south of San Diego may have problems with its labor force under federal immigration law — a common

issue in the context of these types of border plants that are widely used in the garment industry.[11] Alternatively, Galaxy's due diligence review suggests that the plant where Trekker manufactures its skateboards may be subject to liability under relevant environmental laws. How should the parties deal with these issues?

3. Assume that the parties have signed the form of stock purchase agreement included in Appendix C, which includes a representation by the company and certain of the selling shareholders to the effect that there are no undisclosed liabilities. See Article 3 of Trekker's Agreement with Galaxy. During the course of its due diligence, Galaxy learns of potential exposure to environmental liability as a result of operations at Trekker's manufacturing plant.

   a. Can Galaxy refuse to complete the transaction? In other words, can Galaxy "walk away" from the deal?
   b. Assume that Galaxy did not discover the potential environmental liability exposure until after closing on the acquisition. What advice can you give Galaxy as to its rights and remedies under the terms of the parties' agreement?

4. What suggestions can you make to Galaxy on structuring the acquisition and/or the purchase price to address the risk of discovering undisclosed liability *after* the closing?

NOTE

Relationship Between Representations and Due Diligence Process. From Bidder's perspective, the appropriate use of a materiality qualifier requires that the lawyer negotiating the terms of representations and warranties for Bidder have a thorough understanding of the client's business objectives in proposing to acquire Target's business and a firm grasp of what is really important to Bidder about Target's business. Otherwise, Bidder's counsel runs the risk of agreeing to the use of a materiality qualifier as to a particular representation that will operate to rob Bidder of the full business benefits that Bidder hoped to obtain by purchasing Target. In this regard, Bidder often finds it useful to do its diligence review *before* drafting the terms of the acquisition agreement. After its due diligence investigation is completed, Bidder will have a much better understanding of Target's business and where the difficulties and potential business problems; that is, armed with this information, Bidder is in a much better position to negotiate meaningful terms to the representations and warranties to be provided by Target. The difficulty with this strategy is that, in

---

11. This type of issue illustrates the fundamental proposition that M&A law is one of the last places in the modern practice of law where counsel truly must be a Renaissance lawyer; or, to frame the proposition in slightly more perjorative terms, the modern M&A lawyer truly must be "a Jack of all trades, Master of none!"

many cases, Target is simply unwilling to share that level of detail sought by most Bidders in the typical thorough diligence review *unless* Target is confident that a deal has been reached with this Bidder. Or, alternatively, the full benefit of the diligence investigation cannot be obtained because the diligence review is proceeding simultaneous with the parties' negotiations over the terms of the acquisition agreement. The due diligence process is discussed in more detail in the next section.

In any case, the *IBP* decision makes clear that the lawyer who wants to negotiate most effectively for a set of representations that will provide meaningful protection to its business client must go beyond the boilerplate representations that are customarily part of any acquisition agreement. To do this, however, the lawyer must have a firm grasp of the business to be acquired and the importance of the proposed transaction for his/her business client. This is an important task that is time consuming and often left to the junior lawyers as part of the diligence review, particularly in the case of large transactions such as the deal involved in the *IBP* decision. To the extent that diligence is delegated to junior members of the acquisition team, the lawyer responsible for organizing the acquisition process must take care to ensure that the relevant information will be filtered out and directed to those members of the acquisition team who most need to know this information as part of the negotiation process. Although many lawyers think of due diligence as the drudge work — the equivalent of doing windows and ovens in the housekeeping sense — the importance of adequate and thorough due diligence cannot be overstated. The impact of the diligence review will be felt at many stages in the deal process, not the least of which is in connection with negotiating the terms of the representations and warranties to be included in the parties' acquisition agreement.

E.   *Indemnification Provisions and Their Relationship to Representations and Warranties*

As mentioned earlier in this chapter, one of the other important functions of the *representations* and *warranties* section of the acquisition agreement is that these provisions generally will serve as the basis for the *conditions* that must be satisfied at the time of *closing* on the agreement. This same kind of dynamic interaction surfaces again in considering the relationship between the parties' *representations* and the post-closing rights of *indemnification* typically included in any agreement for the acquisition of a privately held company.

The *indemnification* provisions generally give Bidder the express contractual right to recover from the sellers of Target's business. The terms of a typical indemnification provision will grant Bidder an express right of recovery for *all damages, directly or indirectly, resulting from or caused by Target's breach of one (or more) of the representations it made in the acquisition agreement that Bidder did not discover until after closing on the agreement and taking over Target's business.* By insisting on indemnification provisions as part of the acquisition agreement, Bidder is trying to preserve a contractual right to recover from the seller(s) of Target Co. in order to be sure that Bidder gets the benefit of the bargain that it made when it agreed to buy Target's business. Including this right of indemnification in the parties' contract allows Bidder to tailor the scope of the remedy to address the situation presented by the particular facts of its business transaction with Target. Apart from providing an explicit, contractual, financial remedy to the Bidder, indemnification rights also serve the useful purpose of providing Target with a strong motivational incentive to make full disclosure of all relevant information regarding Target's business and financial affairs in order to avoid the fairly draconian financial remedy granted by the terms of the customary indemnification provision.

Usually, Target will be reluctant to agree to rights of indemnification and can be expected to try to narrow the scope of whatever indemnification rights Bidder demands under the terms of the original draft of the parties' contract. Consequently, the indemnification provisions are usually among the more heavily negotiated sections of the parties' agreement for the acquisition of a privately held Target.

With respect to indemnification rights, Target Co. (and its selling shareholders) often have a fairly persuasive argument to avoid including any such provision in the acquisition agreement. Target will contend that it has already disclosed to Bidder's representatives *all* the risk-bearing attributes relevant to its business and financial affairs during the course of Bidder's extensive due diligence process and the resulting negotiations between the parties over the terms of the representations and warranties that ultimately were made part of their acquisition agreement. Since Target has already advised Bidder of all the risks associated with Target's business, Target is likely to claim that it is unfair for Bidder to demand indemnification rights as well, claiming that such rights are tantamount to an insurance policy. Bidder, on the other hand, has a strong incentive to insist on the post-closing financial remedy of indemnification in order to motivate Target to disclose all material facts regarding its business as part of the terms of its representations and warranties including any risks associated with the business on a going forward basis that Target is currently aware of. So Bidder is likely to reject any suggestion that indemnification rights are unfair by asserting that Bidder is *not* buying the business *as is*; rather, Bidder has agreed to buy the business that Target has described under the terms of its representations and warranties. If it should turn out that any of these representations are inaccurate, Bidder has been deprived of the benefit of the bargain that it made with Target. Not surprisingly, Bidder then wants to be able to pursue a financial remedy against Target.

Target is likely to respond that the business was sold to Bidder based on full disclosure of those risks to the business, and therefore, they have already been factored into the agreed-upon purchase price. Based on that reasoning, no financial remedy should be made available to Bidder on a post-closing basis. For its part, Bidder is likely to argue that it must have a financial remedy in order for Target's representations to have any meaning. In other words, Bidder is likely to insist that in order for Target's representation to have any meaning, Bidder must have a financial remedy against Target in case there is a discrepancy between the terms of Target's representations and what turns out to be the true state of affairs—which Bidder will learn about only *after* closing on the acquisition agreement. Most likely, Target will lose the argument on this point and the agreement will grant rights of indemnification to Bidder. At this point,

Target's objective in the negotiations is to limit the scope of indemnification as much as possible.

Use of Baskets. Indemnification provisions typically incorporate a concept known among practicing M&A lawyers as a "basket." The idea of a *basket* is that a certain dollar amount of claims must accumulate (in the "basket") before Bidder triggers rights to be indemnified by Target (or, more likely, the sellers of Target). When agreeing to limit its rights of indemnification by use of a basket, Bidder must take into account the use of any materiality qualifiers, which already serve to limit the scope of Target's potential liability for breach of that representation. In these situations, Bidder must be careful that the basket, when coupled with the materiality qualifier, does not undermine the scope of protection that the parties agreed to as a business matter. If Bidder's counsel is not careful, Bidder may inadvertently allow Target to get a break in two different ways. First, Bidder's counsel must be aware that there is already a materiality standard that must be satisfied in order to establish Target's breach of that particular representation. Second, if a basket is to be incorporated into the indemnification provisions, the amount that must accumulate in the basket before triggering Bidder's right to recover from Target needs to take into account the extent to which small, trivial matters have already been addressed (and excluded) as a threshold matter through the operation of the materiality qualifier. In the experience of most M&A lawyers, the negotiations over the terms of indemnification will get intertwined with the negotiations over the terms of the representations whenever the parties introduce the use of a materiality qualifier to limit the scope of Target's representations and thus limit the scope of protection offered to Bidder by the terms of that particular representation.

QUESTIONS

1. Will any of the representations and warranties contained in the Pfizer/Pharmacia merger agreement (see Appendix B) survive closing? Will these provisions provide the basis for any rights of indemnification on a post-closing basis?

2. Will any of the representations and warranties contained in the stock purchase agreement for Galaxy's acquisition of Trekker (see Appendix C) survive closing? After closing, who will be obligated if there is a breach of representation? If there is a breach of one of these provisions, what remedies are available?

NOTES

1. Waiver of Breach of Representation. As to those provisions that Bidder knows to be inaccurate at the time of closing but Bidder decided to close on the acquisition anyway, should Bidder be able to recover under the indemnification provisions of the agreement? Or, should we treat Bidder's decision to close on the acquisition as a *waiver* of its right to recover for any breach of representation and warranty? This is a vexing question because in this situation, Bidder presumably had a *walk-away right* that was triggered because of the bring-down condition. This condition to closing typically requires Target to attest to the accuracy of its representations as of the date of closing. Target is likely to disclose the inaccuracy before closing and should be prepared that such disclosure will trigger Bidder's right to walk away and refuse to close on the deal. In this case, Target is likely to feel that Bidder has been adequately protected by its right to walk away and therefore no post-closing remedy should be available to the Bidder.

 2. Post-Closing Risk vs. Pre-Closing Risk.   Indemnification addresses post-closing risk allocation, while covenants and conditions address pre-closing risk allocation, which, among other things, includes the risk that the deal will not get completed. From Target's perspective, this is a serious issue because if the deal does not close, then Target (and its selling shareholders) are denied the benefit of the bargain made under the terms of their agreement with Bidder. This is a serious risk because the very process of putting the company up for sale and entering into an agreement with Bidder may leave the company vulnerable. For example, this entire process may have destabilized relationships with key customers, may reduce employee morale (because of the uncertainty about the future), and may have adverse consequences on relationships with vendors and other creditors of the company. The next section, as part of the discussion of the due diligence process, describes steps that Target can take to minimize the risk that the deal will not close.

 3. Liquidated Damages or Termination Fees.   The vast majority of deals involving the acquisition of privately held companies do *not* include break-up fees, termination fees, or liquidated damages provisions. This convention seems to rest on the unspoken assumption of the parties that the deal will proceed to close without any major, unforeseen risks that need to be addressed through break-up fees, unlike the situation presented in a public company deal. It would be unusual to include a break-up fee in a private company M&A acquisition because of the apparent assumption made by the parties that Target (and its owners) is a motivated seller and thus wants to proceed with the transaction. If, for some reason, Target (and/or its selling shareholders) decided at closing that it did not want to sell Target's business to Bidder, then it would seem most likely that Bidder would have a strong claim for breach of contract against Target and/or its owners. Accordingly, it is generally assumed that there is no need to include any type of break-up fee in the acquisition agreement.[12]

---

12. By contrast, in the context of public company deals, break-up fees are widely used. The reason for this practice is explored in more detail in Chapter 7, where we examine the fiduciary duty constraints imposed on management in negotiating the terms of these break-up fees and Bidder's incentive to include such fees in the acquisition agreement.

F.   Due Diligence Procedures

The most important objectives of any due diligence investigation (or due diligence review, as many lawyers like to refer to it) are (i) to learn about the business for the purpose of preparing the acquisition agreement and allocating financial and legal risk as to various matters, (ii) to discover significant problems and material liabilities that may be an impediment to closing on a particular transaction, and (iii) to assist the parties in framing the terms of the representations to be included in the acquisition agreement. In terms of timing, some amount of due diligence review must be done in order for the parties to determine whether to incur the costs of bargaining for the terms of an acquisition. Once the parties determine to proceed with the bargaining process beyond the initial stages, negotiations begin in earnest between Bidder and Target regarding the sharing of sensitive proprietary company information. Assuming appropriate confidentiality agreements are in place, the Bidder will then typically undertake a thorough investigation of Target's business and financial affairs. The information disclosed during the course of this investigation will impact the scope of, and any exclusions to, the terms of the representations to be given by Target to Bidder.

Even the most bare bones of due diligence reviews generally involve a substantial cast of personnel, usually consisting at a minimum of the following: counsel for both Bidder and Target, financial advisors (investment bankers) for both parties, auditors for Target and generally other accounting personnel for both Bidder and Target, and finally, senior management and other internal personnel of both companies. Depending on the nature of Target's business, other experts may be brought into the diligence process. For example, if Target is in the oil and gas industry, petroleum engineers may get involved in the diligence review.

Generally speaking, the diligence process is usually organized by the attorneys with Bidder's lawyer playing a key role in defining the scope of the investigation. The first draft of the due diligence checklist is typically prepared by Bidder's lawyer with substantial assistance from Bidder's management and the company's investment bankers. A sample checklist is attached as Appendix E.

As any experienced M&A lawyer will tell you, there is an ever-present danger that Bidder's diligence procedures may become too routine, thereby impeding the business objectives to be accomplished in the context of any particular investigation. In some situations, the process becomes too mechanical, lacking any careful planning as to the scope of items to be reviewed in order to prioritize those items that are most important to Bidder's decision to purchase Target's business so as to be sure these items are carefully reviewed by competent personnel. Alternatively, the investigation may be too superficial, ignoring key operational details, or the investigation may be conducted by personnel too junior and inexperienced to effectively accomplish the purpose of the investigation. For Bidder's part, the failure to conduct adequate due diligence review may be disastrous because it may result in Bidder overpaying to acquire Target. Alternatively, an inadequate diligence review may result in the failure to successfully integrate Target's business operations with Bidder's in order to produce the synergistic gains that Bidder hoped to achieve through the acquisition of Target. In either case, Bidder will often come to regret that it did not under-take a more thorough and systematic due diligence review of Target.

On Target's side, the process is usually coordinated by company counsel who will, like Bidder, assemble a multidisciplinary team to pull together the materials that are responsive to the items on Bidder's due diligence checklist. While the general rule of thumb is that Bidder can never do too much dili-gence, at the same time, Bidder needs to strike an appropriate balance. Bidder obviously needs to conduct a thorough review of Target's business, yet avoid an overbroad investigation that may result in undue strain on the negotiation process between the parties. If Bidder conducts an overbroad investigation, it runs the risk that Target may view the process as a time-wasting activity that delays closing while simultaneously imposing costs on Target and disrupting its workforce and business operations. On the other hand, Bidder must conduct that level of diligence that allows it to make an informed decision regarding its plans for Target and its ability to realize on the business and financial synergies that Bidder hopes to obtain by acquiring Target's business.

Due Diligence and the Risk of the Deal **Not** *Closing.*   As we have seen in the course of the topics covered in this chapter, there are many risks inherent in the deal process, many of which may lead to the deal *not* closing, even though the acquisition agreement is signed and in place. In addition to the risk that the deal may not close at all, Target also faces the risk that the deal may not close on the financial terms that were originally agreed to by Bidder and Target, usually as the result of a purchase price adjustment that works to the financial detriment of Target. In particular, Target fears that during the course of due diligence and the parties' ongoing negotiations leading up to closing on the transaction, Bidder may learn information that will trigger a right to walk away from the deal. In order to avoid this disastrous result, Target may decide to ini-tiate negotiations to adjust the purchase price to reflect new developments.

How can Target (and its lawyer) mitigate against this type of risk? Essen-tially, there are two ways: First, at the outset of parties' negotiation, Target should aggressively negotiate the terms of its representations and the conditions to closing in order to tailor these provisions as narrowly as possible, thereby giving Target the greatest assurance that the deal will close. Second, Target's lawyer can better protect his/her client from the disastrous consequences of a failed deal by helping his/her client to prepare itself for the diligence review *before* actually putting Target up for sale. There are two preliminary measures that Target can take to minimize the risk that the acquisition will not close. The first precaution that Target can take is to think carefully through the consequences of its decision to put the company on the auction block. Second, once the deci-sion has been reached to sell the business, then Target needs to thoroughly pre-pare the company for sale. By taking steps to clean up its business and financial affairs *before* putting the company on the auction block, Target will minimize the risk that obstacles will surface later that might give Bidder the right to walk away from the deal and thus fail to close on the acquisition. These steps would include, at a minimum, preparation of financial statements (i.e., Target either has audited financials already prepared or it has available financial statements that adequately and accurately reflect the company's financial affairs). In addi-tion, Target should have in place a business plan setting forth business and financial objectives that are realistically attainable within the time period covered by the sale process.

Another suggestion that Target lawyers often recommend to their clients is that Target disclose problems early in the process of negotiating the acquisition agreement. In the experience of many M&A lawyers, Target's bargaining leverage will decline steadily as the negotiations proceed. By disclosing problems early, when Target's bargaining power presumably is at its greatest, Target will likely obtain the most optimal resolution of any problems, thereby allowing the deal to proceed to closing. If disclosure is postponed to a later stage in the deal process, Bidder is likely to have the upper hand and either decide to walk away from the deal, or alternatively, to negotiate for a substantial price reduction, both of which work to Target's disadvantage. If Bidder should determine that it is not interested in buying Target, generally it will terminate the deal process. By terminating early in the deal process, the risk to Target is minimized, both in terms of the disruption to its business as well as the out-of-pocket costs incurred in proceeding with this particular Bidder. This advice—to disclose problems early in the negotiating process—often runs contrary to the businessperson's instinct, which usually is to continue marketing the company as the negotiating process begins by continuing to trump the strong points of the company's business. However, in the experience of many M&A lawyers, the strategy of leaving the bad points to be dealt with at the end of the negotiating process often works to Target's disadvantage, especially where Target is serious about doing a deal with this Bidder and thus wants to minimize the risk that the deal will not close.

Use of Due Diligence Checklists. To illustrate the breadth of business and financial matters typically covered in any thorough due diligence review, consult the checklist in Appendix E. This checklist is fairly representative of the sort that every M&A lawyer uses as the starting point in any given transaction. The lawyer's task then is to tailor this list as appropriate to Target's business and the circumstances of that particular transaction. For example, extensive due diligence as to potential environmental liabilities is usually not warranted in connection with the acquisition of a software development business. Obviously, the same is not true in the case of Bidder's purchase of a local chain of dry cleaning stores.

In developing the due diligence checklist for any particular acquisition, a threshold issue that must be considered by the transaction planners is the question of how far back in time is Target going to be required to search in order to produce information relevant to the items of information requested by Bidder. Again, resolution of this issue will generally depend on the relative bargaining power of the parties, but it usually ranges from one to three to five years. In some areas, most notably tax matters, the appropriate time period often turns out to be the relevant statute of limitations period.

A quick review of the items contained in the sample due diligence checklist in Appendix E reflects the obvious need for counsel to assemble a multidisciplinary team of personnel in order to fulfill the objectives of a due diligence review. This is true for both Target's lawyer and Bidder's lawyer. In order to assemble the information that is responsive to the items on this checklist, Target's lawyer must contact the key staff members of Target, who gather the information that Bidder requests to review. Typically, all this material is then gathered in one place (generally known as the "data room"), and made available for Bidder's inspection. On Bidder's side, counsel will usually be required to assemble a diverse team of experts in order to evaluate competently the information provided by Target.

Impact of Due Diligence on Bidder's Integration Planning. The vital importance of adequate due diligence review to Bidder's strategic planning cannot be overstated. In addition, the due diligence process is also of critical importance to Bidder's ongoing process of planning for the integration of Target's business with Bidder's existing operations. The importance of *integration planning* to the success of any particular M&A strategy is reflected in the planning process undertaken by IBM Corp. in connection with the rapid pace of deal making that this blue-chip company has engaged in over the past decade. From 2000 to 2007, IBM made 69 acquisitions as part of its strategic plan to transform its global business into a leading provider of software and services. As a measure of its success in integrating these acquisitions into IBM's business operations to achieve this transformation, revenue from software and services grew from 54 percent of IBM's total in 2000 to 73 percent in 2007. Given that each acquisition poses its own unique set of integration challenges in order for any particular Bidder to obtain the benefit of the bargain in making the purchase, IBM's track record is quite impressive—regardless of the metric used to measure success. *See* Andrea Orr, *End to End at IBM—Big Blue's Take on Integration*, THE DEAL at 58 (Oct. 12, 2007). However, IBM's

> track record is all the more impressive, considering the historically low success rates for transactions in general. . . . And the quantitative results don't account for other key benefits [to be realized from the acquisition,] such as expanding the company's market presence or helping it accelerate internal product development. . . . In the end, what most sets IBM's integration [efforts] apart is its position as part of a comprehensive acquisition process. It's a process where deals are typically championed by line managers going after products their customers want; supported by an experienced corporate development team; and monitored long after closing by top management equipped with tools to measure whether the acquisition is panning out as planned.

Id. at 59-60.

The Role of Due Diligence in Preventing Bidder Overpayment. In August 2011, Hewlett-Packard (HP) announced its plan to acquire Autonomy Inc. for the eye-popping sum of $11.1 billion, in a deal that HP's management, led by its then-CEO Leo Apotheker, believed would "transform HP from a low-margin producer of printers, PCs, and other hardware into a high-margin, cutting-edge software company." James B. Stewart, *From H.P., A Blunder That Seems to Beat All*, N.Y. TIMES, Nov. 30, 2012, *available at* http://www.nytimes.com/2012/12/01/business/hps-autonmy-blunder-might-be-one-for-the-record-books.html?pagewanted=all$_r=0. "Wall Street's reaction to Hewlett-Packard's announcement was swift and harsh," with many analysts claiming that HP's "decision to purchase Autonomy [was] value-destroying." *Id.* Within days of HP's announcement, HP's CEO responded to the wave of criticism regarding HP's "overly expensive acquisition of Autonomy." *Id.* Apotheker was quoted as saying, "We have a pretty rigorous process inside H.P. that we follow for all our acquisitions, which is a D.C.F.-based [discounted cash flow-based] model. . . . And we try to take a very conservative view." *Id.* Within a year, though, Apotheker was no longer HP's CEO; *and* HP announced that "it was writing down $8.8 billion of its acquisition of Autonomy, in effect admitting that the company" had overpaid by just about a whopping 380 percent. *Id.*

In November 2012, at the time the company announced the write-down, HP attributed more than $5 billion of the write-off to what it called "a willful effort on behalf of certain former Autonomy employees to inflate the underlying financial metrics of the company in order to mislead investors and potential buyers. . . . These representations and lack of disclosure severely impacted HP management's ability to fairly value Autonomy at the time of the deal." Press Release, Hewlett-Packard, HP Issues Statement Regarding Autonomy Impairment Charge (Nov. 20, 2012), *available at* http://www.hp.com/hpinfo/newsroom/press/2012/121120b.html. The founder of Autonomy, Michael Lynch, promptly denied HP's claims of fraud and non-disclosure "and accused Hewlett-Packard of mismanaging the acquisition." James B. Stewart, *From H.P., a Blunder That Seems to Beat All*, N.Y. TIMES, Nov. 30, 2012, *available at* http://www.nytimes.com/2012/12/01/business/hps-autonomy-blunder-might-be-one-for-the-record-books.html?pagewanted=all&_r=0. Other observers, however, pointed out that HP's claims of fraud, "while it may offer a face-saving excuse for at least some of HP's huge write-down, shouldn't obscure the fact that the deal was wildly overpriced from the outset, that at least some people at Hewlett-Packard recognized that, and that H.P.'s chairman, Ray Lane, and the board that approved the deal should be held accountable." *Id.* For other knowledgeable observers, however, the more glaring question is: how did HP's financial due diligence process fail to uncover the accounting issues that ultimately contributed to HP's write-down of its acquisition of Autonomy? Ben Worten, et. al, *Long Before H-P Deal, Autonomy's Red Flags*, WALL ST. J., Nov. 26, 2012, *available at* http://online.wsj.com/article/SB10001424127887324784404578141462744040072.html ("questions are mounting about how H-P failed to uncover the alleged irregularities ahead of buying Autonomy, particularly as some outside analysts raised concerns about Autonomy's accounting for years.").

||6||

Federal Regulation of Stock Purchases: Tender Offers and the Williams Act

We have seen that state law regulates the process of Bidder Co. obtaining control over Target Co.'s business either by way of a merger (whether direct or triangular) or by purchasing all of the assets (and agreeing to assume all (or some) of the liabilities). Either way, certain procedural safeguards are granted, as a matter of state law, primarily for the protection of Target shareholders in the face of this type of fundamental change in their corporation. However, with respect to the stock purchase, this method of acquisition is largely unregulated by state law.[1] As we observed in analyzing the problems in Chapter 2, the public policy premise that underlies this "hands off" approach at the state level is largely based on the notion that no shareholder can be forced (coerced) into selling his/her/its shares by the will of the majority. Rather, each Target shareholder must make the independent decision whether to accept Bidder's offer to buy his/her/its shares and endorse over his/her/its stock certificates to Bidder, thereby surrendering his/her/its equity ownership of Target in exchange for the consideration offered by Bidder.

Consequently, when presented with Bidder's offer to buy Target shares, each Target shareholder must decide whether to accept that offer. At a minimum, the shareholder's decision will depend on whether Bidder is offering "fair value" to acquire Target.[2] The vulnerability of Target shareholders is most

---

1. At the end of this chapter, however, we will describe the recent proliferation of state antitakeover statutes, which do have the effect of regulating this method of acquiring Target Co.

2. It is worth observing that, no matter how fair the offer from Bidder is, at least some Target shareholders can be expected to refuse to sell their shares, either because they think the terms offered are not fair, or they just don't want to sell. Instead, they want to remain invested in Target and its business. As we learned in analyzing the scope and availability of the modern appraisal remedy in the materials and problems in Chapter 2, the modern view is that the will of the majority will prevail, notwithstanding the objections of the minority (dissenting) shareholders. Based on this modern view, the Delaware Supreme Court in *Weinberger* concluded that the controlling shareholder can use the Delaware merger procedure for the sole purpose of cashing out (i.e., eliminating) the minority interest—so long as the transaction satisfies the entire fairness test (i.e., fair price and fair dealing). *Weinberger* thus sets the stage for two-step transactions of the type seen in *Weinberger, supra* at page 166,

acute in those transactions where Bidder offers an all-cash purchase price to acquire Target shares. It is then up to the individual shareholder to bargain for the best price possible, an exercise that depends heavily on the shareholder's ability to access necessary information about Target's business and financial affairs in order to bargain effectively with Bidder.

In this chapter, we consider the information needs of the individual Target shareholders, an issue that invariably comes up in the case of stock purchases because of the agency cost problem, an inherent attribute of modern share ownership. In the modern corporation, the agency costs of separating ownership from management and control of the business operations of Target inevitably results in an information gap that leaves Target shareholders without access to the information they need to make an informed decision about whether to accept Bidder's offer. Here, the distinction between privately held vs. publicly traded corporations becomes important in analyzing this agency cost problem in an acquisition context.

In the closely held corporation, these agency costs are typically addressed as a matter of private ordering at the time the individual invests his/her/its capital to purchase shares of Target Co. At the time of investment in Target, the buyer of these shares (at least if he/she/it is well advised) will bargain for certain rights of control over the business affairs of Target (which may include, among other things, veto rights, election of representative(s) to the board of directors, supermajority quorum or voting requirements, or combinations of these and other types of protections). In the absence of these protections, the investor is at the mercy of the default rules provided by the law of the state where Target is organized, including the fiduciary duty obligations imposed by that jurisdiction. With adequate planning, though, the shareholder of the closely held Target will usually have access to the information needed to make an informed decision whether Bidder's offer constitutes fair value.

By contrast, in those situations where Bidder proposes to issue its stock (or other securities) to acquire Target ,this information gap is mitigated (at least somewhat) by the obligations imposed on Bidder by the Securities Act of 1933 (1933 Act). As we learned in Chapter 4, Bidder Co. must either register the issuance of its securities in exchange for Target Co. stock, or find an exemption for its exchange offer. In the acquisition of a closely held Target, Bidder will often find an exemption for the offering, relying on the statutory private placement exemption or one of the Regulation D exemptions. Either way, the issuer (Bidder Co.) must provide the prospective investor (Target Co. shareholder) sufficient information to allow the Target shareholder to make an informed investment decision whether to accept Bidder's exchange offer by signing the stock purchase agreement. As we saw in analyzing the problems in Chapter 2 involving Nestlé's acquisition of all of the stock of Chef America, Inc. from the Merage brothers,

---

Technicolor, supra at page 199, and *Rabkin, supra* at page 208, involving a stock purchase giving Bidder a controlling interest in Target, which is then followed up by a cash-out merger in the back end, thereby eliminating any minority shares of Target that were not acquired in the first step. See Diagram 12 of Appendix A. The protections offered to the minority by way of the appraisal remedy granted as part of the back-end merger were at issue in *Weinberger* and the efficacy of this remedy was discussed at length in Chapter 2.

this combination of protections offered by state and federal law provided the shareholders of Target (Chef America) with the information they needed to make an informed decision whether to accept Bidder (Nestlé) offer to buy all of their shares for cash, or alternatively, for Bidder's (Nestle's) shares.

More problematic is the situation involving Bidder's offer to buy shares of a *publicly traded* Target for *cash*. Here, the agency costs of separating ownership from control of the business affairs of the modern corporation are most acute. In these cases, Target shareholders first learn of Bidder's offer generally by reading of it in a newspaper of wide circulation (such as the *Wall Street Journal*). It is then up to each Target shareholder—which could be tens of thousands in the case of a very large public company, such as Pharmacia—to decide whether to accept Bidder's offer. As passive investors, these (public) shareholders will usually have little knowledge of the day-to-day business affairs of Target. As a result, they are usually quite vulnerable to the high-pressure sales tactics that characterized the early form of all-cash tender offer, known as the "Saturday night special."

Prior to the adoption of the Williams Act in 1968, Bidder Co. could announce, without any warning to Target Co. or its management, that Bidder was making an all-cash offer to buy Target shares. This tender offer would generally be at a premium over the trading price of Target shares in the open market and usually would be conditioned on obtaining a sufficient number of Target shares to give Bidder control over the company. Additionally, Bidder's offer would typically indicate that those Target shares tendered first would be accepted and all others would be rejected (i.e., first come, first accepted). Such an announcement would generate a stampede effect as Target shareholders raced to tender their shares into Bidder's offer, lest they run the risk of being left behind and thus lose out on the opportunity to cash out their Target shares at a premium. In the case of the "Saturday night special," management of Target would be caught completely off guard, since they had no idea that an unsolicited bid was in the works at Bidder. In the usual case, Target management was left with little time to organize itself in order to erect antitakeover defenses, shop for a better offer, or even notify its stockholders whether Bidder's offer represented fair value. In most of these "Saturday night specials," Bidder was an unrelated third party, not an insider of Target, and therefore was not subject to the disclosure obligations imposed by the antifraud rules of the federal securities laws. Equally important, as an unrelated third party, Bidder did not owe any fiduciary duties, as a matter of state law, to Target or its shareholders.

Consequently, one of the principal advantages of the "Saturday night special" was that it allowed Bidder to announce the all-cash offer to purchase Target shares and then proceed to close quickly on its tender offer, unlike the delay associated with merger procedures that required shareholder approval as a matter of state law. Equally important, at least for Bidder, was that no disclosure was required, either to commence its bid or to complete the all-cash tender offer. The only information Bidder had to disclose (as a matter of contract law) in order to complete the transaction was to set forth the offering price and identify the location where the Target shareholders should tender their stock if they chose to accept Bidder's offer.

However, the advantages of the cash tender offer were substantially eroded, if not eliminated altogether, where the tender offer was made using Bidder's *stock,* rather than an all-cash bid for Target. In the case of a *stock exchange offer,* the 1933 Act required Bidder Co. to register the distribution of its shares to Target Co. shareholders in exchange for the surrender of their stock in the publicly traded Target, since no exemption would be available for this issuance of Bidder stock. As we saw in Chapter 4, the issuer's preparation of a registration statement generally resulted in substantial delay in commencing its bid for Target, and the Securities and Exchange Commission's (SEC) review of the Bidder's registration statement once it was filed usually added further delay to the tender offer process.

This all changed when Congress decided to regulate *cash tender offers* by adopting the Williams Act in 1968, which added subsections (d) and (e) to section 13 and subsections (d) and (e) to section 14 of the Securities Exchange Act of 1934 ("1934 Act"). As originally enacted, §13(d) required the filing of a disclosure document with the SEC whenever any person (or group of persons) acquired more than 10 percent of a class of equity security of a company that was registered under the 1934 Act (commonly known as a *reporting company*). As originally adopted, the 10 percent threshold of §13(d), not surprisingly, was tied to the §16 reporting requirements for beneficial owners of more than 10 percent of the equity securities of a reporting company.[*] Later, in 1970, however, Congress amended the statute to reduce the reporting threshold from 10 percent to 5 percent. Today, §13(d) requires anyone who crosses the 5 percent threshold to file a Schedule 13D within ten days after acquiring the securities. The disclosures required by Schedule 13D include, among other things, the name(s) of the buyer(s), the source of funds for the purchase(s) and the price(s) paid, the number of shares owned, the plans for the company if the buyer(s) intend to gain control of the company, and information about any contracts entered into with respect to the acquired securities. The public policy premise for imposing the filing obligations of §13(d) is discussed in *GAF Corp. v. Milstein, infra,* at page 404.

Whereas §13(d) regulates third-party purchases of Target Co. stock, §13(e) is directed at the issuer's repurchase of its own securities. Congress framed §13(e) as an antifraud provision that delegates broad rulemaking authority to the SEC. Pursuant to this grant of authority, the SEC has adopted Rule 13e-1, which requires issuers that propose to engage in repurchases of their shares during the course of a third party's tender offer to file a disclosure document with the SEC. In addition, where the issuer proposes a self-tender, the issuer must file Schedule 13E-4, which, broadly speaking, imposes disclosure obligations substantially similar to those required of a third party (Bidder Co.) when it commences a tender offer for shares of Target Co.

In addition, the SEC has promulgated Rule 13e-3, which requires the issuer to file required disclosures in the case of a *going private transaction.* In general, a *going private transaction* involves a controlling shareholder who proposes to "take the company private" by purchasing all of the publicly held shares that it does not own. Since the enactment of the Sarbanes-Oxley Act of 2002 (SOX),

---

[*]We discussed the requirements of §16(b) of the 1934 Act as part of the materials in Chapter 4. *See supra,* pages 287-291.

there has been a heightened interest in "taking the (publicly traded) company private" in order to avoid the burden of complying with the enhanced disclosure obligations and other corporate reform measures required by SOX, and the related rules of the SEC, the New York Stock Exchange (NYSE), and other relevant self-regulatory organizations (SROs). We will examine the nature of the SEC's regulation of "going private" transactions later in this chapter, in connection with our discussion of the *Carter, Hawley Hale* case. In addition, as part of the materials in Chapter 7, we will examine the intersection of the disclosure obligations imposed under the federal securities laws and the scope of fiduciary duty obligations imposed under state law with respect to going private transactions.

While §13(d) imposes disclosure obligations in connection with open-market purchases of Target Co.'s stock by a third party, §14(d) imposes disclosure obligations in connection with a *tender offer* by a third party, Bidder Co., for shares of a publicly traded Target. Pursuant to §14(d), the SEC has adopted a substantial set of rules (Regulation 14D), prescribing the requisite procedures for commencing and completing a tender offer as well as the disclosures required of a third-party Bidder in order to make a valid tender offer for shares of a publicly traded Target Co.

As part of the Williams Act, Congress legislated reforms intended to address the plight of the Target shareholder when confronted with Bidder's launch of the "Saturday night special." First, the Williams Act required Bidder to provide detailed disclosures, including, among other things, a description of (i) the source of its funds to finance the cash purchase of Target shares; and (ii) Bidder's plans for Target in the event Bidder gains control over Target as a result of its tender offer. The SEC has adopted a detailed set of rules, set forth in Regulation 14D, that expand on the disclosures and procedures required to commence a tender offer.

In addition, Congress legislated other procedural safeguards designed to alleviate the pressures that Target shareholders typically faced when Bidder launched its "Saturday night special." These include (i) a minimum period of time (now 20 business days) that the tender offer must remain open (known as the "offering period") (Rule 14e-1); (ii) Target shareholders must be given the right to withdraw their shares at any point during the offering period (Rule 14d-7); (iii) if the offer is oversubscribed at the end of the offering period, Bidder must purchase the Target shares pro rata from all the tendering shareholders so that all tendering shareholders have the opportunity to cash in their shares (Rule 14d-8); and, finally, (iv) if the Bidder increases its tender offer price during the offering period, it must pay the increased amount to any shareholder who has previously tendered his/her/its shares into the bid (§14(d)(7) and Rule 14d-10(a)(1)). The general goal of these reforms is to reduce the pressure on the Target shareholder to tender early and thereby afford the Target shareholder the opportunity to make an informed decision as to the merits of Bidder's offer.

As part of the Williams Act, Congress also enacted §14(e), which prohibits material misstatements, omissions, and fraudulent practices in connection with tender offers regardless of whether Target is a 1934 Act reporting company. Patterned after the broad prohibition of §10(b) of the 1934 Act, §14(e) (and the SEC rules promulgated thereunder) has been held to apply to a bid for shares of a company that is not registered under the 1934 Act, and therefore the third party's tender offer is not subject to the filing and disclosure requirements of §14(d) and Regulation 14D promulgated thereunder. Pursuant to §14(e), the SEC has adopted Rule 14e-2, which requires Target management to file a Schedule 14D-9 with the SEC within ten days after Bidder commences its tender offer. As part of its obligations under Rule 14e-2, Target management must send a statement to the shareholders recommending either acceptance or rejection of the tender offer, or, alternatively, expressing no opinion toward the offer and the reasons for management's inability to make a recommendation.

The nature and efficacy of all these reforms, which are not without controversy in M&A literature, are explored in the materials that follow.

A.   Disclosure Requirements of §13(d) of the Williams Act

1.   The Filing Obligations Under §13(d)

GAF Corporation v. Milstein
453 F.2d 709 (2d Cir. 1971)

KAUFMAN, Circuit Judge:

This appeal involves the interpretation of section 13(d) of the Securities Exchange Act, hitherto a largely unnoticed provision[2] added in 1968 by the Williams Act. We write, therefore, on a relatively *tabula rasa*, despite the burgeoning field of securities law. Essentially, section 13(d) requires any person, after acquiring more than 10% (now 5%) of a class of registered equity security, to send to the issuer and the exchanges on which the security is traded and file with the Commission the statement required by the Act. Although the section has not attracted as much comment as section 14(d), also added by the Williams Act and requiring disclosure by persons engaging in tender offers, the section has potential for marked impact on holders, sellers and purchasers of securities.

GAF Corporation filed its complaint in the United States District Court for the Southern District of New York alleging that Morris Milstein, his two sons, Seymour and Paul, and his daughter, Gloria Milstein Flanzer, violated section 13(d) of the Securities Exchange Act first by failing to file the required statements and then by filing false ones. The complaint also alleged violation of sec-

---

2. We are aware of only four other cases which considered the section. Bath Industries, Inc. v. Blot, 305 F. Supp. 526 (E.D. Wis. 1969), aff'd, 427 F.2d 97 (7th Cir. 1970); Ozark Airlines, Inc. v. Cox, 326 F. Supp. 1113 (E.D. Mo. 1971); Sisak v. Wings and Wheels Express, Inc., CCH Fed. Sec. L. Rep. ¶92,991 (S.D.N.Y. Sept. 9, 1970); Grow Chemical Corp. v. Uran, 316 F. Supp. 891 (S.D.N.Y. 1970). *See generally* Comment, Section 13(d) and Disclosure of Corporate Equity Ownership, 119 U. Pa. L. Rev. 853 (1971).

tion 10(b) based on the same false statements and, in addition, market manipulation of GAF stock. The Milsteins moved for dismissal under Rule 12(b)(6), F. R. Civ. P., on the ground that the complaint failed to state a claim on which relief could be granted or, in the alternative, for summary judgment under Rule 56. Judge Pollack aptly framed the issues involved:

> The ultimate issue presented by the defendants' motion to dismiss the first count is whether, organizing a group of stockholders owning more than 10% of a class of equity securities with a view to seeking control is, without more, a reportable event under Section 13(d) of the Exchange Act; and as to the second count, whether in the absence of a connected purchase or sale of securities, the target corporation claiming violation of Section 10 and Rule 10b(5), has standing to seek an injunction against a control contestant for falsity in a Schedule 13D filing. (Footnote omitted.)

324 F. Supp. 1062, 1064-1065 (S.D.N.Y. 1971). Judge Pollack granted the Milsteins' motion to dismiss under Rule 12(b)(6), and GAF has appealed. We disagree with Judge Pollack's determination that GAF failed to state a claim under section 13(d) and Rule 13d-1 promulgated thereunder, and thus reverse his order in this respect, but we affirm the dismissal of the second claim of the complaint on the ground that GAF, as an issuer, has no standing under section 10(b). . . .

The four Milsteins received 324,166 shares of GAF convertible preferred stock, approximately 10.25% of the preferred shares outstanding, when The Ruberoid Company, in which they had substantial holdings, was merged into GAF in May, 1967. They have not acquired any additional preferred shares since the merger.

The complaint informs us that at some time after July 29, 1968, the effective date of the Williams Act, the Milsteins "formed a conspiracy among themselves and other persons to act as a syndicate or group for the purpose of acquiring, holding, or disposing of securities of GAF with the ultimate aim of seizing control of GAF for their own personal and private purposes." It is necessary for our purposes to examine only a few of the nine overt acts GAF alleged were taken in furtherance of this conspiracy.

The complaint alleged that initially the Milsteins sought senior management and board positions for Seymour Milstein with GAF. When this sinecure was not forthcoming, the Milsteins allegedly caused Circle Floor Co., Inc., a company in their control, to reduce its otherwise substantial purchases from GAF. It also charged that the Milsteins thereafter undertook a concerted effort to disparage its management and depress the price of GAF common and preferred stock in order to facilitate the acquisition of additional shares. On May 27, 1970, the Milsteins filed a derivative action in the district court, charging the directors, *inter alia,* with waste and spoliation of corporation assets. A companion action was filed in the New York courts. GAF further alleged that these actions were filed only to disparage management, to depress the price of GAF stock and to use discovery devices to gain valuable information for their takeover conspiracy.

In the meantime, the complaint tells us, Paul and Seymour Milstein purchased respectively 62,000 and 64,000 shares of GAF common stock. When GAF contended that the Milsteins were in violation of section 13(d) because they had not filed a Schedule 13D as required by Rule 13d-1, the Milsteins, although disclaiming any legal obligation under section 13(d), filed such a schedule on September 24, 1970. In their 13D statement (appended to the complaint), the Milsteins disclosed their preferred and common holdings and stated they "at some future time [might] determine to attempt to acquire control of GAF. . . . " They also stated that they had "no present intention as to whether or not any additional securities of GAF [might] be acquired by them in the future. . . . " Indeed, within the next two months, commencing with October 2, Paul and Seymour each purchased an additional 41,650 shares of common. The Milsteins thereafter filed a Restated and Amended Schedule 13D on November 10 to reflect these new purchases.

Then, on January 27, 1971, the Milsteins filed a third Schedule 13D, disclosing their intention to wage a proxy contest at the 1971 annual meeting. Although the statement again disclaimed any present intention to acquire additional shares, Paul purchased 28,300 shares of common stock during February, 1971. These last purchases, which brought the Milsteins' total common holdings to 237,600 shares having a value in excess of $2 million and constituting 1.7% of the common shares outstanding, were reflected in a February 23 amendment to the January 27 Schedule 13D.

The last essential datum for our purposes is the proxy contest. On May 10, 1971, it was announced that GAF management had prevailed at the April 16 meeting by a margin of some 2 to 1. . . .

I.

At the time the conspiracy allegedly was formed, section 13(d)(1) in relevant part provided:

> Any person who, after acquiring directly or indirectly the beneficial ownership of any equity security of a class which is registered pursuant to section 12 of this title . . . , is directly or indirectly the beneficial owner of more than 10 per centum [now 5%] of such class shall, within ten days after such acquisition, send to the issuer of the security at its principal executive office, by registered or certified mail, send to each exchange where the security is traded, and file with the Commission, a statement. . . .

This section, however, exempts from its filing requirements any acquisition which, "together with all other acquisitions by the same person of securities of the same class during the preceding twelve months, does not exceed 2 per centum of that class." Section 13(d)(6)(B). Section 13(d)(3), which is crucial to GAF's claim, further provides that "[w]hen two or more persons act as a partnership, limited partnership, syndicate, or other group for the purpose of acquiring, holding, or disposing of securities of an issuer, such syndicate or group shall be deemed a 'person' for the purposes of [section 13(d)]." On the assumption that the facts alleged in the complaint are true, we cannot conclude other than that the four Milsteins constituted a "group" and thus, as a "person," were subject to the provisions of section 13(d). We also are aware of the charge that the Milsteins agreed after July 29, 1968, to hold their GAF preferred shares for the common purpose of acquiring control of GAF. Furthermore, the individuals collectively or as a "group" held more than 10% of the outstanding preferred shares—a registered class of securities. Since the section requires a "person" to file only if he acquires more than 2% of the class of stock in a 12-month period after July 29, 1968,[12] the principal question presented to us is whether the complaint alleges as a matter of law that the Milstein *group* "acquired" the 324,166 shares of preferred stock owned by its members after that date. We conclude that it does and thus that it states a claim under section 13(d).

The statute refers to "acquiring directly or indirectly the beneficial ownership of securities." Thus, at the outset, we are not confronted with the relatively simple concept of legal title, but rather with the amorphous and occasionally obfuscated concepts of indirect and beneficial ownership which pervade the securities acts.

The Act nowhere explicitly defines the concept of "acquisition" as used in section 13(d). Although we are aware of Learned Hand's warning "not to make a fortress out of the dictionary," Cabell v. Markham, 148 F.2d 737, 739 (2d Cir.), aff'd, 326 U.S. 404, 66 S. Ct. 193, 90 L. Ed. 165 (1945), some light, although dim, is shed by Webster's Third International Dictionary. It tells us that "to acquire" means "to come into possession [or] control." If the allegations in the complaint are true, then the group, which must be treated as an entity separate and distinct from its members, could have gained "beneficial control" of the voting rights of the preferred stock[13] only after its formation, which we must assume occurred after the effective date of the Williams Act. Manifestly, according to the complaint, the group when formed acquired a beneficial interest in the individual holdings of its members. We find ourselves in agreement with the statement of the Court of Appeals for the Seventh Circuit in Bath Industries, Inc. v. Blot, 427 F.2d 97, 112 (7th Cir. 1970), that in the context of the Williams Act, where the principal concern is focused on the battle for corporate control, "voting control of stock is the only relevant element of beneficial ownership." Thus, we hardly can agree with Judge Pollack that the language of the statute compels the conclusion that individual members must acquire shares before the group can be required to file. . . .

The legislative history, as well as the purpose behind section 13(d), bears out our interpretation. Any residual doubt over its soundness is obviated by the following clear statement appearing in both the House and Senate reports accompanying the Williams Act:

> "[Section 13(d)(3)] would prevent a group of persons who seek to pool their voting or other interests in the securities of any issuer from evading the provisions of the statute because no one individual owns more than 10 percent of the securities. *The group would be deemed to have become the beneficial owner, directly or indirectly,*

---

12. The Milsteins concede that their group would have been required to file if the individual members had acquired additional preferred shares after the effective date of the Williams Act and within a 12-month period which amounted to more than 2% of the outstanding shares.

13. The convertible preferred stock votes share-for-share with the common stock. Each share of preferred is convertible into 1.25 shares of common stock.

of more than 10 percent of a class of securities at the time they agreed to act in concert. Consequently, the group would be required to file the information called for in section 13(d)(1) within 10 days after they agree to act together, whether or not any member of the group had acquired any securities at that time." S. Rep. No. 550, 90th Cong., 1st Sess. 8 (1967); H.R. Rep. No. 1711, 90th Cong., 2d Sess. 8-9 (1968), U.S. Code Cong. & Admin. News, p. 2818 (*Emphasis added.*)

Indeed, Professor Loss, one of the foremost scholars of securities law, reached the same interpretation in his treatise, citing this passage. 6 L. Loss, Securities Regulation 3664 (Supp. 1969).

The Senate and House reports and the Act as finally enacted, contrary to appellees' contention,[15] are entirely consistent in our view. This conclusion is buttressed by a consideration of the purpose of the Act. The 1960's on Wall Street may best be remembered for the pyrotechnics of corporate takeovers and the phenomenon of conglomeration. Although individuals seeking control through a proxy contest were required to comply with section 14(a) of the Securities Exchange Act and the proxy rules promulgated by the SEC, and those making stock tender offers were required to comply with the applicable provisions of the Securities Act, before the enactment of the Williams Act there were no provisions regulating cash tender offers or other techniques of securing corporate control. According to the committee reports:

"The [Williams Act] would correct the current gap in our securities laws by amending the Securities Exchange Act of 1934 to provide for full disclosure in connection with cash tender offers and other techniques for accumulating large blocks of equity securities of publicly held companies." S. Rep. No. 550 at 4; H.R. Rep. No. 1711 at 4, U.S. Code Cong. & Admin. News p. 2814.

Specifically, we were told, "the purpose of section 13(d) is to require disclosure of information by persons who have acquired a substantial interest, or increased their interest in the equity securities of a company by a substantial amount, within a relatively short period of time." S. Rep. No. 550 at 7; H.R. Rep. No. 1711 at 8, U.S. Code Cong. & Admin. News p. 2818. Otherwise, investors cannot assess the potential for changes in corporate control and adequately evaluate the company's worth.[16]

That the purpose of section 13(d) is to alert the marketplace to every large, rapid aggregation or accumulation of securities, regardless of technique employed, which might represent a potential shift in corporate control is amply reflected in the enacted provisions. Section 13(d)(1)(C) requires the person filing to disclose any intention to acquire control. If he has such an intention,

---

15. Appellees in their brief "concede" that the 1968 committee reports are "against" them. Professor Loss, co-counsel for the Milsteins both in this and the lower court, informed us at the argument that the view set forth in his treatise was "a mistake" and that this passage is "diametrically opposed to the text of the statute" and the purpose and intent of the Williams Act.

16. The committee reports make it clear that the Act was designed for the benefit of investors and not to tip the balance of regulation either in favor of management or in favor of the person seeking corporate control. *See* S. Rep. No. 550 at 3-4; H.R. Rep. No. 1711 at 4.

he must disclose any plans for liquidating the issuer, selling its assets, merging it with another company or changing substantially its business or corporate structure. It is of some interest, moreover, that section 13(d)(6)(D) empowers the Commission to exempt from the filing requirements "any acquisition . . . as not entered into for the purpose of, and not having the effect of, changing or influencing the control of the issuer *or otherwise* as not comprehended within the purpose of [section 13(d)]." (*Emphasis added.*)

The alleged conspiracy on the part of the Milsteins is one clearly intended to be encompassed within the reach of section 13(d). We have before us four shareholders who together own 10.25% of an outstanding class of securities and allegedly agreed to pool their holdings to effect a takeover of GAF. This certainly posed as great a threat to the stability of the corporate structure as the individual shareholder who buys 10.25% of the equity security in one transaction.[17] A shift in the *loci* of corporate power and influence is hardly dependent on an actual transfer of legal title to shares, and the statute and history are clear on this.

In light of the statutory purpose as we view it, we find ourselves in disagreement with the interpretation of *Bath Industries, supra,* that the group owning more than 10%, despite its agreement to seize control, in addition, must agree to acquire more shares before the filing requirement of section 13(d) is triggered. The history and language of section 13(d) make it clear that the statute was primarily concerned with disclosure of *potential changes* in control resulting from new aggregations of stockholdings and was not intended to be restricted to only individual stockholders who made future purchases and whose actions were, therefore, more apparent.[18] *See* Comment, Section 13(d) and Disclosure of Corporate Equity Ownership, 119 U. Pa. L. Rev. 853, 869-72 (1971). It hardly can be questioned that a group holding sufficient shares can effect a takeover without purchasing a single additional share of stock.

Two "policy" considerations have been advanced against our interpretation. First, the district judge warned that "[t]he inherent difficulty of ascertaining when a group was formed is akin to an attempt to grasp quicksilver." 324 F. Supp. at 1068. This supposed difficulty, however, would not be dissipated even under his view—that individual members must acquire more than 2% after July 29, 1968, before the group can be compelled to file. The court still would be required to determine whether the individuals indeed constituted a "group." But, we hardly envision this as an insuperable obstacle to stating a claim in a complaint. GAF, in order to succeed on the merits, will have to carry its burden

---

17. The appellees correctly argue that section 13(d) was not intended to be retroactive—that is, all persons who held 10% of an outstanding class before July 29, 1968, are not required to file unless they acquire an additional 2% after that date. *Compare* §16(a). But, the Milstein group is not a "person" who held its stock before the effective date of the Williams Act, if the allegations of the complaint are to be accepted. The crucial event under section 13(d) was the formation of the group, which allegedly occurred after the effective date and the purpose of which was to seize control of GAF.

18. Section 13(d)(3) refers to groups formed "for the purpose of acquiring, holding, *or* disposing of securities." *Bath Industries* would read out "holding" and "disposing."

of proof by a fair preponderance of the evidence. It will have to produce evidence establishing that the conspiracy came into being after July 29, 1968, with the purpose of seizing control. If GAF should succeed on the merits, any difficulty in pinpointing the precise date, as distinguished from an approximate time, when the conspiracy was formed and the group became subject to section 13(d) can be one of the elements considered by the district judge in fashioning appropriate equitable relief.

The Milsteins also caution us against throwing our hook into the water and catching too many fish — namely, hundreds of families and other management groups which control companies with registered securities and whose members collectively own more than 5% of a class of the company's stock. Although this problem is not part of the narrow issue we must decide, we cannot close our eyes to the implications of our decision. Upon examination, however, the argument while superficially appealing proves to be totally without substance. Management groups *per se* are not customarily formed for the purpose of "acquiring, holding, or disposing of securities of [the] issuer" and would not be required to file unless the members conspired to pool their securities interests for one of the stated purposes.[20] . . .

QUESTIONS

1. Why did Congress impose the §13(d) filing obligation?

2. Since the Milsteins owned their GAF stock before the Williams Act became effective, what triggered their obligation to file under §13(d)?

3. If §13(d)(6) exempts acquisitions that in the course of the preceding 12 months do not exceed 2 percent of the class, why did the Milsteins' activity with respect to the common stock of GAF trigger a §13(d) filing obligation?

4. What does it take to form a "group"?

5. What is the public policy justification for imposing the disclosure obligation of §13(d) on a "group" who acquires or holds 5 percent of a class of Target's securities? Whose interests are to be protected by this disclosure?

6. What is the regulatory gap that the disclosure obligations imposed under §13(d) of the Williams Act are intended to address?

---

20. The more difficult question, and a question we need not decide on this appeal, is whether management groups which expressly agree to pool their interests to fight a potential takeover are subject to section 13(d). Nor do we intimate any view on whether an insurgent group which has filed under section 13(d) and subsequently is successful in its takeover bid remains subject to the section. In any event, as we have already indicated, the Commission can forestall any untoward effects under the exemptive power conferred upon it by section 13(d)(6)(D).

NOTES

1. Rule 13d-3.   The holding of the principal case has now been codified by the SEC in its Rule 13d-3, reflecting the *GAF* court's "group theory" of beneficial ownership such that will trigger the obligation to file a Schedule 13D.

2. Schedule 13D vs. Schedule 13G Filers.   The SEC's rules permit certain large shareholders to file a more abbreviated form of disclosure on Schedule 13G. In general, Schedule 13G will be filed by "passive shareholders"; that is, shareholders who do not seek to acquire or influence "control" of the issuer and who beneficially own less than 20 percent of the issuer's shares. The SEC's rules also provide that if Schedule 13G filers no longer hold their shares for passive investment purposes (or if their shareholdings exceed 20 percent), then a Schedule 13D must be filed within 10 days. In addition, these passive shareholders must make an annual Schedule 13G filing with the SEC within 45 days after the end of each calendar year.

3. Stock Parking as a Violation of §13(d).   The "parking of shares" can give rise to a violation of §13(d). In the typical *stock parking* arrangement, one trader will agree to buy shares of a publicly traded company on the open market and to hold these shares for the benefit of another trader, whose identity can then be concealed from other market participants. These arrangements will very often include unwritten agreements on the part of the beneficial owner of the shares to protect the buyer of the shares against losses and to share profits. These arrangements to "park shares" in the account of another trading professional allow the beneficial owner to carve up ownership of the company's stock in order to avoid the disclosure requirements of §13(d), which would otherwise be triggered once the beneficial owner crossed the 5 percent threshold. Parking violations were made famous in the 1980s as a result of the SEC's prosecution of Ivan Boesky; as described in more detail in the next chapter, this investigation ultimately led to the downfall of Michael Milken and his firm, Drexel Burnham Lambert.

4. The Role of Risk Arbitrageurs.   Ivan Boesky's firm was known as a "risk arbitrageur," which essentially means that his firm specialized in buying shares of a company that was the target of a takeover. As we have seen in earlier chapters (and as we shall see in the takeover cases that we will read later in this chapter and in Chapter 7), the market, or trading, price of Target's shares is usually less than the share price being offered by the Bidder as part of its tender offer for Target's publicly traded shares. The spread (i.e., the difference) between the trading price and the offering price is largely a function of the market's assessment of the probability of Bidder being able to complete the deal and the timing of the closing on the deal, if it is ultimately completed. Traders (such as Ivan Boesky's firm) are essentially making a "Las Vegas-style" bet that there will be a takeover of Target. Of course, from the perspective of risk arbitrage firms, the downside risk is that the deal falls apart, in which case the arbitrage firm loses the opportunity to "cash in" (i.e., tender) its shares to Bidder and receive the offering price. This type of risk arbitrage activity is today, and always has been, an accepted part of M&A activity. As such, risk arbitrageurs serve the legitimate and useful economic function of allowing professional traders to assume much of the financial risk that is inherent in trading shares of companies who are engaged in takeover battles. However, as we shall see in the takeover cases in this chapter and in the next chapter, arbitrage firms are essentially traders with a very short-term investment horizon, and therefore, are essentially betting on the success of the takeover bid.

   5. Empty Voting.   In 2006, in what has come to be viewed as a groundbreaking and quite provocative article, Professors Henry Hu and Bernard Black described instances involving a phenomenon that they referred to as "empty voting"; that is, the ability to separate a share's voting rights from any economic ownership interest in the company itself—in effect a new form of "vote buying." *See* Henry T. C. Hu and Bernard Black, *Empty Voting and Hidden (Morphable) Ownership: Taxonomy, Implications, and Reforms*, 61 BUSINESS LAWYER 1011 (2006). In this article, they describe the phenomenon of "empty voting" and the related concept of "morphable ownership" as follows:

> Most American publicly held corporations have a one-share, one-vote structure, in which voting power is proportional to economic ownership. This structure gives shareholders economic incentives to exercise their voting power well and helps to legitimate managers' exercise of authority over property the managers do not own. Berle-Means' "separation of ownership and control"[*] suggests that shareholders face large collective action problems in overseeing managers. Even so, mechanisms rooted in the shareholder vote, including proxy fights and takeover bids, constrain managers from straying too far from the goal of shareholder wealth maximization.
>
> In the past few years, the derivatives revolution, hedge fund growth, and other capital market developments have come to threaten this familiar pattern throughout the world. Both outside investors and corporate insiders can now readily decouple economic ownership of shares from voting rights to those shares. This decoupling—which we call "the new vote buying"—is often hidden from public view and is largely untouched by current law and regulation. Hedge funds, sophisticated and largely unfettered by legal rules or conflicts of interest, have been especially aggressive in decoupling. Sometimes they hold more votes than economic ownership, a pattern we call "empty voting." That is, they may have substantial voting power while having limited, zero, or even negative economic ownership. In the extreme situation of negative economic ownership, the empty voter has an incentive to vote in ways that reduce the company's share price. Sometimes hedge funds hold more economic ownership than votes, though often with "morphable" voting rights—the de facto ability to acquire the votes if needed. We call this "hidden (morphable) ownership" because under current disclosure rules, the economic ownership and (de facto) voting ownership are often not disclosed. Corporate insiders, too, can use new vote buying techniques.
>
> This article analyzes the new vote buying and its corporate governance implications. We propose a taxonomy of the new vote buying that unpacks its functional elements. We discuss the implications of decoupling for control contests and other forms of shareholder oversight, and the circumstances in which

---

[*] [By the author] Professors Hu and Black are referring to the seminal work, Adolphe Berle and Gardiner Means, THE MODERN CORPORATION AND PRIVATE PROPERTY (1932).

decoupling could be beneficial or harmful to corporate governance. We also propose a near-term disclosure-based response and sketch longer-term regulatory possibilities.* Our disclosure proposal would simplify and partially integrate five existing, inconsistent share-ownership disclosure regimes, and is worth considering independent of its value with respect to decoupling. In the longer term, other responses may be needed; we briefly discuss possible strategies focused on voting rights, voting architecture, and supply and demand forces in the markets on which the new vote buying relies.

Henry T.C. Hu and Bernard Black, *supra*, 61 Bus. Law. at 1011-1012.

Since this article was first published, increasing attention has been focused on the legal and business issues surrounding empty voting and morphable ownership. *See, e.g.,* Henry T. C. Hu and Bernard Black, *Equity and Debt Decoupling and Empty Voting II: Importance and Extensions,* 156 U. Penn. L. Rev. 625 (2008) (where the authors extend their earlier work to show how the growth of hedge funds and the emergence of over-the-counter (OTC) equity derivatives have greatly facilitated large-scale, low-cost decoupling of shareholder voting rights from shareholder economic interests, and further describe their proposed reforms to address this growing phenomenon); and Jordan M. Barry, John William Hatfield, and Scott Duke Kominers, *On Derivatives Markets and Social Welfare: A Theory of Empty Voting and Hidden Ownership,* BFI Working Paper Series No. 2012-011 (August 22, 2012) *available at* http://ssrn.com/abstract=2134458 (where the authors argue that the present economic evidence contradicts the prevailing view "that derivatives markets simply enable financial markets to incorporate information better and faster . . . thereby increasing the efficiency of the capital markets." Instead, these authors claim that the use of derivatives to allow for empty voting strategies serves to "render financial markets unpredictable, unstable, and inefficient;" their analysis leads these authors to recommend "a robust mandatory disclosure regime" for these empty voting practices). While the implications of empty voting practices and the consequences of hidden ownership have led many commentators to call for the SEC to take action, as of this writing (Fall 2012), no formal action has been adopted by the SEC.

6. *Proposals to Reform Section 13(d)'s "10 Day Window."* In March 2011, the law firm of Wachtel, Lipton, Rosen, and Katz submitted a rule-making proposal to the SEC, asking the commission to close the current "ten-day window between crossing the 5 percent disclosure threshold and the initial filing deadline" for a Schedule 13D. The basis for this proposal centered on "[r]ecent maneuvers by activist investors both in the U.S. and abroad that have demonstrated the extent to which current reporting gaps may be exploited, to the detriment of issuers,

---

* [By the author] In Part III of their article, Professors Hu and Black describe the current disclosure obligations of Section 13(d) and the SEC's rules promulgated thereunder and illustrate how these rules apply to empty voting schemes, thereby exposing gaps in the current regulatory scheme. In Parts IV and V, the authors offer their proposals for reform of existing disclosure rules, as well as other potential regulatory responses to the problem of empty voting and hidden ownership.

other investors, and the market as a whole." Wachtell, Lipton, Rosen, & Katz, *Petition for Rulemaking Under Section 13 of the Securities Exchange Act of 1934,* Mar. 7, 2011, *available at* www.sec.gov/rules/petitions/2011/petn4-624.pdf (Wachtell Lipton Petition). Since this proposal was originally submitted, Wachtell, Lipton has expanded on the public policy premise for its proposed reform measures as follows:

> Our [rule-making] petition included the proposal that the disclosure window in the SEC's rules implementing Section 13(d) be reduced from ten days to one business day. This proposal reflects the reality that the mechanics of accumulation that exist today allow blockholders to accumulate massive stakes in the ten-day window, thereby defeating the statutory purpose of alerting the market to creeping threats to control. The trading world has changed around the rule, with the result that the rule no longer does the work for which the statute was enacted. The [Wachtel Lipton Petition] noted numerous situations in which aggressive investors have taken advantage of the legal loophole to build enormously powerful, control-threatening stakes in their ten-day windows, and further highlighted that other sophisticated securities markets have already taken regulatory steps to reduce the risk of undisclosed rapid accumulations . . . [In addition, the Wachtel Lipton Petition] sought to ensure that the [Section 13(d)] reporting rules would continue to operate in a way broadly consistent with the statute's clear purposes* and that loopholes that have arisen by changing market conditions and practices since the statute's adoption over forty years ago could not continue to be exploited by acquirers, to the detriment of the public markets and security holders. The changes suggested by the [Wachtell Lipton Petition] would bring the U.S. blockholder reporting regime broadly in line with those of virtually all other major developed economies.

Adam O. Emmerich, Theodore N. Mirvis, et al., *Fair Markets and Fair Disclosure: Some Thoughts on the Law and Economics of Blockholder Disclosure, and the Use and Abuse of Shareholder Power,* Columbia Law & Economics Working Paper No. 428 (2012), *available at* http://ssrn.com/abstract=2138945.

Wachtell Lipton's reform proposal has generated considerable controversy. Most notably, Professors Lucian Bebchuk and Robert Jackson, Jr., countered by submitting a letter to the SEC in July 2011, challenging the public policy premise underlying the Wachtell Lipton proposal. *See* Lucian A. Bebchuk & Robert J. Jackson Jr., *Letter to the Securities and Exchange Commission Regarding Commission Examination of Section 13(d) Rules and Rulemaking Petition Submitted by Wachtell, Lipton, Rosen, and Katz, LLP,* (July 11, 2011), *available at* www.sec.gov/comments/4-624/4624-3.pdf. More specifically, they explain that

> [First, there is] significant empirical evidence indicating that the accumulation and holding of outside blocks in public companies benefits shareholders by making incumbent directors and managers more accountable and thereby reducing agency costs and managerial slack.

---

* [By the author] As set forth in the legislature history, the purpose of Section 13(d) is "to alert the marketplace to every large, rapid aggregation or accumulation of securities," *GAF Corp. v. Milstein,* 453 F.2d 709, 717 (2d Cir. 1971), as well as to provide shareholders with "full disclosure when over 5 percent of their company stock is acquired by an outside group." H.R. Rep. No. 91-1125 (1970).

Second, we explain that tightening the rules applicable to outside blockholders can be expected to reduce the returns to blockholders and thereby reduce the incidence and size of outside blocks—and, thus, blockholders' investments in monitoring and engagement, which in turn could result in increased agency costs and managerial slack.

Third, we explain that there is currently no empirical evidence to support [Wachtell Lipton's] assertion that changes in trading technologies and practices have recently led to a significant increase in pre-disclosure accumulations of ownership stakes by outside blockholders.

Fourth, we explain that, since the passage of Section 13, changes in state law—including the introduction of poison pills with low-ownership triggers that impede outside blockholders that are not seeking control—have tilted the playing field against such blockholders.

Finally, we explain that a tightening of the rules [as suggested in Wachtell Lipton's proposal] cannot be justified on the grounds that such tightening is needed to protect investors from the possibility that outside blockholders will capture a control premium at other shareholders' expense.

We conclude by recommending that the [SEC] pursue a comprehensive examination of the rules governing outside blockholders and the empirical questions raised by our analysis. In the meantime, the [SEC] should not adopt new rules that tighten restrictions on outside blockholders. Existing research and available empirical evidence provide no basis for concluding that tightening the rules governing outside blockholders would satisfy the requirement that [SEC] rulemaking protect investors and promote efficiency—and indeed raise concerns that such tightening could harm investors and undermine efficiency.

Id.; see also Lucian A. Bebchuk and Robert J. Jackson, Jr., *The Law and Economics of Blockholder Disclosure*, 2 HARV. BUS. L. REV. 40 (Spring 2012).

In the face of this controversy, the SEC responded in December 2011 by announcing its plans to undertake a comprehensive review of its beneficial reporting rules. *See* Chairwoman Mary L. Schapiro, Remarks at the Transatlantic Corporate Governance Dialogue, U.S. Securities and Exchange Commission, Washington, D.C., Dec. 15, 2011, *available at* www.sec.gov/news/speech/2011/spch121511mls.htm. In making this announcement, the SEC indicated that

> The review process will begin with a concept release and will address whether the 10-day initial filing requirement for Schedule 13D filings should be shortened; whether beneficial ownership reporting of cash-settled equity swaps and other types of derivative instruments should be clarified and strengthened; and how the presentation of information on Schedule 13D and Schedule 13G can be improved.

> Chairwoman Schapiro [also] noted that under the Dodd-Frank Wall Street Reform and Consumer Protection Act, the SEC has new statutory authority to shorten the 10-day filing period for initial Schedule 13D filings, as well as to regulate beneficial ownership reporting of security-based swaps. Specifically, Congress modified § 13(d)(1) of the Exchange Act to read, "within ten days after such acquisition, or *within such shorter time as the Commission may establish by rule.*" With this modification, Congress . . . [has] laid the legislative groundwork for needed reform in this area.

David Katz and Laura McIntosh, *Corporate Governance Update: Section 13(d) Reporting Requirements Need Updating*, NEW YORK LAW JOURNAL (March 22, 2012) (*emphasis in original*).

2.   The Remedy for §13(d) Violations

|| **Rondeau v. Mosinee Paper Corporation**
|| 422 U.S. 49, 95 S. Ct. 2069, 45 L. Ed. 2d 12 (1975)

Mr. Chief Justice BURGER delivered the opinion of the Court.

We granted certiorari in this case to determine whether a showing of irreparable harm is necessary for a private litigant to obtain injunctive relief in a suit under §13(d) of the Securities Exchange Act of 1934, 48 Stat. 894, as added by §2 of the Williams Act, 82 Stat. 454, as amended, 84 Stat. 1497, 15 U.S.C. §78m(d). 419 U.S. 1067, 95 S. Ct. 653, 42 L. Ed. 2d 663 (1974). The Court of Appeals held that it was not. 500 F.2d 1011 (CA7 1974). We reverse.

I

Respondent Mosinee Paper Corp. is a Wisconsin company engaged in the manufacture and sale of paper, paper products, and plastics. Its principal place of business is located in Mosinee, Wis., and its only class of equity security is common stock which is registered under §12 of the Securities Exchange Act of 1934, 15 U.S.C. §78l. At all times relevant to this litigation there were slightly more than 800,000 shares of such stock outstanding.

In April 1971 petitioner Francis A. Rondeau, a Mosinee businessman, began making large purchases of respondent's common stock in the over-the-counter market. . . . By May 17, 1971, petitioner had acquired 40,413 shares of respondent's stock, which constituted more than 5% of those outstanding. He was therefore required to comply with the disclosure provisions of the Williams Act, by filing a Schedule 13D with respondent and the Securities and Exchange Commission within 10 days. That form would have disclosed, among other things, the number of shares beneficially owned by petitioner, the source of the funds used to purchase them, and petitioner's purpose in making the purchases.

Petitioner did not file a Schedule 13D but continued to purchase substantial blocks of respondent's stock. By July 30, 1971, he had acquired more than 60,000 shares. On that date the chairman of respondent's board of directors informed him by letter that his activity had "given rise to numerous rumors" and "seems to have created some problems under the Federal Securities Laws. . . ." Upon receiving the letter petitioner immediately stopped placing orders for respondent's stock and consulted his attorney. On August 25, 1971, he filed a Schedule 13D which, in addition to the other required disclosures, described the "Purpose of Transaction" as follows:

> "Francis A. Rondeau determined during early part of 1971 that the common stock of the Issuer [respondent] was undervalued in the over-the-counter market and represented a good investment vehicle for future income and appreciation. Francis A. Rondeau and his associates presently propose to seek to acquire additional common stock of the Issuer in order to obtain effective control of the Issuer, but such investments as originally determined were and are not necessarily made with this objective in mind. Consideration is currently being given to making

a public cash tender offer to the shareholders of the Issuer at a price which will reflect current quoted prices for such stock with some premium added."

Petitioner also stated that, in the event that he did obtain control of respondent, he would consider making changes in management "in an effort to provide a Board of Directors which is more representative of all of the shareholders, particularly those outside of present management. . . . " One month later petitioner amended the form to reflect more accurately the allocation of shares between himself and his companies.

On August 27 respondent sent a letter to its shareholders informing them of the disclosures in petitioner's Schedule 13D.[3] The letter stated that by his "tardy filing" petitioner had "withheld the information to which you [the shareholders] were entitled for more than two months, in violation of federal law." In addition, while agreeing that "recent market prices have not reflected the real value of your Mosinee stock," respondent's management could "see little in Mr. Rondeau's background that would qualify him to offer any meaning full guidance to a Company in the highly technical and competitive paper industry."

Six days later respondent initiated this suit in the United States District Court for the Western District of Wisconsin. Its complaint named petitioner, his companies, and two banks which had financed some of petitioner's purchases as defendants and alleged that they were engaged in a scheme to defraud respondent and its shareholders in violation of the securities laws. It alleged further that shareholders who had "sold shares without the information which defendants were required to disclose lacked information material to their decision whether to sell or hold," and that respondent "was unable to communicate such information to its stockholders, and to take such actions as their interest required." Respondent prayed for an injunction prohibiting petitioner and his codefendants from voting or pledging their stock and from acquiring additional shares, requiring them to divest themselves of stock which they already owned, and for damages. A motion for a preliminary injunction was filed with the complaint but later withdrawn.

After three months of pretrial proceedings petitioner moved for summary judgment. He readily conceded that he had violated the Williams Act, but contended that the violation was due to a lack of familiarity with the securities laws and that neither respondent nor its shareholders had been harmed. The District Court agreed. It found no material issues of fact to exist regarding petitioner's lack of willfulness in failing to timely file a Schedule 13D, concluding that he discovered his obligation to do so on July 30, 1971, and that there was no basis in the record for disputing his claim that he first considered the possibility of obtaining control of respondent some time after that date. The District Court therefore held that petitioner and his codefendants "did not engage in intentional covert, and conspiratorial conduct in failing to timely file the 13D Schedule." . . .

The Court of Appeals reversed, with one judge dissenting. . . .

---

3. Respondent simultaneously issued a press release containing the same information. Almost immediately the price of its stock jumped to $19-$21 per share. A few days later it dropped back to the prevailing price of $12.50-$14 per share, where it remained.

II

. . . The Court of Appeals' conclusion that respondent suffered "harm" sufficient to require sterilization of petitioner's stock need not long detain us. The purpose of the Williams Act is to insure that public shareholders who are confronted by a cash tender offer for their stock will not be required to respond without adequate information regarding the qualifications and intentions of the offering party.[8] By requiring disclosure of information to the target corporation as well as the Securities and Exchange Commission, Congress intended to do no more than give incumbent management an opportunity to express and explain its position. The Congress expressly disclaimed an intention to provide a weapon for management to discourage takeover bids or prevent large accumulations of stock which would create the potential for such attempts. Indeed, the Act's draftsmen commented upon the "extreme care" which was taken "to avoid tipping the balance of regulation either in favor of management or in favor of the person making the takeover bid." S. Rep. No. 550, 90th Cong., 1st Sess., 3 (1967); H.R. Rep. No. 1711, 90th Cong., 2d Sess., 4 (1968). U.S. Code Cong. & Admin. News 1968, p. 2811. See also Electronic Specialty v. International Controls Corp., 409 F.2d 937, 947 (CA2 1969).

The short of the matter is that none of the evils to which the Williams Act was directed has occurred or is threatened in this case. Petitioner has not attempted to obtain control of respondent, either by a cash tender offer or any other device. Moreover, he has now filed a proper Schedule 13D, and there has been no suggestion that he will fail to comply with the Act's requirement of reporting any material changes in the information contained therein.[9] On this record there is no likelihood that respondent's shareholders will be disadvantaged should petitioner make a tender offer, or that respondent will be unable to adequately place its case before them should a contest for control develop.

---

8. The Senate Report describes the dilemma facing such a shareholder as follows:

"He has many alternatives. He can tender all of his shares immediately and hope they are all purchased. However, if the offer is for less than all the outstanding shares, perhaps only a part of them will be taken. In these instances, he will remain a shareholder in the company, under a new management which he has helped to install without knowing whether it will be good or bad for the company."

"The shareholder, as another alternative, may wait to see if a better offer develops, but if he tenders late, he runs the risk that none of his shares will be taken. He may also sell his shares in the market or hold them and hope for the best. Without knowledge of who the bidder is and what he plans to do, the shareholder cannot reach an informed decision."

S. Rep. No. 550, 90th Cong., 1st Sess., 2 (1967). However, the Report also recognized "that takeover bids should not be discouraged because they serve a useful purpose in providing a check on entrenched but inefficient management." Id., at 3.

9. Because this case involves only the availability of injunctive relief to remedy a §13(d) violation following compliance with the reporting requirements, it does not require us to decide whether or under what circumstances a corporation could obtain a decree enjoining a shareholder who is currently in violation of §13(d) from acquiring further shares, exercising voting rights, or launching a takeover bid, pending compliance with the reporting requirements.

Thus, the usual basis for injunctive relief, "that there exists some cognizable danger of recurrent violation," is not present here. United States v. W.T. Grant, 345 U.S. 629, 633.

Nor are we impressed by respondent's argument that an injunction is necessary to protect the interests of its shareholders who either sold their stock to petitioner at predisclosure prices or would not have invested had they known that a takeover bid was imminent. As observed, the principal object of the Williams Act is to solve the dilemma of shareholders desiring to respond to a cash tender offer, and it is not at all clear that the type of "harm" identified by respondent is redressable under its provisions. In any event, those persons who allegedly sold at an unfairly depressed price have an adequate remedy by way of an action for damages, thus negating the basis for equitable relief.[10] Similarly, the fact that the second group of shareholders for whom respondent expresses concern have retained the benefits of their stock and the lack of an imminent contest for control make the possibility of damage to them remote at best. . . .

Reversed and remanded with directions.

Chromalloy American Corp. v. Sun Chemical Corp.
611 F.2d 240 (8th Cir. 1979)

HENLEY, Circuit Judge.

This case, arising under disclosure provisions of the Securities Exchange Act of 1934, 15 U.S.C. §78m(d) (1977), requires us to decide whether the district court erred in the partial grant and partial denial of preliminary injunctive relief.

Plaintiff-appellant Chromalloy American Corporation (Chromalloy) appeals the denial of injunctive relief which would compel defendant Sun Chemical Corporation to disclose its proposals for control of Chromalloy, and which would halt the purchase of Chromalloy stock by Sun for ninety days. Defendants-appellees Sun Chemical Corporation (Sun) and Norman E. Alexander cross-appeal from the district court's order that Sun disclose an intention to obtain control of Chromalloy. . . .

In January, 1978 Sun Chemical Corporation began purchasing significant amounts of Chromalloy stock on the New York Stock Exchange. Chromalloy is a diversified corporation with revenues in fiscal year 1978 of nearly $1.4 billion and net earnings of $47 million, while Sun is a considerably smaller corporation with 1978 revenues of $394 million and net earnings of $20 million. Norman E. Alexander is Chief Executive Officer and Chairman of Sun's Board of Directors, and has been instrumental in instigating and furthering the purchase of Chromalloy stock by Sun Chemical Corporation.

---

10. The Court was advised by respondent that such a suit is now pending in the District Court and class action certification has been sought. Although we intimate no views regarding the merits of that case, it provides a potential sanction for petitioner's violation of the Williams Act.

By February 5, 1979 Sun had acquired 605,620 shares, or 5.2 percent, of Chromalloy's total outstanding shares. Sun was therefore required to comply with the disclosure provisions of §13(d) of the Securities Exchange Act, 15 U.S.C. §78m(d)(1) (1976). Pursuant to the disclosure requirements, Sun on February 5, 1979 filed its first Schedule 13D. Sun stated that its acquisitions were for investment; that it had no present intention of seeking control of Chromalloy; that it presently intended to continue to increase its holdings; that the amount of such increase had not been determined; that Sun had been discussing with certain directors and members of Chromalloy management the possible increase in Sun's holdings; and that Sun might "at any time determine to seek control of Chromalloy." In four subsequent amendments to the Schedule 13D between April, 1979 and late July, 1979 Sun reported its plans to purchase additional stock, its unsuccessful attempt to gain representation on the Chromalloy Board, and its negotiations regarding a "stand-still" agreement whereby Sun would limit its purchases for a period of time as a condition of representation on the Chromalloy Board. In each of the amendments to its Schedule 13D Sun disclaimed any intent to control Chromalloy.

By late July, 1979 Sun's ownership had increased to nearly ten per cent of Chromalloy's outstanding stock. . . .

Under the provisions of the revised SEC regulations, we are confronted with two distinct questions: first, whether the district court erred in finding that Sun has a disclosable purpose to acquire control, and second, whether the district court abused its discretion in refusing to order disclosure of Sun's proposals for corporate changes aside from Sun's control intent.

In assessing Sun's obligation to disclose a control purpose, we look to the definition of "control" appearing in Rule 12b-2(f), 17 C.F.R. §240.12b-2(f) (1979), made applicable to Schedule 13D filings by 17 C.F.R. §240.12b-1 (1979).[12] Rule 12b-2(f) provides:

> *Control.* The term "control" (including the terms "controlling", "controlled by" and "under common control with") means the possession, directly or indirectly, of the power to direct or cause the direction of the management and policies of a person, whether through the ownership of voting securities, by contract, or otherwise.

17 C.F.R. s 240.12b-2(f) (1979).

---

12. Although revised Item 4 [of Schedule 13D] does not use the term "control", we assume that any control purpose is still measurable against the definition of control appearing in Rule 12b-2(f).

Cases decided before the revision of Item 4 have considered the definition of "control" in Rule 12b-2(f) to be controlling. *TSC Industries, Inc. v. Northway, Inc.,* 426 U.S. 438, 451 n. 13, 96 S. Ct. 2126, 48 L. Ed. 2d 757 (1976); *Graphic Sciences, Inc. v. International Mogul Mines Ltd.,* 397 F. Supp. 112, 125 & n. 37 (D.D.C. 1974). The Southern District of New York, in a case decided after the effective date of the revised form, considered a number of circumstances in determining control intent without reference to the definition of control in Rule 12b-2(f). *Transcon Lines v. A. G. Becker, Inc.,* 470 F. Supp. 356, 376-78 (S.D.N.Y. 1979).

. . . Contrary to Sun's first contention, Sun's desire to influence substantially the policies, management and actions of Chromalloy amounts to a purpose to control Chromalloy. There is ample support in the record for the finding of a control purpose. Sun has disclosed its plans to acquire twenty per cent of Chromalloy's stock, its attempts to gain representation on Chromalloy's Board, and its intention to review continually its position with respect to Chromalloy. The district court further found that Sun has prepared an "acquisition model" with Chromalloy as a "target"; that Norman Alexander first learned of the investment opportunities in Chromalloy when a brokerage firm informed him that the thirty-five per cent of common stock held by insiders was not in a solid management block; that Norman Alexander's private memoranda have been concerned from the start with the split on Chromalloy's Board of Directors as a possible avenue to power; and that according to an investment banker, Sun's projected twenty per cent interest in Chromalloy would be a wise business decision only if Sun is attempting to gain control. Taken together, these facts support the finding that Sun proposes to control Chromalloy through a combination of numbers and influence.

As a matter of law, Rule 12b-2(f) contemplates that influence can be an element of control. Control is defined to include "the [*indirect*] power to . . . cause the direction of . . . policies." Disclosure of a control purpose may be required where the securities purchaser has a perceptible desire to influence substantially the issuer's operations. . . .

Moreover, the Securities Exchange Act is remedial legislation and is to be broadly construed in order to give effect to its intent. . . . To protect the investing public through full and fair disclosure of Sun's intentions, the district court was justified in defining control to include working control and substantial influence. *Graphic Sciences, Inc. v. International Mogul Mines Ltd.*, *supra*, 397 F. Supp. at 125.

Sun next contends that the district court failed to find a "fixed plan" to acquire control of Chromalloy. This fact is not determinative. Item 4 of Schedule 13D requires disclosure of a purpose to acquire control, even though this intention has not taken shape as a fixed plan. We do not agree with Sun's contention that disclosure of Sun's control purpose will mislead investors by overstating the definiteness of Sun's plans. . . . Item 4 specifically requires disclosure of a purpose to acquire control, regardless of the definiteness or even the existence of any plans to implement this purpose.

Finally, we find no merit in Sun's argument that SEC Rule 12b-22 limits the obligation to disclose a control purpose. Rule 12b-22 allows registrants under Sections 13 and 15(d) of the Securities Exchange Act to disclaim the *existence* of control:

> *Disclaimer of control.* If the existence of control is open to reasonable doubt in any instance, the registrant may disclaim the existence of control and any admission thereof; in such case, however, the registrant shall state the material facts pertinent to the possible existence of control.

17 C.F.R. §240.12b-22 (1970). This rule on its face is inapposite to Item 4 of Schedule 13D, since Item 4 requires disclosure of "the *purpose* of the acquisition," while Rule 12b-22 is concerned with *existing* control. We have found no relevant authority, nor has Sun offered any, to support the contention that Rule 12b-22 modifies the obligation of a purchaser to disclose a control purpose.

In sum, we find no error of law and no abuse of discretion in the district court's order that Sun disclose a purpose to seek control of Chromalloy.

We also perceive no abuse of discretion in the district court's refusal to order disclosures beyond Sun's court-approved Schedule 13D. . . .

In the present case, Sun's long-range hopes for certain corporate changes could prove misleading to investors if disclosed as firm proposals. The district court's findings of fact indicate that Sun has made the following tentative overtures towards corporate changes: Norman Alexander once told Moody's Investor Services that any deal with Chromalloy "would be done with Chromalloy's money or they would get out"; Alexander "hoped" Chromalloy would eventually seek to acquire the assets of Sun; Sun commissioned a study to recommend which divisions of Chromalloy are most feasible to sell off; Alexander expressed the opinion that a profit could be realized if a trim-down of Chromalloy were properly executed; and Alexander offered to "take care of" certain Chromalloy Board members in return for their support. Each of these items involves little more than an unconsummated hope, feasibility study, or opinion, not a firm plan or proposal. We note also that Sun and Alexander have to date been denied a seat on Chromalloy's Board of Directors, and are seemingly not in a position to precipitate any of the hoped-for changes.

The degree of specificity with which future plans must be detailed in Schedule 13D filings presents a difficult question. . . . Thus, within the scope of its discretion, the district court might have required further disclosures of Sun. However, given the arguable danger of overstatement and the rule that parties are not required to disclose plans which are contingent or indefinite, we hold that the district court's order refusing further disclosures involved no abuse of discretion.

The final issue on appeal is whether the district court abused its discretion in refusing Chromalloy's request for a cooling-off period, the mailing of a restated Schedule 13D to Chromalloy shareholders at Sun's expense and the publication of a restated Schedule 13D in the press.

We consider the argument for additional injunctive relief in light of the principles set forth by the Supreme Court in *Rondeau v. Mosinee Paper Corp.*, 422 U.S. 49, 95 S. Ct. 2069, 45 L. Ed. 2d 12 (1975). The Court in *Rondeau* considered the availability of injunctive relief to remedy a §13(d) violation following compliance with the reporting requirements. Recognizing that the injunctive process is designed to deter, not to punish, *id.*, at 61, the Court held that injunctive relief under the Williams Act was subject to traditional equitable limitations. Relief beyond compliance with the reporting requirements is justified only if the petitioner can show irreparable harm in the absence of such relief. *Id.*[18]

---

18. Because this case involves only the availability of injunctive relief *following compliance* with §13(d), we are not required to decide what circumstances might justify a decree enjoining a shareholder who is *currently* in violation of §13(d) from acquiring further shares or exercising voting rights, pending compliance with the reporting requirements. The posture of the case is identical to *Rondeau* in this respect. *Rondeau v. Mosinee Paper Corp., supra,* 422 U.S. at 59 n. 9.

We have concluded that the Schedule 13D approved by the district court adequately discloses Sun's control intention. Given Sun's compliance with §13(d), we do not perceive such ongoing harm to Chromalloy or its present shareholders[19] as would justify a cooling-off period or a stockholder mailing. Shareholders who were misinformed by Sun's original Schedule 13D and amendments have been reapprised by the same form of communication. . . .

There is also no precedent for a cooling-off period. In the closely analogous context of misleading tender offers, courts have held that a misleading tender offer is adequately cured by an amended offer. . . .

The disclosure requirements established by Congress are not intended to provide a weapon for current management to discourage takeover bids or prevent large accumulations of stock. . . . Further injunctive relief, particularly a cooling-off period, would in the present case serve largely as a dilatory tool in the hands of current management, and for this reason was properly denied.

In sum, appellant has failed to sustain the burden of demonstrating abuse of discretion in the district court's denial of further disclosures, a cooling-off period, and a stockholder mailing. Appellees likewise fail to convince us that the district court erred as a matter of law in requiring the disclosure of Sun's control purpose.

Affirmed.

QUESTIONS

1. What is the scope of disclosure required by §13(d)? What is the remedy to be imposed if such disclosure is not made in a timely manner?

2. As a public policy matter, is there a risk to imposing the disclosure obligations required under §13(d)?

3. Is there an implied private right of action for §13(d) violations? If so, who has standing to sue?

4. What is the remedy for a violation of §13(d) — damages or injunctive relief?

NOTES

1. Amendments to Schedule 13D.   As to any person (or group) that files a Schedule 13D, Rule 13d-2 requires that any "material" change in the information

---

19. We do not reach the issue of harm to former Chromalloy shareholders who may have sold to Sun without attempting to garner a control premium. Chromalloy on appeal has pressed the interests of present shareholders and the public in requesting additional relief, perhaps recognizing that a cooling-off period and additional dissemination of information cannot redress the harm, if any, suffered by past shareholders who have already sold to Sun. These shareholders have an adequate remedy at law through an action for damages. *Rondeau v. Mosinee Paper Corp., supra,* 422 U.S. at 60, 97 S. Ct. 926; *Missouri Portland Cement Co. v. H.K. Porter,* 535 F.2d 388, 395, 399 (8th Cir. 1976).

disclosed in a Schedule 13D must be filed "promptly." This can lead to some very practical problems in determining whether an amendment is required by the SEC's rules. Some of these problems are described by an experienced practitioner in the following excerpt:

> In general, information is considered material under U.S. securities laws if there is a substantial likelihood that disclosure of the omitted fact would be viewed by a reasonable investor as significantly altering the total mix of information available. [Consequently, if a person] that already has a Schedule 13D on file decides to purchase additional equity securities of the [Target] or merge with the [Target], such information would be considered material under U.S. securities laws. As to the timeliness of the amendment, no bright line test has been adopted by the SEC in order to determine when a Schedule 13D amendment filing is prompt. The question of whether an amendment is prompt is determined based on all of the facts and circumstances surrounding both prior disclosures by the [Schedule 13D filer] and the market's sensitivity to the particular change of fact [that triggers] the obligation to amend. Given the ability to electronically gather and file information with the SEC, [any person who has filed a Schedule 13D] would be hard pressed to explain why a material amendment to its Schedule 13D was not filed with the SEC within two to four business days after its occurrence. [In addition to raising issues as to what constitutes "timely filing" of amendments,] Schedule 13D's requirement to disclose promptly any "plans or proposals" to acquire additional securities of the [Target] or merge with the [Target] has various ramifications . . . [, not the least of which is that there] is no clear formula to determine whether a "plan or proposal" exists. Instead, U.S. courts have used broadly defined concepts to determine when a "plan or proposal" requires disclosure. . . . Case law suggests that the determination of whether a "plan or proposal" exists is a highly fact-specific inquiry and requires a fact-finding investigation. . . .

Stephen D. Bohrer, *When an Acquisition "Plan or Proposal" Requires a Schedule 13D Amendment*, 19 INSIGHTS 17 (August 2005).

2. Recent Examples of Schedule 13D Disclosures.   Below is an excerpt from a Schedule 13D recently filed by Chapman Capital LLC with respect to its investment in Embarcadero Technologies, Inc. (dated March 12, 2007), which provides an example of one of the more outrageous disclosures to be included in a Schedule 13D filing:

Schedule 13D: Embarcadero Technologies, Inc.
Excerpt from Amendment No. 1 to Embarcadero Technologies, Inc., Schedule 13D filed by Chapman Capital L.L.C., dated March 12, 2007

On March 7, 2007, Mr. Chapman communicated to Mr. Shahbazian that the Board's failure to announce a definitive merger agreement no later than March 30, 2007, would result in the filing by the Reporting Persons [Chapman Capital] of an amended Schedule 13D, which should be expected to include as an exhibit a letter to the Board making public the results of Chapman Capital's recently accelerated investigation into the Board and management of the Issuer. Furthermore, in response to certain comments made by Mr. Shahbazian during a conversation later that day, Mr. Chapman conveyed to Mr. Shahbazian Chapman Capital's concern that, according to background checks directed by Chapman Capital, Mr. Shahbazian had been viewed negatively by various shareholders of Niku Corporation, ANDA Networks, Inc. and Walker Interactive, all of which in the past had employed Mr. Shahbazian in the capacity of Chief Financial Officer. *Mr. Shahbazian reacted temperamentally to Mr. Chapman with the eloquent response, "F[***] you!"* Mr. Chapman then forcefully informed Mr. Shahbazian that it was inappropriate and inadvisable for the Chief Financial Officer of a public company to utter such blasphemy to the advisor of a 9.3% ownership stakeholder in the Issuer. [*Emphasis in original.*]

In early 2008, Carl Icahn filed a Schedule 13D with respect to the shares of Motorola Inc. that he and other investors in his group (the "Reporting Persons") had accumulated. The following excerpt from his Schedule 13D reflects the more traditional (and less colorful) disclosure that is customarily included by filers in response to Item 4 of Schedule 13D:

Schedule 13D: Motorola Inc.
Excerpt from Motorola Inc. Schedule 13D, filed by Carl Icahn and other Reporting Persons, dated February 6, 2008

The Reporting Persons acquired their positions in the Shares in the belief that they were undervalued. The Reporting Persons have had, and intend to seek to have further, conversations with members of the Issuer's management and the board of directors to discuss ideas that management, the board of directors and the Reporting Persons may have to enhance shareholder value.

On January 31, 2008 and February 1, 2008, Carl C. Icahn issued press releases concerning Motorola, Inc., . . . [excerpts of which are set forth below].

The Reporting Persons may, from time to time and at any time, acquire additional Shares in the open market or otherwise and reserve the right to dispose of any or all of their Shares in the open market or otherwise, at any time and from time to time, and to engage in any hedging or similar transactions with respect to the Shares.

. . .

[On January 31, 2008, Carl Icahn responded to a public announcement by Motorola Inc. by issuing the following statement:] "For many months I have been publicly advocating the separation of Mobile Devices from Motorola's other business and I am pleased to see that Motorola is finally exploring that proposal. However, we have previously informed Motorola that we expect to run a slate of directors for the upcoming annual meeting and this announcement by Motorola will not deter us from that effort—we believe Motorola is finally moving in the right direction but certainly still has a long way to go."

. . .

[On February 1, 2008,] Carl Icahn announced . . . that his affiliated companies have delivered written notice to Motorola, Inc. (NYSE MOT) for the nomination of Frank Biondi, Jr., William R. Hambrecht, Lionel C. Kimerling and Keith Meister for election as directors at the 2008 annual meeting of stockholders of Motorola. Mr. Icahn stated, "I believe that Frank Biondi and Bill Hambrecht offer unique business insight and experience in the communications and technology arena. Lionel Kimerling is a renowned expert in the processing of semiconductor materials whom I believe can clearly lend needed insight on Motorola's silicon and technology strategy. Keith Meister is a managing director of the Icahn investment entities and offers business and investing insight that I believe will be advantageous at Motorola."[*]

B.   *Regulation of Third Party Tender Offers Under §14(d) of the Williams Act*

1.   What Is a "Tender Offer"?

> **SEC v. Carter Hawley Hale Stores, Inc.**
> 760 F.2d 945 (9th Cir. 1985)

SKOPIL, Circuit Judge:

The issue in this case arises out of an attempt by The Limited ("Limited"), an Ohio corporation, to take over Carter Hawley Hale Stores, Inc. ("CHH"), a publicly-held Los Angeles corporation. The SEC commenced the present action for injunctive relief to restrain CHH from repurchasing its own stock in an attempt to defeat the Limited takeover attempt without complying with the tender offer regulations. The district court concluded CHH's repurchase program was not a tender offer. The SEC appeals from the district court's denial of its motion for a preliminary injunction. We affirm.

FACTS AND PROCEEDINGS BELOW

On April 4, 1984 Limited commenced a cash tender offer for 20.3 million shares of CHH common stock, representing approximately 55% of the total shares outstanding, at $30 per share. Prior to the announced offer, CHH stock was trading at approximately $23.78 per share (pre-tender offer price). Limited disclosed that if its offer succeeded, it would exchange the remaining CHH shares for a fixed amount of Limited shares in a second-step merger. . . .

---

[*] You will recall from Chapter 2 that Motorola did ultimately spin off Motorola Mobility in January 2012, which was then sold later in the year to Google, Inc. *See supra*, pp. 154-165.

While CHH initially took no public position on the offer, it filed an action to enjoin Limited's attempted takeover. *Carter Hawley Hale Stores, Inc. v. The Limited, Inc.*, 587 F. Supp. 246 (C.D. Cal. 1984). CHH's motion for an injunction was denied. *Id.* From April 4, 1984 until April 16, 1984 CHH's incumbent management discussed a response to Limited's offer. During that time 14 million shares, about 40% of CHH's common stock, were traded. The price of CHH stock increased to approximately $29.25 per share. CHH shares became concentrated in the hands of risk arbitrageurs.

On April 16, 1984 CHH responded to Limited's offer. CHH issued a press release announcing its opposition to the offer because it was "inadequate and not in the best interests of CHH or its shareholders." CHH also publicly announced an agreement with General Cinema Corporation ("General Cinema"). . . . Finally, CHH announced a plan to repurchase up to 15 million shares of its own common stock for an amount not to exceed $500 million. . . .

CHH's public announcement stated the actions taken were "to defeat the attempt by Limited to gain voting control of the company and to afford shareholders who wished to sell shares at this time an opportunity to do so." CHH's actions were revealed by press release, a letter from CHH's Chairman to shareholders, and by documents filed with the Securities and Exchange Commission ("SEC") — a Schedule 14D-9 and Rule 13e-1 transaction statement. These disclosures were reported by wire services, national financial newspapers, and newspapers of general circulation. Limited sought a temporary restraining order against CHH's repurchase of its shares. The application was denied. Limited withdrew its motion for a preliminary injunction.

CHH began to repurchase its shares on April 16, 1984. In a one-hour period CHH purchased approximately 244,000 shares at an average price of $25.25 per share. On April 17, 1984 CHH purchased approximately 6.5 million shares in a two-hour trading period at an average price of $25.88 per share. By April 22, 1984 CHH had purchased a total of 15 million shares. It then announced an increase in the number of shares authorized for purchase to 18.5 million.

On April 24, 1984, the same day Limited was permitted to close its offer and start purchasing, CHH terminated its repurchase program having purchased approximately 17.5 million shares, over 50% of the common shares outstanding. On April 25, 1984 Limited revised its offer increasing the offering price to $35.00 per share and eliminating the second-step merger. The market price for CHH then reached a high of $32.00 per share. On May 21, 1984 Limited withdrew its offer. The market price of CHH promptly fell to $20.62 per share, a price below the pre-tender offer price.

On May 2, 1984, two and one-half weeks after the repurchase program was announced and one week after its apparent completion, the SEC filed this action for injunctive relief. The SEC alleged that CHH's repurchase program constituted a tender offer conducted in violation of section 13(e) of the Exchange Act, 15 U.S.C. §78m(e) and Rule 13e-4, 17 C.F.R. §240.13e-4. On May 5, 1984 a temporary restraining order was granted. CHH was temporarily enjoined from further stock repurchases. The district court denied SEC's motion for a preliminary injunction, finding the SEC failed to carry its burden of establishing "the reasonable likelihood of future violations . . . [or] . . . a 'fair chance of success on the merits'. . . . " The court found CHH's repurchase program was not a tender offer because the eight-factor test proposed by the SEC and adopted in *Wellman v. Dickinson*, 475 F. Supp. 783 (S.D.N.Y. 1979), *aff'd on other grounds*, 682 F.2d 355 (2d Cir. 1982), *cert. denied*, 460 U.S. 1069, 103 S. Ct. 1522, 75 L. Ed. 2d 946 (1983), had not been satisfied. The court also refused to adopt, at the urging of the SEC, the alternative test of what constitutes a tender offer as enunciated in *S-G Securities, Inc. v. Fuqua Investment*, 466 F. Supp. 1114 (D. Mass. 1978). On May 9, 1984 the SEC filed an emergency application for an injunction pending appeal to this court. That application was denied.

Discussion

. . . The SEC urges two principal arguments on appeal: (1) the district court erred in concluding that CHH's repurchase program was not a tender offer under the eight-factor *Wellman* test, and (2) the district court erred in declining to apply the definition of a tender offer enunciated in *S-G Securities*, 466 F. Supp. at 1126-27. Resolution of these issues on appeal presents the difficult task of determining whether CHH's repurchase of shares during a third-party tender offer itself constituted a tender offer.

1. THE WILLIAMS ACT

A. Congressional Purposes. The Williams Act amendments to the Exchange Act were enacted in response to the growing use of tender offers to achieve corporate control. Prior to the passage of the Act, shareholders of target companies were often forced to act hastily on offers without the benefit of full disclosure. *See* H.R. Rep. No. 1711, 90th Cong., 2d Sess. (1968), *reprinted in* 1968 U.S. Code, Cong. & Admin. News 2811 (*"House Report 1711"*). The Williams Act was intended to ensure that investors responding to tender offers received full and fair disclosure, analogous to that received in proxy contests. The Act was also designed to provide shareholders an opportunity to examine all relevant facts in an effort to reach a decision without being subject to unwarranted pressure.

This policy is reflected in section 14(d), which governs third-party tender offers, and which prohibits a tender offer unless shareholders are provided with certain procedural and substantive protections including: full disclosure; time in which to make an investment decision; withdrawal rights; and pro rata purchase of shares accepted in the event the offer is oversubscribed.

There are additional congressional concerns underlying the Williams Act. In its effort to protect investors, Congress recognized the need to "avoid favoring either management or the takeover bidder." . . . Congress was also concerned about avoiding undue interference with the free and open market in securities. . . . Each of these congressional concerns is implicated in the determination of whether CHH's issuer repurchase program constituted a tender offer.

B. Issuer Repurchases Under Section 13(e). Issuer repurchases and tender offers are governed in relevant part by section 13(e) of the Williams Act and Rules 13e-1 and 13e-4 promulgated thereunder.

The SEC argues that the district court erred in concluding that issuer repurchases, which had the intent and effect of defeating a third-party tender offer, are authorized by the tender offer rules and regulations. The legislative history of these provisions is unclear. Congress apparently was aware of an intent by the SEC to regulate issuer tender offers to the same extent as third-party offers. At the same time, Congress recognized issuers might engage in "substantial repurchase programs . . . inevitably affect[ing] market performance and price levels." Such repurchase programs might be undertaken for any number of legitimate purposes, including with the intent "to preserve or strengthen . . . control by counteracting tender offer or other takeover attempts. . . . " Congress neither explicitly banned nor authorized such a practice. Congress did grant the SEC authority to adopt appropriate regulations to carry out congressional intent with respect to issuer repurchases. The legislative history of section 13(e) is not helpful in resolving the issues.

There is also little guidance in the SEC Rules promulgated in response to the legislative grant of authority. Rule 13e-1 prohibits an issuer from repurchasing its own stock during a third-party tender offer unless it discloses certain minimal information. The language of Rule 13e-1 is prohibitory rather than permissive. It nonetheless evidences a recognition that not all issuer repurchases during a third-party tender offer are tender offers. In contrast, Rule 13e-4 recognizes that issuers, like third parties, may engage in repurchase activity amounting to a tender offer and subject to the same procedural and substantive safeguards as a third-party tender offer. 17 C.F.R. §240.13e-4 (1984). The regulations do not specify when a repurchase by an issuer amounts to a tender offer governed by Rule 13e-4 rather than 13e-1.[3]

We decline to adopt either the broadest construction of Rule 13e-4, to define issuer tender offers as virtually all substantial repurchases during a third-party tender offer, or the broadest construction of Rule 13e-1, to create an exception from the tender offer requirements for issuer repurchases made during a third-party tender offer. Like the district court, we resolve the question of whether CHH's repurchase program was a tender offer by considering the eight-factor test established in *Wellman*.

To serve the purposes of the Williams Act, there is a need for flexibility in fashioning a definition of a tender offer. The *Wellman* factors seem particularly well suited in determining when an issuer repurchase program during a third-party tender offer will itself constitute a tender offer. *Wellman* focuses, *inter alia*,

---

3. The procedural and substantive requirements that must be complied with under Rule 13e-4 differ from those under Rule 13e-1. An issuer engaged in a repurchase under Rule 13e-1 is required to file a brief statement with the SEC setting forth the amount of shares purchased; the purpose for which the purchase is made; and the source and amount of funds used in making the repurchase. 17 C.F.R. §240.13e-1 (1984). CHH complied with the requirements of Rule 13e-1.

An issuer engaged in a tender offer under Rule 13e-4 must comply with more burdensome regulations. All the substantive and procedural protections for shareholders come into play under Rule 13e-4 including: full disclosure; time in which to make investment decisions; withdrawal rights; and requirements for pro rata [acceptance] of shares. 17 C.F.R. §240.13e-4 (1984). CHH did not comply with Rule 13e-4.

on the manner in which the offer is conducted and whether the offer has the overall effect of pressuring shareholders into selling their stock. Application of the *Wellman* factors to the unique facts and circumstances surrounding issuer repurchases should serve to effect congressional concern for the needs of the shareholder, the need to avoid giving either the target or the offeror any advantage, and the need to maintain a free and open market for securities.

2.   APPLICATION OF THE *WELLMAN* FACTORS

Under the *Wellman* test, the existence of a tender offer is determined by examining the following factors:

> (1) Active and widespread solicitation of public shareholders for the shares of an issuer; (2) solicitation made for a substantial percentage of the issuer's stock; (3) offer to purchase made at a premium over the prevailing market price; (4) terms of the offer are firm rather than negotiable; (5) offer contingent on the tender of a fixed number of shares, often subject to a fixed maximum number to be purchased; (6) offer open only for a limited period of time; (7) offeree subjected to pressure to sell his stock; [and (8)] public announcements of a purchasing program concerning the target company precede or accompany rapid accumulation of a large amount of target company's securities.

Not all factors need be present to find a tender offer; rather, they provide some guidance as to the traditional indicia of a tender offer. . . .

The district court concluded CHH's repurchase program was not a tender offer under *Wellman* because only "two of the eight indicia" were present. The SEC claims the district court erred in applying *Wellman* because it gave insufficient weight to the pressure exerted on shareholders; it ignored the existence of a competitive tender offer; and it failed to consider that CHH's offer at the market price was in essence a premium because the price had already risen above pre-tender offer levels.

A.   *Active and Widespread Solicitation.*   The evidence was uncontraverted that there was "no direct solicitation of shareholders." No active and widespread solicitation occurred. . . . Nor did the publicity surrounding CHH's repurchase program result in a solicitation. The only public announcements by CHH were those mandated by SEC or Exchange rules. . . .

B.   *Solicitation for a Substantial Percentage of Issuer's Shares.*   Because there was no active and widespread solicitation, the district court found the repurchase could not have involved a solicitation for a substantial percentage of CHH's shares. It is unclear whether the proper focus of this factor is the solicitation or the percentage of stock solicited. The district court probably erred in concluding that, absent a solicitation under the first *Wellman* factor, the second factor cannot be satisfied, . . . but we need not decide that here. The solicitation and percentage of stock elements of the second factor often will be addressed adequately in an evaluation of the first *Wellman* factor, which is concerned with solicitation, and the eighth *Wellman* factor, which focuses on the amount of securities accumulated. In this case, CHH did not engage in a solicitation under the first *Wellman* factor but did accumulate a large percentage of stock as defined under the eighth *Wellman* factor. An evaluation of the second *Wellman* factor does not alter the probability of finding a tender offer.

C. Premium Over Prevailing Market Price. The SEC contends that the open-market purchases made by CHH at market prices were in fact made at a premium not over market price, but over the pre-tender offer price. At the time of CHH's repurchases, the market price for CHH's shares (ranging from $24.00 to $26.00 per share) had risen above the pre-tender offer price (approximately $22.00 per share). Given ordinary market dynamics, the price of a target company's stock will rise following an announced tender offer. Under the SEC's definition of a premium as a price greater than the pre-tender offer price, a premium will always exist when a target company makes open market purchases in response to a tender offer even though the increase in market price is attributable to the action of the third-party offeror and not the target company. The SEC definition not only eliminates consideration of this *Wellman* factor in the context of issuer repurchases during a tender offer, but also underestimates congressional concern for preserving the free and open market. The district court did not err in concluding a premium is determined not by reference to pre-tender offer price, but rather by reference to market price. . . .

D. Terms of Offer Not Firm. There is no dispute that CHH engaged in a number of transactions or purchases at many different market prices.

E. Offer Not Contingent on Tender of Fixed Minimum Number of Shares. Similarly, while CHH indicated it would purchase up to 15 million shares, CHH's purchases were not contingent on the tender of a fixed minimum number of shares.

F. Not Open for Only a Limited Time. CHH's offer to repurchase was not open for only a limited period of time but rather was open "during the pendency of the tender offer of The Limited." The SEC argues that the offer was in fact open for only a limited time, because CHH would only repurchase stock until 15 million shares were acquired. The fact that 15 million shares were acquired in a short period of time does not translate into an issuer-imposed time limitation. The time within which the repurchases were made was a product of ordinary market forces, not the terms of CHH's repurchase program.

G-H. Shareholder Pressure and Public Announcements Accompanying a Large Accumulation of Stock. With regard to the seventh *Wellman* factor, following a public announcement, CHH repurchased over the period of seven trading days more than 50% of its outstanding shares. The eighth *Wellman* factor was met.

The district court found that while many shareholders may have felt pressured or compelled to sell their shares, CHH itself did not exert on shareholders the kind of pressure the Williams Act proscribes.

While there certainly was shareholder pressure in this case, it was largely the pressure of the marketplace and not the type of untoward pressure the tender offer regulations were designed to prohibit. . . .

CHH's purchases were made in the open market, at market and not premium prices, without fixed terms and were not contingent upon the tender of a fixed minimum number of shares. CHH's repurchase program had none of the traditional indicia of a tender offer. . . .

The shareholder pressure in this case did not result from any untoward action on the part of CHH. Rather, it resulted from market forces, the third-party offer, and the fear that at the expiration of the offer the price of CHH shares would decrease.

The district court did not abuse its discretion in concluding that under the *Wellman* eight factor test, CHH's repurchase program did not constitute a tender offer.

3.   ALTERNATIVE *S-G SECURITIES* TEST

The SEC finally urges that even if the CHH repurchase program did not constitute a tender offer under the *Wellman* test, the district court erred in refusing to apply the test in *S-G Securities,* 466 F. Supp. at 1114. Under the more liberal *S-G Securities* test, a tender offer is present if there are

(1) A publicly announced intention by the purchaser to acquire a block of the stock of the target company for purposes of acquiring control thereof, and (2) a subsequent rapid acquisition by the purchaser of large blocks of stock through open market and privately negotiated purchases.

Id. at 1126-27.

There are a number of sound reasons for rejecting the *S-G Securities* test. The test is vague and difficult to apply. It offers little guidance to the issuer as to when his conduct will come within the ambit of Rule 13e-4 as opposed to Rule 13e-1. A determination of the existence of a tender offer under *S-G Securities* is largely subjective and made in hindsight based on an *ex post facto* evaluation of the response in the marketplace to the repurchase program. The SEC's contention that these concerns are irrelevant when the issuer's repurchases are made with the intent to defeat a third-party offer is without merit.

The SEC finds further support for its application of the two-pronged *S-G Securities* test in the overriding legislative intent "to ensure that shareholders . . . are adequately protected from pressure tactics . . . [forcing them to make] . . . ill-considered investment decisions." The *S-G Securities* test does reflect congressional concern for shareholders; however, the same can be said of the *Wellman* test. The legislative intent in the context of open-market repurchases during third-party tender offers is, at best, unclear. The *S-G Securities* test, unlike the *Wellman* test, does little to reflect objectively the multiple congressional concerns underlying the Williams Act, including due regard for the free and open market in securities.

We decline to abandon the *Wellman* test in favor of the vague standard enunciated in *S-G Securities.* The district court did not err in declining to apply the *S-G Securities* test or in finding CHH's repurchases were not a tender offer under *Wellman.*

AFFIRMED.

NOTES

1. Rule 13e-1 vs. Rule 13e-4 Transactions.   Section 13(e) of the Williams Act is essentially an antifraud statute that delegates broad rulemaking authority to the SEC to regulate issuers' repurchases of their own shares. Pursuant to this authority, the SEC has promulgated Rule 13e-1, which requires issuers who propose to engage in repurchases of their shares during the course of a third party's tender offer to file a disclosure document with the SEC. In addition, the SEC has adopted Rule 13e-4, which requires issuers who engage in self-tender offers to file disclosures on Schedule 13E-4 and to otherwise comply with rules that impose procedural safeguards that are very similar to the SEC rules that were described earlier in this chapter with respect to the regulation of third-party tender offers under Section 14(d), such as the proration rules and withdrawal rights.

2. Going Private Transactions: The **Weinberger** *Standard of Entire Fairness.* When M&A professionals refer to a going private transaction, they are usually referring to a transaction involving the squeeze-out of minority shareholders in which the controlling shareholder acquires all of the shares of Target, a controlled subsidiary, that the majority shareholder (which is usually the parent company but could be an individual shareholder) does not own. In these transactions, the minority shareholders are eliminated from any further equity participation in the continued growth of Target's business. As we learned in Chapter 2, when we studied the Delaware Supreme Court's landmark decision in *Weinberger*, these squeeze-out transactions are fraught with conflicts of interest, and accordingly, the Delaware Supreme Court imposed an "entire fairness" requirement in connection with freeze-out transactions in order to be sure that the minority shareholders receive adequate consideration for their interest.

As established in *Weinberger*, the concept of entire fairness directs the courts to look at two elements: fair price and fair dealing. Following *Weinberger*, and until quite recently, the Delaware courts consistently applied the entire fairness standard to review squeeze-out transactions of the type that was at issue in *Weinberger*. Indeed, in *Kahn v. Lynch Communication Systems, Inc.*, 638 A.2d 1110 (Del. 1994), the Delaware Supreme Court held that "an approval of [an interested merger] transaction by an independent committee of directors . . . shifts the burden of proof on the issue of fairness from the controlling or dominating shareholder to the challenging shareholder-plaintiff." *Id.* at 1117. The function of a special committee in this setting is to negotiate the price and terms of an interested transaction on behalf of the minority shareholders. In order for the special committee to operate independently for burden-shifting purposes, "[p]articular consideration must be given to evidence of whether the special committee was truly independent, fully informed, and had the freedom to negotiate at arm's length." *Id.* at 1120-1121. Consequently, as was mentioned earlier in the note material following the *Weinberger* decision (*see supra,* pp. 183-184), most practicing M&A lawyers assumed that the entire fairness standard would apply to any transaction where the controlling shareholder sought to eliminate ("squeeze out") the minority interest—regardless of whether the transaction was structured as a long-form merger, a short-form merger, or a two-step transaction involving a tender offer (i.e., stock purchase) to be followed by either a long-form or a short form merger. *See* Diagram 12 in Appendix A.

3. SEC Regulation of Going Private Transactions: Rule 13e-3.   The SEC has adopted Rule 13e-3, which regulates going private transactions. As to those going private transactions that are covered by Rule 13e-3, the controlling shareholder will be required to file a Schedule 13E-3 with the SEC. Since the SEC recognizes the significant potential for abuse of the minority interest that is an inherent attribute of going private transactions, the disclosure requirements of Schedule 13E-3 are rather significant. The Schedule 13E-3 must set forth certain information pertaining to the parties to the transaction, the terms of the transaction, the post-transaction plans of the parties, the source of the funds for the transaction, the purpose of the transaction, and a fairly extensive description of the fairness of the transaction. It is generally this requirement — to provide information with respect to the *fairness* of the proposed transaction — that creates the most difficult disclosure issues for those controlling shareholders proposing to take the company private.

4. Going Private Transactions: Avoiding Majority Shareholders' Duties Under the* Weinberger *Doctrine.   Since a 2001 decision by the Delaware Supreme Court, Delaware courts have chartered a very different path for structuring going private transactions — a path that allows the majority shareholder to avoid the entire fairness doctrine established in *Weinberger* and its progeny. *See Glassman v. Unocal Exploration Corp.,* 777 A.2d 242 (Del. 2001); *In re Pure Resources Shareholders Litigation,* 808 A.2d 421 (Del. Ch. 2002); and *In re Siliconix Inc. Shareholder Litigation,* No. Civ. A. 18700, 2001 WL 716 787 (Del. Ch. June 19, 2001). So, as a matter of Delaware state law, today there are currently two distinct paths that can be used by transaction planners to take a company private. The first is to structure the transaction as a long-form merger, which will be subject to review under the entire fairness standard set forth in *Weinberger.* The second path is the so-called *Siliconix/Pure Resources* transaction, named after the two cases that spawned this second approach to going private transactions. Under this second approach, the controlling shareholder makes a first-step tender offer followed by a second-step short-form merger. The reason to structure the transaction using this two-step approach is that the controlling shareholder can avoid review under the entire fairness standard of *Weinberger* if the transaction is structured to satisfy certain conditions. Given that the Delaware courts have now offered majority shareholders a path to eliminate review of the entire fairness of a going private transaction, this has resulted in an increased emphasis on the scope of disclosures required by SEC Rule 13e-3. And, not surprisingly, the divergent strands of Delaware jurisprudence regarding the scope of fiduciary duty obligations in connection with going private transactions has generated considerable controversy. In Chapter 7, as part of our study of fiduciary duty law, we will examine going private transactions in more detail, with a particular emphasis on the intersection of the controlling shareholder's mandatory fiduciary duty obligations under state law *and* the mandatory disclosure obligations imposed on controlling shareholders under the federal securities laws. S*ee, infra,* Chapter 7 at p. 754.

In another leading case addressing the issue of the definition of "tender offer" in the context of open market purchases of publicly traded shares, the

Second Circuit eschewed the *Wellman* test (used by the Ninth Circuit in *Carter Hawley Hale*) in favor of a very different approach.

Hanson Trust PLC v. SCM Corporation
774 F.2d 47 (2d Cir. 1985)

MANSFIELD, Circuit Judge:

Hanson Trust PLC, HSCM Industries, Inc., and Hanson Holdings Netherlands B.V. (hereinafter sometimes referred to collectively as "Hanson") appeal from an order of the Southern District of New York, 617 F. Supp. 832 (1985), Shirley Wohl Kram, Judge, granting SCM Corporation's motion for a preliminary injunction restraining them, their officers, agents, employees and any persons acting in concert with them, from acquiring any shares of SCM and from exercising any voting rights with respect to 3.1 million SCM shares acquired by them on September 11, 1985. The injunction was granted on the ground that Hanson's September 11 acquisition of the SCM stock through five private and one open market purchases amounted to a "tender offer" for more than 5% of SCM's outstanding shares, which violated §§14(d)(1) and (6) of the Williams Act, 15 U.S.C. §78n(d)(1) and (6) and rules promulgated by the Securities and Exchange Commission (SEC) thereunder. *See* 17 C.F.R. §§240.14(e)(1) and 240.14d-7. We reverse.

The setting is the familiar one of a fast-moving bidding contest for control of a large public corporation: first, a cash tender offer of $60 per share by Hanson, an outsider, addressed to SCM stockholders; next, a counterproposal by an "insider" group consisting of certain SCM managers and their "White Knight," Merrill Lynch Capital Markets (Merrill), for a "leveraged buyout" at a higher price ($70 per share); then an increase by Hanson of its cash offer to $72 per share, followed by a revised SCM-Merrill leveraged buyout offer of $74 per share with a "crown jewel" irrevocable lock-up option to Merrill designed to discourage Hanson from seeking control by providing that if any other party (in this case Hanson) should acquire more than one-third of SCM's outstanding shares (66-2/3% being needed under N.Y. Bus. L. §903(a)(2) to effectuate a merger) Merrill would have the right to buy SCM's two most profitable businesses (consumer foods and pigments) at prices characterized by some as "bargain basement." The final act in this scenario was the decision of Hanson, having been deterred by the SCM-Merrill option (colloquially described in the market as a "poison pill"), to terminate its cash tender offer and then to make private purchases, amounting to 25% of SCM's outstanding shares, leading SCM to seek and obtain the preliminary injunction from which this appeal is taken. A more detailed history of relevant events follows.

SCM is a New York corporation with its principal place of business in New York City. . . .

On August 21, 1985, Hanson publicly announced its intention to make a cash tender of $60 per share for any and all outstanding SCM shares. Five days later [Hanson] filed the tender offer documents required by §14(d)(1) of the Williams Act and regulations issued thereunder. . . . On August 30, 1985, SCM, having recommended to SCM's stockholders that they not accept Hanson's tender offer, announced a preliminary agreement with Merrill under which a new entity, formed by SCM and Merrill, would acquire all SCM shares at $70 per share in a leveraged buyout sponsored by Merrill. . . . On September 3, Hansen increased its tender offer from $60 to $72 cash per share. However, it expressly reserved the right to terminate its offer if SCM granted to anyone any option to purchase SCM assets on terms that Hansen believed to constitute a "lock-up" device.

The next development in the escalating bidding contest for control of SCM occurred on September 10, 1985, when SCM entered into a new leveraged buy-out agreement with its "White Knight," Merrill. The agreement provided for a two-step acquisition of SCM stock by Merrill at $74 per share. The first proposed step was to be the acquisition of approximately 82% of SCM's outstanding stock for cash. Following a merger (which required acquisition of at least 66-2/3%), debentures would be issued for the remaining SCM shares. If any investor or group other than Merrill acquired more than one-third of SCM's outstanding shares, Merrill would have the option to buy SCM's two most profitable businesses, pigments and consumer foods, for $350 and $80 million respectively, prices which Hanson believed to be below their market value.

Hanson, faced with what it considered to be a "poison pill," concluded that even if it increased its cash tender offer to $74 per share it would end up with control of a substantially depleted and damaged company. Accordingly, it announced on the Dow Jones Broad Tape at 12:38 P.M. on September 11 that it was terminating its cash tender offer. A few minutes later, Hanson issued a press release, carried on the Broad Tape, to the effect that "all SCM shares tendered will be promptly returned to the tendering shareholders."

At some time in the late forenoon or early afternoon of September 11 Hanson decided to make cash purchases of a substantial percentage of SCM stock in the open market or through privately negotiated transactions. If Hanson could acquire slightly less than one-third of SCM's outstanding shares it would be able to block the $74 per share SCM-Merrill offer of a leveraged buyout. This might induce the latter to work out an agreement with Hanson, something Hanson had unsuccessfully sought on several occasions since its first cash tender offer.

Within a period of two hours on the afternoon of September 11 Hanson made five privately-negotiated cash purchases of SCM stock and one openmarket purchase, acquiring 3.1 million shares or 25% of SCM's outstanding stock. The price of SCM stock on the NYSE on September 11 ranged from a high of $73.50 per share to a low of $72.50 per share. Hanson's initial private purchase, 387,700 shares from Mutual Shares, was not solicited by Hanson but by a Mutual Shares official, Michael Price, who, in a conversation with Robert Pirie of Rothschild, Inc., Hanson's financial advisor, on the morning of September 11 (before Hanson had decided to make any private cash purchases), had stated that he was interested in selling Mutual's Shares' SCM stock to Hanson. Once Hanson's decision to buy privately had been made, Pirie took Price up on his offer. The parties negotiated a sale at $73.50 per share after Pirie refused Price's asking prices, first of $75 per share and, later, of $74.50 per share. This transaction, but not the identity of the parties, was automatically reported pursuant to NYSE rules on the NYSE ticker at 3:11 P.M. and reported on the Dow Jones Broad Tape at 3:29 P.M.

Pirie then telephoned Ivan Boesky, an arbitrageur who had a few weeks earlier disclosed in a Schedule 13D statement filed with the SEC that he owned approximately 12.7% of SCM's outstanding shares. Pirie negotiated a Hanson purchase of these shares at $73.50 per share after rejecting Boesky's initial demand of $74 per share. At the same time Rothschild purchased for Hanson's account 600,000 SCM shares in the open market at $73.50 per share. An attempt by Pirie next to negotiate the cash purchase of another large block of SCM stock (some 780,000 shares) from Slifka & Company fell through because of the latter's inability to make delivery of the shares on September 12.

Following the NYSE ticker and Broad Tape reports of the first two large anonymous transactions in SCM stock, some professional investors surmised that the buyer might be Hanson. Rothschild then received telephone calls from (1) Mr. Mulhearn of Jamie & Co. offering to sell between 200,000 and 350,000 shares at $73.50 per share, (2) David Gottesman, an arbitrageur at Oppenheimer & Co. offering 89,000 shares at $73.50, and (3) Boyd Jeffries of Jeffries & Co., offering approximately 700,000 to 800,000 shares at $74.00. Pirie purchased the three blocks for Hanson at $73.50 per share. The last of Hanson's cash purchases was completed by 4:35 P.M. on September 11, 1985.

In the early evening of September 11 SCM successfully applied to Judge Kram in the present lawsuit for a restraining order barring Hanson from acquiring more SCM stock for 24 hours. On September 12 and 13 the TRO was extended by consent pending the district court's decision on SCM's application for a preliminary injunction. Judge Kram held an evidentiary hearing on September 12-13, at which various witnesses testified, including Sir Gordon White, Hanson's United States Chairman, two Rothschild representatives (Pirie and Gerald Goldsmith) and stock market risk-arbitrage professionals (Robert Freeman of Goldman, Sachs & Co., Kenneth Miller of Merrill Lynch, and Danial Burch of D.F. King & Co.). Sir Gordon White testified that on September 11, 1985, after learning of the $74 per share SCM-Merrill leveraged buyout tender offer with its "crown jewel" irrevocable "lock-up" option to Merrill, he instructed Pirie to terminate Hanson's $72 per share tender offer, and that only thereafter did he discuss the possibility of Hanson making market purchases of SCM stock. Pirie testified that the question of buying stock may have been discussed in the late forenoon of September 11 and that he had told White that he was having Hanson's New York counsel look into whether such cash purchases were legally permissible.

SCM argued before Judge Kram (and argues here) that Hanson's cash purchases immediately following its termination of its $72 per share tender offer amounted to a *de facto* continuation of Hanson's tender offer, designed to avoid the strictures of §14(d) of the Williams Act, and that unless a preliminary injunction issued SCM and its shareholders would be irreparably injured because Hanson would acquire enough shares to defeat the SCM-Merrill offer. Judge Kram found that the relevant underlying facts (which we have outlined) were not in dispute, and concluded that "[w]ithout deciding what test should ultimately be applied to determine whether Hanson's conduct constitutes a 'tender offer' within the meaning of the Williams Act . . . SCM has demonstrated a likelihood of success on the merits of its contention that Hanson has engaged in a tender offer which violates Section 14(d) of the Williams Act." The district court, characterizing Hanson's stock purchases as "a deliberate attempt to do an 'end run' around the requirements of the Williams Act," made no finding on the question of whether Hanson had decided to make the purchases of SCM before or after it dropped its tender offer but concluded that even if the decision had been made after it terminated its offer preliminary injunctive relief should issue. From this decision Hanson appeals.

Discussion

. . . Since, as the district court correctly noted, the material relevant facts in the present case are not in dispute, this appeal turns on whether the district court erred as a matter of law in holding that when Hanson terminated its offer and immediately thereafter made private purchases of a substantial share of the target company's outstanding stock, the purchases became a "tender offer" within the meaning of §14(d) of the Williams Act. Absent any express definition of "tender offer" in the Act, the answer requires a brief review of the background and purposes of §14(d). . . .

The typical tender offer, as described in the Congressional debates, hearings and reports on the Williams Act, consisted of a general, publicized bid by an individual or group to buy shares of a publicly-owned company, the shares of which were traded on a national securities exchange, at a price substantially above the current market price. . . . The offer was usually accompanied by newspaper and other publicity, a time limit for tender of shares in response to it, and a provision fixing a quantity limit on the total number of shares of the target company that would be purchased.

Prior to the Williams Act a tender offeror had no obligation to disclose any information to shareholders when making a bid. The Report of the Senate Committee on Banking and Currency aptly described the situation: "by using a cash tender offer the person seeking control can operate in almost complete secrecy. At present, the law does not even require that he disclose his identity, the source of his funds, who his associates are, or what he intends to do if he gains control of the corporation." Senate Report, *supra,* at 2. The average shareholder, pressured by the fact that the tender offer would be available for only a short time and restricted to a limited number of shares, was forced "with severely limited information, [to] decide what course of action he should take." *Id.* "Without knowledge of who the bidder is and what he plans to do, the shareholder cannot reach an informed decision. He is forced to take a chance. For no matter what he does, he does it without adequate information to enable him to decide rationally what is the best possible course of action." *Id.*

The purpose of the Williams Act was, accordingly, to protect the shareholders from that dilemma by insuring "that public shareholders who are confronted by a cash tender offer for their stock will not be required to respond without adequate information." . . .

Although §14(d)(1) clearly applies to "classic" tender offers of the type described above, courts soon recognized that in the case of privately negotiated transactions or solicitations for private purchases of stock many of the conditions leading to the enactment of §14(d) for the most part do not exist. The number and percentage of stockholders are usually far less than those involved in public offers. The solicitation involves less publicity than a public tender offer or none. The solicitees, who are frequently directors, officers or substantial stockholders of the target, are more apt to be sophisticated, inquiring or knowledgeable concerning the target's business, the solicitor's objectives, and the impact of the solicitation on the target's business prospects. In short, the solicitee in the private transaction is less likely to be pressured, confused, or ill-informed regarding the businesses and decisions at stake than solicitees who are the subjects of a public tender offer.

These differences between public and private securities transactions have led most courts to rule that private transactions or open market purchases do not qualify as a "tender offer" requiring the purchaser to meet the pre-filing strictures of §14(d). . . . The borderline between public solicitations and privately negotiated stock purchases is not bright and it is frequently difficult to determine whether transactions falling close to the line or in a type of "no man's land" are "tender offers" or private deals. This has led some to advocate a broader interpretation of the term "tender offer" than that followed by us in *Kennecott Copper Corp. v. Curtiss-Wright Corp.,* [449 F. Supp. 951 (S.D.N.Y.), *aff'd in relevant part,* 584 F.2d 1195, 1206-07 (2d Cir. 1978)], and to adopt the eight-factor "test" of what is a tender offer, which was recommended by the SEC and applied by the district court in *Wellman v. Dickinson,* 475 F. Supp. 783, 823-24 (S.D.N.Y. 1979), *aff'd on other grounds,* 682 F.2d 355 (2d Cir. 1982), *cert. denied,* 460 U.S. 1069, 103 S. Ct. 1522, 75 L. Ed. 2d 946 (1983), and by the Ninth Circuit in *SEC v. Carter Hawley Hale Stores, Inc.* . . .

Although many of [these eight] factors are relevant for purposes of determining whether a given solicitation amounts to a tender offer, the elevation of such a list to a mandatory "litmus test" appears to be both unwise and unnecessary. As even the advocates of the proposed test recognize, in any given case a solicitation may constitute a tender offer even though some of the eight factors are absent or, when many factors are present, the solicitation may nevertheless not amount to a tender offer because the missing factors outweigh those present.

We prefer to be guided by the principle followed by the Supreme Court in deciding what transactions fall within the private offering exemption provided by §4(1) of the Securities Act of 1933, and by ourselves in *Kennecott Copper* in determining whether the Williams Act applies to private transactions. That principle is simply to look to the statutory purpose. In *S.E.C. v. Ralston Purina Co.,* 346 U.S. 119, 73 S. Ct. 981, 97 L. Ed. 1494 (1953), the Court stated, "the applicability of §4(1) should turn on whether the particular class of persons affected need the protection of the Act. An offering to those who are shown to be able to fend for themselves is a transaction 'not involving any public offering.'" Similarly, since the purpose of §14(d) is to protect the ill-informed solicitee, the question of whether a solicitation constitutes a "tender offer" within the meaning of §14(d) turns on whether, viewing the transaction in the light of the totality of circumstances, there appears to be a likelihood that unless the pre-acquisition filing strictures of that statute are followed there will be a substantial risk that solicitees will lack information needed to make a carefully considered appraisal of the proposal put before them.

Applying this standard, we are persuaded on the undisputed facts that Hanson's September 11 negotiation of five private purchases and one open market purchase of SCM shares, totaling 25% of SCM's outstanding stock, did not under the circumstances constitute a "tender offer" within the meaning of the Williams Act. Putting aside for the moment the events preceding the purchases, there can be little doubt that the privately negotiated purchases would not, standing alone, qualify as a tender offer, for the following reasons:

(1) In a market of 22,800 SCM shareholders the number of SCM sellers here involved, six in all, was miniscule compared with the numbers involved in public solicitations of the type against which the Act was directed.

(2)   At least five of the sellers were highly sophisticated professionals, knowledgeable in the market place and well aware of the essential facts needed to exercise their professional skills and to appraise Hanson's offer, including its financial condition as well as that of SCM, the likelihood that the purchases might block the SCM-Merrill bid, and the risk that if Hanson acquired more than 33-1/3% of SCM's stock the SCM-Merrill lockup of the "crown jewel" might be triggered. . . .

(3)   The sellers were not "pressured" to sell their shares by any conduct that the Williams Act was designed to alleviate, but by the forces of the market place. Indeed, in the case of Mutual Shares there was no initial solicitation by Hanson; the offer to sell was initiated by Mr. Price of Mutual Shares. Although each of the Hanson purchases was made for $73.50 per share, in most instances this price was the result of private negotiations after the sellers sought higher prices and in one case price protection, demands which were refused. The $73.50 price was not fixed in advance by Hanson. Moreover, the sellers remained free to accept the $74 per share tender offer made by the SCM-Merrill group.

(4)   There was no active or widespread advance publicity or public solicitation, which is one of the earmarks of a conventional tender offer. Arbitrageurs might conclude from ticker tape reports of two large anonymous transactions that Hanson must be the buyer. However, liability for solicitation may not be predicated upon disclosures mandated by Stock Exchange Rules. See *S.E.C. v. Carter-Hawley Hale Stores, Inc., supra,* 760 F.2d at 950.

(5)   The price received by the six sellers, $73.50 per share, unlike that appearing in most tender offers, can scarcely be dignified with the label "premium." The stock market price on September 11 ranged from $72.50 to $73.50 per share. Although risk arbitrageurs sitting on large holdings might reap sizeable profits from sales to Hanson at $73.50, depending on their own purchase costs, they stood to gain even more if the SCM-Merrill offer of $74 should succeed, as it apparently would if they tendered their shares to it. Indeed, the $73.50 price, being at most $1 over market or 1.4% higher than the market price, did not meet the SEC's proposed definition of a premium, which is $2.00 per share or 5% above market price, whichever is greater. SEC Exchange Act Release No. 16,385 (11/29/79) [1979-80] Fed. Sec. L. Rep. ¶82,374.

(6)   Unlike most tender offers, the purchases were not made contingent upon Hanson's acquiring a fixed minimum number or percentage of SCM's outstanding shares. Once an agreement with each individual seller was reached, Hanson was obligated to buy, regardless what total percentage of stock it might acquire. Indeed, it does not appear that Hanson had fixed in its mind a firm limit on the amount of SCM shares it was willing to buy.

(7)   Unlike most tender offers, there was no general time limit within which Hanson would make purchases of SCM stock. Concededly, cash transactions are normally immediate but, assuming an inability on the part of a seller and Hanson to agree at once on a price, nothing

prevented a resumption of negotiations by each of the parties except the arbitrageurs' speculation that once Hanson acquired 33-1/3% or an amount just short of that figure it would stop buying.

In short, the totality of circumstances that existed on September 11 did not evidence any likelihood that unless Hanson was required to comply with §14(d)(1)'s pre-acquisition filing and waiting-period requirements there would be a substantial risk of ill-considered sales of SCM stock by ill-informed shareholders.

There remains the question whether Hanson's private purchases take on a different hue, requiring them to be treated as a "*de facto*" continuation of its earlier tender offer, when considered in the context of Hanson's earlier acknowledged tender offer, the competing offer of SCM-Merrill and Hanson's termination of its tender offer. After reviewing all of the undisputed facts we conclude that the district court erred in so holding.

In the first place, we find no record support for the contention by SCM that Hanson's September 11 termination of its outstanding tender offer was false, fraudulent or ineffective. Hanson's termination notice was clear, unequivocal and straightforward. Directions were given, and presumably are being followed, to return all of the tendered shares to the SCM shareholders who tendered them. Hanson also filed with the SEC a statement pursuant to §14(d)(1) of the Williams Act terminating its tender offer. As a result, at the time when Hanson made its September 11 private purchases of SCM stock it owned no SCM stock other than those shares revealed in its §14(d) preacquisition report filed with the SEC on August 26, 1985.

The reason for Hanson's termination of its tender offer is not disputed: in view of SCM's grant of what Hanson conceived to be a "poison pill" lock-up option to Merrill, Hanson, if it acquired control of SCM, would have a company denuded as the result of its sale of its consumer food and pigment businesses to Merrill at what Hanson believed to be bargain prices. Thus, Hanson's termination of its tender offer was final; there was no tender offer to be "continued." . . .

Nor does the record support SCM's contention that Hanson had decided, before terminating its tender offer, to engage in cash purchases. Judge Kram referred only to evidence that "Hanson had *considered* open market purchases before it announced that the tender offer was dropped" (*emphasis added*) but made no finding to that effect. Absent evidence or a finding that Hanson had decided to seek control of SCM through purchases of its stock, no duty of disclosure existed under the federal securities laws. . . .

It may well be that Hanson's private acquisition of 25% of SCM's shares after termination of Hanson's tender offer was designed to block the SCM-Merrill leveraged buyout group from acquiring the 66-2/3% of SCM's stock needed to effectuate a merger. It may be speculated that such a blocking move might induce SCM to buy Hanson's 25% at a premium or lead to negotiations between the parties designed to resolve their differences. But we know of no provision in the federal securities laws or elsewhere that prohibits such tactics in "hardball" market battles of the type encountered here. *See Treadway Companies, Inc. v. Care Corp.,* 638 F.2d 357, 378-79 (2d Cir. 1980) ("We also see nothing wrong in Care's efforts to acquire one third of Treadway's outstanding stock, and thus to obtain a 'blocking position.'").

Thus the full disclosure purposes of the Williams Act as it now stands appear to have been fully satisfied by Hanson's furnishing to the public, both before and after termination of its tender offer, all of the essential relevant facts it was required by law to supply.

SCM further contends, and in this respect it is supported by the SEC as an amicus, that upon termination of a tender offer the solicitor should be subject to a waiting or cooling-off period (10 days is suggested) before it may purchase any of the target company's outstanding shares. However, neither the Act nor any SEC rule promulgated thereunder prohibits a former tender offeror from purchasing stock of a target through privately negotiated transactions immediately after a tender offer has been terminated. Indeed, it is significant that the SEC's formal proposal for the adoption of such a rule (Proposed Rule 14e-5) has never been implemented even though the SEC adopted a similar prohibition with respect to an *issuer's* making such purchases within 10 days after termination of a tender offer. *See* Rule 13e-4(f)(6). Thus, the existing law does not support the prohibition urged by SCM and the SEC. We believe it would be unwise for courts judicially to usurp what is a legislative or regulatory function by substituting our judgment for that of Congress or the SEC. . . .

In the present case we conclude that since the district court erred in ruling as a matter of law that SCM had demonstrated a likelihood of success on the merits, based on the theory that Hanson's post-tender offer private purchases of SCM constituted a *de facto* tender offer, it was an abuse of discretion to issue a preliminary injunction. Indeed, we do not believe that Hanson's transactions raise serious questions going to the merits that would provide a fair ground for litigation. In view of this holding it becomes unnecessary to rule upon the district court's determination that the balance of hardships tip in favor of SCM and that absent preliminary relief it would suffer irreparable injury. However, our decision is not to be construed as an affirmance of the district court's resolution of these issues. . . .

The order of the district court is reversed, the preliminary injunction against Hanson is vacated, and the case is remanded for further proceedings in accordance with this opinion. The mandate shall issue forthwith.

NOTE

In 1979, the SEC proposed a rule that would provide objective criteria to determine whether a putative Bidder's activity in Target's stock constituted a "tender offer" that would trigger the requirements of the Williams Act. *See* SEC Release No. 33-6159, Proposed Amendments to Tender Offer Rules, 1979 WL 182307 (Nov. 29, 1979). However, the proposed rule was never adopted, primarily because the SEC could not reach a consensus on precisely what activity constitutes a tender offer. "Needless to say, the SEC's preference for flexibility comes at the cost of sleeplessness for transaction planners, who quite naturally quest for certainty for their client's acquisitions." Cox and Hazen, CORPORATIONS (2d Ed. 2003) at p. 676.

QUESTIONS

1. What is the *S-G* test for determining whether a buyer's purchases of stock of the publicly traded company constitute a tender offer? How does this approach differ from the eight-factor *Wellman* test? For example, would the court have reached a different result in *Hanson Trust* if the court had applied the *Wellman* test used by the court in the *Carter Hawley Hale* case?

2. Did Hanson's activity constitute a *de facto* continuation of its earlier tender offer for SCM shares? Why did the court decline to impose a "cooling off" period that would prevent Hanson from making any purchases of SCM stock?

2.   Scope of Disclosure Required Under Regulation 14D and Schedule TO

In Chapter 4, we outlined the disclosure requirements imposed by both the federal proxy rules under the 1934 Act and the registration requirements of the 1933 Act (and the exemptions from registration promulgated thereunder). In addition to these obligations under federal law, the acquisition process is also subject to the disclosure requirements of the Williams Act in those transactions that involve a "tender offer" within the meaning of §14(d) of the 1934 Act.

Although not defined in the statute, nor in any SEC rule, the courts generally follow the eight-factor test (described in the two principal cases) in order to decide whether an acquisition program involves a *tender offer*. If it does constitute a tender offer, then the offeror must file and distribute the disclosure required by §14(d)(1) of the 1934 Act. The specific disclosure required of Bidder Co. to satisfy this statutory mandate is now set forth in Schedule TO, promulgated by the SEC. The disclosure required under the SEC's tender offer rules, which collectively consist of Regulation 14D, Regulation 14E, and Rule 13e-4,[2] was recently revamped and updated by the SEC in the manner described in the following excerpt:

Annual Review of Federal Securities Regulation: Significant 1999 Legislative and Regulatory Developments*
55 Bus. Law. 1505 (2000)

REGULATION OF TAKEOVERS AND SECURITY HOLDER COMMUNICATIONS

The U.S. Securities and Exchange Commission (Commission or SEC) adopted revised rules and regulations applicable to takeover transaction,

---

2. [By the author] The SEC's tender offer rules in Regulations 14D and 14E govern tender offers made by third-party bidders, whereas Rule 13e-4 governs issuer self-tenders; i.e., tender offers by a publicly traded issuer for its own equity securities.

* Prepared by the American Bar Association's Section of Business Law Subcommittee on the Annual Review of the Federal Regulation of Securities Committee.

including mergers, acquisitions, tender offers, and similar business combination transactions.[1] The new rules and amendments, including a new Regulation M-A, became effective January 24, 2000. According to the Commission, the new rules are intended to increase communications with security holders and the marketplace; place cash and stock tender offers on a more equal regulatory footing; and update, clarify, and harmonize disclosure requirements.

REDUCED RESTRICTIONS ON COMMUNICATIONS WITH SECURITY HOLDERS AND THE MARKET

The prior regulatory framework applicable to takeover transactions imposed restrictions on communications before the filing of mandated disclosure documents.[4] The revised regulatory scheme eliminates a number of these restrictions by adopting specific exemptions under the various rules and regulations that apply to business combination transactions. Specifically, the new rules and amendments relax previous restrictions on oral and written communications and permit more communication: (i) regarding a business combination transaction before a registration statement is filed;[6] (ii) before a proxy statement is filed, regardless of whether a business combination transaction is involved;[7] and (iii) regarding a proposed tender offer without formally commencing the offer and triggering filing and information dissemination requirements.[8]

Under this new regulatory scheme, written communications[9] made in reliance on these exemptions must be filed with the Commission. Oral communications are covered by the exemption, but they do not need to be reduced to

---

1. *See* Regulation of Takeovers and Security Holder Communications, Securities Act Release No. 33-7760, Exchange Act Release No. 34-42055, *64 Fed. Reg. 61,408 (1999)* (to be codified in scattered sections of 17 C.F.R.) [hereinafter Takeover Release].

4. These restrictions appeared in the registration, tender offer, and proxy rules.

6. The new and amended rules allow parties to communicate about a proposed business combination before a registration statement is filed, as well as during the waiting period and post-effective period, provided written communications are filed beginning with the first public announcement and ending with the close of the proposed transaction. Securities Act of 1933 (Securities Act) revised Rules 135 and 145 and new Rules 165, 166, and 425 are set forth in the Takeover Release.

7. Revised Rule 14a-12 allows both oral and written communications before a proxy statement is filed, provided all written communications relating to the solicitation are filed on or before the date of first use. This exemption is available regardless of the solicitation's subject matter. The exemption is not limited to business combination transactions.

8. Under the new and revised rules, bidders and targets are permitted to communicate with security holders, provided all written communications related to the offer are filed on the date the communication is made. Exchange Act revised tender offer Rules 14d-2 and 14d-9 are set forth in the Takeover Release.

9. According to the Commission, "written communications include all information disseminated otherwise than orally, including electronic communications and other future applications of changing technology." The release states written communications also include videos, CD-ROMs, transcripts, slides, and other materials shared with investors.

writing or filed.[11] The person making the communication must file all written communications made in connection with or relating to the transaction on or before the date of first use. All written communications must contain a legend advising security holders to read the applicable mandated disclosure document when it is filed, together with any other documents that may be available. Investors must receive the mandated disclosure documents before they are asked to make a voting or investment decision.

Prior rules permitted a proxy statement relating to an acquisition, merger, consolidation, or similar transaction to be filed confidentially with the Commission. The revised rules limit the availability of confidential treatment. Under the amended rules, confidential treatment is available only if the parties to the transaction limit their public comments to the information specified in Rule 135.[17] If the parties publicly disclose information relating to the transaction that goes beyond Rule 135, confidential treatment is not available and all proxy materials related to the transaction must be filed publicly.

LESSENING DISPARITIES IN THE REGULATORY TREATMENT OF CASH AND STOCK TENDER OFFERS

The amendments attempt to place cash and stock tender offers on a more equal regulatory footing. Under previous regulations, a bidder offering securities as consideration in an exchange offer could not commence the offer until the related registration statement was effective. Cash tender offers, however, could commence as soon as a tender offer statement was filed and the required information was disseminated. The revised rules permit exchange offers to commence as early as when the related registration statement is filed.[21] A bidder, however, may not close the transaction and purchase the tendered securities until after the registration statement is declared effective. Bidders also must deliver to all security holders a preliminary prospectus containing all required information in addition to supplements or amendments that disclose material changes from the prospectus previously provided.

---

11. Both oral and written communications made in reliance on these new exemptions continue to be subject to liability under the antifraud rules.

17. Rule 135 permits notices that include the following information: (i) the issuer name; (ii) the title, amount, and basic terms of the securities to be offered, the timing of the offering, and a brief statement of the purpose and manner of the offering; and (iii) any legend required by state law. Also, limited additional information is allowed for specific types of transactions. Revised Rule 135 is set forth in the Takeover Release.

21. New Rule 162 is set forth in the Takeover Release. To commence the tender offer early, the bidder must include in the preliminary prospectus all information necessary for a security holder to make an informed investment decision, including pricing information. Bidders also must distribute the prospectus and related transmittal letters to all investors and file a tender offer statement with the Commission.

UPDATING, CLARIFYING, AND HARMONIZING DISCLOSURE REQUIREMENTS

The Commission has integrated various forms and disclosure requirements relating to tender offers, going-private transactions, and other extraordinary transactions into a new series of rules within Regulation S-K, entitled "Regulation M-A." The new regulatory scheme also combines prior schedules for tender offers into one schedule available for all tender offers, called "Schedule TO." In addition, the new regulations revise the financial statement filing requirements for various business combination transactions. Finally, the new rules allow bidders to provide for a subsequent offering period after completion of a tender offer during which time security holders may tender shares.

QUESTIONS

1.   What information do investors need to know in order to make an informed decision in deciding whether to tender their Target Co. shares into Bidder's public tender offer?

2.   Does your analysis of the scope of required disclosure vary depending on whether Bidder is seeking to acquire any and all shares or is instead making a partial tender offer?

3.   Does your analysis of investors' information needs depend on whether the tender offer consideration consists of all cash or exclusively shares of Bidder's stock?

3.   Rule 14d-10: The Impact of the SEC's Best Price Rule

In 1986, the SEC adopted Rule 14d-10, more popularly known as the Best Price Rule. Consistent with the SEC's mandate of investor protection, the rule requires the tender offeror to pay to all security holders the highest price paid to any security holder in the course of Bidder's tender offer. Although this rule seemed to be relatively straightforward in its terms, by the 1990s, the rule was engulfed in controversy and uncertainty as to its application. The uncertainty largely stemmed from conflicting judicial interpretations as to the scope of Rule 14d-10. "[I]in the early 1990s, some influential courts held that certain compensatory arrangements with officers and other employees of a target who tender shares into a pending tender offer could constitute consideration paid to them by the acquirer.* This led to the virtual demise of the tender offer

---

*   [By the author] *See, e.g., Epstein v. MCA, Inc.,* 50 F.3d 644 (9th Cir. 1995), rev'd on other grounds, *Matsushita Electric Industrial Co. v Epstein,* 516 U.S. 367 (1996) (adopting the "integral element" approach); *see also Lerro v. Quaker Oats Co.,* 84 F.3d 239 (7th Cir. 1996) (adopting the "bright-line" test).

as an acquisition structure in transactions in which the acquiror sought new employment or similar arrangements with target management."* Andrew L. Sommer & Gregory H. Woods, *The Tender Offer Returns: What Does It Mean for Private Equity Buyers?* 7 Debevoise & Plimpton Private Equity Report 1 (Winter/Spring 2007) (copy on file with author).

At the end of 2006, the SEC adopted amendments to its Best Price Rule that were intended to address the uncertainty regarding Rule 14d-10 by clarifying the circumstances in which members of management who tender their Target shares into Bidder's tender offer could also receive new employment agreements or equity-based compensation. "The amended best-price rule now requires that the consideration paid to any security holder 'for securities tendered in the tender offer' be the highest consideration paid to any other security holder 'for securities tendered in the tender offer.' The new phrases are intended to make clear that the rule applies *only* to the consideration paid for securities tendered, not for other arrangements that may be 'integral' to the tender offer[, the test previously applied by a number of courts]. . . . The amendments [also] provide that the best-price rule will *not* prohibit the negotiation, execution, or amendment of an employment compensation, severance, or other employee-benefit arrangement, provided the arrangement is compensation for past or future services or for refraining from performing future services and is not calculated based on the number of securities tendered or to be tendered." *Id.* at 24. (*Emphasis added.*) As a result of these amendments, most commentators believe that it is much less likely that employment-related compensation will trigger claims that a Bidder has violated Rule 14d-10.

The following article comprehensively reviews the practical advantages of the tender offer, as well as the practical impact of the judicial controversy surrounding the scope of Rule 14d-10 and the implications of the SEC's recent amendments to its rule.

---

* [By the author] The "virtual demise of the tender offer" is largely attributable to the devastating financial consequences if a court were to find later that the tender offeror violated Rule 14d-10. "The threat of litigation, . . . [coupled with] the drastic penalties to a bidder for violation of the best price rule (i.e., the mandatory payment of the per share value of the contested [employee compensation] arrangement to *all* security holders), had a chilling effect on tender offers." Marilyn Mooney, et al., *Amendments to the Best Price Tender Offer Rules,* 20 Insights 5 (December 2006) (*emphasis added*). In other words, the damages to be paid if a court were to determine later that Bidder had violated Rule 14d-10 would require the tender offeror to pay every other shareholder (who had tendered their shares into Bidder's tender offer) the same consideration per share that Bidder had paid to the shareholder that received the highest per-share payment. Obviously, this could lead to potentially crushing liability and eliminate the value of the transaction from Bidder's perspective, thereby "chilling" the willingness of prospective Bidders to structure their acquisitions as a tender offer, even in those situations where the tender offer, for other reasons, may have been the preferred deal structure.

David Grinberg & Gordon Bava
A Comeback for Tender Offers?
Mergers & Acquisitions 73-77 (March 2007)

. . . The cloud over the best-price rules resulted in hesitancy among acquirers to utilize tender offers, and they substantially declined over the last several years. . . .

. . .

Tender Offers' Advantages.　Generally, a tender offer is a publicized bid to purchase shares of common stock—usually at a premium over the market price—made directly by a bidder to all of the target's shareholders. As long as the acquisition does not have antitrust or other regulatory approval requirements, a tender can be completed in 20 business days. A complete appreciation of the amendments to the best-price rules is possible only through comparison of the relative advantages of the tender with its primary alternative—the statutory merger.

From a buyer's perspective, the tender offer has four main advantages:

Speedy process.　Because the minimum number of business days that a tender offer must be kept open is only 20, the buyer can purchase a controlling stake in the target in a relatively short period of time, thereby reducing the probability of a competing bid by another potential buyer. If the bidder acquires enough shares to execute a short-form merger—usually 90%—the back-end merger can be consummated promptly without filing a proxy or information statement with the SEC or obtaining shareholder approval. A statutory merger subject to the SEC's proxy rules generally will take at least three to four months to complete.

Speedy completion of the acquisition decreases competition and execution risks and allows the buyer to begin integrating the target rather quickly. A quick closing also minimizes uncertainty and disruption for the target company's business, employees, customers, and business partners.

Direct offer to shareholders.　Tender offers do not require the support of the target's management or its board of directors. Buyers communicate directly with a target's shareholders by requesting them to tender their shares in exchange for cash, stock, or a combination of both.

Telescoping control.　A buyer can gain control of the target without purchasing 100% of the outstanding voting securities, which allows it to achieve its goals at a reduced cost.

Eliminating appraisal rights.　Perhaps most important in today's environment of activist hedge funds, a tender offer eliminates the use of appraisal rights, which may be asserted in an attempt to increase the merger price or disrupt, and even halt, the proposed deal.

The tender offer has two main advantages for the target's shareholders:

- They receive the acquisition currency faster than they would in a statutory merger.
- There is a lower risk that intervening events, such as material adverse changes, will develop.

Significant intervening events could provide the buyer with a basis for terminating the deal or renegotiating the price. In addition, a tender offer usually reduces the time during which the target is operating under certain restrictions contained in a standard acquisition agreement.

Uncertainty Under the Old Rules.   The SEC adopted the best-price rules in 1986 to mandate that all target shareholders must be treated equally during a tender offer. The best-price rules include Exchange Act Rule 14d-10, which applies to third-party tender offers, and Exchange Act Rule 13e-4(f)(8), which applies to self-tenders.

To accomplish the SEC's objective, the best-price rules required the buyer to pay all target shareholders the same price per share. On their face, the best-price rules seemed to be straightforward, but in reality, complying with the rules and their application became anything but simple.

After adoption of the best-price rules, target shareholders, . . . brought lawsuits alleging that employees, directors, and other shareholders had been paid additional amounts during the tender offer in violation of the rules. Typically, the complainants claimed that additional consideration was paid because the buyer entered into new compensation agreements with employees, directors, or other shareholders or adopted the target's existing compensation agreements. Shareholders specifically attacked severance or change-in-control payments to officers, cash retention bonuses, payments for non-competition agreements, and compensation paid in consulting agreements.

Unfortunately for M&A practitioners, federal courts differed in interpreting whether these monetary agreements constituted additional tender offer consideration in violation of the best-price rules. The conflict was between the "integral-part" test and the "bright-line" test.

Courts employing the integral-part test focused on whether the compensation agreement was an integral part of the offer even if it was executed and performed outside of the formal tender offer period—i.e., before the offer began or expired—and if the agreement had any commercial significance of its own outside of the offer.[*] These judges usually concluded that the agreement did in fact constitute an integral part of the tender offer in violation of tender offer rules.

The result of incorporating compensation into the tender price would entitle all other target shareholders to the same level of consideration—often

---

[*] [By the author] *See, e.g., Epstein v. MCA, Inc.,* 50 F.3d 644 (9th Cir. 1995), *rev'd on other grounds, Matsushita Electrical Industrial Co. v. Epstein,* 516 U.S. 367 (1996) (adopting the "integral part" test).

a rather expensive undertaking. For example, suppose the chief executive officer of a target also owned 5,000 shares. In connection with the offer, the buyer agreed to pay the CEO a $500,000 retention bonus to stay on the job for a year after closing.

Under the integral-part test, each target shareholder would be entitled to an additional $100 per share. As a result, legitimate and customary agreements with a target's officers and directors that were designed to ensure a smooth closing or an efficient transition could not be part of a tender offer because of fears that courts would find the compensation in violation of the best-price rules. Because statutory mergers do not have a requirement similar to the best-price rules, an acquisition frequently was structured as a merger. The payments would be disclosed in proxy materials but not precluded.

Courts applying the "bright-line" test, such as the Seventh Circuit Court of Appeals,[*] concentrated on the exact timing of the compensation payments or arrangements. The question was whether they were made during the tender offer—after it was announced and before it closed.

Under the bright-line approach, a disputed deal with a shareholder that was completed before the tender offer began or after it was completed usually was found not to be subject to the best-price rules. Courts following that standard typically held that the compensation agreements and payments did not violate the best-price rules if they had not been made during the formal tender offer period. While affirming the objective of paying all shareholders the highest prices, these courts said that the best-price rules were not intended to capture the amounts paid in compensation under employment or similar agreements.

For several reasons, the split between the federal courts resulted in a drastic reduction in the use of tender offers, even in situations where the speed of a tender offer would have made it the most attractive and preferred acquisition structure. . . .

[The SEC's] Best-Price Rule Amendments. Faced with competing tests regarding the application of the best-price rules and the resulting uncertainty and unintended consequences, the SEC issued amendments through a three-pronged approach that:

- Clarified that the best-price rules apply only to the price paid for securities tendered and not to funds paid to shareholders for other aspects of the acquisition, such as compensatory, severance, or other employee benefit arrangements, as long as these arrangements were not related to purchasing the securities;
- Exempted from the best-price rules any money paid under employment compensation, severance, or other benefit arrangements to shareholders of the target, such as employees and directors, if the money is strictly for performance of service or under non-compete agreements and is not based on the number of securities the shareholder tenders; and

---

[*] [By the author] *Lerro v. Quaker Oats Co.*, 84 F.3d 239 (7th Cir. 1996) (adopting the "bright-line" test).

- Provided a safe harbor so that arrangements approved by independent directors of either the acquirer or target will not be prohibited by the rules.

. . .

[The] Amendments' Lasting Impact.   M&A professionals generally welcome the [SEC's] amendments to the best-price rules because they will reduce disincentives to the structuring of acquisitions as tender offers. By acknowledging that compensation arrangements are frequently important parts of mergers and acquisitions, the amendments ensure that employment and other similar compensation arrangements will be eligible for payment and will alleviate concerns about violating best-price rules.

Potential costs associated with conducting tender offers will be significantly reduced because of a decreased risk of litigation. The structure of a particular transaction will not be dictated by fear of violating the rules and artificial obstacles created by divergent interpretations of the rules. Most influential will be the merits of the structure itself and what is deemed to be in the best interests of the target's shareholders. The SEC stated . . . that it believes that "the interests of security holders are better served when all acquisition structures are viable options."

. . .

Because the amendments will level the playing field between tender offers and statutory mergers in most cases, they may spur a resurgence of tender offers.

QUESTION

1. Given the SEC's amendments to SEC Rule 14d-10, what are the timing advantages of a cash tender offer, as opposed to the other potential deal structures?

4.   Tender Offer Conditions: The Importance of Contract Law

Gilbert v. El Paso Company
575 A.2d 1131 (Del. 1988)

MOORE, Justice.

. . . On the afternoon of December 20, 1982, Travis Petty, El Paso's chairman and chief executive officer, received a telephone call from Richard Bressler, the chairman and chief executive officer of Burlington. Bressler confirmed long-circulating rumors of Burlington's interest in acquiring El Paso, and notified Petty that Burlington's board of directors had recently authorized him to initiate a tender offer to gain control of El Paso. The following day, December 21, 1982, Petty received a letter from Bressler confirming that Burlington had launched a tender offer for up to 25,100,000 common shares of El Paso, representing approximately 49.1% of the company's outstanding common stock. The ownership of these shares, when added to the 537,800 already beneficially owned by Burlington, would give Burlington control of over 51.8% of all outstanding El Paso common shares.

The offer stipulated that tendered shares could be withdrawn until January 12, 1983, and that the offer would expire at 12:00 midnight on January 19, 1983. Burlington stated that if the December offer was oversubscribed, any shares tendered before December 30, 1982 would be entitled to proration rights.[7] Significantly, Burlington revealed no future plans to purchase the remaining 49% of El Paso's common shares upon completion of a fully-subscribed December offer. In fact, Burlington specifically cautioned that any future second-step transaction with El Paso's minority shareholders "might be on terms (including the consideration offered per share) the same as, or more or less favorable than, those of the [December] offer." Additionally, Burlington expressly reserved the right to terminate its highly-conditional offer upon the occurrence of any one of a number of specified events.[8] . . .

Based in part upon these presentations [by its financial advisor (Merrill Lynch) and its legal advisor (Wachtel, Lipton)], the El Paso board unanimously rejected Burlington's December offer, concluding that it was not in the best interests of the company or its shareholders. The directors were principally concerned with the perceived inadequacy of the $24 offering price, the partial nature of the bid, and the potentially adverse impact upon remaining shareholders if the December offer were successful. The directors also adopted several resolutions, upon the recommendation of legal counsel, designed to impede Burlington's bid. These measures included "golden parachute" employment agreements with El Paso's senior managers; amendments to El Paso's by-laws and Employee Savings and Stock Ownership plans; creation of a new series of preferred stock, with detachable share rights intended to forestall any business combination between El Paso and a 25% or greater shareholder without the approval of 90% of the outstanding preferred shares.[9] . . .

---

7. We have previously observed that granting such proration rights, in the absence of adequate protections for the company's remaining or back-end shares, has been universally recognized as a "classic coercive measure designed to stampede shareholders into tendering" their shares. *Unocal* [493 A.2d 946, 956 (Del. 1985)]. This stratagem has primarily been criticized by us and has met a timely demise. *See id. See also* 17 C.F.R. §240.14d-8 (1988).

8. Burlington reserved the right to terminate the offer if: (a) any legal action challenging the offer were instituted or threatened; (b) any governmental body took action which might affect or delay the offer; (c) there were substantial and material changes or threatened changes in the business or assets of El Paso; (d) El Paso authorized or proposed to authorize an extraordinary dividend or the creation of new capital stock; (e) El Paso adopted or proposed to adopt any amendments to its articles of incorporation or By-laws; or (f) El Paso and Burlington entered into a definitive agreement or understanding involving a business combination. Not surprisingly, each of these events occurred at some point during the course of this takeover contest.

9. This novel security, issued as an integral part of a Share Purchase Rights Plan, is generally recognized as the first use and forerunner of the contemporary "poison pill" antitakeover device. *See* M. Johnson, *Takeover: The New Wall Street Warriors* 13, 36-37 (1986).

Throughout the weekend of January 8th and 9th, the parties' financial and legal advisors negotiated the essential components of a possible accord between the companies. Central to these negotiations was the amount which Burlington would ultimately invest in El Paso. Despite the apparent urging of El Paso's representatives, Burlington steadfastly refused to increase its frontend offer beyond the minimal amount required under its December offer to gain control of El Paso—approximately $600,000,000. Therefore, in order to reconcile these conflicting points with both companies' desire to augment El Paso's capital structure, the parties agreed in principle to Burlington's acquisition of a majority of El Paso's common stock through a consensual, two-part transaction. Under this proposal, Burlington was granted an option to purchase 4,166,667 treasury shares directly from El Paso for $100,000,000. These funds would then be used to increase El Paso's equity base. Burlington would then terminate the December offer, and would substitute in its place a new offer (the January offer), for a reduced total of 21,000,000 shares at $24 per share,[16] which would then be open to all El Paso shareholders. Notably, in addition to enhancing the equity base of the company, this arrangement satisfied El Paso's objective that all shareholders should benefit from an improved Burlington offer.

As part of this accord, Burlington agreed in principle to El Paso's demand for enhanced procedural safeguards and protections for El Paso's remaining back-end shareholders. Burlington also agreed that Petty and four other El Paso representatives would continue as directors of El Paso ("the Continuing Directors"). Finally, Burlington acknowledged that any contemplated second step for El Paso's remaining minority shares would be subject to the majority approvals of both the Continuing Directors and El Paso's minority (i.e., non-Burlington) shareholders. . . .

Burlington thereafter terminated its December offer, and on the next day, January 11, 1983, instituted the new January offer for 21,000,000 shares at $24 per share. In response to the January offer, 40,246,853 shares were tendered, including most of the shares owned by El Paso's directors. . . .

II.

Plaintiffs primarily challenge two aspects of the settlement agreement between Burlington and El Paso: the substitution of the January offer for the December offer, and the direct purchase by Burlington of 4,166,667 treasury shares from El Paso. Plaintiffs claim, without dispute from the defendants, that those transactions (i) reduced the number of shares that Burlington directly purchased from El Paso's shareholders and (ii) diluted the proration pool initially established under the December offer by allowing *all* shareholders, including those who were not members of the class, to tender into the January offer. . . .

---

16. It appears that the number of shares to be purchased by Burlington under the January offer was established after Burlington had agreed to directly invest $100,000,000 in El Paso. The record suggests that the parties worked backwards from Burlington's total investment ceiling of $600,000,000, and determined that the remaining $500,000,000 available for Burlington's acquisition effort could be used to purchase approximately 21,000,000 El Paso shares at $24 per share.

III.

. . . We first address the Court of Chancery's decision in *Gilbert I* dismissing the breach of contract allegations against Burlington. The court noted that "[p]laintiffs' principal complaint is that Burlington breached its contractual obligation to complete its December tender offer." *Gilbert I*, [*Gilbert v. El Paso*, 490 A.2d 1050, 1054 (Del. Ch. 1984)]. As characterized, the plaintiffs' breach of contract claim is fundamentally dependent upon their assertion that the class had a recognizable, vested and defendable right to have their shares purchased under the December offer. The plaintiffs' action for contractual breach is contingent upon their presumption that, by tendering their shares into Burlington's highly conditional December offer, the class was vested with certain rights with which neither Burlington nor El Paso could interfere.

It is undisputed that Burlington had conditioned its acceptance of shares tendered into the December offer upon the non-occurrence of a number of specified events, and that *each* of these conditions occurred in the three weeks following the announcement of Burlington's December offer. *See Gilbert I*, 490 A.2d at 1053. It is also well settled that under general contract law an offeror may condition the performance contemplated in his offer upon the occurrence or non-occurrence of specific events. Such conditions may effectively limit the obligation of the promisor to perform. 3A A. Corbin, *Corbin on Contracts* §639 (1960). Under New Jersey law,[26] an offeror has wide latitude over the terms of its offer and is free to engraft any number of conditions or terms upon it. Similarly, in connection with a tender offer, an offeror may specify any number of conditions qualifying its obligation to perform, subject to Securities and Exchange Commission limitations and the requirements established under the Williams Act. These fundamental principles are clear and are apparently uncontested by the plaintiffs.

Among their ancillary contractual claims, however, plaintiffs argue that Burlington deliberately invoked these conditions solely to acquire El Paso on more advantageous terms, and in so doing, breached its implied covenant of good faith and fair dealing with the class. Although an implied covenant of good faith and honest conduct exists in every contract, such subjective standards cannot override the literal terms of an agreement.

As part of the December offer, Burlington expressly reserved the right to terminate the offer upon the occurrence of a number of objective, factual events over which Burlington exercised no discretion or control. Although an implied covenant of good faith may preclude an offeror from escaping its obligations by deliberately causing the occurrence of a condition precedent, there is no evidence of such activity here. We agree with the Vice Chancellor's finding that an offeror "is free to pursue its economic interests through the application of conditions intended to limit the cost of proceeding." In tendering their shares

---

26. The December offer provided for performance (the tender of shares) in Newark, New Jersey. The parties agree that New Jersey law controls the plaintiffs' breach of contract claim. The Vice Chancellor correctly found that New Jersey statutory and case law on this issue is consistent with general principles of contract law.

to Burlington, the class accepted these express limitations and qualifications, and acknowledged that Burlington could be relieved of its promise to perform upon the occurrence of any of the reserved conditions. Thus, Burlington's mere exercise of its contractual right to terminate its tender offer, without more, does not constitute a breach of its implied covenant of good faith and fair dealing.

[In a portion of the Court's opinion that was omitted in this edited excerpt, the Court concluded that the plaintiffs failed to establish that the directors breached their fiduciary duties, relying on *Unocal*'s standard of enhanced judicial scrutiny. *See Unocal Corp. v. Mesa Petroleum, infra,* at page 529. We will discuss the *Unocal* standard of review at length as part of the fiduciary duty materials in Chapter 7.]

QUESTIONS

1. What were the concerns that the El Paso board had with respect to the terms of Burlington's original bid for El Paso?

2. What were the back-end protections that were included in Burlington's revised January offer? How did these protections address the concerns that the El Paso board had with respect to the terms of Burlington's original offer?

3. What is the basis of the plaintiff's complaint with respect to the revised terms of Burlington's offer?

C.   State Antitakeover Statutes: State Regulation of Stock Purchases

Following enactment of the Williams Act in 1968, and as the market for hostile takeovers subsequently heated up, many states responded by adopting statutes regulating tender offers; indeed, by 1982, 37 states had adopted some form of antitakeover statute. *See* Guhan Subramanian, Steven Herscovici, and Brian Barbetta, *Is Delaware's Anti-Takeover Statute Unconstitutional? Evidence from 1988-2008,* 65 Bus. Law. 685 (2010). Broadly speaking, the "intent behind [these state antitakeover statutes] is to protect the incumbent management and to preserve the payrolls of local companies that are potential takeover [targets]." Cox & Hazen, Corporations, at p. 690. Or, as Professor Roberta Romano explains in her book, The Genius of American Corporate Law, at pp. 58-59 (1993):

> Like most pork-barrel legislation such as public works ("rivers and harbors") bills, takeover statutes are almost always unanimously approved [when submitted to state legislatures]. The likely explanation for such legislative unanimity is that the benefits and beneficiaries (real or supposed) of such legislation are highly concentrated—many, if not most, of the target company's managers and workers

reside within the state—while the costs [imposed by these antitakeover statutes] are borne largely by a loosely organized, geographically dispersed group, of shareholders [– many, if not most, of whom are non-residents].

The terms of the earliest generations of these state antitakeover statutes typically imposed requirements that were more stringent than the requirements imposed by federal law. Concern grew whether states could regulate the tender offer process in the face of federal legislation or whether the Williams Act had preempted the field. Another challenge to the constitutionality of these state statutes was based on the Commerce Clause. Here, concern focused on whether the state statute imposed an impermissible burden on interstate commerce. The first generation of the state antitakeover statutes to reach the Supreme Court was Illinois's antitakeover statute, which was declared unconstitutional in *Edgar v. MITE Corp.*, 457 U.S. 624 (1982). Since this case was decided, state antitakeover statutes have continued to evolve through successive generations. "Today, only the second and third generation statutes have survived Constitutional challenge." James D. Cox and Thomas Lee Hazen, CORPORATIONS (2d Ed. 2003) at p. 691. The three generations of state antitakeover statutes are the focus of the following materials.

1.   The First Generation—Disclosure and Fairness Statutes

The Illinois antitakeover statute at issue in *Edgar v. MITE Corp., supra,* covered corporations that were incorporated in Illinois, as well as those *non-Illinois* corporations that had their principal offices in Illinois (or at least 10% of their capital represented within the state), provided further that at least 10% of the shares sought to be acquired in Bidder's tender offer were held by Illinois residents. In addition, the Illinois statute imposed a mandatory 20-day waiting period before Bidder's tender offer could commence and allowed for administrative review (by Illinois state officials) as to the fairness of the terms of Bidder's proposed tender offer. Moreover, there was no fixed timetable for completing this review process, which meant this process potentially could extend for an indefinite period of time.

In a very divided opinion, the Supreme Court ruled that the Illinois statute was unconstitutional on the grounds that the state statute constituted impermissible state interference with interstate commerce. The Illinois statute was also challenged on the grounds that it was preempted by the Williams Act. However, only a plurality of the Court joined in the portion of the *MITE* opinion that found that the Illinois statute was preempted by virtue of the carefully balanced disclosure scheme adopted by Congress in the Williams Act. The Court's decision in "*Edgar v. MITE Corp.* was the death knell for first-generation antitakeover statutes," Cox & Hazen, *supra,* at p. 692, most of which went well "beyond the disclosure philosophy of the Williams Act[7] by giving the state administrator the power to review the merits of the tender offer's terms or the adequacy of

---

7. *See Kennecott Corp. v. Smith,* 507 F. Supp. 1206 (D.N.J. 1981) (New Jersey takeover law frustrates the purpose of the Williams Act by substituting [the state administrator's] view of the offer for the informed judgment of shareholders).

the bidder's disclosures[8]," *id.,* at p. 691, in a manner similar to the terms of the Illinois's antitakeover statute.

Following the Supreme Court's decision in *MITE,* states sought to regulate the tender offer process by exploiting the internal affairs doctrine. "The basic thrust of many of these second-generation statutes is to regulate tender offers through state law rules relating to corporate governance . . . " Cox & Hazen, CORPORATIONS, *supra,* at p. 692. Accordingly, these "second-generation statutes" generally involved amendments to provisions of the state corporation code governing the company's internal affairs. Two types of statutes came to dominate the second-generation statute antitakeover statutes: control share statutes and fair price (or best price) statutes. These statutes are the topic of the next section.

2.   The Second Generation — Control Share and Fair Price Statutes

The *control share statute,* first enacted in Ohio, limited the voting rights of shares held by a control person. Generally speaking, as a prospective Bidder Co. acquires shares of Target Co., it may cross different ownership thresholds; these levels are set forth in the relevant state statute. For example, the Indiana statute at issue in the next case provided that control thresholds are crossed when a person becomes the owner of 20 percent, 33-1/3 percent, or 50 percent of the company's voting stock. After crossing a particular threshold, these statutes typically provide that the acquiring shareholder (i.e., Bidder) cannot vote the shares that it just acquired in the absence of a favorable vote by a majority of the company's other shareholders (i.e., a vote of a majority of the "disinterested shares," as defined in the state's statute). Most of these control share statutes define disinterested shares to exclude the shares held by the acquiring shareholder, as well as those held by the management of Target.

By contrast, the *fair price statutes*—or *best price statutes*—typically provide that any Bidder acquiring a "covered corporation" (i.e., a Target Co. covered by the terms of the fair price statute) must pay to *all* shareholders the best price paid to any Target shareholder. Most of these best price statutes allow for waiver of this requirement either by appropriate vote of Target shareholders or by the company's board of directors. Thus, most best price statutes do not present an obstacle to friendly takeovers (i.e., negotiated acquisitions).

The constitutionality of these so-called second generation statutes was decided by the Supreme Court in the next case.

CTS Corp. v. Dynamics Corp. of America
481 U.S. 69 (1987)

Justice POWELL delivered the opinion of the Court.

These cases present the questions whether the Control Share Acquisitions Chapter of the Indiana Business Corporation Law, Ind. Code §23-1-42-1 *et seq.*

---

8. *E.g.,* La. Rev. Stat. §51:1501(E) (West 1987) (repealed); 70 Pa. Cons. Stat. §74(d) (Supp. 1993) (repealed).

(Supp. 1986), is pre-empted by the Williams Act, or violates the Commerce Clause of the Federal Constitution, Art. I, §8, cl. 3.

I

A

On March 4, 1986, the Governor of Indiana signed a revised Indiana Business Corporation Law, Ind. Code §23-1-17-1 *et seq.* (Supp. 1986). That law included the Control Share Acquisitions Chapter (Indiana Act or Act). Beginning on August 1, 1987, the Act will apply to any corporation incorporated in Indiana, unless the corporation amends its articles of incorporation or bylaws to opt out of the Act. Before that date, any Indiana corporation can opt into the Act by resolution of its board of directors. The Act applies only to "issuing public corporations." The term "corporation" includes only businesses incorporated in Indiana. An "issuing public corporation" is defined as:

> "a corporation that has:
>> "(1) one hundred (100) or more shareholders;
>> "(2) its principal place of business, its principal office, or substantial assets within Indiana; and
>> "(3) either:
>>> "(A) more than ten percent (10%) of its shareholders resident in Indiana;
>>> "(B) more than ten percent (10%) of its shares owned by Indiana residents; or
>>> "(C) ten thousand (10,000) shareholders resident in Indiana."
> §23-1-42-4(a)[1]

The Act focuses on the acquisition of "control shares" in an issuing public corporation. Under the Act, an entity acquires "control shares" whenever it acquires shares that, but for the operation of the Act, would bring its voting power in the corporation to or above any of three thresholds: 20%, 33-1/3%, or 50%. An entity that acquires control shares does not necessarily acquire voting rights. Rather, it gains those rights only "to the extent granted by resolution approved by the shareholders of the issuing public corporation." Section 23-1-42-9(b) requires a majority vote of all disinterested[2] shareholders holding

---

1. These thresholds are much higher than the 5% threshold acquisition requirement that brings a tender offer under the coverage of the Williams Act. See 15 U.S.C. §78n(d)(1).

2. "Interested shares" are shares with respect to which the acquiror, an officer, or an inside director of the corporation "may exercise or direct the exercise of the voting power of the corporation in the election of directors." §23-1-42-3. If the record date passes before the acquiror purchases shares pursuant to the tender offer, the purchased shares will not be "interested shares" within the meaning of the Act; although the acquiror may own the shares on the date of the meeting, it will not "exercise . . . the voting power" of the shares.

As a practical matter, the record date usually will pass before shares change hands. Under Securities and Exchange Commission (SEC) regulations, the shares cannot be purchased

each class of stock for passage of such a resolution. The practical effect of this requirement is to condition acquisition of control of a corporation on approval of a majority of the pre-existing disinterested shareholders.

The shareholders decide whether to confer rights on the control shares at the next regularly scheduled meeting of the shareholders, or at a specially scheduled meeting. The acquiror can require management of the corporation to hold such a special meeting within 50 days if it files an "acquiring person statement,"[4] requests the meeting, and agrees to pay the expenses of the meeting. If the shareholders do not vote to restore voting rights to the shares, the corporation may redeem the control shares from the acquiror at fair market value, but it is not required to do so. Similarly, if the acquiror does not file an acquiring person statement with the corporation, the corporation may, if its bylaws or articles of incorporation so provide, redeem the shares at any time after 60 days after the acquiror's last acquisition.

B

On March 10, 1986, appellee Dynamics Corporation of America (Dynamics) owned 9.6% of the common stock of appellant CTS Corporation, an Indiana corporation. On that day, six days after the Act went into effect, Dynamics announced a tender offer for another million shares in CTS; purchase of those shares would have brought Dynamics' ownership interest in CTS to 27.5%. Also on March 10, Dynamics filed suit in the United States District Court for the Northern District of Illinois, alleging that CTS had violated the federal securities laws in a number of respects no longer relevant to these proceedings. On March 27, the board of directors of CTS, an Indiana corporation, elected to be governed by the provisions of the Act.

Four days later, on March 31, Dynamics moved for leave to amend its complaint to allege that the Act is pre-empted by the Williams Act, and violates the Commerce Clause, Art. I, §8, cl. 3. Dynamics sought a temporary restraining order, a preliminary injunction, and declaratory relief against CTS' use of the Act. On April 9, the District Court ruled that the Williams Act pre-empts the

---

until 20 business days after the offer commences. 17 CFR §240.14e-1(a) (1986). If the acquiror seeks an early resolution of the issue—as most acquirors will—the meeting required by the Act must be held no more than 50 calendar days after the offer commences, about three weeks after the earliest date on which the shares could be purchased. See §23-142-7. The Act requires management to give notice of the meeting "as promptly as reasonably practicable . . . to all shareholders of record as of the record date set for the meeting." §23-1-42-8(a). It seems likely that management of the target corporation would violate this obligation if it delayed setting the record date and sending notice until after 20 business days had passed. Thus, we assume that the record date usually will be set before the date on which federal law first permits purchase of the shares.

4. An "acquiring person statement" is an information statement describing, *inter alia*, the identity of the acquiring person and the terms and extent of the proposed acquisition. See §23-1-42-6.

Indiana Act and granted Dynamics' motion for declaratory relief. . . . A week later, on April 17, the District Court issued an opinion accepting Dynamics' claim that the Act violates the Commerce Clause. This holding rested on the court's conclusion that "the substantial interference with interstate commerce created by the [Act] outweighs the articulated local benefits so as to create an impermissible indirect burden on interstate commerce." . . .

On April 23 — [just] 23 days after Dynamics first contested application of the Act in the District Court — the Court of Appeals issued an order affirming the judgment of the District Court. . . .

II

The first question in these cases is whether the Williams Act pre-empts the Indiana Act. As we have stated frequently, absent an explicit indication by Congress of an intent to pre-empt state law, a state statute is pre-empted only

"'where compliance with both federal and state regulations is a physical impossibility . . . ,' or where the state 'law stands as an obstacle to the accomplishment and execution of the full purposes and objectives of Congress.' . . ." *Ray v. Atlantic Richfield Co.*, 435 U.S. 151, 158, 98 S. Ct. 988, 994, 55 L. Ed. 2d 179 (1978).

Because it is entirely possible for entities to comply with both the Williams Act and the Indiana Act, the state statute can be pre-empted only if it frustrates the purposes of the federal law. . . .

B

The Indiana Act differs in major respects from the Illinois statute that the Court considered in *Edgar v. MITE Corp.*, 457 U.S. 624, 102 S. Ct. 2629, 73 L. Ed. 2d 269 (1982). After reviewing the legislative history of the Williams Act, Justice WHITE, joined by Chief Justice BURGER and Justice BLACKMUN (the plurality), concluded that the Williams Act struck a careful balance between the interests of offerors and target companies, and that any state statute that "upset" this balance was pre-empted.

The plurality then identified three offending features of the Illinois statute. Justice WHITE'S opinion first noted that the Illinois statute provided for a 20-day precommencement period. During this time, management could disseminate its views on the upcoming offer to shareholders, but offerors could not publish their offers. The plurality found that this provision gave management "a powerful tool to combat tender offers." This contrasted dramatically with the Williams Act; Congress had deleted express precommencement notice provisions from the Williams Act. According to the plurality, Congress had determined that the potentially adverse consequences of such a provision on shareholders should be avoided. Thus, the plurality concluded that the Illinois provision "frustrate[d] the objectives of the Williams Act." The second criticized feature of the Illinois statute was a provision for a hearing on a tender offer that, because it set no deadline, allowed management "'to stymie indefinitely a takeover.'" The plurality noted that "'delay can seriously impede a tender offer,'" and that "Congress anticipated that investors and the takeover offeror would be free to go forward without unreasonable delay." Accordingly, the plurality concluded that this provision conflicted with the Williams Act. The third troublesome feature of the Illinois statute was its requirement that the fairness of tender offers would be reviewed by the Illinois Secretary of State. Noting that "Congress intended for investors to be free to make their own decisions," the plurality concluded that "'[t]he state thus offers investor protection at the expense of investor autonomy—an approach quite in conflict with that adopted by Congress.'"

C

As the plurality opinion in *MITE* did not represent the views of a majority of the Court,[6] we are not bound by its reasoning. We need not question that reasoning, however, because we believe the Indiana Act passes muster even under the broad interpretation of the Williams Act articulated by Justice WHITE in *MITE*. As is apparent from our summary of its reasoning, the overriding concern of the *MITE* plurality was that the Illinois statute considered in that case operated to favor management against offerors, to the detriment of shareholders. By contrast, the statute now before the Court protects the independent shareholder against the contending parties. Thus, the Act furthers a basic purpose of the Williams Act, "'plac[ing] investors on an equal footing with the takeover bidder,'" *Piper v. Chris-Craft Industries, Inc.*, 430 U.S., at 30, 97 S. Ct., at 943 (quoting the Senate Report accompanying the Williams Act, S. Rep. No. 550, 90th Cong., 1st Sess., 1 (1967)).

The Indiana Act operates on the assumption, implicit in the Williams Act, that independent shareholders faced with tender offers often are at a disadvantage. By allowing such shareholders to vote as a group, the Act protects them from the coercive aspects of some tender offers. If, for example, shareholders believe that a successful tender offer will be followed by a purchase of nontendering shares at a depressed price, individual shareholders may tender their shares—even if they doubt the tender offer is in the corporation's best interest—to protect themselves from being forced to sell their shares at a depressed price. As the SEC explains: "The alternative of not accepting the tender offer is virtual assurance that, if the offer is successful, the shares will have to be sold in the lower priced, second step." . . . In such a situation under the Indiana Act, the shareholders as a group, acting in the corporation's best interest,

---

6. Justice WHITE's opinion on the pre-emption issue, 457 U.S., at 630-640, 102 S. Ct., at 2634-2640, was joined only by Chief Justice BURGER and by Justice BLACKMUN. Two Justices disagreed with Justice WHITE's conclusion. See *id.*, at 646-647, 102 S. Ct., at 2642-2643 (POWELL, J., concurring in part); *id.*, at 655, 102 S. Ct., at 2647 (STEVENS, J., concurring in part and concurring in judgment). Four Justices did not address the question. See *id.*, at 655, 102 S. Ct., at 2647 (O'CONNOR J., concurring in part); *id.*, at 664, 102 S. Ct., at 2652 (MARSHALL, J., with whom BRENNAN, J., joined, dissenting); *id.*, at 667, 102 S. Ct., at 2653 (REHNQUIST, J., dissenting).

could reject the offer, although individual shareholders might be inclined to accept it. The desire of the Indiana Legislature to protect shareholders of Indiana corporations from this type of coercive offer does not conflict with the Williams Act. Rather, it furthers the federal policy of investor protection.

In implementing its goal, the Indiana Act avoids the problems the plurality discussed in *MITE*. Unlike the *MITE* statute, the Indiana Act does not give either management or the offeror an advantage in communicating with the shareholders about the impending offer. The Act also does not impose an indefinite delay on tender offers. Nothing in the Act prohibits an offeror from consummating an offer on the 20th business day, the earliest day permitted under applicable federal regulations, see 17 CFR §240.14e-1(a) (1986). Nor does the Act allow the state government to interpose its views of fairness between willing buyers and sellers of shares of the target company. Rather, the Act allows *shareholders* to evaluate the fairness of the offer collectively.

D

The Court of Appeals based its finding of pre-emption on its view that the practical effect of the Indiana Act is to delay consummation of tender offers until 50 days after the commencement of the offer. As did the Court of Appeals, Dynamics reasons that no rational offeror will purchase shares until it gains assurance that those shares will carry voting rights. Because it is possible that voting rights will not be conferred until a shareholder meeting 50 days after commencement of the offer, Dynamics concludes that the Act imposes a 50-day delay. This, it argues, conflicts with the shorter 20-business-day period established by the SEC as the minimum period for which a tender offer may be held open. We find the alleged conflict illusory.

The Act does not impose an absolute 50-day delay on tender offers, nor does it preclude an offeror from purchasing shares as soon as federal law permits. If the offeror fears an adverse shareholder vote under the Act, it can make a conditional tender offer, offering to accept shares on the condition that the shares receive voting rights within a certain period of time. The Williams Act permits tender offers to be conditioned on the offeror's subsequently obtaining regulatory approval. . . . There is no reason to doubt that this type of conditional tender offer would be legitimate as well.[9]

Even assuming that the Indiana Act imposes some additional delay, nothing in *MITE* suggested that *any* delay imposed by state regulation, however

---

9. Dynamics argues that conditional tender offers are not an adequate alternative because they leave management in place for three extra weeks, with "free rein to take other defensive steps that will diminish the value of tendered shares." Brief for Appellee 37. We reject this contention. In the unlikely event that management were to take actions designed to diminish the value of the corporation's shares, it may incur liability under state law. But this problem does not control our pre-emption analysis. Neither the Act nor any other federal statute can assure that shareholders do not suffer from the mismanagement of corporate officers and directors. Cf. *Cort v. Ash,* 422 U.S. 66, 84, 95 S. Ct. 2080, 2090-2091, 45 L. Ed. 2d 26 (1975).

short, would create a conflict with the Williams Act. The plurality argued only that the offeror should "be free to go forward without *unreasonable* delay." 457 U.S., at 639, 102 S. Ct., at 2639 (*emphasis added*). In that case, the Court was confronted with the potential for indefinite delay and presented with no persuasive reason why some deadline could not be established. By contrast, the Indiana Act provides that full voting rights will be vested—if this eventually is to occur—within 50 days after commencement of the offer. This period is within the 60-day period Congress established for restitution of withdrawal rights in 15 U.S.C. §78n(d)(5). We cannot say that a delay within that congressionally determined period is unreasonable.

Finally, we note that the Williams Act would pre-empt a variety of state corporate laws of hitherto unquestioned validity if it were construed to pre-empt any state statute that may limit or delay the free exercise of power after a successful tender offer. State corporate laws commonly permit corporations to stagger the terms of their directors. By staggering the terms of directors, and thus having annual elections for only one class of directors each year, corporations may delay the time when a successful offeror gains control of the board of directors. Similarly, state corporation laws commonly provide for cumulative voting. By enabling minority shareholders to assure themselves of representation in each class of directors, cumulative voting provisions can delay further the ability of offerors to gain untrammeled authority over the affairs of the target corporation.

In our view, the possibility that the Indiana Act will delay some tender offers is insufficient to require a conclusion that the Williams Act pre-empts the Act. The longstanding prevalence of state regulation in this area suggests that, if Congress had intended to pre-empt all state laws that delay the acquisition of voting control following a tender offer, it would have said so explicitly. The regulatory conditions that the Act places on tender offers are consistent with the text and the purposes of the Williams Act. Accordingly, we hold that the Williams Act does not pre-empt the Indiana Act.

III

As an alternative basis for its decision, the Court of Appeals held that the Act violates the Commerce Clause of the Federal Constitution. We now address this holding. On its face, the Commerce Clause is nothing more than a grant to Congress of the power "[t]o regulate Commerce . . . among the several States . . . ," Art. I, §8, cl. 3. But it has been settled for more than a century that the Clause prohibits States from taking certain actions respecting interstate commerce even absent congressional action. See, e.g., Cooley v. Board of Wardens, 12 How. 299 (1852). The Court's interpretation of "these great silences of the Constitution," H. P. Hood & Sons, Inc. v. Du Mond, 336 U.S. 525, 535 (1949), has not always been easy to follow. Rather, as the volume and complexity of commerce and regulation have grown in this country, the Court has articulated a variety of tests in an attempt to describe the difference between those regulations that the Commerce Clause permits and those regulations that it prohibits.

The principal objects of dormant Commerce Clause scrutiny are statutes that discriminate against interstate commerce. . . . The Indiana Act is not such a statute. It has the same effects on tender offers whether or not the offeror is a domiciliary or resident of Indiana. Thus, it "visits its effects equally upon both interstate and local business," *Lewis v. BT Investment Managers, Inc.,* [447 U.S. 27, at 36 (1980)].

Dynamics nevertheless contends that the statute is discriminatory because it will apply most often to out-of-state entities. This argument rests on the contention that, as a practical matter, most hostile tender offers are launched by offerors outside Indiana. But this argument avails Dynamics little. "The fact that the burden of a state regulation falls on some interstate companies does not, by itself, establish a claim of discrimination against interstate commerce." . . . Because nothing in the Indiana Act imposes a greater burden on out-of-state offerors than it does on similarly situated Indiana offerors, we reject the contention that the Act discriminates against interstate commerce.

B

This Court's recent Commerce Clause cases also have invalidated statutes that may adversely affect interstate commerce by subjecting activities to inconsistent regulations. . . . The Indiana Act poses no such problem. So long as each State regulates voting rights only in the corporations it has created, each corporation will be subject to the law of only one State. No principle of corporation law and practice is more firmly established than a State's authority to regulate domestic corporations, including the authority to define the voting rights of shareholders. See Restatement (Second) of Conflict of Laws §304 (1971) (concluding that the law of the incorporating State generally should "determine the right of a shareholder to participate in the administration of the affairs of the corporation"). Accordingly, we conclude that the Indiana Act does not create an impermissible risk of inconsistent regulation by different States.

C

The Court of Appeals did not find the Act unconstitutional for either of these threshold reasons. Rather, its decision rested on its view of the Act's potential to hinder tender offers. We think the Court of Appeals failed to appreciate the significance for Commerce Clause analysis of the fact that state regulation of corporate governance is regulation of entities whose very existence and attributes are a product of state law. As Chief Justice MARSHALL explained:

> "A corporation is an artificial being, invisible, intangible, and existing only in contemplation of law. Being the mere creature of law, it possesses only those properties which the charter of its creation confers upon it, either expressly, or as incidental to its very existence. These are such as are supposed best calculated to effect the object for which it was created." *Trustees of Dartmouth College v. Woodward,* 4 Wheat. 518, 636, 4 L. Ed. 518 (1819).

Every State in this country has enacted laws regulating corporate governance. By prohibiting certain transactions, and regulating others, such laws necessarily affect certain aspects of interstate commerce. This necessarily is true with respect to corporations with shareholders in States other than the State of incorporation. Large corporations that are listed on national exchanges, or even regional exchanges, will have shareholders in many States and shares that are traded frequently. The markets that facilitate this national and international participation in ownership of corporations are essential for providing capital not only for new enterprises but also for established companies that need to expand their businesses. This beneficial free market system depends at its core upon the fact that a corporation—except in the rarest situations—is organized under, and governed by, the law of a single jurisdiction, traditionally the corporate law of the State of its incorporation.

These regulatory laws may affect directly a variety of corporate transactions. Mergers are a typical example. In view of the substantial effect that a merger may have on the shareholders' interests in a corporation, many States require supermajority votes to approve mergers. See, *e.g.,* 2 MBCA §73 (requiring approval of a merger by a majority of all shares, rather than simply a majority of votes cast); RMBCA §11.03 (same). By requiring a greater vote for mergers than is required for other transactions, these laws make it more difficult for corporations to merge. State laws also may provide for "dissenters' rights" under which minority shareholders who disagree with corporate decisions to take particular actions are entitled to sell their shares to the corporation at fair market value. See, *e.g.,* 2 MBCA §§80, 81; RMBCA §13.02. By requiring the corporation to purchase the shares of dissenting shareholders, these laws may inhibit a corporation from engaging in the specified transactions.[12]

It thus is an accepted part of the business landscape in this country for States to create corporations, to prescribe their powers, and to define the rights that are acquired by purchasing their shares. A State has an interest in promoting stable relationships among parties involved in the corporations it charters,

---

12. Numerous other common regulations may affect both nonresident and resident shareholders of a corporation. Specified votes may be required for the sale of all of the corporation's assets. See 2 MBCA §79; RMBCA §12.02. The election of directors may be staggered over a period of years to prevent abrupt changes in management. See 1 MBCA §37; RMBCA §8.06. Various classes of stock may be created with differences in voting rights as to dividends and on liquidation. See 1 MBCA §15; RMBCA §6.01 (c). Provisions may be made for cumulative voting. See 1 MBCA §33, ¶ 4; RMBCA §7.28; n. 9, *supra.* Corporations may adopt restrictions on payment of dividends to ensure that specified ratios of assets to liabilities are maintained for the benefit of the holders of corporate bonds or notes. See 1 MBCA §45 (noting that a corporation's articles of incorporation can restrict payment of dividends); RMBCA §6.40 (same). Where the shares of a corporation are held in States other than that of incorporation, actions taken pursuant to these and similar provisions of state law will affect all shareholders alike wherever they reside or are domiciled.

Nor is it unusual for partnership law to restrict certain transactions. For example, a purchaser of a partnership interest generally can gain a right to control the business only with the consent of other owners. See Uniform Partnership Act §27, 6 U.L.A. 353 (1969); Uniform Limited Partnership Act §19 (1916 draft), 6 U.L.A. 603 (1969); Revised Uniform Limited Partnership Act §§702, 704 (1976 draft), 6 U.L.A. 259, 261 (Supp. 1986). These provisions—in force in the great majority of the States—bear a striking resemblance to the Act at issue in this case.

as well as in ensuring that investors in such corporations have an effective voice in corporate affairs.

There can be no doubt that the Act reflects these concerns. The primary purpose of the Act is to protect the shareholders of Indiana corporations. It does this by affording shareholders, when a takeover offer is made, an opportunity to decide collectively whether the resulting change in voting control of the corporation, as they perceive it, would be desirable. A change of management may have important effects on the shareholders' interests; it is well within the State's role as overseer of corporate governance to offer this opportunity. The autonomy provided by allowing shareholders collectively to determine whether the takeover is advantageous to their interests may be especially beneficial where a hostile tender offer may coerce shareholders into tendering their shares.

Appellee Dynamics responds to this concern by arguing that the prospect of coercive tender offers is illusory, and that tender offers generally should be favored because they reallocate corporate assets into the hands of management who can use them most effectively.[13] See generally Easterbrook & Fischel, The Proper Role of a Target's Management in Responding to a Tender Offer, 94 Harv. L. Rev. 1161 (1981). As [previously] indicated, Indiana's concern with tender offers is not groundless. Indeed, the potentially coercive aspects of tender offers have been recognized by the SEC, see SEC Release No. 21079, p. 86,916, and by a number of scholarly commentators, see, e.g., Bradley & Rosenzweig, Defensive Stock Repurchases, 99 Harv. L. Rev. 1377, 1412-1413 (1986); Macey & McChesney, A Theoretical Analysis of Corporate Greenmail, 95 Yale L.J. 13, 20-22 (1985); Lowenstein, 83 Colum. L. Rev., at 307-309. The Constitution does not require the States to subscribe to any particular economic theory. We are not inclined "to second-guess the empirical judgments of lawmakers concerning the utility of legislation," *Kassel v. Consolidated Freightways Corp.*, 450 U.S., at 679, 101 S. Ct., at 1321 (BRENNAN, J., concurring in judgment). In our view, the possibility of coercion in some takeover bids offers additional justification for Indiana's decision to promote the autonomy of independent shareholders.

Dynamics argues in any event that the State has "no legitimate interest in protecting the nonresident shareholders." Brief for Appellee 21 (quoting *Edgar v. MITE Corp.*, 457 U.S., at 644). Dynamics relies heavily on the statement by the *MITE* Court that "[i]nsofar as the . . . law burdens out-of-state transactions, there is nothing to be weighed in the balance to sustain the law." 457 U.S., at 644. But that comment was made in reference to an Illinois law that applied as well to out-of-state corporations as to in-state corporations. We agree that Indiana has no interest in protecting nonresident shareholders *of nonresident*

---

13. It is appropriate to note when discussing the merits and demerits of tender offers that generalizations usually require qualification. No one doubts that some successful tender offers will provide more effective management or other benefits such as needed diversification. But there is no reason to *assume* that the type of conglomerate corporation that may result from repetitive takeovers necessarily will result in more effective management or otherwise be beneficial to shareholders. The divergent views in the literature—and even now being debated in the Congress—reflect the reality that the type and utility of tender offers vary widely. Of course, in many situations the offer to shareholders is simply a cash price substantially higher than the market price prior to the offer.

corporations. But this Act applies only to corporations incorporated in Indiana. We reject the contention that Indiana has no interest in providing for the shareholders of its corporations the voting autonomy granted by the Act. Indiana has a substantial interest in preventing the corporate form from becoming a shield for unfair business dealing. Moreover, unlike the Illinois statute invalidated in *MITE*, the Indiana Act applies only to corporations that have a substantial number of shareholders in Indiana. See Ind. Code §23-1-42-4(a)(3) (Supp. 1986). Thus, every application of the Indiana Act will affect a substantial number of Indiana residents, whom Indiana indisputably has an interest in protecting.

D

Dynamics' argument that the Act is unconstitutional ultimately rests on its contention that the Act will limit the number of successful tender offers. There is little evidence that this will occur. But even if true, this result would not substantially affect our Commerce Clause analysis. We reiterate that this Act does not prohibit any entity—resident or nonresident—from offering to purchase, or from purchasing, shares in Indiana corporations, or from attempting thereby to gain control. It only provides regulatory procedures designed for the better protection of the corporations' shareholders. We have rejected the "notion that the Commerce Clause protects the particular structure or methods of operation in a . . . market." *Exxon Corp. v. Governor of Maryland*, 437 U.S., at 127, 98 S. Ct., at 2215. The very commodity that is traded in the securities market is one whose characteristics are defined by state law. Similarly, the very commodity that is traded in the "market for corporate control"—the corporation—is one that owes its existence and attributes to state law. Indiana need not define these commodities as other States do; it need only provide that residents and nonresidents have equal access to them. This Indiana has done. Accordingly, even if the Act should decrease the number of successful tender offers for Indiana corporations, this would not offend the Commerce Clause.[14]

IV

On its face, the Indiana Control Share Acquisitions Chapter evenhandedly determines the voting rights of shares of Indiana corporations. The Act does not conflict with the provisions or purposes of the Williams Act. To the limited extent that the Act affects interstate commerce, this is justified by the State's interests in defining the attributes of shares in its corporations and in protecting shareholders. Congress has never questioned the need for state regulation

---

14. CTS also contends that the Act does not violate the Commerce Clause—regardless of any burdens it may impose on interstate commerce—because a corporation's decision to be covered by the Act is purely "private" activity beyond the reach of the Commerce Clause. Because we reverse the judgment of the Court of Appeals on other grounds, we have no occasion to consider this argument.

of these matters. Nor do we think such regulation offends the Constitution. Accordingly, we reverse the judgment of the Court of Appeals.

It is so ordered.

Justice SCALIA, concurring in part and concurring in the judgment.

I join Parts I, III-A, and III-B of the Court's opinion. However, having found, as those Parts do, that the Indiana Control Share Acquisitions Chapter neither "discriminates against interstate commerce," *ante,* nor "create[s] an impermissible risk of inconsistent regulation by different States," *ante,* I would conclude without further analysis that it is not invalid under the dormant Commerce Clause. . . .

. . . I also agree with the Court that the Indiana Control Share Acquisitions Chapter is not pre-empted by the Williams Act, but I reach that conclusion without entering into the debate over the purposes of the two statutes. The Williams Act is governed by the antipre-emption provision of the Securities Exchange Act of 1934, 15 U.S.C. §78bb(a), which provides that nothing it contains "shall affect the jurisdiction of the securities commission (or any agency or officer performing like functions) of any State over any security or any person insofar as it does not conflict with the provisions of this chapter or the rules and regulations thereunder." . . .

I do not share the Court's apparent high estimation of the beneficence of the state statute at issue here. But a law can be both economic folly and constitutional. The Indiana Control Share Acquisitions Chapter is at least the latter. I therefore concur in the judgment of the Court.

Justice WHITE, with whom Justice BLACKMUN and Justice STEVENS join as to Part II, dissenting.

The majority today upholds Indiana's Control Share Acquisitions Chapter, a statute which will predictably foreclose completely some tender offers for stock in Indiana corporations. I disagree with the conclusion that the Chapter is neither pre-empted by the Williams Act nor in conflict with the Commerce Clause. The Chapter undermines the policy of the Williams Act by effectively preventing minority shareholders, in some circumstances, from acting in their own best interests by selling their stock. In addition, the Chapter will substantially burden the interstate market in corporate ownership, particularly if other States follow Indiana's lead as many already have done. The Chapter, therefore, directly inhibits interstate commerce, the very economic consequences the Commerce Clause was intended to prevent. The opinion of the Court of Appeals is far more persuasive than that of the majority today, and the judgment of that court should be affirmed. . . .

QUESTIONS

Under the reasoning of the Court's *CTS* opinion, would the following state takeover statutes be held valid?

1.　Excerpt from North Carolina's statute:

Article 9. Shareholder Protection Act—§55-9-02. Voting requirement. Notwithstanding any other provisions of the North Carolina Business Corporation

Act, the affirmative vote of the holders of ninety-five percent (95%) of the voting shares of a corporation, considered for the purposes of this section as one class, shall be required for the adoption or authorization of a business combination with any other entity if, as of the record date for the determination of shareholders entitled to notice thereof and to vote thereon, the other entity is the beneficial owner, directly or indirectly, of more than twenty percent (20%) of the voting shares of the corporation, considered for the purposes of this section as one class.

2.   Excerpt from Maryland's statute:

§3-602. [Business combination] [Prohibited between corporation and interested stock-holder . . .] (a) Unless an exemption under §3-603(c), (d), or (e) of this subtitle applies, a corporation may not engage in any business combination with any interested stockholder . . . for a period of 5 years following the most recent date on which the interested stockholder became an interested stockholder.

(b) Unless an exemption under §3-603 of this subtitle applies, in addition to any vote otherwise required by law or the charter of the corporation, a business combination that is not prohibited by subsection (a) of this section shall be recommended by the board of directors and approved by the affirmative vote of at least:

(1) 80 percent of the votes entitled to be cast by outstanding shares of voting stock of the corporation, voting together as a single voting group; and

(2) Two-thirds of the votes entitled to be cast by holders of voting stock other than voting stock held by the interested stockholder who will . . . be a party to the business combination . . . voting together as a single voting group.

3.   The Third Generation — Business Combination Statutes

The so-called third generation of state takeover statutes is typified by the terms of Delaware's statute, which is codified at §203 of the Delaware General Corporation Law. The terms of this statute prohibit a "business combination" with an "interested stockholder" (defined to be an owner of 15 percent or more of the shares of a company organized under Delaware law) for a period of three years unless either (i) the combination has been approved by the board that was in office *prior to* the interested stockholder's acquisition of its 15 percent stake; (ii) the interested stockholder acquired at least 85 percent of the voting stock of the company (exclusive of shares held by officers or directors or certain types of employee stock plans) at the time that it became an interested stockholder; or (iii) the transaction is approved by the directors *and* by the holders of at least two-thirds of the outstanding stock of the company *not* owned by the interested shareholder. *Query:* Would the Delaware statute be constitutional under the test enunciated by the Supreme Court in *CTS*?

The constitutionality of this type of third-generation state takeover statute is addressed in the next case, although this issue has yet to reach the Supreme Court.

Amanda Acquisition Corp. v. Universal Foods Corp.
877 F.2d 496 (7th Cir. 1989), *cert. denied*, 493 U.S. 955 (1989)

EASTERBROOK, Circuit Judge.

States have enacted three generations of takeover statutes in the last 20 years. Illinois enacted a first-generation statute, which forbade acquisitions of any firm with substantial assets in Illinois unless a public official approved. We concluded that such a statute injures investors, is preempted by the Williams Act, and is unconstitutional under the dormant Commerce Clause. *MITE Corp. v. Dixon*, 633 F.2d 486 (7th Cir. 1980). The Supreme Court affirmed the judgment under the Commerce Clause, *Edgar v. MITE Corp.*, 457 U.S. 624, 643-46 (1982). . . .

Indiana enacted a second-generation statute, applicable only to firms incorporated there and eliminating governmental veto power. Indiana's law provides that the acquiring firm's shares lose their voting power unless the target's directors approve the acquisition or the shareholders not affiliated with either bidder or management authorize restoration of votes. . . .

Wisconsin has a third-generation takeover statute. Enacted after *CTS*, it postpones the kinds of transactions that often follow tender offers (and often are the reason for making the offers in the first place). Unless the target's board agrees to the transaction in advance, the bidder must wait three years after buying the shares to merge with the target or acquire more than 5% of its assets. We must decide whether this is consistent with the Williams Act and Commerce Clause.

I

Amanda Acquisition Corporation is a shell with a single purpose: to acquire Universal Foods Corporation, a diversified firm incorporated in Wisconsin and traded on the New York Stock Exchange. Universal is covered by Wisconsin's anti-takeover law. Amanda is a subsidiary of High Voltage Engineering Corp., a small electronics firm in Massachusetts. Most of High Voltage's equity capital comes from Berisford Capital PLC, a British venture capital firm, and Hyde Park Partners L.P., a partnership affiliated with the principals of Berisford. Chase Manhattan Bank has promised to lend Amanda 50% of the cost of the acquisition, secured by the stock of Universal.

In mid-November 1988 Universal's stock was trading for about $25 per share. On December 1 Amanda commenced a tender offer at $30.50, to be effective if at least 75% of the stock should be tendered.[1] This all-cash, all shares offer has been increased by stages to $38.00.[2] Amanda's financing is contingent

---

1. Wisconsin has, in addition to §180.726, a statute modeled on Indiana's, providing that an acquiring firm's shares lose their votes, which may be restored under specified circumstances. Wis. Stat. §180.25(9). That law accounts for the 75% condition, but it is not pertinent to the questions we resolve.

2. Universal contends that an increase after the district court's opinion makes the case moot, or at least requires a remand. It does not. The parties remain locked in combat. Price has no effect on the operation of the Wisconsin law, and as that is the sole issue we shall decide, there is no need to remand for further proceedings.

on a prompt merger with Universal if the offer succeeds, so the offer is conditional on a judicial declaration that the law is invalid. (It is also conditional on
Universal's redemption of poison pill stock. For reasons that we discuss below,
it is unnecessary to discuss the subject in detail.)

No firm incorporated in Wisconsin and having its headquarters, substantial operations, or 10% of its shares or shareholders there may "engage in a
business combination with an interested stockholder . . . for 3 years after the
interested stockholder's stock acquisition date unless the board of directors of
the [Wisconsin] corporation has approved, before the interested stockholder's
stock acquisition date, that business combination or the purchase of stock,"
Wis. Stat. §180.726(2). An "interested stockholder" is one owning 10% of the
voting stock, directly or through associates (anyone acting in concert with it),
§180.726(1)(j). A "business combination" is a merger with the bidder or any of
its affiliates, sale of more than 5% of the assets to bidder or affiliate, liquidation
of the target, or a transaction by which the target guarantees the bidder's or
affiliates debts or passes tax benefits to the bidder or affiliate, §180.726(1)(e).
The law, in other words, provides for almost hermetic separation of bidder and
target for three years after the bidder obtains 10% of the stock—unless the
target's board consented before then. No matter how popular the offer, the
ban applies: obtaining 85% (even 100%) of the stock held by non-management
shareholders won't allow the bidder to engage in a business combination, as it
would under Delaware law. . . . Wisconsin firms cannot opt out of the law, as
may corporations subject to almost all other state takeover statutes. In Wisconsin it is management's approval in advance, or wait three years. Even when the
time is up, the bidder needs the approval of a majority of the remaining investors, without any provision disqualifying shares still held by the managers who
resisted the transaction. The district court found that this statute "effectively
eliminates hostile leveraged buyouts." As a practical matter, Wisconsin prohibits any offer contingent on a merger between bidder and target, a condition
attached to about 90% of contemporary tender offers.

Amanda filed this suit seeking a declaration that this law is preempted by
the Williams Act and inconsistent with the Commerce Clause. It added a pen-
dent claim that the directors' refusal to redeem the poison-pill rights violates
their fiduciary duties to Universal's shareholders. The district court declined to
issue a preliminary injunction. . . .

II . . .

A

If our views of the wisdom of state law mattered, Wisconsin's takeover statute
would not survive. Like our colleagues who decided *MITE* and *CTS,* we believe
that antitakeover legislation injures shareholders. . . . Managers frequently realize gains for investors via voluntary combinations (mergers). If gains are to
be had, but managers' balk, tender offers are investors' way to go over managers' heads. If managers are not maximizing the firm's value—perhaps because
they have missed the possibility of a synergistic combination, perhaps because
they are clinging to divisions that could be better run in other hands, perhaps

because they are just not the best persons for the job—a bidder that believes it can realize more of the firm's value will make investors a higher offer. Investors tender; the bidder gets control and changes things. . . . The prospect of monitoring by would-be bidders, and an occasional bid at a premium, induces managers to run corporations more efficiently and replaces them if they will not.

Premium bids reflect the benefits for investors. The price of a firm's stock represents investors' consensus estimate of the value of the shares under current and anticipated conditions. Stock is worth the present value of anticipated future returns—dividends and other distributions. Tender offers succeed when bidders offer more. Only when the bid exceeds the value of the stock (however investors compute value) will it succeed. A statute that precludes investors from receiving or accepting a premium offer makes them worse off. It makes the economy worse off too, because the higher bid reflects the better use to which the bidder can put the target's assets. (If the bidder can't improve the use of the assets, it injures itself by paying a premium.) . . .

Although a takeover-*proof* firm leaves investors at the mercy of incumbent managers (who may be mistaken about the wisdom of their business plan even when they act in the best of faith), a takeover-*resistant* firm may be able to assist its investors. An auction may run up the price, and delay may be essential to an auction. Auctions transfer money from bidders to targets, and diversified investors would not gain from them (their left pocket loses what the right pocket gains); diversified investors would lose from auctions if the lower returns to bidders discourage future bids. But from targets' perspectives, once a bid is on the table an auction may be the best strategy. The full effects of auctions are hard to unravel, sparking scholarly debate.[6] Devices giving manager some ability to orchestrate investors' responses, in order to avoid panic tenders in response to front-end-loaded offers, also could be beneficial, as the Supreme Court emphasized in *CTS*, 481 U.S. at 92-93, 107 S.Ct. at 1651-52. ("Could be" is an important qualifier; even from a perspective limited to targets' shareholders given a bid on the table, it is important to know whether managers use this power to augment bids or to stifle them, and whether courts can tell the two apart.)

. . . Investors who prefer to give managers the discretion to orchestrate responses to bids may do so through "fair-price" clauses in the articles of incorporation and other consensual devices. Other firms may choose different strategies. A law such as Wisconsin's does not add options to firms that would like to give more discretion to their managers; instead it destroys the possibility of divergent choices. Wisconsin's law applies even when the investors prefer to

---

6. Compare Lucian Arye Bebchek, *Toward Undistorted Choice and Equal Treatment in Corporate Takeovers*, 98 HARV. L. REV. 1693 (1985), and Ronald J. Gilson, *Seeking Competitive Bids versus Pure Passivity in Tender Offer Defense*, 35 STAN. L. REV. 51 (1982), with Alan Schwartz, *Search Theory and the Tender Offer Auction*, 23 J.L. ECON. & ORG. 229 (1986), and Sanford J. Grossman & Oliver D. Hart, *Takeover Bids, the Free-Rider Problem and the Theory of the Corporation*, 11 BELL J. ECON. 42 (1980). For the most recent round compare Alan Schwartz, *The Fairness of Tender Offer Prices in Utilitarian Theory*, 17 J. LEGAL STUD. 165 (1988), with Lucian Arye Bebchuck, *The Sole Owner Standard for Takeover Policy*, id. at 197, with Schwartz, *The Sole Owner Standard Reviewed*, id. at 231.

leave their managers under the gun, to allow the market full sway. . . . To put this differently, state laws have bite only when investors, given the choice, would deny managers the power to interfere with tender offers (maybe already *have* denied managers that power). *See also,* Roberta Romano, *The Political Economy of Takeover Statutes,* 73 VA. L. REV. 111, 128-31 (1987).

B

Skepticism about the wisdom of a state's law does not lead to the conclusion that the law is beyond the state's power, however. We have not been elected custodians of investors' wealth. States need not treat investors' welfare as their summum bonum. Perhaps they choose to protect managers' welfare instead, or believe that the current economic literature reaches an incorrect conclusion and that despite appearances takeovers injure investors in the long run. Unless a federal statute or the Constitution bars the way, Wisconsin's choice must be respected.

Amanda relies on the Williams Act of 1968, . . . [which] regulates the conduct of tender offers. Amanda believes that Congress created an entitlement for investors to receive the benefit of tender offers, and that because Wisconsin's law makes tender offers unattractive to many potential bidders, it is preempted. . . .

Preemption has not won easy acceptance among the Justices for several reasons. First there is §28(a) of the '34 Act, 15 U.S.C. §78bb(a), which provides that "[n]othing in this chapter shall affect the jurisdiction of the securities commission . . . of any State over any security or any person insofar as it does not conflict with the provisions of this chapter or the rules and regulations thereunder." Although some of the SEC's regulations (particularly the one defining the commencement of an offer) conflict with some state takeover laws, the SEC has not drafted regulations concerning mergers with controlling shareholders, and the Act itself does not address the subject. States have used the leeway afforded by §28(a) to carry out "merit regulation" of securities — "blue sky" laws that allow securities commissioners to forbid sales altogether, in contrast with the federal regimen emphasizing disclosure. So §28(a) allows states to stop some transactions federal law would permit, in pursuit of an approach at odds with a system emphasizing disclosure and investors' choice. Then there is the traditional reluctance of federal courts to infer preemption of "state law in areas traditionally regulated by the States." . . . States have regulated corporate affairs, including mergers and sales of assets, since before the beginning of the nation.

Because Justice White's views of the Williams Act did not garner the support of a majority of the Court in *MITE,* we reexamined that subject in *CTS* and observed that the best argument for preemption is the Williams Act's "neutrality" between bidder and management, a balance designed to leave investors free to choose. . . .

There is a big difference between what Congress *enacts* and what it *supposes* will ensue. Expectations about the consequences of a law are not themselves law. To say that Congress wanted to be neutral between bidder and target — a conclusion reached in many of the Court's opinions, e.g., *Piper v. Chris-Craft*

Industries, Inc., 430 U.S. 1, 97 S. Ct. 926, 51 L. Ed. 2d 124 (1977) — is not to say that it also forbade the states to favor one of these sides. Every law has a stopping point, likely one selected because of a belief that it would be unwise (for now, maybe forever) to do more. . . . Nothing in the Williams Act says that the federal compromise among bidders, targets' managers, and investors is the only permissible one. . . . Like the majority of the Court in *CTS,* however, we stop short of the precipice. . . .

The Williams Act regulates the *process* of tender offers: timing, disclosure, proration if tenders exceed what the bidder is willing to buy, best-price rules. It slows things down, allowing investors to evaluate the offer and management's response. Best-price, proration, and short-tender rules ensure that investors who decide at the end of the offer get the same treatment as those who decide immediately, reducing pressure to leap before looking. After complying with the disclosure and delay requirements, the bidder is free to take the shares. . . .

Any bidder complying with federal law is free to acquire shares of Wisconsin firms on schedule. Delay in completing a second-stage merger may make the target less attractive, and thus depress the price offered or even lead to an absence of bids; it does not, however, alter any of the procedures governed by federal regulation. Indeed Wisconsin's law does not depend in any way on how the acquiring firm came by its stock: open-market purchases, private acquisitions of blocs, and acquisitions via tender offers are treated identically. Wisconsin's law is no different in effect from one saying that for the three years after a person acquires 10% of a firm's stock, a unanimous vote is required to merge. Corporate law once had a generally applicable unanimity rule in major transactions, a rule discarded because giving every investor the power to block every reorganization stopped many desirable changes. (Many investors could use their "hold-up" power to try to engross a larger portion of the gains, creating a complex bargaining problem that often could not be solved.) Wisconsin's more restrained version of unanimity also may block beneficial transactions, but not by tinkering with any of the procedures established in federal law.

Only if the Williams Act gives investors a right to be the beneficiary of offers could Wisconsin's law run afoul of the federal rule. No such entitlement can be mined out of the Williams Act, however. *Schreiber v. Burlington Northern, Inc.,* 472 U.S. 1, 105 S. Ct. 2458, 86 L. Ed. 2d 1 (1985), holds that the cancellation of a pending offer because of machinations between bidder and target does not deprive investors of their due under the Williams Act. The Court treated §14(e) as a disclosure law, so that investors could make informed decisions; it follows that events leading bidders to cease their quest do not conflict with the Williams Act any more than a state law leading a firm not to issue new securities could conflict with the Securities Act of 1933. See also *Panter v. Marshall Field & Co.,* 646 F.2d 271, 283-85 (7th Cir. 1981) . . . Investors have no right to receive tender offers. More to the point — since Amanda sues as bidder rather than as investor seeking to sell — the Williams Act does not create a right to profit from the business of making tender offers. It is not attractive to put bids on the table for Wisconsin corporations, but because Wisconsin leaves the process alone once a bidder appears, its law may co-exist with the Williams Act.

C

The Commerce Clause, Art. I, §8 cl. 3 of the Constitution, grants Congress the power "[t]o regulate Commerce . . . among the several States." For many decades the Court took this to be what it says: a grant to Congress with no implications for the states' authority to act when Congress is silent. . . . The Contract Clause has been held to curtail states' authority over corporations, see *Trustees of Dartmouth College v. Woodward*, 17 U.S. (4 Wheat.) 518, 4 L. Ed. 629 (1819), and it may have something to say about states' ability to limit the transferability of shares after they have been issued. See Henry N. Butler & Larry E. Ribstein, *State Anti-Takeover Statutes and the Contract Clause*, 57 U. Cin. L. Rev. 611 (1988). Broad dicta in *Cooley v. Board of Wardens*, 53 U.S. (12 How.) 299, 13 L. Ed. 996 (1852), eventually led to holdings denying states the power to regulate interstate commerce directly or discriminatorily, or to take steps that had unjustified consequences in other states. Meanwhile the Court began to treat the Contract Clause as if it said that "No State shall pass any *unwise* Law impairing the Obligation of Contracts," so that divergent clauses have become homogenized. *Chicago Board of Realtors, Inc. v. Chicago*, 819 F.2d 732, 742-45 (7th Cir. 1987).

When state law discriminates against interstate commerce expressly — for example, when Wisconsin closes its border to butter from Minnesota — the negative Commerce Clause steps in. The law before us is not of this type: it is neutral between inter-state and intra-state commerce. Amanda therefore presses on us the broader, all-weather, be-reasonable vision of the Constitution. Wisconsin has passed a law that unreasonably injures investors, most of whom live outside of Wisconsin, and therefore it *has* to be unconstitutional, as Amanda sees things. Although *Pike v. Bruce Church, Inc.*, 397 U.S. 137, 90 S. Ct. 844, 25 L. Ed. 2d 174 (1970), sometimes is understood to authorize such general-purpose balancing, a closer examination of the cases may support the conclusion that the Court has looked for discrimination rather than for baleful effects. . . . At all events, although *MITE* employed the balancing process described in *Pike* to deal with a statute that regulated all firms having "contacts" with the state, *CTS* did not even cite that case when dealing with a statute regulating only the affairs of a firm incorporated in the state, and Justice Scalia's concurring opinion questioned its application. 481 U.S. at 95-96, 107 S. Ct. at 1652-53. The Court took a decidedly confined view of the judicial role: "We are not inclined 'to second-guess the empirical judgments of lawmakers concerning the utility of legislation,' *Kassel v. Consolidated Freightways Corp.*, 450 U.S. [662] at 679 [101 S. Ct. 1309, 1320, 67 L. Ed. 2d 580 (1981)] (Brennan, J., concurring in judgment)." Although the scholars whose writings we cited in Part II.A conclude that laws such as Wisconsin's injure investors, Wisconsin is entitled to give a different answer to this empirical question — or to decide that investors' interests should be sacrificed to protect managers' interests or promote the stability of corporate arrangements.

Illinois's law, held invalid in *MITE*, regulated sales of stock elsewhere. Illinois tried to tell a Texas owner of stock in a Delaware corporation that he could not sell to a buyer in California. By contrast, Wisconsin's law, like the Indiana statute sustained by *CTS*, regulates the internal affairs of firms incorporated there. Investors may buy or sell stock as they please. Wisconsin's law differs in this respect not only from that of Illinois but also from that of Massachusetts, which forbade any transfer of shares for one year after the failure to disclose any material fact, a flaw that led the First Circuit to condemn it. *Hyde Park Partners, L.P. v. Connolly*, 839 F.2d 837, 847-48 (1st Cir. 1988)....

. . . Wisconsin, like Indiana, is indifferent to the domicile of the bidder. A putative bidder located in Wisconsin enjoys no privilege over a firm located in New York. So too with investors: all are treated identically, regardless of residence. Doubtless most bidders (and investors) are located outside Wisconsin, but unless the law discriminates according to residence this alone does not matter....

Wisconsin could exceed its powers by subjecting firms to inconsistent regulation. Because §180.726 applies only to a subset of firms incorporated in Wisconsin, however, there is no possibility of inconsistent regulation. Here, too, the Wisconsin law is materially identical to Indiana's. *CTS*, 481 U.S. at 88-89, 107 S. Ct. at 1649-50. This leaves only the argument that Wisconsin's law hinders the flow of interstate trade "too much." *CTS* dispatched this concern by declaring it inapplicable to laws that apply only to the internal affairs of firms incorporated in the regulating state. 481 U.S. at 89-94, 107 S. Ct. at 1649-52. States may regulate corporate transactions as they choose without having to demonstrate under an unfocused balancing test that the benefits are "enough" to justify the consequences....

The three district judges who have considered and sustained Delaware's law delaying mergers did so in large measure because they believed that the law left hostile offers "a meaningful opportunity for success." *BNS, Inc. v. Koppers Co.*, [683 F. Supp. 458, 469 (D. Del. 1988)]. See also *RP Acquisition Corp.* [*v. Staley Continental, Inc.*, 686 F. Supp. 476, 482-484 (D. Del. 1988); *City Capital Associates L.P. v. Inter-Co. Inc.*, 686 F. Supp. 1551, 1555 (D. Del. 1988)]. Delaware allows a merger to occur forthwith if the bidder obtains 85% of the shares other than those held by management and employee stock plans. If the bid is attractive to the bulk of the unaffiliated investors, it succeeds. Wisconsin offers no such opportunity, which Amanda believes is fatal.

Even in Wisconsin, though, options remain. Defenses impenetrable to the naked eye may have cracks. Poison pills are less fatal in practice than in name (some have been swallowed willingly), and corporate law contains self-defense mechanisms. Investors concerned about stock-watering often arranged for firms to issue pre-emptive rights, entitlements for existing investors to buy stock at the same price offered to newcomers (often before the newcomers had a chance to buy in). Poison pills are dilution devices, and so pre-emptive rights ought to be handy countermeasures.[11] So too there are countermeasures to

---

11. Imagine a series of Antidote rights, issued by would-be bidding firms, that detach if anyone exercises flip-over rights to purchase the bidder's stock at a discount. Antidote rights would entitle the bidder's investors, *other than those who exercise flip-over rights,* to purchase the bidder's stock at the same discount available to investors exercising flip-over rights. Antidotes for flip-in rights also could be issued. In general, whenever one firm can issue rights allowing the purchase of cheap stock, another firm can issue the equivalent series of contingent pre-emptive rights that offsets the dilution.

statutes deferring mergers. The cheapest is to lower the bid to reflect the costs of delay. Because every potential bidder labors under the same drawback, the firm placing the highest value on the target still should win. Or a bidder might take down the stock and pledge it (or its dividends) as security for any loans. That is, the bidder could operate the target as a subsidiary for three years. The corporate world is full of partially owned subsidiaries. If there is gain to be had from changing the debt-equity ratio of the target, that can be done consistent with Wisconsin law. The prospect of being locked into place as holders of illiquid minority positions would cause many persons to sell out, and the threat of being locked in would cause many managers to give assent in advance, as Wisconsin allows. (Or bidders might demand that directors waive the protections of state law, just as Amanda believes that the directors' fiduciary duties compel them to redeem the poison pill rights.) Many bidders would find lock-in unattractive because of the potential for litigation by minority investors, and the need to operate the firm as a subsidiary might foreclose savings or synergies from merger. So none of these options is a perfect substitute for immediate merger, but each is a crack in the defensive wall allowing some value-increasing bids to proceed.

At the end of the day, however, it does not matter whether these countermeasures are "enough." The Commerce Clause does not demand that states leave bidders a "meaningful opportunity for success." Maryland enacted a law that absolutely banned vertical integration in the oil business. No opportunities, "meaningful" or otherwise, remained to firms wanting to own retail outlets. *Exxon Corp. v. Governor of Maryland* [, 437 U.S. 117 (1978)], held that the law is consistent with the Commerce Clause, even on the assumption that it injures consumers and investors alike. A state with the power to forbid mergers has the power to defer them for three years. Investors can turn to firms incorporated in states committed to the dominance of market forces, or they can turn on legislators who enact unwise laws. The Constitution has room for many economic policies. "[A] law can be both economic folly and constitutional." *CTS*, 481 U.S. at 96-97, 107 S. Ct. at 1653-54 (SCALIA, J., concurring). Wisconsin's law may well be folly; we are confident that it is constitutional.

AFFIRMED.

QUESTIONS

1. Considering the terms of Delaware's business combination statute, section 203, would it be held constitutional under the reasoning of the Seventh Circuit in *Amanda Acquisition*? *See RP Acquisition v. Staley Continental*, 686 F. Supp. 476 (D. Del. 1988); *BNS v. Koppers*, 683 F. Supp. 454 (D. Del. 1988).

2. Third-generation statutes also include provisions commonly referred to as *stakeholder* or *other constituency* statutes, which generally authorize the board of directors to consider other interests (including those of employees, suppliers, and the local community) as part of its decision-making process. *See, e.g.,* 15 Pa. Cons. Stat. Ann. §1715. While not limited to the takeover context, these statutes were widely regarded as having their genesis in the same set of concerns that led states to adopt other forms of takeover statutes.

Considering the reasoning of *CTS* and *Amanda Acquisition*, are these other constituency statutes constitutionally valid?

3. As a matter of public policy, do you think state law should regulate the tender offer process? What is the proper role for state law?

NOTES

1. More on Delaware Section 203. In 2010, the ABA published a symposium on focusing on Delaware's antitakeover statute. *See* "Symposium," 65 Bus. Law. 685-808 (Issue 3, May 2010). In the lead article, *Is Delaware's Anti-Takeover Statute Constitutional? Evidence from 1988-2008*, the authors presented evidence "that would seem to suggest that the constitutionality of Section 203 is [now] up for grabs," a conclusion that was then challenged in one way or another by the Symposium participants who submitted commentaries that were published as part of the Symposium. In their lead article, the authors summarized their study and its findings as follows:

> Delaware's anti-takeover statute, codified in Section 203 of the Delaware Corporate Code, is by far the most important antitakeover statute in the United States. When it was enacted in 1988, three bidders challenged its constitutionality under the Commerce Clause and the Supremacy Clause of the U.S. Constitution. All three federal district court decisions upheld the constitutionality of Section 203 at the time, relying on evidence indicating that Section 203 gave bidders a "meaningful opportunity for success," but leaving open the possibility that future evidence might change this constitutional conclusion. This Article presents the first systematic empirical evidence since 1988 on whether Section 203 gives bidders a meaningful opportunity for success. The question has become more important in recent years because Section 203's substantive bite has increased, as Exelon's recent hostile bid for NRG illustrates. Using a new sample of all hostile takeover bids against Delaware targets that were announced between 1988 and 2008 and were subject to Section 203 (n=60), we find that no hostile bidder in the past nineteen years has been able to avoid the restrictions imposed by Section 203 by going from less than 15% to more than 85% in its tender offer. At the very least, this finding indicates that the empirical proposition that the federal courts relied upon to uphold Section 203's constitutionality is no longer valid. While it remains possible that courts would nevertheless uphold Section 203's constitutionality on different grounds, the evidence would seem to suggest that the constitutionality of Section 203 is up for grabs. This Article offers specific changes to the Delaware statute that would preempt the constitutional challenge. If instead Section 203 were to fall on constitutional grounds, as Delaware's prior antitakeover statute did in 1987, it would also have implications for similar anti-takeover statutes in thirty-two other U.S. states, which along with Delaware collectively cover 92% of all U.S. corporations.

Guhan Subramanian, et al., *Is Delaware's Anti-Takeover Statute Unconstitutional? Evidence from 1988-2008*, 65 Bus. Law. 685 (2010).

However, these conclusions were vigorously challenged by the commentary of one of the Symposium participants, a leading Delaware M&A lawyer who offered the following observations:

> The [lead] article comes after twenty-two years of vibrant takeover activity in Delaware. According to SDC Platinum[7] from January 1, 1988, through December 31, 2008, there were 1,101 tender offers for Delaware targets, 145 (or 13%) of which were hostile (i.e., the target's board rejected the offer, but the acquirer persisted) or unsolicited (i.e., the acquirer made an offer without prior negotiations with the target board). In at least 73 of the 145 hostile/unsolicited tender offers, the bidder held less than 15% of the target's stock prior to commencing the tender offer and sought to acquire over 85%. Of those seventy-three, twenty-nine (or 40%) were ultimately completed, while forty-three were withdrawn.[8] Moreover, of the forty-three withdrawn, at least twenty-three of those targets agreed to be acquired in a white-knight type transaction. When laid against the reality that a meaningful number of hostile/unsolicited tender offers can and do result in a takeover, without even reaching the question of how many of the unsuccessful offers were not "beneficial" to stockholders, [the lead article] provide[s] no basis, let alone empirical evidence, to support their argument that the constitutionality of Section 203 is "up for grabs." . . .
>
> In the twenty years following the enactment of Section 203, and giving some credence [to the data presented in the lead article], it appears that defensive measures such as the poison pill and independent directors' willingness to negotiate with unsolicited bidders before a tender offer terminates have affected the number of unsolicited/hostile offers that go to conclusion without board intervention to negotiate an optimal resolution. As we have seen, 33% of the unsolicited/hostile offers in [the] meager sample [contained in the lead article], at least 40% of the broader universe of hostile/unsolicited offers when transactions that turned friendly before expiration of the initial tender are added, and least 71% if one also includes subsequent white-knight transactions, resulted in acquisitions. This supports the premise, appropriately from the perspective of stockholders, that unsolicited offers have a meaningful opportunity to result in successful takeovers and the constitutionality of Section 203 is decidedly not "up for grabs." . . .

A. Gilchrist Sparks III and Helen Bowers, *After Twenty-Two Years, Section 203 of the Delaware General Corporation Law Continues to Give Hostile Bidders a Meaningful Opportunity for Success*, 65 Bus. Law. 761, 761-762 and 769 (2010). *Query*: From a public policy perspective, does Delaware Section 203 make sense? What do you think?

2. *Fair Price Clauses and Other Charter Provisions.* In his opinion in *Amanda Acquisitions,* Judge Easterbrook referred to fair price clauses that many

---

7. SDC Platinum is a product of Thompson Reuters, which also owns Thompson One, the database [which was used by the authors of the lead article] for their study. SDC Platinum provides data on approximately 672,000 mergers and acquisitions worldwide from 1985 to the present. We did a search of the database on February 1, 2010.

8. SDC reports the outcome of one of the seventy-three hostile/unsolicited tender offers as "unknown."

companies have included in their articles of incorporation. Generally speaking, a fair price clause is a provision that is included by amending the articles of incorporation, which we learned in Chapter 2 requires approval by both the company's board of directors and its shareholders. These charter (i.e., articles) amendments are often collectively referred to by M&A professionals as "shark repellents." Among the most common shark repellents are supermajority voting requirements coupled with a fair price provision. Management will propose to amend the company's articles to modify the default rule otherwise provided as a matter of state law to increase the percentage vote required for shareholder approval of a merger, often increasing the required vote to two-thirds of the outstanding shares, with some amendments raising the bar to as high as 95 percent of the outstanding shares. The reason that this type of articles amendment is referred to as a "shark repellent" is because of the impact that this type of voting requirement will have on prospective Bidders. Generally speaking, this type of charter provision will require Bidder to purchase sufficient shares to assure passage of the back-end take out merger, thereby presumably increasing the cost to Bidder in completing the takeover of Target, as well as creating the possibility of the problem of a shareholder who holds out for a higher price. Very often, the supermajority provision will be subject to a provision that waives the supermajority vote requirement if the price to be paid by Bidder is "fair." As pointed out by Judge Easterbrook in his opinion, all of these shark repellents take the form of "consensual devices," in that they cannot be implemented unilaterally by existing management; instead, all of these charter provisions require shareholder approval. This is to be contrasted with the types of antitakeover measures adopted by the company's board of directors that are the focus of our analysis in the next chapter.

‖7‖

Fiduciary Duty Law: The Responsibilities of Boards of Directors, Senior Executive Officers, and Controlling Shareholders

A. Introduction to Scope of Fiduciary Duty Obligations

1. Business Judgment Rule: The Duty of Care and the Exercise of Informed Decision Making

In the case of negotiated acquisitions not involving self-dealing or any other form of conflict of interest, *Smith v. Van Gorkom* is the seminal case setting forth the directors' standard of care. In this case, the Delaware Supreme Court is widely credited with giving "teeth" to the more deferential business judgment rule standard of review traditionally invoked by the courts in cases involving what is often described as a naked breach of the duty of care. In analyzing the Delaware Supreme Court's detailed description of the transaction at issue in the *Trans Union* case (as the *Smith v. Van Gorkom* decision is often referred to in the academic literature), consider whether these facts present a "naked breach" of the duty of care. Or, alternatively, does this case involve facts that implicate a breach of the duty of loyalty? If so, how does the Delaware Supreme Court deal with this aspect of the case?

‖ **Smith v. Van Gorkom**
‖ **488 A.2d 858 (Del. 1985)**

HORSEY, Justice (for the majority):

This appeal from the Court of Chancery involves a class action brought by shareholders of the defendant Trans Union Corporation ("Trans Union" or "the Company"), originally seeking rescission of a cash-out merger of Trans Union into the defendant New T Company ("New T"), a wholly-owned subsidiary of the defendant, Marmon Group, Inc. ("Marmon"). Alternate relief in the form of damages is sought against the defendant members of the Board of Directors of Trans Union, New T, and Jay A. Pritzker and Robert A. Pritzker, owners of Marmon.

Following trial, the former Chancellor granted judgment for the defendant directors by unreported letter opinion dated July 6, 1982. Judgment was based on two findings: (1) that the Board of Directors had acted in an informed manner so as to be entitled to protection of the business judgment rule in approving the cash-out merger; and (2) that the shareholder vote approving the merger should not be set aside because the stockholders had been "fairly informed" by the Board of Directors before voting thereon. The plaintiffs appeal.

Speaking for the majority of the Court, we conclude that both rulings of the Court of Chancery are clearly erroneous. Therefore, we reverse and direct that judgment be entered in favor of the plaintiffs and against the defendant directors for the fair value of the plaintiffs' stockholdings in Trans Union, in accordance with *Weinberger v. UOP, Inc.,* Del. Supr., 457 A.2d 701 (1983). . . .

I.

The nature of this case requires a detailed factual statement. The following facts are essentially uncontradicted:

A

Trans Union was a publicly-traded, diversified holding company, the principal earnings of which were generated by its railcar leasing business. During the period here involved, the Company had a cash flow of hundreds of millions of dollars annually. However, the Company had difficulty in generating sufficient taxable income to offset increasingly large investment tax credits (ITCs). Accelerated depreciation deductions had decreased available taxable income against which to offset accumulating ITCs. The Company took these deductions, despite their effect on usable ITCs, because the rental price in the railcar leasing market had already impounded the purported tax savings.

In the late 1970's, together with other capital-intensive firms, Trans Union lobbied in Congress to have ITCs refundable in cash to firms which could not fully utilize the credit. During the summer of 1980, defendant Jerome W. Van Gorkom, Trans Union's Chairman and Chief Executive Officer, testified and lobbied in Congress for refundability of ITCs and against further accelerated depreciation. By the end of August, Van Gorkom was convinced that Congress would neither accept the refundability concept nor curtail further accelerated depreciation.

Beginning in the late 1960's, and continuing through the 1970's, Trans Union pursued a program of acquiring small companies in order to increase available taxable income. In July 1980, Trans Union Management prepared the annual revision of the Company's Five Year Forecast. This report was presented to the Board of Directors at its July, 1980 meeting. The report projected an annual income growth of about 20%. The report also concluded that Trans

Union would have about $195 million in spare cash between 1980 and 1985, "with the surplus growing rapidly from 1982 onward." . . .

B

On August 27, 1980, Van Gorkom met with Senior Management of Trans Union. Van Gorkom reported on his lobbying efforts in Washington and his desire to find a solution to the tax credit problem more permanent than a continued program of acquisitions. Various alternatives were suggested and discussed preliminarily, including the sale of Trans Union to a company with a large amount of taxable income.

Donald Romans, Chief Financial Officer of Trans Union, stated that his department had done a "very brief bit of work on the possibility of a leveraged buy-out." This work had been prompted by a media article which Romans had seen regarding a leveraged buy-out by management. The work consisted of a "preliminary study" of the cash which could be generated by the Company if it participated in a leveraged buy-out. As Romans stated, this analysis "was very first and rough cut at seeing whether a cash flow would support what might be considered a high price for this type of transaction."

On September 5, at another Senior Management meeting which Van Gorkom attended, Romans again brought up the idea of a leveraged buyout as a "possible strategic alternative" to the Company's acquisition program. Romans and Bruce S. Chelberg, President and Chief Operating Officer of Trans Union, had been working on the matter in preparation for the meeting. According to Romans: They did not "come up" with a price for the Company. They merely "ran the numbers" at $50 a share and at $60 a share with the "rough form" of their cash figures at the time. Their "figures indicated that $50 would be very easy to do but $60 would be very difficult to do under those figures." This work did not purport to establish a fair price for either the Company or 100% of the stock. It was intended to determine the cash flow needed to service the debt that would "probably" be incurred in a leveraged buy-out, based on "rough calculations" without "any benefit of experts to identify what the limits were to that, and so forth." These computations were not considered extensive and no conclusion was reached.

At this meeting, Van Gorkom stated that he would be willing to take $55 per share for his own 75,000 shares. He vetoed the suggestion of a leveraged buy-out by Management, however, as involving a potential conflict of interest for Management. Van Gorkom, a certified public accountant and lawyer, had been an officer of Trans Union for 24 years, its Chief Executive Officer for more than 17 years, and Chairman of its Board for 2 years. It is noteworthy in this connection that he was then approaching 65 years of age and mandatory retirement.

For several days following the September 5 meeting, Van Gorkom pondered the idea of a sale. He had participated in many acquisitions as a manager and director of Trans Union and as a director of other companies. He was familiar with acquisition procedures, valuation methods, and negotiations; and he privately considered the pros and cons of whether Trans Union should seek a privately or publicly-held purchaser.

Van Gorkom decided to meet with Jay A. Pritzker, a well-known corporate takeover specialist and a social acquaintance. However, rather than approaching Pritzker simply to determine his interest in acquiring Trans Union, Van Gorkom assembled a proposed per share price for sale of the Company and a financing structure by which to accomplish the sale. Van Gorkom did so without consulting either his Board or any members of Senior Management except one: Carl Peterson, Trans Union's Controller. Telling Peterson that he wanted no other person on his staff to know what he was doing, but without telling him why, Van Gorkom directed Peterson to calculate the feasibility of a leveraged buy-out at an assumed price per share of $55. Apart from the Company's historic stock market price,[5] and Van Gorkom's long association with Trans Union, the record is devoid of any competent evidence that $55 represented the per share intrinsic value of the Company.

Having thus chosen the $55 figure, based solely on the availability of a leveraged buy-out, Van Gorkom multiplied the price per share by the number of shares outstanding to reach a total value of the Company of $690 million. Van Gorkom told Peterson to use this $690 million figure and to assume a $200 million equity contribution by the buyer. Based on these assumptions, Van Gorkom directed Peterson to determine whether the debt portion of the purchase price could be paid off in five years or less if financed by Trans Union's cash flow as projected in the Five Year Forecast, and by the sale of certain weaker divisions identified in a study done for Trans Union by the Boston Consulting Group ("BCG study"). Peterson reported that, of the purchase price, approximately $50-80 million would remain outstanding after five years. Van Gorkom was disappointed, but decided to meet with Pritzker nevertheless.

Van Gorkom arranged a meeting with Pritzker at the latter's home on Saturday, September 13, 1980. Van Gorkom prefaced his presentation by stating to Pritzker: "Now as far as you are concerned, I can, I think, show how you can pay a substantial premium over the present stock price and pay off most of the loan in the first five years. . . . If you could pay $55 for this Company, here is a way in which I think it can be financed."

Van Gorkom then reviewed with Pritzker his calculations based upon his proposed price of $55 per share. Although Pritzker mentioned $50 as a more attractive figure, no other price was mentioned. However, Van Gorkom stated that to be sure that $55 was the best price obtainable, Trans Union should be free to accept any better offer. Pritzker demurred, stating that his organization would serve as a "stalking horse" for an "auction contest" only if Trans Union would permit Pritzker to buy 1,750,000 shares of Trans Union stock at market price which Pritzker could then sell to any higher bidder. After further discussion on this point, Pritzker told Van Gorkom that he would give him a more definite reaction soon.

On Monday, September 15, Pritzker advised Van Gorkom that he was interested in the $55 cash-out merger proposal and requested more information on

---

5. The common stock of Trans Union was traded on the New York Stock Exchange. Over the five year period from 1975 through 1979, Trans Union's stock had traded within a range of a high of $39-1/2 and a low of $24-1/4. Its high and low range for 1980 through September 19 (the last trading day before announcement of the merger) was $38-1/4-$29-1/2.

Trans Union. Van Gorkom agreed to meet privately with Pritzker, accompanied by Peterson, Chelberg, and Michael Carpenter, Trans Union's consultant from the Boston Consulting Group. The meetings took place on September 16 and 17. Van Gorkom was "astounded that events were moving with such amazing rapidity."

On Thursday, September 18, Van Gorkom met again with Pritzker. At that time, Van Gorkom knew that Pritzker intended to make a cash-out merger offer at Van Gorkom's proposed $55 per share. Pritzker instructed his attorney, a merger and acquisition specialist, to begin drafting merger documents. There was no further discussion of the $55 price. However, the number of shares of Trans Union's treasury stock to be offered to Pritzker was negotiated down to one million shares; the price was set at $38 — 75 cents above the per share price at the close of the market on September 19. At this point, Pritzker insisted that the Trans Union Board act on his merger proposal within the next three days, stating to Van Gorkom: "We have to have a decision by no later than Sunday [evening, September 21] before the opening of the English stock exchange on Monday morning." Pritzker's lawyer was then instructed to draft the merger documents, to be reviewed by Van Gorkom's lawyer, "sometimes with discussion and sometimes not, in the haste to get it finished."

On Friday, September 19, Van Gorkom, Chelberg, and Pritzker consulted with Trans Union's lead bank regarding the financing of Pritzker's purchase of Trans Union. The bank indicated that it could form a syndicate of banks that would finance the transaction. On the same day, Van Gorkom retained James Brennan, Esquire, to advise Trans Union on the legal aspects of the merger. Van Gorkom did not consult with William Browder, a Vice-President and director of Trans Union and former head of its legal department, or with William Moore, then the head of Trans Union's legal staff.

On Friday, September 19, Van Gorkom called a special meeting of the Trans Union Board for noon the following day. He also called a meeting of the Company's Senior Management to convene at 11:00 a.m., prior to the meeting of the Board. No one, except Chelberg and Peterson, was told the purpose of the meetings. Van Gorkom did not invite Trans Union's investment banker, Salomon Brothers or its Chicago-based partner, to attend.

Of those present at the Senior Management meeting on September 20, only Chelberg and Peterson had prior knowledge of Pritzker's offer. Van Gorkom disclosed the offer and described its terms, but he furnished no copies of the proposed Merger Agreement. Romans announced that his department had done a second study which showed that, for a leveraged buy-out, the price range for Trans Union stock was between $55 and $65 per share. Van Gorkom neither saw the study nor asked Romans to make it available for the Board meeting.

Senior Management's reaction to the Pritzker proposal was completely negative. No member of Management, except Chelberg and Peterson, supported the proposal. Romans objected to the price as being too low;[6] he was critical

---

6. Van Gorkom asked Romans to express his opinion as to the $55 price. Romans stated that he "thought the price was too low in relation to what he could derive for the company in a cash sale, particularly one which enabled us to realize the values of certain subsidiaries and independent entities."

of the timing and suggested that consideration should be given to the adverse tax consequences of an all-cash deal for low-basis shareholders; and he took the position that the agreement to sell Pritzker one million newly-issued shares at market price would inhibit other offers, as would the prohibitions against soliciting bids and furnishing inside information to other bidders. Romans argued that the Pritzker proposal was a "lock up" and amounted to "an agreed merger as opposed to an offer." Nevertheless, Van Gorkom proceeded to the Board meeting as scheduled without further delay.

Ten directors served on the Trans Union Board, five inside (defendants Bonser, O'Boyle, Browder, Chelberg, and Van Gorkom) and five outside (defendants Wallis, Johnson, Lanterman, Morgan and Reneker). All directors were present at the meeting, except O'Boyle who was ill. Of the outside directors, four were corporate chief executive officers and one was the former Dean of the University of Chicago Business School. None was an investment banker or trained financial analyst. All members of the Board were well informed about the Company and its operations as a going concern. They were familiar with the current financial condition of the Company, as well as operating and earnings projections reported in the recent Five Year Forecast. The Board generally received regular and detailed reports and was kept abreast of the accumulated investment tax credit and accelerated depreciation problem.

Van Gorkom began the Special Meeting of the Board with a twenty-minute oral presentation. Copies of the proposed Merger Agreement were delivered too late for study before or during the meeting.[7] He reviewed the Company's ITC and depreciation problems and the efforts theretofore made to solve them. He discussed his initial meeting with Pritzker and his motivation in arranging that meeting. Van Gorkom did not disclose to the Board, however, the methodology by which he alone had arrived at the $55 figure, or the fact that he first proposed the $55 price in his negotiations with Pritzker.

Van Gorkom outlined the terms of the Pritzker offer as follows: Pritzker would pay $55 in cash for all outstanding shares of Trans Union stock upon completion of which Trans Union would be merged into New T Company, a subsidiary wholly-owned by Pritzker and formed to implement the merger; for a period of 90 days, Trans Union could receive, but could not actively solicit, competing offers; the offer had to be acted on by the next evening, Sunday, September 21; Trans Union could only furnish to competing bidders published information, and not proprietary information; the offer was subject to Pritzker obtaining the necessary financing by October 10, 1980; if the financing contingency were met or waived by Pritzker, Trans Union was required to sell to Pritzker one million newly-issued shares of Trans Union at $38 per share.

Van Gorkom took the position that putting Trans Union "up for auction" through a 90-day market test would validate a decision by the Board that $55 was a fair price. He told the Board that the "free market will have an opportunity

---

7. The record is not clear as to the terms of the Merger Agreement. The Agreement, as originally presented to the Board on September 20, was never produced by defendants despite demands by the plaintiffs. Nor is it clear that the directors were given an opportunity to study the Merger Agreement before voting on it. All that can be said is that Brennan had the Agreement before him during the meeting.

to judge whether $55 is a fair price." Van Gorkom framed the decision before the Board not as whether $55 per share was the highest price that could be obtained, but as whether the $55 price was a fair price that the stockholders should be given the opportunity to accept or reject.[8]

Attorney Brennan advised the members of the Board that they might be sued if they failed to accept the offer and that a fairness opinion was not required as a matter of law.

Romans attended the meeting as chief financial officer of the Company. He told the Board that he had not been involved in the negotiations with Pritzker and knew nothing about the merger proposal until the morning of the meeting; that his studies did not indicate either a fair price for the stock or a valuation of the Company; that he did not see his role as directly addressing the fairness issue; and that he and his people "were trying to search for ways to justify a price in connection with such a [leveraged buy-out] transaction, rather than to say what the shares are worth." Romans testified:

> I told the Board that the study ran the numbers at 50 and 60, and then the subsequent study at 55 and 65, and that was not the same thing as saying that I have a valuation of the company at X dollars. But it was a way—a first step towards reaching that conclusion.

Romans told the Board that, in his opinion, $55 was "in the range of a fair price," but "at the beginning of the range."

Chelberg, Trans Union's President, supported Van Gorkom's presentation and representations. He testified that he "participated to make sure that the Board members collectively were clear on the details of the agreement or offer from Pritzker;" that he "participated in the discussion with Mr. Brennan, inquiring of him about the necessity for valuation opinions in spite of the way in which this particular offer was couched;" and that he was otherwise actively involved in supporting the positions being taken by Van Gorkom before the Board about "the necessity to act immediately on this offer," and about "the adequacy of the $55 and the question of how that would be tested."

The Board meeting of September 20 lasted about two hours. Based solely upon Van Gorkom's oral presentation, Chelberg's supporting representations, Romans' oral statement, Brennan's legal advice, and their knowledge of the market history of the Company's stock,[9] the directors approved the proposed Merger Agreement. However, the Board later claimed to have attached two conditions to its acceptance: (1) that Trans Union reserved the right to accept any better offer that was made during the market test period; and (2) that Trans

---

8. In Van Gorkom's words: The "real decision" is whether to "let the stockholders decide it" which is "all you are being asked to decide today."

9. The Trial Court stated the premium relationship of the $55 price to the market history of the Company's stock as follows:

> . . . the merger price offered to the stockholders of Trans Union represented a premium of 62% over the average of the high and low prices at which Trans Union stock had traded in 1980, a premium of 48% over the last closing price, and a premium of 39% over the highest price at which the stock of Trans Union had traded any time during the prior six years.

Union could share its proprietary information with any other potential bidders. While the Board now claims to have reserved the right to accept any better offer received after the announcement of the Pritzker agreement (even though the minutes of the meeting do not reflect this), it is undisputed that the Board did not reserve the right to actively solicit alternate offers.

The Merger Agreement was executed by Van Gorkom during the evening of September 20 at a formal social event that he hosted for the opening of the Chicago Lyric Opera. Neither he nor any other director read the agreement prior to its signing and delivery to Pritzker. . . .

On February 10, the stockholders of Trans Union approved the Pritzker merger proposal. Of the outstanding shares, 69.9% were voted in favor of the merger; 7.25% were voted against the merger; and 22.85% were not voted.

II.

We turn to the issue of the application of the business judgment rule to the September 20 meeting of the Board.

The Court of Chancery concluded from the evidence that the Board of Directors' approval of the Pritzker merger proposal fell within the protection of the business judgment rule. The Court found that the Board had given sufficient time and attention to the transaction, since the directors had considered the Pritzker proposal on three different occasions, on September 20, and on October 8, 1980 and finally on January 26, 1981. On that basis, the Court reasoned that the Board had acquired, over the four-month period, sufficient information to reach an informed business judgment on the cashout merger proposal. The Court ruled:

> . . . that given the market value of Trans Union's stock, the business acumen of the members of the board of Trans Union, the substantial premium over market offered by the Pritzkers and the ultimate effect on the merger price provided by the prospect of other bids for the stock in question, that the board of directors of Trans Union did not act recklessly or improvidently in determining on a course of action which they believed to be in the best interest of the stockholders of Trans Union. . . .

Applying . . . governing principles of law to the record and the decision of the Trial Court, we conclude that the Court's ultimate finding that the Board's conduct was not "reckless or imprudent" is contrary to the record and not the product of a logical and deductive reasoning process.

The plaintiffs contend that the Court of Chancery erred as a matter of law by exonerating the defendant directors under the business judgment rule without first determining whether the rule's threshold condition of "due care and prudence" was satisfied. The plaintiffs assert that the Trial Court found the defendant directors to have reached an informed business judgment on the basis of "extraneous considerations and events that occurred after September 20, 1980." The defendants deny that the Trial Court committed legal error in relying upon post-September 20, 1980 events and the directors' later acquired knowledge. The defendants further submit that their decision to accept $55 per share was informed because: (1) they were "highly qualified;" (2) they were "well-informed;" and (3) they deliberated over the "proposal" not once but three times. On essentially this evidence and under our standard of review, the defendants assert that affirmance is required. We must disagree.

Under Delaware law, the business judgment rule is the offspring of the fundamental principle, codified in 8 Del. C. §141 (a), that the business and affairs of a Delaware corporation are managed by or under its board of directors. In carrying out their managerial roles, directors are charged with an unyielding fiduciary duty to the corporation and its shareholders. The business judgment rule exists to protect and promote the full and free exercise of the managerial power granted to Delaware directors. The rule itself "is a presumption that in making a business decision, the directors of a corporation acted on an informed basis, in good faith and in the honest belief that the action taken was in the best interests of the company." *Aronson [v. Lewis,* 473 A.2d 805, 812 (Del. 1984)]. Thus, the party attacking a board decision as uninformed must rebut the presumption that its business judgment was an informed one.

The determination of whether a business judgment is an informed one turns on whether the directors have informed themselves "prior to making a business decision, of all material information reasonably available to them." *Id.*

Under the business judgment rule there is no protection for directors who have made "an unintelligent or unadvised judgment." *Mitchell v. Highland-Western Glass,* Del. Ch., 167 A. 831, 833 (1933). A director's duty to inform himself in preparation for a decision derives from the fiduciary capacity in which he serves the corporation and its stockholders. Since a director is vested with the responsibility for the management of the affairs of the corporation, he must execute that duty with the recognition that he acts on behalf of others. Such obligation does not tolerate faithlessness or self-dealing. But fulfillment of the fiduciary function requires more than the mere absence of bad faith or fraud. Representation of the financial interests of others imposes on a director an affirmative duty to protect those interests and to proceed with a critical eye in assessing information of the type and under the circumstances present here.

Thus, a director's duty to exercise an informed business judgment is in the nature of a duty of care, as distinguished from a duty of loyalty. Here, there were no allegations of fraud, bad faith, or self-dealing, or proof thereof. Hence, it is presumed that the directors reached their business judgment in good faith, and considerations of motive are irrelevant to the issue before us. The standard of care applicable to a director's duty of care has also been recently restated by this Court. In *Aronson, supra,* we stated:

> While the Delaware cases use a variety of terms to describe the applicable standard of care, our analysis satisfies us that under the business judgment rule director liability is predicated upon concepts of gross negligence. (footnote omitted)

473 A.2d at 812.

We again confirm that view. We think the concept of gross negligence is also the proper standard for determining whether a business judgment reached by a board of directors was an informed one.

In the specific context of a proposed merger of domestic corporations, a director has a duty under 8 Del. C. §251 (b), along with his fellow directors, to act in an informed and deliberate manner in determining whether to approve an agreement of merger before submitting the proposal to the stockholders. Certainly in the merger context, a director may not abdicate that duty by leaving to the shareholders alone the decision to approve or disapprove the agreement. Only an agreement of merger satisfying the requirements of 8 Del. C. §251(b) may be submitted to the shareholders under §251(c).

It is against those standards that the conduct of the directors of Trans Union must be tested, as a matter of law and as a matter of fact, regarding their exercise of an informed business judgment in voting to approve the Pritzker merger proposal.

III.

The defendants argue that the determination of whether their decision to accept $55 per share for Trans Union represented an informed business judgment requires consideration, not only of that which they knew and learned on September 20, but also of that which they subsequently learned and did over the following four-month period before the shareholders met to vote on the proposal in February, 1981. . . . Thus, the defendants contend that what the directors did and learned subsequent to September 20 and through January 26, 1981, was properly taken into account by the Trial Court in determining whether the Board's judgment was an informed one. We disagree with this *post hoc* approach.

The issue of whether the directors reached an informed decision to "sell" the Company on September 20, 1980 must be determined only upon the basis of the information then reasonably available to the directors and relevant to their decision to accept the Pritzker merger proposal. This is not to say that the directors were precluded from altering their original plan of action, had they done so in an informed manner. What we do say is that the question of whether the directors reached an informed business judgment in agreeing to sell the Company, pursuant to the terms of the September 20 Agreement presents, in reality, two questions: (A) whether the directors reached an informed business judgment on September 20, 1980; and (B) if they did not, whether the directors' actions taken subsequent to September 20 were adequate to cure any infirmity in their action taken on September 20. We first consider the directors' September 20 action in terms of their reaching an informed business judgment.

A

On the record before us, we must conclude that the Board of Directors did not reach an informed business judgment on September 20, 1980 in voting to "sell" the Company for $55 per share pursuant to the Pritzker cash-out merger proposal. Our reasons, in summary, are as follows:

> The directors (1) did not adequately inform themselves as to Van Gorkom's role in forcing the "sale" of the Company and in establishing the per share purchase price; (2) were uninformed as to the intrinsic value of the Company; and (3) given these circumstances, at a minimum, were grossly negligent in approving the "sale" of the Company upon two hours' consideration, without prior notice, and without the exigency of a crisis or emergency.

As has been noted, the Board based its September 20 decision to approve the cash-out merger primarily on Van Gorkom's representations. None of the directors, other than Van Gorkom and Chelberg, had any prior knowledge that the purpose of the meeting was to propose a cash-out merger of Trans Union. No members of Senior Management were present, other than Chelberg, Romans and Peterson; and the latter two had only learned of the proposed sale an hour earlier. Both general counsel Moore and former general counsel Browder attended the meeting, but were equally uninformed as to the purpose of the meeting and the documents to be acted upon.

Without any documents before them concerning the proposed transaction, the members of the Board were required to rely entirely upon Van Gorkom's 20-minute oral presentation of the proposal. No written summary of the terms of the merger was presented; the directors were given no documentation to support the adequacy of $55 price per share for sale of the Company; and the Board had before it nothing more than Van Gorkom's statement of his understanding of the substance of an agreement which he admittedly had never read, nor which any member of the Board had ever seen.

Under 8 Del. C. §141(e), "directors are fully protected in relying in good faith on reports made by officers." The term "report" has been liberally construed to include reports of informal personal investigations by corporate officers, *Cheff v. Mathes*, Del. Supr., 199 A.2d 548, 556 (1964). However, there is no evidence that any "report," as defined under §141(e), concerning the Pritzker proposal, was presented to the Board on September 20. Van Gorkom's oral presentation of his understanding of the terms of the proposed Merger Agreement, which he had not seen, and Romans' brief oral statement of his preliminary study regarding the feasibility of a leveraged buy-out of Trans Union do not qualify as §141(e) "reports" for these reasons: The former lacked substance because Van Gorkom was basically uninformed as to the essential provisions of the very document about which he was talking. Romans' statement was irrelevant to the issues before the Board since it did not purport to be a valuation study. At a minimum for a report to enjoy the status conferred by §141(e), it must be pertinent to the subject matter upon which a board is called to act, and otherwise be entitled to good faith, not blind, reliance. Considering all of the surrounding circumstances—hastily calling the meeting without prior notice of its subject matter, the proposed sale of the Company without any prior consideration of the issue or necessity therefor, the urgent time constraints imposed by Pritzker, and the total absence of any documentation whatsoever—the directors were duty bound to make reasonable inquiry of Van Gorkom and Romans, and if they had done so, the inadequacy of that upon which they now claim to have relied would have been apparent.

The defendants rely on the following factors to sustain the Trial Court's finding that the Board's decision was an informed one: (1) the magnitude of the premium or spread between the $55 Pritzker offering price and Trans Union's current market price of $38 per share; (2) the amendment of the Agreement as submitted on September 20 to permit the Board to accept any better offer during the "market test" period; (3) the collective experience and expertise of the Board's "inside" and "outside" directors; and (4) their reliance on Brennan's legal advice that the directors might be sued if they rejected the Pritzker proposal. We discuss each of these grounds *seriatim:*

(1)

A substantial premium may provide one reason to recommend a merger, but in the absence of other sound valuation information, the fact of a premium alone does not provide an adequate basis upon which to assess the fairness of an offering price. Here, the judgment reached as to the adequacy of the premium was based on a comparison between the historically depressed Trans Union market price and the amount of the Pritzker offer. Using market price as a basis for concluding that the premium adequately reflected the true value of the Company was a clearly faulty, indeed fallacious, premise, as the defendants' own evidence demonstrates.

The record is clear that before September 20, Van Gorkom and other members of Trans Union's Board knew that the market had consistently undervalued the worth of Trans Union's stock, despite steady increases in the Company's operating income in the seven years preceding the merger. The Board related this occurrence in large part to Trans Union's inability to use its ITCs as previously noted. Van Gorkom testified that he did not believe the market price accurately reflected Trans Union's true worth; and several of the directors testified that, as a general rule, most chief executives think that the market undervalues their companies' stock. Yet, on September 20, Trans Union's Board apparently believed that the market stock price accurately reflected the value of the Company for the purpose of determining the adequacy of the premium for its sale.

In the Proxy Statement, however, the directors reversed their position. There, they stated that, although the earnings prospects for Trans Union were "excellent," they found no basis for believing that this would be reflected in future stock prices. With regard to past trading, the Board stated that the prices at which the Company's common stock had traded in recent years did not reflect the "inherent" value of the Company. But having referred to the "inherent" value of Trans Union, the directors ascribed no number to it. Moreover, nowhere did they disclose that they had no basis on which to fix "inherent" worth beyond an impressionistic reaction to the premium over market and an unsubstantiated belief that the value of the assets was "significantly greater" than book value. By their own admission they could not rely on the stock price as an accurate measure of value. Yet, also by their own admission, the Board members assumed that Trans Union's market price was adequate to serve as a basis upon which to assess the adequacy of the premium for purposes of the September 20 meeting.

The parties do not dispute that a publicly-traded stock price is solely a measure of the value of a minority position and, thus, market price represents only the value of a single share. Nevertheless, on September 20, the Board assessed the adequacy of the premium over market, offered by Pritzker, solely by comparing it with Trans Union's current and historical stock price. *(See supra note 5 . . .)*

Indeed, as of September 20, the Board had no other information on which to base a determination of the intrinsic value of Trans Union as a going concern. As of September 20, the Board had made no evaluation of the Company designed to value the entire enterprise, nor had the Board ever previously considered selling the Company or consenting to a buy-out merger. Thus, the adequacy of a premium is indeterminate unless it is assessed in terms of other competent and sound valuation information that reflects the value of the particular business.

Despite the foregoing facts and circumstances, there was no call by the Board, either on September 20 or thereafter, for any valuation study or documentation of the $55 price per share as a measure of the fair value of the Company in a cash-out context. It is undisputed that the major asset of Trans Union was its cash flow. Yet, at no time did the Board call for a valuation study taking into account that highly significant element of the Company's assets.

We do not imply that an outside valuation study is essential to support an informed business judgment; nor do we state that fairness opinions by independent investment bankers are required as a matter of law. Often insiders familiar with the business of a going concern are in a better position than are outsiders to gather relevant information; and under appropriate circumstances, such directors may be fully protected in relying in good faith upon the valuation reports of their management. *See* 8 Del. C. §141(e). *See also Cheff v. Mathes, supra.*

Here, the record establishes that the Board did not request its Chief Financial Officer, Romans, to make any valuation study or review of the proposal to determine the adequacy of $55 per share for sale of the Company. On the record before us: The Board rested on Romans' elicited response that the $55 figure was within a "fair price range" within the context of a leveraged buyout. No director sought any further information from Romans. No director asked him why he put $55 at the bottom of his range. No director asked Romans for any details as to his study, the reason why it had been undertaken or its depth. No director asked to see the study; and no director asked Romans whether Trans Union's finance department could do a fairness study within the remaining 36-hour[18] period available under the Pritzker offer.

Had the Board, or any member, made an inquiry of Romans, he presumably would have responded as he testified: that his calculations were rough and preliminary; and, that the study was not designed to determine the fair value of the Company, but rather to assess the feasibility of a leveraged buy-out financed by the Company's projected cash flow, making certain assumptions as to the purchaser's borrowing needs. Romans would have presumably also informed the Board of his view, and the widespread view of Senior Management, that the timing of the offer was wrong and the offer inadequate.

The record also establishes that the Board accepted without scrutiny Van Gorkom's representation as to the fairness of the $55 price per share for sale of the Company—a subject that the Board had never previously considered. The Board thereby failed to discover that Van Gorkom had suggested the $55 price to Pritzker and, most crucially, that Van Gorkom had arrived at the $55 figure based on calculations designed solely to determine the feasibility of a leveraged

---

18. Romans' department study was not made available to the Board until circulation of Trans Union's Supplementary Proxy Statement and the Board's meeting of January 26, 1981, on the eve of the shareholder meeting; and, as has been noted, the study has never been produced for inclusion in the record in this case.

buy-out.[19] No questions were raised either as to the tax implications of a cash-out merger or how the price for the one million share option granted Pritzker was calculated.

We do not say that the Board of Directors was not entitled to give some credence to Van Gorkom's representation that $55 was an adequate or fair price. Under §141(e), the directors were entitled to rely upon their chairman's opinion of value and adequacy, provided that such opinion was reached on a sound basis. Here, the issue is whether the directors informed themselves as to all information that was reasonably available to them. Had they done so, they would have learned of the source and derivation of the $55 price and could not reasonably have relied thereupon in good faith.

None of the directors, Management or outside, were investment bankers or financial analysts. Yet the Board did not consider recessing the meeting until a later hour that day (or requesting an extension of Pritzker's Sunday evening deadline) to give it time to elicit more information as to the sufficiency of the offer, either from inside Management (in particular Romans) or from Trans Union's own investment banker, Salomon Brothers, whose Chicago specialist in merger and acquisitions was known to the Board and familiar with Trans Union's affairs.

Thus, the record compels the conclusion that on September 20 the Board lacked valuation information adequate to reach an informed business judgment as to the fairness of $55 per share for sale of the Company.

(2)

This brings us to the post-September 20 "market test" upon which the defendants ultimately rely to confirm the reasonableness of their September 20 decision to accept the Pritzker proposal. In this connection, the directors present a two-part argument: (a) that by making a "market test" of Pritzker's $55 per share offer a condition of their September 20 decision to accept his offer, they cannot be found to have acted impulsively or in an uninformed manner on September 20; and (b) that the adequacy of the $17 premium for sale of the Company was conclusively established over the following 90 to 120 days by the most reliable evidence available—the marketplace. Thus, the defendants impliedly contend that the "market test" eliminated the need for the Board to perform any other form of fairness test either on September 20, or thereafter.

---

19. As of September 20 the directors did not know: that Van Gorkom had arrived at the $55 figure alone, and subjectively, as the figure to be used by Controller Peterson in creating a feasible structure for a leveraged buy-out by a prospective purchaser; that Van Gorkom had not sought advice, information or assistance from either inside or outside Trans Union directors as to the value of the Company as an entity or the fair price per share for 100% of its stock; that Van Gorkom had not consulted with the Company's investment bankers or other financial analysts; that Van Gorkom had not consulted with or confided in any officer or director of the Company except Chelberg; and that Van Gorkom had deliberately chosen to ignore the advice and opinion of the members of his Senior Management group regarding the adequacy of the $55 price.

Again, the facts of record do not support the defendants' argument. There is no evidence: (a) that the Merger Agreement was effectively amended to give the Board freedom to put Trans Union up for auction sale to the highest bidder; or (b) that a public auction was in fact permitted to occur. The minutes of the Board meeting make no reference to any of this. Indeed, the record compels the conclusion that the directors had no rational basis for expecting that a market test was attainable, given the terms of the Agreement as executed during the evening of September 20. . . .

(3)

The directors' unfounded reliance on both the premium and the market test as the basis for accepting the Pritzker proposal undermines the defendants' remaining contention that the Board's collective experience and sophistication was a sufficient basis for finding that it reached its September 20 decision with informed, reasonable deliberation.[21] *Compare Gimbel v. Signal Companies, Inc.,* Del. Ch., 316 A.2d 599 (1974), *aff'dper curiam,* Del. Supr., 316 A.2d 619 (1974). . . .

(4)

Part of the defense is based on a claim that the directors relied on legal advice rendered at the September 20 meeting by James Brennan, Esquire, who was present at Van Gorkom's request. Unfortunately, Brennan did not appear and testify at trial even though his firm participated in the defense of this action. There is no contemporaneous evidence of the advice given by Brennan on September 20, only the later deposition and trial testimony of certain directors as to their recollections or understanding of what was said at the meeting. Since counsel did not testify, and the advice attributed to Brennan is hearsay received by the Trial Court over the plaintiffs' objections, we consider it only in the context of the directors' present claims. In fairness to counsel, we make no findings that the advice attributed to him was in fact given. We focus solely on the efficacy of the defendants' claims, made months and years later, in an effort to extricate themselves from liability.

Several defendants testified that Brennan advised them that Delaware law did not require a fairness opinion or an outside valuation of the Company before the Board could act on the Pritzker proposal. If given, the advice was

---

21. Trans Union's five "inside" directors had backgrounds in law and accounting, 116 years of collective employment by the Company and 68 years of combined experience on its Board. Trans Union's five "outside" directors included four chief executives of major corporations and an economist who was a former dean of a major school of business and chancellor of a university. The "outside" directors had 78 years of combined experience as chief executive officers of major corporations and 50 years of cumulative experience as directors of Trans Union. Thus, defendants argue that the Board was eminently qualified to reach an informed judgment on the proposed "sale" of Trans Union notwithstanding their lack of any advance notice of the proposal, the shortness of their deliberation, and their determination not to consult with their investment banker or to obtain a fairness opinion.

correct. However, that did not end the matter. Unless the directors had before them adequate information regarding the intrinsic value of the Company, upon which a proper exercise of business judgment could be made, mere advice of this type is meaningless; and, given this record of the defendants' failures, it constitutes no defense here.[22]

We conclude that Trans Union's Board was grossly negligent in that it failed to act with informed reasonable deliberation in agreeing to the Pritzker merger proposal on September 20; and we further conclude that the Trial Court erred as a matter of law in failing to address that question before determining whether the directors' later conduct was sufficient to cure its initial error.

A second claim is that counsel advised the Board it would be subject to lawsuits if it rejected the $55 per share offer. It is, of course, a fact of corporate life that today when faced with difficult or sensitive issues, directors often are subject to suit, irrespective of the decisions they make. However, counsel's mere acknowledgement of this circumstance cannot be rationally translated into a justification for a board permitting itself to be stampeded into a patently unadvised act. While suit might result from the rejection of a merger or tender offer, Delaware law makes clear that a board acting within the ambit of the business judgment rule faces no ultimate liability. *Pogostin v. Rice, supra.* Thus, we cannot conclude that the mere threat of litigation, acknowledged by counsel, constitutes either legal advice or any valid basis upon which to pursue an uninformed course.

B

We now examine the Board's post–September 20 conduct for the purpose of determining . . . whether it was informed and not grossly negligent . . . . [and, therefore,] whether it was sufficient to legally cure the derelictions of September 20. [In this portion of its opinion, the Delaware Supreme Court concluded that the Board's post-September efforts to canvas the market for other potential bidders did not cure the deficiencies surrounding the Board's initial September 20 decision.]

* * *

V.

The defendants ultimately rely on the stockholder vote of February 10 for exoneration. The defendants contend that the stockholders' "overwhelming" vote approving the Pritzker Merger Agreement had the legal effect of curing any failure of the Board to reach an informed business judgment in its approval of the merger. . . .

---

22. Nonetheless, we are satisfied that in an appropriate factual context a proper exercise of business judgment may include, as one of its aspects, reasonable reliance upon the advice of counsel. This is wholly outside the statutory protections of 8 Del. C. §141(e) involving reliance upon reports of officers, certain experts and books and records of the company.

On this issue the Trial Court summarily concluded "that the stockholders of Trans Union were fairly informed as to the pending merger. . . ." The Court provided no supportive reasoning nor did the Court make any reference to the evidence of record. . . .

The settled rule in Delaware is that "where a majority of fully informed stockholders ratify action of even interested directors, an attack on the ratified transaction normally must fail." *Gerlach v. Gillam,* Del. Ch., 139 A.2d 591, 593 (1958). The question of whether shareholders have been fully informed such that their vote can be said to ratify director action, "turns on the fairness and completeness of the proxy materials submitted by the management to the . . . shareholders." *Michelson v. Duncan, supra* at 220. As this Court stated in *Gottlieb v. Heyden Chemical Corp.,* Del. Supr., 91 A.2d 57, 59 (1952):

> [T]he entire atmosphere is freshened and a new set of rules invoked where a formal approval has been given by a majority of independent, fully informed stockholders. . . .

In *Lynch v. Vickers Energy Corp.,* [91 A.2d 278, 281 (Del. 1978)], this Court held that corporate directors owe to their stockholders a fiduciary duty to disclose all facts germane to the transaction at issue in an atmosphere of complete candor. We defined "germane" in the tender offer context as all "information such as a reasonable stockholder would consider important in deciding whether to sell or retain stock." *Accord Weinberger v. UOP, Inc., supra;* . . . In reality, "germane" means material facts.

Applying this standard to the record before us, we find that Trans Union's stockholders were not fully informed of all facts material to their vote on the Pritzker Merger and that the Trial Court's ruling to the contrary is clearly erroneous. We list the material deficiencies in the proxy materials:

(1) The fact that the Board had no reasonably adequate information indicative of the intrinsic value of the Company, other than a concededly depressed market price, was without question material to the shareholders voting on the merger. . . .

Accordingly, the Board's lack of valuation information should have been disclosed. Instead, the directors cloaked the absence of such information in both the Proxy Statement and the Supplemental Proxy Statement. Through artful drafting, noticeably absent at the September 20 meeting, both documents create the impression that the Board knew the intrinsic worth of the Company . . . Neither in its original proxy statement nor in its supplemental proxy did the Board disclose that it had no information before it, beyond the premium-over-market and the price/earnings ratio, on which to determine the fair value of the Company as a whole. . . .

(2) We find false and misleading the Board's characterization of the Romans report in the Supplemental Proxy Statement. . . . Nowhere does the Board disclose that Romans stated to the Board that his calculations were made in a "search for ways to justify a price in connection with" a leveraged buy-out transaction, "rather than to say what the shares are worth," and that he stated to the Board that his conclusion thus arrived at "was not the same thing as saying that I have a valuation of the Company at X dollars." Such information would have been material to a reasonable shareholder because it tended to invalidate the fairness of the merger price of $55. Furthermore, defendants again failed to disclose the absence of valuation information, but still made repeated reference to the "substantial premium."

(3) We find misleading the Board's references to the "substantial" premium offered. The Board gave as their primary reason in support of the merger the "substantial premium" shareholders would receive. But the Board did not disclose its failure to assess the premium offered in terms of other relevant valuation techniques, thereby rendering questionable its determination as to the substantiality of the premium over an admittedly depressed stock market price.

(4) We find the Board's recital in the Supplemental Proxy of certain events preceding the September 20 meeting to be incomplete and misleading. It is beyond dispute that a reasonable stockholder would have considered material the fact that Van Gorkom not only suggested the $55 price to Pritzker, but also that he chose the figure because it made feasible a leveraged buy-out. The directors disclosed that Van Gorkom suggested the $55 price to Pritzker. But the Board misled the shareholders when they described the basis of Van Gorkom's suggestion. . . .

(5) The Board's Supplemental Proxy Statement, mailed on or after January 27, added significant new matter, material to the proposal to be voted on February 10, which was not contained in the Original Proxy Statement. Some of this new matter was information which had only been disclosed to the Board on January 26; much was information known or reasonably available before January 21 but not revealed in the Original Proxy Statement. Yet, the stockholders were not informed of these facts. . . .

Since we have concluded that Management's Supplemental Proxy Statement does not meet the Delaware disclosure standard of "complete candor" under *Lynch v. Vickers, supra,* it is unnecessary for us to address the plaintiffs' legal argument as to the proper construction of §251(c). . . .

. . . The defendants simply failed in their original duty of knowing, sharing, and disclosing information that was material and reasonably available for their discovery. They compounded that failure by their continued lack of candor in the Supplemental Proxy Statement. While we need not decide the issue here, we are satisfied that, in an appropriate case, a completely candid but belated disclosure of information long known or readily available to a board could raise serious issues of inequitable conduct. *Schnell v. Chris-Craft Industries, Inc.,* Del. Supr., 285 A.2d 437, 439 (1971).

The burden must fall on defendants who claim ratification based on shareholder vote to establish that the shareholder approval resulted from a fully informed electorate. On the record before us, it is clear that the Board failed to meet that burden. *Weinberger v. UOP, Inc., supra* at 703; *Michelson v. Duncan, supra.*

For the foregoing reasons, we conclude that the director defendants breached their fiduciary duty of candor by their failure to make true and correct disclosures of all information they had, or should have had, material to the transaction submitted for stockholder approval.

VI.

To summarize: we hold that the directors of Trans Union breached their fiduciary duty to their stockholders (1) by their failure to inform themselves of all information reasonably available to them and relevant to their decision to recommend the Pritzker merger; and (2) by their failure to disclose all material information such as a reasonable stockholder would consider important in deciding whether to approve the Pritzker offer.

We hold, therefore, that the Trial Court committed reversible error in applying the business judgment rule in favor of the director defendants in this case.

On remand, the Court of Chancery shall conduct an evidentiary hearing to determine the fair value of the shares represented by the plaintiffs' class, based on the intrinsic value of Trans Union on September 20, 1980. Such valuation shall be made in accordance with *Weinberger v. UOP, Inc., supra* at 712-715. Thereafter, an award of damages may be entered to the extent that the fair value of Trans Union exceeds $55 per share.

REVERSED and REMANDED for proceedings consistent herewith. . . .

QUESTIONS

1. What is a "market check"? What is the usefulness—from either a legal or a business perspective—of conducting a market check?

2. Why was the board's determination that the "premium" that the Pritzkers offered (i.e., the spread between the $55 price offered by Pritzkers and the current market price of $38 per share) *not* sufficient to establish that the board reached an informed decision as to the adequacy of the offering price? Do you agree with the court's reasoning on this issue?

3. In light of the overwhelming approval of the transaction by the shareholders of Trans Union, why wasn't this shareholder vote sufficient to establish the fairness of the price? Is the court's decision on this issue in *Trans Union* consistent with its decision in *Weinberger*? (*Hint:* You will recall that we read the Delaware Supreme Court's seminal decision in *Weinberger v. UOP, Inc.,* earlier in Chapter 2 at p. 166).

NOTES

1. The Dissents in **Trans Union.**   The Delaware Supreme Court was sharply divided, with two justices filing strongly worded dissents. The dissenters emphasized that the majority did not extend the usual measure of deference to the findings of the trial court, nor to the judgment and experience of the company's directors. In his dissent, Justice McNeilly pointed out that the five inside directors, who also served as the company's senior executive officers, "had collectively been employed by [Trans Union] for 116 years and had 68 years of combined experience as directors," whereas the five outside directors, all of whom served as CEOs of other companies at least as large as Trans Union, "had 78 years of combined experience as [CEOs], and 53 years cumulative service as Trans Union directors." Based on the experience and qualifications of these ten individuals, Justice McNeilly concluded that

> [d]irectors of this caliber . . . were not taken into this multi-million dollar corporate transaction without being fully informed and aware of [the consequences] as it pertained to the entire corporate panorama of TransUnion. True, even

directors such as these, with their business acumen, interest and expertise, can go astray. I do not believe that to be the case here. These men knew Trans Union like the back of their hands and were more than well qualified to make on the spot informed business judgments concerning the affairs of Trans Union including a 100% sale of the corporation. Lest we forget, the corporate world of then and now operates on what is so aptly referred to as "the fast track". These men were at the time an integral part of that world, all professional business men, not intellectual figureheads.

What do you think? Are you persuaded by the dissent's assertion that these five outside directors "were more than well-qualified to make on the spot informed business judgment" concerning the sale of Trans Union to the Pritzkers for $55 per share?

2. The Fallout from **Trans Union.** The *Trans Union* decision clearly sent shock waves through the corporate bar, leading many lawyers to lament the imminent demise of the business judgment rule as they had learned it in law school. To show how time heals all wounds, many practicing mergers and acquisitions (M&A) lawyers today recommend that board members read the facts of the *Trans Union* decision *carefully* before embarking on any M&A transaction. Why this recommendation? A careful read of the boardroom procedures relied on by the directors of Trans Union Corp. (or, more pointedly, the lack thereof) is strongly recommended because it provides a modern case study of how *not* to execute an M&A transaction.

To the extent that boardroom practices of the type reflected in *Smith v. Van Gorkom* represent the norm 30 years ago, it is abundantly clear that these practices fall far short of the decision-making process expected of board members in today's business environment. In light of the fact that business practices have changed dramatically since *Trans Union* was decided, consider (as you read the remaining materials in this chapter) whether any, all, or some combination of the following are required in order for board members to claim the benefit of business judgment rule protection:

a. Consultation with outside financial advisors?
b. Consultation with senior executive officers of the company and/or other personnel within the company?
c. Careful reading of entire merger agreement?
d. Thorough review of the company's proxy statement soliciting shareholder approval of the transaction?
e. Receipt of fairness opinion from an independent third party?

In considering how to advise the board as to these procedures, does it matter whether the company is privately held or publicly traded?

3. Fairness Opinions After **Trans Union.** As we saw in Chapter 4, fairness opinions are not required under the federal securities laws or the rules of the Securities and Exchange Commission (SEC) promulgated thereunder, nor are they required under the rules of the New York Stock Exchange (NYSE) or the NASDAQ Stock Market. Moreover, as reflected in the Delaware Supreme Court's opinion in *Trans Union,* fairness opinions are not required in order to validly complete the acquisition as a matter of the state's corporation statute. However, in the wake of the *Trans Union* decision, obtaining a fairness opinion "became standard procedure in corporate transactions" based at least in part on the widely held view that Trans Union's board of directors breached its fiduciary duty of care "by approving a merger without adequate information on the transaction, including whether the offering price reflected [the] company's true value." Donna Block, *Honest Opinion*, THE DEAL (August 31, 2007), *available at* http://pipeline.thedeal.com/tdd/ViewArticle.dl?id=1188299409205. In the aftermath of the *Trans Union* decision, many experienced observers of M&A transactions came to believe "that relying in good faith on a fairness opinion is one way directors can demonstrate [that they have satisfied their] duty of care." *Id.* You will recall our extended discussion of fairness opinions earlier in this book in Chapter 4, as part of our discussion of the disclosure obligations imposed under the terms of the SEC's proxy rules. As part of this discussion, we noted that the usual process of preparing fairness opinions is hardly the model of an objective and impartial analysis of the financial terms of the merger in light of the inherent conflicts of interest that arise when fairness "opinions are rendered by [the very same] investment banks that are also advising the merging firms and stand to collect contingency fees if deals go through." *Id.* Given the inherent conflicts of interest, does this call into question the wisdom of relying on fairness opinions to demonstrate whether the board has satisfied its fiduciary duty to bargain on behalf of the company and its shareholders to obtain the best price?

4. *"Staple Financing" and Investment Banker's Conflict of Interest.* On Wall Street, *staple financing* is generally understood to refer to an arrangement made between investment bankers and prospective Bidders whereby the banking firm representing the *seller*, i.e., Target Co., agrees to provide *buy-side financing* in order to allow the prospective Bidder Co. to complete the acquisition of the proposed Target. Of course, very often these staple financing arrangements further provide that the (rather substantial) fees to be paid to the banking firm are contingent on the closing of the proposed acquisition. The name *staple financing* refers to the fact that the financing details (i.e., the principal amount of the loan, any fees, and any loan covenants) are typically "stapled" to the back of the acquisition term sheet.

Many participants in the M&A market believe that the use of staple financing arrangements provides certain benefits in the context of an acquisition. Since Bidder's financing is already in place, Target is often able to generate more timely bids. In addition, since staple financing is in reality a form of preapproved loan, Bidders can avoid the last-minute, often frenzied scramble to secure financing for the proposed acquisition, thereby expediting the deal-making process. However, this financing arrangement does put the investment banker on both sides of the transaction—that is, the banker is providing financial advisory services to Target (for a fee) and is also lending money to Bidder (also for a fee). This has led some market participants to harbor concerns about the conflicts of interest that are inherent in a staple financing arrangement.

One such "stapled financing" arrangement was challenged as part of the leveraged buyout (LBO) transaction that was at issue in *In re Del Monte Foods*

Co. Shareholders Litigation, 25 A.3d 813 (Del. Ch. 2011). Briefly summarized, Vice Chancellor Laster

> found that after the Del Monte board called off a process of exploring a potential sale [of the company] in early 2010, [Del Monte's] investment bankers continued to meet with several of the [prospective] bidders—without the approval or knowledge of Del Monte—ultimately yielding a new joint bid from two buyout firms late in 2010. While still representing the [Del Monte] board and before the parties had reached agreement on price, Del Monte's bankers sought and received permission to provide buy-side financing, which [in turn] required [Del Monte] to retain another investment advisor to render an unconflicted fairness opinion. Del Monte reached a high-premium deal with a "go-shop" provision and deal protection devices including a termination fee and matching rights. The original bankers were then tasked with running Del Monte's go-shop process (which yielded no further offers), although the Court noted [that the bankers] stood to earn a substantial fee from financing the pending acquisition [as a result of the "staple financing" arrangement entered into with the two buyout firms.]
>
> Vice Chancellor Laster was troubled by the investment bank's effort to combine two bidders without consulting the board and in apparent contravention of a "no teaming" provision [that was part of the] confidentiality agreements entered into in connection with the original [deal-making] process. While the Court noted that "the blame for what took place appears at this preliminary stage to lie with [the banker], the buck stops with the Board" because "Delaware law requires that a board take an active and direct role in the sale process." [*Del Monte, supra*, at 835.] The Court also faulted [Del Monte's] board for agreeing to allow the competing bidders to work together and [also for allowing] the bankers to provide buy-side financing (even while overseeing the go-shop period) without "making any effort to obtain a benefit for Del Monte and its stockholders." . . . [Vice Chancellor Laster] warned that "investment banks representing sellers [should] not create the appearance that they desire buy-side work" but instead focus on assisting the target board in fulfilling its fiduciary duties.
>
> In response to these process deficiencies, the Court enjoined the vote on the transaction and the enforcement of the deal protection devices for twenty days, holding that without such relief, "the Del Monte stockholders will be deprived forever of the opportunity to receive a pre-vote topping bid in a process free of taint from [these] improper activities." [*Id.* at 838.] The Court also expressly held open the possibility of a damages remedy against the lead bidder for "colluding" with the bankers.
>
> [Vice Chancellor Laster's decision in *Del Monte*] serves as an important reminder to all participants in M&A transactions that the terms of confidentiality agreements should be properly respected, that bankers should receive and follow clear instructions from [Target] boards, and that bankers should ensure that any conflicts of interest are disclosed in advance, [and] with specificity, to the [Target's] board of directors. . . . [Equally important, Target] boards should pay close attention to how a sales process is managed to avoid findings of favoritism. The [Target] board should lead any sales process and actively supervise [its bankers].

Theodore N. Mirvis, et. al., *Buyout and Deal Protections Enjoined Due to Conflicted Advisor*, Wachtell, Lipton, Rosen, & Katz (law firm memo, Feb. 15, 2011); and Theodore N. Mirvis and Paul K. Rowe, *Settlement of* Del Monte *Buyout Litigation Highlights Risks Where Target Advisors Seek a Buyer-Financing Role*, Wachtell, Lipton, Rosen, & Katz (law firm memo, Oct. 7, 2011).

5. *The Doctrine of Shareholder Ratification.*   In Part V of its opinion in *Trans Union,* the Delaware Supreme Court addressed the defendant directors' claim that overwhelming shareholder approval of the merger agreement served to exonerate the directors from any personal liability on the grounds that the "legal effect" of the shareholder vote was to cure "any failure of the Board to reach an informed business judgment in its approval of the merger." *Smith v. Van Gorkom,* 488 A.2d at 889. The Delaware Supreme Court rejected this affirmative defense of "shareholder ratification" on the grounds that the record failed to show that *Trans Union* stockholders were "fully informed of all facts material to their vote on the Pritzer Merger" agreement, noting several "material deficiencies in the [company's] proxy materials"—thus proving, once again, the truth of that time-honored maxim: the shareholder vote is only as good as the disclosure that informs the vote.

In reaching this conclusion, the Delaware Supreme Court noted in passing that the "settled rule in Delaware is that where a majority of fully informed stockholders ratify an action of even interested directors, an attack on the ratified transaction must fail." *Id.* at 890. Indeed, several years later, the Delaware Chancery Court was presented with a lawsuit brought by plaintiff shareholders claiming that the company's board of directors had failed to inform itself fully with respect to the proposed M&A transaction in violation of the board's duty of care, as well as a claim that the proposed transaction involved a breach of the directors' fiduciary duty of loyalty. *See In re Wheelabrator Technologies, Inc. Shareholders Litigation,* 663 A.2d 1194 (Del. Ch. 1995). In its opinion, the court stated that approval by a fully informed vote of the shareholders constituting a majority of the disinterested shares (i.e., often referred to as a "majority of the minority" vote) would represent shareholder ratification that would require dismissal of the breach of the duty of care claim, in reliance on *Smith v. Van Gorkom* and its progeny. More importantly, the court in *Wheelabrator* held that, with respect to the duty of loyalty claim, the legal "effect of the shareholder vote . . . is to invoke the business judgment standard [of judicial review], which limits [judicial] review to issues of gift or waste with the burden of proof resting upon the plaintiffs." *Id.* at 1200. Based on this precedent, the Delaware Court of Chancery subsequently observed in 2007 that the doctrine of shareholder "ratification, in most situations, *precludes* shareholder claims for breach of fiduciary duty." *See Sample v. Morgan,* 914 A.2d 647, 663 (Del. Ch. 2007) (*emphasis added*). However, in its 2009 opinion in *Gantler v. Stephens,* 965 A.2d 695 (Del. 2009), the Delaware Supreme Court called into question this body of precedent with respect to the doctrine of shareholder ratification:

> Under current Delaware case law, the scope and effect of the common law doctrine of shareholder ratification is unclear, making it difficult to apply that doctrine in a coherent manner. As the Court of Chancery has noted in *In re Wheelabrator Technologies, Inc., Shareholders Litigation:*
>
> > [The doctrine of shareholder ratification] might be thought to lack coherence because the decisions addressing the effect of shareholder "ratification" have fragmented that subject into [different compartments] . . . In its "classic" . . . form, shareholder ratification describes the situation where shareholders approve board action that, legally speaking, could be accomplished without any shareholder approval. . . . "[C]lassic" ratification involves the voluntary addition of an

independent layer of shareholder approval in circumstances where shareholder approval is not legally required. But "shareholder ratification" has also been used to describe the effect of an informed shareholder vote that was statutorily required for the transaction to have legal existence . . . That [the Delaware courts] have used the same term is [sic] such highly diverse sets of factual circumstances, without regard to their possible functional differences, suggests that "shareholder ratification" has now acquired an expanded meaning intended to describe any approval of challenged board action by a fully informed vote of shareholders, irrespective of whether that shareholder vote is legally required for the transaction to attain legal existence.[52]

To restore coherence and clarity to this area of our law, we hold that the scope of the shareholder ratification doctrine must be limited to its so-called "classic" form; that is, to circumstances where a fully informed shareholder vote approves director action that does *not* legally require shareholder approval in order to become legally effective. Moreover, the *only* director action or conduct that can be ratified is that which the shareholders are specifically asked to approve. With one exception, the "cleansing" effect of such a ratifying shareholder vote is to subject the challenged director action to business judgment review, as opposed to "extinguishing" the claim altogether (*i.e.*, obviating *all* judicial review of the challenged action).[54]

Gantler v. Stephens, supra, 965 A. 2d at 712-713 *(emphasis added).*

After *Gantler,* what is the legal effect of shareholder ratification? According to one leading commentator, the Delaware Supreme Court has relegated:

the judicial effect of [shareholder] ratification . . . to doing nothing more than "subject[ing] the challenged director action to business judgment review, as opposed to '*extinguishing*' the claim altogether (*i.e.*, obviating *all* judicial review of the challenged action). . . . While . . . this formulation gives rise to the question [of] what exactly is meant by "business judgment review" in this procedural context, it appears clear that the [Delaware Supreme] Court's intention was to prohibit dismissal of such loyalty claims, as well as duty of care claims, *solely* on the basis of this affirmative defense.

---

52. 663 A.2d 1194, 1202 and n. 4 (Del. Ch. 1995) (citations omitted). *See also Solomon v. Armstrong,* 747 A.2d 1098, 1114-15 (Del. Ch. 1999), *aff'd,* 746 A.2d 277 (Table) (Del. 2000) ("The legal effect of shareholder ratification, as it relates to alleged breaches of the duty of loyalty, may be one of the most tortured areas of Delaware law. A different rule exists for every permutation of facts that fall under the broad umbrella of "duty of loyalty" claims.").

54. To the extent that *Smith v. Van Gorkom* holds otherwise, it is overruled. 488 A.2d 858, 889-90 (Del. 1985). The only species of claim that shareholder ratification can validly extinguish is a claim that the directors lacked the authority to take action that was later ratified. Nothing herein should be read as altering the well-established principle that void acts such as fraud, gift, waste, and *ultra vires* acts cannot be ratified by a less than unanimous shareholder vote. *See Michelson v. Duncan,* 407 A.2d 211, 219 (Del. 1979) ("[W]here a claim of gift or waste of assets, fraud or [u]ltra vires is asserted that a less than unanimous shareholder ratification is not a full defense."); *see also Harbor Fin. Partners v. Huizenga,* 751 A.2d 879, 896 (Del. Ch. 1999) (explaining that *ultra vires,* fraud, and gift or waste of corporate assets are "void" acts that cannot be ratified by less than unanimous shareholder consent); *accord Solomon v. Armstrong,* 747 A.2d at 1115. "Voidable" acts are those beyond management's powers, but where they are performed in the best interest of the corporation, they may be ratified by a majority vote of disinterested shareholders. *See Michelson,* 407 A.2d at 219. . . .

1-11 CORP. & COMMERCIAL PRACTICE IN DE. COURT OF CHANCERY §11.05 (2012 Matthew Bender) (*emphasis added*) (footnote omitted). As of this writing (Fall 2012), it still remains unclear "exactly what is meant" by the Delaware Supreme Court's instruction that business judgment review should apply in the context of an M&A transaction that has received disinterested shareholder approval pursuant to a "majority of the minority vote" as required by the parties' acquisition agreement. So M&A lawyers await further clarification from the Delaware Supreme Court as to the implications of the *Gantler* decision in the context of planning for M&A transactions. *Query:* Since *Gantler* holds that "a majority of the minority" vote does not preclude a claim for breach of fiduciary duty on the part of the board of directors, what should the court examine in subjecting "the challenged board action to business judgment review"? Will it look for allegations of waste that would be sufficient to overcome the otherwise deferential business judgment standard of judicial review?

 6. Procedural Fairness and the Business Judgment Rule. Following *Trans Union*, academic commentary criticized the Delaware Supreme Court's approach as overly emphasizing the process used by the board to approve an acquisition transaction. *See, e.g.*, Daniel R. Fischel, *The Business Judgment Rule and the* Trans Union *Case*, 40 BUS. LAW. 1437, 1455 (1985) (referring to the case as "one of the worst decisions in the history of corporate law"); Bayless Manning, *Reflections and Practical Tips on Life in the Boardroom After* Van Gorkom, 41 BUS. LAW. 1 (1985) ("The Delaware Supreme Court in *Van Gorkom* exploded a bomb. [Moreover, the] corporate bar generally views the decision as atrocious."). Without a doubt, though, in the years since *Trans Union* was decided, we have seen an increasing focus by the board and its advisors on the *process* undertaken in order to adequately document the board's decision to engage in a particular acquisition. Consequently, notwithstanding criticism regarding the "over-proceduralization" of boardroom decision making, it is common practice today to obtain a fairness opinion from an investment banker. In addition to creating more work for investment bankers, the *Trans Union* decision has also led to greater reliance on lawyers to create an adequate "paper trail" for any acquisition decision. Today, it is customary for counsel to get involved early in the acquisition process. By doing so, counsel can advise the constituent corporations to the transaction regarding appropriate board procedures and assist in negotiating and drafting the terms of the acquisition agreement to assure that the board has fulfilled its fiduciary obligations. Despite the practices that have developed over the past two decades since *Trans Union* was decided, controversy continues as to whether the increased focus on the procedures used by the board actually increases the probability of good decisions in the modern corporate boardroom. *See, e.g.*, Fred S. McChesney, *A Bird in the Hand and Liability in the Bush: Why* Van Gorkom *Still Rankles, Probably*, 96 N.W.U. L. REV. 631 (2002); Lynn A. Stout, *In Praise of Procedure: An Economic and Behavioral Defense of* Smith v. Van Gorkom *and the Business Judgment Rule*, 96 N.W.U. L. REV. 675 (2002).

 7. The Legislative Response to the Trans Union *Decision:* **Delaware Section 102(b)(7).** The Delaware legislature reacted swiftly and decisively to the tidal wave of criticism over the *Trans Union* decision. In 1986, the Delaware corporation statute was amended to add section 102(b)(7), which authorizes Delaware corporations to include provisions in their certificates (i.e., articles) of incorporation limiting (or even eliminating altogether) directors' personal liability in money damages for conduct constituting a breach of the duty of care, more popularly referred to as "raincoat provisions." Notably, this exculpatory provision does not extend to directors' conduct involving breach of the duty of loyalty, failure to act in good faith, intentional misconduct, intentional violations of the law, receipt of an improper personal benefit, or directors' decisions approving distributions that are illegal under section 174 of the Delaware Corporations Code. In effect, section 102(b)(7) allows existing Delaware corporations to amend their charters to include "raincoat provisions" that exculpate directors from personal liability for money damages for acts of gross negligence amounting to a breach of the duty of care. The public policy premise for this legislative response to the potential for draconian liability to be imposed on directors as a result of *Trans Union* was succinctly summarized in the following legislative history of section 102(b)(7):

> Section 102(b)(7) and the amendments to Section 145 represent a legislative response to recent changes in the market for directors' liability insurance. Such insurance has become a relatively standard condition of employment for directors. Recent changes in that market, including the unavailability of the traditional policies (and, in many cases, the unavailability of any type of policy from the traditional insurance carriers) have threatened the quality and stability of the governance of Delaware corporations because directors have become unwilling, in many instances, to serve without the protection which such insurance provides and, in other instances, may be deterred by the unavailability of insurance from making entrepreneurial decisions. The amendments are intended to allow Delaware corporations to provide substitute protection, in various forms, to their directors and to limit director liability under certain circumstances.

S. 533, 133d Gen. Assembly 2. 65 Del. Laws ch. 289, §§1-2 (1986) (quoted in Edward P. Welch & Andrew J. Turezyn, FOLK ON THE DELAWARE GENERAL CORPORATION LAW §102, at 14, n. 41 (2004)). The scope of protection offered by these exculpatory provisions has been put to the test in recent Delaware cases, most notably the *Disney* litigation involving claims that directors acted in bad faith, and therefore their conduct fell outside the ambit of Delaware §102(b)(7). *See In re The Walt Disney Derivative Litig.*, 907 A.2d 693 (Del. Ch. 2005); *see also In re Abbott Labs. Derivative Litigation*, 325 F.3d 79 (7th Cir. 2003).

8. The Disney Litigation. In the *Disney* litigation, the plaintiffs brought a shareholder derivative action challenging the controversial hiring and the equally controversial termination of Michael Ovitz as president of the Walt Disney Company. The Disney stockholders claimed that the members of the Disney board did not properly evaluate Ovitz's employment contract, either at the time of his hiring or at the time of his subsequent no-fault termination, which ultimately resulted in the payment of a severance package to Michael Ovitz that was valued at approximately $130 million after only 14 months of employment. At the conclusion of the trial on the plaintiffs' claims, the Delaware Court of Chancery ruled in favor of the Disney directors, confirming that the Disney directors did not violate their fiduciary duties or act in bad faith in connection with the hiring and firing of Michael Ovitz. *See In re Walt Disney Co. Derivative Litigation*, 825 A. 2d 275 (Del. Ch. 2003). In August 2006, a unanimous Delaware Supreme Court affirmed the Chancery Court's lengthy, 174-page opinion, upholding all of the legal and factual conclusions set forth in the Chancery Court's "well-crafted" decision. *See In re Walt Disney Co. Derivative Litigation*, 906 A. 2d 27, 35 (Del. 2006).

In affirming the Chancery Court's ruling, most commentators believe that the Delaware Supreme Court's opinion provides a ringing endorsement of the business judgment rule and the traditional protections that it affords directors and officers of Delaware corporations in their decision making. *See, e.g.*, Akin Gump Law Firm Memo (dated June 26, 2006), titled *Corporate Governance Alert: Delaware Supreme Court Affirms Disney Decision* ("The post-trial *Disney* decisions are powerful judicial endorsements of the business judgment rule . . . [proving that the] business judgment rule is alive, vigorous and working as it should to protect the business decisions of directors and officers of Delaware corporations."). Of course, the protections of the business judgment rule depend on the vigilance of the board members, who continue to be subject to the duty to be informed adequately as to the relevant facts, to discuss and consider the significance of those facts, and to document the board's deliberative process. Although the *Disney* litigation involved board actions concerning executive compensation, its lessons apply with equal vigor in the context of board decision making concerning M&A transactions. The materials in this chapter elaborate in more detail on the scope of the board's fiduciary duty obligations in connection with M&A transactions.

9. Fiduciary Duty Law: Is There a Separate Duty of Good Faith?   One of the more controversial aspects of the *Disney* litigation involves the Delaware Supreme Court's apparent recognition of a separate fiduciary duty of good faith, which the court in *Disney* also recognized is closely connected to the traditional fiduciary duties of care and loyalty that are owed by directors of Delaware corporations. In its 2006 opinion, the Delaware Supreme Court sought to provide much-needed "conceptual guidance to the corporate community" as to the scope of this duty of good faith. However, the Delaware Supreme Court declined to "reach or otherwise address the issue of whether the fiduciary duty to act in good faith is a duty that, like the duties of care and loyalty, can serve as an *independent basis* for imposing liability upon corporate directors and officers." *Disney*, 906 A. 2d 27, 67 at n. 112 (*emphasis added*). This issue proved to be most vexing to legal advisors to Delaware corporations. In fact, within five months after handing down its decision in the *Disney* litigation, this very issue presented itself to the Delaware Supreme Court in the case of *Stone v. Ritter*, 911 A. 2d 362 (Del. 2006).

Stone v. Ritter involved an appeal from the decision of the Delaware Chancery Court dismissing a shareholder derivative action in which the plaintiffs alleged that the directors of AmSouth Bancorporation had failed in good faith to implement sufficient internal controls to guard against violations of federal banking laws and regulations. In upholding the dismissal of the derivative complaint, the Delaware Supreme Court concluded that the directors "discharged their oversight responsibility to establish an information and reporting system" and further, that this "system was designed to permit the

directors to periodically monitor AmSouth's compliance" with federal banking law requirements. *Id.* at 371-72. In reaching this conclusion, the Delaware
Supreme Court held that plaintiffs' claim for oversight liability on the part
of AmSouth's directors failed to satisfy what has come to be known as "the
Caremark standard," a standard which was originally established by Chancellor Allen in his well-known opinion in *In re Caremark International Litigation,*
698 A. 2d 959 (Del. Ch. 1996). Quoting from Chancellor Allen's decision in
Caremark, the Delaware Supreme Court concluded that "the lack of good faith
that is a necessary condition to liability . . . [can be established] only [by] a
sustained or systematic failure of the board to exercise oversight—such as
an utter failure to attempt to assure a reasonable information and reporting
system exists." *Id.* at 971. The significance of the Delaware Supreme Court's
decision in *Stone v. Ritter* has been explained by experienced practitioners as
follows:

> It appears that directorial liability for lack of good faith under *Caremark* may
> be found only in rare circumstances, such as a failure to establish any reporting
> or information system or controls, or, if such a system or controls exist, a con-
> scious absence of any monitoring or oversight of the system. *Caremark,* therefore,
> dissuades acts or omissions by a board that preclude the board from obtaining
> meaningful information about risks or problems requiring its attention.
>
> The Court [in *Stone v. Ritter*] also offered guidance "critical to understand-
> ing fiduciary liability under *Caremark.*" The Court explained that oversight liabil-
> ity amounts to a breach of the duty of good faith. The failure to exercise good
> faith does not in and of itself create liability. Instead, "[t]he failure to act in good
> faith may result in liability because the requirement to act in good faith 'is a sub-
> sidiary element,' i.e., a condition 'of the fundamental duty of loyalty.'" "It follows
> that because a showing of bad faith conduct, in the sense described in *Disney* and
> *Caremark,* is essential to establish director oversight liability, the fiduciary duty
> violated by that conduct is the duty of loyalty."
>
> The Court explained that two principles can be derived from its holding.
> First, although the duty of good faith may be characterized as one of three sets
> of fiduciary duties, along with the duties of care and loyalty, "the obligation to
> act in good faith does not establish an independent fiduciary duty that stands on
> the same footing as the duties of care and loyalty." Second, the duty of loyalty is
> not limited to cases involving conflicts of interest on the part of directors; it also
> includes instances in which the fiduciary "fails to act in good faith."
>
> By addressing the concept of good faith for a second time within just a few
> months after having done so in the *Disney* decision, the Delaware Supreme Court
> has placed additional focus on an area of the law that had until recently not been
> well developed. It is potentially a significant issue, because complaints about lack
> of oversight are categorized as claims for breaches of the duties of loyalty and
> good faith, and under section 102(b)(7) of the Delaware General Corporation
> Law, charter provisions are not permitted to immunize directors from personal
> liability for breaches of the duty of loyalty or for conduct that is not in good
> faith. That might suggest that an increasing number of derivative claims will as-
> sert that directors did not adequately discharge their duties of oversight. Cutting
> against that possibility, however, is the high standard that the derivative plaintiff
> must meet to prevail. The Supreme Court quoted a passage from *Caremark,* in
> which the Court of Chancery stated that a *Caremark* claim remains "possibly the
> most difficult theory in corporation law upon which a plaintiff might hope to win
> judgment."

Phillip T. Mellet and M. Duncan Grant, SECURITIES LITIGATION UPDATE: *Delaware Supreme Court Upholds Caremark Standard for Director Oversight Liability; Clarifies Duty of Good Faith*, (Pepper Hamilton law firm memo, November 21, 2006) (copy on file with author). We will revisit the teachings of *Stone v. Ritter* later in this chapter, as part of our analysis of the more recent Delaware Supreme Court opinion in *Lyondell Chemical Co. v. Ryan*.

10. Recent Increase in Merger-Related Litigation. Without a doubt, litigation challenging M&A transactions has been on the rise in recent years. A March 2012 study reports that, with respect to shareholder litigation related to acquisitions of public companies valued at over $100 million that were announced in 2010 and 2011,

> almost every acquisition of that size elicited multiple lawsuits, which were filed shortly after the deal's announcement and often settled before the deal's closing. Only a small fraction of these lawsuits resulted in payments to shareholders; the majority settled for additional disclosures or, less frequently, changes in merger terms, such as deal protection provisions.

Robert Daines & Olga Koumrian, *Recent Developments in Shareholder Litigation Involving Mergers & Acquisitions*, March 2012 Update, Cornerstone Research (2012). While this study is sharply critical of the effects of merger-related litigation—a topic currently of enormous controversy—not all observers take such a dim view of this type of litigation. For example, another recent study reports a very different set of findings, albeit with respect to a very different set of M&A transactions. Using hand-collected data from M&A deals involving public company targets during 1999 and 2000, the authors report that

> M&A offers [by Bidders that were] subject that to shareholder lawsuits are completed at a significantly lower rate than offers not subject to litigation, after controlling [for a number of different factors]. M&A offers subject to shareholder lawsuits have significantly higher takeover premia in completed deals, after controlling for the same factors. Economically, the expected rise in takeover premia more than offsets the fall in the probability of deal completion, resulting in a positive expected gain to target shareholders. However, in general, target stock price reactions to bid announcements do not appear to fully anticipate the positive expected gain from potential litigation. We find that [during a period where M&A activity was] characterized by friendly single-bidder offers, shareholder litigation substitutes for the presence of a rival bidder by policing low-ball bids and forcing offer price improvements by the bidder.

C. N. V. Krishnan, et al., *Shareholder Litigation in Mergers and Acquisitions*, 18 J. CORP. FIN. 1248 (2012). *See also* Robert Thompson and Randall S. Thomas, *The New Look of Shareholder Litigation: Acquisition-Oriented Class Actions*, 57 VAND. L. REV. 133 (2004) (describing increase in class action litigation in Delaware, and observing that the overwhelming majority of these lawsuits arose in connection with M&A transactions).

As an example of the type of merger-related shareholder litigation that accompanies many M&A transactions, let us remember back to August 2011, when Google announced that it had agreed to buy

Motorola Mobility Holdings Inc. for $12.5 billion in cash, [representing] a 62% premium.* Motorola Inc. had just completed the spinout of its smartphone unit [in January 2011] under pressure from Carl Icahn, who called for Motorola Mobility to maximize the value of its patent portfolio . . . after seeing a group of technology companies led by Apple Inc. shell out $4.5 billion for Nortel Inc.'s patents. Google lost out to its Silicon Valley rival [Apple] in the Nortel auction and needed desperately to strengthen its own patent portfolio. The Motorola Mobility M&A deal was a classic arm's length transaction that seemed perfectly timed to maximize the target's value. Within days, however, various Motorola Mobility shareholders filed lawsuits claiming that the company's directors and senior executives had violated their fiduciary duties to shareholders by approving the transaction. Motorola Mobility is based in Libertyville, Ill., and Mountain View, Calif.-based Google is incorporated in Delaware. The target's shareholders filed at least 17 suits in the Delaware Court of Chancery, Illinois federal court and two Illinois state courts, one of which, in Cook County, will hear the matter.

David Marcus, *Here Comes the Shareholder Litigation*, THE DEAL (May 2012), *available at* http://pipeline.thedeal.com/tdd/ViewBlog.dl?id=46494. Needless to say, there seems to be no end in sight with respect to merger-related litigation, and so the controversy continues.

> ***11. The Duty of Care and the Exercise of Informed Decision Making.*** Notwithstanding the continuing controversy regarding the "over-proceduralization" of boardroom decision making, it is clear that the Delaware Supreme Court's call for the exercise of *informed decision making* by truly *independent directors* is now a staple of the advice given by any good business lawyer advising the board of directors of a company considering an acquisition. In the wake of numerous financial scandals of the early years of the twenty-first century, the meaning of "truly independent directors" and the adequacy of the procedures used to establish that the directors have exercised "informed decision making" have been called into question anew. In response to financial scandals that surfaced following the bursting of the speculative "dot.com bubble," Congress enacted the Sarbanes-Oxley Act of 2002. As was summarized in Chapter 1 (*see supra,* pp. 37-38), this important piece of federal legislation introduced far-reaching reforms addressing, in part, boardroom procedures and practices of publicly traded companies, such as the staffing of board committees and the role of the audit committee. Many of the reforms adopted in the Sarbanes-Oxley Act represent federal intervention into areas of corporate governance that had previously been the exclusive province of state law, most notably Delaware law. Congress obviously felt compelled to intervene in order to address perceived abuses that led to financial scandals on an unprecedented scale. The efficacy of these federal reform measures in restoring investor confidence in our capital markets is a story that is still unfolding, particularly in the wake of the Great Recession. Moreover, there is the further question of whether these reforms of boardroom procedures and practices will improve the overall quality of boardroom decision making.

---

* You will recall reading an excerpt from Motorola's proxy statement as part of the materials in Chapter 2, describing the scope of the appraisal remedy. *See supra*, p. 156.

12. The (Modern) Formulation of the Business Judgment Rule.   In the well-known *Caremark* decision referred to above, then-Chancellor William Allen, a leading Delaware jurist, commented on the traditional formulation of the business judgment rule, as it generally applies to board room decision making, by making the following observation:

> [C]ompliance with a director's duty of care can *never* appropriately be judicially determined by reference to the content of the board decision that leads to a *corporate loss*, apart from consideration of the good faith or rationality of the process employed. That is, whether a judge or jury considering the matter after the fact, believes a decision substantively wrong, or degrees of wrong extending through "stupid" or "egregious" or "irrational," provides *no ground* for director liability, so long as the court determines that the [decision-making] process employed was either rational or employed in a good faith effort to advance corporate interests. . . . Thus, the business judgment rule is *process oriented* and informed by a deep respect for all *good faith* board decisions.

In re *Caremark Int'l Inc., Derivative Lit.*, 698 A.2d 959, 968 (Del. Ch. 1996) (footnotes omitted) (*emphasis added*). In the ensuing years since the Delaware Supreme Court decided *Trans Union*, the Delaware courts have struggled with how to apply the deferential business judgment rule to defensive actions adopted by the board of Target in an effort to resist an unsolicited offer, as well as to board actions in situations involving the sale of the company (such as a merger). The remaining materials in this chapter explore this rather substantial body of case law, a body of case law that is in a constant state of evolution.

2.   Traditional Perspective on Management's Use of Defensive Tactics to Thwart Unsolicited Offer from Bidder

Cheff v. Mathes
199 A.2d 548 (Del. 1964)

CAREY, Justice.

This is an appeal from the decision of the Vice-Chancellor in a derivative suit holding certain directors of Holland Furnace Company liable for loss allegedly resulting from improper use of corporate funds to purchase shares of the company. Because a meaningful decision upon review turns upon a complete understanding of the factual background, a somewhat detailed summary of the evidence is required.

Holland Furnace Company, a corporation of the State of Delaware, manufactures warm air furnaces, air conditioning equipment, and other home heating equipment. At the time of the relevant transactions, the board of directors was composed of the seven individual defendants. Mr. Cheff had been Holland's Chief Executive Officer since 1933, received an annual salary of $77,400, and personally owned 6,000 shares of the company. He was also a director. Mrs. Cheff, the wife of Mr. Cheff, was a daughter of the founder of Holland and had served as a director since 1922. She personally owned 5,804 shares of Holland and owned 47.9 percent of Hazelbank United Interest, Inc. Hazelbank is an

investment vehicle for Mrs. Cheff and members of the Cheff-Landwehr family group, which owned 164,950 shares of the 883,585 outstanding shares of
Holland. As a director, Mrs. Cheff received a compensation of $200.00 for each
monthly board meeting, whether or not she attended the meeting. . . .

Prior to the events in question, Holland employed approximately 8500 persons and maintained 400 branch sales offices located in 43 states. The volume
of sales had declined from over $41,000,000 in 1948 to less than $32,000,000
in 1956. Defendants contend that the decline in earnings is attributable to
the artificial post-war demand generated in the 1946-1948 period. In order to
stabilize the condition of the company, the sales department apparently was
reorganized and certain unprofitable branch offices were closed. By 1957 this
reorganization had been completed and the management was convinced that
the changes were manifesting beneficial results. The practice of the company
was to directly employ the retail salesman, and the management considered
that practice — unique in the furnace business — to be a vital factor in the company's success.

During the first five months of 1957, the monthly trading volume of Holland's stock on the New York Stock Exchange ranged between 10,300 shares to
24,200 shares. In the last week of June 1957, however, the trading increased to
37,800 shares, with a corresponding increase in the market price. In June of
1957, Mr. Cheff met with Mr. Arnold H. Maremont, who was President of Maremont Automotive Products, Inc. and Chairman of the boards of Motor Products Corporation and Allied Paper Corporation. Mr. Cheff testified, on deposition, that Maremont generally inquired about the feasibility of merger between
Motor Products and Holland. Mr. Cheff testified that, in view of the difference
in sales practices between the two companies, he informed Mr. Maremont that
a merger did not seem feasible. In reply, Mr. Maremont stated that, in the light
of Mr. Cheff's decision, he had no further interest in Holland nor did he wish
to buy any of the stock of Holland.

None of the members of the board apparently connected the interest
of Mr. Maremont with the increased activity of Holland stock. However, Mr.
Trenkamp and Mr. Staal, the Treasurer of Holland, unsuccessfully made an
informal investigation in order to ascertain the identity of the purchaser or
purchasers. The mystery was resolved, however, when Maremont called Ames
in July of 1957 to inform the latter that Maremont then owned 55,000 shares
of Holland stock. At this juncture, no requests for change in corporate policy
were made, and Maremont made no demand to be made a member of the
board of Holland.

Ames reported the above information to the board at its July 30, 1957 meeting. Because of the position now occupied by Maremont, the board elected to
investigate the financial and business history of Maremont and corporations
controlled by him. Apart from the documentary evidence produced by this
investigation, which will be considered *infra*, Staal testified, on deposition, that
leading bank officials' had indicated that Maremont 'had been a participant,
or had attempted to be, in the liquidation of a number of companies.' Staal
specifically mentioned only one individual giving such advice, the Vice President of the First National Bank of Chicago. Mr. Cheff testified, at trial, of Maremont's alleged participation in liquidation activities. Mr. Cheff testified that:
'Throughout the whole of the Kalamazoo-Battle Creek area, and Detroit too,

where I spent considerable time, he is well known and not highly regarded by any stretch.' This information was communicated to the board.

On August 23, 1957, at the request of Maremont, a meeting was held between Mr. Maremont and Cheff. At this meeting, Cheff was informed that Motor Products then owned approximately 100,000 shares of Holland stock. Maremont then made a demand that he be named to the board of directors, but Cheff refused to consider it. Since considerable controversy has been generated by Maremont's alleged threat to liquidate the company or substantially alter the sales force of Holland, we believe it desirable to set forth the testimony of Cheff on this point: 'Now we have 8500 men, direct employees, so the problem is entirely different. He indicated immediately that he had no interest in that type of distribution, that he didn't think it was modern, that he felt furnaces could be sold as he sold mufflers, through half a dozen salesmen in a wholesale way.'

Testimony was introduced by the defendants tending to show that substantial unrest was present among the employees of Holland as a result of the threat of Maremont to seek control of Holland. Thus, Mr. Cheff testified that the field organization was considering leaving in large numbers because of a fear of the consequences of a Maremont acquisition; he further testified that approximately '25 of our key men' were lost as the result of the unrest engendered by the Maremont proposal. Staal, corroborating Cheff's version, stated that a number of branch managers approached him for reassurances that Maremont was not going to be allowed to successfully gain control. Moreover, at approximately this time, the company was furnished with a Dun and Bradstreet report, which indicated the practice of Maremont to achieve quick profits by sales or liquidations of companies acquired by him. The defendants were also supplied with an income statement of Motor Products, Inc., showing a loss of $336,121.00 for the period in 1957.

On August 30, 1957, the board was informed by Cheff of Maremont's demand to be placed upon the board and of Maremont's belief that the retail sales organization of Holland was obsolete. The board was also informed of the results of the investigation by Cheff and Staal. Predicated upon this information, the board authorized the purchase of company stock on the market with corporate funds, ostensibly for use in a stock option plan.

Subsequent to this meeting, substantial numbers of shares were purchased and, in addition, Mrs. Cheff made alternate personal purchases of Holland stock. As a result of purchases by Maremont, Holland and Mrs. Cheff, the market price rose. On September 13, 1957, Maremont wrote to each of the directors of Holland and requested a broad engineering survey to be made for the benefit of all stockholders. During September, Motor Products released its annual report, which indicated that the investment in Holland was a 'special situation' as opposed to the normal policy of placing the funds of Motor Products into 'an active company'. On September 4th, Maremont proposed to sell his current holdings of Holland to the corporation for $14.00 a share. However, because of delay in responding to this offer, Maremont withdrew the offer. At this time, Mrs. Cheff was obviously quite concerned over the prospect of a Maremont acquisition, and had stated her willingness to expend her personal resources to prevent it.

On September 30, 1957, Motor Products Corporation, by letter to Mrs. Bowles, made a buy-sell offer to Hazelbank. At the Hazelbank meeting of October 3, 1957, Mrs. Bowles presented the letter to the board. The board took no action, but referred the proposal to its finance committee. Although Mrs. Bowles and Mrs. Putnam were opposed to any acquisition of Holland stock by Hazelbank, Mr. Landwehr conceded that a majority of the board were in favor of the purchase. Despite this fact, the finance committee elected to refer the offer to the Holland board on the grounds that it was the primary concern of Holland.

Thereafter, Mr. Trenkamp arranged for a meeting with Maremont, which occurred on October 14-15, 1957, in Chicago. Prior to this meeting, Trenkamp was aware of the intentions of Hazelbank and Mrs. Cheff to purchase all or portions of the stock then owned by Motor Products if Holland did not so act. As a result of the meeting, there was a tentative agreement on the part of Motor Products to sell its 155,000 shares at $14.40 per share. On October 23, 1957, at a special meeting of the Holland board, the purchase was considered. All directors, except Spatta, were present. The dangers allegedly posed by Maremont were again reviewed by the board. Trenkamp and Mrs. Cheff agree that the latter informed the board that either she or Hazelbank would purchase part or all of the block of Holland stock owned by Motor Products if the Holland board did not so act. The board was also informed that in order for the corporation to finance the purchase, substantial sums would have to be borrowed from commercial lending institutions. A resolution authorizing the purchase of 155,000 shares from Motor Products was adopted by the board. The price paid was in excess of the market price prevailing at the time, and the book value of the stock was approximately $20.00 as compared to approximately $14.00 for the net quick asset value. The transaction was subsequently consummated. The stock option plan mentioned in the minutes has never been implemented. In 1959, Holland stock reached a high of $15.25 a share.

On February 6, 1958, plaintiffs, owners of 60 shares of Holland stock, filed a derivative suit in the court below naming all of the individual directors of Holland, Holland itself and Motor Products Corporation as defendants. The complaint alleged that all of the purchases of stock by Holland in 1957 were for the purpose of insuring the perpetuation of control by the incumbent directors. The complaint requested that the transaction between Motor Products and Holland be rescinded and, secondly, that the individual defendants account to Holland for the alleged damages. Since Motor Products was never served with process, the initial remedy became inapplicable. Ames was never served nor did he enter an appearance.

After trial, the Vice Chancellor found the following facts: (a) Holland directly sells to retail consumers by means of numerous branch offices. There were no intermediate dealers. (b) Immediately prior to the complained-of transactions, the sales and earnings of Holland had declined and its marketing practices were under investigation by the Federal Trade Commission. (c) Mr. Cheff and Trenkamp had received substantial sums as Chief Executive and attorney of the company, respectively. (d) Maremont, on August 23rd, 1957, demanded a place on the board. (e) At the October 14th meeting between Trenkamp, Staal and Maremont, Trenkamp and Staal were authorized to speak for Hazelbank and Mrs. Cheff as well as Holland. Only Mr. Cheff, Mrs. Cheff, Mr. Landwehr, and Mr. Trenkamp clearly understood, prior to the October 23rd meeting, that either Hazelbank or Mrs. Cheff would have utilized their funds to purchase the Holland stock if Holland had not acted. (g) There was no real threat posed by

Maremont and no substantial evidence of intention by Maremont to liquidate Holland. (h) Any employee unrest could have been caused by factors other than Maremont's intrusion and 'only one important employee was shown to have left, and his motive for leaving is not clear.' (i) The Court rejected the stock option plan as a meaningful rationale for the purchase from Maremont or the prior open market purchases.

The Court then found that the actual purpose behind the purchase was the desire to perpetuate control, but because of its finding that only the four above-named directors knew of the 'alternative', the remaining directors were exonerated. No appeal was taken by plaintiffs from that decision. . . .

Under the provisions of 8 Del. C. §160, a corporation is granted statutory power to purchase and sell shares of its own stock. *See Kors v. Carey*, Del. Ch. 158 A.2d 136. Such a right, as embodied in the statute, has long been recognized in this State. The charge here is not one of violation of statute, but the allegation is that the true motives behind such purchases were improperly centered upon perpetuation of control. In an analogous field, courts have sustained the use of proxy funds to inform stockholders of management's views upon the policy questions inherent in an election to a board of directors, but have not sanctioned the use of corporate funds to advance the selfish desires of directors to perpetuate themselves in office. Similarly, if the actions of the board were motivated by a sincere belief that the buying out of the dissident stockholder was necessary to maintain what the board believed to be proper business practices, the board will not be held liable for such decision, even though hindsight indicates the decision was not the wisest course. On the other hand, if the board has acted solely or primarily because of the desire to perpetuate themselves in office, the use of corporate funds for such purposes is improper.

Our first problem is the allocation of the burden of proof to show the presence or lack of good faith on the part of the board in authorizing the purchase of shares. Initially, the decision of the board of directors in authorizing a purchase was presumed to be in good faith and could be overturned only by a conclusive showing by plaintiffs of fraud or other misconduct. *See Bankers Securities Corp. v. Kresge Department Stores, Inc.*, 54 F. Supp. 378 (D. Del. 1944). In *Kors*, cited supra, the court merely indicated that the directors are presumed to act in good faith and the burden of proof to show to the contrary falls upon the plaintiff. However, in *Bennett v. Propp*, [187 A.2d 405, 409 (1926)], we stated:

> "We must bear in mind the inherent danger in the purchase of shares with corporate funds to remove a threat to corporate policy when a threat to control is involved. The directors are of necessity confronted with a conflict of interest, and an objective decision is difficult. . . . Hence, in our opinion, the burden should be on the directors to justify such a purchase as one primarily in the corporate interest." . . .

To say that the burden of proof is upon the defendants is not to indicate, however, that the directors have the same 'self-dealing interest' as is present, for example, when a director sells property to the corporation. The only clear pecuniary interest shown on the record was held by Mr. Cheff, as an executive of the corporation, and Trenkamp, as its attorney. The mere fact that some of the other directors were substantial shareholders does not create a personal pecuniary interest in the decisions made by the board of directors, since all shareholders would presumably share the benefit flowing to the substantial shareholder. Accordingly, these directors other than Trenkamp and Cheff, while called upon to justify their actions, will not be held to the same standard of proof required of those directors having personal and pecuniary interest in the transaction.

As noted above, the Vice Chancellor found that the stock option plan, mentioned in the minutes as a justification for the purchases, was not a motivating reason for the purchases. This finding we accept, since there is evidence to support it; in fact, Trenkamp admitted that the stock option plan was not the motivating reason. The minutes of October 23, 1957 dealing with the purchase from Maremont do not, in fact, mention the option plan as a reason for the purchase. While the minutes of the October 1, 1957 meeting only indicated the stock option plan as the motivating reason, the defendants are not bound by such statements and may supplement the minutes by oral testimony to show that the motivating reason was genuine fear of an acquisition by Maremont.

Plaintiffs urge that the sale price was unfair in view of the fact that the price was in excess of that prevailing on the open market. However, as conceded by all parties, a substantial block of stock will normally sell at a higher price than that prevailing on the open market, the increment being attributable to a 'control premium'. Plaintiffs argue that it is inappropriate to require the defendant corporation to pay a control premium, since control is meaningless to an acquisition by a corporation of its own shares. However, it is elementary that a holder of a substantial number of shares would expect to receive the control premium as part of his selling price, and if the corporation desired to obtain the stock, it is unreasonable to expect that the corporation could avoid paying what any other purchaser would be required to pay for the stock. In any event, the financial expert produced by defendant at trial indicated that the price paid was fair and there was no rebuttal. Ames, the financial man on the board, and was strongly of the opinion that the purchase was a good deal for the corporation. The Vice Chancellor made no finding as to the fairness of the price other than to indicate the obvious fact that the market price was increasing as a result of open market purchases by Maremont, Mrs. Cheff and Holland.

The question then presented is whether or not defendants satisfied the burden of proof of showing reasonable grounds to believe a danger to corporate policy and effectiveness existed by the presence of the Maremont stock ownership. It is important to remember that the directors satisfy their burden by showing good faith and reasonable investigation; the directors will not be penalized for an honest mistake of judgment, if the judgment appeared reasonable at the time the decision was made.

In holding that employee unrest could as well be attributed to a condition of Holland's business affairs as to the possibility of Maremont's intrusions, the Vice Chancellor must have had in mind one or both of two matters: (1) the pending proceedings before the Federal Trade Commission concerning certain sales practices of Holland; (2) the decrease in sales and profits during the preceding several years. Any other possible reason would be pure speculation. In the first place, the adverse decision of the F.T.C. was not announced until *after* the complained-of transaction. Secondly, the evidence clearly shows that the downward trend of sales and profits had reversed itself, presumably because of the reorganization which had then been completed. Thirdly, everyone who testified on the point said that the unrest was due to the possible threat presented by Maremont's purchases of stock. There was, in fact, no *testimony* whatever of any connection between the unrest and either the F.T.C. proceedings or the business picture.

The Vice Chancellor found that there was no substantial evidence of a liquidation posed by Maremont. This holding overlooks an important contention. The fear of the defendants, according to their testimony, was not limited to the possibility of liquidation; it included the alternate possibility of a material change in Holland's sales policies, which the board considered vital to its future success. The *unrebutted* testimony before the court indicated: (1) Maremont had deceived Cheff as to his original intentions, since his open market purchases were contemporaneous with his disclaimer of interest in Holland; (2) Maremont had given Cheff some reason to believe that he intended to eliminate the retail sales force of Holland; (3) Maremont demanded a place on the board; (4) Maremont substantially increased his purchases after having been refused a place on the board; (5) the directors had good reason to believe that unrest among key employees had been engendered by the Maremont threat; (6) the board had received advice from Dun and Bradstreet indicating the past liquidation or quick sale activities of Motor Products; (7) the board had received professional advice from the firm of Merrill Lynch, Fenner & Beane, who recommended that the purchase from Motor Products be carried out; (8) the board had received competent advice that the corporation was over-capitalized; (9) Staal and Cheff had made informal personal investigations from contacts in the business and financial community and had reported to the board of the alleged poor reputation of Maremont. The board was within its rights in relying upon that investigation, since 8 Del. C. §141 (f) allows the directors to reasonably rely upon a report provided by corporate officers.

Accordingly, we are of the opinion that the evidence presented in the court below leads inevitably to the conclusion that the board of directors, based upon direct investigation, receipt of professional advice, and personal observations of the contradictory action of Maremont and his explanation of corporate purpose, believed, with justification, that there was a reasonable threat to the continued existence of Holland, or at least existence in its present form, by the plan of Maremont to continue building up his stock holdings. We find no evidence in the record sufficient to justify a contrary conclusion. The opinion of the Vice Chancellor that employee unrest may have been engendered by other factors or that the board had no grounds to suspect Maremont is not supported in any manner by the evidence.

As noted above, the Vice Chancellor found that the purpose of the acquisition was the improper desire to maintain control, but, at the same time, he exonerated those individual directors whom he believed to be unaware of the possibility of using non-corporate funds to accomplish this purpose. Such a decision is inconsistent with his finding that the motive was improper, within the rule enunciated in Bennett. If the actions were in fact improper because of a desire to maintain control, then the presence or absence of a non-corporate alternative is irrelevant, as corporate funds may not be used to advance an improper purpose even if there is no non-corporate alternative available. Conversely, if the actions were proper because of a decision by the board made in good faith that the corporate interest was served thereby, they are not rendered improper by the fact that some individual directors were willing to advance personal funds if the corporation did not. It is conceivable that the Vice Chancellor considered this feature of the case to be of significance because of his apparent belief that any excess corporate funds should have been used to finance a subsidiary corporation. That action would not have solved the problem of Holland's over-capitalization. In any event, this question was a matter of business judgment, which furnishes no justification for holding the directors personally responsible in this case.

Accordingly, the judgment of the court below is reversed and remanded with instruction to enter judgment for the defendants.

QUESTIONS

1. What is the standard of review that the Delaware Supreme Court used to evaluate the validity of the board's decision in the principal case?

2. In what sense do the facts of the principal case give rise to a conflict of interest?

3. What is the legal relevance of Mrs. Cheff's expressed willingness to spend her own personal funds to buy out Maremont's stock in Holland Furnace?

NOTES

1. Business Judgment Rule.   The traditional approach to the use of defensive tactics is reflected in the early Delaware decision, *Cheff v. Mathes.* To put this decision in historical context, when the dispute in *Cheff* arose, hostile takeovers as we know them now were then in their infancy. When confronted with the hostilities presented by the facts of *Cheff,* the law of fiduciary duty likewise was in its infancy. At that time, the courts framed management's fiduciary obligations in a two-fold manner, embracing both duty of care and a duty of loyalty. For the first half of the twentieth century, the scope of the directors' duty of care was defined under the rather deferential standard of the business judgment rule. But with the advent of the 1960s and an unprecedented wave of M&A activity in the capital markets, commentators began to question the efficacy of this traditional framework for analyzing the board's obligations in the face of both the friendly, negotiated acquisition and the more dramatic situation presented by the development of the hostile takeover, which came into prominence in the deal decade of the 1980s. The Delaware courts were not immune to the pressures created by the increasing use of hostile tender offers.

The remainder of this chapter sketches out the evolution of fiduciary duty law as developed under the jurisprudence of the Delaware courts, the mother lode of case law on this topic. For corporate lawyers, the court of greatest importance is the Delaware Supreme Court, regardless of the state where the lawyer is licensed to practice or the state where the acquisition is to be consummated. Delaware's prominence in this area is quite understandable. It is widely understood that Delaware courts are home to more disputes involving M&A

transactions than any other jurisdiction. As such, Delaware case law usually is consulted by lawyers and courts in other states, at least to frame the starting point in analyzing the fiduciary obligations of management in an acquisition transaction. Occasionally, litigation involving M&A activity will arise in jurisdictions other than Delaware, but often these other jurisdictions will refer to the law of Delaware to frame the analysis even if, in the end, the courts of another state decide to adopt an approach that varies from Delaware law. *See, e.g., First Union Corp. v. SunTrust Bank, Inc.*, 2001 WL 1885686 (N.C. Bus. Ct. August 10, 2001); *Hilton Hotels Corp. v. ITT Corp.*, 978 F. Supp. 1342 (D. Nev. 1997).

2. Migration of Fiduciary Duty Litigation from Delaware Courts to Other Jurisdictions.   Historically, Delaware courts were widely regarded as the principal source of litigation concerning the proper scope of the directors' fiduciary duty obligations in connection with a proposed M&A transaction. However, in recent years, the Delaware courts have seen a migration of such cases to courts of other jurisdictions. This migration of cases has led some to worry about the continued robustness of Delaware caselaw. Under the internal affairs doctrine, these other courts will often be required to interpret and apply Delaware law to the facts of the pending dispute. Will this migration result in a dilution of the efficacy and coherence of Delaware jurisprudence?

> Delaware's expert courts are seen as an integral part of the state's success in attracting incorporation by public companies. However, the benefit that Delaware companies derive from this expertise depends on whether corporate lawsuits against Delaware companies are brought before the Delaware courts. We report evidence that these suits are increasingly brought outside Delaware. . . . We find . . . [an] increase in litigation rates for all companies in large M&A transactions and for Delaware companies in LBO transactions. We also see trends toward (1) suits being filed outside Delaware in both large M&A and LBO transactions and in cases generating opinions; and (2) suits being filed both in Delaware and elsewhere in large M&A transactions. Overall, Delaware courts are losing market share in lawsuits, and Delaware companies are gaining lawsuits, often filed elsewhere. . . . Our evidence suggests that serious as well as nuisance cases are leaving Delaware. The trends we report potentially present a challenge to Delaware's competitiveness in the market for incorporations.

John Armour, et al., *Is Delaware Losing Its Cases?* 9 JOURNAL OF EMPIRICAL LEGAL STUDIES 605 (2012). In other papers, these same authors have offered an explanation for this recent migration of cases out of Delaware. *See* John Armour et al., *Delaware's Balancing Act*, 87 IND. L.J. 1345 (2010); and Brian Cheffins, et al., *Delaware Corporate Litigation and the Fragmentation of the Plaintiff's Bar*, 2012 COLUM. BUS. L. REV. 427 (2012).

3. Conflicts of Interest.   As was mentioned in the *Cheff* case, the courts (including those in Delaware) have consistently taken a very different approach to deciding cases involving a conflict of interest. These cases implicate the fiduciary duty of loyalty, which has always been scrupulously enforced by the courts. At early common law, cases involving self-dealing transactions (between management and his/her/its corporation, whether in an acquisition context or not) were held to be voidable at the option of the corporation. By the mid-twentieth century, however, the courts were willing to enforce the terms of a self-dealing transaction, so long as the terms of the transaction were fair to the corporation. Today, this standard of fairness is enshrined legislatively in statutes such as Delaware §144. *See Marciano v. Nakash*, 535 A.2d 400 (Del. 1987); *see also* Calif. Corp. Code §310. In the acquisition context, transactions involving a conflict of interest are not automatically voidable. Rather, the modern view is to enforce the terms of the transaction, so long as they meet a more exacting standard of judicial scrutiny known as the entire fairness test. After the landmark decision of *Weinberger v. UOP, Inc.,* we know that this test involves a probing judicial scrutiny of both substantive fairness ("fair price") and procedural fairness ("fair dealing"). *See* Chapter 2, *supra,* at p. 166. We will explore the scope of obligations required to fulfill this duty of loyalty as part of the materials later in this chapter.

3.   The Fiduciary Duty of Candor

Without a doubt, the reforms introduced by the Sarbanes-Oxley Act of 2002 continue a trend set in motion by the Delaware Supreme Court in its opinion in *Van Gorkom.* Over the course of the last 25 years, at both the state and federal level, there has been an increased emphasis on transparency of information about publicly traded companies and their business and financial affairs. Thus, even when the decision is made by a truly independent board—not involving any conflict of interest and otherwise acting in good faith—the board may still be faulted for a failure to fulfill what has come to be known as the fiduciary "duty of candor."

By way of general background, our analysis of the problem sets in Chapter 2 reflect that modern state corporation statutes require that shareholders be provided with notice of shareholders' meetings; but beyond this "cursory notice" requirement, these state "statutes do not specify the information that public shareholders are to receive when management solicits their proxies" in connection with voting on a proposed acquisition. Alan A. Palmiter, CORPORATIONS: EXAMPLES AND EXPLANATIONS at pg. 204 (6th Ed. 2009). In addition, as part of our study in Chapter 4 of the various provisions of the federal securities laws that are routinely implicated in planning an M&A transaction, we saw that the SEC's proxy rules obligate management to distribute to the shareholders of a publicly traded company a proxy statement that provides full and adequate disclosure of all "material" facts necessary for the shareholders to make an informed decision with respect to an M&A transaction that requires shareholder approval as a matter of state law. In addition to these disclosure obligations required as a matter of federal law, many state courts (most notably the Delaware courts) have promulgated a body of caselaw that imposes on management what has come to be known as a "duty of candor" (or a "duty of disclosure") that is part of the fiduciary duty obligations of officers and directors. The scope and evolution of this duty of disclosure has been described as follows:

> [In the] seminal Delaware case, *Lynch v. Vickers Energy Corp.*, 383 A.2d 278 (Del. 1977), [the Delaware Supreme Court] imposed on management a "complete candor" duty that explicitly borrows the framework of the federal proxy

fraud action [under SEC Rule 14a-9]. Liability is premised on false or misleading information that "a reasonable shareholder would consider important in deciding whether to [vote]." As is true of federal proxy fraud litigation, challenging shareholders need not show [that] the alleged misinformation would have changed the outcome of the shareholder vote; it is enough that the challenged disclosure was material.

In Delaware, shareholders have used the "complete candor" duty (which subsequent courts have labeled a "duty of disclosure") to successfully challenge mergers, reorganizations, and charter amendments. For many shareholder-plaintiffs, Delaware has become preferable to federal court . . . [because, among other reasons,] attorney fees in Delaware are often computed on the basis of class action results, not the less generous federal "lodestar" method. . . .

In an expansion of the duty of disclosure, the Delaware Supreme Court [subsequently] extended the duty of disclosure to include *all* communications to shareholders, not just those seeking shareholder action. *Malone v. Brincat*, 722 A.2d 5 (Del. 1998) [*emphasis added*]. The case, brought as a class action, involved allegation of an ongoing financial fraud made in SEC filings. The court held that directors who knowingly disseminate false information that results in corporate or shareholder harm violate their fiduciary duty and should be held accountable. But given the existence of federal securities fraud liability, the court refused to adopt a "fraud on the market" theory—thus making individual shareholder reliance an element of the action. As a result, *Malone* has not been heavily used.

Alan R. Palmiter, CORPORATIONS: EXAMPLES AND EXPLANATIONS, 204-205 (6th Ed. 2009).

B. *The Application of the Williams Act to Defensive Tactics Implemented by a Target*

Schreiber v. Burlington Northern, Inc.
472 U.S. 1, 105 S. Ct. 2458 (1985)

Chief Justice BURGER delivered the opinion of the Court.

We granted certiorari to resolve a conflict in the Circuits over whether misrepresentation or nondisclosure is a necessary element of a violation of §14(e) of the Securities Exchange Act of 1934, 15 U.S.C. §78n(e).

I

On December 21, 1982, Burlington Northern, Inc., made a hostile tender offer for El Paso Gas Co. Through a wholly owned subsidiary, Burlington proposed to purchase 25.1 million El Paso shares at $24 per share. Burlington reserved the right to terminate the offer if any of several specified events occurred. El Paso management initially opposed the takeover, but its shareholders responded favorably, fully subscribing the offer by the December 30, 1982, deadline.

Burlington did not accept those tendered shares; instead, after negotiations with El Paso management, Burlington announced on January 10, 1983, the terms of a new and friendly takeover agreement. Pursuant to the new agreement, Burlington undertook, *inter alia,* to (1) rescind the December tender offer, (2) purchase 4,166,667 shares from El Paso at $24 per share, (3) substitute a new tender offer for only 21 million shares at $24 per share, (4) provide procedural protections against a squeeze-out merger[1] of the remaining El Paso shareholders, and (5) recognize "golden parachute" contracts between El Paso and four of its senior officers. By February 8, more than 40 million shares were tendered in response to Burlington's January offer, and the takeover was completed.

The rescission of the first tender offer caused a diminished payment to those shareholders who had tendered during the first offer. The January offer was greatly oversubscribed and consequently those shareholders who retendered were subject to substantial proration. Petitioner Barbara Schreiber filed suit on behalf of herself and similarly situated shareholders, alleging that Burlington, El Paso, and members of El Paso's board of directors violated §14(e)'s prohibition of "fraudulent, deceptive, or manipulative acts or practices . . . in connection with any tender offer." 15 U.S.C. §78n(e). She claimed that Burlington's withdrawal of the December tender offer coupled with the substitution of the January tender offer was a "manipulative" distortion of the market for El Paso stock. Schreiber also alleged that Burlington violated §14(e) by failing in the January offer to disclose the "golden parachutes" offered to four of El Paso's managers. She claims that this January nondisclosure was a deceptive act forbidden by §14(e). . . .

II

A

We are asked in this case to interpret §14(e) of the Securities Exchange Act. The starting point is the language of the statute. Section 14(e) provides:

> "It shall be unlawful for any person to make any untrue statement of a material fact or omit to state any material fact necessary in order to make the statements made, in the light of the circumstances under which they are made, not misleading, or to engage in any fraudulent, deceptive, or manipulative acts or practices, in connection with any tender offer or request or invitation for tenders, or any

---

1. A "squeeze-out" merger occurs when Corporation A, which holds a controlling interest in Corporation B, uses its control to merge B into itself or into a wholly owned subsidiary. The minority shareholders in Corporation B are, in effect, forced to sell their stock. The procedural protection provided in the agreement between El Paso and Burlington required the approval of non-Burlington members of El Paso's board of directors before a squeeze-out merger could proceed. Burlington eventually purchased all the remaining shares of El Paso for $12 cash and one-quarter share of Burlington preferred stock per share. The parties dispute whether this consideration was equal to that paid to those tendering during the January tender offer.

solicitation of security holders in opposition to or in favor of any such offer, request, or invitation. The Commission shall, for the purposes of this subsection, by rules and regulations define, and prescribe means reasonably designed to prevent, such acts and practices as are fraudulent, deceptive, or manipulative."

Petitioner relies on a construction of the phrase, "fraudulent, deceptive, or manipulative acts or practices." Petitioner reads the phrase "fraudulent, deceptive, or manipulative acts or practices" to include acts which, although fully disclosed, "artificially" affect the price of the takeover target's stock. Petitioner's interpretation relies on the belief that §14(e) is directed at purposes broader than providing full and true information to investors.

Petitioner's reading of the term "manipulative" conflicts with the normal meaning of the term. We have held in the context of an alleged violation of §10(b) of the Securities Exchange Act:

> "Use of the word 'manipulative' is especially significant. It is and was virtually a term of art when used in connection with the securities markets. It connotes intentional or willful conduct *designed to deceive or defraud* investors by controlling or artificially affecting the price of securities." *Ernst & Ernst v. Hochfelder*, 425 U.S. 185, 199, 96 S. Ct. 1375, 1384, 47 L. Ed.2d 668 (1976) (*emphasis added*). . . .

She argues, however, that the term "manipulative" takes on a meaning in §14(e) that is different from the meaning it has in §10(b). Petitioner claims that the use of the disjunctive "or" in §14(e) implies that acts need not be deceptive or fraudulent to be manipulative. But Congress used the phrase "manipulative or deceptive" in §10(b) as well, and we have interpreted "manipulative" in that context to require misrepresentation.[6] Moreover, it is a " 'familiar principle of statutory construction that words grouped in a list should be given related meaning.' " *Securities Industry Assn. v. Board of Governors, FRS*, 468 U.S. 207, 218, 104 S. Ct. 3003, 3010, 82 L. Ed. 2d 158 (1984). All three species of misconduct, *i.e.*, "fraudulent, deceptive, or manipulative," listed by Congress are directed at failures to disclose. The use of the term "manipulative" provides emphasis and guidance to those who must determine which types of acts are reached by the statute; it does not suggest a deviation from the section's facial and primary concern with disclosure or congressional concern with disclosure which is the core of the Act.

B

Our conclusion that "manipulative" acts under §14(e) require misrepresentation or nondisclosure is buttressed by the purpose and legislative history of the provision. Section 14(e) was originally added to the Securities Exchange

---

6. *Santa Fe Industries, Inc. v. Green*, 430 U.S. 462, 476-477, 97 S. Ct. 1292, 1302-1303, 51 L. Ed.2d 480 (1977); *Piper v. Chris-Craft Industries, Inc.*, 430 U.S. 1, 43, 97 S. Ct. 926, 950, 51 L. Ed.2d 124 (1977); *Ernst & Ernst v. Hochfelder*, 425 U.S. 185, 199, 96 S. Ct. 1375, 1383, 47 L. Ed.2d 668 (1976).

Act as part of the Williams Act, 82 Stat. 457. "The purpose of the Williams Act is to insure that public shareholders who are confronted by a cash tender offer for their stock will not be required to respond without adequate information." *Rondeau v. Mosinee Paper Corp.*, 422 U.S. 49, 58, 95 S. Ct. 2069, 2075, 45 L. Ed. 2d 12 (1975).

It is clear that Congress relied primarily on disclosure to implement the purpose of the Williams Act. . . .

The expressed legislative intent was to preserve a neutral setting in which the contenders could fully present their arguments. The Senate sponsor went on to say:

> "We have taken extreme care to avoid tipping the scales either in favor of management or in favor of the person making the takeover bids. S. 510 is designed solely to require full and fair disclosure for the benefit of investors. The bill will at the same time provide the offeror and management equal opportunity to present their case." *Ibid.* . . .

While legislative history specifically concerning §14(e) is sparse, the House and Senate Reports discuss the role of §14(e). Describing §14(e) as regulating "fraudulent transactions," and stating the thrust of the section:

> "This provision would affirm the fact that persons engaged in making or opposing tender offers or otherwise seeking to influence the decision of investors or the outcome of the tender offer are under an obligation to make *full disclosure* of material information to those with whom they deal." H.R. Rep. No. 1711, 90th Cong., 2d Sess., 11 (1968), U.S. Code Cong. & Admin. News 1968, pp. 2811, 2821 (*emphasis added*); S. Rep. No. 550, 90th Cong., 1st Sess., 11 (1967) (*emphasis added*).

Nowhere in the legislative history is there the slightest suggestion that §14(e) serves any purpose other than disclosure,[11] or that the term "manipulative" should be read as an invitation to the courts to oversee the substantive fairness of tender offers; the quality of any offer is a matter for the marketplace.

To adopt the reading of the term "manipulative" urged by petitioner would not only be unwarranted in light of the legislative purpose but would be at odds with it. Inviting judges to read the term "manipulative" with their own sense of what constitutes "unfair" or "artificial" conduct would inject uncertainty into the tender offer process. An essential piece of information—whether the court

---

11. The Act was amended in 1970, and Congress added to §14(e) the sentence, "The Commission shall, for the purposes of this subsection, by rules and regulations define, and prescribe means reasonably designed to prevent, such acts and practices as are fraudulent, deceptive, or manipulative." Petitioner argues that this phrase would be pointless if §14(e) was concerned with disclosure only.

We disagree. In adding the 1970 amendment, Congress simply provided a mechanism for defining and guarding against those acts and practices which involve material misrepresentation or nondisclosure. The amendment gives the Securities and Exchange Commission latitude to regulate nondeceptive activities as a "reasonably designed" means of preventing manipulative acts, without suggesting any change in the meaning of the term "manipulative" itself.

would deem the fully disclosed actions of one side or the other to be "manipulative"—would not be available until after the tender offer had closed. This
uncertainty would directly contradict the expressed congressional desire to
give investors full information.

Congress' consistent emphasis on disclosure persuades us that it intended
takeover contests to be addressed to shareholders. In pursuit of this goal, Congress, consistent with the core mechanism of the Securities Exchange Act, created sweeping disclosure requirements and narrow substantive safeguards. The
same Congress that placed such emphasis on shareholder choice would not at
the same time have required judges to oversee tender offers for substantive fairness. It is even less likely that a Congress implementing that intention would
express it only through the use of a single word placed in the middle of a provision otherwise devoted to disclosure.

C

We hold that the term "manipulative" as used in §14(e) requires misrepresentation or nondisclosure. It connotes "conduct designed to deceive or defraud
investors by controlling or artificially affecting the price of securities." *Ernst &
Ernst v. Hochfelder*, 425 U.S., at 199, 96 S. Ct., at 1384. Without misrepresentation or nondisclosure, §14(e) has not been violated.

Applying that definition to this case, we hold that the actions of respondents were not manipulative. The amended complaint fails to allege that the
cancellation of the first tender offer was accompanied by any misrepresentation, nondisclosure, or deception. The District Court correctly found: "All activity of the defendants that could have conceivably affected the price of El Paso
shares was done openly." 568 F. Supp., at 203.

Petitioner also alleges that El Paso management and Burlington entered into
certain undisclosed and deceptive agreements during the making of the second
tender offer. The substance of the allegations is that, in return for certain undisclosed benefits, El Paso managers agreed to support the second tender offer.
But both courts noted that petitioner's complaint seeks only redress for injuries
related to the cancellation of the first tender offer. Since the deceptive and misleading acts alleged by petitioner all occurred with reference to the making of
the second tender offer—when the injuries suffered by petitioner had already
been sustained—these acts bear no possible causal relationship to petitioner's
alleged injuries. The Court of Appeals dealt correctly with this claim.

III

The judgment of the Court of Appeals is *Affirmed*.

NOTE

Although the *Schreiber* decision represents yet another example of the
Supreme Court's unwillingness to invade areas of the law traditionally committed

to the states, that attitude may be changing. By virtue of the well-established choice of law principle known as the internal affairs doctrine, the High Court has adopted a hands-off approach (of the type reflected in *Schreiber)* in a number of other cases, most notably *Santa Fe Indus., Inc. v. Green,* 430 U.S. 462 (1977) (In reversing the court of appeals, the Supreme Court held that a claim for breach of fiduciary duty arising out of a controlling shareholder's decision to cash out the minority shares of a subsidiary in a Delaware short-form merger could not form the basis for a Rule 10b-5 cause of action in the absence of any deception, misrepresentation, or nondisclosure of material facts, emphasizing that the fundamental purpose of the 1934 Act is to implement a "'philosophy of full disclosure'; once full disclosure has occurred, the fairness of the terms of the transaction is at most a tangential concern of the [1934 Act]."). As you remember from the materials in Chapter 1, Congress adopted the Sarbanes-Oxley Act in July 2002, enacting a set of reforms that represent a rather substantial intrusion into matters of corporate governance historically relegated to state law. As part of the inevitable process of interpreting and implementing these reforms, the federal courts will necessarily get involved in resolving disputes over the provisions of SOX (such as the SOX-mandated requirements regarding audit committee independence, adequacy of internal financial controls and board monitoring thereof, and officer certification of quarterly SEC filings, among other things). Although the terms of SOX do not prescribe standards for directors' fiduciary obligations, there is growing commentary as to the impact of these reforms on the future development of fiduciary duty law. Will this continue to be an area committed exclusively (or primarily) to state law? What impact will SOX have on the balance between federal and state law in determining the scope of the board's fiduciary obligations to the company and its shareholders? This story continues to unfold, even as of this writing.

Following the Supreme Court's decision in *Schreiber,* increased importance came to rest on the fiduciary duty obligations of incumbent management (i.e., the directors and senior executive officers) of the company who is the target of an unsolicited takeover bid. As noted above, historically, fiduciary duty obligations have been primarily a matter of state law. The next three sections of this chapter set forth the paradigm cases under Delaware law describing the duties and responsibilities of Target's management in the context of a hostile takeover.

C.   *The Dawn of a New Era of Enhanced Scrutiny*

Early judicial reliance on the business judgment rule to evaluate Target Co. management's response to an unsolicited tender offer from Bidder Co. was criticized by many commentators for overlooking a fundamental tenet of this method for acquiring Target Co. — that Target Co. is *not* a party to the transaction. The question then becomes: Where does the board get the authority to intervene in a transaction that Target is *not* a party to, particularly in those situations where Target's board takes steps to thwart Bidder's efforts to buy Target shares directly from the company's shareholders? That is the central inquiry in the next case, which forms the foundation for the next twenty-five years of Delaware jurisprudence on fiduciary duty law in the M&A context.

In order to fully appreciate the teachings of the Delaware courts in its landmark decisions handed down in the 1980s, it is important to place these cases in some historical context. The 1970s ushered in the first of what came to be known as "hostile takeovers." Prior to the 1970s, most investment banking firms had shunned participating in hostile deals as a matter of generally accepted business practice. However, in the 1970s, hostile deals became a respectable business strategy and thus became part of the culture of "doing business" in corporate America. Indeed, hostile deals became an established part of the business landscape once the well-respected blue-chip firm Morgan Stanley abandoned its earlier refusal to participate in hostile deals and decided to act as financial advisor to a "raider" seeking to acquire control of a target company through a hostile bid.

As the hostile bid came to be an accepted practice on Wall Street in the 1980s, this new frontier broadened its horizons with Michael Milken's "discovery" of the junk bond. The willingness of Milken and his firm, Drexel Burnham, to provide financing to non-strategic buyers (such as T. Boone Pickens) led to enormous financing capacity for would-be bidders who came to be known as "corporate raiders." "Junk bonds" are debt instruments that are below investment grade as determined by one of the rating services (such as Moody's or Standard & Poor's), if they are rated at all. Junk bonds (or "high-yield" bonds as they often (less pejoratively) referred to in today's M&A market) are bonds with a very low credit rating, reflecting the higher yield (i.e., interest rate) because of the significantly higher risk of default associated with junk bonds as compared to investment-grade debt (i.e., debt securities that have received a higher quality rating from Moody's or Standard & Poor's).

In the 1980s, Drexel ushered in a new era of takeover activity by financing takeover deals that came to be known as "boot-strap, bust-up, two-tiered" tender offers. The raider's offer generally would be financed by nothing more than a "highly confident" commitment letter from Drexel; that is to say, the raider would obtain a commitment letter from Drexel in which Drexel would indicate that it was "highly confident" that it could raise the necessary financing on behalf of the raider so that the bidder would have the necessary funding to complete the stock purchase at the time of closing. During the go-go years of the 1980s, junk bonds were sold by Drexel to raise very large amounts of capital—often billions of dollars for takeover bids by raiders. In these highly leveraged situations, it was anticipated that the cash flow generated by the target's business would provide the source of funds to service the debt, often coupled with the sale of target's assets in a "busting up" of Target's business.

Raiders often used the disclosure requirements of §13(d) of the Williams Act to their advantage to seek greenmail payments from the putative target. Raiders would make "toehold" purchases (i.e., accumulating just under 5 percent of Target stock) and threaten to put the company "in play" in order to obtain "greenmail payments" from Target Co. (i.e., the raider gets paid to go away when the company buys back all of the shares of Target that the raider owns). Alternatively, the raider may cross the 5 percent mark and make the required filing under §13(d), thereby putting the company "in play" with the arbitrageurs, who accumulate stock of Target betting that the company will be taken over. The raider then makes money on the spread between the price paid to acquire Target's shares and the premium that will be received when Target gets acquired.

The surge in hostile takeover activity in the 1980s led to the development of takeover defenses, the earliest form of which was litigation, typically brought by Target management and often claiming that the raider was in violation of some aspect of the requirements of the Williams Act (and/or the SEC's rules promulgated thereunder). By bringing this litigation, management of Target bought itself time to mount a further defense in an effort to thwart the raider's takeover bid and thus allow Target to remain independent. This led to a variety of structural defenses, such as providing for staggered terms for the board of directors, eliminating the shareholders' ability to remove directors without cause, and eliminating the shareholders' ability to take action by written consent. Most of these structural defenses required amendments to the company's articles of incorporation, thereby triggering the need to obtain shareholder approval, which was usually forthcoming. However, these structural defenses required advance planning because of the need to obtain shareholder approval, and thus they took time to implement. *Query*: How does the use of staggered boards coupled with a charter provision that permits directors to be removed only for cause work as an antitakeover device?

In the case of an unsolicited offer that takes Target management by surprise, the only real defense that is available in most cases is the negotiated "friendly" deal with a white-knight suitor, or alternatively, the defensive corporate restructuring unilaterally undertaken by Target's management. Thus, in the early years, hostile takeover bids were frequently resisted by Target management leveraging the company's balance sheet and taking on debt to finance the issuer's self-tender and consequent recapitalization of Target's business (*see Carter Hawley Hale, supra,* at p. 426). The M&A market of the 1980s also saw the emergence of the LBO as private equity firms (such as Kohlberg Kravis & Roberts (KKR)) arrived on the scene, willing to provide the beleaguered Target management with a white-knight transaction as an alternative to the raider's hostile takeover bid. By 1988, it is reported that LBOs accounted for over 33 percent of the volume of M&A activity in the United States. Indeed, most observers of the M&A market regard KKR's purchase of RJR Nabisco for $25 billion as the "deal of the decade" in the 1980s, a deal that held the record for the largest LBO transaction for over two decades.

Against this backdrop, Marty Lipton, of the New York law firm Wachtell, Lipton, Rosen, & Katz, invented the "shareholder rights plan," which came to be more popularly known as the "poison pill." The operation of the pill is described by its inventor *infra* at p. 552, and its validity was upheld by the Delaware Supreme Court in the watershed year of 1985, in the landmark decision *Moran v. Household International Inc.* (*see infra* p. 542). In 1985, the Delaware Supreme Court also decided the seminal cases of *Unocal Corp. v. Mesa Petroleum Co.* (*see infra,* at p. 529) and *Revlon, Inc. v. MacAndrews & Forbes Holdings, Inc.* (*see infra* p. 603), which establish new ground rules for hostile takeovers.

By 1989, as the deal decade drew to a close, the takeover boom of the 1980s went bust. In 1989, the insider trading scandal hits Wall Street, resulting in the indictment of Michael Milken on insider trading charges (among other counts) and leading to the demise of his employer, Drexel Burnham, with then-U.S.

attorney Rudy Guiliani as the federal prosecutor making the headlines in the financial press. Likewise, the junk bond market collapsed as junk bonds turn into real junk and the cash buyout craze comes to an abrupt halt as financing for the raiders disappears once their banker of choice, Drexel Burnham, goes under.

With that background in mind, let's review the paradigm fiduciary duty cases that were decided by the Delaware Supreme Court in the watershed year of 1985. Then we will turn our attention to the 1990s and the companion cases of *Time-Warner* (*see infra* p. 634) and *QVC* (*see infra* p. 650), which reflect further developments in the market for M&A activity and further refinements by the Delaware courts as to the scope of fiduciary duty obligations imposed on Target's management in the context of an M&A transaction.

Unocal Corporation v. Mesa Petroleum Co.
493 A.2d 946 (Del. 1985)

MOORE, Justice.

We confront an issue of first impression in Delaware—the validity of a corporation's self-tender for its own shares which excludes from participation a stockholder making a hostile tender offer for the company's stock.

The Court of Chancery granted a preliminary injunction to the plaintiffs, Mesa Petroleum Co., Mesa Asset Co., Mesa Partners II, and Mesa Eastern, Inc. (collectively "Mesa")[1], enjoining an exchange offer of the defendant, Unocal Corporation (Unocal), for its own stock. The trial court concluded that a selective exchange offer, excluding Mesa, was legally impermissible. We cannot agree with such a blanket rule. The factual findings of the Vice Chancellor, fully supported by the record, establish that Unocal's board, consisting of a majority of independent directors, acted in good faith, and after reasonable investigation found that Mesa's tender offer was both inadequate and coercive. Under the circumstances the board had both the power and duty to oppose a bid it perceived to be harmful to the corporate enterprise. On this record we are satisfied that the device Unocal adopted is reasonable in relation to the threat posed, and that the board acted in the proper exercise of sound business judgment. We will not substitute our views for those of the board if the latter's decision can be "attributed to any rational business purpose." *Sinclair Oil Corp. v. Levien*, Del. Supr., 280 A.2d 717, 720 (1971). Accordingly, we reverse the decision of the Court of Chancery and order the preliminary injunction vacated.

I.

The factual background of this matter bears a significant relationship to its ultimate outcome.

---

1. T. Boone Pickens, Jr., is President and Chairman of the Board of Mesa Petroleum and President of Mesa Asset and controls the related Mesa entities.

On April 8, 1985, Mesa, the owner of approximately 13% of Unocal's stock, commenced a two-tier "front loaded" cash tender offer for 64 million shares, or approximately 37%, of Unocal's outstanding stock at a price of $54 per share. The "back-end" was designed to eliminate the remaining publicly held shares by an exchange of securities purportedly worth $54 per share. However, pursuant to an order entered by the United States District Court for the Central District of California on April 26, 1985, Mesa issued a supplemental proxy statement to Unocal's stockholders disclosing that the securities offered in the second-step merger would be highly subordinated, and that Unocal's capitalization would differ significantly from its present structure. Unocal has rather aptly termed such securities "junk bonds".

Unocal's board consists of eight independent outside directors and six insiders. It met on April 13, 1985, to consider the Mesa tender offer. Thirteen directors were present, and the meeting lasted nine and one-half hours. The directors were given no agenda or written materials prior to the session. However, detailed presentations were made by legal counsel regarding the board's obligations under both Delaware corporate law and the federal securities laws. The board then received a presentation from Peter Sachs on behalf of Goldman Sachs & Co. (Goldman Sachs) and Dillon, Read & Co. (Dillon Read) discussing the bases for their opinions that the Mesa proposal was wholly inadequate. Mr. Sachs opined that the minimum cash value that could be expected from a sale or orderly liquidation for 100% of Unocal's stock was in excess of $60 per share. In making his presentation, Mr. Sachs showed slides outlining the valuation techniques used by the financial advisors, and others, depicting recent business combinations in the oil and gas industry. The Court of Chancery found that the Sachs presentation was designed to apprise the directors of the scope of the analyses performed rather than the facts and numbers used in reaching the conclusion that Mesa's tender offer price was inadequate.

Mr. Sachs also presented various defensive strategies available to the board if it concluded that Mesa's two-step tender offer was inadequate and should be opposed. One of the devices outlined was a self-tender by Unocal for its own stock with a reasonable price range of $70 to $75 per share. The cost of such a proposal would cause the company to incur $6.1-6.5 billion of additional debt, and a presentation was made informing the board of Unocal's ability to handle it. The directors were told that the primary effect of this obligation would be to reduce exploratory drilling, but that the company would nonetheless remain a viable entity.

The eight outside directors, comprising a clear majority of the thirteen members present, then met separately with Unocal's financial advisors and attorneys. Thereafter, they unanimously agreed to advise the board that it should reject Mesa's tender offer as inadequate, and that Unocal should pursue a self-tender to provide the stockholders with a fairly priced alternative to the Mesa proposal. The board then reconvened and unanimously adopted a resolution rejecting as grossly inadequate Mesa's tender offer. Despite the nine and one-half hour length of the meeting, no formal decision was made on the proposed defensive self-tender.

On April 15, the board met again with four of the directors present by telephone and one member still absent. This session lasted two hours. Unocal's Vice President of Finance and its Assistant General Counsel made a detailed presentation of the proposed terms of the exchange offer. A price range between $70 and $80 per share was considered, and ultimately the directors agreed upon $72. The board was also advised about the debt securities that would be issued, and the necessity of placing restrictive covenants upon certain corporate activities until the obligations were paid. The board's decisions were made in reliance on the advice of its investment bankers, including the terms and conditions upon which the securities were to be issued. Based upon this advice, and the board's own deliberations, the directors unanimously approved the exchange offer. . . . The board resolution also stated that the offer would be subject to other conditions that had been described to the board at the meeting, or which were deemed necessary by Unocal's officers, including the exclusion of Mesa from the proposal (the Mesa exclusion). Any such conditions were required to be in accordance with the "purport and intent" of the offer.

Unocal's exchange offer was commenced on April 17, 1985, and Mesa promptly challenged it by filing this suit in the Court of Chancery. . . . On April 22, 1985, the Unocal board met again and was advised by Goldman Sachs and Dillon Read . . . that they should tender their own Unocal stock into the exchange offer as a mark of their confidence in it.

Another focus of the board was the Mesa exclusion. Legal counsel advised that under Delaware law Mesa could only be excluded for what the directors reasonably believed to be a valid corporate purpose. The directors' discussion centered on the objective of adequately compensating shareholders at the "back-end" of Mesa's proposal, which the latter would finance with "junk bonds". To include Mesa would defeat that goal, because under the proration aspect of the exchange offer (49%) every Mesa share accepted by Unocal would displace one held by another stockholder. Further, if Mesa were permitted to tender to Unocal, the latter would in effect be financing Mesa's own inadequate proposal.

* * *

[O]n April 22, 1985, Mesa amended its complaint in this action to challenge the Mesa exclusion. . . .

After the May 8 hearing the Vice Chancellor issued an unreported opinion on May 13, 1985 granting Mesa a preliminary injunction. Specifically, the trial court noted that "[t]he parties basically agree that the directors' duty of care extends to protecting the corporation from perceived harm whether it be from third parties or shareholders." The trial court also concluded in response to the second inquiry in the Supreme Court's May 2 order, that "[a]lthough the facts, . . . do not appear to be sufficient to prove that Mesa's principle objective is to be bought off at a substantial premium, they do justify a reasonable inference to the same effect." . . .

II.

The issues we address involve these fundamental questions: Did the Unocal board have the power and duty to oppose a takeover threat it reasonably perceived to be harmful to the corporate enterprise, and if so, is its action here entitled to the protection of the business judgment rule? . . .

III.

We begin with the basic issue of the power of a board of directors of a Delaware corporation to adopt a defensive measure of this type. Absent such authority, all other questions are moot. Neither issues of fairness nor business judgment are pertinent without the basic underpinning of a board's legal power to act.

The board has a large reservoir of authority upon which to draw. Its duties and responsibilities proceed from the inherent powers conferred by 8 Del. C. §141 (a), respecting management of the corporation's "business and affairs".[6] Additionally, the powers here being exercised derive from 8 Del. C. §160(a), conferring broad authority upon a corporation to deal in its own stock.[7] From this it is now well established that in the acquisition of its shares a Delaware corporation may deal selectively with its stockholders, provided the directors have not acted out of a sole or primary purpose to entrench themselves in office. . . .

Finally, the board's power to act derives from its fundamental duty and obligation to protect the corporate enterprise, which includes stockholders, from harm reasonably perceived, irrespective of its source. . . . Thus, we are satisfied that in the broad context of corporate governance, including issues of fundamental corporate change, a board of directors is not a passive instrumentality.[8]

Given the foregoing principles, we turn to the standards by which director action is to be measured. In *Pogostin v. Rice,* Del. Supr., 480 A.2d 619 (1984), we held that the business judgment rule, including the standards by which director conduct is judged, is applicable in the context of a takeover. *Id.* at 627. The business judgment rule is a "presumption that in making a business decision the directors of a corporation acted on an informed basis, in good faith and in the honest belief that the action taken was in the best interests of the company."

---

6. The general grant of power to a board of directors is conferred by 8 Del. C. § 141 (a), which provides:

   (a) The business *and affairs* of every corporation organized under this chapter shall be managed by or under the direction of a board of directors, except as may be otherwise provided in this chapter or in its certificate of incorporation. If any such provision is made in the certificate of incorporation, the powers and duties conferred or imposed upon the board of directors by this chapter shall be exercised or performed to such extent and by such person or persons as shall be provided in the certificate of incorporation. (Emphasis added.)

7. This power under 8 Del. C. § 160(a), with certain exceptions not pertinent here, is as follows:

   (a) Every corporation may purchase, redeem, receive, take or otherwise acquire, own and hold, sell, lend, exchange, transfer or otherwise dispose of, pledge, use and otherwise deal in and with its own shares; . . .

8. Even in the traditional areas of fundamental corporate change, i.e., charter, amendments [8 Del. C. §242(b)], mergers [8 Del. C. §§251(b), 252(c), 253(a), and 254(d)], sale of assets [8 Del. C. §271(a)], and dissolution [8 Del. C. §275(a)], director action is a prerequisite to the ultimate disposition of such matters. *See also, Smith v. Van Gorkom,* Del. Supr., 488 A.2d 858, 888 (1985).

Aronson v. Lewis, Del. Supr., 473 A.2d 805, 812 (1984) (citations omitted). A hallmark of the business judgment rule is that a court will not substitute its judgment for that of the board if the latter's decision can be "attributed to any rational business purpose." *Sinclair Oil Corp. v. Levien,* Del. Supr., 280 A.2d 717, 720 (1971).

When a board addresses a pending takeover bid it has an obligation to determine whether the offer is in the best interests of the corporation and its shareholders. In that respect a board's duty is no different from any other responsibility it shoulders, and its decisions should be no less entitled to the respect they otherwise would be accorded in the realm of business judgment.[9] *See also Johnson v. Trueblood,* 629 F.2d 287, 292-293 (3d Cir. 1980). There are, however, certain caveats to a proper exercise of this function. Because of the omnipresent specter that a board may be acting primarily in its own interests, rather than those of the corporation and its shareholders, there is an enhanced duty which calls for judicial examination at the threshold before the protections of the business judgment rule may be conferred. This Court has long recognized that:

> We must bear in mind the inherent danger in the purchase of shares with corporate funds to remove a threat to corporate policy when a threat to control is involved. The directors are of necessity confronted with a conflict of interest, and an objective decision is difficult.

Bennett v. Propp, Del. Supr., 187 A.2d 405, 409 (1962). In the face of this inherent conflict directors must show that they had reasonable grounds for believing that a danger to corporate policy and effectiveness existed because of another person's stock ownership. *Cheff v. Mathes,* 199 A.2d at 554-55. However, they satisfy that burden "by showing good faith and reasonable investigation. . . ." *Id.* at 555. Furthermore, such proof is materially enhanced, as here, by the approval of a board comprised of a majority of outside independent directors who have acted in accordance with the foregoing standards. . . .

IV.

A.

In the board's exercise of corporate power to forestall a takeover bid our analysis begins with the basic principle that corporate directors have a fiduciary duty to act in the best interests of the corporation's stockholders. *Guth*

---

9. This is a subject of intense debate among practicing members of the bar and legal scholars. Excellent examples of these contending views are: Block & Miller, *The Responsibilities and Obligations of Corporate Directors in Takeover Contests,* 11 Sec. Reg. L.J. 44 (1983); Easterbrook & Fischel, *Takeover Bids, Defensive Tactics, and Shareholders' Welfare,* 36 Bus. Law. 1733 (1981); Easterbrook & Fischel, *The Proper Role of a Target's Management in Responding to a Tender Offer,* 94 Harv. L. Rev. 1161 (1981). Herzel, Schmidt & Davis, *Why Corporate Directors Have a Right to Resist Tender Offers,* 3 Corp. L. Rev. 107 (1980); Lipton, *Takeover Bids in the Target's Boardroom,* 35 Bus. Law. 101 (1979).

v. Loft, Inc., Del. Supr., 5 A.2d 503, 510 (1939). As we have noted, their duty of care extends to protecting the corporation and its owners from perceived harm whether a threat originates from third parties or other shareholders.[10] But such powers are not absolute. A corporation does not have unbridled discretion to defeat any perceived threat by any Draconian means available.

The restriction placed upon a selective stock repurchase is that the directors may not have acted solely or primarily out of a desire to perpetuate themselves in office. *See Cheff v. Mathes*, 199 A.2d at 556; *Kors v. Carey*, 158 A.2d at 140. Of course, to this is added the further caveat that inequitable action may not be taken under the guise of law. *Schnell v. Chris-Craft Industries, Inc.*, Del. Supr., 285 A.2d 437, 439 (1971). The standard of proof established in *Cheff v. Mathes* and discussed *supra* at page 16, is designed to ensure that a defensive measure to thwart or impede a takeover is indeed motivated by a good faith concern for the welfare of the corporation and its stockholders, which in all circumstances must be free of any fraud or other misconduct. *Cheff v. Mathes*, 199 A.2d at 554-55. However, this does not end the inquiry.

B.

A further aspect is the element of balance. If a defensive measure is to come within the ambit of the business judgment rule, it must be reasonable in relation to the threat posed. This entails an analysis by the directors of the nature of the takeover bid and its effect on the corporate enterprise. Examples of such concerns may include: inadequacy of the price offered, nature and timing of the offer, questions of illegality, the impact on "constituencies" other than shareholders (i.e., creditors, customers, employees, and perhaps even the community generally), the risk of nonconsummation, and the quality of securities being offered in the exchange. *See* Lipton and Brownstein, *Takeover Responses and Directors' Responsibilities: An Update*, p. 7, ABA National Institute on the Dynamics of Corporate Control (December 8, 1983). While not a controlling factor, it also seems to us that a board may reasonably consider the basic stockholder interests at stake, including those of short term speculators, whose actions may have fueled the coercive aspect of the offer at the expense of the long term investor. Here, the threat posed was viewed by the Unocal board as a grossly inadequate two-tier coercive tender offer coupled with the threat of greenmail.

Specifically, the Unocal directors had concluded that the value of Unocal was substantially above the $54 per share offered in cash at the front end. Furthermore, they determined that the subordinated securities to be exchanged in Mesa's announced squeeze out of the remaining shareholders in the "back-end" merger were "junk bonds" worth far less than $54. It is now well recognized that such offers are a classic coercive measure designed to stampede shareholders

---

10. It has been suggested that a board's response to a takeover threat should be a passive one. Easterbrook & Fischel, *supra*, 36 Bus. Law. at 1750. However, that clearly is not the law of Delaware, and as the proponents of this rule of passivity readily concede, it has not been adopted either by courts or state legislatures. Easterbrook & Fischel, *supra*, 94 Harv. L. Rev. at 1194.

into tendering at the first tier, even if the price is inadequate, out of fear of what they will receive at the back end of the transaction. Wholly beyond the coercive aspect of an inadequate two-tier tender offer, the threat was posed by a corporate raider with a national reputation as a "greenmailer."[13]

In adopting the selective exchange offer, the board stated that its objective was either to defeat the inadequate Mesa offer or, should the offer still succeed, provide the 49% of its stockholders, who would otherwise be forced to accept "junk bonds," with $72 worth of senior debt. We find that both purposes are valid.

However, such efforts would have been thwarted by Mesa's participation in the exchange offer. First, if Mesa could tender its shares, Unocal would effectively be subsidizing the former's continuing effort to buy Unocal stock at $54 per share. Second, Mesa could not, by definition, fit within the class of shareholders being protected from its own coercive and inadequate tender offer.

Thus, we are satisfied that the selective exchange offer is reasonably related to the threats posed. It is consistent with the principle that "the minority stockholder shall receive the substantial equivalent in value of what he had before." *Sterling v. Mayflower Hotel Corp.*, Del. Supr., 93 A.2d 107, 114 (1952). This concept of fairness, while stated in the merger context, is also relevant in the area of tender offer law. Thus, the board's decision to offer what it determined to be the fair value of the corporation to the 49% of its shareholders, who would otherwise be forced to accept highly subordinated "junk bonds," is reasonable and consistent with the directors' duty to ensure that the minority stockholders receive equal value for their shares.

V.

Mesa contends that it is unlawful, and the trial court agreed, for a corporation to discriminate in this fashion against one shareholder. It argues correctly that no case has ever sanctioned a device that precludes a raider from sharing in a benefit available to all other stockholders. However, as we have noted earlier, the principle of selective stock repurchases by a Delaware corporation is neither unknown nor unauthorized. . . . The only difference is that heretofore the approved transaction was the payment of "greenmail" to a raider or dissident posing a threat to the corporate enterprise. All other stockholders were denied such favored treatment, and given Mesa's past history of greenmail, its claims here are rather ironic.

However, our corporate law is not static. It must grow and develop in response to, indeed in anticipation of, evolving concepts and needs. Merely because the General Corporation Law is silent as to a specific matter does not

---

13. The term "greenmail" refers to the practice of buying out a takeover bidder's stock at a premium that is not available to other shareholders in order to prevent the takeover. The Chancery Court noted that "Mesa has made tremendous profits from its takeover activities although in the past few years it has not been successful in acquiring any of the target companies on an unfriendly basis." Moreover, the trial court specifically found that the actions of the Unocal board were taken in good faith to eliminate both the inadequacies of the tender offer and to forestall the payment of "greenmail."

mean that it is prohibited. In the days when *Cheff, Bennett, Martin* and *Kors* were decided, the tender offer, while not an unknown device, was virtually unused, and little was known of such methods as two-tier "front-end" loaded offers with their coercive effects. Then, the favored attack of a raider was stock acquisition followed by a proxy contest. Various defensive tactics, which provided no benefit whatever to the raider, evolved. Thus, the use of corporate funds by management to counter a proxy battle was approved. . . . Litigation, supported by corporate funds, aimed at the raider has long been a popular device.

More recently, as the sophistication of both raiders and targets has developed, a host of other defensive measures to counter such ever mounting threats has evolved and received judicial sanction. These include defensive charter amendments and other devices bearing some rather exotic, but apt, names: Crown Jewel, White Knight, Pac Man, and Golden Parachute. Each has highly selective features, the object of which is to deter or defeat the raider.

Thus, while the exchange offer is a form of selective treatment, given the nature of the threat posed here the response is neither unlawful nor unreasonable. If the board of directors is disinterested, has acted in good faith and with due care, its decision in the absence of an abuse of discretion will be upheld as a proper exercise of business judgment.

To this Mesa responds that the board is not disinterested, because the directors are receiving a benefit from the tender of their own shares, which because of the Mesa exclusion, does not devolve upon *all* stockholders equally. *See Aronson v. Lewis*, Del. Supr., 473 A.2d 805, 812 (1984). However, Mesa concedes that if the exclusion is valid, then the directors and all other stockholders share the same benefit. The answer of course is that the exclusion is valid, and the directors' participation in the exchange offer does not rise to the level of a disqualifying interest. The excellent discussion in *Johnson v. Trueblood*, [629 F.2d 287, 292-293 (3rd Cir. 1980)], of the use of the business judgment rule in takeover contests also seems pertinent here.

Nor does this become an "interested" director transaction merely because certain board members are large stockholders. As this Court has previously noted, that fact alone does not create a disqualifying "personal pecuniary interest" to defeat the operation of the business judgment rule. *Cheff v. Mathes*, 199 A.2d at 554.

Mesa also argues that the exclusion permits the directors to abdicate the fiduciary duties they owe it. However, that is not so. The board continues to owe Mesa the duties of due care and loyalty. But in the face of the destructive threat Mesa's tender offer was perceived to pose, the board had a supervening duty to protect the corporate enterprise, which includes the other shareholders, from threatened harm.

Mesa contends that the basis of this action is punitive, and solely in response to the exercise of its rights of corporate democracy.[14] Nothing precludes Mesa,

---

14. This seems to be the underlying basis of the trial court's principal reliance on the unreported Chancery decision of *Fisher v. Moltz*, Del. Ch. No. 6068 (1979), published in 5 Del. J. Corp. L. 530 (1980). However, the facts in *Fisher* are thoroughly distinguishable. There, a corporation offered to repurchase the shares of its former employees, except those of the plaintiffs, merely because the latter were then engaged in lawful competition with the company. No threat to the enterprise was posed, and at best it can be said that the exclusion was motivated by pique instead of a rational corporate purpose.

as a stockholder, from acting in its own self-interest. . . . However, Mesa, while pursuing its own interests, has acted in a manner which a board consisting of a majority of independent directors has reasonably determined to be contrary to the best interests of Unocal and its other shareholders. In this situation, there is no support in Delaware law for the proposition that, when responding to a perceived harm, a corporation must guarantee a benefit to a stockholder who is deliberately provoking the danger being addressed. There is no obligation of self-sacrifice by a corporation and its shareholders in the face of such a challenge.

Here, the Court of Chancery specifically found that the "directors' decision [to oppose the Mesa tender offer] was made in the good faith belief that the Mesa tender offer is inadequate." Given our standard of review under *Levitt v. Bouvier*, Del. Supr., 287 A.2d 671, 673 (1972), and *Application of Delaware Racing Association*, Del. Supr., 213 A.2d 203, 207 (1965), we are satisfied that Unocal's board has met its burden of proof. *Cheff v. Mathes*, 199 A.2d at 555.

VI.

In conclusion, there was directorial power to oppose the Mesa tender offer, and to undertake a selective stock exchange made in good faith and upon a reasonable investigation pursuant to a clear duty to protect the corporate enterprise. Further, the selective stock repurchase plan chosen by Unocal is reasonable in relation to the threat that the board rationally and reasonably believed was posed by Mesa's inadequate and coercive two-tier tender offer. Under those circumstances the board's action is entitled to be measured by the standards of the business judgment rule. Thus, unless it is shown by a preponderance of the evidence that the directors' decisions were primarily based on perpetuating themselves in office, or some other breach of fiduciary duty such as fraud, overreaching, lack of good faith, or being uninformed, a Court will not substitute its judgment for that of the board.

In this case that protection is not lost merely because Unocal's directors have tendered their shares in the exchange offer. Given the validity of the Mesa exclusion, they are receiving a benefit shared generally by all other stockholders except Mesa. In this circumstance the test of *Aronson v. Lewis*, 473 A.2d at 812, is satisfied. *See also Cheff v. Mathes*, 199 A.2d at 554. If the stockholders are displeased with the action of their elected representatives, the powers of corporate democracy are at their disposal to turn the board out. *Aronson v. Lewis*, Del. Supr., 473 A.2d 805, 811 (1984). *See also* 8 Del. C. §§141(k) and 211(b).

With the Court of Chancery's findings that the exchange offer was based on the board's good faith belief that the Mesa offer was inadequate, that the board's action was informed and taken with due care, that Mesa's prior activities justify a reasonable inference that its principle objective was greenmail, and implicitly, that the substance of the offer itself was reasonable and fair to the corporation and its stockholders if Mesa were included, we cannot say that the Unocal directors have acted in such a manner as to have passed an "unintelligent and unadvised judgment." *Mitchell v. Highland-Western Glass Co.*, Del. Ch., 167 A. 831, 833 (1933). The decision of the Court of Chancery is therefore REVERSED, and the preliminary injunction is VACATED.

QUESTIONS

1. What is the perceived threat posed by the terms of Mesa's offer to acquire Unocal?

2. What is "greenmail"?

3. Given the board's fiduciary duty to manage the business for the benefit of *all* shareholders, why is it permissible for the board to discriminate against one of its own shareholders (here, T. Boone Pickens and his investment vehicle, Mesa)?

4. As a public policy matter, why allow Target's (here, Unocal's) board to get involved when Target (Unocal) itself is not a party to the transaction? What is the "passivity theory"? Why did the Delaware Supreme Court refused to adopt the "passivity theory"? In thinking about this issue, consider the following perspective by leading scholars advocating the "passivity theory":

> Under existing federal and state law, a corporation's managers can resist and often defeat a premium tender offer without liability to either the corporation's shareholders or the unsuccessful tender offeror. Professors Easterbrook and Fischel argue that resistance by a corporation's managers to premium tender offers, even if it triggers a bidding contest, ultimately decreases shareholder welfare. Shareholders would be better off, the authors claim, were such resistance all but proscribed. The authors consider, but find wanting, a number of potential criticisms of their analysis; they conclude by proposing a rule of managerial passivity. . . .

Frank Easterbrook & Daniel Fischel, *The Proper Role of Target's Management in Responding to a Tender Offer*, 94 HARV. L. REV. 1161, 1194 (1981).

NOTES

1. The Market for Corporate Control.   Those commentators who advocate the passivity theory often rely on the seminal writings of Professor Henry Manne to support their views. In his path-breaking article, *Mergers and the Market for Control*, Professor Manne offered the following introduction to the "market for corporate control":

> [As explained by Professor Manne in this article,] the market for corporate control gives . . . shareholders both power and protection commensurate with their interest in corporate affairs.
>
> A fundamental premise underlying the market for corporate control is the existence of a high positive correlation between corporate managerial efficiency and the market price of shares of that company. As an existing company is poorly managed—in the sense of not making as great a return for the shareholders as could be accomplished under other feasible managements—the market price of the shares declines relative to the values of other companies on the same industry or relative to the market as a whole. . . . The lower the stock price, relative to what it could be with more efficient management, the more attractive the take-over

becomes to those who believe that they can manage the company more efficiently. And the potential return from the successful take-over and revitalization of the company can be enormous.

[T]he greatest benefits of the take-over . . . probably inure to those least conscious of it. Apart from the stock market, we have no objective standard of managerial efficiency. Courts, as indicated by the so-called business-judgment rule, are loath to second guess business decisions or remove directors from office. Only the take-over . . . provides some assurance of competitive efficiency among corporate managers and therefore affords strong protection to the interests of vast numbers of small non-controlling shareholders. Compared to this mechanism, the efforts of the SEC and the courts to protect shareholders through the development of a fiduciary duty concept and the shareholder's derivative suit seem small indeed. It is true that sales by dissatisfied shareholders are necessary to trigger the mechanism and that these shareholders may suffer considerable losses. On the other hand, even greater capital losses are prevented by the existence of a competitive market for corporate control.

Henry Manne, *Mergers and the Market for Corporate Control,* 73 JOURNAL OF POLITICAL ECONOMY 110, 117 (1965). In this article, Professor Manne then goes on to describe the three basic techniques for taking over control of corporations—the proxy fight, the direct purchase of shares, and the merger—and to evaluate the "costs, practical difficulties, and legal consequences" of each of these approaches. The modern sets of legal considerations that regulate each of these "three basic techniques" have been set forth in the materials contained in the prior chapters of the casebook. In this chapter, therefore, we will build on our understanding of the modern rules and regulations for these "three basic techniques" by analyzing the interaction of the relevant legal rules and regulations (as set forth in the prior chapters of this book) with the ongoing evolution of fiduciary duty law.

2. Development of an Intermediate Standard of Judicial Review for Takeover Cases.   The Delaware Supreme Court's pronouncement in *Unocal* of a new, intermediate standard of judicial review was not without its critics. On the fifteenth anniversary of the *Unocal* decision, a leading scholar of corporate law observed:

> A natural inclination towards stocktaking accompanies the new millennium. It coincidences [sic] with the fifteenth anniversary of the Delaware Supreme Court's announcement in *Unocal Corp. v. Mesa Petroleum Co.* of a new approach to takeover law provides an appropriate occasion to step back and evaluate a remarkable experiment in corporate law—the Delaware Supreme Court's development of an intermediate standard for evaluating defensive tactics.
>
> This experiment began with, and was surely a response to, an earlier and extremely controversial takeover wave. . . .
>
> . . . I have been quite negative in my assessment of the fifteen-year *Unocal* experiment. However, no cloud is without a silver lining, and in this case the silver lining is substantial even if accidental.
>
> Given the decision to take on the task of distinguishing between good and bad defensive tactics, the manner in which the Delaware courts have carried out that charge is interesting. A fair reading of the supreme court's intermediate

standard decisions, buttressed by the chancery court's and especially Chancellor Allen's repeated dicta about the critical role of independent directors in management buyouts, is that independent directors are expected to be the controlling parties in a target company's conduct of its defense. Only when the directors appear to have abdicated their role to management—think of *Van Gorkom, Macmillan,* and *QVC*—will the court intervene.

As I have made clear to this point, I think this is the wrong approach; evaluating target board conduct misses the question of who should be making the decision in the first place. But, it seems to me, there has been at least one beneficial, if unintended, consequence of this focus on director performance. The role the Delaware Supreme Court has assigned independent directors in connection with takeovers is quite different than the role directors assigned to themselves prior to the turbulent 1980s. At least in the takeover arena, independent directors, the Delaware courts have stated pointedly, are not merely advisers to management, who have no stake in whether their advice is followed. In the takeover arena, independent directors must be the *real* decision-makers and courts will expect them to play a central role in conducting the target's response to a hostile or competing offer.

Ronald J. Gilson, Unocal *Fifteen Years Later* (*And What We Can Do About It*), 26 DEL. J. CORP. L. 491, 491-492, and 513 (2001) (*emphasis in original*).

Professor Gilson's concern highlights one of the central public policy issues raised by the takeover wave of the 1980s and the ensuing caselaw that came out of this period: *Who should decide when and on what terms a publicly held company is for sale?* This question goes to the fundamental balance of power between the board of directors, the senior executive officers (most notably, the CEO), and the company's stockholders. The remaining materials in this chapter explore the various considerations implicated in Delaware case law over the past 25 years addressing this issue of modern corporate governance, a matter that continues to be of considerable importance in the wake of the recent financial scandals (and one of continuing controversy as well).

3. The SEC's Response: Regulation of Issuer Self-Tenders. The SEC filed an amicus brief in *Unocal* opposing the discriminatory self-tender undertaken by Target. Following the decision in *Unocal,* the SEC responded by adopting what is known as the "all-holders rule," Rule 13e-4 and Rule 14d-10. *See* Securities Exchange Act Rel. No. 23421 (1986). Under the SEC's all-holders rule, both issuer and third-party tender offers must be open to all shareholders and the best price paid by the acquiror to any tendering shareholder must be paid to all other tendering shareholders (the latter aspect of this SEC rule is often referred to as the "best price" rule). The practical effect of this SEC rulemaking is to eliminate the exclusionary self-tender as a viable defensive strategy, thereby nullifying the Delaware Supreme Court decision in *Unocal.* Even though the defensive strategy undertaken in *Unocal* has been consigned to the scrap heap as a result of this SEC rulemaking, the standard of review first enunciated in *Unocal* lives on, spawning a new era of judicial decision making. The *Unocal* progeny are considered in the remaining cases in this chapter.

D.   The "Poison Pill": Addressing the Risk of Selling Target Co. "Too Cheaply"

In order to set the stage for the competing considerations that are central to the reasoning of the Delaware Supreme Court in connection with its caselaw addressing the validity of the "poison pill," consider the public policy implications presented by the facts of the following hypothetical involving a proposed change of control transaction:

> . . . Assume an acquiring company buys 25% of the target's stock in a small number of privately negotiated transactions. It then commences a public tender offer for 26% of the company stock at a cash price that the board, in good faith, believes is inadequate. Moreover, the acquiring corporation announces that it may or may not do a second-step merger, but if it does one, the consideration will be junk bonds that will have a value, when issued, in the opinion of its own investment banker, of no more than the cash being offered in the tender offer. In the face of such an offer, the board may have a duty to seek to protect the company's shareholders from the coercive effects of this inadequate offer. Assume, for purposes of the hypothetical, that neither newly amended Section 203, nor any defensive device available to the target specifically, offers protection. Assume that the target's board turns to the market for corporate control to attempt to locate a more fairly priced alternative that would be available to all shareholders. And assume that just as the tender offer is closing, the board locates an all cash deal for all shares at a price materially higher than that offered by the acquiring corporation. Would the board of the target corporation be justified in issuing sufficient shares to the second acquiring corporation to dilute the 51% stockholder down so that it no longer had a practical veto over the merger or sale of assets that the target board had arranged for the benefit of all shares? It is not necessary to now hazard an opinion on that abstraction. . . .

Blasius Industries, Inc. v. Atlas Corp., 564 A.2d 651, 658 fn. 5 (Del. Ch. 1988). Although Chancellor Allen declined to present his views on the hypothetical that he posed in this footnote to his opinion in *Blasius,* the facts of this proposed change of control transaction crystallize the vexing public policy issues that the courts must grapple with in deciding the proper role for Target's board of directors when faced with an unsolicited tender offer from Bidder.

Since the *Unocal* decision, these public policy considerations have surfaced most prominently in connection with the development (and continued evolution) of the poison pill defense, which is the focus of the cases in this section. We begin our consideration of "poison pills" by examining the landmark case of *Moran v. Household Int'l, Inc.,* decided the same year as *Unocal,* a watershed year in the development of modern fiduciary duty law in Delaware.

In order to put these cases into some context, a bit of general background is in order. You will recall that our analysis of the problem sets in Chapter 2 reflected that the stock purchase agreement is a contract entered into between the buyer, Bidder Co., and the selling shareholders of Target Co. in the case of a closely held Target. In the case of a publicly traded Target Co., however, the process for Bidder to make a contract offer to purchase Target's outstanding shares directly from the company's stockholders is regulated by the provisions of the federal securities laws known as the Williams Act, which we studied in Chapter 6. The materials and problems in these two chapters underscore that this deal structure is the *only* method available to Bidder to acquire Target *without* obtaining approval from Target's board of directors. The hypothetical fact pattern that Chancellor Allen posed above highlights the fundamental question presented by the development of the "poison pill" defense: *What is the proper role for Target's board?* With the development of the poison pill, this takeover defense results in giving Target's board a "seat at the negotiating table," a point that is made in the next case in which the Delaware Supreme Court upholds the validity of the "shareholder rights plan," *aka* the "poison pill."

1.   Delaware Supreme Court Establishes the Validity of the Poison Pill

Moran v. Household International, Inc.
500 A.2d 1346 (Del. 1985)

McNEILLY, Justice:

This case presents to this Court for review the most recent defensive mechanism in the arsenal of corporate takeover weaponry—the Preferred Share Purchase Rights Plan ("Rights Plan" or "Plan"). The validity of this mechanism has attracted national attention. *Amici curiae* briefs have been filed in support of appellants by the Security [sic] and Exchange Commission ("SEC")[1] and the Investment Company Institute. An *amicus curiae* brief has been filed in support of appellees ("Household") by the United Food and Commercial Workers International Union.

In a detailed opinion, the Court of Chancery upheld the Rights Plan as a legitimate exercise of business judgment by Household. *Moran v. Household International, Inc.,* Del. Ch., 490 A.2d 1059 (1985). We agree, and therefore, affirm the judgment below.

I

The facts giving rise to this case have been carefully delineated in the Court of Chancery's opinion. *Id.* at 1064-69. A review of the basic facts is necessary for a complete understanding of the issues.

On August 14, 1984, the Board of Directors of Household International, Inc. adopted the Rights Plan by a fourteen to two vote.[2] The intricacies of the

---

1. The SEC split 3-2 on whether to intervene in this case. The two dissenting Commissioners have publicly disagreed with the other three as to the merits of the Rights Plan. 17 Securities Regulation & Law Report 400; The Wall Street Journal, March 20, 1985, at 6.

2. Household's Board has ten outside directors and six who are members of management. Messrs. Moran (appellant) and Whitehead voted against the Plan. The record reflects that Whitehead voted against the Plan not on its substance but because he thought it was novel and would bring unwanted publicity to Household.

Rights Plan are contained in a 48-page document entitled "Rights Agreement." Basically, the Plan provides that Household common stockholders are entitled to the issuance of one Right per common share under certain triggering conditions. There are two triggering events that can activate the Rights. The first is the announcement of a tender offer for 30 percent of Household's shares ("30% trigger") and the second is the acquisition of 20 percent of Household's shares by any single entity or group ("20% trigger").

If an announcement of a tender offer for 30 percent of Household's shares is made, the Rights are issued and are immediately exercisable to purchase 1/100 share of new preferred stock for $100 and are redeemable by the Board for $.50 per Right. If 20 percent of Household's shares are acquired by anyone, the Rights are issued and become non-redeemable and are exercisable to purchase 1/100 of a share of preferred. If a Right is not exercised for preferred, and thereafter, a merger or consolidation occurs, the Rights holder can exercise each Right to purchase $200 of the common stock of the tender offeror for $100. This "flip-over" provision of the Rights Plan is at the heart of this controversy.

Household is a diversified holding company with its principal subsidiaries engaged in financial services, transportation and merchandising. HFC, National Car Rental and Vons Grocery are three of its wholly-owned entities.

Household did not adopt its Rights Plan during a battle with a corporate raider, but as a preventive mechanism to ward off future advances. The Vice Chancellor found that as early as February 1984, Household's management became concerned about the company's vulnerability as a takeover target and began considering amending its charter to render a takeover more difficult. After considering the matter, Household decided not to pursue a fair price amendment.[3]

In the meantime, appellant Moran, one of Household's own Directors and also Chairman of the Dyson-Kissner-Moran Corporation, ("D-K-M") which is the largest single stockholder of Household, began discussions concerning a possible leveraged buy-out of Household by D-K-M. D-K-M's financial studies showed that Household's stock was significantly undervalued in relation to the company's break-up value. It is uncontradicted that Moran's suggestion of a leveraged buy-out never progressed beyond the discussion stage.

Concerned about Household's vulnerability to a raider in light of the current takeover climate, Household secured the services of Wachtell, Lipton, Rosen and Katz ("Wachtell, Lipton") and Goldman, Sachs & Co. ("Goldman, Sachs") to formulate a takeover policy for recommendation to the Household Board at its August 14 meeting. After a July 31 meeting with a Household Board member and a pre-meeting distribution of material on the potential takeover problem and the proposed Rights Plan, the Board met on August 14, 1984.

Representatives of Wachtell, Lipton and Goldman, Sachs attended the August 14 meeting. The minutes reflect that Mr. Lipton explained to the Board that his recommendation of the Plan was based on his understanding that the

---

3. A fair price amendment to a corporate charter generally requires supermajority approval for certain business combinations and sets minimum price criteria for mergers. *Moran,* 490 A.2d at 1064, n. 1.

Board was concerned about the increasing frequency of "bust-up"[4] takeovers, the increasing takeover activity in the financial service industry, such as Leucadia's attempt to take over Arco, and the possible adverse effect this type of activity could have on employees and others concerned with and vital to the continuing successful operation of Household even in the absence of any actual bust-up takeover attempt. Against this factual background, the Plan was approved.

Thereafter, Moran and the company of which he is Chairman, D-K-M, filed this suit. On the eve of trial, Gretl Golter, the holder of 500 shares of Household, was permitted to intervene as an additional plaintiff. The trial was held, and the Court of Chancery ruled in favor of Household. Appellants now appeal from that ruling to this Court.

II

The primary issue here is the applicability of the business judgment rule as the standard by which the adoption of the Rights Plan should be reviewed. Much of this issue has been decided by our recent decision in *Unocal Corp. v. Mesa Petroleum*, Del. Supr., 493 A.2d 946 (1985). In *Unocal*, we applied the business judgment rule to analyze Unocal's discriminatory self-tender. We explained:

> When a board addresses a pending takeover bid it has an obligation to determine whether the offer is in the best interests of the corporation and its shareholders. In that respect a board's duty is no different from any other responsibility it shoulders, and its decisions should be no less entitled to the respect they otherwise would be accorded in the realm of business judgment.

Id. at 954 (citation and footnote omitted).

Other jurisdictions have also applied the business judgment rule to actions by which target companies have sought to forestall takeover activity they considered undesirable. *See Gearhart Industries, Inc. v. Smith International*, 5th Cir., 741 F.2d 707 (1984) (sale of discounted subordinate debentures containing springing warrants); *Treco, Inc. v. Land of Lincoln Savings and Loan*, 7th Cir., 749 F.2d 374 (1984) (amendment to by-laws); *Panter v. Marshall Field*, 7th Cir., 646 F.2d 271 (1981) (acquisitions to create antitrust problems); *Johnson v. Trueblood*, 3d Cir., 629 F.2d 287 (1980), *cert. denied*, 450 U.S. 999, 101 S. Ct. 1704, 68 L. Ed. 2d 200 (1981) (refusal to tender); *CrouseHinds Co. v. InterNorth, Inc.*, 2d Cir., 634 F.2d 690 (1980) (sale of stock to favored party); *Treadway v. Cane Corp.*, 2d Cir., 638 F.2d 357 (1980) (sale to White Knight); *Enterra Corp. v. SGS Associates*, E.D. Pa., 600 F. Supp. 678 (1985) (standstill agreement); *Buffalo Forge Co. v. Ogden Corp.*, W.D.N.Y., 555 F. Supp. 892, *aff'd*, (2d Cir.) 717 F.2d 757, *cert. denied*, 464 U.S. 1018, 104 S. Ct. 550, 78 L. Ed. 2d 724 (1983) (sale of treasury shares and grant of stock option to White Knight); *Whittaker Corp. v. Edgar*, N.D. Ill., 535 F. Supp. 933 (1982) (disposal of valuable assets); *Martin Marietta Corp. v. Bendix Corp.*, D. Md., 549 F. Supp. 623 (1982) (Pac-Man defense).

---

4. "Bust-up" takeover generally refers to a situation in which one seeks to finance an acquisition by selling off pieces of the acquired company.

This case is distinguishable from the ones cited, since here we have a defensive mechanism adopted to ward off possible future advances and not a mechanism adopted in reaction to a specific threat. This distinguishing factor does not result in the Directors losing the protection of the business judgment rule. To the contrary, pre-planning for the contingency of a hostile takeover might reduce the risk that, under the pressure of a takeover bid, management will fail to exercise reasonable judgment. Therefore, in reviewing a pre-planned defensive mechanism it seems even more appropriate to apply the business judgment rule. *See Warner Communications v. Murdoch*, D. Del., 581 F. Supp. 1482, 1491 (1984).

Of course, the business judgment rule can only sustain corporate decision making or transactions that are within the power or authority of the Board. Therefore, before the business judgment rule can be applied it must be determined whether the Directors were authorized to adopt the Rights Plan.

III

Appellants vehemently contend that the Board of Directors was unauthorized to adopt the Rights Plan. First, appellants contend that no provision of the Delaware General Corporation Law authorizes the issuance of such Rights. Secondly, appellants, along with the SEC, contend that the Board is unauthorized to usurp stockholders' rights to receive hostile tender offers. Third, appellants and the SEC also contend that the Board is unauthorized to fundamentally restrict stockholders' rights to conduct a proxy contest. We address each of these contentions in turn.

A

While appellants contend that no provision of the Delaware General Corporation Law authorizes the Rights Plan, Household contends that the Rights Plan was issued pursuant to 8 Del. C. §§151 (g) and §157. It explains that the Rights are authorized by §157[7] and the issue of preferred stock underlying the Rights is authorized by §151.[8] Appellants respond by making several attacks upon the authority to issue the Rights pursuant to §157.

---

7. The power to issue rights to purchase shares is conferred by 8 Del. C. §157 which provides in relevant part:

> Subject to any provisions in the certificate of incorporation, every corporation may create and issue, whether or not in connection with the issue and sale of any shares of stock or other securities of the corporation, rights or options entitling the holders thereof to purchase from the corporation any shares of its capital stock of any class or classes, such rights or options to be evidenced by or in such instrument or instruments as shall be approved by the board of directors.

8. Del. C. §151(g) provides in relevant part:

> When any corporation desires to issue any shares of stock of any class or of any series of any class of which the voting powers, designations, preferences and relative, participating, optional or other rights, if any, or the qualifications, limitations or restrictions thereof, if any, shall not have been set forth in the certificate of incorporation or in any amendment thereto but shall be provided for in a resolution or resolutions adopted by the board of directors pursuant to authority

Appellants begin by contending that §157 cannot authorize the Rights Plan since §157 has never served the purpose of authorizing a takeover defense. Appellants contend that §157 is a corporate financing statute, and that nothing in its legislative history suggests a purpose that has anything to do with corporate control or a takeover defense. Appellants are unable to demonstrate that the legislature, in its adoption of §157, meant to limit the applicability of §157 to only the issuance of Rights for the purposes of corporate financing. Without such affirmative evidence, we decline to impose such a limitation upon the section that the legislature has not. As we noted in *Unocal:*

> [O]ur corporate law is not static. It must grow and develop in response to, indeed in anticipation of, evolving concepts and needs. Merely because the General Corporation Law is silent as to a specific matter does not mean that it is prohibited.

493 A.2d at 957. *See also Cheff v. Mathes,* Del. Supr., 199 A.2d 548 (1964).

Secondly, appellants contend that §157 does not authorize the issuance of sham rights such as the Rights Plan. They contend that the Rights were designed never to be exercised, and that the Plan has no economic value. In addition, they contend the preferred stock made subject to the Rights is also illusory, citing *Telvest, Inc. v. Olson,* Del. Ch., C.A. No. 5798, Brown, V.C. (March 8, 1979).

Appellants' sham contention fails in both regards. As to the Rights, they can and will be exercised upon the happening of a triggering mechanism, as we have observed during the current struggle of Sir James Goldsmith to take control of Crown Zellerbach. *See* Wall Street Journal, July 26, 1985, at 3, 12. As to the preferred shares, we agree with the Court of Chancery that they are distinguishable from sham securities invalidated in *Telvest, supra.* The Household preferred, issuable upon the happening of a triggering event, have superior dividend and liquidation rights.

Third, appellants contend that §157 authorizes the issuance of Rights "entitling holders thereof to purchase from the corporation any shares of *its* capital stock of any class . . ." (*emphasis added*). Therefore, their contention continues, the plain language of the statute does not authorize Household to issue rights to purchase another's capital stock upon a merger or consolidation.

Household contends, *inter alia,* that the Rights Plan is analogous to "antidestruction" or "anti-dilution" provisions which are customary features of a wide variety of corporate securities. While appellants seem to concede that "anti-destruction" provisions are valid under Delaware corporate law, they seek to distinguish the Rights Plan as not being incidental, as are most "anti-destruction" provisions, to a corporation's statutory power to finance itself. We find no merit to such a distinction. We have already rejected appellants' similar contention that §157 could only be used for financing purposes. We also reject that distinction here.

---

expressly vested in it by the provisions of the certificate of incorporation or any amendment thereto, a certificate setting forth a copy of such resolution or resolutions and the number of shares of stock of such class or series shall be executed, acknowledged, filed, recorded, and shall become effective, in accordance with §103 of this title.

"Anti-destruction" clauses generally ensure holders of certain securities of the protection of their right of conversion in the event of a merger by giving them the right to convert their securities into whatever securities are to replace the stock of their company. *See Broad v. Rockwell International Corp.*, 5th Cir., 642 F.2d 929, 946, *cert. denied*, 454 U.S. 965, 102 S. Ct. 506, 70 L. Ed. 2d 380 (1981); *Wood v. Coastal States Gas Corp.*, Del. Supr., 401 A.2d 932, 937-39 (1979); *B.S.F. Co. v. Philadelphia National Bank*, Del. Supr., 204 A.2d 746, 750-51 (1964). The fact that the rights here have as their purpose the prevention of coercive two-tier tender offers does not invalidate them. . . .

Having concluded that sufficient authority for the Rights Plan exists in 8 Del. C. §157, we note the inherent powers of the Board conferred by 8 Del. C. §141 (a), concerning the management of the corporation's "business and *affairs*" (*emphasis added*), also provides the Board additional authority upon which to enact the Rights Plan. *Unocal*, 493 A.2d at 953.

B

Appellants contend that the Board is unauthorized to usurp stockholders' rights to receive tender offers by changing Household's fundamental structure. We conclude that the Rights Plan does not prevent stockholders from receiving tender offers, and that the change of Household's structure was less than that which results from the implementation of other defensive mechanisms upheld by various courts.

Appellants' contention that stockholders will lose their right to receive and accept tender offers seems to be premised upon an understanding of the Rights Plan which is illustrated by the SEC *amicus* brief which states: "The Chancery Court's decision seriously understates the impact of this plan. In fact, as we discuss below, the Rights Plan will deter not only two-tier offers, but virtually all hostile tender offers."

The fallacy of that contention is apparent when we look at the recent takeover of Crown Zellerbach, which has a similar Rights Plan, by Sir James Goldsmith. Wall Street Journal, July 26, 1985, at 3, 12. The evidence at trial also evidenced many methods around the Plan ranging from tendering with a condition that the Board redeem the Rights, tendering with a high minimum condition of shares and Rights, tendering and soliciting consents to remove the Board and redeem the Rights, to acquiring 50% of the shares and causing Household to self-tender for the Rights. One could also form a group of up to 19.9% and solicit proxies for consents to remove the Board and redeem the Rights. These are but a few of the methods by which Household can still be acquired by a hostile tender offer.

In addition, the Rights Plan is not absolute. When the Household Board of Directors is faced with a tender offer and a request to redeem the Rights, they will not be able to arbitrarily reject the offer. They will be held to the same fiduciary standards any other board of directors would be held to in deciding to adopt a defensive mechanism, the same standard as they were held to in originally approving the Rights Plan. *See Unocal*, 493 A.2d at 954-55, 958.

In addition, appellants contend that the deterrence of tender offers will be accomplished by what they label "a fundamental transfer of power from the stockholders to the directors." They contend that this transfer of power, in itself, is unauthorized.

The Rights Plan will result in no more of a structural change than any other defensive mechanism adopted by a board of directors. The Rights Plan does not destroy the assets of the corporation. The implementation of the Plan neither results in any outflow of money from the corporation nor impairs its financial flexibility. It does not dilute earnings per share and does not have any adverse tax consequences for the corporation or its stockholders. The Plan has not adversely affected the market price of Household's stock.

Comparing the Rights Plan with other defensive mechanisms, it does less harm to the value structure of the corporation than do the other mechanisms. Other mechanisms result in increased debt of the corporation. *See Whittaker Corp. v. Edgar, supra* (sale of "prize asset"), *Cheff v. Mathes, supra,* (paying greenmail to eliminate a threat), *Unocal Corp. v. Mesa Petroleum Co., supra,* (discriminatory self-tender).

There is little change in the governance structure as a result of the adoption of the Rights Plan. The Board does not now have unfettered discretion in refusing to redeem the Rights. The Board has no more discretion in refusing to redeem the Rights than it does in enacting any defensive mechanism.

The contention that the Rights Plan alters the structure more than do other defensive mechanisms because it is so effective as to make the corporation completely safe from hostile tender offers is likewise without merit. As explained above, there are numerous methods to successfully launch a hostile tender offer.

C

Appellants' third contention is that the Board was unauthorized to fundamentally restrict stockholders' rights to conduct a proxy contest. Appellants contend that the "20% trigger" effectively prevents any stockholder from first acquiring 20% or more shares before conducting a proxy contest and further, it prevents stockholders from banding together into a group to solicit proxies if, collectively, they own 20% or more of the stock.[12] In addition, at trial, appellants contended that read literally, the Rights Agreement triggers the Rights upon the mere acquisition of the right to vote 20% or more of the shares through a proxy solicitation, and thereby precludes any proxy contest from being waged.[13]

Appellants seem to have conceded this last contention in light of Household's response that the receipt of a proxy does not make the recipient the "beneficial owner" of the shares involved which would trigger the Rights. In essence, the Rights Agreement provides that the Rights are triggered when

---

12. Appellants explain that the acquisition of 20% of the shares trigger the Rights, making them non-redeemable, and thereby would prevent even a future friendly offer for the ten-year life of the Rights.

13. The SEC still contends that the mere acquisition of the right to vote 20% of the shares through a proxy solicitation triggers the rights. We do not interpret the Rights Agreement in that manner.

someone becomes the "beneficial owner" of 20% or more of Household stock. Although a literal reading of the Rights Agreement definition of "beneficial owner" would seem to include those shares which one has the right to vote, it has long been recognized that the relationship between grantor and recipient of a proxy is one of agency, and the agency is revocable by the grantor at any time. Henn, *Corporations* §196, at 518. Therefore, the holder of a proxy is not the "beneficial owner" of the stock. As a result, the mere acquisition of the right to vote 20% of the shares does not trigger the Rights.

The issue, then, is whether the restriction upon individuals or groups from first acquiring 20% of shares before waging a proxy contest fundamentally restricts stockholders' right to conduct a proxy contest. Regarding this issue the Court of Chancery found:

> Thus, while the Rights Plan does deter the formation of proxy efforts of a certain magnitude, it does not limit the voting power of individual shares. On the evidence presented it is highly conjectural to assume that a particular effort to assert shareholder views in the election of directors or revisions of corporate policy will be frustrated by the proxy feature of the Plan. Household's witnesses, Troubh and Higgins described recent corporate takeover battles in which insurgents holding less than 10% stock ownership were able to secure corporate control through a proxy contest or the threat of one.

Moran, 490 A.2d at 1080.

We conclude that there was sufficient evidence at trial to support the Vice Chancellor's finding that the effect upon proxy contests will be minimal. Evidence at trial established that many proxy contests are won with an insurgent ownership of less than 20%, and that very large holdings are no guarantee of success. There was also testimony that the key variable in proxy contest success is the merit of an insurgent's issues, not the size of his holdings.

IV

Having concluded that the adoption of the Rights Plan was within the authority of the Directors, we now look to whether the Directors have met their burden under the business judgment rule.

The business judgment rule is a "presumption that in making a business decision the directors of a corporation acted on an informed basis, in good faith and in the honest belief that the action taken was in the best interests of the company." *Aronson v. Lewis,* Del. Supr., 473 A.2d 805, 812 (1984) (citations omitted). Notwithstanding, in *Unocal* we held that when the business judgment rule applies to adoption of a defensive mechanism, the initial burden will lie with the directors. The "directors must show that they had reasonable grounds for believing that a danger to corporate policy and effectiveness existed. . . . [T]hey satisfy that burden 'by showing good faith and reasonable investigation. . . .'" *Unocal,* 493 A.2d at 955 (citing *Cheff v. Mathes,* 199 A.2d at 554-55). In addition, the directors must show that the defensive mechanism was "reasonable in relation to the threat posed." *Unocal,* 493 A.2d at 955. Moreover, that proof is materially enhanced, as we noted in *Unocal,* where, as here, a majority of the board favoring the proposal consisted of outside independent directors who have acted in accordance with the foregoing standards. *Unocal,* 493 A.2d at 955; *Aronson,* 473 A.2d at 815. Then, the burden shifts back to the plaintiffs who have the ultimate burden of persuasion to show a breach of the directors' fiduciary duties. *Unocal,* 493 A.2d at 958.

There are no allegations here of any bad faith on the part of the Directors' action in the adoption of the Rights Plan. There is no allegation that the Directors' action was taken for entrenchment purposes. Household has adequately demonstrated, as explained above, that the adoption of the Rights Plan was in reaction to what it perceived to be the threat in the market place of coercive two-tier tender offers. Appellants do contend, however, that the Board did not exercise informed business judgment in its adoption of the Plan.

Appellants contend that the Household Board was uninformed since they were, *inter alia,* told the Plan would not inhibit a proxy contest, were not told the plan would preclude all hostile acquisitions of Household, and were told that Delaware counsel opined that the plan was within the business judgment of the Board.

As to the first two contentions, as we explained above, the Rights Plan will not have a severe impact upon proxy contests and it will not preclude all hostile acquisitions of Household. Therefore, the Directors were not misinformed or uninformed on these facts.

Appellants contend the Delaware counsel did not express an opinion on the flip-over provision of the Rights, rather only that the Rights would constitute validly issued and outstanding rights to subscribe to the preferred stock of the company.

To determine whether a business judgment reached by a board of directors was an informed one, we determine whether the directors were grossly negligent. *Smith v. Van Gorkom,* Del. Supr., 488 A.2d 858, 873 (1985). Upon a review of this record, we conclude the Directors were not grossly negligent. The information supplied to the Board on August 14 provided the essentials of the Plan. The Directors were given beforehand a notebook which included a three-page summary of the Plan along with articles on the current takeover environment. The extended discussion between the Board and representatives of Wachtell, Lipton and Goldman, Sachs before approval of the Plan reflected a full and candid evaluation of the Plan. Moran's expression of his views at the meeting served to place before the Board a knowledgeable critique of the Plan. The factual happenings here are clearly distinguishable from the actions of the directors of Trans Union Corporation who displayed gross negligence in approving a cash-out merger. *Id.*

In addition, to meet their burden, the Directors must show that the defensive mechanism was "reasonable in relation to the threat posed". The record reflects a concern on the part of the Directors over the increasing frequency in the financial services industry of "boot-strap" and "bust-up" takeovers. The Directors were also concerned that such takeovers may take the form of two-tier offers.[14] In addition, on August 14, the Household Board was aware of Moran's overture on behalf of D-K-M. In sum, the Directors reasonably believed

---

14. We have discussed the coercive nature of two-tier tender offers in *Unocal,* 493 A.2d at 956, n. 12. We explained in *Unocal* that a discriminatory self-tender was reasonably related to the threat of two-tier tender offers and possible greenmail.

Household was vulnerable to coercive acquisition techniques and adopted a reasonable defensive mechanism to protect itself.

V

In conclusion, the Household Directors receive the benefit of the business judgment rule in their adoption of the Rights Plan.

The Directors adopted the Plan pursuant to statutory authority in 8 Del. C. §§141, 151, 157. We reject appellants' contentions that the Rights Plan strips stockholders of their rights to receive tender offers, and that the Rights Plan fundamentally restricts proxy contests.

The Directors adopted the Plan in the good faith belief that it was necessary to protect Household from coercive acquisition techniques. The Board was informed as to the details of the Plan. In addition, Household has demonstrated that the Plan is reasonable in relation to the threat posed. Appellants, on the other hand, have failed to convince us that the Directors breached any fiduciary duty in their adoption of the Rights Plan.

While we conclude for present purposes that the Household Directors are protected by the business judgment rule, that does not end the matter. The ultimate response to an actual takeover bid must be judged by the Directors' actions at that time, and nothing we say here relieves them of their basic fundamental duties to the corporation and its stockholders. *Unocal,* 493 A.2d at 954-55, 958; *Smith v. Van Gorkom,* 488 A.2d at 872-73; *Aronson,* 473 A.2d at 812-13; *Pogostinv. Rice,* Del. Supr., 480 A.2d 619, 627 (1984). Their use of the Plan will be evaluated when and if the issue arises.

AFFIRMED.

QUESTIONS

1. What is the source of the board's authority to adopt the poison pill?

2. What is the "flip-over" feature of the pill at issue in *Moran?*

3. What is the basis for the plaintiff's claim that the board's decision to adopt a poison pill usurps the shareholders of their right to receive tender offers? Do you agree with the court's reasoning on this issue?

4. Why does the plaintiff claim that the mere adoption of the poison pill involves a fundamental transfer of power from the company's shareholders to its board of directors?

5. What are the objectives that the board of directors hopes to accomplish by adopting the poison pill? How does the poison pill serve to implement those objectives?

6. Why did the board of directors in *Moran* include a redemption provision as part of the terms of the poison pill that it adopted?

7. What is the standard of review used by the *Moran* court to determine the validity of the board's decision to adopt the poison pill?

NOTES

1. Introduction to the Terms of a "Shareholder Rights Plan"—Or, What Is a "Poison Pill"?   The primary architect of the *poison pill* defense is Martin Lipton of the well-known New York law firm of Wachtell, Lipton, Rosen, & Katz. The development and efficacy of the pill is described in the firm's own words as follows:

Wachtell, Lipton, Rosen & Katz (1996)
THE SHARE PURCHASE RIGHTS PLAN

Background of the Rights Plan

The basic objectives of the rights plan are to deter abusive takeover tactics by making them unacceptably expensive to the raider and to encourage prospective acquirors to negotiate with the board of directors of the target rather than to attempt a hostile takeover.

The plan includes a "flip-in" feature designed to deter creeping accumulations of a company's stock. The "flip-in" feature is structured to be available from a 10% to a 20% ownership threshold. If triggered, the flip-in feature would give shareholders, other than the holder triggering the flip-in, the right to purchase shares of the company at a discount to market price (thereby diluting the triggering shareholder). The plan also has a "flip-over" feature which provides shareholders protection against a squeeze-out. The flip-over feature would give shareholders the right to purchase shares of the acquiring company at a discount in the event of a freeze-out merger or similar transaction (thereby diluting the acquiring company).

The rights issued pursuant to the plan are redeemable for a nominal amount prior to the acquisition of a large block of the target's shares. Thus, the effect of the plan is to force potential acquirors to deal with the company's board of directors (or conduct a proxy contest to replace directors) before acquiring shares in excess of the threshold levels. This increases the negotiating power of the Board. Part II contains a summary of the terms of our recommended plan.

The rights plan was designed not to interfere, and has not interfered, with the day to day operations of the companies that have adopted it. Prior to its being activated by an acquisition of a large block of the target company's shares, it has no effect on a company's balance sheet or income statement and it has no tax effect on the company or the shareholders. Companies have split their stock without interference from the plan. While the plan requires special care in such transactions, it has not hindered public offerings of common stock or SEC clearance of pooling of interests mergers.

The efficacy of the rights plan has made it a common feature among U.S. corporations. Over 1,700 companies have adopted a rights plan, including half of the Business Week 1000 companies and Fortune 500 companies and approximately two-thirds of the Fortune 200 companies. Indeed, in upholding the adoption rights plan as a proportionate response to a tender offer in the recent *Unitrin* case, the Delaware Supreme Court commented that the rights plan is an "effective takeover device" that has resulted in a "remarkable transformation in the market for corporate control."

Rights plans are also now well established in case law and statutory law. Starting with the Delaware Supreme Court's 1985 decision in the *Household* case, upholding one of the first right's plans to be adopted, the Delaware courts and courts in other jurisdictions, have widely recognized the legality and legitimate uses of a variety of rights plans. In each of the few jurisdictions in which a rights plan has been held invalid under the state's corporation law (because of the discriminatory flip in feature), the state legislature has amended the corporation law to establish clearly the legality of the flip-in feature of the rights plan.

The *Household* case and subsequent case law establish that adoption of a plan does not change the fiduciary standards to be followed by a board of directors in responding to a takeover bid. In the event of a specific takeover bid, the plan and its operation will have to be assessed in light of the response that the board decides is appropriate based on the advice at that time of the company's financial advisors and legal counsel. Much of the case law since *Household* has focused on how the board uses the rights plan in the face of a takeover bid, particularly on the decision whether to redeem the rights in response to a particular takeover bid. Some early Delaware Chancery Court cases suggested that a board would have an obligation to redeem a rights plan following an opportunity to search for alternatives where the bid offered a higher value than or was close in value to the identified alternatives. However, [subsequent] Delaware case law *(e.g.,* the Delaware Supreme Court decisions in *Paramount v. Time, QVC v. Paramount* and *Unitrin v. American General)* supports the view that, where the board has not made a decision to sell the company, the board may "just say no" and refuse to redeem the rights if the board determines in its business judgment that the bid is not in the best interests of the shareholders and would interfere with the company's long-term business plans and strategy.

The Flip-In Plan

The rights plan combines the flip-over with a flip-in that is triggered by an acquisition at the 20% level. The flip-in at a 20% threshold provides protection against takeover abuses involving partial and creeping accumulations. The plan also allows the board of directors to lower the threshold to not less than 10% if appropriate in light of specific circumstances.

If the flip-in is triggered, each holder of rights (other than the raider, whose rights become void) will be able to exercise the rights for common stock of the target having a market value, at the time the raider crosses the 20% threshold, of twice the right's exercise price. This would result in dilution to the raider both economically and in terms of its percentage ownership of the target's shares. The exact level of the dilution would depend on the market value of the target's common stock in relation to the exercise price of the rights.

The rights plan also contains a feature that gives the board of directors the option, after the flip-in is triggered by an acquisition at the 20% level (or such lower threshold down to 10% as has been set by the board) but before there has been a 50% acquisition, to exchange one new share of common stock of the company for each then valid right (which would exclude rights held by the raider that have become void). This provision will have an economically dilutive effect on the acquiror, and provide a corresponding benefit to the remaining rightsholders, that is comparable to the flip-in without requiring shareholders to go through the process and expense of exercising their rights. . . .

The Debate over Rights Plan

Rights plans have been anathema to the efficient market theorists of the Chicago School whose concept of a free market for corporate control is used as a policy justification by the opponents of plans. The evidence, however, does not support their argument that rights plans hurt shareholder values.

* * *

Institutional Investor Activists

[In recent] years, institutions such as the College Retirement Equities Fund and the California Public Employees Retirement System, several union pension funds and other shareholder activists have submitted resolutions to several companies each year, generally those with institutions holding a majority of the outstanding shares, requesting rescission of their plans unless submitted to a shareholder vote and approved by a majority of the shares. Although these proposals often receive significant support, only a few proposals have been approved. A 1995 report by the Investor Responsibility Research Center indicates that the frequency of these proposals has continued to decline in recent years, with the twelve such proposals presented to shareholders in 1994 the lowest number since they were first introduced in 1987. In addition, a few companies have agreed to either redeem their rights plans in three to four years or seek shareholder ratification. Several other companies, including Texaco, have solicited and received shareholder ratification of their rights plans. A few companies voluntarily redeemed rights plans when takeover activity lessened in the early 1990s. Time-Warner, which have redeemed its rights plan in response to institutional shareholder pressure, reinstituted a rights plan with a 15% threshold in response to open market purchases by Seagrams. Many institutional investors have come to recognize that a rights plan can be an effective negotiating tool for a responsible board of directors.

Conclusion

Takeover activity continues and the dynamics of takeovers are constantly changing. While the rights plan decreases the potential of hostile takeover activity, it will not, and is not intended to, make a company takeover-proof. The rights plan protects against takeover abuses, it gives all parties an increased period of time in which to make decisions on such a fundamentally important question as a takeover, and it strengthens the ability of the board of directors of a Target to fulfill its fiduciary duties to obtain the best result for the shareholders. We recommend that the Company adopt the rights plan.

TERMS OF RIGHTS PLAN[1]

Issuance: One right to buy 1/100th of a share of a new series-of preferred stock as a dividend on each outstanding share of common stock of the company. Until the rights become exercisable, all further issuances of common stock, including common stock issuable upon exercise of outstanding options, would include issuance of rights.

Term: 10 years.

Exercise price: An amount per 1/100th of a share of the preferred stock which approximates the board's view of the long-term value of the company's common stock. Factors to be considered in setting the exercise price include the company's business and prospects, its long-term plans and market conditions. For most companies that have adopted rights plans, the exercise price has been

---

1. These terms are as they would be set by a company that uses authorized blank check preferred stock, with terms that make 1/100th of a share of the preferred stock the economic equivalent of one share of common stock, as the security for which the rights are exercisable.

between three and five times current market price. The exercise price is subject to certain anti-dilution adjustments. For illustration only, assume an exercise price of $150 per 1/100th of a share.

Rights detach and become exercisable: The rights are not exercisable and are not transferable apart from the company's common stock until the tenth day after such time as a person or group acquires beneficial ownership of 20% or more of the company's common stock or the tenth business day (or such later time as the board of directors may determine) after a person or group announces its intention to commence or commences a tender or exchange offer the consummation of which would result in beneficial ownership by a person or group of 20% or more of the company' common stock. As soon as practicable after the rights become exercisable, separate right certificates would be issued and the rights would become transferable apart from the company's common stock.

Protection against squeezeout: If, after the rights have been triggered, an acquiring company were to merge or otherwise combine with the company, or the company were to sell 50% or more of its assets or earning power, each right than outstanding would "flip over" and thereby would become a right to buy that number of shares of common stock of the acquiring company which at the time of such transaction would have a market value of two times the exercise price of the rights. Thus, if the acquiring company's common stock at the time of such transaction were trading at $75 per share and the exercise price at the rights at such time were $150, each right would thereafter be exercisable $150 for four shares (*i.e.,* the number of shares that could be purchased for $300, or two times the exercise price of the rights) of the acquiring company's common stock.

Protection against creeping acquisition/open market purchases: In the event a person or group were to acquire a 20% or greater position in the company, each right then outstanding would "flip in" and become a right to buy that number of shares of common stock of the company which at the time of the 20% acquisition had a market value of two times the exercise price of the rights. The acquiror who triggered the rights would be excluded from the "flip-in" because his rights would have become null and void upon his triggering acquisition. Thus, if the company's common stock at the time of the "flip-in" were trading at $75 per share and the exercise price of the rights at such time were $150, each right would thereafter be exercisable at $150 for four shares of the company's common stock. As described below, the amendment provision of the Rights Agreement provides that the 20% threshold can be lowered to not less than 10%. The board can utilize this provision to provide additional protection against creeping accumulations.

Exchange: At any time after the acquisition by a person or group of affiliated or associated persons of beneficial ownership of 20% or more of the outstanding common stock of the company and before the acquisition by a person or group of 50% or more of the outstanding common stock of the company, the board of directors may exchange the rights (other than rights owned by such person or group, which have become avoid), in whole or in part, at an exchange ratio of one share of the company's common stock (or 1/100th of a share of junior participating preferred stock) per right, subject to adjustment.

Redemption: The rights are redeemable by the company's board of directors at a price of $.01 per right at any time prior to the acquisition by a person or group of beneficial ownership of 20% or more of the company's common stock. The redemption of the rights may be made effective at such time, on such basis, and with such conditions as the board of directors in its sole discretion may establish. Thus, the rights would not interfere with a negotiated merger or a white knight transaction, even after a hostile tender offer has been commenced. The rights may prevent a white knight transaction after a 20% acquisition (unless the exchange feature described above is used to eliminate the rights and the white knight's price is adjusted for the issuance of the additional shares).

Voting: The rights would not have any voting rights.

Terms of preferred stock: The preferred stock issuable upon exercise of the rights would be non-redeemable and rank junior to all other series of the company's preferred stock. The dividend, liquidation and voting rights, and nonredemption features of the preferred stock are designed so that the value of the 1/100th interest in a share of new preferred stock purchasable with each right will approximate the value of the one share of common stock. Each whole share of preferred stock would be entitled to receive a quarterly preferential dividend of $1 per share but would be entitled to receive, in the aggregate, a dividend of 100 times the dividend declared on the common stock. In the event of liquidation, the holders of the new preferred stock would be entitled to receive a preferential liquidation payment of $100 per share but would be entitled to receive, in the aggregate, a liquidation payment equal to 100 times the payment made per share of common stock. Each share of preferred stock would have 100 votes, voting together with the common stock. Finally, in the event of any merger, consolidation or other transaction in which shares of common stock are exchanged for or changed into other stock or securities, cash and/or other property, each share of preferred stock would be entitled to receive 100 times the amount received per share of common stock. The foregoing rights are protected against dilution in the event of additional shares of common stock are issued. Since the "out of the money" rights would not be exercisable immediately, registration of the preferred stock issuable upon exercise of the rights with the Securities and Exchange Commission need not be effective until the rights become exercisable and are "in the money" or are so close to being "in the money" so as to make exercise economically possible. . . .

Miscellaneous: The Rights Agreement provides that the company may not enter into any transaction of the sort which would give rise to the "flip-over" right if in connection therewith there are outstanding securities or there are agreements or arrangements intended to counteract the protective provisions of the rights. The Rights Agreement may be amended from time to time in any manner prior to the acquisition of a 20% position. . . .

2. How Does the Pill Work as a Takeover Defense?   The essential features and the basic mechanics of the terms that are typically included as part of most modern shareholder rights plans (*aka* poison pills) have been briefly summarized as follows:

> Stockholder right plans were born in the 1980s in response to the proliferation of corporate raiders making hostile bids for public companies, and were designed to provide public company boards of directors with a "poison pill" with which to defend themselves against hostile takeover bids. Stockholder rights plans allow the target board of directors time and leverage to negotiate for a control premium or other alternatives to hostile bids. Typically, a stockholder rights plan provides rights to all holders of common stock that, if fully activated, will give all stockholders, other than the hostile bidder, the right to buy additional stock at a substantial discount. The rights initially trade together with the common stock, do not have separate certificates and are not exercisable.
>
> A poison pill typically has two triggers that will cause the rights to be distributed separately from the common stock and to become exercisable. The date this occurs is usually called the "distribution date."
>
> One trigger occurs when a potential acquirer launches a tender offer for the purchase of at least a specified percentage of the stock of the target company.

Upon this trigger, the rights are distributed and become exercisable. Upon a distribution for this trigger, one right is usually exercisable to purchase the equivalent of one share of common stock at a fixed price (the "exercise price"), which is customarily set at a price representing the hypothetical appreciation of the stock over the duration of the plan. Often, a board seeks the advice of an investment bank on setting the exercise price.

The second trigger occurs when someone actually acquires beneficial ownership of stock over a specified percentage. When this occurs, the holder is usually given some time to divest itself of excess holdings, and if it does not, the rights undergo what is called a "flip-in." On a flip-in, each right other than rights held by the holder that triggered the flip-in becomes exercisable for the number of shares equal to the exercise price divided by one-half the then-current trading price of the stock. For example, if a company's stock is trading at $15 per share at a time when someone triggers a flip-in by acquiring 25 percent of the outstanding shares, and the rights have a $30 per share exercise price, each right, other than those held by the triggering holder, will enable the purchase of 4 common stock equivalents for $30, which is an effective price per share of $7.50. Assuming all the rights are exercised, the holdings of the holder that triggered the rights will decrease from 25 percent to 6.25 percent. Typically, upon a flip-in event, the board can elect to exchange each right for one (or more) common stock equivalents in lieu of permitting the rights to be exercised for cash.

Louis Lehot, et al., *The Return of the Poison Pill — Lessons Learned in 2010 from the* Selectica *and* Barnes & Noble *Cases*, 21 INSIGHTS, 23-24 (December 2010).

3. The Validation of the Poison Pill Is a Game-Changing Event. The validation of the poison pill by the Delaware Supreme Court revolutionized the takeover defense practices of incumbent corporate managers. The development of the shareholder rights plan (aka "the pill") solved many of the problems that were associated with several of the takeover defenses that were widely employed at the time (before the *Moran* case was decided). Notably, and as was seen in the *Moran* case, the poison pill could be implemented unilaterally by management and without obtaining shareholder approval; moreover, adoption of the pill generally had no effect on the company's capital structure, its accounting, or its fundamental value, and yet it provided Target management with a potent tool to ward off the unsolicited Bidder. As such, company managers no longer felt as though they were sitting ducks; instead, the implementation of the poison pill gave the board of directors a seat at the bargaining table by leaving the board in control of the acquisition process. Consequently, the determined Bidder was left to negotiate with Target management, or alternatively, replace the recalcitrant directors, usually by mounting a proxy fight.

4. The Pill Becomes Widely Adopted as a Takeover Defense. Following the Delaware Supreme Court's ruling in *Moran*, the poison pill became a staple in the arsenal of takeover defenses erected by public companies. Indeed, by "the mid-1990s, poison pills had been widely adopted by public companies in the United States, and were a key structural defense, or 'shark repellent' to hostile corporate raiders. By the end of 1993, approximately 1,375 companies had poison pills in place. Adoptions and extensions of poison pills continued and by the end of 2001, approximately 2,200 companies had poison pills in force."

Louis Lehot, et al., *The Return of the Poison Pill—Lessons Learned from the* Selectica *and* Barnes & Noble *Cases,* 24 INSIGHTS 23, at 24 (December 2010).

5. *The Continuing Evolution of the Pill.*   Shareholder rights plans (or "poison pills" as they are more popularly known) are widely regarded as one of the most effective, if not the most effective, device developed yet to protect the company from an inadequate bid or other types of abusive takeover tactics. Since the invention of the poison pill in 1984, these rights plan have continued to evolve. Although the key features of a rights plan continue to be the "flip-in" and the "flip-over" provisions, modern versions of the poison pill have added other features designed to address specific concerns or specific types of Bidder tactics. Thus, today, modern variations of rights plans include dead-hand pills, no-hand pills, and chewable pills. The operation of these modern variations and their validity under modern fiduciary duty law are addressed in the cases in the next section. *See Carmody v. Toll Bros, Inc., infra,* at p. 581; and *Quickturn Design Systems, Inc., infra,* at p. 590.

6. *The Poison Pill Is a Very Potent Defense.*   With respect to the early generation of "flip-over" pill, the only case that I am aware of where this type of pill has been triggered is the Crown-Zellerbach situation (as described in the *Moran* opinion), where Sir Jimmy Goldsmith triggered the company's pill, leaving him a substantial shareholder in the company. Once Sir Jimmy Goldsmith acquired 51 percent of the stock of Crown-Zellerbach, the board's power to redeem the pill was terminated. At this point, the controlling shareholder could not undertake a second-step, takeout merger without triggering the devastating consequences of the flip-over rights of the poison pill. The moral of this story was obvious: a poison pill with flip-over rights generally will operate to prevent a second-step merger, but it will not necessarily prevent a change in control of the company. To discourage this type of open-market purchase activity that allowed a prospective bidder to accumulate a sizeable stake in the Target company, the pill evolved to include a "flip-in" feature. The evolution of the "flip-in" pill is supported by the Delaware Supreme Court's decision in *Unocal,* where the Delaware Supreme Court upheld the discriminatory self-tender. Based on this, the inventor of the pill was emboldened to include a "flip-in" provision, which depends (as it must to be effective) on a discriminatory feature. To the best of my knowledge, no one has ever willingly triggered a "flip-in" pill. While the pill is a potent deterrent to an unsolicited bid and thus encourages Bidders to negotiate with Target management, it bears emphasizing that the pill does not provide the Target with an impenetrable defense against the unsolicited takeover. That is, the poison pill does not erect a bulletproof shield that operates to prevent hostile takeovers. Instead, the Bidder is encouraged to come to the bargaining table and negotiate with Target management, and the option of "going hostile" usually becomes the Bidder's tool of last resort.

7. *Fair Price Provisions and Other Charter Amendments.*   In footnote 3 of the *Moran* opinion, the Delaware Supreme Court describes the fair price provisions that some companies have included in their corporate charter, i.e, in the company's articles of incorporation, or in the case of Delaware companies, in the company's certificate of incorporation, although these provisions may in some cases be made part of the company's by-laws. Other types of charter provisions—that also operate as antitakeover devices—include staggered terms for the company's board of directors (sometimes referred to as a "classified board"), a provision that a board can be removed only for cause, and limitations on the use of special meetings of the shareholders and the setting of the date for shareholder meetings. Collectively, these various types of charter provisions are often colloquially referred to as "shark repellants," a reference to the fact that these provisions are designed not only to protect the company's shareholders from certain harmful effects that may accompany a change in control of the company, but are also designed to discourage prospective bidders from launching an unsolicited bid seeking control of the company. *Query*: How do these various types of charter provisions work to achieve these objectives?

8. Recent Activist Shareholder Movement Questions the Wisdom of the Pill. The development of the poison pill defense has not been without its critics. Almost from its inception, controversy surrounded the wisdom of implementing a pill. *See, e.g.,* Gregg Jarrell and Michael Ryngaert, Office of the Chief Economist of the Securities and Exchange Commission, *The Effect of Poison Pills on the Wealth of Target Shareholders* (Oct. 23, 1986); and the controversy continues; *see, e.g.,* John C. Coates IV, *The Contestability of Corporate Control: A Critique of the Scientific Evidence on Takeover Defenses*, 79 Tex. L. Rev. 271 (2000). In the wake of unprecedented financial scandals involving some of the largest corporations in the United States, the dawn of the twenty-first century saw institutional shareholders once again take to the offensive. Following the collapse of the tech bubble in 2002 and the end of the dot-com era, hedge funds began to join other institutional shareholder activists in advocating the dismantling of many antitakeover measures. These shareholders frequently used the SEC's shareholder proposal rule (Rule 14a-8 of Regulation 14A, the federal proxy rules) to bring their reform proposals before the shareholders for a nonbinding vote; one of the more popular proposals that the proponents would put forth recommended termination of the shareholder rights plan. As these proposals started meeting with success at the ballot box, companies quietly began dismantling the takeover defenses that had been so carefully erected in the past, rather than face the prospect of defeat at the ballot box. In the post-SOX era, these activist shareholders were further emboldened as investors generally grew more skeptical of incumbent management; and, as management's often quite lavish pay packages came under greater scrutiny, this resulted in ever greater shareholder disenchantment with incumbent management. So, not surprisingly:

> The last decade saw major corporate scandals from Enron to WorldCom to Tyco, the adoption of the Sarbanes-Oxley Act of 2002 and the rise of organized institutional investor voting and corporate governance metrics. Stockholder activists and proxy advisory firms rallied against poison pills, arguing that they often resulted in the entrenchment of management and the loss of stockholder value. With these changes came declines in the annual number of pill adoptions and extensions, with annual decreased activity each year. By the end 2007, the number of companies with poison pills in place had declined to the levels seen in 1994. By the third quarter of 2009, boards of directors of established public companies had largely allowed their stockholder rights plans to expire, companies in registration ceased adopting stockholder rights plans in the course of going public and less than a third of S&P 1,500 companies had a poison pill in place.

Louis Lehot, et al., *The Return of the Poison Pill—Lessons Learned from the* Selectica *and* Barnes & Noble *Cases,* 24 INSIGHTS 23 at 27 (December 2010). Consequently, by 2011, "only about 900 U.S. publicly traded companies had a [poison pill] in place—a nearly 60% drop over the last ten years." John F. Grossbauer and Pamela L. Millard, *Stockholder Rights, Plans in Negotiated Mergers: Issues of Delaware Law,* 44 SEC. & COMMODITIES REG. 269 (Dec. 2011).

Even more importantly, the explosive growth of institutional investment in the stock markets has led to a dramatic power shift to shareholders and away from the dominance of management that was prevalent in the 1970s. This shift has resulted in focusing increasing attention on the most basic of corporate tenets: Will this seeming power shift to shareholders (most notably, institutional shareholders, including the explosive growth of hedge funds over the past decade) fundamentally change the long-standing paradigm that directors—not shareholders—manage the business affairs of the modern corporation? This is the question that is currently being hotly debated by the practicing M&A bar, by the regulators, and in the academic literature—a question that as of this writing has no readily discernible answer.

9. Proxy Contests Mounted by Activist Shareholders.   Historically, corporate raiders who disagreed with a particular company's business strategy (such as Carl Icahn and T. Boone Pickens) would purchase a controlling interest in the company (typically through a tender offer) and then "squeeze out" the remaining shareholders by engaging in a second-step, back-end merger. The raider, as the new owner of the company, would then implement a different business strategy, which might include "busting up" the company by selling off its assets. Reflecting that business practices of M&A transactions are continually evolving, a very different strategy is often employed today by those investors who disagree with the business strategy of a particular company. Now activist shareholders are purchasing as little as 2 percent or 3 percent of a Target's stock and then undertaking a proxy campaign to elect the insurgent shareholders' slate of nominees to the Target's board. If an activist shareholder succeeds in electing its nominees to the board, the investor "can often effectively [gain] control of the target [company], without purchasing any additional shares, without payment of a control premium to the existing shareholders and, if the board seats are received in settlement of a proxy contest [as where the activist shareholder reaches an agreement with target company's management to appoint the investors' nominees to the company's board of directors] without receiving a single vote in an election of directors." Gary D. Gilson and Michelle Torline, *Control for the Taking: Activist Shareholder Election Contests,* 5. BOARDROOM BRIEFING 33 (Summer 2008, a publication of Directors & Boards Magazine and GRID Media LLC).* In light of the recent market activity of these activist investors,

---

* As a reflection of how the times have changed—and how the market for M&A activity continues to evolve in our post-Enron world—Carl Icahn has been quoted as saying publicly, "What's changed is the perception. Now, instead of being called a corporate raider, I'm an activist." [This quote was included in the materials submitted by James C. Morphy as part of his presentation at the Twentieth Annual Tulane Corporate Law Institute on April 4, 2008; see p. 21 of his slide presentation, a copy of which is on file with the author.] Indeed,

not surprisingly many experienced market participants are revisiting the long-standing debate over the wisdom of implementing (or dismantling, as the case may be) defensive measures such as shareholder rights plans and staggered boards. *See, e.g.,* Martin Lipton, *Shareholder Activism and the "Eclipse" of the Public Corporation: Is the Current Wave of Activism Causing Another Tectonic Shift in the American Corporate World?*, Keynote Address, The 2008 Directors Forum of the University of Minnesota Law School, June 25, 2008; and David A. Katz and Laura A. McIntosh, *Corporate Governance: Advice on Coping with Hedge Fund Activism,* (Wachtell, Lipton, Rosen, & Katz Law Firm Publication, dated May 25, 2006).

2.   The Continuing Evolution of Delaware's Standard of "Enhanced Scrutiny" and Further Development of the "Poison Pill" Defense

Unitrin, Inc. v. American General Corp.
651 A.2d 1361 (Del. 1995)

HOLLAND, Justice.

This is an appeal from the Court of Chancery's entry of a preliminary injunction on October 13, 1994, upon plaintiffs' motions in two actions: American General Corporation's ("American General") suit against Unitrin, Inc. ("Unitrin") and its directors; and a parallel class action brought by Unitrin stockholders. An interlocutory appeal was certified by the Court of Chancery on October 24, 1994. This Court accepted the appeal on October 27, 1994.

American General, which had publicly announced a proposal to merge with Unitrin for $2.6 billion at $50-3/8 per share, and certain Unitrin shareholder plaintiffs, filed suit in the Court of Chancery, *inter alia,* to enjoin Unitrin from repurchasing up to 10 million shares of its own stock (the "Repurchase Program"). On August 26, 1994, the Court of Chancery temporarily restrained Unitrin from making any further repurchases. After expedited discovery, briefing and argument, the Court of Chancery preliminarily enjoined Unitrin from making further repurchases on the ground that the Repurchase Program was a disproportionate response to the threat posed by American General's inadequate all cash for all shares offer, under the standard of this Court's holding in *Unocal Corp. v. Mesa Petroleum Co.,* Del. Supr., 493 A.2d 946 (1985) *("Unocal").*

Carl Icahn deployed this very strategy (as described in the accompanying text) on several recent occasions. One high-profile example is his recent run at Motorola, which resulted in Carl Icahn negotiating a compromise with the company to end his proxy context. "In April [2008], Motorola, Inc. caved in to Mr. Icahn's demands by agreeing to add two Icahn associates to its board and to consult with him on naming a new leader for its troubled handset division." Merissa Marr and Jessica E. Vascellaro, *Icahn Ends Feud with Yahoo, Setting up an Uneasy Truce,* WALL STREET JOURNAL, July 22, 2008 at A1.

UNITRIN'S CONTENTIONS

Unitrin has raised several issues in this appeal. First, it contends that the Court of Chancery erred in assuming that the outside directors would subconsciously act contrary to their substantial financial interests as stockholders and, instead, vote in favor of a subjective desire to protect the "prestige and perquisites" of membership on Unitrin's Board of Directors. Second, it contends that the Court of Chancery erred in holding that the adoption of the Repurchase Program would materially affect the ability of an insurgent stockholder to win a proxy contest. According to Unitrin, that holding is unsupported by the evidence, is based upon a faulty mathematical analysis, and disregards the holding of *Moran v. Household Int'l, Inc.,* Del. Supr., 500 A.2d 1346, 1355 (1985). Furthermore, Unitrin argues that the Court of Chancery erroneously substituted its own judgment for that of Unitrin's Board, contrary to this Court's subsequent interpretations of *Unocal* in *Paramount Communications, Inc. v. QVC Network, Inc.,* Del. Supr., 637 A.2d 34, 45-46 (1994), and *Paramount Communications, Inc. v. Time, Inc.* Del. Supr., 571 A.2d 1140 (1990). Third, Unitrin submits that the Court of Chancery erred in finding that the plaintiffs would be irreparably harmed absent an injunction (a) because the Court of Chancery disregarded Unitrin's proffered alternative remedy of sterilizing the increased voting power of the stockholder directors and (b) because there was no basis for finding that stockholders who sold into the market during the pendency of the Repurchase Program would be irreparably harmed.

THIS COURT ULTIMATE DISPOSITION

This Court has concluded that the Court of Chancery erred in applying the proportionality review *Unocal* requires by focusing upon whether the Repurchase Program was an "unnecessary" defensive response. *See Paramount Communications, Inc. v. QVC Network, Inc.,* 637 A.2d at 45-46. The Court of Chancery should have directed its enhanced scrutiny: first, upon whether the Repurchase Program the Unitrin Board implemented was draconian, by being either preclusive or coercive and; second, if it was not draconian, upon whether it was within a range of reasonable responses to the threat American General's Offer posed. Consequently, the interlocutory preliminary injunctive judgment of the Court of Chancery is reversed. This matter is remanded for further proceedings in accordance with this opinion.

THE PARTIES

American General is the largest provider of home service insurance. On July 12, 1994, it made a merger proposal to acquire Unitrin for $2.6 billion at $50-3/8 per share. Following a public announcement of this proposal, Unitrin shareholders filed suit seeking to compel a sale of the company. American General filed suit to enjoin Unitrin's Repurchase Program.

Unitrin is also in the insurance business. It is the third largest provider of home service insurance. The other defendants-appellants are the members of Unitrin's seven person Board of Directors (the "Unitrin Board" or "Board"). Two directors are employees, Richard C. Vie ("Vie"), the Chief Executive Officer, and Jerrold V. Jerome ("Jerome"), Chairman of the Board. The five remaining directors are not and have never been employed by Unitrin. . . .

The record reflects that [five out of the seven] non-employee directors each receive a fixed annual fee of $30,000. They receive no other significant financial benefit from serving as directors. At the offering price proposed by American General, the value of Unitrin's non-employee directors' stock exceeded $450 million.

AMERICAN GENERAL'S OFFER

In January 1994, James Tuerff ("Tuerff"), the President of American General, met with Richard Vie, Unitrin's Chief Executive Officer. Tuerff advised Vie that American General was considering acquiring other companies. Unitrin was apparently at or near the top of its list. Tuerff did not mention any terms for a potential acquisition of Unitrin. Vie replied that Unitrin had excellent prospects as an independent company and had never considered a merger. Vie indicated to Tuerff that Unitrin was not for sale.

According to Vie, he reported his conversation with Tuerff at the next meeting of the Unitrin Board in February 1994. The minutes of the full Board meeting do not reflect a discussion of Tuerff's proposition. Nevertheless, the parties agree that the Board's position in February was that Unitrin was not for sale. It was unnecessary to respond to American General because no offer had been made.

On July 12, 1994, American General sent a letter to Vie proposing a consensual merger transaction in which it would "purchase all of Unitrin's 51.8 million outstanding shares of common stock for $50-3/8 per share, in cash" (the "Offer"). The Offer was conditioned on the development of a merger agreement and regulatory approval. The Offer price represented a 30% premium over the market price of Unitrin's shares. In the Offer, American General stated that it "would consider offering a higher price" if "Unitrin could demonstrate additional value." American General also offered to consider tax-free "[a]lternatives to an all cash transaction."

UNITRIN'S REJECTION

Upon receiving the American General Offer, the Unitrin Board's Executive Committee (Singleton, Vie, and Jerome) engaged legal counsel and scheduled a telephonic Board meeting for July 18. At the July 18 special meeting, the Board reviewed the terms of the Offer. The Board was advised that the existing charter and bylaw provisions might not effectively deter all types of takeover strategies. It was suggested that the Board consider adopting a shareholder rights plan and an advance notice provision for shareholder proposals.

The Unitrin Board met next on July 25, 1994 in Los Angeles for seven hours.[3] All directors attended the meeting. The principal purpose of the meeting was to discuss American General's Offer.

Vie reviewed Unitrin's financial condition and its ongoing business strategies. The Board also received a presentation from its investment advisor, Morgan Stanley & Co. ("Morgan Stanley"), regarding the financial adequacy of American General's proposal. Morgan Stanley expressed its opinion that the Offer was financially inadequate.[4] Legal counsel expressed concern that the combination of Unitrin and American General would raise antitrust complications due to the resultant decrease in competition in the home service insurance markets.

The Unitrin Board unanimously concluded that the American General merger proposal was not in the best interests of Unitrin's shareholders and voted to reject the Offer. The Board then received advice from its legal and financial advisors about a number of possible defensive measures it might adopt, including a shareholder rights plan ("poison pill") and an advance notice bylaw provision for shareholder proposals. Because the Board apparently thought that American General intended to keep its Offer private, the Board did not implement any defensive measures at that time.

AMERICAN GENERAL'S PUBLICITY
UNITRIN'S INITIAL RESPONSES

On August 2, 1994, American General issued a press release announcing its Offer to Unitrin's Board to purchase all of Unitrin's stock for $50-3/8 per share. The press release also noted that the Board had rejected American General's Offer. After that public announcement, the trading volume and market price of Unitrin's stock increased.

At its regularly scheduled meeting on August 3, the Unitrin Board discussed the effects of American General's press release. The Board noted that the market reaction to the announcement suggested that speculative traders or arbitrageurs were acquiring Unitrin stock. The Board determined that American General's public announcement constituted a hostile act designed to coerce the sale of Unitrin at an inadequate price. The Board unanimously approved the poison pill and the proposed advance notice bylaw that it had considered previously.

Beginning on August 2 and continuing through August 12, 1994, Unitrin issued a series of press releases to inform its shareholders and the public market:

---

3. Prior to the meeting, Unitrin's outside counsel, Irell & Manella ("Irell"), sent Unitrin a draft press release and script for the meeting. These documents contemplated the adoption of the poison pill, advance notice provision and the Repurchase Program. American General argues that this shows that the Board action was a *fait accompli*. The Unitrin defendants argue that it was contingency planning.

4. Eric Daut, who prepared these materials for Morgan Stanley under extreme time pressure, had never prepared such information previously and did not rely on firm figures. Morgan Stanley, in turn, did not investigate these figures.

first, that the Unitrin Board believed Unitrin's stock was worth more than the $50-3/8 American General offered; second, that the Board felt that the price of American General's Offer did not reflect Unitrin's long term business prospects as an independent company; third, that "the true value of Unitrin [was] not reflected in the [then] current market price of its common stock," and that because of its strong financial position, Unitrin was well positioned "to pursue strategic and financial opportunities;" fourth, that the Board believed a merger with American General would have anticompetitive effects and might violate antitrust laws and various state regulatory statutes; and fifth, that the Board had adopted a shareholder rights plan (poison pill) to guard against undesirable takeover efforts.

UNITRIN'S REPURCHASE PROGRAM

The Unitrin Board met again on August 11, 1994. The minutes of that meeting indicate that its principal purpose was to consider the Repurchase Program. At the Board's request, Morgan Stanley had prepared written materials to distribute to each of the directors. Morgan Stanley gave a presentation in which alternative means of implementing the Repurchase Program were explained. Morgan Stanley recommended that the Board implement an open market stock repurchase. The Board voted to authorize the Repurchase Program for up to ten million shares of its outstanding stock.

On August 12, Unitrin publicly announced the Repurchase Program. The Unitrin Board expressed its belief that "Unitrin's stock is undervalued in the market and that the expanded program will tend to increase the value of the shares that remain outstanding." The announcement also stated that the director stockholders were not participating in the Repurchase Program, and that the repurchases "will increase the percentage ownership of those stockholders who choose not to sell."

Unitrin's August 12 press release also stated that the directors owned 23% of Unitrin's stock, that the Repurchase Program would cause that percentage to increase, and that Unitrin's certificate of incorporation included a supermajority voting provision. The following language from a July 22 draft press release revealing the antitakeover effects of the Repurchase Program was omitted from the final press release:

> Under the [supermajority provision], the consummation of the expanded repurchase program would enhance the ability of nonselling stockholders, including the directors, to prevent a merger with a greater-than-15% stockholder if they did not favor the transaction.

Unitrin sent a letter to its stockholders on August 17 regarding the Repurchase Program which stated:

> Your Board of Directors has authorized the Company to repurchase, in the open market or in private transactions, up to 10 million of Unitrin's 51.8 million outstanding common shares. This authorization is intended to provide an additional measure of liquidity to the Company's shareholders in light of the unsettled market conditions resulting from American General's unsolicited

acquisition proposal. The Board believes that the Company's stock is undervalued and that this program will tend to increase the value of the shares that remain outstanding.

Between August 12 and noon on August 24, Morgan Stanley purchased nearly 5 million of Unitrin's shares on Unitrin's behalf. The average price paid was slightly above American General's Offer price. . . .

* * *

UNOCAL IS PROPER REVIEW STANDARD

* * *

The Court of Chancery held that all of the Unitrin Board's defensive actions merited judicial scrutiny according to *Unocal*. The record supports the Court of Chancery's determination that the Board perceived American General's Offer as a threat and adopted the Repurchase Program, along with the poison pill and advance notice bylaw, as defensive measures in response to that threat. Therefore, the Court of Chancery properly concluded the facts before it required an application of *Unocal* and its progeny.

UNOCAL'S STANDARD
BUSINESS JUDGMENT RULE
ENHANCED JUDICIAL SCRUTINY

. . . In *Unocal*, this Court reaffirmed "the application of the business judgment rule in the context of a hostile battle for control of a Delaware corporation where board action is taken to the exclusion of, or in limitation upon, a valid stockholder vote." *Stroud v. Grace*, 606 A.2d at 82. . . .

The enhanced judicial scrutiny mandated by *Unocal* is not intended to lead to a structured, mechanistic, mathematical exercise. Conversely, it is not intended to be an abstract theory. The *Unocal* standard is a flexible paradigm that jurists can apply to the myriad of "fact scenarios" that confront corporate boards.

PARTIES' BURDENS SHIFT
JUDICIAL REVIEW STANDARDS DIFFER
BUSINESS JUDGMENT RULE AND UNOCAL

The correct analytical framework is essential to a proper review of challenges to the decision-making process of a corporate Board. The ultimate question in applying the *Unocal* standard is: what deference should the reviewing court give "to the decisions of directors in defending against a takeover?" E. Norman Veasey, *The New Incarnation of the Business Judgment Rule in Takeover Defenses*, 11 Del. J. Corp. L. 503, 504-05 (1986). The question is usually presented to the Court of Chancery, as in the present case, in an injunction proceeding, a posture which is known as "transactional justification." *Id.* To answer the question, the enhanced judicial scrutiny *Unocal* requires implicates both the substantive and procedural nature of the business judgment rule. . . .

[I]n transactional justification cases involving the adoption of defenses to takeovers, the director's actions invariably implicate issues affecting stockholder rights. *See Revlon, Inc. v. MacAndrews & Forbes Holdings, Inc.,* Del. Supr., 506 A.2d 173, 180 n. 10 (1986). In transactional justification cases, the directors' decision is reviewed judicially and the burden of going forward is placed on the directors. *See* Joseph Hinsey, IV, *Business Judgment and the American Law Institute's Corporate Governance Project: the Rule, the Doctrine and the Reality,* 52 Geo. Wash. L. Rev., 609, 611-13 (1984). If the directors' actions withstand *Unocal's* reasonableness and proportionality review, the traditional business judgment rule is applied to shield the directors' defensive decision rather than the directors themselves. *Id.*

The litigation between Unitrin, American General, and the Unitrin shareholders in the Court of Chancery is a classic example of a transactional justification case. The Court of Chancery's determination that the conduct of Unitrin's Board was subject to *Unocal's* enhanced judicial scrutiny required it to evaluate each party's ability to sustain its unique burden in the procedural context of a preliminary injunction proceeding. The plaintiff's burden in such a proceeding is to demonstrate a reasonable probability of success after trial.

In general, to effectively defeat the plaintiff's ability to discharge that burden, a board must sustain its burden of demonstrating that, even under *Unocal's* standard of enhanced judicial scrutiny, its actions deserved the protection of the traditional business judgment rule. Thus, the plaintiff's likelihood of success in obtaining a preliminary injunction was initially dependent upon the inability of the Unitrin Board to discharge the burden placed upon it first by *Unocal.* Accordingly, having concluded that the Board's actions were defensive, the Court of Chancery logically began with an evaluation of the Unitrin Board's evidence.

AMERICAN GENERAL THREAT
REASONABLENESS BURDEN SUSTAINED

The first aspect of the *Unocal* burden, the reasonableness test, required the Unitrin Board to demonstrate that, after a reasonable investigation, it determined in good faith, that American General's Offer presented a threat to Unitrin that warranted a defensive response. This Court has held that the presence of a majority of outside independent directors will materially enhance such evidence. *Unocal,* 493 A.2d at 955. . . .

The Unitrin Board identified two dangers it perceived the American General Offer posed: inadequate price and antitrust complications. The Court of Chancery characterized the Board's concern that American General's proposed transaction could never be consummated because it may violate antitrust laws and state insurance regulations as a "makeweight excuse" for the defensive measure. It determined, however, that the Board reasonably believed that the American General Offer was inadequate and also reasonably concluded that the Offer was a threat to Unitrin's uninformed stockholders.

The Court of Chancery held that the Boards evidence satisfied the first aspect or reasonableness test under *Unocal*. The Court of Chancery then noted, however, that the threat to the Unitrin stockholders from American General's inadequate opening bid was "mild," because the Offer was negotiable both in price and structure.[16] The court then properly turned its attention to *Unocal's* second aspect, the proportionality test because "[i]t is not until both parts of the *Unocal* inquiry have been satisfied that the business judgment rule attaches to defensive actions of a board of directors." *Paramount Communications, Inc. v. Time, Inc.*, 571 A.2d at 1154.

PROPORTIONALITY BURDEN
CHANCERY APPROVES POISON PILL

The second aspect or proportionality test of the initial *Unocal* burden required the Unitrin Board to demonstrate the proportionality of its response to the threat American General's Offer posed. The record reflects that the Unitrin Board considered three options as defensive measures: the poison pill, the advance notice bylaw, and the Repurchase Program. . . .

On August 2, American General made a public announcement of its offer to buy all the shares of Unitrin for $2.6 billion at $50-3/8 per share. The Unitrin Board had already concluded that the American General offer was inadequate. It also apparently feared that its stockholders did not realize that the long term value of Unitrin was not reflected in the market price of its stock.

On August 3, the Board met to decide whether any defensive action was necessary. The Unitrin Board decided to adopt defensive measures to protect Unitrin's stockholders from the inadequate American General Offer in two stages: first, it passed the poison pill and the advance notice bylaw; and, a week later, it implemented the Repurchase Program.

With regard to the second aspect or proportionality test of the initial *Unocal* burden, the Court of Chancery analyzed each stage of the Unitrin Board's defensive responses separately. . . . The Court of Chancery concluded that Unitrin's Board believed in good faith that the American General Offer was inadequate and properly employed a poison pill as a proportionate defensive response to protect its stockholders from a "low ball" bid.

No cross-appeal was filed in this expedited interlocutory proceeding. Therefore, the Court of Chancery's ruling that the Unitrin Board's adoption of a poison pill was a proportionate response to American General's Offer is not now directly at issue. Nevertheless, to the extent the Unitrin Board's prior adoption of the poison pill influenced the Court of Chancery's proportionality review of the Repurchase Program, the Board's adoption of the poison pill is also a factor to be considered on appeal by this Court.

---

16. A board's response to an offer to merge is traditionally tested by the business judgment rule since a statutory prerequisite (8 Del. C. §251(b)) to a merger transaction is approval by the Board before any stockholder action. *See Paramount Communications, Inc. v. Time, Inc.*, 571 A.2d at 1142.

PROPORTIONALITY BURDEN
CHANCERY ENJOINS REPURCHASE PROGRAM

The Court of Chancery did not view either its conclusion that American General's Offer constituted a threat, or its conclusion that the poison pill was a reasonable response to that threat, as requiring it, *a fortiori*, to conclude that the Repurchase Program was also an appropriate response. The Court of Chancery then made two factual findings: first, the Repurchase Program went beyond what was "necessary" to protect the Unitrin stockholders from a "low ball" negotiating strategy; and second, it was designed to keep the decision to combine with American General within the control of the members of the Unitrin Board, as stockholders, under virtually all circumstances. Consequently, the Court of Chancery held that the Unitrin Board failed to demonstrate that the Repurchase Program met the second aspect or proportionality requirement of the initial burden *Unocal* ascribes to a board of directors.

The Court of Chancery framed the ultimate question before it as follows:

> This case comes down to one final question: Is placing the decision to sell the company in the hands of stockholders who are also directors a disproportionate response to a low price offer to buy all the shares of the company for cash?

The Court of Chancery then answered that question:

> I conclude that because the only threat to the corporation is the inadequacy of an opening bid made directly to the board, and the board has already taken actions that will protect the stockholders from mistakenly falling for a low ball negotiating strategy, a repurchase program that intentionally provides members of the board with a veto of any merger proposal is not reasonably related to the threat posed by American General's negotiable all shares, all cash offer.

In explaining its conclusion, the Court of Chancery reasoned that:

> I have no doubt that a hostile acquiror can make an offer high enough to entice at least some of the directors that own stock to break ranks and sell their shares. Yet, these directors undoubtedly place a value, probably a substantial one, on their management of Unitrin, and will, at least subconsciously, reject an offer that does not compensate them for that value. . . . The prestige and perquisites that accompany managing Unitrin as a member of its Board of directors, even for the non-officer directors that do not draw a salary, may cause these stockholder directors to reject an excellent offer unless it includes this value in its "price parameter."

The Court of Chancery concluded that, although the Unitrin Board had properly perceived American General's inadequate Offer as a threat and had properly responded to that threat by adopting a "poison pill," the additional defensive response of adopting the Repurchase Program was unnecessary and disproportionate to the threat the Offer posed. Accordingly, it concluded that the plaintiffs had "established with reasonable probability that the [Unitrin Board] violated its duties under *Unocal* [by authorizing the Repurchase Program]" because the Board had not sustained its burden of demonstrating that the Repurchase Program was a proportionate response to American General's Offer. Therefore, the Court of Chancery held that the plaintiffs proved a likelihood of success on that issue and granted the motion to preliminarily enjoin the Repurchase Program.[18]

PROXY CONTEST
SUPERMAJORITY VOTE
REPURCHASE PROGRAM

Before the Repurchase Program began, Unitrin's directors collectively held approximately 23% of Unitrin's outstanding shares. Unitrin's certificate of incorporation already included a "shark-repellent"[19] provision barring any business combination with a more-than-15% stockholder unless approved by a majority of continuing directors or by a 75% stockholder vote ("Supermajority Vote"). Unitrin's shareholder directors announced publicly that they would not participate in the Repurchase Program and that this would result in a percentage increase of ownership for them, as well as for any other shareholder who did not participate.

The Court of Chancery found that by not participating in the Repurchase Program, the Board "expected to create a 28% voting block to support the Board's decision to reject [a future] offer by American General." From this underlying factual finding, the Court of Chancery concluded that American General might be "chilled" in its pursuit of Unitrin:

> Increasing the board members' percentage of stock ownership, combined with the supermajority merger provision, does more than protect uninformed stockholders from an inadequate offer, it chills any unsolicited acquiror from making an offer.

The parties are in substantial disagreement with respect to the Court of Chancery's ultimate factual finding that the Repurchase Program was a disproportionate response under *Unocal*. Unitrin argues that American General or another potential acquiror can theoretically prevail in an effort to obtain control of Unitrin through a proxy contest. . . . The stockholder-plaintiffs argue that even if it can be said, as a matter of law, that it is acceptable under certain circumstances to leave potential bidders with a proxy battle as the sole avenue for acquiring an entity, the Court of Chancery correctly determined, as a factual matter, that the Repurchase Program was disproportionate to the threat American General's Offer posed.

---

18. We note that the directors' failure to carry their initial burden under *Unocal* does not, *ipso facto*, invalidate the board's actions. Instead, once the Court of Chancery finds the business judgment rule does not apply, the burden remains on the directors to prove "entire fairness." *See Cede & Co. v. Technicolor, Inc.*, Del. Supr., 634 A.2d 345, 361 (1993); . . .

19. A "shark-repellent" is a provision in a company's by-laws or articles of incorporation that is intended to deter a bidder's interest in that company as a target for a takeover. *See* Ellen S. Friedenberg, Jaws III: *The Impropriety of Shark-Repellent Amendments as a Takeover Defense*, 7 Del. J. Corp. L. 32 (1982).

PROPORTIONALITY TEST
SHAREHOLDER FRANCHISE

This Court has been and remains assiduous in its concern about defensive actions designed to thwart the essence of corporate democracy by disenfranchising shareholders. *Paramount Communications, Inc. v. QVC Network, Inc.,* Del. Supr., 637 A.2d 34, 42 n. 11 (1994). *See also Stroud v. Grace,* Del. Supr., 606 A.2d 75 (1992). . . .

Nevertheless, this Court has upheld the propriety of adopting poison pills in given defensive circumstances. Keeping a poison pill in place may be inappropriate, however, when those circumstances change dramatically. *See Moran v. Household Int'l, Inc.,* Del. Supr., 500 A.2d 1346, 1355 (1985). *Cf. Revlon, Inc. v. MacAndrews & Forbes Holdings, Inc.,* Del. Supr., 506 A.2d 173, 179 (1986). Similarly, this Court has recognized the propriety of implementing certain repurchase programs (as in *Unocal* itself), as well as the unreasonableness and non-proportionality of responding defensively to a takeover bid with a coercive and preclusive partial self-tender offer. *See Paramount Communications, Inc. v. Time, Inc.,* Del. Supr., 571 A.2d 1140, 1154 (1990).

More recently, this Court stated: "we accept the basic legal tenets," set forth in *Blasius Indus., Inc. v. Atlas Corp.,* Del. Ch., 564 A.2d 651 (1988),[21] that "[w]here boards of directors deliberately employ [ ]. . . legal strategies either to frustrate or completely disenfranchise a shareholder vote, . . . [t]here can be no dispute that such conduct violates Delaware law." *Stroud v. Grace,* 606 A.2d at 91. . . .

TAKEOVER STRATEGY
TENDER OFFER/PROXY CONTEST

We begin our examination of Unitrin's Repurchase Program mindful of the special import of protecting the shareholder's franchise within *Unocal's* requirement that a defensive response be reasonable and proportionate. For many years the "favored attack of a [corporate] raider was stock acquisition followed by a proxy contest." *Unocal,* 493 A.2d at 957. Some commentators have noted that the recent trend toward tender offers as the preferable alternative to proxy contests appears to be reversing because of the proliferation of sophisticated takeover defenses. Lucian A. Bebchuk & Marcel Kahan, *A Framework for Analyzing Legal Policy Towards Proxy Contests,* 78 Cal. L. Rev. 1071, 1134 (1990). In fact, the same commentators have characterized a return to proxy contests

---

21. In *Blasius,* the Court of Chancery held that board actions done primarily for the purpose of impeding the exercise of stockholder voting power are not invalid *per se.* "Rather, . . . in such a case, the board bears the heavy burden of demonstrating a compelling justification for such action." *Blasius Indus., Inc. v. Atlas Corp.,* Del. Ch., 564 A.2d 651, 661 (1988). *See also* Robert J. Klein, *The Case for Heightened Scrutiny in Defense of the Shareholders' Franchise Right,* 44 Stan. L. Rev. 129 (1991).

as "the only alternative to hostile takeovers to gain control against the will of the incumbent directors." *Id.*[24]

The Court of Chancery, in the case *subjudice,* was obviously cognizant that the emergence of the "poison pill" as an effective takeover device has resulted in such a remarkable transformation in the market for corporate control that hostile bidders who proceed when such defenses are in place will usually "have to couple proxy contests with tender offers." Joseph A. Grundfest, *Just Vote No: A Minimalist Strategy for Dealing with Barbarians Inside the Gates,* 45 Stan. L. Rev. 857, 858 (1993).[25] The Court of Chancery concluded that Unitrin's adoption of a poison pill was a proportionate response to the threat its Board reasonably perceived from American General's Offer. Nonetheless, the Court of Chancery enjoined the additional defense of the Repurchase Program as disproportionate and "unnecessary."

The record reflects that the Court of Chancery's decision to enjoin the Repurchase Program is attributable to a continuing misunderstanding, i.e., that in conjunction with the longstanding Supermajority Vote provision in the Unitrin charter, the Repurchase Program would operate to provide the director shareholders with a "veto" to preclude a successful proxy contest by American General. The origins of that misunderstanding are three premises that are each without record support. Two of those premises are objective misconceptions and the other is subjective.

DIRECTORS' MOTIVES
"PRESTIGE AND PERQUISITES"
SUBJECTIVE DETERMINATION

The subjective premise was the Court of Chancery's *sua sponte* determination that Unitrin's outside directors, who are also substantial stockholders, would not vote like other stockholders in a proxy contest, *i.e.,* in their own best economic interests. At American General's Offer price, the outside directors held Unitrin shares worth more than $450 million. Consequently, Unitrin argues the stockholder directors had the same interest as other Unitrin stockholders generally, when voting in a proxy contest, to wit: the maximization of the value of their investments.

In rejecting Unitrin's argument, the Court of Chancery stated that the stockholder directors would be "subconsciously" motivated in a proxy contest to vote against otherwise excellent offers which did not include a "price parameter" to compensate them for the loss of the "prestige and perquisites" of membership

---

24. "Proxy fights (including consent solicitations) have become a critical weapon of raiders who rely on them as an accessory to, and means of facilitating, a tender offer." 1 Arthur Fleischer, Jr., et al., *Takeover Defenses* X.C. at 653 (4th ed. 1990).

25. Another legal scholar states that, as a defensive tactic, the poison pill "warrants special attention chiefly because its preclusive effect frequently exceeds that of other takeover defensive tactics. . . . [and] make it effective even in circumstances where other defensive tactics may not work." Jeffrey N. Gordon, *Corporations, Markets, and Courts,* 91 Colum. L. Rev. 1931, 1946 (1991). *See also* Randall S. Thomas, *Judicial Review of Defensive Tactics in Proxy Contests: When Is Using a Rights Plan Right?* 46 Vand. L. Rev. 503 (1993).

on Unitrin's Board. The Court of Chancery's subjective determination that the *stockholder directors* of Unitrin would reject an "excellent offer," unless it compensated them for giving up the "prestige and perquisites" of directorship, appears to be subjective and without record support. It cannot be presumed.

It must be the subject of proof that the Unitrin directors' objective in the Repurchase Program was to forego the opportunity to sell their stock at a premium. In particular, it cannot be presumed that the prestige and perquisites of holding a director's office or a motive to strengthen collective power prevails over a stockholder-director's economic interest. Even the shareholder-plaintiffs in this case agree with the legal proposition Unitrin advocates on appeal: stockholders are presumed to act in their own best economic interests when they vote in a proxy contest.

WITHOUT REPURCHASE PROGRAM
ACTUAL VOTING POWER EXCEEDS 25%

The first objective premise relied upon by the Court of Chancery, unsupported by the record, is that the shareholder directors needed to implement the Repurchase Program to attain voting power in a proxy contest equal to 25%. The Court of Chancery properly calculated that if the Repurchase Program was completed, Unitrin's shareholder directors would increase their absolute voting power to 25%. It then calculated the odds of American General marshalling enough votes to defeat the Board and its supporters.

The Court of Chancery and all parties agree that proxy contests do not generate 100% shareholder participation. The shareholder plaintiffs argue that 80-85% may be a usual turnout. Therefore, *without* the Repurchase Program, the director shareholders' absolute voting power of 23% would already constitute *actual voting power greater than* 25% in a proxy contest with normal shareholder participation below 100%.

SUPERMAJORITY VOTE
NO REALISTIC DETERRENT

The second objective premise relied upon by the Court of Chancery, unsupported by the record, is that American General's ability to succeed in a proxy contest depended on the Repurchase Program being enjoined because of the Supermajority Vote provision in Unitrin's charter. Without the approval of a target's board, the danger of activating a poison pill renders it irrational for bidders to pursue stock acquisitions above the triggering level.[30] Instead, "bidders

---

30. "The . . . flip-in and flip-over features [of a poison pill] stop individual shareholders or shareholder groups from accumulating large amounts of the target company's stock. No potential acquiror or other shareholder will risk triggering a [poison pill] by accumulating more than the threshold level of shares because of the threat of massive discriminatory dilution. The trigger level therefore effectively sets a ceiling on the amount of stock that any shareholder can accumulate before launching a proxy contest." Randall S. Thomas, *Judicial Review of Defensive Tactics in Proxy Contests: When is Using a Rights Plan Right?* 46 Vand. L. Rev. 503, 512 (1993).

intent on working around a poison pill must launch and win proxy contests to elect new directors who are willing to redeem the target's poison pill." Joseph A. Grundfest, *Just Vote No: A Minimalist Strategy for Dealing with Barbarians Inside the Gates,* 45 Stan. L. Rev. 857, 859 (1993).

As American General acknowledges, a less than 15% stockholder bidder need not proceed with acquiring shares to the extent that it would ever implicate the Supermajority Vote provision. In fact, it would be illogical for American General or any other bidder to acquire more than 15% of Unitrin's stock because that would not only trigger the poison pill, but also the constraints of 8 Del. C. §203. If American General were to initiate a proxy contest *before* acquiring 15% of Unitrin's stock, it would need to amass only 45.1% of the votes assuming a 90% voter turnout. If it commenced a tender offer at an attractive price contemporaneously with its proxy contest, it could seek to acquire 50.1% of the outstanding voting stock.

The record reflects that institutional investors own 42% of Unitrin's shares. Twenty institutions own 33% of Unitrin's shares. It is generally accepted that proxy contests have re-emerged with renewed significance as a method of acquiring corporate control because "the growth in institutional investment has reduced the dispersion of share ownership." Lucian A. Bebchuk & Marcel Kahan, *A Framework for Analyzing Legal Policy Towards Proxy Contests,* 78 Cal. L. Rev. 1071, 1134 (1990). "Institutions are more likely than other shareholders to vote at all, more likely to vote against manager proposals, and more likely to vote for proposals by other shareholders." Bernard S. Black, *The Value of Institutional Investor Monitoring: The Empirical Evidence,* 39 UCLA L. Rev. 895, 925 (1992). *See also* John Pound, *Shareholder Activism and Share Values: The Causes and Consequences of Countersolicitations Against Management Antitakeover Proposals,* 32 J.L. & Econ. 357, 368 (1989).

WITH SUPERMAJORITY VOTE AFTER REPURCHASE PROGRAM PROXY CONTEST APPEARS VIABLE

The assumptions and conclusions American General sets forth in this appeal for a different purpose are particularly probative with regard to the effect of the institutional holdings in Unitrin's stock. American General's two predicate assumptions are a 90% stockholder turnout in a proxy contest and a bidder with 14.9% holdings, i.e., the maximum the bidder could own to avoid triggering the poison pill and the Supermajority Vote provision. American General also calculated the votes available to the Board or the bidder with and without the Repurchase Program[.]

[T]o prevail in a proxy contest with a 90% turnout, the percentage of additional shareholder votes a 14.9% shareholder bidder needs to prevail is 30.2% for directors and 35.2% in a subsequent merger. The record reflects that institutional investors held 42% of Unitrin's stock and 20 institutions held 33% of the stock. Thus, American General's own assumptions and calculations in the record support the Unitrin Board's argument that "it is hard to imagine a company more readily susceptible to a proxy contest concerning a pure issue of dollars."[33]

---

33. That institutions held a high percentage of Unitrin's stock is not as significant as the fact that the relatively concentrated percentage of stockholdings would facilitate a bidder's ability to communicate the merits of its position.

The conclusion of the Court of Chancery that the Repurchase Program would make a proxy contest for Unitrin a "theoretical" possibility that American General could not realistically pursue may be erroneous and appears to be inconsistent with its own earlier determination that the "repurchase program strengthens the position of the Board of Directors to defend against a hostile bidder, but will not deprive the public stockholders of the 'power to influence corporate direction through the ballot.'" Even a complete implementation of the Repurchase Program, in combination with the pre-existing Supermajority Vote provision, would not appear to have a preclusive effect upon American General's ability successfully to marshall enough shareholder votes to win a proxy contest. *Accord Shamrock Holdings, Inc. v. Polaroid Corp.*, Del. Ch., 559 A.2d 278 (1989). A proper understanding of the record reflects that American General or any other 14.9% shareholder bidder could apparently win a proxy contest with a 90% turnout.

The key variable in a proxy contest would-be the merit of American General's issues, not the size of its stockholdings. If American General presented an attractive price as the cornerstone of a proxy contest, it could prevail, irrespective of whether the shareholder directors' absolute voting power was 23% or 28%. . . .

Consequently, a proxy contest apparently remained a viable alternative for American General to pursue notwithstanding Unitrin's poison pill, Supermajority Vote provision, and a fully implemented Repurchase Program.

SUBSTANTIVE COERCION
AMERICAN GENERAL'S THREAT

This Court has recognized "the prerogative of a board of directors to resist a third party's unsolicited acquisition proposal or offer." *Paramount Communications, Inc. v. QVC Network, Inc.*, Del. Supr., 637 A.2d 34, 43 n. 13 (1994). The Unitrin Board did not have unlimited discretion to defeat the threat it perceived from the American General Offer by any draconian means available. *See Unocal*, 493 A.2d at 955. Pursuant to the *Unocal* proportionality test, the nature of the threat associated with a particular hostile offer sets the parameters for the range of permissible defensive tactics. Accordingly, the purpose of enhanced judicial scrutiny is to determine whether the Board acted reasonably in "relation to the threat which a particular bid allegedly poses to stockholder interests." *Mills Acquisition Co. v. Macmillan, Inc.*, Del. Supr., 559 A.2d 1261, 1288 (1989).

"The obvious requisite to determining the reasonableness of a defensive action is a clear identification of the nature of the threat." *Paramount Communications, Inc. v. Time, Inc.*, Del. Supr., 571 A.2d 1140, 1154 (1990). Courts, commentators and litigators have attempted to catalogue the threats posed by hostile tender offers. *Id.* at 1153. Commentators have categorized three types of threats:

> (i) *opportunity loss* . . . [where] a hostile offer might deprive target shareholders of the opportunity to select a superior alternative offered by target management [or, we would add, offered by another bidder]; (ii) *structural coercion,* . . . the risk that disparate treatment of non-tendering shareholders might

distort shareholders' tender decisions; and (iii) *substantive coercion,* . . . the risk that shareholders will mistakenly accept an underpriced offer because they disbelieve management's representations of intrinsic value.

Id. at 1153 n. 17 (*quoting* Ronald J. Gilson & Reinier Kraakman, *Delaware's Intermediate Standard for Defensive Tactics: Is There Substance to Proportionality Review?*, 44 Bus. Law. 247, 267 (1989)).

    This Court has held that the "inadequate value" of an all cash for all shares offer is a "legally cognizable threat." *Paramount Communications, Inc. v. Time, Inc.,* 571 A.2d at 1153. In addition, this Court has specifically concluded that inadequacy of value is *not* the only legally cognizable threat from "an all-shares, all-cash offer at a price below what a target board in good faith deems to be the present value of its shares." *Id.* at 1152-53. In making that determination, this Court held that the Time board of directors had reasonably determined that inadequate value was not the only threat that Paramount's all cash for all shares offer presented, but was *also* reasonably concerned that the Time stockholders might tender to Paramount in ignorance or based upon a mistaken belief, *i.e.,* yield to substantive coercion.

    The record reflects that the Unitrin Board perceived the threat from American General's Offer to be a form of substantive coercion. The Board noted that Unitrin's stock price had moved up, on higher than normal trading volume, to a level slightly below the price in American General's Offer. The Board also noted that some Unitrin shareholders had publicly expressed interest in selling at or near the price in the Offer. The Board determined that Unitrin's stock was undervalued by the market at current levels and that the Board considered Unitrin's stock to be a good long-term investment. The Board also discussed the speculative and unsettled market conditions for Unitrin stock caused by American General's public disclosure. The Board concluded that a Repurchase Program would provide additional liquidity to those stockholders who wished to realize short-term gain, and would provide enhanced value to those stockholders who wished to maintain a long-term investment. Accordingly, the Board voted to authorize the Repurchase Program for up to ten million shares of its outstanding stock on the open market.

    In *Unocal,* this Court noted that, pursuant to Delaware corporate law, a board of directors' duty of care required it to respond actively to protect the corporation and its shareholders from perceived harm. *Unocal,* 493 A.2d at 955. In *Unocal,* when describing the proportionality test, this Court listed several examples of concerns that boards of directors should consider in evaluating and responding to perceived threats. Unitrin's Board deemed three of the concerns exemplified in *Unocal* relevant in deciding to authorize the Repurchase Program: first, the inadequacy of the price offered; second, the nature and timing of American General's Offer; and third, the basic stockholder interests at stake, including those of short-term speculators whose actions may have fueled the coercive aspect of the Offer at the expense of the long-term investor. *Unocal,* 493 A.2d at 955-56. *Accord Ivanhoe Partners v. Newmont Mining Corp.,* Del. Supr., 535 A.2d 1334, 1341-42 (1987).

    The record appears to support Unitrin's argument that the Board's justification for adopting the Repurchase Program was its reasonably perceived risk of substantive coercion, *i.e.,* that Unitrin's shareholders might accept American General's inadequate Offer because of "ignorance or mistaken belief regarding the Board's assessment of the long-term value of Unitrin's stock. *See Shamrock Holdings, Inc. v. Polaroid Corp.,* Del. Ch., 559 A.2d 278, 290 (1989). In this case, the Unitrin Board's letter to its shareholders specifically reflected those concerns in describing its perception of the threat from American General's Offer. The adoption of the Repurchase Program also appears to be consistent with this Court's holding that economic inadequacy is not the only threat presented by an all cash for all shares hostile bid, because the threat of such a hostile bid could be exacerbated by shareholder "ignorance or . . . mistaken belief." *Paramount Communications, Inc. v. Time, Inc.,* 571 A.2d at 1153.

RANGE OF REASONABLENESS
PROPER PROPORTIONALITY BURDEN

. . . We have already noted that the Court of Chancery made a factual finding unsupported by the record, *i.e.,* that the increase in the percentage of ownership by the stockholder directors from 23% to 28%, resulting from the completed Repurchase Program, would make it merely theoretically possible for an insurgent to win a proxy contest. . . .

The Court of Chancery applied an incorrect legal standard when it ruled that the Unitrin decision to authorize the Repurchase Program was disproportionate because it was "unnecessary." The Court of Chancery stated:

> Given that the Board had already implemented the poison pill and the advance notice provision, the repurchase program was unnecessary to protect Unitrin from an inadequate bid.

In *QVC,* this Court recently elaborated upon the judicial function in applying enhanced scrutiny, citing *Unocal* as authority, albeit in the context of a sale of control and the target board's consideration of one of several reasonable alternatives. That teaching is nevertheless applicable here:

> a court applying enhanced judicial scrutiny should be deciding whether the directors made *a reasonable* decision, not *a perfect* decision. If a board selected one of several reasonable alternatives, a court should not second guess that choice even though it might have decided otherwise or subsequent events may have cast doubt on the board's determination. Thus, courts will not substitute their business judgment for that of the directors, but will determine if the directors' decision was, on balance, within a range of reasonableness. *See Unocal,* 493 A.2d at 955-56; *Macmillan,* 559 A.2d at 1288; *Nixon,* 626 A.2d at 1378.

Paramount Communications, Inc. v. QVC Network, Inc., Del. Supr., 637 A.2d 34, 45-46 (1994) (*emphasis in original*). The Court of Chancery did not determine whether the Unitrin Board's decision to implement the Repurchase Program fell within a "range of reasonableness." . . .

The Court of Chancery's determination that the Unitrin Board's adoption of the Repurchase Program was unnecessary constituted a substitution of its business judgment for that of the Board, contrary to this Court's "range of reasonableness" holding in *Paramount Communications, Inc. v. QVC Network, Inc.*, 637 A.2d at 45-46. . . .

DRACONIAN DEFENSES
COERCIVE OR PRECLUSIVE
RANGE OF REASONABLENESS

In assessing a challenge to defensive actions by a target corporation's board of directors in a takeover context, this Court has held that the Court of Chancery should evaluate the board's overall response, including the justification for each contested defensive measure, and the results achieved thereby. Where all of the target board's defensive actions are inextricably related, the principles *of Unocal* require that such actions be scrutinized collectively as a unitary response to the perceived threat. *Gilbert v. El Paso Co.*, Del. Supr., 575 A.2d 1131, 1145 (1990). Thus, the Unitrin Board's adoption of the Repurchase Program, in addition to the poison pill, must withstand *Unocal's* proportionality review. *Id.*

In *Unocal*, the progenitor of the proportionality test, this Court stated that the board of directors' "duty of care extends to protecting the corporation and its [stockholders] from perceived harm whether a threat originates from third parties or other shareholders." *Unocal*, 493 A.2d at 955. We then noted that "such powers are not absolute." *Id.* Specifically, this Court held that the board "does not have unbridled discretion to defeat any perceived threat by any Draconian means available." *Id.* Immediately following those observations in *Unocal*, when exemplifying the parameters of a board's authority in adopting a restrictive stock repurchase, this Court held that "the directors may not have acted *solely* or *primarily* out of a desire to perpetuate themselves in office" (preclusion of the stockholders' corporate franchise right to vote) and, further, that the stock repurchase plan must not be inequitable. *Unocal*, 493 A.2d at 955 (*emphasis added*). . . .

More than a century before *Unocal* was decided, Justice Holmes observed that the common law must be developed through its application and "cannot be dealt with as if it contained only the axioms and corollaries of a book of mathematics." Oliver Wendell Holmes, Jr., *The Common Law* 1 (1881). As common law applications *of Unocal's* proportionality standard have evolved, at least two characteristics of draconian defensive measures taken by a board of directors in responding to a threat have been brought into focus through enhanced judicial scrutiny. In the modern takeover lexicon, it is now clear that since *Unocal*, this Court has consistently recognized that defensive measures which are either preclusive or coercive are included within the common law definition of draconian.

If a defensive measure is not draconian, however, because it is not either coercive or preclusive, the *Unocal* proportionality test requires the focus of enhanced judicial scrutiny to shift to "the range of reasonableness." Proper and proportionate defensive responses are intended and permitted to thwart perceived threats. When a corporation is not for sale, the board of directors is the defender of the metaphorical medieval corporate bastion and the protector of the corporation's shareholders. The fact that a defensive action must not be coercive or preclusive does not prevent a board from responding defensively before a bidder is at the corporate bastion's gate.[38]

The *ratio decidendi* for the "range of reasonableness" standard is a need of the board of directors for latitude in discharging its fiduciary duties to the corporation and its shareholders when defending against perceived threats. The concomitant requirement is for judicial restraint. Consequently, if the board of directors' defensive response is not draconian (preclusive or coercive) and is within a "range of reasonableness," a court must not substitute its judgment for the board's. *Paramount Communications, Inc. v. QVC Network, Inc.*, 637 A.2d at 45-46.

THIS CASE
REPURCHASE PROGRAM
PROPORTIONATE WITH POISON PILL

In this case, the initial focus of enhanced judicial scrutiny for proportionality requires a determination regarding the defensive responses by the Unitrin Board to American General's offer. We begin, therefore, by ascertaining whether the Repurchase Program, as an addition to the poison pill, was draconian by being either coercive or preclusive.

A limited nondiscriminatory self-tender, like some other defensive measures, may thwart a current hostile bid, but is not inherently coercive. Moreover, it does not necessarily preclude future bids or proxy contests by stockholders who decline to participate in the repurchase. A selective repurchase of shares in a public corporation on the market, such as Unitrin's Repurchase Program, generally does not discriminate because all shareholders can voluntarily realize the same benefit by selling. *See* Larry E. Ribstein, *Takeover Defenses and the Corporate Contract*, 78 Geo. L.J. 71, 129-31 (1989). *See also* Michael Bradley & Michael Rosenzweig, *Defensive Stock Repurchases*, 99 Harv. L. Rev. 1377 (1986). Here, there is no showing on this record that the Repurchase Program was coercive.

We have already determined that the record in this case appears to reflect that a proxy contest remained a viable (if more problematic) alternative for American General even if the Repurchase Program were to be completed in its entirety. Nevertheless, the Court of Chancery must determine whether Unitrin's Repurchase Program would only inhibit American General's ability to wage a proxy fight and institute a merger or whether it was, in fact, preclusive[39]

---

38. This Court's choice of the term draconian in *Unocal* was a recognition that the law affords boards of directors substantial latitude in defending the perimeter of the corporate bastion against perceived threats. . . . Stated more directly, depending upon the circumstances, the board may respond to a reasonably perceived threat by adopting individually or sometimes in combination: advance notice by-laws, supermajority voting provisions, shareholder rights plans, repurchase programs, etc.

39. The record in this case, when properly understood, appears to reflect that the Repurchase Program's effect on a proxy contest would not be preclusive. *Accord Moran v. Household Int'l, Inc.*, Del. Supr., 500 A.2d 1346, 1355 (1985). If the stockholders of Unitrin are "displeased with the action of their elected representatives, the powers of corporate democracy" remain available as a viable alternative to turn the Board out in a proxy contest. *Unocal*, 493 A.2d at 959.

because American General's success would either be mathematically impossible or realistically unattainable. If the Court of Chancery concludes that the Unitrin Repurchase Program was not draconian because it was not preclusive, one question will remain to be answered in its proportionality review: whether the Repurchase Program was within a range of reasonableness?

The Court of Chancery found that the Unitrin Board reasonably believed that American General's Offer was inadequate and that the adoption of a poison pill was a proportionate defensive response. Upon remand, in applying the correct legal standard to the factual circumstances of this case, the Court of Chancery may conclude that the implementation of the limited Repurchase Program was also within a range of reasonable additional defensive responses available to the Unitrin Board. In considering whether the Repurchase Program was within a range of reasonableness the Court of Chancery should take into consideration whether: (1) it is a statutorily authorized form of business decision which a board of directors may routinely make in a non-takeover context; (2) as a defensive response to American General's Offer it was limited and corresponded in degree or magnitude to the degree or magnitude of the threat, (*i.e.,* assuming the threat was relatively "mild," was the response relatively "mild?"); (3) with the Repurchase Program, the Unitrin Board properly recognized that all shareholders are not alike, and provided immediate liquidity to those shareholders who wanted it.

* * *

REMAND TO CHANCERY

In this case, the Court of Chancery erred by substituting its judgment, that the Repurchase Program was unnecessary, for that of the Board. The Unitrin Board had the power and the duty, upon reasonable investigation, to protect Unitrin's shareholders from what it perceived to be the threat from American General's inadequate all-cash for all-shares Offer. *Unocal,* 493 A.2d at 958. The adoption of the poison pill *and* the limited Repurchase Program was not coercive and the Repurchase Program may not be preclusive. Although each made a takeover more difficult, individually and collectively, if they were not coercive or preclusive the Court of Chancery must determine whether they were within the range of reasonable defensive measures available to the Board. *Accord Cheff v. Mathes,* Del. Supr., 199 A.2d 548, 554-56 (1964).

If the Court of Chancery concludes that individually and collectively the poison pill and the Repurchase Program were proportionate to the threat the Board believed American General posed, the Unitrin Board's adoption of the Repurchase Program and the poison pill is entitled to review under the traditional business judgment rule. The burden will then shift "back to the plaintiffs who have the ultimate burden of persuasion [in a preliminary injunction proceeding] to show a breach of the directors' fiduciary duties." *Moran v. Household Int'l, Inc.,* Del. Supr., 500 A.2d 1346, 1356 (1985) *(citing Unocal,* 493 A.2d at 958). In order to rebut the protection of the business judgment rule, the burden on the plaintiffs will be to demonstrate, "by a preponderance of the evidence that the directors' decisions were *primarily* based on [(1)] perpetuating themselves in office or [(2)] some other breach of fiduciary duty such as fraud, overreaching, lack of good faith, or [(3)] being uninformed." *Unocal*, 493 A.2d at 958 (*emphasis added*).

* * *

CONCLUSION

We hold that the Court of Chancery correctly determined that the *Unocal* standard of enhanced judicial scrutiny applied to the defensive actions of the Unitrin defendants in establishing the poison pill and implementing the Repurchase Program. The Court of Chancery's finding, that the Repurchase Program was a disproportionate defensive response, was based on faulty factual predicates, unsupported by the record. This error was exacerbated by its application of an erroneous legal standard of "necessity" to the Repurchase Program as a defensive response.

The interlocutory judgment of the Court of Chancery, in favor of American General, is REVERSED. This matter is REMANDED for further proceedings in accordance with this opinion.

Carmody v. Toll Brothers, Inc.
723 A.2d 1180 (Del. Ch. 1998)

JACOBS, Vice Chancellor.

At issue on this Rule 12(b)(6) motion to dismiss is whether a most recent innovation in corporate anti-takeover measures—the so-called "dead hand" poison pill rights plan—is subject to legal challenge on the basis that it violates the Delaware General Corporation Law and/or the fiduciary duties of the board of directors who adopted the plan. As explained more fully below, a "dead hand" rights plan is one that cannot be redeemed except by the incumbent directors who adopted the plan or their designated successors. As discussed below, the Court finds that the "dead hand" feature of the rights plan as described in the complaint (the "Rights Plan") is subject to legal challenge on both statutory and fiduciary grounds, and that because the complaint states legally cognizable claims for relief, the pending motion to dismiss must be denied.

I.   FACTS

A.   BACKGROUND LEADING TO ADOPTION OF THE PLAN

The firm whose rights plan is being challenged is Toll Brothers (sometimes referred to as "the company"), a Pennsylvania-based Delaware corporation that designs, builds, and markets single family luxury homes in thirteen states and five regions in the United States. The company was founded in 1967 by brothers Bruce and Robert Toll, who are its Chief Executive and Chief Operating Officers, respectively, and who own approximately 37.5% of Toll Brothers' common stock. The company's board of directors has nine members, four of whom (including Bruce and Robert Toll) are senior executive officers. The remaining five members of the board are "outside" independent directors.[2]

From its inception in 1967, Toll Brothers has performed very successfully, and "went public" in 1986. . . .

B.   THE RIGHTS PLAN

The Rights Plan was adopted on June 12, 1997, at which point Toll Brothers' stock was trading at approximately $18 per share—near the low end of its established price range of $16-3/8 to $25-3/16 per share. After considering the industry economic and financial environment and other factors, the Toll Brothers board concluded that other companies engaged in its lines of business might perceive the company as a potential target for an acquisition. The Rights Plan was adopted with that problem in mind, but not in response to any specific takeover proposal or threat. The company announced that it had done that to protect its stockholders from "coercive or unfair tactics to gain control of the Company" by placing the stockholders in a position of having to accept or reject an unsolicited offer without adequate time.

1.   The Rights Plan's "Flip In" and "Flip Over" Features

The Rights Plan would operate as follows: there would be a dividend distribution of one preferred stock purchase right (a "Right") for each outstanding share of common stock as of July 11, 1997. Initially the Rights would attach to the company's outstanding common shares, and each Right would initially entitle the holder to purchase one thousandth of a share of a newly registered series Junior A Preferred Stock for $100. The Rights would become exercisable, and would trade separately from the common shares, after the "Distribution Date," which is defined as the earlier of (a) ten business days following a public announcement that an acquiror has acquired, or obtained the right to acquire, beneficial ownership of 15% or more of the company's outstanding common shares (the "Stock Acquisition Date"), or (b) ten business days after the commencement of a tender offer or exchange offer that would result in a person or group beneficially owning 15% or more of the company's outstanding common shares. Once exercisable, the Rights remain exercisable until their Final Expiration Date (June 12, 2007, ten years after the adoption of the Plan), unless the Rights are earlier redeemed by the company.

The dilutive mechanism of the Rights is "triggered" by certain defined events. One such event is the acquisition of 15% or more of Toll Brothers' stock by any person or group of affiliated or associated persons. Should that occur, each Rights holder (except the acquiror and its affiliates and associates)

---

2. One board member is a partner of a Philadelphia law firm that acted as counsel to the company in various matters, and that received approximately $128,000 in fees from the company in 1996. Because of that relationship, the plaintiff challenges the independence of that particular director. That issue is not reached on this motion.

becomes entitled to buy two shares of Toll Brothers common stock or other securities at half price. That is, the value of the stock received when the Right is exercised is equal to two times the exercise price of the Right. In that manner, this so-called "flip in" feature of the Rights Plan would massively dilute the value of the holdings of the unwanted acquiror.[5]

The Rights also have a standard "flip over" feature, which is triggered if after the Stock Acquisition Date, the company is made a party to a merger in which Toll Brothers is not the surviving corporation, or in which it is the surviving corporation and its common stock is changed or exchanged. In either event, each Rights holder becomes entitled to purchase common stock of the acquiring company, again at half-price, thereby impairing the acquiror's capital structure and drastically diluting the interest of the acquiror's other stockholders.

The complaint alleges that the purpose and effect of the company's Rights Plan, as with most poison pills, is to make any hostile acquisition of Toll Brothers prohibitively expensive, and thereby to deter such acquisitions unless the target company's board first approves the acquisition proposal. The target board's "leverage" derives from another critical feature found in most rights plans: the directors' power to redeem the Rights at any time before they expire, on such conditions as the directors "in their sole discretion" may establish. To this extent there is little to distinguish the company's Rights Plan from the "standard model." What is distinctive about the Rights Plan is that it authorizes only a specific, defined category of directors—the "Continuing Directors"—to redeem the Rights. The dispute over the legality of this "Continuing Director" or "dead hand" feature of the Rights Plan is what drives this lawsuit.

2.   The "Dead Hand" Feature of the Rights Plan

In substance, the "dead hand" provision operates to prevent any directors of Toll Brothers, except those who were in office as of the date of the Rights Plan's adoption (June 12, 1997) or their designated successors, from redeeming the Rights until they expire on June 12, 2007. That consequence flows directly from the Rights Agreement's definition of a "Continuing Director," which is:

> (i) any member of the Board of Directors of the Company, while such person is a member of the Board, who is not an Acquiring Person, or an Affiliate [as defined] or Associate [as defined] of an Acquiring Person, or a representative or

---

5. The "flip-in" feature of a rights plan is triggered when the acquiror crosses the specified ownership threshold, regardless of the acquiror's intentions with respect to the use of the shares. At that point, rights vest in all shareholders other than the acquiror, and as a result, those holders become entitled to acquire additional shares of voting stock at a substantially discounted price, usually 50% of the market price. Commonly, rights plans also contain a "flip-over" feature entitling target company shareholders (again, other than the acquiror) to purchase shares of the acquiring company at a reduced price. That feature is activated when, after a "flip-in" triggering event, the acquiror initiates a triggering event, such as a merger, self-dealing transaction, or sale of assets. *See* Shawn C. Lese, *Note, Preventing Control From the Grave: A Proposal for Judicial Treatment of Dead Hand Provisions in Poison Pills,* 96 Colum. L. Rev. 2175, 2180-81 (1996).

nominee of an Acquiring Person or of any such Affiliate or Associate, and was a member of the Board prior to the date of this agreement, or (ii) any Person who subsequently becomes a member of the Board, while such Person is a member of the Board, who is not an Acquiring Person, or an Affiliate [as defined] or Associate [as defined] of an Acquiring Person, or a representative or nominee of an Acquiring Person or of any such Affiliate or Associate, if such Person's nomination for election or election to the Board is recommended or approved by a majority of the Continuing Directors.

According to the complaint, this "dead hand" provision has a twofold practical effect. First, it makes an unsolicited offer for the company more unlikely by eliminating a proxy contest as a useful way for a hostile acquiror to gain control, because even if the acquiror wins the contest, its newly-elected director representatives could not redeem the Rights. Second, the "dead hand" provision disenfranchises, in a proxy contest, all shareholders that wish the company to be managed by a board empowered to redeem the Rights, by depriving those shareholders of any practical choice except to vote for the incumbent directors. Given these effects, the plaintiff claims that the only purpose that the "dead hand" provision could serve is to discourage future acquisition activity by making any proxy contest to replace incumbent board members an exercise in futility.

II. OVERVIEW OF THE PROBLEM AND THE PARTIES' CONTENTIONS . . .

A. OVERVIEW

The critical issue on this motion is whether a "dead hand" provision in a "poison pill" rights plan is subject to legal challenge on the basis that it is invalid as *ultra vires,* or as a breach of fiduciary duty, or both. Although that issue has been the subject of scholarly comment,[9] it has yet to be decided under Delaware law, and to date it has been addressed by only two courts applying the law of other jurisdictions.[10]

---

9. *See, e.g.,* Shawn C. Lese, *Note, Preventing Control From the Grave: A Proposal for Judicial Treatment of Dead Hand Provisions in Poison Pills,* 96 Col. L. Rev. 2175 (1996) (cited herein as "Lese"); Jeffrey N. Gordon, *"Just Say Never" Poison Pills, Deadhand Pills and Shareholder Adopted By-Laws: An Essay for Warren Buffett,* 19 Cardozo L. Rev. 511 (1997) (cited herein as "Gordon"); Daniel A. Neff, *The Impact of State Statutes and Continuing Director Rights Plans,* 51 U. Miami L. Rev. 663 (1997) (cited herein as "Neff"); and Meredith M. Brown and William D. Regner, *2 Shareholder Rights Plans: Recent Toxopharmological Developments, Insights* (Aspen, Law & Business, Oct., 1997) (cited herein as "Brown and Regner").

10. The jurisdictions that have directly addressed the legality of the dead hand poison pill are New York, *see Bank of New York Co., Inc. v. Irving Bank Corp., et. al.,* N.Y. Sup. Ct., 139 Misc. 2d 665, 528 N.Y.S.2d 482 (1988), and the United States District Court for the Northern District of Georgia, *see Invacare Corp. v. Healthdyne Technologies. Inc.,* N.D. Ga., 968 F. Supp. 1578 (1997) (applying Georgia law). In Delaware, the issue arose in *Davis Acquisition, Inc. v. NWA, Inc.,* Del. Ch., C.A. No. 10761, Allen, C., 1989 WL 40845 (Apr. 25,1989), but was not decided because the preliminary injunction motion was resolved on other grounds. In *Sutton*

Some history may elucidate the issue by locating its relevance within the dynamic of state corporate takeover jurisprudence. Since the 1980s, that body of law, largely judge-made, has been racing to keep abreast of the ever evolving and novel tactical and strategic developments so characteristic of this important area of economic endeavor that is swiftly becoming a permanent part of our national (and international) economic landscape.

For our purposes, the relevant history begins in the early 1980s with the advent of the "poison pill" as an antitakeover measure. That innovation generated litigation focused upon the issue of whether any poison pill rights plan could validly be adopted under state corporation law. The seminal case, *Moran v. Household International, Inc.*, answered that question in the affirmative. . . .

It being settled that a corporate board could permissibly adopt a poison pill, the next litigated question became: under what circumstances would the directors' fiduciary duties require the board to redeem the rights in the face of a hostile takeover proposal? That issue was litigated, in Delaware and elsewhere, during the second half of the 1980s. The lesson taught by that experience was that courts were extremely reluctant to order the redemption of poison pills on fiduciary grounds. The reason was the prudent deployment of the pill proved to be largely beneficial to shareholder interests: it often resulted in a bidding contest that culminated in an acquisition on terms superior to the initial hostile offer.

Once it became clear that the prospects were unlikely for obtaining judicial relief mandating a redemption of the poison pill, a different response to the pill was needed. That response, which echoed the Supreme Court's suggestion in *Moran*, was the foreseeable next step in the evolution of takeover strategy: a tender offer coupled with a solicitation for shareholder proxies to remove and replace the incumbent board with the acquiror's nominees who, upon assuming office, would redeem the pill.[15] Because that strategy, if unopposed, would enable hostile offerors to effect an "end run" around the poison pill, it again was predictable and only a matter of time that target company boards would develop counter-strategies. With one exception—the "dead hand" pill—these counter-strategies proved "successful" only in cases where the purpose was to delay the process to enable the board to develop alternatives to the hostile offer. The counterstrategies were largely unsuccessful, however, where the goal was to stop the proxy contest (and as a consequence, the hostile offer) altogether.

For example, in cases where the target board's response was either to (i) amend the by-laws to delay a shareholders meeting to elect directors, or (ii) delay an annual meeting to a later date permitted under the bylaws, so

---

Holding Corp. v. DeSoto, Inc., Del. Ch., C.A. No. 12051, Allen, C, 1991 WL 80223 (May 13, 1991) the validity of a "continuing director" provision was presented indirectly (but again was not decided) in the context of an amendment to a pension plan prohibiting its termination or a reduction of benefits in the event of a "change of control." That term was defined as a new, substantial shareholder becoming the beneficial owner of 35% or more of the corporation's voting stock without the prior approval of two thirds of the board and a majority of the "continuing directors."

15. *See, Unitrin, Inc. v. American General Corp.*, Del. Supr., 651 A.2d 1361, 1379 (1995); *Kidsco, Inc. v. Dinsmore*, Del. Ch., 674 A.2d 483, 490 (1995), *aff'd*, 670 A.2d 1338 (1995).

that the board and management would be able to explore alternatives to the hostile offer (but not entrench themselves), those responses were upheld.[16] On the other hand, where the target board's response to a proxy contest (coupled with a hostile offer) was (i) to move the shareholders meeting to a later date to enable the incumbent board to solicit revocations of proxies to defeat the apparently victorious dissident group, or (ii) to expand the size of the board, and then fill the newly created positions so the incumbents would retain control of the board irrespective of the outcome of the proxy contest, those responses were declared invalid.[17]

This litigation experience taught that a target board, facing a proxy contest joined with a hostile tender offer, could, in good faith, employ nonpreclusive defensive measures to give the board time to explore transactional alternatives. The target board could not, however, erect defenses that would either preclude a proxy contest altogether or improperly bend the rules to favor the board's continued incumbency.

In this environment, the only defensive measure that promised to be a "show stopper" (*i.e.*, had the potential to deter a proxy contest altogether) was a poison pill with a "dead hand" feature. The reason is that if only the incumbent directors or their designated successors could redeem the pill, it would make little sense for shareholders or the hostile bidder to wage a proxy contest to replace the incumbent board. Doing that would eliminate from the scene the only group of persons having the power to give the hostile bidder and target company shareholders what they desired: control of the target company (in the case of the hostile bidder) and the opportunity to obtain an attractive price for their shares (in the case of the target company stockholders). It is against that backdrop that the legal issues presented here, which concern the validity of the "dead hand" feature, attain significance.

* * *

---

16. *See, e.g., Stahl v. Apple Bancorp, Inc.*, Del. Ch., 579 A.2d 1115 (1990) (upholding post-ponement of annual meeting to a later date permitted by bylaws to enable target board to explore alternatives to hostile offer); *Kidsco Inc. v. Dinsmore*, n. 15, *supra*, (upholding amend-ment of bylaws to give target board an additional 25 days before calling a shareholder-initiated special meeting, to enable shareholders to vote on a pending merger proposal, and, if the proposal were defeated, to enable the board to explore other alternatives).

17. *See, Aprahamian v. HBO & Co.*, Del. Ch., 531 A.2d 1204 (1987) (shareholders' meet-ing moved to later date for the purpose of defeating the apparent victors in proxy contest. Held: invalid); *Blasius Indus. v. Atlas Corp.*, Del. Ch., 564 A.2d 651 (1988) (in response to an announced proxy contest, target board amended bylaws to create two new board positions, then filled those positions to retain board control, irrespective of outcome of proxy contest. Held: invalid).

Another statutorily permissible defensive device—the "staggered" or classified board—was useful, but still of limited effectiveness. Because only one third of a classified board would stand for election each year, a classified board would delay—but not prevent—a hostile acquiror from obtaining control of the board, since a determined acquiror could wage a proxy contest and obtain control of two thirds of the target board over a two year period, as opposed to seizing control in a single election.

III. ANALYSIS

* * *

B. THE VALIDITY OF THE "DEAD HAND" PROVISION

1. The Invalidity Contentions

The plaintiff's complaint attacks the "dead hand" feature of the Toll Brothers poison pill on both statutory and fiduciary duty grounds. The statutory claim is that the "dead hand" provision unlawfully restricts the powers of future boards by creating different classes of directors—those who have the power to redeem the poison pill, and those who do not. Under 8 Del. C. §§141(a) and (d), any such restrictions and director classifications must be stated in the certificate of incorporation. The complaint alleges that because those restrictions are not stated in the Toll Brothers charter, the "dead hand" provision of the Rights Plan is ultra vires and, consequently, invalid on its face.

The complaint also alleges that even if the Rights Plan is not *ultra vires,* its approval constituted a breach of the Toll Brothers board's fiduciary duty of loyalty in several respects. It is alleged that the board violated its duty of loyalty because (a) the "dead hand" provision was enacted solely or primarily for entrenchment purposes; (b) it was also a disproportionate defensive measure, since it precludes the shareholders from receiving tender offers and engaging in a proxy contest, in contravention of the principles of *Unocal Corp. v. Mesa Petroleum Co. ("Unocal"),* as elucidated in *Unitrin, Inc. v. American General Corp. ("Unitrin")* and (c) the "dead hand" provision purposefully interferes with the shareholder voting franchise without any compelling justification, in derogation of the principles articulated in *Blasius Indus. v. Atlas Corp. ("Blasius")* [Del. Ch., 564 A.2d 651, 662-63 (1988)]. . . .

2. The Statutory Invalidity Claims

Having carefully considered the arguments and authorities marshaled by both sides, the Court concludes that the complaint states legally sufficient claims that the "dead hand" provision of the Toll Brothers Rights Plan violates 8 Del. C. §§141(a) and (d). There are three reasons.

First, it cannot be disputed that the Rights Plan confers the power to redeem the pill only upon some, but not all, of the directors. But under §141(d), the power to create voting power distinctions among directors exists only where there is a classified board, and where those voting power distinctions are expressed in the certificate of incorporation. Section 141 (d) pertinently provides:

> . . . *The certificate of incorporation may confer upon holders of any class or series of stock the right to elect 1 or more directors who shall serve for such term, and have such voting powers as shall be stated in the certificate of incorporation.* The terms of office and voting powers of the directors elected in the manner so provided in the certificate of incorporation may be greater than or less than those of any other director or class of directors. . . . (*emphasis added*)

The plain, unambiguous meaning of the quoted language is that if one category or group of directors is given distinctive voting rights not shared by the other directors, those distinctive voting rights must be set forth in the certificate of incorporation. In the case of Toll Brothers (the complaint alleges), they are not.

Second, §141(d) mandates that the "right to elect 1 or more directors who shall . . . have such [greater] voting powers" is reserved to the stockholders, not to the directors or a subset thereof. Absent express language in the charter, nothing in Delaware law suggests that some directors of a public corporation may be created less equal than other directors, and certainly not by unilateral board action. Vesting the pill redemption power exclusively in the Continuing Directors transgresses the statutorily protected shareholder right to elect the directors who would be so empowered. For that reason, and because it is claimed that the Rights Plan's allocation of voting power to redeem the Rights is nowhere found in the Toll Brothers certificate of incorporation, the complaint states a claim that the "dead hand" feature of the Rights Plan is *ultra vires,* and hence, statutorily invalid under Delaware law.

Third, the complaint states a claim that the "dead hand" provision would impermissibly interfere with the directors' statutory power to manage the business and affairs of the corporation. That power is conferred by 8 Del. C. §141(a), which mandates:

> The business and affairs of every corporation organized under this chapter shall be managed by or under the direction of a board of directors, *except as may be otherwise provided in this chapter or in its certificate of incorporation. . . . (emphasis added)*

The "dead hand" poison pill is intended to thwart hostile bids by vesting shareholders with preclusive rights that cannot be redeemed except by the Continuing Directors. Thus, the one action that could make it practically possible to redeem the pill — replacing the entire board — could make that pill redemption legally impossible to achieve. The "dead hand" provision would jeopardize a newly-elected future board's ability to achieve a business combination by depriving that board of the power to redeem the pill without obtaining the consent of the "Continuing Directors," who (it may be assumed) would constitute a minority of the board. In this manner, it is claimed, the "dead hand" provision would interfere with the board's power to protect fully the corporation's (and its shareholders') interests in a transaction that is one of the most fundamental and important in the life of a business enterprise.

* * *

The defendants offer two arguments in response. First, they contend that the Rights Plan does not facially preclude or interfere with proxy contests as a means to gain control, or coerce shareholders to vote for or against any particular director slate. The second argument is that the "dead hand" provision is tantamount to a delegation to a special committee, consisting of the Continuing Directors, of the power to redeem the pill.

Neither contention has merit. The first is basically an argument that the Rights Plan does not violate any fiduciary duty of the board. That is unresponsive to the statutory invalidity claim. The second argument rests upon an analogy that has no basis in fact. In adopting the Rights Plan, the board did not, nor did it purport to, create a special committee having the exclusive power to redeem the pill. The analogy also ignores fundamental structural differences between the creation of a special board committee and the operation of the "dead hand" provision of the Rights Plan. The creation of a special committee would not impose long term structural power-related distinctions between different groups of directors of the same board. The board that creates a special committee may abolish it at any time, as could any successor board. On the other hand, the Toll Brothers "dead hand" provision, if legally valid, would embed structural power-related distinctions between groups of directors that no successor board could abolish until after the Rights expire in 2007.

For these reasons, the statutory invalidity claims survive the motion to dismiss.

3.   The Fiduciary Duty Invalidity Claims

Because the plaintiffs statutory invalidity claims have been found legally cognizable, the analysis arguably could end at this point. But the plaintiff also alleges that the board's adoption of the "dead hand" feature violated its fiduciary duty of loyalty. For the sake of completeness, that claim is addressed as well.

* * *

b)   The *Unocal/Unitrin* Fiduciary Duty Claim

[In this section, the court addresses] whether the complaint states a legally cognizable claim that the inclusion of the "dead hand" provision in the Rights Plan was an unreasonable defensive measure within the meaning of *Unocal* [and thus, constitutes a claim that the Board breached its fiduciary duty]. I conclude that it does.

As a procedural matter, it merits emphasis that a claim under *Unocal* requires enhanced judicial scrutiny. In that context, the board has the burden to satisfy the Court that the board (1) "had reasonable grounds for believing that a danger to corporate policy and effectiveness existed," and (2) that its "defensive response was reasonable in relation to the threat posed."[46] Such scrutiny is, by its nature, fact-driven and requires a factual record. For that reason, as the Supreme Court recently observed, enhanced scrutiny "will usually not be satisfied by resting on a defense motion merely attacking the pleadings." Only "conclusory complaints without well-pleaded facts [may] be dismissed early under Chancery Rule 12."[47]

The complaint at issue here is far from conclusory. Under *Unitrin,* a defensive measure is disproportionate (*i.e.,* unreasonable) if it is either coercive or

---

46. *Unitrin,* 651 A.2d at 1373 (citing *Unocal,* 493 A.2d at 955).
47. *In re Santa Fe Pacific Corp. Shareholder Lit.,* Del. Supr., 669 A.2d 59, 72 (1995).

preclusive. The complaint alleges that the "dead hand" provision "disenfranchises shareholders by forcing them to vote for incumbent directors or their designees if shareholders want to be represented by a board entitled to exercise its full statutory prerogatives." That is sufficient to claim that the "dead hand" provision is coercive. The complaint also alleges that that provision "makes an offer for the Company much more unlikely since it eliminates use of a proxy contest as a possible means to gain control. . . [because]. . . any directors elected in such a contest would still be unable to vote to redeem the pill"; and "renders future contests for corporate control of Toll Brothers prohibitively expensive and effectively impossible." A defensive measure is preclusive if it makes a bidder's ability to wage a successful proxy contest and gain control either "mathematically impossible" or "realistically unattainable."[51] These allegations are sufficient to state a claim that the "dead hand" provision makes a proxy contest "realistically unattainable," and therefore, disproportionate and unreasonable under *Unocal*.

IV. CONCLUSION

The Court concludes that for the reasons discussed above, the complaint states claims under Delaware law upon which relief can be granted.[52] Accordingly, the defendants' motion to dismiss is denied. IT IS SO ORDERED.

Quickturn Design Systems, Inc. v. Shapiro
721 A.2d 1281 (Del. 1998)

HOLLAND, Justice:

This is an expedited appeal from a final judgment entered by the Court of Chancery. The dispute arises out of an ongoing effort by Mentor Graphics Corporation ("Mentor"), a hostile bidder, to acquire Quickturn Design Systems, Inc. ("Quickturn"), the target company. The plaintiffs-appellees are Mentor[1] and an unaffiliated stockholder of Quickturn. The named defendants-appellants are Quickturn and its directors.

---

51. *Unitrin*, 651 A.2d at 1388-89; *see also, Gordon*, 19 Cardozo L. Rev. at 541.

52. For the sake of clarity, it must be emphasized that the "dead hand" provision at issue here is of unlimited duration; that is, it remains effective during the entire life of the poison pill. There are also "dead hand" provisions of limited duration (*e.g.*, six months), which are sometimes referred to as "diluted" or "deferred redemption" provisions. Some commentators have urged that such limited duration "dead hand" provisions stand on a different footing and should be upheld; others have argued the contrary. *See Lese*, 96 Col. L. Rev. at 2210; and *Gordon*, 19 Cardozo L. Rev. at 542. In any event, this case does not involve the validity of a "dead hand" provision of limited duration, and nothing in this Opinion should be read as expressing a view or pronouncement on that subject.

1. Mentor and MGZ Corp., a wholly owned Mentor subsidiary specially created as a vehicle to acquire Quickturn, are referred to collectively as "Mentor." Unless otherwise indicated, Mentor and Howard Shapiro, the shareholder plaintiff in Court of Chancery Civil Action No. 16588, are referred to collectively as "Mentor."

In response to Mentor's tender offer and proxy contest to replace the Quickturn board of directors, as part of Mentor's effort to acquire Quickturn, the Quickturn board enacted two defensive measures. First, it amended the Quickturn shareholder rights plan ("Rights Plan") by adopting a "no hand" feature of limited duration (the "Delayed Redemption Provision" or "DRP"). Second, the Quickturn board amended the corporation's by-laws to delay the holding of any special stockholders meeting requested by stockholders for 90 to 100 days after the validity of the request is determined (the "Amendment" or "By-Law Amendment").

Mentor filed actions for declarative and injunctive relief in the Court of Chancery challenging the legality of both defensive responses by Quickturn's board. The Court of Chancery conducted a trial on the merits. It determined that the By-Law Amendment is valid. It also concluded, however, that the DRP is invalid on fiduciary duty grounds.

In this appeal, Quickturn argues that the Court of Chancery erred in finding that Quickturn's directors breached their fiduciary duty by adopting the Delayed Redemption Provision. We have concluded that, as a matter of Delaware law, the Delayed Redemption Provision was invalid. Therefore, on that alternative basis, the judgment of the Court of Chancery is affirmed.

STATEMENT OF FACTS

THE PARTIES

Mentor (the hostile bidder) is an Oregon corporation, headquartered in Wilsonville, Oregon, whose shares are publicly traded on the NASDAQ national market system. Mentor manufactures, markets, and supports electronic design automation ("EDA") software and hardware. . . .

Quickturn, the target company, is a Delaware corporation, headquartered in San Jose, California. Quickturn has 17,922,518 outstanding shares of common stock that are publicly traded on the NASDAQ national market system. Quickturn invented, and was the first company to successfully market, logic emulation technology, which is used to verify the design of complex silicon chips and electronics systems. Quickturn is currently the market leader in the emulation business, controlling an estimated 60% of the worldwide emulation market and an even higher percentage of the United States market. Quickturn maintains the largest intellectual property portfolio in the industry, which includes approximately twenty-nine logic emulation patents issued in the United States, and numerous other patents issued in foreign jurisdictions. Quickturn's customers include the world's leading technology companies, among them Intel, IBM, Sun Microsystems, Texas Instruments, Hitachi, Fujitsu, Siemens, and NEC.

Quickturn's board of directors consists of eight members, all but one of whom are outside, independent directors. All have distinguished careers and significant technological experience. Collectively, the board has more than 30 years of experience in the EDA industry and owns one million shares (about 5%) of Quickturn's common stock.

Since 1989, Quickturn has historically been a growth company, having experienced increases in earnings and revenues during the past seven years. Those favorable trends were reflected in Quickturn's stock prices, which reached a high of $15.75 during the first quarter of 1998, and generally traded in the $15.875 to $21.25 range during the year preceding Mentor's hostile bid.

Since the spring of 1998, Quickturn's earnings, revenue growth, and stock price levels have declined, largely because of the downturn in the semiconductor industry and more specifically in the Asian semiconductor market. Historically, 30%-35% of Quickturn's annual sales (approximately $35 million) had come from Asia, but in 1998, Quickturn's Asian sales declined dramatically with the downturn of the Asian market.[5] Management has projected that the negative impact of the Asian market upon Quickturn's sales should begin reversing itself sometime between the second half of 1998 and early 1999.

QUICKTURN-MENTOR PATENT LITIGATION

Since 1996, Mentor and Quickturn have been engaged in patent litigation that has resulted in Mentor being barred from competing in the United States emulation market. Because its products have been adjudicated to infringe upon Quickturn's patents, Mentor currently stands enjoined from selling, manufacturing, or marketing its emulation products in the United States. Thus, Mentor is excluded from an unquestionably significant market for emulation products. . . .

MENTOR'S INTEREST IN ACQUIRING QUICKTURN

Mentor began exploring the possibility of acquiring Quickturn. If Mentor owned Quickturn, it would also own the patents, and would be in a position to "unenforce" them by seeking to vacate Quickturn's injunctive orders against Mentor in the patent litigation. . . .

In December 1997, Mentor retained Salomon Smith Barney ("Salomon") to act as its financial advisor in connection with a possible acquisition of Quickturn. Salomon prepared an extensive study which it reviewed with Mentor's senior executives in early 1998. The Salomon study concluded that although a Quickturn acquisition could provide substantial value for Mentor, Mentor could not afford to acquire Quickturn at the then-prevailing market price levels. Ultimately, Mentor decided not to attempt an acquisition of Quickturn during the first half of 1998.

After Quickturn's stock price began to decline in May 1998, however, Gregory Hinckley, Mentor's Executive Vice President, told Dr. Walden Rhines, Mentor's Chairman, that "the market outlook being very weak due to the Asian crisis made it a good opportunity" to try acquiring Quickturn for a cheap price.

---

5. By the summer of 1998, Quickturn's stock price had declined to $6 per share. On August 11, 1998, the closing price was $8.00 It was in this "trough" period that Mentor, which had designs upon Quickturn since the fall of 1997, saw an opportunity to acquire Quickturn for an advantageous price.

Mr. Hinckley then assembled Mentor's financial and legal advisors, proxy solicitors, and others, and began a three month process that culminated in Mentor's
August 12, 1998 tender offer.

MENTOR TENDER OFFER AND PROXY CONTEST

On August 12, 1998, Mentor announced an unsolicited cash tender offer
for all outstanding common shares of Quickturn at $12.125 per share, a price
representing an approximate 50% premium over Quickturn's immediate pre-
offer price, and a 20% discount from Quickturn's February 1998 stock price
levels. Mentor's tender offer, once consummated, would be followed by a second
step merger in which Quickturn's nontendering stockholders would receive, in
cash, the same $12.125 per share tender offer price.

Mentor also announced its intent to solicit proxies to replace the board at
a special meeting. Relying upon Quickturn's then-applicable by-law provision
governing the call of special stockholders meetings, Mentor began soliciting
agent designations from Quickturn stockholders to satisfy the by-law's stock
ownership requirements to call such a meeting.[11]

QUICKTURN BOARD MEETINGS

Under the Williams Act, Quickturn was required to inform its shareholders
of its response to Mentor's offer no later than ten business days after the offer
was commenced. During that ten day period, the Quickturn board met three
times, on August 13, 17, and 21, 1998. During each of those meetings, it considered Mentor's offer and ultimately decided how to respond.

The Quickturn board first met on August 13, 1998, the day after Mentor publicly announced its bid. All board members attended the meeting,
for the purpose of evaluating Mentor's tender offer. The meeting lasted for
several hours. Before or during the meeting, each board member received a
package that included (i) Mentor's press release announcing the unsolicited
offer; (ii) Quickturn's press release announcing its board's review of Mentor's
offer; (iii) Dr. Rhines's August 11 letter to Mr. Antle; (iv) the complaints filed by
Mentor against Quickturn and its directors; and (v) copies of Quickturn's then
current Rights Plan and by-laws.

* * *

During the balance of the meeting, the board discussed for approximately
one or two hours (a) the status, terms, and conditions of Mentor's offer; (b) the
status of Quickturn's patent litigation with Mentor; (c) the applicable rules and
regulations that would govern the board's response to the offer required by
the Securities Exchange Act of 1934 (the "34 Act"); (d) the board's fiduciary

---

11. The applicable by-law (Article II, §2.3) authorized a call of a special stockholders
meeting by shareholders holding at least 10% of Quickturn's shares. . . .

duties to Quickturn and its shareholders in a tender offer context; (e) the scope of defensive measures available to the corporation if the board decided that the offer was not in the best interests of the company or its stockholders; (f) Quickturn's then-current Rights Plan and special stockholders meeting by-law provisions; (g) the need for a federal antitrust filing; and (h) the potential effect of Mentor's offer on Quickturn's employees. The board also instructed management and H & Q to prepare analyses to assist the directors in evaluating Mentor's offer, and scheduled two board meetings, August 17, and August 21, 1998.

The Quickturn board next met on August 17, 1998. That meeting centered around financial presentations by management and by Hambrecht & Quist (H & Q), Quickturn's investment banker, financial advisor. . . .

The Quickturn board held its third and final meeting in response to Mentor's offer on August 21, 1998. Again, the directors received extensive materials and a further detailed analysis performed by H & Q. The focal point of that analysis was a chart entitled "Summary of Implied Valuation." That chart compared Mentor's tender offer price to the Quickturn valuation ranges generated by H & Q's application of five different methodologies.[14] The chart showed that Quickturn's value under all but one of those methodologies was higher than Mentor's $12.125 tender offer price.

QUICKTURN'S BOARD REJECTS MENTOR'S OFFER AS INADEQUATE

After hearing the presentations, the Quickturn board concluded that Mentor's offer was inadequate, and decided to recommend that Quickturn shareholders reject Mentor's offer. The directors based their decision upon: (a) H & Q's report; (b) the fact that Quickturn was experiencing a temporary trough in its business, which was reflected in its stock price; (c) the company's leadership in technology and patents and resulting market share; (d) the likely growth in Quickturn's markets (most notably, the Asian market) and the strength of Quickturn's new products (specifically, its Mercury product); (e) the potential value of the patent litigation with Mentor; and (f) the problems for Quickturn's customers, employees, and technology if the two companies were combined as the result of a hostile takeover.

QUICKTURN'S DEFENSIVE MEASURES

At the August 21 board meeting, the Quickturn board adopted two defensive measures in response to Mentor's hostile takeover bid. First, the board amended Article II, §2.3 of Quickturn's by-laws, which permitted stockholders holding 10% or more of Quickturn's stock to call a special stockholders

---

14. The five methodologies and the respective price ranges were: Historical Trading Range ($6.13-$21.63); Comparable Public Companies ($2.55-$15.61); Comparable M&A Transactions ($6.00-$31.36); Comparable Premiums Paid ($9.54-$ 10.72); and Discounted Cash Flow Analysis ($11.88-$57.87).

meeting. The By-Law Amendment provides that if any such special meeting is requested by shareholders, the corporation (Quickturn) would fix the record date for, and determine the time and place of, that special meeting, which must take place not less than 90 days nor more than 100 days after the receipt and determination of the validity of the shareholders' request.

Second, the board amended Quickturn's shareholder Rights Plan by eliminating its "dead hand" feature and replacing it with the Deferred Redemption Provision, under which no newly elected board could redeem the Rights Plan for six months after taking office, if the purpose or effect of the redemption would be to facilitate a transaction with an "Interested Person" (one who proposed, nominated or financially supported the election of the new directors to the board).[15] Mentor would be an Interested Person.

The effect of the By-Law Amendment would be to delay a shareholder called special meeting for at least three months. The effect of the DRP would be to delay the ability of a newly-elected, Mentor-nominated board to redeem the Rights Plan or "poison pill" for six months, in any transaction with an Interested Person. Thus, the combined effect of the two defensive measures would be to delay any acquisition of Quickturn by Mentor for at least nine months. . . .

QUICKTURN'S DELAYED REDEMPTION PROVISION

At the time Mentor commenced its bid, Quickturn had in place a Rights Plan that contained a so-called "dead hand" provision. That provision had a limited "continuing director" feature that became operative only if an insurgent that owned more than 15% of Quickturn's common stock successfully waged a proxy contest to replace a majority of the board. In that event, only the "continuing directors" (those directors in office at the time the poison pill was adopted) could redeem the rights.

During the same August 21, 1998 meeting at which it amended the special meeting by-law, the Quickturn board also amended the Rights Plan to eliminate its "continuing director" feature, and to substitute a "no hand" or "delayed redemption provision" into its Rights Plan. The Delayed Redemption Provision provides that, if a majority of the directors are replaced by stockholder action, the newly elected board cannot redeem the rights for six months if the purpose or effect of the redemption would be to facilitate a transaction with an "Interested Person."

It is undisputed that the DRP would prevent Mentor's slate, if elected as the new board majority, from redeeming the Rights Plan for six months following their election, because a redemption would be "reasonably likely to have the purpose or effect of facilitating a Transaction" with Mentor, a party

---

15. . . . An "Interested Person" is defined under the amended Rights Plan as "any Person who (i) is or will become an Acquiring Person if such Transaction were to be consummated or an Affiliate or Associate of such a Person, and (ii) is, or directly or indirectly proposed, nominated or financially supported, a director of [Quickturn] in office at the time of consideration of such Transaction who was elected at an annual or special meeting of stockholders."

that "directly or indirectly proposed, nominated or financially supported" the election of the new board. Consequently, by adopting the DRP, the Quickturn board built into the process a six month delay period in addition to the 90 to 100 day delay mandated by the By-Law Amendment.

COURT OF CHANCERY
INVALIDATES DELAYED REDEMPTION PROVISION

When the board of a Delaware corporation takes action to resist a hostile bid for control, the board of directors' defensive actions are subjected to "enhanced" judicial scrutiny. For a target board's actions to be entitled to business judgment rule protection, the target board must first establish that it had reasonable grounds to believe that the hostile bid constituted a threat to corporate policy and effectiveness; and second, that the defensive measures adopted were "proportionate," that is, reasonable in relation to the threat that the board reasonably perceived. The Delayed Redemption Provision was reviewed by the Court of Chancery pursuant to that standard.

The Court of Chancery found: "the evidence, viewed as a whole, shows that the perceived threat that led the Quickturn board to adopt the DRP, was the concern that Quickturn shareholders might mistakenly, in ignorance of Quickturn's true value, accept Mentor's inadequate offer, and elect a new board that would prematurely sell the company before the new board could adequately inform itself of Quickturn's fair value and before the shareholders could consider other options." The Court of Chancery concluded that Mentor's combined tender offer and proxy contest amounted to substantive coercion. Having concluded that the Quickturn board reasonably perceived a cognizable threat, the Court of Chancery then examined whether the board's response—the Delayed Redemption Provision—was proportionate in relation to that threat.

In assessing a challenge to defensive measures taken by a target board in response to an attempted hostile takeover, enhanced judicial scrutiny requires an evaluation of the board's justification for each contested defensive measure and its concomitant results. The Court of Chancery found that the Quickturn board's "justification or rationale for adopting the Delayed Redemption Provision was to force *any* newly elected board to take sufficient time to become familiar with Quickturn and its value, and to provide shareholders the opportunity to consider alternatives, before selling Quickturn to *any* acquiror." The Court of Chancery concluded that the Delayed Redemption Provision could not pass the proportionality test. Therefore, the Court of Chancery held that "the DRP cannot survive scrutiny under *Unocal* and must be declared invalid."

DELAYED REDEMPTION PROVISION
VIOLATES FUNDAMENTAL DELAWARE LAW

In this appeal, Mentor argues that the judgment of the Court of Chancery should be affirmed because the Delayed Redemption Provision is invalid as a matter of Delaware law. According to Mentor, the Delayed Redemption

Provision, like the "dead hand" feature in the Rights Plan that was held to be invalid in *Toll Brothers*,[29] will impermissibly deprive any newly elected board of both its statutory authority to manage the corporation under 8 Del. C. §141 (a) and its concomitant fiduciary duty pursuant to that statutory mandate. We agree.

Our analysis of the Delayed Redemption Provision in the Quickturn Rights Plan is guided by the prior precedents of this Court with regard to a board of directors authority to adopt a Rights Plan or "poison pill." In *Moran*, this Court held that the "inherent powers of the Board conferred by 8 Del. C. §141 (a) concerning the management of the corporation's 'business and affairs' provides the Board additional authority upon which to enact the Rights Plan." Consequently, this Court upheld the adoption of the Rights Plan in *Moran* as a legitimate exercise of business judgment by the board of directors. In doing so, however, this Court also held "the rights plan is not absolute":

> When the Household Board of Directors is faced with a tender offer and a request to redeem the Rights [Plan], they will not be able to arbitrarily reject the offer. They will be held to the same fiduciary standards any other board of directors would be held to in deciding to adopt a defensive mechanism, the same standards as they were held to in originally approving the Rights Plan.[33]

In *Moran*, this Court held that the "ultimate response to an actual takeover bid must be judged by the Directors' actions at the time and nothing we say relieves them of their fundamental duties to the corporation and its shareholders." Consequently, we concluded that the use of the Rights Plan would be evaluated when and if the issue arises.

One of the most basic tenets of Delaware corporate law is that the board of directors has the ultimate responsibility for managing the business and affairs of a corporation. Section 141 (a) requires that any limitation on the board's authority be set out in the certificate of incorporation. The Quickturn certificate of incorporation contains no provision purporting to limit the authority of the board in any way. The Delayed Redemption Provision, however, would prevent a newly elected board of directors from *completely* discharging its fundamental management duties to the corporation and its stockholders for six months. While the Delayed Redemption Provision limits the board of directors' authority in only one respect, the suspension of the Rights Plan, it nonetheless restricts the board's power in an area of fundamental importance to the shareholders—negotiating a possible sale of the corporation. Therefore, we hold that the Delayed Redemption Provision is invalid under Section 141 (a), which confers upon any newly elected board of directors *full* power to manage and direct the business and affairs of a Delaware corporation.

---

29. *Carmody v. Toll Brothers, Inc.*, Del. Ch., C.A. No. 15983, Jacobs, V.C. 1998 WL 418896 (July 24, 1998) ("*Toll Brothers*"). . . .

33. [*Moran v. Household Intl., Inc.*, 500 A.2d 1346, 1354 (Del. 1985)]; *See also Unocal Corp. v. Mesa Petroleum Co.*, 493 A.2d at 954-55, 958.

In discharging the statutory mandate of Section 141 (a), the directors have a fiduciary duty to the corporation and its shareholders. This unremitting obligation extends equally to board conduct in a contest for corporate control. The Delayed Redemption Provision prevents a newly elected board of directors from completely discharging its fiduciary duties to protect fully the interests of Quickturn and its stockholders.

This Court has recently observed that "although the fiduciary duty of a Delaware director is unremitting, the exact course of conduct that must be charted to properly discharge that responsibility will change in the specific context of the action the director is taking with regard to either the corporation or its shareholders."[42] This Court has held "[t]o the extent that a contract, or a provision thereof, purports to require a board to act *or not act* in such a fashion as to limit the exercise of fiduciary duties, it is invalid and unenforceable."[43] The Delayed Redemption Provision "tends to limit in a substantial way the freedom of [newly elected] directors' decisions on matters of management policy."[44] Therefore, "it violates the duty of each [newly elected] director to exercise his own best judgment on matters coming before the board."[45]

In this case, the Quickturn board was confronted by a determined bidder that sought to acquire the company at a price the Quickturn board concluded was inadequate. Such situations are common in corporate takeover efforts. In *Revlon,* this Court held that no defensive measure can be sustained when it represents a breach of the directors' fiduciary duty. *A fortiori,* no defensive measure can be sustained which would require a new board of directors to breach its fiduciary duty. In that regard, we note Mentor has properly acknowledged that in the event its slate of directors is elected, those newly elected directors will be required to discharge their unremitting fiduciary duty to manage the corporation for the benefit of Quickturn and its stockholders.

CONCLUSION

The Delayed Redemption Provision would prevent a new Quickturn board of directors from managing the corporation by redeeming the Rights Plan to facilitate a transaction that would serve the stockholders' best interests, even under circumstances where the board would be required to do so because of its fiduciary duty to the Quickturn stockholders. Because the Delayed Redemption Provision impermissibly circumscribes the board's statutory power under Section 141 (a) and the directors' ability to fulfill their concomitant fiduciary duties, we hold that the Delayed Redemption Provision is invalid. On that alternative basis, the judgment of the Court of Chancery is AFFIRMED.

---

42. *Malone v. Brincat,* Del. Supr., 722 A.2d 5 (1998).

43. *See Paramount Communications, Inc. v. QVC Network, Inc.,* 637 A.2d at 51 (*emphasis added*). . . .

44. *Abercrombie v. Davies,* Del. Ch., 123 A.2d 893, 899 (1956), *rev'd on other grounds,* Del. Supr., 130 A.2d 338 (1957).

45. *Id.*

NOTES

1. The Influence of Proxy Advisory Firms.   Many institutional investors rely on the advisory services of firms such Institutional Shareholder Services (ISS), to make recommendations to their clients regarding how to vote their shares of publicly traded U.S. corporations. In connection with the annual election of directors, ISS has promulgated guidelines that recommend, among other things, that shareholders vote against the entire board of directors of a company if it, among other things, adopts a stockholder rights plan with a term longer than 12 months without prior shareholder approval. The ISS has adopted other more specific guidelines with respect to voting recommendations where a company seeks shareholder approval of a poison pill. Taken together,

> . . . [In today's world of corporate governance,] ISS's voting policies create a [powerful] disincentive to adopt a poison pill that does not meet ISS's specifications and that is not submitted for stockholder ratification. Poison pills may be adopted once a particular threat has emerged, and at such a time, the board may be less concerned with ISS voting policies. Because a hostile bidder may emerge without warning and may quickly seek to take control through a hostile tender offer, boards should consider having a "pill-on-the-shelf" that will be ready to be implemented quickly in response to a specific threat. The work involved in drafting and implementing a poison pill is not trivial, and the need to do so "from scratch" in the face of an actual threat can distract the board and its advisors at a time when resources are already under pressure from the threat itself.

Louis Lehot, et al., *The Return of the Poison Pill—Lessons Learned from the* Selectica *and* Barnes & Noble *Cases*, 24 INSIGHTS 24, at 27 (December 2010).

2. Recent Poison Pill Cases.   In 2010, the Delaware Supreme Court decided an important (and well-known) case involving the enforceability of poison pills: *Versata Enterprises Inc., v. Selectica, Inc.*, 5 A. 3d 586 (Del. 2010) (involving the use of poison pill to protect the company's Net Operating Losses (NOLs)). Later that same year, the Delaware Chancery Court decided another important case regarding the enforceability of a poison pill. *See, Yucaipa American Alliance Fund II, L.P. v. Riggo, et al.*, 1 A.3d 310 (Del. Ch. 2010) (involving validity of a poison pill adopted as a defense to a hostile takeover bid). These two recent cases are described in the excerpt below.

**Louis Lehot, Kevin Rooney, John Tishler,
and Camille Formosa**
**The Return of the Poison Pill: Lessons Learned From
the *Selectica* and *Barnes & Noble* Cases,**
24 Insights 27 (December 2010)

RECENT DEVELOPMENTS

* * *

SELECTICA

In December 2008, Versata Enterprises, Inc. intentionally triggered an NOL poison pill adopted by Selectica, Inc., marking the first intentional triggering of a modern poison pill. In response to share accumulations earlier in 2008 by Versata, a direct competitor of Selectica, Selectica's board reduced the trigger threshold of its existing rights plan from 15 percent to 4.99 percent. Stockholders owning more than five percent at the time of this action, including Versata, were grandfathered in under the poison pill, subject to a trigger threshold of half a percent above their then-current ownership. Versata's intentional triggering of the poison pill in turn triggered a 10-day period during which the board of directors could negotiate and, if beneficial, waive the triggering acquisition, thereby avoiding the dilutive effects of the pill. Selectica declined to grant a waiver and instead decided to exercise the exchange feature in its poison pill, thereby avoiding potential threats to use of its NOLs presented by a flip-in. Selectica then instated a new poison pill, again with a 4.99 percent threshold. In the ensuing litigation, the Delaware Chancery Court determined that the poison pill was not preclusive, that the Selectica directors had showed that they had reasonable grounds for believing that a danger to corporate policy and effectiveness existed because of another person's stock ownership and had acted reasonably in relation to the threat posed by Versata. The court upheld each of the initial poison pill, the adopted replacement poison pill and the exchange. The Delaware Supreme Court affirmed the lower court's decision on October 4, 2010.

BARNES & NOBLE

In November of 2009, following failed discussions regarding company strategy and policies between investor Ronald Burkle and Barnes & Noble's founder and largest stockholder, Leonard Riggio, Yucaipa, and several other investment funds affiliated with Burkle increased their 8 percent ownership stock in Barnes & Noble to 17.8 percent and indicated in a Schedule 13D filing the possibility of Yucaipa acquiring Barnes & Noble. In response to the rapid accumulation of shares by Yucaipa, the board of directors of Barnes & Noble adopted a stockholder rights plan. The rights plan had a 20 percent trigger, but grandfathered Riggio's significantly higher stake from triggering the plan, which, together with family members, equaled almost 30 percent. In the ensuing lawsuit brought by Burkle, the Delaware Court of Chancery applied the *Unocal* standard and upheld the Barnes & Noble rights plan as a reasonable and proportionate response to the threat posed by Yucaipa. On November 17, 2010, the stockholders of Barnes & Noble overwhelmingly approved the poison pill at the 20 percent threshold.

[THE IMPLICATIONS OF *SELECTICA* AND *BARNES & NOBLE*]

BOARD DECISION-MAKING PROCESS

In *Selectica* and *Barnes & Noble*, the courts painstakingly reviewed the board's decision-making processes that resulted in the determination that an identifiable threat to a legitimate corporate purpose warranted the adoption of a poison pill, including the involvement of independent and interested directors in the decision-making process and the board's reliance on outside experts. Despite ultimately upholding the decisions of the Barnes & Noble board, the court faulted the board and its advisors for failing to exclude Riggio from the boardroom when discussing Riggio's motivations and interests and for the selection of outside experts to advise the board (certain of the advisors selected had previously advised Riggio on business and personal matters). The court in *Selectica* affirmed the board's determination that the NOLs had potential value, despite noted skepticism, because the board reasonably relied on outside experts to analyze the potential value of the NOLs and the potential threat that an ownership change presented to the NOL asset. These decisions reiterate the importance of independent directors, outside advisors that are free of relationships with interested directors and thorough documentation of the board process.

TRIGGERING THRESHOLD

In determining the reasonableness of the triggering threshold, courts have generally focused on whether it is so low that it would preclude a holder from undertaking and winning a proxy contest. Traditionally, the triggering threshold for poison pills has hovered between 10 percent and 20 percent. Delaware's anti-takeover statute has a 15 percent threshold percentage and, . . . ISS policy has a minimum 20 percent trigger under its guidelines. Allowing accumulations up to a larger trigger make it easier for a bidder to win a proxy contest.

The Selectica pill's triggering threshold was 4.99 percent due to Internal Revenue Service regulations with respect to NOLs, which provide that if a five percent stockholder increases its ownership by more than 50 percent, an "ownership change" is triggered and a company's ability to use its NOLs following an "ownership change" is limited. The *Selectica* court examined evidence from proxy solicitors and others as to the feasibility of running a proxy contest against a company of Selectica's size from a 4.99 percent ownership position. The court found that there was evidence that bidders had succeeded in winning proxy contests from that position, and hence the threshold was not preclusive. The court made this determination without reviewing whether running a proxy contest was possible in Versata's particular circumstances. Despite a range of acceptable thresholds from 10 percent to 20 percent, a threshold as low as 4.99 percent will be upheld, provided it meets the *Unocal/Unitrin* test. The new 2011 ISS guidelines regarding NOL poison pills acknowledge the general five percent threshold for NOL poison pills.

In the *Barnes & Noble* case the threshold was 20 percent—in line with ISS guidelines. However, Burkle initially argued that the 20 percent trigger was preclusive, since Riggio, who was adverse to Burkle, already held 30 percent of the outstanding shares. The court found that, due to the make-up of the stockholders other than Riggio and the activity of proxy advisory firms, Burkle's fund Yucaipa could win a proxy contest (as it turned out, Burkle lost the proxy contest in September 2010).

These cases demonstrate the importance of the board keeping a record to show that the poison pill will not prevent someone from winning a proxy contest.

* * *

DELAYED TRIGGER

Many poison pills include a window of time, commonly 10 days, after a stockholder purchases above the triggering threshold and before the activation of the rights occurs. The window gives the board fiduciary flexibility to ensure the pill wasn't triggered inadvertently, or to negotiate with the triggering stockholder and potentially amend the rights plan or redeem the rights. However, the existence of a delay in triggering can create pressure for the board to amend the plan rather than allow the draconian result of allowing the rights to activate. Boards should carefully weigh the benefits and detriments of the delayed trigger for a particular company's situation.

EXCHANGE FEATURE

As discussed above, poison pills typically permit the board to exchange the rights for common stock equivalents upon a flip-in event. The exchange is most commonly one share of common stock or common stock equivalent for each right, but some poison pills provide for an exchange that equates to a cashless exercise of the flip-in option. That is, each holder of the right receives the net number of shares it would receive if it sold shares to pay the exercise price. For Selectica, the dilution that would have been caused by the flip-in posed potential threats to the company's use of its NOLs, which was the very corporate asset the poison pill was designed to protect. To avoid the threat, Selectica chose to use the exchange feature in its poison pill, exchanging each right for one share of common stock. The exchange feature may avoid the need to register under the Securities Act of 1933 the sale of securities upon exercise of the rights and it may also avoid a situation where receipt of the exercise price would put unwanted cash on the company's balance sheet.

CONCLUSION

[In today's world of turbulent economic conditions,] unsolicited deal activity [will often] cause many companies to reconsider the [usefulness of a] poison pill. Whether a company is renewing or restoring a poison pill or putting one in place for the first time, it can expect that:

- a poison pill adopted in good faith by independent directors advised by outside experts with the intention of maximizing shareholder value is a valid defensive measure;
- Delaware courts will review carefully the board's decision making and record keeping processes in the context of a challenged poison pill;

- poison pills will be an available tool for protecting a company's NOLs; and
- design features will have a significant effect on the poison pill's effectiveness at achieving its desired goals.

E.   The Board's Decision to Sell the Company: The Duty to "Auction" the Firm

Revlon, Inc. v. MacAndrews & Forbes Holdings, Inc.
506 A.2d 173 (Del. 1985)

MOORE, Justice:

In this battle for corporate control of Revlon, Inc. (Revlon), the Court of Chancery enjoined certain transactions designed to thwart the efforts of Pantry Pride, Inc. (Pantry Pride) to acquire Revlon.[1] The defendants are Revlon, its board of directors, and Forstmann Little & Co. and the latter's affiliated limited partnership (collectively, Forstmann). The injunction barred consummation of an option granted Forstmann to purchase certain Revlon assets (the lock-up option), a promise by Revlon to deal exclusively with Forstmann in the face of a takeover (the no-shop provision), and the payment of a $25 million cancellation fee to Forstmann if the transaction was aborted. The Court of Chancery found that the Revlon directors had breached their duty of care by entering into the foregoing transactions and effectively ending an active auction for the company. The trial court ruled that such arrangements are not illegal *per se* under Delaware law, but that their use under the circumstances here was impermissible. We agree. *See MacAndrews & Forbes Holdings, Inc. v. Revlon, Inc.*, Del. Ch., 501 A.2d 1239 (1985). Thus, we granted this expedited interlocutory appeal to consider for the first time the validity of such defensive measures in the face of an active bidding contest for corporate control. Additionally, we address for the first time the extent to which a corporation may consider the impact of a takeover threat on constituencies other than shareholders. *See Unocal Corp. v. Mesa Petroleum Co.*, Del. Supr., 493 A.2d 946, 955 (1985).

In our view, lock-ups and related agreements are permitted under Delaware law where their adoption is untainted by director interest or other breaches of fiduciary duty. The actions taken by the Revlon directors, however, did not meet this standard. Moreover, while concern for various corporate constituencies is proper when addressing a takeover threat, that principle is limited by the requirement that there be some rationally related benefit accruing to the stockholders. We find no such benefit here.

---

1. The nominal plaintiff, MacAndrews & Forbes Holdings, Inc., is the controlling stockholder of Pantry Pride. For all practical purposes their interests in this litigation are virtually identical, and we hereafter will refer to Pantry Pride as the plaintiff.

Thus, under all the circumstances we must agree with the Court of Chancery that the enjoined Revlon defensive measures were inconsistent with the directors' duties to the stockholders. Accordingly, we affirm.

I.

The somewhat complex maneuvers of the parties necessitate a rather detailed examination of the facts. The prelude to this controversy began in June 1985, when Ronald O. Perelman, chairman of the board and chief executive officer of Pantry Pride, met with his counterpart at Revlon, Michel C. Bergerac, to discuss a friendly acquisition of Revlon by Pantry Pride. Perelman suggested a price in the range of $40-50 per share, but the meeting ended with Bergerac dismissing those figures as considerably below Revlon's intrinsic value. All subsequent Pantry Pride overtures were rebuffed, perhaps in part based on Mr. Bergerac's strong personal antipathy to Mr. Perelman.

Thus, on August 14, Pantry Pride's board authorized Perelman to acquire Revlon, either through negotiation in the $42-$43 per share range, or by making a hostile tender offer at $45. Perelman then met with Bergerac and outlined Pantry Pride's alternate approaches. Bergerac remained adamantly opposed to such schemes and conditioned any further discussions of the matter on Pantry Pride executing a standstill agreement prohibiting it from acquiring Revlon without the latter's prior approval.

On August 19, the Revlon board met specially to consider the impending threat of a hostile bid by Pantry Pride.[3] At the meeting, Lazard Freres, Revlon's investment banker, advised the directors that $45 per share was a grossly inadequate price for the company. Felix Rohatyn and William Loomis of Lazard Freres explained to the board that Pantry Pride's financial strategy for acquiring Revlon would be through "junk bond" financing followed by a break-up of Revlon and the disposition of its assets. With proper timing, according to the experts, such transactions could produce a return to Pantry Pride of $60 to $70 per share, while a sale of the company as a whole would be in the "mid 50" dollar range. Martin Lipton, special counsel for Revlon, recommended two defensive measures: first, that the company repurchase up to 5 million of its nearly 30 million outstanding shares; and second, that it adopt a Note Purchase Rights Plan. Under this plan, each Revlon shareholder would receive as a dividend one Note Purchase Right (the Rights) for each share of common stock, with the Rights entitling the holder to exchange one common share for a $65 principal Revlon note at 12% interest with a one-year maturity. The Rights would become effective whenever anyone acquired beneficial ownership of 20% or more of Revlon's shares, unless the purchaser acquired all the

---

3. There were 14 directors on the Revlon board. Six of them held senior management positions with the company, and two others held significant blocks of its stock. Four of the remaining six directors were associated at some point with entities that had various business relationships with Revlon. On the basis of this limited record, however, we cannot conclude that this board is entitled to certain presumptions that generally attach to the decisions of a board whose majority consists of truly outside independent directors.

company's stock for cash at $65 or more per share. In addition, the Rights would not be available to the acquiror, and prior to the 20% triggering event the Revlon board could redeem the rights for 10 cents each. Both proposals were unanimously adopted.

Pantry Pride made its first hostile move on August 23 with a cash tender offer for any and all shares of Revlon at $47.50 per common share and $26.67 per preferred share, subject to (1) Pantry Pride's obtaining financing for the purchase, and (2) the Rights being redeemed, rescinded or voided.

The Revlon board met again on August 26. The directors advised the stockholders to reject the offer. Further defensive measures also were planned. On August 29, Revlon commenced its own offer for up to 10 million shares, exchanging for each share of common stock tendered one Senior Subordinated Note (the Notes) of $47.50 principal at 11.75% interest, due 1995, and one-tenth of a share of $9.00 Cumulative Convertible Exchangeable Preferred Stock valued at $100 per share. Lazard Freres opined that the notes would trade at their face value on a fully distributed basis.[4] Revlon stockholders tendered 87 percent of the outstanding shares (approximately 33 million), and the company accepted the full 10 million shares on a pro rata basis. The new Notes contained covenants which limited Revlon's ability to incur additional debt, sell assets, or pay dividends unless otherwise approved by the "independent" (non-management) members of the board.

At this point, both the Rights and the Note covenants stymied Pantry Pride's attempted takeover. The next move came on September 16, when Pantry Pride announced a new tender offer at $42 per share, conditioned upon receiving at least 90% of the outstanding stock. Pantry Pride also indicated that it would consider buying less than 90%, and at an increased price, if Revlon removed the impeding Rights. While this offer was lower on its face than the earlier $47.50 proposal, Revlon's investment banker, Lazard Freres, described the two bids as essentially equal in view of the completed exchange offer.

The Revlon board held a regularly scheduled meeting on September 24. The directors rejected the latest Pantry Pride offer and authorized management to negotiate with other parties interested in acquiring Revlon. Pantry Pride remained determined in its efforts and continued to make cash bids for the company, offering $50 per share on September 27, and raising its bid to $53 on October 1, and then to $56.25 on October 7.

In the meantime, Revlon's negotiations with Forstmann and the investment group Adler & Shaykin had produced results. The Revlon directors met on October 3 to consider Pantry Pride's $53 bid and to examine possible alternatives to the offer. Both Forstmann and Adler & Shaykin made certain proposals to the board. As a result, the directors unanimously agreed to a leveraged buyout by Forstmann. The terms of this accord were as follows: each stockholder would get $56 cash per share; management would purchase stock in

---

4. Like bonds, the Notes actually were issued in denominations of $1,000 and integral multiples thereof. A separate certificate was issued in a total principal amount equal to the remaining sum to which a stockholder was entitled. Likewise, in the esoteric parlance of bond dealers, a Note trading at par ($1,000) would be quoted on the market at 100.

the new company by the exercise of their Revlon "golden parachutes";[5] Forstmann would assume Revlon's $475 million debt incurred by the issuance of the Notes; and Revlon would redeem the Rights and waive the Notes covenants for Forstmann or in connection with any other offer superior to Forstmann's. The board did not actually remove the covenants at the October 3 meeting, because Forstmann then lacked a firm commitment on its financing, but accepted the Forstmann capital structure, and indicated that the outside directors would waive the covenants in due course. Part of Forstmann's plan was to sell Revlon's Norcliff Thayer and Reheis divisions to American Home Products for $335 million. Before the merger, Revlon was to sell its cosmetics and fragrance division to Adler & Shaykin for $905 million. These transactions would facilitate the purchase by Forstmann or any other acquiror of Revlon.

When the merger, and thus the waiver of the Notes covenants, was announced, the market value of these securities began to fall. The Notes, which originally traded near par, around 100, dropped to 87.50 by October 8. One director later reported (at the October 12 meeting) a "deluge" of telephone calls from irate noteholders, and on October 10 the Wall Street Journal reported threats of litigation by these creditors.

Pantry Pride countered with a new proposal on October 7, raising its $53 offer to $56.25, subject to nullification of the Rights, a waiver of the Notes covenants, and the election of three Pantry Pride directors to the Revlon board. On October 9, representatives of Pantry Pride, Forstmann and Revlon conferred in an attempt to negotiate the fate of Revlon, but could not reach agreement. At this meeting Pantry Pride announced that it would engage in fractional bidding and top any Forstmann offer by a slightly higher one. It is also significant that Forstmann, to Pantry Pride's exclusion, had been made privy to certain Revlon financial data. Thus, the parties were not negotiating on equal terms.

Again privately armed with Revlon data, Forstmann met on October 11 with Revlon's special counsel and investment banker. On October 12, Forstmann made a new $57.25 per share offer, based on several conditions.[6] The principal demand was a lock-up option to purchase Revlon's Vision Care and National Health Laboratories divisions for $525 million, some $100-$175 million below the value ascribed to them by Lazard Freres, if another acquiror got 40% of Revlon's shares. Revlon also was required to accept a no-shop provision. The Rights and Notes covenants had to be removed as in the October 3 agreement. There would be a $25 million cancellation fee to be placed in escrow, and released to Forstmann if the new agreement terminated or if another acquiror got more than 19.9% of Revlon's stock. Finally, there would be no participation by Revlon management in the merger. In return, Forstmann agreed to support

---

5. In the takeover context "golden parachutes" generally are understood to be termination agreements providing substantial bonuses and other benefits for managers and certain directors upon a change in control of a company.

6. Forstmann's $57.25 offer ostensibly is worth $1 more than Pantry Pride's $56.25 bid. However, the Pantry Pride offer was immediate, while the Forstmann proposal must be discounted for the time value of money because of the delay in approving the merger and consummating the transaction. The exact difference between the two bids was an unsettled point of contention even at oral argument.

the par value of the Notes, which had faltered in the market, by an exchange of new notes. Forstmann also demanded immediate acceptance of its offer, or it would be withdrawn. The board unanimously approved Forstmann's proposal because: (1) it was for a higher price than the Pantry Pride bid, (2) it protected the noteholders, and (3) Forstmann's financing was firmly in place.[7] The board further agreed to redeem the rights and waive the covenants on the preferred stock in response to any offer above $57 cash per share. The covenants were waived, contingent upon receipt of an investment banking opinion that the Notes would trade near par value once the offer was consummated.

Pantry Pride, which had initially sought injunctive relief from the Rights plan on August 22, filed an amended complaint on October 14 challenging the lock-up, the cancellation fee, and the exercise of the Rights and the Notes covenants. Pantry Pride also sought a temporary restraining order to prevent Revlon from placing any assets in escrow or transferring them to Forstmann. Moreover, on October 22, Pantry Pride again raised its bid, with a cash offer of $58 per share conditioned upon nullification of the Rights, waiver of the covenants, and an injunction of the Forstmann lock-up.

On October 15, the Court of Chancery prohibited the further transfer of assets, and eight days later enjoined the lock-up, no-shop, and cancellation fee provisions of the agreement. The trial court concluded that the Revlon directors had breached their duty of loyalty by making concessions to Forstmann, out of concern for their liability to the noteholders, rather than maximizing the sale price of the company for the stockholders' benefit. *MacAndrews & Forbes Holdings, Inc. v. Revlon, Inc.*, 501 A.2d at 1249-50.

II.

To obtain a preliminary injunction, a plaintiff must demonstrate both a reasonable probability of success on the merits and some irreparable harm which will occur absent the injunction. . . . Additionally, the Court shall balance the conveniences of and possible injuries to the parties.

A

We turn first to Pantry Pride's probability of success on the merits. The ultimate responsibility for managing the business and affairs of a corporation falls on its board of directors. In discharging this function the directors owe fiduciary duties of care and loyalty to the corporation and its shareholders. *Guth v. Loft, Inc.*, 23 Del. Supr. 255, 5 A.2d 503, 510 (1939); *Aronson v. Lewis,*

---

7. Actually, at this time about $400 million of Forstmann's funding was still subject to two investment banks using their "best efforts" to organize a syndicate to provide the balance. Pantry Pride's entire financing was not firmly committed at this point either, although Pantry Pride represented in an October 11 letter to Lazard Freres that its investment banker, Drexel Burnham Lambert, was highly confident of its ability to raise the balance of $350 million. Drexel Burnham had a firm commitment for this sum by October 18.

Del. Supr., 473 A.2d 805, 811 (1984). These principles apply with equal force when a board approves a corporate merger pursuant to 8 Del. C. §251(b);[9] *Smith v. Van Gorkom,* Del. Supr., 488 A.2d 858, 873 (1985); and of course they are the bedrock of our law regarding corporate takeover issues. . . . While the business judgment rule may be applicable to the actions of corporate directors responding to takeover threats, the principles upon which it is founded—care, loyalty and independence—must first be satisfied.

If the business judgment rule applies, there is a "presumption that in making a business decision the directors of a corporation acted on an informed basis, in good faith and in the honest belief that the action taken was in the best interests of the company." *Aronson v. Lewis,* 473 A.2d at 812. However, when a board implements anti-takeover measures there arises "the omnipresent specter that a board may be acting primarily in its own interests, rather than those of the corporation and its shareholders. . ." *Unocal Corp. v. Mesa Petroleum Co.,* 493 A.2d at 954. This potential for conflict places upon the directors the burden of proving that they had reasonable grounds for believing there was a danger to corporate policy and effectiveness, a burden satisfied by a showing of good faith and reasonable investigation. In addition, the directors must analyze the nature of the takeover and its effect on the corporation in order to ensure balance—that the responsive action taken is reasonable in relation to the threat posed. *Id.*

B

The first relevant defensive measure adopted by the Revlon board was the Rights Plan, which would be considered a "poison pill" in the current language of corporate takeovers—a plan by which shareholders receive the right to be bought out by the corporation at a substantial premium on the occurrence of a stated triggering event. *See generally Moran v. Household International, Inc.,* Del. Supr., 500 A.2d 1346 (1985). By 8 Del. C. §§141 and 122(13),[11] the board clearly had the power to adopt the measure. *See Moran v. Household International, Inc.,* 500 A.2d at 1351. Thus, the focus becomes one of reasonableness and purpose.

The Revlon board approved the Rights Plan in the face of an impending hostile takeover bid by Pantry Pride at $45 per share, a price which Revlon reasonably concluded was grossly inadequate. Lazard Freres had so advised the

---

9. The statute provides in pertinent part:

   (b) The board of directors of each corporation which desires to merge or consolidate shall adopt a resolution approving an agreement of merger or consolidation. 8 Del. C. §251(b).

11. The relevant provision of Section 122 is:

   Every corporation created under this chapter shall have power to: (13) Make contracts, including contracts of guaranty and suretyship, incur liabilities, borrow money at such rates of interest as the corporation may determine, issue its notes, bonds and other obligations, and secure any of its obligations by mortgage, pledge or other encumbrance of all or any of its property, franchises and income, . . . 8 Del. C. §122(13).

directors, and had also informed them that Pantry Pride was a small, highly leveraged company bent on a "bust-up" takeover by using "junk bond" financing to buy Revlon cheaply, sell the acquired assets to pay the debts incurred, and retain the profit for itself.[12] In adopting the Plan, the board protected the shareholders from a hostile takeover at a price below the company's intrinsic value, while retaining sufficient flexibility to address any proposal deemed to be in the stockholders' best interests.

To that extent the board acted in good faith and upon reasonable investigation. Under the circumstances it cannot be said that the Rights Plan as employed was unreasonable, considering the threat posed. Indeed, the Plan was a factor in causing Pantry Pride to raise its bids from a low of $42 to an eventual high of $58. At the time of its adoption the Rights Plan afforded a measure of protection consistent with the directors' fiduciary duty in facing a takeover threat perceived as detrimental to corporate interests. *Unocal,* 493 A.2d at 954-55. Far from being a "show-stopper," as the plaintiffs had contended in *Moran,* the measure spurred the bidding to new heights, a proper result of its implementation. *See Moran,* 500 A.2d at 1354, 1356-67.

Although we consider adoption of the Plan to have been valid under the circumstances, its continued usefulness was rendered moot by the directors' actions on October 3 and October 12. At the October 3 meeting the board redeemed the Rights conditioned upon consummation of a merger with Forstmann, but further acknowledged that they would also be redeemed to facilitate any more favorable offer. On October 12, the board unanimously passed a resolution redeeming the Rights in connection with any cash proposal of $57.25 or more per share. Because all the pertinent offers eventually equaled or surpassed that amount, the Rights clearly were no longer any impediment in the contest for Revlon. This mooted any question of their propriety under *Moran* or *Unocal.*

c

The second defensive measure adopted by Revlon to thwart a Pantry Pride takeover was the company's own exchange offer for 10 million of its shares. The directors' general broad powers to manage the business and affairs of the corporation are augmented by the specific authority conferred under 8 Del. C. §160(a), permitting the company to deal in its own stock.[13] *Unocal,* 493 A.2d at 953-54. However, when exercising that power in an effort to forestall a hostile takeover, the board's actions are strictly held to the fiduciary standards outlined in *Unocal.* These standards require the directors to determine the best

---

12. As we noted in *Moran,* a "bust-up" takeover generally refers to a situation in which one seeks to finance an acquisition by selling off pieces of the acquired company, presumably at a substantial profit. *See Moran,* 500 A.2d at 1349, n. 4.

13. The pertinent provision of this statute is:

(a) Every corporation may purchase, redeem, receive, take or otherwise acquire, own and hold, sell, lend, exchange, transfer or otherwise dispose of, pledge, use and otherwise deal in and with its own shares. 8 Del. C. §160(a).

interests of the corporation and its stockholders, and impose an enhanced duty to abjure any action that is motivated by considerations other than a good faith concern for such interests. *Unocal*, 493 A.2d at 954-55.

The Revlon directors concluded that Pantry Pride's $47.50 offer was grossly inadequate. In that regard the board acted in good faith, and on an informed basis, with reasonable grounds to believe that there existed a harmful threat to the corporate enterprise. The adoption of a defensive measure, reasonable in relation to the threat posed, was proper and fully accorded with the powers, duties, and responsibilities conferred upon directors under our law. *Unocal*, 493 A.2d at 954.

D

However, when Pantry Pride increased its offer to $50 per share, and then to $53, it became apparent to all that the break-up of the company was inevitable. The Revlon board's authorization permitting management to negotiate a merger or buyout with a third party was a recognition that the company was for sale. The duty of the board had thus changed from the preservation of Revlon as a corporate entity to the maximization of the company's value at a sale for the stockholders' benefit. This significantly altered the board's responsibilities under the *Unocal* standards. It no longer faced threats to corporate policy and effectiveness, or to the stockholders' interests, from a grossly inadequate bid. The whole question of defensive measures became moot. The directors' role changed from defenders of the corporate bastion to auctioneers charged with getting the best price for the stockholders at a sale of the company.

III.

This brings us to the lock-up with Forstmann and its emphasis on shoring up the sagging market value of the Notes in the face of threatened litigation by their holders. Such a focus was inconsistent with the changed concept of the directors' responsibilities at this stage of the developments. The impending waiver of the Notes covenants had caused the value of the Notes to fall, and the board was aware of the noteholders' ire as well as their subsequent threats of suit. The directors thus made support of the Notes an integral part of the company's dealings with Forstmann, even though their primary responsibility at this stage was to the equity owners.

The original threat posed by Pantry Pride—the break-up of the company—had become a reality which even the directors embraced. Selective dealing to fend off a hostile but determined bidder was no longer a proper objective. Instead, obtaining the highest price for the benefit of the stockholders should have been the central theme guiding director action. Thus, the Revlon board could not make the requisite showing of good faith by preferring the noteholders and ignoring its duty of loyalty to the shareholders. The rights of the former already were fixed by contract. The noteholders required no further protection, and when the Revlon board entered into an auction-ending lock-up agreement with Forstmann on the basis of impermissible considerations at the expense of the shareholders, the directors breached their primary duty of loyalty.

The Revlon board argued that it acted in good faith in protecting the note-holders because *Unocal* permits consideration of other corporate constituen-cies. Although such considerations may be permissible, there are fundamental limitations upon that prerogative. A board may have regard for various constit-uencies in discharging its responsibilities, provided there are rationally related benefits accruing to the stockholders. *Unocal,* 493 A.2d at 955. However, such concern for non-stockholder interests is inappropriate when an auction among active bidders is in progress, and the object no longer is to protect or maintain the corporate enterprise but to sell it to the highest bidder.

Revlon also contended that by *Gilbert v. El Paso Co.,* Del. Ch., 490 A.2d 1050, 1054-55 (1984), it had contractual and good faith obligations to consider the noteholders. However, any such duties are limited to the principle that one may not interfere with contractual relationships by improper actions. Here, the rights of the noteholders were fixed by agreement, and there is nothing of sub-stance to suggest that any of those terms were violated. The Notes covenants specifically contemplated a waiver to permit sale of the company at a fair price. The Notes were accepted by the holders on that basis, including the risk of an adverse market effect stemming from a waiver. Thus, nothing remained for Rev-lon to legitimately protect, and no rationally related benefit thereby accrued to the stockholders. Under such circumstances we must conclude that the merger agreement with Forstmann was unreasonable in relation to the threat posed.

A lock-up is not *per se* illegal under Delaware law. Its use has been approved in an earlier case. *Thompson v. Enstar Corp.,* Del. Ch., __ A.2d __ (1984). Such options can entice other bidders to enter a contest for control of the corpo-ration, creating an auction for the company and maximizing shareholder profit. Current economic conditions in the takeover market are such that a "white knight" like Forstmann might only enter the bidding for the target company if it receives some form of compensation to cover the risks and costs involved. . . . However, while those lock-ups which draw bidders into the battle benefit shareholders, similar measures which end an active auction and fore-close further bidding operate to the shareholders' detriment. . . .

Recently, the United States Court of Appeals for the Second Circuit invali-dated a lock-up on fiduciary duty grounds similar to those here.[15] *Hanson Trust PLC, et al. v. ML SCM Acquisition Inc., et al.,* 781 F.2d 264 (2nd Cir. 1986). Citing *Thompson v. Enstar Corp., supra,* with approval, the court stated:

> In this regard, we are especially mindful that some lock-up options may be ben-eficial to the shareholders, such as those that induce a bidder to compete for con-trol of a corporation, while others may be harmful, such as those that effectively preclude bidders from competing with the optionee bidder. 781 F.2d at 274.

---

15. The federal courts generally have declined to enjoin lock-up options despite argu-ments that lock-ups constitute impermissible "manipulative" conduct forbidden by Section 14(e) of the Williams Act [15 U.S.C. §78n(e)]. *See Buffalo Forge Co. v. Ogden Corp., Ill* F.2d 757 (2nd Cir. 1983), *cert. denied,* 464 U.S. 1018, 104 S. Ct. 550, 78 L. Ed. 2d 724 (1983); *Data Probe Acquisition Corp. v. Datatab, Inc.,* 7²2 F.2d 1 (2nd Cir. 1983); *cert. denied* 465 U.S. 1052, 104 S. Ct. 1326, 79 L. Ed. 2d 722 (1984); *but see Mobil Corp. v. Marathon Oil Co.,* 669 F.2d 366 (6th Cir. 1981). The cases are all federal in nature and were not decided on state law grounds.

In *Hanson Trust,* the bidder, Hanson, sought control of SCM by a hostile cash tender offer. SCM management joined with Merrill Lynch to propose a leveraged buy-out of the company at a higher price, and Hanson in turn increased its offer. Then, despite very little improvement in its subsequent bid, the management group sought a lock-up option to purchase SCM's two main assets at a substantial discount. The SCM directors granted the lock-up without adequate information as to the size of the discount or the effect the transaction would have on the company. Their action effectively ended a competitive bidding situation. The Hanson Court invalidated the lock-up because the directors failed to fully inform themselves about the value of a transaction in which management had a strong self-interest. "In short, the Board appears to have failed to ensure that negotiations for alternative bids were conducted by those whose only loyalty was to the shareholders." *Id.* at 277.

The Forstmann option had a similar destructive effect on the auction process. Forstmann had already been drawn into the contest on a preferred basis, so the result of the lock-up was not to foster bidding, but to destroy it. The board's stated reasons for approving the transactions were: (1) better financing, (2) noteholder protection, and (3) higher price. As the Court of Chancery found, and we agree, any distinctions between the rival bidders' methods of financing the proposal were nominal at best, and such a consideration has little or no significance in a cash offer for any and all shares. The principal object, contrary to the board's duty of care, appears to have been protection of the noteholders over the shareholders' interests.

While Forstmann's $57.25 offer was objectively higher than Pantry Pride's $56.25 bid, the margin of superiority is less when the Forstmann price is adjusted for the time value of money. In reality, the Revlon board ended the auction in return for very little actual improvement in the final bid. The principal benefit went to the directors, who avoided personal liability to a class of creditors to whom the board owed no further duty under the circumstances. Thus, when a board ends an intense bidding contest on an insubstantial basis, and where a significant by-product of that action is to protect the directors against a perceived threat of personal liability for consequences stemming from the adoption of previous defensive measures, the action cannot withstand the enhanced scrutiny which *Unocal* requires of director conduct. *See Unocal,* 493 A.2d at 954-55.

In addition to the lock-up option, the Court of Chancery enjoined the no-shop provision as part of the attempt to foreclose further bidding by Pantry Pride. *MacAndrews & Forbes Holdings, Inc. v. Revlon, Inc.,* 501 A.2d at 1251. The no-shop provision, like the lock-up option, while not *per se* illegal, is impermissible under the *Unocal* standards when a board's primary duty becomes that of an auctioneer responsible for selling the company to the highest bidder. The agreement to negotiate only with Forstmann ended rather than intensified the board's involvement in the bidding contest.

It is ironic that the parties even considered a no-shop agreement when Revlon had dealt preferentially, and almost exclusively, with Forstmann throughout the contest. After the directors authorized management to negotiate with other parties, Forstmann was given every negotiating advantage that Pantry Pride had been denied: cooperation from management, access to financial data, and the exclusive opportunity to present merger proposals directly to the board of directors. Favoritism for a white knight to the total exclusion of a hostile bidder might be justifiable when the latter's offer adversely affects shareholder interests, but when bidders make relatively similar offers, or dissolution of the company becomes inevitable, the directors cannot fulfill their enhanced *Unocal* duties by playing favorites with the contending factions. Market forces must be allowed to operate freely to bring the target's shareholders the best price available for their equity.[16] Thus, as the trial court ruled, the shareholders' interests necessitated that the board remain free to negotiate in the fulfillment of that duty.

The court below similarly enjoined the payment of the cancellation fee, pending a resolution of the merits, because the fee was part of the overall plan to thwart Pantry Pride's efforts. We find no abuse of discretion in that ruling.

IV.

Having concluded that Pantry Pride has shown a reasonable probability of success on the merits, we address the issue of irreparable harm. The Court of Chancery ruled that unless the lock-up and other aspects of the agreement were enjoined, Pantry Pride's opportunity to bid for Revlon was lost. The court also held that the need for both bidders to compete in the marketplace outweighed any injury to Forstmann. Given the complexity of the proposed transaction between Revlon and Forstmann, the obstacles to Pantry Pride obtaining a meaningful legal remedy are immense. We are satisfied that the plaintiff has shown the need for an injunction to protect it from irreparable harm, which need outweighs any harm to the defendants.

V.

In conclusion, the Revlon board was confronted with a situation not uncommon in the current wave of corporate takeovers. A hostile and determined bidder sought the company at a price the board was convinced was inadequate. The initial defensive tactics worked to the benefit of the shareholders, and thus the board was able to sustain its *Unocal* burdens in justifying those measures. However, in granting an asset option lock-up to Forstmann, we must conclude that under all the circumstances the directors allowed considerations other than the maximization of shareholder profit to affect their judgment, and followed a course that ended the auction for Revlon, absent court intervention, to the ultimate detriment of its shareholders. No such defensive measure can be sustained when it represents a breach of the directors' fundamental duty of care. *See Smith v. Van Gorkom*, Del. Supr., 488 A.2d 858, 874 (1985). In that context the board's action is not entitled to the deference accorded it by the business judgment rule. The measures were properly enjoined. The decision of the Court of Chancery, therefore, is
AFFIRMED. . . .

---

16. By this we do not embrace the "passivity" thesis rejected in *Unocal. See* 493 A.2d at 954-55, nn. 8-10. The directors' role remains an active one, changed only in the respect that they are charged with the duty of selling the company at the highest price attainable for the stockholders' benefit.

QUESTIONS

1. In light of the facts involved in *Revlon,* why did Revlon management propose to engage in a self-tender (i.e., issuer repurchase of its shares)? What did management hope to accomplish through this repurchase of Revlon shares?

2. What are the terms of the poison pill (i.e., Note Purchase Rights Plan) adopted by the Revlon board?

3. What are the conditions to Pantry Pride's original tender offer?

4. Did the Revlon board satisfy the *Unocal* standard when they decided to adopt the pill? Did the pill work the way the board intended? In other words, did the pill serve its stated business objective?

5. Why was the board's decision to approve the repurchase of $10 million of its shares protected by the *Unocal* standard? Why was this board decision subject to judicial review under the *Unocal* standard rather than the more protective, traditional business judgment rule standard of review?

6. This decision of the Delaware Supreme Court coined a new expression in the growing lexicon related to M&A defensive strategies: the "*Revlon* mode" or, as it sometimes is referred to, the "auction mode." When did the company (Revlon) enter the auction mode? What is the board's responsibility once the company enters the *Revlon* mode? Once the company enters the *Revlon* mode, is the board's responsibility (as described by the *Revlon* decision) consistent with the Delaware court's steadfast refusal to adopt the passivity theory?

7. What is a "no-shop" clause?

8. What is a "crown jewel lock-up" option? Why did the granting of this option end up working as a "showstopper"—that is to say, operate to end the competitive bidding process in *Revlon?*

9. What is "change of control" compensation (aka "golden parachutes")? (*Hint:* Refer to footnote 5 of the *Revlon* opinion.) What are the arguments in favor of these executive compensation packages that take effect on a change of control of Target Co.? Who might oppose this form of executive compensation and why?

10. According to *Revlon,* are all lock-up options *per se* invalid? If not, then under what circumstances can Target's board of directors grant a valid and enforceable lock-up option?

11. As a public policy matter, what are the competing interests to be balanced in deciding whether to invalidate or enforce a lock-up option?

12. Who should decide whether a particular lock-up option is valid?

13. According to *Revlon,* what is the relevance of the interests of "other constituencies" in deciding how Target's board should respond to an unsolicited takeover bid?

14. What is the nature of the Delaware Supreme Court's public policy concern regarding the "preclusive effect" of granting a "lock-up" option to a "white knight" Bidder?

15. What was the Revlon board's stated reason(s) for approving the revised Forstman LBO at its meeting on October 12? In invalidating this decision of the Revlon board, is the Delaware Supreme Court substituting its business judgment for that of the Revlon board?

NOTES

1. What Qualifies as Appropriate Auction Procedures? The holding in *Revlon* makes clear that the fiduciary obligations of the board of directors of Target Co. are especially significant when the company is for sale. In those cases where management decides to put the company up for sale (to put the company "on the auction block," so to speak), *Revlon* requires that Target's board of directors must take reasonable steps to maximize shareholder value, and further, must take care to place the interests of the company and all of its stockholders ahead of (what may often be) the divergent personal interests of the directors and/or senior executive officers. Subsequent Delaware cases also make clear that there is no definitive set of procedures — "no single blueprint" — that the board is required to follow in order to demonstrate that Target's board has fulfilled its duties under *Revlon*. Thus, *Revlon* "does not require, for example, that before every corporate merger agreement can be validly entered into, the constituent corporations must be 'shopped' or, more radically, an auction process undertaken, even though the merger may be regarded as a sale of the company." *City Capital Associates v. Interco, Inc.*, 551 A. 2d 787, 802 (Del. Ch. 1988). Rather, post-*Revlon* case law reflects that directors' duties in the context of the sale of Target are very fact specific and further reflects that the board has fairly broad latitude to fashion the direction and structure of the sale ("auction") process.

Although Delaware courts confer broad discretion on the board, the courts also make clear that the board of directors cannot enter into a definitive merger agreement without obtaining information about other potential transactions. "There must be a reasonable basis for the board . . . to conclude that the transaction involved is in the best interests of the shareholders. This involves having information about possible alternatives. The essence of rational choice is an assessment of costs and benefits and the consideration of alternatives." *Id.* Several recent cases underscore that Target's board of directors (and their legal and financial advisors) must take care that the board's decisions in connection with the sale of the company are custom-tailored to the factual setting of Target's particular situation, which is vitally important in light of the willingness of the Delaware courts to scrutinize the sale process carefully to determine compliance with the board's duties under *Revlon*. See, e.g., *In re Toys "R" Us, Inc. Shareholder Litigation*, 877 A. 2d 975 (Del. Ch. 2005); *In re Netsmart Technologies, Inc. Shareholder Litigation*, 924 A. 2d 171; *In re Lear Corporation Shareholder Litigation*, 926 A. 2d 94 (Del. Ch. 2007); and *In re Topps Company Shareholders Litigation*, 926 A. 2d 58 (Del. Ch. 2007). We will examine one of these cases (*Topps*) in more detail later in this section, as part of our discussion of the validity of various types of deal protection measures under Delaware law.

2. *What Are Lock-Up Options?* The court in *Revlon* referred to the use of *lock-up options*. What is a "lock-up option"?

> When confronted by two or more opposing [i.e., competing] bids for control, target management sometimes enters into an arrangement with one of the bidders that has the effect of conferring on that bidder a strategic advantage in the contest for control vis-a-vis the other bidders. These arrangements can take several forms, such as an option by the preferred bidder to acquire significant target assets at a favorable price (called a "lock-up option"), an agreement not to seek other bidders (called a "no shop clause"), the payment of a significant fee if that bidder's offer does not result in the bidder obtaining control (called a "termination fee," "hello fee," or "goodbye fee"), . . .

James D. Cox and Thomas Lee Hazen, CORPORATIONS §23.07 at p. 661 (2d ed. 2003) We will explore the use of lock-up options, and the validity of this and other forms of deal protection measures, as part of our discussion of the fiduciary duty cases in the next section of this chapter.

3. *Use of "Termination" Fees.* In public company deals, similar to the provisions found in an agreement for the acquisition of a private company, the parties' agreement will typically provide that the deal will terminate if the Target shareholders vote it down, if Bidder shareholders vote it down (in those cases where Bidder shareholders get the right to vote on the deal), if a nonappealable order or injunction is entered prohibiting the consummation of the transaction, or if there are breaches of certain representations and warranties or, alternatively, the occurrence of a "material adverse change." The occurrence of one of these events (i.e., conditions to closing) will typically trigger payment of a termination ("or break-up") fee (usually in cash) in the amount specified in the agreement.

4. *Use of "Break-up" Fees.* In the context of an acquisition of a publicly traded Target Co., the parties' agreement will usually provide for payment of a break-up fee that is triggered in the event that Target jilts Bidder Co., usually in favor of some other acquiror. Bidder typically will insist on a break-up fee as part of the parties' definitive agreement for the acquisition of a publicly held Target out of concern that Bidder may otherwise turn out to be a stalking horse. In other words, Bidder is concerned that when its proposal to acquire Target is publicly announced, some other third-party bidder will come forward offering Target and its shareholders a better offer. In this case, Bidder wants to be compensated for its expenses and lost opportunity in the event that this kind of "topping bid" comes along (i.e., a third party's superior offer is often called a "topping bid"). In negotiating the terms of a break-up fee to be paid in the event that Target walks away from the deal with Bidder, there are several issues that must be addressed, most important of which are:

a.   What triggers a break-up fee?
b.   How large can the break-up fee be?
c.   When in the deal process will the break-up fee become payable?

Break-up fees can be used in connection with any of the different methods for structuring an acquisition (mergers—direct or triangular, as well as two-step acquisitions involving a front-end tender offer followed by a back-end merger). How these terms get fixed will vary from deal to deal, but in the end, the Target board's discretion in negotiating these terms is limited by its fiduciary duty obligations to Target shareholders. The manner in which fiduciary duty law constrains management's discretion in this important area is examined in the materials later in this chapter regarding the use of "deal protection devices," such as termination fees and break-up fees.

5. Use of "No-Shop" Clauses.   Under the terms of a *no-shop* provision, the board of Target promises Bidder that to the extent that Target is currently engaged in ongoing discussions with a competing third-party bidder, any further discussions with this third party will cease as soon as an agreement with Bidder is signed. In addition, a no-shop clause will typically provide that Target's board will not do anything to initiate discussions in the future with a competing bidder, nor will Target do anything to assist (or facilitate) another bidder in proposing a competing offer/transaction. Of course, Bidder and Target will usually engage in extensive negotiations as to what qualifies as a "competing transaction." For example, will a proposed sale of assets trigger the no-shop provision, or will Target's board be allowed to proceed with the sale without violating the terms of the no-shop clause?

From Bidder's perspective, the goal of the no-shop provision is not only to prevent Target from sharing information with another prospective bidder, but also to eliminate the ability of Target's board to extend any assistance to a third party in an effort to encourage or facilitate a competing offer. Of course, what qualifies as "facilitation" or "encouragement" will also be heavily negotiated by the parties. Bidder's objective in these negotiations usually is to create as many obstacles as possible in order to minimize the likelihood that Target will receive a competing offer that will jeopardize Bidder's ability to close on its proposed transaction with Target. At the same time, Target's board is under considerable pressure in these negotiations with Bidder over the terms of a no-shop clause to reserve for itself enough flexibility so that Target's board can fulfill its fiduciary obligations to Target shareholders. If the terms of the no-shop clause (or other form of deal protection device) are so draconian as to eliminate (or unreasonably limit) the board's freedom to take those actions necessary to fulfill the fiduciary duty obligations that they owe to Target Co. shareholders, then Bidder runs the risk that the deal protection device will be declared invalid and therefore unenforceable on the grounds that the provision violates the board's fiduciary duties. As a result, there is an inherent tension in negotiating the terms of any deal protection measure, including a no-shop clause.

6. Use of "Golden Parachutes."   In footnote 5 of its *Revlon* opinion, the Delaware Supreme Court refers to the "golden parachute" agreements that were in place for certain Revlon executives; these arrangements may also be referred to (somewhat less pejoratively) as "management retention agreements," "severance agreements," "change of control agreements," or occasionally, " 'evergreen' employment agreements." Generally speaking, this type of agreement involves an employment contract between a company and one of its executives that calls for the payment of benefits (in often a quite generous amount) if there is a change in control (i.e., ownership) of the company (in what is known as a "single trigger"); or alternatively, such payment may be required if there is a change of control *and* the executive's continued employment is either actually or "constructively" terminated (in what is known as a "double trigger"). "Constructive termination" is customarily a defined term in the employment contract that, in its typical form, allows the executive to resign following a change in the control of the company that results in the executive being demoted, or relocated, or experiencing other changes in the terms of his employment that the executive negotiated as part of his employment contract — such changes being viewed as an attempt to force the executive out. It is important to bear in mind that these payments were to be made to the executive only *after* an event constituting a change in control of the company. As such, these compensation arrangements have the effect of keeping the executive in office until the change of control event occurs, all of which has led some observers to refer to these arrangements as management retention contracts. In the words of one leading M&A lawyer, golden parachute agreements generally do not operate as "a takeover defense because they do not cost the buyer enough to be a significant economic deterrent. In fact, they may be an important factor in helping to mitigate the natural inclination [of the company's managers] to resist" a hostile takeover effort by an unsolicited suitor. *See* David A. Katz, Wachtell, Lipton, Rosen, & Katz, *Glossary of M&A Terms*, 15TH ANNUAL NATIONAL INSTITUTE ON NEGOTIATING BUSINESS ACQUISITIONS, Nov. 2010 at p. 24. *Query*: In what way do these executive compensation plans work "to mitigate [managers'] natural inclination to resist" hostile bids? Is there any advantage to the company by including "change of control" provisions in their contracts with senior executives?

Notwithstanding the suggested benefits that "golden parachutes" may provide to Target Co. in the event of an unsolicited bid, by the mid-1980s, there was growing criticism of what many perceived to be the quite generous (even lavish) payments that were paid to a handful of Target's senior executives in the event of a change of control. The large size of these headline-grabbing "golden parachute" payments angered many and eventually led Congress to adopt Section 280G of the Internal Revenue Code of 1986 in an effort to discourage use of "golden parachutes." In a rather complex set of provisions, Congress sought to impose punitive treatment on "excess parachute payments," which are defined to be payments in excess of three years of compensation for an executive. In general, the company will lose the deduction for the amount of "excess parachute payments" and, in addition, the employee will be subject to a 20 percent excise tax on receipt of such payments.

Another more recent development that may also have an impact on the use of "golden parachutes" is the executive pay reforms adopted by Congress as part of the Dodd-Frank Act. You will recall from the materials in Chapter 1 discussing the provisions of the Dodd-Frank Act (*see supra*, pp. 38-39), that Congress mandated a shareholder vote with respect to "golden parachute" payments in a change of control transaction. And, again, in Chapter 2 (at pp. 154-165), we saw that Motorola Mobility was required by the Dodd-Frank Act (as part of the company's proxy solicitation materials) to obtain shareholder approval of compensation to be paid to the company's senior executives (including its CEO, Dr. Sanjay Jha) as part of Google's proposed acquisition of Motorola Mobility. More specifically, Dodd-Frank (and the SEC rules implementing these provisions of the Dodd-Frank Act) mandated an advisory vote of Motorola Mobility's shareholders with respect to any severance payments (i.e., "golden parachute" compensation) that would be triggered by the acquisition and which payments had not previously been approved by an appropriate "say-on-pay" vote of Motorola Mobility's shareholders.

City Capital Associates v. Interco, Inc.
551 A.2d 787 (Del. Ch. 1988)

ALLEN, Chancellor.

This case, before the court on an application for a preliminary injunction, involves the question whether the directors of Interco Corporation are breaching their fiduciary duties to the stockholders of that company in failing to now redeem certain stock rights originally distributed as part of a defense against unsolicited attempts to take control of the company. In electing to leave Interco's "poison pill" in effect, the board of Interco seeks to defeat a tender offer for all of the shares of Interco for $74 per share cash, extended by plaintiff Cardinal Acquisition Corporation [which is wholly owned by City Capital Associates (CCA), a Delaware limited partnership]. The $74 offer is for all shares and the offeror expresses an intent to do a back-end merger at the same price promptly if its offer is accepted. Thus, plaintiffs' offer must be regarded as noncoercive.

As an alternative to the current tender offer, the board is endeavoring to implement a major restructuring of Interco that was formulated only recently. The board has grounds to conclude that the alternative restructuring transaction may have a value to shareholders of at least $76 per share. The restructuring does not involve a Company self-tender, a merger or other corporate action requiring shareholder action or approval.

It is significant that the question of the board's responsibility to redeem or not to redeem the stock rights in this instance arises at what I will call the end-stage of this takeover contest. That is, the negotiating leverage that a poison pill confers upon this company's board will, it is clear, not be further utilized by the board to increase the options available to shareholders or to improve the terms of those options. Rather, at this stage of this contest, the pill now serves the principal purpose of "protecting the restructuring"—that is, precluding the shareholders from choosing an alternative to the restructuring that the board finds less valuable to shareholders.

Accordingly, this case involves a further judicial effort to pick out the contours of a director's fiduciary duty to the corporation and its shareholders when the board has deployed the recently innovated and powerful antitakeover device of flip-in or flip-over stock rights. That inquiry is, of course, necessarily a highly particularized one.

In Moran v. Household International, Inc., Del. Supr., 500 A.2d 1346 (1985), our Supreme Court acknowledged that a board of directors of a Delaware corporation has legal power to issue corporate securities that serve principally not to raise capital for the firm, but to create a powerful financial disincentive to accumulate shares of the firm's stock . . . In upholding the board's power under

Sections 157 and 141 of our corporation law to issue such securities or rights, the court, however, noted that:

> When the Household Board of Directors is faced with a tender offer and a request to redeem rights, they will not be able to arbitrarily reject the offer. They will be held to the same fiduciary standards any other board of directors would be held to in deciding to adopt a defensive mechanism, the same standard they were held to in originally approving the Rights Plan. *See Unocal*, 493 A.2d at 954-55, 958.

Moran v. Household International, Inc., Del. Supr., 500 A.2d at 1354. Thus, the Supreme Court in *Moran* has directed us specifically to its decision in *Unocal Corp. v. Mesa Petroleum Co.*, Del. Supr., 493 A.2d 946 (1985) as supplying the appropriate legal framework for evaluation of the principal question posed by this case.[1]

In addition to seeking an order requiring the Interco board to now redeem the Company's outstanding stock rights, plaintiffs seek an order restraining any steps to implement the Company's alternative restructuring transaction.

For the reasons that follow, I hold that the board's determination to leave the stock rights in effect is a defensive step that, in the circumstances of this offer and at this stage of the contest for control of Interco, cannot be justified as reasonable in relationship to a threat to the corporation or its shareholders posed by the offer; that the restructuring itself does represent a reasonable response to the perception that the offering price is "inadequate"; and that the board, in proceeding as it has done, has not breached any duties derivable from the Supreme Court's opinion in *Revlon v. MacAndrews & Forbes Holdings, Inc.*, Del. Supr., 506 A.2d 173 (1986).

I turn first to a description of the general background facts. . . .

I.

INTERCO INCORPORATED

Interco is a diversified Delaware holding company that comprises 21 subsidiary corporations in four major business areas: furniture and home furnishings, footwear, apparel and general retail merchandising. Its principal offices are located in St. Louis, Missouri. The Company's nationally recognized brand names include London Fog raincoats; Ethan Allen, Lane and Broyhill furniture; Converse All Star athletic shoes and Le Tigre and Christian Dior sportswear. . . .

---

1. In saying that *Unocal* supplies the framework for decision of this aspect of the case, I reject plaintiffs' argument that the board bears a burden to demonstrate the entire fairness of its decision to keep the pill in place while its recapitalization is effectuated. *Ivanhoe Partners v. Newmont Mining Corp.*, Del. Supr., 535 A.2d 1334, 1341 (1987). While the recapitalization does represent a transaction in which the 14 person board (and most intensely, its seven inside members) has an interest—in the sense referred to in *Unocal*—it does not represent a self-dealing transaction in the sense necessary to place upon the board the heavy burden of the intrinsic fairness test. *See Weinberger v. U.O.P., Inc.*, Del. Supr., 457 A.2d 701 (1983); *Sinclair Oil Corp. v. Levien*, Del. Supr., 280 A.2d 717 (1971).

. . . Owing to the lack of integration between its operating divisions, the Company is, in management's opinion, particularly vulnerable to a highly leveraged "bust-up" takeover of the kind that has become prevalent in recent years. To combat this perceived danger, the Company adopted a common stock rights plan, or poison pill, in late 1985, which included a "flip-in" provision.

The board of directors of Interco is comprised of 14 members, seven of whom are officers of the Company or its subsidiaries.

THE RALES BROTHERS' ACCUMULATION OF INTERCO STOCK; THE INTERCO BOARD'S RESPONSE

In May, 1988, Steven and Mitchell Rales began acquiring Interco stock through CCA. The stock had been trading in the low 40's during that period. Alerted to the unusual trading activity taking place in the Company's stock, the Interco board met on July 11, 1988, to consider the implications of that news. At that meeting, the board redeemed the rights issued pursuant to the 1985 rights plan and adopted a new rights plan that contemplated both "flip-in" and "flip-over" rights.

In broad outline, the "flip-in" provision contained in the rights plan adopted on July 11 provides that, if a person reaches a threshold shareholding of 30% of Interco's outstanding common stock, rights will be exercisable entitling each holder of a right to purchase from the Company that number of shares per right as, at the triggering time, have a market value of twice the exercise price of each right.[3] The "flip-over" feature of the rights plan provides that, in the event of a merger of the Company or the acquisition of 50% or more of the Company's assets or earning power, the rights may be exercised to acquire common stock of the acquiring company having a value of twice the exercise price of the right. The exercise price of each right is $160. The redemption price is $.01 per share.

On July 15, 1988, soon after the adoption of the new rights plan, a press release was issued announcing that the Chairman of the Company's board, Mr. Harvey Saligman, intended to recommend a major restructuring of Interco to the board at its next meeting.

On July 27, 1988, the Rales brothers filed a Schedule 13D with [the SEC] disclosing that, as of July 11, they owned, directly or indirectly, 3,140,300 shares, or 8.7% of Interco's common stock. On that day, CCA offered to acquire the Company by merger for a price of $64 per share in cash, conditioned upon the availability of financing. On August 8, before the Interco board had responded to this offer, CCA increased its offering price to $70 per share, still contingent upon receipt of the necessary financing.

At the Interco board's regularly scheduled meeting on August 8, Wasserstein Perella, Interco's investment banker, informed the board that, in its view,

---

3. Rights, however, will not be exercisable in the event that an acquiror who holds 20% or less of Interco's common stock acquires not less than 80% of its outstanding stock in a single transaction.

the $70 CCA offer was inadequate and not in the best interests of the Company and its shareholders. This opinion was based on a series of analyses, including discounted cash flow, comparable transaction analysis, and an analysis of premiums paid over existing stock prices for selected tender offers during early 1988. Wasserstein Perella also performed an analysis based upon selling certain Interco businesses and retaining and operating others. This analysis generated a "reference range" for the Company of $68-$80 per share. Based on all of these analyses, Wasserstein Perella concluded the offer was inadequate. The board then resolved to reject the proposal. Also at that meeting, the board voted to decrease the threshold percentage needed to trigger the flip-in provision of the rights plan from 30% to 15% and elected to explore a restructuring plan for the Company.

THE INITIAL TENDER OFFER FOR INTERCO STOCK

On August 15, the Rales brothers announced a public tender offer for all of the outstanding stock of Interco at $70 cash per share. The offer was conditioned upon (1) receipt of financing, (2) the tender of sufficient shares to give the offeror a total holding of at least 75% of the Company's common stock on a fully diluted basis at the close of the offer, (3) the redemption of the rights plan, and (4) a determination as to the inapplicability of 8 Del. C. §203.[4]

The board met to consider the tender offer at a special meeting a week later on August 22. Wasserstein Perella had engaged in further studies since the meeting two weeks earlier. It was prepared to give a further view about Interco's value. Now the studies showed a "reference range" for the whole Company of $74-$87. The so-called reference ranges do not purport to be a range of fair value; but just what they purport to be is (deliberately, one imagines) rather unclear.

In all events, after hearing the banker's opinion, the Interco board resolved to recommend against the tender offer. In rejecting the offer, the board also declined to redeem the rights plan or to render 8 Del. C. §203 inapplicable to the offer. Finally, the board refused to disclose confidential information requested by CCA in connection with its tender offer unless and until CCA indicated a willingness to enter into a confidentiality and standstill agreement with the Company.[5]

The remainder of the meeting was devoted to an exploration of strategic alternatives to the CCA proposal. Wasserstein Perella presented the board with a detailed valuation of each operating component of the Company. The board adopted a resolution empowering management ". . . to explore all appropriate

---

4. CCA sued Interco in the federal district court for a determination that Section 203 [Delaware's antitakeover statute] was an invalid enactment under the federal Constitution. It was unsuccessful in that attempt. *See City Capital Associates LP v. Interco Incorporated,* 696 F. Supp. 1551 (D. Del. 1988).

5. The standstill agreement would commit CCA not to make any tender offer for three years unless asked to do so by the Company; it apparently does not have an out should CCA seek to make an offer for all shares at a price higher than an offer endorsed by the board.

alternatives to the CCA offer, including, without limitation, the recapitalization, restructuring or other reorganization of the company, the sale of assets of the company in addition to the Apparel Manufacturing Group, and other extraordinary transactions, to maximize the value of the company to the stockholders. . . ."

On August 23, 1988, a letter was sent to CCA informing it that Interco intended to explore alternatives to the offer and planned to make confidential information available to third parties in connection with that endeavor. Interco informed CCA that it would not disclose information to it absent compliance with a confidentiality agreement and a standstill agreement. (*See* fn. 5). Interco's proposal was met with an August 26, 1988 counterproposal by CCA suggesting an alternative confidentiality agreement—without standstill provisions.

Apart from the exchange of letters, there were no communications between CCA and Interco between the time the $70 offer was made on August 22 and a later, higher offer at $72 per share was made on September 10. . . .

[O]n September 10, the Rales brothers did amend their offer, increasing the price offered to $72 per share. The Interco board did not consider that offer until September 19 when its investment banker was ready to report on a proposed restructuring. At that meeting, the board rejected the $72 offer on grounds of financial inadequacy and adopted the restructuring proposal.

THE PROPOSED RESTRUCTURING

Under the terms of the restructuring designed by Wasserstein Perella, Interco would sell assets that generate approximately one-half of its gross sales and would borrow $2.025 billion. It would make very substantial distributions to shareholders, by means of a dividend, amounting to a stated aggregate value of $66 per share. The $66 amount would consist of (1) a $25 dividend payable November 7 to shareholders of record on October 13, consisting of $14 in cash and $11 in face amount of senior subordinated debentures, and (2) a second dividend, payable no earlier than November 29, which was declared on October 19, of (a) $24.15 in cash, (b) $6.80 principal amount of subordinated discount debentures, (c) $5.44 principal amount of junior subordinated debentures, (d) convertible preferred stock with a liquidation value of $4.76, and (e) a remaining equity interest or stub that Wasserstein Perella estimates (based on projected earnings of the then remaining businesses) will trade at a price of at least $10 per share. Thus, the total value of the restructuring to shareholders would, in the opinion of Wasserstein Perella, be at least $76 per share on a fully distributed basis.

The board had agreed to a compensation arrangement with Wasserstein Perella that gives that firm substantial contingency pay if its restructuring is successfully completed. Thus, Wasserstein Perella has a rather straightforward and conventional conflict of interest when it opines that the inherently disputable value of its restructuring is greater than the all cash alternative offered by plaintiffs. The market has not, for whatever reason, thought the prospects of the Company quite so bright. It has, in recent weeks consistently valued Interco stock at about $70 a share. [. . . , which is the] value at which Drexel Burnham has valued the restructuring in this litigation. Steps have now been taken to effectuate the restructuring. On September 15, the Company announced its plans to sell the Ethan Allen furniture division, which is said by the plaintiffs to be the Company's "crown jewel." Ethan Allen, the Company maintains, has a unique marketing approach which is not conductive to integration of that business with Interco's other furniture businesses, Lane and Broyhill. Moreover, the Company says that Ethan Allen is not a suitable candidate for the cost cutting measures which must be undertaken in connection with the proposed restructuring.

THE PRESENT CCA OFFER AND THE INTERCO BOARD'S REACTION

In its third supplemental Offer to Purchase dated October 18, 1988, CCA raised its bid to $74. Like the preceding bid, the proposal is an all cash offer for all shares with a contemplated back-end merger for the same consideration.

At its October 19, 1988 board meeting, the board rejected the $74 offer as inadequate and agreed to recommend that shareholders reject the offer. The board based its rejection both on its apparent view that the price was inadequate and on its belief that the proposed restructuring will yield shareholder value of at least $76 per share.

II.

This case was filed on July 27, 1988. Following extensive discovery, it was presented on plaintiffs' application for a preliminary injunction on October 24, 1988. As indicated above, the relief now sought has two principal elements. First, CCA seeks an order requiring the Interco board to redeem the defensive stock rights and effectively give the Interco shareholders the opportunity to choose as a practical matter. Second, it seeks an order restraining further steps to implement the restructuring, including any steps to sell Ethan Allen.

In order to justify that relief, plaintiffs offer several theories. First, it is their position that this case involves an interested board which has acted to entrench itself at the expense of the stockholders of the Company. Second, because they assert that the board comprises interested directors, plaintiffs also assert that the proposed restructuring transaction involves self-dealing, and that the board is therefore obligated, under *Weinberger v. U.O.P., Inc.*, Del. Supr., 457 A.2d 701 (1983), to establish the entire fairness of the restructuring and its refusal to rescind the stock rights, which plaintiffs assert it cannot do. Third, plaintiffs urge that under the approach first adopted by the Delaware Supreme Court in *Unocal*, the board's action is said *not* to be reasonable in relation to any threat posed by the plaintiffs because, they say, their noncoercive, all cash offer does not pose a threat. Fourth and last, plaintiffs claim that the proposed restructuring does not importantly differ from a sale of the Company, and that under *Revlon v. MacAndrews & Forbes Holdings, Inc.*, Del. Supr., 506 A.2d 173 (1986), the Interco directors have a duty to obtain the highest available price for the Company's stockholders in the market, which the directors have not done.

Interco answers that only the *Unocal* standard applies in this case. Defendants urge that the *Weinberger* entire fairness test is inapposite because there has been no self-dealing. *(See* n. 1, *supra.)* Similarly, defendants claim that no *Revlon* duties have arisen because the restructuring does not amount to a sale of the Company and the Company is not, in fact, for sale. Defendants state that the Interco board is proceeding in good faith to protect the best interests of the Company's stockholders. The board believes that CCA's offer is inadequate, and therefore constitutes a threat to the Company's stockholders; it is their position that the restructuring and the poison pill are, therefore, reasonable reactions to the threat posed. Moreover, defendants assert that leaving the pill in place to protect the restructuring is reasonable because the restructuring will achieve better value for stockholders than will be garnered by shareholders' acceptance of the plaintiffs' inadequate offer. . . .

III.

The pending motion purports to seek a preliminary injunction. The test for the issuance of such a provisional remedy is well established. It is necessary for the applicant to demonstrate both a reasonable probability of ultimate success on the claims asserted and, most importantly, the threat of an injury that will occur before trial which is not remediable by an award of damages or the later shaping of equitable relief. Beyond that, it is essential for the court to consider the offsetting equities, if any, including the interests of the public and other innocent third parties, as well as defendants. . . .

It is appropriate, therefore, before subjecting the board's decision not to redeem the pill to the form of analysis mandated by *Unocal,* to identify what relevant facts are not contested or contestable, and what relevant facts may appropriately be assumed against the party prevailing on this point. They are as follows:

First. The value of the Interco restructuring is inherently a debatable proposition, most importantly (but not solely) because the future value of the stub share is unknowable with reasonable certainty.

Second. The board of Interco believes in good faith that the restructuring has a value of "at least" $76 per share.

Third. The City Capital offer is for $74 per share cash.

Fourth. The board of Interco has acted prudently to inform itself of the value of the Company.

Fifth. The board believes in good faith that the City Capital offer is for a price that is "inadequate."

Sixth. City Capital cannot, as a practical matter, close its tender offer while the rights exist; to do so would be to self-inflict an enormous financial injury that no reasonable buyer would do.

Seventh. Shareholders of Interco have differing liquidity preferences and different expectations about likely future economic events.

Eighth. A reasonable shareholder could prefer the restructuring to the sale of his stock for $74 in cash now, but a reasonable shareholder could prefer the reverse.

Ninth. The City Capital tender offer is in no respect coercive. It is for all shares, not for only a portion of shares. It contemplates a prompt follow-up merger, if it succeeds, not an indefinite term as a minority shareholder. It proposes identical consideration in a follow-up merger, not securities or less money.

Tenth. While the existence of the stock rights has conferred time on the board to consider the City Capital proposals and to arrange the restructuring, the utility of those rights as a defensive technique has, given the time lines for the restructuring and the board's actions to date, now been effectively exhausted except in one respect: the effect of those rights continues to "protect the restructuring."

These facts are sufficient to address the question whether the board's action in electing to leave the defensive stock rights plan in place qualifies for the deference embodied in the business judgment rule.

IV.

I turn then to the analysis contemplated by *Unocal,* the most innovative and promising case in our recent corporation law. That case, of course, recognized that in defending against unsolicited takeovers, there is an "omnipresent specter that a board may be acting primarily in its own interest." 493 A.2d at 954. That fact distinguishes takeover defense measures from other acts of a board which, when subject to judicial review, are customarily upheld once the court finds the board acted in good faith and after an appropriate investigation. *E.g., Aronson v. Lewis,* Del. Supr., 473 A.2d 805 (1984). *Unocal* recognizes that human nature may incline *even one acting in subjective good faith* to rationalize as right that which is merely personally beneficial. Thus, it created a new intermediate form of judicial review to be employed when a transaction is neither self-dealing nor wholly disinterested. That test has been helpfully referred to as the "proportionality test."[8]

The test is easy to state. Where it is employed, it requires a threshold examination "before the protections of the business judgment rule may be conferred." 493 A.2d 954. That threshold requirement is in two parts. First, directors claiming the protections of the rule "must show that they had reasonable grounds for believing that a danger to corporate policy and effectiveness existed." The second element of the test is the element of balance. "If a defensive measure is to come within the ambit of the business judgment rule, it must be reasonable in relationship to the threat posed." 493 A.2d 955.

Delaware courts have employed the *Unocal* precedent cautiously.[9] The promise of that innovation is the promise of a more realistic, flexible and, ultimately, more responsible corporation law. The danger that it poses is, of course, that courts—in

---

8. *See* Gilson & Kraakman, *Delaware's Intermediate Standard for Defensive Tactics: Is There Substance to the Proportionality Review?,* John M. Olin Program in Law & Economics, Stanford Law School (Working Paper No. 45, August, 1988), 44 Bus. Law. [247] (forthcoming February, 1989). Professors Gilson and Kraakman offer a helpful structure for reviewing problems of this type and conclude with a perceptive observation concerning the beneficial impact upon corporate culture that the *Unocal* test might come to have.

9. Only two cases have found defensive steps disproportionate to a threat posed by a takeover attempt. *See AC Acquisitions Corp. v. Anderson, Clayton & Co.,* Del. Ch., 519 A.2d 103 (1986); *Robert M. Bass Group, Inc. v. Evans,* Del. Ch., C.A. No. 9953, Jacobs, V.C. (July 14, 1988) [1988 WL 73744].

exercising some element of substantive judgment—will too readily seek to assert the primacy of their own view on a question upon which reasonable, completely disinterested minds might differ. Thus, inartfully applied, the *Unocal* form of analysis could permit an unraveling of the well-made fabric of the business judgment rule in this important context. Accordingly, whenever, as in this case, this court is required to apply the *Unocal* form of review, it should do so cautiously, with a clear appreciation for the risks and special responsibility this approach entails.

A.

Turning to the first element of the *Unocal* form of analysis, it is appropriate to note that, in the special case of a tender offer for all shares, the threat posed, if any, is not importantly to corporate policies (as may well be the case in a stock buy-back case such as *Cheff v. Mathes,* Del. Supr., 199 A.2d 548 (1964) or a partial tender offer case such as *Unocal* itself), but rather the threat, if any, is most directly to shareholder interests. Broadly speaking, threats to shareholders in that context may be of two types: threats to the voluntariness of the choice offered by the offer, and threats to the substantive, economic interest represented by the stockholding.

1.   Threats to voluntariness.

It is now universally acknowledged that the structure of an offer can render mandatory in substance that which is voluntary in form. The so-called "front-end" loaded partial offer—already a largely vanished breed—is the most extreme example of this phenomenon. An offer may, however, be structured to have a coercive effect on a rational shareholder in any number of different ways. Whenever a tender offer is so structured, a board may, or perhaps should, perceive a threat to a stockholder's interest in exercising choice to remain a stockholder in the firm. The threat posed by structurally coercive offers is typically amplified by an offering price that the target board responsibly concludes is substantially below a fair price.[10]

Each of the cases in which our Supreme Court has addressed a defensive corporate measure under the *Unocal* test involved the sharp and palpable threat to shareholders posed by a coercive offer. *See Unocal Corp. v. Mesa Petroleum Co.,* Del. Supr., 493 A.2d 946 (1985); *Moran v. Household International, Inc.,* Del. Supr., 500 A.2d 1346 (1985); *Ivanhoe Partners v. Newmont Mining Corp.,* Del. Supr., 535 A.2d 1334 (1987).

2.   Threats from "inadequate" but noncoercive offers.

The second broad classification of threats to shareholder interests that might be posed by a tender offer for all shares relates to the "fairness" or "adequacy"

---

10. A different form of threat relating to the voluntariness of the shareholder's choice would arise in a structurally noncoercive offer that contained false or misleading material information.

of the price. It would not be surprising or unreasonable to claim that where an offer is not coercive or deceptive (and, therefore, what is in issue is essentially whether the consideration it offers is attractive or not), a board—even though it may expend corporate funds to arrange alternatives or to inform shareholders of its view of fair value—is not authorized to take preclusive action. By preclusive action I mean action that, as a practical matter, withdraws from the shareholders the option to choose between the offer and the status quo or some other board sponsored alternative.

Our law, however, has not adopted that view and experience has demonstrated the wisdom of that choice. We have held that a board is not required simply by reason of the existence of a noncoercive offer to redeem outstanding poison pill rights. [Citations to cases omitted.] The reason is simple. Even where an offer is noncoercive, it may represent a "threat" to shareholder interests in the special sense that an active negotiator with power, in effect, to refuse the proposal may be able to extract a higher or otherwise more valuable proposal, or may be able to arrange an alternative transaction or a modified business plan that will present a more valuable option to shareholders. Our cases, however, also indicate that in the setting of a noncoercive offer, absent unusual facts, there may come a time when a board's fiduciary duty will require it to redeem the rights and to permit the shareholders to choose.

B.

In this instance, there is no threat of shareholder coercion. The threat is to shareholders' economic interests posed by an offer the board has concluded is "inadequate." If this determination is made in good faith (as I assume it is here), it alone will justify leaving a poison pill in place, even in the setting of a noncoercive offer, for a period while the board exercises its good faith business judgment to take such steps as it deems appropriate to protect and advance shareholder interests in light of the significant development that such an offer doubtless is. That action may entail negotiation on behalf of shareholders with the offeror, the institution of a *Revlon*-style auction for the Company, a recapitalization or restructuring designed as an alternative to the offer, or other action.[13]

Once that period has closed, and it is apparent that the board does not intend to institute a *Revlon*-style auction,[14] or to negotiate for an increase in the unwanted offer, and that it has taken such time as it required in good faith to arrange an alternative value-maximizing transaction, then, in most instances, the legitimate role of the poison pill in the context of a noncoercive offer will

---

13. I leave aside the rare but occasionally encountered instance in which the board elects to do nothing at all with respect to an any and all tender offer.

14. If a board elects to conduct an auction of a company, the deployment or continuation of a poison pill will serve as a method to permit the board to act as an effective auctioneer.

have been fully satisfied.[15] The only function then left for the pill at this end-stage is to preclude the shareholders from exercising a judgment about their own interests that differs from the judgment of the directors, who will have some interest in the question. What then is the "threat" in this instance that might justify such a result? Stating that "threat" at this stage of the process most specifically, it is this: *Wasserstein Perella may be correct in their respective valuations of the offer and the restructuring but a majority of the Interco shareholders may not accept that fact and may be injured as a consequence.* [*emphasis in original*]

C.

Perhaps there is a case in which it is appropriate for a board of directors to in effect permanently foreclose their shareholders from accepting a noncoercive offer for their stock by utilization of the recent innovation of "poison pill" rights. If such a case might exist by reason of some special circumstance, a review of the facts here show[s] this not to be it. The "threat" here, when viewed with particularity, is far too mild to justify such a step in this instance.

Even assuming Wasserstein Perella is correct that when received (and following a period in which full distribution can occur), each of the debt securities to be issued in the restructuring will trade at par, that the preferred stock will trade at its liquidation value, and that the stub will trade initially at $10 a share, the difference in the values of these two offers is only 3%, and the lower offer is all cash and sooner. Thus, the threat, at this stage of the contest, cannot be regarded as very great even on the assumption that Wasserstein Perella is correct.

More importantly, it is incontestable that the Wasserstein Perella value is itself a highly debatable proposition. Their prediction of the likely trading range of the stub share represents one obviously educated guess. Here, the projections used in that process were especially prepared for use in the restructuring. Plaintiffs claim they are rosy to a fault, citing, for example, a $75 million cost reduction from remaining operations once the restructuring is fully implemented. This cost reduction itself is $2 per share; 20% of the predicted value of the stub. The Drexel Burnham analysis, which offers no greater claim to correctness, estimates the stub will trade at between $4.53 and $5.45. Moreover, Drexel opines that the whole package of restructure consideration has a value between $68.28 and $70.37 a share, which, for whatever reason, is quite consistent with the stock market price of a share of Interco stock during recent weeks.

The point here is not that, in exercising some restrained substantive review of the board's decision to leave the pill in place, the court finds Drexel's opinion more persuasive than Wasserstein Perella's. I make no such judgment. What is apparent—indeed inarguable—is that one could do so. More importantly,

---

15. The role of a poison pill in an auction setting may presumably be affected by provisions in the bid documents. For example, should a disinterested board or committee agree in good faith to a provision requiring that a pill remain in place following bidding (which they might do in order to elicit bidders), such a commitment would presumably validly bind the corporation.

without access to Drexel Burnham's particular analysis, a shareholder could prefer a $74 cash payment now to the complex future consideration offered through the restructuring. The defendants understand this; it is evident.

The information statement sent to Interco shareholders to inform them of the terms of the restructuring accurately states and repeats the admonition:

> There can be no assurances as to actual trading values of [the stub shares]. . . .
>
> It should be noted that the value of securities, including newly-issued securities and equity securities in highly leveraged companies, are subject to uncertainties and contingencies, all of which are difficult to predict and therefore any valuation [of them] may not necessarily be indicative of the price at which such securities will actually trade.

October 1, 1988 Interco Information Statement, at 3.

Yet, recognizing the relative closeness of the values and the impossibility of knowing what the stub share will trade at, the board, having arranged a value maximizing restructuring, elected to preclude shareholder choice. It did so not to buy time in order to negotiate or arrange possible alternatives, but asserting in effect a right and duty to save shareholders from the consequences of the choice they might make, if permitted to choose.

Without wishing to cast any shadow upon the subjective motivation of the individual defendants, I conclude that reasonable minds not affected by an inherent, entrenched interest in the matter, could not reasonably differ with respect to the conclusion that the CCA $74 cash offer did not represent a threat to shareholder interests sufficient in the circumstances to justify, in effect, foreclosing shareholders from electing to accept that offer.

Our corporation law exists, not as an isolated body of rules and principles, but rather in a historical setting and as a part of a larger body of law premised upon shared values. To acknowledge that directors may employ the recent innovation of "poison pills" to deprive shareholders of the ability effectively to choose to accept a noncoercive offer, after the board has had a reasonable opportunity to explore or create alternatives, or attempt to negotiate on the shareholders' behalf, would, it seems to me, be so inconsistent with widely shared notions of appropriate corporate governance as to threaten to diminish the legitimacy and authority of our corporation law.

I thus conclude that the board's decision not to redeem the rights following the amendment of the offer to $74 per share cannot be justified in the way *Unocal* requires. This determination does not rest upon disputed facts and I conclude that affirmative relief is therefore permissible at this stage. . . .

VII.

Having concluded, under the *Unocal* analysis, that—putting aside the question of the poison pill—the restructuring appears at this stage to be a reasonable response to the CCA offer that is perceived as inadequate, it is necessary to address briefly CCA's argument that the implementation of that restructuring in this setting constitutes a violation of the board's fiduciary duty under *Revlon v. MacAndrews & Forbes Holdings, Inc.*, Del. Supr., 506 A.2d 173 (1986). That argument, in essence, is that the restructuring—which involves the sale of assets generating about one-half of Interco's sales; massive borrowings; and the distribution to shareholders of cash and debt securities (excluding the preferred stock) per share equal to approximately 85% of the market value of Interco's stock[19]—in effect involves the breakup and sale of the Company as it has existed. This argument contends that such a transaction, even if not in form a sale, necessarily involves a duty recognized in *Revlon* to sell the Company, through an auction, only for the best available price.

To this assertion, the defendants reply that Interco is not for sale and, in any event, the board intends to force upon the stockholders the best available transaction anyway. In authorizing management to discuss the terms on which the Company might be sold (which the board did), the board was only fulfilling its obligation to be informed; it has never made a determination that it was in the best interests of the shareholders to sell the Company. Thus, it is said that the teaching of *Revlon*, even if it is presumed to reach every sale of a Company, is not implicated here.

I agree that the board of Interco has no duty, in the circumstances as they now appear, to conduct an auction sale of the Company. I do not think this question, however, is answered by merely referring to a board resolve to try to keep the Company independent.

The contours of a board's duties in the face of a takeover attempt are not, stated generally, different from the duties the board always bears: to act in an informed manner and in the good faith pursuit of corporate interests and only for that purpose. . . .

Revlon should not, in my opinion, be interpreted as representing a sharp turn in our law. It does not require, for example, that before every corporate merger agreement can validly be entered into, the constituent corporations must be "shopped" or, more radically, an auction process undertaken, even though a merger may be regarded as a sale of the Company. But mergers or recapitalizations or other important corporate transactions may be authorized by a board only advisedly. There must be a reasonable basis for the board of directors involved to conclude that the transaction involved is in the best interest of the shareholders. This involves having information about possible alternatives. The essence of rational choice is an assessment of costs and benefits and the consideration of alternatives.

Indeed, the central obligation of a board (*assuming it acts in good faith*—an assumption that would not hold for *Revlon*) is to act in an informed manner. When the transaction is so fundamental as the restructuring here (or a sale or merger of the Company), the obligation to be informed would seem to require that reliable information about the value of alternative transactions be explored. . . .

When, as in *Revlon*, two bidders are actively contesting for control of a company, the most reliable source of information as to what may be the best available transaction will come out of an open contest or auction. . . .

When the transaction is a defensive recapitalization, a board may not proceed, consistently with its duty to be informed, without appropriately

---

19. That is, the value (using Wasserstein Perella numbers) of the distribution of cash and debt is approximately $60 and the market price of the stock is approximately $70.

considering relevant information relating to alternatives.[21] But if a board does probe prudently to ascertain possible alternative values, and thus is in a position to act advisedly, I do not understand the *Revlon* holding as requiring it to turn to an auction alternative, if it has arrived at a good faith, informed determination that a recapitalization or other form of transaction is more beneficial to shareholders. Should the board produce a reactive recapitalization, any steps it may take to implement it in the face of an offer for all stock may, as here, be judicially tested not under *Revlon,* but under the *Unocal* form of judicial review.

Here, given the significance of the restructuring and its character as an alternative to an all cash tender offer, the requirement to inform oneself of possible alternatives may be seen as demanding. It appears, however, that defendants have appropriately informed themselves. . . .

Accordingly, I can detect no basis to conclude that the board did not proceed prudently and in good faith to pursue the restructuring as an alternative to the CCA offer. I do not read *Revlon* as requiring it to follow any different course.

QUESTIONS

1. Why does Chancellor Allen treat CCA's offer as "non-coercive"?

2. What is the procedural posture of this case? What relief does the plaintiff (Bidder/CCA) seek?

3. What are the terms of the "flip-in" feature of the poison pill adopted by the Interco Board?

4. In deciding to apply *Unocal* to the actions taken by the Interco Board, why did Chancellor Allen reject use of the "entire fairness" standard of judicial review?

5. Why does Chancellor Allen conclude that Interco is not in the *Revlon* mode?

6. How does Chancellor Allen apply the two-pronged *Unocal* standard to the actions taken by the Interco board? What is the nature of Chancellor Allen's concern regarding the preclusive effect of the decision of the Interco board not to redeem the pill? How does this concern fit into the two-pronged *Unocal* standard of review? (*Hint:* You may want to reconsider your analysis of this question after you read the next set of Delaware Supreme Court decisions and again after we analyze Chancellor Chandler's opinion in *Airgas, Inc., v. Air Products, Inc.,* at the end of the materials in this chapter.)

---

21. A delicate question is how far a board must go to satisfy its obligation to inform itself, with respect to the question whether the bidder would pay more. Must it disclose information? Must it negotiate? Surely it need not enter into negotiations if it has not reached a decision to sell the Company, but its duty to shareholders may not permit the board to simply ignore the offeror. This issue may come down to the reasonableness of the terms of a confidentiality and standstill agreement. These agreements which always play an important role for a period in cases of this kind rarely get litigated.

NOTES

1. The Delaware Supreme Court's Response to **Interco.**   Following Chancellor Allen's decision in the principal case, the Rales brothers decided not to proceed with a takeover bid for Interco. Accordingly, the Delaware Supreme Court was not presented with the opportunity to review the Chancery Court's *Unocal* analysis as to the validity of the decision of the Interco board of directors to implement a poison pill defense (*see* Part IV of Chancellor Allen's opinion). Nonetheless, the Delaware Supreme Court broadly hinted at how it might have decided such an appeal from the Chancery Court's poison pill ruling as part of the Court's opinion in the next case. In *Paramount Communications, Inc. v. Time, Inc., infra,* the Delaware Supreme Court made the following (rather pointed) observations as to the reasoning used by Chancellor Allen with regard to the application of the *Unocal* analysis to a poison pill defense:

> . . . [T]he Court of Chancery has [previously] suggested that an all-cash, all-shares offer, falling within a range of values that a shareholder might reasonably prefer, *cannot* constitute a legally recognized "threat" to shareholder interests sufficient to withstand a *Unocal* analysis. *See* . . . [e.g., *City Capital Associates v. Interco. Inc.,* Del. Ch., 551 A.2d 787 (1988)]. In those cases, the Court of Chancery determined that whatever threat existed related only to the shareholders and only to price and not to the corporation.
>
> From those decisions by our Court of Chancery, Paramount and the individual plaintiffs extrapolate a rule of law that an all-cash, all-shares offer with values reasonably in the range of acceptable price *cannot* pose any objective threat to a corporation or its shareholders. Thus, Paramount would have us hold that *only* if the value of Paramount's offer were determined to be clearly inferior to the value created by management's plan to merge with Warner could the offer be viewed—objectively—as a threat.
>
> Implicit in the plaintiffs' argument is the view that a hostile tender offer can pose only two types of threats: the threat of coercion that results from a two-tier offer promising unequal treatment for nontendering shareholders; and the threat of inadequate value from an all-shares, all-cash offer at a price below what a target board in good faith deems to be the present value of its shares. *See, e.g., Interco,* 551 A.2d at 797; *see also BNS, Inc. v. Koppers,* D. Del., 683 F. Supp. 458 (1988). Since Paramount's offer was all cash, the only conceivable "threat," plaintiffs argue, was inadequate value. We disapprove of such a narrow and rigid construction of *Unocal,* . . .
>
> Plaintiffs' position represents a fundamental misconception of our standard of review under *Unocal* principally because it would involve the court in substituting its judgment as to what is a "better" deal for that of a corporation's board of directors. To the extent that the Court of Chancery has recently done so in certain of its opinions, we hereby reject such approach as not in keeping with a proper *Unocal* analysis. *See, e.g., Interco,* 551 A.2d 787, and its progeny; . . .

Paramount Communications, Inc. v. Time Inc., 571 A.2d 1140, 1152-53 (Del. 1989) (*emphasis added*). We will revisit this tension between the perspective of Chancellor Allen and the subsequent, more critical perspective of the Delaware Supreme Court (with respect to the *Unocal* analysis of the poison pill defense in Chancellor Allen's well-known *Interco* opinion) later in this chapter when we examine Chancellor Chandler's 2011 decision in *Air Products and Chemicals, Inc. v. Airgas, Inc.*

2. The Era of the "Merger of Equals."   With the collapse of the junk bond market, the most viable players left at the dawn of the 1990s were the strategic buyers. The prevailing sentiment at the time frowned on the use of borrowed capital and the leveraging of the company's balance sheet. In this market, stock for stock deals became the order of the day, a trend that was further encouraged as the stock market rebounded in the 1990s into a robust bull market, thereby making stock a favored form of acquisition currency. "Merger of equals" became the new buzzword, thereby allowing for even bigger strategic deals, which were often accompanied by lower premiums. It was in this climate that the Delaware Supreme Court decided the following case (which is widely referred to as the *Time-Warner* decision), and, as we shall see in the subsequent *QVC* case (*see infra* p. 650), the Time-Warner deal became the harbinger of things to come.

Paramount Communications, Inc. v. Time, Inc.
571 A.2d 1140 (Del. 1989)

HORSEY, Justice:

Paramount Communications, Inc. ("Paramount") and two other groups of plaintiffs ("Shareholder Plaintiffs"), shareholders of Time Incorporated ("Time"), a Delaware corporation, separately filed suits in the Delaware Court of Chancery seeking a preliminary injunction to halt Time's tender offer for 51 % of Warner Communication, Inc.'s ("Warner") outstanding shares at $70 cash per share. The court below consolidated the cases and, following the development of an extensive record, after discovery and an evidentiary hearing, denied plaintiffs' motion. In a 50-page unreported opinion and order entered July 14, 1989, the Chancellor refused to enjoin Time's consummation of its tender offer, concluding that the plaintiffs were unlikely to prevail on the merits. . . .

The principal ground for reversal, asserted by all plaintiffs, is that Paramount's June 7, 1989 uninvited all-cash, all-shares, "fully negotiable" (though conditional) tender offer for Time triggered duties under *Unocal Corp. v. Mesa Petroleum Co.*, Del. Supr., 493 A.2d 946 (1985), and that Time's board of directors, in responding to Paramount's offer, breached those duties. As a consequence, plaintiffs argue that in our review of the Time board's decision of June 16, 1989 to enter into a revised merger agreement with Warner, Time is not entitled to the benefit and protection of the business judgment rule.

Shareholder Plaintiffs also assert a claim based on *Revlon v. MacAndrews & Forbes Holdings, Inc.*, Del. Supr., 506 A.2d 173 (1986). They argue that the original Time-Warner merger agreement of March 4, 1989 resulted in a change of control which effectively put Time up for sale, thereby triggering *Revlon* duties. Those plaintiffs argue that Time's board breached its *Revlon* duties by failing, in the face of the change of control, to maximize shareholder value in the immediate term.

Applying our standard of review, we affirm the Chancellor's ultimate finding and conclusion under *Unocal*. We find that Paramount's tender offer was reasonably perceived by Time's board to pose a threat to Time and that the Time board's "response" to that threat was, under the circumstances, reasonable and proportionate. Applying *Unocal*, we reject the argument that the only corporate threat posed by an all-shares, all-cash tender offer is the possibility of inadequate value.

We also find that Time's board did not by entering into its initial merger agreement with Warner come under a *Revlon* duty either to auction the company or to maximize short-term shareholder value, notwithstanding the unequal share exchange. Therefore, the Time board's original plan of merger with Warner was subject only to a business judgment rule analysis. *See Smith v. Van Gorkom,* Del. Supr., 488 A.2d 858, 873-74 (1985).

I

Time is a Delaware corporation with its principal offices in New York City. Time's traditional business is publication of magazines and books; however, Time also provides pay television programming through its Home Box Office, Inc. and Cinemax subsidiaries. In addition, Time owns and operates cable television franchises through its subsidiary, American Television and Communication Corporation. During the relevant time period, Time's board consisted of sixteen directors. Twelve of the directors were "outside," nonemployee directors. Four of the directors were also officers of the company. . . .

As early as 1983 and 1984, Time's executive board began considering expanding Time's operations into the entertainment industry. . . .

The board's consensus was that a merger of Time and Warner was feasible, but only if Time controlled the board of the resulting corporation and thereby preserved a management committed to Time's journalistic integrity. To accomplish this goal, the board stressed the importance of carefully defining in advance the corporate governance provisions that would control the resulting entity. Some board members expressed concern over whether such a business combination would place Time *"in play."* The board discussed the wisdom of adopting further defensive measures to lessen such a possibility.[5] . . .

From the outset, Time's board favored an all-cash or cash and securities acquisition of Warner as the basis for consolidation. Bruce Wasserstein, Time's financial advisor, also favored an outright purchase of Warner. However, Steve Ross, Warner's CEO, was adamant that a business combination was only practicable on a stock-for-stock basis. Warner insisted on a stock swap in order to preserve its shareholders' equity in the resulting corporation. Time's officers, on the other hand, made it abundantly clear that Time would be the acquiring corporation and that Time would control the resulting board. Time refused to permit itself to be cast as the "acquired" company.

Eventually Time acquiesced in Warner's insistence on a stock-for-stock deal, but talks broke down over corporate governance issues. . . .

Warner and Time resumed negotiations in January 1989. The catalyst for the resumption of talks was a private dinner between Steve Ross and Time

---

5. Time had in place a panoply of defensive devices, including a staggered board, a "poison pill" preferred stock rights plan triggered by an acquisition of 15% of the company, a fifty-day notice period for shareholder motions, and restrictions on shareholders' ability to call a meeting or act by consent.

outside director, Michael Dingman. Dingman was able to convince Ross that the transitional nature of the proposed co-CEO arrangement did not reflect a lack of confidence in Ross. Ross agreed that this course was best for the company and a meeting between Ross and Munro resulted. Ross agreed to retire in five years and let Nicholas succeed him. Negotiations resumed and many of the details of the original stock-for-stock exchange agreement remained intact. In addition, Time's senior management agreed to long-term contracts.

Time insider directors Levin and Nicholas met with Warner's financial advisors to decide upon a stock exchange ratio. Time's board had recognized the potential need to pay a premium in the stock ratio in exchange for dictating the governing arrangement of the new Time-Warner. Levin and outside director Finkelstein were the primary proponents of paying a premium to protect the "Time Culture." The board discussed premium rates of 10%, 15% and 20%. Wasserstein also suggested paying a premium for Warner due to Warner's rapid growth rate. The market exchange ratio of Time stock for Warner stock was .38 in favor of Warner. Warner's financial advisors informed its board that any exchange rate over .400 was a fair deal and any exchange rate over .450 was "one hell of a deal." The parties ultimately agreed upon an exchange rate favoring Warner of .465. On that basis, Warner stockholders would have owned approximately 62% of the common stock of Time-Warner.

On March 3, 1989, Time's board, with all but one director in attendance, met and unanimously approved the stock-for-stock merger with Warner. Warner's board likewise approved the merger. The agreement called for Warner to be merged into a wholly-owned Time subsidiary with Warner becoming the surviving corporation. The common stock of Warner would then be converted into common stock of Time at the agreed upon ratio. Thereafter, the name of Time would be changed to Time-Warner, Inc.

The rules of the New York Stock Exchange required that Time's issuance of shares to effectuate the merger be approved by a vote of Time's stockholders. The Delaware General Corporation Law required approval of the merger by a majority of the Warner stockholders. Delaware law did not require any vote by Time stockholders. The Chancellor concluded that the agreement was the product of "an arms-length negotiation between two parties seeking individual advantage through mutual action."

The resulting company would have a 24-member board, with 12 members representing each corporation. The company would have co-CEO's, at first Ross [CEO of Warner] and Munro [CEO of Time], then Ross and Nicholas [an executive of Time], and finally, after Ross' retirement, by Nicholas alone. The board would create an editorial committee with a majority of members representing Time. A similar entertainment committee would be controlled by Warner board members. A two-thirds supermajority vote was required to alter CEO successions but an earlier proposal to have supermajority protection for the editorial committee was abandoned. Warner's board suggested raising the compensation levels for Time's senior management under the new corporation. Warner's management, as with most entertainment executives, received higher salaries than comparable executives in news journalism. Time's board, however, rejected Warner's proposal to equalize the salaries of the two management teams.

At its March 3, 1989 meeting, Time's board adopted several defensive tactics. Time entered an automatic share exchange agreement with Warner. Time would receive 17,292,747 shares of Warner's outstanding common stock (9.4%) and Warner would receive 7,080,016 shares of Time's outstanding common stock (11.1%). Either party could trigger the exchange. Time sought out and paid for "confidence" letters from various banks with which it did business. In these letters, the banks promised not to finance any third-party attempt to acquire Time. Time argues these agreements served only to preserve the confidential relationship between itself and the banks. The Chancellor found these agreements to be inconsequential and futile attempts to "dry up" money for a hostile takeover. Time also agreed to a "no-shop" clause, preventing Time from considering any other consolidation proposal, thus relinquishing its power to consider other proposals, regardless of their merits. Time did so at Warner's insistence. Warner did not want to be left "on the auction block" for an unfriendly suitor, if Time were to withdraw from the deal.

Time's board simultaneously established a special committee of outside directors, Finkelstein, Kearns, and Opel, to oversee the merger. The committee's assignment was to resolve any impediments that might arise in the course of working out the details of the merger and its consummation.

Time representatives lauded the lack of debt to the United States Senate and to the President of the United States. Public reaction to the announcement of the merger was positive. Time-Warner would be a media colossus with international scope. The board scheduled the stockholder vote for June 23; and a May 1 record date was set. On May 24, 1989, Time sent out extensive proxy statements to the stockholders regarding the approval vote on the merger. In the meantime, with the merger proceeding without impediment, the special committee had concluded, shortly after its creation, that it was not necessary either to retain independent consultants, legal or financial, or even to meet. Time's board was unanimously in favor of the proposed merger with Warner; and, by the end of May, the Time-Warner merger appeared to be an accomplished fact.

On June 7, 1989, these wishful assumptions were shattered by Paramount's surprising announcement of its all-cash offer to purchase all outstanding shares of Time for $175 per share. The following day, June 8, the trading price of Time's stock rose from $126 to $170 per share. Paramount's offer was said to be "fully negotiable."[8]

Time found Paramount's "fully negotiable" offer to be in fact subject to at least three conditions. First, Time had to terminate its merger agreement and stock exchange agreement with Warner, and remove certain other of its defensive devices, including the redemption of Time's shareholder rights. Second, Paramount had to obtain the required cable franchise transfers from Time in a fashion acceptable to Paramount in its sole discretion. Finally, the offer depended upon a judicial determination that section 203 of the General

---

8. Subsequently, it was established that Paramount's board had decided as early as March 1989 to move to acquire Time. However, Paramount management intentionally delayed publicizing its proposal until Time had mailed to its stockholders its Time-Warner merger proposal along with the required proxy statements.

Corporate Law of Delaware (The Delaware Anti-Takeover Statute) was inapplicable to any Time-Paramount merger. While Paramount's board had been privately advised that it could take months, perhaps over a year, to forge and consummate the deal, Paramount's board publicly proclaimed its ability to close the offer by July 5, 1989. Paramount executives later conceded that none of its directors believed that July 5th was a realistic date to close the transaction.

On June 8, 1989, Time formally responded to Paramount's offer. Time's chairman and CEO, J. Richard Munro, sent an aggressively worded letter to Paramount's CEO, Martin Davis. Munro's letter attacked Davis' personal integrity and called Paramount's offer "smoke and mirrors." Time's nonmanagement directors were not shown the letter before it was sent. However, at a board meeting that same day, all members endorsed management's response as well as the letter's content.

Over the following eight days, Time's board met three times to discuss Paramount's $175 offer. The board viewed Paramount's offer as inadequate and concluded that its proposed merger with Warner was the better course of action. Therefore, the board declined to open any negotiations with Paramount and held steady its course toward a merger with Warner.

In June, Time's board of directors met several times. During the course of their June meetings, Time's outside directors met frequently without management, officers or directors being present. At the request of the outside directors, corporate counsel was present during the board meetings and, from time to time, the management directors were asked to leave the board sessions. During the course of these meetings, Time's financial advisors informed the board that, on an auction basis, Time's per share value was materially higher than Warner's $175 per share offer. After this advice, the board concluded that Paramount's $175 offer was inadequate.

At these June meetings, certain Time directors expressed their concern that Time stockholders would not comprehend the long-term benefits of the Warner merger. Large quantities of Time shares were held by institutional investors. The board feared that even though there appeared to be wide support for the Warner transaction, Paramount's cash premium would be a tempting prospect to these investors. In mid-June, Time sought permission from the New York Stock Exchange to alter its rules and allow the TimeWarner merger to proceed without stockholder approval. Time did so at Warner's insistence. The New York Stock Exchange rejected Time's request on June 15; and on that day, the value of Time stock reached $182 per share.

The following day, June 16, Time's board met to take up Paramount's offer. The board's prevailing belief was that Paramount's bid posed a threat to Time's control of its own destiny and retention of the "Time Culture." Even after Time's financial advisors made another presentation of Paramount and its business attributes, Time's board maintained its position that a combination with Warner offered greater potential for Time [and thus decided to reject Paramount's offer]. Warner provided Time a much desired production capability and an established international marketing chain. Time's advisors suggested various options, including defensive measures. . . .

At the same meeting, Time's board decided to recast its consolidation with Warner into an outright cash and securities acquisition of Warner by Time; and Time so informed Warner. Time accordingly restructured its proposal to acquire Warner as follows: Time would make an immediate all-cash offer for 51% of Warner's outstanding stock at $70 per share. The remaining 49% would be purchased at some later date for a mixture of cash and securities worth $70 per share. To provide the funds required for its outright acquisition of Warner, Time would assume 7-10 billion dollars worth of debt, thus eliminating one of the principal transaction-related benefits of the original merger agreement.

Warner agreed. . . .

On June 23, 1989, Paramount raised its all-cash offer to buy Time's outstanding stock to $200 per share. Paramount still professed that all aspects of the offer were negotiable. Time's board met on June 26, 1989 and formally rejected Paramount's $200 per share second offer. The board reiterated its belief that, despite the $25 increase, the offer was still inadequate. The Time board maintained that the Warner transaction offered a greater long-term value for the stockholders and, unlike Paramount's offer, did not pose a threat to Time's survival and its "culture." Paramount then filed this action in the Court of Chancery.

II

The Shareholder Plaintiffs first assert a *Revlon* claim. They contend that the March 4 Time-Warner agreement effectively put Time up for sale, triggering *Revlon* duties, requiring Time's board to enhance short-term shareholder value and to treat all other interested acquirors on an equal basis. The Shareholder Plaintiffs base this argument on two facts: (i) the ultimate Time-Warner exchange ratio of .465 favoring Warner, resulting in Warner shareholders' receipt of 62% of the combined company; and (ii) the subjective intent of Time's directors as evidenced in their statements that the market might perceive the Time-Warner merger as putting Time up "for sale" and their adoption of various defensive measures.

The Shareholder Plaintiffs further contend that Time's directors, in structuring the original merger transaction to be "takeover-proof," triggered *Revlon* duties by foreclosing their shareholders from any prospect of obtaining a control premium. In short, plaintiffs argue that Time's board's decision to merge with Warner imposed a fiduciary duty to maximize immediate share value and not erect unreasonable barriers to further bids. Therefore, they argue, the Chancellor erred in finding: that Paramount's bid for Time did not place Time "for sale"; that Time's transaction with Warner did not result in any transfer of control; and that the combined Time-Warner was not so large as to preclude the possibility of the stockholders of Time-Warner receiving a future control premium.

Paramount asserts only a *Unocal* claim in which the shareholder plaintiffs join. Paramount contends that the Chancellor, in applying the first part of the *Unocal* test, erred in finding that Time's board had reasonable grounds to believe that Paramount posed both a legally cognizable threat to Time shareholders and a danger to Time's corporate policy and effectiveness. Paramount also contests the court's finding that Time's board made a reasonable and objective investigation of Paramount's offer so as to be informed before rejecting it. Paramount further claims that the court erred in applying *Unocal's* second part in finding Time's response to be "reasonable." Paramount points primarily to the preclusive effect of the revised agreement which denied Time shareholders the opportunity both to vote on the agreement and to respond to Paramount's tender offer. Paramount argues that the underlying motivation of Time's board in adopting these defensive measures was management's desire to perpetuate itself in office.

The Court of Chancery posed the pivotal question presented by this case to be: Under what circumstances must a board of directors abandon an in place plan of corporate development in order to provide its shareholders with the option to elect and realize an immediate control premium? As applied to this case, the question becomes: Did Time's board, having developed a strategic plan of global expansion to be launched through a business combination with Warner, come under a fiduciary duty to jettison its plan and put the corporation's future in the hands of its shareholders?

While we affirm the result reached by the Chancellor, we think it unwise to place undue emphasis upon long-term versus short-term corporate strategy. Two key predicates underpin our analysis. First, Delaware law imposes on a board of directors the duty to manage the business and affairs of the corporation. 8 Del. C. §141 (a). This broad mandate includes a conferred authority to set a corporate course of action, including time frame, designed to enhance corporate profitability. Thus, the question of "long-term" versus "short-term" values is largely irrelevant because directors, generally, are obliged to chart a course for a corporation which is in its best interests without regard to a fixed investment horizon. Second, absent a limited set of circumstances as defined under *Revlon,* a board of directors, while always required to act in an informed manner, is not under any *per se* duty to maximize shareholder value in the short term, even in the context of a takeover.[12] In our view, the pivotal question presented by this case is: "Did Time, by entering into the proposed merger with Warner, put itself up for sale?" A resolution of that issue through application of *Revlon* has a significant bearing upon the resolution of the derivative *Unocal* issue.

A.

We first take up plaintiffs' principal *Revlon* argument, summarized above. In rejecting this argument, the Chancellor found the original Time-Warner merger agreement not to constitute a "change of control" and concluded that the transaction did not trigger *Revlon* duties. The Chancellor's conclusion is premised on a finding that "[b]efore the merger agreement was signed, control of the corporation existed in a fluid aggregation of unaffiliated shareholders representing a voting majority—in other words, in the market." The

---

12. Thus, we endorse the Chancellor's conclusion that it is not a breach of faith for directors to determine that the present stock market price of shares is not representative of true value or that there may indeed be several market values for any corporation's stock. We have so held in another context. *See Van Gorkom,* 488 A.2d at 876.

Chancellor's findings of fact are supported by the record and his conclusion is correct as a matter of law. However, we premise our rejection of plaintiffs' *Revlon* claim on different grounds, namely, the absence of any substantial evidence to conclude that Time's board, in negotiating with Warner, made the dissolution or break-up of the corporate entity inevitable, as was the case in *Revlon*.

Under Delaware law there are, generally speaking and without excluding other possibilities, two circumstances which may implicate *Revlon* duties. The first, and clearer one, is when a corporation initiates an active bidding process seeking to sell itself or to effect a business reorganization involving a clear break-up of the company. *See, e.g., Mills Acquisition Co. v. Macmillan, Inc,* Del. Supr., 559 A.2d 1261 (1988). However, *Revlon* duties may also be triggered where, in response to a bidder's offer, a target abandons its long-term strategy and seeks an alternative transaction involving the breakup of the company. Thus, in *Revlon*, when the board responded to Pantry Pride's offer by contemplating a "bust-up" sale of assets in a leveraged acquisition, we imposed upon the board a duty to maximize immediate shareholder value and an obligation to auction the company fairly. If, however, the board's reaction to a hostile tender offer is found to constitute only a defensive response and not an abandonment of the corporation's continued existence, *Revlon* duties are not triggered, though *Unocal* duties attach.[14]

The plaintiffs insist that even though the original Time-Warner agreement may not have worked "an objective change of control," the transaction made a "sale" of Time inevitable. Plaintiffs rely on the subjective intent of Time's board of directors and principally upon certain board members' expressions of concern that the Warner transaction *might* be viewed as effectively putting Time up for sale. Plaintiffs argue that the use of a lock-up agreement, a no-shop clause, and so-called "dry-up" agreements prevented shareholders from obtaining a control premium in the immediate future and thus violated *Revlon*.

We agree with the Chancellor that such evidence is entirely insufficient to invoke *Revlon* duties; and we decline to extend *Revlon*'s application to corporate transactions simply because they might be construed as putting a corporation either "in play" or "up for sale." . . .

Finally, we do not find in Time's recasting of its merger agreement with Warner from a share exchange to a share purchase a basis to conclude that Time had either abandoned its strategic plan or made a sale of Time inevitable. The Chancellor found that although the merged Time-Warner company would be large (with a value approaching approximately $30 billion), recent takeover cases have proven that acquisition of the combined company might nonetheless be possible. . . .

---

14. Within the auction process, any action taken by the board must be reasonably related to the threat posed or reasonable in relation to the advantage sought, *See Mills Acquisition Co. v. Macmillian, Inc.,* Del. Supr., 559 A.2d 1261, 1288 (1988). Thus, a *Unocal* analysis may be appropriate when a corporation is in a *Revlon* situation and *Revlon* duties may be triggered by a defensive action taken in response to a hostile offer. Since *Revlon*, we have stated that differing treatment of various bidders is not actionable when such action reasonably relates to achieving the best price available for the stockholders. *Macmillian,* 559 A.2d at 1286-87.

B.

We turn now to plaintiffs' *Unocal* claim. We begin by noting, as did the Chancellor, that our decision does not require us to pass on the wisdom of the board's decision to enter into the original Time-Warner agreement. That is not a court's task. Our task is simply to review the record to determine whether there is sufficient evidence to support the Chancellor's conclusion that the initial Time-Warner agreement was the product of a proper exercise of business judgment.

We have purposely detailed the evidence of the Time board's deliberative approach, beginning in 1983-84, to expand itself. Time's decision in 1988 to combine with Warner was made only after what could be fairly characterized as an exhaustive appraisal of Time's future as a corporation. After concluding in 1983-84 that the corporation must expand to survive, and beyond journalism into entertainment, the board combed the field of available entertainment companies. By 1987 Time had focused upon Warner; by late July 1988 Time's board was convinced that Warner would provide the best "fit" for Time to achieve its strategic objectives. The record attests to the zealousness of Time's executives, fully supported by their directors, in seeing to the preservation of Time's "culture," i.e., its perceived editorial integrity in journalism. We find ample evidence in the record to support the Chancellor's conclusion that the Time board's decision to expand the business of the company through its March 3 merger with Warner was entitled to the protection of the business judgment rule.

The Chancellor reached a different conclusion in addressing the Time-Warner transaction as revised three months later. He found that the revised agreement was defense-motivated and designed to avoid the potentially disruptive effect that Paramount's offer would have had on consummation of the proposed merger were it put to a shareholder vote. Thus, the court declined to apply the traditional business judgment rule to the revised transaction and instead analyzed the Time board's June 16 decision under *Unocal*. The court ruled that *Unocal* applied to all director actions taken, following receipt of Paramount's hostile tender offer, that were reasonably determined to be defensive. Clearly that was a correct ruling and no party disputes that ruling.

In *Unocal*, we held that before the business judgment rule is applied to a board's adoption of a defensive measure, the burden will lie with the board to prove (a) reasonable grounds for believing that a danger to corporate policy and effectiveness existed; and (b) that the defensive measure adopted was reasonable in relation to the threat posed. *Unocal*, 493 A.2d 946. Directors satisfy the first part of the *Unocal* test by demonstrating good faith and reasonable investigation. We have repeatedly stated that the refusal to entertain an offer may comport with a valid exercise of a board's business judgment. . . .

Unocal involved a two-tier, highly coercive tender offer. In such a case, the threat is obvious: shareholders may be compelled to tender to avoid being treated adversely in the second stage of the transaction. In subsequent cases, the Court of Chancery has suggested that an all-cash, all-shares offer, falling within a range of values that a shareholder might reasonably prefer, cannot constitute a legally recognized "threat" to shareholder interests sufficient to withstand a *Unocal* analysis. . . . [*See City Capital Associates v. Interco, Inc.*, Del. Ch., 551 A.2d 787 (1988)] . . .

From those decisions by our Court of Chancery, Paramount and the individual plaintiffs extrapolate a rule of law that an all-cash, all-shares offer with values reasonably in the range of acceptable price cannot pose any objective threat to a corporation or its shareholders. Thus, Paramount would have us hold that only if the value of Paramount's offer were determined to be clearly inferior to the value created by management's plan to merge with Warner could the offer be viewed—objectively—as a threat.

Implicit in the plaintiffs' argument is the view that a hostile tender offer can pose only two types of threats: the threat of coercion that results from a two-tier offer promising unequal treatment for nontendering shareholders; and the threat of inadequate value from an all-shares, all-cash offer at a price below what a target board in good faith deems to be the present value of its shares. Since Paramount's offer was all-cash, the only conceivable "threat," plaintiffs argue, was inadequate value. We disapprove of such a narrow and rigid construction of *Unocal,* for the reasons which follow.

Plaintiffs' position represents a fundamental misconception of our standard of review under *Unocal* principally because it would involve the court in substituting its judgment as to what is a "better" deal for that of a corporation's board of directors. To the extent that the Court of Chancery has recently done so in certain of its opinions, we hereby reject such approach as not in keeping with a proper *Unocal* analysis. See, e.g., [*City Capital Associates v. Interco., Inc.,* 551 A.2d 787, 797 (Del. Ch. 1988] and its progeny, . . .

The usefulness of *Unocal* as an analytical tool is precisely its flexibility in the face of a variety of fact scenarios. *Unocal* is not intended as an abstract standard; neither is it a structured and mechanistic procedure of appraisal. Thus, we have said that directors may consider, when evaluating the threat posed by a takeover bid, the "inadequacy of the price offered, nature and timing of the offer, questions of illegality, the impact on 'constituencies' other than shareholders . . . the risk of nonconsummation, and the quality of securities being offered in the exchange." 493 A.2d at 955. The open-ended analysis mandated by *Unocal* is not intended to lead to a simple mathematical exercise: that is, of comparing the discounted value of Time-Warner's expected trading price at some future date with Paramount's offer and determining which is the higher. Indeed, in our view, precepts underlying the business judgment rule militate against a court's engaging in the process of attempting to appraise and evaluate the relative merits of a long-term versus a short-term investment goal for shareholders. To engage in such an exercise is a distortion of the *Unocal* process and, in particular, the application of the second part of *Unocal's* test, discussed below.

In this case, the Time board reasonably determined that inadequate value was not the only legally cognizable threat that Paramount's all-cash, all-shares offer could present. Time's board concluded that Paramount's eleventh hour offer posed other threats. One concern was that Time shareholders might elect to tender into Paramount's cash offer in ignorance or a mistaken belief of the strategic benefit which a business combination with Warner might produce. Moreover, Time viewed the conditions attached to Paramount's offer as introducing a degree of uncertainty that skewed a comparative analysis. Further, the timing of Paramount's offer to follow issuance of Time's proxy notice was viewed as arguably designed to upset, if not confuse, the Time stockholders' vote. Given this record evidence, we cannot conclude that the Time board's decision of June 6 that Paramount's offer posed a threat to corporate policy and effectiveness was lacking in good faith or dominated by motives of either entrenchment or self-interest.

Paramount also contends that the Time board had not duly investigated Paramount's offer. Therefore, Paramount argues, Time was unable to make an informed decision that the offer posed a threat to Time's corporate policy. Although the Chancellor did not address this issue directly, his findings of fact do detail Time's exploration of the available entertainment companies, including Paramount, before determining that Warner provided the best strategic "fit." In addition, the court found that Time's board rejected Paramount's offer because Paramount did not serve Time's objectives or meet Time's needs. Thus, the record does, in our judgment, demonstrate that Time's board was adequately informed of the potential benefits of a transaction with Paramount. We agree with the Chancellor that the Time board's lengthy pre-June investigation of potential merger candidates, including Paramount, mooted any obligation on Time's part to halt its merger process with Warner to reconsider Paramount. Time's board was under no obligation to negotiate with Paramount. Time's failure to negotiate cannot be fairly found to have been uninformed. The evidence supporting this finding is materially enhanced by the fact that twelve of Time's sixteen board members were outside independent directors. *Unocal*, 493 A.2d at 955; *Moran v. Household Intern., Inc.*, Del. Supr., 500 A.2d 1346, 1356 (1985).

We turn to the second part of the *Unocal* analysis. The obvious requisite to determining the reasonableness of a defensive action is a clear identification of the nature of the threat. As the Chancellor correctly noted, this "requires an evaluation of the importance of the corporate objective threatened; alternative methods of protecting that objective; impacts of the 'defensive' action, and other relevant factors." It is not until both parts of the *Unocal* inquiry have been satisfied that the business judgment rule attaches to defensive actions of a board of directors. *Unocal*, 493 A.2d at 954.[18] As applied to the facts of this case, the question is whether the record evidence supports the Court of Chancery's conclusion that the restructuring of the Time-Warner transaction, including the adoption of several preclusive defensive measures, was a *reasonable response* in relation to a perceived threat.

Paramount argues that, assuming its tender offer posed a threat, Time's response was unreasonable in precluding Time's shareholders from accepting the tender offer or receiving a control premium in the immediately foreseeable future. Once again, the contention stems, we believe, from a fundamental misunderstanding of where the power of corporate governance lies. Delaware law confers the management of the corporate enterprise to the stockholders' duly elected board representatives. 8 Del. C. §141(a). The fiduciary duty to manage

---

18. Some commentators have criticized *Unocal* by arguing that once the board's deliberative process has been analyzed and found not to be wanting in objectivity, good faith or deliberateness, the so-called "enhanced" business judgment rule has been satisfied and no further inquiry is undertaken. *See generally* Johnson & Siegel, *Corporate Mergers: Redefining the Role of Target Directors*, 136 U. Pa. L. Rev. 315 (1987). We reject such views.

a corporate enterprise includes the selection of a time frame for achievement of corporate goals. That duty may not be delegated to the stockholders. *Van Gorkom,* 488 A.2d at 873. Directors are not obliged to abandon a deliberately conceived corporate plan for a short-term shareholder profit unless there is clearly no basis to sustain the corporate strategy. *See, e.g., Revlon,* 506 A.2d 173.

Although the Chancellor blurred somewhat the discrete analyses required under *Unocal,* he did conclude that Time's board reasonably perceived Paramount's offer to be a significant threat to the planned Time-Warner merger and that Time's response was not "overly broad." We have found that even in light of a valid threat, management actions that are coercive in nature or force upon shareholders a management-sponsored alternative to a hostile offer may be struck down as unreasonable and nonproportionate responses.

Here, on the record facts, the Chancellor found that Time's responsive action to Paramount's tender offer was not aimed at "cramming down" on its shareholders a management-sponsored alternative, but rather had as its goal the carrying forward of a pre-existing transaction in an altered form. Thus, the response was reasonably related to the threat. The Chancellor noted that the revised agreement and its accompanying safety devices did not preclude Paramount from making an offer for the combined Time-Warner company or from changing the conditions of its offer so as not to make the offer dependent upon the nullification of the Time-Warner agreement. Thus, the response was proportionate. We affirm the Chancellor's rulings as clearly supported by the record. Finally, we note that although Time was required, as a result of Paramount's hostile offer, to incur a heavy debt to finance its acquisition of Warner, that fact alone does not render the board's decision unreasonable so long as the directors could reasonably perceive the debt load not to be so injurious to the corporation as to jeopardize its well being.

C.

Conclusion

Applying the test for grant or denial of preliminary injunctive relief, we find plaintiffs failed to establish a reasonable likelihood of ultimate success on the merits. Therefore, we affirm. . . .

QUESTIONS

1. With the benefit of hindsight, do you think that the Time-Warner merger proved to be a good deal for the Time shareholders? This inevitably leads to the vexing question that commentators are still grappling with in the wake of the Time-Warner business combination—indeed, that we have grappled with throughout our study of M & A law—*Who should decide the fate of the company: Time's board of directors or Time's shareholders?*

2. According to the Delaware Supreme Court, what triggers the *Revlon* duties? In other words, how does the legal advisor to the company determine when the company is in the *Revlon* mode?

3. In light of the numerous financial scandals that have marked the dawn of
    the twenty-first century, does reliance on independent outside directors
    continue to be as compelling as it was for the Delaware Supreme Court in its
    Time-Warner decision? In the wake of the Great Recession, do you find the
    Delaware Supreme Court's reasoning on this issue persuasive as a matter of
    public policy?

4. What are the public policy concerns that the Delaware Supreme Court iden-
    tified in connection with the decision of Time's board to take on debt (i.e.,
    leverage the company's balance sheet) in order to finance the acquisition
    of Warner on a cash basis?

5. What standard of review applies to the decision of Time's board of directors
    to restructure the transaction from a single-step, reverse triangular merger
    into a two-step acquisition? How does the Delaware Supreme Court apply
    that standard of review to determine whether Time's board of directors has
    fulfilled its fiduciary duty obligations?

NOTES

1. *The Aftermath of the* Time-Warner *Decision.* Following the Delaware
Supreme Court's decision, the trading price of Time shares fell to $93 per share,
a far cry from the lofty cash offer of $200 per share that Paramount offered
Time's shareholders, leading to considerable criticisms of the Court's decision. As succinctly described by one leading commentator: "In [*Time-Warner*],
the Delaware court let incumbent directors block an any-and-all tender offer
paying a 100 percent premium. So preposterous was its opinion that it quickly
became the target of massive ridicule." J. Mark Ramseyer, BUSINESS ORGANIZA-
TIONS 375 (2012).

2. *The "Just Say No" Defense.* The *Time-Warner* decision gave rise to what
is popularly referred to as the "just say no" defense. "[M]any commentators
concluded that [the *Time-Warner* decision] validated the 'just say no' defense,
pursuant to which the target's board simply refuses to allow the firm to be
acquired, backing up that refusal by a poison pill or other takeover defenses."
Stephen M. Bainbridge, MERGERS & ACQUISITIONS 227 (2d Ed. 2009). It is important to note that at least one court had previously rejected the "just say no"
defense, at least implicitly. You will recall that Chancellor Allen's opinion in *City
Capital Associates, supra,* at pg. 619, "at least implicitly rejected the 'just say no'
defense. . . . Chancellor Allen indicated that 'in most instances' the use of takeover defenses was only legitimate in connection with attempts by the board to
negotiate with unsolicited bidder or to assemble an alternative transaction. *City
Capital Assoc. Ltd. Partnership v. Interco Inc.,* 551 A.2d 787, 798 (Del. Ch. 1988). In
other words, the [Target] Board cannot simply just say no." Bainbridge, *supra,*
at p. 227, n. 83. However, in its *Time-Warner* opinion, the Delaware Supreme
Court rejected the view "that an all-cash, all-shares offer, falling within a range
of values that a shareholder might reasonably prefer, *cannot* constitute a legally
recognized 'threat' to shareholder interests sufficient to withstand scrutiny
under the first prong of *Unocal's* intermediate standard of judicial scrutiny."

Time-Warner, supra at p. 1152 (*emphasis added*). *Query*: Should the Target board be able to "just say no" to an unsolicited Bidder?

3. *Long-Term vs. Short-Term Perspective.*   In recent years, there has been considerable public controversy over excessive executive compensation, particularly with respect to the continued use of change-of-control compensation (i.e., golden parachutes) in connection with M&A transactions involving publicly traded companies. The important public policy issues that are presented by this modern controversy, especially with respect to management's incentives to manage the company's business affairs in order to maximize gain in the short run or the long run, were recently highlighted by Chancellor Strine:

> During the last quarter century, the compensation of top executives, particularly CEOs, has grown enormously. There is a heated argument about why that is the case and whether, on balance, that increase is largely attributable to demands by the institutional investor community that the takeover market operate with great vibrancy, that underperforming management be replaced, that executive compensation take the form of stock options, and that top executives engage in measures (such as job cutting and outsourcing) that they may find distasteful but which increase corporate bottom lines.[59] Arguably, these pressures to manage to an avaricious market, greatly decreased job security, and a change in the public perception of CEOs of public companies from being community leaders running important societal institutions into being ruthless sharpies willing to do whatever it takes to increase the corporation's stock price, have led CEOs to seek much greater compensation.[60] Ironically, some say, the one corporate constituency that has little to complain about executive compensation are stockholders, whose returns have largely tracked the increases in CEO pay, while returns to ordinary corporate workers in the form of wages and returns to society in the form of increases in median family income have stagnated. On the other hand, even institutional investors, such as labor pension funds, who do invest for the long term are concerned about executive compensation, believing that it is excessive and often tied to counterproductive ends, such as short-term stock price movements, rather than the sound generation of corporate wealth over the long run. And, many corporate advisors and mid-level executives privately admit that many CEOs have grabbed for and gotten compensation packages that are far in excess of what market forces would generate.

Leo E. Strine, Jr., *One Fundamental Corporate Governance Question We Face: Can Corporations Be Managed for the Long Term Unless Their Power Electorates Also Act and Think Long Term?*, 66 Bus. Law. 1, 19-20 (2010).

In this essay, Chancellor Strine poses the fundamental "question of how corporations can be managed to promote long term growth if their

---

59. *Compare* Steven N. Kaplan, *Are U.S. CEOs Overpaid?* 22 Acad. Mgmt. Persp. 1 (2008), with Lucian A. Bebhuk & Jesse M. Fried, *Pay Without Performance: An Overview of the Issues*, 30 J. Corp. L. 647 (2005).

60. *See* Richard A. Posner, *Are American CEOs Overpaid, and, If So, What If Anything Should Be Done About It?* 58 Duke L.J. 1013, 1022 (2009) ("Because business executives, as distinct from entrepreneurs, do not like risk, they will demand a higher wage if the wage has a substantial risky component; and stock options are risky.").

stockholders do not act and think with the long term in mind." *Id.* at 1. In addition to his concerns regarding excessive executive compensation, he points to other "underlying facts regarding how *short* a time most stockholders, including institutional investors hold their shares," all of which often gives rise to what Chancellor Strine views as "a myopic concern for *short-term* performance," *id.* at 10 (*emphasis added*), particularly on the part of "institutional investors who now control nearly 70 percent of U.S. publicly traded equities." *Id.* Adding to his concerns, Chancellor Strine points to a riveting statistic: Given the trading practices of institutional investors—most notably, hedge funds, mutual funds, and pension funds—their open-market trading in equities "consistently results in annualized turnover of stocks traded on the [NYSE] of well over 100 percent, with turnover approaching 138 percent in 2008." *Id.* at 11 (citing to *NYSE Facts and Figures: NYSE Group Turnover 2000-2009*, NYX Data.com, *available at* http://www.nyxdata.com/nysedata/asp/factbook/viewer_edition.asp?_mode=table&key=2992&category=3).

From Chancellor Strine's perspective, these trends in investor behavior and trading practices serve to highlight "the tension between the institutional investors' incentive to think short term and the best interests of not only the corporations in which these investors buy stock, but also with the best interests of the institutional investors' own clients, who are saving to pay for college for their kids and for their own retirement." *Id.* at 1. As an observer of the U.S. capital markets, and more specifically, a student of the M&A markets, what do you think of this question posed by Chancellor Strine: "[S]hould we expect [the managers of modern] corporations to chart a sound long-term course of economic growth, if the so-called investors who determine the fate of their managers do not themselves act or think with the long term in mind?" *Id.* at 1-2. This tension in our system of corporate governance that Chancellor Strine describes surfaces most acutely in M&A transactions as policy makers, including the Delaware judiciary, face the fundamental question: *Who should decide when and on what terms the corporation should be sold?*

4. *The Director Primacy Model of Corporate Governance.* In *Unocal*, the Delaware Supreme Court firmly rejected the "passivity theory"; that is to say, the board of Target is not a "passive instrumentality" when faced with an unsolicited takeover bid. Instead, as subsequent Delaware cases have made clear, the board of Target is to serve as "the defender of the metaphorical medieval corporate bastion and the protector of the corporation's shareholders." *Unitrin, Inc., v. Am. Gen. Corp.*, 651 A.2d 1361, 1388 (Del. 1995). Thus, *Unocal* and its progeny have led some scholars to suggest that modern U.S. corporate law follows a model of "director primacy" to address one of the most fundamental questions that scholars of modern corporate governance struggle with:

> Who decides whether a transaction is beneficial for the corporation? Although questions of this sort pervade corporate governance, few transactions present it so starkly as does an unsolicited tender offer. Are such transactions mere "transfers of stock by stockholders to a third party" that do not "implicate the internal affairs of the target company"?[1] Or, as with most aspects of corporate

---

1. Edgar v. MITE Corp., 457 U.S. 624, 645 (1982).

governance, does the target company's board of directors have a gatekeeping function?

In statutory acquisitions, such as mergers or asset sales, the target's board of directors' gatekeeping function is established by statute. If the board rejects a proposed transaction, the shareholders are neither invited to, nor entitled to, pass on the merits of that decision.[3] Only if the target's board of directors approves the transaction are the shareholders invited to ratify that decision.[4]

In nonstatutory acquisitions, such as tender offers, the answer is more complicated. A tender offer enables the bidders to go directly to the shareholders of the target corporation, bypassing the board of directors.[5] When the hostile tender offer emerged in the 1970s as an important acquirer tool, lawyers and investment bankers working for target boards responded by developing defensive tactics designed to impede such offers.[6] Takeover defenses reasserted the target board's primacy by extending the board's gatekeeping function to the nonstatutory acquisition setting.

The Delaware Supreme Court came down in favor of a target board gatekeeping function in *Unocal Corp. v. Mesa Petroleum Co.*[7] . . .

[*Unocal* and its progeny make clear that] control [in the sense of authority to manage the business affairs of a corporation] is vested not in the hands of the firm's so-called owners, the shareholders, who exercise virtually no control over either day-to-day operations or long-term policy, but in the hands of the board of directors and their subordinate professional managers. On the other hand, the separation of ownership and control in modern public corporations obviously implicates important accountability concerns, which corporate law must also address. . . .

[In order to answer the fundamental question of who should decide when and on what terms the company should be sold, one must first consider some basic principles:] What is the nature of the corporation? What is the nature of the shareholders' relationship to the corporation? What is the proper role and function of the board of directors? And so on.[24]

---

3. *See* Jennifer J. Johnson & Mary Siegel, *Corporate Mergers: Redefining the Role of Target Directors*, 136 U. Pa. L. Rev. 315, 321-322 (1987) (explaining corporate law vests the decision to reject a merger in the unilateral discretion of the target corporation's board of directors).

4. *See, e.g.,* 3 Model Bus. Corp. Act Ann. §11.04(b) (3d ed. Supp. 2000-2002) (providing that "*after* adopting the plan of merger . . . the board of directors must submit the plan to the shareholders for their approval") (*emphasis added*).

5. *See* Roberta Romano, *Competition for Corporate Charters and the Lesson of Takeover Statutes*, 61 Fordham L. Rev. 843, 844 (1993) (explaining "takeovers . . . , in contrast to mergers, are achieved by tender offers to the shareholders, and thus bypass incumbent management's approval").

6. *See generally,* Patrick A. Gaughan, Mergers, Acquisitions, and Corporate Restructurings 167-234 (3d ed. 2002) (tracing the development of takeover defenses).

7. 493 A.2d 946 (Del. 1985).

24. The analysis in this [article] draws heavily on my recent work on director primacy. *See, e.g.,* Stephen M Bainbridge, *Director Primacy: The Means and Ends of Corporate Governance*, 97 Nw. U. L. Rev. 547 (2003) [hereinafter Bainbridge, *Director Primacy*]; Stephen M. Bainbridge, *The Board of Directors as Nexus of Contracts*, 88 Iowa L. Rev. 1 (2002) [hereinafter Bainbridge, *Board as Nexus*]. . . . For a constructive critique of my director primacy model, *see* Wayne O. Hanewicz, *Director Primacy*, *Omnicare*, *and the Function of Corporate Law*, 71 Tenn L. Rev. 511 (2004). For an instructive application of the model to shareholder voting, see Harry G. Hutchison, *Director Primacy and Corporate Governance: Shareholder Voting Rights Captured by the Accountability/Authority Paradigm*, 36 Loy. U. Chi. L.J. 111 (2005).

Stephen M Bainbridge, Unocal *at 20: Director Primacy in Corporate Takeovers,* 31 Del. J. Corp Law 769, 771-775 (2006). Professor Bainbridge has written extensively on the "director primacy model," strongly advocating

> that the power and right to exercise decisionmaking fiat is vested neither in the shareholders nor the managers, but in the board of directors. According to this director primacy model, the board of directors is not a mere agent of the shareholders, but rather is a sort of Platonic guardian serving as the nexus of the various contracts making up the corporation. As a positive theory of corporate governance, the director primacy model strongly emphasizes the role of fiat—i.e., the centralized decisionmaking authority possessed by the board of directors. As a normative theory of corporate governance, director primacy claims that resolving the resulting tension between authority and accountability is the central problem of corporate law. The substantial virtues of fiat can be realized only by preserving the board's decisionmaking authority from being trumped by either shareholders or courts. Achieving an appropriate balance between authority and accountability is a daunting but necessary task. Ultimately, authority and accountability cannot be reconciled. At some point, greater accountability necessarily makes the decisionmaking process less efficient, while highly efficient decisionmaking structures necessarily reduce accountability. In general, that tension is resolved in favor of authority. Because only shareholders are entitled to elect directors, boards of public corporations are insulated from pressure by nonshareholder corporate constituencies, such as employees or creditors. At the same time, the diffuse nature of U.S. stockownership and regulatory impediments to investor activism insulate directors from shareholder pressure. Accordingly, the board has virtually unconstrained freedom to exercise business judgment. . . . Hence the term "director primacy," which reflects the board's sovereignty.

Stephen M. Bainbridge, *Director Primacy: The Means and the Ends of Corporate Governance,* 97 Nw. U.L. Rev. 547, 605 (2003). *Query:* In considering the decisions in *Time-Warner* and *QVC* (which follows), does the Delaware Supreme Court seem to be adopting the director primacy model?

Paramount Communications, Inc. v. QVC Network, Inc.
637 A.2d 34 (Del. 1994)

VEASEY, Chief Justice.

In this appeal we review an order of the Court of Chancery dated November 24, 1993 (the "November 24 Order"), preliminarily enjoining certain defensive measures designed to facilitate a so-called strategic alliance between Viacom Inc. ("Viacom") and Paramount Communications Inc. ("Paramount") approved by the board of directors of Paramount (the "Paramount Board" or the "Paramount directors") and to thwart an unsolicited, more valuable, tender offer by QVC Network Inc. ("QVC"). In affirming, we hold that the sale of control in this case, which is at the heart of the proposed strategic alliance, implicates enhanced judicial scrutiny of the conduct of the Paramount Board under *Unocal Corp. v. Mesa Petroleum Co.,* Del. Supr., 493 A.2d 946 (1985), and *Revlon, Inc. v. MacAndrews & Forbes Holdings, Inc.,* Del. Supr., 506 A.2d 173 (1986). We further hold that the conduct of the Paramount Board was not reasonable as to process or result.

. . . This action arises out of a proposed acquisition of Paramount by Viacom through a tender offer followed by a second-step merger (the "Paramount-Viacom transaction"), and a competing unsolicited tender offer by QVC. The Court of Chancery granted a preliminary injunction. . . .

The Court of Chancery found that the Paramount directors violated their fiduciary duties by favoring the Paramount-Viacom transaction over the more valuable unsolicited offer of QVC. The Court of Chancery preliminarily enjoined Paramount and the individual defendants (the "Paramount defendants") from amending or modifying Paramount's stockholder rights agreement (the "Rights Agreement"), including the redemption of the Rights, or taking other action to facilitate the consummation of the pending tender offer by Viacom or any proposed second-step merger, including the Merger Agreement between Paramount and Viacom dated September 12, 1993 (the "Original Merger Agreement"), as amended on October 24, 1993 (the "Amended Merger Agreement"). Viacom and the Paramount defendants were enjoined from taking any action to exercise any provision of the Stock Option Agreement between Paramount and Viacom dated September 12, 1993 (the "Stock Option Agreement"), as amended on October 24, 1993. The Court of Chancery did not grant preliminary injunctive relief as to the termination fee provided for the benefit of Viacom in Section 8.05 of the Original Merger Agreement and the Amended Merger Agreement (the "Termination Fee").

Under the circumstances of this case, the pending sale of control implicated in the Paramount-Viacom transaction required the Paramount Board to act on an informed basis to secure the best value reasonably available to the stockholders. Since we agree with the Court of Chancery that the Paramount directors violated their fiduciary duties, we have AFFIRMED the entry of the order of the Vice Chancellor granting the preliminary injunction and have REMANDED these proceedings to the Court of Chancery for proceedings consistent herewith.

We also have attached an Addendum to this opinion addressing serious deposition misconduct by counsel who appeared on behalf of a Paramount director at the time that director's deposition was taken by a lawyer representing QVC.[2]

I. FACTS

. . . Paramount is a Delaware corporation with its principal offices in New York City. Approximately 118 million shares of Paramount's common stock are outstanding and traded on the New York Stock Exchange. The majority of Paramount's stock is publicly held by numerous unaffiliated investors.

---

2. It is important to put the Addendum in perspective. This Court notes and has noted its appreciation of the outstanding judicial workmanship of the Vice Chancellor and the professionalism of counsel in this matter in handling this expedited litigation with the expertise and skill which characterize Delaware proceedings of this nature. The misconduct noted in the Addendum is an aberration which is not to be tolerated in any Delaware proceeding. [Addendum omitted]

Paramount owns and operates a diverse group of entertainment businesses, including motion picture and television studios, book publishers, professional sports teams, and amusement parks.

There are 15 persons serving on the Paramount Board. Four directors are officer-employees of Paramount: Martin S. Davis ("Davis"), Paramount's Chairman and Chief Executive Officer since 1983; Donald Oresman ("Oresman"), Executive Vice-President, Chief Administrative Officer, and General Counsel; Stanley R. Jaffe, President and Chief Operating Officer; and Ronald L. Nelson, Executive Vice President and Chief Financial Officer. Paramount's 11 outside directors are distinguished and experienced business persons who are present or former senior executives of public corporations or financial institutions.

Viacom is a Delaware corporation with its headquarters in Massachusetts. Viacom is controlled by Sumner M. Redstone ("Redstone"), its Chairman and Chief Executive Officer, who owns indirectly approximately 85.2 percent of Viacom's voting Class A stock and approximately 69.2 percent of Viacom's nonvoting Class B stock through National Amusements, Inc. ("NAI"), an entity 91.7 percent owned by Redstone. Viacom has a wide range of entertainment operations, including a number of well-known cable television channels such as MTV, Nickelodeon, Showtime, and The Movie Channel. Viacom's equity coinvestors in the Paramount-Viacom transaction include NYNEX Corporation and Blockbuster Entertainment Corporation.

QVC is a Delaware corporation with its headquarters in West Chester, Pennsylvania. QVC has several large stockholders, including Liberty Media Corporation, Comcast Corporation, Advance Publications, Inc., and Cox Enterprises Inc. Barry Diller ("Diller"), the Chairman and Chief Executive Officer of QVC, is also a substantial stockholder. QVC sells a variety of merchandise through a televised shopping channel. . . .

Beginning in the late 1980s, Paramount investigated the possibility of acquiring or merging with other companies in the entertainment, media, or communications industry. Paramount considered such transactions to be desirable, and perhaps necessary, in order to keep pace with competitors in the rapidly evolving field of entertainment and communications. Consistent with its goal of strategic expansion, Paramount made a tender offer for Time Inc. in 1989, but was ultimately unsuccessful. *See Paramount Communications, Inc. v. Time Inc.*, Del. Supr., 571 A.2d 1140 (1990) *("Time-Warner")*.

Although Paramount had considered a possible combination of Paramount and Viacom as early as 1990, recent efforts to explore such a transaction began at a dinner meeting between Redstone and Davis on April 20, 1993. Robert Greenhill ("Greenhill"), Chairman of Smith Barney Shearson Inc. ("Smith Barney"), attended and helped facilitate this meeting. After several more meetings between Redstone and Davis, serious negotiations began taking place in early July.

It was tentatively agreed that Davis would be the chief executive officer and Redstone would be the controlling stockholder of the combined company, but the parties could not reach agreement on the merger price and the terms of a stock option to be granted to Viacom. With respect to price, Viacom offered a package of cash and stock (primarily Viacom Class B nonvoting stock) with a market value of approximately $61 per share, but Paramount wanted at least $70 per share.

Shortly after negotiations broke down in July 1993, two notable events occurred. First, Davis apparently learned of QVC's potential interest in Paramount, and told Diller over lunch on July 21, 1993, that Paramount was not for sale. Second, the market value of Viacom's Class B nonvoting stock increased from $46.875 on July 6 to $57.25 on August 20. QVC claims (and Viacom disputes) that this price increase was caused by open market purchases of such stock by Redstone or entities controlled by him.

On August 20, 1993, discussions between Paramount and Viacom resumed when Greenhill arranged another meeting between Davis and Redstone. . . .

On September 12, 1993, the Paramount Board met again and unanimously approved the Original Merger Agreement whereby Paramount would merge with and into Viacom. The terms of the merger provided that each share of Paramount common stock would be converted into 0.10 shares of Viacom Class A voting stock, 0.90 shares of Viacom Class B nonvoting stock, and $9.10 in cash. In addition, the Paramount Board agreed to amend its "poison pill" Rights Agreement to exempt the proposed merger with Viacom. The Original Merger Agreement also contained several provisions designed to make it more difficult for a potential competing bid to succeed. We focus, as did the Court of Chancery, on three of these defensive provisions: a "no-shop" provision (the "No-Shop Provision"), the Termination Fee, and the Stock Option Agreement.

First, under the No-Shop Provision, the Paramount Board agreed that Paramount would not solicit, encourage, discuss, negotiate, or endorse any competing transaction unless: (a) a third party "makes an unsolicited written, bona fide proposal, which is not subject to any material contingencies relating to financing"; and (b) the Paramount Board determines that discussions or negotiations with the third party are necessary for the Paramount Board to comply with its fiduciary duties.

Second, under the Termination Fee provision, Viacom would receive a $100 million termination fee if: (a) Paramount terminated the Original Merger Agreement because of a competing transaction; (b) Paramount's stockholders did not approve the merger; or (c) the Paramount Board recommended a competing transaction.

The third and most significant deterrent device was the Stock Option Agreement, which granted to Viacom an option to purchase approximately 19.9 percent (23,699,000 shares) of Paramount's outstanding common stock at $69.14 per share if any of the triggering events for the Termination Fee occurred. In addition to the customary terms that are normally associated with a stock option, the Stock Option Agreement contained two provisions that were both unusual and highly beneficial to Viacom: (a) Viacom was permitted to pay for the shares with a senior subordinated note of questionable marketability instead of cash, thereby avoiding the need to raise the $1.6 billion purchase price (the "Note Feature"); and (b) Viacom could elect to require Paramount to pay Viacom in cash a sum equal to the difference between the purchase price and the market price of Paramount's stock (the "Put Feature"). Because the Stock Option Agreement was not "capped" to limit its maximum dollar value, it had the potential to reach (and in this case did reach) unreasonable levels.

After the execution of the Original Merger Agreement and the Stock Option Agreement on September 12, 1993, Paramount and Viacom announced their proposed merger. In a number of public statements, the parties indicated that the pending transaction was a virtual certainty. Redstone described it as a "marriage" that would "never be torn asunder" and stated that only a "nuclear attack" could break the deal. Redstone also called Diller and John Malone of Tele-Communications Inc., a major stockholder of QVC, to dissuade them from making a competing bid.

Despite these attempts to discourage a competing bid, Diller sent a letter to Davis on September 20, 1993, proposing a merger in which QVC would acquire Paramount for approximately $80 per share, consisting of 0.893 shares of QVC common stock and $30 in cash. QVC also expressed its eagerness to meet with Paramount to negotiate the details of a transaction. When the Paramount Board met on September 27, it was advised by Davis that the Original Merger Agreement prohibited Paramount from having discussions with QVC (or anyone else) unless certain conditions were satisfied. In particular, QVC had to supply evidence that its proposal was not subject to financing contingencies. The Paramount Board was also provided information from Lazard describing QVC and its proposal.

On October 5, 1993, QVC provided Paramount with evidence of QVC's financing. The Paramount Board then held another meeting on October 11, and decided to authorize management to meet with QVC. . . .

On October 21, 1993, QVC filed this action and publicly announced an $80 cash tender offer for 51 percent of Paramount's outstanding shares (the "QVC tender offer"). Each remaining share of Paramount common stock would be converted into 1.42857 shares of QVC common stock in a second-step merger. The tender offer was conditioned on, among other things, the invalidation of the Stock Option Agreement, which was worth over $200 million by that point.[5] QVC contends that it had to commence a tender offer because of the slow pace of the merger discussions and the need to begin seeking clearance under federal antitrust laws.

Confronted by QVC's hostile bid, which on its face offered over $10 per share more than the consideration provided by the Original Merger Agreement, Viacom realized that it would need to raise its bid in order to remain competitive. . . .

At a special meeting on October 24, 1993, the Paramount Board approved the Amended Merger Agreement and an amendment to the Stock Option Agreement. The Amended Merger Agreement was, however, essentially the same as the Original Merger Agreement, except that it included a few new provisions. One provision related to an $80 per share cash tender offer by Viacom for 51 percent of Paramount's stock, and another changed the merger consideration so that each share of Paramount would be converted into 0.20408 shares of Viacom Class A voting stock, 1.08317 shares of Viacom Class B nonvoting stock, and 0.20408 shares of a new series of Viacom convertible preferred stock. The Amended Merger Agreement also added a provision giving Paramount the right not to amend its Rights Agreement to exempt Viacom if the Paramount Board determined that such an amendment would be inconsistent

---

5. By November 15, 1993, the value of the Stock Option Agreement had increased to nearly $500 million based on the $90 QVC bid.

with its fiduciary duties because another offer constituted a "better alternative." Finally, the Paramount Board was given the power to terminate the Amended Merger Agreement if it withdrew its recommendation of the Viacom transaction or recommended a competing transaction.

Although the Amended Merger Agreement offered more consideration to the Paramount stockholders and somewhat more flexibility to the Paramount Board than did the Original Merger Agreement, the defensive measures designed to make a competing bid more difficult were not removed or modified. . . .

Viacom's tender offer commenced on October 25, 1993, and QVC's tender offer was formally launched on October 27, 1993. Diller sent a letter to the Paramount Board on October 28 requesting an opportunity to negotiate with Paramount, and Oresman responded the following day by agreeing to meet. The meeting, held on November 1, was not very fruitful, however, after QVC's proposed guidelines for a "fair bidding process" were rejected by Paramount on the ground that "auction procedures" were inappropriate and contrary to Paramount's contractual obligations to Viacom.

On November 6, 1993, Viacom unilaterally raised its tender offer price to $85 per share in cash and offered a comparable increase in the value of the securities being proposed in the second-step merger. At a telephonic meeting held later that day, the Paramount Board agreed to recommend Viacom's higher bid to Paramount's stockholders.

QVC responded to Viacom's higher bid on November 12 by increasing its tender offer to $90 per share and by increasing the securities for its secondstep merger by a similar amount. In response to QVC's latest offer, the Paramount Board scheduled a meeting for November 15, 1993. Prior to the meeting, Oresman sent the members of the Paramount Board a document summarizing the "conditions and uncertainties" of QVC's offer. One director testified that this document gave him a very negative impression of the QVC bid.

At its meeting on November 15, 1993, the Paramount Board determined that the new QVC offer was not in the best interests of the stockholders. The purported basis for this conclusion was that QVC's bid was excessively conditional. The Paramount Board did not communicate with QVC regarding the status of the conditions because it believed that the No-Shop Provision prevented such communication in the absence of firm financing. Several Paramount directors also testified that they believed the Viacom transaction would be more advantageous to Paramount's future business prospects than a QVC transaction.[7] Although a number of materials were distributed to the Paramount Board describing the Viacom and QVC transactions, the only quantitative analysis of the consideration to be received by the stockholders under each proposal was based on then-current market prices of the securities involved, not on the anticipated value of such securities at the time when the stockholders would receive them.

---

7. This belief may have been based on a report prepared by Booz-Allen and distributed to the Paramount Board at its October 24 meeting. The report, which relied on public information regarding QVC, concluded that the synergies of a Paramount-Viacom merger were significantly superior to those of a Paramount-QVC merger. QVC has labeled the Booz-Allen report as a "joke."

The preliminary injunction hearing in this case took place on November 16, 1993. On November 19, Diller wrote to the Paramount Board to inform it that QVC had obtained financing commitments for its tender offer and that there was no antitrust obstacle to the offer. On November 24, 1993, the Court of Chancery issued its decision granting a preliminary injunction in favor of QVC and the plaintiff stockholders. This appeal followed.

II.   APPLICABLE PRINCIPLES OF ESTABLISHED DELAWARE LAW

The General Corporation Law of the State of Delaware (the "General Corporation Law") and the decisions of this Court have repeatedly recognized the fundamental principle that the management of the business and affairs of a Delaware corporation is entrusted to its directors, who are the duly elected and authorized representatives of the stockholders. 8 Del. C. §141(a). Under normal circumstances, neither the courts nor the stockholders should interfere with the managerial decisions of the directors. The business judgment rule embodies the deference to which such decisions are entitled.

Nevertheless, there are rare situations which mandate that a court take a more direct and active role in overseeing the decisions made and actions taken by directors. In these situations, a court subjects the directors' conduct to enhanced scrutiny to ensure that it is reasonable.[9] The decisions of this Court have clearly established the circumstances where such enhanced scrutiny will be applied. *E.g., Unocal,* 493 A.2d 946; *Moran v. Household Int'l, Inc.,* Del. Supr., 500 A.2d 1346 (1985); *Revlon,* 506 A.2d 173; *Mills Acquisition Co. v. Macmillan, Inc.,* Del. Supr., 559 A.2d 1261 (1989); *Gilbert v. El Paso Co.,* Del. Supr., 575 A.2d 1131 (1990). The case at bar implicates two such circumstances: (1) the approval of a transaction resulting in a sale of control, and (2) the adoption of defensive measures in response to a threat to corporate control.

A.   THE SIGNIFICANCE OF A SALE OR CHANGE OF CONTROL

When a majority of a corporation's voting shares are acquired by a single person or entity, or by a cohesive group acting together, there is a significant diminution in the voting power of those who thereby become minority stockholders. Under the statutory framework of the General Corporation Law, many of the most fundamental corporate changes can be implemented only if they are approved by a majority vote of the stockholders. Such actions include elections of directors, amendments to the certificate of incorporation, mergers, consolidations, sales of all or substantially all of the assets of the corporation, and dissolution. 8 Del. C. §§211, 242, 251-258, 263, 271, 275. Because of the overriding importance of voting rights, this Court and the Court of Chancery

---

9. Where actual self-interest is present and affects a majority of the directors approving a transaction, a court will apply even more exacting scrutiny to determine whether the transaction is entirely fair to the stockholders. *E.g., Weinberger v. UOP, Inc.,* Del. Supr., 457 A.2d 701, 710-11 (1983); *Nixon v. Blackwell,* Del. Supr., 626 A.2d 1366, 1376 (1993).

have consistently acted to protect stockholders from unwarranted interference with such rights.

In the absence of devices protecting the minority stockholders, stockholder votes are likely to become mere formalities where there is a majority stockholder. For example, minority stockholders can be deprived of a continuing equity interest in their corporation by means of a cash-out merger. *Weinberger,* 457 A.2d at 703. Absent effective protective provisions, minority stockholders must rely for protection solely on the fiduciary duties owed to them by the directors and the majority stockholder, since the minority stockholders have lost the power to influence corporate direction through the ballot. The acquisition of majority status and the consequent privilege of exerting the powers of majority ownership come at a price. That price is usually a control premium which recognizes not only the value of a control block of shares, but also compensates the minority stockholders for their resulting loss of voting power.

In the case before us, the public stockholders (in the aggregate) currently own a majority of Paramount's voting stock. Control of the corporation is not vested in a single person, entity, or group, but vested in the fluid aggregation of unaffiliated stockholders. In the event the Paramount-Viacom transaction is consummated, the public stockholders will receive cash and a minority equity voting position in the surviving corporation. Following such consummation, there will be a controlling stockholder who will have the voting power to: (a) elect directors; (b) cause a break-up of the corporation; (c) merge it with another company; (d) cash-out the public stockholders; (e) amend the certificate of incorporation; (f) sell all or substantially all of the corporate assets; or (g) otherwise alter materially the nature of the corporation and the public stockholders' interests. Irrespective of the present Paramount Board's vision of a long-term strategic alliance with Viacom, the proposed sale of control would provide the new controlling stockholder with the power to alter that vision.

Because of the intended sale of control, the Paramount-Viacom transaction has economic consequences of considerable significance to the Paramount stockholders. Once control has shifted, the current Paramount stockholders will have no leverage in the future to demand another control premium. As a result, the Paramount stockholders are entitled to receive, and should receive, a control premium and/or protective devices of significant value. There being no such protective provisions in the Viacom-Paramount transaction, the Paramount directors had an obligation to take the maximum advantage of the current opportunity to realize for the stockholders the best value reasonably available.

B.   THE OBLIGATIONS OF DIRECTORS IN A SALE OR CHANGE OF CONTROL TRANSACTION

The consequences of a sale of control impose special obligations on the directors of a corporation. In particular, they have the obligation of acting reasonably to seek the transaction offering the best value reasonably available to the stockholders. The courts will apply enhanced scrutiny to ensure that the directors have acted reasonably. . . .

In the sale of control context, the directors must focus on one primary objective — to secure the transaction offering the best value reasonably available for the stockholders—and they must exercise their fiduciary duties to further that end. The decisions of this Court have consistently emphasized this goal. *Revlon*, 506 A.2d at 182 ("The duty of the board . . . [is] the maximization of the company's value at a sale for the stockholders' benefit."); *Macmillan*, 559 A.2d at 1288 ("[I]n a sale of corporate control the responsibility of the directors is to get the highest value reasonably attainable for the shareholders."). . . .

In pursuing this objective, the directors must be especially diligent. . . . In particular, this Court has stressed the importance of the board being adequately informed in negotiating a sale of control. . . . This requirement is consistent with the general principle that "directors have a duty to inform themselves, prior to making a business decision, of all material information reasonably available to them." *Aronson*, 473 A.2d at 812. *See also Cede & Co. v. Technicolor, Inc.*, Del. Supr., 634 A.2d 345, 367 (1993); *Smith v. Van Gorkom*, Del. Supr., 488 A.2d 858, 872 (1985). Moreover, the role of outside, independent directors becomes particularly important because of the magnitude of a sale of control transaction and the possibility, in certain cases, that management may not necessarily be impartial. *See Macmillan*, 559 A.2d at 1285 (requiring "the intense scrutiny and participation of the independent directors"). . . .

In determining which alternative provides the best value for the stockholders, a board of directors is not limited to considering only the amount of cash involved, and is not required to ignore totally its view of the future value of a strategic alliance. *See Macmillan*, 559 A.2d at 1282 n. 29. Instead, the directors should analyze the entire situation and evaluate in a disciplined manner the consideration being offered. Where stock or other non-cash consideration is involved, the board should try to quantify its value, if feasible, to achieve an objective comparison of the alternatives. In addition, the board may assess a variety of practical considerations relating to each alternative, including:

> [an offer's] fairness and feasibility; the proposed or actual financing for the offer, and the consequences of that financing; questions of illegality; . . . the risk of non-consum[m]ation; . . . the bidder's identity, prior background and other business venture experiences; and the bidder's business plans for the corporation and their effects on stockholder interests.

Macmillan, 559 A.2d at 1282 n.29. These considerations are important because the selection of one alternative may permanently foreclose other opportunities. While the assessment of these factors may be complex, the board's goal is straightforward: Having informed themselves of all material information reasonably available, the directors must decide which alternative is most likely to offer the best value reasonably available to the stockholders.

C.   ENHANCED JUDICIAL SCRUTINY OF A SALE OR CHANGE OF CONTROL TRANSACTION

Board action in the circumstances presented here is subject to enhanced scrutiny. Such scrutiny is mandated by: (a) the threatened diminution of the current stockholders' voting power; (b) the fact that an asset belonging to public stockholders (a control premium) is being sold and may never be available again; and (c) the traditional concern of Delaware courts for actions which impair or impede stockholder voting rights . . . In *MacMillan,* this Court held:

> When *Revlon* duties devolve upon directors, this Court will continue to exact an enhanced judicial scrutiny at the threshold, as in *Unocal,* before the normal presumptions of the business judgment rule will apply.[15]

559 A.2d at 1288. The *Macmillan* decision articulates a specific two-part test for analyzing board action where competing bidders are not treated equally:[16]

> In the face of disparate treatment, the trial court must first examine whether the directors properly perceived that shareholder interests were enhanced. In any event the board's action must be reasonable in relation to the advantage sought to be achieved, or conversely, to the threat which a particular bid allegedly poses to stockholder interests.

Id. . . .

The key features of an enhanced scrutiny test are: (a) a judicial determination regarding the adequacy of the decisionmaking process employed by the directors, including the information on which the directors based their decision; and (b) a judicial examination of the reasonableness of the directors' action in light of the circumstances then existing. The directors have the burden of proving that they were adequately informed and acted reasonably.

Although an enhanced scrutiny test involves a review of the reasonableness of the substantive merits of a board's actions,[17] a court should not ignore the complexity of the directors' task in a sale of control. There are many business and financial considerations implicated in investigating and selecting the best value reasonably available. The board of directors is the corporate decisionmaking body best equipped to make these judgments. Accordingly, a court applying enhanced judicial scrutiny should be deciding whether the directors made *a reasonable* decision, not *a perfect* decision. If a board selected one of several reasonable alternatives, a court should not second-guess that choice even though it might have decided otherwise or subsequent events may have cast doubt on the board's determination. Thus, courts will not substitute their business judgment for that of the directors, but will determine if the directors' decision was,

---

15. Because the Paramount Board acted unreasonably as to process and result in this sale of control situation, the business judgment rule did not become operative.

16. Before this test is invoked, "the plaintiff must show, and the trial court must find, that the directors of the target company treated one or more of the respective bidders on unequal terms." *Macmillian,* 559 A.2d at 1288.

17. It is to be remembered that, in cases where the traditional business judgment rule is applicable and the board acted with due care, in good faith, and in the honest belief that they are acting in the best interests of the stockholders (which is not this case), the Court gives great deference to the substance of the directors' decision and will not invalidate the decision, will not examine its reasonableness, and "will not substitute our views for those of the board if the latter's decision can be 'attributed to any rational business purpose.'" *Unocal,* 493 A.2d at 949 (*quoting Sinclair Oil Corp. v. Levien,* Del.Supr., 280 A.2d 717, 720 (1971)). *See Aronson,* 473 A.2d at 812.

on balance, within a range of reasonableness. *See Unocal,* 493 A.2d at 955-56; *Macmillan,* 559 A.2d at 1288; *Nixon,* 626 A.2d at 1378.

D.   *REVLON* AND *TIME-WARNER* DISTINGUISHED

The Paramount defendants and Viacom assert that the fiduciary obligations and the enhanced judicial scrutiny discussed above are not implicated in this case in the absence of a "break-up" of the corporation, and that the order granting the preliminary injunction should be reversed. This argument is based on their erroneous interpretation of our decisions in *Revlon* and *Time-Warner.*

In *Revlon,* we reviewed the actions of the board of directors of Revlon, Inc. ("Revlon"), which had rebuffed the overtures of Pantry Pride, Inc. and had instead entered into an agreement with Forstmann Little & Co. ("Forstmann") providing for the acquisition of 100 percent of Revlon's outstanding stock by Forstmann and the subsequent break-up of Revlon. Based on the facts and circumstances present in *Revlon,* we held that "[t]he directors' role changed from defenders of the corporate bastion to auctioneers charged with getting the best price for the stockholders at a sale of the company." We further held that "when a board ends an intense bidding contest on an insubstantial basis, . . . [that] action cannot withstand the enhanced scrutiny which *Unocal* requires of director conduct."

It is true that one of the circumstances bearing on these holdings was the fact that "the break-up of the company . . . had become a reality which even the directors embraced." It does not follow, however, that a "break-up" must be present and "inevitable" before directors are subject to enhanced judicial scrutiny and are required to pursue a transaction that is calculated to produce the best value reasonably available to the stockholders. In fact, we stated in *Revlon* that "when bidders make relatively similar offers, or dissolution of the company becomes inevitable, the directors cannot fulfill their enhanced *Unocal* duties by playing favorites with the contending factions." *Revlon* thus does not hold that an inevitable dissolution or "breakup" is necessary.

The decisions of this Court following *Revlon* reinforced the applicability of enhanced scrutiny and the directors' obligation to seek the best value reasonably available for the stockholders where there is a pending sale of control, regardless of whether or not there is to be a break-up of the corporation. In *Macmillan,* this Court held:

> We stated in *Revlon,* and again here, that *in a sale of corporate control* the responsibility of the directors is to get the highest value reasonably attainable for the shareholders.

559 A.2d at 1288 (*emphasis added*). . . .

Although *Macmillan* and *Barkan* are clear in holding that a change of control imposes on directors the obligation to obtain the best value reasonably available to the stockholders, the Paramount defendants have interpreted our decision in *Time-Warner* as requiring a corporate break-up in order for that obligation to apply. The facts in *Time-Warner,* however, were quite different from the facts of this case, and refute Paramount's position here. In *Time-Warner*, the Chancellor held that there was no change of control in the original stock-for-stock merger between Time and Warner because Time would be owned by a fluid aggregation of unaffiliated stockholders both before and after the merger. . . . Moreover, the transaction actually consummated in *Time-Warner* was not a merger, as originally planned, but a sale of Warner's stock to Time.

In our affirmance of the Court of Chancery's well-reasoned decision, this Court held that "The Chancellor's findings of fact are supported by the record and *his conclusion is correct as a matter of law.*" 571 A.2d at 1150 (*emphasis added*). Nevertheless, the Paramount defendants here have argued that a break-up is a requirement and have focused on the following language in our *Time-Warner* decision:

> However, we premise our rejection of plaintiffs' *Revlon* claim on different grounds, namely, the absence of any substantial evidence to conclude that Time's board, in negotiating with Warner, made the dissolution or break-up of the corporate entity inevitable, as was the case in *Revlon.*
>
> Under Delaware law there are, generally speaking and *without excluding other possibilities,* two circumstances which may implicate *Revlon* duties. The first, and clearer one, is when a corporation *initiates an active bidding process seeking to sell itself* or to effect a business reorganization involving a clear breakup of the company. However, *Revlon* duties may also be triggered where, in response to a bidder's offer, a target abandons its long-term strategy and seeks an alternative transaction involving the breakup of the company.

Id. at 1150 (*emphasis added*) (citation and footnote omitted).

The Paramount defendants have misread the holding of *Time-Warner*. Contrary to their argument, our decision in *Time-Warner* expressly states that the two general scenarios discussed in the above-quoted paragraph are not the *only* instances where "*Revlon* duties" may be implicated. The Paramount defendants' argument totally ignores the phrase "without excluding other possibilities." Moreover, the instant case is clearly within the first general scenario set forth in *Time-Warner*. The Paramount Board, albeit unintentionally, had "initiate[d] an active bidding process seeking to sell itself" by agreeing to sell control of the corporation to Viacom in circumstances where another potential acquiror (QVC) was equally interested in being a bidder.

The Paramount defendants' position that *both* a change of control *and* a break-up are *required* must be rejected. Such a holding would unduly restrict the application *of Revlon,* is inconsistent with this Court's decisions in *Barkan* and *Macmillan,* and has no basis in policy. There are few events that have a more significant impact on the stockholders than a sale of control or a corporate break-up. Each event represents a fundamental (and perhaps irrevocable) change in the nature of the corporate enterprise from a practical standpoint. It is the significance of *each* of these events that justifies: (a) focusing on the directors' obligation to seek the best value reasonably available to the stockholders; and (b) requiring a close scrutiny of board action which could be contrary to the stockholders' interests.

Accordingly, when a corporation undertakes a transaction which will cause: (a) a change in corporate control; or (b) a break-up of the corporate entity, the directors' obligation is to seek the best value reasonably available to the stockholders. This obligation arises because the effect of the Viacom-Paramount transaction, if consummated, is to shift control of Paramount from the public stockholders to a controlling stockholder, Viacom. Neither *Time-Warner* nor any other decision of this Court holds that a "break-up" of the company is essential to give rise to this obligation where there is a sale of control.

III. BREACH OF FIDUCIARY DUTIES BY PARAMOUNT BOARD

We now turn to duties of the Paramount Board under the facts of this case and our conclusions as to the breaches of those duties which warrant injunctive relief.

A. THE SPECIFIC OBLIGATIONS OF THE PARAMOUNT BOARD

Under the facts of this case, the Paramount directors had the obligation: (a) to be diligent and vigilant in examining critically the Paramount-Viacom transaction and the QVC tender offers; (b) to act in good faith; (c) to obtain, and act with due care on, all material information reasonably available, including information necessary to compare the two offers to determine which of these transactions, or an alternative course of action, would provide the best value reasonably available to the stockholders; and (d) to negotiate actively and in good faith with both Viacom and QVC to that end.

Having decided to sell control of the corporation, the Paramount directors were required to evaluate critically whether or not all material aspects of the Paramount-Viacom transaction (separately and in the aggregate) were reasonable and in the best interests of the Paramount stockholders in light of current circumstances, including: the change of control premium, the Stock Option Agreement, the Termination Fee, the coercive nature of both the Viacom and QVC tender offers, the No-Shop Provision, and the proposed disparate use of the Rights Agreement as to the Viacom and QVC tender offers, respectively.

These obligations necessarily implicated various issues, including the questions of whether or not those provisions and other aspects of the Paramount-Viacom transaction (separately and in the aggregate): (a) adversely affected the value provided to the Paramount stockholders; (b) inhibited or encouraged alternative bids; (c) were enforceable contractual obligations in light of the directors' fiduciary duties; and (d) in the end would advance or retard the Paramount directors' obligation to secure for the Paramount stockholders the best value reasonably available under the circumstances.

The Paramount defendants contend that they were precluded by certain contractual provisions, including the No-Shop Provision, from negotiating with QVC or seeking alternatives. Such provisions, whether or not they are presumptively valid in the abstract, may not validly define or limit the directors' fiduciary duties under Delaware law or prevent the Paramount directors from carrying out their fiduciary duties under Delaware law. To the extent such provisions are inconsistent with those duties, they are invalid and unenforceable. *See Revlon,* 506 A.2d at 184-85.

Since the Paramount directors had already decided to sell control, they had an obligation to continue their search for the best value reasonably available to the stockholders. This continuing obligation included the responsibility, at the October 24 board meeting and thereafter, to evaluate critically both the QVC tender offers and the Paramount-Viacom transaction to determine if: (a) the QVC tender offer was, or would continue to be, conditional; (b) the QVC tender offer could be improved; (c) the Viacom tender offer or other aspects of the Paramount-Viacom transaction could be improved; (d) each of the respective offers would be reasonably likely to come to closure, and under what circumstances; (e) other material information was reasonably available for consideration by the Paramount directors; (f) there were viable and realistic alternative courses of action; and (g) the timing constraints could be managed so the directors could consider these matters carefully and deliberately.

B.   THE BREACHES OF FIDUCIARY DUTY BY THE PARAMOUNT BOARD

The Paramount directors made the decision on September 12, 1993, that, in their judgment, a strategic merger with Viacom on the economic terms of the Original Merger Agreement was in the best interests of Paramount and its stockholders. Those terms provided a modest change of control premium to the stockholders. The directors also decided at that time that it was appropriate to agree to certain defensive measures (the Stock Option Agreement, the Termination Fee, and the No-Shop Provision) insisted upon by Viacom as part of that economic transaction. Those defensive measures, coupled with the sale of control and subsequent disparate treatment of competing bidders, implicated the judicial scrutiny of *Unocal, Revlon, Macmillan,* and their progeny. We conclude that the Paramount directors' process was not reasonable, and the result achieved for the stockholders was not reasonable under the circumstances.

When entering into the Original Merger Agreement, and thereafter, the Paramount Board clearly gave insufficient attention to the potential consequences of the defensive measures demanded by Viacom. The Stock Option Agreement had a number of unusual and potentially "draconian"[19] provisions, including the Note Feature and the Put Feature. Furthermore, the Termination Fee, whether or not unreasonable by itself, clearly made Paramount less attractive to other bidders, when coupled with the Stock Option Agreement. Finally, the No-Shop Provision inhibited the Paramount Board's ability to negotiate with other potential bidders, particularly QVC which had already expressed an interest in Paramount.[20]

---

19. The Vice Chancellor so characterized the Stock Option Agreement. Court of Chancery Opinion, 635 A.2d 1245, 1272. We express no opinion whether a stock option agreement of essentially this magnitude, but with a reasonable "cap" and without the Note and Put Features, would be valid or invalid under other circumstances. *See Hecco Ventures v. Sea-Land Corp.,* Del. Ch., C.A. No. 8486, 1986 WL 5840, Jacobs, V.C. (May 19, 1986) (21.7 percent stock option); *In re Vitalink Communications Corp. Shareholders Litig.,* Del. Ch., C.A. No. 12085, Chandler, V.C. (May 16, 1990) (19.9 percent stock option).

20. We express no opinion whether certain aspects of the No-Shop Provision here could be valid in another context. Whether or not it could validly have operated here at an early stage solely to prevent Paramount from actively "shopping" the company, it could not prevent

Throughout the applicable time period, and especially from the first QVC merger proposal on September 20 through the Paramount Board meeting on November 15, QVC's interest in Paramount provided the *opportunity* for the Paramount Board to seek significantly higher value for the Paramount stockholders than that being offered by Viacom. QVC persistently demonstrated its intention to meet and exceed the Viacom offers, and frequently expressed its willingness to negotiate possible further increases.

The Paramount directors had the opportunity in the October 23-24 time frame, when the Original Merger Agreement was renegotiated, to take appropriate action to modify the improper defensive measures as well as to improve the economic terms of the Paramount-Viacom transaction. Under the circumstances existing at that time, it should have been clear to the Paramount Board that the Stock Option Agreement, coupled with the Termination Fee and the No-Shop Clause, were impeding the realization of the best value reasonably available to the Paramount stockholders. Nevertheless, the Paramount Board made no effort to eliminate or modify these counterproductive devices, and instead continued to cling to its vision of a strategic alliance with Viacom. Moreover, based on advice from the Paramount management, the Paramount directors considered the QVC offer to be "conditional" and asserted that they were precluded by the No-Shop Provision from seeking more information from, or negotiating with, QVC.

By November 12, 1993, the value of the revised QVC offer on its face exceeded that of the Viacom offer by over $1 billion at then current values. This significant disparity of value cannot be justified on the basis of the directors' vision of future strategy, primarily because the change of control would supplant the authority of the current Paramount Board to continue to hold and implement their strategic vision in any meaningful way. Moreover, their uninformed process had deprived their strategic vision of much of its credibility.

When the Paramount directors met on November 15 to consider QVC's increased tender offer, they remained prisoners of their own misconceptions and missed opportunities to eliminate the restrictions they had imposed on themselves. Yet, it was not "too late" to reconsider negotiating with QVC. The circumstances existing on November 15 made it clear that the defensive measures, taken as a whole, were problematic: (a) the No-Shop Provision could not define or limit their fiduciary duties; (b) the Stock Option Agreement had become "draconian"; and (c) the Termination Fee, in context with all the circumstances, was similarly deterring the realization of possibly higher bids. Nevertheless, the Paramount directors remained paralyzed by their uninformed

---

the Paramount directors from carrying out their fiduciary duties in considering unsolicited bids or in negotiating for the best value reasonably available to the stockholders. *Macmillan,* 559 A.2d at 1287. As we said in *Barkan:* "Where a board has no reasonable basis upon which to judge the adequacy of a contemplated transaction, a no-shop restriction gives rise to the inference that the board seeks to forestall competing bids." 567 A.2d at 1288. *See also Revlon,* 506 A.2d at 184 (holding that "[t]he no-shop provision, like the lock-up option, while not *per se* illegal, is impermissible under the *Unocal* standards when a board's primary duty becomes that of an auctioneer responsible for selling the company to the highest bidder").

belief that the QVC offer was "illusory." This final opportunity to negotiate on the stockholders' behalf and to fulfill their obligation to seek the best value reasonably available was thereby squandered.

IV.   VIACOM'S CLAIM OF VESTED CONTRACT RIGHTS

Viacom argues that it had certain "vested" contract rights with respect to the No-Shop Provision and the Stock Option Agreement. In effect, Viacom's argument is that the Paramount directors could enter into an agreement in violation of their fiduciary duties and then render Paramount, and ultimately its stockholders, liable for failing to carry out an agreement in violation of those duties. Viacom's protestations about vested rights are without merit. This Court has found that those defensive measures were improperly designed to deter potential bidders, and that such measures do not meet the reasonableness test to which they must be subjected. They are consequently invalid and unenforceable under the facts of this case.

The No-Shop Provision could not validly define or limit the fiduciary duties of the Paramount directors. To the extent that a contract, or a provision thereof, purports to require a board to act or not act in such a fashion as to limit the exercise of fiduciary duties, it is invalid and unenforceable. Despite the arguments of Paramount and Viacom to the contrary, the Paramount directors could not contract away their fiduciary obligations. Since the No-Shop Provision was invalid, Viacom never had any vested contract rights in the provision.

As discussed previously, the Stock Option Agreement contained several "draconian" aspects, including the Note Feature and the Put Feature. While we have held that lock-up options are not *per se* illegal, *see Revlon*, 506 A.2d at 183, no options with similar features have ever been upheld by this Court. Under the circumstances of this case, the Stock Option Agreement clearly is invalid. Accordingly, Viacom never had any vested contract rights in that Agreement.

Viacom, a sophisticated party with experienced legal and financial advisors, knew of (and in fact demanded) the unreasonable features of the Stock Option Agreement. It cannot be now heard to argue that it obtained vested contract rights by negotiating and obtaining contractual provisions from a board acting in violation of its fiduciary duties. As the Nebraska Supreme Court said in rejecting a similar argument in *ConAgra, Inc. v. Cargill, Inc.*, 222 Neb. 136, 382 N.W.2d 576, 587-88 (1986), "To so hold, it would seem, would be to get the shareholders coming and going." Likewise, we reject Viacom's arguments and hold that its fate must rise or fall, and in this instance fall, with the determination that the actions of the Paramount Board were invalid.

V.   CONCLUSION

The realization of the best value reasonably available to the stockholders became the Paramount directors' primary obligation under these facts in light of the change of control. That obligation was not satisfied, and the Paramount Board's process was deficient. The directors' initial hope and expectation for a strategic alliance with Viacom was allowed to dominate their decisionmaking process to the point where the arsenal of defensive measures established at the outset was perpetuated (not modified or eliminated) when the situation was dramatically altered. QVC's unsolicited bid presented the opportunity for significantly greater value for the stockholders and enhanced negotiating leverage for the directors. Rather than seizing those opportunities, the Paramount directors chose to wall themselves off from material information which was reasonably available and to hide behind the defensive measures as a rationalization for refusing to negotiate with QVC or seeking other alternatives. Their view of the strategic alliance likewise became an empty rationalization as the opportunities for higher value for the stockholders continued to develop. . . .

For the reasons set forth herein, the November 24, 1993, Order of the Court of Chancery has been AFFIRMED, and this matter has been REMANDED for proceedings consistent herewith, as set forth in the December 9, 1993, Order of this Court.

QUESTIONS

1. Why does the proposed transaction between Paramount and Viacom constitute a change of control? Why is it legally significant that this transaction involves a change of control?

2. How does the Delaware Supreme Court reconcile the reasoning of its decision in *Time-Warner* with the result that it reaches in this case and the reasoning that it uses to support this result? *Query*: In light of the Court's holding in this case, was there a sale of control in *Time-Warner*?

3. What happened to the duties imposed on the board under *Revlon*? After *QVC*, what triggers the board's duties under *Revlon*? In other words, based on the result reached in this case, when is the company in the "*Revlon* mode"?

4. What standard of judicial review should apply to the original decision of the Paramount board to merge with Viacom? Business judgement rule? *Unocal*? *Revlon*? Entire fairness?

NOTES

1. ***Dual-Class Stock Structure.***   The facts of this case reflect another type of shark repellant (i.e., a charter provision that operates as an antitakeover device). Viacom is a publicly traded, Delaware-based company that has two classes of stock outstanding: Class A shares and Class B shares. As described in the case, Sumner Redstone, Viacom's chairman and CEO, controls approximately 85 percent of the company's voting Class A shares and approximately 70 percent of the company's non-voting Class B stock. *Query*: How does this capital structure operate as an antitakeover device? It is worth noting that this type of dual-class structure is not without some controversy. *See generally*, Stephen Bainbridge, *The Short Life and Resurrection of SEC Rule 19c-4*, 69 WASH. U. L.Q. 565 (1991); and George W. Dent, *Dual Class Capitalization: A Reply to Professor Seligman*, 54 GEO. WASH. L. REV. 725 (1986). In fact, during the go-go years of

M&A activity in the 1980s, the SEC adopted a one-share/one-vote rule (Rule 19c-4), which was immediately challenged in the courts as exceeding the SEC's authority to regulate stock exchange practices and as an encroachment on the province of state corporate law. The rule was ultimately invalidated in *Business Roundtable v. SEC*, 905 F. 2d 406 (D.C. Cir. 1990), although, in the end, the SEC's view prevailed. Under considerable pressure from the SEC, among others, the NYSE voluntarily agreed to adopt a one-share/one-vote standard similar to Rule 19c-4. *See* NYSE Listed Company Manual §313.10. However, the NYSE's provision includes a "grandfather clause" for companies with a dual-class voting structure in place at the time the company lists its shares for trading with the NYSE. As a result, many companies have taken advantage of this grandfather clause by going public with a dual-class voting structure in place at the time of the company's initial public offering (IPO), as was the case with Google's IPO back in 2004, as just one high-profile example.

2. *Recent Criticism of the Dual-Class Capital Structure.* In 2004, Google went public with a dual-class capital structure in place that gave co-founders Larry Page and Sergey Brin two-thirds of the voting power. "While Google had to overcome opposition [from investment bankers and prospective investors] at the time, [Mark] Zukerberg [faced] less resistance [at the time Facebook, Inc. went public in 2011]." Jeff Green and Ari Levy, *Zuckerberg Grip Becomes New Normal in Silicon Valley*, May 7, 2012, *available at* http://bloomberg.com/news/print/2012-05-07/zuckerberg-stock-grip-becomes-new-normal-in-silicon-valley-tech.html. While other technology companies (such as Groupon, Inc., Zillow Inc., and Linked In, Corp.) have since gone public with dual-class capital structures in place, arguments over the merits of these capital structures have been "heating up":

> as institutional investors have complained about the increasing number of IPO companies (Facebook, Groupon, Zynga being the most notable) who have gone public as dual class stock companies[, thereby] limiting the rights and influence of shareholders and turning them into economic bystanders.

* * *

Institutional investors raise the point that dual class shares limit their ability to press boards and managements to make corrections or changes through the use of the shareholder vote. Those limits, investors allege, create an economic imbalance between management insiders, who usually hold the high voting rights shares and ordinary shareholders whose voting rights are essentially proscribed. Thus insulated, the board and management may engage in (or ignore) value destroying behavior—i.e., News Corp in the phone-hacking scandal or company insiders whose proposed transactions may appear, to some investors, to lack value for all shareholders and could be seen as questionable.

Companies with dual class structures argue that the insulation provides boards and management with an ability to plan and execute for the long-term, lessening the harsh power of quarterly earnings analysis and the short-term challenge of "making the numbers". Dual class stock schemes also create a permanent level of protection against hostile takeovers by short-term holders. The advocates for the use of dual structures state that institutions with concerns about stock performance or shareholder rights can simply sell the stock and walk away.

Both sides cite studies defending their points of view. Governance advocates claim that companies with dual class structures trade at a discount to their non-dual class peers and create less value for ordinary shareholders in the long-term. Dual class companies point to their stock performance refuting the charge they underperform or are perceived by the market as discounted.

In reality institutional investors—the mutual fund complexes, the large public pension funds and the institutional asset managers—with their large pools of indexed capital—are limited in the nature of the responses they can undertake. Simply selling the stock, the "Wall Street Walk" is not a viable option.

Divestment is a difficult process especially for the public pension funds that would need to manage the cost of financial and legal opinions, and lost opportunity cost to the fund's equity portfolios.

So the question, from the governance advocate perspective, is what to do about this trend? Well the answer may be, as posited by some investor[s], to force changes in regulation via Congress, the SEC, the stock exchanges or at the index creators, the Russell Indexes.

What are the prospects for those changes? [Legislative changes by Congress and regulatory changes via either the SEC or the stock exchanges remain highly doubtful following the November 2012 presidential election] . . . [Consequently], the new campaign against dual class structures is one we will be hearing more about in the [future].

Francis H. Bryd, *Dual Class Share Structures: The Next Campaign*, Harvard Law School Forum on Corporate Governance & Financial Regulation (Sept. 16, 2012 10:18 a.m.), *available at* http://blogs.law.harvard.edu/corpgov/2012/09/16/dual-class-share-structures-the-next-campaign/.

The next case is the Delaware Supreme Court's most recent pronouncement on *Revlon* issues. In the course of its opinion, the court provides important insight and guidance about what a board *must* do in order to satisfy its *Revlon* duties.

Lyondell Chemical Co. v. Ryan
970 A.2d 235 (Del. 2009)

BERGER, Justice.

We accepted this interlocutory appeal to consider a claim that directors failed to act in good faith in conducting the sale of their company. The Court of Chancery decided that "unexplained inaction" permits a reasonable inference that the directors may have consciously disregarded their fiduciary duties. The trial court expressed concern about the speed with which the transaction was consummated; the directors' failure to negotiate better terms; and their failure to seek potentially superior deals. But the record establishes that the directors were disinterested and independent; that they were generally aware of the company's value and its prospects; and that they considered the offer, under the time constraints imposed by the buyer, with the assistance of financial and legal advisors. At most, this record creates a triable issue of fact on the question of whether the directors exercised due care. There is no evidence, however, from which to infer that the directors knowingly ignored their responsibilities, thereby breaching their duty of loyalty. Accordingly, the directors are entitled to the entry of summary judgment.

FACTUAL AND PROCEDURAL BACKGROUND

Before the merger at issue, Lyondell Chemical Company ("Lyondell") was the third largest independent, publicly traded chemical company in North America. Dan Smith ("Smith") was Lyondell's Chairman and CEO. Lyondell's other ten directors were independent and many were, or had been, CEOs of other large, publicly traded companies. Basell AF ("Basell") is a privately held Luxembourg company owned by Leonard Blavatnik ("Blavatnik") through his ownership of Access Industries. Basell is in the business of polyolefin technology, production and marketing.

In April 2006, Blavatnik told Smith that Basell was interested in acquiring Lyondell. A few months later, Basell sent a letter to Lyondell's board offering $26.50-$28.50 per share. Lyondell determined that the price was inadequate and that it was not interested in selling. During the next year, Lyondell prospered and no potential acquirors expressed interest in the company. In May 2007, an Access affiliate filed a Schedule 13D with the Securities and Exchange Commission disclosing its right to acquire an 8.3% block of Lyondell stock owned by Occidental Petroleum Corporation. The Schedule 13D also disclosed Blavatnik's interest in possible transactions with Lyondell.

In response to the Schedule 13D, the Lyondell board immediately convened a special meeting. The board recognized that the 13D signaled to the market that the company was "in play,"[3] but the directors decided to take a "wait and see" approach. A few days later, Apollo Management, L.P. contacted Smith to suggest a management-led LBO, but Smith rejected that proposal. In late June 2007, Basell announced that it had entered into a $9.6 billion merger agreement with Huntsman Corporation ("Huntsman"), a specialty chemical company. Basell apparently reconsidered, however, after Hexion Specialty Chemicals, Inc. made a topping bid for Huntsman. Faced with competition for Huntsman, Blavatnik returned his attention to Lyondell.

On July 9, 2007, Blavatnik met with Smith to discuss an all-cash deal at $40 per share. Smith responded that $40 was too low, and Blavatnik raised his offer to $44-$45 per share. Smith told Blavatnik that he would present the proposal to the board, but that he thought the board would reject it. Smith advised Blavatnik to give Lyondell his best offer, since Lyondell really was not on the market. The meeting ended at that point, but Blavatnik asked Smith to call him later in the day. When Smith called, Blavatnik offered to pay $48 per share. Under Blavatnik's proposal, Basell would require no financing contingency, but Lyondell would have to agree to a $400 million break-up fee and sign a merger agreement by July 16, 2007.

---

3. On the day that the 13D was made public, Lyondell's stock went from $33 to $37 per share.

Smith called a special meeting of the Lyondell board on July 10, 2007 to review and consider Basell's offer. The meeting lasted slightly less than one hour, during which time the board reviewed valuation material that had been prepared by Lyondell management for presentation at the regular board meeting, which was scheduled for the following day. The board also discussed the Basell offer, the status of the Huntsman merger, and the likelihood that another party might be interested in Lyondell. The board instructed Smith to obtain a written offer from Basell and more details about Basell's financing.

Blavatnik agreed to the board's request, but also made an additional demand. Basell had until July 11 to make a higher bid for Huntsman, so Blavatnik asked Smith to find out whether the Lyondell board would provide a firm indication of interest in his proposal by the end of that day. The Lyondell board met on July 11, again for less than one hour, to consider the Basell proposal and how it compared to the benefits of remaining independent. The board decided that it was interested, authorized the retention of Deutsche Bank Securities, Inc. ("Deutsche Bank") as its financial advisor, and instructed Smith to negotiate with Blavatnik.

Basell then announced that it would not raise its offer for Huntsman, and Huntsman terminated the Basell merger agreement. From July 12-July 15 the parties negotiated the terms of a Lyondell merger agreement; Basell conducted due diligence; Deutsche Bank prepared a "fairness" opinion; and Lyondell conducted its regularly scheduled board meeting. The Lyondell board discussed the Basell proposal again on July 12, and later instructed Smith to try to negotiate better terms. Specifically, the board wanted a higher price, a go-shop provision,[4] and a reduced break-up fee. As the trial court noted, Blavatnik was "incredulous." He had offered his best price, which was a substantial premium, and the deal had to be concluded on his schedule. As a sign of good faith, however, Blavatnik agreed to reduce the break-up fee from $400 million to $385 million.

On July 16, 2007, the board met to consider the Basell merger agreement. Lyondell's management, as well as its financial and legal advisers, presented reports analyzing the merits of the deal. The advisors explained that, notwithstanding the no-shop provision in the merger agreement, Lyondell would be able to consider any superior proposals that might be made because of the "fiduciary out" provision. In addition, Deutsche Bank reviewed valuation models derived from "bullish" and more conservative financial projections. Several of those valuations yielded a range that did not even reach $48 per share, and Deutsche Bank opined that the proposed merger price was fair. Indeed, the bank's managing director described the merger price as "an absolute home run." Deutsche Bank also identified other possible acquirors and explained why it believed no other entity would top Basell's offer. After considering the presentations, the Lyondell board voted to approve the merger and recommend it to the stockholders. At a special stockholders' meeting held on November 20, 2007, the merger was approved by more than 99% of the voted shares. . . .

---

4. A "go-shop" provision allows the seller to seek other buyers for a specified period after the agreement is signed.

DISCUSSION

The class action complaint challenging this $13 billion cash merger alleges that the Lyondell directors breached their "fiduciary duties of care, loyalty and candor . . . and . . . put their personal interests ahead of the interests of the Lyondell shareholders." Specifically, the complaint alleges that: 1) the merger price was grossly insufficient; 2) the directors were motivated to approve the merger for their own self-interest;[5] 3) the process by which the merger was negotiated was flawed; 4) the directors agreed to unreasonable deal protection provisions; and 5) the preliminary proxy statement omitted numerous material facts. The trial court rejected all claims except those directed at the process by which the directors sold the company and the deal protection provisions in the merger agreement.

The remaining claims are but two aspects of a single claim, under *Revlon v. MacAndrews & Forbes Holdings, Inc.,*[6] that the directors failed to obtain the best available price in selling the company. As the trial court correctly noted, *Revlon* did not create any new fiduciary duties. It simply held that the "board must perform its fiduciary duties in the service of a specific objective: maximizing the sale price of the enterprise."[7] The trial court reviewed the record, and found that Ryan might be able to prevail at trial on a claim that the Lyondell directors breached their duty of care. But Lyondell's charter includes an exculpatory provision, pursuant to 8 *Del. C.* §102(b)(7), protecting the directors from personal liability for breaches of the duty of care. Thus, this case turns on whether any arguable shortcomings on the part of the Lyondell directors also implicate their duty of loyalty, a breach of which is not exculpated. Because the trial court determined that the board was independent and was not motivated by self-interest or ill will, the sole issue is whether the directors are entitled to summary judgment on the claim that they breached their duty of loyalty by failing to act in good faith.

This Court examined "good faith"[8] in two recent decisions. In *In re Walt Disney Co. Deriv. Litig.,*[9] the Court discussed the range of conduct that might be characterized as bad faith, and concluded that bad faith encompasses not only an intent to harm but also intentional dereliction of duty:

> [A]t least three different categories of fiduciary behavior are candidates for the "bad faith" pejorative label. The first category involves so-called "subjective

---

5. The directors' alleged financial interest is the fact that they would receive cash for their stock options.

6. 506 A.2d 173, 182 (Del. 1986).

7. *Malpiede v. Townson,* 780 A.2d 1075, 1083 (Del. 2001).

8. Our corporate decisions tend to use the terms "bad faith" and "failure to act in good faith" interchangeably, although in a different context we noted that, "[t]he two concepts-bad faith and conduct not in good faith are not necessarily identical." 25 *Massachusetts Avenue Property LLC v. Liberty Property Limited Partnership,* Del.Supr., No. 188, 2008, Order at p. 5 (November 25, 2008). For purposes of this appeal, we draw no distinction between the terms.

9. 906 A.2d 27, [at 64-66] (Del. 2006).

bad faith," that is, fiduciary conduct motivated by an actual intent to do harm. . . . [S]uch conduct constitutes classic, quintessential bad faith. . . .

The second category of conduct, which is at the opposite end of the spectrum, involves lack of due care—that is, fiduciary action taken solely by reason of gross negligence and without any malevolent intent. . . . [W]e address the issue of whether gross negligence (including failure to inform one's self of available material facts), without more, can also constitute bad faith. The answer is clearly no.

* * *

That leaves the third category of fiduciary conduct, which falls in between the first two categories. . . . This third category is what the Chancellor's definition of bad faith—intentional dereliction of duty, a conscious disregard for one's responsibilities—is intended to capture. The question is whether such misconduct is properly treated as a non-exculpable, nonindemnifiable violation of the fiduciary duty to act in good faith. In our view, it must be. . . .

The *Disney* decision expressly disavowed any attempt to provide a comprehensive or exclusive definition of "bad faith."

A few months later, in *Stone v. Ritter*,[11] this Court addressed the concept of bad faith in the context of an "oversight" claim. We adopted the standard articulated ten years earlier, in *In re Caremark Int'l Deriv. Litig.*:[12]

[W]here a claim of directorial liability for corporate loss is predicated upon ignorance of liability creating activities within the corporation . . . only a sustained or systematic failure of the board to exercise oversight—such as an utter failure to attempt to assure a reasonable information and reporting system exists—will establish the lack of good faith that is a necessary condition to liability.

The *Stone* Court explained that the *Caremark* standard is fully consistent with the *Disney* definition of bad faith. *Stone* also clarified any possible ambiguity about the directors' mental state, holding that "imposition of liability requires a showing that the directors knew that they were not discharging their fiduciary obligations."[13]

The Court of Chancery recognized these legal principles, but it denied summary judgment in order to obtain a more complete record before deciding whether the directors had acted in bad faith. Under other circumstances, deferring a decision to expand the record would be appropriate. Here, however, the trial court reviewed the existing record under a mistaken view of the applicable law. Three factors contributed to that mistake. First, the trial court imposed *Revlon* duties on the Lyondell directors before they either had decided to sell, or before the sale had become inevitable. Second, the court read *Revlon* and its progeny as creating a set of requirements that must be satisfied during the sale process. Third, the trial court equated an arguably imperfect attempt to carry out *Revlon* duties with a knowing disregard of one's duties that constitutes bad faith.

---

11. 911 A.2d 362 (Del. 2006).
12. 698 A.2d 959, 971 (Del. Ch. 1996).
13. *Stone*, 911 A.2d at 370.

. . . The Court of Chancery identified several undisputed facts that would support the entry of judgment in favor of the Lyondell directors: the directors were "active, sophisticated, and generally aware of the value of the Company and the conditions of the markets in which the Company operated." They had reason to believe that no other bidders would emerge, given the price Basell had offered and the limited universe of companies that might be interested in acquiring Lyondell's unique assets. Smith negotiated the price up from $40 to $48 per share-a price that Deutsche Bank opined was fair. Finally, no other acquiror expressed interest during the four months between the merger announcement and the stockholder vote.

Other facts, however, led the trial court to "question the adequacy of the Board's knowledge and efforts. . . ." After the Schedule 13D was filed in May, the directors apparently took no action to prepare for a possible acquisition proposal. The merger was negotiated and finalized in less than one week, during which time the directors met for a total of only seven hours to consider the matter. The directors did not seriously press Blavatnik for a better price, nor did they conduct even a limited market check. Moreover, although the deal protections were not unusual or preclusive, the trial court was troubled by "the Board's decision to grant considerable protection to a deal that may not have been adequately vetted under *Revlon*."

The trial court found the directors' failure to act during the two months after the filing of the Basell Schedule 13D critical to its analysis of their good faith. The court pointedly referred to the directors' "two months of slothful indifference despite *knowing* that the Company was in play," and the fact that they "languidly awaited overtures from potential suitors. . . ." In the end, the trial court found that it was this "failing" that warranted denial of their motion for summary judgment: . . .

The problem with the trial court's analysis is that *Revlon* duties do not arise simply because a company is "in play."[23] The duty to seek the best available price applies only when a company embarks on a transaction—on its own initiative or in response to an unsolicited offer—that will result in a change of control. Basell's Schedule 13D did put the Lyondell directors, and the market in general, on notice that Basell was interested in acquiring Lyondell. The directors responded by promptly holding a special meeting to consider whether Lyondell should take any action. The directors decided that they would neither put the company up for sale nor institute defensive measures to fend off a possible hostile offer. Instead, they decided to take a "wait and see" approach. That decision was an entirely appropriate exercise of the directors' business judgment. The time for action under *Revlon* did not begin until July 10, 2007, when the directors began negotiating the sale of Lyondell.

The Court of Chancery focused on the directors' two months of inaction, when it should have focused on the one week during which they considered Basell's offer. During that one week, the directors met several times; their CEO tried to negotiate better terms; they evaluated Lyondell's value, the price offered and the likelihood of obtaining a better price; and then the directors approved

---

23. *Paramount Communications, Inc. v. Time, Inc.*, 571 A.2d 1140, 1151 (Del. 1989).

the merger. The trial court acknowledged that the directors' conduct during those seven days might not demonstrate anything more than lack of due care.[25] But the court remained skeptical about the directors' good faith—at least on the present record. That lingering concern was based on the trial court's synthesis of the *Revlon* line of cases, which led it to the erroneous conclusion that directors must follow one of several courses of action to satisfy their *Revlon* duties.

There is only one *Revlon* duty—to "[get] the best price for the stockholders at a sale of the company."[26] No court can tell directors exactly how to accomplish that goal, because they will be facing a unique combination of circumstances, many of which will be outside their control. As we noted in *Barkan v. Amsted Industries, Inc.,* "there is no single blueprint that a board must follow to fulfill its duties."[27] That said, our courts have highlighted both the positive and negative aspects of various boards' conduct under *Revlon*.[28] The trial court drew several principles from those cases: directors must "engage actively in the sale process," and they must confirm that they have obtained the best available price either by conducting an auction, by conducting a market check, or by demonstrating "an impeccable knowledge of the market."

The Lyondell directors did not conduct an auction or a market check, and they did not satisfy the trial court that they had the "impeccable" market knowledge that the court believed was necessary to excuse their failure to pursue one of the first two alternatives. As a result, the Court of Chancery was unable to conclude that the directors had met their burden under *Revlon*. In evaluating the totality of the circumstances, even on this limited record, we would be inclined to hold otherwise. But we would not question the trial court's decision to seek additional evidence if the issue were whether the directors had exercised due care. Where, as here, the issue is whether the directors failed to act in good faith, the analysis is very different, and the existing record mandates the entry of judgment in favor of the directors.

As discussed above, bad faith will be found if a "fiduciary intentionally fails to act in the face of a known duty to act, demonstrating a conscious disregard for his duties."[31] The trial court decided that the *Revlon* sale process must follow one of three courses, and that the Lyondell directors did not discharge that "known set of [*Revlon*] 'duties'." But, as noted, there are no legally prescribed steps that directors must follow to satisfy their *Revlon* duties. Thus, the directors' failure to take any specific steps during the sale process could not have demonstrated a conscious disregard of their duties. More importantly, there is a vast difference between an inadequate or flawed effort to carry out fiduciary duties and a conscious disregard for those duties.

---

25. [*Ryan v. Lyondell Chemical Co.,* WL 4174038 at *4 (Del. Ch. 2008).]

26. *Revlon,* 506 A.2d at 182.

27. 567 A.2d 1279, 1286 (Del. 1989).

28. *See, e.g.: Barkan v. Amsted Industries, Inc.,* 567 A.2d at 1287 (Directors need not conduct a market check if they have reliable basis for belief that price offered is best possible.); *Paramount Communications, Inc. v. QVC Network, Inc.,* 637 A.2d 34, 49 (Del. 1994) (No-shop provision impermissibly interfered with directors' ability to negotiate with another known bidder); *In re Netsmart Technologies, Inc., Shareholders Litig.,* 924 A.2d 171, 199 (Del. Ch. 2007) (Plaintiff likely to succeed on claim based on board's failure to consider strategic buyers.)

31. *Disney* at 67.

Directors' decisions must be reasonable, not perfect.[33] "In the transactional context, [an] extreme set of facts [is] required to sustain a disloyalty claim premised on the notion that disinterested directors were intentionally disregarding their duties."[34] The trial court denied summary judgment because the Lyondell directors' "unexplained inaction" prevented the court from determining that they had acted in good faith. But, if the directors failed to do all that they should have under the circumstances, they breached their duty of care. Only if they knowingly and completely failed to undertake their responsibilities would they breach their duty of loyalty. The trial court approached the record from the wrong perspective. Instead of questioning whether disinterested, independent directors did everything that they (arguably) should have done to obtain the best sale price, the inquiry should have been whether those directors utterly failed to attempt to obtain the best sale price.

Viewing the record in this manner leads to only one possible conclusion. The Lyondell directors met several times to consider Basell's premium offer. They were generally aware of the value of their company and they knew the chemical company market. The directors solicited and followed the advice of their financial and legal advisors. They attempted to negotiate a higher offer even though all the evidence indicates that Basell had offered a "blowout" price. Finally, they approved the merger agreement, because "it was simply too good not to pass along [to the stockholders] for their consideration." We assume, as we must on summary judgment, that the Lyondell directors did absolutely nothing to prepare for Basell's offer, and that they did not even consider conducting a market check before agreeing to the merger. Even so, this record clearly establishes that the Lyondell directors did not breach their duty of loyalty by failing to act in good faith. In concluding otherwise, the Court of Chancery reversibly erred.

CONCLUSION

Based on the foregoing, the decision of the Court of Chancery is reversed and this matter is remanded for entry of judgment in favor of the Lyondell directors. Jurisdiction is not retained.

NOTE

The Implications of **Lyondell** *for Future M&A Transactions.* The legal significance of the Delaware Supreme Court's decision in *Lyondell* has been the subject of considerable commentary. In the words of one leading M&A law firm:

> In an important decision, the Delaware Supreme Court [in *Lyondell*] has firmly rejected post-merger stockholder claims that directors failed to act in good faith in selling the company, even if it were assumed that they did nothing to prepare for an impending offer and did not even consider conducting a market check before entering into a merger agreement (at a substantial premium to market)

---

33. *Paramount Communications, Inc. v. QVC Network, Inc.,* 637 A.2d at 45.
34. *In re Lear Corp. S'holder Litig.,* 2008 WL 4053221 at *11 (Del.Ch.).

containing a no-shop provision and a 3.2% break-up fee. The *en banc* decision, authored by Justice Berger, is a sweeping rejection of attempts to impose personal liability on directors for their actions in responding to acquisition proposals, and reaffirms the board's wide discretion in managing a sale process.

* * *

The key to the Supreme Court's opinion was its unremitting focus on the effect of the charter exculpation provision [*see* Del. §102(b)(7)] foreclosing liability for duty of care claims, leaving only the possibility of duty of loyalty claims based on a failure to act in good faith—which requires a court to find a "conscious disregard" of "known duties." [*See Stone v. Ritter*, 911 A.2d 362 (Del. 2006); and *In re Caremark Int'l. Derivative Litigation*, 698 A.2d 959 (Del. Ch. 1996).] The Court made clear that hindsight debate about whether directors should have done something more or differently will not suffice to create a possibility of posttransaction personal liability . . .

The Supreme Court's opinion is a powerful statement that courts appreciate the complex decisions directors must make in selling the company, and will not allow post hoc process attacks to be deemed indicative of bad faith. Stockholders can still seek a preliminary injunction against a merger. But disinterested, independent directors will not face the threat of personal monetary liability unless truly egregious circumstances are shown in which the directors consciously disregard their known duties by utterly failing to attempt to obtain the best available sale price.

In this fundamental sense, the Supreme Court's decision [in *Lyondell*] fully implements Delaware's legislative policy, reflected in Section 102(b)(7), of protecting directors from personal liability for what are essentially duty of care claims, whether pleaded in that form or not. The need for the legislation was itself created by the Court's 1985 decision in *Smith v. Van Gorkom*, imposing person liability on directors for failing to devote sufficient care to approval of an arms-length, premium-to-market merger agreement subject to an open stockholder vote. *Lyondell* shows that the legislative response to *Van Gorkom* has worked as intended: the Delaware courts will not permit plaintiffs to plead around it.

Theodore N. Mirvis, et al., *Delaware Supreme Court Rejects Claims Against Directors Challenging Sale Process* (Wachtell Lipton, Rosen, & Katz, law firm memo, March 26, 2009) at p. 2 (copy on file with author). *Query*: What do you think—did the Delaware Supreme Court reach the correct result in *Lyondell*? Is the decision in *Lyondell* consistent with the result and reasoning of the Delaware Supreme Court's decision in *Smith v. Van Gorkom*? Is the decision in *Lyondell* consistent with the standards established in *Revlon* and its progeny?

F. *Board Approval of Acquisition Agreements and the Use of "Deal Protection Devices"*

Deal protection measures come in various forms, including no-shop clauses, lock-up options, and termination fees (also referred to as *break-up fees*). Generally speaking, the essence of these deal protection measures is to allow Bidder Co. to prevent the Target Co. board from taking any steps that would encourage a competing bidder to come forward with a superior offer for Target. With the rise of strategic mergers in the M&A market of the 1990s, the use of deal protection measures took on increasing importance. This leads to an inherent tension because the board of Target owes a fiduciary duty to the company's shareholders; the board's fiduciary obligations may constrain the board's ability to agree to limit its conduct in the manner that Bidder demands under the terms of whatever deal protection device Bidder proposes to include in the parties' acquisition agreement. At the same time, the dilemma from the Bidder's perspective is that Target may terminate the fully negotiated transaction in the event that a better offer should appear—what is known as a *topping bid*. This leads to the very real concern that Bidder may invest considerable resources in negotiating a deal, incurring expenses to perform the necessary due diligence, retaining and paying legal and financial advisors—only to see the deal evaporate once a topping bid appears later. So not surprisingly, Bidder will generally seek some form of protection to guard against this disappointment.

In the case of a publicly traded Target, the use of deal protection devices is an important element of modern M&A deals in that these devices allow Bidder to address the inherent risk that the deal will not close (i.e., the risk of non-consummation). In the case of M&A transactions, there are a number of reasons that a fully negotiated transaction may not close, not the least of which is that Target shareholders may decide not to approve the transaction. Other recurring risks of non-consummation are summarized in the following excerpt:

> . . . [Deal protection measures, including lock-ups and termination fees] developed as a response to the substantial risk that the parties entering a negotiated merger agreement will not consummate the merger. This risk is inherent in the negotiated acquisition process. A two to four month delay typically transpires between the signing of the merger agreement and the closing[3], which provides ample opportunity for intervening events to hinder the merger. Changes in the business environment occasionally may lead the target board to renege. Competition is an even greater risk. Another other party may approach the target board with an alternative, presumably higher-priced, acquisition proposal; indeed, target management might initiate negotiations with a second party before presenting the initial bid to the shareholders. Alternatively, a competing bidder may directly present its proposal to target shareholders by making a tender offer for their shares.
>
> The substantial risk of nonconsummation is especially important to the prospective acquirer, which incurs substantial up-front costs in making the initial offer. Depending on the circumstances, the initial bidder may incur significant search costs to identify an appropriate target. Once an appropriate target is identified, preparation of the offer typically requires the services of outside legal, accounting, and financial advisers. If the bidder will pay all or part of the

---

3. This delay period is necessitated by, among other things, the need to obtain shareholder, and perhaps also regulatory, approval, prepare and file a detailed proxy statement, register and list any securities to be issued in connection with the acquisition, and take other necessary steps. Although the delay between signing the merger agreement and closing the transaction can be reduced by efficient execution of those steps, it cannot be eliminated in light of various statutory time limits. *See, e.g.,* 17 C.F.R. § 240.14a-6(a) (1990) (proxy statement may not be mailed until at least 10 days after the preliminary statement is filed with the Securities and Exchange Commission (SEC)); DEL. CODE ANN., tit. 8, § 251(c) (1988) (requiring at least 20 days notice before shareholder meeting may be held). . . .

purchase price from sources other than cash reserves, a likely scenario, the bidder also incurs commitment and other financing fees. Finally, the bidder may pass up other acquisition opportunities while negotiating with the target. Although the bidder will recover these up-front costs if the parties consummate the merger, the emergence of a competing bid may eliminate or reduce the bidder's expected return on its sunk costs[.]

Stephen M. Bainbridge, *Exclusive Merger Agreements and Lock-Ups in Negotiated Corporate Acquisitions*, 75 MINN. L. REV. 239, 241-243 (1990). Today Bidders address this inherent risk of non-consummation by seeking to include deal protection provisions as part of the acquisition agreement, which are (broadly speaking) designed to "discourage[] the target board from reneging on the . . . agreement or, at the least, reimburse[] the . . . bidder's up-front costs if the parties do not consummate the merger." *Id.*

In an early (non-Delaware) case, *Jewel Companies, Inc. v. Pay Less Drug Stores Northwest, Inc.*, 741 F.2d. 1555 (9th Cir. 1984), the court struggled with the (rather metaphysical) question of the "legal effect" of "a merger agreement [including any deal protection provisions] entered into by the boards of two corporations . . . *prior* to shareholder approval." *Id.* at 1560 (*emphasis added*). The Ninth Circuit concluded that the merger provisions of the California Corporations Code "contemplate[] that the boards of two corporations seeking [to merge] . . . may enter into a *binding* merger agreement governing the conduct of the parties pending submission of the agreement to the shareholders for approval." *Id.* at 1561 (*emphasis added*). Although the merger transaction could not be validly consummated without obtaining the necessary the shareholder approval, the Ninth Circuit concluded that:

> In light of California's statutory scheme preserving the board's traditional management function in the case of corporate control transactions, we see no reason to conclude that the drafters of the Corporate Code intended to deprive a corporate board of the authority to agree to refrain from negotiating or accepting competing offers until the shareholders have considered an initial offer [a provision that today is widely referred to as a "no-shop" clause]. . . .
>
> We do, of course, recognize that a board may not lawfully divest itself of its fiduciary obligations in a contract . . . However, to permit a board of directors to decide that a proposed merger transaction is in the best interests of its shareholders at a given point in time, and to agree to refrain from entering into competing contracts until the shareholders consider the proposal, does not conflict in any way with the board's fiduciary obligation . . .
>
> . . . While the board can bind itself to exert its best efforts to consummate the merger under California law,[11] it can only bind the corporation temporarily, and in limited areas,[12] pending shareholder approval. The shareholders retain

---

11. It is not necessary for us to delineate the full scope of a board's "best efforts" obligation. The term does, however, include at a minimum a duty to act in good faith toward the party to whom it owes a "best efforts" obligation.

12. The board can bind the corporation temporarily with provisions like those included in the Jewel-Pay Less agreement, which essentially require the board of the target firm to refrain from entering any contract outside the ordinary course of business or from altering the corporation's capital structure. Such provisions are intended, essentially, to preserve the status quo until the shareholders consider the offer.

the ultimate control over the corporation's assets. They remain free to accept or reject the merger proposal presented by the board, to respond to a merger proposal or tender offer made by another firm subsequent to the board's execution of exclusive merger agreement, or to hold out for a better offer. Given the benefits that may accrue to shareholders from an exclusive merger agreement, we fail to see how such an agreement would compromise their legal rights. . . .

We therefore hold that the district court erred in ruling that a merger agreement between boards of directors is of no legal effect prior to shareholder approval. To the contrary, we hold that under California law a corporate board of directors may lawfully bind itself in a merger agreement to forbear from negotiating or accepting competing offers until the shareholders have had an opportunity to consider the initial proposal.[13]

Jewel Companies, Inc., supra, at 1562-64.

Since this case was decided by the Ninth Circuit in 1984, it has become accepted practice in fully negotiated M&A transactions to include deal protection devices as part of the terms of the acquisition agreement. A no-shop clause (sometimes today this provision may be referred to as a "no-talk" clause) of the type at issue in *Jewel Companies* is now commonly used.

QUESTIONS

1. Can the parties' acquisition agreement delineate the entire scope of the board's fiduciary duty? For example, can the terms of a no-shop clause included in the parties' agreement prescribe precisely what steps Target's board must undertake in order for it to conclude that a third-party competing Bidder is offering a superior proposal? Or, is there some residual layer of fiduciary duty law that survives notwithstanding the parties' efforts to define contractually the scope of the board's fiduciary duty to the company and its shareholders?

2. Should the courts treat a no-shop/no-talk clause differently when it is made a binding provision in a letter of intent signed by the parties, as opposed to including such a provision in the definitive agreement to be signed by both Bidder and Target? Is there a public policy justification for treating a no-shop clause that is fairly stringent in its terms as valid in a letter of intent but invalid when made part of the parties' definitive merger agreement?

In the case of a publicly traded Target Co., it is accepted practice today for Bidder Co. to seek payment of a termination fee by Target in the event that Target decides to terminate the original deal with Bidder in order to accept a competing bid offering superior terms. The validity of termination fees, another form of deal protection, is the subject of the next case.

---

13. We do not decide the question whether upon the unsolicited receipt of a more favorable offer after signing a merger agreement, the board still must recommend to its shareholders that they approve the initial proposal.

Brazen v. Bell Atlantic Corporation
695 A.2d 43 (Del. 1997)

VEASEY, Chief Justice:

In this appeal, the issues facing the Court surround the question of whether a two-tiered $550 million termination fee in a merger agreement is a valid liquidated damages provision or whether the termination fee was an invalid penalty and tended improperly to coerce stockholders into voting for the merger.

Although there are judgmental aspects involved in the traditional liquidated damages analysis applicable here, we do not apply the business judgment rule as such. We hold that the termination fee should be analyzed as a liquidated damages provision because the merger agreement specifically so provided. Under the appropriate test for liquidated damages, the provisions at issue here were reasonable in the context of this case. We further find that the fee was not a penalty and was not coercive. Accordingly, we affirm the judgment of the Court of Chancery, but upon an analysis that differs somewhat from the rationale of that Court.

FACTS

In 1995, defendant below-appellee, Bell Atlantic Corporation, and NYNEX Corporation entered into merger negotiations. In January 1996, NYNEX circulated an initial draft merger agreement that included a termination fee provision. Both parties to the agreement determined that the merger should be a stock-for-stock transaction and be treated as a merger of equals. Thus, to the extent possible, the provisions of the merger agreement, including the termination fee, were to be reciprocal.

Representatives of Bell Atlantic and NYNEX agreed that a two-tiered $550 million termination fee was reasonable for compensating either party for damages incurred if the merger did not take place because of certain enumerated events. The termination fee was divided into two parts. First, either party would be required to pay $200 million if there were both a competing acquisition offer for that party and either (a) a failure to obtain stockholder approval, or (b) a termination of the agreement. Second, if a competing transaction were consummated within eighteen months of termination of the merger agreement, the consummating party would be required to pay an additional $350 million to its disappointed merger partner.

In the negotiations where such a fee was discussed, the parties took into account the losses each would have suffered as a result of having focused attention solely on the merger to the exclusion of other significant opportunities for mergers and acquisitions in the telecommunications industry. The parties concluded that, with the recent passage of the national Telecommunications Act of 1996, the entire competitive landscape had been transformed for the regional Bell operating companies, creating a flurry of business combinations. The parties further concluded that the prospect of missing out on alternative transactions due to the pendency of the merger was very real. The "lost opportunity" cost issue loomed large. The negotiators also considered as factors in determining the size of the termination fee (a) the size of termination fees in other merger agreements found reasonable by Delaware courts, and (b) the lengthy period during which the parties would be subject to restrictive covenants under the merger agreement while regulatory approvals were sought.

Bell Atlantic and NYNEX decided that $550 million, which represented about 2% of Bell Atlantic's approximately $28 billion market capitalization, would serve as a "reasonable proxy" for the opportunity cost and other losses associated with the termination of the merger. In addition, senior management advised Bell Atlantic's board of directors that the termination fee was at a level consistent with percentages approved by Delaware courts in earlier transactions, and that the likelihood of a higher offer emerging for either Bell Atlantic or NYNEX was very low. . . .

In addition, section 9.2(e) of the merger agreement states,

> NYNEX and Bell Atlantic agree that the agreements contained in Sections 9.2(b) and (c) above are an integral part of the transactions contemplated by this Agreement and constitute liquidated damages and not a penalty. If one Party fails to promptly pay to the other any fee due under such Sections 9.2(b) and (c), the defaulting Party shall pay the costs and expenses (including legal fees and expenses) in connection with any action, including the filing of any lawsuit or other legal action, taken to collect payment, together with interest on the amount of any unpaid fee at the publicly announced prime rate of Citibank, N.A. from the date such fee was required to be paid.

Finally, section 9.2(a), also pertinent to this appeal, states,

> In the event of termination of this Agreement as provided in Section 9.1 hereof, and subject to the provisions of Section 10.1 hereof, this Agreement shall forthwith become void and there shall be no liability on the part of any of the Parties except (i) as set forth in this Section 9.2 . . . and (ii) nothing herein shall relieve any Party from liability for any willful breach hereof.

Plaintiff below-appellant, Lionel L. Brazen, a Bell Atlantic stockholder, filed a class action against Bell Atlantic and its directors for declaratory and injunctive relief. Plaintiff alleged that the termination fee was not a valid liquidated damages clause because it failed to reflect an estimate of actual expenses incurred in preparation for the merger. Plaintiffs alleged that the $550 million payment was "an unconscionably high termination or 'lockup' fee," employed "to restrict and impair the exercise of the fiduciary duty of the Bell Atlantic board and coerce the shareholders to vote to approve the proposed merger. . . . "

The parties filed cross-motions for summary judgment. Bell Atlantic sought a declaration that the decision to include and structure the termination fee was a valid exercise of business judgment. The Court of Chancery denied the relief sought by plaintiff after concluding that the termination fee structure and terms were protected by the business judgment rule and that plaintiff failed to rebut its presumptions. . . .

TERMINATION FEE AS LIQUIDATED DAMAGES

The Court of Chancery determined that the proper method for analyzing the termination fee in this merger agreement was to employ the business judgment rule rather than the test accepted by Delaware courts for analyzing the validity of liquidated damages provisions. In arriving at this determination, the

Court of Chancery concluded that a liquidated damages analysis was not appropriate in this case because, notwithstanding section 9.2(e) of the merger agreement, which states that the $550 million fee constitutes liquidated damages,

> the event which triggers payment of the fees is not a breach but a termination. Liquidated damages, by definition, are damages paid in the event of a breach. . . . In addition, the Merger Agreement clearly provides that nothing in the Agreement (including the payment of termination fees) "shall relieve any Party from liability for any willful breach hereof." Accordingly, the Boards' decision to include these termination fees, which are triggered by a *termination* of the Merger Agreement and payment of which will not hinder either party's ability to recover damages from a breach, is protected by the business judgment rule and the fees will not be struck down unless plaintiff demonstrates that their inclusion was the result of disloyal or grossly negligent acts.

Plaintiff argued below and argues again here that the proper analysis for determining the validity of the termination fee in section 9.2(c) of the merger agreement is to analyze it as a liquidated damages clause employing a test different from the business judgment rule. We agree.

The express language in section 9.2(e) of the agreement unambiguously states that the termination fee provisions "constitute liquidated damages and not a penalty."[9] The Court of Chancery correctly found that liquidated damages, by definition, are damages paid in the event of a breach of a contract. While a breach of the merger agreement is not the only event that would trigger payment of the termination fee, the express language of section 9.2(c) states that a party's breach of section 7.2 (which provides that the parties are required to take all action necessary to convene a stockholders' meeting and use all commercially reasonable efforts to secure proxies to be voted in favor of the merger), coupled with other events, may trigger a party's obligation to pay the termination fee.

Thus, we find no compelling justification for treating the termination fee in this agreement as anything but a liquidated damages provision, in light of the express intent of the parties to have it so treated.

ANALYZING THE VALIDITY OF LIQUIDATED DAMAGES

In *Lee Builders v. Wells*, a case involving a liquidated damages provision equal to 5% of the purchase price in a contract for the sale of land, the Court of Chancery articulated the following two-prong test for analyzing the validity of the amount of liquidated damages: "Where the damages are uncertain and the amount agreed upon is reasonable, such an agreement will not be disturbed."[12]

---

9. At oral argument in this Court, counsel for Bell Atlantic explained that the liquidated damages language was "boilerplate" terminology for termination fees in merger transactions such as this one. So be it, but in our view, the drafters of corporate documents bear the responsibility for the selection of appropriate and clear language. *See Kaiser v. Matheson,* Del. Supr., 681 A.2d 392, 398-99 (1996). Accordingly, the parties to this merger cannot disown their own language.

12. *Lee Builders v. Wells,* Del. Ch., 103 A.2d 918, 919 (1954); *accord Wilmington Housing Authority v. Pan Builders, Inc.,* D. Del., 665 F. Supp. 351, 354, (1987); RESTATEMENT (SECOND) OF CONTRACTS §356 (1981).

Plaintiff argues that the termination fee, if properly analyzed as liquidated damages, fails the *Lee Builders* test because both portions of the fee are punitive rather than compensatory, having nothing to do with actual damages but instead being designed to punish Bell Atlantic stockholders and the subsequent third-party acquirer if Bell Atlantic were ultimately to agree to merge with another entity. We find, however, that the termination fee safely passes both prongs of the *Lee Builders* test.

To be a valid liquidated damages provision under the first prong of the test, the damages that would result from a breach of the merger agreement must be uncertain or incapable of accurate calculation. Plaintiff does not attack the fee on this ground. Given the volatility and uncertainty in the telecommunications industry due to enactment of the Telecommunications Act of 1996 and the fast pace of technological change, one is led ineluctably to the conclusion that advance calculation of actual damages in this case approaches near impossibility.

Plaintiff contends, however, that the $550 million fee violates the second prong of the *Lee Builders* test, i.e., that it is not a reasonable forecast of actual damages, but rather a penalty intended to punish the stockholders of Bell Atlantic for not approving the merger. Plaintiff's attack is without force.

Two factors are relevant to a determination of whether the amount fixed as liquidated damages is reasonable. The first factor is the anticipated loss by either party should the merger not occur. The second factor is the difficulty of calculating that loss: the greater the difficulty, the easier it is to show that the amount fixed was reasonable. In fact, where the level of uncertainty surrounding a given transaction is high, "[e]xperience has shown that . . . the award of a court or jury is no more likely to be exact compensation than is the advance estimate of the parties themselves."[14] Thus, to fail the second prong of *Lee Builders*, the amount at issue must be unconscionable or not rationally related to any measure of damages a party might conceivably sustain.

Here, in the face of significant uncertainty, Bell Atlantic and NYNEX negotiated a fee amount and a fee structure that take into account the following: (a) the lost opportunity costs associated with a contract to deal exclusively with each other; (b) the expenses incurred during the course of negotiating the transaction; (c) the likelihood of a higher bid emerging for the acquisition of either party; and (d) the size of termination fees in other merger transactions. The parties then settled on the $550 million fee as reasonable given these factors. Moreover, the $550 million fee represents 2% of Bell Atlantic's market capitalization of $28 billion. This percentage falls well within the range of termination fees upheld as reasonable by the courts of this State.[17] We hold that it is within a range of reasonableness and is not a penalty.

---

14. 5 Arthur L. Corbin, Corbin on Contracts §1060, at 348 (1964).

17. *See, e.g., Kysor,* 674 A.2d at 897 (where the Superior Court held that a termination fee of 2.8% of Kysor's offer was reasonable); *Roberts v. General Instrument Corp.,* Del. Ch., C.A. No. 11639, slip op. at 21, Allen, C., 1990 WL 118356 (Aug. 13, 1990) (breakup fee of 2% described as "limited"); *Lewis v. Leaseway Transp. Corp.,* Del. Ch., C.A. No. 8720, slip op. at 6, Chandler, V.C., 1990 WL 67383 (May 16, 1990) (dismissing challenge to a transaction which included a breakup fee and related expenses of approximately 3% of transaction value); *Braunschweiger v. American Home Shield Corp.,* Del. Ch., C.A. No. 10755, slip op. at 19-20, Allen, C., 1989 WL 128571 (Oct. 26, 1989) (2.3% breakup fee found not to be onerous).

This is not strictly a business judgment rule case. If it were, the Court would not be applying a reasonableness test. . . .

Since we are applying the liquidated damages rubric, and not the business judgment rule, it is appropriate to apply a reasonableness test, which in some respects is analogous to some of the heightened scrutiny processes employed by our courts in certain other contexts. Even then, courts will not substitute their business judgment for that of the directors, but will examine the decision to assure that it is, "on balance, within a range of reasonableness."[20] Is the liquidated damages provision here within the range of reasonableness? We believe that it is, given the undisputed record showing the size of the transaction, the analysis of the parties concerning lost opportunity costs, other expenses and the arms-length negotiations.

Plaintiff further argues that the termination fee provision was coercive. Plaintiff contends that (a) the stockholders never had an option to consider the merger agreement without the fee, and (b) regardless of what the stockholders thought of the merits of the transaction, the stockholders knew that if they voted against the transaction, they might well be imposing a $550 million penalty on their company. Plaintiff contends that the termination fee was so enormous that it "influenced" the vote. Finally, plaintiff argues that the fee provision was meant to be coercive because the drafters deliberately crafted the termination fees to make them applicable when Bell Atlantic's stockholders decline to approve the transaction as opposed to a termination resulting from causes other than the non-approval of the Bell Atlantic stockholders. We find plaintiff's arguments unpersuasive.

First, the Court of Chancery properly found that the termination fee was not egregiously large. Second, the mere fact that the stockholders knew that voting to disapprove the merger may result in activation of the termination fee does not by itself constitute stockholder coercion. Third, we find no authority to support plaintiff's proposition that a fee is coercive because it can be triggered upon stockholder disapproval of the merger agreement, but not upon the occurrence of other events resulting in termination of the agreement.

In *Williams v. Geier*, this Court enunciated the test for stockholder coercion. Wrongful coercion that nullifies a stockholder vote may exist "where the board or some other party takes actions which have the effect of causing the stockholders to vote in favor of the proposed transaction for some reason other

---

20. *QVC*, 637 A.2d at 45. It is to be noted that, in *QVC*, the termination fee of $100 million, which was 1.2% of the original merger agreement, was upheld by the Vice Chancellor because it "represents a fair liquidated amount to cover Viacom's expenses should the Paramount-Viacom merger not be consummated." *QVC Network, Inc. v. Paramount Communications, Inc.*, Del. Ch., 635 A.2d 1245, 1271 (1993), *aff'd on other grounds, Paramount Communications, Inc. v. QVC Network, Inc.*, Del. Supr., 637 A.2d at 50 n. 22 and accompanying text (termination fee considered in context with other measures in that case was problematic, but termination fee, standing alone, was not considered by Supreme Court since there was no cross-appeal to present the issue). *See also In re J.P. Stevens & Co., Inc. Shareholders Litigation*, Del. Ch., 542 A.2d 770, 783 (1988), *interlocutory appeal refused*, Del. Supr., 1988 WL 35145, 1988 DEL. LEXIS 103 (Apr. 12, 1988) (reasonable termination fee negotiated in good faith upheld as conventional and not product of disloyal action).

than the merits of that transaction."[21] But we also stated in *Williams v. Geier* that "[i]n the final analysis . . . the determination of whether a particular stockholder vote has been robbed of its effectiveness by impermissible coercion depends on the facts of the case."

In this case, the proxy materials sent to stockholders described very clearly the terms of the termination fee. Since the termination fee was a valid, enforceable part of the merger agreement, disclosure of the fee provision to stockholders was proper and necessary.[23] Plaintiff has not produced any evidence to show that the stockholders were forced into voting for the merger for reasons other than the merits of the transaction. To the contrary, it appears that the reciprocal termination fee provisions, drafted to protect both Bell Atlantic and NYNEX in the event the merger was not consummated, were an integral part of the merits of the transaction. Thus, we agree with the finding of the Court of Chancery that, although the termination fee provision may have influenced the stockholder vote, there were "no structurally or situationally coercive factors" that made an otherwise valid fee provision impermissibly coercive in this setting.[24]

CONCLUSION

Because we find that actual damages in this case do not lend themselves to reasonably exact calculation, and because we further find that the $550 million termination fee was a reasonable forecast of damages and that the fee was neither coercive nor unconscionable, we hold that the fee is a valid liquidated damages provision in this merger agreement.

In light of the foregoing, we affirm, albeit on somewhat different grounds, the judgment of the Court of Chancery.

QUESTIONS

1. What standard should courts use to review the validity of any termination fee included as part of an acquisition agreement (such as the merger agreement before the court in *Brazen*)? Why not review this contract provision under the traditional formulation of the business judgment rule?

2. How does the liquidated damages analysis used by the *Brazen* court differ from the application of the business judgment rule standard of review to these facts? In other words, would you get a different result had the Delaware court analyzed the validity of the termination fee under the business judgment rule?

---

21. *Williams v. Geier*, Del. Supr., 671 A.2d 1368, 1382-83 (1996) (citations omitted).

23. *Id.* (The board is "required to disclose the reality of the situation . . . [and] could not couch these disclosures in vague or euphemistic language, or in terms that would deprive stockholders of their right to choose.")

24. *Brazen v. Bell Atlantic Corp.*, Del. Ch., C.A. No. 14976, slip op. at 14 (Mar. 19, 1997).

3. In what way is the termination fee at issue in *Brazen* "coercive"? Why is its "coerciveness" (or lack thereof) legally significant?

4. What is the source of the board's authority to bind the company to a no-shop clause or a termination fee as part of the acquisition agreement, even though the consummation of the transaction itself is conditioned on obtaining shareholder approval of the transaction?

5. With respect to determining the *amount* of "termination fees," how does the analysis of this issue vary under *Unocal's* two-pronged test versus the analysis required to determine the validity of a liquidated damages clause? Would the court have reached a different outcome if the court had applied the traditional business judgment rule standard of review to assess the validity of the amount of the termination fee in *Brazen*?

NOTES

1. The Use of Lock-up Options: Another Form of Deal Protection. While termination fees are a common form of deal protection sought by Bidder to address the inherent risk of non-consummation, another type of deal protection involves the use of "lock-up options":

> Three types of lockups[2] can be distinguished. Stock lockups give the acquirer [Bidder] a call option on a specified number of shares of the target at a specified strike price. Asset lockups give the acquirer a call option on certain assets of the target at a specified price. Breakup fees give the acquirer a cash payment from the target if a specified event occurs. An acquirer's rights under each type of lockup are "triggered" by specified events that vary but usually make completion of the original deal unlikely or impossible.[16] More than one type of lockup may be included in a deal, and in mergers both parties may obtain one or more lockups.[17] . . .

John C. Coates IV and Guhan Subramanian, *A Buy-Side Model of M&A Lock-Ups: Theory and Evidence*, 53 STANFORD L. REV. 307, 314 (2000).

---

2. The very word "lockup" can be controversial in the M&A context, since it implies the agreement is designed to ensure that an M&A transaction is completed. Many "lockups" do not provide complete insurance of that sort, and would be illegal if they did. [In this article, we] follow industry practice in using "lockup" to mean a term in an agreement related to an M&A transaction involving a public company target that provides value to the bidder in the event that the transaction is not consummated due to specified conditions ("trigger events"). "Lockup" thus includes asset options, stock options, breakup fees, and expense reimbursement.

16. Standard trigger events include an agreement for a business combination with a third party, rejection of the first bidder's deal by target shareholders after a bust-up bid, or acquisition of a block of target stock by a third party. Some lockups contain "dual triggers," which extend the life of the lockup if other events occur. Fees payable upon events unrelated to bust-up risk (such as regulatory denials) are sometimes called "breakup" fees, but raise distinct practical and policy issues.

17. In hostile deals, lockups are by definition not available.

2. Use of "Shareholder Lock-ups."   In M&A deals where the publicly traded Target has a controlling shareholder, "it is legal, advisable, and hence common for a bidder to obtain a binding agreement [often called a "voting agreement"] from the controlling shareholder [obligating the shareholder] to vote for (or tender into) the deal, and to oppose other bids. Unlike merger agreements, such shareholder lockups are not generally subject to approval by other shareholders or regulators, or other significant conditions, so that shareholder lockups greatly if not completely reduce the odds of competing bids." Coates and Subramanian, *supra*, at 314-15 n. 18. If a shareholder lockup is used in connection with a fully negotiated merger, the merger agreement will often contain a "fiduciary out," of the type discussed below.

3. Fixing the Amount of the Termination Fee.   In light of the fact that termination fees are routinely sought by Bidders in order to protect the deal that they entered into with their Targets, the next logical question is what should be the *amount* of the fee to be paid in the event that Target jilts Bidder in favor of accepting a "topping bid." In other words, when is the amount of the fee "too much"? The following excerpt offers helpful guidelines in considering this recurring issue:

> During the course of negotiations of every public company deal, inevitably the conversation will turn to the amount of the breakup fee payable by a target company to a buyer if the deal is terminated under certain circumstances. Because U.S. corporate law generally requires a target company to retain the ability to consider post-signing superior proposals, a breakup fee is an important element of the suite of deal protection devices . . . that an initial buyer [seeks in order] to protect its position as the favored suitor. Speaking broadly, a breakup fee will increase the cost to a topping bidder as it will also need to cover the expense of the fee payable to the first buyer. However, with respect to deal protection terms in general, as well as the amount of breakup fees in particular, courts have indicated that they cannot be so tight or so large as to be preclusive of a true superior proposal. Starting from this somewhat ambiguous principle, the negotiations therefore turn to the appropriate amount for the breakup fee given the particular circumstances of the deal at hand.
>
> Unquestionably, precedent often informs the discussion, and there is a significant amount of statistical data to back up a general proposition that fees "usually" fall in the 3% to 4% range. A variety of studies has shown that median termination fees as a percentage of transaction or equity value consistently fell between 3.2% and 3.4% over the course of the last four years. Fees measured by enterprise value have been similarly stable between 3.1% and 3.3% over the same period. Studies have also shown that, as deal size goes up, fees, measured on a percentage basis, tend to go down. This inverse correlation between deal and fee size is probably a function of the optics resulting from the absolute, rather than relative (percentage), amount of the fees in megadeals. As then VC Strine admonished in the *Toys "R" Us* decision, [*In re Toys "R" Us, Inc. Shareholder Litigation*, 877 A.2d 975 (Del. Ch. 2005)], regardless of historical precedent for accepted ranges, when dealmakers are working with very large numbers they can run afoul of the "preclusive differences between termination fees starting with a 'b' rather than an 'm'."
>
> While the statistical data have some baseline value, not least because of their consistency over long periods of time, dealmakers should be cognizant that the Delaware courts have resisted providing a bright line or range test for reasonableness of breakup fees. In a relatively consistent set of rulings, Delaware courts

have upheld breakup fees falling within the statistically supported 3% to 4% range . . . That said, the Delaware courts have regularly taken the position that acceptability of a breakup fee is a highly fact specific inquiry, [and] not a function of consistency with statistical ranges. . . .

Beyond the simple question of the percentage of the breakup fee, parties will often discuss the appropriate denominator for the exercise—specifically whether it is measured as a percentage of equity value or of enterprise value. As to this question, the Delaware courts generally have taken a similar fact-specific approach. The court has avoided stating that one metric is appropriate to all situations. . . .

Despite the surface appeal of relying on statistical and court precedent, deal-makers must resist the temptation to rely solely on these data. The amount of a breakup fee is not a matter that can be viewed in isolation from other factors such as the other deal protection devices (including any separate expense reimbursements), the circumstances in which the fee is payable and the history of the sale process. Historical ranges may have value as one reference point for a discussion, but a more nuanced, fact-specific and tailored approach to setting a breakup fee is required for each deal.

Kirkland & Ellis, LLP, *M&A Update: Break-Up Fees—Picking Your Number* (law firm memo, Sept. 6, 2012) (copy on file with author).

4. Use of "Reverse" Termination Fees. With the advent of the private equity boom of 2005-2007, the M&A markets saw increasing use of a new form of deal protection device—what came to be known as the "reverse" termination fee. The origins and expansion of the reverse termination fee are described in the following excerpt:

Acquisition agreements are peppered with various provisions designed to mitigate, allocate, or address the ramifications of deal risk.[1] The potential for deal risk is particularly pronounced in acquisition transactions involving public companies, which generally entail a significant interim period between the date of the signing of the acquisition agreement and the date of the completion of the transaction.[2] . . .

---

1. Deal risk includes all the factors that could prevent or delay the closing of an announced acquisition transaction. For an overview of deal risks in business combinations, see Robert T. Miller, *The Economics of Deal Risk: Allocating Risk Through MAC Clauses in Business Combination Agreements*, 50 WM. & MARY L. REV. 2007, 2015-34 (2009), and Albert H. Choi & George G. Triantis, *Strategic Vagueness in Contract Design: The Case of Corporate Acquisitions*, 119 YALE L.J. 848, 851-54 (2010).

2. *See* Lou R. Kling, Eileen Nugent Simon & Michael Goldman, *Summary of Acquisition Agreements* 51 U. MIAMI L. REV. 779, 781 (1997) (explaining corporate and regulatory reasons for delay between signing and closing, including stockholder approval by [Target's] and/or [Bidder's] shareholders, antitrust filings under the Hart-Scott-Rodino Antitrust Improvements Act of 1976 or other needed regulatory approvals, and time needed to line up financing, if necessary). Various corporate and regulatory requirements may mean that acquisition transactions can take months to complete. In transactions with a significant regulatory component, the time between signing and closing can take over six months. *See* Miller, *supra* note 1, at 2029 (discussing possible time frames for transactions).

Perhaps the most obvious deal risk is of one party abandoning the transaction. One of the primary ways of dealing with this risk is through termination fee provisions. Typically, acquisition agreements provide for a standard termination fee ("STF") to be paid by the [Target] in the event that [Target] does not complete the transaction due to specific triggers. These triggers commonly involve situations where a third-party bidder for [Target] emerges. In an increasing number of transactions, acquisition agreements provide for a reverse termination fee ("RTF") — that is, a payment [made] by the [Bidder] in the event the [Bidder] cannot or does not complete the acquisition as specified in the agreement.[4]

. . . RTFs came under focus following the private equity[16] acquisition boom of 2005-2007.[7] While RTFs were seldom used prior to 2005, in an unprecedented manner, private equity buyers used RTF provisions to either renegotiate pending deals or to abandon deals altogether.[8] While the private equity RTF structure ultimately proved problematic for public company sellers, it may have paved a way for innovation in strategic deals entered into during the economic crisis.[9] . . .

An analysis of RTF provisions is particularly timely. In part due to the [onset of the Great Recession and the ensuing difficult economic environment], the payment of such fees and their role as an exclusive remedy in acquisition agreements have recently been at the center of debate among parties in broken deals and the subject of heated litigation in the Delaware courts.[10] . . .

The RTF structure also raises important questions regarding the appropriate level of review of a board of director's decision to enter an acquisition agreement with an RTF. The ability of shareholders for either the [Bidder] or the [Target] to bring RTF-related fiduciary duty and disclosure claims against boards is a matter of considerable importance. . . .

In general. . . . both [Bidders] and [Targets] . . . have been less than forthcoming with the shareholders in public disclosure about the role of the RTF in the transaction. [Targets] have touted that they entered into a "definitive agreement" to be acquired, focusing on the value of the transaction and the premium to be received by the company's stockholders, but rarely including much relevant information from which one could decipher whether the agreement included

---

4. RTFs are also referred to as "reverse breakup fees," "bidder termination fees," and "acquirer termination fees."

16. The term "private equity" as used in this Article refers to privately held partnerships, which acquire and "take private" publicly held companies, primarily using a leveraged financing structure. *See* Brian Cheffins & John Armour, *The Eclipse of Private Equity* 33 DEL. J. CORP. L. 1, 9 (2008) (using similar terminology).

7. According to practitioner surveys, in 2005-2006, over sixty percent of all private equity buyouts had reverse termination fees. Franci J. Blassberg & Kyle A. Pasewark, *Trendwatch: Deal Terms*, DEBEVOISE & PLIMPTON PRIVATE EQUITY REP., Winter 2006, at 11; DOUG WARNER & ALISON HAMPTON, WEIL, GOTSHAL & MANGES, LLP, SURVEY OF SPONSOR-BACKED GOING PRIVATE TRANSACTIONS 15 (2006).

8. For an excellent account of the rise of RTFs in private equity deals and their contribution to the demise of some of these deals, see generally Steven M. Davidoff, *The Failure of Private Equity*, 82 S. CAL. L. REV. 481, 482-87 (2008).

9. Strategic acquisition transactions are deals where the buyer and seller are both operating companies and agree to the transaction in order to achieve operating synergies, market power or empire building.

10. *See, e.g.*, United Rentals, Inc., v. RAM Holdings, Inc., 937 A.2d 810, 822 (Del. Ch. 2007) (discussing a party's payment of reverse break-up fees as its exclusive remedy).

an RTF. In fact, even experienced practitioners have noted that, while acquisition agreements are presented to the [Target's] shareholders and the public as a
committed agreement by the [Bidder] to complete the acquisition, one can determine if the agreement actually gives the [Bidder] an option to pay the fee and
walk away from the transaction without further liabilities "only by carefully pars-
ing the [reverse termination fee] and remedies provisions of the merger agreement. . . . " [Bidders] have been similarly circumspect in their disclosure about
RTF provisions in acquisition transactions.

The lack of effective disclosure could lead to potential liability for disclosure
violations under state and federal law relating to the [Bidder's] or [Target's] public statements about the transaction.[240] In an economic environment filled with
uncertainty, courts have been heavily focused on shareholder disclosure in connection with acquisition transactions. . . .

RTFs may also implicate board fiduciary duties for both the [Bidder] and
[Target] boards. A failed transaction resulting in the payment of a high RTF may
potentially create significant cash flow problems for a [Bidder]. Furthermore, a
[Bidder] board could arguably use an RTF provision as a form of takeover defense to prevent a hostile acquisition of the [Bidder] by another third-party bidder. When used in this manner, the RTF is analogous to the Customer Assurance
Program ("CAP") used by PeopleSoft to deter the hostile bid from Oracle in their
heated 2005 acquisition.[243] The CAP, which required a significant contractual
rebate to PeopleSoft customers in the event an acquirer discontinued new sales
of the PeopleSoft product line or "materially reduce[d] support services" for the
company's products, has been described as a "perfect defense" that would cost a
potential acquirer hundreds of million, if not billions, of dollars. Like the CAP,
the RTF has two important features. First, it is a contract term embedded in an acquisition agreement that cannot be easily renegotiated and used as a bargaining
chip against a third-party hostile bidder for the buyer in exchange for a higher
price. Second, although the size of the RTF is dependent on arm's length bargaining between the [Bidder] and the [Target] in the initial acquisition agreement,
when used as a poison pill, both the [Bidder] and the [Target] would clearly
prefer a higher RTF amount.

The Delaware courts have yet to address directly RTF provisions in acquisition
agreements, and there is much uncertainty regarding the nature of such review. In
general, the Delaware courts are extremely reluctant to question the substantive
decisions of boards, particularly [Bidder] boards, to enter into acquisition transaction.[246] In fact, in a recent decision arising out of a shareholder derivative claim
against the board of directors of Dow Chemical regarding its acquisition of Rohm
& Haas, the court appeared unwilling not only to question the decision to enter

---

240. Disclosure-related litigation has been identified by Delaware practitioners and
scholars as an emerging battle ground in fiduciary duty litigations. *See* Lloyd L. Drury III, *Private Equity and the Heightened Fiduciary Duty of Disclosure*, 6 N.Y.U. J. L. & Bus. 33, 35 (2009).

243. For a more detailed description of the Customer Assurance Program used by PeopleSoft, *see* David Millstone & Guhan Subramanian, *Oracle v. PeopleSoft: A Case Study*, 12 Harv.
Negot. L. Rev. 1, 12 (2007).

246. *See, e.g.*, Ash v. McCall, No. 17132, 2000 WL 1370341 (Del. Ch. Sept. 15, 2000). In
Ash v. McCall, the Delaware Court of Chancery dismissed the plaintiff's allegations that the
board had breached its duties and committed waste by failing to detect accounting irregu-
larities at the selling company during its due diligence investigation. The *Ash* court refused
to second-guess the good faith business judgment of a board which approved an acquisition
based on expert advice and a thorough board process. *Id.* at *8.

into the transaction, but also to question substantive buy-side decisions, including how to structure the transaction and what terms to include in an acquisition agreement.[247] However, given the growing complexities of RTF provisions, one can certainly envision RTF arrangements that would implicate board fiduciary duties.

Afra Afsharipour, *Transforming the Allocation of Deal Risk Through Reverse Termination Fees*, 63 VAND. L. REV. 1161 (2010); *see also* Brian JM Quinn, *Optionality in Merger Agreements*, 35 DEL. J. CORP. L. 789 (2010).

5. The "Optionality" Nature of the "Reverse" Termination Fee. From Target's perspective, the use of reverse termination fees will often implicate fiduciary duty concerns. When private equity funds make an offer for a publicly traded Target, they will generally need to arrange financing in order to close on the transaction and complete the purchase of Target. Thus, private-equity Bidders often condition their bids on their ability to arrange financing. This led to the very real concern on the part of Target that the acquisition would not close because the private-equity Bidder would not be able to secure the requisite financing. So Targets began to seek contractual provisions designed to address this risk of non-consummation. Eventually, the structure of private equity deals (i.e., LBOs) evolved to include bridge financing, which is interim financing that is put in place on the closing of the transaction in order to "bridge" the gap in financing until the private-equity firm (and its bankers) could arrange permanent debt financing. The use of bridge financing had the advantage of providing Target with greater certainty that the transaction would close in the event the private-equity firm's bankers were unable to arrange permanent debt financing by the date of closing on the acquisition transaction. As described in more detail in the following excerpt, with the onset of the private-equity boom of 2005-2007, the use of financing conditions (i.e., "financing out") dropped off and the use of reverse termination fees concomitantly increased.

> . . . In its purest form the reverse termination fee structure created an option. The private equity firm had the discretion to exercise this option and, if the firm did so, it could terminate the transaction and pay the reverse termination fee. A private equity acquirer [Bidder] thus could assess the benefits of the transaction before completion and decide whether it was more economical to complete the transaction or otherwise pay the reverse termination fee and terminate the acquisition agreement.
>
> This option was not calculated according to any option pricing method. Nor did it appear to be calculated by reference to the damage incurred by an acquiree [Target] in the event that it was exercised by the private equity firm. The amount ultimately paid also did not deter acquirers from exercising the option in many instances. Rather, the amount of the reverse termination fee was normatively set by reference to the termination fee typically paid by acquirees, making for a symmetrical penalty.

---

247. *See In Re Dow Chem. Derivative Litig.*, Cons. No. 4339, 2010 WL 66769, at *9 (Del. Ch., Jan. 11, 2010) ("[S]ubstantive second-guessing of the merits of a business decision . . . is precisely the kind of inquiry that the business judgment rule prohibits.").

The fact [is] that each of these penalties existed for different reasons and worked differently. . . . The reverse termination fee provided a liquidated damages remedy equivalent to the termination fee paid by acquirees. This latter fee was capped by Delaware case law and was designed to deter competing bids and to compensate bidders for the costs associated with making a trumped offer. But the same principles did not apply in the reverse termination fee context. In a number of prominent instances, the [the amount of the reverse termination] fee did not deter exercise of the option and, in hindsight, the amount appeared to undercompensate acquirees [i.e., Targets] for the losses incurred by the acquiree company and its shareholders. . . .

Steven M. Davidoff, *The Failure of Private Equity*, 82 S. CAL. L. REV. 481, 515-516 (2009). *Query*: In light of the option nature of the reverse termination fee, what factors do you think the Target board should take into account in negotiating the terms of such a fee? Does your analysis of this question depend on whether Bidder is a strategic buyer or a financial buyer? *See, e.g., United Rentals, Inc. v. RAM Holdings, Inc.*, 937 A.2d 810 (Del. Ch. 2007).

In sum, these reverse termination fee provisions operate to limit the liability of the private equity fund to paying a fixed amount in the event that the fund decides not to close (i.e., to "walk away from the deal") — no matter whether the decision to "walk away" constitutes an intentional breach of the acquisition agreement or not.

And, these provisions exclude the possibility of specific performance to require the private equity firm to consummate the transaction. So, the net effect is to give the private equity [fund] a walk-away right with a cap on their liability at a fixed dollar amount. . . . These clauses essentially give the private equity fund an "option" on the acquired company. They can rationally assess at the time of closing whether it is worth it to close in numerical dollar terms. This makes for a very interesting calculus, particularly in these [difficult economic] times. Private equity firms who have negotiated these clauses must be making some hard, number-crunching decisions. No one likes to pay the size of these possible payments [ranging in amounts from $900 million up to $1 billion in deals that failed to close in 2007, at the time of the onset of the Great Recession], tarnish their reputation as a bad player or admit to your investors that you made a bad decision, but sometimes cutting your losses is the better part of valor. . . .

Brian Quinn, *Private Equity's Option to Buy*, M&A Law Prof. Blog, *available at* http://lawprofessors.typepad.com/mergers/2007/08/private-equitys.html (Aug. 16, 2007).

6. Use of "Fiduciary Out" Clauses. The term *fiduciary out* is customarily used to refer to a provision in an acquisition agreement that allows the board of Target to terminate the agreement if Target's board, usually on the advice of counsel, concludes that its fiduciary duties require the board to accept an offer from a competing bidder, most often because the competing bid offers superior terms. The most recent pronouncement of the Delaware Supreme Court concerning the importance of fiduciary out provisions is offered in the next case, *Omnicare, Inc. v. NCS Healthcare, Inc.*

Omnicare, Inc. v. NCS Healthcare, Inc.
818 A.2d 914 (Del. 2003)

HOLLAND, Justice, for the majority:

NCS Healthcare, Inc. ("NCS"), a Delaware corporation, was the object of competing acquisition bids, one by Genesis Health Ventures, Inc. ("Genesis"), a Pennsylvania corporation, and the other by Omnicare, Inc. ("Omnicare"), a Delaware corporation. The proceedings before this Court were expedited due to exigent circumstances, including the pendency of the stockholders' meeting to consider the NCS/Genesis merger agreement. The determinations of this Court were set forth in a summary manner following oral argument to provide clarity and certainty to the parties going forward. Those determinations are explicated in this opinion.

OVERVIEW OF OPINION

The board of directors of NCS, an insolvent publicly traded Delaware corporation, agreed to the terms of a merger with Genesis. Pursuant to that agreement, all of the NCS creditors would be paid in full and the corporation's stockholders would exchange their shares for the shares of Genesis, a publicly traded Pennsylvania corporation. Several months after approving the merger agreement, but before the stockholder vote was scheduled, the NCS board of directors withdrew its prior recommendation in favor of the Genesis merger.

In fact, the NCS board recommended that the stockholders reject the Genesis transaction after deciding that a competing proposal from Omnicare was a superior transaction. The competing Omnicare bid offered the NCS stockholders an amount of cash equal to more than twice the then current market value of the shares to be received in the Genesis merger. The transaction offered by Omnicare also treated the NCS corporation's other stakeholders on equal terms with the Genesis agreement.

The merger agreement between Genesis and NCS contained a provision authorized by Section 251 (c) [now codified at Section 146] of Delaware's corporation law. It required that the Genesis agreement be placed before the corporation's stockholders for a vote, even if the NCS board of directors no longer recommended it. At the insistence of Genesis, the NCS board also agreed to omit any effective fiduciary clause from the merger agreement. In connection with the Genesis merger agreement, two stockholders of NCS, who held a majority of the voting power, agreed unconditionally to vote all of their shares in favor of the Genesis merger. Thus, the combined terms of the voting agreements and merger agreement guaranteed, *ab initio*, that the transaction proposed by Genesis would obtain NCS stockholder's approval.

The Court of Chancery ruled that the voting agreements, when coupled with the provision in the Genesis merger agreement requiring that it be presented to the stockholders for a vote pursuant to 8 Del. C. §251(c), constituted defensive measures within the meaning of *Unocal Corp. v. Mesa Petroleum Co.* After applying the *Unocal* standard of enhanced judicial scrutiny, the Court of Chancery held that those defensive measures were reasonable. We have concluded that, in the absence of an effective fiduciary out clause, those defensive measures are both preclusive and coercive. Therefore, we hold that those defensive measures are invalid and unenforceable.

The Parties

The defendant, NCS, is a Delaware corporation headquartered in Beachwood, Ohio. NCS is a leading independent provider of pharmacy services to long-term care institutions including skilled nursing facilities, assisted living facilities and other institutional healthcare facilities. NCS common stock consists of Class A shares and Class B shares. The Class B shares are entitled to ten votes per share and the Class A shares are entitled to one vote per share. The shares are virtually identical in every other respect.

The defendant Jon H. Outcalt is Chairman of the NCS board of directors. Outcalt owns 202,063 shares of NCS Class A common stock and 3,476,086 shares of Class B common stock. The defendant Kevin B. Shaw is President, CEO and a director of NCS. At the time the merger agreement at issue in this dispute was executed with Genesis, Shaw owned 28,905 shares of NCS Class A common stock and 1,141,134 shares of Class B common stock. [Collectively, Shaw and Outcalt own over 65 percent of the voting power of NCS stock.]

The NCS board has two other members, defendants Boake A. Sells and Richard L. Osborne. Sells is a graduate of the Harvard Business School. He was Chairman and CEO at Revco Drugstores in Cleveland, Ohio from 1987 to 1992, when he was replaced by new owners. Sells currently sits on the boards of both public and private companies. Osborne is a full-time professor at the Weatherhead School of Management at Case Western Reserve University. He has been at the university for over thirty years. Osborne currently sits on at least seven corporate boards other than NCS.

The defendant Genesis is a Pennsylvania corporation with its principal place of business in Kennett Square, Pennsylvania. It is a leading provider of healthcare and support services to the elderly. The defendant Geneva Sub, Inc., a wholly owned subsidiary of Genesis, is a Delaware corporation formed by Genesis to acquire NCS.

The plaintiffs in the class action own an unspecified number of shares of NCS Class A common stock. They represent a class consisting of all holders of Class A common stock. As of July 28, 2002, NCS had 18,461,599 Class A shares and 5,255,210 Class B shares outstanding.

Omnicare is a Delaware corporation with its principal place of business in Covington, Kentucky. Omnicare is in the institutional pharmacy business, with annual sales in excess of $2.1 billion during its last fiscal year. Omnicare purchased 1000 shares of NCS Class A common stock on July 30, 2002. . . .

Factual Background

The parties are in substantial agreement regarding the operative facts. They disagree, however, about the legal implications. . . .

NCS SEEKS RESTRUCTURING ALTERNATIVES

Beginning in late 1999, changes in the timing and level of reimbursements by government and third-party providers adversely affected market conditions in the health care industry. As a result, NCS began to experience greater difficulty in collecting accounts receivables, which led to a precipitous decline in the market value of its stock. NCS common shares that traded above $20 in January 1999 were worth as little as $5 at the end of that year. By early 2001, NCS was in default on approximately $350 million in debt, including $206 million in senior bank debt and $102 million of its 5-3/4% Convertible Subordinated Debentures (the "Notes"). After these defaults, NCS common stock traded in a range of $0.09 to $0.50 per share until days before the announcement of the transaction at issue in this case.

NCS began to explore strategic alternatives that might address the problems it was confronting. As part of this effort, in February 2000, NCS retained UBS Warburg, L.L.C. to identify potential acquirers and possible equity investors. UBS Warburg contacted over fifty different entities to solicit their interest in a variety of transactions with NCS. UBS Warburg had marginal success in its efforts. By October 2000, NCS had only received one non-binding indication of interest valued at $190 million, substantially less than the face value of NCS's senior debt. This proposal was reduced by 20% after the offeror conducted its due diligence review.

NCS FINANCIAL DETERIORATION

In December 2000, NCS terminated its relationship with UBS Warburg and retained Brown, Gibbons, Lang & Company as its exclusive financial advisor. During this period, NCS's financial condition continued to deteriorate. In April 2001, NCS received a formal notice of default and acceleration from the trustee for holders of the Notes. As NCS's financial condition worsened, the Noteholders formed a committee to represent their financial interests (the "Ad Hoc Committee"). At about that time, NCS began discussions with various investor groups regarding a restructuring in a "prepackaged" bankruptcy. NCS did not receive any proposal that it believed provided adequate consideration for its stakeholders. At that time, full recovery for NCS's creditors was a remote prospect, and any recovery for NCS stockholders seemed impossible.

OMNICARE'S INITIAL NEGOTIATIONS

In the summer of 2001, NCS invited Omnicare, Inc. to begin discussions with Brown Gibbons regarding a possible transaction. On July 20, Joel Gemunder, Omnicare's President and CEO, sent Shaw a written proposal to acquire NCS in a bankruptcy sale under Section 363 of the Bankruptcy Code. This proposal was for $225 million subject to satisfactory completion of due diligence. NCS asked Omnicare to execute a confidentiality agreement so that more detailed discussions could take place.[3]

In August 2001, Omnicare increased its bid to $270 million, but still proposed to structure the deal as an asset sale in bankruptcy. Even at $270 million, Omnicare's proposal was substantially lower than the face value of NCS's outstanding debt. It would have provided only a small recovery for Omnicare's Noteholders and no recovery for its stockholders. In October 2001, NCS sent Glen Pollack of Brown Gibbons to meet with Omnicare's financial advisor, Merrill Lynch, to discuss Omnicare's interest in NCS. Omnicare responded that it was not interested in any transaction other than an asset sale in bankruptcy.

There was no further contact between Omnicare and NCS between November 2001 and January 2002. Instead, Omnicare began secret discussions with Judy K. Mencher, a representative of the Ad Hoc Committee. In these discussions, Omnicare continued to pursue a transaction structured as a sale of assets in bankruptcy. In February 2002, the Ad Hoc Committee notified the NCS board that Omnicare had proposed an asset sale in bankruptcy for $313,750,000. [Omnicare's offer was for an amount that was lower than the face value of NCS's outstanding debt and provided for no recovery for NCS shareholders.]

NCS INDEPENDENT BOARD COMMITTEE

In January 2002, Genesis was contacted by members of the Ad Hoc Committee concerning a possible transaction with NCS. Genesis executed NCS's standard confidentiality agreement and began a due diligence review. Genesis had recently emerged from bankruptcy because, like NCS, it was suffering from dwindling government reimbursements.

Genesis previously lost a bidding war to Omnicare in a different transaction. This led to bitter feelings between the principals of both companies. More importantly, this bitter experience for Genesis led to its insistence on exclusivity agreements and lock-ups in any potential transaction with NCS.

NCS FINANCIAL IMPROVEMENT

NCS's operating performance was improving by early 2002. As NCS's performance improved, the NCS directors began to believe that it might be possible for NCS to enter into a transaction that would provide some recovery for NCS stockholders' equity. In March 2002, NCS decided to form an independent committee of board members who were neither NCS employees nor major NCS stockholders (the "Independent Committee"). The NCS board thought

---

3. Discovery had revealed that, at the same time, Omnicare was attempting to lure away NCS's customers through what it characterized as the "NCS Blitz." The "NCS Blitz" was an effort by Omnicare to target NCS's customers. Omnicare has engaged in an "NCS Blitz" a number of times, most recently while NCS and Omnicare were in discussions in July and August 2001.

this was necessary because, due to NCS's precarious financial condition, it felt that fiduciary duties were owed to the enterprise as a whole rather than solely to NCS stockholders.

Sells and Osborne were selected as the members of the committee, and given authority to consider and negotiate possible transactions for NCS. The entire four member NCS board, however, retained authority to approve any transaction. The Independent Committee retained the same legal and financial counsel as the NCS board.

The Independent Committee met for the first time on May 14, 2002. At that meeting Pollack suggested that NCS seek a "stalking-horse merger partner" to obtain the highest possible value in any transaction. The Independent Committee agreed with the suggestion.

GENESIS INITIAL PROPOSAL

Two days later, on May 16, 2002, [representatives of Brown Gibbons, and Boake Sells met with representatives of Genesis]. At that meeting, Genesis made it clear that if it were going to engage in any negotiations with NCS, it would not do so as a "stalking horse." . . . Thus, Genesis "wanted a degree of certainty that to the extent [it] w[as] willing to pursue a negotiated merger agreement . . . , [it] would be able to consummate the transaction [it] negotiated and executed."

In June 2002, Genesis proposed a transaction that would take place outside the bankruptcy context. . . . As discussions continued, the terms proposed by Genesis continued to improve. On June 25, the economic terms of the Genesis proposal included repayment of the NCS senior debt in full, full assumption of trade credit obligations, an exchange offer or direct purchase of the NCS Notes providing NCS Noteholders with a combination of cash and Genesis common stock equal to the par value of the NCS Notes (not including accrued interest), and $20 million in value for the NCS common stock. Structurally, the Genesis proposal continued to include consents from a significant majority of the Noteholders as well as support agreements from stockholders owning a majority of the NCS voting power.

GENESIS EXCLUSIVITY AGREEMENT

NCS's financial advisors and legal counsel met again with Genesis and its legal counsel on June 26, 2002, to discuss a number of transaction-related issues. At this meeting, Pollack asked Genesis to increase its offer to NCS stockholders. Genesis agreed to consider this request. Thereafter, Pollack and Hager had further conversations. Genesis agreed to offer a total of $24 million in consideration for the NCS common stock, or an additional $4 million, in the form of Genesis common stock.

At the June 26 meeting, Genesis's representatives demanded that, before any further negotiations take place, NCS agree to enter into an exclusivity agreement with it. As Hager from Genesis explained it: "[I]f they wished us to continue to try to move this process to a definitive agreement, that they would need to do it on an exclusive basis with us. We were going to, and already had incurred significant expense, but we would incur additional expenses . . . , both internal and external, to bring this transaction to a definitive signing. We wanted them to work with us on an exclusive basis for a short period of time to see if we could reach agreement." On June 27, 2002, Genesis's legal counsel delivered a draft form of exclusivity agreement for review and consideration by NCS's legal counsel.

The Independent Committee met on July 3, 2002, to consider the proposed exclusivity agreement. Pollack presented a summary of the terms of a possible Genesis merger, which had continued to improve. The then-current Genesis proposal included (1) repayment of the NCS senior debt in full, (2) payment of par value for the Notes (without accrued interest) in the form of a combination of cash and Genesis stock, (3) payment to NCS stockholders in the form of $24 million in Genesis stock, plus (4) the assumption, because the transaction was to be structured as a merger, of additional liabilities to trade and other unsecured creditors.

NCS director Sells testified, Pollack told the Independent Committee at a July 3, 2002 meeting that Genesis wanted the Exclusivity Agreement to be the first step towards a completely locked up transaction that would preclude a higher bid from Omnicare . . .

After NCS executed the exclusivity agreement, Genesis provided NCS with a draft merger agreement, a draft Noteholders' support agreement, and draft voting agreements for Outcalt and Shaw, who together held a majority of the voting power of the NCS common stock. Genesis and NCS negotiated the terms of the merger agreement over the next three weeks. During those negotiations, the Independent Committee and the Ad Hoc Committee persuaded Genesis to improve the terms of its merger.

The parties were still negotiating by July 19, and the exclusivity period was automatically extended to July 26. At that point, NCS and Genesis were close to executing a merger agreement and related voting agreements. Genesis proposed a short extension of the exclusivity agreement so a deal could be finalized. On the morning of July 26, 2002, the Independent Committee authorized an extension of the exclusivity period through July 31.

OMNICARE PROPOSES NEGOTIATIONS

By late July 2002, Omnicare came to believe that NCS was negotiating a transaction, possibly with Genesis or another of Omnicare's competitors, that would potentially present a competitive threat to Omnicare. Omnicare also came to believe, in light of a run-up in the price of NCS common stock, that whatever transaction NCS was negotiating probably included a payment for its stock. Thus, the Omnicare board of directors met on the morning of July 26 and, on the recommendation of its management, authorized a proposal to acquire NCS that did not involve a sale of assets in bankruptcy.

On the afternoon of July 26, 2002, Omnicare faxed to NCS a letter outlining a proposed acquisition. The letter suggested a transaction in which Omnicare would retire NCS's senior and subordinated debt at par plus accrued interest, and pay the NCS stockholders $3 cash for their shares. Omnicare's proposal, however, was expressly conditioned on negotiating a merger agreement, obtaining certain third party consents, and completing its due diligence.

Mencher [a member of the Ad Hoc Committee of Noteholders] saw the July 26 Omnicare letter and realized that, while its economic terms were attractive, the "due diligence" condition substantially undercut its strength. In an effort to get a better proposal from Omnicare, Mencher telephoned Gemunder [Omnicare's CEO] and told him that Omnicare was unlikely to succeed in its bid unless it dropped the "due diligence outs." She explained this was the only way a bid at the last minute would be able to succeed. Gemunder considered Mencher's warning "very real," and followed up with his advisors. They, however, insisted that he retain the due diligence condition "to protect [him] from doing something foolish." Taking this advice to heart, Gemunder decided not to drop the due diligence condition.

Late in the afternoon of July 26, 2002, NCS representatives received voice-mail messages from Omnicare asking to discuss the letter. The exclusivity agreement prevented NCS from returning those calls. In relevant part, that agreement precluded NCS from "engag[ing] or particpat[ing] in any discussions or negotiations with respect to a Competing Transaction or a proposal for one." The July 26 letter from Omnicare met the definition of a "Competing Transaction."

Despite the exclusivity agreement, the Independent Committee met to consider a response to Omnicare. It concluded that discussions with Omnicare about its July 26 letter presented an unacceptable risk that Genesis would abandon merger discussions. The Independent Committee believed that, given Omnicare's past bankruptcy proposals and unwillingness to consider a merger, as well as its decision to negotiate exclusively with the Ad Hoc Committee, the risk of losing the Genesis proposal was too substantial. Nevertheless, the Independent Committee instructed Pollack to use Omnicare's letter to negotiate for improved terms with Genesis.

GENESIS MERGER AGREEMENT AND VOTING AGREEMENTS

Genesis responded to the NCS request to improve its offer as a result of the Omnicare fax the next day. On July 27, Genesis proposed substantially improved terms. First, it proposed to retire the Notes in accordance with the terms of the indenture, thus eliminating the need for Noteholders to consent to the transaction. This change involved paying all accrued interest plus a small redemption premium. Second, Genesis increased the exchange ratio for NCS common stock to one-tenth of a Genesis common share for each NCS common share, an 80% increase. Third, it agreed to lower the proposed termination fee in the merger agreement from $10 million to $6 million. In return for these concessions, Genesis stipulated that the transaction had to be approved by midnight the next day, July 28, or else Genesis would terminate discussions and withdraw its offer.

The Independent Committee and the NCS board both scheduled meetings for July 28. The committee met first. Although that meeting lasted less than an hour, the Court of Chancery determined the minutes reflect that the directors were fully informed of all material facts relating to the proposed transaction.

After concluding that Genesis was sincere in establishing the midnight deadline, the committee voted unanimously to recommend the transaction to the full board.

The full board met thereafter. After receiving similar reports and advice from its legal and financial advisors, the board concluded that "balancing the potential loss of the Genesis deal against the uncertainty of Omnicare's letter, results in the conclusion that the only reasonable alternative for the Board of Directors is to approve the Genesis transaction." The board first voted to authorize the voting agreements with Outcalt and Shaw, for purposes of Section 203 of the Delaware General Corporation Law ("DGCL"). The board was advised by its legal counsel that "under the terms of the merger agreement and because NCS shareholders representing in excess of 50% of the outstanding voting power would be *required* by Genesis to enter into stockholder voting agreements contemporaneously with the signing of the merger agreement, and would agree to vote their shares in favor of the merger agreement, shareholder approval of the merger would be assured even if the NCS Board were to withdraw or change its recommendation. *These facts would prevent NCS from engaging in any alternative or superior transaction in the future.*" (*emphasis added*).

After listening to a *summary* of the merger terms, the board then resolved that the merger agreement and the transactions contemplated thereby were advisable and fair and in the best interests of all the NCS stakeholders. The NCS board further resolved to recommend the transactions to the stockholders for their approval and adoption. A definitive merger agreement between NCS and Genesis and the stockholder voting agreements were executed later that day. The Court of Chancery held that it was not *a per se* breach of fiduciary duty that the NCS board never read the NCS/Genesis merger agreement word for word.[4]

NCS/GENESIS MERGER AGREEMENT

Among other things, the NCS/Genesis merger agreement provided the following:

- NCS stockholders would receive 1 share of Genesis common stock in exchange for every 10 shares of NCS common stock held;
- NCS stockholders could exercise appraisal rights under 8 Del. C. §262;
- NCS would redeem NCS's Notes in accordance with their terms;
- NCS would submit the merger agreement to NCS stockholders regardless of whether the NCS board continued to recommend the merger;
- NCS would not enter into discussions with third parties concerning an alternative acquisition of NCS, or provide non-public information to such parties, unless (1) the third party provided an unsolicited, *bona fide* written proposal documenting the terms of the acquisition; (2) the NCS board believed in good faith that the proposal was or was likely to result

---

4. *See, e.g., Smith v. Van Gorkom,* 488 A.2d 858, 883 n. 25 (Del. 1985).

in an acquisition on terms superior to those contemplated by the NCS/ Genesis merger agreement; and (3) before providing non-public information to that third party, the third party would execute a confidentiality agreement at least as restrictive as the one in place between NCS and Genesis; and

- If the merger agreement were to be terminated, under certain circumstances NCS would be required to pay Genesis a $6 million termination fee and/or Genesis's documented expenses, up to $5 million.

VOTING AGREEMENTS

Outcalt and Shaw, in their capacity as NCS stockholders, entered into voting agreements with Genesis. NCS was also required to be a party to the voting agreements by Genesis. Those agreements provided, among other things, that:

- Outcalt and Shaw were acting in their capacity as NCS stockholders in executing the agreements, not in their capacity as NCS directors or officers;
- Neither Outcalt nor Shaw would transfer their shares prior to the stockholder vote on the merger agreement;
- Outcalt and Shaw agreed to vote all of their shares in favor of the merger agreement; and
- Outcalt and Shaw granted to Genesis an irrevocable proxy to vote their shares in favor of the merger agreement.
- The voting agreement was specifically enforceable by Genesis.

The merger agreement further provided that if either Outcalt or Shaw breached the terms of the voting agreements, Genesis would be entitled to terminate the merger agreement and potentially receive a $6 million termination fee from NCS. Such a breach was impossible since Section 6 provided that the voting agreements were specifically enforceable by Genesis.

OMNICARE'S SUPERIOR PROPOSAL

On July 29, 2002, hours after the NCS/Genesis transaction was executed, Omnicare faxed a letter to NCS restating its conditional proposal and attaching a draft merger agreement. Later that morning, Omnicare issued a press release publicly disclosing the proposal.

On August 1, 2002, Omnicare filed a lawsuit attempting to enjoin the NCS/ Genesis merger, and announced that it intended to launch a tender offer for NCS's shares at a price of $3.50 per share. On August 8, 2002, Omnicare began its tender offer. By letter dated that same day, Omnicare expressed a desire to discuss the terms of the offer with NCS. Omnicare's letter continued to condition its proposal on satisfactory completion of a due diligence investigation of NCS.

On August 8, 2002, and again on August 19, 2002, the NCS Independent Committee and full board of directors met separately to consider the Omnicare tender offer in light of the Genesis merger agreement. NCS's outside legal counsel and NCS's financial advisor attended both meetings. The board was unable to determine that Omnicare's expressions of interest were likely to lead to a "Superior Proposal," as the term was defined in the NCS/Genesis merger agreement. On September 10, 2002, NCS requested and received a waiver from Genesis allowing NCS to enter into discussions with Omnicare without first having to determine that Omnicare's proposal was a "Superior Proposal."

On October 6, 2002, Omnicare irrevocably committed itself to a transaction with NCS. Pursuant to the terms of its proposal, Omnicare agreed to acquire all the outstanding NCS Class A and Class B shares at a price of $3.50 per share in cash. As a result of this irrevocable offer, on October 21, 2002, the NCS board withdrew its recommendation that the stockholders vote in favor of the NCS/Genesis merger agreement. NCS's financial advisor withdrew its fairness opinion of the NCS/Genesis merger agreement as well.

GENESIS REJECTION IMPOSSIBLE

The Genesis merger agreement permits the NCS directors to furnish non-public information to, or enter into discussions with, "any Person in connection with an unsolicited bona fide written Acquisition Proposal by such person" that the board deems likely to constitute a "Superior Proposal." That provision has absolutely no effect on the Genesis merger agreement. Even if the NCS board "changes, withdraws or modifies" its recommendation, as it did, it must still submit the merger to a stockholder vote.

A subsequent filing with the Securities and Exchange Commission ("SEC") states: "the NCS independent committee and the NCS board of directors have determined to withdraw their recommendations of the Genesis merger agreement and recommend that the NCS stockholders vote against the approval and adoption of the Genesis merger." In that same SEC filing, however, the NCS board explained why the success of the Genesis merger had already been predetermined. "Notwithstanding the foregoing, the NCS independent committee and the NCS board of directors recognize that (1) the existing contractual obligations to Genesis currently prevent NCS from accepting the Omnicare irrevocable merger proposal; and (2) the existence of the voting agreements entered into by Messrs. Outcalt and Shaw, whereby Messrs. Outcalt and Shaw agreed to vote their shares of NCS Class A common stock and NCS Class B common stock in favor of the Genesis merger, ensure NCS stockholder approval of the Genesis merger." This litigation was commenced to prevent the consummation of the inferior Genesis transaction.

LEGAL ANALYSIS

BUSINESS JUDGMENT OR ENHANCED SCRUTINY

The "defining tension" in corporate governance today has been characterized as "the tension between deference to directors' decisions and the scope of judicial review."[5] The appropriate standard of judicial review is dispositive of which party has the burden of proof as any litigation proceeds from stage to stage until there is a substantive determination on the merits. Accordingly, identification of the correct analytical framework is essential to a proper judicial review of challenges to the decision-making process of a corporation's board of directors.[7]

* * *

The prior decisions of this Court have identified the circumstances where board action must be subjected to enhanced judicial scrutiny before the presumptive protection of the business judgment rule can be invoked. One of those circumstances was described in *Unocal:* when a board adopts defensive measures in response to a hostile takeover proposal that the board reasonably determines is a threat to corporate policy and effectiveness. In *Moran v. Household,* we explained why a *Unocal* analysis also was applied to the adoption of a stockholder's rights plan, even in the absence of an immediate threat. Other circumstances requiring enhanced judicial scrutiny give rise to what are known as *Revlon* duties, such as when the board enters into a merger transaction that will cause a change in corporate control, initiates an active bidding process seeking to sell the corporation, or makes a break up of the corporate entity inevitable.[17]

MERGER DECISION REVIEW STANDARD

The first issue decided by the Court of Chancery addressed the standard of judicial review that should be applied to the decision by the NCS board to merge with Genesis. This Court has held that a board's decision to enter into a merger transaction that does not involve a change in control is entitled to judicial deference pursuant to the procedural and substantive operation of the business judgment rule.[18] When a board decides to enter into a merger transaction that will result in a change of control, however, enhanced judicial scrutiny under *Revlon* is the standard of review.

The Court of Chancery concluded that, because the stock-for-stock merger between Genesis and NCS did not result in a change of control, the NCS directors' duties under *Revlon* were not triggered by the decision to merge with Genesis. The Court of Chancery also recognized, however, that *Revlon* duties are imposed "when a corporation initiates an active bidding process seeking to sell itself." The Court of Chancery then concluded, alternatively, that *Revlon* duties

---

5. E. Norman Veasey, *The Defining Tension in Corporate Governance in America,* 52 Bus. Law. 393, 403 (1997).

7. *Unitrin, Inc. v. Am. Gen. Corp.,* [651 A.2d 1361, at 1374 (Del. 1995)].

17. *Paramount Communications Inc. v. QVC Network Inc.* [637 A.2d 34, 47 (Del. 1993)]; *Revlon, Inc. v. MacAndrews & Forbes Holdings, Inc.,* 506 A.2d 173, 182 (Del. 1986).

18. *Paramount Communications, Inc. v. Time Inc.,* 571 A.2d 1140, 1152 (Del. 1989).

had not been triggered because NCS did not start an active bidding process, and the NCS board "abandoned" its efforts to sell the company when it entered into an exclusivity agreement with Genesis.

After concluding that the *Revlon* standard of enhanced judicial review was completely inapplicable, the Court of Chancery then held that it would examine the decision of the NCS board of directors to approve the Genesis merger pursuant to the business judgment rule standard. After completing its business judgment rule review, the Court of Chancery held that the NCS board of directors had not breached their duty of care by entering into the exclusivity and merger agreements with Genesis. The Court of Chancery also held, however, that "even applying the more exacting *Revlon* standard, the directors acted in conformity with their fiduciary duties in seeking to achieve the highest and best transaction that was reasonably available to [the stockholders]."

The appellants argue that the Court of Chancery's *Revlon* conclusions are without factual support in the record and contrary to Delaware law for at least two reasons. First, they submit that NCS did initiate an active bidding process. Second, they submit that NCS did not "abandon" its efforts to sell itself by entering into the exclusivity agreement with Genesis. The appellants contend that once NCS decided "to initiate a bidding process seeking to maximize short-term stockholder value, it cannot avoid enhanced judicial scrutiny under *Revlon* simply because the bidder it selected [Genesis] happens to have proposed a merger transaction that does not involve a change of control."

The Court of Chancery's decision to review the NCS board's decision to merge with Genesis under the business judgment rule rather than the enhanced scrutiny standard of *Revlon* is not outcome determinative for the purposes of deciding this appeal. We have assumed arguendo that the business judgment rule applied to the decision by the NCS board to merge with Genesis.[23] We have also assumed arguendo that the NCS board exercised due care when it: abandoned the Independent Committee's recommendation to pursue a stalking horse strategy, without even trying to implement it; executed an exclusivity agreement with Genesis; acceded to Genesis' twenty-four hour ultimatum for making a final merger decision; and executed a merger agreement that was summarized but never completely read by the NCS board of directors.[24]

DEAL PROTECTION DEVICES REQUIRE ENHANCED SCRUTINY

The dispositive issues in this appeal involve the defensive devices that protected the Genesis merger agreement. The Delaware corporation statute provides that the board's management decision to enter into and recommend a merger transaction can become final only when ownership action is taken by a vote of the stockholders. Thus, the Delaware corporation law expressly provides for a balance of power between boards and stockholders which makes merger transactions a shared enterprise and ownership decision. Consequently, a board of directors' decision to adopt defensive devices to protect a merger agreement

---

23 *Paramount Communications, Inc. v. Time Inc.*, 571 A.2d 1140, 1152 (Del. 1989).

24. *But see Smith v. Van Gorkom*, 488 A.2d 858 (Del. 1985).

may implicate the stockholders' right to effectively vote contrary to the initial recommendation of the board in favor of the transaction.[25] . . .

It is well established that conflicts of interest arise when a board directors acts to prevent stockholders from effectively exercising their to vote contrary to the will of the board. The "omnipresent specter" of conflict may be present whenever a board adopts defensive devices to protect a merger agreement. The stockholders' ability to effectively reject a merger agreement is likely to bear an inversely proportionate relationship to the structural and economic devices that the board has approved to protect the transaction.

In *Paramount v. Time,* the original merger agreement between Time and Warner did not constitute a "change of control." The plaintiffs in *Paramount v. Time* argued that, although the original Time and Warner merger agreement did not involve a change of control, the use of a lock-up, no-shop clause, and "dry-up" provisions violated the Time board's *Revlon* duties. This Court held that "[t]he adoption of structural safety devices alone does not trigger *Revlon*. Rather, as the Chancellor stated, *such devices are properly subject to a* Unocal *analysis.*"

In footnote 15 of *Paramount v. Time,* we stated that legality of the structural safety devices adopted to protect the original merger agreement between Time and Warner were not a central issue on appeal. That is because the issue on appeal involved the "Time's board [decision] to recast its consolidation with Warner into an outright cash and securities acquisition of Warner by Time." Nevertheless, we determined that there was substantial evidence on the record to support the conclusions reached by the Chancellor in applying a *Unocal* analysis to each of the structural devices contained in the original merger agreement between Time and Warner.

There are inherent conflicts between a board's interest in protecting a merger transaction it has approved, the stockholders' statutory right to make the final decision to either approve or not approve a merger, and the board's continuing responsibility to effectively exercise its fiduciary duties at all times after the merger agreement is executed. These competing considerations require a threshold determination that board-approved defensive devices protecting a merger transaction are within the limitations of its statutory authority and consistent with the directors' fiduciary duties. Accordingly, in *Paramount v. Time,* we held that the business judgment rule applied to the Time board's original decision to merge with Warner. We further held, however, that defensive devices adopted by the board to protect the original merger transaction must withstand enhanced judicial scrutiny under the *Unocal* standard of review, even when that merger transaction does not result in a change of control.[34]

ENHANCED SCRUTINY GENERALLY

In *Paramount v. QVC,* this Court identified the key features of an enhanced judicial scrutiny test. The first feature is a "judicial determination regarding

---

25. *See MM Companies v. Liquid Audio, Inc.,* 813 A.2d Co., 1118, 1120 (Del. 2003).

34. *Id.* at 1151-55; *Unocal Corp. v. Mesa Petroleum Co.,* 493 A.2d 946 (Del. 1985); *see In re Santa Fe Pacific Corp. Shareholder Litigation,* 669 A.2d 59 (Del. 1995).

the adequacy of the decisionmaking process employed by the directors, including the information on which the directors based their decision." The second feature is "a judicial examination of the reasonableness of the directors' action in light of the circumstances then existing." We also held that "the directors have the burden of proving that they were adequately informed and acted reasonably."

* * *

In *Unitrin*, we explained the "*ratio decidendi* for the 'range of reasonableness' standard"[41] when a court applies enhanced judicial scrutiny to director action pursuant to our holding in *Unocal*. It is a recognition that a board of directors needs "latitude in discharging its fiduciary duties to the corporation and its shareholders when defending against perceived threats." "The concomitant requirement is for judicial restraint." Therefore, if the board of directors' collective defensive responses are not draconian (preclusive or coercive) and are "within a 'range of reasonableness,' a court must not substitute its judgment for the board's [judgment]." The same *ratio decidendi* applies to the "range of reasonableness" when courts apply *Unocal's* enhanced judicial scrutiny standard to defensive devices intended to protect a merger agreement that will not result in a change of control.

A board's decision to protect its decision to enter a merger agreement with defensive devices against uninvited competing transactions that may emerge is analogous to a board's decision to protect against dangers to corporate policy and effectiveness when it adopts defensive measures in a hostile takeover contest. In applying *Unocal's* enhanced judicial scrutiny in assessing a challenge to defensive actions taken by a target corporation's board of directors in a takeover context, this Court held that the board "does not have unbridled discretion to defeat perceived threats by any Draconian means available".[46] Similarly, just as a board's statutory power with regard to a merger decision is not absolute, a board does not have unbridled discretion to defeat any perceived threat to a merger by protecting it with any draconian means available.

Since *Unocal*, "this Court has consistently recognized that defensive measures which are either preclusive or coercive are included within the common law definition of draconian."[47] In applying enhanced judicial scrutiny to defensive actions under *Unocal*, a court must "evaluate the board's overall response, including the justification for each contested defensive measure, and the results achieved thereby." If a "board's defensive actions are inextricably related, the principles of *Unocal* require that such actions be scrutinized collectively as a unitary response to the perceived threat."

Therefore, in applying enhanced judicial scrutiny to defensive devices designed to protect a merger agreement, a court must first determine that those measures are not preclusive or coercive *before* its focus shifts to the "range of reasonableness" in making a proportionality determination. If the

---

41. *Unitrin, Inc. v. Am. Gen. Corp.*, 651 A.2d at 1388.
46. *Unocal Corp. v. Mesa Petroleum Co.*, 493 A.2d. at 955.
47. *Unitrin, Inc. v. Am. Gen. Corp.*, 651 A.2d at 1387.

trial court determines that the defensive devices protecting a merger are not preclusive or coercive, the proportionality paradigm of *Unocal* is applicable. The board must demonstrate that it has reasonable grounds for believing that a danger to the corporation and its stockholders exists if the merger transaction is not consummated. That burden is satisfied "by showing good faith and reasonable investigation." Such proof is materially enhanced if it is approved by a board comprised of a majority of outside directors or by an independent committee.

When the focus of judicial scrutiny shifts to the range of reasonableness, *Unocal* requires that any defensive devices must be proportionate to the perceived threat to the corporation and its stockholders if the merger transaction is not consummated. Defensive devices taken to protect a merger agreement executed by a board of directors are intended to give that agreement an advantage over any subsequent transactions that materialize before the merger is approved by the stockholders and consummated. This is analogous to the favored treatment that a board of directors may properly give to encourage an initial bidder when it discharges its fiduciary duties under *Revlon*. . . .

The latitude a board will have in either maintaining or using the defensive devices it has adopted to protect the merger it approved will vary according to the degree of benefit or detriment to the stockholders' interests that is presented by the value or terms of the subsequent competing transaction.

GENESIS' ONE DAY ULTIMATUM

The record reflects that two of the four NCS board members, Shaw and Outcalt, were also the *same* two NCS stockholders who combined to control a majority of the stockholder voting power. Genesis gave the four person NCS board less than twenty-four hours to vote in favor of its proposed merger agreement. Genesis insisted the merger agreement include a Section 251(c) clause, mandating its submission for a stockholder vote even if the board's recommendation was withdrawn. Genesis further insisted that the merger agreement omit any effective fiduciary out clause.

Genesis also gave the two stockholder members of the NCS board, Shaw and Outcalt, the same accelerated time table to personally sign the proposed voting agreements. These voting agreements committed them irrevocably to vote their majority power in favor of the merger and further provided in Section 6 that the voting agreements be specifically enforceable. Genesis also required that NCS execute the voting agreements.

Genesis' twenty-four hour ultimatum was that, *unless both* the merger agreement and the voting agreements were signed with the terms it requested, its offer was going to be withdrawn. According to Genesis' attorneys, these "were unalterable conditions to Genesis' willingness to proceed." Genesis insisted on the execution of the interlocking voting rights and merger agreements because it feared that Omnicare would make a superior merger proposal. The NCS board signed the voting rights and merger agreements, without any effective fiduciary out clause, to expressly guarantee that the Genesis merger would be approved, even if a superior merger transaction was presented from Omnicare or any other entity.

DEAL PROTECTION DEVICES

Defensive devices, as that term is used in this opinion, is a synonym for what are frequently referred to as "deal protection devices." Both terms are used interchangeably to describe any measure or combination of measures that are intended to protect the consummation of a merger transaction. Defensive devices can be economic, structural, or both.

Deal protection devices need not all be in the merger agreement itself. In this case, for example, the Section 251(c) provision in the merger agreement was combined with the separate voting agreements to provide a structural defense for the Genesis merger agreement against any subsequent superior transaction. Genesis made the NCS board's defense of its transaction absolute by insisting on the omission of any effective fiduciary out clause in the NCS merger agreement.

Genesis argues that stockholder voting agreements cannot be construed as deal protection devices taken by a board of directors because stockholders are entitled to vote in their own interest. Genesis cites *Williams v. Geier*[57] and *Stroud v. Grace*[58] for the proposition that voting agreements are not subject to the *Unocal* standard of review. Neither of those cases, however, holds that the operative effect of a voting agreement must be disregarded *per se* when a *Unocal* analysis is applied to a comprehensive and combined merger defense plan.

In this case, the stockholder voting agreements were inextricably intertwined with the defensive aspects of the Genesis merger agreement. In fact, the voting agreements with Shaw and Outcalt were the linchpin of Genesis' proposed tripartite defense. Therefore, Genesis made the execution of those voting agreements a non-negotiable condition precedent to its execution of the merger agreement. In the case before us, the Court of Chancery held that the acts which locked-up the Genesis transaction were the Section 251(c) provision and "the execution of the *voting agreement* by Outcalt and Shaw."

With the assurance that Outcalt and Shaw would irrevocably agree to exercise their majority voting power in favor of its transaction, Genesis insisted that the merger agreement reflect the other two aspects of its concerted defense, i.e., the inclusion of a Section 251(c) provision and the omission of any effective fiduciary out clause. Those dual aspects of the merger agreement would not have provided Genesis with a complete defense in the absence of the voting agreements with Shaw and Outcalt.

THESE DEAL PROTECTION DEVICES UNENFORCEABLE

In this case, the Court of Chancery correctly held that the NCS directors' decision to adopt defensive devices to *completely* "lock up" the Genesis merger mandated "special scrutiny" under the two-part test set forth in *Unocal*. That conclusion is consistent with our holding in *Paramount v. Time* that "safety devices" adopted to protect a transaction that did not result in a change of

---

57. *Williams v. Geier*, 671 A.2d 1368 (Del. 1996).
58. *Stroud v. Grace*, 606 A.2d 75 (Del. 1992).

control are subject to enhanced judicial scrutiny under a *Unocal* analysis. The record does not, however, support the Court of Chancery's conclusion that the defensive devices adopted by the NCS board to protect the Genesis merger were reasonable and proportionate to the threat that NCS perceived from the potential loss of the Genesis transaction.

Pursuant to the judicial scrutiny required under *Unocal's* two-stage analysis, the NCS directors must first demonstrate "that they had reasonable grounds for believing that a danger to corporate policy and effectiveness existed. . . . " To satisfy that burden, the NCS directors are required to show they acted in good faith after conducting a reasonable investigation. The threat identified by the NCS board was the possibility of losing the Genesis offer and being left with no comparable alternative transaction.

The second stage of the *Unocal* test requires the NCS directors to demonstrate that their defensive response was "reasonable in relation to the threat posed." This inquiry involves a two-step analysis. The NCS directors must first establish that the merger deal protection devices adopted in response to the threat were not "coercive" or "preclusive," and then demonstrate that their response was within a "range of reasonable responses" to the threat perceived.[64] In *Unitrin,* we stated:

- A response is "coercive" if it is aimed at forcing upon stockholders a management-sponsored alternative to a hostile offer.
- A response is "preclusive" if it deprives stockholders of the right to receive all tender offers or precludes a bidder from seeking control by fundamentally restricting proxy contests or otherwise.

This aspect of the *Unocal* standard provides for a disjunctive analysis. If defensive measures are either preclusive or coercive they are draconian and impermissible. In this case, the deal protection devices of the NCS board were *both* preclusive and coercive.

This Court enunciated the standard for determining stockholder coercion in the case of *Williams v. Geier.* A stockholder vote may be nullified by wrongful coercion "where the board or some other party takes actions which have the effect of causing the stockholders to vote in favor of the proposed transaction for some reason other than the merits of that transaction." In *Brazen v. Bell Atlantic Corporation,* we applied that test for stockholder coercion and held "that although the termination fee provision may have influenced the stockholder vote, there were 'no structurally or situationally coercive factors' that made an otherwise valid fee provision impermissibly coercive" under the facts presented.

In *Brazen,* we concluded "the determination of whether a particular stockholder vote has been robbed of its effectiveness by impermissible coercion depends on the facts of the case." In this case, the Court of Chancery did not expressly address the issue of "coercion" in its *Unocal* analysis. It did find as a fact, however, that NCS's public stockholders (who owned 80% of NCS and overwhelmingly supported Omnicare's offer) will be forced to accept the Genesis merger because of the structural defenses approved by the NCS board.

---

64. *Unitrin, Inc. v. Am. Gen. Corp.,* 651 A.2d 1361, 1387-88 (Del. 1995).

Consequently, the record reflects that any stockholder vote would have been robbed of its effectiveness by the impermissible coercion that predetermined the outcome of the merger without regard to the merits of the Genesis transaction at the time the vote was scheduled to be taken. Deal protection devices that result in such coercion cannot withstand *Unocal's* enhanced judicial scrutiny standard of review because they are not within the range of reasonableness.

Although the minority stockholders were not forced to vote for the Genesis merger, they were required to accept it because it was *a fait accompli.* The record reflects that the defensive devices employed by the NCS board are preclusive and coercive in the sense that they accomplished *a fait accompli.* In this case, despite the fact that the NCS board has withdrawn its recommendation for the Genesis transaction and recommended its rejection by the stockholders, the deal protection devices approved by the NCS board operated in concert to have a preclusive and coercive effect. Those tripartite defensive measures — the Section 251(c) provision, the voting agreements, and the absence of an effective fiduciary out clause — made it "mathematically impossible" and "realistically unattainable" for the Omnicare transaction or any other proposal to succeed, no matter how superior the proposal.[72]

The deal protection devices adopted by the NCS board were designed to coerce the consummation of the Genesis merger and preclude the consideration of any superior transaction. The NCS directors' defensive devices are not within a reasonable range of responses to the perceived threat of losing the Genesis offer because they are preclusive and coercive. Accordingly, we hold that those deal protection devices are unenforceable.

EFFECTIVE FIDUCIARY OUT REQUIRED

The defensive measures that protected the merger transaction are unenforceable not only because they are preclusive and coercive but, alternatively, they are unenforceable because they are invalid as they operate in this case. Given the specifically enforceable irrevocable voting agreements, the provision in the merger agreement requiring the board to submit the transaction for a stockholder vote and the omission of a fiduciary out clause in the merger agreement completely prevented the board from discharging its fiduciary responsibilities to the minority stockholders when Omnicare presented its superior transaction. "To the extent that a [merger] contract, or a provision thereof, purports to require a board to act or not act in such a fashion as to limit the exercise of fiduciary duties, it is invalid and unenforceable."[74]

---

72. *See Unitrin, Inc. v. Am. Gen. Corp.,* 651 A.2d at 1388-89; *see also Carmody v. Toll Bros., Inc.,* 723 A.2d 1180, 1195 (Del. Ch. 1998) (citations omitted).

74. *Paramount Communications Inc. v. QVC Network Inc.,* 637 A.2d 34, 51 (Del. 1993) (citation omitted). *Restatement (Second) of Contracts* §193 explicitly provides that a "promise by a fiduciary to violate his fiduciary duty *or a promise that tends to induce such a violation is unenforceable on grounds of public policy.*" The comments to that section indicate that "[d]irectors and other officials of a corporation act in a fiduciary capacity and are subject to the rule stated in this Section." Restatement (Second) of Contracts §193 (1981) (*emphasis added*).

In *QVC,* this Court recognized that "[w]hen a majority of a corporation's voting shares are acquired by a single person or entity, or by *a cohesive group acting together* [as in this case], there is a significant diminution in the voting power of those who thereby become minority stockholders." Therefore, we acknowledged that "[i]n the absence of devices protecting the minority stockholders, stockholder votes are likely to become mere formalities," where a cohesive group acting together to exercise majority voting powers have already decided the outcome. Consequently, we concluded that since the minority stockholders lost the power to influence corporate direction through the ballot, "minority stockholders must rely for protection solely on the fiduciary duties owed to them by the directors."

Under the circumstances presented in this case, where a cohesive group of stockholders with majority voting power was irrevocably committed to the merger transaction, "[e]ffective representation of the financial interests of the minority shareholders imposed upon the [NCS board] an affirmative responsibility to protect those minority shareholders' interests."[79] The NCS board could not abdicate its fiduciary duties to the minority by leaving it to the stockholders alone to approve or disapprove the merger agreement because two stockholders had already combined to establish a majority of the voting power that made the outcome of the stockholder vote a foregone conclusion.

The Court of Chancery noted that Section 251(c) of the Delaware General Corporation Law now permits boards to agree to submit a merger agreement for a stockholder vote, even if the Board later withdraws its support for that agreement and recommends that the stockholders reject it.[80] The Court of Chancery also noted that stockholder voting agreements are permitted by Delaware law. In refusing to certify this interlocutory appeal, the Court of Chancery stated "it is simply nonsensical to say that a board of directors abdicates its duties to manage the 'business and affairs' of a corporation under Section 141 (a) of the DGCL by agreeing to the inclusion in a merger agreement of a term authorized by §251(c) of the same statute."

Taking action that is otherwise legally possible, however, does not *ipso facto* comport with the fiduciary responsibilities of directors in all circumstances. The synopsis to the amendments that resulted in the enactment of Section 251(c) in the Delaware corporation law statute specifically provides: "the amendments are not intended to address the question of whether such a submission requirement is appropriate in any particular set of factual circumstances." Section 251 provisions, like the no-shop provision examined in *QVC,* are "presumptively valid in the abstract." Such provisions in a merger agreement may not, however, "validly define or limit the directors' fiduciary duties under Delaware law or prevent the [NCS] directors from carrying out their fiduciary duties under Delaware law."

---

79. *McMullin v. Beran,* 765 A.2d 910, 920 (Del. 2000).

80. Section 251(c) was amended in 1998 to allow for the inclusion in a merger agreement of a term requiring that the agreement be put to a vote of stockholders whether or not their directors continue to recommend the transaction. Before this amendment, Section 251 was interpreted as precluding a stockholder vote if the board of directors, after approving the merger agreement but before the stockholder vote, decided no longer to recommend it. *See Smith v. Van Gorkom,* 488 A.2d 858, 887-88 (Del. 1985).

Genesis admits that when the NCS board agreed to its merger conditions, the NCS board was seeking to assure that the NCS creditors were paid in full and that the NCS stockholders received the highest value available for their stock. In fact, Genesis defends its "bulletproof merger agreement on that basis. We hold that the NCS board did not have authority to accede to the Genesis demand for an absolute "lock-up."

The directors of a Delaware corporation have a continuing obligation to discharge their fiduciary responsibilities, as future circumstances develop, after a merger agreement is announced. Genesis anticipated the likelihood of a superior offer after its merger agreement was announced and demanded defensive measures from the NCS board that *completely* protected its transaction.[84] Instead of agreeing to the absolute defense of the Genesis merger from a superior offer, however, the NCS board was required to negotiate a fiduciary out clause to protect the NCS stockholders if the Genesis transaction became an inferior offer. By acceding to Genesis' ultimatum for complete protection *in futuro,* the NCS board disabled itself from exercising its own fiduciary obligations at a time when the board's own judgment is most important,[85] i.e. receipt of a subsequent superior offer.

Any board has authority to give the proponent of a recommended merger agreement reasonable structural and economic defenses, incentives, and fair compensation if the transaction is not completed. To the extent that defensive measures are economic and reasonable, they may become an increased cost to the proponent of any subsequent transaction. Just as defensive measures cannot be draconian, however, they cannot limit or circumscribe the directors' fiduciary duties. Notwithstanding the corporation's insolvent condition, the NCS board had no authority to execute a merger agreement that subsequently prevented it from effectively discharging its ongoing fiduciary responsibilities.

The stockholders of a Delaware corporation are entitled to rely upon the board to discharge its fiduciary duties at all times. The fiduciary duties of a director are unremitting and must be effectively discharged in the specific context of the actions that are required with regard to the corporation or its stockholders as circumstances change. The stockholders with majority voting power, Shaw and Outcalt, had an absolute right to sell or exchange their shares with a third party at any price. This right was not only known to the other directors of NCS, it became an integral part of the Genesis agreement. In its answering brief, Genesis candidly states that its offer "came with a condition—Genesis would not be a stalking horse and would not agree to a transaction to which NCS's controlling shareholders were not committed."

The NCS board was required to contract for an effective fiduciary out clause to exercise its continuing fiduciary responsibilities to the minority

---

84. The marked improvements in NCS's financial situation during the negotiations with Genesis strongly suggests that the NCS board should have been alert to the prospect of competing offers or, as eventually occurred, a bidding contest.

85. *See Malone v. Brincat,* 722 A.2d 5, 10 (Del. 1998) (directors' fiduciary duties do not operate intermittently). *See also Moran v. Household Int'l, Inc.,* 500 A.2d 1346 (Del. 1985).

stockholders.[88] The issues in this appeal do not involve the general validity of either stockholder voting agreements or the authority of directors to insert a Section 251(c) provision in a merger agreement. In this case, the NCS board combined those two otherwise valid actions and caused them to operate in concert as an absolute lock up, in the absence of an effective fiduciary out clause in the Genesis merger agreement.

In the context of this preclusive and coercive lock up case, the protection of Genesis' contractual expectations must yield to the supervening responsibility of the directors to discharge their fiduciary duties on a continuing basis. The merger agreement and voting agreements, as they were combined to operate in concert in this case, are inconsistent with the NCS directors' fiduciary duties. To that extent, we hold that they are invalid and unenforceable. . . .

VEASEY, Chief Justice, with whom STEELE, Justice, joins dissenting.

The beauty of the Delaware corporation law, and the reason it has worked so well for stockholders, directors and officers, is that the framework is based on an enabling statute with the Court of Chancery and the Supreme Court applying principles of fiduciary duty in a common law mode on a case-by-case basis. Fiduciary duty cases are inherently fact-intensive and, therefore, unique. This case is unique in two important respects. First, the peculiar facts presented render this case an unlikely candidate for substantial repetition. Second, this is a rare 3-2 split decision of the Supreme Court.[90]

* * *

The process by which this merger agreement came about involved a joint decision by the controlling stockholders and the board of directors to secure what appeared to be the only value-enhancing transaction available for a company on the brink of bankruptcy. The Majority adopts a new rule of law that imposes a prohibition on the NCS board's ability to act in concert with controlling stockholders to lock up this merger. The Majority reaches this conclusion by analyzing the challenged deal protection measures as isolated board actions. The Majority concludes that the board owed a duty to the NCS minority stockholders to refrain from acceding to the Genesis demand for an irrevocable lock-up notwithstanding the compelling circumstances confronting the board

---

88. *See Paramount Communications Inc. v. QVC Network Inc.*, 637 A.2d at 42-43. Merger agreements involve an ownership decision and, therefore, cannot become final without stockholder approval. Other contracts do not require a fiduciary out clause because they involve business judgments that are *within the exclusive* province of the board of directors' power to manage the affairs of the corporation. *See Grimes v. Donald*, 673 A.2d 1207, 1214-15 (Del. 1996).

90. Split decisions by this Court, especially in the field of corporation law, are few and far between. One example is our decision in *Smith v. Van Gorkom*, 488 A.2d 858 (Del.1985), where only three Justices supported reversing the Court of Chancery's decision. As Justice Holland and David Skeel recently noted, while our decisionmaking process fosters consensus, dissenting opinions "illustrate that principled differences of opinion about the law [are] . . . never compromised for the sake of unanimity." Randy J. Holland & David A. Skeel, Jr., *Deciding Cases Without Controversy*, 5 Del. L. Rev. 115, 118 (2002).

and the board's disinterested, informed, good faith exercise of its business judgment.

Because we believe this Court must respect the reasoned judgment of the board of directors and give effect to the wishes of the controlling stockholders, we respectfully disagree with the Majority's reasoning that results in a holding that the confluence of board and stockholder action constitutes a breach of fiduciary duty. The essential fact that must always be remembered is that this agreement and the voting commitments of Outcalt and Shaw concluded a lengthy search and intense negotiation process in the context of insolvency and creditor pressure where no other viable bid had emerged. Accordingly, we endorse the Vice Chancellor's well-reasoned analysis that the NCS board's action before the hostile bid emerged was within the bounds of its fiduciary duties under these facts.

We share with the Majority and the independent NCS board of directors the motivation to serve carefully and in good faith the best interests of the corporate enterprise and, thereby, the stockholders of NCS. It is now known, of course, after the case is over, that the stockholders of NCS will receive substantially more by tendering their shares into the topping bid of Omnicare than they would have received in the Genesis merger, as a result of the post-agreement Omnicare bid and the injunctive relief ordered by the Majority of this Court. Our jurisprudence cannot, however, be seen as turning on such ex post felicitous results. Rather, the NCS board's good faith decision must be subject to a real-time review of the board action before the NCS-Genesis merger agreement was entered into.

AN ANALYSIS OF THE PROCESS LEADING TO THE LOCK-UP REFLECTS A QUINTESSENTIAL, DISINTERESTED AND INFORMED BOARD DECISION REACHED IN GOOD FAITH

The Majority has adopted the Vice Chancellor's findings and has assumed arguendo that the NCS board fulfilled its duties of care, loyalty, and good faith by entering into the Genesis merger agreement. Indeed, this conclusion is indisputable on this record. The problem is that the Majority has removed from their proper context the contractual merger protection provisions. The lock-ups here cannot be reviewed in a vacuum. A court should review the entire bidding process to determine whether the independent board's actions permitted the directors to inform themselves of their available options and whether they acted in good faith.[92]

Going into negotiations with Genesis, the NCS directors knew that, up until that time, NCS had found only one potential bidder, Omnicare. Omnicare had refused to buy NCS except at a fire sale price through an asset sale in bankruptcy. Omnicare's best proposal at that stage would not have paid off all creditors and would have provided nothing for stockholders. The Noteholders,

---

92. *See, e.g., Malpiede v. Townson*, 780 A.2d 1075, 1089 (Del. 2001) (concluding that the board made an informed decision to refrain from returning to a rival bidder to solicit another offer because the board conducted a "lengthy sale process" that spanned one year).

represented by the Ad Hoc Committee, were willing to oblige Omnicare and force NCS into bankruptcy if Omnicare would pay in full the NCS debt. Through the NCS board's efforts, Genesis expressed interest that became increasingly attractive. Negotiations with Genesis led to an offer paying creditors off and conferring on NCS stockholders $24 million-an amount infinitely superior to the prior Omnicare proposals.

But there was, understandably, a sine qua non. In exchange for offering the NCS stockholders a return on their equity and creditor payment, Genesis demanded certainty that the merger would close. If the NCS board would not have acceded to the Section 251(c) provision, if Outcalt and Shaw had not agreed to the voting agreements and if NCS had insisted on a fiduciary out, there would have been no Genesis deal! Thus, the only value-enhancing transaction available would have disappeared. NCS knew that Omnicare had spoiled a Genesis acquisition in the past, and it is not disputed by the Majority that the NCS directors made a reasoned decision to accept as real the Genesis threat to walk away.[94]

When Omnicare submitted its conditional eleventh-hour bid, the NCS board had to weigh the economic terms of the proposal against the uncertainty of completing a deal with Omnicare. Importantly, because Omnicare's bid was conditioned on its satisfactorily completing its due diligence review of NCS, the NCS board saw this as a crippling condition, as did the Ad Hoc Committee. As a matter of business judgment, the risk of negotiating with Omnicare and losing Genesis at that point outweighed the possible benefits. The lock-up was indisputably a sine qua non to any deal with Genesis.

A lock-up permits a target board and a bidder to "exchange certainties." Certainty itself has value. The acquirer may pay a higher price for the target if the acquirer is assured consummation of the transaction. The target company also benefits from the certainty of completing a transaction with a bidder because losing an acquirer creates the perception that a target is damaged goods, thus reducing its value.

While the present case does not involve an attempt to hold on to only one interested bidder, the NCS board was equally concerned about "exchanging certainties" with Genesis. If the creditors decided to force NCS into bankruptcy, which could have happened at any time as NCS was unable to service its obligations, the stockholders would have received nothing. The NCS board also did not know if the NCS business prospects would have declined again, leaving NCS less attractive to other bidders, including Omnicare, which could have changed its mind and again insisted on an asset sale in bankruptcy.

Situations will arise where business realities demand a lock-up so that wealth-enhancing transactions may go forward. Accordingly, any bright-line rule prohibiting lock-ups could, in circumstances such as these, chill otherwise permissible conduct.

---

94. In *Citron v. Fairchild Camera & Instrument Corp.*, we noted that "whether the constraints are self-imposed or attributable to bargaining tactics of an adversary seeking a final resolution of a belabored process must be considered" in analyzing the target's decision to accept an ultimatum from a bidder. 569 A.2d 53, 67 (Del. 1989). Based on Genesis's prior dealings with Omnicare, NCS had good reason to take the Genesis ultimatum seriously.

OUR JURISPRUDENCE DOES NOT COMPEL THIS COURT TO INVALIDATE THE JOINT ACTION OF THE BOARD AND THE CONTROLLING STOCKHOLDERS

The Majority invalidates the NCS board's action by announcing a new rule that represents an extension of our jurisprudence. That new rule can be narrowly stated as follows: A merger agreement entered into after a market search, before any prospect of a topping bid has emerged, which locks up stockholder approval and does not contain a "fiduciary out" provision, is per se invalid when a later significant topping bid emerges. As we have noted, this bright-line, per se rule would apply regardless of (1) the circumstances leading up to the agreement and (2) the fact that stockholders who control voting power had irrevocably committed themselves, *as stockholders,* to vote for the merger. Narrowly stated, this new rule is a judicially-created "third rail" that now becomes one of the given "rules of the game," to be taken into account by the negotiators and drafters of merger agreements. In our view, this new rule is an unwise extension of existing precedent.

Although it is debatable whether *Unocal* applies—and we believe that the better rule in this situation is that the business judgment rule should apply[102]—we will, nevertheless, assume arguendo—as the Vice Chancellor did—that *Unocal* applies. Therefore, under *Unocal* the NCS directors had the burden of going forward with the evidence to show that there was a threat to corporate policy and effectiveness and that their actions were reasonable in response to that threat. The Vice Chancellor correctly found that they reasonably perceived the threat that NCS did not have a viable offer from Omnicare—or anyone else—to pay off its creditors, cure its insolvency and provide some payment to stockholders. The NCS board's actions—as the Vice Chancellor correctly held—were reasonable in relation to the threat because the Genesis deal was the "only game in town," the NCS directors got the best deal they could from Genesis and—but-for the emergence of Genesis on the scene—there would have been no viable deal.

The Vice Chancellor held that the NCS directors satisfied *Unocal.* He even held that they would have satisfied *Revlon,* if it had applied, which it did not. . . . We agree fully with the Vice Chancellor's findings and conclusions, and we would have affirmed the judgment of the Court of Chancery on that basis.

---

102. The basis for the *Unocal* doctrine is the "omnipresent specter" of the board's self-interest to entrench itself in office. *Unocal Corp. v. Mesa Petroleum Co.,* 493 A.2d 946, 954 (Del. 1985). NCS was not plagued with a specter of self-interest. Unlike the *Unocal* situation, a hostile offer did not arise here until *after* the market search and the locked-up deal with Genesis. The *Unocal* doctrine applies to unilateral board actions that are defensive and reactive in nature. Thus, a *Unocal* analysis was necessary in *Paramount Communications v. Time Inc.* because Time and Warner restructured their original transaction from a merger to an acquisition *in response* to the Paramount bid. 571 A.2d 1140, 1148 (Del. 1989). In *Time,* the original Time-Warner stock-for-stock merger, which this Court held was entitled to the presumption of the business judgment rule, was jettisoned by the parties in the face of Paramount's topping bid. *Id.* at 1152. The merger was replaced with a new transaction which was an all cash tender offer by Time to acquire 51% of the Warner stock. It was the revised agreement, not the original merger agreement, that was found to be "defense-motivated" and subject to *Unocal. Id.*

In our view, the Majority misapplies the *Unitrin* concept of "coercive and preclusive" measures to preempt a proper proportionality balancing. Thus, the Majority asserts that "in applying *enhanced judicial scrutiny* to *defensive devices* designed to protect a merger agreement, . . . a court must . . . determine that those measures are not preclusive or coercive. . . . " Here, the deal protection measures were not adopted unilaterally by the board to fend off an existing hostile offer that threatened the corporate policy and effectiveness of NCS.[105] They were adopted because Genesis—the "only game in town"—would not save NCS, its creditors and its stockholders without these provisions.

The very measures the Majority cites as "coercive" were approved by Shaw and Outcalt through the lens of their independent assessment of the merits of the transaction. The proper inquiry in this case is whether the NCS board had taken actions that "have the effect of causing the stockholders to vote in favor of the proposed transaction for some reason other than the merits of that transaction."[109] Like the termination fee upheld as a valid liquidated damages clause against a claim of coercion in *Brazen v. Bell Atlantic Corp.,* the deal protection measures at issue here were "an integral part of the merits of the transaction" as the NCS board struggled to secure—and did secure—the only deal available.

Outcalt and Shaw were fully informed stockholders. As the NCS controlling stockholders, they made an informed choice to commit their voting power to the merger. The minority stockholders were deemed to know that when controlling stockholders have 65% of the vote they can approve a merger without the need for the minority votes. Moreover, to the extent a minority stockholder may have felt "coerced" to vote for the merger, which was already a *fait accompli,* it was a meaningless coercion—or no coercion at all—because the controlling votes, those of Outcalt and Shaw, were already "cast." Although the fact that the controlling votes were committed to the merger "precluded" an overriding vote against the merger by the Class A stockholders, the pejorative "preclusive" label applicable in a *Unitrin* fact situation has no application here. Therefore, there was no meaningful minority stockholder voting decision to coerce.

In applying *Unocal* scrutiny, we believe the Majority incorrectly preempted the proportionality inquiry. In our view, the proportionality inquiry must account for the reality that the contractual measures protecting this merger

---

105. The Majority states that our decisions in *Williams v. Geier* and *Stroud v. Grace* do not hold that "the operative effect of a voting agreement must be disregarded *per se* when a *Unocal* analysis is applied to a comprehensive and combined merger defense plan." *Majority Opinion* at 934. In *Stroud v. Grace,* however, we noted that "The record clearly indicates, and [plaintiff] . . . concedes, that over 50% of the outstanding shares of . . . [the corporation] are under the direct control of [the defendants]. . . . These directors controlled the corporation in fact and law. *This obviates any threat contemplated by* Unocal. . . . " 606 A.2d 75, 83 (Del. 1992) (*emphasis supplied*). According to *Stroud,* then, Shaw's and Outcalt's decision to enter into the voting agreements should not be subject to a *Unocal* analysis because they controlled the corporation "in fact and law." *Id.* Far from a breach of duty, the joint action of the stockholders and directors here represents "the highest and best form of corporate democracy." *Williams v. Geier,* 671 A.2d 1368, 1381 (Del. 1996).

109. *Geier,* 671 A.2d at 1382-83 (citations omitted).

agreement were necessary to obtain the Genesis deal. The Majority has not demonstrated that the director action was a disproportionate response to the threat posed. Indeed, it is clear to us that the board action to negotiate the best deal reasonably available with the only viable merger partner (Genesis) who could satisfy the creditors and benefit the stockholders, was reasonable in relation to the threat, by any practical yardstick.

AN ABSOLUTE LOCK-UP IS NOT A PER SE VIOLATION OF FIDUCIARY DUTY

We respectfully disagree with the Majority's conclusion that the NCS board breached its fiduciary duties to the Class A stockholders by failing to negotiate a "fiduciary out" in the Genesis merger agreement. What is the practical import of a "fiduciary out?" It is a contractual provision, articulated in a manner to be negotiated, that would permit the board of the corporation being acquired to exit without breaching the merger agreement in the event of a superior offer.

In this case, Genesis made it abundantly clear early on that it was willing to negotiate a deal with NCS but only on the condition that it would not be a "stalking horse." Thus, it wanted to be certain that a third party could not use its deal with NCS as a floor against which to begin a bidding war. As a result of this negotiating position, a "fiduciary out" was not acceptable to Genesis. The Majority Opinion holds that such a negotiating position, if implemented in the agreement, is invalid per se where there is an absolute lock-up. We know of no authority in our jurisprudence supporting this new rule, and we believe it is unwise and unwarranted.

The Majority relies on our decision in *QVC* to assert that the board's fiduciary duties prevent the directors from negotiating a merger agreement without providing an escape provision. Reliance on *QVC* for this proposition, however, confuses our statement of a board's responsibilities when the directors confront a superior transaction and turn away from it to lock up a less valuable deal with the very different situation here, where the board committed itself to the *only* value-enhancing transaction available. The decision in *QVC* is an extension of prior decisions in *Revlon* and *Mills* that prevent a board from ignoring a bidder who is willing to match and exceed the favored bidder's offer. The Majority's application of "continuing fiduciary duties" here is a further extension of this concept and thus permits, wrongly in our view, a court to second-guess the risk and return analysis the board must make to weigh the value of the only viable transaction against the prospect of an offer that has not materialized.

The Majority also mistakenly relies on our decision in *QVC* to support the notion that the NCS board should have retained a fiduciary out to save the minority stockholder from Shaw's and Outcalt's voting agreements. Our reasoning in *QVC*, which recognizes that minority stockholders must rely for protection on the fiduciary duties owed to them by directors, does not create a *special* duty to protect the minority stockholders from the consequences of a controlling stockholder's ultimate decision unless the controlling stockholder stands on both sides of the transaction, which is certainly not the case here. Indeed, the discussion of a minority stockholders' lack of voting power in *QVC* notes the importance of enhanced scrutiny in change of control transactions *precisely because* the minority stockholders' interest in the *newly merged entity* thereafter will hinge on the course set by the controlling stockholder. In *QVC,* Sumner Redstone owned 85% of the voting stock of Viacom, the surviving corporation. Unlike the stockholders who are confronted with a transaction that will relegate them to a minority status in the corporation, the Class A stockholders of NCS purchased stock knowing that the Charter provided Class B stockholders voting control.

CONCLUSION

It is regrettable that the Court is split in this important case. One hopes that the Majority rule announced here—though clearly erroneous in our view—will be interpreted narrowly and will be seen as *sui generis.* By deterring bidders from engaging in negotiations like those present here and requiring that there must always be a fiduciary out, the universe of potential bidders who could reasonably be expected to benefit stockholders could shrink or disappear. Nevertheless, if the holding is confined to these unique facts, negotiators may be able to navigate around this new hazard.

Accordingly, we respectfully dissent.

STEELE, Justice, dissenting.

I respectfully dissent from the majority opinion, join the Chief Justice's dissent in all respects and dissent separately in order to crystallize the central focus of my objection to the majority view.

I would affirm the Vice Chancellor's holding denying injunctive relief.

Here the board of directors acted selflessly pursuant to a careful, fair process and determined in good faith that the benefits to the stockholders and corporation flowing from a merger agreement containing reasonable deal protection provisions outweigh any speculative benefits that might result from entertaining a putative higher offer. A court asked to examine the decisionmaking process of the board should decline to interfere with the consummation and execution of an otherwise valid contract.

In my view, the Vice Chancellor's unimpeachable factual findings preclude further judicial scrutiny of the NCS board's business judgment that the hotly negotiated terms of its merger agreement were necessary in order to save the company from financial collapse, repay creditors and provide some benefits to NCS stockholders. . . .

In my opinion, Delaware law mandates deference under the business judgment rule to a board of directors' decision that is free from self interest, made with due care and in good faith. . . .

Importantly, *Smith v. Van Gorkom,* correctly casts the focus on any court review of board action challenged for alleged breach of the fiduciary duty of care "only upon the basis of the information then reasonably available to the directors and relevant to their decision. . . ." Though criticized particularly for the imposition of personal liability on directors for a breach of the duty of care, *Van Gorkom* still stands for the importance of recognizing the limited circumstances for court intervention and the importance of focusing on the timing of the decision attacked. . . .

In the factual context of this case, the NCS board had thoroughly canvassed the market in an attempt to find an acquirer, save the company, repay creditors and provide some financial benefit to stockholders. They did so in the face of silence, tepid interest to outright hostility from Omnicare. The only *bona fide,* credible merger partner NCS could find during an exhaustive process was Genesis, a company that had experienced less than desirable relations with Omnicare in the past. Small wonder NCS' only viable merger partner made demands *and concessions* to acquire contract terms that enhanced assurance that the merger would close. The NCS board agreed to lock up the merger with contractual protection provisions in order to avoid the prospect of Genesis walking away from the deal leaving NCS in the woefully undesirable position of negotiating with a company that had worked for months against NCS' interests by negotiating with NCS' creditors. Those negotiations suggested no regard for NCS' stockholders' interests, and held out only the hope of structuring a purchase of NCS in a bankruptcy environment.

The contract terms that NCS' board agreed to included no insidious, camouflaged side deals for the directors or the majority stockholders nor transparent provisions for entrenchment or control premiums. At the time the NCS board and the majority stockholders agreed to a voting lockup, the terms were the best reasonably available for all the stockholders, balanced against a genuine risk of no deal at all. The cost benefit analysis entered into by an independent committee of the board, approved by the full board and independently agreed to by the majority stockholders cannot be second guessed by courts with no business expertise that would qualify them to substitute their judgment for that of a careful, selfless board or for majority stockholders who had the most significant economic stake in the outcome.

* * *

I believe that the absence of a suggestion of self-interest or lack of care compels a court to defer to what is a business judgment that a court is not qualified to second guess. However, I recognize that another judge might prefer to view the reasonableness of the board's action through the *Unocal* prism before deferring. Some flexible, readily discernible standard of review must be applied no matter what it may be called. Here, one deferring or one applying *Unocal* scrutiny would reach the same conclusion. When a board agrees rationally, in good faith, without conflict and with reasonable care to include provisions in a contract to preserve a deal in the absence of a better one, their business judgment should not be second-guessed in order to invalidate or declare unenforceable an otherwise valid merger agreement. The fact that majority stockholders free of conflicts have a choice and every incentive to get the best available deal and then make a rational judgment to do so as well neither unfairly impinges upon minority shareholder choice or the concept of a shareholder "democracy" nor has it any independent significance bearing on the reasonableness of the board's separate and distinct exercise of judgment.

* * *

Therefore, I respectfully dissent.

QUESTIONS

1. Why would Genesis insist on an exclusivity agreement? What is required under the terms of this exclusivity agreement?

2. Who insisted that the agreement prevent NCS from meeting with Omnicare while negotiating with NCS?

3. What is a "force the vote" provision? Why is that provision considered a "deal protection" measure?

4. Why would Genesis grant a waiver of the type described by the *Omnicare* court? Is it because they have nothing to lose since Genesis has secured voting agreements from 65 percent of Omnicare shareholders?

5. Does *Revlon* apply? In other words, did Omnicare enter the *Revlon* mode?

6. What is the analytical approach used by the Delaware Supreme Court to decide the validity of the deal protection devices used here? Is it the same (consistent with) the analytical approach used in prior takeover cases involving breach of fiduciary claims? For example, is the reasoning used in *Omnicare* consistent with the court's analytical approach in *Brazen*?

7. What standard of review would the dissent apply to these facts?

8. How does the combination of deal protection devices that were at issue in *Omnicare* differ from the use of a dual-capital structure of the type in place at Google, Inc.? *See supra,* at pp. 666-668.

9. Generally speaking, Delaware case law does not draw a distinction between directors of privately held and publicly held companies in defining the scope of directors' duties to the corporation. Well-established Delaware case law makes it clear that the same fiduciary duties of due care, good faith, and loyalty are applicable to all companies incorporated in Delaware. However, is there any reason to distinguish acquisitions of private companies from those involving public companies? Based on the reasoning in *Omnicare,* do you think the Delaware courts would reach the same result in the case of an acquisition of a privately held Target in which a majority of the voting shares were locked up (i.e., committed to vote in favor of the proposed transaction with Bidder) at the time the acquisition agreement was signed? Is there any principled way to validate the kind of lock-up arrangement involved in *Omnicare* in the context of the acquisition of a privately held Target in order to reach a different result than *Omnicare*? Does it affect your analysis if Target has only two shareholders (such as the two Merage brothers who own all of Chef America) as opposed to a privately held company involving 30-40 shareholders, many of whom are also employees of Target Co.?

10. Delaware §203 applied to the facts involved in *Omnicare,* and thus board approval was required for the proposed transaction. Does the application of Delaware §203 present a principled basis on which to distinguish public company deals from those involving private company targets?

11. Can the written consent procedure available under Delaware law (*see* DGCL §228) be used to avoid the result in *Omnicare?* Is a written consent distinguishable from a voting agreement of the type used in *Omnicare?* (*Hint:* A "sign-and-consent" shareholder approval structure in a merger transaction typically requires that Target's shareholders provide "written consent" (pursuant to DGCL §228) approving the merger transaction shortly *after* the signing of the merger agreement.)

12. Does the court in *Omnicare* suggest that the coerciveness and/or preclusiveness analysis must be done before analyzing the validity of a deal protection measure under the two-pronged *Unocal* standard? In other words, how does the court's concern about the preclusiveness and/or coerciveness of a particular defensive measure fit into the *Unocal* standard of intermediate scrutiny?

13. After *Omnicare,* can controlling shareholders do whatever they want with their shares (i.e., vote their shares as they see fit)? Does that type of property-based theory of share ownership continue to hold true under Delaware law after the *Omnicare* decision?

14. What is a "fiduciary out"? Why does the Delaware Supreme Court require use of a "fiduciary out"? Does *Omnicare* stand for the proposition that *all* acquisition agreements (or perhaps just those involving publicly traded targets) *must* include a fiduciary out?

NOTES

1. "Force the Vote" Provision.   As a result of provisions that were originally made part of Delaware GCL §251(c), and which are now codified in Delaware GCL §146,* the board is no longer required to recommend the merger to the company's shareholders; all that is now required is that the board initially conclude that it is advisable to submit the merger to Target shareholders. Under what is commonly referred to as a "force the vote" provision, many merger agreements now include a provision that requires a merger transaction be submitted to a vote of Target's shareholders even in those cases where Target's board has withdrawn its recommendation. Although rare, there have been instances (such as *Omnicare)* where Target's board has withdrawn its recommendation but still proceeded to submit the transaction to a vote of the company's shareholders. In general, most proxy statements will include a section setting forth the basis for the board's recommendation that shareholders approve a transaction and that the board recommends that shareholders vote to approve the transaction.

---

* "Section 146 was added to the [Delaware GCL] in 2003. Under this section, directors may authorize the corporation to agree with another person to submit a matter to the stockholders, but the directors reserve the ability to change their recommendation of the matter. Prior to the 2003 amendment, a rule similar to that set forth in section 146 was codified at section 251(c) and applied to mergers and consolidations. Section 146 was enacted to clarify that the rule previously set forth in section 251(c) applies to *any* matter submitted to stockholders." Edward R. Welch and Andrew J. Turezyn, FOLK ON THE DELAWARE GENERAL CORPORATION LAW §146.1 at p. 276 (FUNDAMENTALS 2006 ed.) (*emphasis added*).

2. Sharply Divided Opinion. The *Omnicare* decision was the result of a rather unusual 3-2 split of the Delaware Supreme Court, with two very sharply worded dissents being filed by Chief Justice Veasey and Justice Steele. This split, which is highly unusual for the Delaware Supreme Court (a court that is widely regarded as striving to reach its decisions on a unanimous basis) has led many observers to speculate whether this decision will be further refined or modified by the Delaware court in the near future, which was the hope clearly expressed by the both of the dissents. Speculation that the court will revisit the issues raised in this case has been further fueled in light of the subsequent appointment of Justice Steele (who filed a dissent in *Omnicare*) to serve as chief justice of the Delaware Supreme Court, following the retirement in 2004 of Chief Justice Veasey (who authored the other dissent in *Omnicare*). To make matters even more intriguing, Justice Walsh, who was in the majority in *Omnicare*, has since retired from the Delaware Supreme Court.

3. The Fall-Out from Omnicare. Since the Delaware Supreme Court decided *Omnicare* almost ten years ago, controversy has surrounded its decision, with criticism coming from both practicing M&A lawyers and academic lawyers. Although the decision remains controversial, with many experienced observers opining that the Delaware Supreme Court will eventually overturn its ruling, *Omnicare* "remains the common law of Delaware with respect to the precise facts in that case—a fully locked-up deal that was a *fait accompli*." The Deal Lawyer, *Webcast Transcript, M&A Deal Protections: The Latest Developments and Techniques*, Sept. 18, 2012, *available at* http://www.deallawyers.com/member/Programs/Webcast/2012/09_18/transcript.html. While *Omnicare* remains the law of the land, the Delaware Chancery courts have nonetheless "sought to narrow the reach of *Omnicare*" by distinguishing the facts at issue in subsequent cases in order "to find *Omnicare* inapplicable. . . . In the wake of *Omnicare*, a variety of deal structures have emerged to avoid replicating the facts [of *Omnicare*] where the [prospective M&A] deal involves a controller [i.e., controlling shareholder] or a majority selling block [of Target shares]." *Id.* As a general proposition, the strategy to avoid "replicating" *Omnicare* centers on "the fact that there are three legs to it": the force-the-vote provision, the shareholder voting agreements and the failure to include a "fiduciary out" clause. So, the strategy is to "kick-out any of one of those [three] legs [in order to] distinguish *Omnicare*." *Id.* One commonly accepted strategy "is to not have a voting agreement that gets you to the level of a *fait accompli*. What level is that? That's up for debate when it's not a majority [of the shares]. But how close can you get to a majority is one issue that gets debated. And it tends to be . . . [very] fact specific." *Id.*

4. Omnicare and the "Revlon" Mode. It bears emphasizing that the Delaware Supreme Court in *Omnicare* applied *Unocal* as the appropriate standard of judicial review, not *Revlon*.

> The directors' *Revlon* obligations were not triggered because the NCS-Genesis merger agreement did not involve a sale of control. The deal was a stock-for-stock combination. Genesis was a public, listed company that had no controller or control group. So, in the *Paramount v. Time* sense, stockholders of NCS were going to receive shares that traded in a fluid, changing and changeable market. [For

many commentators, this has left] a bit of fuzziness after *Omnicare*, as a result of the dissent in this 3-2 decision and the criticism surrounding the appropriateness of using *Unocal* and *Unitrin* [*Unitrin, Inc. v. American General Corp.*, 651 A.2d 1361 (Del. 1995)] as the judicial review standard to assess the validity of deal protections in a friendly merger transaction. This may be more of an academic point with no meaningful distinction, but there's still a question . . . of whether deal protections in transactions where *Revlon* applies should be reviewed under the *Revlon* standard or whether, in all contexts, deal protections should be reviewed under the *Unocal* and *Unitrin* standard. In any case, [it would seem that] after *Omnicare* . . . heightened scrutiny is the prevailing judicial review standard for [analyzing the validity of] deal protection [devices].

THE DEAL LAWYER, *Webcast Transcript, supra. Query*: What do you think? What should be the standard of review in determining the validity of deal protection measures in the context of an M&A transaction involving a change of control: *Revlon* or *Unocal*?

5. The Deal-Making Process in M&A Transactions Continues to Evolve.   Starting with our description of the "flow of a deal" in Chapter 1, which details the deal-making process typically involved in an M&A transaction, we have observed that the life cycle of an M&A transaction continues to evolve, responding to ever-changing market conditions. In addition, starting with the problem sets in Chapter 2, we have seen how the legal constraints imposed on M&A transactions—as a matter of both state and federal law—have contributed to the further evolution of the deal-making process. Most notably, since the tumultuous period of the mid-1980s, when the Delaware Supreme Court decided the seminal cases of *Unocal, Moran,* and *Revlon,* "deal-makers have devised various tactics and sale methods in response [to these landmark Delaware decisions and their progeny] . . . Similar to Delaware's takeover jurisprudence, corporate sale methods are not formed in a vacuum, but are products of the periods in which they are developed." Christina M. Sautter, *Shopping During Extended Store Hours: From No Shops to Go Shops,* 73 BROOK. L. REV. 525, 526 (2008). The next two Delaware cases move us into a new era of M&A deal making. These cases also offer the opportunity to further reflect on how the Delaware courts are continually refining their takeover jurisprudence in order to address the fiduciary duty concerns presented by the facts of this new deal making trend broadly referred to as "going private" deals.

In re The Topps Company Shareholders Litigation
926 A.2d 58 (Del. Ch. 2007)

STRINE, Vice Chancellor.

I.   INTRODUCTION

The Topps Company, Inc. is familiar to all sports-loving Americans. Topps makes baseball and other cards (think Pokemon), this is Topps's so-called "Entertainment Business." It also distributes Bazooka bubble gum and other old-style confections, this is Topps's "Confectionary Business." Arthur Shorin, the son of Joseph Shorin, one of the founders of Topps and the inspiration for "Bazooka Joe," is Topps's current Chairman and Chief Executive Officer. Shorin has served in those positions since 1980 and has worked for Topps for more than half a century, though he owns only about 7% of Topps's equity. Shorin's son-in-law, Scott Silverstein, is his second-in-command, serving as Topps's President and Chief Operating Officer.

Despite its household name, Topps is not a large public company. Its market capitalization is less than a half billion dollars and its financial performance has, as a general matter, flagged over the past five years.

In 2005, Topps was threatened with a proxy contest. It settled that dispute by a promise to explore strategic options, including a sale of its Confectionary Business. Topps tried to auction off its Confectionary Business, but a serious buyer never came forward. Insurgents reemerged the next year, in a year when Shorin was among the three directors up for re-election to Topps's classified board. With the ballots about to be counted, and defeat a near certainty for the management nominees, Shorin cut a face-saving deal, which expanded the board to ten and involved his re-election along with the election of all of the insurgent nominees.

Before that happened, former Disney CEO and current private equity investor Michael Eisner had called Shorin and offered to be "helpful." Shorin understood Eisner to be proposing a going private transaction.

Once the insurgents were seated, an "Ad Hoc Committee" was formed of two insurgent directors and two "Incumbent Directors" to evaluate Topps's strategic direction. Almost immediately, the insurgent directors and the incumbent directors began to split on substantive and, it is fair to say, stylistic grounds. The insurgents then became "Dissident Directors."

In particular, the Ad Hoc Committee divided on the issue of whether and how Topps should be sold. The Dissident Directors waxed and waned on the advisability of a sale, but insisted that if a sale was to occur, it should involve a public auction process. The Incumbent Directors were also ambivalent about a sale, but were resistant to the idea that Topps should again begin an auction process, having already failed once in trying to auction its Confectionary Business.

From the time the insurgents were seated, Eisner was on the scene, expressing an interest in making a bid. Two other financial buyers also made a pass. But Topps's public message was that it was not for sale.

Eventually, the other bidders dropped out after making disappointingly low value expressions of interest. Eisner was told by a key Incumbent Director that the Incumbent Directors might embrace a bid of $10 per share. Eisner later bid $9.24 in a proposal that envisioned his retention of existing management, including Shorin's son-in-law. Eisner was willing to tolerate a post-signing Go Shop process, but not a pre-signing auction.

The Ad Hoc Committee split 2-2 over whether to negotiate with Eisner. Although offered the opportunity to participate in the negotiation process, the apparent leader of the Dissidents refused, favoring a public auction. One of the Incumbent Directors who was an independent director took up the negotiating oar, and reached agreement with Eisner on a merger at $9.75 per share. The "Merger Agreement" gave Topps the chance to shop the bid for 40 days after signing, and the right to accept a "Superior Proposal" after that, subject only to Eisner's receipt of a termination fee and his match right.

The Topps board approved the Merger Agreement in a divided vote, with the Incumbent Directors all favoring the Merger, and the Dissidents all dissenting. Because of the dysfunctional relations on the Ad Hoc Committee, that Committee was displaced from dealing with the Go Shop process by an Executive Committee comprised entirely of Incumbent Directors.

Shortly before the Merger Agreement was approved, Topps's chief competitor in the sports cards business, plaintiff The Upper Deck Company, expressed a willingness to make a bid. That likely came as no surprise to Topps since Upper Deck had indicated its interest in Topps nearly a year and half earlier. In fact, Upper Deck had expressed an unrequited ardor for a friendly deal with Topps since 1999, and Shorin knew that. But Topps signed the Merger Agreement with Eisner without responding to Upper Deck's overture. Shortly after the Merger was approved, Topps's investment banker began the Go Shop process, contacting more than 100 potential strategic and financial bidders, including Upper Deck, who was the only serious bidder to emerge.

Suffice it to say that Upper Deck did not move with the clarity and assiduousness one would ideally expect from a competitive rival seeking to make a topping bid. Suffice it also to say that Topps's own reaction to Upper Deck's interest was less than welcoming. Instead of an aggressive bidder and a hungry seller tangling in a diligent, expedited way over key due diligence and deal term issues, the story that emerges from the record is of a slow-moving bidder unwilling to acknowledge Topps's legitimate proprietary concerns about turning over sensitive information to its main competitor and a seller happy to have a bid from an industry rival go away, even if that bid promised the Topps's stockholders better value.

By the end of the Go Shop period, Upper Deck had expressed a willingness to pay $10.75 per share in a friendly merger, subject to its receipt of additional due diligence and other conditions. Although having the option freely to continue negotiations to induce an even more favorable topping bid by finding that Upper Deck's interest was likely to result in a Superior Proposal, the Topps board, with one Dissident Director dissenting, one abstaining, and one absent, voted not to make such a finding.

After the end of the Go Shop period, Upper Deck made another unsolicited overture, expressing a willingness to buy Topps for $10.75 without a financing contingency and with a strong come hell or high water promise to deal with manageable (indeed, mostly cosmetic) antitrust issues. The bid, however, limited Topps to a remedy for failing to close limited to a reverse break-up fee in the same amount ($12 million) Eisner secured as the only recourse against him. Without ever seriously articulating why Upper Deck's proposal for addressing the antitrust issue was inadequate and without proposing a specific higher reverse break-up fee, the Topps Incumbent Directors have thus far refused to treat Upper Deck as having presented a Superior Proposal, a prerequisite to putting the onus on Eisner to match that price or step aside.

In fact, Topps went public with a disclosure about Upper Deck's bid, but in a form that did not accurately represent that expression of interest and disparaged Upper Deck's seriousness. Topps did that knowing that it had required Upper Deck to agree to a contractual standstill (the "Standstill Agreement") prohibiting Upper Deck from making public any information about its discussions with Topps or proceeding with a tender offer for Topps shares without permission from the Topps board.

The Topps board has refused Upper Deck's request for relief from the Standstill Agreement in order to allow Upper Deck to make a tender offer and to tell its side of events. A vote on the Eisner Merger is scheduled to occur within a couple of weeks.

A group of "Stockholder Plaintiffs" and Upper Deck (collectively, the "moving parties") have moved for a preliminary injunction. They contend that the upcoming Merger vote will be tainted by Topps's failure to disclose material facts about the process that led to the Merger Agreement and about Topps's subsequent dealings with Upper Deck. Even more, they argue that Topps is denying its stockholders the chance to decide for themselves whether to forsake the lower-priced Eisner Merger in favor of the chance to accept a tender offer from Upper Deck at a higher price. Regardless of whether the Topps board prefers the Eisner Merger as lower risk, the moving parties contend that the principles animating *Revlon, Inc. v. MacAndrews & Forbes Holdings, Inc.*[1] prevent the board from denying the stockholders the chance to make a mature, uncoerced decision for themselves.

In this decision, I conclude that a preliminary injunction against the procession of the Eisner Merger vote should issue until such time as: (1) the Topps board discloses several material facts not contained in the corporation's "Proxy Statement," including facts regarding Eisner's assurances that he would retain existing management after the Merger; and (2) Upper Deck is released from the standstill for purposes of: (a) publicly commenting on its negotiations with Topps; and (b) making a non-coercive tender offer on conditions as favorable or more favorable than those it has offered to the Topps board.

The moving parties have established a reasonable probability of success that the Topps board is breaching its fiduciary duties by misusing the Standstill in order to prevent Upper Deck from communicating with the Topps stockholders and presenting a bid that the Topps stockholders could find materially more favorable than the Eisner Merger. Likewise, the moving parties have shown a likelihood of success on their claim that the Proxy Statement is materially misleading in its current form.

The injunction that issues is warranted to ensure that the Topps stockholders are not irreparably injured by the loss of an opportunity to make an informed decision and to avail themselves of a higher-priced offer that they might find more attractive.

II. A READER'S ROADMAP TO THE OPINION

The briefs of the Stockholder Plaintiffs and Upper Deck advance arguments so numerous that it is realistically impossible for the court to address them all in the time frame in which a decision of this kind should issue; nor, frankly, do the briefs treat all these arguments in a substantive manner that

---

1. 506 A.2d 173 (Del. 1986).

comports with requirements for fair presentation. Given this reality, I focus my attention solely on the arguments that are substantial enough to possibly support the issuance of a preliminary injunction.

In examining those issues, I divide my consideration of the merits along a traditional dividing line, which separates my consideration of disclosure claims from my resolution of claims premised on the defendants' compliance with their *Revlon* duties. The standards of review relevant to such claims are familiar and need not be dilated on at length.

When directors of a Delaware corporation seek approval for a merger, they have a duty to provide the stockholders with the material facts relevant to making an informed decision.[3] In that connection, the directors must also avoid making materially misleading disclosures, which tell a distorted rendition of events or obscure material facts. In determining whether the directors have complied with their disclosure obligations, the court applies well-settled standards of materiality, familiar to practitioners of our law and federal securities law.

The so-called *Revlon* standard is equally familiar. When directors propose to sell a company for cash or engage in a change of control transaction, they must take reasonable measures to ensure that the stockholders receive the highest value reasonably attainable.[6] Of particular pertinence to this case, when directors have made the decision to sell the company, any favoritism they display toward particular bidders must be justified solely by reference to the objective of maximizing the price the stockholders receive for their shares. When directors bias the process against one bidder and toward another not in a reasoned effort to maximize advantage for the stockholders, but to tilt the process toward the bidder more likely to continue current management, they commit a breach of fiduciary duty.

* * *

III.   FACTUAL BACKGROUND

A.   THE EISNER MERGER AGREEMENT

Eisner proposes to acquire Topps through a private equity firm he controls, The Tornante Company, LLC, in an alliance with another private equity group, Madison Dearborn Capital Partners, LLC. For simplicity's sake, I refer to Eisner and his private equity partners simply as "Eisner."

Eisner and Topps executed the Merger Agreement on March 5, 2006, under which Eisner will acquire Topps for $9.75 per share or a total purchase price of about $385 million. The Merger Agreement is not conditioned on Eisner's ability to finance the transaction, and contains a representation that Eisner has the ability to obtain such financing. But the only remedy against Eisner if he breaches his duties and fails to consummate the Merger is his responsibility to pay a $12 million reverse break-up fee.

---

3. *E.g., Arnold v. Society for Savings Bancorp., Inc.,* 650 A.2d 1270, 1277 (Del. 1994).

6. *E.g., Revlon,* 506 A.2d at 184 n.16; accord *Paramount Communications, Inc. v. QVC Network, Inc.,* 637 A.2d 34, 44 (Del. 1994).

The "Go Shop" provision in the Merger Agreement works like this. For a period of forty days after the execution of the Merger Agreement, Topps was authorized to solicit alternative bids and to freely discuss a potential transaction with any buyer that might come along. Upon the expiration of the "Go Shop Period," Topps was required to cease all talks with any potential bidders unless the bidder had already submitted a "Superior Proposal," or the Topps board determined that the bidder was an "Excluded Party," which was defined as a potential bidder that the board considered reasonably likely to make a Superior Proposal. If the bidder had submitted a Superior Proposal or was an Excluded Party, Topps was permitted to continue talks with them after the expiration of the Go Shop Period.

The Merger Agreement defined a Superior Proposal as a proposal to acquire at least 60% of Topps that would provide more value to Topps stockholders than the Eisner Merger. The method in which the 60% measure was to be calculated, however, is not precisely defined in the Merger Agreement, but was sought by Eisner in order to require any topping bidder to make an offer for all of Topps, not just one of its Businesses.

Topps was also permitted to consider unsolicited bids after the expiration of the 40-day Go Shop period if the unsolicited bid constituted a Superior Proposal or was reasonably likely to lead to one. Topps could terminate the Merger Agreement in order to accept a Superior Proposal, subject only to Eisner's right to match any other offer to acquire Topps.

The Eisner Merger Agreement contains a two-tier termination fee provision. If Topps terminated the Eisner Merger Agreement in order to accept a Superior Proposal during the Go Shop Period, Eisner was entitled to an $8 million termination fee (plus a $3.5 million expense reimbursement), in total, or approximately 3.0% of the transaction value. If Topps terminates the Merger Agreement after the expiration of the Go Shop Period, Eisner is entitled to a $12 million termination fee (plus a $4.5 million expense reimbursement), or approximately 4.6% of the total deal value.

The Eisner Merger Agreement is subject to a number of closing conditions, such as consent to the transaction by regulatory authorities and the parties to certain of Topps's material contracts, such as its licenses with Major League Baseball and other sports leagues.

In connection with the Eisner Merger Agreement, Shorin and Eisner entered into a letter agreement pursuant to which Shorin agreed to retire within sixty days after the consummation of the Merger and to surrender $2.8 million to which he would otherwise be entitled under his existing employment agreement in the event of a change of control of Topps. Shorin would remain a consultant to Topps for several years with sizable' benefits, consistent with his existing employment agreement.

* * *

IV.   THE ESSENCE OF THE *REVLON* CLAIMS

The *Revlon* arguments advanced by the Stockholder Plaintiffs and Upper Deck differ a bit in their focus. I begin with the Stockholder Plaintiffs' *Revlon* arguments, which are premised on the notion that the Incumbent Directors

who constitute a majority of the Topps board have been motivated by a desire
to ensure that Topps remains under the control of someone friendly to the
Shorin family and who will continue Shorin family members in the top leadership position. Since Shorin was forced into a face-saving settlement adding the
Dissidents to the board, Shorin has known that time was running out on him.
Therefore, he was motivated to find a buyer who was friendly to him and would
guarantee that Shorin and Silverstein, his son-in-law, would continue to play
leading roles at Topps. If Shorin didn't strike a deal to that effect before the
2007 annual meeting, he faced the prospect of having a new board majority
oust him and his son-in-law from their managerial positions, and being relegated to a mere 7% stockholder of the company his father and uncles started,
and that he has personally managed as CEO for more than a quarter century. According to the Stockholder Plaintiffs, Eisner was the answer to Shorin's
dilemma, as he promised to be "helpful" by taking Topps private and retaining
Silverstein as CEO.

To the supposed end of helping Shorin meet his personal objectives, the
Topps board majority resisted the Dissidents' desire for a public auction of
Topps, and signed up a deal with Eisner without any effort to shop the company
beforehand. Not only that, the Stockholder Plaintiffs contend that defendant
Greenberg capped the price that could be extracted from Eisner by making an
ill-advised and unauthorized decision to mention to Eisner that a $10 per share
bid was likely to command the support of the non-Dissident directors.

The Stockholder Plaintiffs also complain that the deal protection measures
in the Merger Agreement precluded any effective post-signing market check.
Although the Stockholder Plaintiffs admit the Merger Agreement contained
a Go Shop provision allowing Topps to shop the company for forty days, the
Stockholder Plaintiffs contend that that time period was too short and that the
break-up fee and match right provided to Eisner were, in combination, too bid-
chilling. Therefore, although Topps approached over 100 financial and strategic bidders to solicit their interest, the Stockholder Plaintiffs say that effort
was bound to fail from the get-go, especially given the market's justifiable sus-
picions that Shorin and the board majority wanted to do a deal with Eisner to
preserve the Shorin family's managerial influence.

It is at this stage that the arguments of the Stockholder Plaintiffs and Upper
Deck intersect. Although Upper Deck does not stress the failure of Topps to
seek out a bid from it before signing up a deal with Eisner, it does contend
that the Topps board's lack of responsiveness to its expression of interest in
presenting a bid at $10.75 per share evidences the entrenchment motivations
highlighted by the Stockholder Plaintiffs.

Upper Deck contends that the Topps board unjustifiably delayed its access
to, and the scope of, due diligence materials. Upper Deck argues that the Topps
board manufactured pretextual excuses not to decide before the end of the
Go Shop Period that Upper Deck had presented a proposal reasonably likely
to result in a Superior Proposal. By that decision, the Topps board gave up its
ability freely to continue discussions with Upper Deck.

When Upper Deck refused to lose heart and continued to press ahead by
making a formal unsolicited bid at $10.75 per share, Upper Deck says it met
with further resistance, in the form of withheld due diligence and unsubstantiated concerns about Upper Deck's ability and commitment to closing a deal.

Finally, Upper Deck found itself publicly criticized by the Topps board for having failed to act as a diligent, serious bidder.

When it met those obstacles, Upper Deck asked to be released from the Standstill so that it could: (1) present a tender offer directly to the Topps stockholders; and (2) present its own version of events to the Topps stockholders to correct the misstatements allegedly made by Topps about Upper Deck. But Topps refused, despite its undisputed right under the Eisner Merger Agreement to grant such a relief if the board believed its fiduciary duties so required.

According to Upper Deck (and the Stockholder Plaintiffs), by this pattern of behavior, the Topps board majority has clearly abandoned any pretense of trying to secure the highest price reasonably available. Instead of using the Standstill Agreement for a proper value-maximizing purpose, the Topps board majority is using that Agreement to leave the Topps stockholders with only one viable alternative, Eisner's bid, based on a skewed informational base. Unless injunctive relief issues to prevent the Merger vote, Upper Deck (and the Stockholder Plaintiffs) contend that the Topps stockholders face irreparable injury because they will vote on the Merger in ignorance of Upper Deck's version of events and, even more important, without the chance to accept a tender offer from Upper Deck at a price higher than Eisner's offer.

These are in essence, the key *Revlon* arguments made by the Stockholder Plaintiffs and Upper Deck in support of their application for a preliminary injunction.

V.   RESOLUTION OF THE *REVLON* CLAIMS AND DECISION ON THE SCOPE OF THE INJUNCTION

Upper Deck and the Stockholder Plaintiffs have moved for a preliminary injunction seeking to (1) stop the shareholder vote on the Eisner Merger; (2) require Topps to correct material misstatements in the Proxy Statement; and (3) prevent Topps from using the Standstill Agreement to preclude Upper Deck from publicly discussing its bid for Topps or from making a non-coercive tender offer directly to the Topps stockholders. In the previous sections, I addressed the moving parties' disclosure claims and identified the additional and corrective disclosures that are required before the Eisner Merger vote may proceed.* The only task remaining therefore is to determine whether the moving parties' *Revlon* claims warrant the broader injunctive relief sought.

The legal standard governing the resolution of that question is well settled. In order to warrant injunctive relief, the moving parties must prove that (1) they are likely to succeed on the merits of their *Revlon* claims; (2) they will suffer

---

* [By the author] The complaint alleged a number of disclosure deficiencies in the Proxy Statement soliciting shareholder approval of the Eisner merger. In a portion of the opinion that has been omitted, the court considered a number of "problems with the Proxy Statement." Most importantly, the court agreed with plaintiffs' assertion that the Proxy Statement did not communicate all material facts regarding Eisner's assurances during the course of the merger negotiations that his bid is "friendly to [Topps' incumbent] management and [that his bid] depends on their retention."

imminent irreparable harm if an injunction is not granted; and (3) the balance of the equities weighs in favor of issuing the injunction. I turn to those issues now, dividing the analysis in two parts. First, I address the decisions of the Topps board leading up to the signing of the Merger Agreement with Eisner. I then turn to the Topps board's dealings with Upper Deck after the Merger Agreement was executed.

The Stockholder Plaintiffs have largely taken the lead on the first time period. They argue that the Incumbent Directors unreasonably resisted the desire of the Dissident Directors to conduct a full auction before signing the Merger Agreement, that Greenberg capped the price Eisner could be asked to pay by mentioning that a $10 per share price would likely command support from the Incumbent Directors, that the Incumbent Directors unfairly restricted the Dissident Director's ability to participate in the Merger negotiation and consideration process, and that the Incumbent Directors foreclosed a reasonable possibility of obtaining a better bid during the Go Shop Period by restricting that time period and granting Eisner excessive deal protections. For its part, Upper Deck echoes these arguments, and supplements them with a contention that Upper Deck had made its desire to make a bid known in 2005, before Eisner ever made a formal bid, and was turned away.

Although these arguments are not without color, they are not vibrant enough to convince me that they would sustain a finding of breach of fiduciary duty after trial. A close reading of the record reveals that a spirited debate occurred between the two members of the Ad Hoc Committee who were Incumbent Directors, Greenberg and Feder, and the two who were Dissident Directors, Ajdler and Brog. After examining the record, I am not at all convinced that Greenberg and Feder were wrong to resist the Dissidents' demand for a full auction. Topps had run an auction for its Confectionary Business in 2005, without success.

The market knew that Topps, which had no poison pill in place, had compromised a proxy fight in 2006, with the insurgents clearly prevailing. . . . [O]ne must assume that Upper Deck is run by adults. As Topps's leading competitor, it knew the stress the Dissident Directors would be exerting on Shorin to increase shareholder value. If Upper Deck wanted to make a strong move at that time, it could have contacted Shorin directly . . . , written a bear hug letter, or made some other serious expression of interest, as it had several years earlier. The fact that it did not, inclines me toward the view that the defendants are likely correct in arguing that Upper Deck was focused on acquiring and then digesting another company, Fleer, during 2005 and 2006, and therefore did not make an aggressive run at (a clearly reluctant) Topps in those years.

Given these circumstances, the belief of the Incumbent Directors on the Ad Hoc Committee, and the full board, that another failed auction could damage Topps, strikes me, on this record, as a reasonable one.

* * *

Likewise, I am not convinced that the Incumbent Directors treated the Dissident Directors in a manner that adversely affected the ability of the board to obtain the highest value. The Dissident Directors were full of ideas — ideas that diverged widely. Their views of Topps's value do not suggest that the Topps board's approach was off the mark. . . .

In the end, I perceive no unreasonable flaw in the approach that the Topps board took to negotiating the Merger Agreement with Eisner. I see no evidence that another bidder who expressed a serious interest to get in the game during 2006 was fended off. There is no suggestion by even the Stockholder Plaintiffs that the two other private equity firms who discussed making a bid with Topps were inappropriately treated.

Most important, I do not believe that the substantive terms of the Merger Agreement suggest an unreasonable approach to value maximization. The Topps board did not accept Eisner's $9.24 bid. They got him up to $9.75 per share—not their desired goal but a respectable price, especially given Topps's actual earnings history and the precarious nature of its business.

Critical, of course, to my determination is that the Topps board recognized that they had not done a pre-signing market check. Therefore, they secured a 40-day Go Shop Period and the right to continue discussions with any bidder arising during that time who was deemed by the board likely to make a Superior Proposal. Furthermore, the advantage given to Eisner over later arriving bidders is difficult to see as unreasonable. He was given a match right, a useful deal protection for him, but one that has frequently been overcome in other real-world situations. Likewise, the termination fee and expense reimbursement he was to receive if Topps terminated and accepted another deal—an eventuality more likely to occur after the Go Shop Period expired than during it—was around 4.3% of the total deal value. Although this is a bit high in percentage terms, it includes Eisner's expenses, and therefore can be explained by the relatively small size of the deal. At 42 cents a share, the termination fee (including expenses) is not of the magnitude that I believe was likely to have deterred a bidder with an interest in materially outbidding Eisner. In fact, Upper Deck's expression of interest seems to prove that point—the termination fee is not even one of the factors it stresses.

Although a target might desire a longer Go Shop Period or a lower break fee, the deal protections the Topps board agreed to in the Merger Agreement seem to have left reasonable room for an effective post-signing market check. For 40 days, the Topps board could shop like Paris Hilton. Even after the Go Shop Period expired, the Topps board could entertain an unsolicited bid, and, subject to Eisner's match right, accept a Superior Proposal. The 40-day Go Shop Period and this later right work together, as they allowed interested bidders to talk to Topps and obtain information during the Go Shop Period with the knowledge that if they needed more time to decide whether to make a bid, they could lob in an unsolicited Superior Proposal after the Period expired and resume the process.

In finding that this approach to value maximization was likely a reasonable one, I also take into account the potential utility of having the proverbial bird in hand. Although it is true that having signed up with Eisner at $9.75 likely prevented Topps from securing another deal at $10, the $9.75 bird in hand might be thought useful in creating circumstances where other bidders would feel more comfortable paying something like Upper Deck now says it is willing to bid. Because a credible buying group—comprised not only of Eisner, an experienced buyer of businesses for Disney, but also the experienced private equity firm, Madison Dearborn—had promised to pay $9.75, other bidders could take some confidence in that and have some form of "sucker's insurance" for considering a bid higher than that. Human beings, for better or worse, like cover. We tend to feel better about being wrong, if we can say others made the same mistake. Stated more positively, recognizing our own limitations, we often, quite rationally, take comfort when someone whose acumen and judgment we respect validates our inclinations. A credible, committed first buyer serves that role.

In this regard, Topps's decision to enter into the Merger Agreement with Eisner despite its having received an unsolicited indication of interest from Upper Deck a few days before the signing was also likely not an unreasonable one. This is perhaps a closer call, but the suggestion of Dissident Director Brog to respond to Upper Deck only after inking the Eisner deal bolsters this conclusion. Although the facts on this point are less than clear, as discussed, Topps appears to have had rational reason to be suspicious of Upper Deck's sincerity. Upper Deck had made proposals before, but had often appeared flaky. Moreover, Upper Deck was only expressing an interest in the Entertainment Business, not the whole company at that point. A sale of the Entertainment Business would have left Topps with a floundering Confectionary Business that it had already tried to sell once, without success. Signing up a sure thing with Eisner forced Upper Deck to get serious about the whole company, and set a price floor that Upper Deck knew it had to beat by a material amount.

For all these reasons, I cannot buttress the issuance of an injunction on the alleged unreasonableness of the Topps's board decision to sign up the Merger Agreement. I now turn to the more troubling claims raised, which are about the board's conduct after the Merger Agreement was consummated.

The parties have presented competing versions of the events surrounding Topps's discussions with Upper Deck during the Go Shop Period, beginning with a fight over who was the first to contact the other and when the parties began discussing the Standstill Agreement, which was not executed until the start of the third week of the Go Shop Period. Neither party emerges from these arguments in an entirely positive light. Regardless of whose version of events is correct, the Topps board was hardly as receptive as one would expect in a situation where it received an unsolicited overture from a competitor who had long expressed interest in buying Topps in a friendly deal and who, given the likely synergies involved in a combination of the two businesses, might, if serious about doing a deal, be able to pay a materially higher price than a financial buyer like Eisner. And when Upper Deck actually suggested a price materially higher than Eisner, the Topps Incumbent Directors controlling the process did not evince enthusiasm about the possibilities for the stockholders; rather, they seemed more bent on coming up with obstacles to securing that higher value. This regrettably suggests that the Topps Incumbent Directors favored Eisner, who they perceived as a friendly suitor who had pledged to retain management and would continue Shorin and his family in an influential role.

At the same time, Upper Deck hardly moved with the speed expected of an interested buyer that has a limited time in which to secure a deal. Rather, Upper Deck initially acted in a manner that created rational questions about its seriousness and whether it was simply looking to poke around in Topps's files. To that point, Upper Deck failed to acknowledge Topps's legitimate concerns about entering into serious discussions with its only baseball card competitor. Upper Deck overreached when it asked for a provision in the Standstill Agreement obligating Topps to turn over to it the same information it provided to Eisner and the other bidders. Upper Deck was not the same as the other bidders and Topps had good reason to be skeptical of Upper Deck's intentions. Topps had to balance its concerns about the possibility that Upper Deck might use the Go Shop process as a pretext for gaining access to Topps's proprietary information with the possibility that Upper Deck might be willing to make higher bid than Eisner. There is a colorable argument that in the weeks that followed, Topps did not balance those concerns properly and rather relied on Upper Deck's status as a competitor as a pretext to keep Upper Deck at bay in order to preserve its friendly deal with Eisner. At the same time, Upper Deck's contention that it was delayed in submitting an actual bid for Topps by due diligence gamesmanship is undermined by the fact that Upper Deck claims (hotly disputed by Topps) to have made a blind, unsolicited bid for Topps at $11 a share in 2005. If it was able to make a blind bid then, why not in 2007?

In any event, I need not obsess over the behavior of the parties during the Go Shop Period. Upper Deck did finally make a formal bid for Topps at $10.75 per share two days before the close of the Go Shop. The Topps board had a fiduciary obligation to consider that bid in good faith and to determine whether it was a Superior Proposal or reasonably likely to lead to one. That is especially the case because the Topps board was duty bound to pursue the highest price reasonably attainable, given that they were recommending that the stockholders sell their shares to Eisner for cash.

Because of the final-hour nature of the bid, the Topps board had to determine whether to treat Upper Deck as an Excluded Party under the Merger Agreement so that it could continue negotiations with it after the close of the Go Shop Period. The Topps board's decision not to do so strikes me as highly questionable. In reaching that conclusion, I recognize that Topps had legitimate concerns about Upper Deck's bid. Although there was no financing contingency in the proposal, Topps had reason for concern because Upper Deck has proposed to limit its liability under its proposed deal to $12 million in the event it was not able to close the transaction. Underlying Topps's skepticism of the seriousness of Upper Deck's proposal was perhaps the suspicion that Upper Deck was willing to pay $12 million simply to blow up Topps's deal with Eisner. Topps had to consider the possibility that Upper Deck was afraid that Eisner, by leveraging his reputation in the entertainment community, might be able to turn Topps into a stronger competitor than it had previously been.

Moreover, Upper Deck's initial proposal arguably did not address Topps's concerns that Upper Deck's proposal raised antitrust concerns. In its initial unsolicited overture to Topps before the Eisner deal was signed, Upper Deck acknowledged that there might be some antitrust issues associated with a merger of the two firms. Yet, in its initial bid, Upper Deck proposed placing virtually all of the antitrust risk on Topps. True, Topps had been down this road itself before, and won, but the lack of any more substantial antitrust assurance in Upper Deck's initial bid arguably gave Upper Deck too easy an out in the event that regulators raised even a minor objection because of the optics of the transaction.

That said, Upper Deck was offering a substantially higher price, and rather than responding to Upper Deck's proposal by raising these legitimate concerns, the Topps board chose to tie its hands by failing to declare Upper Deck an

Excluded Party in a situation where it would have cost Topps nothing to do so. Eisner would have had no contractual basis to complain about a Topps board decision to treat Upper Deck as an Excluded Party in light of Upper Deck's 10% higher bid price.

Upper Deck's first bid may not have been a Superior Proposal. But Topps had no reason to believe that the terms of Upper Deck's bid were non-negotiable, and it would have been reasonable for the Topps directors to have believed that their financing and antitrust concerns were manageable ones that could and, indeed, should have been capable of reasonable resolution in subsequent negotiating rounds. Topps could have gone back to Upper Deck with a proposal to increase the reverse termination fee and could have proposed a reasonable provision to deal with the antitrust concerns. By declaring Upper Deck an Excluded Party, the Topps board would have preserved maximum flexibility to negotiate freely with Upper Deck. The downside of such a declaration is hard to perceive.

The only advantage I can perceive from the decision not to continue talking with Upper Deck was if that decision was intended to signal Topps's insistence on a better bid that satisfied its concerns. But the behavior of the Topps's Incumbent Directors and their advisors, as revealed in this record, does not suggest such a motivation. The decision of Brog to abstain from the vote on that issue is an oddment, I admit, which lends support to the decision, but is consistent with the Dissident Directors' enigmatic behavior and possibly a refusal by Brog to vote on the issue, given his exclusion from the sale process. The reason I remain troubled by the decision is that the behavior of the Topps Incumbent Directors after this point inspires no confidence that their prior actions were motivated by a desire to advance the interests of Topps stockholders.

Upper Deck came back a month later with an improved unsolicited bid. That bid again offered a price materially higher than Eisner's: $10.75 per share. That bid also was, again, not any more financially contingent than Eisner's bid; there was no financial contingency, but Topps's remedy was limited to a $12 million reverse break-up fee. This time, to address Topps's antitrust concerns, Upper Deck offered a strong "come hell or high water" provision offering to divest key licenses if required by antitrust regulators, as well as an opinion by a respected antitrust expert addressing Topps's still unspecified antitrust concerns.

Although the Topps Incumbent Directors did obtain a waiver from Eisner to enter discussions with Upper Deck about this bid, they did not pursue the potential for higher value with the diligence and genuineness expected of directors seeking to get the best value for stockholders. Topps made no reasonable counter-offer on the antitrust issue and failed to identify why the transaction proposed a genuine antitrust concern. Instead, Topps insisted that Upper Deck agree to accept any condition, however extreme, proposed by antitrust regulators, and Topps never acknowledged its own past antitrust victories. Although Topps felt free to negotiate price with Eisner when he was promising to pay a materially lower price, cap his liability at $12 million, and condition his deal on approval by Topps licensors (which Upper Deck did not), it never made reasonable suggestions to Upper Deck about a higher reverse break-up fee, antitrust issues, or price. Furthermore, although it did a deal with Eisner with only very limited remedial recourse if he breached, largely one senses, because of the reputational damage Eisner would suffer if he failed to close, the Topps board never seems to have taken into account the reputational damage Upper Deck would suffer if it did the same, despite its knowledge that Upper Deck has acquired other businesses in the past (remember Fleer?) and may therefore wish to continue to do so.

This behavior is consistent with a record that indicates that Shorin was never enthusiastic about the idea of having his family company end up in the hands of an upstart rival. That possible motivation is one that I do not approach in the same reductivist manner as the moving parties. Quite frankly, neither of the moving parties has made the case that Shorin and Silverstein are not skilled, competent, hard-working executives. More important, it is often the case that founders (and sons of founders) believe that their businesses stand for something more than their stock price. Founders therefore often care how their family legacy—in the form of a corporate culture that treats workers and consumers well, or a commitment to product quality—will fare if the corporation is placed under new stewardship.

The record before me clearly evidences Shorin's diffidence toward Upper Deck and his comparatively much greater enthusiasm for doing a deal with Eisner. Eisner's deal is premised on continuity of management and involvement of the Shorin family in the firm's business going forward. Upper Deck is in the same business line and does not need Shorin or his top managers.

Although Shorin and the other defendants claim that they truly desire to get the highest value and want nothing more than to get a topping bid from Upper Deck that they can accept, their behavior belies those protestations. In reaching that conclusion, I rely not only on the defendants' apparent failure to undertake diligent good faith efforts at bargaining with Upper Deck, I also rely on the misrepresentations of fact about Upper Deck's offer that are contained in Topps's public statements.

This raises the related issue of how the defendants have used the Standstill. Standstills serve legitimate purposes. When a corporation is running a sale process, it is responsible, if not mandated, for the board to ensure that confidential information is not misused by bidders and advisors whose interests are not aligned with the corporation, to establish rules of the game that promote an orderly auction, and to give the corporation leverage to extract concessions from the parties who seek to make a bid.

But standstills are also subject to abuse. Parties like Eisner often, as was done here, insist on a standstill as a deal protection. Furthermore, a standstill can be used by a target improperly to favor one bidder over another, not for reasons consistent with stockholder interest, but because managers prefer one bidder for their own motives.

In this case, the Topps board reserved the right to waive the Standstill if its fiduciary duties required. That was an important thing to do, given that there was no shopping process before signing with Eisner.

The fiduciary out here also highlights a reality. Although the Standstill is a contract, the Topps board is bound to use its contractual power under that contract only for proper purposes. On this record, I am convinced that Upper Deck has shown a reasonable probability of success on its claim that the Topps board is misusing the Standstill. As I have indicated, I cannot read the record as indicating that the Topps board is using the Standstill to extract reasonable

concessions from Upper Deck in order to unlock higher value. The Topps
board's negotiating posture and factual misrepresentations are more redolent
of pretext, than of a sincere desire to comply with their *Revlon* duties.

Frustrated with its attempt to negotiate with Topps, Upper Deck asked for
a release from the Standstill to make a tender offer on the terms it offered
to Topps and to communicate with Topps's stockholders. The Topps board
refused. That refusal not only keeps the stockholders from having the chance
to accept a potentially more attractive higher priced deal, it keeps them in the
dark about Upper Deck's version of important events, and it keeps Upper Deck
from obtaining antitrust clearance, because it cannot begin the process without either a signed merger agreement or a formal tender offer.

Because the Topps board is recommending that the stockholders cash out,
its decision to foreclose its stockholders from receiving an offer from Upper
Deck seems likely, after trial, to be found a breach of fiduciary duty. If Upper
Deck makes a tender at $10.75 per share on the conditions it has outlined,
the Topps stockholders will still be free to reject that offer if the Topps board
convinces them it is too conditional. Indeed, Upper Deck is not even asking for
some sort of prior restraint preventing the Topps board from implementing a
rights plan in the event of a tender offer (although Upper Deck has indicated
that will begin round two of this litigation if Topps does). What Upper Deck
is asking for is release from the prior restraint on it, a prior restraint that prevents Topps's stockholders from choosing another higher-priced deal. Given
that the Topps board has decided to sell the company, and is not using the
Standstill Agreement for any apparent legitimate purpose, its refusal to release
Upper Deck justifies an injunction. Otherwise, the Topps stockholders may be
foreclosed from ever considering Upper Deck's offer, a result that, under our
precedent, threatens irreparable injury.[29]

Similarly, Topps went public with statements disparaging Upper Deck's bid
and its seriousness but continues to use the Standstill to prevent Upper Deck
from telling its own side of the story. The Topps board seeks to have the Topps
stockholders accept Eisner's bid without hearing the full story. That is not a
proper use of a standstill by a fiduciary given the circumstances presented here.
Rather, it threatens the Topps stockholders with making an important decision
on an uninformed basis, a threat that justifies injunctive relief.

As this reasoning recognizes, one danger of an injunction based on the
Topps board's refusal to waive the Standstill is that it will reduce the board's
leverage to bargain with Upper Deck. Because this record suggests no genuine
desire by the board to use the Standstill for that purpose, that danger is minimal. To address it, however, the injunction I will issue will not allow Upper Deck
to go backwards as it were. The Merger vote will be enjoined until after Topps
has granted Upper Deck a waiver of the Standstill to: (1) make an all shares,
non-coercive tender offer of $10.75 cash or more per share, on conditions as
to financing and antitrust no less favorable to Topps than contained in Upper
Deck's most recent offer; and (2) communicate with Topps stockholders about
its version of relevant events. The parties shall settle the order in good faith so

---

29. *E.g., MacAndrews & Forbes Holdings, Inc. v. Revlon, Inc.,* 501 A.2d 1239, 1251 (Del. Ch.
1985), *aff'd,* 506 A.2d 173 (Del. 1986).

as to avoid any timing inequities to either Eisner or Upper Deck, and therefore to the Topps stockholders. The injunction will not permit Upper Deck any relief from its obligations not to misuse Topps's confidential information.

In reaching a remedy, I also take into account unsolicited correspondence I received from the defendants today at a time when this decision was being finalized for imminent issuance. That correspondence suggests that the Topps incumbent directors, facing the possibility of an injunction, have now begun to negotiate more earnestly with Upper Deck and to make more serious overtures. Regrettably, Topps did not consult with Upper Deck before sending in the correspondence, has not put off the Eisner Merger vote, and has not obtained Upper Deck's agreement that a delay in issuing this decision is in order. That leaves me in an uncomfortable place. Given the record as it existed as of midday, I conclude that an injunction of the kind I have outlined above remains in order. By its terms, that injunction will not prevent Topps from keeping the Standstill in place but if it chooses to do so, it will not be able to proceed with the Merger vote.

The other danger of an injunction of this kind is premised on a fear that stockholders will make an erroneous decision. In this regard, it is notable that nothing in this decision purports to compel the Topps board to enter a merger agreement with Upper Deck that it believes to be unduly conditional. What this decision does conclude is that, on this record, there is no reasonable basis for permitting the Topps board to deny its stockholders the chance to consider for themselves whether to prefer Upper Deck's higher-priced deal, taking into account its unique risks, over Eisner's lower-priced deal, which has its own risks. If the Topps board sees the Upper Deck tender offer and believes it should not be accepted, it can tell the stockholders why. It can even consider the use of a rights plan to prevent the tender offer's procession, if it can square use of such a plan with its obligations under *Revlon* and *Unocal*. But it cannot at this point avoid an injunction on the unsubstantiated premise that the Topps stockholders will be unable, after the provision of full information, rationally to decide for themselves between two competing, non-coercive offers.

Consistent with this reasoning, the vote on the Eisner Merger will also be enjoined until Topps issues corrective disclosures addressing the problems identified earlier in this decision.

VI.   CONCLUSION

For all these reasons, the moving parties' motion for a preliminary injunction is GRANTED.

QUESTIONS

1. Why is Topps in the *Revlon* mode?

2. What is a "go-shop clause"? As a negotiating strategy, what does Chancellor Strine suggest are the advantages of relying on a go-shop clause rather than engaging in a full auction process before signing the merger agreement with the Bidder (here, Michael Eisner)?

3. What is the nature of the problem that Chancellor Strine identifies regarding the behavior of the Topps board of directors during the post-signing go-shop period?

4. Is the decision (and the court's reasoning) in the *Topps* case consistent with the result reached in *Omnicare* and the reasoning of the Delaware Supreme Court's opinion in that case?

NOTES

1. Go-Shop Clauses.   What is a go-shop clause? These provisions represent an important recent development in the evolution of M&A transactions. As explained by one experienced M&A practitioner:

> A new trend is emerging on the mergers and acquisitions landscape. While M&A deals frequently include no-shop clauses that prevent boards from soliciting higher offers, some companies are now negotiating provisions that allow for the opposite result. These provisions are aptly named go-shop clauses. . . .
> The no-shop clause prohibits the target company from soliciting bids from other buyers. However, in order to ensure the board of directors of the target company is not in breach of its fiduciary duties, no-shop clauses generally allow the board to respond to superior unsolicited bids. In such cases, the target company usually gives the original buyer the opportunity to match the bid. If the original bidder does not match the superior bid, merger agreements generally provide for break [up] fees to be paid to the original buyer.
>
> * * *
>
> A go-shop clause allows the target board to actively shop for additional buyers that will pay a higher price after the board has agreed to deal with an initial buyer. In concept, this provides the opportunity for the target company to obtain better value for its shareholders by using the initial bid as a floor price in the market. Go-shop clauses developed, in part, from the skepticism shareholders have for management-led buyouts. They are meant to reassure shareholders that the target company's board is fulfilling its fiduciary duties and getting the best deal possible. Go-shop clauses have the benefit of promoting greater transparency and openness by allowing the target board to actively seek offers, as opposed to restricting the company to only reacting to unsolicited competing offers.

Blair Horn, *No Shop vs. Go Shop: New Trends in Mergers and Acquisitions*, MERGERS & ACQUISITIONS (May 2007), at p. 55. What are the business motivations that might prompt the parties to include a no-shop clause as part of the acquisition agreement? Notwithstanding the advantages described above regarding a go-shop clause, who might object to the use of a go-shop clause?

2. The Use of "Go-Shops."   In Chapter 2, we described the private equity boom of 2005-2007. *See supra,* pp. 72-75. During this period, financial buyers, such as Eisner in the *Topps* case, made use of "an important new deal making technology" that emerged in this period: the go-shop clause. *See* Guhan Subramanian, *Go-Shops vs. No-Shops in Private Equity Deals: Evidence and Implications,* 63 BUS. LAW. 729, 730 (2008). The emerging importance of the go-shop clause in the M&A deal-making process has been described by Professor Subramanian as follows:

> The "go-shop" clause has emerged as an important new deal-making technology during the private equity boom of 2005-2007. Under the so-called *Revlon* duty, the seller's board of directors must obtain the highest possible price in the sale of the company. Traditionally, the board would satisfy its *Revlon* duty by canvassing the market (through investment bankers), identifying serious bidders, holding a formal or informal auction among them, and signing a deal with the winning bidder. The merger agreement would typically include a "no-shop" clause, which would prevent the target from talking to potential "deal jumpers," unless the target board's fiduciary duty required it to do so (a "fiduciary out"). The go-shop clause turns this traditional approach on its head: rather than canvassing the marketplace first, the seller negotiates with a single bidder, announces the deal, and then has thirty to fifty days to "go shop" to find a higher bidder. At the highest level, then, the traditional route involves a market canvass followed by exclusivity with the winning bidder; while the go-shop route in its pure form involves . . . exclusivity with a bidder followed by a market canvass.

Id. at 729. Based on the empirical evidence collected and analyzed by Professor Subramanian, involving all going private deals between January 2006 and August 2007 that included a private equity buyer, Professor Subramanian reached the following conclusions:

> that go-shop provisions, appropriately structured, can satisfy target board's *Revlon* duties . . . and that private equity firms are not stealing companies from the public shareholders at low-ball prices through go-shops, as some commentators suggest; . . . rather, the go-shop process includes a full price from the first bidder, which is meaningfully shopped post-signing . . . While the evidence presented [in this article] suggests no reason for categorical skepticism of go-shops, the data does indicate some reason to be wary in the specific context of management buyouts ("MBOs") . . . Taken as a whole, these findings have implications for how sell-side boards should structure a meaningful go-shop process, and where the Delaware courts should focus their attention in determining whether a particular go-shop satisfies the selling board's *Revlon* duties. To date, practitioners and courts have focused on the length of the go-shop window and the magnitude of the breakup fee in assessing the viability of the go-shop process. The analysis presented here suggests additional features that boards should negotiate for and courts should look for, particularly in the context of MBOs: bifurcated breakup fees, no contractual match right or (even better) no ability to participate in the post-signing auction, a contractual commitment for the initial bidder to sell in to any higher offer that emerges during the go-shop period, and ex ante inducement fees for subsequent bidders, among other deal features. This proposal tracks the Delaware courts' general approach to conflict [of interest] transactions, which begins with substantive fairness review[9] but gives up fairness review if appropriate procedural protections are in place.[10]

---

9. *See Weinberger v. UOP, Inc.*, 457 A.2d 701, 710-11 (Del. 1983); *Kahn v. Lynch Commc'ns Sys., Inc.*, 638 A.2d 1110, 1115 (Del. 1994).

10. *See* Faith Stevelman, *Going Private at the Intersection of the Market and the Law*, 62 BUS. LAW. 777, 783 (2007).

Id. at 730-731. *See also* Kirkland & Ellis, LLP, *M&A Update: Test-Driving a Hybrid Go-Shop,* (law firm memo, Oct. 28, 2010) ("With the return of private equity dealmaking beginning in 2009, it has quickly become apparent that the predilection towards go-shops . . . is undiminished.") (copy on file with author); and Sacha Jamal, et al., *Private Equity Alert: The Latest Tips You Must Know Before You Go-Shop,* Weil Gotshal, & Manges, LLP (law firm memo, October 2010) (copy on file with author).

G. Management Buyouts: The Duty of Loyalty and Conflicts of Interest

For many observers of recent M&A market activity, the deal at issue in the *Topps* case typifies the type of management buyout (MBO) that came to dominate the private equity boom period that prevailed during 2005-2007. During this period, private equity buyers (such as Michael Eisner and his buyout firm) took advantage of the cheap financing that was available because of the then-prevailing low interest rates. Using substantial amounts of borrowed capital, these financial buyers would then team up with Target's management to propose acquiring Target Co. As Chancellor Strine pointed out, these MBO deals are fraught with conflicts of interest that will, at a minimum, result in the Delaware courts carefully scrutinizing the sale process and its participants. The next case involves a deal where the board of directors decided to undertake a "going private recapitalization" as an alternative to an acquisition. *Query:* Do the facts of the deal at issue in *Gantler v. Stephens* present the same concerns that Chancellor Strine emphasized in his opinion in the *Topps* case? Does the Delaware Supreme Court rely on the same standard of review as did the court in *Topps*?

Gantler v. Stephens
965 A. 2d 695 (Del. 2009)

JACOBS, Justice.

The plaintiffs in this breach of fiduciary duty action, who are certain shareholders of First Niles Financial, Inc. ("First Niles" or the "Company"), appeal from the dismissal of their complaint by the Court of Chancery. The complaint alleges that the defendants, who are officers and directors of First Niles, violated their fiduciary duties by rejecting a valuable opportunity to sell the Company, deciding instead to reclassify the Company's shares in order to benefit themselves, and by disseminating a materially misleading proxy statement to induce shareholder approval. We conclude that the complaint pleads sufficient facts to overcome the business judgment presumption, and to state substantive fiduciary duty and disclosure claims. We therefore reverse the Court of Chancery's judgment of dismissal and remand the case for further proceedings consistent with this Opinion.

FACTUAL AND PROCEDURAL BACKGROUND

A.   THE PARTIES

First Niles, a Delaware corporation headquartered in Niles, Ohio, is a holding company whose sole business is to own and operate the Home Federal Savings and Loan Association of Niles ("Home Federal" or the "Bank"). The Bank is a federally chartered stock savings association that operates a single branch in Niles, Ohio.

The plaintiffs (Leonard T. Gantler and his wife, Patricia A. Cetrone; John and Patricia Gernat; and Paul and Marsha Mitchell) collectively own 121,715 First Niles shares. Plaintiff Gantler was a First Niles director from April 2003 until April 2006.

Defendant William L. Stephens is the Chairman of the Board, President and CEO of both First Niles and the Bank, and has been employed by the Bank since 1969. Defendant P. James Kramer, a director of First Niles and the Bank since 1994, is president of William Kramer & Son, a heating and air conditioning company in Niles that provides heating and air conditioning services to the Bank. Defendant William S. Eddy has been a director of First Niles and the Bank since 2002. Defendant Daniel E. Csontos has been a director of First Niles and the Bank since April 2006. Csontos has also been a full-time employee, serving as compliance officer and corporate secretary of both institutions since 1996 and 2003, respectively. Defendant Robert I. Shaker, who became a director of First Niles and the Bank in January of 2006 after former director Ralph A. Zuzolo passed away, is a principal of a law firm in Niles, Ohio. Defendant Lawrence Safarek is the Treasurer and Vice President of both First Niles and the Bank.

Until his death in August of 2005, Mr. Zuzolo (who is not a party) was a director and corporate board secretary of First Niles and the Bank. Zuzolo was also both a principal in the law firm of Zuzolo, Zuzolo & Zuzolo, and the CEO and sole owner of American Title Services, Inc., a real estate title company in Niles, Ohio. Zuzolo's law firm frequently provided legal services to the Bank, and American Title provided title services for nearly all of the Bank's real estate closings.

B.   EXPLORING A POTENTIAL SALE OF FIRST NILES

In late 2003, First Niles was operating in a depressed local economy, with little to no growth in the Bank's assets and anticipated low growth for the future. At that time Stephens, who was Chairman, President, CEO and founder of First Niles and the Bank, was beyond retirement age and there was no heir apparent among the Company's officers. The acquisition market for banks like Home Federal was brisk, however, and First Niles was thought to be an excellent acquisition for another financial institution. Accordingly, the First Niles Board sought advice on strategic opportunities available to the Company, and in August 2004, decided that First Niles should put itself up for sale (the "Sales Process").

After authorizing the sale of the Company, the First Niles Board specially retained an investment bank, Keefe, Bruyette & Woods (the "Financial Advisor"), and a law firm, Silver, Freedman & Taft ("Legal Counsel"). At the next Board meeting in September 2004, Management advocated abandoning the Sales Process in favor of a proposal to "privatize" the Company. Under Management's proposal, First Niles would delist its shares from the NASDAQ Small-Cap Market, convert the Bank from a federally chartered to a state chartered bank, and reincorporate in Maryland. The Board did not act on that proposal, and the Sales Process continued.

In December 2004, three potential purchasers—Farmers National Banc Corp. ("Farmers"), Cortland Bancorp ("Cortland"), and First Place Financial Corp. ("First Place")—sent bid letters to Stephens. Farmers stated in its bid letter that it had no plans to retain the First Niles Board, and the Board did not further pursue the Farmers' offer. In its bid letter, Cortland offered $18 per First Niles share, 49% in cash and 51% in stock, representing a 3.4% premium over the current First Niles share price. Cortland also indicated that it would terminate all the incumbent Board members, but would consider them for future service on Cortland's board. First Place's bid letter, which made no representation regarding the continued retention of the First Niles Board, proposed a stock-for-stock transaction valued at $18 to $18.50 per First Niles Share, representing a 3.4% to 6.3% premium.

The Board considered these bids at its next regularly scheduled meeting in December 2004. At that meeting the Financial Advisor opined that all three bids were within the range suggested by its financial models, and that accepting the stock-based offers would be superior to retaining First Niles shares. The Board took no action at that time. Thereafter, at that same meeting, Stephens also discussed in further detail Management's proposed privatization.

On January 18, 2005, the Board directed the Financial Advisor and Management to conduct due diligence in connection with a possible transaction with First Place or Cortland. The Financial Advisor met with Stephens and Safarek, and all three reviewed Cortland's due diligence request. Stephens and Safarek agreed to provide the materials Cortland requested and scheduled a due diligence session for February 6. Cortland failed to receive the materials it requested, canceled the February 6 meeting, and demanded the submission of those materials by February 8. The due diligence materials were never furnished, and Cortland withdrew its bid for First Niles on February 10. Management did not inform the Board of these due diligence events until after Cortland had withdrawn its bid.

First Place made its due diligence request on February 7, 2005, and asked for a due diligence review session the following week. Initially, Stephens did not provide the requested materials to First Place and resisted setting a date for a due diligence session. After Cortland withdrew its bid, however, Stephens agreed to schedule a due diligence session.

First Place began its due diligence review on February 13, 2005, and submitted a revised offer to First Niles on March 4. As compared to its original offer, First Place's revised offer had an improved exchange ratio. Because of a decline in First Place's stock value, the revised offer represented a lower implied price per share ($17.25 per First Niles share), but since First Niles' stock price had also declined, the revised offer still represented an 11% premium over market price. The Financial Advisor opined that First Place's revised offer was within an acceptable range, and that it exceeded the mean and median comparable multiples for previous acquisitions involving similar banks.

On March 7, 2005, at the next regularly scheduled Board meeting, Stephens informed the directors of First Place's revised offer. Although the Financial Advisor suggested that First Place might again increase the exchange ratio, the Board did not discuss the offer. Stephens proposed that the Board delay considering the offer until the next regularly scheduled Board meeting. After the Financial Advisor told him that First Place would likely not wait two weeks for a response, Stephens scheduled a special Board meeting for March 9 to discuss the First Place offer.

On March 8, First Place increased the exchange ratio of its offer to provide an implied value of $17.37 per First Niles share. At the March 9 special Board meeting, Stephens distributed a memorandum from the Financial Advisor describing First Place's revised offer in positive terms. Without any discussion or deliberation, however, the Board voted 4 to 1 to reject that offer, with only Gantler voting to accept it. After the vote, Stephens discussed Management's privatization plan and instructed Legal Counsel to further investigate that plan.

C.   THE RECLASSIFICATION PROPOSAL

Five weeks later, on April 18, 2005, Stephens circulated to the Board members a document describing a proposed privatization of First Niles ("Privatization Proposal"). That Proposal recommended reclassifying the shares of holders of 300 or fewer shares of First Niles common stock into a new issue of Series A Preferred Stock on a one-to-one basis (the "Reclassification"). The Series A Preferred Stock would pay higher dividends and have the same liquidation rights as the common stock, but the Preferred holders would lose all voting rights except in the event of a proposed sale of the Company. The Privatization Proposal claimed that the Reclassification was the best method to privatize the Company because it allowed maximum flexibility for future capital management activities, such as open market purchases and negotiated buy-backs. Moreover, First Niles could achieve the Reclassification without having to buy back shares in a fair market appraisal.

On April 20, 2005, the Board appointed Zuzolo to chair a special committee to investigate issues relating to the Reclassification, specifically: (1) reincorporating in a state other than Delaware, (2) changing the Bank's charter from a federal to a state charter, (3) deregistering from NASDAQ, and (4) delisting. However, Zuzolo passed away before any other directors were appointed to the special committee.

On December 5, 2005, Powell Goldstein, First Niles' outside counsel specially retained for the Privatization ("Outside Counsel"), orally presented the Reclassification proposal to the Board. The Board was not furnished any written materials. After the presentation, the Board voted 3 to 1 to direct Outside Counsel to proceed with the Reclassification program. Gantler cast the only dissenting vote.

Thereafter, the makeup of the Board changed. Shaker replaced Zuzolo in January of 2006, and Csontos [a full-time employee of First Niles, who also served as the company's compliance officer and corporate secretary] replaced Gantler in April of 2006. From that point on, the Board consisted of Stephens, Kramer, Eddy, Shaker and Csontos.

On June 5, 2006, the Board determined, based on the advice of Management and First Niles' general counsel, that the Reclassification was fair both to the First Niles shareholders who would receive newly issued Series A Preferred Stock, and to those shareholders who would continue to hold First Niles common stock. On June 19, the Board voted unanimously to amend the Company's certificate of incorporation to reclassify the shares held by owners of 300 or fewer shares of common stock into shares of Series A Preferred Stock that would have the features and terms described in the Privatization Proposal.

D. THE RECLASSIFICATION PROXY AND THE SHAREHOLDER VOTE

On June 29, 2006, the Board submitted a preliminary proxy to the United States Securities and Exchange Commission ("SEC"). An amended version of the preliminary proxy was filed on August 10. Plaintiffs initiated this lawsuit after the amended filing, claiming that the preliminary proxy was materially false and misleading in various respects. On November 16, 2006, the Board, after correcting some of the alleged deficiencies, disseminated a definitive proxy statement ("Reclassification Proxy" or "Proxy") to the First Niles shareholders. On November 20, the plaintiffs filed an amended complaint, alleging (inter alia) that the Reclassification Proxy contained material misstatements and omissions.

In the Reclassification Proxy, the Board represented that the proposed Reclassification would allow First Niles to "save significant legal, accounting and administrative expenses" relating to public disclosure and reporting requirements under the Exchange Act. The Proxy also disclosed the benefits of deregistration as including annual savings of $142,500 by reducing the number of common shareholders, $81,000 by avoiding Sarbanes-Oxley related compliance costs, and $174,000 by avoiding a one-time consulting fee to design a system to improve the Company's internal control structure. The negative features and estimated costs of the transaction included $75,000 in Reclassification-related expenses, reduced liquidity for both the to-be-reclassified preferred and common shares, and the loss of certain investor protections under the federal securities laws.

The Reclassification Proxy also disclosed alternative transactions that the Board had considered, including a cash-out merger, a reverse stock-split, an issue tender offer, expense reduction and a business combination. The Proxy stated that each of the directors and officers of First Niles had "a conflict of interest with respect to [the Reclassification] because he or she is in a position to structure it in such a way that benefits his or her interests differently from the interests of unaffiliated shareholders." The Proxy further disclosed that the Company had received one firm merger offer, and that "[a]fter careful deliberations, the board determined in its business judgment the proposal was not in the best interests of the Company or our shareholders and rejected the proposal."

The Company's shareholders approved the Reclassification on December 14, 2006. Taking judicial notice of the Company's Rule 13e-3 Transaction Statement,[5] the trial court concluded that of the 1,384,533 shares outstanding

---

5. Rules promulgated under the Exchange Act require the filing of a Rule 13e–3 transaction statement for any transaction that may result in a company reclassifying any of its securities. *See* 17 C.F.R. § 240.13e–3 (2008) ("Going Private Transactions by Certain Issuers or Their Affiliates").

and eligible to vote, 793,092 shares (or 57.3%) were voted in favor and 11,060 shares abstained. Of the unaffiliated shares, however, the proposal passed by a bare 50.28% majority vote[.]

E.   PROCEDURAL HISTORY

The amended complaint asserts three separate claims. Count I alleges that the defendants breached their fiduciary duties to the First Niles shareholders by rejecting the First Place merger offer and abandoning the Sales Process. Count II alleges that the defendants breached their fiduciary duty of disclosure by disseminating a materially false and misleading Reclassification Proxy. Count III alleges that the defendants breached their fiduciary duties by effecting the Reclassification.

The defendants moved to dismiss the complaint in its entirety. Defendants argued that Counts I and III were legally deficient for failure to allege facts sufficient to overcome the business judgment presumption; that Count II failed to state a claim that the Reclassification Proxy was materially false and misleading; and that Count III should also be dismissed because the First Niles shareholders had "ratified" the Board's decision to reclassify the First Niles shares. The Court of Chancery credited these arguments and dismissed the complaint. This appeal followed.

ANALYSIS

* * *

I.   THE COURT OF CHANCERY ERRONEOUSLY DISMISSED COUNT I
OF THE COMPLAINT

Count I of the complaint alleges that the defendants breached their duties of loyalty and care as directors and officers of First Niles by abandoning the Sales Process. Specifically, plaintiffs claim that the defendants improperly: (1) sabotaged the due diligence aspect of the Sales Process, (2) rejected the First Place offer, and (3) terminated the Sales Process, all for the purpose of retaining the benefits of continued incumbency.

In his opinion, the Vice Chancellor concluded that *Unocal* did not apply, because the complaint did not allege any "defensive" action by the Board. . . . [On appeal, the Delaware Supreme Court agreed with the Chancellor's decision that *Unocal* did not apply, observing that the Board's decision to reject "an acquisition offer, without more, is not a defensive action under *Unocal*." The Delaware Supreme Court then proceeded to consider the ruling of the Chancery Court, holding the plaintiff had failed to rebut the business judgment rule.]

. . . Because the Board had "initiated the Sales Process on its own accord, seemingly as a market check as part of an exploration of strategic alternatives[,]" that supported the Board's stated business purpose—to reduce corporate expense associated with federal securities law compliance. The Vice

Chancellor also concluded that the complaint failed to plead facts sufficient to infer disloyalty, and that given the Board's extensive discussions with, and receipt of reports from, the Financial Advisor, and given the involvement of specially retained Outside Counsel, the alleged facts were insufficient to establish a violation of the duty of care. The court therefore concluded that the challenged conduct was entitled to business judgment protection, which required the dismissal of Count I.

* * *

B.　THE COURT OF CHANCERY MISAPPLIED THE BUSINESS JUDGMENT STANDARD

The plaintiffs next claim that the legal sufficiency of Count I should have been reviewed under the entire fairness standard. That claim is assessed within the framework of the business judgment standard, which is "a presumption that in making a business decision the directors of a corporation acted on an informed basis, in good faith and in the honest belief that the action taken was in the best interests of the company."

Procedurally, the plaintiffs have the burden to plead facts sufficient to rebut that presumption. On a motion to dismiss, the pled facts must support a reasonable inference that in making the challenged decision, the board of directors breached either its duty of loyalty or its duty of care. If the plaintiff fails to satisfy that burden, "a court will not substitute its judgment for that of the board if the . . . decision can be 'attributed to any rational business purpose.' "[27]

We first consider the sufficiency of Count I as against the Director Defendants. That Count alleges that those defendants (together with non-party director Zuzolo) improperly rejected a value-maximizing bid from First Place and terminated the Sales Process. Plaintiffs allege that the defendants rejected the First Place bid to preserve personal benefits, including retaining their positions and pay as directors, as well as valuable outside business opportunities. The complaint further alleges that the Board failed to deliberate before deciding to reject the First Place bid and to terminate the Sales Process. Indeed, plaintiffs emphasize, the Board retained the Financial Advisor to advise it on the Sales Process, yet repeatedly disregarded the Financial Advisor's advice.

A board's decision not to pursue a merger opportunity is normally reviewed within the traditional business judgment framework. In that context the board is entitled to a strong presumption in its favor, because implicit in the board's statutory authority to propose a merger, is also the power to decline to do so.[29]

---

27. *Unocal v. Mesa Petroleum Co.*, 493 A.2d 946, 954 (Del. 1985) (quoting *Sinclair Oil Corp. v. Levien*, 280 A.2d 717, 720 (Del. 1971)).

29. *See* 8 *Del. C.* §251 for the grant of authority to enter into a merger; *see also* [*TW Servs., Inc. v. SWT Acquisition Corp.*, 1989 WL 20290, at *10–11 [(Del. Ch. March 2, 1989)]; *see generally Kahn v. MSB Bancorp, Inc.*, 1998 WL 409355 (Del. Ch. July 16, 1998), *af'd*, 734 A.2d 158 (Table) (Del. 1999) (describing a board's power under Section 251 and reviewing a decision not to negotiate a merger under the business judgment standard).

Our analysis of whether the Board's termination of the Sales Process merits the business judgment presumption is two pronged. First, did the Board reach its decision in the good faith pursuit of a legitimate corporate interest? Second, did the Board do so advisedly? For the Board's decision here to be entitled to the business judgment presumption, both questions must be answered affirmatively.

We consider first whether Count I alleges a cognizable claim that the Board breached its duty of loyalty. In *TW Services v. SWT Acquisition Corporation,* the Court of Chancery recognized that a board's decision to decline a merger is often rooted in distinctively corporate concerns, such as enhancing the corporation's long term share value, or "a plausible concern that the level of debt likely to be borne by [the target company] following any merger would be detrimental to the long term function of th[at] [c]ompany." A good faith pursuit of legitimate concerns of this kind will satisfy the first prong of the analysis.

Here, the plaintiffs allege that the Director Defendants had a disqualifying self-interest because they were financially motivated to maintain the status quo. A claim of this kind must be viewed with caution, because to argue that directors have an entrenchment motive solely because they could lose their positions following an acquisition is, to an extent, tautological. By its very nature, a board decision to reject a merger proposal could always enable a plaintiff to assert that a majority of the directors had an entrenchment motive. For that reason, the plaintiffs must plead, in addition to a motive to retain corporate control, other facts sufficient to state a cognizable claim that the Director Defendants acted disloyally.[32]

The plaintiffs have done that here. At the time the Sales Process was terminated, the Board members were Stephens, Kramer, Eddy, Zuzolo and Gantler. Only Gantler voted to accept the First Place merger bid. The pled facts are sufficient to establish disloyalty of at least three (*i.e.,* a majority) of the remaining directors, which suffices to rebut the business judgment presumption. First, the Reclassification Proxy itself admits that the Company's directors and officers had "a conflict of interest with respect to [the Reclassification] because he or she is in a position to structure it in a way that benefits his or her interests differently from the interest of the unaffiliated stockholders." Second, a director-specific analysis establishes (for Rule 12(b)(6) purposes) that a majority of the Board was conflicted.

Stephens: Aside from Stephens losing his long held positions as President, Chairman and CEO of First Niles and the Bank, the plaintiffs have alleged specific conduct from which a duty of loyalty violation can reasonably be inferred. Stephens never responded to Cortland's due diligence request. The Financial

---

32. *See Pogostin v. Rice,* 480 A.2d 619, 627 (Del. 1984), *overruled on other grounds by Brehm v. Eisner,* 746 A.2d 244 (Del. 2000) ("plaintiffs have failed to plead any facts supporting their claim[s] that the . . . board rejected the . . . offer solely to retain control. Rather, plaintiffs seek to establish a motive or primary purpose to retain control only by showing that the . . . board opposed a tender offer. Acceptance of such an argument would condemn any board, which successfully avoided a takeover, regardless of whether that board properly determined that it was acting in the best interests of the shareholders.").

Advisor noted that Stephens' failure to respond had caused Cortland to withdraw its bid. Even after Cortland had offered First Niles an extension, Stephens did not furnish the necessary due diligence materials, nor did he inform the Board of these due diligence problems until after Cortland withdrew. Cortland had also explicitly stated in its bid letter that the incumbent Board would be terminated if Cortland acquired First Niles. From these alleged facts it may reasonably be inferred that what motivated Stephens' unexplained failure to respond promptly to Cortland's due diligence request was his personal financial interest, as opposed to the interests of the shareholders. That same inference can be drawn from Stephens' response to the First Place bid: Count I alleges that Stephens attempted to "sabotage" the First Place due diligence request in a manner similar to what occurred with Cortland.

Thus, the pled facts provide a sufficient basis to conclude, for purposes of a Rule 12(b)(6) motion to dismiss, that Stephens acted disloyally.

Kramer: Director Kramer's alleged circumstances establish a similar disqualifying conflict. Kramer was the President of William Kramer & Son, a heating and air conditioning company in Niles that provided heating and air conditioning services to the Bank. It is reasonable to infer that Kramer feared that if the Company were sold his firm would lose the Bank as a client. The loss of such a major client would be economically significant, because the complaint alleges that Kramer was a man of comparatively modest means, and that his company had few major assets and was completely leveraged. Because Kramer would suffer significant injury to his personal business interest if the Sales Process went forward, those pled facts are sufficient to support a reasonable inference that Kramer disloyally voted to terminate the Sales Process and support the Privatization Proposal.

Zuzolo: As earlier noted, Director Zuzolo was a principal in a small law firm in Niles that frequently provided legal services to First Niles and the Bank. Zuzolo was also the sole owner of a real estate title company that provided title services in nearly all of Home Federal's real estate transactions. Because Zuzolo, like Kramer, had a strong personal interest in having the Sales Process not go forward, the same reasonable inferences that flow from Kramer's personal business interest can be drawn in Zuzolo's case.

In summary, the plaintiffs have alleged facts sufficient to establish, for purposes of a motion to dismiss, that a majority of the First Niles Board acted disloyally. Because a cognizable claim of disloyalty rebuts the business judgment presumption, we need not reach the separate question of whether, in deciding to terminate the Sales Process, the Director Defendants acted advisedly (*i.e.,* with due care). Because the claim of disloyalty was subject to entire fairness review, the Court of Chancery erred in dismissing Count I as to the Director Defendants on the basis of the business judgment presumption.

In dismissing Count I as to the Officer Defendants, the Court of Chancery similarly erred. The Court of Chancery has held, and the parties do not dispute, that corporate officers owe fiduciary duties that are identical to those owed by corporate directors. That issue—whether or not officers owe fiduciary duties identical to those of directors—has been characterized as a matter of first impression for this Court. In the past, we have implied that officers of Delaware corporations, like directors, owe fiduciary duties of care and loyalty, and that the fiduciary duties of officers are the same as those of directors.[36] We now explicitly so hold.[37] The only question presented here is whether the complaint alleges sufficiently detailed acts of wrongdoing by Stephens and Safarek to state a claim that they breached their fiduciary duties as officers. We conclude that it does.

Stephens and Safarek were responsible for preparing the due diligence materials for the three firms that expressed an interest in acquiring First Niles. The alleged facts that make it reasonable to infer that Stephens violated his duty of loyalty as a director, also establish his violation of that same duty as an officer. It also is reasonably inferable that Safarek aided and abetted Stephens' separate loyalty breach. Safarek, as First Niles' Vice President and Treasurer, depended upon Stephen's continued good will to retain his job and the benefits that it generated. Because Safarek was in no position to act independently of Stephens, it may be inferred that by assisting Stephens to "sabotage" the due diligence process, Safarek also breached his duty of loyalty.

The Court of Chancery found otherwise. Having characterized Safarek's actions as causing "a delay of a matter of days, or at most a couple of weeks," the Vice Chancellor observed that he could not see how that "conceivably could be a breach of Safarek's fiduciary duties." This analysis is inappropriate on a motion to dismiss. The complaint alleges that Safarek never responded to Cortland's due diligence requests and that as a result, Cortland withdrew a competitive bid for First Niles. Those facts support a reasonable inference that Safarek and Stephens attempted to sabotage the Cortland and First Place due diligence process. On a motion to dismiss, the Court of Chancery was not free to disregard that reasonable inference, or to discount it by weighing it against other, perhaps contrary, inferences that might also be drawn. By dismissing Count I as applied to Stephens and Safarek as officers of First Niles, the trial court erred.

II. The Court of Chancery Erroneously Dismissed Count II of the Complaint

In granting defendants' motion to dismiss Count II, the Court of Chancery ruled that the defendants' allegedly misleading disclosures and non-disclosures relating to the Sales Process and Reclassification were immaterial, because they did not alter the "total mix" of information available to shareholders. . . .

---

36. That officers and directors of Delaware corporations have identical fiduciary duties has long been an articulated principle of Delaware law. *See, e.g., Guth v. Loft, Inc.,* 5 A.2d 503, 510 (Del. 1939) (discussing the duty of loyalty applicable to officers and directors); *Cede & Co. v. Technicolor, Inc.,* 634 A.2d 345, 361 (Del. 1993) (same).

37. That does not mean, however, that the consequences of a fiduciary breach by directors or officers, respectively, would necessarily be the same. Under 8 *Del. C.* §102(b)(7), a corporation may adopt a provision in its certificate of incorporation exculpating its directors from monetary liability for an adjudicated breach of their duty of care. Although legislatively possible, there currently is no statutory provision authorizing comparable exculpation of corporate officers.

We conclude that the Proxy disclosures concerning the Board's deliberations about the First Place bid were materially misleading. Because we reverse
the dismissal of Count II on that basis, we do not reach the plaintiffs' remaining
disclosure claims.

III. THE COURT OF CHANCERY ERRONEOUSLY DISMISSED COUNT III OF THE COMPLAINT

Finally, we address the issues generated by the dismissal of Count III. That
Count alleges that the defendants breached their duty of loyalty by recommending the Reclassification Proposal to the shareholders for purely self-interested
reasons (to enlarge their ability to engage in stock buy-backs and to trigger their
ESOP put and appraisal rights). The Court of Chancery determined that the relevant Board for analytical purposes was the June 2006 Board that voted to effect
the Reclassification, because at any earlier time the Board could have decided
to abandon the transaction. The Vice Chancellor then concluded that the complaint sufficiently alleged that a majority of the directors that approved the
Reclassification Proposal lacked independence. Despite having so concluded,
the court dismissed the claim on the ground that a disinterested majority of the
shareholders had "ratified" the Reclassification by voting to approve it.

The plaintiffs claim that this ratification ruling is erroneous as a matter of
law. They argue that because the Proxy disclosures were materially misleading,
no fully informed shareholder vote took place. The plaintiffs also urge that in
determining the number of unaffiliated shares that were voted, the Court of
Chancery took improper judicial notice of shares owned by the defendants. The
defendants respond that the Vice Chancellor's ratification ruling is correct and
should be upheld. Alternatively, they argue that we should overturn the Vice
Chancellor's determination that the Board had a disqualifying self-interest.

We conclude that the Court of Chancery legally erred in upholding Count
III on shareholder ratification grounds, . . . [because] the Reclassification
Proxy contained a material misrepresentation, [which] eliminates an essential
predicate for applying the doctrine, namely, that the shareholder vote was fully
informed.

* * *

The Court of Chancery held that although Count III of the complaint pled
facts establishing that the Reclassification Proposal was an interested transaction not entitled to business judgment protection, the shareholders' fully
informed vote "ratifying" that Proposal reinstated the business judgment presumption. That ruling was legally erroneous, . . . because we have determined
that the complaint states a cognizable claim that the Reclassification Proxy was
materially misleading (*see* Part II, *supra,* of this Opinion), that precludes ruling at this procedural juncture, as a matter of law, that the Reclassification was
fully informed. Therefore, the approving shareholder vote did not operate as a
"ratification" of the challenged conduct in any legally meaningful sense.

Alternatively, the defendants urge that, apart from ratification, Count III
was properly dismissed because the Board was not interested, and that the Vice
Chancellor's contrary ruling is erroneous. That argument lacks merit both

procedurally and substantively. Procedurally it lacks merit because the Court of Chancery expressly determined that a majority of the Board was interested, and the Defendants have not cross-appealed from that ruling. Substantively, the argument lacks merit, because the defendants concede that Stephens and Csontos were interested in the Reclassification, and our earlier analysis of Kramer's alleged disloyalty with respect to Count I applies equally to Count III.[56] These allegations require that the Vice Chancellor's determination that a majority of the Board was interested be sustained.

We conclude that the Court of Chancery erroneously dismissed Count III of the complaint.

CONCLUSION

For the foregoing reasons, the judgment of the Court of Chancery is reversed as to all counts and remanded for proceedings consistent with the rulings in this Opinion.

NOTES

1. The Doctrine of Shareholder Ratification. With respect to the doctrine of shareholder ratification, the Delaware Supreme Court held in *Gantler* "that the fact that First Nile's shareholders . . . approved the [recapitalization transaction] was irrelevant because the proxy statement distributed in connection with the [shareholder] vote was materially misleading[. As a result, the shareholder vote] was not fully informed and [therefore,] could not operate to ratify board action." *See WSGR Alert: Delaware Court Clarifies Fiduciary Duties of Officers and Directors,* Wilson, Sonsini, Goodrich, & Rosati (law firm memo, February 2009) at p. 1. In this respect, the ruling in *Gantler* is entirely consistent with the Delaware Supreme Court's earlier landmark decision in *Smith v. Van Gorkom.* In both of these cases, the defendant officers and directors sought to rely on a shareholder vote to exonerate them for actions that were alleged to be in breach of their fiduciary duties. In both cases, however, the (cleansing) vote of the shareholders failed to ratify the transaction because of material deficiencies in the company's proxy materials (i.e., the disclosure materials). However, the *Gantler* court also sought to further clarify the doctrine of shareholder ratification as established in *Smith v. Van Gorkom* and its progeny. You will recall that this rather confusing portion of the *Gantler* opinion was described earlier in this chapter, as part of the note material following *Smith v. Van Gorkom. See supra* at pp. 503-505.

2. The Scope of Fiduciary Duty Obligations of Officers. Until the decision in *Gantler,* Delaware caselaw was unclear regarding the contours of the fiduciary

---

56. The complaint's allegations support a reasonable inference that Kramer was motivated by the prospect of preserving the Bank as a client for his heating and air conditioning company, and thus, voted for Reclassification to keep the Bank as a client.

duty obligations of company officers, especially in the context of pending M&A transactions. The *Gantler* opinion establishes that the fiduciary duties owed by officers are the *same* as those owed by directors. "It is important to note that, unlike directors, officers are not protected by Delaware's exculpatory statute. [*See* Del. §102(b)(7).] Whether that distinction could have significant implications for directors who also serve as officers remains to be seen." Hunton Williams, LLP, *Corporate Law Update: Delaware Supreme Court Addresses M&A Process, Officers' Duties and Stockholder Ratification*, (law firm memo, Feb. 2009) (copy on file with author).

   3. "Going Private" Transactions.   In the next section, we will explore in more detail the conflicts of interest that are inherent in the case of a "going private" transaction of the type that was at issue in the *Gantler* case. Since the enactment of the Sarbanes-Oxley Act (SOX), the reform legislation adopted by Congress in 2002, "going private" transactions have been on the rise as many public companies seek to avoid the costs associated with the reforms imposed by SOX on publicly traded companies.

> The number of . . . going private transactions is increasing . . . The driving forces behind the . . . increase in going private transactions include . . . [t]he regulatory costs and burdens associated with being a public company[, which in turn,] often contribute to the determination by a board of directors and management of public companies, particularly smaller cap public companies, to consider going private. The disclosure, compliance and corporate governance requirements of a public company results in increased costs, both in terms of hard dollars and management time, not to mention the increased risk of personal liability to both directors and officers. Whether it is debating proper amounts of disclosure, increasing internal controls, revamping audit committees or rebalancing risks, the costs for a public company have increased considerably since the enactment of the Sarbanes Oxley Act and the related stock exchange requirements.

Michael Weisser and Lindsay Germano, *Private Equity Alert: Going . . . Going . . . Going . . . Gone Private,* Weil, Gotshal, & Manges, LLP, (law firm memo, August 2006) (copy on file with author). Given the increasing prevalence of "going private" transactions, it is important to understand the framework of state and federal regulation of these transactions, which is the focus of the materials in the next section.

H.   "Going Private" Transactions: "Squeeze Outs" of Minority Interests and the Scope of Fiduciary Duty Obligations

In this section, we "bring it all home" by returning to study in more detail the modern regulatory and judicial framework of the "freeze-out" transaction that we first encountered in Chapter 2 as part of our analysis of the Delaware

Supreme Court's opinion in *Weinberger v. UOP, Inc., supra*, at p. 166. The Delaware caselaw developments since *Weinberger* are described in the following excerpt, which also provides general background that is important to a thorough understanding of the issues that were before the Delaware Supreme Court in the opinion that follows, *Glassman v. Unocal Exploration Corporation*.

Guhan Subramanian
Fixing Freeze-outs
115 Yale L.J. 2 (2005)

I. BACKGROUND

* * *

B. DEVELOPMENT OF PROCEDURAL PROTECTION

1. Weinberger v. UOP

The seminal case on freezeouts in the modern era is *Weinberger v. UOP*, handed down by the Delaware Supreme Court in 1983. *Weinberger* involved a freezeout of UOP's minority shareholders by its 50.5% shareholder, Signal Companies. Minority shareholders brought suit alleging that the price paid, $21 per share in cash, was not fair to them. The Delaware Chancery Court held for the defendant directors, who were affiliated with both UOP and Signal. The Delaware Supreme Court reversed, finding that the deal process did not meet the entire fairness standard, and remanded the case to the chancery court for an inquiry into the fair value of the minority shares.

While *Weinberger* did several notable things, [for present purposes] its most important contribution was the identification of the procedural protections that minority shareholders should receive in freezeout mergers. The Court began by noting that entire fairness review required both "fair dealing" and "fair price," and clarified what each of these entailed. . . .

In assessing the transaction at hand, the [*Weinberger*] court found several aspects problematic under this standard. First, the court criticized the fact that a valuation report prepared by two officers of Signal, who were also directors of UOP, was shared only with the Signal board and not with UOP. This report was "of obvious significance to both Signal and UOP" because it indicated that any price up to $24 per share (14% higher than the $21 per share that was actually paid) would have been a good investment for Signal. Second, the court noted the casualness of the fairness opinion rendered by Lehman Brothers to the UOP board. Among other deficiencies, the Lehman partner seemed to have reviewed the opinion only on the flight to the UOP board meeting, and, even at this late stage, the actual price being assessed by Lehman had been left blank. Finally, the Court criticized James Crawford, President and CEO of UOP, for failing to negotiate in response to Signal's first offer of $21.

But in the midst of its litany of criticisms of Signal's freezeout process, the *Weinberger* court paused to provide crucial guidance for transactional lawyers. In a much-noticed footnote [footnote 7], the court stated:

> Although perfection is not possible, or expected, the result here could have been entirely different if UOP had appointed an independent negotiating committee of its outside directors to deal with Signal at arm's length. Since fairness in this context can be equated to conduct by a theoretical, wholly independent, board of directors acting upon the matter before them, it is unfortunate that this course apparently was neither considered nor pursued. Particularly in a parent-subsidiary context, a showing that the action taken was as though each of the contending parties had in fact exerted its bargaining power against the other at arm's length is strong evidence that the transaction meets the test of fairness.

Transactional lawyers took the hint: An SC [i.e., special committee] of independent directors quickly became standard practice in freezeout mergers.[47]

Two opposing concerns developed in response to the *Weinberger* SC mechanism. The first, voiced primarily by judges and academics, is that an SC can never be truly independent from the controlling shareholder because the controller is an "800-pound gorilla"[48] who inevitably will dominate the independent directors.[49] Among those who hold this view, some (generally academics) conclude that SCs should not warrant significant deference from the courts as suggested by *Weinberger*, while others (generally judges) conclude that, even if soft ties exist between the controller and the SC, at least some judicial deference to an SC process is warranted because courts are not well-positioned to assess questions of value.

The second concern, diametrically opposite from the first and voiced primarily by practitioners, is that SCs are too independent from the controller. As described by Charles Nathan, global co-chair of the mergers and acquisitions group at Latham & Watkins: "There are a number of times the committee turns down perfectly fine deals, or drags things out for months, because they can't get their act together. And it's a very, very frustrating experience." Under this view, the *Weinberger* SC roadmap actually works to the detriment of minority shareholders by allowing independent directors with imperfect incentives to veto [value-creating] transactions.

---

47. *See* Donald J. Wolfe, Jr., & Janine M. Salomone, *Pure Resources, Printcafe and the Pugnacious Special Committee*, M&A Law., May 2003, at 10, 10 ("Since [Weinberger], the use of special negotiating committees has become commonplace. . . . ").

48. *See* Leo E. Strine, Jr., *The Inexcapably Empirical Foundation of the Common Law of Corporations*, 27 DEL. J. CORP. L. 499, 509 (2002) ("[T]his strain of thought was premised on the notion that when an 800-pound gorilla wants the rest of the bananas, little chimpanzees, like independent directors and minority stockholders, cannot be expected to stand in the way, even if the gorilla putatively gives them veto power.").

49. *See, e.g., Kahn v. Tremont Corp.*, 694 A.2d 422, 428 (Del. 1997) ("Entire fairness remains applicable even when an independent committee is utilized because the underlying factors which raise the specter of impropriety can never be completely eradicated and still require careful judicial scrutiny."); William T. Allen, et al., *Function over Form: A Reassessment of Standards of Review in Delaware Corporation Law*, 56 BUS. LAW. 1287, 1308 (2001) (noting that outside directors "are not hermetically sealed off from the inside directors").

2. Kahn v. Lynch Communication Systems

In the years following *Weinberger*, these opposing views on the wisdom and efficacy of SCs, invoking fundamental questions of human nature and organizational behavior, manifested themselves in the Delaware courts as a narrow, but crucial, legal question: What level of deference should courts afford to a freezeout merger that was approved by an SC of independent directors? Footnote 7 of Weinberger was vague on this critical question. In the absence of guidance, judges on the Delaware Chancery Court divided in their approaches in the late 1980s and early 1990s. In *In re Trans World Airlines, Inc. Shareholders Litigation*, for example, Chancellor Bill Allen held that SC approval changed the standard of review for a freezeout merger from entire fairness to highly deferential business judgment review.[53] In contrast, . . . [in] *Rabkin v. Olin Corp.*,[55] . . . [Vice Chancellor Bill Chandler] held that SC approval only shifted the burden on entire fairness review from the defendant to the plaintiff.

These competing approaches were reconciled by the Delaware Supreme Court eleven years after *Weinberger* in *Kahn v. Lynch Communication Systems*.[56] *Lynch* involved a freezeout of the minority shareholders in Lynch Communications by Lynch's controlling shareholder, Alcatel. Following the *Weinberger* roadmap, the Lynch board established an SC of independent directors to negotiate with Alcatel. Unlike the UOP representatives in *Weinberger*, the Lynch SC was not spineless: Alcatel proposed $14 per share in cash; the Lynch SC counter-offered $17; Alcatel responded with offers of $15, $15.25, and then a "final offer" of $15.50, all rejected by the Lynch SC. To break the stalemate, Alcatel informed the SC that it was "'ready to proceed with an unfriendly tender [directly to the minority shareholders] at a lower price' if the $15.50 per share price was not recommended." In the face of this threat, the Lynch SC caved and unanimously recommended approval of the $15.50 offer.

Minority shareholders in *Lynch* brought suit seeking entire fairness review. The chancery court entered judgment for the defendants Alcatel and Lynch Communications, and the plaintiffs appealed. The Delaware Supreme Court reversed on the grounds that the Lynch SC did not have the "power to say no" when faced with Alcatel's tender offer threat.[62] The court remanded the case to the Delaware Chancery Court with the burden on the defendants to demonstrate the entire fairness of the transaction.

One of the interesting features in *Lynch* is that Alcatel did not threaten to execute a statutory merger unilaterally—which it had the legal ability to do because it controlled Lynch's board—but only threatened to go directly to the minority shareholders through a tender offer. Because Alcatel held only 43% of the Lynch shares, it would have needed 83% support from the minority

---

53. Civ. A. No. 9844, 1988 WL 111271, at *7 (Del. Ch. Oct. 21, 1988), abrogated by *Kahn v. Lynch Commc'n Sys.*, 638 A.2d 1110 (Del. 1994).

55. C.A. No. 7547, 1990 WL 47648, at *6 (Del. Ch. Apr. 17, 1990), *aff'd*, 586 A.2d 1202 (Del. 1990).

56. 638 A.2d 1110 (Del. 1994).

62. *Lynch*, 638 A.2d at 1119-20.

shareholders (47% out of the remaining 57%) to achieve the 90% control that would then have allowed a short-form back-end merger. Therefore, Alcatel's "threat" was nothing more than an invocation of Alcatel's otherwise legal walk-away alternative, in which Alcatel would have had to achieve overwhelming support from the minority in order to be successful. The *Lynch* court ignored this point, making clear the extent to which a controller must behave nicely in its negotiations with the SC.

And what exactly does the controller get from behaving nicely? Here too the *Lynch* court provided an unsatisfying answer from the controller's perspective. *Lynch* resolved the two strands of Delaware Chancery Court cases noted above by holding that even a pristine SC process only shifts the burden of proof to the plaintiff on entire fairness review. Thus, *Lynch* implicitly endorses the view that independent directors cannot be truly independent from the controlling shareholder, and that courts still need to scrutinize freezeout transactions for entire fairness because of the inability to replicate an arm-length process between the controlling shareholder and the SC.

* * *

To summarize, while *Weinberger* provides the procedural roadmap for freezeout transactions, *Lynch* limits the benefits of this route by requiring a "Caesar's wife" SC process, and *Lynch* and *Rosenblatt* [*v. Getty Oil*], 493 A.2d 929 (Del. 1985), taken] together hold that even an SC/MOM condition [i.e., approval by a majority of the minority (MOM) shareholders (a "MOM condition")] combination does not eliminate entire fairness review. From a transactional lawyer's perspective, merger-freezeout doctrine after *Lynch* and *Rosenblatt* represents the worst of all possible worlds: a fully empowered SC and a feisty negotiation with the controller, to be followed nevertheless with entire fairness review by the court, even if [disinterested] minority shareholders have approved the deal. Of course, the potential beneficiaries of this approach are the minority shareholders, who should gain from both the procedural protections that *Weinberger* encourages and the judicial scrutiny that *Lynch* and *Rosenblatt* mandate.

In effect, the *Weinberger*-to-*Rosenblatt*-to-*Lynch* trajectory represents the Delaware courts' gradual approach to the problem of inadequate minority shareholder protections that presented itself in the 1970s. This gradual trajectory would be disrupted by the *Siliconix* and *Glassman* combination in 2001. I now turn to this latest doctrinal contour.

C. DISRUPTIVE TECHNOLOGY: THE TENDER OFFER FREEZEOUT

A statutory merger is not the only way to execute a freezeout; it can also be executed through a reverse stock split or an asset acquisition, though these methods are rare in practice. Another method that began to appear in the 1990s was a freezeout via [a] tender offer. In this route, the controlling shareholder would begin, or announce its intention to begin, a tender offer directly to the minority shareholders. The target [company] would form an SC of independent directors to assess the transaction, negotiate with the controller, and issue a Schedule 14D-9 recommendation to the minority (*e.g.*, approve, reject, neutral, or unable to take a position). If the controller gained sufficient shares

in its tender offer to get to 90% voting control of the target, it would then execute a short-form merger, which does not require a shareholder vote, in order to
eliminate the remaining (nontendering) minority shareholders. Because 90%
is the critical threshold in a tender offer freezeout, the controller would typically condition its offer on getting to 90% control (a "90% condition")....

Historically, [M & A lawyers] assumed that tender offer freezeouts would
also be subject to entire fairness review, because they achieved the same end
result as merger freezeouts, namely, the elimination of the minority shareholders. As a result there was no obvious benefit to be gained from a tender offer
freezeout, and the merger form continued to dominate in practice [, until the
2001 decision of the Delaware chancery court in] *In re Siliconix Inc. Shareholders
Litigation*, [No. Civ. A. 18700, 2001 WL 716 787 (Del. Ch. June 19, 2001)].

* * *

... *Siliconix* involved Vishay Intertechnology's freezeout of the minority shareholders in Siliconix. Vishay, which owned 80.4% of Siliconix, announced a tender
offer for the minority shares at $28.82 cash per share. With Vishay's encourage-
ment, Siliconix appointed an SC of two independent directors to negotiate with
Vishay. The SC hired legal and financial advisors and concluded that the offer
price was inadequate. After three months of negotiations, Vishay switched from a
cash tender offer to a stock exchange offer at a ratio of 1.5 Vishay shares for every
Siliconix share. Minority shareholders brought suit alleging that the exchange
ratio being offered was unfair.... [T]he Delaware Chancery Court declined to
apply entire fairness review to the tender offer freezeout: "Because . . . there were
no disclosure violations and the tender [offer] is not coercive, Vishay was not
obligated to offer a fair price in its tender...." [*Id.* at *6.]

The remaining piece of this emerging two-step strategy to "squeeze out"
the minority interest—the back-end, short-form merger—was addressed by
the Delaware Supreme Court in the next case.

Glassman v. Unocal Exploration Corp.
777 A. 2d 242 (Del. 2001)

BERGER, Justice.

In this appeal, we consider the fiduciary duties owed by a parent corporation to the subsidiary's minority stockholders in the context of a "short-form"
merger. Specifically, we take this opportunity to reconcile a fiduciary's seemingly absolute duty to establish the entire fairness of any self-dealing transaction with the less demanding requirements of the short-form merger statute.
The statute authorizes the elimination of minority stockholders by a summary
process that does not involve the "fair dealing" component of entire fairness.
Indeed, the statute does not contemplate any "dealing" at all. Thus, a parent
corporation cannot satisfy the entire fairness standard if it follows the terms of
the short-form merger statute without more.

Unocal Corporation addressed this dilemma by establishing a special negotiating committee and engaging in a process that it believed would pass muster under traditional entire fairness review. We find that such steps were unnecessary. By enacting a statute that authorizes the elimination of the minority without notice, vote, or other traditional indicia of procedural fairness, the General Assembly effectively circumscribed the parent corporation's obligations to the minority in a short-form merger. The parent corporation does not have to establish entire fairness, and, absent fraud or illegality, the only recourse for a minority stockholder who is dissatisfied with the merger consideration is appraisal.

I. FACTUAL AND PROCEDURAL BACKGROUND

Unocal Corporation is an earth resources company primarily engaged in the exploration for and production of crude oil and natural gas. At the time of the merger at issue, Unocal owned approximately 96% of the stock of Unocal Exploration Corporation ("UXC"), an oil and gas company operating in and around the Gulf of Mexico. In 1991, low natural gas prices caused a drop in both companies' revenues and earnings. Unocal investigated areas of possible cost savings and decided that, by eliminating the UXC minority, it would reduce taxes and overhead expenses.

In December 1991 the boards of Unocal and UXC appointed special committees to consider a possible merger. The UXC committee consisted of three directors who, although also directors of Unocal, were not officers or employees of the parent company. The UXC committee retained financial and legal advisors and met four times before agreeing to a merger exchange ratio of .54 shares of Unocal stock for each share of UXC. Unocal and UXC announced the merger on February 24, 1992, and it was effected, pursuant to 8 *Del. C.* §253, on May 2, 1992. The Notice of Merger and Prospectus stated the terms of the merger and advised the former UXC stockholders of their appraisal rights.

Plaintiffs filed this class action, on behalf of UXC's minority stockholders, on the day the merger was announced. They asserted, among other claims, that Unocal and its directors breached their fiduciary duties of entire fairness and full disclosure. The Court of Chancery conducted a two day trial and held that: (i) the Prospectus did not contain any material misstatements or omissions; (ii) the entire fairness standard does not control in a short-form merger; and (iii) plaintiffs' exclusive remedy in this case was appraisal. The decision of the Court of Chancery is affirmed.

II. DISCUSSION

The short-form merger statute, as enacted in 1937, authorized a parent corporation to merge with its wholly-owned subsidiary by filing and recording a certificate evidencing the parent's ownership and its merger resolution. In 1957, the statute was expanded to include parent/subsidiary mergers where the parent company owns at least 90% of the stock of the subsidiary. The 1957 amendment also made it possible, for the first time and only in a short-form merger, to pay the minority cash for their shares, thereby eliminating their ownership interest in the company. In its current form, which has not changed significantly since 1957, 8 *Del. C.* §253 provides in relevant part:

> (a) In any case in which at least 90 percent of the outstanding shares of each class of the stock of a corporation . . . is owned by another corporation, . . . the corporation having such stock ownership may . . . merge the other corporation . . . into itself . . . by executing, acknowledging and filing, in accordance with §103 of this title, a certificate of such ownership and merger setting forth a copy of the resolution of its board of directors to so merge and the date of the adoption; provided, however, that in case the parent corporation shall not own all the outstanding stock of . . . the subsidiary corporation[ ], . . . the resolution . . . shall state the terms and conditions of the merger, including the securities, cash, property or rights to be issued, paid delivered or granted by the surviving corporation upon surrender of each share of the subsidiary corporation. . . .

* * *

> (d) In the event that all of the stock of a subsidiary Delaware corporation . . . is not owned by the parent corporation immediately prior to the merger, the stockholders of the subsidiary Delaware corporation party to the merger shall have appraisal rights as set forth in Section 262 of this Title.

This Court first reviewed §253 in *Coyne v. Park & Tilford Distillers Corporation.*[1] There, minority stockholders of the merged-out subsidiary argued that the statute could not mean what it says because Delaware law "never has permitted, and does not now permit, the payment of cash for whole shares surrendered in a merger and the consequent expulsion of a stockholder from the enterprise in which he has invested." The *Coyne* court held that §253 plainly does permit such a result and that the statute is constitutional.

The next question presented to this Court was whether any equitable relief is available to minority stockholders who object to a short-form merger. In *Stauffer v. Standard Brands Incorporated,*[3] minority stockholders sued to set aside the contested merger or, in the alternative, for damages. They alleged that the merger consideration was so grossly inadequate as to constitute constructive fraud and that Standard Brands breached its fiduciary duty to the minority by failing to set a fair price for their stock. The Court of Chancery held that appraisal was the stockholders' exclusive remedy, and dismissed the complaint. This Court affirmed, but explained that appraisal would not be the exclusive remedy in a short-form merger tainted by fraud or illegality:

> [T]he exception [to appraisal's exclusivity] . . . refers generally to all mergers, and is nothing but a reaffirmation of the ever-present power of equity to deal with illegality or fraud. But it has no bearing here. No illegality or overreaching is shown. The dispute reduces to nothing but a difference of opinion as to value. Indeed it is difficult to imagine a case under the short merger statute in which there could be such actual fraud as would entitle a minority to set aside the merger. This is so because the very purpose of the statute is to provide the parent corporation

---

1. Del.Supr., 154 A.2d 893 (1959).
3. Del.Supr., 187 A.2d 78 (1962).

with a means of eliminating the minority shareholder's interest in the enterprise. Thereafter the former stockholder has only a monetary claim.

The *Stauffer* doctrine's viability rose and fell over the next four decades. Its holding on the exclusivity of appraisal took on added significance in 1967, when the long-form merger statute—§251—was amended to allow cash-out mergers. In *David J. Greene & Co. v. Schenley Industries, Inc.,*[5] the Court of Chancery applied *Stauffer* to a long-form cash-out merger. *Schenley* recognized that the corporate fiduciaries had to establish entire fairness, but concluded that fair value was the plaintiff's only real concern and that appraisal was an adequate remedy. The court explained:

> While a court of equity should stand ready to prevent corporate fraud and any overreaching by fiduciaries of the rights of stockholders, by the same token this Court should not impede the consummation of an orderly merger under the Delaware statutes, an efficient and fair method having been furnished which permits a judicially protected withdrawal from a merger by a disgruntled stockholder.

In 1977, this Court started retreating from *Stauffer* (and *Schenley*). *Singer v. Magnavox Co.*[7] held that a controlling stockholder breaches its fiduciary duty if it effects a cash-out merger under §251 for the sole purpose of eliminating the minority stockholders. The *Singer* court distinguished *Stauffer* as being a case where the only complaint was about the value of the converted shares. Nonetheless, the Court cautioned:

> [T]he fiduciary obligation of the majority to the minority stockholders remains and proof of a purpose, other than such freeze-out, without more, will not necessarily discharge it. In such case the Court will scrutinize the circumstances for compliance with the *Sterling* [*v. Mayflower Hotel Corp.*, Del.Supr., 93 A.2d 107 (1952)] rule of "entire fairness" and, if it finds a violation thereof, will grant such relief as equity may require. Any statement in *Stauffer* inconsistent herewith is held inapplicable to a §251 merger.

Singer's business purpose test was extended to short-form mergers two years later in *Roland International Corporation v. Najjar.*[9] The *Roland* majority wrote:

> The short form permitted by §253 does simplify the steps necessary to effect a merger, and does give a parent corporation some certainty as to result and control as to timing. But we find nothing magic about a 90% ownership of outstanding shares which would eliminate the fiduciary duty owed by the majority to the minority.

* * *

As to *Stauffer,* we agree that the purpose of §253 is to provide the parent with a means of eliminating minority shareholders in the subsidiary but, as

---

5. Del.Ch., 281 A.2d 30 (1971).

7. Del.Supr., 380 A.2d 969 (1977).

9. Del.Supr., 407 A.2d 1032 (1979).

we observed in *Singer*, we did "not read the decision [*Stauffer*] as approving a merger accomplished solely to freeze-out the minority without a valid business purpose." We held that any statement in *Stauffer* inconsistent with the principles restated in *Singer* was inapplicable to a §251 merger. Here we hold that the principles announced in *Singer* with respect to a §251 merger apply to a §253 merger. It follows that any statement in *Stauffer* inconsistent with that holding is overruled.[10]

After *Roland*, there was not much of *Stauffer* that safely could be considered good law. But that changed in 1983, in *Weinberger v. UOP, Inc.*,[11] when the Court dropped the business purpose test, made appraisal a more adequate remedy, and said that it was "return[ing] to the well established principles of *Stauffer* . . . and *Schenley* . . . mandating a stockholder's recourse to the basic remedy of an appraisal." *Weinberger* focused on two subjects — the "unflinching" duty of entire fairness owed by self-dealing fiduciaries, and the "more liberalized appraisal" it established.

With respect to entire fairness, the [*Weinberger*] Court explained that the concept includes fair dealing (how the transaction was timed, initiated, structured, negotiated, disclosed and approved) and fair price (all elements of value); and that the test for fairness is not bifurcated. On the subject of appraisal, the Court made several important statements: (i) courts may consider "proof of value by any techniques or methods which are generally considered acceptable in the financial community and otherwise admissible in court . . . ;" (ii) fair value must be based on "all relevant factors," which include not only "elements of future value . . . which are known or susceptible of proof as of the date of the merger" but also, when the court finds it appropriate, "damages, resulting from the taking, which the stockholders sustain as a class;" and (iii) "a plaintiff's monetary remedy ordinarily should be confined to the more liberalized appraisal proceeding herein established. . . . "

By referencing both *Stauffer* and *Schenley*, one might have thought that the *Weinberger* court intended appraisal to be the exclusive remedy "ordinarily" in non-fraudulent mergers where "price . . . [is] the preponderant consideration outweighing other features of the merger." In *Rabkin v. Philip A. Hunt Chemical Corp.*,[18] however, the Court dispelled that view. The *Rabkin* plaintiffs claimed that the majority stockholder breached its fiduciary duty of fair dealing by waiting until a one year commitment to pay $25 per share had expired before effecting a cash-out merger at $20 per share. The Court of Chancery dismissed the complaint, reasoning that, under *Weinberger*, plaintiffs could obtain full relief for the alleged unfair dealing in an appraisal proceeding. This Court reversed, holding that the trial court read *Weinberger* too narrowly and that appraisal is the exclusive remedy only if stockholders' complaints are limited to "judgmental factors of valuation."

---

10. 407 A.2d at 1036 (Citations omitted). Justice Quillen dissented, saying that the majority created "an unnecessary damage forum" for a plaintiff whose complaint demonstrated that appraisal would have been an adequate remedy. *Id.* at 1039–40.

11. Del.Supr., 457 A.2d 701 (1983).

18. Del.Supr., 498 A.2d 1099 (1985).

Rabkin, through its interpretation of *Weinberger,* effectively eliminated appraisal as the exclusive remedy for any claim alleging breach of the duty of entire fairness. But *Rabkin* involved a long-form merger, and the Court did not discuss, in that case or any others, how its refinement of *Weinberger* impacted short-form mergers. Two of this Court's more recent decisions that arguably touch on the subject are *Bershad v. Curtiss–Wright Corp.*[20] and *Kahn v. Lynch Communication Systems, Inc.,*[21] both long-form merger cases. In *Bershad,* the Court included §253 when it identified statutory merger provisions from which fairness issues flow:

> In parent-subsidiary merger transactions the issues are those of fairness—fair price and fair dealing. These flow from the statutory provisions permitting mergers, 8 *Del.C.* §§ 251-253 (1983), and those designed to ensure fair value by an appraisal, 8 *Del.C.* § 262 (1983) . . . ;

and in *Lynch,* the Court described entire fairness as the "exclusive" standard of review in a cash-out, parent/subsidiary merger.

Mindful of this history, we must decide whether a minority stockholder may challenge a short-form merger by seeking equitable relief through an entire fairness claim. Under settled principles, a parent corporation and its directors undertaking a short-form merger are self-dealing fiduciaries who should be required to establish entire fairness, including fair dealing and fair price. The problem is that §253 authorizes a summary procedure that is inconsistent with any reasonable notion of fair dealing. In a short-form merger, there is no agreement of merger negotiated by two companies; there is only a unilateral act—a decision by the parent company that its 90% owned subsidiary shall no longer exist as a separate entity. The minority stockholders receive no advance notice of the merger; their directors do not consider or approve it; and there is no vote. Those who object are given the right to obtain fair value for their shares through appraisal.

The equitable claim plainly conflicts with the statute. If a corporate fiduciary follows the truncated process authorized by §253, it will not be able to establish the fair dealing prong of entire fairness. If, instead, the corporate fiduciary sets up negotiating committees, hires independent financial and legal experts, etc., then it will have lost the very benefit provided by the statute—a simple, fast and inexpensive process for accomplishing a merger. We resolve this conflict by giving effect the intent of the General Assembly. In order to serve its purpose, §253 must be construed to obviate the requirement to establish entire fairness.[25]

Thus, we again return to *Stauffer,* and hold that, absent fraud or illegality, appraisal is the exclusive remedy available to a minority stockholder who objects to a short-form merger. In doing so, we also reaffirm *Weinberger's* statements about the scope of appraisal. The determination of fair value must be

---

20. Del.Supr., 535 A.2d 840 (1987).

21. Del.Supr., 638 A.2d 1110 (1994).

25. We do not read *Lynch* as holding otherwise; this issue was not before the Court in *Lynch.*

based on *all* relevant factors, including damages and elements of future value, where appropriate. So, for example, if the merger was timed to take advantage of a depressed market, or a low point in the company's cyclical earnings, or to precede an anticipated positive development, the appraised value may be adjusted to account for those factors. We recognize that these are the types of issues frequently raised in entire fairness claims, and we have held that claims for unfair dealing cannot be litigated in an appraisal.[26] But our prior holdings simply explained that equitable claims may not be engrafted onto a statutory appraisal proceeding; stockholders may not receive rescissionary relief in an appraisal. Those decisions should not be read to restrict the elements of value that properly may be considered in an appraisal.

Although fiduciaries are not required to establish entire fairness in a short-form merger, the duty of full disclosure remains, in the context of this request for stockholder action.[27] Where the only choice for the minority stockholders is whether to accept the merger consideration or seek appraisal, they must be given all the factual information that is material to that decision.[28] The Court of Chancery carefully considered plaintiffs' disclosure claims and applied settled law in rejecting them. We affirm this aspect of the appeal on the basis of the trial court's decision.[29]

III. CONCLUSION

Based on the foregoing, we affirm the Court of Chancery and hold that plaintiffs' only remedy in connection with the short-form merger of UXC into Unocal was appraisal.

NOTES

1. Regulation of "Going Private" Transactions Under SEC's Rule 13e-3. In 1979, the SEC adopted Rule 13e-3, which imposes significant disclosure obligations on market participants engaged in a so-called Rule 13e-3 Transaction, which is a defined term under the rule. *See* Rule 13e-3(a)(3), 17 C.F.R. §240.13e-3 (2012). The definition of a Rule 13e-3 transaction has two components—a structural standard and a results standard—both of which must be satisfied. Structurally, a transaction will be subject to the Rule if it meets any of the following three criteria:

- A *purchase* of any equity security by the issuer of such security or by an *affiliate* of such issuer [i.e., a controlling shareholder];

---

26. *Alabama By-Products Corporation v. Neal,* Del.Supr., 588 A.2d 255, 257 (1991).

27. *See Malone v. Brincat,* Del.Supr., 722 A.2d 5 (1998) ("No stockholder action was requested, but [the] Court recognized that even in such a case, directors breach [their] duty of loyalty and good faith by knowingly disseminating false information to stockholders").

28. *McMullin v. Beran,* Del.Supr., 765 A.2d 910 (2000).

29. *In re Unocal Exploration Corporation Shareholders Litigation,* Del. Ch. 2001 WL 823376 (2000).

- A *tender offer* for or request or invitation for tenders of any equity security made by the issuer of such class of securities or by an affiliate of such issuer; or
- A *solicitation subject to Regulation 14A of any proxy, consent, or authorization of, or a distribution subject to Regulation 14C of information statements* to, any equity security holder by the issuer of the class of securities or by an affiliate of such issuer, in connection with: a merger, consolidation, reclassification, recapitalization, reorganization or similar corporate transaction of an issuer or between an issuer (or its subsidiaries) and its affiliate; a sale of substantially all the assets of an issuer to its affiliate or group of affiliates; or a reverse stock split of any class of equity securities of the issuer involving the purchase of fractional interests.

In addition to satisfying this structure standard, the transaction must produce one of the following effects (i.e., the results standard) in order to trigger the disclosure obligations of Rule 13e-3:

- Cause any class of equity securities of the issuer that is subject to section 12(g) or section 15(d) of the Securities Exchange Act to be held of record by *less than* 300 persons; or
- Cause any class of equity securities of the issuer that is either listed on a national securities exchange or authorized to be quoted in an inter-dealer quotation system of a registered national securities association *to be neither listed on any national securities exchange nor authorized to be quoted on an inter-dealer quotation system* of any registered national securities association.

In adopting Rule 13e-3, it is clear that the SEC was worried about protecting minority shareholders:

> . . . The nature of and methods utilized in effecting going private transactions present an opportunity for overreaching of unaffiliated security holders by an issuer or its affiliates [i.e., controlling shareholder(s)]. This is due, in part, to the lack of arm's length bargaining and the inability of unaffiliated security holders [i.e., minority shareholders] to influence corporate decisions to enter into such transactions. Additionally, such transactions have a coercive effect in that [minority shareholders] confronted by a going private transaction are faced with the prospects of an illiquid market, termination of the protections under the federal securities laws and further efforts by the proponent to eliminate their equity interest. Because of the potential for harm to [the minority interest], particularly small investors, and the need for full and timely disclosure, the Commission continues to believe that Rule 13e-3 is necessary and appropriate for the public interest and the protection of investors.

SEC Release No. 34-17719 (April 13, 1981).

While the disclosure obligations of Rule 13e-3 are considerable, for our purposes, the most important item of disclosure—unique to Rule 13e-3 going private transactions—obligates the directors in a going private transaction to disclose their view regarding the "fairness" of the terms of the proposed squeeze-out transaction. This disclosure requirement stands in stark contrast to the usual and customary premise underlying the SEC's disclosure philosophy, which (as we saw in the materials in Chapter 4) is to require full disclosure of all material facts in order to let the shareholders evaluate the merits of a proposed transaction. Here, in a marked departure to its usual approach, the SEC specifically requires Target's directors to express their view as to the merits (i.e., the fairness) of a proposed freeze-out transaction. *Query*: Given the potential for conflict of interest inherent in these transactions, how much protection does the SEC's disclosure requirement provide to the minority shareholders?

2. "Two Paths" to "Squeeze Out" the Minority Interest. In the wake of the Delaware Supreme Court's holding in *Glassman*, transaction planners were left with a clear path to *avoid* judicial review of a freeze-out transaction under the entire fairness standard. Under *Siliconix*, the controlling shareholder could commence a tender offer to purchase the minority interest, and the tender would be exempt from entire fairness review—although it would be subject to the disclosure requirements of SEC Rule 13e-3. Moreover, if the controlling shareholder held 90 percent of the voting shares, then *Glassman* instructed that the back-end, short-form merger would also be exempt from entire fairness review. Thus, transaction planners were left with two paths to going private—tender offer freeze-outs and merger freeze-outs—each involving very different standards of judicial review for what are essentially two functionally equivalent transactional forms. This disparity has led to further doctrinal developments under Delaware caselaw, which are described in the following excerpt that then sets the stage for the next case, *Cox Communications*.

Guhan Subramanian
Fixing Freeze-outs
115 Yale L.J. 2 (2005)

[Following the Delaware Supreme Court's decision in *Glassman*, Vice Chancellor Strine decided *In re Pure Resources Shareholder Litigation*, 808 A.2d 421 (Del. Ch. 2002).] *Pure Resources* involved Unocal Exploration (again) [commencing a tender offer] for the 35% of Pure Resources that it did not own. Minority shareholders (again) brought suit alleging unfairness. After an extensive discussion of the "two strands of authority that answer these questions differently," Vice Chancellor Leo Strine, . . . declined to apply entire fairness review to Unocal's freezeout tender offer. However, in a clear effort to close some of the gap between the two [very different] doctrinal strands, Vice Chancellor Strine noted that the exemption . . . from entire fairness review only applied to tender offers that were noncoercive to the minority. The court [then] seized on this qualification to establish three procedural conditions that must be met in order for a tender offer to be noncoercive: (1) the offer must be subject to a nonwaivable MOM condition [i.e., requiring approval by a "majority of the minority" shareholders]; (2) the controller must guarantee to consummate a prompt short-form merger at the same price if it obtains 90% or more of the shares; and (3) the controller must make no "retributive threats" in its negotiations with the SC. The *Pure Resources* court confirmed, however, that if these conditions were met then a tender offer freezeout would not be subject to entire fairness review. . . .

To summarize, Delaware law currently offers a controlling shareholder two transactional forms for a freezeout: the statutory merger route and the tender offer route. These two forms appear similar at the outset. In each case the process begins when the controller informs the target board of its intention to freeze out the minority, and the target board responds by establishing an SC of independent directors. But at this point the similarity disappears. While the SC in a merger freezeout has veto power over the transaction and in theory can negotiate indefinitely, the SC in a tender offer freezeout cannot veto the transaction and has only ten days to issue its [Schedule] 14D-9 recommendation to the minority. The difference continues in the standard of judicial review imposed: entire fairness review for merger freezeouts compared to business judgment review for tender offer freezeouts. Perhaps not surprisingly in view of this procedural divergence, the substantive outcomes differ significantly as well: Controlling shareholders pay less to the minority, on average, in tender offer freezeouts than in merger freezeouts. I now review the academic and practitioner commentary that has developed in response to this state of play [under Delaware case law].

D. Prior Literature

Commentators have divided on the *Weinberger*-to-*Pure Resources* line of cases. These responses can be divided into three categories: those who advocate convergence in standards of judicial review by subjecting tender offer freezeouts to entire fairness review; those who defend the status quo; and those who propose hybrid approaches. This Section summarizes and assesses each of these positions in turn.

1. Advocating Entire Fairness Review for Tender Offer Freezeouts

At one end of the spectrum, some commentators argue for doctrinal convergence through entire fairness review for tender offer freezeouts on the grounds of doctrinal coherence. Although this simple solution has some superficial appeal, there are two problems with it. First, it does not take into account the costs of judicial intervention. Because courts are not well positioned to engage in the difficult task of valuation, entire fairness review should be deployed sparingly. In fact, part of the explanation for the dramatic doctrinal gap between *Lynch* (a Delaware Supreme Court decision) and *Siliconix* (a Delaware chancery court decision) may be the fact that chancery judges "personally face the daunting task of valuation" and, therefore, may be "institutionally inclined to avoid it wherever they can do so responsibly."[107] This aspect of judicial realism suggests that the simple solution of applying entire fairness review may not adequately

---

107. [William T. Allen and Reinier Kraakman, Commentaries and Cases on the Law of Business Organizations 312 (2003).]

account for institutional realities and may introduce judicial costs that outweigh the benefits of doctrinal convergence.

Second, and more importantly, entire fairness review for all freezeouts does not necessarily follow from the general argument in favor of doctrinal convergence. The argument for convergence "up" focuses on providing adequate procedural protections to minority shareholders, but an important counterargument is that entire fairness review for all freezeouts may deter some value-creating transactions. In an important article published just before *Siliconix* [was decided], two sitting Vice-Chancellors and a former Chancellor proposed convergence "down" to business judgment review for all freezeouts that received SC approval, in effect proposing a reconsideration of the rule in *Lynch*.[108] The question of convergence "up" or convergence "down" cannot be resolved on a theoretical level. But at the very least it is clear that arguments for convergence only invite the larger question of convergence to what. Commentators who support entire fairness review for all freezeouts do not adequately address this issue.

2. DEFENDING THE STATUS QUO

A second group of commentators defend the doctrinal contour that *Siliconix* and *Glassman* establish. [In support of this view, these commentators argue that] Delaware corporate law provides an important role for a target board in a statutory merger but no role for the board in a tender offer. Therefore, judicial scrutiny of a tender offer is not warranted because there is no corporate action. This argument was central to the court's reasoning in *Siliconix*: "[T]ender offers essentially represent the sale of shareholders' separate property and such sales—even when aggregated into a single change in control transaction—require no 'corporate action' and do not involve distinctively corporate interests." The problem with this argument, . . . is that it ignores one of the most important strands of Delaware corporate law of the past twenty years, which is precisely about articulating the board's role in a tender offer: the degree to which a target board may adopt defensive measures against a hostile tender offer. Thus, this argument creates a tension, if not outright contradiction, between the board's role in freezeout tender offers (none) and the board's role in hostile tender offers (substantial). If the distinguishing feature is the nature of the bidder (controlling shareholder versus hostile bidder), then it would seem that minority shareholders should receive more protection in the freezeout case, rather than less, because in a freezeout there is no market check on the bidder's actions.

* * *

3. PROPOSING DOCTRINAL CONVERGENCE THROUGH HYBRID APPROACHES

Two sets of commentators have taken middle-ground approaches. Ronald Gilson and Jeff Gordon proposed business judgment review if the controller

---

108. *See* [William T. Allen, et al., *Function Over Form: A Reassessment of Standards of Review in Delaware Corporation Law*, 56 Bus. Law. 1287, 1306-1309 (2001)].

has complied with the procedural protections identified in *Pure Resources* and the SC has veto power over the transaction (i.e., a reconsideration of *Lynch*), but would impose entire fairness review if the controller goes directly to shareholders through a tender offer without gaining SC approval (i.e., a reconsideration of *Siliconix*).[127] Prominent Delaware practitioner Frank Balotti, with two colleagues, also proposed a hybrid approach, urging a "limited fairness hearing" for freezeout tender offers, or an amendment to the Delaware appraisal statute requiring the controller to pay all minority shareholders the appraised [value] of their shares.[128]

These approaches are well considered in that they seek to balance the competing concerns of protecting minority shareholders and facilitating value-creating transactions. . . .

———————————————

As it stands, Delaware caselaw has created two paths for controlling shareholders to "squeeze out" the minority interest. The implications (and commentators' criticisms) of these judicial developments are explored at length in the next case. As you read through this case, consider whether the court's reasoning reflects "doctrinal convergence," and if so, convergence to what.

In re Cox Communications, Inc. Shareholders Litigation
879 A.2d 604 (Del. Ch. 2005)

STRINE, Vice Chancellor.

I. INTRODUCTION

This decision addresses an objection to a request for attorneys' fees. The plaintiffs seeking the fee award filed premature, hastily-drafted, makeweight complaints attacking a fully negotiable proposal by the Cox family[1] to enter into

———————————————

127. *See* Ronald J. Gilson and Jeffrey N. Gordon, *Controlling Controlling Shareholders*, 152 U. PA. L. REV. 785 (2003).

128. [Bradley R. Aronstam, et al., *Delaware's Going Private Dilemma: Fostering Protection for Minority Shareholders in the Wake of* Siliconix *and* Unocal Exploration, 58 BUS. LAW. 519 (2003)]; Bradley R. Aronstam, et al., *Revisiting Delaware's Going-Private Dilemma Post-*Pure Resources, 59 BUS. LAW. 1459 (2004).

1. The Cox family owns a controlling stake of Cox Communications, Inc. ("Cox") primarily through a family-owned holding company, Cox Enterprises, Inc. (hereinafter, members of the Cox family and their holding company itself are collectively defined as the "Family").

a merger whereby they would buy all the public's shares in Cox Communications, Inc. The Family's proposal was specifically conditioned on agreement to final merger terms with a special committee of independent directors. Its $32 per share bid constituted a 14% premium over the pre-existing average market price for Cox shares for the 30 calendar days before the announcement.

After vigorous negotiations, the Family and the special committee reached tentative agreement on a merger at $34.75 per share that would be subject to approval by a majority of the minority stockholders. The tentative agreement was conditioned on settlement of the outstanding lawsuits, receipt of a final fairness opinion, and agreement on the terms of a final merger agreement. After the tentative agreement with the special committee, the family's litigation counsel gave the plaintiffs the $34.75 per share and minority approval condition as a "best and absolutely final offer." The plaintiffs settled with the Family agreeing that the pendency of the litigation had contributed to their decision to increase their bid to the final price it reached.

In this opinion, I address the dueling arguments about whether the plaintiffs' requested fee of $4.95 million should be awarded and describe the legal landscape from which those arguments grow. Rather than attempt to recite that back and forth in summary form here, I instead will summarize my conclusions.

Initially, I conclude that complaints challenging fully negotiable, all cash, all shares merger proposals by controlling stockholders are not meritorious when filed under the *Chrysler Corp. v. Dann*[2] standard. For reasons I explain, this does not prevent the court from approving a class action settlement and a reasonable award of attorneys' fees in a case when the party bearing the fee agrees to pay it and there is no plausible injury to the class from a fee award, but it should, and does here, influence the size of the fees awarded.

Relatedly, I consider the non-coincidental relationship between the premature filing of cases like this and the standard of review articulated in *Kahn v. Lynch Communication Systems, Inc.*[3] Because that standard (as heretofore understood by practitioners and courts) makes it impossible for a controlling stockholder ever to structure a transaction in a manner that will enable it to obtain dismissal of a complaint challenging the transaction, each *Lynch* case has settlement value, not necessarily because of its merits but because it cannot be dismissed.

For that reason, plaintiffs and defendants both have an incentive to settle non-meritorious, premature suits attacking negotiable, going-private proposals. For their part, plaintiffs' lawyers can get sizable fees by "contributing" to the successful work of a special committee and by settling at the same level that the special committee achieved. Meanwhile, defendants can avoid the otherwise unavoidable costs of discovery and lost executive time involved in getting rid of any later ripe challenge under *Lynch* to the financial fairness of the final deal negotiated with a special committee. So neatly has this incentive system worked that the plaintiffs cannot cite one example of a *Lynch* case in which plaintiffs sued attacking a negotiable proposal, and refused to settle on the same (or worse) terms than the special committee extracted from the controller.

---

2. 223 A.2d 384 (Del. 1966).
3. 638 A.2d 1110 (Del. 1994).

For reasons I detail, I therefore award a substantially smaller fee than the plaintiffs have requested. I perceive the plaintiffs to have taken no appreciable risk, because they knew the Family would have to materially increase its bid to satisfy the special committee. Moreover, I cannot give credence to the notion that the litigation had a substantially important impact on the pricing of the transaction because the plaintiffs' claims were not meritorious when filed and it is most probable that the defendants settled simply because they had, under *Lynch,* no other economically efficient option for disposal of the lawsuit.

More generally, I conclude that no risk premium should be awarded in fee applications in cases of this kind, when a plaintiff suing on a proposal settles at the same level as the special committee. Even further, if a controller and a special committee ignore a prematurely filed suit and conclude final merger terms, there should be no presumed entitlement to a fee by the plaintiffs, if the plaintiffs attempt to argue that their unripe claims are now moot and that the pendency of those claims influenced the controller to offer the special committee fair terms.

On a more fundamental level, I observe that Delaware law would improve the protections it offers to minority stockholders and the integrity of the representative litigation process by reforming and extending *Lynch* in modest but important ways. The reform would be to invoke the business judgment rule standard of review when a going private merger with a controlling stockholder was effected using a process that mirrored *both* elements of an arms-length merger: 1) approval by disinterested directors; and 2) approval by disinterested stockholders. The two elements are complementary and not substitutes. The first element is important because the directors have the capability to act as effective and active bargaining agents, which disaggregated stockholders do not. But, because bargaining agents are not always effective or faithful, the second element is critical, because it gives the minority stockholders the opportunity to reject their agents' work. Therefore, when a merger with a controlling stockholder was: 1) negotiated and approved by a special committee of independent directors; and 2) conditioned on an affirmative vote of a majority of the minority stockholders, the business judgment standard of review should presumptively apply, and any plaintiff ought to have to plead particularized facts that, if true, support an inference that, despite the facially fair process, the merger was tainted because of fiduciary wrongdoing. This reform to *Lynch* would not permit a controller to obtain business judgment rule protection merely by using a special committee or a majority of the minority vote; in that case, *Lynch* in its current form would still govern. To invoke the business judgment rule standard of review, the controller would have to replicate fully both elements of the arms-length merger process.

Through this modification, there would be an incentive for transactional planners to use the transactional structure that virtually all informed commentators believe is most advantageous to minority stockholders. At the same time, by giving defendants the real option to get rid of cases on the pleadings, the integrity of the representative litigation process would be improved, as those cases that would be filed would involve plaintiffs and plaintiffs' lawyers who knew that they could only succeed by filing and actually prosecuting meritorious claims, and not by free riding on a special committee's work.

To provide even greater coherence to our law, the equitable standards governing going-private transactions with controlling stockholders could be sensibly unified through an extension of this reformed *Lynch* standard. That is, in the context of going-private transactions implemented by tender offers by controlling stockholders—so called *Siliconix*[4] transactions—the protections of *Pure Resources*[5] should be supplemented by subjecting the controlling stockholder to the entire fairness standard if a special committee recommended that the minority not tender. Because *Pure Resources* already requires the equivalent of an informed, uncoerced majority of the minority vote condition for a controller to avoid entire fairness review, the additional step of triggering fairness review when a controller proceeded against the views of the special committee would bring together both lines of our going-private jurisprudence in a sensible manner, providing stockholders with substantial procedural guarantees of fairness that work in tandem while minimizing the rote filing of makeweight cases. Reform of our common law in this manner also honors our law's traditions, by respecting the informed business judgment of disinterested directors and stockholders.

II. FACTUAL BACKGROUND

Cox is one of the nation's largest broadband communications companies, with a particularly strong cable television franchise. Throughout its history, the eponymous Cox has been controlled by its founding family, the Coxes. At various times, the Family has found it convenient to take Cox public, in order to raise money from the public capital markets. At other times, the Family has found it preferable to run Cox as a private company.

As of the summer of 2004, Cox was a public company, whose shares were listed on the New York Stock Exchange. The Cox Family controlled 74% of Cox's voting power. By summer 2004, the Family decided that it would be in its best interest to acquire the remaining shares of Cox that it did not own—some 245.5 million shares—and to take Cox private again. This idea was broached with top management of Cox by Family representatives on the Cox board, including the Chairman James C. Kennedy. On August 1, 2004, a Cox board meeting was held at which the Family previewed its intention to offer to pay $32 per share as an initial bid in a merger transaction whereby the Family would acquire all of the public shares of Cox (the "Proposal"). In a letter that followed the meeting, the Family made clear that it expected that Cox would form a special committee of independent Cox directors (the "Special Committee") to respond to and negotiate its Proposal. Indeed, the Proposal specifically required approval by the Special Committee. The Family did not threaten to change the board in order to pursue a merger if the Special Committee did not find favor with its Proposal. But the Family did state that it would not sell its Cox shares or support a sale of Cox to a third party.

At 4:06 a.m. on the next morning, August 2, the Proposal was announced publicly before the markets opened. The Proposal set in course two separate

---

4. *See In re Siliconix Inc. Shareholders Litig.*, 2001 WL 716787 (Del. Ch. June 19, 2001).
5. *In re Pure Resources, Inc., Shareholders Litig.*, 808 A.2d 421 (Del. Ch. 2002).

strands of activity. One involved the formation and start of work by the Special Committee. The other involved a race to the courthouse by various plaintiffs. I describe the latter activity first because it took place largely without any consideration of what the Special Committee was planning to do. After describing the initial jockeying among the plaintiffs, I will return to discuss the key events that led to an actual transaction between the Family and Cox, and the settlement of this litigation.

A.   THE PLAINTIFFS RUSH TO COURT TO CHALLENGE THE NEGOTIABLE PROPOSAL

Beginning at 8:36 a.m. on August 2, and continuing throughout the day, a flurry of hastily drafted complaints were filed with this court. The first of the complaints consisted of paragraphs cobbled together from public documents, and rested on the core premises that Cox was poised for growth, that the Family's Proposal undervalued the company, that the offer was timed to allow the Family to reap for itself Cox's expected profits from heavy capital investments made in recent years, and that the directors of Cox were acquiescing to the Family's wishes. At 9:28 a.m., the Abbey Gardy firm, which is lead counsel in this action, filed its initial complaint, the second complaint filed that morning. That complaint was even less meaty than the first filed complaint. It is exemplary of hastily-filed, first-day complaints that serve no purpose other than for a particular law firm and its client to get into the medal round of the filing speed (also formerly known as the lead counsel selection) Olympics. The complaint's allegations were entirely boilerplate, with no particular relevance to the situation facing Cox. Most notably, the complaint's strained accusations of wrongdoing reflected, but did not maturely and thoughtfully confront, the reality that the Family's Proposal was just that, a proposal, subject to the expected evaluation of a Special Committee of independent directors, which would soon be formed and have the chance to hire advisors.

By the end of the day, six complaints of this ilk were filed in this court.[6] . . .

A food fight then ensued among the plaintiffs' firms for lead counsel status. The Prickett Jones firm filed motions to expedite and to consolidate the cases under a committee structure it would lead. The rest of the filing plaintiffs lined up behind Abbey Gardy. The fight was resolved at a hearing on August 24, and confirmed in an order dated August 30, in which the court determined that Abbey Gardy would be lead counsel. . . .

The court largely denied the motion to expedite, for the obvious reason that there was as yet no transaction to enjoin. The only thing on the table was a Proposal by the Family that was subject to ongoing examination and negotiation by the Cox board through its Special Committee. For the convenience of the court and the parties, including the defendants, the court encouraged the defendants to provide a rolling production of documents that would not

---

6. Eventually, thirteen complaints were filed in Delaware, and three in Georgia.

compromise the special committee's negotiating position. This admonition merely reflected a desire to avoid an unnecessary time crunch later in the event of either a challenge to whatever deal resulted or a settlement. The court's encouragement also reflected the reality that any amended complaint that the plaintiffs' might file against an ultimate merger agreement could not be dismissed, per the teachings of *Kahn v. Lynch Communication Systems, Inc.,*[7] if the plaintiffs could plausibly allege unfairness.

As it turns out, the denial of the motion to expedite was the last substantial activity that would occur in the litigation challenging the Proposal until the consideration of the settlement itself. All the important events were transpiring on the business front, even those that involved the plaintiffs themselves. I therefore describe the course of those events next.

B. GETTING TO A DEAL AND A SETTLEMENT: A TALE OF TWO NEGOTIATION PATHS LEADING TO THE SAME PLACE AT THE SAME TIME

After the public announcement of the Proposal, the Cox board formed the Special Committee as anticipated in the Family's Proposal. It was comprised of three Cox directors who were not employees or officers of Cox, or otherwise affiliates of the Family, including Janet M. Clarke who was the Chairwoman. The board resolution creating the Special Committee specifically stated that the Cox board would not authorize or recommend any transaction with the Family unless the transaction was recommended to the full board by the Special Committee.

On August 5, 2004, the Special Committee selected Fried, Frank, Harris, Shriver & Jacobson LLP as its legal counsel. On August 16, the Special Committee retained Goldman, Sachs & Co. as its financial advisor. After that, the Special Committee, with the aid of its advisors, gathered public and non-public financial information about Cox and its prospects, including non-public projections of the company's future performance. The Special Committee did so for the evident purposes of considering the attractiveness of Cox's opening bid and determining how to respond to that bid. During this stage, the Special Committee communicated with representatives of the Family to understand the basis for the Proposal and to hear their views about value. Goldman Sachs used this input and other information to develop valuation information to help its clients develop a bargaining position.

By late September, the Special Committee had worked with Goldman Sachs to develop a presentation to the Family's financial advisors. That presentation was designed to impress upon the Family the Special Committee's view that Cox had a bright future and should be valued much higher than the Proposal's $32 per share price. In other words, the presentation was a negotiation document designed to help the Special Committee convince the Family of the sincerity of its view that it should substantially increase its initial bid. After the meeting with the financial advisors, Fried Frank met with the Family's legal advisors and

---

7. 638 A.2d 1110 (Del. 1994).

expressed the Special Committee's desire that any merger or tender offer transaction be subject to a non-waivable majority of minority approval condition or "Minority Approval Condition."

On October 4, 2004, the Special Committee initiated the beginning of real negotiations by sending a letter to the Family unanimously rejecting the $32 price as unacceptable. Various rounds of discussions were had, at which the Family's and the Special Committee's financial advisors jousted over value. On October 11, the Family raised its bid to $33.50 per share and hinted that this might be its final bid. The next day, the Special Committee communicated to the Family that if the $33.50 bid was the Family's final bid, it would be rejected, and if that bid was intended to lead to a deal at $35.00, then the Family should know that the Special Committee would reject that price as well.

By this time, the plaintiffs in this case, through their lead counsel, Arthur N. Abbey of Abbey Gardy, had been invited into the negotiation dance by the Family's litigation counsel, Kevin G. Abrams of Richards Layton & Finger, but on a separate track from the Special Committee. On October 12, the plaintiffs' counsel and their financial advisor, Richard L. Smithline, met with the financial and legal advisors for the Family. Smithline presented valuation materials designed to support the plaintiffs' position that the Family should raise its bid to at least $38 per share. The plaintiffs were not informed, apparently, that the Family had already told the Special Committee that it was prepared to raise its bid to $33.50.

This established a pattern. The Special Committee dealt with the Family in a direct manner: Clarke had direct contact with the Family's key representative, Kennedy, as well as through communications between the Special Committee's advisors and the Family's advisors. By contrast, the plaintiffs, as might be expected, dealt exclusively with litigation counsel for the Family, aside from the one meeting at which the plaintiffs' financial advisors were given the opportunity to make a presentation to the Family's financial advisors. Litigation counsel for the Family decided what, if any, information the plaintiffs would be told about the bargaining dynamic between the Special Committee and the Family.

Consistent with this pattern, on October 12, Kennedy called Clarke and told her that the Family would withdraw its $33.50 offer unless an in-person meeting between principals for the Family and the Special Committee members themselves resulted in an agreement. It was eventually agreed that this meeting would occur on October 15.

Meanwhile, on October 13, Abrams told Abbey that the Family might raise its offer to $33.50 and might agree to a majority of the minority condition. Later that day, Abbey told Abrams that the plaintiffs would accept a settlement at $37 per share with a Minority Approval Condition.

On October 15, Kennedy and one of his top subordinates for the Family's Holding Company met with the Special Committee. No advisors were present. After some discussion, Kennedy indicated that the Family might raise its offer to $34 per share. After even more talk, Kennedy signaled a willingness to offer $34.50 with the proviso that if the Special Committee did not accept that price, the Family would cease consideration of taking Cox private.

The Special Committee adjourned to caucus with their advisors. Upon their return, Clarke told Kennedy that the Special Committee would not recommend a price lower than $35.25 per share. Kennedy responded that if that was the Special Committee's position, the Family would withdraw its Proposal.

The Special Committee then caucused again with its advisors. Clarke was empowered to negotiate the best obtainable price, subject to a confirming opinion as to financial fairness by Goldman Sachs, agreement to a Minority Approval Condition, settlement of this litigation, and negotiation of a merger agreement.

Clarke met with Kennedy later that day. She said the Special Committee would accept a deal at $35 per share. Naturally, having framed the bidding this way, Clarke opened the door to Kennedy offering to split the difference between his previous $34.50 overture and her $35 price. Kennedy did so and Clarke agreed that the Special Committee would recommend that $34.75 per share price, subject to the conditions described.

After that occurred, Abrams was informed of the state of play. He called Abbey and told him that the Family's "best and final offer" was $34.75 per share and that the Family would not settle this case at any higher price. Abbey remembers being told that this was the Family's "best and absolutely final offer." I have little doubt that, without being explicitly told so, Abbey knew that this meant that the Family had likely reached the end of its bargaining process with the Special Committee. As Abrams stated in court, he told Abbey that the Family was "prepared to proceed with this transaction without you." As Abrams also noted, "[Mr. Abbey] knows that when I say best and final, that's it, and he was not going to get an additional penny from me." In other words, Abbey was told that the proverbial "train was leaving the station."

Abbey told Abrams that he would consider the offer in consultation with the plaintiffs' financial advisor but that the deal would also have to include a Minority Approval Condition. The next morning Abbey orally agreed to these terms. Abrams promptly informed the Special Committee's lawyers and the transactional counsel for the Family that the litigation was settled in principle and that a formal Memorandum of Understanding [MOU] would be prepared.

As of that time, the Special Committee's financial advisors were finalizing their analysis in advance of determining whether they could deliver a fairness opinion. The Special Committee and the Family were also negotiating the terms of the actual merger agreement.

By October 18, the Special Committee and the Family reached accord on a final merger contract. The Special Committee met and received a favorable fairness presentation from Goldman Sachs. After receiving that, the Special Committee unanimously recommended the merger to the full board. At a later meeting, the full Cox board also voted to approve the deal based upon the recommendation of the Special Committee.

That same day, Abrams and Abbey reached agreement on an MOU stating that the Family acknowledged that the desirability of settling this action and the efforts of the plaintiffs' counsel in this action were causal factors that led to the Family increasing its bid to $34.75, and agreeing to the Minority Approval Condition. A similar MOU was also executed with a group of plaintiffs who had filed similar actions in Georgia. The negotiations involving those plaintiffs are not described in the record before me in any detail.

The next day, October 19, Cox and the Family signed the merger agreement.

C.   THE SETTLEMENT IS PRESENTED TO THE COURT FOR APPROVAL
     AND THE MERGER CLOSES

The parties moved promptly to complete confirmatory discovery and negotiate a final stipulation of settlement. Only after that was done, they swear, was
there any discussion of the amount of attorneys' fees the plaintiffs' counsel
would seek.

In the attorneys' fee negotiations, the Family eventually agreed not to
oppose a fee request of up to $4.95 million. Separately, the Family forged a deal
by which it agreed not to oppose a fee request from the Georgia plaintiffs of
more than $1.25 million. In both cases, the Family agreed to pay whatever fee
was awarded rather than to require that any fee award be withheld from the
merger consideration to be paid to the public stockholders of Cox. According
to the plaintiffs' counsel Arthur Abbey, he would have sought a fee much larger
than $4.95 million had the defendants refused to agree not to oppose a fee
request up to that amount.

The Stipulation of Settlement was presented to the court on November 10,
2004. Notice was promptly issued to the public stockholders on November 24,
2004. By that time, the Family had already commenced their tender offer at
$34.75 per share.

On December 2, 2004, the tender offer expired. Approximately 189.7 million of Cox's 245.5 million public shares were tendered, satisfying the Minority
Approval Condition and giving the Family over 90% of the Cox shares. On
December 8, 2004, a back end, short-form merger was executed taking Cox
private.

III.   OBJECTORS TO THE PLAINTIFFS' FEE EMERGE

When the deadline to object to the proposed settlement expired, no objections to the settlement itself had been filed. But an objection was made to the
plaintiffs' counsel request for an award of attorneys' fees. . . .

One senses, moreover, that the objectors were not entirely self-motivated
but rather were inspired to object by one of their attorneys, Elliott J. Weiss,
a Professor of Law at the University of Arizona Law School. In recent years,
Weiss has himself appeared as an objecting stockholder to fee requests in this
court. And much of his recent scholarship has focused on what he regards to be
failures in the integrity and efficiency of corporate and securities class action
litigation.[13] . . .

. . . I highlight the [VANDERBILT] article because Weiss's advocacy on behalf
of the objectors as an attorney, which includes his filing of an affidavit by his
co-author White attaching their article, essentially consists of the conversion
of a particular part of his article into a brief to this court. The points that the

---

13. *E.g.*, Elliott J. Weiss & John S. Beckerman, *Let the Money Do The Monitoring: How
Institutional Investors Can Reduce Agency Costs in Securities Class Actions,* 104 YALE L.J. 2053
(1995) [; *see also*, Elliott J. Weiss and Lawrence J. White *File Early, Then Free Ride: How Delaware Law (Mis)Shapes Shareholder Class Actions,* 57 VAND. L. REV. 1797 (2004).]

objectors make, in other words, have less to do with this case in particular, and more to do with concerns about how the common law rules that Delaware uses to govern mergers with controlling stockholders create inefficient incentives for plaintiffs' lawyers and corporate defense counsel, leading to lawsuits that exist, in Weiss's view, almost entirely as a vehicle for the payment of attorneys' fees and the entry of a judgment of the court providing the defendants with a broad release from any future lawsuits relating to the underlying transactions. At oral argument, Weiss conceded that his client's objection to the fee in this particular case was not driven by anything unusual about the Cox merger but rather by their objection to the perpetuation of a pattern of settlements and fee requests like this one, and that their objection had reform of the law as its principle objective.

For that reason, it is important to set forth in some detail the objectors' argument that no fee should be awarded, a task that requires a description of the legal framework within which settlements of this type arise.

IV. LEGAL ANALYSIS

A. THE DELAWARE LAW OF MERGERS WITH CONTROLLING STOCKHOLDERS

It would not be much of a stretch to say that the central idea of Delaware's approach to corporation law is the empowerment of centralized management, in the form of boards of directors and the subordinate officers they choose, to make disinterested business decisions. The business judgment rule exemplifies and animates this idea.

But this idea also presents to corporate law makers — of both the statutory and common law variety — a correlative challenge that has occupied most of the last century of American corporation law: how to regulate transactions between corporations and their own directors, officers, or controlling stockholders. And, with the later emergence of a vibrant market for corporate control, came the need to address the extent to which certain corporate transactions with, or defensive reactions towards, third parties sufficiently implicate the self-interest of directors and officers as to cast doubt on their ability to pursue their corporations' best interests with unconflicted fidelity. . . .

. . . To that end, §144 of the DGCL says that a transaction between a corporation and an officer or director is not per se voidable so long as the transaction is approved, after full disclosure, either by: 1) a majority of the disinterested directors; or 2) a good faith vote of the stockholders. By those methods, respect for the business judgment of the board can be maintained with integrity, because the law has taken into account the conflict and required that the business judgment be either proposed by the disinterested directors or ratified by the stockholders it affects. In the absence of those protections, the transaction is presumed voidable absent a demonstration, by the interested party, that the transaction is fair.

But the common law of corporations also was centered on the idea of the business judgment rule and its approach to interested transactions looked much like that codified in §144. The approval by a majority of the disinterested directors of an interested transaction was held to invoke the business judgment rule standard of review, and to relieve the proponents of the burden to show that the transaction was entirely fair to the corporation. But a good example of the distinction between §144 and the common law of corporations is their disparate approach to stockholder ratification. By its own terms, §144 alleviates the possibility of per se invalidity by a vote of stockholders, without any explicit requirement that a majority of the disinterested stockholders approve. The common law, by contrast, only gives ratification effect to approval of the interested transaction by a majority of the disinterested stockholders.

This example helps make another point, which is the continuing struggle in our law to determine how to balance the goals of respecting business judgments made by boards and protecting stockholders from abuse from self-interested fiduciaries. In the 1980s, much of what was most compelling and urgent in corporation law, was the judiciary's articulation of the freedom that directors had to address hostile takeover bids. At least in our law, what emerged were common law rules that encouraged boards to invest decision-making primacy in outside directors rather than insiders, because it was presumed that outside directors, as opposed to CEOs and CFOs who had their primary jobs at stake, would be less likely to resist a takeover simply to remain directors of a public company. When independent directors were given substantial authority, the law was more willing to conclude that the board's actions in resisting a takeover were permissible. But even then, the "omnipresent specter that a board may be acting in its own interest, rather than those of the corporation and its shareholders" subjected defensive actions to heightened scrutiny, under a reasonableness form of review that was tighter than the bare rationality test of the business judgment rule.

For present purposes, what is most critical is how the Delaware Supreme Court addressed the standard of review that would apply to a very particular type of interested transaction: a merger in which a controlling stockholder acquires the rest of the shares it did not control. . . .

In the important case of *Kahn v. Lynch Communication, Inc.*,[26] the Delaware Supreme Court resolved this doctrinal debate. In its decision, the Supreme Court held that regardless of the procedural protections employed, a merger with a controlling stockholder would always be subject to the entire fairness standard. Even if the transaction was 1) negotiated and approved by a special committee of independent directors; and 2) subject to approval by a majority of the disinterested shares (i.e., those shares not held by the controller or its affiliates), the best that could be achieved was a shift of the burden of persuasion on the issue of fairness from the defendants to the plaintiffs. In reaching this decision, the Supreme Court expressly relied on *Citron's* reasoning about the implicit coercion thought to be felt by minority stockholders in this transactional context. Less clear is why the Supreme Court refused to give weight to independent director approval, given that *Aronson v. Lewis*[28] had held that independent directors were presumed to be capable of exercising a disinterested business judgment in deciding whether to cause the company to sue a

---

26. 638 A.2d 1110 (Del. 1994).
28. 473 A.2d 805 (Del. 1984).

controlling stockholder. In part, *Lynch's* decision on this score seemed to turn on a vestigial concept from a discarded body of case law; namely, that because there no longer needed to be a "business purpose" for a merger with a controlling stockholder,[29] it was somehow not a "business judgment" for independent directors to conclude that a merger was in the best interests of the minority stockholders.

That is an odd and unsatisfying rationale, which, if taken seriously, would have implications for all decisions by directors who agree to cash mergers. All in all, it is perhaps fairest and more sensible to read *Lynch* as being premised on a sincere concern that mergers with controlling stockholders involve an extraordinary potential for the exploitation by powerful insiders of their informational advantages and their voting clout. Facing the proverbial 800 pound gorilla who wants the rest of the bananas all for himself, chimpanzees like independent directors and disinterested stockholders could not be expected to make sure that the gorilla paid a fair price.[31] Therefore, the residual protection of an unavoidable review of the financial fairness whenever plaintiffs could raise a genuine dispute of fact about that issue was thought to be a necessary final protection. But, in order to encourage the use of procedural devices such as special committees and Minority Approval Conditions that tended to encourage fair pricing, the Court did give transactional proponents a modest procedural benefit—the shifting of the burden of persuasion on the ultimate issue of fairness to the plaintiffs—if the transaction proponents proved, in a factually intensive way, that the procedural devices had, in fact, operated with integrity. In the case of a special committee, later case law held that the defendants would only be relieved of the burden of proving fairness if it first proved that "the committee function[ed] in a manner which indicates that the controlling shareholder did not dictate the terms of the transaction and that the committee exercised real bargaining power." In the case of a Minority Approval Condition, the defendants had the usual ratification burden—to show that all material facts had been disclosed and the absence of coercive threats. But in either event, or in the exceedingly rare case in which both protections were employed in advance of, and not as part of a negotiated settlement, the most the defendants could get was a burden shift.

Although it is an undeniable reality that *Lynch* stated that any merger with a controlling stockholder, however structured, was subject to a fairness review, it would be unfair not to make explicit another reality. No defendant in *Lynch*, and no defendant since, has argued that the use of an independent special committee *and* a Minority Approval Condition sufficiently alleviates any implicit coercion as to justify invocation of the business judgment rule. For this reason, it is important not to assume that the Supreme Court has already rejected this more precisely focused contention.

---

29. *Weinberger* eliminated this requirement, which was the rule of *Singer v. Magnavox Co.*, 380 A.2d 969 (Del. 1977). *See Weinberger [v. UOP, Inc.*, 457 A.2d 701, 715 (Del. 1983)].

31. *See Pure Resources*, 808 A.2d 421, 436 (Del. Ch. 2002); Leo E. Strine, Jr., *The Inescapably Empirical Foundation of the Common Law of Corporations*, 27 Del. J. Corp. L. 499, 509 (2002) (both describing the evolution of this thinking).

**B. A TEMPERED DESCRIPTION OF THE OBJECTORS' CRITICISM
    OF THE INCENTIVE EFFECTS CREATED BY *LYNCH***

The incentive effects created by *Lynch* are largely what inspire the objectors' position. . . .

Initially, it cannot be ignored that *Lynch* created a strong incentive for the use of special negotiating committees in addressing mergers with controlling stockholders. This is a very useful incentive. In the main, the experience with such committees has been a positive one. Independent directors have increasingly understood and aggressively undertaken the burdens of acting as a guarantor of the minority's interest, by undertaking a deep examination of the economics of the transactions they confront and developing effective negotiation strategies to extract value for the minority from the controller. . . .

These steps are in important ways complements and not substitutes. A good board is best positioned to extract a price at the highest possible level because it does not suffer from the collective action problem of disaggregated stockholders. But boards are rarely comprised of independent directors whose own financial futures depend importantly on getting the best price and, history shows, are sometimes timid, inept, or . . . , well, let's just say worse. Although stockholders are not well positioned to use the voting process to get the last nickel out of a purchaser, they are well positioned to police bad deals in which the board did not at least obtain something in the amorphous "range" of financial fairness.

In the context of a merger with [a] controlling stockholder, the complementary role of disinterested director and disinterested stockholder approval is difficult to conceive of as less important. For a variety of obvious reasons (e.g., informational asymmetries, the possibility that the outside directors might be more independent in appearance than in substance, or might lack the savvy to effectively counter the controller), the integrity-enforcing utility of a Minority Approval Condition seems hard to dispute. And, with increasingly active institutional investors and easier information flows, stockholders have never been better positioned to make a judgment as to whether a special committee has done its job. At the same time, the ability of disaggregated stockholders to reject by a binary up or down vote obviously "unfair" deals does not translate into their ability to do what an effective special committee can do, which is to negotiate effectively and strike a bargain much higher in the range of fairness. As a practical matter, however, the effect of *Lynch* in the real world of transactions was to generate the use of special committees alone.

The incentive system that *Lynch* created for plaintiffs' lawyers is its most problematic feature, however, and the consequence that motivates the objectors' contentions here. . . .

Unlike any other transaction one can imagine—even a *Revlon* deal—it was impossible after *Lynch* to structure a merger with a controlling stockholder in a way that permitted the defendants to obtain a dismissal of the case on the pleadings. . . .

For both the proponents of mergers with controlling stockholders (i.e., controllers and the directors involved in the transactions, all of whom become defendants in lawsuits attacking those transactions) and the plaintiffs' lawyers who file suits, this incentive effect of *Lynch* manifested itself in a unique approach to "litigation." Instead of suing once a controller actually signs up a merger agreement with a special committee of independent directors, plaintiffs sue as soon as there is a public announcement of the controller's intention to propose a merger.

This case is typical of that phenomenon because the plaintiffs sued the same day that the Family announced it was prepared to buy the rest of the Cox shares. The suits were filed despite the express indication that the Family was going to negotiate its $32 per share opening bid with a special committee of independent directors and the absence of any attempt to coerce that committee or to rush it in its work.

In this regard, this case is paradigmatic. And that is what bothers the objectors.

* * *

As the objectors point out and this court has often noted in settlement hearings regarding these kind of cases in the past, the ritualistic nature of a process almost invariably resulting in the simultaneous bliss of three parties—the plaintiffs' lawyers, the special committee, and the controlling stockholders—is a jurisprudential triumph of an odd form of tantra. I say invariably because the record contains a shocking omission—the inability of the plaintiffs, despite their production of expert affidavits, to point to one instance in the precise context of a case of this kind (i.e., cases started by attacks on negotiable going-private proposals) of the plaintiffs' lawyers refusing to settle once a special committee has agreed on price with a controller.

That bears repeating. In no instance has there been a situation when the controller's lawyer told the plaintiffs' lawyer this is my best and final offer and received the answer, "sign up your deal with the special committee, and we'll meet you in the Chancellor's office for the scheduling conference on our motion to expedite." Rather, in every instance, the plaintiffs' lawyers have concluded that the price obtained by the special committee was sufficiently attractive, that the acceptance of a settlement at that price was warranted.[39]

The objectors use this admittedly material fact to buttress another argument they make about *Lynch*. That argument, which is again something members of this court have grasped for some time, rests in the ease for the plaintiffs' lawyers of achieving "success" in this ritual. When a controlling stockholder announces a "proposal" to negotiate a going private merger, the controller is, like any bidder, very unlikely to present his full reserve price as its opening bid. Moreover, given the nature of *Lynch* and its progeny, and their emphasis on the effectiveness of the special committee as a bargaining agent, the controller knows, and special committee members will demand, that real price negotiations proceed after the opening bid, and that those negotiations will almost certainly result in any consummated deal occurring at a higher price.

For plaintiffs' lawyers, the incentives are obvious.[40] By suing on the proposal, the plaintiffs' lawyers can claim that they are responsible, in part, for price

---

39. *See* Elliott J. Weiss & Lawrence J. White, *File Early, Then Free Ride: How Delaware Law (Mis)Shapes Shareholder Class Actions,* 57 Vand. L.Rev. 1797, 1820 & n. 84, 1833–34 (2004); . . .

40. *Cf.* Weiss & White, 57 Vand. L.Rev. at 1857 n. 183 (stating that the rule of *Lynch* "appears to have had the effect of encouraging plaintiffs' attorneys to settle cases challenging squeeze outs, largely without regard to whether the merger terms agreed to by an SNC [special negotiating committee] are entirely fair").

increases in a deal context in which price increases are overwhelmingly likely to occur. Added to this incentive is the fact that the plaintiffs' lawyers know that the *Lynch* standard gives them the ability, on bare satisfaction of notice pleading standards and Rule 11, to defeat a motion to dismiss addressed to any complaint challenging an actual merger agreement with a special committee, even one conditioned on Minority Approval. Because of this ability, the plaintiffs' claims always have settlement value because of the costs of discovery and time to the defendants. Add to this another important ingredient, which is that once a special committee has negotiated a material price increase with the aid of well-regarded financial and legal advisors, the plaintiffs' lawyers can contend with a straight-face that it was better to help get the price up to where it ended than to risk that the controller would abandon the deal. Abandonment of the deal, the plaintiffs' lawyers will say with accuracy, will result in the company's stock price falling back to its pre-proposal level, which is always materially lower as it does not reflect the anticipation of a premium-generating going private transaction. Having vigorously aided the special committee to get into the range of fairness and having no reason to suspect that the special committee was disloyal to its mission, the plaintiffs' lawyers can say, in plausible good faith, that it was better for the class to take this improved bid, which is now well within the range of fairness, rather than to risk abandonment of the transaction. Moreover, for those stockholders who wish to challenge the price, appraisal still remains an option.

* * *

C. *SILICONIX*: ANOTHER ROAD TO GOING PRIVATE IS PAVED

Of course, things cannot be quite that simple. And they are not. To describe why, I must add more jurisprudential context and then bring in the arguments raised by the plaintiffs' experts.

Under Delaware law, the doctrine of independent legal significance exists. That doctrine permits corporations to take, if the DGCL permits it, a variety of transactional routes to the same destination. For years, there had existed a strand of Delaware law that stated that a controlling stockholder who made a tender offer—as opposed to a merger proposal—to acquire the rest of the controlled company's shares had no duty to offer a fair price. So long as the controller did not actually coerce the minority stockholders or commit a disclosure violation, its tender offer was immune from equitable intervention for breach of fiduciary duty. *Lynch v. Vickers Energy Corp.*[44] stands for this basic proposition, which was reaffirmed in *Solomon v. Pathe Communications Corp.*,[45] less than two years after *Lynch* was decided. In the tender offer context, the doctrine of implicit coercion that *Lynch* is premised upon was unrecognized, but the form of the transaction, rather than any reasoned analysis, apparently formed the implicit justification for the discrepancy.

The opportunity that the tender offer line of cases presented for transactional planners interested in deal certainty was tempered, however, by the

---

44. 351 A.2d 570 (Del. Ch. 1976), *rev'd on other grounds,* 383 A.2d 278 (Del. 1977).
45. 672 A.2d 35, 39 (Del. 1996).

unsettled nature of a related question. By their very nature, going private trans-actions involve the desire by a controlling stockholder to acquire all of the com-pany and to avoid the costs that come with having other equity holders. In most tender offers, at least some percentage of the shares will not tender, not necessarily because the offer was too low, but for other reasons (lack of focus, administrative failures by brokers, etc.). At the controller's disposal was the short-form merger technique, which permitted a controller, without a formal process, to merge out the remaining stockholders if the controller's owner-ship had increased to 90% through the tender offer. But the uncertainty was whether the short-form merger would be subject to the *Lynch* standard. In *In re Unocal Exploration Corp. Shareholders Litigation*,[46] that uncertainty was resolved, with the Court of Chancery, and then the Supreme Court, holding that the short-form merger statute specifically contemplated the absence of any negotia-tion process and that to impose the entire fairness standard on such mergers would therefore intrude on the transactional freedom authorized by §253. In that transactional context, stockholders who believed that the price was unfair had an exclusive remedy: appraisal.

After *Unocal Exploration* was decided by this court, transactional lawyers put together the *Solomon* strand of authority with that new certainty and gener-ated a new, and less negotiation-and-litigation-intensive route to going private: a front tender offer designed to get the controller 90% of the shares, coupled with a back-end short form merger. In subsequent cases in this Court, it was held that this method of transaction—which came to be known by the first written decision addressing it—*In re Siliconix Inc. Shareholders Litigation*[47]—did not trigger entire fairness review so long as the offer was not actually coercive and there was full disclosure. In the later case of *Pure Resources*,[48] this Court held that the mere fact that the controller had taken the *Siliconix* route did not relieve it of fiduciary duties. Although those duties did not include a duty to pay a fair price, the court held that a *Siliconix* transaction could be subject to fair-ness review to protect the minority unless:

   (i)   the offer is subject to a nonwaivable majority of the minority tender condition,
   (ii) the controlling shareholder commits to consummate a short-form merger promptly after increasing its holdings above ninety percent,
   (iii) the controlling shareholder "has made no retributive threats," and
   (iv) the independent directors are given complete discretion and sufficient time "to react to the tender offer, by (at the very least) hiring their own ad-visors," providing a recommendation to the non-controlling shareholders, and disclosing adequate information to allow the non-controlling share-holders an opportunity for informed decision making.[50]

---

46. 793 A.2d 329 (Del. Ch. 2000), *aff'd*, 777 A.2d 242 (Del. 2001).

47. 2001 WL 716787 (Del. Ch. June 19, 2001).

48. 808 A.2d 421 (Del. Ch. 2002).

50. Ronald J. Gilson & Jeffrey N. Gordon, *Controlling Controlling Stockholders*, 152 U. Pa. L.Rev. 785, 827–28 (2003) (paraphrasing and distilling the holdings of *Pure Resources*, 808 A.2d at 445).

In *Pure Resources,* the relationship between the *Lynch* and *Siliconix* forms of transactions was explored in depth and the logical tension between our common law's disparate approach to the form of equitable review for those forms was acknowledged. Rather than subject the *Siliconix* form to the rigid *Lynch* standard, this court decided that it was better to formulate protective standards that were more flexible, with the hope that at a later stage the two strands could be made coherent, in a manner that addressed not only the need to protect minority stockholders but also the utility of providing a non-litigious route to effecting transactions that often were economically efficient both for the minority who received a premium and in the sense of creating more rationally organized corporations.

Since *Siliconix* was decided, controllers have therefore had two different transactional methods to choose between in attempting to go private. One can imagine various reasons why a controller might prefer one route or the other, depending on variables like the controller's ownership stake, the extent of the public float, the presence of big holders, the desire for certainty and closure, and which route might yield the best price for it. For example, the further a controller was from 90% to begin with, the more attractive the merger route might be, and vice versa, simply for efficiency reasons in both cases.

D.   THE PLAINTIFFS' EXPERT COUNTER ATTACK

For present purposes, however, what is relevant is the empirical evidence that the plaintiffs have submitted to counter the objectors' position. To confront the scholarly work of Weiss and White, who are of the view that litigation of this kind is of no material benefit to minority stockholders, the plaintiffs have submitted an affidavit from Professor Guhan Subramanian of the Harvard Law School.

Subramanian makes two major arguments. First, Subramanian cites to his own recent scholarly studies to support his view that the *Lynch* form of transaction results, on average, in going private transactions that pay the minority a higher premium in comparison to the pre-announcement market price than do *Siliconix* deals. Second, Subramanian attempts to show that the filing of lawsuits under *Lynch* challenging going private merger proposals by controlling stockholders are a material factor in producing these more favorable results.

I will now explain in summary form Subramanian's arguments and explain why I conclude that the first of his arguments is his strongest, and that his other point is less convincing. . . .

In recent work, Professor Subramanian studied the prices at which going-private transactions occurred since *Siliconix,* breaking them down between merger, or *Lynch,* transactions and tender offer, or *Siliconix,* transactions. Subramanian finds that the final premium paid over the pre-announcement market price was on average higher in *Lynch* deals than *Siliconix* deals, and that the difference was statistically significant.[52] Likewise, he finds that controllers,

---

52. Subramanian, *Post–Siliconix Freeze-Outs: Theory & Evidence,* at Table 1 (Working Draft, Jan. 2005).

on average, increase their opening bids more when pursuing a *Lynch* merger than a *Siliconix* tender offer and that the difference is statistically significant.[53] Subramanian, after controlling for other possible factors, concludes that these outcomes differ primarily because of the stronger bargaining hand given to the special committee in the *Lynch* context versus the *Siliconix* context. Because the *Lynch* transaction can only proceed with the special committee's approval unless the controller wants to take on the affirmative burden to prove fairness and because a merger transaction presupposes a negotiated price and a tender offer does not, Subramanian believes that minority stockholders do better in *Lynch* deals.

The active bargaining agency of the special committee is, Subramanian concludes, the critically absent feature in *Siliconix* deals. In those deals, the special committee is usually making, at most, a recommendation rather than acting as a necessary approving force and the (disaggregated) minority stockholders are required to make a binary choice between accepting or rejecting the tender offer, without a prior process of negotiation by a bargaining agent on their behalf. Subramanian posits that even when any structural coercion is removed, the stockholders are poorly positioned to extract the controllers' best price. They might protect themselves against unfair prices but are not in a good position to bargain the price up in the same manner as a good special committee in a *Lynch* deal. . . .

. . . Subramanian infers that the controller can pay a lower price in the *Siliconix* context because the weaker hand of the special committee and plaintiffs, *combined,* will enable controllers to keep more nickels in their pockets and still close deals. For that reason, Subramanian thinks *Lynch,* and the role that it provides to plaintiffs as a watchdog, "polices the worst control shareholder deals, and benefits target company shareholders. . . ."[54]

* * *

F. THE COURT'S DISTILLATION OF THE EXPERT INPUT

Where does this leave us? By this point, the reader has probably accurately sensed that I have been dragged into an academic debate of considerable complexity. The lawyers did not ask for an opportunity for the experts to testify and the experts' dueling over minutia in affidavits has been less than clear and helpful. That is not to say that the input they have provided is without decisional utility. It has value if used with appropriate caution. And from it I make the following observations.

First, the record supports the proposition that *Lynch* deals tend to generate higher final premiums than *Siliconix* deals. One would suspect that this would be so for several reasons, including: 1) the greater leverage that the form of transaction gives to special committees; 2) the fact that the governing standard of review always gives the plaintiffs settlement value; 3) the reality that signing

---

54. Subramanian Aff. ¶ 31 (quoting Robert B. Thompson & Randall S. Thomas, *The New Look of Shareholder Litigation: Acquisition Oriented Class Actions,* 57 Vand. L.Rev. 133, 202 (2004)).

up a merger when the votes are locked up results in the greatest certainty for
a controller; and 4) signing up a merger with a special committee and a settlement with plaintiffs' lawyers provides not only deal certainty, but a broad
release and the most effective discouragement of appraisal claims. One cannot
tell, of course, how important each of them is as a factor, but one awkward fact
strongly suggests that the threat of bare knuckles litigation over fairness is not
as important as the special committee's role as an negotiating force.

That awkward fact is the absence of evidence that "traditional" plaintiffs'
lawyers, who attacked going private proposals by controllers, have ever refused
to settle once they have received the signal that the defendants have put on the
table their best and final offer—i.e., an offer that is acceptable to the special
committee. There are examples of when the plaintiffs have settled at a lower
price than the special committee demanded,[58] but no examples of when the
iron fist of the plaintiffs' bar demanded more than the velvet glove of the special committee. The plaintiffs' bar would say, of course, this is because they did
such a good job in each case that the price concessions they helped the special
committee extract was of such inarguable fairness that it would been silly to
fight on.

Perhaps what can be most charitably said is that the pendency of litigation
and the theoretical threat that the plaintiffs will press on provides special committee members with additional clout that they wield to get good results, and
that gives lawyers for controllers leverage to get their clients to pay a higher
price to ensure deal closure and the utmost reduction of litigation risk.

Second, there is much that remains to be explored about the actual price
differences between *Lynch* and *Siliconix* deals. Many *Siliconix* deals are quite
small and involve very troubled companies. . . .

Third, litigation under *Lynch* never seems to involve actual litigation conflict if the lawsuit begins with a suit attacking a negotiable proposal. These cases
almost invariably settle or are dismissed voluntarily by the plaintiffs. In those
instances when there is actual litigation conflict in an "attack" on a going private transaction that has occurred because the complaint actually sought to stop
a real transaction—an agreed-upon merger or a tender offer that was actively
been pressed. In those situations, it is also much more likely that a plaintiff with
a large stake who has hired a non-traditional law firm will mount a challenge.
The *Pure Resources* and *Emerging Communications* [*In re Emerging Communications,
Inc. Shareholders Litigation*, 2005 WL1305745 (Del. Ch. 2003)] transactions are
good examples of these realities. Indeed, in *Emerging Communications*, the original plaintiffs pressed forward with a settlement after confirmatory discovery
that would have resulted in a final price of $10.25 binding those stockholders
who did not seek appraisal to the same price negotiated by the special committee. Only after objection by a large holder represented by a very large firm

---

58. *See, e.g., In re Donna Karan Int'l Inc. Shareholders Litigation*, C.A. No. 18559, Tr. (Del.
Ch. Sept. 10, 2002) (following an initial proposal of $8.50 per share, plaintiffs agreed in
principle to settle at $10.50 per share, but the special committee refused to consummate the
transaction at that price and ultimately secured a $10.75 per share price).

that more usually represents corporate defendants than stockholders was the settlement abandoned. The ultimate result was an award of damages based on a $38.05 per share value, in a detailed opinion by Vice Chancellor (Justice) Jacobs that found glaringly obvious procedural and substantive problems with the special committee process.

Fourth, minority stockholders seem to be doing more than tolerably well under both the *Lynch* and *Siliconix* regimes. Even if premiums to market are lower in *Siliconix* transactions, the premiums paid are large in comparison to the routine, day-to-day trading prices, in which minority and liquidity discounts will be suffered. For that reason, at every settlement, the plaintiffs' lawyers say that they could not risk pushing farther, lest the controller decide not to press on and offer a deal, and the stockholders suffer the fate of continuing as owners of minority shares in a going concern. After all, events that generate liquidity for all minority stockholders at substantial premiums are usually welcomed by stockholders.

* * *

V.   ARE THE PLAINTIFFS ENTITLED TO AN AWARD OF ATTORNEYS' FEES AND IN WHAT AMOUNT?

Having completed a lengthy predicate describing the legal context in which this request for attorneys' fees arises, and the arguments of the plaintiffs and the objectors about that context and its relevance, I will now turn to the ultimate resolution of this dispute.

* * *

Put simply, when the plaintiffs filed their complaint they were not attacking any completed fiduciary decision. They were attacking a target that, by its very nature, was moving. The only purpose of their complaints was to act as a placeholder for a possible later attack on an actual fiduciary judgment of the Cox board to enter into a formal merger agreement with the Family. The complaints were therefore unripe and without merit.

* * *

Put simply, because this case is characteristic of *Lynch* cases involving suits on mere proposals, there was not much work to be done, except in negotiating and later conducting confirmatory discovery of a settlement. There is no special complexity to the case; indeed, it is entirely characteristic of prior going private cases attacking negotiable proposals.

For all these reasons, I conclude that the fee sought [$4.95 million] is well in excess of what can reasonably be justified. . . .

For those reasons—the size of the benefit and the negotiation of the fee by defendants—I have awarded a fee larger than I otherwise would have. I do so by awarding a total award of fees and expenses of $1.275 million. That could be translated into an award of $500 per hour for 2000 hours worked, plus the full payment of expenses. Given the factors outlined above, that is a more than generous award.

VI. A Coda on the Jurisprudential Elephant in the Corner

Before concluding, I feel obliged to add a coda. The present case illustrates, in my view, the need to adjust our common law of corporations to take appropriate account of the positive and negative consequences flowing from the standard of review governing going private mergers.

Lynch is a well-motivated decision that belies any contention that Delaware law blindly favors management. The incentive it creates for the use of well-functioning special committees is useful and has benefited minority stockholders. But its failure to provide any additional incentive for the use of Minority Approval Conditions—except as a settlement add-on—is less useful. . . .

In the plaintiffs' submissions, much has been made of the notion that even if lawsuits filed on mere proposals are not ripe and have no merit, having the presence of plaintiffs' lawyers around during the negotiation process has led to good results and that the law should therefore tolerate the continuation of this phenomenon. In *Bird v. Lida, Inc.*, Chancellor Allen noted that arguments of this kind have not and should never be deemed sufficient by courts of law.[81] The judicial process should be invoked when a party has a genuine claim of injury. Particularly in the representative litigation context, where there are deep concerns about the agency costs imposed by plaintiffs' attorneys, our judiciary must be vigilant to make sure that the incentives we create promote integrity and that we do not, by judicial doctrine, generate the need for defendants to settle simply because they have no viable alternative, even when they have done nothing wrong. This vigilance is appropriate not because the representative litigation process is not important to our corporate law's ability to protect stockholders against fiduciary wrongdoing, but precisely because it is so important. That process should not be one that we permit to be seen as lacking in integrity and therefore vulnerable to elimination.

In this corner of our law, a relatively modest alteration of *Lynch* would do much to ensure this type of integrity, while continuing to provide important, and I would argue, *enhanced,* protections for minority stockholders. That alteration would permit the invocation of the business judgment rule for a going private merger that involved procedural protections that mirrored what is contemplated in an arms-length merger under §251—independent, disinterested director *and* stockholder approval. Put simply, if a controller proposed a merger, subject from inception to negotiation and approval of the merger by an independent special committee *and* a Minority Approval Condition, the business judgment rule should presumptively apply. In that situation, the controller and the directors of the affected company should be able to obtain dismissal of a complaint unless: 1) the plaintiffs plead particularized facts that the special committee was not independent or was not effective because of its own breach of fiduciary duty or wrongdoing by the controller (e.g., fraud on the committee); or 2) the approval of the minority stockholders was tainted by misdisclosure, or actual or structural coercion.

---

81. 681 A.2d 399, 407 (Del. Ch. 1996).

This alteration would promote the universal use of a transactional structure that is very favorable to minority stockholders — one that deploys an active, disinterested negotiating agent to bargain for the minority coupled with an opportunity for the minority to freely decide whether to accept or reject their agent's work product. Indeed, the plaintiffs' own expert, Professor Subramanian, supports reform of precisely this kind. And *Lynch* in its current form could be retained to govern any merger in which the controller refuses to use both of these techniques from the inception of the process, allowing for the controller to proceed, get appropriate burden-shifting credit for use of special committee or a Minority Approval Condition, but remain subject to the entire fairness standard.

Importantly, this revised standard would not diminish the integrity-enforcing potential of litigation in any material way, in my view. Plaintiffs who believed that a special committee breached its fiduciary duties in agreeing to a merger would continue to have the practical ability to press a claim; . . .

This standard would also encourage the filing of claims only by plaintiffs and plaintiffs' lawyers who genuinely believed that a wrong had been committed. The chance to free ride on the expected increase in the controller's original proposal would be eliminated and therefore litigation would only be filed by those who believed that they possessed legal claims with value.

Importantly, a revision along these lines would leave in place another remedial option that is viable for stockholders who believe that the ultimate price paid in a negotiated merger is unfair — appraisal. Appraisal permits a stockholder to receive a fair value determination regardless of the procedural fairness leading to a merger. Particularly for institutional investors with large stakes, appraisal can be a potent remedy, . . .

Therefore, this revision would have much to offer minority stockholders. Minority stockholders would continue to receive the benefits of the mechanism that most commentators believe is responsible for the bulk of the premiums paid in the going privates, the negotiating power of special committees, but backed up by an incentive system that would give them, through an up-front Minority Approval Condition, the right to turn down their negotiating agent's work. At the same time, they would retain viable litigation options that would also operate to deter overreaching by controllers.

Of course, a revision in *Lynch* alone is arguably not complete. The plaintiffs have presented a cogent argument that the negotiating leverage wielded by special committees in mergers with controlling stockholders results in better outcomes for stockholders than does the ability of stockholders to reject a structurally non-coercive tender offer made by a controlling stockholder. The jarring doctrinal inconsistency between the equitable principles of fiduciary duty that apply to *Lynch* and *Siliconix* deals has been noted by this court before in *Pure Resources* and *Cysive*. [*See In re Cysive, Inc. Shareholders Litigation*, 836 A.2d 531 (Del. Ch. 2003).] It was thought preferable in *Pure Resources* to keep the strands separate until there is an alteration in *Lynch,* lest the less than confidence inspiring pattern of "*Lynch* litigation" replicate itself across-the-board in all going private transactions, thereby deterring the procession of offers that provide valuable liquidity to minority stockholders and efficiency for the economy in general.

A principled reconciliation of the two lines of authority could center on much the same solution articulated above, as Professors Gilson and Gordon have suggested in an important scholarly article.[92] In the case of a tender offer by a controlling stockholder, the controlling stockholder could be relieved of the burden of proving entire fairness if: 1) the tender offer was recommended by an independent special committee; 2) the tender offer was structurally non-coercive in the manner articulated by *Pure Resources*; and 3) there was a disclosure of all material facts. In that case, the transaction should be immune from challenge in a breach of fiduciary duty action unless the plaintiffs pled particularized facts from which it could be inferred that the special committee's recommendation was tainted by a breach of fiduciary duty or that there was a failure in disclosure. That is, an alteration on the *Lynch* line could be accompanied by a strengthening of equitable review in the *Siliconix* line. But in both cases, there would remain a strong incentive for controllers to afford stockholders the procedural protection *of both* a special committee with real clout and of non-coerced, fully informed approval by the minority stockholders.

As important, this incentive would enable transactional planners to know that they can structure transactions in a way that affords them the opportunity to obtain a dismissal on the complaint. In this way, the alteration brings this area of our law into harmony with the rest of Delaware corporate law that gives substantial deference to decisions made by disinterested, independent directors and approved by disinterested, non-coerced stockholders. That deference is consistent with the central notion of our law, which respects business judgments made by impartial directors and approved by unconflicted stockholders. . . .

NOTES

So . . . where do we stand today? More importantly, as Delaware caselaw continues to evolve, what should be the state of Delaware law with respect to "freeze-out" transactions? In thinking about this question, consider the following recent assessment:

> Determination of the appropriate approach to [judicial] review [of] controlling stockholder/minority buyout transactions—i.e., where a controlling stockholder acquires the "minority" shares that it does not already own—requires resolution of the tension between deference to business judgment and protection against self-dealing and coercion. Delaware courts, along with legal practitioners and academics have been fascinated with this tension in the context of minority buyouts, and the debate continues without resolution. This Article critiques the progress of the effort to resolve this tension against a compilation of real-world data points collected from actual controlling stockholder buyout transactions. This data shows that the Delaware Court of Chancery's efforts to make progress toward a more efficient and coherent approach to judicial review of minority buyout transactions are having *de minimis*, if any, impact, and that market forces, rather than existing case law, are the participants' primary drivers when deciding how to structure these type of transactions and how to respond to related litigation.

* * *

---

92. Ronald J. Gilson & Jeffrey N. Gordon, *Controlling Controlling Stockholders*, 152 U. Pa. L.Rev. 785, 827–28 (2003).

Delaware courts have sought to create a framework for analyzing controlling stockholder buyout transactions that balance traditional deference for business judgment with the need to discourage self-dealing by the controlling stockholder. The courts' efforts have given rise to two different analytical frameworks: (1) the heightened "entire fairness" review of transactions pursuant to negotiated merger agreements; and (2) deferential business judgment review where the controlling stockholder pursues the buyout of the unaffiliated or "minority" shares through a unilateral tender offer (i.e., outside the context of a negotiated agreement with the target's board). [T]hese two standards have converged somewhat over the last ten years.

The justification for the two different approaches arose from the courts' perception that the process of negotiating a merger agreement threatened unaffiliated stockholders' interests in a way that pursuing a unilateral tender offer did not. The negotiated merger agreement evoked a scene of opaque backroom deliberations, in which a controlling stockholder—an "800 pound gorilla" with "informational advantages and . . . voting clout"—could promise reward or threaten retributive action against the target board with whom it was negotiating. In such a situation, the courts perceived "extraordinary potential for . . . exploitation" by the controlling stockholder, in the form of a strong temptation for both the controlling stockholder and the target board to prioritize the controlling stockholder's interests ahead of those of the unaffiliated stockholders.

* * *

From time to time over the last decade, the Delaware Court of Chancery has questioned whether Delaware's bifurcated approach to these two types of controlling stockholder buyout transactions is justified. After all, from the point of view of the basic structural outcome of the transactions, the negotiated merger and the unilateral tender offer are no different. The transactions are "economically similar" but are treated as "categorically different simply because the method by which the controlling stockholder proceeds varies." [*Pure Resources*, 808 A.2d at 435.]

More significantly, the Court of Chancery has challenged the underlying assumptions regarding the relative necessity of stockholder protection in each of the two transaction structures, identifying the stockholder in a tender offer context not as the free market participant described in earlier cases, but rather one of many "disaggregated stockholders" who must "decide whether to tender quickly, pressured by the risk of being squeezed out in a short-form merger at a different price later or being left as part of a much smaller public minority." [*Id.*] The stockholder contemplating whether to participate in a tender offer may well be placed under at least the same pressure to accept the terms of the "800-pound gorilla" as the target board contemplating whether to adopt a negotiated merger agreement. If this is true, the Court of Chancery has reasoned, then the minority stockholders deciding whether to participate in a tender offer required more protection than the Delaware courts had been providing.

As the Court of Chancery considered whether Delaware courts were providing too little protection to unaffiliated stockholders in the unilateral tender offer context, it also began to express concern that the *Kahn v. Lynch* "entire fairness" framework provided too much "protection" to stockholders in the negotiated merger context. The court noted, in *dicta*, that the negotiated merger participants' inability to seek dismissal on the pleadings, once a merger agreement was challenged and subjected to "entire fairness" review, generated a troubling pattern of free-riding plaintiffs' litigation; litigation that predictably followed the announcement of each transaction, but that did not actually serve the interests of the unaffiliated stockholders. [*Cox Communications*, 879 A.2d at 619-20.]

As identified by then-Vice Chancellor Strine in *Cox Communications*, and still accurate today, it has become inevitable that plaintiff-stockholders react to the announcement of a controlling stockholder's proposal to negotiate a merger agreement at a specified price by filing suit purportedly on behalf of the general class of unaffiliated stockholders. The target board then appoints a special committee and dual negotiations commence — one set of negotiations between the special committee and the controlling stockholder that is real and hard fought, and a parallel set of phantom negotiations that involve the plaintiff-stockholders. Eventually, the special committee and controlling stockholder reach and announce a deal (on improved terms from those originally proposed) and, in the spirit of settling the plaintiffs' litigation, volunteer to recognize some contribution of plaintiffs in securing the improved terms (generally formalized in a Memorandum of Understanding). The plaintiffs readily agree to settle the case (subject to perfunctory confirmatory discovery) and plaintiffs' counsel petitions for fees to remunerate them for their "work" and the improved terms they "earned" for the stockholders. Plaintiffs' counsel receive their fees (on occasion reduced by the Court), and the merger moves forward, with the controlling stockholder/ acquiror absorbing the cost of these fees as the price of settlement.

Then-Vice Chancellor Strine highlighted in *Cox Communications* the absence of a single instance in which plaintiffs rejected the terms negotiated by the special committee as inadequately beneficial for the unaffiliated stockholders: "[I]n every instance, the plaintiffs' lawyers have concluded that the price obtained by the special committee was sufficiently attractive, that the acceptance of a settlement at that price was warranted." The key takeaway from *Cox* is that if plaintiffs' counsel adds no value to what the special committee already achieves once the special committee's process concludes, then the special committee process is sufficient to protect the unaffiliated stockholders, and application of "entire fairness," in depriving defendants of a way to demonstrate this and secure dismissal on the pleadings, serves solely to line the pockets of plaintiffs' lawyers and clog up the [court's] docket.

Suneela Kim, et al., *Examining Data Points in Minority Buy-Outs: A Practitioners' Report*, 36 DEL J. CORP. LAW 939, 940-46 (2011). *Query:* What do you think of the bifurcated approach taken by the Delaware courts? Do you think there should be a "unified standard" for judicial review of freeze-out transactions? As a public policy matter, what do you think is the appropriate standard of judicial review of a freeze-out transaction by a controlling stockholder? Does the current state of Delaware law place increasing importance on the disclosure obligations of the federal securities laws? If so, does the SEC requirement of full and adequate disclosure of all material facts provide sufficient protection to the minority interest in a going private transaction?

I.   The Ongoing Public Policy Debate: What Is the Proper Role for Target's Management?

The following opinion offers a summary of Delaware caselaw and the continuing controversy surrounding the appropriate balance of the competing interests that are central to any court's analysis of the fiduciary obligations of the board of directors of the modern publicly traded corporation in the context of an M&A transaction. By way of general background, Chancellor Chandler issued this opinion and then shortly thereafter announced his retirement from the Delaware judiciary, following eight years of service as Vice Chancellor and fourteen years of service as Chancellor. For many observers of the Delaware judiciary, this opinion was something of a swan song for the esteemed Delaware jurist. His decision is seen "as the most important ruling on the [use of a] poison pill since the mid-1990s . . . and also is viewed as something of "a coda to [Chancellor] Chandler's quarter-century on the bench. . . . The [*Airgas*] case gave [Chancellor] Chandler the rare opportunity to consider a body of doctrine that has developed largely in his time as a judge [on the Delaware Chancery Court] and he took full advantage with a 153-page opinion [with over 500 footnotes] in which he commented on the caselaw, [and] evaluated the enormous body of scholarship on it . . ." David Marcus, *A Pill of a Swan Song*, THE DEAL (Feb. 18, 2011).

Air Products and Chemicals, Inc. v. Airgas, Inc.
16 A.3d 48 (Del. Ch. 2011)

CHANDLER, Chancellor.

This case poses the following fundamental question: Can a board of directors, acting in good faith and with a reasonable factual basis for its decision, when faced with a structurally non-coercive, all-cash, fully financed tender offer directed to the stockholders of the corporation, keep a poison pill in place so as to prevent the stockholders from making their own decision about whether they want to tender their shares-even after the incumbent board has lost one election contest, a full year has gone by since the offer was first made public, and the stockholders are fully informed as to the target board's views on the inadequacy of the offer? If so, does that effectively mean that a board can "just say never" to a hostile tender offer?

The answer to the latter question is "no." A board cannot "*just* say no" to a tender offer. Under Delaware law, it must first pass through two prongs of exacting judicial scrutiny by a judge who will evaluate the actions taken by, and the motives of, the board. Only a board of directors found to be acting in good faith, after reasonable investigation and reliance on the advice of outside advisors, which articulates and convinces the Court that a hostile tender offer poses a legitimate threat to the corporate enterprise, may address that perceived threat by blocking the tender offer and forcing the bidder to elect a board majority that supports its bid.

In essence, this case brings to the fore one of the most basic questions animating all of corporate law, which relates to the allocation of power between directors and stockholders. That is, "when, if ever, will a board's duty to 'the corporation and its shareholders' require [the board] to abandon concerns for 'long term' values (and other constituencies) and enter a current share value maximizing mode?"[1] More to the point, in the context of a hostile tender offer, who gets to decide when and if the corporation is for sale?

---

1. *TW Servs., Inc. v. SWT Acquisition Corp.*, 1989 WL 20290, at *8 (Del. Ch. Mar. 2, 1989).

Since the Shareholder Rights Plan (more commonly known as the "poison pill") was first conceived and throughout the development of Delaware corporate takeover jurisprudence during the twenty-five-plus years that followed, the debate over who ultimately decides whether a tender offer is adequate and should be accepted—the shareholders of the corporation or its board of directors—has raged on. Starting with *Moran v. Household International, Inc.*[2] in 1985, when the Delaware Supreme Court first upheld the adoption of the poison pill as a valid takeover defense, through the hostile takeover years of the 1980s, and in several recent decisions of the Court of Chancery and the Delaware Supreme Court,[3] this fundamental question has engaged practitioners, academics, and members of the judiciary, but it has yet to be confronted head on.

For the reasons much more fully described in the remainder of this Opinion, I conclude that, as Delaware law currently stands, the answer must be that the power to defeat an inadequate hostile tender offer ultimately lies with the board of directors. As such, I find that the Airgas board has met its burden under *Unocal* to articulate a legally cognizable threat (the allegedly inadequate price of Air Products' offer, coupled with the fact that a majority of Airgas's stockholders would likely tender into that inadequate offer) and has taken defensive measures that fall within a range of reasonable responses proportionate to that threat. I thus rule in favor of defendants. Air Products' and the Shareholder Plaintiffs' requests for relief are denied, and all claims asserted against defendants are dismissed with prejudice.

INTRODUCTION

This is the Court's decision after trial, extensive post-trial briefing, and a supplemental evidentiary hearing in this long-running takeover battle between Air Products & Chemicals, Inc. ("Air Products") and Airgas, Inc. ("Airgas"). The now very public saga began quietly in mid-October 2009 when John McGlade, President and CEO of Air Products, privately approached Peter McCausland, founder and CEO of Airgas, about a potential acquisition or combination. After McGlade's private advances were rebuffed, Air Products went hostile in February 2010, launching a public tender offer for all outstanding Airgas shares.

Now, over a year since Air Products first announced its all-shares, all-cash tender offer, the terms of that offer (other than price) remain essentially unchanged. After several price bumps and extensions, the offer currently stands at $70 per share and is set to expire today, February 15, 2011—Air Products' stated "best and final" offer. The Airgas board unanimously rejected that offer as being "clearly inadequate." The Airgas board has repeatedly expressed the view that Airgas is worth at least $78 per share in a sale transaction—and at any rate, far more than the $70 per share Air Products is offering.

---

2. 490 A.2d 1059 (Del.1985).

3. *See, e.g., Yucaipa Am. Alliance Fund II, L.P. v. Riggio,* 1 A.3d 310, 351 n.229 (Del. Ch. 2010); *eBay Domestic Holdings, Inc. v. Newmark,* 2010 WL 3516473 (Del. Ch. Sept. 9, 2010); *Versata Enters., Inc. v. Selectica, Inc.,* 5 A.3d 586 (Del. 2010).

So, we are at a crossroads. Air Products has made its "best and final" offer—apparently its offer to acquire Airgas has reached an end stage. Meanwhile, the Airgas board believes the offer is clearly inadequate and its value in a sale transaction is at least $78 per share. At this stage, it appears, neither side will budge. Airgas continues to maintain its defenses, blocking the bid and effectively denying shareholders the choice whether to tender their shares. Air Products and Shareholder Plaintiffs now ask this Court to order Airgas to redeem its poison pill and other defenses that are stopping Air Products from moving forward with its hostile offer, and to allow Airgas's stockholders to decide for themselves whether they want to tender into Air Products' (inadequate or not) $70 "best and final" offer.

* * *

Although I have a hard time believing that inadequate price alone (according to the target's board) in the context of a non-discriminatory, all-cash, all-shares, fully financed offer poses any "threat"—particularly given the wealth of information available to Airgas's stockholders at this point in time—under existing Delaware law, it apparently does. Inadequate price has become a form of "substantive coercion" as that concept has been developed by the Delaware Supreme Court in its takeover jurisprudence. That is, the idea that Airgas's stockholders will disbelieve the board's views on value (or in the case of merger arbitrageurs who may have short-term profit goals in mind, they may simply ignore the board's recommendations), and so they may mistakenly tender into an inadequately priced offer. Substantive coercion has been clearly recognized by our Supreme Court as a valid threat.

Trial judges are not free to ignore or rewrite appellate court decisions. Thus, for reasons explained in detail below, I am constrained by Delaware Supreme Court precedent to conclude that defendants have met their burden under *Unocal* to articulate a sufficient threat that justifies the continued maintenance of Airgas's poison pill. That is, assuming defendants have met their burden to articulate a legally cognizable threat (prong 1), Airgas's defenses have been recognized by Delaware law as reasonable responses to the threat posed by an inadequate offer—even an all-shares, all-cash offer (prong 2).

In my personal view, Airgas's poison pill has served its legitimate purpose. Although the "best and final" $70 offer has been on the table for just over two months (since December 9, 2010), Air Products' advances have been ongoing for over sixteen months, and Airgas's use of its poison pill—particularly in combination with its staggered board—has given the Airgas board over a full year to inform its stockholders about its view of Airgas's intrinsic value and Airgas's value in a sale transaction. It has also given the Airgas board a full year to express its views to its stockholders on the purported opportunistic timing of Air Products' repeated advances and to educate its stockholders on the inadequacy of Air Products' offer. It has given Airgas *more time than any litigated poison pill in Delaware history*—enough time to show stockholders four quarters of improving financial results, demonstrating that Airgas is on track to meet its projected goals. And it has helped the Airgas board push Air Products to raise its bid by $10 per share from when it was first publicly announced to what Air Products has now represented is its highest offer. The record at both the

October trial and the January supplemental evidentiary hearing confirm that Airgas's stockholder base is sophisticated and well-informed, and that essentially all the information they would need to make an informed decision is available to them. In short, there seems to be no threat here—the stockholders know what they need to know (about both the offer and the Airgas board's opinion of the offer) to make an informed decision.

That being said, however, as I understand binding Delaware precedent, I may not substitute my business judgment for that of the Airgas board.[9] The Delaware Supreme Court has recognized inadequate price as a valid threat to corporate policy and effectiveness.[10] The Delaware Supreme Court has also made clear that the "selection of a time frame for achievement of corporate goals . . . may not be delegated to the stockholders."[11] Furthermore, in powerful dictum, the Supreme Court has stated that "[d]irectors are not obliged to abandon a deliberately conceived corporate plan for a short-term shareholder profit unless there is clearly no basis to sustain the corporate strategy."[12] Although I do not read that dictum as eliminating the applicability of heightened *Unocal* scrutiny to a board's decision to block a non-coercive bid as underpriced, I do read it, along with the actual holding in *Unitrin*, as indicating that a board that has a good faith, reasonable basis to believe a bid is inadequate may block that bid using a poison pill, irrespective of stockholders' desire to accept it.

Here, even using heightened scrutiny, the Airgas board has demonstrated that it has a reasonable basis for sustaining its long term corporate strategy—the Airgas board is independent, and has relied on the advice of three different outside independent financial advisors in concluding that Air Products' offer is inadequate. Air Products' *own three nominees* who were elected to the Airgas board in September 2010 have joined wholeheartedly in the Airgas board's determination, and when the Airgas board met to consider the $70 "best and final" offer in December 2010, it was one of those Air Products Nominees who said, "We have to protect the pill." Indeed, one of Air Products' *own directors* conceded at trial that the Airgas board members had acted within their fiduciary duties in their desire to "hold out for the proper price," and that "if an offer was made for Air Products that [he] considered to be unfair to the stockholders of Air Products . . . [he would likewise] use every legal mechanism available" to hold out for the proper price as well. Under Delaware law, the Airgas directors have complied with their fiduciary duties. Thus, as noted above, and for the reasons more fully described in the remainder of this Opinion, I am constrained to deny Air Products' and the Shareholder Plaintiffs' requests for relief.

---

9. *Paramount Commc'ns, Inc. v. Time, Inc.*, 571 A.2d 1140, 1154 (Del. 1990); *see City Capital Assocs. Ltd. P'ship v. Interco, Inc.*, 551 A.2d 787 (Del. Ch. 1988); *Grand Metro. Pub. Ltd. Co. v. Pillsbury Co.*, 558 A.2d 1049 (Del. Ch.1988).

10. *See Unitrin, Inc. v. Am. Gen. Corp.*, 651 A.2d 1361, 1384 (Del. 1995) ("This Court has held that the 'inadequate value' of an all cash for all shares offer is a 'legally cognizable threat.'") (quoting *Paramount Commc'ns, Inc. v. Time, Inc.*, 571 A.2d 1140, 1153 (Del. 1990)).

11. *Paramount*, 571 A.2d at 1154.

12. *Id.*

I.   FACTS

These are the facts as I find them after trial, several rounds of post-trial briefing, and the supplemental evidentiary hearing. Because facts material to this dispute continued to unfold after the October trial had ended, I first describe the general background facts leading up to Air Products' $70 "best and final" offer. The facts developed in the supplemental evidentiary hearing specifically necessary to determine whether Air Products' $70 offer presents a cognizable threat and whether Airgas's defensive measures are reasonable in relation to that threat are set forth beginning in Section I.*P* (under the heading "Facts Developed at the Supplemental Evidentiary Hearing").

* * *

A.   THE PARTIES

Plaintiff Air Products is a Delaware corporation headquartered in Allentown, Pennsylvania that serves technology, energy, industrial and healthcare customers globally. It offers a unique portfolio of products, services and solutions that include atmospheric gases, process and specialty gases, performance materials, equipment and services. Air Products is the world's largest supplier of hydrogen and helium, and it has also built leading positions in growth markets. . . . Air Products currently owns approximately 2% of Airgas outstanding common stock.

The Shareholder Plaintiffs are Airgas stockholders. Together, they own 15,159 shares of Airgas common stock, and purport to represent all other stockholders of Airgas who are similarly situated.

Airgas is a Delaware corporation headquartered in Radnor, Pennsylvania. Founded in 1982 by Chief Executive Officer Peter McCausland, it is a domestic supplier and distributor of industrial, medical and specialty gases and related hardgoods. . . .

Before its September 15, 2010 annual meeting, Airgas was led by a nine-member staggered board of directors, divided into three equal classes with one class (three directors) up for election each year.[29] Other than McCausland, the rest of the board members are independent outside directors. At the time of the September 15 annual meeting (and at the time this lawsuit was initiated), the eight outside directors were: W. Thacher Brown; James W. Hovey; Richard C. Ill; Paula A. Sneed; David M. Stout; Lee M. Thomas; John C. van Roden, Jr. and Ellen C. Wolf (together with McCausland, "director defendants," and collectively with Airgas, "defendants").

At the 2010 annual meeting, three Airgas directors (McCausland, Brown, and Ill) lost their seats on the board when three Air Products nominees were elected. On September 23, 2010, Airgas expanded the size of its board to ten members and reappointed McCausland to fill the new seat. Thus, Airgas is now

---

29. Airgas Amended and Restated Certificate of Incorporation at Art. V, §1; Airgas Amended and Restated Bylaws (amended through April 7, 2010) at Art. III, §1.

led by a ten-member staggered board of directors, nine of whom are independent. To be clear, references to the Airgas board in the section of this Opinion discussing the factual background from October 2009 through September 15, 2010 means the entire Airgas board as it was constituted before the September 15 annual meeting. After the September 15, 2010 meeting, I will discuss in detail the facts relating to Air Products' $70 offer and the actions of the "new" Airgas board, including the three Air Products nominees.

As of the record date for the 2010 annual meeting, Airgas had 83,629,731 shares outstanding. From October 2009 (when Air Products privately approached Airgas about a potential deal) until today, Airgas's stock price has ranged from a low of $41.64[35] to a high of $71.28.[36] For historical perspective, before then it had been trading in the $40s and $50s (with a brief stint in the $60s) through most of 2007-2008, until the financial crisis hit in late 2008. The stock price dropped as low as $27 per share in March of 2009, but quickly recovered and jumped back into the mid-$40s. In the board's unanimous view, the company is worth at least $78 in a sale transaction at this time ($60-ish unaffected stock price plus a 30% premium), and left alone, most of the Airgas directors "would say the stock will be worth north of $70 by next year." In the professional opinion of one of Airgas's independent financial advisors, the fair value of Airgas as of January 26, 2011 is "in the mid to high seventies, and well into the mid eighties." McCausland currently owns approximately 9.5% of Airgas common stock. The other directors collectively own less than 2% of the outstanding Airgas stock. Together, the ten current Airgas directors own approximately 11% of Airgas's outstanding stock.

B. AIRGAS'S ANTI-TAKEOVER DEVICES

As a result of Airgas's classified board structure, it would take two annual meetings to obtain control of the board. In addition to its staggered board, Airgas has three main takeover defenses: (1) a shareholder rights plan ("poison pill") with a 15% triggering threshold, (2) Airgas has not opted out of Delaware General Corporation Law ("DGCL") § 203, which prohibits business combinations with any interested stockholder for a period of three years following the time that such stockholder became an interested stockholder, unless certain conditions are met, and (3) Airgas's Certificate of Incorporation includes a supermajority merger approval provision for certain business combinations. Namely, any merger with an "Interested Stockholder" (defined as a stockholder who beneficially owns 20% or more of the voting power of Airgas's outstanding voting stock) requires the approval of 67% or more of the voting power of the then-outstanding stock entitled to vote, unless approved by a majority of the disinterested directors or certain fair price and procedure requirements are met.

Together, these are Airgas's takeover defenses that Air Products and the Shareholder Plaintiffs challenge and seek to have removed or deemed inapplicable to Air Products' hostile tender offer.

---

35. Jan. 29, 2010. As of today, Airgas's 52-week low is $59.26.
36. Nov. 2, 2010.

C.   AIRGAS'S FIVE-YEAR PLAN

In the regular course of business, Airgas prepares a five-year strategic plan approximately every eighteen months, forecasting the company's financial performance over a five year horizon. In the fall of 2007, Airgas developed a five-year plan predicting the company's performance through fiscal year 2012. The 2007 plan included two scenarios: a strong economy case and a weakening economy case. Airgas generally has a history of meeting or beating its strategic plans, but it fell behind its 2007 plan when the great recession hit. At the time of the October trial, Airgas was running about six months behind the weakening economy case, and about a year and a half behind the strong economy case.

In the summer of 2009, Airgas management was already working on an updated five-year plan . . .

D.   AIR PRODUCTS PRIVATELY EXPRESSES INTEREST IN AIRGAS

1.   The $60 All-Stock Offer

Air Products first became interested in a transaction with Airgas in 2007, but did not pursue a transaction at that time because Airgas's stock price was too high. Then the global recession hit, and in the spring or summer of 2009, Air Products' interest in Airgas was reignited. On September 17, 2009, the Air Products board of directors authorized [John McGlade, Air Products' CEO, President and Chairman of the board,] to approach McCausland and discuss a possible transaction between the two companies. The codename for the project was "Flashback," because Air Products had previously been in the packaged gas business and wanted to "flash back" into it.

On October 15, 2009, McGlade and McCausland met at Airgas's headquarters. At the meeting, McGlade conveyed Air Products' interest in a potential business combination with Airgas and proposed a $60 per share all equity deal. After the meeting, McCausland reported the substance of his conversation with McGlade to Les Graff, Airgas's Senior Vice President for Corporate Development, who took typewritten notes which he called "Thin Air." As Graff's notes corroborate, during the meeting McGlade communicated Air Products' views on the strategic benefits and synergies that a transaction could yield, noting that a combination would be immediately accretive. McCausland told McGlade that it was "not a good time" to sell the company but that he would nevertheless convey the proposal to the Airgas board.

Shortly thereafter, McCausland telephoned Thacher Brown, Airgas's then-presiding director, to inform him of the offer and ask whether he thought it was necessary to call a special meeting of the board to consider Air Products' proposal. Brown said he did not think so, since the entire board was already scheduled to meet a few weeks later for its strategic planning retreat. McCausland suggested that he would reach out to Airgas's legal and financial advisors to solicit their advice, which Brown thought was a good idea.

At its three-day strategic planning retreat from November 5-7, 2009, in Kiawah, South Carolina, the full board first learned of Air Products' proposal. In advance of the retreat, the board had received copies of the five-year strategic plan, which served as the basis for the board's consideration of the $60 offer. The board also relied on a "discounted future stock price analysis" (the "McCausland Analysis") that had been prepared by management at McCausland's request to show the value of Airgas in a change-of-control transaction.

After reviewing the numbers, the board's view on the inadequacy of the offer was not even a close call. The board agreed that $60 was "just so far below what we thought fair value was" that it would be harmful to Airgas's stockholders if the board sat down with Air Products. In the board's view, the offer was so "totally out of the range" of what might be reasonable that beginning negotiations at that price would send the wrong message—that Airgas would be willing to sell the company at a price that is well below its fair value. Thus, the board unanimously concluded that Airgas was "not interested in a transaction." No one on the Airgas board thought it made sense to have any further discussions with Air Products at that point. On November 11, McCausland called McGlade to inform him of the board's decision.

* * *

2. The $62 Cash-Stock Offer

On December 17, 2009, McGlade sent McCausland a revised proposal, raising Air Products' offer to an implied value of $62 per share in a cash-and-stock transaction, and reiterating Air Products' "continued strong interest in a business combination with Airgas." McGlade explained that Air Products' original proposal of structuring a potential combination as an all-stock deal was intended to allow Airgas's stockholders to share in the "expected appreciation of Air Products' stock as the synergies of the combined companies are realized." Nonetheless, to address Airgas's concern that Air Products' stock was an "unattractive currency" for a potential transaction, Air Products was "prepared to offer cash for up to half of the $62 per share" they were offering.

* * *

The Airgas board held a two-part meeting to consider this revised proposal. First, a special telephonic meeting was held on December 21, 2009. Graff discussed the financial aspects of the $62 offer. He noted that the offer price remained low, and explained that with a 50/50 cash-stock split, Air Products could bid well into the $70s and still maintain its credit rating. The call lasted about thirty-five minutes. The board reconvened (again, by telephone) on January 4, 2010 and the discussion resumed. Again, Graff presented financial analyses of the December 17 proposal based on discussions he and other members of management had had with Airgas's investment bankers. He advised the board that the bankers agreed the offer was inadequate and well below the company's intrinsic value, and the board unanimously agreed with management's recommendation to reject the offer.

On January 4, 2010, McCausland sent a letter to McGlade communicating the Airgas board's view that Air Products' offer "grossly undervalues Airgas." The letter continued: "[T]he [Airgas] Board is not interested in pursuing your company's proposal and continues to believe there is no reason to meet."

On January 5, 2010, McCausland exercised 300,000 stock options, half of which were set to expire in May 2010, and half of which were set to expire in May 2011.

E.   AIR PRODUCTS GOES PUBLIC

By late January 2010, it was becoming clear that Air Products' private attempts to negotiate with the Airgas board were going nowhere. The Airgas board felt that it was "precisely the wrong time" to sell the company and thus it continued to reject Air Products' advances. So, Air Products decided to take its offer directly to the Airgas stockholders . . .

Shortly thereafter, Air Products did just that. On February 4, 2010, Air Products sent a public letter to the Airgas board announcing its intention to proceed with a fully-financed, all-cash offer to acquire all outstanding shares of Airgas for $60 per share. The letter closed with McGlade again reiterating Air Products' full commitment to completing a transaction with Airgas, and emphasizing Air Products' "willingness to reflect in our offer any incremental value you can demonstrate."

On February 8-9, 2010, the Airgas board met in Philadelphia, Pennsylvania. The board's financial advisors from Goldman Sachs and Bank of America Merrill Lynch provided written materials and made presentations to the board regarding Air Products' proposal. The bankers reviewed Airgas management's financial projections, research analysts' estimates for Airgas, discounted cash flow valuations of Airgas using various EBITDA multiples and discount rates, historical stock prices, and the fact that Airgas generally emerges later from economic recessions than Air Products. At the meeting, the board unanimously agreed that the $60 price tag was too low, and that it "significantly undervalued Airgas and its future prospects." The board also unanimously authorized McCausland to convey the board's decision to reject the offer to McGlade, which he did the following day.

F.   THE $60 TENDER OFFER

On February 11, 2010, Air Products launched its tender offer for all outstanding shares of Airgas common stock on the terms announced in its February 4 letter—$60 per share, all-cash, structurally non-coercive, non-discriminatory, and backed by secured financing. The tender offer is conditioned, among other things, upon the following:

(1)   a majority of the total outstanding shares tendering into the offer;
(2)   the Airgas board redeeming its rights plan or the rights otherwise having been deemed inapplicable to the offer;
(3)   the Airgas board approving the deal under DGCL §203 or DGCL §203 otherwise having been deemed inapplicable to the offer;
(4)   the Airgas board approving the deal under Article VI of Airgas's charter or Article VI otherwise being inapplicable to the offer;
(5)   certain regulatory approvals having been met; and
(6)   the Airgas board not taking certain action (i.e., entering into a third-party agreement or transaction) that would have the effect of impairing Air Products' ability to acquire Airgas.

Air Products' stated purpose in commencing its tender offer is "to acquire control of, and the entire equity interest in, Airgas." To that end, it is Air Products' current intention, "as soon as practicable after consummation of the Offer," to seek to have Airgas consummate a proposed merger with Air Products valued at an amount in cash equal to the highest price per share paid in the offer. Air Products also announced its intention to run a proxy contest to nominate a slate of directors for election to Airgas's board at the Airgas 2010 annual meeting.

On February 20, 2010, the Airgas board held another special telephonic meeting to discuss Air Products' tender offer. Airgas's financial advisors from Goldman Sachs and Bank of America Merrill Lynch reviewed the bankers' presentations with the board, which were similar to the presentations that had been made to the board on February 8, and concluded that the offer "was inadequate from a financial point of view."

In a [Schedule] 14D-9 filed with the SEC on February 22, 2010, Airgas recommended that its shareholders not tender into Air Products' offer because it "grossly undervalues Airgas." In explaining its reasons for recommending that shareholders not accept Air Products' offer, Airgas's filing stated that the timing of the offer was "extremely opportunistic . . . in light of the depressed value of the Airgas Common shares prior to the announcement of the Offer," so while the timing was excellent for Air Products, it was disadvantageous to Airgas. The filing went on to explain that Airgas had received inadequacy opinions from its financial advisors, Goldman Sachs and Bank of America Merrill Lynch. In addition, Airgas expressed its view that the offer was highly uncertain and subject to significant regulatory concerns. Finally, attached to the filing was a fifty-page slide presentation entitled "Our Rejection of Air Products' Proposals."

G.   THE PROXY CONTEST

On March 13, 2010, Air Products nominated its slate of three independent directors for election at the Airgas 2010 annual meeting. The three Air Products nominees were:

- John P. Clancey;
- Robert L. Lumpkins; and
- Ted B. Miller, Jr. (together, the "Air Products Nominees").

Air Products made clear in its proxy materials that its nominees to the Airgas board were independent and would act in the Airgas stockholders' best interests. Air Products told the Airgas stockholders that "the election of the Air Products Nominees . . . will establish an Airgas Board that is more likely to act in your best interests." Air Products actively promoted the independence of its slate, saying that its three nominees:

- "are independent and do not have any prior relationship with Airgas or its founder, Chairman and Chief Executive Officer, Peter McCausland;"
- "will consider without any bias [the Air Products] Offer;"

- "will be willing to be outspoken in the boardroom about their views on these issues;" and
- "are highly qualified to serve as directors on the Airgas Board."

In addition to its proposed slate of directors, Air Products also announced that it was seeking approval by Airgas stockholders of three bylaw proposals that would:

(1) Amend Airgas's bylaws to require Airgas to hold its 2011 annual meeting and all subsequent annual shareholder meetings in the month of January;

(2) Amend Airgas' bylaws to limit the Airgas Board's ability to reseat directors not elected by Airgas shareholders at the annual meeting (excluding the CEO); and

(3) Repeal all bylaw amendments adopted by the Airgas Board after April 7, 2010.

Over the next several months leading up to Airgas's 2010 annual meeting, both Air Products and Airgas proceeded to engage in a protracted "high-visibility proxy contest widely covered by the media," during which the parties aggressively made their respective cases to the Airgas stockholders. Both Airgas and Air Products made numerous SEC filings, press releases and public statements regarding their views on the merits of Air Products' offer.

H. AIRGAS DELAYS ANNUAL MEETING

In April 2010, the Airgas board amended Article II of the company's bylaws (which addressed the timing of Airgas's annual meetings), giving the board the ability to push back Airgas's 2010 annual meeting. Previously, the bylaws required that the annual meeting be held within five months of the end of Airgas's fiscal year—March—which would make August the annual meeting deadline. The amendment allowed the meeting to be held "on such date as the Board of Directors shall fix." In other words, the board gave itself full discretion to set the date of the annual meeting as it saw fit. As it turns out, the reason the board pushed back the meeting date was to buy itself more time to "provide information to stockholders" before the annual meeting, as well as more time to "demonstrate performance of the company." The annual meeting was scheduled for September 15, 2010.

I. THE $63.50 OFFER

On July 8, 2010, Air Products raised its offer to $63.50. Other than price, all other material terms of the offer remained unchanged. The following day, McGlade sent a letter to the Airgas board reiterating (once again) Air Products' willingness to negotiate, and inviting the Airgas board and its advisors to sit down with Air Products "to discuss completing the transaction in the best interests of the shareholders of both companies."

The Airgas board held two special telephonic meetings to consider the revised $63.50 offer. The first was held on July 15, 2010. McLaughlin updated the board on Airgas's performance for the first quarter of fiscal year 2011 and the financial advisors provided updated financial analyses. On the second call, held on July 20, 2010, Rensky and Carr each described their respective opinions that the $63.50 offer was "inadequate to the [Airgas] stockholders from a financial point of view," and the financial advisors issued written inadequacy opinions to that effect.

The next day, McCausland sent a public letter to McGlade rejecting Air Products' revised offer and invitation to meet because $63.50 "is not a sensible starting point for any discussions or negotiations." Also on July 21, 2010, Airgas filed an amendment to its [Schedule] 14D-9, rejecting the $63.50 offer as "grossly inadequate" and recommending that Airgas stockholders not tender their shares. In this filing, Airgas set out many of the reasons for its recommendation, including its view that the offer "grossly undervalue[d]" Airgas because it did not reflect the value of Airgas's future prospects and strategic plans, the fact that Airgas tends to lag in entering into, and emerging from, economic recessions, Airgas's extraordinary historical results, Airgas's unrivaled platform in the packaged gas business, the "extremely opportunistic" timing of Air Products' offer, the inadequacy opinions provided to the board by Airgas's financial advisors, and many other reasons . . .

* * *

K. THE $65.50 OFFER

On September 6, 2010, Air Products further increased its offer to $65.50 per share. Again, the rest of the terms and conditions of the February 11, 2010 offer remained the same. In connection with this increased offer, Air Products threatened to walk if the Airgas stockholders did not elect the three Air Products Nominees to the Airgas board and vote in favor of Air Products' proposed bylaw amendments at the 2010 annual meeting.[159]

The next day, the Airgas board met to consider Air Products' revised offer. The board received updated analyses from McLaughlin and inadequacy opinions from its bankers. The board unanimously rejected the $65.50 offer as inadequate, saying that it was "not an appropriate value or a sensible starting point for negotiations to achieve such a value." Airgas also filed an amendment to its Schedule 14D-9 on September 8, 2010, recommending that stockholders reject the offer and not tender their shares.

L. "WITH $65.50 ON THE TABLE, THE STOCKHOLDERS WANTED THE PARTIES TO ENGAGE."

On September 10, in advance of the annual meeting, McCausland, Thomas, and Brown (along with Airgas's financial advisors, Renksy and Carr,

---

159. *Id.* ("If Airgas shareholders do not elect these three nominees and approve all of our proposals, we will conclude that shareholders do not want a sale of Airgas at this time- and we will therefore terminate our offer and move on to the many other attractive growth opportunities available to Air Products around the world.").

and representatives of Airgas's proxy solicitor, Innisfree) held a series of meetings with about 25-30 Airgas stockholders—mostly arbs, hedge funds, and institutional holders. At every meeting, the sentiment was the same, "Why don't you guys go negotiate, sit down with Air Products." The answer was simple: the offer was unreasonably low; it was not a place to begin any serious negotiations about fair value. If Air Products "were to offer $70, with an indication that they were ready to sit down and have a full and fair discussion about real value and negotiate from that, what we both could agree was fair value for the company, [Thomas], for one, would be prepared to have that sit-down discussion." Brown and McCausland said the same thing. During the course of two days of meetings with stockholders, McCausland expressed this view to "[m]aybe a hundred" people—he expected word to get back to Air Products.

Although none of the stockholders attending these meetings said that they wanted Airgas to do a deal with Air Products at $65.50, the general sentiment was not, "Hell, no, we don't want you to even talk to these people if they're at 65.50"—rather, the "clear message [was:] With 65.50 on the table, the stockholders wanted the parties to engage."

Rather than engaging with each other directly (i.e. McGlade and McCausland), Air Products' financial advisors at J.P. Morgan (Rodney Miller) and Perella Weinberg (Andrew Bednar) called Airgas's financial advisors (Rensky and Carr). Word had gotten back to Bednar and Miller that some Airgas board members had indicated that there might be "reason to sit down together" if Air Products made an offer at "$70 with the willingness to negotiate upwards from there." Airgas's advisors welcomed a revised offer, but over that weekend before the annual meeting, none came. Air Products' bankers at that point "could not get to $70 a share . . . Air Products was not at that number."

* * *

M.   THE ANNUAL MEETING

On September 15, 2010, Airgas's 2010 annual meeting was held. The Airgas stockholders elected all three of the Air Products Nominees to the board, and all three of Air Products' bylaw proposals were adopted by a majority of the shares voted. On September 23, 2010, John van Roden was unanimously appointed Chairman of the Airgas board, and McCausland was unanimously reappointed to the board.

N.   THE BYLAW QUESTION

After the annual meeting results were preliminarily calculated, Airgas immediately filed suit against Air Products in the Delaware Court of Chancery to invalidate the January meeting bylaw. Briefing was completed on an expedited basis, and oral arguments on cross-motions for summary judgment were heard on October 8, 2010. That afternoon, the Court issued its decision upholding the validity of the January meeting bylaw. Airgas appealed, and ultimately the Delaware Supreme Court reversed the decision, invalidating the bylaw and holding that annual meetings must be spaced "approximately" one year apart. Airgas's current expectation is that its 2011 annual meeting will be held in August or early September 2011.

O.   THE OCTOBER TRIAL

As a result of both sides having aggressively campaigned for months leading up to Airgas's 2010 annual meeting, the evidence presented at the October trial made clear that, at the time of the September annual meeting, the Airgas stockholders had all of the information they needed to evaluate Air Products' $65.50 offer. The testimony from Airgas's own directors and management demonstrated as much. . . .

* * *

The evidence at trial also incontrovertibly demonstrated that $65.50 was not as high as Air Products was willing to go. As Huck unequivocally stated, "65.50 is not our best and final offer."

* * *

In addition, Air Products made clear that if Airgas were stripped of its defenses at that point, Air Products would seek to close on that $65.50 offer. So Air Products was moving forward with an offer that admittedly was not its highest and aggressively seeking to remove Airgas's defensive impediments standing in its way. At the same time, Airgas's stockholders arguably knew all of this, and knew whatever information they needed to know in order to make an informed decision on whether they wanted to tender into Air Products' "grossly inadequate" and not-yet-best offer.

FACTS DEVELOPED AT THE SUPPLEMENTAL EVIDENTIARY HEARING

* * *

P.   REPRESENTATIVES FROM AIRGAS AND AIR PRODUCTS MEET

On October 26, 2010, after announcing strong second-quarter earnings earlier that day, Airgas Chairman John van Roden sent a letter to McGlade. In the letter, van Roden reiterated that each of Airgas's ten directors — *including the three newly-elected Air Products Nominees* — "is of the view that the current Air Products offer of $65.50 per share is grossly inadequate." . . .

* * *

. . . On November 4, 2010, principals from both companies met in person to discuss their views on the value of Airgas. The Airgas representatives and the Air Products representatives had differences of opinion regarding some of the assumptions each other had made underlying their respective valuations of Airgas. The meeting lasted for an hour and a half. At the conclusion of the meeting, the parties issued a disclosure stating that "no further meetings are planned." Although perhaps not the result the parties had hoped for, I conclude based on the evidence presented at the supplemental hearing that the November 4 meeting was in fact a legitimate attempt between the parties to reach some sort of meeting of the minds despite their disagreements over Airgas's value (as opposed to a litigation sham designed by defendants), and that both sides acted in good faith.

Q. **MORE POST-TRIAL FACTUAL DEVELOPMENTS**

* * *

1. The Air Products Nominees and the November 1-2 Airgas Board Meeting

At the supplemental evidentiary hearing, John Clancey, one of the Air Products Nominees, explained his views coming onto the Airgas board following the 2010 annual meeting. Without any other information, his initial impression of Airgas's position with respect to Air Products' offer was that, quite simply, "[i]t was no." Back during the course of the proxy contest, Clancey had met with ISS, who had asked what he would do if elected to the Airgas board, focusing on who he thought he would represent and what skills he would bring to the table. "[I]f I was elected," he told them, "I would immediately represent all the shareholders of Airgas."[215] His perspective from the outset was that there was a lot of information he wanted to drill down on. He wanted the benefit of meeting with management and hearing from the financial advisors working on the situation to inform his understanding, but he came to the board with no agenda other than wanting to see if a deal could be done.

A new-director orientation session for Clancey was held on November 1, 2010. New director orientation for Lumpkins and Miller was held on September 23, 2010. The newly-elected Air Products Nominees were given written materials in advance of their orientation sessions. Clancey came at the board at all different angles at the November 1 orientation. He challenged the board's economic assumptions in its five-year plan, probed Molinini about the SAP implementation, and asked other questions he felt were important to fully understand the situation. In the end, he was "very impressed."

* * *

---

215. . . . Clancey concedes that his duty to represent *all* of the Airgas stockholders includes representing the interests of the Airgas stockholders who happen to be arbitrageurs and those who have shorter-term rather than longer-term investment horizons and who may want to sell their shares . . . Lumpkins similarly understood his role if elected to the Airgas board. At his deposition, he explained, "I believe [ ] that as a director of Airgas, my fiduciary duties, including a duty of care and loyalty, run to Airgas, and that in carrying out those duties I was representing all of the shareholders of Airgas."

2. December 7-8 Airgas Board Letters

On December 7, 2010, the three new directors sent a letter to van Roden formally requesting the Airgas board to authorize their retention of independent outside legal counsel and financial advisors of their choice to assist them in the event Air Products raised its offer. The letter also suggested that statements about the "unanimous" views of the board on issues relating to Air Products' offer may have "become misleading."

Specifically, the three Air Products Nominees sought to clarify their view regarding the statement in the November 2, 2010 letter from van Roden to McGlade that "the [Airgas] board has unanimously concluded that it believes that the value of Airgas in a sale is at least $78 per share." The Air Products Nominees explained:

> We do not believe that such an unequivocal statement is accurate. Any discussion about the $78 valuation must be framed in the context in which that number was actually discussed at the November, 2010 board meeting. Specifically, in the context of a board discussion about what should be the next steps in responding to Air Products, we expressed our beliefs that proposing a price (any price, within reason) would be more likely to generate a constructive dialogue between the two companies and potentially result in an increased offer from Air Products than would a figurative "stiff arm." It was in that context, and only in that context, that we agreed to communicate a $78 price to Air Products.
>
> To be clear, at no time did any of us take the position that a $78 offer price was the price of admission to having any discussions with Air Products, nor did we agree that $78 was the minimum per share price at which Airgas might be purchased, and it would be wrong for you to insinuate otherwise to the Court.

Van Roden responded by letter to the three Air Products Nominees the next day, stating that all of the statements that Airgas has made to the Court and publicly have been accurate. The letter also stated that while all of the other directors were satisfied with the analyses performed by Airgas's two outside financial advisors, the board agreed to the retention of a third independent financial advisor to advise the Airgas board, to be selected by the nine independent directors.

* * *

. . . The nine independent directors unanimously agreed to retain Credit Suisse as a third independent financial advisor to represent the full board. The three new directors were satisfied with the choice of Credit Suisse, and Air Products' own representatives harbored no reason to doubt Credit Suisse's qualifications or independence. In addition, the Air Products Nominees retained their own independent counsel — Skadden, Arps, Slate, Meagher & Flom, LLP — and the board agreed to reimburse the reasonable costs of Skadden's past work for the new directors and to pay Skadden's fees going forward.

Moreover, the Air Products Nominees publicly disavowed any real disagreement that may have allegedly existed on the board before the November 2, 2010 letter to Air Products. The December 7 and December 8 letters were made publicly available on December 13, 2010, along with a statement by the three new directors:

In response to reports of division on the Airgas Board of Directors, we the newly elected directors of Airgas, affirm that the Board is functioning effectively in the discharge of its duties to Airgas stockholders. We deny the charges of division on the Board, we condemn the spread of unproductive rumors, and we strongly disagree with the notion that we were unaware of the November 2nd letter to Air Products.

In any event, as will be explained in greater detail below, by December 21, 2010 the new Air Products Nominees seem to have changed their tune and fully support the view that Airgas is worth *at least* $78 in a sale transaction.

R.   THE $70 "BEST AND FINAL" OFFER

Meanwhile, over at Air Products, the board was considering its position with respect to its outstanding tender offer, and on December 9, 2010, the board met to discuss its options. Specifically, question 1 in the Court's December 2 Letter asked: "Is $65.50 per share the price that Air Products wants this Court to rely upon in addressing the 'threat' analysis under *Unocal?*" The Court also recognized that Air Products had made clear that $65.50 was not its best offer — it was a "floor" from which Air Products was willing to negotiate higher.

After reviewing recent events with the board (including the Supreme Court's reversal on the bylaw issue) and noting the looming December 10 response deadline to my December 2 letter, Huck explained Air Products' options at that point:

(1)   withdraw the tender offer and walk away;

(2)   seek to call a special meeting of the Airgas stockholders to remove the board; or

(3)   "[b]ring the issues around removal of the poison pill to a head by making the Company's best and final offer."

Huck walked the board through each of the three alternatives, noting that the first would effectively eliminate any possibility of a transaction, and the second was "as a practical matter impossible" (and could take several months as well). As for the third, Huck said that "while most of the record [in this case] was fully developed, increasing the offer to the Company's best and final price could strengthen the case for removal of the poison pill." Accordingly, on December 9, 2010 — the day before the parties filed their Supplemental Post-Trial Briefs in response to the Court's December 2 Letter — Air Products made its "best and final" offer for Airgas, raising its offer price to $70 per share.

In its filing and related press release, Air Products said:

This is Air Products' best and final offer for Airgas and will not be further increased. It provides a 61% premium to Airgas' closing price on February 4, 2010, the day before Air Products first announced an offer to acquire Airgas. . . .

The Airgas board, in initially considering the $70 offer, did not really believe that $70 was actually Air Products' "best and final" offer, despite Air Products' public statements saying as much.

* * *

Air Products has repeatedly represented, both in publicly available press releases, public filings with the SEC, and submissions to this Court, that $70 per share is its "best and final" offer. The testimony offered by representatives of Air Products at the supplementary evidentiary hearing regarding the $70 offer provides further evidence to this Court that Air Products' offer is now, as far as this Court is concerned, at its end stage.

* * *

. . . Thus, for purposes of my analysis and the context of this litigation, based on the representations made in public filings and under oath to this Court, I treat $70, as a matter of fact, as Air Products' "best and final" offer.

* * *

S.   THE AIRGAS BOARD UNANIMOUSLY REJECTS THE $70 OFFER

* * *

On December 21, the Airgas board met to consider Air Products' "best and final" offer. Management kicked off the meeting by presenting an updated five-year plan to the board. McCausland gave an overview of the refreshed plan, and then McLaughlin addressed key financial highlights. Molinini and Graff discussed other aspects of the company's growth. This was followed by presentations by the three financial advisors. Carr went first, then Rensky. Both Bank of America Merrill Lynch and Goldman Sachs "were of the opinion that the Air Products' $70 offer was inadequate from a financial point of view."

Then they turned the floor over to David DeNunzio of Credit Suisse, Airgas's newly-retained third independent financial advisor. DeNunzio explained how Credit Suisse had performed its analysis, and how its analysis differed from that of Goldman Sachs and Bank of America Merrill Lynch. He observed that "Airgas's SAP plan is the most detailed plan he and his team had come across in 25-30 years." In summary, DeNunzio said that Air Products' offer "was only slightly above what [Airgas] should trade at, was below most selected transactions and was well below the value of the Company on the basis of a DCF analysis, which was the analysis to which Credit Suisse gave the most weight." In the end, Credit Suisse "easily concluded that the $70 offer was inadequate from a financial point of view."

After considering Airgas's updated five-year plan and the inadequacy opinions of all three of the company's financial advisors, the Airgas board unanimously—including the Air Products Nominees—rejected the $70 offer. Interestingly, the Air Products Nominees were some of the most vocal opponents to the $70 offer. After the bank presentations, John Clancey, one of the three Air Products Nominees concluded that "the offer was not adequate," and that even "an increase to an amount which was well below a $78 per share price was not going to 'move the needle.'" He said to the rest of the board, "We have to protect the pill." When asked what he meant by that comment, Clancey testified:

> That we have a company . . . that is worth, *in my mind, worth in excess of 78, and I wanted, as a fiduciary, I wanted all shareholders to have an opportunity to realize that.*

[Protecting the pill was important to achieve that objective because] I don't believe 70 is the correct number. And if there was no pill, it is always feasible, possible, that 51 percent of the people tender, and the other 49 percent don't have a
lot of latitude.

This was Air Products' own nominee saying this. The other two Air Products Nominees—Lumpkins and Miller—have expressed similar views on what
Airgas would be worth in a sale transaction. So what changed their minds? Why
do they now all believe that the $70 offer is so inadequate? In McCausland's
words:

[I]t doesn't reflect the fundamental value—intrinsic value of the company. Airgas can create tremendous value for its shareholders through executing its management plan—value that's far superior to the offer on the table. That's one. I
would say that I also, you know, listened to three investment bankers, including
Credit Suisse, who came in and took a fresh look. And every one of those bankers has opined that the offer is inadequate. The undisturbed stock price that we
just talked about in the low to mid sixties—and that's not some wishful thinking,
that's just applying our average five-year multiples, comparing what other companies in our peer group are doing vis-a-vis their five-year multiples. And if you
were to apply an appropriate premium for a strategic acquisition like this, in the
35 to 40 percent range, you would end up with a price in the mid to high eighties.
There's the DCF valuations that the bankers presented to us. I mean, there's a lot
of reasons why this bid is inadequate.

McCausland testified that he and the rest of the board are "[a]bsolutely not"
opposed to a sale of Airgas—but they are opposed to $70 because it is an in-
adequate bid.

The next day, December 22, 2010, Airgas filed another amendment to its
[Schedule] 14D-9, announcing the board's unanimous rejection of Air Products' $70 offer as "clearly inadequate" and recommending that Airgas stock-
holders not tender their shares. The board reiterated once more that the value
of Airgas in a sale is at least $78 per share. In this filing, Airgas listed numer-
ous reasons for its recommendation, in two pages of easy-to-read bullet points.
These reasons included the Airgas board's knowledge and experience in the
industry; the board's knowledge of Airgas's financial condition and strategic
plans, including current trends in the business and the expected future benefits of SAP and returns on other substantial capital investments that have yet to
be realized; Airgas's historical trading prices and strong position in the industry; the potential benefits of the transaction for Air Products, including synergies and accretion; the board's consideration of views expressed by various
stockholders; and the inadequacy opinions of its financial advisors. All three
of the outside financial advisors' written inadequacy opinions were attached to
the filing.

Once again, the evidence presented at the supplemental evidentiary hearing was that the Airgas stockholders are a sophisticated group, and that they
had an extraordinary amount of information available to them with which to
make an informed decision about Air Products' offer. Although a few of the
directors expressed the view that they understood the potential benefits of
SAP and the details of the five-year plan better than stockholders could, the

material information underlying management's assumptions has been released to stockholders through SEC filings and is reflected in public analysts' reports as well. . . .

* * *

In addition, numerous independent analysts' reports on Airgas are publicly available (and the numbers are very similar to Airgas's projections). Stockholders can read those reports; they can read the testimony presented during the October trial and the January supplementary hearing. . . . They can read the three inadequacy opinions of the independent financial advisors. In short, "[a]ll the information they could ever want is available."

II. STANDARD OF REVIEW

A. THE *UNOCAL* STANDARD

Because of the "omnipresent specter" of entrenchment in takeover situations, it is well-settled that when a poison pill is being maintained as a defensive measure and a board is faced with a request to redeem the rights, the *Unocal* standard of enhanced judicial scrutiny applies.[291] Under that legal framework, to justify its defensive measures, the target board must show (1) that it had "reasonable grounds for believing a danger to corporate policy and effectiveness existed" (i.e., the board must articulate a legally cognizable threat) and (2) that any board action taken in response to that threat is "reasonable in relation to the threat posed."[292]

The first hurdle under *Unocal* is essentially a process-based review: "Directors satisfy the first part of the *Unocal* test by demonstrating good faith and reasonable investigation."[293] Proof of good faith and reasonable investigation is "materially enhanced, as here, by the approval of a board comprised of a majority of outside independent directors."[294]

But the inquiry does not end there; process alone is not sufficient to satisfy the first part of *Unocal* review—"under *Unocal* and *Unitrin* the defendants have the burden of showing the reasonableness of their investigation, the reasonableness of their process and *also of the result that they reached*."[295] That is, the "process" has to lead to the finding of a threat. Put differently, no matter

---

291. *Unocal Corp. v. Mesa Petroleum Co.*, 493 A.2d 946 (Del.1985), *see also Yucaipa Am. Alliance Fund II, L.P. v. Riggio,* 1 A.3d 310, 335 (Del. Ch. 2010) ("[I]t is settled law that the standard of review to be employed to address whether a poison pill is being exercised consistently with a board's fiduciary duties is [ ] *Unocal.*").

292. *Unitrin, Inc. v. Am. Gen. Corp.*, 651 A.2d 1361 (Del. 1995) (citing *Unocal*, 493 A.2d at 955).

293. *Paramount Commc'ns, Inc. v. Time, Inc.,* 571 A.2d 1140, 1152 (Del.1990); *see also Unocal,* 493 A.2d at 955.

294. *Unocal,* 493 A.2d at 955.

295. *Chesapeake Corp. v. Shore,* 771 A.2d 293, 301 n. 8 (Del. Ch. 2000) (internal citation omitted) (*emphasis added*).

how exemplary the board's process, or how independent the board, or how reasonable its investigation, to meet their burden under the first prong of *Unocal* defendants must actually articulate some legitimate threat to corporate policy and effectiveness.

Once the board has reasonably perceived a legitimate threat, *Unocal* prong 2 engages the Court in a substantive review of the board's defensive actions: Is the board's action taken in response to that threat proportional to the threat posed? In other words, "[b]ecause of the omnipresent specter that directors could use a rights plan improperly, even when acting subjectively in good faith, *Unocal* and its progeny require that this Court also review the use of a rights plan objectively." This proportionality review asks first whether the board's actions were "draconian, by being either preclusive or coercive."[299] If the board's response was not draconian, the Court must then determine whether it fell "within a range of reasonable responses to the threat" posed.[300]

B.   *UNOCAL*—NOT THE BUSINESS JUDGMENT RULE—APPLIES HERE

Defendants argue that "*Unocal* does not apply in a situation where the bidder's nominees agree with the incumbent directors after receiving advice from a new investment banker." This, they say, is because the "sole justification for *Unocal's* enhanced standard of review is the 'omnipresent specter that a board may be acting primarily in its own interests, rather than those of the corporation and its shareholders,'" and that in "the absence of this specter, a board's 'obligation to determine whether [a takeover] offer is in the best interests of the corporation and its shareholders . . . is no different from any other responsibility it shoulders, and its decisions should be no less entitled to the respect they otherwise would be accorded in the realm of business judgment.'" Thus, they argue, because Airgas has presented overwhelming evidence that the directors—particularly now including the three new Air Products Nominees—are independent and have acted in good faith, the "theoretical specter of disloyalty does not exist" and therefore "*Unocal's* heightened standard of review does not apply here."

That is simply an incorrect statement of the law. What the Supreme Court actually said in *Unocal*, without taking snippets of quotes out of context, was the following:

> When a board addresses a pending takeover bid it has an obligation to determine whether the offer is in the best interests of the corporation and its shareholders. In that respect a board's duty is no different from any other responsibility it shoulders, and its decisions should be no less entitled to the respect they otherwise would be accorded in the realm of business judgment. *There are, however, certain caveats to a proper exercise of this function. Because of the omnipresent specter that a board may be acting primarily in its own interests, rather than those of the corporation and*

---

299. *Unitrin, Inc. v. Am. Gen. Corp.*, 651 A.2d 1361, 1367 (Del. 1995).
300. *Id.*

*its shareholders, **there is an enhanced duty which calls for judicial examination at the threshold before the protections of the business judgment rule may be conferred.***[305]

Because the Airgas board is taking defensive action in response to a pending takeover bid, the "theoretical specter of disloyalty" *does* exist—indeed, it is the very reason the Delaware Supreme Court in *Unocal* created an intermediate standard of review applying enhanced scrutiny to board action before directors would be entitled to the protections of the business judgment rule. In articulating this intermediate standard, the Supreme Court in *Unocal* continued:

> [Even when] a defensive measure to thwart or impede a takeover is indeed motivated by a good faith concern for the welfare of the corporation and its stockholders, which in all circumstances must be free of any fraud or other misconduct . . . this does not end the inquiry. A further aspect is the element of balance. If a defensive measure is to come within the ambit of the business judgment rule, it must be reasonable in relation to the threat posed.[306]

The idea that boards may be acting in their own self-interest to perpetuate themselves in office is, in and of itself, the "omnipresent specter" justifying enhanced judicial scrutiny. There is "no doubt that the basis for the omnipresent specter is the interest of incumbent directors, both insiders and outsiders, in retaining the 'powers and perquisites' of board membership."[307] To pass muster under this enhanced scrutiny, those directors bear the burden of proving that they were acting in good faith and have articulated a legally cognizable threat *and* that their actions were reasonable in response to that perceived threat—not simply that they were independent and acting in good faith.[308] To wit:

> In *Time*, [the Delaware Supreme Court] expressly rejected the proposition that once the board's deliberative process has been analyzed and found not to be wanting in objectivity, good faith or deliberativeness, the so-called

---

305. *Unocal,* 493 A.2d at 954 (internal footnote and citation omitted) (*emphasis added*).

306. *Id.* at 955 (internal citation omitted).

307. J. Travis Laster, *Exorcising the Omnipresent Specter: The Impact of Substantial Equity Ownership by Outside Directors on* Unocal *Analysis,* 55 Bus. Law. 109, 116 (1999); *see also Kahn v. Roberts,* 679 A.2d 460, 465 (Del.1996) ("Where [] the board takes defensive action in response to a threat to the board's control of the corporation's business and policy direction, a heightened standard of judicial review applies because of the temptation for directors to seek to remain at the corporate helm in order to protect their own powers and perquisites. Such self-interested behavior may occur even when the best interests of the shareholders and corporation dictate an alternative course.").

308. Defendants further argue that there is less justification for *Unocal's* approach today than when *Unocal* was decided because boards are more independent now and stockholders are better able to keep boards in check. Whether or not this is true does not have any bearing on whether *Unocal* applies, though. *Unocal* applies to both independent outside directors, as well as insiders, whenever a board is taking defensive measures to thwart a takeover. Independence certainly bears heavily on the first prong of *Unocal,* but it is not outcome-determinative; the burden of proof is still on the directors to show that their actions are reasonable in relation to a perceived threat (that is, they still must meet *Unocal* prong 2 before they are back under the business judgment rule).

'enhanced' business judgment rule has been satisfied and no further inquiry is undertaken.[309]

Accordingly, defendants are wrong. The *Unocal* standard of enhanced judicial scrutiny—not the business judgment rule—is the standard of review that applies to a board's defensive actions taken in response to a hostile takeover. This is how Delaware has always interpreted the *Unocal* standard. There has never been any doubt about this, and as recently as four months ago the Delaware Supreme Court reaffirmed this understanding in *Selectica*.[310]

C. A BRIEF POISON PILL PRIMER — *MORAN* AND ITS PROGENY

This case unavoidably highlights what former-Chancellor Allen has called "an anomaly" in our corporation law.[311] The anomaly is that "[p]ublic tender offers are, or rather can be, change in control transactions that are functionally similar to merger transactions with respect to the critical question of control over the corporate enterprise."[312] Both tender offers and mergers are "extraordinary" transactions that "threaten [ ] equivalent impacts upon the corporation and all of its constituencies including existing shareholders."[313] But our corporation law statutorily views the two differently—under DGCL §251, board approval and recommendation is required before stockholders have the opportunity to vote on or even consider a merger proposal, while traditionally the board has been given no statutory role in responding to a public tender offer. The poison pill was born "as an attempt to address the flaw (as some would see it) in the corporation law" giving boards a critical role to play in the merger context but no role to play in tender offers.

These "functionally similar forms of change in control transactions," however, have received disparate legal treatment—on the one hand, a decision not to pursue a merger proposal (or even a decision not to engage in negotiations at all) is reviewed under the deferential business judgment standard, while on the other hand, a decision not to redeem a poison pill in the face of a hostile tender offer is reviewed under "intermediate scrutiny" and must be "reasonable in relation to the threat posed" by such offer.

---

309. *Unitrin v. Am. Gen. Corp.*, 651 A.2d 1361, 1376 (Del. 1995) (quoting *Paramount Commc'ns v. Time, Inc.*, 571 A.2d at 1154 n. 8).

310. *See Versata Enters., Inc. v. Selectica, Inc.*, 5 A.3d 586, 599 (Del. 2010) ("Delaware courts have approved the adoption of a Shareholder Rights Plan as an antitakeover device, and have applied the *Unocal* test to analyze a board's response to an actual or potential hostile takeover threat.").

311. *TW Servs., Inc. v. SWT Acquisition Corp.*, 1989 WL 20290, at *9 (Del. Ch. Mar. 2, 1989).

312. *Id.* Here, Air Products' tender offer would almost certainly result in a "change of control" transaction, as the offer would likely succeed in achieving greater than 50% support from Airgas's stockholders, which largely consist of merger arbitrageurs and hedge funds who would gladly tender into Air Products' offer. . . .

313. 1989 WL 20290, at *10.

In *Moran v. Household International, Inc.*, written shortly after the *Unocal* decision in 1985, the Delaware Supreme Court first upheld the legality of the poison pill as a valid takeover defense. Specifically, in *Moran,* the Household board of directors "react[ed] to what it perceived to be the threat in the market place of coercive two-tier tender offers" by adopting a stockholder rights plan that would allow the corporation to protect stockholders by issuing securities as a way to ward off a hostile bidder presenting a structurally coercive offer. . . .

The Court went on to say that "[t]he Board does not now have unfettered discretion in refusing to redeem the Rights. The Board has no more discretion in refusing to redeem the Rights than it does in enacting any defensive mechanism." Accordingly, while the Household board's adoption of the rights plan was deemed to be made in good faith, and the plan was found to be reasonable in relation to the threat posed by the "coercive acquisition techniques" that were prevalent at the time, the pill at that point was adopted merely as a preventive mechanism to ward off future advances. The "ultimate response to an actual takeover," though, would have to be judged by the directors' actions taken at that time, and the board's "use of the Plan [would] be evaluated when and if the issue [arose]."

Notably, the pill in *Moran* was considered reasonable in part because the Court found that there were many methods by which potential acquirers could get around the pill. One way around the pill was the "proxy out"—bidders could solicit consents to remove the board and redeem the rights. In fact, the Court did "not view the Rights Plan as much of an impediment on the tender offer process" at all. After all, the board in *Moran* was not classified, and so the entire board was up for reelection annually[324]—meaning that all of the directors could be replaced in one fell swoop and the acquiror could presumably remove any impediments to its tender offer fairly easily after that.

* * *

Two scholars at the time penned an article[325] suggesting that there were three types of threats that could be recognized under *Unocal:* (1) structural coercion—"the risk that disparate treatment of non-tendering shareholders might distort shareholders' tender decisions" (i.e., the situation involving a two-tiered offer where the back end gets less than the front end); (2) opportunity loss—the "dilemma that a hostile offer might deprive target shareholders of the opportunity to select a superior alternative offered by target management;" and (3) substantive coercion—"the risk that shareholders will mistakenly accept an underpriced offer because they disbelieve management's representations of intrinsic value."

Recognizing that substantive coercion was a "slippery concept" that had the potential to be abused or misunderstood, the professors explained:

> To note abstractly that management *might* know shareholder interests better than shareholders themselves do cannot be a basis for rubber-stamping management's pro forma claims in the face of market skepticism and the enormous

---

324. *Moran v. Household Int'l, Inc.*, 490 A.2d 1059, 1064 (Del. Ch. 1985).

325. Ronald Gilson & Reinier Kraakman, *Delaware's Intermediate Standard for Defensive Tactics: Is There Substance to Proportionality Review?* 44 Bus. Law. 247, 258, 267 (1989).

opportunity losses that threaten target shareholders when hostile offers are defeated. Preclusive defensive tactics are gambles made on behalf of target shareholders by presumptively self-interested players. Although shareholders may win or lose in each transaction, they would almost certainly be better off on average if the gamble were never made in the absence of meaningful judicial review. By minimizing management's ability to further its self-interest in selecting its response to a hostile offer, an effective proportionality test can raise the odds that management resistance, when it does occur, will increase shareholder value.[329]

Gilson & Kraakman believed that, if used correctly, an effective proportionality test could properly incentivize management, protect stockholders and ultimately increase value for stockholders in the event that management does resist a hostile bid—but only if a real "threat" existed. To demonstrate the existence of such a threat, management must show (in detail) how its plan is better than the alternative (the hostile deal) for the target's stockholders. Only then, if management met that burden, could it use a pill to block a "substantively coercive," but otherwise non-coercive bid.

The test proposed by the professors was taken up, and was more or less adopted, by then-Chancellor Allen in *City Capital Associates v. Interco*.[330] There, the board of Interco had refused to redeem a pill that was in place as a defense against an unsolicited tender offer to purchase all of Interco's shares for $74 per share. The bid was non-coercive (structurally), because the offer was for $74 both on the front and back end, if accepted. As an alternative to the offer, the board of Interco sought to effect a restructuring that it claimed would be worth at least $76 per share.

After pointing out that every case in which the Delaware Supreme Court had, to that point, addressed a defensive corporate measure under *Unocal* involved a structurally coercive offer (i.e. a threat to voluntariness), the Chancellor recognized that "[e]ven where an offer is noncoercive, it may represent a 'threat' to shareholder interests" because a board with the power to refuse the proposal and negotiate actively may be able to obtain higher value from the bidder, or present an alternative transaction of higher value to stockholders. Although he declined to apply the term "substantive coercion" to the threat potentially posed by an "inadequate" but non-coercive offer, Chancellor Allen clearly addressed the concept. . . .

The Chancellor held that the "mild threat" posed by the tender offer (a difference of approximately $2 per share, when the tender offer was for all cash and the value of management's alternative was less certain) did not justify the board's decision to keep the pill in place, effectively precluding stockholders from exercising their own judgment—despite the board's good faith belief that the offer was inadequate and keeping the pill in place was in the best interests of stockholders.

In *Paramount Communications, Inc. v. Time, Inc.*, however, the Delaware Supreme Court explicitly rejected an approach to *Unocal* analysis that "would

---

329. *Id.* at 274.

330. *City Capital Assocs. Ltd. P'ship v. Interco Inc.*, 551 A.2d 787 (Del. Ch. 1988).

involve the court in substituting its judgment as to what is a 'better' deal for that of a corporation's board of directors."[335] . . .

As the Supreme Court put it, the case presented them with the following question: "Did Time's board, having developed a [long-term] strategic plan . . . come under a fiduciary duty to jettison its plan and put the corporation's future in the hands of its stockholders?" Key to the Supreme Court's ruling was the underlying pivotal question in their mind regarding the Time board's specific long-term plan—its proposed merger with Warner—and whether by entering into the proposed merger, Time had essentially "put itself up for sale."[337] This was important because, so long as the company is *not* "for sale," then *Revlon* duties do not kick in and the board "is not under any *per se* duty to maximize shareholder value in the short term, even in the context of a takeover." The Supreme Court held that the Time board had not abandoned its long-term strategic plans; thus *Revlon* duties were not triggered and *Unocal* alone applied to the board's actions.

In evaluating the Time board's actions under *Unocal*, the Supreme Court embraced the concept of substantive coercion, agreeing with the Time board that its stockholders might have tendered into Paramount's offer "in ignorance or a mistaken belief of the strategic benefit which a business combination with Warner might produce."[340] Stating in no uncertain terms that "in our view, precepts underlying the business judgment rule militate against a court's engaging in the process of attempting to appraise and evaluate the relative merits of a long-term versus a short-term investment goal for shareholders" (as to do so would be "a distortion of the *Unocal* process"), the Supreme Court held that Time's response was proportionate to the threat of Paramount's offer. Time's defensive actions were not aimed at "cramming down" a management-sponsored alternative to Paramount's offer, but instead, were simply aimed at furthering a pre-existing long-term corporate strategy. This, held the Supreme Court, comported with the board's valid exercise of its fiduciary duties under *Unocal*.

Five years later, the Supreme Court further applied the "substantive coercion" concept in *Unitrin, Inc. v. American General Corp.*[343] There, a hostile acquirer (American General) wanted Unitrin (the target corporation) to be enjoined from implementing a stock repurchase and poison pill adopted in response to American General's "inadequate" all-cash offer. Recognizing that previous cases had held that "inadequate value" of an all-cash offer could be a valid threat (i.e., *Interco*), the Court also reiterated its conclusion in *Paramount* that inadequate value is not the only threat posed by a non-coercive, all-cash offer. The *Unitrin* Court recited that "the Time board of directors had reasonably determined that inadequate value was not the only threat that Paramount's all

---

335. *Paramount Commc'ns, Inc. v. Time Inc.*, 571 A.2d 1140, 1153 (Del. 1990).

337. *Id.* at 1150. In other words, would the board's actions be judged under the *Unocal* standard or under the *Revlon* standard of review?

340. *Id.* at 1153. The Court also noted other potential threats posed by Paramount's all-cash, all-shares offer, including (1) that the conditions attached to the offer introduced some uncertainty into the deal, and (2) that the timing of the offer was designed to confuse Time stockholders.

343. 651 A.2d 1361 (Del. 1995).

cash for all shares offer presented, but was *also* reasonably concerned that the Time stockholders might tender to Paramount in ignorance or based upon a mistaken belief, i.e., yield to substantive coercion."

* * *

D. A NOTE ON *TW SERVICES*

TW Services, Inc. v. SWT Acquisition Corp.[354] is an often overlooked case that is, in my view, an illuminating piece in this takeover puzzle. The case was another former-Chancellor Allen decision, decided just after *Interco* and *Pillsbury,* and right before *Paramount.* . . .

* * *

. . . [As] the Supreme Court later did in *Paramount,* Chancellor Allen grappled with the following "critical question[:] *when* is a corporation in a *Revlon* mode?" It is not until the board is under *Revlon* that its duty "narrow[s]" to getting the best price reasonably available for stockholders in a sale of the company. The reason the board's duty shifts at that point to maximizing shareholder value is simple: "In such a setting, for the present shareholders, *there is no long run.*"[361] This is not so when the board is under *Unocal,* the company is not for sale, and the board is instead pursuing long run corporate interests. Accordingly, the Chancellor asked,

> But what of a situation in which the board resists a sale? May a board find itself thrust involuntarily into a *Revlon* mode in which is it required to take only steps designed to maximize current share value and in which it must desist from steps that would impede that goal, even if they might otherwise appear sustainable as an arguable step in the promotion of "long term" corporate or share values?

Chancellor Allen does not directly answer the question. Instead, he continues with another follow-up question: Does a director's duty of loyalty to "the corporation and its shareholders" require a board—in light of the fact that a majority of shares may wish to tender into a current share value maximizing transaction now—to enter into *Revlon* mode? Again, he leaves the answer for another day and another case. But the most famous quote from *TW Services* was embedded in a footnote following that last question. Namely, in considering whether the duty of loyalty could force a board into *Revlon* mode, the Chancellor mused:

> Questions of this type call upon one to ask, what is our model of corporate governance? "Shareholder democracy" is an appealing phrase, and the notion of

---

354. 1989 WL 20290 (Del. Ch. Mar. 2, 1989).

361. *Id.* (*emphasis added*). Chancellor Allen continued, "The rationale for recognizing that non-contractual claims of other corporate constituencies are cognizable by boards, *or the rationale that recognizes the appropriateness of sacrificing achievable share value today in the hope of greater long term value,* is not present when all of the current shareholders will be removed from the field by the contemplated transaction." *Id.* (*emphasis added*).

shareholders as the ultimate voting constituency of the board has obvious pertinence, but that phrase would not constitute the only element in a well articulated model. While corporate democracy is a pertinent concept, *a corporation is
not a New England town meeting; directors, not shareholders, have responsibilities to
manage the business and affairs of the corporation,* subject however to a fiduciary
obligation.[363]

Second, Chancellor Allen shed light on two then-recent cases where the
Court of Chancery had attempted to order redemption of a poison pill. He
noted that the boards in those cases (i.e., *Pillsbury*[364] and *Interco*[365]) had "elected
to pursue a defensive restructuring that in form and effect was (so far as the
corporation itself was concerned) a close approximation of and an alternative
to a pending all cash tender offer for all shares."[366] In other words, in *Pillsbury*
and *Interco,* the boards were responding to a hostile offer by proposing "a management endorsed breakup transaction that, realistically viewed, constituted a
functional alternative to the resisted sale." Importantly, "[t]hose cases *did not
involve circumstances in which a board had in good faith . . . elected to continue managing the enterprise in a long term mode and not to actively consider an extraordinary
transaction of any type.*" The issue presented by a board that responds to a tender
offer with a major restructuring or recapitalization is fundamentally different
than that posed by a board which "just says no" and maintains the status quo.

Thus, it seemed, the Chancellor endorsed the view that so long as a corporation is not for sale, it is not in *Revlon* mode and is free to pursue its long run
goals. In essence, *TW Services* appeared to support the view that a well-informed
board acting in good faith in response to a reasonably perceived threat may, in
fact, be able to "just say no" to a hostile tender offer.

The foregoing legal framework describes what I believe to be the current
legal regime in Delaware. With that legal superstructure in mind, I now apply
the *Unocal* standard to the specific facts of this case.

III. ANALYSIS

A. HAS THE AIRGAS BOARD ESTABLISHED THAT IT REASONABLY PERCEIVED THE EXISTENCE OF A LEGALLY COGNIZABLE THREAT?

1. Process

Under the first prong of *Unocal,* defendants bear the burden of showing
that the Airgas board, "after a reasonable investigation . . . determined in good
faith, that the [Air Products offer] presented a threat . . . that warranted a
defensive response."[369] I focus my analysis on the defendants' actions in response

---

363. *Id.* at *8 n.14 (*emphasis added*).
364. *Grand Metro. Pub. Ltd. Co. v. Pillsbury Co.,* 558 A.2d 1049 (Del. Ch. 1988).
365. *City Capital Assocs. Ltd. P'ship v. Interco Inc.,* 551 A.2d 787 (Del. Ch. 1988).
366. 1989 WL 20290, at *9.
369. *Chesapeake v. Shore,* 771 A.2d 293, 330 (Del. Ch. 2000) (citing *Unitrin,* 651 A.2d at 1375).

to Air Products' current $70 offer, but I note here that defendants would have cleared the *Unocal* hurdles with greater ease when the relevant inquiry was with respect to the board's response to the $65.50 offer.[370]

In examining defendants' actions under this first prong of *Unocal,* "the presence of a majority of outside independent directors coupled with a showing of reliance on advice by legal and financial advisors, 'constitute[s] a prima facie showing of good faith and reasonable investigation.'"[371] Here, it is undeniable that the Airgas board meets this test.

First, it is currently comprised of a majority of outside independent directors—including the three recently-elected insurgent directors who were nominated to the board by Air Products. Air Products does not dispute the independence of the Air Products Nominees, and the evidence at trial showed that the rest of the Airgas board, other than McCausland, are outside, independent directors who are not dominated by McCausland.

Second, the Airgas board relied on not one, not two, but three outside independent financial advisors in reaching its conclusion that Air Products' offer is "clearly inadequate." . . . In addition, the Airgas board has relied on the advice of legal counsel, and the three Air Products Nominees have retained their own additional independent legal counsel (Skadden, Arps). In short, the Airgas board's process easily passes the smell test.

2.   What Is the "Threat?"

Although the Airgas board meets the threshold of showing good faith and reasonable investigation, the first part of *Unocal* review requires more than that; it requires the board to show that its good faith and reasonable investigation ultimately gave the board "grounds for concluding that a threat to the corporate enterprise existed."[377] In the supplemental evidentiary hearing, Airgas (and its lawyers) attempted to identify numerous threats posed by Air Products' $70 offer: It is coercive. It is opportunistically timed. It presents the stockholders with a "prisoner's dilemma." It undervalues Airgas—it is a "clearly inadequate" price. The merger arbitrageurs who have bought into Airgas need to be "protected from themselves." The arbs are a "threat" to the minority. The list goes on.

The reality is that the Airgas board discussed essentially none of these alleged "threats" in its board meetings, or in its deliberations on whether to accept or reject Air Products' $70 offer, or in its consideration of whether to keep the pill in place. The board did not discuss "coercion" or the idea that Airgas's stockholders would be "coerced" into tendering. The board did not discuss

---

370. There are a number of reasons for this. For example, the inadequacy of the price was even greater at $65.50. More importantly, Air Products had openly admitted that it was willing to pay more for Airgas. The pill was serving an obvious purpose in providing leverage to the Airgas board. The collective action problem is lessened when the bidder has made its "best and final" offer, provided it is in fact its best and final offer.

371. *Selectica Inc. v. Versata Enters., Inc.,* 2010 WL 703062, at *12 (Del. Ch. Feb. 26, 2010).

377. *Versata Enters., Inc. v. Selectica, Inc.,* 5 A.3d 586, 599 (Del. 2010).

the concept of a "prisoner's dilemma." The board did not discuss Air Products' offer in terms of any "danger" that it posed to the corporate enterprise. In the October trial, Airgas had likewise failed to identify threats other than that Air Products' offer undervalues Airgas. In fact, there has been no specific board discussion since the October trial over whether to keep the poison pill in place (other than Clancey's "protect the pill" line).

Airgas's board members testified that the concepts of coercion, threat, and the decision whether or not to redeem the pill were nonetheless "implicit" in the board's discussions due to their knowledge that a large percentage of Airgas's stock is held by merger arbitrageurs who have short-term interests and would be willing to tender into an inadequate offer. But the only threat that the board discussed—the threat that has been the central issue since the beginning of this case—is the inadequate price of Air Products' offer. Thus, inadequate price, coupled with the fact that a majority of Airgas's stock is held by merger arbitrageurs who might be willing to tender into such an inadequate offer, is the only real "threat" alleged. In fact, Airgas directors have admitted as much. . . .

In the end, it really is "All About Value." Airgas's directors and Airgas's financial advisors concede that the Airgas stockholder base is sophisticated and well-informed, and that they have all the information necessary to decide whether to tender into Air Products' offer.

a. Structural Coercion

Air Products' offer is not structurally coercive. A structurally coercive offer involves "the risk that disparate treatment of non-tendering shareholders might distort shareholders' tender decisions."[390] *Unocal*, for example, "involved a two-tier, highly coercive tender offer" where stockholders who did not tender into the offer risked getting stuck with junk bonds on the back end.[391] "In such a case, the threat is obvious: shareholders may be compelled to tender *to avoid being treated adversely* in the second stage of the transaction."[392]

Air Products' offer poses no such structural threat. It is for all shares of Airgas, with consideration to be paid in all cash. The offer is backed by secured financing. There is regulatory approval. The front end will get the same consideration as the back end, in the same currency, as quickly as practicable. Air Products is committed to promptly paying $70 in cash for each and every share of Airgas and has no interest in owning less than 100% of Airgas. Air Products would seek to acquire any non-tendering shares "[a]s quick[ly] as the law would allow." It is willing to commit to a subsequent offering period. In light of that, any stockholders who believe that the $70 offer is inadequate simply *would not*

---

390. Ronald Gilson & Reinier Kraakman, *Delaware's Intermediate Standard for Defensive Tactics: Is There Substance to Proportionality Review?* 44 Bus. Law. 247, 258 (1989).

391. *Unocal*, 493 A.2d at 956 ("It is now well recognized that such offers are a classic coercive measure designed to stampede shareholders into tendering at the first tier, even if the price is inadequate, out of fear of what they will receive at the back end of the transaction.").

392. *Paramount Commc'ns, Inc. v. Time, Inc.*, 571 A.2d 1140, 1152 (Del. 1990) (*emphasis added*).

tender into the offer—they would risk nothing by not tendering because if a majority of Airgas shares did tender, any non-tendering shares could tender into the subsequent offering period and receive the exact same consideration ($70 per share in cash) as the front end. In short, if there were an antonym in the dictionary for "structural coercion," Air Products' offer might be it.

As former-Vice Chancellor, now Justice Berger noted, "[c]ertainly an inadequate [structurally] coercive tender offer threatens injury to the stockholders . . . [but i]t is difficult to understand how, as a general matter, an inadequate all cash, all shares tender offer, with a back end commitment at the same price in cash, can be considered a continuing threat under *Unocal*."[400] I agree. As noted above, though, the Supreme Court has recognized other "threats" that can be posed by an inadequately priced offer. One such potential continuing threat has been termed "opportunity loss," which appears to be a time-based threat.

b. Opportunity Loss

Opportunity loss is the threat that a "hostile offer might deprive target stockholders of the opportunity to select a superior alternative offered by target management or . . . offered by another bidder."[401] As then-Vice Chancellor Berger (who was also one of the Justices in *Unitrin*) explained in *Shamrock Holdings*:

> An inadequate, non-coercive offer may [ ] constitute a threat for some reasonable period of time after it is announced. The target corporation (or other potential bidders) may be inclined to provide the stockholders with a more attractive alternative, but may need some additional time to formulate and present that option. During the interim, the threat is that the stockholders might choose the inadequate tender offer only because the superior option has not yet been presented. . . . However, *where there has been sufficient time for any alternative to be developed and presented* and for the target corporation to inform its stockholders of the benefits of retaining their equity position, the "threat" to the stockholders of an inadequate, non-coercive offer seems, in most circumstances, to be without substance.[402]

As such, Air Products' offer poses no threat of opportunity loss. The Airgas board has had, at this point, over sixteen months to consider Air Products' offer and to explore "strategic alternatives going forward as a company." After all that time, there is no alternative offer currently on the table, and counsel for defendants represented during the October trial that "we're not asserting that we need more time to explore a specific alternative." The "superior alternative" Airgas is pursuing is simply to "continue[ ] on its current course and execute[ ] its strategic [five-year, long-term] plan."

---

400. *Shamrock Holdings, Inc. v. Polaroid Corp.*, 559 A.2d 278, 289 (Del. Ch. 1989).

401. *Unitrin, Inc. v. Am. Gen. Corp.*, 651 A.2d 1361, 1384 (Del. 1995) (quoting Ronald Gilson & Reinier Kraakman, *Delaware's Intermediate Standard for Defensive Tactics: Is There Substance to Proportionality Review?* 44 Bus. Law. 247, 267 (1989)).

402. *Shamrock Holdings*, 559 A.2d at 289 (internal citations omitted).

c. Substantive Coercion

Inadequate price and the concept of substantive coercion are inextricably related. The Delaware Supreme Court has defined substantive coercion, . . . as "the risk that [Airgas's] stockholders might accept [Air Products'] inadequate Offer because of 'ignorance or mistaken belief' regarding the Board's assessment of the long-term value of [Airgas's] stock."[406] In other words, if management advises stockholders, in good faith, that it believes Air Products' hostile offer is inadequate because in its view the future earnings potential of the company is greater than the price offered, Airgas's stockholders might nevertheless reject the board's advice and tender.

In the article that gave rise to the concept of "substantive coercion," Professors Gilson and Kraakman argued that, in order for substantive coercion to exist, two elements are necessary: (1) management must actually expect the value of the company to be greater than the offer—and be correct that the offer is in fact inadequate, and (2) the stockholders must reject management's advice or "*believe* that management will not deliver on its promise."[407] Both elements must be present because "[w]ithout the first element, shareholders who accept a structurally non-coercive offer have not made a mistake. Without the second element, shareholders will believe management and reject underpriced offers."

Defendants' argument involves a slightly different take on this threat, based on the particular composition of Airgas's stockholders (namely, its large "short-term" base). In essence, Airgas's argument is that "the substantial ownership of Airgas stock by these short-term, deal-driven investors poses a threat to the company and its shareholders"—the threat that, because it is likely that the arbs would support the $70 offer, "shareholders will be coerced into tendering into an inadequate offer." The threat of "arbs" is a new facet of substantive coercion, different from the substantive coercion claim recognized in *Paramount*.[410] There, the hostile tender offer was purposely timed to confuse the stockholders. The terms of the offer could cause stockholders to mistakenly tender if they did not believe or understand (literally) the value of the merger with Warner as compared with the value of Paramount's cash offer. The terms of the offer introduced uncertainty. In contrast, here, defendants' claim is not about "confusion" or "mistakenly tendering" (or even "disbelieving" management)—Air Products' offer has been on the table for over a year, Airgas's stockholders have been barraged with information, and there is no alternative offer to choose that might cause stockholders to be confused about the terms of Air Products' offer. Rather, Airgas's claim is that it needs to maintain its defensive measures to prevent control from being surrendered for an unfair or inadequate price.

---

406. *Unitrin, Inc. v. Am. Gen. Corp.*, 651 A.2d 1361, 1385 (Del. 1995).

407. Ronald Gilson & Reinier Kraakman, *Delaware's Intermediate Standard for Defensive Tactics: Is There Substance to Proportionality Review?* 44 Bus. Law. 247, 260 (1989).

410. *Paramount Commc'ns, Inc. v. Time, Inc.*, 571 A.2d 1140 (Del. 1990). Similar concerns about short-term investors were noted in *Paramount*, however: "Large quantities of Time shares were held by institutional investors. The board feared that even though there appeared to be wide support for the Warner transaction, Paramount's cash premium would be a tempting prospect to these investors." *Id.* at 1148.

The argument is premised on the fact that a large percentage (almost half) of Airgas's stockholders are merger arbitrageurs—many of whom bought into the stock when Air Products first announced its interest in acquiring Airgas, at a time when the stock was trading much lower than it is today—who would be willing to tender into an inadequate offer because they stand to make a significant return on their investment even if the offer grossly undervalues Airgas in a sale. "They don't care a thing about the fundamental value of Airgas."[411] In short, the risk is that a majority of Airgas's stockholders will tender into Air Products' offer despite its inadequate price tag, leaving the minority "coerced" into taking $70 as well. The defendants do not appear to have come to grips with the fact that the arbs bought their shares from long-term stockholders who viewed the increased market price generated by Air Products' offer as a good time to sell.[413]

The threat that merger arbs will tender into an inadequately priced offer is only a legitimate threat if the offer is indeed inadequate.[414] "The only way to protect stockholders [from a threat of substantive coercion] is for courts to

---

411. [Trial Testimony of McCausland] ("They don't care a thing about the fundamental value of Airgas. I know that. I naively spent a lot of time trying to convince them of the fundamental value of Airgas in the beginning. But I'm quite sure now, given that experience, that they have no interest in the long-term.").

413. *See Mercier v. Inter-Tel (Delaware), Inc.,* 929 A.2d 786, 815 (Del. Ch. 2007) ("[T]he bad arbs and hedge funds who bought in, had obviously bought their shares from folks who were glad to take the profits that came with market prices generated by the Merger and Vector Capital's hint of a higher price. These folks, one can surmise, had satisfied whatever long-term objective they had for their investment in Inter-Tel.").

414. Otherwise, as Gilson and Kraakman have articulated it, there will have been no "coercion" because the first element will be missing—that is, stockholders who tendered into an "adequate" offer will not have made a mistake. Airgas also belatedly tries to make the argument that the typical "disbelieve management and tender" form of substantive coercion exists as well, because there is nonpublic information that Airgas's stockholders do not have access to (for example, the detailed valuation information that goes into the five-year plan, and other sensitive competitive and strategic information). In support of this argument, they point to Clancey, who believed that all the information stockholders could want is available, yet it was not until he gained access to the nonpublic information that he joined in the board's view on value. This argument fails for at least two reasons. First, this argument was simply made too late in the game. Almost every witness during the October trial—and even in the January supplemental hearing—testified that Airgas's stockholders had all the information they need to make an informed decision. *See* Section I.*O.* (*The October Trial*); Section I.*S.* (*The Airgas Board Unanimously Rejects the $70 Offer*) at 73-76. Second, Airgas stockholders *know* this about Clancey, Lumpkins, and Miller. They know that the three Air Products Nominees were skeptical of management's projections initially (after all, these were Air Products' nominees who got onto the board for the purpose of seeing if a deal could get done!), but they changed their tune once they studied the board's information and heard from the board's advisors. This is why stockholders elect directors to the board. The fact that Air Products' own three nominees fully support the rest of the Airgas board's view on value, in my opinion, makes it even less likely that stockholders will disbelieve the board and tender into an inadequate offer. The articulated risk that does exist, however, is that arbitrageurs with no long-term horizon in Airgas will tender, *whether or not* they believe the board that $70 clearly undervalues Airgas.

ensure that the threat is real and that the board asserting the threat is not imag-
ining or exaggerating it."[415] Air Products and Shareholder Plaintiffs attack two
main aspects of Airgas's five-year plan — (1) the macroeconomic assumptions
relied upon by management, and (2) the fact that Airgas did not consider what
would happen if the economy had a "double-dip" recession.

Plaintiffs argue that reasonable stockholders may disagree with the board's
optimistic macroeconomic assumptions. McCausland did not hesitate to admit
during the supplemental hearing that he is "very bullish" on Airgas. "It's an
amazing company," he said. He testified that the company has a shot at making
its 2007 five year plan "despite the fact that the worst recession since the Great
Depression landed right in the middle of that period. [W]e're in a good business, and we have a unique competitive advantage in the U.S. market." And it's
not just Airgas that McCausland is bullish about — he's "bullish on the United
States [ ] economy" as well.

So management presented a single scenario in its revised five-year
plan — no double dip recession; reasonably optimistic macroeconomic growth
assumptions. Everyone at trial agreed that "reasonable minds can differ as to
the view of future value." But nothing in the record supported a claim that Airgas fudged any of its numbers, nor was there evidence that the board did not
act at all times in good faith and in reasonable reliance on its outside advisors.
The Air Products Nominees found the assumptions to be "reasonable." They do
not see "any indication of a double-dip recession."

The next question is, if a majority of stockholders *want* to tender into an
inadequately priced offer, is that substantive coercion? Is that a threat that justifies continued maintenance of the poison pill? Put differently, is there evidence
in the record that Airgas stockholders are so "focused on the short-term" that
they would "take a smaller harvest in the swelter of August over a larger one
in Indian Summer"? Air Products argues that there is none whatsoever. They
argue that there is "no evidence in the record that [Airgas's short-term] holders [i.e., arbitrageurs and hedge funds] would not [ ] reject the $70 offer if it
was viewed by them to be inadequate. . . . Defendants have not demonstrated a
single fact supporting their argument that a threat to Airgas stockholders exists
because the Airgas stock is held by investors with varying time horizons."

But there is at least some evidence in the record suggesting that this risk
may be real.[424] Moreover, both Airgas's expert and well as *Air Products' own expert*

---

415. *Chesapeake Corp. v. Shore,* 771 A.2d 293, 326 (Del. Ch. 2000).

424. For example, on December 8, 2010, one stockholder who claimed to represent
"the views of Airgas stockholders generally" sent a letter to the Airgas board urging them
to negotiate with Air Products — when the $65.50 offer was still on the table. *See . . .* (Letter
from P. Schoenfeld Asset Management LP to Airgas Board of Directors (Dec. 8, 2010)). . . . At
various points in time, Peter Schoenfeld urged the board to take $65.50, $67, $70. He would
be happy, it seemed, to see a deal done at *any* price (presumably above what he bought into
the stock at). Schoenfeld wrote, "We hope that the demand for $78 per share is a negotiating
position. As an Airgas stockholder, we strongly believe that the Airgas board could accept a
significant discount from $78 per share and still get a good deal for the Airgas stockholders."
Certainly, I can safely assume that Schoenfeld (and similarly situated stockholders) likely
would tender into Air Products' $70 offer.

testified that a large number—if not all—of the arbitrageurs who bought into Airgas's stock at prices significantly below the $70 offer price would be happy to tender their shares at that price regardless of the potential long-term value of the company. Based on the testimony of both expert witnesses, I find sufficient evidence that a majority of stockholders might be willing to tender their shares regardless of whether the price is adequate or not—thereby ceding control of Airgas to Air Products. This is a clear "risk" under the teachings of *TW Services*[426] and *Paramount*[427] because it would essentially thrust Airgas into *Revlon* mode.

Ultimately, it all seems to come down to the Supreme Court's holdings in *Paramount* and *Unitrin*. In *Unitrin*, the Court held: "[T]he directors of a Delaware corporation have the prerogative to determine that the market undervalues its stock and to protect its stockholders from offers that do not reflect the long-term value of the corporation under its present management plan."[428] When a company is not in *Revlon* mode, a board of directors "is not under any *per se* duty to maximize shareholder value in the short term, even in the context of a takeover."[429] The Supreme Court has unequivocally "endorse[d the] conclusion that it is not a breach of faith for directors to determine that the present stock market price of shares is not representative of true value or that there may indeed be several market values for any corporation's stock."[430] As noted

---

426. *TW Servs., Inc. v. SWT Acquisition Corp.*, 1989 WL 20290 (Del. Ch. Mar. 2, 1989).

427. Airgas's board is not under "a fiduciary duty to jettison its plan and put the corporation's future in the hands of its stockholders." *Paramount Commc'ns, Inc. v. Time, Inc.*, 571 A.2d 1140, 1149-50 (Del. 1990).

428. *Unitrin*, 651 A.2d 1361, 1376 (citing *Paramount*, 571 A.2d at 1153). Vice Chancellor Strine has pointed out that "[r]easonable minds can and do differ on whether it is appropriate for a board to consider an all cash, all shares tender offer as a threat that permits any response greater than that necessary for the target board to be able to negotiate for or otherwise locate a higher bid and to provide stockholders with the opportunity to rationally consider the views of both management and the prospective acquiror before making the decision to sell their personal property." *In re Gaylord Container Corp. S'holders Litig.*, 753 A.2d 462, 478 n. 56 (Del. Ch. 2000). But the Supreme Court cited disapprovingly to the approach taken in *City Capital Associates v. Interco, Inc.*, 551 A.2d 787 (Del. Ch. 1988), which had suggested that an all-cash, all-shares bid posed a limited threat to stockholders that justified leaving a poison pill in place only for some period of time while the board protects stockholder interests, but "[o]nce that period has closed . . . and [the board] has taken such time as it required in good faith to arrange an alternative value-maximizing transaction, then, in most instances, the legitimate role of the poison pill in the context of a noncoercive offer will have been fully satisfied." The Supreme Court rejected that understanding as "not in keeping with a proper *Unocal* analysis."

429. *Paramount*, 571 A.2d at 1150.

430. *Id.* at 1150 n. 12. I admit empirical studies show that corporate boards are subject to error in firm value projections, usually on the overconfident side of the equation. I also admit that markets are imperfect, most often on the side of overvaluing a company. *See generally* Bernard Black and Reinier Kraakman, *Delaware's Takeover Law: The Uncertain Search for Hidden Value*, 96 Nw. U.L.Rev. 565 (2001-02) (describing the "hidden value" model on which managers and directors rely as the basis for resisting takeover offers, and contrasting it with the "visible value" model animating stockholders and potential acquirers). In this case, the

above, based on all of the facts presented to me, I find that the Airgas board acted in good faith and relied on the advice of its financial and legal advisors in coming to the conclusion that Air Products' offer is inadequate. And as the Supreme Court has held, a board that in good faith believes that a hostile offer is inadequate may "properly employ[ ] a poison pill as a proportionate defensive response to protect its stockholders from a 'low ball' bid."

B. IS THE CONTINUED MAINTENANCE OF AIRGAS'S DEFENSIVE MEASURES PROPORTIONATE TO THE "THREAT" POSED BY AIR PRODUCTS' OFFER?

Turning now to the second part of the *Unocal* test, I must determine whether the Airgas board's defensive measures are a proportionate response to the threat posed by Air Products' offer. Where the defensive measures "are inextricably related, the principles of *Unocal* require that [they] be scrutinized collectively as a unitary response to the perceived threat." Defendants bear the burden of showing that their defenses are not preclusive or coercive, and if neither, that they fall within a "range of reasonableness."

1.   Preclusive or Coercive

A defensive measure is coercive if it is "aimed at 'cramming down' on its shareholders a management-sponsored alternative."[434] Airgas's defensive measures are certainly not coercive in this respect, as Airgas is specifically *not* trying to cram down a management sponsored alternative, but rather, simply wants to maintain the status quo and manage the company for the long term.

A response is preclusive if it "makes a bidder's ability to wage a successful proxy contest and gain control [of the target's board] . . . 'realistically unattainable.'"[435] Air Products and Shareholder Plaintiffs argue that Airgas's defensive measures are preclusive because they render the possibility of an effective proxy contest realistically unattainable. What the argument boils down to, though, is that Airgas's defensive measures make the possibility of Air Products obtaining control of the Airgas board and removing the pill realistically unattainable *in the very near future*, because Airgas has a staggered board in place. Thus, the real issue posed is whether defensive measures are "preclusive" if they make

---

Airgas board (relying on the "hidden value" model described by Black and Kraakman) is strongly positing that the market has seriously erred in the opposite direction, by dramatically underestimating Airgas's intrinsic value. I do not share the Airgas board's confidence in its strategic analysis and I do not agree with their claims to superior inside information, but I am bound by Delaware Supreme Court precedent that, in my opinion, drives the result I reach.

434. *Selectica*, 5 A.3d at 601 (quoting *Unitrin*, 651 A.2d at 1387).

435. *Id.* (citing *Carmody v. Toll Bros., Inc.*, 723 A.2d 1180, 1195 (Del. Ch. 1998)). Until *Selectica*, the preclusive test asked whether defensive measures rendered an effective proxy contest "'mathematically impossible' or 'realistically unattainable,'" but since "realistically unattainable" subsumes "mathematically impossible," the Supreme Court in *Selectica* explained that there is really "only one test of preclusivity: 'realistically unattainable.'" *Id.*

gaining control of the board realistically unattainable in the short term (but still realistically attainable sometime in the future), or if "preclusive" actually means "preclusive"—i.e. forever unattainable. In reality, or perhaps I should say in practice, these two formulations ("preclusive for now" or "preclusive forever") may be one and the same when examining the combination of a staggered board plus a poison pill, because no bidder to my knowledge has ever successfully stuck around for two years and waged two successful proxy contests to gain control of a classified board in order to remove a pill.[436] So does that make the combination of a staggered board and a poison pill preclusive?

This precise question was asked and answered four months ago in *Versata Enterprises, Inc. v. Selectica, Inc.* There, Trilogy (the hostile acquiror) argued that in order for the target's defensive measures not to be preclusive: (1) a successful proxy contest must be realistically attainable, and (2) the successful proxy contest must result in gaining control of the board at the next election. The Delaware Supreme Court rejected this argument, stating that "[i]f that preclusivity argument is correct, then it would apply whenever a corporation has both a classified board and a Rights Plan. . . . *[W]e hold that the combination of a classified board and a Rights Plan do not constitute a preclusive defense.*"[437]

The Supreme Court explained its reasoning as follows:

> Classified boards are authorized by statute and are adopted for a variety of business purposes. Any classified board also operates as an antitakeover defense by preventing an insurgent from obtaining control of the board in one election. More than a decade ago, in *Carmody [v. Toll Brothers, Inc.]*, the Court of Chancery noted "because only one third of a classified board would stand for election each year, a classified board would *delay—but not prevent—a hostile acquiror from obtaining control of the board,* since a determined acquiror could wage a proxy contest and obtain control of two thirds of the target board over a two year period, as opposed to seizing control in a single election."[438]

The Court concluded: "The fact that a combination of defensive measures makes it more difficult for an acquirer to obtain control of a board does not make such measures realistically unattainable, i.e., preclusive."[439] Moreover,

---

436. Indeed, Airgas's own expert testified that no bidder has ever replaced a majority of directors on a staggered board by winning two consecutive annual meeting elections.

437. *Selectica,* 5 A.3d 586, 604 (Del. 2010) (*emphasis added*).

438. *Id.* (quoting *Carmody v. Toll Bros., Inc.,* 723 A.2d 1180. 1186 n.17 (Del. Ch. 1998)).

439. *Id.* (citing *In re Gaylord Container Corp. S'holders Litig.,* 753 A.2d 462, 482 (Del. Ch. 2000)). Of course, the target company in the case the Supreme Court cited for that proposition, *In re Gaylord Container Corp. Shareholders Litigation,* did *not* have a staggered board (all directors were up for election annually). The combination of the defensive measures in *Gaylord Container* combined to make obtaining control "more difficult" because an acquiror could only obtain control once a year, at the annual meeting, but the defensive measures were found not to be preclusive because "[b]y taking out the target company's board through a proxy fight or a consent solicitation, the acquiror could obtain control of the board room, redeem the pill, and open the way for consummation of its tender offer." *Gaylord Container,* 753 A.2d at 482. Vice Chancellor Strine noted, however, that "[t]hese provisions are far less preclusive than a staggered board provision, which can delay an acquiror's ability to take over a board for several years." *Id.*

citing *Moran*, the Supreme Court noted that pills do not fundamentally restrict proxy contests, explaining that a "Rights Plan will not have a severe impact upon proxy contests and it will not *preclude* all hostile acquisitions of Household."[440] Arguably the combination of a staggered board plus a pill is at least *more* preclusive than the use of a rights plan by a company with a pill alone (where all directors are up for election annually, as in *Gaylord Container* and *Moran*, because the stockholders could replace the entire board at once and redeem the pill). In any event, though, the Supreme Court in *Selectica* suggests that this is a distinction without a significant difference, and very clearly held that the combination of a classified board and a Rights Plan is not preclusive, and that the combination may only "delay—but not prevent—a hostile acquiror from obtaining control of the board."

The Supreme Court reinforced this holding in its Airgas bylaw decision related to this case, when it ruled that directors on a staggered board serve "three year terms" and Airgas could thus not be forced to push its annual meeting from August/September 2011 up to January 2011.[442] There, the Supreme Court cited approvingly to the "historical understanding" of the impact of staggered boards:

> "By spreading the election of the full board over a period of three years, the classified board forces the successful [tender] offeror to wait, in theory at least, two years before assuming working control of the board of directors."[443]
>
> * * *
>
> "A real benefit to directors on a [staggered] board is that it would take two years for an insurgent to obtain control in a proxy contest."[444]

In addition, the Supreme Court cited its *Selectica* decision where, as noted above, it had held that "a classified board would *delay—but not prevent—a hostile acquiror from obtaining control of the board,* since **a determined acquiror could wage a proxy contest and obtain control of two thirds of the target board over a two year period,** as opposed to seizing control in a single election."[445]

I am thus bound by this clear precedent to proceed on the assumption that Airgas's defensive measures are not preclusive if they delay Air Products from obtaining control of the Airgas board (even if that delay is significant) so long as obtaining control at some point in the future is realistically attainable. I now examine whether the ability to obtain control of Airgas's board in the future is realistically attainable.

---

440. *Selectica,* 5 A.3d at 604 (quoting *Moran v. Household Int'l, Inc.,* 500 A.2d at 1357). Again, in the case the Supreme Court is quoting from (*Moran*), the entire Household board was subject to election *annually;* the company did *not* have a staggered board.

442. *See Airgas, Inc. v. Air Prods. & Chems., Inc.,* 8 A.3d 1182 (Del. 2010).

443. 8 A.3d 1182, 1192 n.27 (Del. 2010) (quoting Lewis S. Black, Jr. & Craig B. Smith, *Antitakeover Charter Provisions: Defending Self-Help for Takeover Targets,* 36 Wash. & Lee L.Rev. 699, 715 (1979)) (alteration in original).

444. *Id.* (quoting 1 R. Franklin Balotti & Jesse A. Finkelstein, The Delaware Law of Corporations and Business Organizations § 4.6 (2010)) (alteration in original).

445. [8 A.3d. at 1190 n. 18 (*emphasis added*).]

Air Products has already run one successful slate of insurgents. Their three independent nominees were elected to the Airgas board in September. Airgas's next annual meeting will be held sometime around September 2011. Accordingly, if Airgas's defensive measures remain in place, Air Products has two options if it wants to continue to pursue Airgas at this time:[446] (1) It can call a special meeting and remove the entire board with a supermajority vote of the outstanding shares, or (2) It can wait until Airgas's 2011 annual meeting to nominate a slate of directors. I will address the viability of each of these options in turn.

a.   Call a Special Meeting to Remove the Airgas Board by a 67% Supermajority Vote

Airgas's charter allows for 33% of the outstanding shares to call a special meeting of the stockholders, and to remove the entire board without cause by a vote of 67% of the outstanding shares. Defendants make much of the fact that "[o]f the 85 Delaware companies in the Fortune 500 with staggered boards, only six (including Airgas) have charter provisions that permit shareholders to remove directors without cause between annual meetings (i.e., at a special meeting and/or by written consent)." This argument alone is not decisive on the issue of preclusivity, although it does distinguish the particular facts of this case from the typical case of a company with a staggered board.[449] Ultimately, though, it does not matter how many or how few companies in the Fortune 500 with staggered boards allow shareholders to remove directors by calling a special meeting; what matters is the "realistic attainability" of actually achieving a 67% vote of the outstanding Airgas shares in the context of Air Products' hostile tender offer (which equates to achieving approximately 85-86% of the unaffiliated voting shares), or whether, instead, Airgas's continued use of its defensive measures is preclusive because it is a near "impossible task."

The fact that something might be a theoretical possibility does not make it "realistically attainable." In other words, what the Supreme Court in *Unitrin* and *Selectica* meant by "realistically attainable" must be something more than a mere "mathematical possibility" or "hypothetically conceivable chance" of circumventing a poison pill. One would think a sensible understanding of

---

446. I say at this time because Air Products has indicated that if Airgas's defenses remain in place, it may walk away from a deal now, but it may be willing to bid for Airgas at some point in the future. . . .

449. It also distinguishes this case from the paradigmatic case posited by Professors Bebchuk, Coates, and Subramanian in 54 Stan. L.Rev. 887 (2002). In their article, the professors write: "Courts should not allow managers to continue blocking a takeover bid after they lose one election conducted over an acquisition offer." *Id.* at 944. In essence, the professors argue that corporations with an "effective staggered board" ("ESB"), defined as one in which a bidder "must go through two annual meetings in order to gain majority control of the target's board," should be required to redeem their pill after losing one election cycle. *Id.* at 912-14, 944. But, the professors concede, "without an ESB, no court intervention is necessary." *Id.* at 944. Airgas does not have an ESB as described by the professors because of its charter provision allowing removal of the entire board without consent at any time by a 67% vote.

the phrase would be that an insurgent has a reasonably meaningful or real world shot at securing the support of enough stockholders to change the target board's composition and remove the obstructing defenses.[452] It does not mean that the insurgent has a right to win or that the insurgent must have a highly probable chance or even a 50-50 chance of prevailing. But it must be more than just a theoretical possibility, given the required vote, the timing issues, the shareholder profile, the issues presented by the insurgent and the surrounding circumstances.

The real-world difficulty of a judge accurately assessing the "realistically attainable" factor, however, was made painfully clear during the January supplemental evidentiary hearing through the lengthy and contentious testimony of two "proxy experts." Airgas offered testimony from Peter C. Harkins, the President and CEO of D.F. King & Co. Inc. and Air Products presented testimony by Joseph J. Morrow, the founder and CEO of Morrow & Co., LLC. Both experts have extensive experience advising corporate clients in contested proxy solicitations and corporate takeover contests, as well as extensive (and lucrative) experience opining in courtrooms as experts on stockholder voting and investment behavior. Ultimately, and despite Harkins' pseudo-scientific "bottoms-up analysis" and Morrow's anecdotal approach, I found both experts' testimony essentially unhelpful and unconvincing on the fundamental question whether a 67% vote of Airgas stockholders at a special meeting is realistically attainable. . . .

* * *

Thus, the expert opinions proffered on how stockholders are likely to vote at a special meeting called to remove the entire Airgas board were unhelpful and not persuasive. The expert witnesses neither took the time nor made the effort to speak with any Airgas stockholders—whether retail, index, institutional investors who subcontract voting to ISS, long or short hedge funds, dual stockholders or event-driven stockholders—about how they might vote if such a special stockholder meeting were actually convened. To that extent, each expert failed to support his conclusions in a manner that a judge would find reliable. In short, I am not persuaded by Harkins that 67% is realistically attainable, especially given the absence of any historical instance where a bidder achieved such a margin in a contested election. Both experts essentially admitted, moreover, that one cannot really know how an election will turn out until it is held and that, generally speaking, it is easier to obtain investor support for electing a minority insurgent slate than for a controlling slate of directors.

* * *

But what seems clear to me, quite honestly, is that a poison pill is assuredly preclusive in the everyday common sense meaning of the word; indeed, its *rasion d'etre* is preclusion—to stop a bid (or *this* bid) from progressing. That is

---

452. *Yucaipa Am. Alliance Fund II, L.P. v. Riggio*, 1 A.3d 310, 337 n.182 (Del. Ch. 2010).

what it is intended to do and that is what the Airgas pill has done successfully for over sixteen months. Whether it is realistic to believe that Air Products can, at some point in the future, achieve a 67% vote necessary to remove the entire Airgas board at a special meeting is (in my opinion) impossible to predict given the host of variables in this setting, but the sheer lack of historical examples where an insurgent has ever achieved such a percentage in a contested control election must mean something. Commentators who have studied actual hostile takeovers for Delaware companies have, at least in part, essentially corroborated this common sense notion that such a victory is not realistically attainable.[474] Nonetheless, while the special meeting may not be a realistically attainable mechanism for circumventing the Airgas defenses, that assessment does not end the analysis under existing precedent.

b.   Run Another Proxy Contest

Even if Air Products is unable to achieve the 67% supermajority vote of the outstanding shares necessary to remove the board in a special meeting, it would only need a simple majority of the voting stockholders to obtain control of the board at next year's annual meeting. Air Products has stated its unwillingness to wait around for another eight months until Airgas's 2011 annual meeting. There are legitimately articulated reasons for this—Air Products' stockholders, after all, have been carrying the burden of a depressed stock price since the announcement of the offer. But that is a business determination by the Air Products board. The reality is that obtaining a simple majority of the voting stock is significantly less burdensome than obtaining a supermajority vote of the outstanding shares, and considering the current composition of Airgas's stockholders (and the fact that, as a result of that shareholder composition, a majority of the voting shares today would likely tender into Air Products' $70 offer), if Air Products and those stockholders choose to stick around, an Air Products victory at the next annual meeting is very realistically attainable.

Air Products certainly realized this. It had actually intended to run an insurgent slate at Airgas's 2011 annual meeting—when everyone thought that meeting was going to be held in January. The Supreme Court has now held, however, that each annual meeting must take place "approximately" one year after the last annual meeting. If Air Products is unwilling to wait another eight months to run another slate of nominees, that is a business decision of the Air Products board, but as the Supreme Court has held, waiting until the next annual meeting "delay[s] — but [does] not prevent — [Air Products] from obtaining control

---

474. *See* Guhan Subramanian, et al., *Is Delaware's Antitakeover Statute Unconstitutional?* 65 Bus. Law. 685 (2010). *But see* A. Gilchrist Sparks & Helen Bowers, *After Twenty-Two Years, Section 203 of the Delaware General Corporation Law Continues to Give Hostile Bidders a Meaningful Opportunity for Success,* 65 Bus. Law. 761 (2010).

of the board."[479] I thus am constrained to conclude that Airgas's defensive measures are not preclusive.[480]

2. Range of Reasonableness

"If a defensive measure is neither coercive nor preclusive, the *Unocal* proportionality test requires the focus of enhanced judicial scrutiny to shift to the range of reasonableness."[481] The reasonableness of a board's response is evaluated in the context of the specific threat identified — the "specific nature of the threat [ ] 'sets the parameters for the range of permissible defensive tactics' at any given time."[482]

Here, the record demonstrates that Airgas's board, composed of a majority of outside, independent directors, acting in good faith and with numerous outside advisors[483] concluded that Air Products' offer clearly undervalues Airgas in a sale transaction. The board believes in good faith that the offer price is inadequate by no small margin. Thus, the board is responding to a legitimately articulated threat.

This conclusion is bolstered by the fact that the three Air Products Nominees on the Airgas board have now wholeheartedly joined in the board's determination — what is more, they believe it is their fiduciary duty to keep Airgas's defenses in place. And Air Products' *own directors* have testified that (1) they have no reason to believe that the Airgas directors have breached their fiduciary duties, (2) even though plenty of information has been made available to the stockholders, they "agree that Airgas management is in the best position to understand the intrinsic value of the company," and (3) if the shoe were on the other foot, they would act in the same way as Airgas's directors have.

In addition, Air Products made a tactical decision to proceed with its offer for Airgas in the manner in which it did. First, Air Products made a choice to

---

479. *Selectica*, 5 A.3d at 604. Although the three Air Products Nominees from the September 2010 election all have joined the rest of the Airgas board in its current views on value, if Air Products nominated another slate of directors who were elected, there is no question that it would have "control" of the Airgas board — i.e. it will have nominated and elected the majority of the board members. There is no way to know at this point whether or not those three hypothetical New Air Products Nominees would join the rest of the board in its view, or whether the entire board would then decide to remove its defensive measures. The preclusivity test, though, is whether obtaining control of the board is realistically unattainable, and here I find that it is not. Considering whether some future hypothetical Air-Products-Controlled Airgas board would vote to redeem the pill is not the relevant inquiry.

480. Our law would be more credible if the Supreme Court acknowledged that its later rulings have modified *Moran* and have allowed a board acting in good faith (and with a reasonable basis for believing that a tender offer is inadequate) to remit the bidder to the election process as its only recourse. The tender offer is in fact precluded and the only bypass of the pill is electing a new board. If that is the law, it would be best to be honest and abandon the pretense that preclusive action is *per se* unreasonable.

481. *Selectica*, 5 A.3d at 605 (internal quotations omitted).

482. *Id.* at 606 (quoting *Unitrin*, 651 A.2d at 1384).

483. *See* 8 *Del. C.* § 141(e) (the board may rely in good faith upon the advice of advisors selected with reasonable care).

launch a proxy contest in connection with its tender offer. It could have — at that point, in February 2010 — attempted to call a special meeting to remove the entire board. The 67% vote requirement was a high hurdle that presented uncertainty, so it chose to proceed by launching a proxy contest in connection with its tender offer.

Second, Air Products chose to replace a minority of the Airgas board with three *independent directors* who promised to take a "fresh look." Air Products ran its nominees expressly premised on that independent slate. It could have put up three nominees premised on the slogan of "shareholder choice." It could have run a slate of nominees who would promise to remove the pill if elected.[487] It could have gotten three directors elected who were resolved to fight back against the rest of the Airgas board.

Certainly what occurred here is not what Air Products expected to happen. Air Products ran its slate on the promise that its nominees would "consider without any bias [the Air Products] Offer," and that they would "be willing to be outspoken in the boardroom about their views on these issues." Air Products *got what it wanted.* Its three nominees got elected to the Airgas board and then questioned the directors about their assumptions. (They got answers.) They looked at the numbers themselves. (They were impressed.) They requested outside legal counsel. (They got it.) They requested a third outside financial advisor. (They got it.) And in the end, they *joined in the board's view* that Air Products' offer was inadequate. John Clancey, one of the Air Products Nominees, grabbed the flag and championed Airgas's defensive measures, telling the rest of the board, "*We have to protect the pill.*" David DeNunzio, Airgas's new independent financial advisor from Credit Suisse who was brought in to take a "fresh look" at the numbers, concluded in his professional opinion that the fair value of Airgas is in the "mid to high seventies, and well into the mid eighties." In Robert Lumpkins' opinion (one of the Air Products Nominees), "the company on its own, its own business will be worth $78 or more in the not very distant future because of its own earnings and cash flow prospects . . . as a standalone company."

The Supreme Court has clearly held that "the 'inadequate value' of an all cash for all shares offer is a 'legally cognizable threat.'"[492] Moreover, "[t]he fiduciary duty to manage a corporate enterprise includes the selection of a time

---

487. That is, Air Products could have chosen three "independent" directors who may have a different view of value than the current Airgas board, who could act in a manner that would still comport with their exercise of fiduciary duties, but would perhaps better align their interests with those of the short-term arbs, for instance. As an example, Air Products could have proposed a slate of three Lucian Bebchuks (let's say Lucian Bebchuk, Alma Cohen, and Charles Wang) for election. In exercising their business judgment if elected to the board, these three academics might have reached different conclusions than Messrs. Clancey, Miller, and Lumpkins did — businessmen with years of experience on boards who got in there, saw the numbers, and realized that the intrinsic value of Airgas in their view far exceeded Air Products' offer. Maybe Bebchuk, et al. would have been more skeptical. Or maybe they would have gotten in, seen the numbers, and acted just as the three Air Products Nominees did. But the point is, Air Products chose to put up the slate that it did.

492. *Unitrin, Inc. v. Am. Gen. Corp.,* 651 A.2d 1361, 1384 (Del. 1995) (quoting *Paramount*).

frame for achievement of corporate goals. *That duty may not be delegated to the stockholders.*"[493] The Court continued, "Directors are not obligated to abandon a deliberately conceived corporate plan for a short-term shareholder profit unless there is clearly no basis to sustain the corporate strategy." Based on all of the foregoing factual findings, I cannot conclude that there is "clearly no basis" for the Airgas board's belief in the sustainability of its long-term plan.

On the contrary, the maintenance of the board's defensive measures must fall within a range of reasonableness here. The board is not "cramming down" a management-sponsored alternative—or *any* company-changing alternative. Instead, the board is simply maintaining the status quo, running the company for the long-term, and consistently showing improved financial results each passing quarter. The board's actions do not *forever* preclude Air Products, or any bidder, from acquiring Airgas or from getting around Airgas's defensive measures if the price is right. In the meantime, the board is preventing a change of control from occurring at an inadequate price. This course of action has been clearly recognized under Delaware law: "directors, when acting deliberately, in an informed way, and in the good faith pursuit of corporate interests, may follow a course designed to achieve long-term value even at the cost of immediate value maximization."

Shareholder plaintiffs argue in their Post-Supplemental Hearing brief that Delaware law adequately protects any non-tendering shareholders in the event a majority of Airgas shareholders did tender into Air Products' offer because, as a result of McCausland and the Airgas board and management's ownership positions in Airgas, there is no way that Air Products would be able to effect a short-form merger under DGCL § 253 at the inadequate $70 price.[498] They argue that when Air Products would then seek to effect a long-form merger on the back end—as it has stated is its intention—any deal would be subject to entire fairness and claims for appraisal rights.

But this protection may not be adequate for several reasons. First, despite Air Products' stated intention to consummate a merger "as soon as practicable" by acquiring any non-tendered shares "as quick as the law would allow,"[499] there

---

493. *Paramount Commc'ns, Inc. v. Time, Inc.*, 571 A.2d 1140, 1154 (Del. 1990) (*emphasis added*).

498. Specifically, because McCausland and the other directors and officers of Airgas together own greater than 10% of the outstanding shares, there is essentially no way for Air Products to obtain greater than 90% of the outstanding shares in a tender offer. Under DGCL §253, a bidder who acquires 90% of the outstanding stock of a corporation could effect a short-form merger to freeze out the remaining less-than-10%, without a vote of the minority. Short of obtaining 90% of the outstanding shares, though, Air Products would be left as a majority stockholder in Airgas, and would have to effect any merger under 8 *Del. C.* §251, which would require the affirmative vote of both the Airgas board and Airgas's minority stockholders.

499. . . . Air Products' representatives made clear, however, that they do not intend to retain a majority interest in Airgas. [Trial Testimony] (Huck) "Q. Does Air Products have any interest in owning less than 100 percent of Airgas? A. No, we do not."). Thus, the non-tendering minority Airgas stockholders would likely receive $70 in a back-end transaction with Air Products, or else Air Products would at that point sell its interest and leave Airgas alone, resulting in a depressed stock price for some period of time before it resumes its unaffected stock price.

are no guarantees; there is a risk that no back end deal will take place. Second, and more importantly, on the back end, control will have already been conveyed to Air Products.[500] The enormous value of synergies will not be factored into any appraisal.[501] Additionally, much of the projected value in Airgas's five year plan is based on the expected returns from substantial investments that Airgas has already made—e.g., substantial capital investments, the SAP implementation. There is no guarantee (in fact it is unlikely) a fair value appraisal today would account for that projected value—value which Airgas's newest outside financial advisor describes as "orders of magnitude greater than what's been assumed and which would give substantially higher values."

C.   PILLS, POLICY AND PROFESSORS (AND HYPOTHETICALS)

When the Supreme Court first upheld the use of a rights plan in *Moran,* it emphasized that "[t]he Board does not now have unfettered discretion in refusing to redeem the Rights."[503] And in the most recent "pill case" decided just this past year, the Supreme Court reiterated its view that, "[a]s we held in *Moran,* the adoption of a Rights Plan is not absolute."[504] The poison pill's limits, however, still remain to be seen.

---

500. *See Golden Telecom, Inc. v. Global GT LP,* 2010 WL 5387589, at *2 (Dec. 29, 2010) ("[I]n determining 'fair value,' the [appraisal] statute [DGCL §262] instructs that the court 'shall take into account all relevant factors.' Importantly, [the Delaware Supreme] Court has defined 'fair value' as the value to a stockholder of the firm as a going concern, as opposed to the firm's value in the context of an acquisition or other transaction.") (internal footnote and citations omitted); *see also M.P.M. Enters., Inc. v. Gilbert,* 731 A.2d 790, 795 (Del. 1999) ("Section 262(h) requires the trial court to 'appraise the shares, determining their fair value exclusive of any element of value arising from the accomplishment or expectation of the merger or consolidation.' Fair value, as used in §262(h), is more properly described as the value of the company to the stockholder as a going concern, rather than its value to a third party as an acquisition.").

501. *See Golden Telecom,* 2010 WL 5387589, at *3 ("[P]ublic companies distribute data to their stockholders to convince them that a tender offer price is 'fair.' In the context of a merger, this 'fair' price accounts for various transactional factors, such as synergies between the companies. Requiring public companies to stick to transactional data in an appraisal proceeding would pay short shrift to the difference between valuation at the tender offer stage—seeking 'fair price' under the circumstances of the transaction—and valuation at the appraisal stage—seeking 'fair value' as a going concern.").

503. *Moran v. Household Int'l, Inc.,* 500 A.2d 1346, 1354 (Del. 1985).

504. *Versata Enters., Inc. v. Selectica, Inc.,* 5 A.3d 586, 607 (Del.2010) (citing *Moran,* 500 A.2d at 1354). Marty Lipton himself has written that "the pill was neither designed nor intended to be an absolute bar. It was always contemplated that the possibility of a proxy fight to replace the board would result in the board's taking shareholder desires into account, but that the delay and uncertainty as to the outcome of a proxy fight would give the board the negotiating position it needed to achieve the best possible deal for all the shareholders, which in appropriate cases could be the target's continuing as an independent company. . . . A board cannot say 'never,' but it can say 'no' in order to obtain the best deal for its shareholders." Martin Lipton, *Pills, Polls, and Professors Redux,* 69 U. Chi. L.Rev. 1037, 1054

The merits of poison pills, the application of the standards of review that should apply to their adoption and continued maintenance, the limitations (if any) that should be imposed on their use, and the "anti-takeover effect" of the combination of classified boards plus poison pills have all been exhaustively written about in legal academia.[505] Two of the largest contributors to the literature are Lucian Bebchuk (who famously takes the "shareholder choice" position that pills should be limited and that classified boards reduce firm value) on one side of the ring, and Marty Lipton (the founder of the poison pill, who continues to zealously defend its use) on the other.[506]

The contours of the debate have morphed slightly over the years, but the fundamental questions have remained. Can a board "just say no"? If so, when? How should the enhanced judicial standard of review be applied? What are the pill's limits? And the ultimate question: Can a board "just say never"? In a 2002 article entitled *Pills, Polls, and Professors Redux*, Lipton wrote the following:

> As the pill approaches its twentieth birthday, it is under attack from [various] groups of professors, each advocating a different form of shareholder poll, but each intended to eviscerate the protections afforded by the pill. . . . Upon reflection, I think it fair to conclude that the [ ] schools of academic opponents of the pill are not really opposed to the idea that the staggered board of the target of a hostile takeover bid may use the pill to "just say no." Rather, their *fundamental disagreement is with the theoretical possibility that the pill may enable a staggered board to "just say never."* However, as . . . almost every [situation] in which a takeover bid was combined with a proxy fight show, the incidence of a target's actually saying

---

(2002) (citing Marcel Kahan & Edward Rock, *How I Learned to Stop Worrying and Love the Pill: Adaptive Responses to Takeover Law*, 69 U. Chi. L.Rev. 871, 910 (2002) ("[T]he ultimate effect of the pill is akin to 'just say wait.'")). As it turns out, for companies with a "pill plus staggered board" combination, it might actually be that a target board can "just say wait . . . a very long time," because the Delaware Supreme Court has held that having to wait two years is not preclusive.

505. I will not cite them all here, but a sampling of just the early generation of articles includes: Martin Lipton, *Takeover Bids in the Target's Boardroom*, 35 Bus. Law. 101 (1979); Frank Easterbrook & Daniel Fischel, *Takeover Bids, Defensive Tactics, and Shareholders' Welfare*, 36 Bus. Law. 1733 (1981); Martin Lipton, *Takeover Bids in the Target's Boardroom: An Update After One Year*, 36 Bus. Law. 1017 (1981); Frank Easterbrook & Daniel Fischel, *The Proper Role of a Target's Management in Responding to a Tender Offer*, 94 Harv. L.Rev. 161 (1981); Martin Lipton, *Takeover Bids in the Target's Boardroom: A Response to Professors Easterbrook and Fischel*, 55 N.Y.U. L.Rev. 1231 (1980); Ronald J. Gilson, *A Structural Approach to Corporations: The Case Against Defensive Tactics in Tender Offers*, 33 Stan. L.Rev. 819 (1981); Lucian Arye Bebchuk, *The Case for Facilitating Competing Tender Offers*, 95 Harv. L.Rev. 1028 (1982).

506. In addition, Lipton often continues to argue that the deferential business judgment rule should be the standard of review that applies, despite the fact that that suggestion was squarely rejected in *Moran* and virtually every pill case since, which have consistently applied the *Unocal* analysis to defensive measures taken in response to hostile bids. Accordingly, although it is not the law in Delaware, Lipton's "continued defense of an undiluted application of the business judgment rule to defensive conduct" has been aptly termed "tenacious." Ronald Gilson & Reinier Kraakman, *Delaware's Intermediate Standard for Defensive Tactics: Is There Substance to Proportionality Review?* 44 Bus. Law. 247, 247 n.1 (1989).

"never" is so rare as not to be a real-world problem. While [the various] professors' attempts to undermine the protections of the pill is argued with force and considerable logic, none of their arguments comes close to overcoming the cardinal rule of public policy—particularly applicable to corporate law and corporate finance—"If it ain't broke, don't fix it."[507]

Well, in this case, the Airgas board has continued to say "no" even after one proxy fight. So what Lipton has called the "largely theoretical possibility of continued resistance after loss of a proxy fight" is now a real-world situation.[508] . . .

* * *

CONCLUSION

Vice Chancellor Strine recently suggested that:

> The passage of time has dulled many to the incredibly powerful and novel device that a so-called poison pill is. That device has no other purpose than to give the board issuing the rights the leverage to prevent transactions it does not favor by diluting the buying proponent's interests.[513]

There is no question that poison pills act as potent anti-takeover drugs with the potential to be abused. Counsel for plaintiffs (both Air Products and Shareholder Plaintiffs) make compelling policy arguments in favor of redeeming the pill in this case—to do otherwise, they say, would essentially make all companies with staggered boards and poison pills "takeover proof." The argument is an excellent sound bite, but it is ultimately not the holding of this fact-specific case, although it does bring us one step closer to that result.

As this case demonstrates, in order to have any effectiveness, pills do not—and can not—have a set expiration date. To be clear, though, this case does not endorse "just say never." What it does endorse is Delaware's long-understood respect for reasonably exercised managerial discretion, so long as boards are found to be acting in good faith and in accordance with their fiduciary duties (after rigorous judicial fact-finding and enhanced scrutiny of their defensive actions). The Airgas board serves as a quintessential example.

Directors of a corporation still owe fiduciary duties to *all stockholders*—this undoubtedly includes short-term as well as long-term holders. At the same time, a board cannot be forced into *Revlon* mode any time a hostile bidder makes a tender offer that is at a premium to market value. The mechanisms in place to get around the poison pill—even a poison pill in combination with a staggered board, which no doubt makes the process prohibitively more difficult—have been in place since 1985, when the Delaware Supreme Court first decided to

---

507. Martin Lipton, *Pills, Polls, and Professors Redux,* 69 U. Chi. L.Rev. 1037, 1065 (2002) (*emphasis added*).

508. *Id.* at 1058.

513. *Hollinger Int'l, Inc. v. Black,* 844 A.2d 1022, 1083 (Del. Ch. 2004).

uphold the pill as a legal defense to an unwanted bid. That is the current state of Delaware law until the Supreme Court changes it.

For the foregoing reasons, Air Products' and the Shareholder Plaintiffs' requests for relief are denied, and all claims asserted against defendants are dismissed with prejudice. The parties shall bear their own costs.

QUESTIONS

1. Why does Chancellor Chandler decide that *Unocal* applies, rather than the more deferential business judgment rule standard of judicial review?

2. According to Chancellor Chandler, where do the public policy concerns regarding "coerciveness and preclusiveness" of shareholder voting fit into the two-pronged *Unocal* standard of review?

3. Was Airgas in the *Revlon* mode?

4. Can the duty of loyalty force Target's board into the *Revlon* mode? In other words, can a fully financed, "any and all shares," all-cash offer by a Bidder put Target "in play" (i.e., in the *Revlon* mode)?

5. What are the defensive measures that Airgas had in place that are at issue in this case?

6. How does Chancellor Chandler rule on the validity of these defensive measures?

7. Does the decision Chancellor Chandler reached in *Airgas* mean that boards of directors can "just say no" to a prospective bidder?

8. After considering Chancellor Chandler's review of Delaware jurisprudence and the analytical approach that he ultimately adopted in *Airgas*, what do you think is the appropriate framework for judicial decision making in this area? In other words, we return to the fundamental question that we have grappled with throughout the materials in this casebook: *Who should decide whether and on what terms a publicly traded company should be sold?* Does your analysis of this issue change in the case of a sale of a privately held company?

9. As the Supreme Court observed in *CTS Corp. v. Dynamics Corp. of America*, 481 U.S. 69, 88 (1987), "[n]o principle of corporation law and practice is more firmly established that a State's authority to regulate domestic corporations," which has resulted in the design of the modern American system of corporate governance being left to the states. While that may very well have been true from a historical perspective, it is clear that the reforms introduced by the passage of the Sarbanes-Oxley Act (SOX) in July 2002 have sorely tested the continuing vitality of this proposition. In considering the views expressed by Chancellor Chandler in his *Airgas* opinion, should future development of corporate governance systems be left to the states? If so, what are the relative merits of committing this to the states rather than the federal government? Do the recent financial scandals and the ensuing Great Recession influence your thinking on this issue?

10. How does your assessment of the public policy to be served by providing for judicial review of the board's actions in this area compare with your assessment of the efficacy of the modern appraisal remedy that we studied at the end of Chapter 2 and the court's role in enforcing this statutorily authorized remedy?

NOTES

1. The "Strange Case" of Delaware Section 203.   Because Chancellor Chandler "reluctantly endorsed the Airgas Board's use of the [poison] pill to thwart a hostile bid" from Air Products, the implications of Delaware's antitakeover statute, Section 203, in the context of this hostile deal were not fully considered by Chancellor Chandler in his opinion. "But the maneuverings of the parties in the battle for Airgas" raised the possibility that Delaware Section 203 "might have posed an important obstacle to the Air Products bid had [Chancellor Chandler] ordered Airgas to redeem its pill." David Marcus, *The Strange Case of Section 203*, THE DEAL, March 2011, *available at* http://www.thedeal .com/magazine/ID/038635/2011/the-strange-case-of-section-203.php. *Query*: In what way would the terms of Delaware Section 203 present "an obstacle" to Air Products' bid for Airgas? Should Chancellor Chandler have evaluated the terms of Delaware Section 203 as part of the total array of takeover defenses that Airgas had in place? Should the board's decision whether or not to waive application of Delaware Section 203 be subject to a fiduciary duty challenge, much in the way that the decision of the Airgas board not to redeem the pill was subject to a claim of breach of the board's fiduciary duties?

2. The "Linguistic Box" of Delaware Fiduciary Duty Case Law.   One of the leading commentaries on the "linguistic box"* that has resulted from the evolution of judicial standards of review under Delaware case law over the past two decades is an article written by three esteemed (current and former) members of the Delaware judiciary. *See* William T. Allen, Jack B. Jacobs, and Leo E. Strine, *Function over Form: A Reassessment of Standards of Review in Delaware Corporation Law*, 56 BUS. LAW 1287 (2001). In their article, the authors address *Unocal* and its progeny:

> This article focuses on a central aspect of the protean growth in the conceptual vocabulary of the Delaware corporation law since 1985—judicial standards of review. Our thesis is that certain key Delaware decisions articulated and applied standards of review without adequately taking into account the policy purposes those standards were intended to achieve. Moreover, new standards of review proliferated when a smaller number of functionally-thought-out standards

---

* *See First Union Corporation Suntrust Banks, Inc.,* 2001 WL 1885686 at *18 (N.C. Bus. Ct., August 10, 2001) (Following an extensive review of the development of Delaware fiduciary duty case law over the past twenty years, the North Carolina court observes that the evolution of Delaware law has resulted in "trapping" counsel "in the linguistic box of Delaware [fiduciary duty] law.").

would have provided a more coherent framework. In this Article, we suggest a closer alignment between the standards of judicial review used in Delaware corporate law and the underlying policies that that body of law seeks to achieve. In our view, a rigorous functional evaluation of existing corporate law standards of review will clarify their application, reduce their number, and facilitate the task of corporate advisors and courts. . . .

Our analysis concludes by proposing that the corporation law can function most effectively with three basic standards of judicial review: (i) a gross negligence standard of review for claims that directors are liable for damages caused by their inattention—a standard that would require plaintiff to prove both a breach of the duty and the fact and extent of any damages caused by the breach; (ii) a rehabilitated entire fairness standard to address duty of loyalty claims; and (iii) an intermediate standard of review to govern challenges to director decisions arguably influenced by an entrenchment motive, *e.g.*, the adoption of anti-takeover defense measures or the approval of a change in control.

Id. at 1293. *Query:* Which of the three standards proposed by the authors should be used to analyze the facts of the *Airgas* case? What result would you obtain using that standard of judicial review?

|8|

Tax, Accounting, and Antitrust Considerations Related to Mergers and Acquisition Transactions

A. Overview of Taxable Transactions vs. Tax-Deferred Reorganizations

The conventional wisdom (in the mergers and acquisitions (M&A) field) is that tax consequences are the primary driver in the selection of M&A deal structures. Thus, any seasoned tax lawyer is likely to advise that tax considerations are the single most important factor in determining whether an acquisition will be structured as a merger, an asset purchase, or a stock purchase. While many corporate lawyers may dismiss this as a bit of an overstatement, it is undoubtedly true that the tax treatment of a proposed acquisition will be one of the major considerations that influence how the deal will be structured. Under the provisions of §368 of the Internal Revenue Code (IRC), transactions may be structured so as to avoid (defer) immediate tax consequences and hence are generally referred to as *nontaxable* (or *tax-free*) *deals*. However, the criteria used under IRC §368 to classify methods of reorganization is a bit different from the basic types of deal structures authorized under the terms of modern state corporation codes. A brief summary of the provisions of IRC §368 is provided below, although this general overview is certainly no substitute for a law school course that analyzes in detail the requirements that must be satisfied for an acquisition to qualify as a tax-deferred transaction.

The statutory requirements of the IRC, like federal securities laws and state corporation statutes, are subject to further development through the promulgation of regulations and by the courts. One of the most important judicially developed principles is generally known as the *continuity of interest doctrine*. The continuity of interest doctrine is central to the law of tax-deferred transactions. At the risk of oversimplification, a transaction is not likely to qualify for tax-deferred treatment unless the investment interest of the shareholders of Target Co. is carried over as a similar investment in Bidder Co. (or the surviving business) without the opportunity for the shareholder to cash out as a part of the acquisition transaction. This judicially developed requirement is now included in the regulations under §368.

The tax treatment of an acquisition is usually of most concern to Target Co. and its shareholders. The tax liability associated with the recognition of gain (or loss, as the case may be) by either Target Co. or the shareholders of Target may have significant financial consequences for these shareholders, which may heavily influence the attractiveness of Bidder's offer. The tax attributes of an acquisition generally do not loom as large for Bidder Co. From a tax perspective, Bidder is usually most worried about two things: first, determining its basis in Target's assets once Bidder acquires Target's business; and second, avoiding liability for any of Target's existing tax problems.

A taxable M&A transaction usually consists of the purchase of stock or assets of Target for consideration—usually consisting of cash or Bidder's debt securities—that precludes the transaction from being able to qualify as a tax-free reorganization under IRC §368. This section first describes the taxable forms of acquisition structures, and then briefly describes the criteria that must be satisfied under §368 for a transaction to qualify as a tax-free acquisition.

1. Taxable Acquisitions

Stock Purchase for Cash. If Bidder Co. purchases Target shares directly from the stockholders for cash, Target shareholders would be required to recognize a gain (or loss) on the sale of their shares. Generally speaking, Target shareholders will qualify for a long-term capital gain or loss if the shares were held as a capital asset for more than one year. On Bidder's side, its tax basis in the shares will usually be equal to the price paid (plus acquisition expenses). In the hands of Bidder, the tax basis of the underlying assets of Target Co. will generally be carried over since the corporate form of the entity (Target Co.) essentially remains untouched. However, Bidder Co. may make an election under IRC §338, which will allow Bidder a step up in its basis in the acquired assets, but at the cost of a tax on the unrealized appreciation in its assets.

Asset Purchase for Cash. If Bidder Co. buys all (or substantially all) of Target's assets for cash, then Target Co. would be subject to a tax at the corporate level *and* generally there would be a second level of tax imposed on Target shareholders when the proceeds of this asset sale are distributed to the shareholders in the liquidation of Target Co. If no second-step dissolution is contemplated, then generally speaking, Target's sale of its assets has no effect on the company's stockholders. In the likely event of a complete liquidation of Target, this liquidating distribution to Target's shareholders will be treated as a sale of Target Co. stock by its shareholders, requiring the shareholders to recognize a capital gain (or loss) at the time of the distribution in the liquidation of Target Co. (assuming that the individual shareholders qualify for capital gain treatment).

2. Tax-Deferred Reorganizations

To qualify as a tax-free acquisition (or, more properly, tax-deferred reorganization), the transaction must conform to the rather technical terms of one of the specific definitions of tax-free reorganization under §368(a). The rather technical requirements of the different types of reorganizations are summarized below. In addition, the transaction must pass muster under the additional gloss imposed by the courts and the applicable regulations on transactions seeking to qualify as tax-free under §368: continuity of interest, continuity of business enterprise, and business purpose.

First, continuity of interest usually means that the shareholders of Target Co. must receive a substantial equity interest in Bidder Co. (the acquiring company), thereby maintaining a continuing ownership interest in Target's business operations. The continuity of business enterprise test usually requires Bidder to continue to operate a historic business of Target Co., or, alternatively, use all (or a significant portion of) Target's historic business assets in its business operations. Finally, the transaction must be entered into for a valid business purpose.

Assuming that these requirements are all satisfied, the transaction must satisfy one of the different types of reorganizations set forth under §368(a), the terms of which are briefly summarized below. Generally speaking, the parties to an acquisition will obtain an opinion of counsel (or a letter ruling from the IRS) as to the tax-free nature of the transaction.

Statutory Merger—the "A" Reorganization.   An "A" reorganization is an acquisition transaction that is structured as a merger (or consolidation) pursuant to the laws of a particular state. This is the most flexible of the §368(a) reorganization definitions in terms of the allowable type of acquisition consideration because Bidder can pay Target shareholders up to approximately half of the purchase price in cash, property, or debt securities (all of which are collectively referred to in tax parlance as "boot"—that is, nonqualifying (taxable) consideration under the terms of §368(a)) and the remainder of the purchase price can be paid using any class of Bidder's stock (permitting use of voting or nonvoting shares). As for the tax effects, the shareholders of Target Co. must recognize any realized gain to the extent of money plus the fair market value of any other boot (nonqualifying consideration) received. Generally speaking, Bidder recognizes no taxable gain or loss and usually takes a basis in the assets acquired that is equal to the basis of these assets in the hands of Target Co.

Stock for Stock Exchange Offer—the "B" Reorganization.   This transaction is defined as Bidder's acquisition of Target Co. shares directly from the company's shareholders *solely* in exchange for voting stock of Bidder Co. *if* immediately after the transaction, Bidder has at least 80 percent control of Target Co. The *sole* consideration allowed under this type of reorganization is voting stock of Bidder Co., although voting preferred stock can be used so long as the voting rights afford the former Target shareholders significant participation in the management of Bidder. For purposes of "B" reorganizations, "control" is defined as requiring Bidder to acquire at least 80 percent of Target's voting stock and at least 80 percent of each other class of Target stock outstanding.

Acquisition of Assets in Exchange for Stock—the "C" Reorganization.   Where Bidder acquires "substantially all" of Target's assets (which usually means that Bidder must purchase at least 90 percent of the fair market value of Target's net assets and 70 percent of the fair market value of the gross assets held by Target immediately prior to the transaction) *solely* in exchange for Bidder's voting stock, the acquisition qualifies as a tax-deferred "C" reorganization. As was the case with a "B" reorganization, the only form of acquisition consideration allowed is voting stock of Bidder Co. At least 80 percent of the consideration must consist of Bidder's voting stock, although the remainder of the purchase price may be paid in cash, property, or debt securities, provided that the total amount of such nonqualifying consideration *plus* the amount of Target liabilities that Bidder agrees to assume do not constitute more than 20 percent of the total consideration paid by Bidder. Generally speaking, Target Co. must be liquidated immediately following this type of reorganization, thereby distributing the acquisition consideration to its shareholders as part of the orderly dissolution of Target. As for Target's shareholders, there is no taxable gain or loss to the extent that the acquisition consideration consists of Bidder's voting stock. However, Target's shareholders do incur a tax to the extent of the "boot" (nonqualifying consideration) received in the transaction. Bidder Co. usually recognizes no taxable gain or loss and generally takes a tax basis in the acquired assets equal to the basis of these assets in the hands of Target Co. Target Co. generally recognizes no taxable gain or loss, either at the time of closing on the sale of substantially all of its assets to Bidder or at the time of dissolution of Target.

Forward Triangular (Subsidiary) Merger — the "D" Reorganization.   In those cases where Target is merged into a subsidiary of Bidder Co. ("NewCo") with NewCo as the surviving corporation (forward triangular merger), the transaction will qualify as an "(a)(2)(D)" reorganization, so long as it results in NewCo acquiring "substantially all" of Target's assets. To determine if NewCo holds "substantially all" of Target's assets, the same standard must be satisfied as for "C" reorganizations. However, unlike a "C" reorganization, Bidder is not as limited in the type of acquisition consideration that it may use to fund the purchase price. So, a forward triangular merger may still qualify as a tax-free reorganization, even though consideration other than Bidder's voting stock is used (such as cash), so long as the form of consideration is authorized by the relevant merger statute. Recall, though, that the transaction still must satisfy the continuity of interest requirement to qualify for tax-deferred treatment under the terms of §368. The tax consequences of this form of reorganization are essentially the same as for an "A" reorganization.

Reverse Triangular (Subsidiary) Merger — the "E" Reorganization.   This provision covers those cases where Target Co. is to merge with a subsidiary of Bidder Co. and the merger agreement calls for Target to survive (reverse triangular merger). The transaction will qualify for tax-deferred treatment so long as, *after* the transaction is completed, Target (as the surviving company) continues to own "substantially all" of its assets. In addition, Bidder Co. must exchange its voting stock for an amount of Target Co. stock constituting control of Target (using the 80 percent definition of §368(c)), although the remaining consideration may consist of boot. In this way, the transaction is analogous to a "B" reorganization in that Bidder must acquire "control" of Target "solely" in exchange for its voting stock. However, unlike a "B" reorganization, there is greater flexibility in the type of consideration that may be used since Bidder must acquire only 80 percent of Target's stock in exchange for voting stock of Bidder, and the remaining 20 percent of Target's stock can be acquired for other nonqualifying consideration (boot). The tax effects of this type of reorganization are essentially the same as in the case of an "A" reorganization.

B.   Accounting for Business Combinations: Purchase Accounting and Elimination of Pooling-of-Interests Accounting

The following article provides useful background regarding the issues that routinely arise in connection with accounting for business combinations. As this article makes clear, these accounting issues often are an important influence on the transaction planner's decision as to how to structure a particular acquisition.

Takeover Law and Practice
David Silk & David Katz
(PLI Program — Doing Deals 2003 at 327-329)

Until recently, the parties to a merger were required to decide whether to structure it, for accounting purposes, as a purchase of one company by the other or as a pooling of interests of the two companies. The pooling-of-interests accounting method assumed that the combining companies had been merged from their inception, and their balance sheets were simply added together with no additional goodwill created. However, the Financial Accounting Standards Board has issued Statement No. 141, Business Combinations, which eliminates pooling of interests as an acquisition accounting method altogether, so that all business combinations initiated after June 30, 2001 must be accounted for as purchases. Any business combination accounted for as a pooling of interests that was initiated on or prior to that date will be grandfathered. In addition, the FASB issued Statement No. 142, Goodwill and Other Intangible Assets, which requires that goodwill created in purchase transactions no longer be amortized to earnings. Instead, acquired goodwill will be recognized as an asset and will only be expensed against earnings in the periods in which that goodwill is impaired. Amortization of goodwill ceased upon adoption of Statement No. 142, effective January 1, 2002 for most companies. Goodwill will be tested for impairment annually, as well as when certain triggering events occur. . . .

Practical Impact of Elimination of Pooling-of-Interests Accounting. A significant portion of merger activity over the past several years has been in the form of strategic stock-for-stock mergers accounted for as pooling of interests transactions. The change in the applicable accounting method for such transactions going forward will likely have a significant impact on transaction structures and "deal technology." Given the stringent requirements associated with pooling-of-interests transactions, there was little variety in deal structure that was permitted in the context of 100% stock-for-stock pooling of interests (other than slight variations on exchange ratios, collars and walk-aways). There was also limited potential to mount aggressive hostile acquisitions given the relative ease of defeating a hostile bid conditioned upon pooling-of-interests accounting. . . . In a post-pooling world, all transaction structural options will be open.

Pros and Cons of New Purchase Accounting. Under the new purchase accounting rules, most acquirors will be able to avoid heavy amortization charges in the context of a purchase transaction at a high premium to book value. It is yet to be determined how common it will be for companies to take impairment charges if the assumptions underlying an acquisition premium prove to have been too optimistic with the benefit of hindsight. Even absent future goodwill impairment charges, however, some acquirors will still face significant earnings charges to the extent they are required to write-up tangible, and certain classes of intangible, assets and depreciate or amortize such write-ups over the useful lives of the respective asset classes. For example, in the case of an acquisition of a depository institution, it is clear that a portion of the purchase price premium will need to be allocated to the core deposits intangible, which premium will need to be written off over a useful life that could be as short as eight or less years. Companies will likely face increasing pressure from accounting authorities to allocate purchase price premiums to identifiable assets (including intangibles) other than goodwill, resulting in potentially significant non-cash charges in connection with high premium acquisitions in certain industries. . . .

     . . . On the plus side, acquirors will no longer need to engage in artificially constrained behavior in order to satisfy the rigid requirements of pooling-of-interest accounting. . . .

C.   Federal Antitrust Law and the Hart-Scott-Rodino Antitrust Improvement Act: An Overview of Hart-Scott-Rodino Requirements

"The Hart-Scott-Rodino Anti-Trust Improvement Act of 1976, as amended (the HSR Act), generally requires parties to notify the FTC [Federal Trade Commission] and the DOJ [Department of Justice] of certain proposed [acquisition] transactions that meet the HSR Act's jurisdictional thresholds and to observe certain statutory waiting periods while a review of the competitive impact of the [proposed] transaction is performed by those agencies." Patrick S. Convery, *Changes to Disclosure Requirements for Hart-Scott-Rodino Premerger Notification Rules and Form, available at* http://www.natlawreview.com/article/changes-to-disclosure-requirements-hart-scott-rodino-premerger-notification-rules-and-form. The nature (and implications) of this HSR Act filing obligation is the focus of the next case.

Heublein, Inc. v. Federal Trade Commission
539 F. Supp. 123 (D. Conn. 1982)

CLARIE, Chief Judge:

I. FACTUAL BACKGROUND

A. THE PARTIES

1. Plaintiff Heublein, is a Connecticut corporation having its principal place of business at Farmington, Connecticut. Heublein is engaged in the production and distribution of distilled spirits and wines, the operation and franchising of Kentucky Fried Chicken, H. Salt and Zantigo Mexican-American quick service restaurants, and the production and distribution of other specialty food products.

2. Defendant Federal Trade Commission ("Commission") is an agency of the United States and . . . is one of two federal agencies responsible for administering the premerger notification program established by the Hart-Scott-Rodino Antitrust Improvements Act of 1976 ("H-S-R Act").

3. Defendant James C. Miller, III is Chairman, and defendants David A. Clanton, Michael Pertschuk and Patricia P. Bailey are members of the Federal Trade Commission. Defendant Thomas J. Campbell is Director of the Bureau of Competition of the Federal Trade Commission. The Bureau of Competition is the organizational unit of the Commission responsible for administering the premerger notification program under the H-S-R Act. The Commission has delegated to the Director of the Bureau of Competition the power to permit persons to consummate acquisitions which are subject to the H-S-R Act prior to the expiration of the waiting period prescribed in that Act.

B. HART-SCOTT-RODINO ACT AND PREMERGER NOTIFICATION
REGULATIONS RELEVANT TO THIS CASE

4. Title II of the H-S-R Act, enacted in 1976, added section 7A to the Clayton Act, which established a new premerger notification program governing certain acquisitions of voting securities or assets. The legislative purposes of Title II were to provide the Commission and the Antitrust Division of the United States Department of Justice ("Department"), in advance of an acquisition: (a) information concerning both the nature of the particular transaction and the competitive effects of the acquisition and (b) sufficient time to analyze the competitive effects of the acquisition to determine whether to challenge the acquisition prior to its consummation.

5. If a stock acquisition is subject to the H-S-R Act, both the acquiring and acquired parties must: (a) file with the Commission and the Department a premerger notification form and exhibits, which report the required information concerning their businesses and the details of the particular transaction; and (b) wait a prescribed period before consummating the acquisition, subject to the Commission's authority to extend or reduce that waiting period.

6. After a premerger notification form and exhibits have been filed by an acquiring party with both the Commission and the Department, personnel of

those agencies confer and decide which agency will assume responsibility for analyzing those materials to determine whether the particular acquisition is likely to lessen competition or whether additional information or documents are required to make that determination.

7. In the case of an acquisition of voting securities on the open market through a national securities exchange or through private transactions, the waiting period under the Commission's premerger notification rules expires on the thirtieth day after the acquiring party has filed its premerger notification form and exhibits, unless: (a) the waiting period is terminated, by the Commission and the Department, prior to the expiration of the thirty-day period; or (b) prior to the expiration of the thirty-day period, the Commission or the Department (as the case may be) requests additional information or documents from either the acquiring or the acquired party. Such a request for additional information or documents extends the H-S-R waiting period until the twentieth day following the agencies' receipt of such additional information or documents.

8. As amended by the H-S-R Act, section 7A(b)(2) of the Clayton Act expressly authorizes the Commission and the Department to reduce the H-S-R Act waiting period "and allow any person to proceed with any acquisition subject to" the H-S-R Act. The Commission's premerger notification rules expressly provide that "early termination" of the waiting period may be granted either upon written request by a party to the acquisition or sua sponte by the Commission or the Department.

9. A Formal Interpretation of those rules and regulations, issued by the Bureau of Competition on April 10, 1979, identifies the principles governing the Bureau's consideration of "early termination" requests. This Interpretation states that such requests will not be granted unless the Commission has concluded that it will not take any further action within the waiting period and unless the requesting party demonstrates "some special business reason that warrants early termination of the waiting period," such as a "need to complete the transaction before the waiting period would normally expire." . . .

C.   CINEMA'S REQUEST FOR PERMISSION TO ACQUIRE UP TO 49.9% OF HEUBLEIN'S STOCK

12. General Cinema Corporation ("Cinema") is a Delaware corporation, having its principal place of business in Chestnut Hill, Massachusetts, and is primarily engaged in bottling and marketing carbonated soft drinks and in the exhibition of motion pictures.

13. On February 4, 1982, Cinema filed with the Commission and the Department a premerger notification form and exhibits, in which Cinema sought approval from the Commission and the Department to acquire, through open market and private transactions, up to 49.9% of Heublein's common stock. Upon the filing of Cinema's premerger notification form, it was determined that the Commission, rather than the Department, would assume responsibility for evaluating the competitive effects of Cinema's proposed acquisition of up to 49.9% of Heublein's stock.

14. On February 19, 1982, Heublein filed the premerger notification form and exhibits required to be submitted by parties whose stock may be acquired in a transaction subject to the H-S-R Act.

15. Upon receipt of Cinema's and Heublein's premerger notification filings, the Commission reviewed Cinema's proposed acquisition of up to 49.9% of Heublein's stock and determined to allow Cinema to consummate the acquisition. Under the Commission's premerger notification rules, Cinema's waiting period expired at 11:59 p.m. on March 6, 1982, and, effective at that time, the Commission permitted Cinema to acquire up to 49.9% of Heublein stock.

D.   HEUBLEIN'S REQUEST FOR PERMISSION TO ACQUIRE UP TO 49.9% OF CINEMA'S STOCK

16. On March 2, 1982, Heublein filed a premerger notification form and exhibits in which Heublein sought approval to acquire, through open market or private transactions, up to 49.9% of Cinema's common stock. Under the Commission's premerger notification rules, the H-S-R Act waiting period with respect to Heublein's acquisition of up to 49.9% of Cinema's stock will not expire until 11:59 p.m. on April 2, 1981 unless reduced by the Commission pursuant to its authority to grant an "early termination" of the waiting period.

17. By letter dated March 2, 1981, submitted pursuant to section 7A(b)(2) of the Clayton Act, as amended by the H-S-R Act, Heublein requested that the Commission terminate the H-S-R Act waiting period with respect to Heublein's acquisition of up to 49.9% of Cinema's stock as soon as possible, but no later than the expiration of the waiting period with respect to Cinema's acquisition of up to 49.9% of Heublein's stock. As grounds for early termination of its H-S-R Act waiting period, Heublein's letter of March 2, 1982 stated:

(a) That there is no likelihood that Heublein's acquisition of Cinema stock will lessen competition in any line of commerce in any section of the country;
(b) That unless Heublein's waiting period was terminated simultaneously with Cinema's, Cinema would be permitted to acquire up to 49.9% of Heublein's stock, while Heublein would not be permitted to acquire up to 49.9% of Cinema stock, and that such a result would be contrary to the legislative history and policies of the H-S-R Act.

E.   THE COMMISSION'S DENIAL OF HEUBLEIN'S REQUEST FOR PERMISSION TO ACQUIRE CINEMA'S STOCK SIMULTANEOUSLY WITH CINEMA'S ACQUISITION OF HEUBLEIN'S STOCK

18. On Thursday, March 4, 1982, the Bureau of Competition denied Heublein's request for early termination not because of any concern about the competitive effects of Heublein's acquisition of up to 49.9% of Cinema's stock, but because, in its view, Heublein had not demonstrated the existence of a "special business reason" in accordance with the Bureau's Formal Interpretation, dated April 10, 1979. The Bureau's position was that a "special business reason" was not shown by the fact that early termination was necessary so that Heublein

would be free to acquire up to 49.9% of Cinema's stock at the same time that Cinema would be free to acquire up to 49.9% of Heublein's stock. The Bureau believed it should to remain "neutral" with respect to contested acquisitions and believed that to grant early termination to Heublein in this case would be to favor Heublein and disfavor Cinema. . . .

F. CINEMA'S EFFORTS TO DETER HEUBLEIN'S ACQUISITION OF UP TO 49.9% OF CINEMA'S STOCK

20. On March 9, 1982, Cinema was reported to have announced that it intended to acquire up to three million shares of its own common stock. Wall Street Journal, March 9, 1982 at 52. It was reported that Cinema's acquisition of three million of its shares would increase the holdings of Cinema's chairman, vice chairman and their families to 47.5% of Cinema's then-outstanding shares. On March 12, 1982, Cinema was reported to have purchased on the open market 1,060,800 of its shares and increased its borrowing capacity from $160 million to $300 million. On that date, a share of Cinema's stock was reportedly priced on the open market at $42, the highest price of such stock in the previous fifty-two weeks. Wall Street Journal, dated March 12, 1982 at 46.

CONCLUSIONS OF LAW . . .

III. STANDARD FOR GRANTING A TEMPORARY RESTRAINING ORDER . . .

IV. IRREPARABLE HARM TO HEUBLEIN

4. As a Connecticut corporation, Heublein has the right to acquire and sell property and to invest corporate funds. . . .

5. If Heublein's right to invest is to be preserved, Heublein must be permitted to invest now. Already, as a result of the Commission's actions described above, nine days have elapsed since Cinema became free to acquire up to 49.9% of Heublein's stock, and during this time Heublein has been prohibited from acquiring a like amount of Cinema's stock. The favorable market opportunities which, absent the Commission's action, would have been available to Heublein during that period, have been irretrievably lost. Moreover, Heublein cannot be compensated for such lost opportunities by money damages. Hence, Heublein has already been irreparably harmed as a result of the Commission's action and it has no adequate remedy at law.

6. In addition, as each day passes during which Heublein is prohibited from acquiring up to 49.9% of Cinema's stock, Heublein loses the favorable market opportunities which would be available to Heublein were it able immediately to acquire up to 49.9% of Cinema's stock. In addition, Cinema's purchases of its own stock, and other actions which Cinema, as a target company, may take to defeat Heublein's effort to purchase Cinema's stock, are further evidence of the likelihood that Heublein will be irreparably harmed unless it is immediately permitted to consummate its proposed acquisition of Cinema's stock. . . .

V.   THE BALANCE OF HARDSHIPS TIPS DECIDEDLY
IN HEUBLEIN'S FAVOR

8. The balance of hardships in this case decidedly favors issuance of a temporary restraining order to Heublein.

9. Neither defendants nor the public interest will be harmed if Heublein is permitted to acquire up to 49.9% of Cinema's stock, because defendants have determined to allow consummation of that acquisition.

10. Since neither the defendants nor the public interest will be harmed by issuance of the requested temporary restraining order and Heublein will be irreparably harmed absent such relief, the balance of hardships tips decidedly in favor of Heublein.

VI.   HEUBLEIN IS LIKELY TO SUCCEED ON THE MERITS
OF THIS ACTION

A.   HEUBLEIN IS LIKELY TO SUCCEED IN SHOWING THAT THE
COMMISSION EXCEEDED ITS STATUTORY JURISDICTION AND
AUTHORITY IN DENYING HEUBLEIN'S REQUEST FOR EARLY
TERMINATION OF THE H-S-R WAITING PERIOD

11. Sections 702 and 704 of the Administrative Procedure Act, 5 U.S.C. ss 701 et seq. provide for judicial review of the Commission's denial of Heublein's early termination request.

12. Under §706(2)(C) of the APA, agency action must be set aside if it exceeds the agency's statutory jurisdiction or authority.

13. The Commission's denial of Heublein's early termination request exceeded the Commission's jurisdiction and authority for each of several reasons. First, the H-S-R Act is intended to permit the antitrust enforcement agencies to evaluate the competitive effects of a transaction and the purpose of the H-S-R waiting period is to provide those agencies sufficient time, in advance of an acquisition, to conduct that analysis. But Heublein was denied early termination on a ground unrelated to competitive considerations. Hence, the Commission's denial of Heublein's request was contrary to the H-S-R Act's purpose and, therefore, beyond its jurisdiction and authority and serves no governmental purpose under the Act.

14. Second, Heublein was denied early termination because the Commission believed that Heublein's request was governed by the standards set forth in the Bureau of Competition's Formal Interpretation, dated April 10, 1979. That Formal Interpretation states that an early termination will not be granted unless the requesting party demonstrates a "special business reason" justifying early termination. However, neither the H-S-R Act nor its legislative history justifies a requirement that a "special business reason" be shown in order to obtain an early termination. If, as here, the Commission has determined well prior to the expiration of the waiting period that the particular transaction will not likely lessen competition and if, as here, Heublein has presented a lawful business reason for early termination, it is beyond the Commission's authority not to grant early termination on the ground that a "special business reason" has not been shown.

15. Third, Heublein's request was denied not because of any concern about the competitive effects of Heublein's acquisition of Cinema's stock, but because

the Commission believed that it must remain "neutral" with respect to contested acquisitions and that to grant early termination to Heublein would be to favor Heublein and disfavor Cinema. This rationale is wrong because if the Commission intends to remain "neutral" with respect to the Heublein-Cinema acquisitions, it should grant Heublein early termination to permit Heublein to acquire Cinema's stock at the same time as Cinema is acquiring Heublein's stock. . . .

17. For these reasons, Heublein is likely to succeed in establishing that the Commission's denial of Heublein's early termination request exceeded its jurisdiction and authority and must, therefore, be set aside.

B. HEUBLEIN IS LIKELY TO SUCCEED IN SHOWING THAT THE COMMISSION WAS ARBITRARY, CAPRICIOUS AND ABUSED ITS DISCRETION IN DENYING HEUBLEIN'S REQUEST FOR EARLY TERMINATION OF THE H-S-R WAITING PERIOD

18. Section 706(2)(A) of the APA provides that on review of agency action:

> The reviewing court shall— (2) hold unlawful and set aside agency action, findings and conclusions found to be—
> (A) arbitrary, capricious, an abuse of discretion, or otherwise not in accordance with law. . . .

In reviewing agency action under this standard, the court must determine whether the agency's decision was based on a consideration of relevant factors and whether it is consistent with the overall policy of the governing Act.

19. For several reasons, Heublein is likely to succeed in establishing that the Commission's denial of Heublein's early termination request was arbitrary, capricious and an abuse of discretion. First, the H-S-R Act is intended to permit the antitrust enforcement agencies to evaluate the competitive effects of a transaction and to provide those agencies sufficient time to conduct that analysis. Heublein, however, was denied early termination on a ground unrelated to competitive considerations. Second, there appears to be no rational basis for the Bureau's requirement that a "special business reason" be shown in order to justify an early termination. Third, the Commission has granted a large number of early termination requests including many involving acquisitions among large companies. Fourth, there appears to be no rational basis for the Bureau's position that it must remain "neutral" with respect to contested acquisitions and that to grant early termination to Heublein would be to favor Heublein and disfavor Cinema. If the Commission intends to remain "neutral" with respect to the Heublein-Cinema acquisitions, it should grant Heublein early termination to permit Heublein to acquire Cinema's stock at the same time as Cinema is acquiring Heublein's stock. Finally, the Commission has applied its policy prohibiting early terminations in contested acquisitions in a discriminatory fashion. "In this instance, to maintain a neutral posture, it is incumbent upon the Commission to grant an early termination, because to deny the same places it is an active posture against the petitioner corporation, Heublein."

20. For all of these reasons, Heublein will likely succeed in showing that Heublein's early termination request was arbitrary, capricious and an abuse of discretion.

Appendices

Diagrams of Deal Structures to Be Analyzed

DIAGRAM 1
Traditional Form of Stock for Stock Direct (Statutory) Merger

• **BEFORE Transaction** •

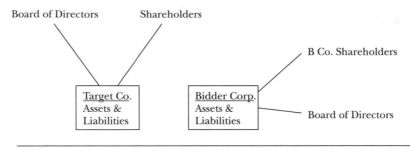

Board of Directors   Shareholders

B Co. Shareholders

Target Co.
Assets &
Liabilities

Bidder Corp.
Assets &
Liabilities

Board of Directors

• **The Transaction** •

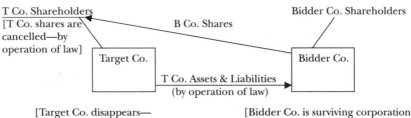

T Co. Shareholders
[T Co. shares are
cancelled—by
operation of law]

B Co. Shares

Bidder Co. Shareholders

Target Co.

Bidder Co.

T Co. Assets & Liabilities
(by operation of law)

[Target Co. disappears—
by operation of law]

[Bidder Co. is surviving corporation—
by operation of law]

• **AFTER Transaction** •

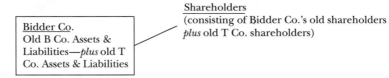

Bidder Co.
Old B Co. Assets &
Liabilities—*plus* old T
Co. Assets & Liabilities

Shareholders
(consisting of Bidder Co.'s old shareholders
plus old T Co. shareholders)

DIAGRAM 2
Stock for Cash Merger
(Cash Out Merger)

• **BEFORE Transaction** •

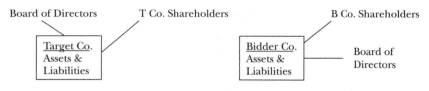

Board of Directors   T Co. Shareholders   B Co. Shareholders

Target Co.   Bidder Co.   Board of
Assets &   Assets &   Directors
Liabilities   Liabilities

• **The Transaction** •

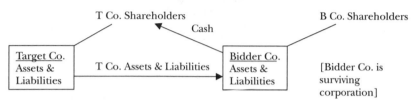

T Co. Shareholders   B Co. Shareholders
                            Cash

Target Co.   Bidder Co.   [Bidder Co. is
Assets &   T Co. Assets & Liabilities   Assets &   surviving
Liabilities   Liabilities   corporation]

[Target Co. disappears—extinguished by operation of law]

• **AFTER Transaction** •

                                          Old B Co. Shareholders

[Target Co. shareholders hold   Bidder Co.
cash—no stock]   Old B Co. Assets &
                                       Liabilities—*plus* old T
                                       Co. Assets & Liabilities

DIAGRAM 3
Short Form Merger

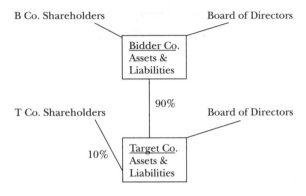

• BEFORE Transaction •

B Co. Shareholders   Board of Directors

Bidder Co.
Assets &
Liabilities

90%

T Co. Shareholders   Board of Directors

10%

Target Co.
Assets &
Liabilities

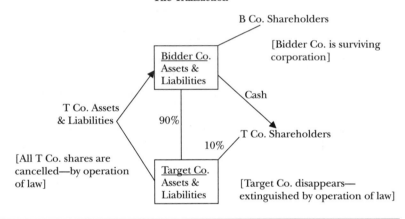

• The Transaction •

B Co. Shareholders

Bidder Co.
Assets &
Liabilities

[Bidder Co. is surviving
corporation]

T Co. Assets
& Liabilities

Cash

90%

T Co. Shareholders

10%

[All T Co. shares are
cancelled—by operation
of law]

Target Co.
Assets &
Liabilities

[Target Co. disappears—
extinguished by operation of law]

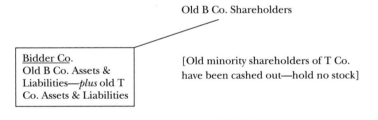

• AFTER Transaction •

Old B Co. Shareholders

Bidder Co.
Old B Co. Assets &
Liabilities—*plus* old T
Co. Assets & Liabilities

[Old minority shareholders of T Co.
have been cashed out—hold no stock]

DIAGRAM 4
Traditional Form of Asset Purchase for Cash:
Sale of Substantially All of Target Co. Assets for Cash—Followed by Dissolution
of Target Co.

• **BEFORE Transaction** •

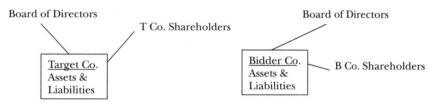

• **FIRST Step: Sale of Target Co. Assets to Bidder Co.** •

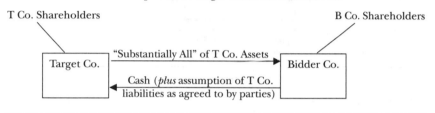

• **AFTER Sale of Substantially All of Target Co. Assets** •

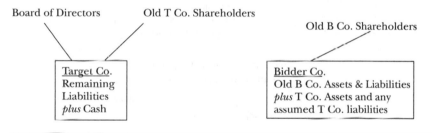

• **SECOND Step: Dissolution of Target Co.** •

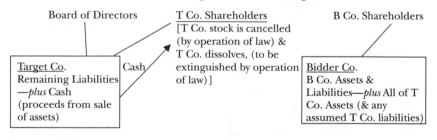

• **AFTER Second Step Dissolution** •

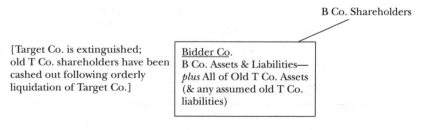

DIAGRAM 5
Asset Acquisition for Stock

• **BEFORE Transaction** •

Board of Directors   T Co. Shareholders   Board of Directors

Target Co.   Bidder Co.
Assets &   Assets &
Liabilities   Liabilities

B Co. Shareholders

• **The Transaction** •

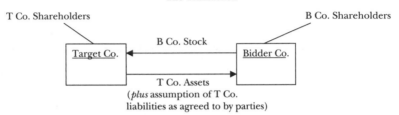

T Co. Shareholders   B Co. Shareholders

Target Co.   B Co. Stock   Bidder Co.

T Co. Assets
(*plus* assumption of T Co.
liabilities as agreed to by parties)

• **AFTER Transaction** •

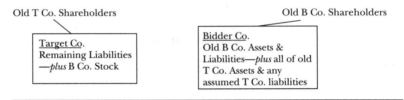

Old T Co. Shareholders   Old B Co. Shareholders

Target Co.   Bidder Co.
Remaining Liabilities   Old B Co. Assets &
—*plus* B Co. Stock   Liabilities—*plus* all of old
                                    T Co. Assets & any
                                    assumed T Co. liabilities

Step 2: Dissolution of Target Co.
• **BEFORE Dissolution** •

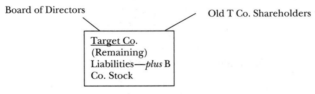

Board of Directors   Old T Co. Shareholders

Target Co.
(Remaining)
Liabilities—*plus* B
Co. Stock

• **The Transaction** •

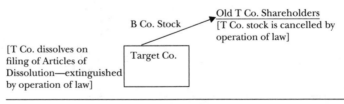

Old T Co. Shareholders
B Co. Stock   [T Co. stock is cancelled by
                     operation of law]

[T Co. dissolves on
filing of Articles of   Target Co.
Dissolution—extinguished
by operation of law]

• **AFTER Dissolution** •

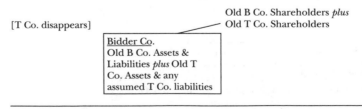

Old B Co. Shareholders *plus*
Old T Co. Shareholders

[T Co. disappears]

Bidder Co.
Old B Co. Assets &
Liabilities *plus* Old T
Co. Assets & any
assumed T Co. liabilities

DIAGRAM 6
Traditional Form of Stock Purchase for Cash

• **BEFORE Transaction** •

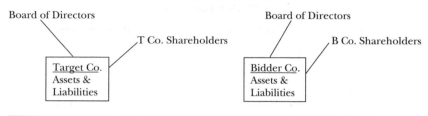

• **The Transaction** •

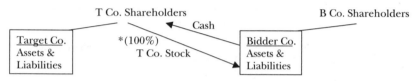

*It is possible (but often not likely) that all (100%) of Target Co. stock is exchanged for cash in this transaction.

• **AFTER Transaction** •

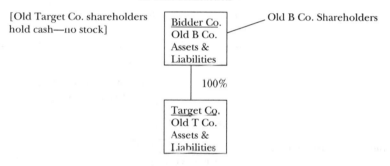

DIAGRAM 7
Stock for Stock Acquisition
(Stock Exchange Offer)

• **BEFORE Transaction** •

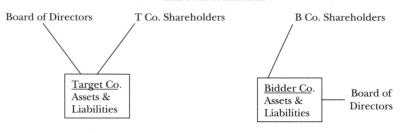

Board of Directors   T Co. Shareholders   B Co. Shareholders

Target Co.   Bidder Co.   Board of
Assets &   Assets &   Directors
Liabilities   Liabilities

• **The Transaction** •

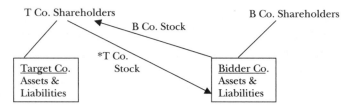

T Co. Shareholders   B Co. Shareholders
                              B Co. Stock

Target Co.   *T Co.   Bidder Co.
Assets &   Stock   Assets &
Liabilities   Liabilities

*(This assumes that all (100%) of Target Co. Shareholders accept the offer and exchange
their T Co. shares for B Co. stock.)

• **AFTER Transaction** •

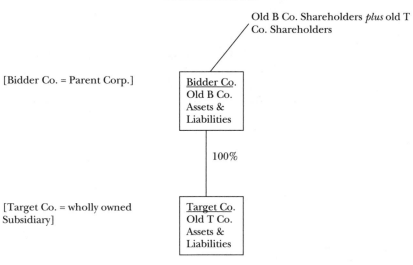

Old B Co. Shareholders *plus* old T
Co. Shareholders

[Bidder Co. = Parent Corp.]   Bidder Co.
                                   Old B Co.
                                   Assets &
                                   Liabilities

                                       100%

[Target Co. = wholly owned   Target Co.
Subsidiary]   Old T Co.
                                   Assets &
                                   Liabilities

DIAGRAM 8
Forward Triangular Merger
(Using *stock* as merger consideration)

• **BEFORE Transaction** •

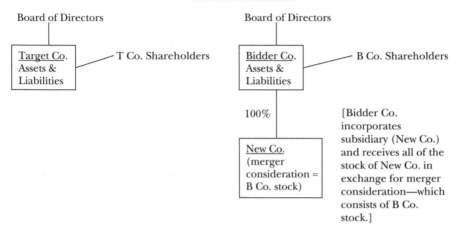

Board of Directors   Board of Directors

Target Co.   T Co. Shareholders   Bidder Co.   B Co. Shareholders
Assets &   Assets &
Liabilities   Liabilities

                                          100%

                                          New Co.   [Bidder Co.
                                          (merger   incorporates
                                          consideration = subsidiary (New Co.)
                                          B Co. stock)   and receives all of the
                                                           stock of New Co. in
                                                           exchange for merger
                                                           consideration—which
                                                           consists of B Co.
                                                           stock.]

• **The Transaction** •
(Target Co. Merges into New Co.)

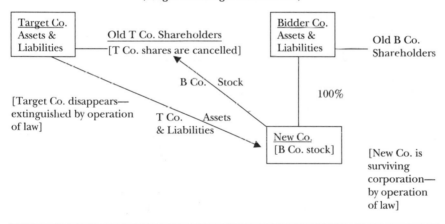

Target Co.   Bidder Co.
Assets &   Old T Co. Shareholders   Assets &   Old B Co.
Liabilities   [T Co. shares are cancelled] Liabilities Shareholders

                        B Co. Stock

[Target Co. disappears—   100%
extinguished by operation   T Co.   Assets
of law]   & Liabilities

                                          New Co.
                                          [B Co. stock]   [New Co. is
                                                           surviving
                                                           corporation—
                                                           by operation
                                                           of law]

• **AFTER Transaction is Completed** •

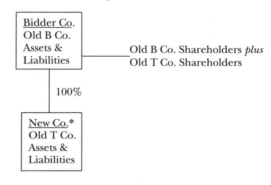

                  Bidder Co.
                  Old B Co.
                  Assets &   Old B Co. Shareholders *plus*
                  Liabilities   Old T Co. Shareholders

                  100%

                  New Co.*
                  Old T Co.
                  Assets &
                  Liabilities

*New Co. may undertake the transaction costs associated with changing name to "Target Co."

DIAGRAM 9
Forward Triangular Merger
(Using *cash* as merger consideration)

• **BEFORE Transaction** •

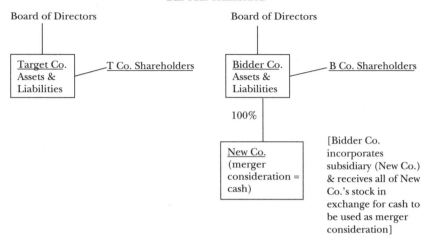

Board of Directors   Board of Directors

Target Co.
Assets &
Liabilities   T Co. Shareholders

Bidder Co.
Assets &
Liabilities   B Co. Shareholders

100%

New Co.
(merger
consideration =
cash)

[Bidder Co.
incorporates
subsidiary (New Co.)
& receives all of New
Co.'s stock in
exchange for cash to
be used as merger
consideration]

• **The Transaction** •
(Target Co. Merges into New Co.)

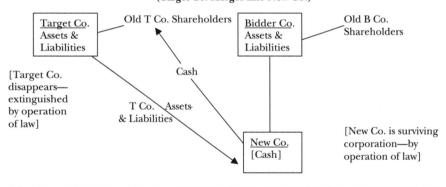

Target Co.
Assets &
Liabilities

Old T Co. Shareholders

Bidder Co.
Assets &
Liabilities

Old B Co.
Shareholders

[Target Co.
disappears—
extinguished
by operation
of law]

Cash

T Co. Assets
& Liabilities

New Co.
[Cash]

[New Co. is surviving
corporation—by
operation of law]

• **AFTER Transaction Is Consummated** •

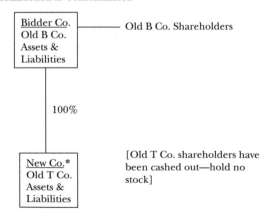

Bidder Co.
Old B Co.
Assets &
Liabilities   Old B Co. Shareholders

100%

New Co.*
Old T Co.
Assets &
Liabilities

[Old T Co. shareholders have
been cashed out—hold no
stock]

*New Co. may undertake the transaction costs associated with changing name to "Target
Co."

DIAGRAM 10
Reverse Triangular Merger
(Using *stock* as merger consideration)

• **BEFORE** Transaction •

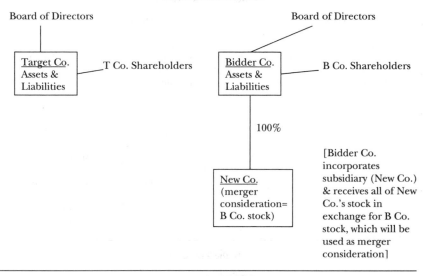

Board of Directors   Board of Directors

Target Co.
Assets &
Liabilities   ⎯ T Co. Shareholders   Bidder Co.
Assets &
Liabilities   ⎯ B Co. Shareholders

100%

New Co.
(merger
consideration=
B Co. stock)

[Bidder Co.
incorporates
subsidiary (New Co.)
& receives all of New
Co.'s stock in
exchange for B Co.
stock, which will be
used as merger
consideration]

• **In the Transaction** •
(New Co. Merges into Target Co.)

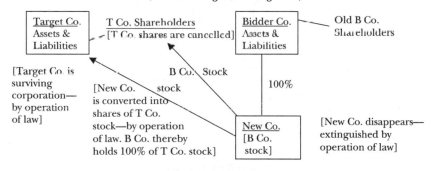

Target Co.
Assets &
Liabilities   T Co. Shareholders
⎯ [T Co. shares are cancelled]   Bidder Co.
Assets &
Liabilities   ⎯ Old B Co.
Shareholders

[Target Co. is
surviving
corporation—
by operation
of law]

B Co. Stock

[New Co.   stock
is converted into
shares of T Co.
stock—by operation
of law. B Co. thereby
holds 100% of T Co. stock]

100%

New Co.
[B Co.
stock]

[New Co. disappears—
extinguished by
operation of law]

• **AFTER the Transaction** •

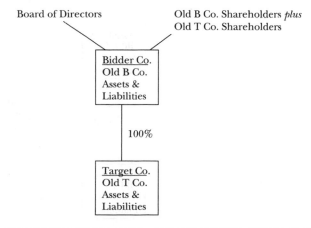

Board of Directors   Old B Co. Shareholders *plus*
Old T Co. Shareholders

Bidder Co.
Old B Co.
Assets &
Liabilities

100%

Target Co.
Old T Co.
Assets &
Liabilities

DIAGRAM 11
Reverse Triangular Merger
(Using *cash* as consideration)

• BEFORE the Transaction •

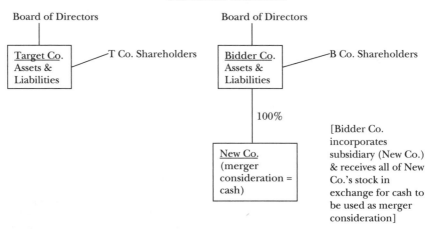

Board of Directors

Board of Directors

Target Co.
Assets &
Liabilities

—T Co. Shareholders

Bidder Co.
Assets &
Liabilities

—B Co. Shareholders

100%

New Co.
(merger
consideration =
cash)

[Bidder Co.
incorporates
subsidiary (New Co.)
& receives all of New
Co.'s stock in
exchange for cash to
be used as merger
consideration]

• In the Transaction •

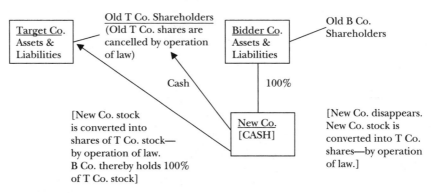

Target Co.
Assets &
Liabilities

Old T Co. Shareholders
(Old T Co. shares are
cancelled by operation
of law)

Bidder Co.
Assets &
Liabilities

Old B Co.
Shareholders

Cash

100%

[New Co. stock
is converted into
shares of T Co. stock—
by operation of law.
B Co. thereby holds 100%
of T Co. stock]

New Co.
[CASH]

[New Co. disappears.
New Co. stock is
converted into T Co.
shares—by operation
of law.]

• AFTER the Transaction •

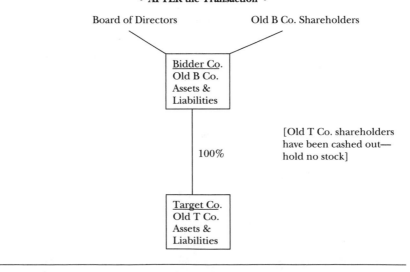

Board of Directors

Old B Co. Shareholders

Bidder Co.
Old B Co.
Assets &
Liabilities

[Old T Co. shareholders
have been cashed out—
hold no stock]

100%

Target Co.
Old T Co.
Assets &
Liabilities

DIAGRAM 12

TWO STEP TRANSACTION: Stock Purchase Followed
by Squeeze Out/Cash Out Merger
(Using either a reverse *or* a forward triangular merger)

STEP ONE: Stock Purchase
• BEFORE Stock Purchase •

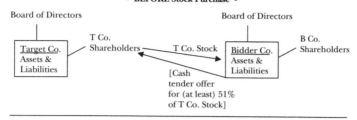

• AFTER Stock Purchase •

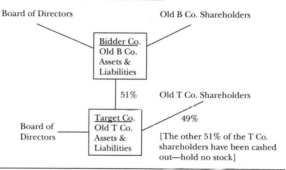

STEP TWO: Squeeze-Out (Cash-Out) Merger
(Using *Reverse* Triangular Merger)
• BEFORE the Transaction •

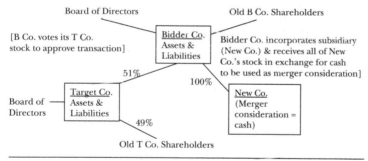

• In the Transaction •

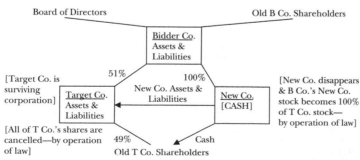

(continued)

DIAGRAM 12
Continued

• AFTER the Squeeze Out Merger •
(Using *Reverse* Triangular Merger)

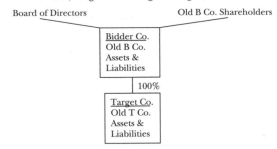

[Old T Co. Shareholders have been cashed out—hold no stock]

ALTERNATIVE SECOND STEP: Squeeze-Out (Cash-Out) Merger
(Using *Forward* Triangular Merger)
• BEFORE the Transaction •

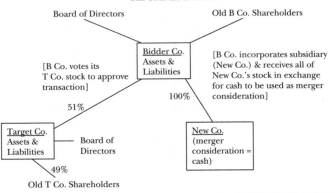

• In the Transaction •

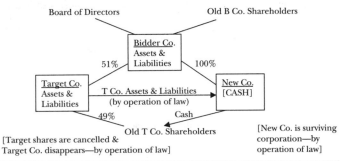

• AFTER the Squeeze Out Merger •
(Using *Forward* Triangular Merger)

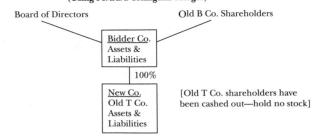

||B||

Pfizer/Pharmacia Merger Agreement

AGREEMENT AND PLAN OF MERGER

Dated as of July 13, 2002

among

PFIZER INC.,

PILSNER ACQUISITION SUB CORP.

and

PHARMACIA CORPORATION

TABLE OF CONTENTS

ARTICLE I
THE MERGER; CERTAIN RELATED MATTERS

ARTICLE II
EXCHANGE OF CERTIFICATES

ARTICLE III
REPRESENTATIONS AND WARRANTIES

ARTICLE IV
COVENANTS RELATING TO CONDUCT OF BUSINESS

ARTICLE V
ADDITIONAL AGREEMENTS

ARTICLE VI
CONDITIONS PRECEDENT

ARTICLE VII
TERMINATION AND AMENDMENT

ARTICLE VIII
GENERAL PROVISIONS

LIST OF EXHIBITS

[Exhibits have been omitted.]

AGREEMENT AND PLAN OF MERGER, dated as of July 13, 2002 (this "Agreement"), among PFIZER INC., a Delaware corporation ("Parent"), PILSNER ACQUISITION SUB CORP., a Delaware corporation and a direct wholly-owned subsidiary of Parent ("Merger Sub"), and PHARMACIA CORPORATION, a Delaware corporation (the "Company" and collectively with Parent and Merger Sub, the "parties").

WITNESSETH:

WHEREAS, the respective Boards of Directors of the Company and Parent deem it advisable and in the best interests of each corporation and its respective stockholders that the Company and Parent engage in a business combination in order to advance the long-term strategic business interests of the Company and Parent;

WHEREAS, the combination of the Company and Parent shall be effected by the terms of this Agreement through a merger as outlined below (the "Merger");

WHEREAS, in furtherance thereof, the respective Boards of Directors of the Company and Parent have approved the Merger, upon the terms and subject to the conditions set forth in this Agreement, pursuant to which each share of common stock, par value $2.00 per share, of the Company ("Company Common Stock") issued and outstanding immediately prior to the Effective Time (as defined in *Section 1.3*), other than shares owned or held directly or indirectly by Parent or directly or indirectly by the Company, together with the associated Company Rights (as defined in *Section 3.2(b)*) will be converted into the right to receive shares of common stock, par value $0.05 per share, of Parent ("Parent Common Stock") as set forth in *Section 1.8* . . .

WHEREAS, for Federal income tax purposes, it is intended that the Merger shall qualify as a reorganization within the meaning of Section 368 (a) of the Internal Revenue Code of 1986, as amended (the "Code"), and the regulations promulgated thereunder; and

NOW, THEREFORE, in consideration of the foregoing and the respective representations, warranties, covenants and agreements set forth in this Agreement, and intending to be legally bound hereby, the parties agree as follows:

ARTICLE I
THE MERGER; CERTAIN RELATED MATTERS

Section 1.1   The Merger.   Upon the terms and subject to the conditions set forth in this Agreement, and in accordance with the Delaware General Corporation Law (the "DGCL"), Merger Sub shall be merged with and into the Company at the Effective Time. Following the Merger, the separate corporate existence of Merger Sub shall cease and the Company shall continue as the surviving corporation (the "Surviving Corporation").

Section 1.2   Closing.   Upon the terms and subject to the conditions set forth in *Article VI*, and the termination rights set forth in *Article VII*, the closing of the Merger (the "Closing") will take place on the first Business Day after the satisfaction or waiver (subject to applicable law) of the conditions (excluding conditions that, by their nature, cannot be satisfied until the Closing Date, but subject to the fulfillment or waiver of those conditions) set forth in *Article VI*, unless this Agreement has been previously terminated pursuant to its terms or unless another time or date is agreed to in writing by the parties (the actual time and date of the Closing being referred to herein as the "Closing Date"). The Closing shall be held at the offices of Cadwalader, Wickersham & Taft, 100 Maiden Lane, New York, New York, 10038, unless another place is agreed to in writing by the parties.

Section 1.3   Effective Time.   As soon as practicable following the satisfaction or waiver (subject to applicable law) of the conditions set forth in *Article VI*, at the Closing the parties shall (i) file a certificate of merger (the "Certificate of Merger") in such form as is required by, and executed in accordance with, the relevant provisions of the DGCL and (ii) make all other filings or recordings required under the DGCL. The Merger shall become effective at such time as the Certificate of Merger is duly filed with the Delaware Secretary of State or at such subsequent time as Parent and the Company shall agree and as shall be specified in the Certificate of Merger (the date and time the Merger becomes effective being the "Effective Time").

Section 1.4   Effects of the Merger.   At and after the Effective Time, the Merger will have the effects set forth in the DGCL. Without limiting the generality of the foregoing, and subject thereto, at the Effective Time all the property, rights, privileges, powers and franchises of the Company and Merger Sub shall be vested in the Surviving Corporation, and all debts, liabilities and duties of the Company and Merger Sub shall become the debts, liabilities and duties of the Surviving Corporation.

Section 1.5   Certificate of Incorporation.   The certificate of incorporation of the Company, as in effect immediately prior to the Effective Time, shall be the certificate of incorporation of the Surviving Corporation, until thereafter changed or amended as provided therein or by applicable law . . .

Section 1.7   Officers and Directors.   From and after the Effective Time, until successors are duly elected or appointed and qualified in accordance with applicable law, (i) the directors of Merger Sub at the Effective Time shall be the directors of the Surviving Corporation and (ii) the officers of the Company at the Effective Time shall be the officers of the Surviving Corporation.

Section 1.8   Effect on Capital Stock.
   (a)   At the Effective Time, by virtue of the Merger and without any action on the part of the holder thereof, each share of Company Common Stock issued and outstanding immediately prior to the Effective Time (other than

shares of Company Common Stock owned by Parent or Merger Sub or held by the Company, all of which shall be canceled as provided in *Section 1.8(d)*), together with the associated Company Rights (as defined in *Section 3.2(b)*), shall be converted into 1.4 validly issued, fully paid and non-assessable shares of Parent Common Stock (the "Exchange Ratio") . . . (together with any cash in lieu of fractional shares of Parent Common Stock to be paid pursuant to *Section 2.5*, the "Common Stock Merger Consideration") . . .

(c) As a result of the Merger and without any action on the part of the holders thereof, at the Effective Time, all shares of Company Common Stock (together with the associated Company Rights) . . . shall cease to be outstanding and shall be canceled and retired and shall cease to exist, and each holder of a certificate or certificates which immediately prior to the Effective Time represented any such shares of Company Common Stock ("Common Certificates [or Certificates]") . . . shall thereafter cease to have any rights with respect to such shares of Company Common Stock (together with the associated Company Rights) . . . except as provided herein or by law.

(d) Each share of Company Common Stock . . . owned by Parent, Merger Sub or any other wholly-owned Subsidiary of Parent or held by the Company at the Effective Time shall, by virtue of the Merger, cease to be outstanding and shall be canceled and retired and no stock of Parent or other consideration shall be delivered in exchange therefor.

(e) At the Effective Time, by virtue of the Merger and without any action on the part of the holder thereof, each share of common stock, par value $0.01 per share, of Merger Sub issued and outstanding immediately prior to the Effective Time, shall be converted into one validly issued, fully paid and non-assessable share of common stock, par value $2.00 per share, of the Surviving Corporation . . .

Section 1.10 Certain Adjustments. If, between the date of this Agreement and the Effective Time, the outstanding Parent Common Stock or Company Common Stock shall have been changed into a different number of shares or different class by reason of any reclassification, recapitalization, stock split, split-up, combination or exchange of shares or a stock dividend or dividend payable in any other securities shall be declared with a record date within such period, or any similar event shall have occurred, the Exchange Ratio shall be appropriately adjusted to provide to the holders of Company Common Stock the same economic effect as contemplated by this Agreement prior to such event; *provided, however*, that there shall be no adjustment as a result of any dividend or distribution to the Company's stockholders of the stock of Monsanto Company ("Monsanto") pursuant to the spin-off of Monsanto as described in the Company's Annual Report on Form 10-K for the year ended December 31, 2001 (the "Monsanto Spin-Off").

Section 1.11 Associated Rights. References in *Article I* and *Article II* of this Agreement to Company Common Stock shall include, unless the context requires otherwise, the associated Company Rights and references in *Article I* and *Article II* of this Agreement to Parent Common Stock shall include, unless the context requires otherwise, the associated Parent Rights . . .

ARTICLE II
EXCHANGE OF CERTIFICATES

Section 2.1   Exchange Fund.   Prior to the Effective Time, Parent shall appoint a commercial bank or trust company to act as exchange agent hereunder (which entity shall be reasonably acceptable to the Company) for the purpose of exchanging Certificates for the Merger Consideration (the "Exchange Agent"). At or prior to the Effective Time, Parent shall deposit with the Exchange Agent, in trust for the benefit of holders of shares of Company Common Stock . . . certificates representing the Parent Common Stock issuable pursuant to *Section 1.8* in exchange for outstanding shares of Company Common Stock . . . Parent agrees to make available directly or indirectly to the Exchange Agent from time to time as needed, cash sufficient to pay cash in lieu of fractional shares pursuant to *Section 2.5* and any dividends and other distributions pursuant to *Section 2.3*. Any cash and certificates of Parent Common Stock . . . deposited with the Exchange Agent shall hereinafter be referred to as the "Exchange Fund."

Section 2.2   Exchange Procedures.   Promptly after the Effective Time, the Surviving Corporation shall cause the Exchange Agent to mail to each holder of record of a Certificate (i) a letter of transmittal which shall specify that delivery shall be effected, and risk of loss and title to the Certificates shall pass, only upon proper delivery of the Certificates to the Exchange Agent, and which letter shall be in customary form and have such other provisions as Parent may reasonably specify (such letter to be reasonably acceptable to the Company prior to the Effective Time) and (ii) instructions for effecting the surrender of such Certificates in exchange for the applicable Merger Consideration. Upon surrender of a Certificate to the Exchange Agent together with such letter of transmittal, duly executed and completed in accordance with the instructions thereto, and such other documents as may reasonably be required by the Exchange Agent, the holder of such Certificate shall be entitled to receive in exchange therefor (i) in the case of holders of Common Certificates (A) one or more shares of Parent Common Stock (which shall be in uncertificated book-entry form unless a physical certificate is requested) representing, in the aggregate, the whole number of shares that such holder has the right to receive pursuant to *Section 1.8* (after taking into account all shares of Company Common Stock then held by such holder) and (B) a check in the amount equal to the cash that such holder has the right to receive pursuant to the provisions of this Article II, consisting of cash in lieu of any fractional shares of Parent Common Stock pursuant to *Section 2.5* and dividends and other distributions pursuant to *Section 2.3* . . .

Section 2.3   Distributions with Respect to Unexchanged Shares; Voting.
(a)   All shares of Parent Common Stock and Parent Convertible Preferred Stock to be issued pursuant to the Merger shall be deemed issued and outstanding as of the Effective Time . . .
(b)   For a period of one year following the Closing, holders of unsurrendered Certificates shall be entitled to vote at any meeting of Parent stockholders

the number of whole shares of Parent Common Stock . . . represented by such Certificates, regardless of whether such holders have exchanged their Certificates.

Section 2.4   *No Further Ownership Rights in Company Common Stock.* All shares of Parent Common Stock . . . issued and cash paid upon conversion of shares of Company Common Stock . . . in accordance with the terms of *Article I* and this *Article II* (including any cash paid pursuant to *Section 2.3* or *2.5*) shall be deemed to have been issued or paid in full satisfaction of all rights pertaining to the shares of Company Common Stock . . .

Section 2.5   *No Fractional Shares of Parent Common Stock.*

(a)   No certificates or scrip or shares of Parent Common Stock representing fractional shares of Parent Common Stock or book-entry credit of the same shall be issued upon the surrender for exchange of Certificates and such fractional share interests will not entitle the owner thereof to vote or to have any rights of a stockholder of Parent or a holder of shares of Parent Common Stock.

(b)   Notwithstanding any other provision of this Agreement, each holder of shares of Company Common Stock exchanged pursuant to the Merger who would otherwise have been entitled to receive a fraction of a share of Parent Common Stock (after taking into account all Certificates delivered by such holder) shall receive, in lieu thereof, cash (without interest) in an amount equal to the product of (i) such fractional part of a share of Parent Common Stock multiplied by (ii) the closing price for a share of Parent Common Stock on the New York Stock Exchange, Inc. ("NYSE") Composite Transactions Tape on the date of the Effective Time . . . Such payment of cash consideration in lieu of fractional shares of Parent Common Stock is not expected to exceed, in the aggregate, 1% of the total Merger Consideration.

(c)   As promptly as practicable after the determination of the amount of cash, if any, to be paid to holders of fractional interests, the Exchange Agent shall so notify Parent, and Parent shall deposit or cause the Surviving Corporation to deposit such amount with the Exchange Agent and shall cause the Exchange Agent to forward payments to such holders of fractional interests subject to and in accordance with the terms hereof.

Section 2.6   *Termination of Exchange Fund.* Any portion of the Exchange Fund which remains undistributed to the holders of Certificates for six months after the Effective Time shall be delivered to Parent or otherwise on the instruction of Parent, and any holders of the Certificates who have not theretofore complied with this *Article II* shall thereafter look only to Parent for the Merger Consideration with respect to the shares of Company Common Stock . . . formerly represented thereby to which such holders are entitled pursuant to *Section 1.8* and *Section 2.2*, [and] any cash in lieu of fractional shares of Parent Common Stock to which such holders are entitled pursuant to *Section 2.5* . . . Any such portion of the Exchange Fund remaining unclaimed by holders of shares of Company Common Stock . . . five years after the Effective Time (or such earlier date immediately prior to such time as such amounts would otherwise escheat to or become property of any Governmental

Entity (as defined in *Section 3.1(c)(iii)*) shall, to the extent permitted by law, become the property of the Surviving Corporation free and clear of any claims or interest of any Person previously entitled thereto.

Section 2.7　No Liability.　None of Parent, Merger Sub, the Company, the Surviving Corporation or the Exchange Agent shall be liable to any Person in respect of any Merger Consideration from the Exchange Fund delivered to a public official pursuant to any applicable abandoned property, escheat or similar law.

Section 2.8　Investment of the Exchange Fund.　The Exchange Agent shall invest any cash included in the Exchange Fund as directed by Parent on a daily basis; *provided*, that no such gain or loss thereon shall affect the amounts payable to the Company stockholders pursuant to *Article I* and the other provisions of this *Article II*. Any interest and other income resulting from such investments shall promptly be paid to Parent . . .

Section 2.11　Further Assurances.　After the Effective Time, the officers and directors of the Surviving Corporation will be authorized to execute and deliver, in the name and on behalf of the Company or Merger Sub, any deeds, bills of sale, assignments or assurances and to take and do, in the name and on behalf of the Company or Merger Sub, any other actions and things to vest, perfect or confirm of record or otherwise in the Surviving Corporation any and all right, title and interest in, to and under any of the rights, properties or assets acquired or to be acquired by the Surviving Corporation as a result of, or in connection with, the Merger.

Section 2.12　Stock Transfer Books.　The stock transfer books of the Company shall be closed immediately upon the Effective Time and there shall be no further registration of transfers of shares of Company Common Stock . . . thereafter on the records of the Company . . .

Section 2.13　Affiliates.　Notwithstanding anything to the contrary herein, to the fullest extent permitted by law, no certificates representing shares of Parent Common Stock or cash shall be delivered to a Person who may be deemed an "affiliate" of the Company in accordance with *Section 5.12* hereof for purposes of Rule 145 under the Securities Act of 1933, as amended (the "Securities Act"), and applicable rules and regulations of the Securities and Exchange Commission (the "SEC") until such Person has executed and delivered an Affiliate Agreement (as defined in *Section 5.12*) to Parent.

ARTICLE III
REPRESENTATIONS AND WARRANTIES

Section 3.1　Representations and Warranties of Parent.　Except as set forth in the Parent disclosure schedule delivered by Parent to the Company prior to the execution of this Agreement (the "Parent Disclosure Schedule") (each section of which qualifies the correspondingly numbered representation and warranty or covenant and any other representation or warranty, if the disclosure set forth in the Parent Disclosure Schedule is readily applicable to such other representation or warranty), Parent represents and warrants to the Company as follows:

(a) *Organization, Standing and Power; Subsidiaries.*

(i) Each of Parent and each of its Subsidiaries (as defined in *Section 8.11*) is duly organized, validly existing and in good standing under the laws of its jurisdiction of incorporation or organization, has the requisite corporate (or similar) power and authority to own, lease and operate its properties and to carry on its business as now being conducted, except where the failures to be so organized, existing and in good standing or to have such power and authority, in the aggregate, would not reasonably be expected to have a Material Adverse Effect (as defined in *Section 8.11*) on Parent, and is duly qualified and in good standing to do business in each jurisdiction in which the nature of its business or the ownership or leasing of its properties makes such qualification necessary other than in such jurisdictions where the failures so to qualify or to be in good standing, in the aggregate, would not reasonably be expected to have a Material Adverse Effect on Parent. The copies of the certificate of incorporation and bylaws of Parent which were previously furnished or made available to the Company are true, complete and correct copies of such documents as in effect on the date of this Agreement.

(ii) Exhibit 21 to Parent's Annual Report on Form 10K for the year ended December 31, 2001 ("Parent Exhibit 21") includes all the Subsidiaries of Parent which as of the date of this Agreement are Significant Subsidiaries (as defined in Rule 1-02 of Regulation S-X of the SEC) . . .

(b) *Capital Structure.*

(i) As of March 31, 2002, the authorized capital stock of Parent consisted of (A) 9,000,000,000 shares of Parent Common Stock of which 6,254,532,591 shares were outstanding and 539,225,789 shares were held in the treasury of Parent and (B) 12,000,000 shares of Preferred Stock, no par value, . . . Since March 31, 2002 to the date of this Agreement, there have been no issuances of shares of the capital stock of Parent or any other securities of Parent other than issuances of shares of Parent Common Stock pursuant to options or rights outstanding as of March 31, 2002 under the Benefit Plans (as defined in *Section 8.11*) of Parent. All issued and outstanding shares of the capital stock of Parent are, and when shares of Parent Common Stock . . . are issued in the Merger . . . such shares will be, duly authorized, validly issued, fully paid and nonassessable and free of any preemptive rights . . . *Section 3.1 (b)* of the Parent Disclosure Schedule sets forth a complete and correct list, as of March 31, 2002, of the number of shares of Parent Common Stock subject to Parent Stock Options or other rights to purchase or receive Parent Common Stock granted under the Parent Benefit Plans or otherwise, the dates of grant and the exercise prices thereof. No options or warrants or other rights to acquire capital stock from Parent have been issued or granted since March 31, 2002 to the date of this Agreement.

(ii) No bonds, debentures, notes or other indebtedness of Parent having the right to vote (or convertible into or exercisable for securities having the right to vote) on any matters on which holders of capital stock of Parent may vote ("Parent Voting Debt") are issued or outstanding.

(iii) Except as otherwise set forth in this *Section 3.1 (b)* and as contemplated by *Section 1.8* and *Section 1.9*, as of the date of this Agreement, there are no securities, options, warrants, calls, rights, commitments, agreements, arrangements or undertakings of any kind to which Parent or any of its Subsidiaries is a party or by which any of them is bound obligating Parent or any of its Subsidiaries to issue, deliver or sell, or cause to be issued, delivered or sold, additional shares of capital stock or other voting securities of Parent or any of its Subsidiaries or obligating Parent or any of its Subsidiaries to issue, grant, extend or enter into any such security, option, warrant, call, right, commitment, agreement, arrangement or undertaking . . .

(c)   *Authority; No Conflicts.*

(i) Parent has all requisite corporate power and authority to enter into this Agreement and to consummate the transactions contemplated hereby, subject to obtaining the requisite stockholder approval of the issuance of the shares of Parent Common Stock to be issued in the Merger (the "Share Issuance") and the amendment to the Parent Restated Certificate of Incorporation to increase the authorized share capital (the "Certificate Amendment"), in each case, by the votes set forth in *Section 3.1 (g)* hereof (such votes as set forth in such *Section 3.1 (g)* collectively being the "Parent Stockholder Approval"). The execution and delivery of this Agreement and the consummation of the transactions contemplated hereby have been duly authorized by all necessary corporate action on the part of Parent, subject to obtaining the Parent Stockholder Approval. This Agreement has been duly executed and delivered by Parent and constitutes a valid and binding agreement of Parent, enforceable against it in accordance with its terms, except as such enforceability may be limited by bankruptcy, insolvency, reorganization, moratorium and similar laws relating to or affecting creditors generally or by general equity principles (regardless of whether such enforceability is considered in a proceeding in equity or at law).

(ii) The execution and delivery of this Agreement by Parent does not or will not, as the case may be, and the consummation by Parent of the Merger and the other transactions contemplated hereby will not, conflict with, or result in any violation of, or constitute a default (with or without notice or lapse of time, or both) under, or give rise to a right of, or result by its terms in the, termination, amendment, cancellation or acceleration of any obligation or the loss of a material benefit under, or the creation of a lien, pledge, security interest, charge or other encumbrance on, or the loss of, any assets, including Intellectual Property (as defined in *Section 3.1(p)*) (any such conflict, violation, default, right of termination, amendment, cancellation or acceleration, loss or creation, a "Violation") pursuant to: (A) any provision of the certificate of incorporation or bylaws of Parent or any Significant Subsidiary (as defined in Rule 1-02 of Regulation S-X of the SEC) of Parent, or (B) except as, in the aggregate, would not reasonably be expected to have a Material Adverse Effect on Parent, or subject to obtaining or making the consents, approvals, orders, authorizations, registrations, declarations and filings referred to in paragraph (iii) below, any loan or credit agreement, note, mortgage, bond, indenture, lease, benefit plan or other agreement, obligation, instrument, permit, concession, franchise, license, judgment, order, decree, statute, law, ordinance, rule or regulation applicable to Parent or any Subsidiary of Parent or their respective properties or assets.

(iii) No consent, approval, order or authorization of, clearance by, or registration, declaration or filing with, any supranational, national, state, municipal, local or foreign government, any instrumentality, subdivision, court, administrative agency or commission or other authority thereof, or any quasi-governmental or private body exercising any regulatory, taxing, importing or other governmental or quasi-governmental authority (a "Governmental Entity"), is required by or with respect to Parent or any Subsidiary of Parent in connection with the execution and delivery of this Agreement by Parent or Merger Sub or the consummation of the Merger and the other transactions contemplated hereby, except for those required under or in relation to (A) the Hart-Scott-Rodino Antitrust Improvements Act of 1976, as amended (the "HSR Act"), (B) state securities or "blue sky" laws (the "Blue Sky Laws"), (C) the Securities Act, (D) the Exchange Act, (E) the DGCL with respect to the filing of the Certificate of Merger, (F) rules and regulations of the NYSE, (G) antitrust or other competition laws, of the European Union or other jurisdictions, and (H) such other consents, approvals, orders, authorizations, registrations, declarations and filings the failures of which to make or obtain, in the aggregate, would not reasonably be expected to have a Material Adverse Effect on Parent. Consents, approvals, orders, authorizations, registrations, declarations and filings required under or in relation to any of the foregoing *clauses (A) through (G)* are hereinafter referred to as "Necessary Consents."

(d)   *Reports and Financial Statements.*

(i) Parent has filed all required registration statements, prospectuses, reports, schedules, forms, statements and other documents required to be filed by it with the SEC since January 1, 2000 (collectively, including all exhibits thereto, the "Parent SEC Reports"). No Subsidiary of Parent is required to file any form, report, registration statement, prospectus or other document with the SEC. None of the Parent SEC Reports, as of their respective dates (and, if amended or superseded by a filing prior to the date of this Agreement or the Closing Date, then on the date of such filing), contained or will contain any untrue statement of a material fact or omitted or will omit to state a material fact required to be stated therein or necessary to make the statements therein, in light of the circumstances under which they were made, not misleading. Each of the financial statements (including the related notes and schedules) included or incorporated by reference in the Parent SEC Reports presents fairly, or will present fairly, in all material respects, the consolidated financial position and consolidated results of operations, retained earnings and cash flows of Parent and its consolidated Subsidiaries as of the respective dates or for the respective periods set forth therein, all in conformity with generally accepted accounting principles ("GAAP") consistently applied during the periods involved except as otherwise noted therein, and subject, in the case of the unaudited interim financial statements, to the absence of notes and normal year-end adjustments that have not been and are not expected to be material in amount. All of such Parent SEC Reports, as of their respective dates (and as of the date of any amendment to the respective Parent SEC Report), complied as to form in all material respects with the applicable requirements of the Securities Act and the Exchange Act and the rules and regulations promulgated thereunder.

(ii) Except as disclosed in the Parent SEC Reports filed prior to the date hereof, Parent and its Subsidiaries have not incurred any liabilities that are of a nature that would be required to be disclosed on a balance sheet of Parent and its Subsidiaries or the footnotes thereto prepared in conformity with GAAP, other than (A) liabilities incurred in the ordinary course of business or (B) liabilities that, in the aggregate, would not reasonably be expected to have a Material Adverse Effect on Parent.

(e)   *Information Supplied*.

(i) None of the information supplied or to be supplied by Parent for inclusion or incorporation by reference in (A) the Form S-4 (as defined in *Section 5.1*) will, at the time the Form S-4 is filed with the SEC, at any time it is amended or supplemented or at the time it becomes effective under the Securities Act, contain any untrue statement of a material fact or omit to state any material fact required to be stated therein or necessary to make the statements therein not misleading and (B) the Joint Proxy Statement/ Prospectus (as defined in *Section 5.1*) will, on the date it is first mailed to the Company stockholders or Parent stockholders or at the time of the Company Stockholders Meeting or the Parent Stockholders Meeting (each as defined in *Section 5.1*), contain any untrue statement of a material fact or omit to state any material fact required to be stated therein or necessary in order to make the statements therein, in light of the circumstances under which they were made, not misleading. The Form S-4 and the Joint Proxy Statement/Prospectus will comply as to form in all material respects with the requirements of the Exchange Act and the Securities Act and the rules and regulations of the SEC thereunder.

(ii) Notwithstanding the foregoing provisions of this *Section 3.1(e)*, no representation or warranty is made by Parent with respect to statements made or incorporated by reference in the Form S-4 or the Joint Proxy Statement/Prospectus based on information supplied by the Company for inclusion or incorporation by reference therein.

(f)   *Board Approval*.   The Board of Directors of Parent, by resolutions duly adopted by unanimous vote at a meeting duly called and held and not subsequently rescinded or modified in any way (the "Parent Board Approval"), has duly (i) determined that this Agreement and the Merger are advisable and are fair to and in the best interests of Parent and its stockholders, (ii) approved this Agreement, the Merger, the Certificate Amendment and the Share Issuance and (iii) recommended that the stockholders of Parent approve the Share Issuance and Certificate Amendment and directed that the Share Issuance and the Certificate Amendment be submitted for consideration by Parent's stockholders at the Parent Stockholders Meeting.

(g)   *Vote Required*.   The affirmative vote of a majority of the votes cast by the holders of Parent Common Stock, *provided* that the total votes cast represents a majority of the outstanding shares of Parent Common Stock, is the only vote of the holders of any class or series of Parent capital stock necessary to consummate the Share Issuance. The affirmative vote of a majority of the outstanding shares of Parent Common Stock is the only vote of the holders of any class or series of Parent capital stock necessary to consummate the Certificate Amendment. Other than the votes set forth in this *Section 3.1(g)*, there are no votes of the holders of any class or series of Parent capital stock necessary to consummate any of the transactions contemplated hereby.

(h) *Litigation; Compliance with Laws.*

(i) Except as disclosed in the Parent SEC Reports filed prior to the date of this Agreement, there are no suits, actions or proceedings (collectively "Actions") pending or, to the knowledge of Parent, threatened, against or affecting Parent or any Subsidiary of Parent which, in the aggregate, would reasonably be expected to have a Material Adverse Effect on Parent, nor are there any judgments, decrees, injunctions, rules or orders of any Governmental Entity or arbitrator outstanding against Parent or any Subsidiary of Parent which, in the aggregate, would reasonably be expected to have a Material Adverse Effect on Parent.

(ii) Except as disclosed in the Parent SEC Reports filed prior to the date of this Agreement and except as, in the aggregate, would not reasonably be expected to have a Material Adverse Effect on Parent, Parent and its Subsidiaries hold all permits, licenses, variances, exemptions, orders and approvals of all Governmental Entities which are necessary for the operation of the businesses of Parent and its Subsidiaries, taken as a whole (the "Parent Permits"). Parent and its Subsidiaries are in compliance with the terms of the Parent Permits, except where the failures to so comply, in the aggregate, would not reasonably be expected to have a Material Adverse Effect on Parent. Except as disclosed in the Parent SEC Reports filed prior to the date of this Agreement, neither Parent nor any of its Subsidiaries is in violation of, and Parent and its Subsidiaries have not received any notices of violations with respect to, any laws, ordinances or regulations of any Governmental Entity, except for violations which, in the aggregate, would not reasonably be expected to have a Material Adverse Effect on Parent.

(i) *Absence of Certain Changes or Events.* Except for liabilities incurred in connection with this Agreement or the transactions contemplated hereby, except as disclosed in the Parent SEC Reports filed prior to the date of this Agreement, and except as permitted by *Section 4.1*, since March 31, 2002, (i) Parent and its Subsidiaries have conducted their business only in the ordinary course; (ii) through the date hereof, there has not been any declaration, setting aside or payment of any dividend or other distribution in cash, stock or property in respect of Parent's capital stock, except for dividends or other distributions on its capital stock publicly announced prior to the date hereof; (iii) there has not been any action taken by Parent or any of its Subsidiaries during the period from March 31, 2002 through the date of this Agreement that, if taken during the period from the date of this Agreement through the Effective Time would constitute a breach of *Section 4.1*; and (iv) except as required by GAAP, there has not been any change by Parent in accounting principles, practices or methods. Except as disclosed in the Parent SEC Reports filed prior to the date of this Agreement, since March 31, 2002, there have not been any changes, circumstances or events (including changes, circumstances or events involving, impacting or related to development stage products of Parent) which, in the aggregate, have had, or would reasonably be expected to have, a Material Adverse Effect on Parent.

(j) *Brokers or Finders.* No agent, broker, investment banker, financial advisor or other firm or Person is or will be entitled to any broker's or finder's fee or any other similar commission or fee in connection with any of the transactions contemplated by this Agreement, based upon arrangements made by or on behalf of Parent, except Lazard Freres & Co. LLC and Bear, Stearns & Co. Inc., whose fees and expenses will be paid by Parent.

(k) *Opinions of Parent Financial Advisors.* Parent has received the opinions of Lazard Freres & Co. LLC and Bear, Stearns & Co. Inc., each dated the date of this Agreement, to the effect that, as of such date, the Exchange Ratio is fair to Parent, from a financial point of view, copies of which opinions will be promptly delivered to the Company in connection with the preparation of the necessary regulatory filings.

(l) *Employee Benefit Plans.* Except as disclosed in the Parent SEC Reports, there are no Benefit Plans maintained by Parent covering only Parent executive officers. Each Benefit Plan maintained by Parent has been operated and administered in accordance with its terms and applicable law, except where failure to do so would not reasonably be expected to have a Material Adverse Effect on Parent. The execution of this Agreement and the consummation of the Merger will not constitute an event under any Benefit Plan maintained by Parent that will or may result in any payment, acceleration, forgiveness of indebtedness, vesting, distribution, increase in compensation or benefits or obligation to fund benefits with respect to any Parent employee which, in the aggregate, have had, or would reasonably be expected to have, a Material Adverse Effect on Parent.

(m) *Foreign Corrupt Practices and International Trade Sanctions.* To Parent's knowledge, neither Parent, nor any of its Subsidiaries, nor any of their respective directors, officers, agents, employees or any other Persons acting on their behalf has, in connection with the operation of their respective businesses, (i) used any corporate or other funds for unlawful contributions, payments, gifts or entertainment, or made any unlawful expenditures relating to political activity to government officials, candidates or members of political parties or organizations, or established or maintained any unlawful or unrecorded funds in violation of Section 104 of the Foreign Corrupt Practices Act of 1977, as amended, (the "FCPA") or any other similar applicable foreign, Federal or state law, (ii) paid, accepted or received any unlawful contributions, payments, expenditures or gifts, or (iii) violated or operated in noncompliance with any export restrictions, anti-boycott regulations, embargo regulations or other applicable domestic or foreign laws and regulations, except, in each case, which will not have a Material Adverse Effect on Parent.

(n) *No Restrictions on the Merger; Takeover Statutes.* The Board of Directors of Parent has taken all necessary action to render Section 203 of the DGCL, and any other potentially applicable anti-takeover or similar statute or regulation or provision of the certificate of incorporation or by-laws, or other organizational or constitutive document or governing instruments of Parent or any of its Subsidiaries, inapplicable to this Agreement and the transactions contemplated hereby.

(o) *Environmental Matters.*

(i) Except as, in the aggregate, would not reasonably be expected to have a Material Adverse Effect on Parent and except as disclosed in the Parent SEC Reports filed prior to the date of this Agreement, (i) the operations of Parent and its Subsidiaries have been and are in compliance with all Environmental Laws and with all licenses required by Environmental Laws, (ii) there are no pending or, to the knowledge of Parent, threatened, Environmental Claims under or pursuant to Environmental Laws against Parent or its Subsidiaries or involving any real property currently or, to the knowledge of Parent, formerly owned, operated or leased by Parent or its Subsidiaries, (iii) to the knowledge of Parent, Parent and its Subsidiaries have not incurred any Environmental Liabilities and no facts, circumstances or conditions relating to, arising from, associated with or attributable to any real property currently or, to the knowledge of Parent, formerly owned, operated or leased by Parent or its Subsidiaries or operations thereon would reasonably be expected to result in Environmental Liabilities, (iv) all real property owned and, to the knowledge of Parent, all real property operated or leased by Parent or its Subsidiaries is free of contamination from Hazardous Material that would have an adverse effect on human health or the environment and (v) other than in compliance with any Environmental Laws, there is not now, nor, to the knowledge of Parent, has there been in the past, on, in or under any real property owned, leased or operated by Parent or any of its predecessors (A) any underground storage tanks, regulated pursuant to 40 C.F.R. Part 280 or delegated state programs, dikes or impoundments containing more than a reportable quantity of Hazardous Materials, (B) any friable asbestos-containing materials or (c) any polychlorinated biphenyls.

(ii) For purposes of this *Section 3.1(o)* and *Section 3.2(j)* the following terms shall have the following meanings:

"Environmental Claim" shall mean any and all administrative, regulatory or judicial actions, suits, demands, demand letters, directives, orders, claims, liens, investigations, requests for information, proceedings, or notices of noncompliance or violation (written or oral) by any person (including, without limitation, any governmental authority) alleging liability or potential liability arising out of, based on or resulting from (A) the presence release or disposal or threatened release or disposal, of any Hazardous Materials at any location, or (B) circumstances forming the basis of any violation or alleged violation of any Environmental Law or permit thereunder, or (C) any and all claims by any third party seeking damages, contribution, indemnification, cost recovery, compensation or injunctive relief resulting from exposure to or the presence, release, or disposal or threat thereof of any Hazardous Materials.

"Environmental Law" means any applicable law, regulation, code, license, permit, order, judgment, decree or injunction promulgated by any Governmental Entity, (A) for the protection of the environment (including air, water, soil and natural resources) or (B) regulating the use, storage, handling, release or disposal of any chemical, material, waste or hazardous substance.

"Hazardous Material" means any substance listed, defined, designated or regulated pursuant to any applicable Environmental Law including petroleum products and byproducts, asbestos and polychlorinated biphenyls.

"Environmental Liabilities" means all liabilities, actions, remedial obligations, losses, damages, fines, penalties and sanctions arising under any Environmental Law.

(p) *Intellectual Property.*   Except as, in the aggregate, would not reasonably be expected to have a Material Adverse Effect on Parent and except as disclosed in the Parent SEC Reports filed prior to the date of this Agreement, (i) Parent and each of its Subsidiaries owns, or is licensed to use (in each case, free and clear of any Liens), all Intellectual Property used in or necessary for the conduct of its business as currently conducted; (ii) to the knowledge of Parent, the use of any Intellectual Property by Parent and its Subsidiaries does not infringe on or otherwise violate the rights of any Person and is in accordance with any applicable license pursuant to which Parent or any Subsidiary acquired the right to use any Intellectual Property; (iii) to the knowledge of Parent, no Person is challenging, infringing on or otherwise violating any right of Parent or any of its Subsidiaries with respect to any Intellectual Property owned by and/ or licensed to Parent or itsSubsidiaries; and (iv) neither Parent nor any of its Subsidiaries has received any written notice or otherwise has knowledge of any pending claim, order or proceeding with respect to any Intellectual Property used by Parent and its Subsidiaries and to its knowledge no Intellectual Property owned and/or licensed by Parent or its Subsidiaries is being used or enforced in a manner that would reasonably be expected to result in the abandonment, cancellation or unenforceability of such Intellectual Property. For purposes of this Agreement, "Intellectual Property" shall mean trademarks, service marks, brand names, certification marks, trade dress and other indications of origin, the goodwill associated with the foregoing and registrations in any domestic or foreign jurisdiction of, and applications in any such jurisdiction to register, the foregoing, including any extension, modification or renewal of any such registration or application; inventions, discoveries and ideas, whether patentable or not, in any domestic or foreign jurisdiction; patents, applications for patents (including, without limitation, divisions, continuations, continuations in part and renewal applications), and any renewals, extensions or reissues thereof, in any such jurisdiction; nonpublic information, trade secrets and confidential information and rights in any domestic or foreign jurisdiction to limit the use or disclosure thereof by any person; writings and other works, whether copyrightable or not, in any such jurisdiction; and registrations or applications for registration of copyrights in any domestic or foreign jurisdiction, and any renewals or extensions thereof; and any similar intellectual property or proprietary rights.

(q) *Taxes*

(i) Parent and each of its Subsidiaries has timely filed, or has caused to be timely filed, all Tax Returns required to be filed, and all such Tax Returns are true, complete and accurate, except to the extent any failure to file or any inaccuracies in any filed Tax Returns would not, individually or in the aggregate, have a Material Adverse Effect on Parent. All Taxes shown to be due on such Tax Returns, or otherwise owed, have been or will be timely paid, except to the extent that any failure to pay, individually or in the aggregate, has not had and would not reasonably be expected to have a Material Adverse Effect on Parent.

(ii) The most recent financial statements contained in the Parent SEC Reports reflect an adequate reserve for all Taxes payable by Parent and its Subsidiaries for all Taxable periods and portions thereof through the date of such financial statements . . .

(vi) For purposes of this Agreement:

(A) "Taxes" includes all forms of taxation, whenever created or imposed, and whether of the United States or elsewhere, and whether imposed by a local, municipal, governmental, state, foreign, Federal or other Governmental Entity, or in connection with any agreement with respect to Taxes, including all interest, penalties and additions imposed with respect to such amounts.

(B) "Tax Return" means all Federal, state, local, provincial and foreign Tax returns, declarations, statements, reports, schedules, forms and information returns and any amended Tax return relating to Taxes.

Section 3.2 Representations and Warranties of the Company. Except as set forth in the Company Disclosure Schedule delivered by the Company to Parent prior to the execution of this Agreement (the "Company Disclosure Schedule") (each section of which qualifies the correspondingly numbered representation and warranty or covenant and any other representation or warranty, if the disclosure set forth in the Company Disclosure Schedule is readily applicable to such other representation or warranty), the Company represents and warrants to Parent as follows:

(a) *Organization, Standing and Power; Subsidiaries . . .*

(b) *Capital Structure.*

(i) As of March 31, 2002, the authorized capital stock of the Company consisted of (A) 3,000,000,000 shares of Company Common Stock, of which 1,295,761,753 shares were outstanding and 189,041,409 shares were held in the treasury of the Company, . . . and (C) 1,500,000 shares of Preferred Stock, no par value, which have been designated Series A Junior Participating Preferred Stock and reserved for issuance upon exercise of the rights (the "Company Rights") distributed to the holders of Company Common Stock pursuant to the Amended and Restated Rights Agreement dated as of February 20, 2001, between the Company and Mellon Investor Services LLC (the "Company Rights Agreement"). Since March 31, 2002 to the date of this Agreement, there have been no issuances of shares of the capital stock of the Company or any other securities of the Company . . . All issued and outstanding shares of the capital stock of the Company are duly authorized, validly issued, fully paid and nonassessable, and no class of capital stock is entitled to preemptive rights . . .

(ii) No bonds, debentures, notes or other indebtedness of the Company having the right to vote (or convertible into or exercisable for securities having the right to vote) on any matters on which holders of capital stock of the Company may vote ("Company Voting Debt") are issued or outstanding . . .

(c) *Authority; No Conflicts.*

(i) The Company has all requisite corporate power and authority to enter into this Agreement and to consummate the transactions contemplated hereby, subject in the case of the consummation of the Merger to the adoption of this Agreement by the Company Stockholder Approval (as defined in *Section 3.2(g)*). The execution and delivery of this Agreement and the consummation of the transactions contemplated hereby have been duly authorized by all necessary corporate action on the part of the Company, subject in the case of the consummation of the Merger to the adoption of this Agreement by the Company Stockholder Approval. This Agreement has been duly executed and delivered by the Company and constitutes a valid and binding agreement of the Company, enforceable against it in accordance with its terms, except as such enforceability may be limited by bankruptcy, insolvency, reorganization, moratorium and similar laws relating to or affecting creditors generally or by general equity principles (regardless of whether such enforceability is considered in a proceeding in equity or at law) . . .

(d) *Reports and Financial Statements* . . .

(e) *Information Supplied* . . .

(f) *Board Approval.* The Board of Directors of the Company, by resolutions duly adopted by unanimous vote of those voting at a meeting duly called and held and not subsequently rescinded or modified in any way (the "Company Board Approval"), has duly (i) determined that this Agreement and the Merger are advisable and are fair to and in the best interests of the Company and its stockholders, (ii) approved this Agreement and the Merger and (iii) recommended that the stockholders of the Company adopt this Agreement and directed that this Agreement and the transactions contemplated hereby be submitted for consideration by the Company's stockholders at the Company Stockholders Meeting.

(g) *Vote Required.* The affirmative vote of the holders of a majority of the outstanding shares of Company Common Stock . . . to adopt this Agreement (the "Company Stockholder Approval") is the only vote of the holders of any class or series of the Company capital stock necessary to consummate the transactions contemplated hereby.

(h) *Litigation; Compliance with Laws.* . . .

(i) *Absence of Certain Changes or Events* . . .

(j) *Environmental Matters* . . .

(k) *Intellectual Property* . . .

(l) *Brokers or Finders.* No agent, broker, investment banker, financial advisor or other firm or Person is or will be entitled to any broker's or finder's fee or any other similar commission or fee in connection with any of the transactions contemplated by this Agreement, based upon arrangements made by or on behalf of the Company, except Goldman, Sachs & Co., whose fees and expenses will be paid by the Company.

(m) *Opinions of the Company Financial Advisor.* The Company has received the opinion of Goldman, Sachs & Co., dated the date of this Agreement, to the effect that, as of such date, the Exchange Ratio is fair, from a financial point of view, to the holders of Company Common Stock, copies of which opinions will promptly be provided to Parent.

(n) *Taxes* . . .

(o) *Certain Contracts.* As of the date hereof, except as set forth in the Company SEC Reports filed prior to the date of this Agreement or set forth on *Section 3.2(o)* of the Company Disclosure Schedule, neither the Company nor any of its Subsidiaries is a party to or bound by any "material contracts" (as such term is defined in Item 601 (b) (10) of Regulation S-K of the SEC). Except as set forth on *Schedule 3.2(o)* of the Company Disclosure Schedule, neither the Company nor any of its Subsidiaries is a party to or bound by any noncompetition agreements or any other agreements or arrangements that limit or otherwise restrict the Company or any of its Subsidiaries or any of their respective affiliates or any successor thereto or that would, after the Effective Time, to the knowledge of the Company, limit or restrict Parent or any of its affiliates (including the Surviving Corporation) or any successor thereto, from engaging or competing in any line of business or in any geographic area or, in the case of the pharmaceutical business, any therapeutic area, class of drugs or mechanism of action, that relate to the top 25 marketed products or any development stage product currently in Phase III.

(p) *Employee Benefit Plans.* Section 3.2(p) of the Company Disclosure Schedule, sets forth all U.S. Benefit Plans maintained by the Company or any of its Subsidiaries; all Benefit Plans maintained by the Company or any of its Subsidiaries outside the U.S. will be listed on *Schedule 3.2(p)* by the Company within seven (7) Business Days of the date of this Agreement. Except as disclosed in the Company SEC Reports, there are no Benefit Plans maintained by the Company (each, a "Company Benefit Plan") covering only the Company executive officers. Each Company Benefit Plan has been operated and administered in accordance with its terms and applicable law, except where failure to do so would not reasonably be expected to have a Material Adverse Effect on the Company. The execution of this Agreement and the consummation of the Merger will not constitute an event under any Company Benefit Plan that will or may result in any payment, acceleration, termination, forgiveness of indebtedness, vesting, distribution, increase in compensation or benefits or obligation to fund benefits with respect to any Company employee which, in the aggregate, have had, or would reasonably be expected to have, a Material Adverse Effect on the Company.

(q) *Labor Matters.* Except where failure to comply would not reasonably be expected to have a Material Adverse Effect on the Company, the Company is and has been in compliance with all applicable laws of the United States, or of any state or local government or any subdivision thereof or of any foreign government respecting employment and employment practices, terms and conditions of employment and wages and hours, including, without limitation, ERISA, the Code, the Immigration Reform and Control Act, the WARN Act, any laws respecting employment discrimination, sexual harassment, disability rights or benefits, equal opportunity, plant closure issues, affirmative action, workers' compensation, employee benefits, severance payments, COBRA, labor relations, employee leave issues, wage and hour standards, occupational safety and health requirements and unemployment insurance and related matters, and is not engaged in any unfair labor practices.

(r) *Foreign Corrupt Practices and International Trade Sanctions . . .*

(s) *Company Stockholder Rights Plan.* The Board of Directors of the Company has amended the Company Rights Agreement (the "Rights Agreement Amendment") in accordance with its terms to render it inapplicable to the transactions contemplated by this Agreement. The Company has delivered to the Parent a true and correct copy of the Rights Agreement Amendment.

(t) *Compliance with Co-Promotion Agreements.* The Company has delivered to Parent all material documents filed with governmental authorities as required to be provided to Parent pursuant to the terms of the U.S. Collaboration Agreement (Second Generation), dated as of February 18, 1998, by and among, Parent, the Company (as successor to Monsanto Company) and G.D. Searle & Co., the U.S. Collaboration Agreement (Celocoxib), dated as of February 18, 1998, by and among, Parent, the Company (as successor to Monsanto Company) and G.D. Searle & Co., and any other agreements among Parent, the Company and G.D. Searle & Co. with respect to Cox-2 Second Generation drugs and Celocoxib (collectively, the "Co-Promotion Agreements"). To the knowledge of the Company, these documents comprise all information that would be material to an evaluation of the safety and efficacy of the Cox-2 Second Generation drugs and Celocoxib.

(u) *Monsanto Documents.*   All material agreements (whether written or oral) between the Company and Monsanto have been disclosed in the Company SEC Reports and there has not been any material amendment or change to any such agreements and the Company has not entered into any new material agreements (whether written or oral) with Monsanto since March 31, 2002.

(v) *No Restrictions on the Merger; Takeover Statutes.*   The Board of Directors of the Company has taken all necessary action to render Section 203 of the DGCL, and any other potentially applicable anti-takeover or similar statute or regulation or provision of the certificate of incorporation or by-laws, or other organizational or constitutive document or governing instruments of the Company or any of its Subsidiaries, inapplicable to this Agreement and the transactions contemplated hereby.

Section 3.3   *Representations and Warranties of Parent and Merger Sub.*   Parent and Merger Sub represent and warrant to the Company as follows:

(a) *Organization.*   Merger Sub is a corporation duly incorporated, validly existing and in good standing under the laws of Delaware. Merger Sub is a direct wholly-owned subsidiary of Parent.

(b) *Corporate Authorization.*   Merger Sub has all requisite corporate power and authority to enter into this Agreement and to consummate the transactions contemplated hereby. The execution, delivery and performance by Merger Sub of this Agreement and the consummation by Merger Sub of the transactions contemplated hereby have been duly authorized by all necessary corporate action on the part of Merger Sub. This Agreement has been duly executed and delivered by Merger Sub and constitutes a valid and binding agreement of Merger Sub, enforceable against it in accordance with its terms, except as such enforceability may be limited by bankruptcy, insolvency, reorganization, moratorium and other similar laws relating to or affecting creditors generally or by general equity principles (regardless of whether such enforceability is considered in a proceeding in equity or at law). The copies of the certificate of incorporation and bylaws of Merger Sub which were previously furnished or made available to the Company are true, complete and correct copies of such documents as in effect on the date of this Agreement.

(c) *Non-Contravention.*   The execution, delivery and performance by Merger Sub of this Agreement and the consummation by Merger Sub of the transactions contemplated hereby do not and will not contravene or conflict with the certificate of incorporation or bylaws of Merger Sub or any law binding on Merger Sub.

(d) *No Business Activities.*   Merger Sub has not conducted any activities other than in connection with the organization of Merger Sub, the negotiation and execution of this Agreement and the consummation of the transactions contemplated hereby. Merger Sub has no Subsidiaries.

(e) *Capitalization of Merger Sub.*   The authorized capital stock of Merger Sub consists of 1,000 shares of common stock, par value $0.01 per share, all of which are validly issued and outstanding. All of the issued and outstanding capital stock of Merger Sub is, and at the Effective Time will be, owned by Parent, and there are (i) no other shares of capital stock or voting securities of

Merger Sub, (ii) no securities of Merger Sub convertible into or exchangeable for shares of capital stock or voting securities of Merger Sub and (iii) no options or other rights to acquire from Merger Sub, and no obligations of Merger Sub to issue, any capital stock, voting securities or securities convertible into or exchangeable for capital stock or voting securities of Merger Sub.

ARTICLE IV
COVENANTS RELATING TO CONDUCT OF BUSINESS

Section 4.1   Covenants of Parent.   During the period from the date of this Agreement and continuing until the Effective Time, Parent agrees as to itself and its Subsidiaries that (except as expressly contemplated or permitted by this Agreement or as disclosed in the Parent Disclosure Schedule or as required by a Governmental Entity of competent jurisdiction or to the extent that the Company shall otherwise consent in writing):

(a)   *Ordinary Course.*   Parent and its Subsidiaries shall carry on their respective businesses in the usual, regular and ordinary course in all material respects, in substantially the same manner as heretofore conducted, and shall use reasonable best efforts to preserve intact their present lines of business, maintain their rights and franchises and preserve their relationships with customers, suppliers and others having business dealings with them; . . .

(b)   *Dividends.*   Parent shall not, and shall not permit any of its Subsidiaries to, and shall not propose to, declare or pay any dividends or distributions on or make other distributions in respect of any of its capital stock, except (i) the declaration and payment of regular quarterly cash dividends not in excess of the amount set forth in *Section 4.1 (b)* of the Parent Disclosure Schedule per share of Parent Common Stock with usual record and payment dates for such dividends in accordance with past dividend practice and (ii) for dividends by wholly owned Subsidiaries of Parent.

(c)   *Governing Documents.*   Except to the extent required to comply with applicable law or their obligations hereunder, Parent and Merger Sub shall not amend or propose to so amend their respective certificates of incorporation, bylaws or other governing documents.

(d)   *No Acquisitions.*   Other than (i) acquisitions disclosed on the Parent Disclosure Schedule and (ii) acquisitions for cash in existing or related lines of business of Parent the fair market value of the total consideration (including the value of indebtedness acquired or assumed) for which does not exceed the amount that would be material to the business and assets of the Parent and its Subsidiaries, taken as a whole, Parent shall not, and shall not permit any of its Subsidiaries to, acquire or agree to acquire by merging or consolidating with, or by purchasing a substantial equity interest in or a substantial portion of the assets of, or by any other manner, any business (including by acquisition of assets) or any corporation, partnership, association or business organization or division thereof; . . .

(e)   *Accounting Methods.*   Except as disclosed in Parent SEC Reports filed prior to the date of this Agreement, or as required by a Governmental Entity, Parent shall not change its methods of accounting in effect at March 31, 2002, except as required by changes in GAAP as concurred in by Parent's independent public accountants . . .

Section 4.2   Covenants of the Company.   During the period from the date of this Agreement and continuing until the Effective Time, the Company agrees as to itself and its Subsidiaries that (except as expressly contemplated or permitted by this Agreement, as disclosed in the Company Disclosure Schedule or as required by a Governmental Entity of competent jurisdiction or to the extent that Parent shall otherwise consent in writing):

(a)   *Ordinary Course.*

(i) The Company and its Subsidiaries shall carry on their respective businesses in the usual, regular and ordinary course in all material respects, in substantially the same manner as heretofore conducted, and shall use reasonable best efforts to preserve intact their present lines of business, maintain their rights and franchises and preserve their relationships with customers, suppliers and others having business dealings with them; . . .

(ii) Other than in connection with acquisitions and activities permitted by *Section 4.2(e)*, the Company shall not, and shall not permit any of its Subsidiaries to, (A) enter into any licensing agreement, except for licensing agreements set forth in *Section 4.2(a) (ii)* of the Company Disclosure Schedule and, subject to *Section 4.2(e)*, any licensing agreement relating to the non-pharmaceutical licenses of the Company entered into in the ordinary course of business, (B) enter into or terminate any "material contract" as such term is defined in Item 601 (b) (10) of Regulation S-K of the SEC or agreement or make any change in any material lease or contract, other than in the ordinary course of business; (C) enter into any new line of business; (D) incur or commit to any capital expenditures or any obligations or liabilities in connection therewith other than Permitted Capital Expenditures (as defined below) and obligations or liabilities in connection therewith, (E) with respect to the pharmaceutical and consumer healthcare businesses, enter into any contract, agreement or other arrangement for the sale of products or inventories or for the furnishing of services by the Company or any of its Subsidiaries which contract, agreement or other arrangement involves amounts or expenditures in excess of $20 million or which may give rise to commitments which may extend beyond twelve months from the date of such contract, agreement or arrangement, unless, such contract, agreement or arrangement can be terminated by the Company or its Subsidiary, as the case may be, by giving less than 60 days' notice and without incurring an obligation to pay any material premium or penalty or suffering any other material detriment, or (F) with respect to the pharmaceutical business, enter into an agreement to provide rebates or discounts to public, governmental, or private entities, unless such agreement is able to be terminated within one year without penalty and the rebates or discounts therein do not differ significantly from prior arrangements or agreements. As used herein, a "Permitted Capital Expenditure" is a capital expenditure which (i) is set forth on a Capital Expenditure Schedule to be delivered by the Company as contemplated by the Company Disclosure Schedule or (ii) is (A) less than $20 million in the case of any single expenditure or related series of expenditures and (B) $100 million in the aggregate for all capital expenditures incurred pursuant to this clause (ii) and not clause (i). The Company will deliver to Parent on a quarterly basis a schedule of actual capital expenditures made.

(b) *Dividends, Changes in Share Capital.* The Company shall not, and shall not permit any of its Subsidiaries to, and shall not propose to, (i) declare or pay any dividends on or make other distributions in respect of any of its capital stock, except (A) the declaration and payment of regular quarterly cash dividends not in excess of $0.135 per share of Company Common Stock . . . in accordance with past dividend practice; (B) dividends or distributions by wholly owned Subsidiaries of the Company, (C) dividends or distributions from Monsanto to the Company, and (D) any stock dividend or distribution by the Company to effect the Monsanto Spin-Off; (ii) split, combine or reclassify any of its capital stock or issue or authorize or propose the issuance of any other securities in respect of, in lieu of or in substitution for, shares of its capital stock, except for any such transaction by a wholly owned Subsidiary of the Company which remains a wholly owned Subsidiary after consummation of such transaction, . . .

(c) *Issuance of Securities.* The Company shall not, and shall not permit any of its Subsidiaries to, issue, deliver or sell, or authorize or propose the issuance, delivery or sale of, any shares of its capital stock of any class, any Company Voting Debt or any securities convertible into or exercisable for, or any rights, warrants, calls or options to acquire, any such shares or Company Voting Debt, . . .

(d) *Governing Documents.* Except to the extent required to comply with its obligations hereunder or with applicable law, the Company shall not amend or propose to so amend its certificate of incorporation or bylaws.

(e) *No Acquisitions.* Other than (i) acquisitions disclosed on the Company Disclosure Schedule and (ii) acquisitions for cash in existing or related lines of business of the Company and its Subsidiaries, the fair market value of the total consideration (including the value of indebtedness acquired or assumed) for which does not exceed $20 million for any individual acquisition, or $100 million in the aggregate for all such acquisitions, the Company shall not, and shall not permit any of its Subsidiaries to, acquire or agree to acquire by merging or consolidating with, or by purchasing a substantial equity interest in or a substantial portion of the assets of, or by any other manner, any business (including by acquisition of assets) or any corporation, partnership, association or other business organization or division thereof; . . .

(f) *No Dispositions.* Other than (i) internal reorganizations or consolidations involving existing Subsidiaries of the Company, (ii) dispositions referred to in the Company SEC Reports filed prior to the date of this Agreement, (iii) as may be required by or in conformance with law or regulation in order to permit or facilitate the consummation of the transactions contemplated hereby or the transactions disclosed in the Company Disclosure Schedule, (iv) the sale or disposition of assets or stock of Monsanto, or (v) the Monsanto Spin-Off, the Company shall not, and shall not permit any of its Subsidiaries to, sell, lease or otherwise dispose of, or agree to sell, lease or otherwise dispose of, any of its assets (including capital stock of Subsidiaries of the Company but excluding inventory in the ordinary course of business), if the fair market value of the total consideration (including the value of the indebtedness acquired or assumed) therefor exceeds $20 million for any individual disposition, or $100 million in the aggregate for all such dispositions.

(g) *Investments, Indebtedness . . .*

(h) *Compensation.* Other than as contemplated by *Sections 4.2 (c)* or *4.2 (h)* of the Company Disclosure Schedule, the Company shall not increase the amount of compensation of any director, executive officer or employee, make any increase in or commitment to increase any employee benefits, . . . and, in the case of any of the foregoing, except, in any case, in the ordinary course of business consistent with past practice or as required by an existing agreement.

(i) *Accounting Methods; Income Tax Elections.* Except as disclosed in the Company SEC Reports filed prior to the date of this Agreement, or as required by a Governmental Entity, the Company shall not change its methods of accounting in effect at March 31, 2002, except as required by changes in GAAP as concurred in by the Company's independent public accountants. The Company shall not (i) change its fiscal year or (ii) make or change any material tax election, settle or compromise any material tax liability or claim for refund, without the prior written consent of Parent.

(j) *Certain Agreements . . .*

(k) *Monsanto Separation Agreements.* Neither the Company nor its Subsidiaries shall amend, modify, alter, supplement or terminate the Separation Agreement, the Tax Sharing Agreement, the Corporate Agreement, the Intellectual Property Transfer Agreement, the Services Agreement or the Employee Benefits and Compensation Allocation Agreement, each agreement dated as of September , 2000 and by and between the Company and Monsanto and the Protocol Agreement, dated as of July 1, 2002, by and among the Company, Monsanto and Solutia Inc. (collectively and each as amended through the date hereof, the "Separation Agreements"), other than, in any such case, for technical or ministerial amendments necessary or appropriate to effect the Monsanto SpinOff.

(l) *Settlement of Litigation.* The Company shall not settle or compromise any material action, suit or claim, or enter into any consent decree, injunction or similar restraint or form of equitable relief in settlement of any material action, suit or claim . . .

Section 4.3 Monsanto Indebtedness.

(a) The Company will use its reasonable best efforts consistent with its obligation to effectuate the Monsanto Spin-Off, to collect all outstanding indebtedness from Monsanto and Monsanto's subsidiaries and the release of all guarantees of other Monsanto obligations to other parties (collectively, "Monsanto Indebtedness"), other than current obligations for services provided to Monsanto pursuant to any agreements between the Company and Monsanto for the provision of services. The amount of Monsanto Indebtedness as of the date hereof is not greater than $650 million. The Company shall not invest in or lend any additional funds or extend further guarantees to Monsanto or to third parties on behalf of Monsanto . . .

Section 4.4 Governmental Filings. Each party shall (a) confer on a regular basis with the other and (b) report to the other (to the extent permitted by law or regulation or any applicable confidentiality agreement) on material operational matters . . .

Section 4.5 Control of Other Party's Business. Nothing contained in this Agreement shall give the Company, directly or indirectly, the right to control or direct Parent's operations prior to the Effective Time. Nothing contained in this Agreement shall give Parent, directly or indirectly, the right to control or direct the Company's operations prior to the Effective Time. Prior to the Effective Time, each of the Company and Parent shall exercise, consistent with the terms and conditions of this Agreement, complete control and supervision over its respective operations . . .

ARTICLE V
ADDITIONAL AGREEMENTS

Section 5.1 Preparation of Proxy Statement; Stockholders Meetings.
(a) As promptly as reasonably practicable following the date hereof, Parent and the Company shall prepare and file with the SEC mutually acceptable proxy materials which shall constitute the Joint Proxy Statement/ Prospectus (such proxy statement/prospectus, and any amendments or supplements thereto, the "Joint Proxy Statement/Prospectus") and Parent shall prepare and file a registration statement on Form S-4 with respect to the issuance of Parent Common Stock in the Merger (the "Form S-4"). The Joint Proxy Statement/Prospectus will be included in and will constitute a part of the Form S-4 as Parent's prospectus. The Form S-4 and the Joint Proxy Statement/Prospectus shall comply as to form in all material respects with the applicable provisions of the Securities Act and the Exchange Act and the rules and regulations thereunder. Each of Parent and the Company shall use reasonable best efforts to have the Form S-4 declared effective by the SEC as promptly as practicable after the date hereof and to keep the Form S-4 effective as long as is necessary to consummate the Merger and the transactions contemplated thereby. Parent and the Company shall, as promptly as practicable after receipt thereof, provide the other party copies of any written comments and advise the other party of any oral comments, with respect to the Joint Proxy Statement/Prospectus received from the SEC. Parent shall provide the Company with a reasonable opportunity to review and comment on any amendment or supplement to the Form S-4 prior to filing such with the SEC, and will promptly provide the Company with a copy of all such filings made with the SEC. Notwithstanding any other provision herein to the contrary, no amendment or supplement (including by incorporation by reference) to the Joint Proxy Statement/Prospectus or the Form S-4 shall be made without the approval of both parties, which approval shall not be unreasonably withheld or delayed; *provided*, that with respect to documents filed by a party which are incorporated by reference in the Form S-4 or Joint Proxy Statement/Prospectus, this right of approval shall apply only with respect to information relating to the other party or its business, financial condition or results of operations; and *provided, further*, that Parent, in connection with a Change in the Parent Recommendation (as defined in *Section 5.1(c)*), and the Company, in connection with a Change in the Company Recommendation (as defined in *Section 5.1(b)*), may amend or supplement the Joint Proxy

Statement/Prospectus or Form S-4 (including by incorporation by reference) pursuant to a Qualifying Amendment (as defined below) to effect such a Change, and in such event, this right of approval shall apply only with respect to information relating to the other party or its business, financial condition or results of operations, and shall be subject to the right of each party to have its Board of Directors' deliberations and conclusions accurately described. A "Qualifying Amendment" means an amendment or supplement to the Joint Proxy Statement/Prospectus or Form S-4 (including by incorporation by reference) to the extent it contains (i) a Change in the Parent Recommendation or a Change in the Company Recommendation (as the case may be), (ii) a statement of the reasons of the Board of Directors of Parent or the Company (as the case may be) for making such Change in the Parent Recommendation or Change in the Company Recommendation (as the case may be) and (iii) additional information reasonably related to the foregoing. Parent will use reasonable best efforts to cause the Joint Proxy Statements/Prospectus to be mailed to Parent stockholders, and the Company will use reasonable best efforts to cause the Joint Proxy Statement/Prospectus to be mailed to the Company's stockholders, in each case, as soon as reasonably practicable after the Form S-4 is declared effective under the Securities Act. Parent shall also take any action (other than qualifying to do business in any jurisdiction in which it is not now so qualified or to file a general consent to service of process) required to be taken under any applicable state securities laws in connection with the Share Issuance and the Company shall furnish all information concerning the Company and the holders of Company Common Stock as may be reasonably requested in connection with any such action . . .

(b)   The Company shall duly take (subject to compliance with the provisions of *Section 3.1(e)* and *Section 3.2(e)* (*provided* that the Company shall have used reasonable best efforts to ensure that such representations are true and correct)) all lawful action to call, give notice of, convene and hold a meeting of its stockholders on a date as soon as reasonably practicable (the "Company Stockholders Meeting") for the purpose of obtaining the Company Stockholder Approval with respect to the adoption of this Agreement and shall take all lawful action to solicit the adoption of this Agreement by the Company Stockholder Approval; and the Board of Directors of the Company shall recommend adoption of this Agreement by the stockholders of the Company to the effect as set forth in *Section 3.2(f)* (the "Company Recommendation"), and shall not withdraw, modify or qualify (or propose to withdraw, modify or qualify) (a "Change") in any manner adverse to Parent such recommendation or take any action or make any statement in connection with the Company Stockholders Meeting inconsistent with such recommendation (collectively, a "Change in the Company Recommendation"); *provided* the foregoing shall not prohibit accurate disclosure (and such disclosure shall not be deemed to be a Change in the Company Recommendation) of factual information regarding the business, financial condition or results of operations of Parent or the Company or the fact that an Acquisition Proposal has been made, the identity of the party making such proposal or the material terms of such proposal (*provided*, that the Board of Directors of the Company does not withdraw, modify or qualify (or propose to withdraw, modify or qualify) in any manner adverse to Parent its recommendation) in the Form S-4 or the Joint Proxy

Statement/Prospectus or otherwise, to the extent such information, facts, identity or terms is required to be disclosed under applicable law; and, *provided further*, that the Board of Directors of the Company may make a Change in the Company Recommendation (x) pursuant to *Section 5.4* hereof or (y) prior to the Company Stockholders Meeting if the Board of Directors of the Company determines in good faith that a Material Adverse Effect has occurred with respect to Parent. Notwithstanding any Change in the Company Recommendation, this Agreement shall be submitted to the stockholders of the Company at the Company Stockholders Meeting for the purpose of adopting the Agreement and approving the Merger, *provided* that this Agreement shall not be required to be submitted to the stockholders of the Company at the Company Stockholders Meeting if this Agreement has been terminated pursuant to *Section 7.1* hereof.

(c)   Parent shall duly take (subject to compliance with the provisions of *Section 3.2(e)* and *Section 3.1(e)* (*provided* that Parent shall have used reasonable best efforts to ensure that such representations are true and correct)) all lawful action to call, give notice of, convene and hold a meeting of its stockholders on a date as soon as reasonably practicable (the "Parent Stockholders Meeting") for the purpose of obtaining the Parent Stockholder Approval with respect to the approval of the Share Issuance and Certificate Amendment and shall take all lawful action to solicit the approval of the Share Issuance and Certificate Amendment by the Parent Stockholder Approval and the Board of Directors of Parent shall recommend approval of each of the Share Issuance and Certificate Amendment by the stockholders of Parent to the effect as set forth in *Section 3.1(f)* (the "Parent Recommendation"), and shall not Change in any manner adverse to the Company such recommendation or take any action or make any statement in connection with the Parent Stockholders Meeting inconsistent with such recommendation (collectively, a "Change in the Parent Recommendation"); *provided* the foregoing shall not prohibit accurate disclosure (and such disclosure shall not be deemed to be a Change in the Parent Recommendation) of factual information regarding the business, financial condition or operations of Parent or the Company (*provided*, that the Board of Directors of Parent does not withdraw, modify or qualify (or propose to withdraw, modify or qualify) in any manner adverse to the Company its recommendation) in the Form S-4 or the Joint Proxy Statement/Prospectus or otherwise, to the extent such information, facts, identity or terms is required to be disclosed under applicable law; and *provided further*, that the Board of Directors of Parent may make a Change in the Parent Recommendation prior to the Parent Stockholders Meeting if the Board of Directors of Parent determines in good faith that a Material Adverse Effect has occurred with respect to the Company. Notwithstanding any Change in the Parent Recommendation, a proposal to approve the Share Issuance and Certificate Amendment shall be submitted to the stockholders of Parent at the Parent Stockholders Meeting for the purpose of obtaining the Parent Stockholder Approval; *provided* that this Agreement shall not be required to be submitted to the stockholders of Parent at the Parent Stockholders Meeting if this Agreement has been terminated pursuant to *Section 7.1* hereof.

(d)   For purposes of this Agreement, a Change in the Company Recommendation shall be deemed to include, without limitation, a recommendation by the Company Board of Directors of a third party Acquisition Proposal with respect to the Company.

Section 5.2   Access to Information/Employees.

(a) Upon reasonable notice, each party shall (and shall cause its Subsidiaries to) afford to the officers, employees, accountants, counsel, financial advisors and other authorized representatives of the other party reasonable access during normal business hours, during the period prior to the Effective Time, to all its properties, books, contracts, commitments, records, officers and employees . . . Any such information obtained pursuant to this *Section 5.2* ("Confidential Information") will be used solely for the purpose of consideration or performance of the transactions contemplated by this Agreement or any other agreement related hereto and will be kept confidential by the party obtaining such information and all persons obtaining such information on such party's behalf or who obtain such information from such party . . . In the event of termination of this Agreement, each party will promptly return to the other party all Confidential Information in its possession (including all written materials prepared or supplied by or on its behalf containing or reflecting any Confidential Information) and will not retain any copies, extracts or other reproductions in whole or in part of any Confidential Information. Any work papers, memoranda or other writings prepared by a party or its Representatives derived from or incorporating any Confidential Information shall be destroyed promptly upon termination of this Agreement, with such destruction confirmed to the other party in writing. Any oral Confidential Information will continue to be subject to the terms of this *Section 5.2* . . . In the event of any conflict between the terms of this *Section 5.2* and the terms of the Confidentiality Agreement, the terms of the Confidentiality Agreement shall control.

(b) After the date hereof, Parent and the Company shall establish a mechanism reasonably acceptable to both parties by which Parent will be permitted, prior to the Effective Time and subject to applicable law, to communicate directly with the Company employees regarding employee related matters after the Effective Time.

Section 5.3   Reasonable Best Efforts.

(a) Subject to the terms and conditions of this Agreement, each party will use its reasonable best efforts to take, or cause to be taken, all actions and to do, or cause to be done, all things necessary, proper or advisable under this Agreement and applicable laws and regulations to consummate the Merger and the other transactions contemplated by this Agreement as soon as practicable after the date hereof, including (i) preparing and filing as promptly as practicable all documentation to effect all necessary applications, notices, petitions, filings, tax ruling requests and other documents and to obtain as promptly as practicable all consents, clearances, waivers, licenses, orders, registrations, approvals, permits, tax rulings and authorizations necessary or advisable to be obtained from any third party and/or any Governmental Entity in order to consummate the Merger or any of the other transactions contemplated by this Agreement and (ii) taking all reasonable steps as may be necessary to obtain all such material consents, clearances, waivers, licenses, registrations, permits, authorizations, tax rulings, orders and approvals. In furtherance and not in limitation of the foregoing, each party hereto agrees to make an appropriate filing of a Notification and Report Form pursuant to the HSR Act and any other Regulatory Law (as defined in *Section 5.3(b)* below) with respect to the transactions contemplated hereby as promptly as practicable after the date hereof and to supply as promptly as practicable any additional information and documentary material that may be requested pursuant to the HSR Act and any other Regulatory Law and to take all other actions necessary to cause the expiration or termination of the applicable waiting periods under the HSR Act as soon as practicable . . .

(b) To the extent permissible under applicable law or any rule, regulation or restriction of a Governmental Entity, each of Parent and the Company shall, in connection with the efforts referenced in *Section 5.3(a)* to obtain all requisite material approvals, clearances and authorizations for the transactions contemplated by this Agreement under the HSR Act or any other Regulatory Law, use its reasonable best efforts to (i) cooperate in all respects with each other in connection with any filing or submission and in connection with any investigation or other inquiry, including any proceeding initiated by a private party, (ii) promptly inform the other party of any communication received by such party from, or given by such party to, the Antitrust Division of the Department of Justice (the "DOJ"), the Federal Trade Commission (the "FTC") or any other Governmental Entity and of any material communication received or given in connection with any proceeding by a private party, in each case regarding any of the transactions contemplated hereby, (iii) permit the other party, or the other party's legal counsel, to review any communication given by it to, and consult with each other in advance of any meeting or conference with, the DOJ, the FTC or any such other Governmental Entity or, in connection with any proceeding by a private party, with any other Person and (iv) give the other party the opportunity to attend and participate in such meetings and conferences. For purposes of this Agreement, "Regulatory Law" means the Sherman Act, as amended, Council Regulation No. 4064/89 of the European Community, as amended (the "EC Merger Regulation") the Clayton Act, as amended, the HSR Act, the Federal Trade Commission Act, as amended, and all other Federal, state and foreign, if any, statutes, rules, regulations, orders, decrees, administrative and judicial doctrines and other laws that are designed or intended to prohibit, restrict or regulate (i) foreign investment or (ii) actions having the purpose or effect of monopolization or restraint of trade or lessening of competition.

(c) If any objections are asserted with respect to the transactions contemplated hereby under any Regulatory Law or if any suit is instituted by any Governmental Entity or any private party challenging any of the transactions contemplated hereby as violative of any Regulatory Law, each of Parent and the Company shall use its reasonable best efforts to resolve any such objections or challenge as such Governmental Entity or private party may have to such transactions under such Regulatory Law so as to permit consummation of the transactions contemplated by this Agreement.

Section 5.4 Acquisition Proposals. The Company agrees that neither it nor any of its Subsidiaries nor any of the officers and directors of it or its

Subsidiaries shall, and that it shall use its reasonable best efforts to cause its and its Subsidiaries' employees, agents and representatives (including any investment banker, attorney or accountant retained by it or any of its Subsidiaries) not to, directly or indirectly, initiate, solicit, encourage or knowingly facilitate (including by way of furnishing information) any inquiries or the making of any proposal or offer with respect to a merger, reorganization, share exchange, consolidation, business combination, recapitalization, liquidation, dissolution or similar transaction involving it, or any purchase or sale of the consolidated assets (including without limitation stock of Subsidiaries) of the Company and its Subsidiaries, taken as a whole, having an aggregate value equal to 15% or more of the market capitalization of the Company, or any purchase or sale of, or tender or exchange offer for, 15% or more of the equity securities of the Company (any such proposal or offer (other than a proposal or offer made by the other party or an affiliate thereof) being hereinafter referred to as an "Acquisition Proposal"). The Company further agrees that neither it nor any of its Subsidiaries nor any of the officers and directors of it or its Subsidiaries shall, and that it shall use its reasonable best efforts to cause its and its Subsidiaries' employees, agents and representatives (including any investment banker, attorney or accountant retained by it or any of its Subsidiaries) not to, directly or indirectly, have any discussion with or provide any confidential information or data to any Person relating to an Acquisition Proposal, or engage in any negotiations concerning an Acquisition Proposal, or knowingly facilitate any effort or attempt to make or implement an Acquisition Proposal or (subject to *Section 7.1(h)*) accept an Acquisition Proposal. Notwithstanding anything in this Agreement to the contrary, the Company and the Company's Board of Directors shall be permitted to (A) to the extent applicable, comply with Rule 14d-9 and Rule 14e-2 promulgated under the Exchange Act with regard to an Acquisition Proposal, (B) effect a Change in the Company Recommendation, or (C) engage in any discussions or negotiations with, or provide any information to, any Person in response to an unsolicited bona fide written Acquisition Proposal by any such Person, if and only to the extent that, with respect to the actions contemplated by *clauses (B)* or *(C)*, (i) the Company's Stockholders Meeting shall not have occurred, (ii) (x) in the case of *clause (B)* above, (I) such change is permitted by *clause (y)* of the second proviso of the first sentence of *Section 5.1 (b)* or (II) the Company has received an unsolicited bona fide written Acquisition Proposal from a third party and the Company's Board of Directors concludes in good faith that such Acquisition Proposal constitutes a Superior Proposal (as defined in *Section 8.11*) and (y) in the case of *clause (C)* above, the Company's Board of Directors concludes in good faith that there is a reasonable likelihood that such Acquisition Proposal could result in a Superior Proposal, (iii) in the case of *clause (C)* above, prior to providing any information or data to any Person in connection with an Acquisition Proposal by any such Person, the Company's Board of Directors receives from such Person an executed confidentiality agreement containing terms at least as stringent as those contained in *Section 5.2* and (iv) in the case of *clause (C)* above, prior to providing any information or data to any Person or entering into discussions or negotiations with any Person, the Company notifies Parent promptly of such inquiries, proposals or offers received by, any such information requested from, or any such discussions or negotiations sought to be initiated or continued with, any of its representatives indicating, in connection with such notice, the name of such Person and the material terms and conditions of any inquiries, proposals or offers. The Company agrees that it will promptly keep Parent informed of the status and terms of any such proposals or offers and the status and terms of any such discussions or negotiations. The Company agrees that it will, and will cause its officers, directors and representatives to, immediately cease and cause to be terminated any activities, discussions or negotiations existing as of the date of this Agreement with any parties conducted heretofore with respect to any Acquisition Proposal. The Company agrees that it will use reasonable best efforts to promptly inform its directors, officers, key employees, agents and representatives of the obligations undertaken in this *Section 5.4*. Nothing in this *Section 5.4* shall (x) permit Parent or the Company to terminate this Agreement (except as specifically provided in *Article VII* hereof) or (y) affect any other obligation of Parent or the Company under this Agreement.

Section 5.5 *Employee Benefits Matters.*

(a) At the Effective Time, Parent shall provide employment to, or shall cause the Surviving Corporation to provide employment to, employees who were employed by the Company or its Subsidiaries as of the Effective Time ("Continuing Employees"). Nothing contained herein shall be deemed to guarantee employment for any period of time or preclude the Parent's ability to terminate any Continuing Employee for any reason subsequent to the Effective Time. Except as may be otherwise required by law, nothing contained herein shall require Parent to continue any particular Company Benefit Plan or compensation plan, program or arrangement, or prevent the amendment, modification or termination thereof; *provided* that Parent shall not take any action or cause the Surviving Corporation to take any action (by way of amendment, termination or otherwise) which is in violation of the terms of any Company Benefit Plan. From and after the Effective Time until the second anniversary of the Effective Time (the "Benefits Continuation Period"), Parent shall provide, or shall cause the Surviving Corporation to provide compensation and employee benefits to the Continuing Employees and former employees of the Company and its Subsidiaries ("Former Employees") which are substantially comparable in the aggregate to those provided to such individuals by the Company and its Subsidiaries immediately prior to the Effective Time; provided, however, that with respect to employees who are subject to collective bargaining, compensation and benefits shall be provided in accordance with the applicable collective bargaining agreements. Following the Benefits Continuation Period, Parent shall provide, or shall cause the Surviving Corporation to provide, compensation and benefits that are substantially comparable in the aggregate to those provided to similarly situated employees of Parent.

(b) During the Benefits Continuation Period, Parent shall continue, or shall cause the Surviving Corporation to continue, the severance and post-retirement medical and dental benefits provided by the Company and its Subsidiaries immediately prior to the Effective Time as provided in the Pharmacia Separation Benefit Plans, as amended through July 9, 2002 . . .

(d)   From and after the Effective Time, Parent shall honor, fulfill and discharge and shall cause the Surviving Corporation to honor, fulfill and discharge, in accordance with its terms, each Company Benefit Plan and related funding arrangement, including each employment, change in control, severance and' termination agreement between the Company or any of its Subsidiaries and any officer, director or employee of such company, including without limitation (i) all legal and contractual obligations pursuant to outstanding retirement plans, salary and bonus deferral plans, vested and accrued benefits and similar employment and benefit arrangements and agreements in effect as of the Effective Time, including all the "change in control" provisions under the Company Benefit Plans, and (ii) all vacation, personal and sick days accrued by Continuing Employees and Former Employees as of the Effective Time.

Section 5.6   Fees and Expenses.   Subject to *Section 7.2*, whether or not the Merger is consummated, all Expenses incurred in connection with this Agreement and the transactions contemplated hereby shall be paid by the party incurring such Expenses, except (a) if the Merger is consummated, the Surviving Corporation or its relevant Subsidiary shall pay, or cause to be paid, any and all property or transfer taxes imposed on the Company or its Subsidiaries and (b) Expenses incurred in connection with the filing, printing and mailing of the Joint Proxy Statement/Prospectus, which shall be paid 50% by Parent and 50% by the Company. As used in this Agreement, "Expenses" includes all out-of-pocket expenses (including, without limitation, all fees and expenses of counsel, accountants, investment bankers, experts and consultants to a party hereto and its affiliates) incurred by a party or on its behalf in connection with or related to the authorization, preparation, negotiation, execution and performance of this Agreement and the transactions contemplated hereby, including the preparation, printing, filing and mailing of the Joint Proxy Statement/ Prospectus and the solicitation of stockholder approvals and all other matters related to the transactions contemplated hereby.

Section 5.7   Directors' and Officers' Indemnification and Insurance.
(a)   From and after the Effective Time the Parent agrees that it will (i) indemnify and hold harmless, against any costs or expenses (including attorney's fees), judgments, fines, losses, claims damages or liabilities incurred in connection with any claim, action, suit, proceeding or investigation, whether civil, criminal, administrative or investigative, and provide advancement of expenses to, all past and present directors, officers and employees of the Company and its Subsidiaries (in all of their capacities) (a) to the same extent such persons are indemnified or have the right to advancement of expenses as of the date of this Agreement by the Company pursuant to the Company's certificate of incorporation, bylaws and indemnification agreements, if any, in existence on the date hereof with any directors, officers and employees of the Company and its Subsidiaries and (b) without limitation to *clause (a)*, to the fullest extent permitted by law, in each case, for acts or omissions at or prior to the Effective Time (including for acts or omissions occurring in connection with the approval of this Agreement and the consummation of the transactions contemplated hereby), (ii) include and cause to

be maintained in effect in the Surviving Corporation's (or any successor's) certificate of incorporation and bylaws for a period of six years after the Effective Time, the current provisions regarding elimination of liability of directors, indemnification of officers, directors and employees and advancement of expenses contained in the certificate of incorporation and bylaws of the Company and (iii) cause to be maintained for a period of six years after the Effective Time the current policies of directors' and officers' liability insurance and fiduciary liability insurance maintained by the Company (*provided* that Parent (or any successor) may substitute therefor policies of at least the same coverage and amounts containing terms and conditions which are, in the aggregate, no less advantageous to the insured) with respect to claims arising from facts or events that occurred on or before the Effective Time (including for acts or omissions occurring in connection with the approval of this Agreement and the consummation of the transactions contemplated hereby). The obligations of Parent under this *Section 5.7* shall not be terminated or modified in such a manner as to adversely affect any indemnitee to whom this *Section 5.7* applies without the consent of such affected indemnitee (it being expressly agreed that the indemnities to whom this *Section 5.7* applies shall be third party beneficiaries of this *Section 5.7*).

(b)   If Parent or any of its successors or assigns (i) shall consolidate with or merge into any other corporation or entity and shall not be the continuing or surviving corporation or entity of such consolidation or merger or (ii) shall transfer all or substantially all of its properties and assets to any individual, corporation or other entity, then, and in each such case, proper provisions shall be made so that the successors and assigns of Parent shall assume all of the obligations set forth in this *Section 5.7.*

Section 5.8 Public Announcements. Parent and the Company shall use reasonable best efforts to develop a joint communications plan and each party shall use reasonable best efforts (i) to ensure that all press releases and other public statements with respect to the transactions contemplated hereby shall be consistent with such joint communications plan, and (ii) unless otherwise required by applicable law or by obligations pursuant to any listing agreement with or rules of any securities exchange, to consult with each other before issuing any press release or, to the extent practical, otherwise making any public statement with respect to this Agreement or the transactions contemplated hereby . . .

Section 5.9 Accountant's Letters.

(a) Parent shall use reasonable best efforts to cause to be delivered to the Company two letters from Parent's independent public accountants, one dated approximately the date on which the Form S-4 shall become effective and one dated the Closing Date, each addressed to Parent and the Company, in form reasonably satisfactory to the Company and customary in scope for comfort letters delivered by independent public accountants in connection with registration statements similar to the Form S-4.

(b)   The Company shall use reasonable best efforts to cause to be delivered to Parent two letters from the Company's independent public accountants, one dated approximately the date on which the Form S-4 shall become effective and one dated the Closing Date, each addressed to the Company and Parent, in form reasonably satisfactory to Parent and customary in scope for comfort letters delivered by independent public accountants in connection with registration statements similar to the Form S-4.

Section 5.10   *Listing of Shares of Parent Common Stock*. Parent shall use its reasonable best efforts to cause the shares of Parent Common Stock to be issued in the Merger and the shares of Parent Common Stock to be reserved for issuance upon exercise of the Company Stock Options to be approved for listing on the NYSE, subject to official notice of issuance, prior to the Closing Date.

Section 5.11   *Dividends*. After the date of this Agreement, each of Parent and the Company shall coordinate with the other the payment of dividends with respect to the Parent Common Stock and Company Common Stock and the record dates and payment dates relating thereto, it being the intention of the parties that holders of Parent Common Stock and Company Common Stock shall not receive two dividends, or fail to receive one dividend, for any single calendar quarter with respect to their shares of Parent Common Stock and/or Company Common Stock or any shares of Parent Common Stock that any such holder receives in exchange for such shares of Company Common Stock in the Merger. Notwithstanding the foregoing, such coordination shall not in any manner affect the Company's ability to declare a dividend on the shares of Common Stock to effect the Monsanto Spin-Off.

Section 5.12   *Affiliates*. Not less than 45 days prior to the Effective Time, the Company shall deliver to Parent a letter identifying all persons who, in the judgment of the Company, may be deemed at the time this Agreement is submitted for adoption by the stockholders of the Company, "affiliates" of the Company for purposes of Rule 145 under the Securities Act and applicable SEC rules and regulations, and such list shall be updated as necessary to reflect changes from the date thereof. The Company shall use reasonable best efforts to cause each person identified on such list to deliver to Parent not less than 30 days prior to the Effective Time, a written agreement substantially in the form attached as *Exhibit 5.12* hereto (an "Affiliate Agreement").

Section 5.13   *Section 16 Matters*. Prior to the Effective Time, each of Parent and the Company shall take all such steps as may be required to cause any dispositions of Company Common Stock (including derivative securities with respect to Company Common Stock) or acquisitions of Parent Common Stock (including derivative securities with respect to Parent Common Stock) resulting from the transactions contemplated by *Article I* or *Article II* of this Agreement by each individual who is subject to the reporting requirements of Section 16(a) of the Exchange Act with respect to the Company, to be exempt under Rule 16b-3 promulgated under the Exchange Act, such steps to be taken in accordance with the No-Action Letter dated January 12, 1999, issued by the SEC to Skadden, Arps, Slate, Meagher & Flom LLP.

Section 5.14   *Tax Treatment*. Parent and the Company intend the Merger to qualify as a reorganization under Section 368(a) of the Code. Each of Parent and the Company, and each of their respective affiliates shall, to the extent consistent with their rights and obligations under this Agreement, use their reasonable best efforts to cause the Merger to so qualify and to obtain the opinions of Cadwalader, Wickersham & Taft and Sullivan & Cromwell referred to in *Section 6.2 (c)* and *6.3(c)* of this Agreement . . .

Section 5.15   Tax Certificates.   The Company shall deliver to Parent at the time of the Monsanto Spin-Off, unless the Monsanto Sale Transaction (as defined in *Section 5.16*) shall have occurred, a representation letter in the form of *Exhibit 5.15* hereto, dated as of the date of the Monsanto Spin-Off.

Section 5.16   Completion of Spin-off or Sale of Monsanto.   The Company shall cause either (i) the Monsanto Spin-Off, (ii) the sale of all or substantially all of the assets of Monsanto and transfer of all its liabilities to an entity no less creditworthy than Monsanto followed by the liquidation and dissolution of Monsanto, or (iii) the sale of all of the Company's equity interest in Monsanto (any of *clauses (ii)* or *(iii)*, the "Monsanto Sale Transaction") to occur.

Section 5.17   Restructure of Transaction.   In the event that either of Cadwalader, Wickersham & Taft or Sullivan & Cromwell is unable to render its opinion pursuant to *Sections 6.2(c)* or *6.3(c)*, respectively, Parent and the Company shall negotiate in good faith to revise the structure of the business combination between the Company and Parent such that each of Cadwalader, Wickersham & Taft and Sullivan & Cromwell will be able to render such opinion, *provided* that no such revision to the structure of the Merger shall (a) result in any change in the Merger Consideration, (b) be adverse to the interests of Parent, the Company, Merger Sub, the holders of shares of Parent Common Stock or the holders of shares of Company Common Stock . . . or (c) unreasonably impede or delay consummation of the Merger. If the structure of the Merger is so revised, this Agreement shall be amended by the parties as appropriate to give effect to the revised structure of the Merger with each party executing a written amendment to this Agreement as necessary to reflect the foregoing.

Section 5.18   Election to Parent's Board of Directors.   Prior to the Effective Time, Parent shall (i) cause Mr. Frederick Hassan to be appointed to Parent's board of directors at the Effective Time and (ii) take all action necessary so that, at the Effective Time and so long as he is willing and able to serve, Mr. Hassan shall be appointed the Vice-Chairman of Parent.

ARTICLE VI
CONDITIONS PRECEDENT

Section 6.1   Conditions to Each Party's Obligation to Effect the Merger.   The respective obligations of the Company, Parent and Merger Sub to effect the Merger are subject to the satisfaction or waiver on or prior to the Closing Date of the following conditions:

(a) *Stockholder Approval.* (i) The Company shall have obtained the Company Stockholder Approval in connection with the adoption of this

Agreement by the stockholders of the Company and (ii) Parent shall have obtained the Parent Stockholder Approval in connection with the approval of each of the Share Issuance and the Certificate Amendment by the stockholders of Parent.

(b) *No Injunctions or Restraints, Illegality.*   No Laws shall have been adopted or promulgated, and no temporary restraining order, preliminary or permanent injunction or other order, judgment, decision, opinion or decree issued by a court or other Governmental Entity of competent jurisdiction in the United States or the European Union shall be in effect, having the effect of making the Merger illegal or otherwise prohibiting consummation of the Merger.

(c) *HSR Act; EC Merger Regulation.*   Each of (i) the waiting period (and any extension thereof) applicable to the Merger under the HSR Act shall have been terminated or shall have expired, and any investigation opened by means of a second request for additional information or otherwise shall have been terminated or closed, and (ii) the approval of the Merger by the European Commission shall have been granted pursuant to the EC Merger Regulation.

(d) *NYSE Listing.*   The shares of Parent Common Stock to be issued in the Merger and such other shares to be reserved for issuance in connection with the Merger shall have been approved for listing on the NYSE, subject to official notice of issuance.

(e) *Effectiveness of the Form S-4.*   The Form S-4 shall have been declared effective by the SEC under the Securities Act. No stop order suspending the effectiveness of the Form S-4 shall have been issued by the SEC and no proceedings for that purpose shall have been initiated or threatened by the SEC.

(f) *Governmental and Regulatory Approvals.*   Other than the filing provided for under *Section 1.3* and filings pursuant to the HSR Act and EC Merger Regulation (which are addressed in *Section 6.1(c)*), all consents, clearances, approvals and actions of, filings with and notices to any Governmental Entity required of Parent, the Company or any of their Subsidiaries in connection with the execution and delivery of this Agreement and the consummation of the Merger, the Share Issuance and the other transactions contemplated hereby shall have been made or obtained (as the case may be), except for those the failure of which to be made or obtained, individually or in the aggregate, would not reasonably be expected to have a Material Adverse Effect on Parent and its Subsidiaries (including the Surviving Corporation and its Subsidiaries), taken together after giving effect to the Merger.

(g) *Blue Sky Approvals.*   Parent shall have received all state securities and "blue sky" permits and approvals necessary to consummate the transactions contemplated hereby.

Section 6.2   *Additional Conditions to Obligations of Parent and Merger Sub.*   The obligations of Parent and Merger Sub to effect the Merger are subject to the satisfaction of, or waiver by Parent, on or prior to the Closing Date of the following conditions:

(a) *Representations and Warranties.*   Each of the representations and warranties of the Company set forth in this Agreement that is qualified as to

Material Adverse Effect shall be true and correct, and each of the representations and warranties of the Company set forth in this Agreement that is not so qualified shall be true and correct, except where the failure to be so true and correct, individually or in the aggregate, would not have a Material Adverse Effect on the Company, in each case, as of the date of this Agreement and as of the Closing Date as though made on and as of the Closing Date (except to the extent in either case that such representations and warranties speak as of another date), and Parent shall have received a certificate of the chief executive officer and the chief financial officer of the Company to such effect.

(b) *Performance of Obligations of the Company.*   The Company shall have performed or complied with all agreements and covenants required to be performed by it under this Agreement at or prior to the Closing Date that are qualified as to Material Adverse Effect and shall have performed or complied in all material respects with all other material agreements and covenants required to be performed by it under this Agreement at or prior to the Closing Date and Parent shall have received a certificate of the chief executive officer and the chief financial officer of the Company to such effect.

(c) *Tax Opinions.*   Parent shall have received from Cadwalader, Wickersham & Taft, counsel to Parent, on or before the date the Form S-4 shall become effective, and subsequently, on the Closing Date, written opinions dated as of such dates substantially in the form of *Exhibit 6.2(c) (1).* In rendering such opinions, counsel to Parent shall be entitled to rely upon representations provided by Parent and the Company substantially in the form of *Exhibits 6.2(c) (2)* and *6.2(c) (3)* (allowing for such amendments to the representations as counsel to Parent deems reasonably necessary).

(d) *Tax Certificates.*   The Company shall have delivered to Parent at the time of the Monsanto Spin-Off, unless the Monsanto Sale Transaction shall have occurred, a representation letter in the form of *Exhibit 5.15* hereto, dated as of the date of the Monsanto Spin-Off.

(e) *The Company Rights Agreement.*   No Share Acquisition Date or Distribution Date (as such terms are defined in Company Rights Agreement) shall have occurred pursuant to Company Rights Agreement.

(f) *Events Related to Monsanto.* The Monsanto Sale Transaction or the Monsanto Spin-Off shall have been completed.

(g) *No Material Change.*   The Company and its Subsidiaries shall not have suffered from the date of this Agreement any change that would reasonably be expected to have a Material Adverse Effect on the Company.

Section 6.3   *Additional Conditions to Obligations of the Company.* The obligations of the Company to effect the Merger are subject to the satisfaction of, or waiver by the Company, on or prior to the Closing Date of the following additional conditions:

(a) *Representations and Warranties.*   Each of the representations and warranties of Parent set forth in this Agreement that is qualified as to Material Adverse Effect shall be true and correct, and each of the representations and warranties of Parent set forth in this Agreement that is not so qualified shall be true and correct, except where the failure to be so true and correct, individually or in the aggregate, would not have a Material Adverse Effect on Parent, in each case, as of the date of this Agreement and as of the Closing Date as though made on and as of the Closing Date (except to the extent in either case that such representations and warranties speak as of another date), and the Company shall have received a certificate of the chief executive officer and the chief financial officer of Parent to such effect.

(b) *Performance of Obligations of Parent.*   Parent shall have performed or complied with all agreements and covenants required to be performed by it under this Agreement at or prior to the Closing Date that are qualified as to Material Adverse Effect and shall have performed or complied in all material respects with all other material agreements and covenants required to be performed by it under this Agreement at or prior to the Closing Date, and the Company shall have received a certificate of the chief executive officer and the chief financial officer of Parent to such effect.

(c) *Tax Opinions.*   The Company shall have received from Sullivan & Cromwell, counsel to the Company, on or before the date the Form S-4 shall become effective, and subsequently, on the Closing Date, written opinions dated as of such dates substantially in the form of *Exhibit 6.3(c) (1)*. In rendering such opinion, counsel to the Company shall be entitled to rely upon representations provided by Parent and the Company substantially in the form of *Exhibits 6.2(c) (2)* and *6.2(c) (3)* (allowing for such amendments to the representations as counsel to the Company deems reasonably necessary).

(d) *Events Related to Monsanto.*   The Monsanto Sale Transaction or the Monsanto Spin-Off shall have been completed; provided, that the Company shall not be entitled to assert this condition to Closing if it has not complied with the terms of *Section 5.16* hereof.

(e) *Parent Rights Agreement.*   No Stock Acquisition Date or Distribution Date (as such terms are defined in the Parent Rights Agreement) shall have occurred pursuant to the Parent Rights Agreement.

(f) *No Material Changes.*   Parent and its Subsidiaries shall not have suffered from the date of this Agreement any change that would reasonably be expected to have a Material Adverse Effect on Parent.

ARTICLE VII
TERMINATION AND AMENDMENT

Section 7.1 General. This Agreement may be terminated and the transactions contemplated hereby may be abandoned at any time prior to the Effective Time notwithstanding approval thereof by the stockholders of the Company:

(a) by mutual written consent duly authorized by the Boards of the Company and Parent;

(b) by the Company or Parent if the Closing shall not have occurred on or before April 15, 2003 (the "Termination Date" which term shall include the date of any extension under this *Section 7.1 (b)); provided, however*, that if on the Termination Date the conditions to Closing set forth in *Sections 6.1(c)* and *6.1(f)* shall not have been fulfilled but all other conditions to Closing shall or shall be capable of being fulfilled then the Termination Date shall be automatically extended to July 15, 2003 (the "Extended Termination Date"); and *provided, further*, that the right to terminate this Agreement under this *Section 7.1(b)* shall not be available to any party whose failure to fulfill any material obligation under this Agreement has been the cause of, or resulted in, the failure of the Closing to occur before such date;

(c)   by the Company, if Parent shall have breached in any material respect any of its representations or warranties or failed to perform in any material respect any of its covenants or other agreements contained in this Agreement, which breach or failure to perform (1) is incapable of being cured by Parent prior to the Termination Date and (2) renders the condition set forth in *Section 6.3(a)* or *6.3(b)* incapable of being satisfied prior to the Termination Date;

(d)   by Parent, if the Company shall have breached in any material respect any of its representations or warranties or failed to perform in any material respect any of its covenants or other agreements contained in this Agreement, which breach or failure to perform (1) is incapable of being cured by the Company prior to the Termination Date and (2) renders the condition set forth in *Section 6.2(a)* or *6.2(b)* incapable of being satisfied prior to the Termination Date;

(e)   by the Company or Parent, upon written notice to the other party, if a Governmental Entity of competent jurisdiction in the United States or of the European Union shall have issued an order, judgment, decision, opinion, decree or ruling or taken any other action (which the party seeking to terminate shall have used its reasonable best efforts to resist, resolve, annul, quash, or lift, as applicable, subject to the provisions of *Section 5.3*) permanently enjoining or otherwise prohibiting the consummation of the transactions contemplated by this Agreement, and such order, decree, ruling or action shall have become final and non-appealable; *provided, however*, that the party seeking to terminate this Agreement pursuant to this clause (e) has fulfilled its obligations under *Section 5.3*;

(f)   by the Company if (i) the Board of Directors of Parent shall have withdrawn or changed or modified the Parent Recommendation in a manner adverse to the Company or (ii) for any reason Parent fails to call or hold the Parent Stockholders Meeting within six months of the date hereof (provided that if the Form S-4 shall not have become effective for purposes of the Federal securities laws by the date that is 20 business days prior to the date that is five months from the date hereof, then such six month period shall be extended by the number of days from that elapse from the end of the five-month period until the effective date of the Form S-4);

(g)   by Parent if (i) the Board of Directors of the Company shall have withdrawn or changed or modified the Company Recommendation in a manner adverse to Parent or (ii) for any reason the Company fails to call or hold the Company Stockholders Meeting within six months of the date hereof (provided that if the Form S-4 shall not have become effective for purposes of the Federal securities laws by the date that is 20 business days prior to the date that is five months from the date hereof, then such six month period shall be extended by the number of days from that elapse from the end of the five-month period until the effective date of the Form S-4);

(h)   by the Company, if the (i) Board of Directors of the Company authorizes the Company, subject to complying with the terms of this Agreement, to enter into a binding written agreement concerning a transaction that constitutes a Superior Proposal to the Company and the Company notifies Parent in writing that it intends to enter into such an agreement, attaching the most current version of such agreement (or a description of all material terms and conditions thereof) to such notice, (ii) Parent does not make, within five business days of receipt of the Company's written notification of its intention to enter into a binding agreement for such Superior Proposal, an offer that the Board of Directors of the Company determines, in good faith after consultation with a financial advisor of nationally recognized reputation, is at least as favorable to the Company's stockholders as such Superior Proposal, it being understood that the Company shall not enter into any such binding agreement during such fiveday period, and (iii) the Company, at or prior to any termination pursuant to this *Section 7.1(h)*, pays Parent the Termination Fee (as defined below) set forth in *Section 7.2*;

(i)   by the Company or Parent, if the Parent Stockholder Approval shall not have been received at a duly held meeting of the stockholders of Parent called for such purpose (including any adjournment or postponement thereof); and

(j)   by the Company or Parent, if the Company Stockholder Approval shall not have been received at a duly held meeting of the stockholders of the Company called for such purpose (including any adjournment or postponement thereof).

Section 7.2   *Obligations in Event of Termination.*

(a)   In the event of any termination of this Agreement as provided in Section 7.1, this Agreement shall forthwith become wholly void and of no further force and effect (except with respect to *Section 3.1(j)*, *Section 3.2(1)*, *Section 5.2*, *Section 5.6*, this *Section 7.2* and *Article VIII*, which shall remain in full force and effect) and there shall be no liability on the part of the Company or Parent; provided, however, that termination shall not preclude any party from suing the other party for, or relieve any party hereto from any liability arising from a, willful breach of this Agreement; and, provided, further, however, that if this Agreement is terminated for any reason, other than a termination (1) by Parent pursuant to *Section 7.1 (g)* (but only if the reason for the termination was based on a Change in the Company Recommendation pursuant to the terms of *Section 5.4*) or *(2)* by the Company pursuant to *Section 7.1(h)*, then the provisions of the sixth paragraph of the Confidentiality Agreement shall continue to apply following the termination of the Merger Agreement and the date set forth in the definition of "Standstill Period" set forth in the last sentence of the sixth paragraph of the Confidentiality Agreement shall be modified to be the date that is two (2) years from the date of the termination of the Merger Agreement; *provided, however*, that the provisions of the sixth paragraph of the Confidentiality Agreement shall terminate on the date that an event described in clause (y) of such paragraph shall occur and *provided further* that the Company agrees to notify Parent not later than 48 hours prior to entering into any agreement with respect to a Business Combination.

(b)   If this Agreement is terminated (i) by Parent pursuant to *Section 7.1 (g)* (but only if, on or before the date this Agreement is terminated, there shall have been made an offer or proposal for, or any announcement of any intention with respect to (including the filing of a statement of beneficial ownership on Schedule 13D discussing the possibility of or reserving the right to engage in), a transaction that would constitute a Business Combination involving the Company (whether or not such offer, proposal, announcement or agreement will have been rejected or withdrawn prior to the date this Agreement is terminated)); (ii) by Parent or the Company pursuant to *Section 7.1 (j)* because of the failure to obtain the Company Stockholder Approval (but only if, after the date hereof and prior to the Company Stockholder Meeting, there shall have been made public to a significant number of the Company's stockholders an offer or proposal for, or any public announcement of any intention with respect to (including the filing of a statement of beneficial ownership on Schedule 13D discussing the possibility of or reserving the right to engage in), a transaction that would constitute a Business Combination involving the Company (whether or not such offer, proposal, announcement or agreement will have been rejected or withdrawn prior to the date of the Company Stockholder Meeting)); (iii) by Parent or the Company pursuant to *Section 7.1 (b)* because the Merger shall not have been consummated at or prior to the Termination Date or the Extended Termination Date, as the case may be, and, at the time of the termination, (x) the Company Stockholder Approval shall not have been obtained and (y) after the date hereof and prior to the Termination Date or the Extended Termination Date, as the case may be, there shall have been made an offer or proposal for, or an announcement of any intention with respect to (including the filing of a statement of beneficial ownership on Schedule 13D discussing the possibility of or reserving the right to engage in), a transaction that would constitute a Business Combination involving the Company (whether or not such offer, proposal, announcement or agreement will have been rejected or withdrawn prior to the Termination Date or the Extended Termination Date, as the case may be); or (iv) by the Company pursuant to *Section 7.1(h)*, then (A) in the case of *clauses (b) (i), (b) (ii)*, and *(b) (iii)* if within twelve months of termination of this Agreement, the Company enters into a definitive agreement with any Person (other than Parent or any of Parent's affiliates) with respect to a Business Combination or any Business Combination with respect to the Company is consummated, then the Company shall pay to Parent, not later than one business day after the earlier of the date such agreement is entered into or such Business Combination is consummated, a termination fee of $1,600,000,000 (the "Termination Fee") and (B) in the case of *clauses (b) (iv)*, the Company shall pay to Parent, at or prior to such termination pursuant to *Section 7.1(h)*, the Termination Fee. Notwithstanding the foregoing, no Termination Fee shall be payable by the Company to Parent if the Parent stockholders do not approve the Share Issuance or Certificate Amendment.

(c)   For the purposes of this *Section 7.2*, "Business Combination" means with respect to the Company, (i) a merger, reorganization, consolidation, share exchange, business combination, recapitalization, liquidation, dissolution or similar transaction involving such party as a result of which either (A) the Company's stockholders prior to such transaction (by virtue of their ownership of such party's shares) in the aggregate cease to own at least 50% of the voting securities of the entity surviving or resulting from such transaction (or the ultimate parent entity thereof) or, regardless of the percentage of voting securities held by such stockholders, if any Person shall beneficially own, directly or indirectly, at least 40% of the voting securities of such ultimate parent entity or (B) the individuals comprising the board of directors of the Company prior to such transaction do not constitute a majority of the board of directors of such ultimate parent entity, (ii) a sale, lease, exchange, transfer or other disposition of at least 40% of the assets of the Company and its Subsidiaries, taken as a whole, in a single transaction or a series of related transactions, or (iii) the acquisition, directly or indirectly, by a Person of beneficial ownership of 40% or more of the common stock of the Company whether by merger, consolidation, share exchange, business combination, tender or exchange offer or otherwise (other than a merger, reorganization, consolidation, share exchange, business combination, recapitalization, liquidation, dissolution or similar transaction upon the consummation of which the Company's stockholders would in the aggregate beneficially own greater than 50% of the voting securities of such Person).

(d)   All payments under this *Section 7.2* shall be made by wire transfer of immediately available funds to an account designated by Parent.

(e)   The parties each agree that the agreements contained in *Section 7.2(b)* are an integral part of the transaction contemplated by this Agreement and constitute liquidated damages and not a penalty. If the Company fails to promptly pay Parent any fee due under such *Section 7.2(b)*, the Company shall pay the costs and expenses of Parent (including legal fees and expenses) in connection with any action, including the filing of any lawsuit or legal action, taken to collect payment.

Section 7.3   Amendment.   This Agreement may be amended by the parties, by action taken or authorized by their respective Boards of Directors, at any time before or after approval of the matters presented in connection with the Merger by the stockholders of the Company and Parent, but, after any such approval, no amendment shall be made which by law or in accordance with the rules of any relevant stock exchange requires further approval by such stockholders without such further approval. This Agreement may not be amended except by an instrument in writing signed on behalf of each of the parties.

Section 7.4   Extension; Waiver.   At any time prior to the Effective Time, the parties, by action taken or authorized by their respective Boards of Directors, may, to the extent legally allowed, (i) extend the time for the performance of any of the obligations or other acts of the other parties, (ii) waive any inaccuracies in the representations and warranties contained herein or in any document delivered pursuant hereto and (iii) waive compliance with any of the agreements or conditions contained herein. Any agreement on the part of a party hereto to any such extension or waiver shall be valid only if set forth in a written instrument signed on behalf of such party. The failure of any party to this Agreement to assert any of its rights under this Agreement or otherwise shall not constitute a waiver of those rights . . .

Article VIII
General Provisions

Section 8.1 Non-Survival of Representations, Warranties and Agreements. None of the representations, warranties, covenants and other agreements in this Agreement or in any instrument delivered pursuant to this Agreement, including any rights arising out of any breach of such representations, warranties, covenants and other agreements, shall survive the Effective Time, except for those covenants and agreements contained herein and therein (including *Section 5.7*) that by their terms apply or are to be performed in whole or in part after the Effective Time and this *Article VIII*.

Section 8.2 Notices. All notices and other communications hereunder shall be in writing and shall be deemed duly given (a) on the date of delivery if delivered personally, or by telecopy or telefacsimile, upon confirmation of receipt, (b) on the first Business Day following the date of dispatch if delivered by a recognized next-day courier service, or (c) on the tenth Business Day following the date of mailing if delivered by registered or certified mail, return receipt requested, postage prepaid. All notices hereunder shall be delivered as set forth below, or pursuant to such other instructions as may be designated in writing by the party to receive such notice:

(a) if to Parent or Merger Sub, to:

Pfizer Inc.
235 East 42nd Street
New York, New York 10017
Fax: (212) 808-8924
Attention: Jeffrey Kindler, Esq.

with a copy to:

Cadwalader, Wickersham & Taft
100 Maiden Lane
New York, New York 10038
Fax: (212) 504-6666
Attention: Dennis J. Block, Esq.

(b) if to the Company to:

Pharmacia Corporation
100 Route 206 North Peapack,
New Jersey 07977
Fax: (908) 901-1810
Attention: Richard T. Collier, Esq.

with a copy to:

Sullivan & Cromwell
125 Broad Street
New York, New York 10004
Fax: (212) 558-3588
Attention: Neil T. Anderson, Esq.
          Keith A. Pagnani, Esq.

Section 8.3   Interpretation.   When a reference is made in this Agreement to Sections, Exhibits or Schedules, such reference shall be to a Section of or Exhibit or Schedule to this Agreement unless otherwise indicated. The table of contents and headings contained in this Agreement are for reference purposes only and shall not affect in any way the meaning or interpretation of this Agreement. Whenever the words "include", "includes" or "including" are used in this Agreement, they shall be deemed to be followed by the words "without limitation".

Section 8.4   Counterparts.   This Agreement may be executed in one or more counterparts, all of which shall be considered one and the same agreement and shall become effective when one or more counterparts have been signed by each of the parties and delivered to the other party, it being understood that both parties need not sign the same counterpart.

Section 8.5   Entire Agreement; No Third Party Beneficiaries.
   (a)   This Agreement (including the Exhibits and Schedules hereto) and the Confidentiality Agreement constitute the entire agreement, and supersede all prior agreements and understandings, both written and oral, among the parties with respect to the subject matter hereof and thereof.
   (b)   This Agreement shall be binding upon and inure solely to the benefit of each party hereto, and nothing in this Agreement, express or implied, is intended to or shall confer upon any other Person any right, benefit or remedy of any nature whatsoever under or by reason of this Agreement, other than *Section 5.7* (which is intended to be for the benefit of the Persons covered thereby and may be enforced by such Persons).

Section 8.6   Governing Law.   This Agreement shall be governed and construed in accordance with the laws of the State of New York (without giving effect to choice of law principles thereof).

Section 8.7   Severability.   If any term or other provision of this Agreement is invalid, illegal or incapable of being enforced by any law or public policy, all other terms and provisions of this Agreement shall nevertheless remain in full force and effect so long as the economic or legal substance of the transactions contemplated hereby is not affected in any manner materially adverse to any party. Notwithstanding the foregoing, upon such determination that any term or other provision is invalid, illegal or incapable of being enforced, the parties shall negotiate in good faith to modify this Agreement so as to effect the original intent of the parties as closely as possible in an acceptable manner in order that the transactions contemplated hereby are consummated as originally contemplated to the greatest extent possible.

Section 8.8 Assignment. Neither this Agreement nor any of the rights, interests or obligations hereunder shall be assigned by any of the parties, in whole or in part (whether by operation of law or otherwise), without the prior written consent of the other party, and any attempt to make any such assignment without such consent shall be null and void, except that Merger Sub may assign, in its sole discretion, any or all of its rights, interests and obligations under this Agreement to any direct wholly owned Subsidiary of Parent without the consent of the Company, but no such assignment shall relieve Merger Sub of any of its obligations under this Agreement. Subject to the preceding sentence, this Agreement will be binding upon, inure to the benefit of and be enforceable by the parties and their respective successors and assigns.

Section 8.9 Submission to Jurisdiction; Waivers. Each of Parent and the Company irrevocably agrees that any legal action or proceeding with respect to this Agreement or for recognition and enforcement of any judgment in respect hereof brought by the other party hereto or its successors or assigns may be brought and determined in the Chancery or other Courts of the State of Delaware, and each of Parent and the Company hereby irrevocably submits with regard to any such action or proceeding for itself and in respect to its property, generally and unconditionally, to the nonexclusive jurisdiction of the aforesaid courts. Each of Parent and the Company hereby irrevocably waives, and agrees not to assert, by way of motion, as a defense, counterclaim or otherwise, in any action or proceeding with respect to this Agreement, (a) any claim that it is not personally subject to the jurisdiction of the above-named courts for any reason other than the failure to lawfully serve process (b) that it or its property is exempt or immune from jurisdiction of any such court or from any legal process commenced in such courts (whether through service of notice, attachment prior to judgment, attachment in aid of execution of judgment, execution of judgment or otherwise), and (c) to the fullest extent permitted by applicable law, that (i) the suit, action or proceeding in any such court is brought in an inconvenient forum, (ii) the venue of such suit, action or proceeding is improper and (iii) this Agreement, or the subject matter hereof, may not be enforced in or by such courts.

Section 8.10 Enforcement. The parties agree that irreparable damage would occur in the event that any of the provisions of this Agreement were not performed in accordance with their specific terms. It is accordingly agreed that the parties shall be entitled to specific performance of the terms hereof, this being in addition to any other remedy to which they are entitled at law or in equity.

Section 8.11 Definitions. As used in this Agreement:
(a) "beneficial ownership" or "beneficially own" shall have the meaning under Section 13(d) of the Exchange Act and the rules and regulations thereunder.

(b)   "Benefit Plans" means, with respect to any Person, each employee benefit plan, program, policy, arrangement and contract (including, without limitation, any "employee benefit plan," as defined in Section 3(3) of the Employee Retirement Income Security Act of 1974, as amended ("ERISA") and any bonus, deferred compensation, stock bonus, stock purchase, restricted stock, stock option, employment, termination, stay agreement or bonus, change in control and severance plan, program, policy, arrangement and contract, written or oral) in effect on the date of this Agreement or disclosed on the Company Disclosure Schedule or the Parent Disclosure Schedule, as the case may be, to which such Person or its Subsidiary is a party, which is maintained or contributed to by such Person, or with respect to which such Person could incur material liability under Section 4069, 4201 or 4212(c) of ERISA.

(c)   "Board of Directors" means the Board of Directors of any specified Person and any committees thereof.

(d)   "Business Day" means any day on which banks are not required or authorized to close in the City of New York.

(e)   "Confidentiality Agreement" means the letter agreement, dated June 27, 2002 between Parent and the Company.

(f)   "known" or "knowledge" means, with respect to any party, the actual knowledge of such party's executive officers and senior management as listed on such party's annual report to its shareholders and such knowledge as would be reasonably expected to be known by such executive officers in the ordinary and usual course of the performance of their professional responsibilities to such party.

(g)   "Material Adverse Effect" means, with respect to any entity, any event, change, circumstance or effect that is or is reasonably likely to be materially adverse to (i) the business, financial condition or results of operations of such entity and its Subsidiaries, taken as a whole, other than any event, change, circumstance or effect relating (w) to the economy or financial markets in general, (x) in general to the industries in which such entity operates and not specifically relating to (or having the effect of specifically relating to or having a materially disproportionate effect (relative to most other industry participants) on) such entity, (y) to changes in applicable law or regulations or in GAAP or (z) to the announcement of this Agreement or the transactions contemplated hereby or (ii) the ability of such entity to consummate the transactions contemplated by this Agreement. Except as specifically set forth in this Agreement, all references to Material Adverse Effect on Parent or its Subsidiaries contained in this Agreement shall be deemed to refer solely to Parent and its Subsidiaries without including its ownership of the Company and its Subsidiaries after the Merger.

(h)   "other party" means, with respect to the Company, Parent and means, with respect to Parent, the Company, unless the context otherwise requires.

(i)   "Person" means an individual, corporation, limited liability company, partnership, association, trust, unincorporated organization, other entity or group (as defined in the Exchange Act).

(j)   "Subsidiary" when used with respect to any party means any corporation or other organization, whether incorporated or unincorporated, (i) of which such party or any other Subsidiary of such party is a general partner (excluding partnerships, the general partnership interests of which held by such party or any Subsidiary of such party do not have a majority of the voting interests in such partnership) or (ii) at least a majority of the securities or other interests of which having by their terms ordinary voting power to elect a majority of the Board of Directors or others performing similar functions with respect to such corporation or other organization is directly or indirectly owned or controlled by such party or by any one or more of its Subsidiaries, or by such party and one or more of its Subsidiaries; *provided*, that the parties agree that notwithstanding any other provision of this Agreement, the term "Subsidiary" shall not, with respect to the Company and for the purposes of (x) *Section 6.2(a)* (as it relates to the accuracy of the Company's representations and warranties as of the Closing Date only), but only if the Monsanto Spin-Off shall have occurred, and (y) *Article IV* (except as to the ability of the Company to control or prohibit action of Monsanto pursuant to the Separation Agreements or otherwise), *Article V* (except as to the ability of the Company to control or prohibit action of Monsanto pursuant to the Separation Agreements or otherwise) and *Section 7.1 (d)* only, include Monsanto Company.

(k) "Superior Proposal" means with respect to the Company, a bona fide written proposal made by a third party which is (I) (i) for a sale, lease, exchange, transfer or other disposition of at least 40% of the assets of the Company and its Subsidiaries, taken as a whole, in a single transaction or a series of related transactions, or (ii) for the acquisition, directly or indirectly, by such third party of beneficial ownership of 30% or more of the common stock of the Company whether by merger, consolidation, share exchange, business combination, tender or exchange offer or otherwise, and which is (II) otherwise on terms which the Board of Directors of the Company in good faith concludes (after consultation with its financial advisors and outside counsel), taking into account, among other things, all legal, financial, regulatory and other aspects of the proposal and the third party making the proposal, (i) would, if consummated, result in a transaction that is more favorable to its stockholders (in their capacities as stockholders), from a financial point of view, than the transactions contemplated by this Agreement and (ii) is reasonably capable of being completed.

IN WITNESS WHEREOF, Parent, Merger Sub and the Company have caused this Agreement to be signed by their respective officers thereunto duly authorized, all as of the date first written above.

PFIZER INC.

By: /s/ Henry A. McKinnell
Henry A. McKinnell
Chairman of the Board and
Chief Executive Officer

PILSNER ACQUISITION SUB CORP.

By: /s/ David Shedlarz
David Shedlarz
President

PHARMACIA CORPORATION

By: */s/ Fred Hassan*
      Fred Hassan
      Chairman and
      Chief Executive Officer

Stock Purchase Agreement

[ESCROW]
[DEFERRED NOTES]
[SHAREHOLDER REPRESENTATIVE]

DRAFT __/__/04

STOCK PURCHASE AGREEMENT

by and among

THE STOCKHOLDERS NAMED HEREIN

TREKKER MARKETING, INC.
A California Corporation

THE MANAGEMENT STOCKHOLDERS NAMED HEREIN

and

GALAXY INTERNATIONAL CORP.
or its Nominee

for

all of the outstanding capital stock of

TREKKER MARKETING, INC.
A California Corporation

dated as of

April __, 2004

TABLE OF CONTENTS

GLOSSARY OF DEFINED TERMS

[EXHIBITS OMITTED]

GLOSSARY OF DEFINED TERMS

STOCK PURCHASE AGREEMENT (this **"Agreement"**), dated as of June___, 20___, by and among the Stockholders listed on <u>Annex I</u> attached hereto (collectively **"Stockholders"**), Trekker Marketing, Inc. (**"Company"**), and Galaxy International Corp., a Delaware corporation, or its Nominee (**"Buyer"**), and Stanley Rockledge and Fred Merlin in their capacity as Management Stockholders (**"Management Stockholders"**).

RECITALS:

1.   The Company and the Company Subsidiaries (as defined in Section 3.1 (c) hereof) design, manufacture and market high-end proprietary branded skateboards, snowboards, surfboards, apparel and related accessories through specialty retailers and a network of distributors worldwide (the **"Business"**).

2.   The Stockholders own all of the issued outstanding shares of capital stock of the Company as described and identified on <u>Annex I</u> (the **"Shares"**).

3.   Pursuant to the Company's Stock Option Plan (**"Stock Option Plan"**), 1,200,000 common stock options (**"Stock Options"**) are outstanding as of the date hereof.

4.   The Board of Directors of the Company believes that it is in the best interest of the Company and the Stockholders to enter into a transaction for the sale of the Company and that it is in the best interest of the Stockholders to structure a sale of the Company as provided in this Agreement. In consideration for Buyer entering into this Agreement Buyer has required the Company to enter into this Agreement and to make various representations and warranties and agree to take certain actions.

5.   Stockholders desire to sell to Buyer, and Buyer desires to purchase from the Stockholders, all of the Shares. Company intends to cause the Stock Options to be cancelled in exchange for the consideration to be paid to holders of options by Buyer.

6.   The Stockholders have appointed the Representative (as defined in Section 10.1) hereof) to take such actions, and accept such deliveries as provided herein to be taken or accepted by Stockholders other than the representations, warranties and covenants made by the Stockholders.

NOW, THEREFORE, in consideration of the foregoing and the respective representations, warranties, covenants, agreements, undertakings and obligations set forth herein, and intending to be legally bound hereby, the parties agree as follows:

ARTICLE I
SALE AND PURCHASE OF SHARES

Section 1.1   Sale and Purchase of Shares.   Upon the terms and subject to the conditions set forth in this Agreement and on the basis of the representations, warranties, covenants, agreements, undertakings and obligations contained herein, at the Closing (as defined in Section 2.1 hereof), Stockholders hereby agree to sell to Buyer, and Buyer hereby agrees to purchase from Stockholders, the Shares, free and clear of any and all Liens (as defined in Section 3.2(b) hereof) and Company shall cancel the Stock Options, for the consideration specified in this Article I.

Section 1.2   Purchase Price.   The purchase price (the **"Purchase Price"**) for the Shares and Stock Options shall consist of the following:

(a) $30.0 million, subject to any adjustment pursuant to Section 1.5(b), payable in cash and in shares of Galaxy International Corp. (**"Galaxy"**) common stock (**"Galaxy Shares"**) as more fully described in Annex II (the **"Initial Purchase Price"**);

(b) $5.0 million evidenced by promissory notes payable in four semi-annual equal cash payments, plus accrued interest, commencing April 1, 2005, bearing simple interest of 7.25% per annum from the Closing Date (the **"Deferred Notes"**); and

(c)   Up to an additional US $7.0 million of Earnout Payments (as defined in Annex II attached hereto).

Section 1.3   Delivery of Shares and Purchase Price.   At the Closing:

(a)   The Stockholders, as holders of all outstanding certificates representing the Shares, shall upon surrender of such certificates to Buyer, be entitled to receive their respective allocation of the Initial Purchase Price and Deferred Notes determined pursuant to Section 1.2 and as set forth in Annex II, less $___ (the **"Escrow Amount"**) to be deposited in the Escrow Account (as defined in Section 1.4(a)) pursuant to Section 1.4. The Escrow Amount shall be allocated among the Stockholders as set forth on Annex II.

(b)   The cash portion of the Initial Purchase Price and any subsequent cash payments to be made by Buyer shall be paid by wire transfer in immediately available funds to the accounts designated in writing three (3) business days prior to Closing by each Stockholder.

(c)   Any Galaxy Shares issued toward payment of the Purchase Price shall be subject to the execution of the Stock Issuance Agreement between the Stockholder receiving the Galaxy Shares and Galaxy International Corp. in the form attached hereto as Exhibit 1.3(c) (**"Stock Issuance Agreement"**).

(d)   The Deferred Notes issued toward payment of the Purchase Price shall be in the form attached hereto as Exhibit 1.3(d).

(e)   None of the Purchase Price shall be delivered until the certificates or affidavits of lost shares and assignment, as applicable, representing 100% of the Shares have been surrendered by all of the Stockholders, provided that Buyer in its sole and absolute discretion may waive this provision.

(f)   Each issued and outstanding Option issued under the Company's Stock Option Plan shall be cancelled and converted into the right to receive the cash consideration set forth on Annex II.

Section 1.4   Escrow.

(a)   On the Closing Date, Buyer, Company and the Stockholders shall enter into an escrow agreement in the form attached hereto as Exhibit 1.4(a) (the **"Escrow Agreement"**) with a bank or a licensed escrow agent (the **"Escrow Agent"**), and Buyer, on behalf of the **Stockholders**, shall deposit into an interest bearing account in escrow (**"Escrow Account"**), pursuant to the Escrow Agreement, the Escrow Amount. The Escrow Amount will stand as security for, but not as a limitation on, any and all claims for Damages (as defined in Section 9.2 hereof) (the **"Claims"**) and breached prior to or on the periods set forth in the Escrow Agreement (the **"Determination Period"**). The Escrow Amount shall also be available to Buyer for any Purchase Price adjustments due Buyer under Section 1.5. From time to time, the Escrow Agent will pay to the Buyer such amounts as may be required by the Escrow Agreement. On the fifteenth (15th) day following the expiration of the Determination Period, the Escrow Agent shall pay to the Stockholders, on a pro rata basis on their ownership percentages, the excess of (i) any Escrow Amount which has not already been paid to Buyer in respect of Claims over (ii) the aggregate amount of all Claims then pending. Claims made by Buyer against the Escrow Amount may be made at any time prior to the expiration of the Determination Period.

(b) It is understood that the provisions of this Section 1.4 in no way limit the amount and timing of any claims made by the Buyer against the Company, Management Stockholders or Stockholders under this Agreement.

(c) Buyer and the Stockholders will each pay one-half of the Escrow Agent's fees. Interest earned on the Escrow Amount shall be distributed pro rata in the same proportion that the principal is distributed to the parties under the Escrow Agreement.

Section 1.5 Determination of Shareholders Equity.

(a) <u>Definition of Shareholders Equity</u>. The term **"Shareholders Equity"** shall mean the dollar amount by which the net book value of the assets of Company exceeds the net book value of the liabilities of Company, as reflected in the Closing Balance Sheet (as defined in Section 1.5(b)).

(b) <u>Closing Balance Sheet</u>. A balance sheet of Company prepared as of the Closing Date (**"Closing Balance Sheet"**) and certified by Buyer's independent accountants (**"Buyer's Accountants"**) shall be prepared as follows:

(i) Within forty-five (45) days after the Closing Date, Buyer (with the assistance of the Company and the Stockholders) shall deliver to the Stockholders an unaudited balance sheet of Company as of the Closing Date, prepared in accordance with GAAP (as defined in Section 3.3(b) hereof) from the books and records of Company, on a basis consistent with the generally accepted accounting principles theretofore followed by Company in the preparation of the Balance Sheet (as defined in Section 3.6(a) hereof) and in accordance with this Section 1.5(b), and fairly presenting the financial position of Company as of the Closing Date. The balance sheet shall be accompanied by detailed schedules of the assets and liabilities and by a report of Buyer's Accountants (1) setting forth the amount of Shareholder Equity (as defined above) reflected in the balance sheet, and (2) stating that the examination of the balance sheet has been prepared in accordance with GAAP, on a basis consistent with the accounting principles theretofore followed by Company.

(ii) Within thirty (30) days following the delivery of the balance sheet referred to in (i) above, the Stockholders' Representative or its independent accountants (**"Stockholders Accountants"**) may object to any of the information contained in said balance sheet or accompanying schedules which could affect the necessity or amount of any payment by Buyer or Company pursuant to Section 1.5(d) hereof. Any such objection shall be made in writing, shall state the particular objection(s) and the basis therefor, and shall state the Stockholder's determination of the amount of the Shareholders Equity.

(iii) In the event of a dispute or disagreement relating to the balance sheet or schedules which Buyer and Stockholders' Representative are unable to resolve within thirty (30) days following Buyer's receipt of Stockholders' Representative objection, either party may elect to have all such disputes or disagreements resolved by _____ (the **"Third Accounting Firm"**). Each party will furnish to the Third Accounting Firm such work papers and other documents and information as the Third Accounting Firm may request and are available to that party and will be afforded the opportunity to present to the Third Accounting Firm any material relating to the determination and to discuss the determination with the Third Party Accounting Firm. The Third Accounting Firm shall make a resolution of the disputed items of the balance sheet of Company as of the Closing Date and re-calculate the Shareholders Equity in order to reflect the resolution of such disputed items, which shall be final and binding for purposes of this Section 1.5. The Third Accounting Firm shall be instructed to use every reasonable effort to perform its services within fifteen (15) days of submission of the balance sheet to it and, in any case, as soon as practicable after such submission. The fees and expenses for the services of the Third Accounting Firm shall be shared equally by Buyer and Stockholders.

(iv) Buyer and Stockholders agree that they will, and agree to cause their respective independent accountants to, cooperate and assist in the preparation of the Closing Balance Sheet and the calculation of Shareholders Equity and in the conduct of the audits and reviews referred to in this Section 1.5, including making available to the extent reasonably required books, records, work papers and personnel.

(c) <u>Adjustment of Final Cash Purchase Price</u>. On or before the fifth business day following the final determination of the Closing Balance Sheet pursuant to this Section 1.5 (such date being hereinafter referred to as the **"Settlement Date"**), either (i) Buyer shall be paid from the Escrow Account the amount, if any, by which Shareholders Equity as reflected on the Balance Sheet (as defined in Section 3.6(a) hereof) exceeds Shareholders Equity as reflected on the Closing Balance Sheet, together with interest on the amount being paid from the Closing Date to the date of the payment at a rate per annum equal to seven percent (7%); or (ii) Buyer shall pay to the Stockholders pro rata according to their respective ownership of Common Stock as set forth in Annex I the amount, if any, by which Shareholders Equity as reflected on the Closing Balance Sheet, exceeds Shareholders Equity as reflected on the Balance Sheet, together with interest on the amount being paid from the Closing Date to the date of payment at a rate per annum equal to seven percent (7%) per annum.

ARTICLE II
THE CLOSING

Section 2.1   Closing. The closing (the **"Closing"**) of the sale and purchase of the Shares (the **"Stock Purchase"**) and the other transactions provided for herein shall take place at the offices of Bigar, Strong & Wise, a professional corporation, at 5000 Wilshire Blvd., Los Angeles, California, at 10:00 A.M. (Los Angeles time) on the fifth (5 th) business day following satisfaction or, if permissible, waiver of the conditions set forth in Article VII of this Agreement (excluding those conditions which by their nature are to be satisfied as a part of the Closing) or at such other place, time or date as the parties hereto may agree (the time and date of the Closing being herein referred to as the **"Closing Date"**).

Section 2.2 Deliveries by Stockholders to Buyer. On the Closing Date, Stockholders (or the Stockholders' Representative and Company, as applicable) shall deliver, or cause to be delivered, to Buyer the following:

(a) an original certificate or certificates evidencing all of the Shares, duly endorsed in blank or accompanied by stock powers duly executed in blank, in proper form for transfer, or affidavits of lost shares and assignment, as applicable;

(b) the certificates, opinions, agreements and other documents and instruments to be delivered pursuant to Section 7.1 hereof;

(c) a long-form "good standing" certificate for the Company and each Company Subsidiary (as defined in Section 3.1(e) hereof, and a copy of the Articles of Incorporation or Certificate of Incorporation and all amendments thereto (or equivalent document) of the Company and each Company Subsidiary, in each case certified by the Secretary of State of the jurisdiction of incorporation, each dated as of a date within five days prior to the Closing Date and certification to the good standing of such entities and listing all documents on file;

(d) the Stock Issuance Agreements;

(e) the Subordinated Note Agreement (as defined in Section 7.1(k) hereof);

(f) the Stockholder Releases (as defined in Section 7.1(o)); and

(g) such other closing documents as Stockholders' Representative, Company and Buyer shall reasonably agree.

Section 2.3 Deliveries by Buyer to Stockholders. On the Closing Date, Buyer shall deliver, or cause to be delivered, to the Stockholders the following:

(a) cash in immediately available funds and certificates representing the Galaxy Shares that comprise the Initial Purchase Price in accordance with Annex II (which shall be distributed by the Stockholders' Representative);

(b) the Deferred Notes in accordance with Annex II;

(c) the certificates, opinions, agreements and other documents and instruments to be delivered pursuant to Section 7.2 hereof; and

(d) such other closing documents as Stockholders' Representative, Company and Buyer shall reasonably agree.

Section 2.4 Deliveries by Buyer to Escrow Account. On the Closing Date, Buyer shall deliver, or cause to be delivered, to the Escrow Account the Escrow Amount in accordance with Section 1.3(a) hereof.

Section 2.5 Conversion of the Options; Other Securities.
(a) On the Closing Date, each Option shall be exercised in full, and if not exercised shall be terminated as of the Closing Date (including the Options issued under the Company's Stock Option Plan).

(b)   The Company shall promptly take all actions necessary to ensure that following the Closing Date no holder of the Options or rights pursuant to, nor any participant in, the Stock Option Plan or any other plan, programs or arrangement providing for the issuance or grant of any interest in respect of the capital stock of the Company and any Subsidiary of the Company will have any right thereunder to acquire equity securities, or any right to payment in respect of the equity securities, of the Company, or any subsidiary of the Company.

ARTICLE III
REPRESENTATIONS AND WARRANTIES OF COMPANY AND MANAGEMENT STOCKHOLDERS

Company and the Management Stockholders hereby represent and warrant to Buyer that the statements contained in this Article III are correct and complete as of the date of this Agreement and will be correct and complete as of the Closing Date (as though made then and as though the Closing Date were substituted for the date of this Agreement), except (i) as set forth in the Company's disclosure schedule accompanying this Agreement as the same may be modified or amended in accordance with Section 6.10 hereof (the **"Disclosure Schedule"**), or (ii) to the extent that such representations and warranties are expressly made as of a specified date.

Section 3.1   Organization and Good Standing; Company Subsidiaries.
(a)   Each of Company and each Company Subsidiary (as defined in Section 3.1(c)) is a corporation duly organized, validly existing and in good standing under the laws of their respective jurisdiction of incorporation, with full power and authority to conduct its business as it is now being conducted, to own or use the properties or assets that it purports to own or use, and to perform all of its respective obligations under all Applicable Contracts (as defined in Section 3.5(c) hereof). The Company and each Company Subsidiary is duly qualified or licensed to do business as a foreign corporation and is in good standing as a foreign corporation in each jurisdiction in which either the ownership or use of the properties owned or used by it, or the nature of the activities conducted by it, requires such licensing, qualification or good standing.

(b)   Company has made available or delivered to Buyer a true, complete and correct copy of the Company's and each Company Subsidiary's Certificate of Incorporation, and Articles of Incorporation and By-laws, each as amended to date (collectively, the **"Company's Organizational Documents"**). Neither the Company nor any Company Subsidiary are in violation of any of the provisions of the Company's Organizational Documents and, to the Knowledge (as defined in Section 11(b) hereof) of the Company, no condition exists that could reasonably be expected to constitute or result in such a violation. The Company's Organizational Documents so delivered are in full force and effect.

   (c) Schedule 3.1 (c) of the Disclosure Schedule sets forth a true, complete and correct list of all Subsidiaries (as defined below) of the Company (each hereinafter referred to individually as a **"Company Subsidiary"** and collectively as the **"Company Subsidiaries"**). For purposes of this Agreement, the term **"Subsidiary"** shall mean with respect to any Person (as defined in Section 3.2(c) hereof), any corporation or other entity of which such Person has, directly or indirectly, ownership of securities or other interests having the power to elect a majority of such corporation's Board of Directors (or similar governing body), or otherwise having the power to direct the business and policies of that corporation. Schedule 3.1(c) of the Disclosure Schedule states, with respect to the Company each jurisdiction in which it is qualified to do business, and with respect to each Company Subsidiary, its jurisdiction of incorporation or organization, its authorized capital stock, its outstanding and issued shares of such capital stock, the percentage of each class of its capital stock owned by the Company and any other Persons and jurisdictions in which it is qualified to do business.

   (d) The minute books of the Company and each Company Subsidiary are up to date and contain accurate and complete records of all meetings held of and corporate action taken by the stockholders, and the Board of Directors.

Section 3.2 Capitalization.

   (a) The authorized capital stock of the Company consists solely of (i) 40,000,000 shares of Common Stock, $.001 par value (**"Common Stock"**), of which 12,000,000 shares of Common Stock are issued and outstanding, (ii) 11,000,000 shares of Series A Preferred Stock, $.001 par value, (**"Series A Preferred Stock"**), of which 1,000,000 shares of Series A Preferred Stock are issued and outstanding, (iii) 5,000,000 shares of Series B Preferred Stock, $.001 par value, (**"Series B Preferred Stock"**) of which 4,000,000 shares of Series B Preferred Stock are issued and outstanding. The Company's Common Stock, Series A Preferred Stock and Series B Preferred Stock is collectively referred to as **"Company Stock."** All of the issued and outstanding shares of Company Stock and the capital stock of each Company Subsidiary have been duly authorized and are validly issued, fully paid and nonassessable. All of the issued and outstanding shares of Company Stock have been issued in compliance with state and federal securities laws. Schedule 3.2(a) of the Disclosure Schedule sets forth a true and complete list of the holders of record shares of Company Stock and the number of such shares owned of record and beneficially by each such holder. Schedule 3.2(a) of the Disclosure Schedule sets forth a true and complete list of the Options, outstanding as of the date hereof, including the name of each holder thereof, the number of shares of Company Stock subject to each such Option, the per share exercise price for each such Option, the grant date of each such Option and whether each such Option was intended at the time of issuance to be an incentive stock option or a non-qualified stock option.

   (b) The Company is and shall be on the Closing Date the sole record and beneficial holder of all the issued and outstanding shares of capital stock of each Company Subsidiary, free and clear of all Liens. For purposes of this Agreement, the term **"Liens"** shall mean any charges, claims, community property interests, conditions, conditional sale or other title retention agreements, covenants, easements, encumbrances, equitable interests, exceptions, liens, mortgages, options, pledges, rights of first refusal, building use restrictions, rights of way, security interests, servitudes, statutory liens, variances, or restrictions of any kind, including any restrictions on use, voting, transfer, alienation, receipt of income, or exercise of any other attribute of ownership.

(c) Except as set forth in <u>Schedule 3.2(c)</u> of the Disclosure Schedule and the Options listed on <u>Annex I</u>, there are no shares of capital stock or other securities of the Company or any Company Subsidiary (i) reserved for issuance or (ii) subject to preemptive rights or any outstanding subscriptions, options, warrants, calls, rights, convertible securities or other agreements or other instruments outstanding or in effect giving any Person the right to acquire any shares of capital stock or other securities of the Company or any Company Subsidiary or any commitments of any character relating to the issued or unissued capital stock or other securities of the Company or any Company Subsidiary. The Company does not have outstanding any bonds, debentures, notes or other obligations the holders of which have the right to vote (or convertible into or exercisable for securities having the right to vote) with the stockholders of the Company on any matter. For purposes of this Agreement, the term **"Person"** shall mean any individual, corporation (including any non-profit corporation), general or limited partnership, limited liability company, Governmental Entity (as defined in Section 3.4 hereof), joint venture, estate trust, association, organization or other entity of any kind or nature.

Section 3.3 Authority. Company has the full legal right, requisite corporate power and authority and has taken all corporate action necessary in order to execute, deliver and perform fully, its obligations under this Agreement and to consummate the transactions contemplated herein. The execution and delivery of this Agreement by the Company and the consummation by the Company of the transactions contemplated herein have been duly authorized and approved by the Board of Directors of the Company and no other corporate proceeding with respect to the Company is necessary to authorize this Agreement or the transactions contemplated herein. This Agreement has been duly executed and delivered by Company and constitutes a valid and binding agreement of Company, enforceable against Company in accordance with its terms, except as such enforceability may be limited by general principles of bankruptcy, insolvency, reorganization and moratorium and other similar laws relating to creditor's rights (the **"Bankruptcy Exceptions"**).

Section 3.4 Governmental Filings and Consents. Except as set forth in <u>Schedule 3.4</u> of the Disclosure Schedule, no notices, reports, submissions or other filings are required to be made by, and no consents, registrations, approvals, declarations, permits, expiration of any applicable waiting periods or authorizations are required to be obtained by, (collectively, **"Consents"**) the Company or any Company Subsidiary from, any foreign, federal, state, local, municipal, county or other governmental, quasi-governmental, administrative or regulatory authority, body, agency, court, tribunal, commission or other similar entity (including any branch, department or official thereof) (**"Governmental Entity"**), in connection with the execution or delivery of this Agreement by Company, the performance by Company of its obligations hereunder or the consummation by Company of the transactions contemplated herein.

Section 3.5   No Violations.   Assuming the obtaining of the Consents set forth in <u>Schedule 3.4</u> and <u>Schedule 3.5</u> of the Disclosure Schedule, the execution and delivery of this Agreement by Company does not, and the performance and consummation by Company of any of the transactions contemplated herein will not, with respect to the Company and each Company Subsidiary, directly or indirectly (with or without the giving of notice or the lapse of time or both);

(a)   contravene, conflict with, or constitute or result in a breach or violation of, or a default under any provision of the Company's Organizational Documents;

(b)   contravene, conflict with, or constitute or result in a breach or violation of, or a default under, or the acceleration of, or the triggering of any payment or other obligations pursuant to any existing Benefit Plan (as defined in Section 3.10(a) hereof) or any grant or award made under any Benefit Plan;

(c)   contravene, conflict with, or constitute or result in a breach or violation of, or a default under, or the cancellation, modification or termination of, or the acceleration of, or the creation of a Lien on any properties or assets owned or used by the Company or any Company Subsidiary pursuant to, or require the making of any filing or the obtaining of any Consent under, any provision of any agreement, license, lease, understanding, contract, loan, note, mortgage, indenture, promise, undertaking or other commitment or obligation (whether written or oral and express or implied) (a **"Contract"**), under which the Company or any Company Subsidiary is or may become bound or is or may become subject to any obligation or Liability (as defined in Section 3.23 hereof) or by which any of their respective assets owned or used are or may become bound (an **"Applicable Contract"**), in each case other than as set forth in <u>Schedule 3.5</u> of the Disclosure Schedule;

(d)   contravene, conflict with, or constitute or result in a breach or violation of, any securities laws of any state, or any other federal, state, local, municipal, foreign, international, multinational, or other constitution, law, rule, standard, requirement, administrative ruling, order, ordinance, principle of common law, legal doctrine, code, regulation, statute, treaty or process (**"Law"**) or any award, decision, injunction, judgment, decree, settlement, order, process, or ruling, (whether temporary, preliminary or permanent) entered, issued, made or rendered by any court, administrative agency, arbitrator, Governmental Entity or other tribunal of competent jurisdiction (**"Order"**) or give any Governmental Entity or any other Person the right to challenge any of the transactions contemplated herein or to exercise any remedy or obtain any relief under, any Law or any Order to which the Company or any Company Subsidiary, or any of the assets owned or used by the Company or any Company Subsidiary, are subject; or

(e)   contravene, conflict with, or constitute or result in a breach or violation of, or a default under, any provision of, or give any Governmental Entity the right to revoke, withdraw, suspend, cancel, terminate or modify, any approval, franchise, certificate of authority, order, consent, judgment, decree, license, permit, waiver or other authorization issued, granted, given or otherwise made available by or under the authority of any Governmental Entity or pursuant to any Law (**"Governmental Authorization"**) that is held by the Company or any Company Subsidiary or that otherwise relates to the Business or any of the assets owned or used by the Company or any Company Subsidiary.

Section 3.6   Financial Statements.   (a)   The Company has previously furnished to Buyer the following financial statements (collectively, the **"Financial Statements"**): (i) audited consolidated balance sheet of the Company and each Company Subsidiary as at December 31, 2002 and December 31, 2001, and the audited consolidated statements of income, changes in stockholders' equity and cash flow for each of the fiscal years then ended, together with the report thereon of Ernst & Young, independent certified public accountants, (ii) audited consolidated balance sheet of the Company and each Company Subsidiary as at December 31, 2003 (including the notes thereto, the **"Balance Sheet"**), and the related audited consolidated statements of income, changes in stockholders' equity and cash flow for the fiscal year then ended, together with the report thereon of Ernst & Young, independent certified public accountants, and (iii) an unaudited consolidated balance sheet of the Company and each Company Subsidiary as at March 31, 2004 (the **"Interim Balance Sheet"**) and the related unaudited consolidated statements of income, changes in stockholders' equity and cash flow for the three months then ended, including in each case the notes thereto.

(b)   The Financial Statements and notes fairly present, the financial condition and the results of operations, changes in stockholders' equity and cash flow of the Company and the Company Subsidiaries as at the respective dates of and for the periods referred to in such Financial Statements, and have been in accordance with United States generally accepted accounting principles (**"GAAP"**) applied on a consistent basis during the periods presented, subject in the case of unaudited financial statements, to normal recurring year-end adjustments (which adjustments shall not in any event result in a Material Adverse Effect) and absence of footnotes. No financial statements of any Person other than the Company and the Company Subsidiaries are required by GAAP to be included in the consolidated financial statements of the Company.

(c)   The Financial Statements were compiled from and are in accordance with the books and records of the Company and each Company Subsidiary, as the case may be. The books and records (including the books of account and other records) of the Company and each Company Subsidiary, all of which have been made available to Buyer, are true, complete and correct, have been maintained in accordance with sound business practices and accurately present and reflect in all material respects all of the transactions and actions therein described. At the Closing, all of those books and records shall be in the possession of the Company and each Company Subsidiary.

Section 3.7   Absence of Certain Changes and Events.   Except as set forth in Schedule 3.7 of the Disclosure Schedule, since the date of the Balance Sheet, the Company and each Company Subsidiary has conducted the Business only in, and has not engaged in any transaction other than according to, the ordinary and usual course of such business in a manner consistent with its past practice (**"Ordinary Course of Business"**), and there has not been any:

(a) change in the business, operations, properties, prospects, assets, or condition of the Company or any Company Subsidiary that is reasonably likely to have a Material Adverse Effect (as defined in Section 11.1(a) hereof) on the Company:

(b) (i) material increase in salary, bonus or other compensation (other than compensation increases in the Ordinary Course of Business of any employee, director or consultant of the Company or any Company Subsidiary; or (ii) increase in benefits, material waivers or variations for the benefit of any such employee, director or consultant, material amendments, or payments or grants of awards that were not required, under any Benefit Plan), or adoption or execution of any new Benefit Plan;

(c) (i) damage to or destruction or loss of any material asset or property of the Company or any Company Subsidiary, whether or not covered by insurance;

(d) payment of, accrual or commitment for, capital expenditures in excess of $25,000 individually or $100,000 in the aggregate;

(e) (i) making of any loans or advances to any Person (other than intercompany receivables extensions of credit to customers in the Ordinary Course of Business); or (ii) payment, discharge or satisfaction of Liabilities reflected or reserved against in the Financial Statements or subsequently incurred in the Ordinary Course of Business;

(f) (i) change in the authorized or issued capital stock of the Company or any Company Subsidiary; (ii) grant of any stock option, warrant, or other right to purchase shares of capital stock of the Company or any Company Subsidiary; (iii) issuance of any security convertible into the capital stock of the Company or any Company Subsidiary; (iv) grant of any registration rights in respect of the capital stock of the Company or any Company Subsidiary; (v) reclassification, combination, split, subdivision, purchase, redemption, retirement, issuance, sale, or any other acquisition or disposition, directly or indirectly, by the Company or any Company Subsidiary of any shares of the capital stock of the Company or any Company Subsidiary; (vi) any amendment of any material term of any outstanding security of the Company or any Company Subsidiary; (vii) declaration, setting aside or payment of any dividend (whether in cash, securities or other property) or other distribution or payment in respect of the shares of the capital stock of the Company or any Company Subsidiary, except in respect of satisfaction of intercompany payables and receivables; or (viii) sale or pledge of any stock or other equity interests owned by the Company in the Company Subsidiaries;

(g) sale of any material asset or property of the Company or a Company Subsidiary;

(h) material change in accounting methods used by the Company; or

(i) agreement (whether written or oral and express or implied) by the Company or any Company Subsidiary to do any of the foregoing.

Section 3.8 Actions; Orders.

(a) Except as set forth in <u>Schedule 3.8</u> of the Disclosure Schedule, there are no civil, criminal, administrative, investigative, quasi-judicial or informal actions, audits, demands, suits, claims, arbitrations, hearings, litigations, disputes, investigations or other proceedings of any kind or nature in any federal, state, local or foreign jurisdiction or before any arbitrator at law, in equity or otherwise (**"Actions"**) filed, commenced, pending or, to the Knowledge of the Company, or Management Stockholders, Threatened (as defined in Section 11.1(c) hereof), against the Company or any Company Subsidiary or any of their respective assets.

(b)   Except as set forth in <u>Schedule 3.8(b)</u> of the Disclosure Schedule, neither the Company nor any Company Subsidiary or any of the assets owned or used by the Company or Company Subsidiary is subject to any Order.

(c)   None of the matters set forth in <u>Schedule 3.8 (a)</u> or <u>(b)</u> of the Disclosure Schedule are reasonably expected to result in a Material Adverse Effect on the Company. To the Knowledge of the Company or the Managing Stockholders, no Action or Order has been Threatened and no event has occurred or circumstance exists that is reasonably likely to give rise to or serve as a basis for the commencement of any such Action or the issuance of any such Order of the nature described in Section 3.8(a) or 3.8(b). Company has delivered or made available to Buyer copies of all pleadings, correspondence and other documents relating to each Action and Order listed in <u>Schedule 3.8(a)</u> or <u>3.8(b)</u> of the Disclosure Schedule.

Section 3.9   Taxes.

(a)   Except as set forth in <u>Schedule 3.9(a)</u> of the Disclosure Schedule, (i) all Tax Returns (defined in Section 3.9(j) hereof) that are or were required to be filed by or with respect to the Company and each Company Subsidiary, either separately or as a member of an affiliated, combined, consolidated or unitary group of corporations, have been filed on a timely basis (taking into account all extensions of due dates) in accordance with applicable Law, (ii) all Tax Returns referred to in clause (i) are true complete and correct in all material respects, (iii) all Taxes (defined in Section 3.9(j) due for the periods covered by such Tax Returns, including any Taxes payable pursuant to any assessment made by the Internal Revenue Service or other relevant taxing authority in respect of such periods, have been paid in full, and (iv) all estimated Taxes required to be paid in respect of the Company and each Company Subsidiary have been paid in full when due in accordance with applicable Law. Company has delivered or made available to Buyer true and correct copies of all Tax Returns filed by the Company, each Company Subsidiary, and any affiliated, combined, consolidated or unitary group of which the Company or any Company Subsidiary is or was a member (insofar as such Tax Returns relate to the Company or any Company Subsidiary).

(b)   Except as set forth in <u>Schedule 3.9(b)</u> of the Disclosure Schedule, (i) the Tax Returns referred to in Section 3.9(a) have been examined by the Internal Revenue Service or the appropriate state, local or foreign taxing authority, or the period for assessment of the Taxes in respect of which such Tax Returns were filed has expired under the applicable statute of limitations (after giving effect to all extensions and waivers), (ii) all deficiencies asserted or assessments made as a result of such examinations have been paid in full, and no issues that were raised by the Internal Revenue Service or other relevant taxing authority, in connection with any such examination are currently pending, and (iii) none of Seller nor the Company nor any Company Subsidiary has given or been requested to give a waiver or extension (or is or could be subject to a waiver or extension given by any other Person) of any statute of limitations relating to the payment of Taxes of the Company or any Company Subsidiary or for which the Company or any Company Subsidiary is or is reasonably likely to be liable.

(c)   Except as set forth in <u>Schedule 3.9(c)</u> of the Disclosure Schedule, the charges, accruals and reserves with respect to Taxes provided in the Balance Sheet and the Interim Balance Sheet are adequate (determined in accordance with GAAP on a basis consistent with that of the preceding period) to cover the aggregate liability of the Company and each Company Subsidiary for Taxes in respect of all Pre-Closing Tax Periods (defined in Section 3.9(j)) for which Tax Returns have not yet been filed or for which Taxes are not yet due and payable.

(d)   There is no Tax sharing agreement, contract or intercompany account system in existence that would require any payment by the Company or any Company Subsidiary after the date of this Agreement. Neither the Company nor any Company Subsidiary has any liability for indemnification of third parties with respect to Taxes or any liability for Taxes as a transferee.

(e)   The Company is not a "foreign person" within the meaning of Section 1445 of the Code.

(f)   Neither the Company nor any Company Subsidiary is a party to any agreement, contract, arrangement or plan that has resulted or would result, separately or in the aggregate, in the payment of any "excess parachute payment" within the meaning of Section 280G of the Code.

(g)   There are no Liens for Taxes (other than Liens for current Taxes not yet due and payable) upon the assets of the Company or any Company Subsidiary. There is no basis for the assertion of any claim for Taxes which, if adversely determined, would or is reasonably likely to result in the imposition of any Lien on the assets of the Company for any Company Subsidiary or otherwise adversely affect Buyer, the Company or any Company Subsidiary or their use of such assets.

(h)   All Taxes that the Company or any Company Subsidiary is or was required by Law to withhold or collect have been duly withheld or collected and, to the extent required by applicable Law, have been paid to the proper Governmental Entity or other Person.

(i)   Company has provided or made available to Buyer copies of all record retention agreements currently in effect between the Company or any Company Subsidiary and any taxing authority.

(j)   For purposes of this Agreement, the following terms shall have the following meanings:

"Code" means the Internal Revenue Code of 1986, as amended.

"Pre-Closing Tax Period" means any taxable year or period that ends on or before the Closing Date and, with respect to any taxable year or period beginning before and ending after the Closing Date, the portion of such taxable year or period ending on and including the Closing Date.

"Tax" means any Federal, state, local or foreign income, gross receipts, license, severance, occupation, capital gains, premium, environmental, customs, duties, profits, disability, registration, alternative or add on minimum, estimated, withholding, payroll, employment, unemployment, insurance, social security (or similar), excise, production, sales, use, value-added, occupancy, franchise, real property, personal property, business and occupation, mercantile, windfall profits, capital stock, stamp, transfer, workmen's compensation or other tax, of any kind whatsoever, including any interest, penalties, additions, assessments or deferred liability with respect thereto, and any interest in respect of such penalties, additions, assessments or deferred liability, whether or not disputed.

"Tax Return" means any return, report, notice, form, declaration, claim for refund, estimate, election, or information statement or other document relating to any Tax, including any Schedule or attachment thereto, and any amendment thereof.

Section 3.10   Employee Benefits: ERISA.

(a)   Schedule 3.10(a) of the Disclosure Schedule sets forth a true, complete and correct list of, each profit-sharing, pension, severance, thrift, savings, incentive change of control, employment, retirement, bonus, deferred compensation, group life and health insurance other employee benefit plan, agreement, arrangement or commitment, which is maintained, contributed to or required to be contributed to by the Company or any Company Subsidiary on behalf of any current or former employee, director or consultant of the Company or any Company Subsidiary (all of which are hereinafter referred to as the **"Benefit Plans"**). Schedule 3.10(a) identifies each of the Benefit Plans which constitutes an "employee benefit plan" as defined in Section 3(3) of the Employee Retirement Income Security Act of 1974, as amended (**"ERISA"**). Neither the Company nor any Company Subsidiary has any formal commitment, or intention communicated to employees, to create any additional Benefit Plan or modify or change any existing Benefit Plan.

(b)   With respect to each of the Benefit Plans, the Company has delivered to Buyer true, complete and correct copies of each of the following documents, if applicable: (i) the plan document (including all amendments thereto); (ii) trust documents and insurance contracts (iii) the annual report for the last two years (iv) the actuarial report for the last two years; (v) the most recent summary plan description, together with each summary of material modifications; (vi) the most recent determination letter received from the Internal Revenue Service; (vii) the most recent nondiscrimination tests performed under ERISA and the Code (including 401(k) and 401(m) tests).

(c)   Each Benefit Plan has been operated and administered in accordance with its terms and with applicable law including, but not limited to, ERISA and the Code, and all notices filings and disclosures required by ERISA or the Code have been timely made. Each Benefit Plan which is an "employee pension benefit plan" within the meaning of Section 3(2) of ERISA (a **"Pension Plan"**) and which is intended to be qualified under Section 401 (a) of the Code has received a favorable determination letter from the Internal Revenue Service for "TRA" (as defined in Rev. Proc. 93-39), or will file for such a determination letter prior to the expiration of the remedial amendment period for such Benefit Plan and, to the Knowledge of the Company or Management Stockholders, there are no circumstances that are reasonably likely to result in revocation of any such favorable determination letter. There is no pending or, to the Knowledge of the Company, Threatened litigation relating to any of the Benefit Plans. None of the Company or any Company Subsidiary has engaged in a transaction with respect to any Benefit Plan that, assuming the taxable period of such transaction expired as of the date hereof, could subject the Company or any Company Subsidiary or any Benefit Plan to a Tax or penalty imposed by ERISA. No action has been taken with respect to any of the Benefit Plans to either terminate any of such Benefit Plans or to cause distributions, other than in the Ordinary Course of Business to participants under such Benefit Plans.

(d)   None of the Pension Plans is a "multiemployer plan" (within the meaning of Section 4001(a)(3) of ERISA) and neither the Company nor any Company Subsidiary (or any current ERISA Affiliate) has contributed to or had any obligation to contribute to a multiemployer plan during the six-year period immediately preceding the date hereof. Neither the Company nor any Company Subsidiary has formerly contributed to, or had an obligation to contribute to a multi-employer plan.

(e)   All contributions required to be made under the terms of any Benefit Plan have been timely made when due. No Pension Plan has an "accumulated funding deficiency" (whether or not waived) within the meaning of Section 412 of the Code or Section 302 of ERISA and none of the Company, any Company Subsidiary or any ERISA Affiliate has an outstanding funding waiver.

(f)   The consummation of the transactions contemplated by this Agreement will not (or will not upon termination of employment within a fixed period of time following such consummation) (i) entitle any employee, director or consultant to severance pay, unemployment compensation or any other payment or (ii) accelerate the time of payment or vesting or increase the amount of payment with respect to any compensation due to any employee, director or consultant.

Section 3.11   Labor Matters; Employees.   Except as set forth in Schedule 3.11 of the Disclosure Schedule:

(a)   The Company and each Company Subsidiary has not been a party to, and is not bound by, any collective bargaining agreement or other labor Contract nor is any collective bargaining agreement or other labor Contract currently being negotiated, nor, to the Knowledge of the Company or Management Stockholders, are there any activities or proceedings of any labor union or labor organization to organize any of the employees of the Company or any Company Subsidiary Threatened.

(b)   There has not been, there is not presently pending or existing and, to the Knowledge of the Company or Management Stockholders, there is not threatened and there has not occurred any event or circumstance that is reasonably likely to provide the basis for, any strike, slowdown, picketing, work stoppage, labor difficulty, labor arbitration or other proceeding in respect of the grievance of any employee, application or complaint filed by an employee or union with the National Labor Relations Board or any comparable Governmental Entity and none of the employment policies or practices of the Company or a Company Subsidiary is currently being audited or investigated by any federal, state or local government agency.

(c)   There is no labor strike, dispute, claim, charge, lawsuit, proceeding, labor slowdown or stoppage pending or Threatened against or involving the Company or any Company Subsidiary.

(d) To Knowledge of Company and Management Stockholders no key employee of the Company or any Company Subsidiary, intends to terminate his or her employment following the Closing. Since December 31, 2003, neither the Company nor any Company Subsidiary has experienced any difficulties in obtaining any qualified personnel necessary for the operations of its business. The Company is not a party to any employment Contract with any individual or employee. There is not pending or existing or to the Knowledge of the Company, any Action Threatened against or affecting the Company or any Company Subsidiary relating to the alleged violation of any Law pertaining to labor relations or employment matters. To the Knowledge of the Company no event has occurred or circumstances exist that could provide the basis for such Action. The Company and each Company Subsidiary has complied in all respects with all Laws relating to employment, equal employment opportunity, nondiscrimination, immigration ages, hours, benefits, collective bargaining, the payment of social security and similar taxes, occupational safety and health. The Company is not subject to any settlement or consent decree with any present or former employee, employee representative or any Governmental Entity relating to claims of discrimination or other claims in respect to employment practices and policies; and no Governmental Entity has issued a judgment, order, decree or finding with respect to the labor and employment practices (including practices relating to discrimination) of the Company or any Company Subsidiary. Since December 31, 2001 the Company has not incurred any liability or obligation under the Worker Adjustment and Retraining Notification Act or similar state laws; and neither Company nor any Company Subsidiary has laid off more than ten percent (10%) of its employees at any single site of employment in any ninety (90) day period during the twelve (12) month period ending at the Closing Date.

(e) The Company is in compliance in all respects with the provisions of the Americans with Disabilities Act.

(f) The consummation of the transactions contemplated by this Agreement will not (or will not upon termination of employment within a fixed period of time following such consummation) (i) entitle any employee, director or consultant to severance pay, unemployment compensation or any other payment or (ii) accelerate the time of payment or vesting or increase the amount of payment with respect to any compensation due to any employee, director or consultant.

Section 3.12 Compliance with Laws; Governmental Authorizations; etc.

(a) Except as set forth in <u>Schedule 13.12(a)</u> of the Disclosure Schedule, the Company and each Company Subsidiary is in compliance in all material respects with all applicable Laws.

(b) Except as set forth in <u>Schedule 3.12(b)</u> of the Disclosure Schedule, the Company and each Company Subsidiary hold and maintain in full force and effect all Governmental Authorizations required to conduct the Business in the manner and in all suchjurisdictions as it is currently conducted and to permit the Company and the Company Subsidiaries to own and use their respective properties and assets in the manner in which they currently own and use such assets.

(i)   The Company and each Company Subsidiary is, and at all times has been, in full in compliance with all of the terms and requirements of each such Governmental Authorization;

(ii)   no event has occurred or circumstance exists that is reasonably likely to (with or without the giving of notice or the lapse of time or both) (A) constitute or result, directly or indirectly, in a violation of, or a failure to comply with, any term or requirement of any such Governmental Authorization, or (B) result, directly or indirectly, in the revocation, withdrawal, suspension, cancellation, or termination of, or any modification to, any such Governmental Authorization;

(iii)   neither the Company nor any Company Subsidiary has received, at any time since December 31, 2001 any notice or other communication from any Governmental Entity or any other Person regarding (A) any actual, alleged, possible or potential violation of, or failure to comply with, any term or requirement of any Governmental Authorization or Law, or (B) any actual, proposed, possible, or potential revocation, withdrawal, suspension, cancellation, termination of, or modification to any Governmental Authorization or Law;

(iv)   all applications required to have been filed for the renewal of each such Governmental Authorization have been duly filed on a timely basis with the appropriate Governmental Entity, and all other filings required to have been made with respect to each such Governmental Authorizations have been duly made on a timely basis with the appropriate Governmental Entity.

Section 3.13   Title to Properties.   The Company and each Company Subsidiary has good and marketable title to all real and personal properties and assets owned by the Company or such Company Subsidiary, free and clear of any Lien, except for (i) liens for Taxes not yet due and payable or for Taxes that the taxpayer is contesting in good faith through appropriate proceedings, (ii) purchase money liens and liens securing rental payments under capital lease arrangements, and (iii) other minor imperfections of title that do not have any material impact with respect to the ownership or use of the applicable property (**"Permitted Exceptions"**). All properties held under lease by the Company or any Company Subsidiary are held under valid, subsisting and enforceable leases.

Section 3.14   Real and Personal Property.

(a)   Real Property.   Neither the Company nor any Company Subsidiary owns or hold any interest in real property other than as set forth in Schedule 3.14(a) to the Disclosure Schedule (the **"Real Property"**). Except as set forth on such schedule, the Company and each Company Subsidiary, as applicable, has good and marketable title to all Real Property and none of the Real Property is subject to any Lien, except for Permitted Exceptions.

(b)   Personal Property.   Except as set forth on Schedule 3.14(b) of the Disclosure Schedule and except for inventory, supplies and other personal property disposed of or consumed, and accounts receivable collected or written off, and cash utilized, all in the Ordinary Course of Business consistent with past practice, the Company and each Subsidiary, as applicable owns all of its inventory, equipment and other personal property (both tangible and intangible) reflected on the Balance Sheet free and clear of any Liens, except for Permitted Exceptions. All of the assets presently owned by the Company and its subsidiaries are sufficient to operate the Business as currently conducted.

(c) <u>Condition of Properties</u>. Except as set forth on <u>Schedule 13.14(c)</u> of the Disclosure Schedule, the tangible personal property owned or leased by the Company and each Company Subsidiary, as applicable, is structurally sound, free of defects and deficiencies and in good operating condition and repair, (ordinary wear and tear excepted).

(d) <u>Compliance</u>. The continued ownership, operation, use and occupancy of the Real Property and the improvements thereto, and the continued use and occupancy of the leasehold estates the subject of the Real Property Leases (as defined in Section 3.15 hereof) as currently operated, used and occupied will not violate any zoning, building, health, flood control, fire or other law, ordinance, order or regulation or any restrictive covenant. There are no violations of any Law affecting any portion of the Real Property or the leasehold estates and no written notice of any such violation has been issued by any Governmental Entity.

Section 3.15 Real Property Leases; Options. <u>Schedule 3.15</u> to the Disclosure Schedule sets forth a list by common address and description of lease parties (i) all leases and subleases under which the Company and each Company Subsidiary is lessor or lessee or sublessor or sublessee of any real property, together with all amendments, supplements, nondisturbance agreements, brokerage and commission agreements and other agreements pertaining thereto (**"Real Property Leases"**); (ii) all material options held by the Company and each Company Subsidiary or contractual obligations on the part of the Company and each Company Subsidiary to purchase or acquire any interest in real property; and (iii) all options granted by the Company and each Company Subsidiary or contractual obligations on the part of the Company and each Company Subsidiary to sell or dispose of any material interest in real property. Copies of all Real Property Leases and such options and contractual obligations have been delivered to Buyer. The Company and each Company Subsidiary has not assigned any Real Property Leases or any such options or obligations. There are no disputes, oral agreements or forbearance programs in effect as to any Real Property Lease; all facilities leased under the Real Property Leases (including alternations constructed by the Company and each Company Subsidiary and shelving installed by the Company and each Company Subsidiary) have received all approvals of Governmental Entities (including licenses and permits) required in connection with the operation thereof; and all facilities leased under the Real Property Leases are supplied with utilities and other services necessary for the operation of said facilities. There are no Liens on the interest of the Company and each Company Subsidiary in the Real Property Leases except for Permitted Exceptions. The Real Property Leases and options and contractual obligations listed on <u>Schedule 3.15</u> to the Disclosure Schedule are in full force and effect (subject to Bankruptcy Exceptions) and constitute binding obligations of the Company and each Company Subsidiary, as applicable, and (x) there are no defaults thereunder by the Company or the applicable Company Subsidiary and (y) no event has occurred that with notice, lapse of time or both would constitute a default by the Company or the applicable Company Subsidiary, as applicable, or, to the Knowledge of the Company and the Management Shareholders, by any other party thereto.

Section 3.16 *Intellectual Property Rights.*

(a) For purposes of this Agreement, the following terms shall have the following meanings:

"Intellectual Property" means (whether international or United States) (a) all trademarks, service marks, trade dress, logos, trade names, and corporate names (whether registered or unregistered), together with all translations, adaptations, derivations, and combinations thereof and including all goodwill associated therewith, and all applications, registrations, and renewals in connection therewith (**"Marks"**), (b) all copyrightable works, all copyrights (whether or registered or unregistered), and all applications, registrations, and renewals in connection therewith (**"Copyrights"**), (c) all mask works and all applications, registrations, and renewals in connection therewith, (d) all trade secrets and confidential business information (including ideas, research and development, know-how, formulas, compositions, manufacturing and production processes and techniques, technical data, designs, drawings, specifications, customer and supplier lists, pricing and cost information, and business and marketing plans and proposals), (e) all computer software (including data and related documentation), all inventions (whether patentable or unpatentable and whether or not reduced to practice), all improvements thereto, (f) all URL's and domain names, and (g) all patents, patent applications, and patent disclosures, together with all reissuances, continuations, continuations-in-part, revisions, extensions, and reexaminations thereof (**"Patents"**), (h) all other proprietary rights relating to the foregoing, and (i) all copies and tangible embodiments thereof (in whatever form or medium).

"Company Intellectual Property" shall mean any Intellectual Property that is owned by or licensed to the Company or any Company Subsidiary (other than mass marketed software licensed to the Company or any Company subsidiary) or used thereby (collectively, the "Intellectual Property").

"Company Registered Intellectual Property" means Company Intellectual Property consisting of (i) Patents, (ii) registered Marks, and (iii) registered Copyrights, (and in each case applications for registration), and (iv) any other Company Intellectual and Property that is the subject of an application, certificate, filing, registration or other document issued by, filed with, or recorded by any Governmental Entity.

(b) Schedule 3.16(b) of the Disclosure Schedule lists the Company Registered Intellectual Property. Each item of Registered Intellectual Property registered with a Governmental Entity is valid and subsisting; all necessary registration, maintenance and renewal fees currently due in connection with such Registered Intellectual Property have been made and all necessary documents, recordations and certificates in connection with such Registered Intellectual Property have been filed with the relevant patent, copyrights, trademark authorities in the United States or foreign jurisdictions, as the case may be, for the purpose of maintaining such Company Registration Intellectual Property.

(c)   The Company owns and has good and marketable title to, or has the right to use pursuant to a written license, sublicense, agreement or other permission, exclusive right and title to each item of Company Intellectual Property free and clear of any Lien (excluding non-exclusive licenses and related restrictions granted in the Ordinary Course of Business). Except as stated on Schedule 3.16(c) of the Disclosure Schedule, there are no pending proceedings or adverse claims made or, to the Knowledge of the Company or Management Stockholders, Threatened against the Company or any Company Subsidiary with respect to Company Intellectual Property; and there has been no litigation commenced or Threatened in writing within the past five (5) years with respect to Company Registered Intellectual Property or the rights of the Company or a Company Subsidiary therein. The Company Intellectual Property or the use thereof by the Company or a Company Subsidiary does not conflict with or infringe any Intellectual Property of any other Person (**"Third Party Intellectual Property"**), (ii) such Third Party Intellectual Property or its use by others or any other conduct of a third party does not conflict with or infringe upon any Company Registered Intellectual Property or its use by the Company or any Company Subsidiary.

(d)   To the Knowledge of the Company and Management Stockholders, none of the Company's or any Company Subsidiary's key employees is in violation of any term of any employment contract, patent disclosure agreement, confidential agreement or any other Contract relating to the relationship of any such employee with the Company or any Company Subsidiary or any other party the result of which has had or is reasonably likely to have a Material Adverse Effect.

Section 3.17   Inventory.   The inventory of the Company and each Company Subsidiary consists of raw materials and supplies, manufactured and purchased parts, goods on order and in process, and finished goods, all of which is merchantable and fit for the purpose for which it was procured or manufactured (including all inventory, that is reflected on the Interim Balance Sheet) is of such qualify and quantity as to be saleable and useable by the Company and Companies subsidiaries in the Ordinary Course of Business, and none of the inventory is slow moving and obsolete (including without limitation, inventory of a type which has not had substantial sales during the past 12 months), damaged or defective, except as accounted for in the reserve for inventory writedown reflected in the Interim Balance Sheet as adjusted for the passage of time through the Closing Date in accordance with the past custom and practice of the Company.

Section 3.18   Accounts Receivable.   Except as set forth in Schedule 3.18 of the Disclosure Schedule, all accounts receivable of the Company and each Company Subsidiary presented in the Balance Sheet and the Interim Balance Sheet and those arising since the date thereof are (a) reflected properly on their respective books and records, (b) are valid and genuine, (c) arise out of bona fide performance of services or transactions, (d) are not subject to setoffs, defenses or counterclaims, (e) are current and collectable, and will be collected in accordance with their terms at their recorded amounts (except as set forth as reserves on the Interim Balance Sheet.

Section 3.19 Contracts; No Default.

(a) Except as set forth in Schedule 3.19(a) of the Disclosure Schedule, neither the Company nor any Company Subsidiary is a party to or bound by any Contract (excluding in each case policies of insurance issued in the Ordinary Course of Business):

(i)   evidencing indebtedness for borrowed money or pursuant to which the Company or any Company Subsidiary has guaranteed (including guarantees by way of acting as surety, co-signer, endorser, co-maker, indemnitor or otherwise) any obligation of any other Person;

(ii)   prohibiting or limiting the ability of the Company or any Company Subsidiary (A) to engage in any line of business, (B) to compete with any Person, (C) to carry on or expand the nature or geographical scope of the Business anywhere in the world or (D) to disclose any confidential information in the possession of the Company or any Company Subsidiary (and not otherwise generally available to the public) that is reasonably likely to have a Material Adverse Effect on the Company or any Company Subsidiary in the conduct of the Business which relates to the use of an item of Intellectual Property;

(iii)   pursuant to which it (A) leases or licenses from or to any other Person any tangible personal property providing for lease payments in excess of $10,000 per annum or (B) purchases or sells materials, supplies, equipment or services outside the Ordinary Course of Business;

(iv)   which is a partnership agreement, joint venture agreement, profit sharing or other Contract (however named);

(v)   providing for the acquisition or disposition after the date of this Agreement of any portion of the Business or assets of the Company or any Company Subsidiary other than in the Ordinary Course of Business;

(vi)   providing for team rider agreements, or sponsorship agreements;

(vii)   provides for a distribution or seller representative agreement or arrangement;

(viii)   pursuant to which the Company or a Company Subsidiary has the right to use an item of Third Party Intellectual Property;

(ix)   pursuant to which the Company or a Company Subsidiary has granted a Person to use an item of Company Intellectual Property.

(x)   involving a payment after the date hereof of an amount of money in excess of $10,000 and continuing (including mandatory renewals or extensions which do not require the consent of the Company or any Company Subsidiary) more than one year from its date and not made in the Ordinary Course of Business;

(xi)   a mortgage, pledge, security agreement, deed of trust or other document granting a Lien over any real or personal asset or property owned by the Company or any Company Subsidiary.

Company has delivered or made available to Buyer a true, complete and correct copy of each Contracts identified or required to be identified in Schedule 3.19(a) of the Disclosure Schedule and each such Contract is in full force and effect and is valid and enforceable in accordance with its terms.

(b)   Except as set forth in Schedule 3.19(b) of the Disclosure Schedule,

(i)   the Company and each Company Subsidiary is in substantial compliance with all applicable material terms and requirements of each Contract identified or required to be identified in Schedule 3.19(a) of the Disclosure Schedule;

(ii)　to the knowledge of the Company and the Management Stockholders, each other Person that has or had any obligation or Liability under any Contract identified or required to be identified in <u>Schedule 3.19(a)</u> of the Disclosure Schedule is in substantial compliance with all applicable terms and requirements of each such Contract;

(iii)　no event has occurred or circumstance exists (presently or as a result of the change in control of Company by this Agreement) that is reasonably likely to (with or without the giving of notice or the lapse of time or both) contravene, conflict with, or result in a violation or breach of, or give the Company or any Company Subsidiary or other Person the right to declare a default or exercise any remedy under, or to accelerate the maturity or performance of, or to cancel, terminate, or modify, any Contract identified or required to be identified in <u>Schedule 3.19(a)</u> of the Disclosure Schedule.

Section 3.20　*Environmental Matters.*

(a)　Except as set forth in <u>Schedule 3.20</u> of the Disclosure Schedule,

(i)　the Company and each Company Subsidiary has conducted the Business in full compliance with all applicable Environmental Laws (as defined in Section 3.20(b) hereof), including having all permits, licenses and other approvals and Governmental Authorizations necessary or appropriate for the Business under any Environmental Law;

(ii)　neither the Company nor any Company Subsidiary has, in connection with the Business, disposed of or released any Hazardous Substances (as defined in Section 3.18(c) hereof) or hazardous wastes on any properties presently or formerly owned, operated or used by the Company or any Company Subsidiary (including soil, groundwater or surface water on, under or emanating from the properties, and buildings thereon) (the **"Properties"**) in violation of applicable Environmental Law;

(iii)　the Company and each Company Subsidiary has not received any notices, demand letter, claim, notice of violation noncompliance letter or request for information from any Governmental Entity or any third party indicating that the Company or any Company Subsidiary may be in violation of, or liable under, any Environmental Law;

(iv)　there are no Actions pending or Threatened against the Company or any Company Subsidiary with respect to the Company, any Company Subsidiary or the Properties relating to any violation or alleged violation of or liability under any Environmental Law;

(v)　no reports reports or notifications have been filed, or are required to be filed, by the Company or any Company Subsidiary concerning the release of any Hazardous Substance or the threatened or actual violation of any Environmental Law on or at the Properties;

(vi)　no Hazardous Substance or any waste has been disposed of, transferred released or transported from any of the Properties during the time such property was owned or leased or operated by the Company or any Company Subsidiary, other than as permitted by, and would not be expected to result in Liability under, applicable Environmental Law;

(vii)　there have been no environmental investigations, studies, audits, tests, reviews or other analyses conducted by, in the possession of, or otherwise available to the Company or any Company Subsidiary relating to the Company, any Company Subsidiary or the Properties which have not been delivered to Buyer prior to the date hereto; and

(viii) the Company and each Company Subsidiary has not incurred, and none of the Properties are subject to, any Liabilities (fixed or contingent) including those relating to any Action or Order, arising under any Environmental Law.

(b) **"Environmental Law"** means (i) any Law or Governmental Authorization, (x) relating to the protection, preservation or restoration of the environment (including air, water vapor, surface water, groundwater, drinking water supply, surface land, subsurface land, structures or any natural resource), or to human health or safety, or (y) the exposure to, or the use, storage, recycling, treatment, generation, transportation, processing, handling, labeling, production, release or disposal of Hazardous Substances, in each case as amended and as now or hereafter in effect. The term Environmental Law includes, without limitation, the federal Comprehensive Environmental Response Compensation and Liability Act of 1980, the Superfund Amendments and Reauthorization Act, the Federal Water Pollution Control Act of 1972, the federal Clean Air Act, the federal Clean Water Act, the federal Resource Conservation and Recovery Act of 1976 (including the Hazardous and Solid Waste Amendments thereto), the federal Solid Waste Disposal and the federal Toxic Substance Control Act, the Federal Insecticide, Fungicide and Rodenticide Act, the Federal Occupational Safety and Health Act of 1970 and any similar state or local law, each as amended and as now or hereafter in effect, and (ii) any common law or equitable doctrine (including, without, limitation, injunctive relief and tort doctrines such as negligence, nuisance, trespass and strict liability) that may impose Liability or obligations for injuries or damages due to, or threatened as a result of, the presence of or exposure to any Hazardous Substance.

(c) **"Hazardous Substance"** means any substance presently or hereafter listed, defined, designated or classified, as hazardous, toxic, radioactive or dangerous, or otherwise regulated, under any Environmental Law, whether by type or by quantity, including any substance containing any such substance as a component. Hazardous Substance includes, without limitation, any carcinogen, mutagen, teratogen, waste, pollutant, contaminant, hazardous substance, toxic substance, hazardous waste, special waste, industrial substance or petroleum or any derivative or by-product thereof, radon, radioactive material, asbestos, asbestos containing material, urea formaldehyde insulation, lead and polychlorinated biphenyl.

Section 3.21 Insurance.

(a) Schedule 3.21(a) of the Disclosure Schedule sets forth a true, complete and correct list of all insurance policies or binders of fire, liability, workmen's compensation, motor vehicle, directors' and officers' liability, property, casualty, life and other forms of insurance owned, held by, or applied for, or the premiums for which are paid by the Company or any Company Subsidiary. Company and each Company Subsidiary has delivered or made available to Buyer (i) true, complete and correct copies of such policies and binders and all pending applications for any such policies or binders and (ii) any statement by the auditors of the Financial Statements with regard to the adequacy of the coverage or of the reserves for claims. Notwithstanding anything to the contrary contained herein, the assets of the Company and the Company Subsidiaries shall include any proceeds of any such policy and any benefits thereunder, and any claims by the Company or any Company Subsidiary in respect thereof, to the extent arising out of any such casualty to any asset of the Company or any Company Subsidiary occurring after the date hereof and prior to the Closing, and no such proceeds shall be divided, distributed or otherwise paid out of said Company or any Company Subsidiary.

(b)   Except as set forth in <u>Schedule 3.21(b)</u> of the Disclosure Schedule, (i) the Company and each Company Subsidiary maintains insurance coverage for the Business that is customary and consistent with past practice, (ii) the Company and each Company Subsidiary is, and since December 31, 1998 has been, covered on an uninterrupted basis by valid and effective insurance policies or binders which are in the aggregate reasonable in scope and amount in light of the risks attendant to the business in which the Company or any Company Subsidiary is or has been engaged, (iii) all such policies or binders are in full force and effect, no notice of cancellation, termination, revocation or limitation that any insurance policy is no longer in full force or effect or that the issuer of any policy is not willing or able to perform its obligations thereunder, has been received with respect to any such policy and all premiums due and payable thereon have been paid in full on a timely basis; and will continue in full force and effect through and following the Closing, (iv) there are no pending or, to the Knowledge of the Company Threatened, material claims against such insurance by the Company or any Company Subsidiary as to which the insurers have denied liability, and (iv) there exist no material claims under such insurance policies or binders that have not been properly and timely submitted by the Company or any Company Subsidiary to its insurers.

Section 3.22   *Brokers and Finders*.   Except as set forth in <u>Schedule 3.22</u> of the Disclosure Schedule, no agent, brokers investment banker, intermediary, finder, Person or firm acting on behalf of the Company or any Company Subsidiary or which has been retained by or is authorized to act on behalf of the Company or any Company Subsidiary is or would be entitled to any broker's or finder's fee or any other commission or similar fee, directly or indirectly, from any of the parties hereto in connection with the execution of this Agreement or upon consummation of the transactions contemplated herein.

Section 3.23   *No Undisclosed Liabilities*.   Except as set forth in <u>Schedule 3.23</u> of the Disclosure Schedule, since the Date of the Interim Balance Sheet, neither the Company nor any Company Subsidiary has incurred any Liabilities other than Liabilities for performance under contracts or agreements to which the Company or any Company Subsidiary is a party, (ii) Liabilities which are reflected or reserved against in the Closing Balance Sheet, or (iii) Liabilities incurred in the Ordinary Course of Business. For purposes of this Agreement, the term **"Liability"** shall mean any indebtedness, debt, liability, commitment, guaranty, claim, loss, deficiency, cost, expense, obligation, liability or obligation of any kind, character or nature whatsoever, whether known or unknown, choate or inchoate, secured or unsecured, matured or unmatured, accrued, fixed, absolute, contingent or otherwise, and whether due or to become due.

Section 3.24 Bank Accounts. Schedule 3.24 of the Disclosure Schedule hereto sets forth a list of the bank names, locations and account numbers of all bank and safe deposit box accounts of the Company and each Company Subsidiary including any custodial accounts for securities owned by the Company or any Company Subsidiary and the names of all persons authorized to draw thereon or to have access thereto.

Section 3.25 Intercompany Accounts. Schedule 3.25 of the Disclosure Schedule contains a complete list of all intercompany account balances as of the date of the Balance Sheet the Company and each Company Subsidiary.

Section 3.26 Suppliers and Customers. Schedule 3.26 of the Disclosure Schedule sets forth a list of (a) the ten largest suppliers of materials or services to the Company by value during the twelve (12) month period ended December 31, 2003 (**"Major Suppliers"**) and (b) the ten largest wholesale customers of Products (as defined in Section 3.27 hereof) or services of the Company by value during the twelve (12) month period ended December 31, 2003 (the **"Major Customers"**). Except as set forth on Schedule 3.26 of the Disclosure Schedule, no Major Supplier or Major Customer of the Company has during the last twelve (12) months decreased materially or, to the Knowledge of the Company (or Management Stockholders), Threatened to decrease or limit materially its purchase of products, provision of services or supplies to the Company. To the Knowledge of the Company and the Management Stockholders the Management Stockholders there is no termination, cancellation or limitation of, or any material modification or change in, the business relationships of the Company with any Major Supplier or Major Customer. To the Knowledge of the Company and Management Stockholders, there will not be any such change in relations with Major Suppliers or Major Customers of the Company or triggering of any right of termination, cancellation or penalty or other payment in connection with or as a result of transactions contemplated by this Agreement which would or could reasonably be expected to have a Material Adverse Effect.

Section 3.27 Products; Business. Except as set forth on Schedule 3.27 of the Disclosure Schedule, during the most recent three (3) years, there are and will be no Actions or Orders by any Governmental Entity stating that any product manufactured, sold, designed, distributed or marketed by the Company (**"Products"**) is defective or unsafe or fails to meet any standards promulgated by any Governmental Entity. Except as set forth on Schedule 3.27 of the Disclosure Schedule, there is no (a) duty to recall any product or a duty to warn customers of a defect in any Product, (b) latent or overt design, manufacturing or other defect in any Product or (c) Liability for warranty claims or returns with respect to any Product. None of the Products has been subject to recall. All Products sold by the Company or a Company Subsidiary comply in all material respects with all industry and trade association standards applicable to such Products, including, without limitation, consumer product, manufacturing, labeling, quality, purity and safety laws of the United States and each state in which the Company or a Company Subsidiary sells its Products and each other jurisdiction in which the Company sells its Products. Schedule 3.27 of the Disclosure Schedule sets forth a complete and correct list of all Products currently manufactured or sold by the Company or a Company Subsidiary or manufactured or sold by the Company or a Company Subsidiary in the past twelve (12) months, or for which the Company is currently engaged in planning or product development.

Section 3.28   Promotions.   Schedule 3.31 of the Disclosure Schedule contains a complete and accurate description of the Company's material accounting policies with respect to discounts, allowances, rebates, bill-backs, price concessions, advertising fund payments, bonuses, incentives, trade deals, slotting fees, any other trade promotion program, or extended payment terms (collectively, **"Promotions"**).

Section 3.29   Sales Representatives.   Schedule 3.31 of the Disclosure Schedule sets forth a complete and correct list of each sales representative, agent, broker, distributor or other Person who has received commissions or other consideration in respect of the sale of any Product of the Company at any time from March 1, 2003. Schedule 3.31 also sets forth with respect to each such Person (a) the amount of sales generated during such time period, (b) the time period during which such sales were generated, and an indication of whether such Person is still affiliated with the Company as of the date hereof, (c) the commission rate and any other consideration paid or payable with respect to such sales, and (d) any geographic territory or customer with respect to which such Person held exclusive rights. Except as set forth on Schedule 3.31 of the Disclosure Schedule, no Person listed on Schedule 3.31 of the Disclosure Schedule was an employee of the Company during the period in which such Person generated the sales listed on Schedule 3.31 of the Disclosure Schedule. Except as set forth on Schedule 3.31 of the Disclosure Schedule, any domestic commitment in effect on the date hereof between any person listed on Schedule 3.31 of the Disclosure Schedule and the Company is terminable by the Company upon no more than 60 days notice, without any additional obligation to the Company, except for commissions or payments earned but not yet paid through the date of any such termination. Except as set forth on Schedule 3.31 of the Disclosure Schedule, any international commitment in effect on the date hereof between any Person listed on Schedule 3.31 of the Disclosure Schedule and the Company is terminable by the Company upon no more than 180 days notice, without any additional obligation to the Company, except for commissions or payments earned but not yet paid through the date of any such termination.

Section 3.30   Foreign Corrupt Practices Act.   Neither the Company nor any officer or employee has at any time made or committed to make any payments for illegal political contributions or made any bribes, kickback payments or other illegal payments. The Company has not made, offered or agreed to offer anything of value to any governmental official, political party or candidate for governmental office (or any person that the Company knows or has reason to know, will offer anything of value to any governmental official, political party or candidate for political office), such that the Company or its subsidiaries have violated the Foreign Corrupt Practices Act of 1987, as amended from time to time, and all applicable rules and regulations promulgated thereunder. There is not now nor has there ever been any employment by the Company of any governmental or political official in any country while such official was in office.

Section 3.31   Related Party Transactions.   Except as set forth in Schedule 3.31 of the Disclosure Schedule or the Financial Statements: (a) no Related Party (as defined in Section 11.1 (d) hereof) has, and no Related party has at any time since December 31, 2001 had, any direct or indirect interest of any nature in any asset used in or otherwise relating to the business of any of the Company or the Company Subsidiaries; (b) no Related Party is indebted to the Company or the Company Subsidiaries; (c) since December 31, 2001, no Related party has entered into, or has had any direct or indirect financial interest in, any Applicable Contract, or any of the transaction or business dealing of any nature involving any of the Company or the Company Subsidiaries; (d) no Related Party is competing, or has at any time since December 31, 2001 competed, directly or indirectly, with any of the Company or the Company Subsidiaries in any market served by any of the Company or the Company Subsidiaries; (e) no Related Party has any claim or right against any of the Company or the Company Subsidiaries for borrowed money or money owed for past services (other than normal compensation and reimbursement); and (f) no event has occurred, and no condition or circumstance exists, that might (with or without notice or lapse of time) give rise to or serve as a basis for any claim or right in favor of any Related Party against the Company or the Company Subsidiaries.

Section 3.32   Disclosure.   No representation or warranty by the Company or Management Stockholders herein, the Disclosure Schedule, or any certificate or annex furnished or to be furnished by any of them pursuant to this Agreement or in connection with the transactions contemplated herein, contains or will contain any untrue statement of a material fact, or omits, or will omit to state a material fact necessary to make the statements contained herein or therein, in light of the circumstances in which they were made, not misleading.

Article IV
Representations and Warranties of Buyer

Buyer hereby represents and warrants to Company and Stockholders that the statements contained in this Article IV are correct and complete as of the date of this Agreement and will be correct and complete as of the Closing Date (as though made then and as though the Closing Date were substituted for the date of this Agreement), except as set forth in the Buyer's disclosure schedule accompanying this Agreement (the **"Buyer Disclosure Schedule"**):

Section 4.1   Organization and Good Standing.   Buyer is a corporation duly organized, validly existing and in good standing under the laws of its jurisdiction of incorporation.

Section 4.2   Corporate Authority.   Buyer has the full corporate power and authority and has taken all corporate action necessary in order to execute, deliver and perform fully, its obligations under, this Agreement and to consummate the transactions contemplated herein. The execution and delivery of this Agreement by the Buyer and the consummation by the Buyer of the transactions contemplated herein have been duly authorized and approved by the Board of Directors of the Buyer and no other corporate proceeding with respect to the Buyer is necessary to authorize this Agreement or the transactions contemplated herein. This Agreement has been duly executed and delivered by Buyer and constitutes a valid and binding agreement of Buyer, enforceable against Buyer in accordance with its terms, except for the Bankruptcy Exception.

Section 4.3   Governmental Filings and Consents; No Violations.
(a)   No Consents are required to be obtained by Buyer from any Governmental Entity in connection with the execution or delivery of this Agreement by Buyer, the performance by Buyer of its obligations hereunder or the consummation by Buyer of the transactions contemplated herein.
(b)   The execution and delivery of this Agreement by Buyer does not, and the performance and consummation by Buyer of any of the transactions contemplated herein will not, with respect to Buyer, directly or indirectly (with or without the giving of notice or the lapse of time or both):
  (i)   contravene, conflict with, or constitute or result in a breach or violation of, or a default under any provision of the charter documents, Certificate of Incorporation or By-laws (or equivalent documents) of Buyer;
  (ii)   require Buyer to make any filing with or obtain any Consent from any Person under any Contract binding upon Buyer; or
  (iii)   contravene, conflict with, or constitute or result in a breach or violation of, any Law or Order to which Buyer, or any of the assets owned or used by Buyer, are subject.

Section 4.4   Securities Act.   Buyer is acquiring the Shares for its own account and not with a view to their distribution within the meaning of Section 2(11) of the Securities Act of 1933, as amended (the **"Securities Act"**) in any manner that would be in violation of the Securities Act.

Section 4.5   Brokers and Finders.   No agent, broker, investment banker, intermediary, finder, Person or firm acting on behalf of Buyer or which has been retained by or is authorized to act on behalf of Buyer is or would be entitled to any broker's or finder's fee or any other commission or similar fee, directly or indirectly, from any of the parties hereto in connection with the execution of this Agreement or upon consummation of the transactions contemplated herein.

Section 4.6   Galaxy Shares.   Galaxy Shares to be issued as part of the Purchase Price shall be upon satisfaction of the conditions of this Agreement validly, issued, fully paid and non accessible common shares of Galaxy International Corp. Based on the representations made by the recipients of the Galaxy Shares made in the Stock Issuance Agreement, the Galaxy Shares will be issued in compliance with the securities laws of the United States.

ARTICLE V
REPRESENTATIONS AND WARRANTIES OF STOCKHOLDERS

Each Stockholder hereby represents and warrants severally for themselves and not jointly with any other Stockholder to Buyer that the statements contained in this Article V are correct and complete as of the date of this Agreement and will be correct and complete as of the Closing Date (as though made then and as though the Closing Date were substituted for the date of this Agreement), except as set forth in the Stockholders' disclosure schedule accompanying this Agreement (the **"Stockholders Disclosure Schedule"**):

Section 5.1   Title to Shares.   Such Stockholder has good and valid title to and is the record and beneficial owner of the Shares listed for such Stockholder in <u>Annex I</u> free and clear of all Liens with full right, power and authority to enter into this Agreement and to sell, assign, transfer and deliver to Buyer the Shares to be transferred by such Stockholder to the Buyer, and upon delivery of and payment for the Shares, the Buyer will acquire valid right and title to the Shares to be transferred by the Stockholder to the Buyer.

Section 5.2   Authority.   Such Stockholder has the absolute and unrestricted right, power and authority or capacity to enter into and perform such Stockholder's obligations under this Agreement and to consummate the transactions contemplated herein. The respective spouses of such Stockholders have the absolute and unrestricted right, power and capacity to execute and deliver and to perform their obligations under the spousal consents being executed by them. Said spousal consents constitute their legal, valid and binding obligations, enforceable against them in accordance with their terms. If applicable, the execution and delivery of this Agreement by such Stockholder and the consummation by such Stockholder of the transactions contemplated herein have been duly authorized and approved by the Board of Directors (or similar governing body) of such Stockholder and no other corporate proceeding with respect to the Buyer is necessary to authorize this Agreement or the transactions contemplated herein.

Section 5.3   Enforceability.   This Agreement has been duly executed and delivered by such Stockholder and constitutes a valid and binding agreement of such Stockholder, enforceable against such Stockholder in accordance with its terms, subject to general equitable principles and to Bankruptcy Exceptions.

Section 5.4 Governmental Filings and Consents; No Violations.

(a)   No filings are required to be made by such Stockholder with, nor are any Consents required to be obtained by such Stockholder from, any Governmental Entity, in connection with the execution or delivery of this Agreement by such Stockholder, the performance by such Stockholder of its obligations hereunder or the consummation by such Stockholder of the transactions contemplated herein.

(b)   The execution and delivery of this Agreement by such Stockholder does not, and the performance and consummation by such Stockholder of any of the transactions contemplated herein will not, with respect to such Stockholder, directly or indirectly (with or without the giving of notice or the lapse of time or both):

(i)   contravene, conflict with, or constitute or result in a breach or violation of, or a default under any provision of the charter documents or Bylaws (or equivalent documents) of such Stockholder;

(ii)   require such Stockholder to make any filing with or obtain any Consent from any Person under any Contract binding upon such Stockholder; or

(iii)   contravene, conflict with, or constitute or result in a breach or violation of, any Law or Order to which such Stockholder is subject.

Section 5.5 Other Contracts.

No Stockholder is a party to: (i) any Contract under which any of the Company or Stockholders is or may become obligated to sell or otherwise issue any shares of his or its capital stock, or any other securities or interest; (ii) any Contract that may give rise to or provide a basis for the assertion of a claim by any Person to the effect that such person is entitled to repurchase, acquire or receive or reacquire any shares of capital stock, partnership interest, or other securities or interest of any of the Company (whether from the Company or the Stockholders); or (iii) any other Contract relating to the Shares, the voting of, or any other rights associated with, the Shares or any other shares of capital stock, partnership interest, or other securities or interest of any Company, including any buy-sell agreements, voting agreements, proxies, rights of first refusal, tag along rights, bring along rights, shareholder agreements, repurchase agreements, co-sale agreements, stock transfer agreements or similar Contracts.

Section 5.6 Brokers and Finders.

No agent, broker, investment banker, intermediary, finder, Person or firm acting on behalf of Buyer or which has been retained by or is authorized to act on behalf of Stockholder is or would be entitled to any broker's or finder's fee or any other commission or similar fee, directly or indirectly, from any of the parties hereto in connection with the execution of this Agreement or upon consummation of the transactions contemplated herein.

Section 5.7 Stockholder Claims Against Company or a Company Subsidiary.

Such Stockholder has no claims outstanding that would result in a Liability against the Company or a Company Subsidiary, and no facts exists which could reasonably be likely to result in such a claim by such Stockholder against the Company or a Company Subsidiary.

Section 5.8 Brokers and Finders. No agent, broker, investment banker, intermediary, finder, Person or firm acting on behalf of Buyer or which has been retained by or is authorized to act on behalf of such Stockholder is or would be entitled to any broker's or finder's fee or any other commission or similar fee, directly or indirectly, from any of the parties hereto in connection with the execution of this Agreement or upon consummation of the transactions contemplated herein.

Section 5.9 Stockholder Claims Against Company or a Company Subsidiary. Stockholder has no claims outstanding that would result in a Liability against the Company or a Company Subsidiary, and no facts exist which could reasonably be likely to result in such a claim by the Stockholder against the Company or a Company Subsidiary.

ARTICLE VI
COVENANTS

Section 6.1 Conduct of Business by Company. During the period from the date of this Agreement and continuing until the earlier of the termination of this Agreement pursuant to its terms or the Closing Date, Company shall, and covenants and agrees to cause each Company Subsidiary to use commercially reasonable efforts to carry on its business, in the Ordinary Course of Business, in substantially the same manner as heretofore conducted and in compliance with all applicable laws and regulations, pay its debts and taxes when due subject to good faith disputes over such debts or taxes, pay or perform other material obligations when due, and use its commercially reasonable efforts consistent with past practices and policies to (i) preserve intact its present business organization, (ii) keep available the services of its present officers and employees and (iii) preserve its relationships with customers, suppliers, manufactures, distributors, licensors, licensees, and others with which it has business dealings. In addition, Company will promptly notify Buyer of any material event involving its business or operations or the business or operations of the Company Subsidiary.

In addition, except as expressly permitted by the terms of this Agreement or as set forth in <u>Schedule 6.1</u> of the Disclosure Schedule, without the prior written consent of Buyer (with [_____] acknowledged as the point person who can authorize such actions), during the period from the date of this Agreement and continuing until the earlier of the termination of this Agreement pursuant to its terms or the Closing Date, Company shall not, and covenants and agrees to cause each Company Subsidiary not to do any of the following:

(a) Waive any stock repurchase rights, accelerate, amend or change the period of exercisability of options or restricted stock, or reprice options granted under any employee, consultant, director or other stock plans or authorize cash payments in exchange for any options granted under any of such plans;

(b)   Grant any severance or termination pay to any officer or employee except pursuant to written agreements outstanding, or policies existing, on the date hereof and as previously disclosed in writing or made available to Buyer, or adopt any new severance plan;

(c)   Transfer or license to any person or entity or otherwise extend, amend or modify any rights to Intellectual Property, or enter into grants to transfer or license to any person future patent rights other than extensions, amendments, modifications, transfers or licenses in the Ordinary Course of Business in connection with the sale of commercially available Company Products through the Company's standard distribution channels consistent with past practices, provided that in no event shall Company license on an exclusive basis or sell any Intellectual Property;

(d)   Declare, set aside or pay any dividends on or make any other distributions (whether in cash, stock, equity securities or property) in respect of any capital stock or split, combine or reclassify any capital stock or issue or authorize the issuance of any other securities in respect of, in lieu of or in substitution for any capital stock;

(e)   Purchase, redeem or otherwise acquire, directly or indirectly, any shares of capital stock of Company or any Company Subsidiary;

(f)   Issue, deliver, sell, authorize, pledge or otherwise encumber or propose any of the foregoing with respect to, any shares of capital stock or any securities convertible into shares of capital stock, or subscriptions, rights, warrants or options to acquire any shares of capital stock or any securities convertible into shares of capital stock, or enter into other agreements or commitments of any character obligating it to issue any such shares or convertible securities, other than the issuance, delivery and/or sale of shares of Company Common Stock pursuant to the exercise of stock options outstanding as of the date of this Agreement;

(g)   Cause, permit or propose any amendments to the Company's Organizational Documents;

(h)   Acquire or agree to acquire by merging or consolidating with, or by purchasing any equity interest in or a portion of the assets of, or by any other manner, any business or any corporation, partnership, association or other business organization or division thereof, or otherwise acquire or agree to acquire any assets, other than in the Ordinary Course of Business or enter into any joint ventures, strategic partnerships or alliances;

(i)   Sell, lease, license, encumber or otherwise dispose of any properties or assets except (A) sales of inventory in the Ordinary Course of Business, and (B) for the sale, lease or disposition (other than through licensing) of property or assets which are not material, individually or in the aggregate, to the Company and the Company Subsidiaries;

(j)   Incur any indebtedness for borrowed money or guarantee any such indebtedness of another person (other than borrowings under the Company's existing credit facility), issue or sell any debt securities or options, warrants, calls or other rights to acquire any debt securities of Company, enter into any "keep well" or other agreement to maintain any financial statement condition or enter into any arrangement having the economic effect of any of the foregoing other than in connection with the financing of ordinary course trade payables in the Ordinary Course of Business;

(k) Except as required under applicable Law or in the Ordinary Course of Business, adopt or amend any employee benefit plan, policy or arrangement, any employee stock purchase or employee stock option plan, or enter into any employment contract or collective bargaining agreement (other than offer letters and letter agreements entered into in the Ordinary Course of Business with employees who are terminable "at will"), pay any special bonus or special remuneration to any director or employee, or increase the salaries or wage rates or fringe benefits (including rights to severance or indemnification) of its directors, officers, employees or consultants;

(l) (i) Pay, discharge, settle or satisfy any claims, liabilities or obligations (absolute, accrued, asserted or unasserted, contingent or otherwise), or litigation (whether or not commenced prior to the date of this Agreement) other than the payment, discharge, settlement or satisfaction, in the Ordinary Course of Business, or (ii) waive the benefits of, agree to modify in any manner, terminate, release any person from or fail to enforce any confidentiality or similar agreement to which Company or any Company Subsidiary is a party or of which Company or any Company Subsidiary is a beneficiary;

(m) Make, or incur any obligation to make, any individual or series of related payments outside of the Ordinary Course of Business other than payments to legal, accounting, and other professional service advisors and other expenses in connection with the negotiation and closing of the transactions contemplated hereby;

(n) Except in the Ordinary Course of Business, modify, amend or terminate any material contract or agreement to which Company or any Company Subsidiary is a party or waive, delay the exercise of, release or assign any material rights or claims thereunder;

(o) Except in the Ordinary Course of Business, enter into or materially modify any contracts, agreements, or obligations relating to the distribution, sale, license, sponsorship or marketing by third parties of Company's Products or products licensed by Company;

(p) Revalue any of its assets or, except as required by GAAP, make any change in accounting methods, principles or practices;

(q) Incur or enter into any agreement, contract or commitment in excess of $50,000 individually, except in the Ordinary Course of Business;

(r) Make any tax election or settle or compromise any material income tax liability; or

(s) Agree in writing or otherwise to take any of the actions described in Section 6.1 (a) through (r) above.

Section 6.2 *Acquisition Proposals.*

(a) The Company agrees that it shall not, and shall cause each Company Subsidiary and each of its and their respective directors officers, employees, agents, consultants, advisors or other representatives of such Person, including legal counsel, accountants and financial advisors (collectively, **"Representatives"**) not to, directly or indirectly, solicit, initiate, encourage, or otherwise facilitate, any inquiries or the making of any proposals or offers from, discuss or negotiate with, provide any confidential information or data to, or consider the merits of any unsolicited inquiries, proposals or offers from, any Person (other than Buyer) relating to any transaction involving the sale of the Company, Business or assets (other than in the Ordinary Course of Business) of the Company or any Company Subsidiary, or any of its capital stock, or any merger, consolidation, business combination, or similar transaction involving the Company or any Company Subsidiary (any such inquiry, proposal or offer being hereinafter referred to as an **"Acquisition Proposal"**).

(b)   The Company shall, and shall cause each Company Subsidiary and each of their respective Representatives to, immediately cease and cause to be terminated any existing activities, discussions or negotiations with any parties conducted heretofore with respect to any of the foregoing. Company shall promptly notify Buyer if any such inquiries, proposals or offers are received by, any such information is requested from, or any such negotiations or discussions are sought to be initiated or continued with or about the Company and shall promptly request each Person which has heretofore executed a confidentiality agreement in connection with its consideration of acquiring the Company or any Company Subsidiary or the Business or assets (other than in the Ordinary Course of Business) of the Company to return all confidential information heretofore furnished to such person by or on behalf of the Company or any Company Subsidiary.

Section 6.3   Access.   Between the date of this Agreement and the Closing Date, Company shall, and shall cause the Company Subsidiaries and each of their respective Representatives to, (i) afford Buyer and its Representatives full access, upon prior notice, at all reasonable times during normal business hours and in a manner so as not to interfere with the normal business operations of Company and each Company Subsidiary, to the Company's and each Company Subsidiary's personnel, premises, properties, Contracts, books and records, and other documents and data, (ii) furnish Buyer and its Representatives with copies of all such Contracts, books and records, and other existing documents and data as Buyer may reasonably request, (iii) furnish Buyer and its Representatives with such additional financial, operating, and other data and information as Buyer may reasonably request and (iv) otherwise cooperate with the investigation by Buyer and its Representatives of the Company and each Company Subsidiary and shall authorize the Company's independent certified public accountants to permit Buyer and its independent certified public accountants to examine all accounting records and working papers pertaining to the Financial Statements (subject to appropriate indemnifications). No investigation pursuant to this Section 6.3 shall affect or be deemed to modify any representation or warranty made by Company, the Management Stockholders or Stockholders. All requests for information made pursuant to this Section 6.3 shall be directed to an executive officer of the Company or such other persons as may be designated by Seller.

Section 6.4   Required Approvals.   Each party to this Agreement hereby agrees to cooperate with each other party and use its commercially reasonable efforts to promptly prepare and file all necessary filings and other documents and to obtain as promptly as practicable all necessary Consents of all third parties and Governmental Entities necessary or advisable to consummate the transactions contemplated herein. Each party shall have the right to review in advance and to the extent practicable each will consult the other on, in each case subject to applicable Laws relating to the exchange of information, all the information relating to Buyer, or the Company or any Company Subsidiary, as the case may be, that appear in any filing made with, or other written materials submitted to, any third party or Governmental Entity in connection with the transactions contemplated in this Agreement. In exercising the foregoing right, each of Buyer and Company shall act reasonably and as promptly as practicable. Buyer and Company agree that they will keep the other apprised of the status of matters relating to completion of the transactions contemplated herein, including promptly furnishing the other with copies of notice or other communications received by Buyer or the Company or any Company Subsidiary, as the case may be, from any third party or Governmental Entity with respect to the transactions contemplated herein.

Section 6.5 *Commercially Reasonable Best Efforts.* Between the date of this Agreement and the Closing Date, each of the parties hereto shall use their respective commercially reasonable best efforts to cause the conditions in Sections 7.1 and 7.2 to be satisfied.

Section 6.6 *Publicity.* The initial press release announcing the transactions contemplated herein shall be released jointly after consultation between the Buyer and the Company and the parties hereto shall consult with each other prior to issuing any press releases or otherwise making public announcements with respect to the transactions contemplated herein and prior to making any filings with any Governmental Entity, except as may be required by Law. Any press release or announcement shall conform to New York Stock Exchange Rules and Delaware Corporate laws.

Section 6.7 *Confidentiality.*

(a) Each of Buyer and the Stockholders, after the Closing Date, Buyer, Company and Stockholders shall maintain in confidence, and shall cause its Representatives to maintain in confidence, and not use to the detriment of any other party hereto any written, oral or other information relating to another party (including, without limitation, information about processes, procedures, techniques, know-how, financial or sales and marketing matters, and other similar proprietary and confidential information). Notwithstanding the foregoing a party shall be free to discuss (i) any such information that is or becomes generally available to the public other than as a result of disclosure by any other Party or any of its Representatives, (ii) any such information that is required to be disclosed to a Governmental Entity of competent jurisdiction or (iii) any such information that was or becomes available on a non-confidential basis and from a source (other than a party to this Agreement or any Representative of such party) that is not bound by a confidentiality obligation to the Buyer Company, any Company Subsidiary or any Stockholder as applicable, or (iv) such information if it is necessary or appropriate in making any filing or obtaining any Consent required for the consummation of the transactions contemplated herein, and each party shall instruct its respective Representatives having access to such information of such obligation of confidentiality and such party shall be legally responsible for any violation or breach of the foregoing obligations of confidentiality. If for any reason this Agreement is terminated, or the transactions contemplated herein are abandoned, the provisions of this Section 6.7 shall remain in full force and effect and Buyer, Company and Stockholders, as applicable, shall return to the appropriate party, or at such party's option, destroy all copies of material containing confidential or proprietary information disclosed to such party. The redelivery or destruction of such material shall not relieve a party of its obligations regarding confidentiality.

Section 6.8 Expenses. Except as otherwise expressly provided in Section 8.2, whether or not the transactions contemplated herein are consummated, all costs and expenses incurred in connection with this Agreement and the transactions contemplated herein shall be paid by the party incurring such expense. In the event of termination of this Agreement, the obligation of each party to pay its own expenses will be subject to any rights of such party arising from a breach of this Agreement by another party. Stockholders shall be liable for all stock transfer taxes arising from the sale of the Shares.

Section 6.9 Further Assurances. At any time and from time to time after the Closing Date, the parties hereto agree to (a) furnish upon request to each other such further assurances, information documents, instruments of transfer or assignment, files and books and records, (b) promptly execute, acknowledge, and deliver any such further assurances, documents, instruments of transfer or assignment, files and books and records, and (c) subject to the provisions of this Section 6.9 hereof, do all such further acts and things, all as such other party may reasonably request for the purpose of carrying out the intent of this Agreement and the documents referred to herein.

Section 6.10 Notification. Between the date of this Agreement and the Closing Date, Company and the Management Stockholders shall promptly notify Buyer in writing if the Company or Management Stockholders becomes aware of any fact or condition that causes or constitutes a breach of any of Company's or the Management Stockholder's representations and warranties as of the date of this Agreement, or if the Company or the Management Stockholders becomes aware of the occurrence after the date of this Agreement of any fact or condition that could (except as expressly contemplated herein) cause or constitute a breach of any such representation or warranty had such representation or warranty been made as of the time of occurrence or discovery of such fact or condition. Should any such fact or condition require any change in the Disclosure Schedule if the Disclosure Schedule were dated the date of the occurrence or discovery of any such fact or condition, Company and the Management Stockholder shall promptly deliver to Buyer a supplement to the Disclosure Schedule specifying such change. During the same period, Company shall promptly notify Buyer of the occurrence of any breach of any covenant, agreement, undertaking or obligation of Company in this Article VI or of the occurrence of any event that may make the satisfaction of the conditions in Section 7.1 not reasonably likely. No supplement to the Disclosure Schedule or notification to Buyer made pursuant to the requirements of this Section 6.10 shall have any effect for the purpose of determining the satisfaction of the conditions in Section 7.1 or for the purpose of determining the right of Buyer to claim or obtain indemnification or set off from the Stockholders under Article IX.

Section 6.11 *[Alternative Notification].*

(a) Between the date of this Agreement and the Closing Date, Company and the Management Stockholders shall promptly notify Buyer in writing if the Company or Management Stockholders becomes aware of any fact or condition (i) not disclosed in this Agreement or the Disclosure Schedule which existed on or prior to the date of this Agreement and whose existence causes or constitutes a breach of any of Company's representations and warranties as of the date of this Agreement, or (ii) not disclosed in this Agreement or the Disclosure Schedule which did not come into existence until after the date of this Agreement, or, in the case of a representation or warranty by its terms qualified by a reference to Knowledge, become required to be disclosed until after the date of this Agreement, that would, were it not for the provisions of this Schedule 6.10 cause or constitute a breach of Company's representations or warranties had such representations or warranties been made as of the time of occurrence or discovery of such fact or condition. If any such fact or condition in (i) or (ii) would have required any change in the Disclosure Schedule if the Disclosure Schedule were dated the date of the occurrence or discovery of any such fact or condition, Company and the Management Stockholder shall promptly deliver to Buyer a supplement to the Disclosure Schedule specifying such change. During the same period, Company shall promptly notify Buyer of the occurrence of any breach of any covenant, agreement, undertaking or obligation of Company in this Article VI or of the occurrence of any event that may make the satisfaction of the conditions in Section 7.1 not reasonably likely.

(b) No supplement to the Disclosure Schedule or notification to Buyer made pursuant to Section 6.10(a)(i) of this Section 6.10 shall have any effect for the purpose of determining the satisfaction of the conditions in Section 7.1 or for the purpose of determining the right of Buyer to claim or obtain indemnification or set off from the Stockholders under Article IX. Any supplement to the Disclosure Schedule provided in accordance with Section 6.10(a)(ii) shall, unless the Buyer has the right to terminate this Agreement pursuant to Section 8.1 (b) below by the reason of the existence of a fact or condition required to be disclosed pursuant to Section 6.10(a)(ii), and actually exercises such right within five (5) business days of being notified of the Disclosure Schedule supplement, be deemed to have amended the Disclosure Schedule and to have qualified the representations and warranties contained in Article III and to have cured any misrepresentations or breach of warranty that otherwise might have existed by reason of the existence of such fact or condition.

ARTICLE VII
CONDITIONS TO CLOSING

Section 7.1 *Conditions to Obligations of Buyer.* The obligation of Buyer to consummate the transactions contemplated by this Agreement and to take the other actions to be taken by Buyer at the Closing is subject to the satisfaction, at or prior to the Closing, of each of the following conditions (any of which may be waived in whole or in part by Buyer):

(a) <u>Representations and Warranties</u>. All of the representations and warranties of the Stockholders and the Managing Stockholders and the Company set forth in this Agreement shall be true and correct (considered individually and collectively) in all material respects as of the date of this Agreement and as of the Closing Date, with the same effect as though such representations and warranties had been made on and as of the Closing Date, without giving effect to any supplement to the Disclosure Schedule (delivered to Buyer in accordance with Section 6.10 hereof), except (i) that such representations and warranties that are made as of a specific date need only be true in all material respects as of such date, (ii) each of the representation and warranties in Section 3.2, 3.6, 5.1, 5.3 and 5.4 shall be true and correct in all respects, and (iii) any representation and warranty qualified by "material" or "Material Adverse Effect" shall be true and correct in all respects.

(b) <u>Covenants</u>. All of the covenants, agreements, undertakings and obligations that Company or Stockholders are required to perform or to comply with pursuant to this Agreement at or prior to the Closing, shall have been duly performed.

(c) <u>Officer's Certificate</u>. Company shall have delivered to Buyer a certificate dated as of the Closing Date and signed by a senior executive officer or officers of Company, representing that the conditions referred to in Sections 7.1 (a) and 7.1(b) have been satisfied and the changes set forth in 7.1(i) have not occurred; provided, however, that such senior executive officer or officers shall have no personal liability on account of the delivery of such certificate.

(d) <u>Secretary's Certificate</u>. Buyer shall have received copies of the resolutions of the Board of Directors (or other similar governing body) of the Company, authorizing the execution, delivery and performance of this Agreement. Buyer also shall have received a certificates of the secretary or assistant secretary of the Company, dated as of the Closing Date, to the effect that such resolutions were duly adopted and are in full force and effect, that each officer of the Company who executed and delivered this Agreement and any other document delivered in connection with the consummation of the transactions contemplated by this Agreement was at the respective times of such execution and delivery and is now duly elected or appointed, qualified and acting as such officer, and that the signature of each such officer appearing on such document is his or her genuine signature.

(e) <u>No Action or Order</u>. No Action or Order shall be issued or pending which (i) involves a challenge to or seeks to or does prohibit, prevent, restrain, restrict, delay, make illegal or otherwise interfere with the consummation of any of the transactions contemplated herein, (ii) seeks or imposes damages in connection with the consummation of any of the transactions contemplated herein, (iii) questions the validity or legality of any of the transactions contemplated herein or (iv) seeks to impose conditions upon the ownership or operations of the Company or any Company Subsidiary or the operations of the Buyer reasonably deemed unduly burdensome by Buyer.

(f) <u>Receipt of Shares</u>. Buyer shall have received from the Stockholders an original certificate or certificates evidencing 100% of the Shares, duly endorsed in blank or accompanied by stock powers duly executed in blank in proper form for transfer or affidavits of lost shares and assignments, as applicable. There shall not have been made or Threatened by any Person any claim asserting that such Person (i) is the holder or the beneficial owner of, or has the right to acquire or to obtain beneficial ownership of, any stock of, or any other voting, equity, or ownership interest in, the Company or any Company Subsidiary, or (ii) is entitled to all or any portion of the Purchase Price payable for the Shares.

(g) _Consents_. Each of the Consents set forth in Schedule 3.4 and Schedule 3.5 of the Disclosure Schedule and or otherwise required for consummation of the transactions contemplated by this Agreement shall have been obtained and must be in full force and effect provided, however, that such Consents (i) shall not contain one or more terms or conditions that individually or in the aggregate in Buyer's reasonable judgement could be expected to have a Material Adverse Effect, or (ii) materially and adversely impair the economic benefits of the transaction contemplated by this Agreement to Buyer.

(h) _Opinion of Counsel_. Buyer shall have received an opinion, dated as of the Closing Date, of Klever & Sharp, counsel for the Company, as to the matters referred to in Exhibit 6.1(h) attached hereto.

(i) _No Material Adverse Effect_. There shall not have occurred any change in the business, operations, properties, prospects, assets, or condition of the Company or any Company Subsidiary since the date of the Interim Balance Sheet that is reasonably likely to constitute a Material Adverse Effect on the Company and the Company Subsidiaries (taken as a whole), and no event has occurred or circumstance exists that is reasonably likely to result in such a Material Adverse Effect.

(j) _Stock Options_. (i) Buyer shall have received evidence of the cancellation of each outstanding Option issued by the Company pursuant to its Stock Option Plan, and (ii) Buyer shall have received evidence of the repayment of each loan made by the Company to an option holder for the exercise price of an option under the Company's Stock Option Plan.

(k) _Subordinated Notes_. Company shall have entered into an agreement with each holder of its issued and outstanding subordinated notes (the **"Subordinated Notes"**) in the form attached hereto as Exhibit 7.1(k) (**"Subordinated Note Agreement"**).

(l) _Financing_. Buyer shall have obtained financing for transactions contemplated herein on terms it believes, in its sole discretion, are reasonable to Buyer [, provided, that a placement of ordinary shares of Galaxy at up to a [____]% discount average closing price during the preceding ____ day period, shall be deemed reasonable]. **[Galaxy to Consider.]**

(m) _Escrow Agreement_. The Company and Stockholders shall have executed and delivered the Escrow Agreement.

(n) _Employment Contracts_. Each of the Employment Agreements shall have been executed and delivered.

(o) _Stockholder Releases_. Buyer shall have received the Stockholder Releases for each Stockholder in the form attached hereto as Exhibit 7.1(o) (the **"Stockholder Releases"**).

(p) _Noncompete Agreements_. Each of the Noncompete Agreements shall have been executed and delivered.

(q) <u>Execution of Closing Documents</u>.   Each of the Closing documents described in Section 2.2 hereof shall have been executed and delivered by each of the named parties (other than Buyer).

(r) <u>Other Documentation</u>.   Buyer shall have received such other documents, certificates, opinions or statements as Buyer may reasonably request.

Section 7.2   Conditions to Obligations of Stockholders and Company.   The obligation of the Stockholders and the Company to consummate the transaction contemplated by this Agreement and to take the other actions to be taken by the Stockholders and the Company at the Closing is subject to the satisfaction, at or prior to the Closing, of each of the following conditions (any of which may be waived in whole or in part by the Stockholders' Representative or the Company):

(a) <u>Representations and Warranties</u>.   All of the representations and warranties of Buyer set forth in this Agreement, shall be true and correct (considered individually and collectively) in all material respects as of the date of this Agreement and as of the Closing Date, with the same effect as though such representations and warranties had been made on and as of the Closing Date, without giving effect to any supplement to the Disclosure Scheduled (delivered to Company in accordance with Section 6.10 hereof), except (i) that such representations and warranties that are made as of a specific date need only be true in all material respects as of such date, and (ii) any representation and warranty qualified by "material" or "Material Adverse Effect" shall be true and correct in all respects.

(b) <u>Covenants</u>.   All of the covenants, agreements, undertakings and obligations that Buyer is required to perform or to comply with pursuant to this Agreement at or prior to the Closing, shall have been duly performed.

(c) <u>Officer's Certificate</u>.   Buyer shall have delivered to Company and the Stockholders' Representative a certificate, dated as of the Closing Date and signed by a senior executive officer or officers of Buyer, representing that the conditions referred to in Sections 7.2(a) and 7.2(b) have been satisfied; provided, however, that such senior executive officer or officers shall have no personal liability on account of the delivery of such certificate.

(d) <u>Secretary's Certificate</u>.   Company and the Stockholders' Representative shall have received copies of the resolutions of the Board of Directors (or other similar governing body) of Buyer authorizing the execution, delivery and performance of this Agreement. Company and the Stockholders' Representative also shall have received a certificate of the secretary or assistant secretary of Buyer dated as of the Closing Date, to the effect that such resolutions were duly adopted and are in full force and effect, that each officer of the Buyer who executed and delivered this Agreement and any other document delivered in connection with the consummation of the transactions contemplated by this Agreement was at the respective times of such execution and delivery and is now duly elected or appointed, qualified and acting as such officer, and that the signature of each such officer appearing on such document is his genuine signature.

(e) <u>No Action or Order</u>.   No Action or Order shall be issued or pending which (i) involves a challenge to or seeks to or does prohibit, prevent, restrain, restrict, delay, make illegal or otherwise interfere with the consummation of any of the transactions contemplated herein, (ii) seeks or imposes damages in connection with the consummation of any of the transactions contemplated herein, or (iii) questions the validity or legality of any of the transactions contemplated herein.

(f) <u>Payment of Initial Purchase Price and Escrow Amount</u>. Stockholders shall have received from Buyer the Initial Purchase Price as provided in Section 1.2 and <u>Annex II</u>, including as applicable, the Galaxy Shares and Deferred Notes.

(g) <u>Opinion of Counsel</u>. Seller shall have received an opinion, dated as of the Closing Date, of Bigar, Strong & Wise, a professional corporation.

(h) <u>Escrow Agreement</u>. Buyer shall have executed and delivered the Escrow Agreement.

(i) <u>Execution of Closing Documents</u>. Each of the Closing documents described in Section 2.2 hereof shall have been executed and delivered by Buyer.

(j) <u>Other Documentation</u>. Company and the Stockholders' Representative shall have received such other documents, certificates, opinions or statements as Company or the Stockholders' Representative may reasonably request.

ARTICLE VIII
TERMINATION

Section 8.1   Termination. Notwithstanding anything in this Agreement to the contrary, this Agreement and the transactions contemplated herein may, by written notice given at any time prior to the Closing, be terminated:

(a)   by mutual written consent of Buyer, Company, and the Stockholders' Representative;

(b)   by the Buyer, if a material breach of a representation or warranty or any other provision of this Agreement has been committed by any of the Stockholders or the Company and such breach has not been waived or cured within five (5) business days after written notice; or by Company or Stockholders' Representative if a material breach of a representation or warranty or any other provision of this Agreement has been committed by the Buyer and such breach has not been waived or cured within five (5) business days after written notice; provided, however, that termination pursuant to this Section 8.1 (b) shall not relieve the breaching party of liability for such breach or otherwise;

(c)   by Buyer, if any of the conditions set forth in Section 7.1 has not been satisfied as of_____, 2004 or if satisfaction of such a condition is or becomes impossible (other than through the failure of Buyer to fully comply with its obligations hereunder) and Buyer has not waived such condition on or before _____, 2004; or

(d)   by Buyer if the Company or its Board of Directors shall have recommended to the Stockholders an Acquisition Proposal (as defined in Section 6.2 hereof).

(e)   by Company and Stockholders' Representative if any of the conditions set forth in Section 7.2 has not been satisfied as of_____, 2004 or if satisfaction of such a condition is or becomes impossible (other than through the failure of Company or the Stockholders to fully comply with their obligations hereunder) and Company and Stockholders' Representative have not waived such condition on or before_____, 2004.

Section 8.2   Effect of Termination.   Termination of this Agreement pursuant to Section 8.1 shall not in any way terminate, limit or restrict the rights and remedies of any party hereto against any party which has related, breached or failed to satisfy any of the representations, warranties, covenants or other provisions of this Agreement prior to termination hereof; provided, however, that (i) Company shall within five (5) business days after termination of this Agreement by Buyer pursuant to Sections 8.1(b), (c) or (d) shall pay Buyer a fee of $500,000 in cash by wire transfer and (ii) Buyer shall within five (5) days after termination of this Agreement by Company and Stockholders' Representative pursuant to Section 8.1(b) or (e) pay the Company an amount equal to its reasonable expenses not to exceed $_____.

ARTICLE IX
INDEMNIFICATION; REMEDIES

Section 9.1   Survival.   Notwithstanding (a) any investigation or examination conducted with respect to, or any knowledge acquired (or capable of being acquired) about the accuracy or inaccuracy of or compliance with, any representation, warranty, covenant, agreement, undertaking or obligation made by or on behalf of the parties hereto, (b) the waiver of any condition based on the accuracy of any representation or warranty, or on the performance of or compliance with any covenant, agreement, undertaking or obligation, or (c) the Closing hereunder;

(i)   All of the representations and warranties of the parties contained in this Agreement, the Disclosure Schedule, the supplements to the Disclosure Schedule (delivered to Buyer in accordance with Section 6.10), and any other certificate or document delivered pursuant to this Agreement shall survive the Closing until 36 months after the Closing Date, except for the representations and warranties contained in (A) Section 3.2 (Capitalization) and Section 5.1 (Title to Shares), each of which shall survive the execution and delivery of this Agreement and the Closing indefinitely, and (B) Section 3.20 (Environmental Matters), Section 3.9 (Taxes) and Section 3.10 (Employee Benefits; ERISA) which shall survive the execution and delivery of this Agreement and the Closing until the expiration of all relevant statutes of limitations (including any extensions).

(ii)   All of the covenants, agreements, undertakings and obligations of the parties contained in this Agreement, the Disclosure Schedule, the supplements to the Disclosure Schedule (delivered to Buyer in accordance with Section 6.10 hereof), and any other certificate or document delivered pursuant to this Agreement shall survive until fully performed or fulfilled, unless non-compliance with such covenants, agreements, undertakings or obligations is waived in writing by the party or parties entitled to such performance.

No claim for indemnification, reimbursement or any other remedy pursuant to Sections 9.2 or 9.3 hereof may be brought with respect to breaches of representations or warranties contained herein after the applicable expiration date set forth in this Section 9.1; provided, however, that if, prior to such applicable date, a party hereto shall have notified the other party hereto in writing of a claim for indemnification under this Article IX (whether or not formal legal action shall have been commenced based upon such claim), such claim shall continue to be subject to indemnification in accordance with this Article IX notwithstanding such expiration date.

Section 9.2 Indemnification and Reimbursement by Stockholders. Subject to Section 1.4, Section 9.4 and Section 9.6 hereof, Stockholders shall indemnify and hold harmless and defend Buyer and its respective successors, assigns, stockholders, subsidiaries, controlling persons, affiliates, officers and directors and the Representatives of each of them (collectively, the **"Buyer Indemnified Persons"**) from and against, and shall reimburse the Buyer Indemnified Persons for, any and all losses, Liabilities, Actions, deficiencies, diminution of value, expenses (including costs of investigation and defense and reasonable attorneys' and accountants' fees and expenses), or damages (excluding punitive damages consequential damages and lost profits) of any kind or nature whatsoever, whether or not involving a third-party claim (collectively, **"Damages"**), incurred thereby or caused thereto, directly or indirectly, based on, arising out of, resulting from relating to, or in connection with:

(a)   any breach of or inaccuracy in any representation or warranty made by the Company or the Management Stockholders in Article III of this Agreement, without giving effect to any supplement to the Disclosure Schedule), the Disclosure Schedule, the supplements to the Disclosure Schedule (delivered to Buyer in accordance with Section 6.10 hereof).

(b)   any breach or violation of or failure to fully perform any covenant, agreement, undertaking or obligation of the Company (to the extent to be performed prior to Closing), set forth in this Agreement.

(c)   any breach of or inaccuracy in any representation or warranty made by the Stockholders in Article V of this Agreement (without giving effect to any supplement to the Disclosure Schedule), the Disclosure Schedule, the supplements to the Disclosure Schedule (delivered to Buyer in accordance with Section 6.10 hereof);

(d)   any breach or violation of or failure to fully perform any covenant, agreement, undertaking or obligation of Stockholders (to the extent to be performed prior to Closing) set forth in this Agreement.

(e)   Any Taxes arising out of or in connection with the transaction contemplated by this Agreement.

For purposes of this Article IX and for purposes of determining whether Buyer is entitled to indemnification from Stockholders pursuant to this Section 9.2 hereof, any breach of or inaccuracy in any representation or warranty of Company or Stockholders shall be determined without regard to any materiality qualifications set forth in such representation or warranty, and all references to the terms "material", "materially", "materiality", "Material Adverse Effect" or any similar terms shall be ignored for purposes of determining whether such representation or warranty was true and correct when made.

The matters set forth in Sections 9.2(a) and (b) are joint obligations of the Stockholders. This means that with respect to each indemnification claim thereunder, each Stockholder shall be responsible for a pro rata share of any Damages a Buyer Indemnified Person may suffer based on his, her or its respective holding of Common Stock as set forth in Annex I. Each Stockholder's liability shall be limited to his, her or its respective proportion of the overall limit on indemnification claims set forth in Section 9.4(b) hereof.

The matters set forth in Sections 9.2(c) and (d) are individual and several obligations of each Stockholder. This means that with respect to each indemnification claim thereunder, the particular Stockholder shall be solely responsible for any Damages a Buyer Indemnified Person may suffer. Buyer acknowledges and agrees that no Stockholder shall be liable for any breach of a representation, warranty, covenant or agreement of any other Stockholder.

The matters set forth in Section 9.2(e) shall be joint and several obligations of the Stockholders.

Section 9.3   Indemnification and Reimbursement by Buyer. Buyer shall indemnify and hold harmless and defend Stockholders from and against, and shall reimburse Stockholders for, any and all Damages incurred thereby or caused thereto, directly or indirectly, based on, arising out of, resulting from, relating to, or in connection with:

(a)   any breach of or inaccuracy in any representation or warranty made by Buyer in this Agreement, the Buyer Disclosure Schedule or any other certificate or document delivered by, or on behalf of, Buyer pursuant to this Agreement, or

(b)   any breach or violation of or failure to fully perform any covenant, agreement, undertaking or obligation of Buyer set forth in this Agreement.

For purposes of this Article IX and for purposes of determining whether Stockholders is entitled to indemnification from Buyer pursuant to Section 9.3 (a) or Section 9.3(b) hereof, any breach of or inaccuracy in any representation or warranty of Buyer shall be determined without regard to any materiality qualifications set forth in such representation or warranty, and all references to the terms "material", "materially", "materiality", "Material Adverse Effect" or any similar terms shall be ignored for purposes of determining whether such representation or warranty was true and correct when made.

Section 9.4   Limitations on Amount — Stockholders.

(a)   The Stockholders shall not be liable for Damages arising in connection with its indemnification obligations under Section 9.2 hereof until the amount of such Damages exceeds $[_____] in the aggregate. If the aggregate amount of such Damages exceeds $[_____], the Stockholders shall be liable for all such Damages including the first $1.00 thereof.

(b)   Notwithstanding anything to the contrary contained herein, except for Damages based on, arising out of, resulting from, or relating to any breach of the representations and warranties contained in Section 3.2 (Capitalization), Section 3.9 (Taxes) Section 3.20 (Environmental Matters), Section 3.22 (Brokers and Finders), Section 5.1 (Title to Shares), or resulting from Section 9.2(e), Stockholders shall have no liability for Damages under this Article IX in excess of [$_____]. Notwithstanding any other provision of this Agreement, for purposes of any indemnification liability with respect to Damages based on, arising out of, resulting from, or relating to any breach of the representations and warranties contained in Section 3.2 (Capitalization), Section 3.9 (Taxes), Section 3.20 (Environmental Matters), Section 3.22 (Brokers and Finders), Section 5.1 (Title to Shares), or resulting from Section 9.2(e), there shall be no limit on the amount of Damages for which Stockholders shall be liable.

(c)   The limitations set forth in this Section 9.4 will not apply to any breach of any of the representations and warranties of which Stockholders had knowledge at any time prior to the date on which such representation and warranty is made or any intentional or willful breach by Stockholders or Company of any covenant, agreement, undertaking or obligation, and shall be liable for all Damages with respect to such breach or breaches.

Section 9.5   Limitations on Amount — Buyer.

(a)   Buyer shall not be liable for Damages arising in connection with its indemnification obligations under Section 9.3 hereof until the amount of such Damages exceeds $[_____] in the aggregate. If the aggregate amount of such Damages exceeds $[_____], Buyer shall be liable for all such Damages including the first $1.00 thereof.

(b)   The limitations set forth in this Section 9.5 will not apply to any breach of any of Buyer's representations and warranties of which Buyer had knowledge at any time prior to the date on which such representation and warranty is made or any intentional breach by Buyer of any covenant, agreement, undertaking or obligation, and Buyer shall be liable for all Damages with respect to such breach or breaches.

Section 9.6   Other Limitations.

(a)   The Stockholders' indemnification obligations to the Buyer Indemnified Persons in respect of Damages for which indemnification is provided under this Agreement (**"Stockholder Indemnified Damages"**) will be reduced by any amounts actually received by or on behalf of the Buyer Indemnified Persons from third parties (net of deductible amounts, costs and expenses (including reasonable legal fees and expenses) incurred by such Buyer Indemnified Persons in connection with seeking to collect and collecting such amounts), in respect to such Stockholder Indemnified Damages (such amounts are referred to herein as **"Indemnity Reduction Amounts"**). If any Buyer Indemnified Persons receives any Indemnity Reduction Amounts in respect of Stockholder Indemnified Damages after the full amount of such Stockholder Indemnified Damages has been set off against the Deferred Notes or disclosure from the Escrow Account pursuant to Section 9.6 hereof, then either the amount of such set off will be reduced (and the underlying debt obligation shall be revised) by an amount equal to the Indemnity Reduction Amount, or Buyer shall refund the Escrow Account with the amount of the Indemnity Reduction Amount. No insurer or other third party who would otherwise be obligated to pay any claim shall be relieved of the responsibility with respect to such claim or, solely by virtue of the indemnification provisions hereof, have any subrogation rights with respect to such claim. The parties agree that the indemnification provisions hereof shall not confirm any benefit upon an insurer or any other third party which such insurer or other third party would not be entitled to receive in the absence of indemnification provisions. Buyer will, or will cause each Buyer Indemnified Person to, use its reasonable best efforts to pursue any claims or rights it may have against all third parties which would reduce the amount of Stockholder Indemnified Damages.

(b) The parties hereto acknowledge and agree that the foregoing indemnification provisions in this Article IX shall be the sole and exclusive remedy of an Indemnified Party (as defined in Section 9.7(a) hereof) with respect to the transactions contemplated by this Agreement and any and all claims for any breach or liability arising under, or in connection with, this Agreement or any of the agreements ancillary hereto, or otherwise relating to the subject matter of this Agreement and the transactions contemplated hereby and thereby shall be treated solely in accordance with, and limited by, the indemnification provisions set forth in this Article IX, provided, however, that, nothing contained in Article IX shall in any way limit, impair, modify or otherwise effect the rights of an Indemnified Party (including rights available under the Securities Exchange Act of 1934, as amended or the Securities Act of 1933, as amended) nor shall there be any limitation of liability of any Indemnified Party (as defined in Section 9.7 (a) hereof) to bring any claim, demand, suit or cause of action otherwise available to an Indemnified Person based upon an allegation or allegations that the Company or an Indemnified Party had an intent to defraud or made a willful, intentions or reckless misrepresentations or willful omission of a material fact in connection with this Agreement and the transactions contemplated hereby.

Section 9.7   *Notice and Payment of Claims; Set Off.*

(a) <u>Notice</u>. The party entitled to indemnification pursuant to this Article IX (the **"Indemnified Party"**) shall notify the party liable for indemnification pursuant to this Article IX (the **"Indemnifying Party"**) within a reasonable period of time after becoming aware of, and shall provide to the Indemnifying Party as soon as practicable thereafter all information and documentation necessary to support and verify, any Damages that the Indemnified Party shall have determined to have given or may give rise to a claim for indemnification hereunder. Notwithstanding the foregoing, the failure to so notify the Indemnifying Party shall not relieve the Indemnifying Party of any Liability that it may have not any Indemnified Party, except to the extent that the Indemnifying Party demonstrates that it is prejudiced by the Indemnified Party's failure to give such notice.

(b) <u>Payment; Set Off</u>. The Indemnifying Party shall satisfy its obligations hereunder within five (5) days after receipt of a notice of a claim. Any amount not paid to the Indemnified Party by such date shall bear interest at a rate equal to ten percent (10%) per annum from the date due until the date paid. Buyer agrees and acknowledges that before it may demand payment for Damages under this Article IX it must seek reimbursement from the following, and in the following priority: FIRST up to an aggregate of $_____ for all claims under this Article IX, by reducing the principal amount (and any accrued interest to date) pro rata according to each Stockholder's respective obligation set forth in Section 9.4(a) and (b), which shall affect the timing and amounts required under the Deferred Notes in the same manner as if Buyer had made a permitted prepayment without premium or penalty thereunder, and SECOND, by submitting a claim to the Escrow Agent for reimbursement from the Escrow Account in accordance with the terms of the Escrow Agreement.

Section 9.8 *Procedure for Indemnification — Third Party Claims.*

(a)   Upon receipt by an Indemnified Party of notice of the commencement of any Action by a third party (a **"Third Party Claim"**) against it, such Indemnified Party shall, if a claim is to be made against an Indemnifying Party under this Article IX, give notice to (and in any event within five (5) business days) the Indemnifying Party of the commencement of such Third Party Claim as soon as practicable, but the failure to so notify the Indemnifying Party shall not relieve the Indemnifying Party of any Liability that it may have to any Indemnified Party, except to the extent that the Indemnifying Party demonstrates that the defense of such Third Party Claim is prejudiced by the Indemnified Party's failure to give such notice.

(b)   If a Third Party Claim is brought against an Indemnified Party and it gives proper notice to the Indemnifying Party of the commencement of such Third Party Claim, the Indemnifying Party will be entitled to participate in such Third Party Claim (unless (i) the Indemnifying Party is also a party to such Third Party Claim and the Indemnified Party determines in good faith that joint representation would be inappropriate or (ii) the Indemnifying Party fails to provide reasonable assurance to the Indemnified Party of its financial capacity to defend such Third Party Claim and provide indemnification with respect to such Third Party Claim) and, to the extent that it elects to assume the defense of such Third Party Claim with counsel satisfactory to the Indemnified Party and provides notice to the Indemnified Party of its election to assume the defense of such Third Party Claim, the Indemnifying Party shall not, as long as it diligently conducts such defense, be liable to the Indemnified Party under this Article IX for any fees of other counsel or any other expenses with respect to the defense of such Third Party Claim, in each case subsequently incurred by the Indemnified Party in connection with the defense of such Third Party Claim, other than reasonable costs of investigation.

If the Indemnifying Party assumes the defense of a Third Party Claim, (i) it shall be conclusively established for purposes of this Agreement that the claims made in such Third Party Claim are within the scope of and subject to indemnification; (ii) no compromise, discharge or settlement of, or admission of Liability in connection with, such claims may be effected by the Indemnifying Party without the Indemnified Party's written consent (which consent shall not be unreasonably withheld or delayed) unless (A) there is no finding or admission of any violation of Law or any violation of the rights of any Person and no effect on any other claims that may be made against the Indemnified Party, and (B) the sole relief provided is monetary damages that are paid in full by the Indemnifying Party; (ii) the Indemnifying Party shall have no Liability with respect to any compromise or settlement of such claims effected without its written consent; and (iv) the Indemnified Party shall cooperate in all reasonable respects with the Indemnifying Party in connection with such defense, and shall have the right to participate in such defense, with counsel selected by it. If proper notice is given to an Indemnifying Party of the commencement of any Third Party Claim and the Indemnifying Party does not, within ten (10) days after the Indemnified Party's notice is given, give notice to the Indemnified Party of its election to assume the defense of such Third Party Claim, the Indemnifying Party shall be bound by any determination made in such Third Party Claim or any compromise or settlement effected by the Indemnified Party.

(c) Notwithstanding the foregoing, if an Indemnified Party determines in good faith that there is a reasonable probability that a Third Party Claim may adversely affect it or its directors, officers, subsidiaries, controlling persons or affiliates other than as a result of monetary damages for which it could be entitled to indemnification under this Agreement, the Indemnified Party may, by notice to the Indemnifying Party, assume the exclusive right to defend, compromise, or settle such Third Party Claim.

Section 9.9 Company Representations and Warranties. Anything contained herein to the contrary notwithstanding, the representations and warranties of the Company contained in this Agreement (including, without limitation, the Disclosure Schedule and any supplements thereto pursuant to Section 6.10 hereof) (a) are being given by the Company on behalf of the Stockholders and for the purpose of binding the Stockholders to the terms and provisions of Article IX and the Escrow Agreement, and as an inducement to Buyer to enter into this Agreement (and the Company acknowledges that Buyer have expressly relied thereon) and (ii) are solely for the benefit of the Indemnified Persons and each of them. Accordingly, no third party (including, without limitation, the Stockholders or anyone acting on behalf of any thereof) other than the Indemnified Persons, and each of them, shall be a third party or other beneficiary of such representations and warranties and no such third party shall have any rights of contribution against the Company or any Company Subsidiary with respect to such representations or warranties or any matter subject to or resulting in indemnification by such third party under Article IX or otherwise.

Section 9.10 Tax Indemnification.

(a) Stockholders and Deferred Optionholders shall indemnify the Buyer and hold it harmless from and against Taxes of the Company and each Company Subsidiary for all Pre-Closing Tax Periods, but only to the extent that such Taxes are in excess of the amount, if any, reserved for such Taxes (excluding any reserve for deferred Taxes established to reflect timing differences between book and Tax income) on the face of the Final Closing Balance Sheet. Stockholders and Deferred Optionholders shall reimburse Buyer for any Taxes of the Company and each Company Subsidiary which are the responsibility of Stockholders and Deferred Optionholders pursuant to this Section 9.9 within fifteen (15) business days after payment of such Taxes by Buyer or the Company or a Company Subsidiary.

(b) In the case of any taxable period that includes but does not end on the Closing Date, the amount of any Taxes for such period shall be determined based on an interim closing of the books as of the close of business on the Closing Date (and for such purposes, the Taxable period of any partnership or other pass-through entity in which the Company or a Company Subsidiary holds a beneficial interest shall be deemed to terminate at such time).

(c)   Buyer shall prepare and file or cause to be prepared and filed all Tax Returns for the Company and each Company Subsidiary which are filed after the Closing Date. Buyer shall permit Stockholders' Representative to review and comment on each such Tax Return described in the preceding sentence prior to filing and shall make such revisions to such Tax Returns as are reasonably requested by Stockholders' Representative.

(d)   Any Tax refunds that are received by Buyer or the Company or a Company Subsidiary, and any amounts credited against Tax to which the Company or a Company Subsidiary becomes entitled, that relate to Pre-Closing Tax Periods shall be for the account of Stockholders, and Buyer shall pay over to Stockholders any such refunds or the amount of any such credits within fifteen (15) days after receipt or entitlement thereto. In addition, to the extent that a claim for refund or a proceeding results in a payment or credit against Tax by a taxing authority to Buyer or the Company or a Company Subsidiary of any amount accrued on the Final Closing Balance Sheet, Buyer shall pay such amount to Stockholders within fifteen (15) days after receipt or entitlement thereto.

(e)   Buyer, the Company, each Company Subsidiary, and Stockholders shall cooperate fully, as and to the extent reasonably requested by the other party, in connection with the filing of Tax Returns pursuant to this Section 9.9 and any audit, litigation, or other proceeding with respect to Taxes. Such cooperation shall include the retention and (upon the other party's request) the provision of records and information which are reasonably relevant to any such audit, litigation, or other proceeding and making employees available on a mutually convenient basis to provide additional information and explanation of any material provided hereunder. The Company, each Company Subsidiary, and Stockholders agree (A) to retain all books and records with respect to Tax matters pertinent to the Company or a Company Subsidiary relating to any Pre-Closing Tax Period until the expiration of the statute of limitations (and, to the extent notified by Buyer or Stockholders' Representative, any extensions thereof) of the respective taxable periods and to abide by all record retention agreements entered into with any taxing authority, and (B) to give the other party reasonable written notice prior to transferring, destroying, or discarding any such books and records and, if the other party so requests, Buyer, the Company, a Company Subsidiary, or Stockholders, as the case may be, shall allow the other party to take possession of such books and records.

(f)   Buyer and Stockholders agree, upon request, to use their commercially reasonable efforts to obtain any certificate or other document from any Governmental Entity or any other Person as may be necessary to mitigate, reduce, or eliminate any Tax that could be imposed (including, but not limited to, with respect to the transactions contemplated by this Agreement).

ARTICLE X
REPRESENTATIVE

Section 10.1 Appointment. The Stockholders hereby irrevocably make, constitute and appoint [_____] as their agent and representative (the

"Stockholders' Representative") for all purposes under this Agreement. In the event of the death, resignation or incapacity of the Stockholders' Representative, the Stockholders shall promptly designate another individual to act as their representative under this Agreement so that at all time there will be a Stockholders Representative with the authority provided in this Article X. Such successor Stockholders' Representative shall be designated by the Stockholders by an instrument in writing signed by the Stockholders (or their successors in interest) holding a "required interest" of the Shares, and such appointment shall become effective as to the successor Stockholders Representative when such instrument shall have been delivered to him or her and a copy thereof delivered to the Buyer and Company. For purposes of this Agreement, **"a required interest"** of the Shares or Stockholders means the holders of [_____] percent (_____%) of the Company's Common Stock on as converted and fully diluted basis.

Section 10.2 Authorization. Stockholders hereby authorize the Stockholders' Representative, on their behalf and in their name to:

(a) receive all notice or documents given or to be given to the Stockholders pursuant hereto or in connection herewith and to receive and accept service of legal process in connection with any suit or proceeding arising under this Agreement. The Stockholders' Representative shall promptly forward a copy of such notice of process to each Stockholder.

(b) deliver at the Closing the certificates for the Shares or affidavits of lost shares and assignment, as applicable, in exchange for their respective portion of the Purchase Price, including the Galaxy Shares and Deferred Notes;

(c) deliver to Buyer at the Closing all certificates and documents to be delivered to Buyer by the Stockholders pursuant to this Agreement, together with any other certificates and documents executed by the Stockholders and deposited with the Stockholders' Representative for such purpose;

(d) [act as disbursement agent for distribution of the Purchase Price (including the Galaxy shares and Deferred Notes) to the Stockholders in accordance with <u>Annex II</u>];

(e) engage counsel, and such accountants and other advisors for the Stockholders and incur such other expenses on behalf of the Stockholders in connection with this Agreement and the transactions contemplated hereby as the Stockholders' Representative may deem appropriate;

(f) take such action on behalf of the Stockholders as the Stockholders' Representative may deem appropriate in respect of:

(i) waiving any inaccuracies in the representations or warranties of Buyer contained in this Agreement or in any document delivered by Buyer pursuant hereto;

(ii) waiving the fulfillment of any of the conditions precedent to the Stockholders' obligations hereunder; or terminating this Agreement if Buyer fails to satisfy its obligations under Section 7.2 hereof;

(iii) taking such other action as the Stockholders' Representative is authorized to take under this Agreement or on written instructions executed by a required interest of Stockholders;

(iv) receiving all documents or certificates or notices and making all determinations on behalf of the Stockholders required under this Agreement;

(v) all such other matters as the Stockholders' Stockholders' Representative may deem necessary or appropriate to consummate this Agreement and the transactions contemplated hereby;

(vi) negotiating, representing or entering into settlements and compromises of any disputes arising in connection with this Agreement and the transactions contemplated hereby; and

(vii) taking all such action as may be necessary after the date hereof to carry out any of the transactions contemplated by this Agreement.

Section 10.3 *Irrevocable Appointment.* The appointment of the Stockholders' Representative hereunder is irrevocable and any action taken by the Stockholders' Representative pursuant to the authority granted in this Article X shall be effective and absolutely binding on each Stockholders notwithstanding any contrary action of, or direction from, an Stockholder, except for actions taken by the Stockholders' Representative which are in bad faith or grossly negligent. The death or incapacity of a Stockholder shall not terminate the prior authority and agency of the Stockholders' Representative.

Section 10.4 *Exculpation and Indemnification.*

(a) In performing any of his, her or its duties as Stockholders' Representative under this Agreement, the Stockholders' Representative shall not incur any Liability to any Person, except for Liability caused by the Stockholders' Representative's gross or willful misconduct. Accordingly, the Stockholders' Representative shall not incur any such Liability for (i) any action that is taken or omitted in good faith regarding any questions relating to the duties and responsibilities of the Stockholders' Representative under this Agreement, or (ii) any action taken or omitted to be taken in reliance upon any instrument that the Stockholders' Representative shall in good faith believe to be genuine, to have been signed or delivered by a proper Person and to conform with the provisions of this Agreement.

(b) The Stockholders, jointly and severally, shall indemnify, defend and hold harmless the Stockholders' Representative against, from and in respect of any Liability arising out of or resulting from the performance of his or her or its duties hereunder or in connection with this Agreement (except for Liabilities arising from the gross negligence or willful misconduct of the Stockholders' Representative). Neither the Buyer nor the Company shall be liable to the Stockholders for dealing with the Stockholders' Representative in good faith (other than as a result of the gross negligence or willful misconduct of Company or Buyer).

Section 10.5 *Actions of Stockholders.* Whenever this Agreement requires the Stockholders to take any action, such requirement shall be deemed to involve an undertaking by the Stockholders to cause the Stockholders' Representative to take such action on their behalf.

ARTICLE XI
MISCELLANEOUS

Section 11.1   Certain Definitions.
(a)   As used herein, the term **"Material Adverse Effect"** means with respect to the Company (i) any occurrence, condition, or effect that individually or in the aggregate is or reasonably likely to be materially adverse to (ii) the assets, properties, business, operations, prospects, results of operations, or conditions (financial or otherwise) of the Company and the Company Subsidiaries, taken as a whole.

(b)   When references are made in this agreement of information being **"to the Knowledge of the Company"** or similar language it shall be deemed to have "knowledge" of a particular fact or other matter if: (a) such individual is actually aware of such fact or other matter; or (b) a prudent individual could be expected to discover or otherwise become aware of such fact or other matter in the course of conducting a reasonable investigation concerning the existence of such fact or other matter.

(c)   When reference is made to **"Threatened"** such term shall be deemed to mean any demand or statement that has been made (orally or in writing) or any notice has been given that would lead a prudent Person to conclude that such a claim, event Action or Order is likely to be asserted, commenced, or taken in the future.

(d)   As used in this Agreement **"Related Party"** means (i) each of the Stockholders; (ii) each individual who is, or who has at any time since December 28, 1999 has been, an officer or any of the Company or any Company Subsidiary; (iii) each spouse, parent, child or sibling of each of the individuals referred to in clauses "(i)" and "(i)" hereof; and (iv) any Person entity (other than the Company or Company Subsidiaries) in which any one of the individuals referred to in clauses "(i)", "(ii)" and "(iii)" above hereof (or in which more than one of such individuals collectively hold), beneficially or otherwise, a material voting, proprietary or equity interest.

Section 11.2   Assignment; Successors; No Third Party Rights.   No party may assign any of its rights under this Agreement (including by merger or other operation of law) without the prior written consent of the other parties hereto (which may not be unreasonably withheld or delayed), and any purported assignment without such consent shall be void, except that Stockholders and Buyer hereby agree that Buyer may assign all of its rights and obligations under this Agreement to a wholly-owned direct or indirect subsidiary of Buyer (in any or all of which cases Buyer nonetheless shall remain responsible for the performance of its obligation hereunder. Upon Buyer's sale, disposition or other transfer, in whole or in part, of the Business or assets or properties of the Company or any Company Subsidiary, Stockholders and Company hereby agree that Buyer may assign, in whole or in part, any of Buyer's indemnification and set-off rights related thereto set forth in Article IX hereof, without the consent of the Company or Stockholders. Subject to the foregoing, this Agreement and all of the provisions hereof shall apply to, be binding upon, and inure to the benefit of the parties hereto and their successors and permitted assigns and the parties indemnified pursuant to Article IX. This Agreement and all of its provisions and conditions are for the sole and exclusive benefit of the parties to this Agreement and their successors and permitted assigns and nothing in this Agreement, express or implied, is intended to confer upon any Person other than the parties hereto any rights or remedies of any nature whatsoever under or by reason of this Agreement or any provision of this Agreement, provided however, that the Stockholders' Representative shall be a third party beneficiary to the provisions of Article X.

Section 11.3 Entire Agreement. This Agreement, including the Disclosure Schedule, Buyer Disclosure Schedule, <u>Annex I</u> and <u>Annex II</u>, and Exhibits hereto and the other agreements and written understandings referred to herein or otherwise entered into by the parties hereto on the date hereof, constitute the entire agreement and understanding and supersede all other prior covenants, agreements, undertakings, obligations, promises, arrangements, communications, representations and warranties, whether oral or written, by any party hereto or by any director, officer, employee, agent, or Representative of any party hereto, other than [Confidentiality Agreement].

Section 11.4 Amendment or Modification. This Agreement may be amended or modified only by written instrument signed by the Buyer, the Company and the Stockholders' Representative all of the parties hereto.

Section 11.5 Notices. All notices, requests, instructions, claims, demands, consents and other communications required or permitted to be given hereunder shall be in writing and shall be deemed to have been duly given on the date delivered by hand or by courier service such as Federal Express, or by other messenger (or, if delivery is refused, upon presentment) or if by facsimile transmission upon receipt of confirmation, or upon delivery by registered or certified mail (return receipt requested), postage prepaid, to the parties at the following addresses:

(a) If to Buyer:

> Galaxy International Corp.
> 100 Melbourne Ave
> Brooklyn, New York 10001
> Tel: 212-222-2222
> Facsimile: 212-222-2223
> Attn: Michael Sherman
>   Chief Financial Officer

with copy to:

> Bigar, Strong & Wise
> 5000 Wilshire Blvd.
> Los Angeles, California 90017
> Tel: (213) 789-4321
> Facsimile: (213) 789-1234
> Attn: Mark A. Bigar

(b)   If to Company:

>Trekker Marketing, Inc.
>333 Surfside Road
>San Diego, California 90001
>Tel: (619) 222-9876
>Facsimile: (619) 222-6789
>Attn: Frank Merlin
>   Chief Executive Officer

with copy to:

>Klever & Coolidge
>100 Hollywood Blvd.
>Los Angeles, California 90002
>Tel: (213) 678-7654
>Facsimile: (213) 678-4567
>Attn: Julie Hartbreaker

(c)   If to Stockholder:

>[Stockholders Representative]

>_____
>_____
>_____
>_____

with a copy to:

>_____
>_____
>_____
>_____

Section 11.6   Actions of the Company and the Company Subsidiaries.   Whenever this Agreement requires the Company or any Company Subsidiary to take any action, such requirement shall be deemed to involve, with respect to actions to be taken to or prior to the Closing, an undertaking on the part of Management Stockholders and Stockholders to cause the Company or any Company Subsidiary to take such action.

Section 11.7   Descriptive Headings; Construction.   The descriptive headings herein are inserted for convenience of reference only and are not intended to be part of, or to affect the meaning, construction or interpretation of, this Agreement. Unless otherwise expressly provided, the word "including" does not limit the preceding words or terms.

Section 11.8   Counterparts.   For the convenience of the parties hereto, this Agreement may be executed in any number of counterparts, each such counterpart being deemed to be an original instrument, and all such counterparts shall together constitute the same agreement.

Section 11.9 Governing Law; Contest to Jurisdiction. **THIS AGREEMENT SHALL BE CONSTRUED IN ACCORDANCE WITH THE LAWS OF THE STATE OF CALIFORNIA WITHOUT GIVING EFFECT TO ANY CHOICE OR CONFLICT OF LAW PROVISIONS OR RULES THAT COULD CAUSE THE APPLICATION OF THE LAWS OF ANY JURISDICTION OTHER THAN THE STATE OF CALIFORNIA. THE PARTIES HERETO EXPRESSLY CONSENT AND AGREE THAT ANY DISPUTE, CONTROVERSY, LEGAL ACTION OR OTHER PROCEEDING THAT ARISES UNDER, RESULTS FROM, CONCERNS OR RELATES TO THIS AGREEMENT MAY BE BROUGHT IN THE FEDERAL AND STATE COURTS IN AND OF THE STATE OF CALIFORNIA AND ACKNOWLEDGE THAT THEY WILL ACCEPT SERVICE OF PROCESS BY REGISTERED OR CERTIFIED MAIL OR THE EQUIVALENT DIRECTED TO THEIR LAST KNOWN ADDRESS AS DETERMINED BY THE OTHER PARTY IN ACCORDANCE WITH THIS AGREEMENT OR BY WHATEVER OTHER MEANS ARE PERMITTED BY SUCH COURTS. THE PARTIES HERETO HEREBY ACKNOWLEDGE THAT SAID COURTS HAVE JURISDICTION OVER ANY SUCH DISPUTE OR CONTROVERSY, AND THAT THEY HEREBY WAIVE ANY OBJECTION TO PERSONAL JURISDICTION OR VENUE IN THESE COURTS OR THAT SUCH COURTS ARE AN INCONVENIENT FORUM.**

Section 11.10   Exercise of Rights and Remedies.   Except as otherwise provided herein, no delay of or omission in the exercise of any right, power or remedy accruing to any party as a result of any breach or default by any other party under this Agreement shall impair any such right, power or remedy, nor shall it be construed as a waiver of or acquiescence in any such breach or default, or of any similar breach or default occurring later; nor shall any waiver of any single breach or default be deemed a waiver of any other breach or default occurring before or after that waiver.

Section 11.11   Reformation and Severability.   In case any provision of this Agreement shall be invalid, illegal or unenforceable, it shall, to the extent possible, be modified in such manner as to be valid, legal and enforceable but so as to most nearly retain the intent of the parties, and if such modification is not possible, such provision shall be severed from this Agreement, and in either case the validity, legality and enforceability of the remaining provisions of this Agreement shall not in any way be affected or impaired thereby.

Section 11.12   Specific Performance; Other Rights and Remedies.   Each party recognizes and agrees that in the event the other party or parties should refuse to perform any of its or their obligations under this Agreement, the remedy at law would be inadequate and agrees that for breach of such provisions, each party shall, in addition to such other remedies as may be available to it at law or in equity, be entitled to injunctive relief and to enforce its rights by an action for specific performance to the extent permitted by applicable law. Each party hereby waives any requirement for security or the posting of any bond or other surety in connection with any temporary or permanent award of injunctive, mandatory or other equitable relief.

Section 11.13   Stockholder Parties.   [In the event that not all of the Stockholders execute this Agreement and become a party thereto, then this Agreement shall nevertheless be binding on only those Stockholders who become a party hereto, provided that such executing Stockholders constitute or own at least ninety percent (90%) of each of the Common Stock, Series A Preferred Stock and Series B Preferred Stock. In addition, the Buyer, the Company and the executing Stockholders agree to amend this Agreement as may be reasonably necessary to reflect that not all of the Shares are being sold and that not all of the Stockholders are a party to the Agreement.]

IN WITNESS WHEREOF, the parties hereto have caused this Stock Purchaser Agreement to be executed by their officers duly authorized, if applicable as of the date first written above.

TREKKER MARKETING, INC.

By: _____
Name: Fred Merlin
Title: Chief Executive Officer

GALAXY INTERNATIONAL Corp.

By: _____
Name: Robert Halfacre
Title: Chief Executive Officer

By: _____
Name: [_____]
Title: Secretary

MANAGEMENT STOCKHOLDERS[1]

_____

Stanley Rockledge

_____

Fred Merlin

STOCKHOLDERS:

SWIFT ROHN CAPITAL LLC

By: _____
Name:
Title:

YORK LIFE FUND III, LLC

By:_____

FRED MERLIN

_____

---

1.   Please revise stockholder names to reflect stock ledger which we believe is in your possession.

STANLEY ROCKLEDGE

_____

RANDY MOSES

_____

JAMES KILJOY

_____

MELVIN KIRKPATRICK

_____

CHARLES TEALEAF

_____

LAWRENCE BROAD

_____

ROBERT ALLSTOCK

_____

STOCKHOLDERS' REPRESENTATIVE:

[_____]

By: _____
Name:
Title:

ANNEX I

TO THAT CERTAIN
STOCK PURCHASE AGREEMENT
DATED AS OF APRIL ___, 2004
BY AND AMONG
THE STOCKHOLDERS NAMED THEREIN
THE MANAGEMENT STOCKHOLDERS NAMED THEREIN
TREKKER MARKETING, INC.
AND
GALAXY INTERNATIONAL CORP.

STOCK HOLDERS

NAME AND ADDRESS	SHARES OF COMMON STOCK	SHARES OF SERIES A PREFERRED STOCK	SHARES OF SERIES B PREFERRED STOCK	OPTIONS	PERCENTAGE OWNERSHIP OF COMMON STOCK

ANNEX II

**TO THAT CERTAIN
STOCK PURCHASE AGREEMENT
AND COMPANY
DATED AS OF APRIL __, 2004
BY AND AMONG
THE STOCKHOLDERS NAMED THEREIN
THE MANAGEMENT STOCKHOLDERS NAMED THEREIN
TREKKER MARKETING, INC.
AND
GALAXY INTERNATIONAL CORP.**

Aggregate consideration to be paid to the Stockholders:[2]

Cash — $____, including $___ of such amount to be held by the Escrow Agent pursuant to the Escrow Agreement pursuant to Section 1.4 hereof for the purchase of Common Stock and Preferred Stock and for the cancellation of Stock Options.

Galaxy Shares — [____] shares of Galaxy Shares ($[___] in value)[3] for the purchase of a portion of the Shares. The issuance of the Galaxy Shares shall be subject to execution by the recipient of a Stock Issuance Agreement.

Deferred Notes — $5.0 million principal amount for the purchase of a portion of the Shares.

Aggregate consideration to be allocated among the Stockholders and holders of Options as follows:

[Add Chart]

(a) <u>Earnout</u>. Buyer will pay the Stockholders an earnout as set forth below (**"Earnout Payments"**):

(i) For the year ended December 31, 2004, $1.75 million if the Company's EBITDA (as defined below) equals $8 million and rising at a linear rate to $3.5 million if EBITDA equals or exceeds $10.5 million; and

(ii) For the year ended December 31, 2005, $1.75 million if the Company's EBITDA equals $9 million and rising at a linear rate to $3.5 million of EBITDA equals or exceeds $11.5 million.

(b) The Earnout Payments, if any, shall be allocated 57.14% equally among [NAMES OF SENIOR MANAGEMENT] (collectively **"Senior Management"**), and 42.86% among the Stockholders (other than Senior Management) pro rata in relationship to their ownership of Shares.

---

2. Subject to upward or downward adjustment to the extent that the Shareholders' Equity of the Company on the Closing Date as calculated in accordance with GAAP and on a basis consistent with past practices as set forth on Section 1.5 hereof.

3. Determined by reference to the weighted average price per share of Galaxy Shares for the six (6) months ending on the date this Agreement is executed less 10% for the Earnout Payments. The payments at closing are to be valued at the same price granted by Galaxy in stock sales made immediately prior to closing to fund this transaction.

For purposes of this *Annex II* **"EBITDA"** shall mean the earnings before interest, taxes, depreciation and amortization of the Company before calculation of the Earnout (as defined below) if any, based in accordance with upon GAAP and on a basis consistent with past practice.

(c) <u>General</u>. In calculating EBITDA, actual reported results of the Company:

(i) Shall neither be reduced by Buyer corporate allocations, except for direct services provided by the Company at cost (not to exceed the cost of the same services performed on an out-sourced basis);

(ii) Shall be reduced by the interest expense associated with any capital that Buyer or any affiliate will be required to infuse into the Company in order for the Company to reach its targeted EBITDA objectives at an assumed interest rate of 10%;

(iii) Assumes operating expenses will include total lease costs if leases do not meet the criteria for a capital lease or will include appropriate depreciation and interest expenses related to lease equipment if such leases do not meet the criteria for a capital lease;

(iv) Shall be reduced by the costs (if any) of additional administrative staff which the Company and Buyer determine shall be necessary to meet reporting and administrative requirements of the Company while relieving the Company management and other personnel from certain administrative duties to allow them to focus more of their efforts on business development; and

(v) Shall be reduced by profit-sharing contributions, increases in compensation packages paid to the Company's Senior Management under employment agreements that might be put in place as a result of this transaction other than the agreements required in this Agreement.

(vi) Shall not be reduced by any Damages for which the Buyer recovered in accordance with Article IX, however, to the extent any Damages are not reimbursed in accordance with Article IX then actual results shall be reduced by such amount.

(vii) [other Adjustments to be discussed]

The Buyer agrees that subsequent to the Closing Date and until the expiration of the time period related to the Earnout Payments, it shall maintain the separate corporate existence of the Company as a wholly-owned direct or indirect subsidiary of Buyer and shall maintain separate books of account in order to calculate the Earnout Payments.

The Company and Buyer shall use all reasonable efforts to prepare financial statements necessary for calculation of the Earnout Payments as soon as practicable and in any event within thirty (30) days following expiration of the applicable 12-month period. After calculation of the Earnout, if any, the Company shall provide the Stockholders' Representative with copies of all workpapers and other relevant documents to verify the calculation of such Earnout Payments, if any. In addition, Company will provide the Stockholders' Representative with annual financial statements of the Company. In the event of any dispute or controversy concerning the calculation of the Earnout Payments, the parties to the Agreement shall use their reasonable best efforts to resolve the matter to the reasonable satisfaction of the parties within sixty (60) days following such calculation of the Earnout Payments. Any dispute or controversy with respect to the Earnout Payments that is not resolved within such sixty-day period shall be settled exclusively by arbitration, conducted before a panel of three arbitrators in Los Angeles, California, in accordance with the rules of the American Arbitration Association then in effect. The arbitrators shall not have the authority to add to, detract from, or modify any provision of this Agreement nor to award punitive damages. A decision by a majority of the arbitration panel shall be final and binding, and judgment may be entered on the arbitrators' award in any court having jurisdiction. The costs of any arbitration proceeding shall be borne by the party or parties not prevailing in such arbitration as determined by the arbitrators.

Payment of the Earnout Payments, if any, will be made within sixty (60) days following preparation of the financial statements described above, if applicable, or promptly upon the determination by the arbitrators. Any amounts paid pursuant to the shall be paid in cash to the Stockholders pro rata in the same proportion as their ownership of Shares (other than Senior Management) and in Galaxy Shares to Senior Management (valued for this purpose based on the volume weighted average per shares of Galaxy Shares for the six (6) months ending prior to the date on which the Company's audited financial statements are issued, less 10%). Any issuance of Galaxy Shares will be subject to the execution of a Stock Issuance Agreement.

||D||

Letter of Intent

February 1, 2004

Mr. Fred Merlin
Chief Executive Officer
Trekker Marketing, Inc.
333 Surfside Road
San Diego, CA 90001

Dear Fred:

Introduction

We are writing to you following the discussions between Galaxy International Corporation ("Galaxy") and J.B. Hubble and yourself regarding Trekker Marketing, Inc. ("Trekker").

This letter confirms the interest of Galaxy in acquiring Trekker, and reflects our understanding of the key issues of the non-binding proposal as discussed by us in our teleconference of February 1, 2004.

Non-binding Proposal

The terms of Galaxy's non-binding proposal to acquire Trekker are:

Galaxy or its nominee will acquire 100% of the issued capital of Trekker, comprised of common and preference shares and outstanding options for $42 million, of which $30 million will be payable on completion, and $5 million will be payable in four semi-annual equal payments commencing in the second quarter of calendar 2005, bearing simple interest of 7% per year. Galaxy to have the right to prepay at any time and from time to time part or all of the deferred consideration without penalty. Specified Trekker Senior Management will be required to accept Galaxy shares in respect of their common and preference share holdings in Trekker.

In addition there may be up to $7 million of contingent payments, (of which up to $3 million will be paid to the fully diluted Common Stock owners of Trekker and up to $4 million to specified Trekker Senior Management as specified by Galaxy. These contingent payments would be based on the hurdles proposed by Galaxy:

     (i)   In the year to December 31, 2005, Trekker must achieve EBITDA of $8 million to trigger a payment of $1.75 million, rising at a linear rate to $3.5 million on achieving EBITDA of $10.5 million.

     (ii)   In the year to December 31, 2006, Trekker must achieve EBITDA of $9 million to trigger a payment of $1.75 million, rising at a linear rate to $3.5 million on achieving EBITDA of $11.5 million;

Of this $7 million contingent payment the up to $3.0 million payment to the Common stock owners would be paid in cash and the up to $4.0 million payment to Trekker Senior Management would be satisfied by the issuance of Galaxy shares of that value. The Galaxy shares would be valued at a 10% discount to the volume weighted average price of Galaxy shares over the six-month period prior to the signing of the accounts in respect of the year which is the subject of the additional consideration. All shares issued would be subject to three-month escrow;

     (iii)   An additional $1.0 million will be paid to specific Trekker Senior Management in respect of four year Service Agreements and Non-Compete Agreements. The payment would be made with cash paid in four annual equal installments on 4/05, 4/06, 4/07, and 4/08. These payments are of a capital nature as are all other payments referred to in this letter proposal save for interest payments and Galaxy will require the purchase agreement to be structured to reflect that fact;

     (iv)   Settlement amount to be adjusted for rise and fall in balance sheet items between December 31, 2003 accounts and completion; and,

     (v)   Trekker's existing subordinated notes to be rescheduled as follows: principal repayments to cease at the effective date of the completion of the acquisition of Trekker ("Effective Date"); 50% of the remaining principal to be repaid on July 1, 2005; 25% to be repaid July 1, 2006; and, the residual 25% to be repaid July 1, 2007. The coupon of the existing notes will be reduced to 7.0% and interest in arrears on the outstanding balance will be paid monthly to noteholders. Galaxy to have the right of early repayment of part of any or all of the notes at any time or from time to time without penalty. Trekker's payment obligations to noteholders will be guaranteed by Galaxy. Galaxy will need to review the other terms of the notes and may seek additional amendments to those terms.

Financing

Galaxy proposes to finance the cash component of any acquisition of Trekker from a combination of three sources. These are, first, the existing cash resources of Galaxy; second, borrowings by Galaxy; and, third, the proceeds of a placement of common shares in Galaxy to be completed if Galaxy is successful in acquiring Trekker. The mix of these forms of financing is yet to be determined by Galaxy.

Timing

Galaxy is in a position to complete the acquisition of Trekker once agreement is reached and due diligence is satisfactorily completed. Under Delaware law, the proposed acquisition does not require Galaxy shareholder approval.

Any placement of ordinary shares by Galaxy necessary to fund a part of the proposed acquisition consideration of Trekker does not require approval of Galaxy shareholders.

Galaxy requires exclusive rights for 60 days to negotiate with Trekker and its shareholders during the due diligence period.

Conditions Precedent

This preliminary proposal is subject to the following conditions precedent:

1. Approval of the Galaxy Board of Directors to the final terms of any transaction to acquire Trekker;

2. The entering into by selected members of the management team of Trekker of employment contracts and non compete contracts to the satisfaction of Galaxy;

3. The entering into by members of the Trekker sponsored riding team of satisfactory sponsorship contracts and/or non compete contracts to the satisfaction of Galaxy;

4. The assets of Trekker to be acquired by Galaxy are to include the Dud and Druids brands currently owned by Mirage, Inc. It is understood that Trekker owns or will own, inter alia, the businesses or entities: Dwarf; Mirage; and Green Hat;

5. The satisfactory completion by Galaxy of a due diligence review of Trekker including the financial and other information concerning Trekker; and,

6. The completion by Galaxy of any new placement of ordinary shares in Galaxy necessary in order to fund the completion of the proposed acquisition of Trekker.

Level of Review

This non-binding proposal to acquire Trekker has received review from the senior executive team of Galaxy. The Board of Directors of Galaxy will be required to review and approve the terms of any definitive proposal by Galaxy to acquire Trekker.

Conclusion

We look forward to welcoming Trekker to the Galaxy International, Corp., and we are very excited about working with Trekker management to grow Trekker and Galaxy over the long term to be the world's premier skate-board equipment and apparel company.

Yours sincerely,
For and on behalf of Galaxy International, Corp.

Robert Halfacre   Date:_____
Chief Executive Officer

Agreed and Accepted:
For and on behalf of Trekker Marketing, Inc.

Fred Merlin   Date:_____
Chief Executive Officer

Due Diligence Checklist

GENERAL DUE DILIGENCE CHECKLIST

What follows is an itemized outline of certain of the documents and materials we would initially like to review concerning the business of the Company (the "Business"). All references to the Company apply to any members of the affiliated group of companies having as its ultimate parent Company. To the extent any requested documents are available as part of filings made by the Company with the SEC, in lieu of providing the document you may reference the applicable filing.

A. CORPORATE MATTERS

1. A corporate structure chart depicting the various entities within the Company conducting the Business, and the ownership and relationship of those entities.
2. A list of jurisdictions in which the Business is being conducted indicating the entity conducting the Business in each jurisdiction.
3. A list of any governmental (federal, state, or local) approvals, permits, certificates, registrations, concessions, exemptions, etc., required for the Company to conduct the Business in every jurisdiction in which the Business is conducted.
4. Audited and/or unaudited financial statements for the last 3 years, and current budgets and projections for each Company engaged in any aspect of the Business.
5. Independent accountants' management letters on internal controls and contingent liabilities (if any) for the last 3 years for each financial statement provided in response to item A.6.
6. Agreements relating to the ownership and control of each Company involved in the Business (if any), including all shareholder agreements, voting trusts and voting agreements, proxies, transfer restriction agreements, registration agreements, stock purchase rights (including the Company's current rights plan) and warrants.

7. Agreements to which the Company is a party relating to any completed or proposed business acquisitions, mergers, sales or purchases of substantial assets, equity financings, reorganizations and other material transactions outside of the ordinary course of business for each Company involved in the Business with in the last 3 years.
8. Agreements relating to ownership of or investments in any business or enterprise, including investments in joint ventures and minority equity investments.

B.   MATERIAL CONTRACTS

1. Descriptions of arrangements between each Company involved in the Business and the 50 largest customers and 50 largest suppliers of the Company.
2. All sales distribution agreements, sales representative agreements, franchise agreements and advertising agreements involving each Company related to the Business.
3. All service contracts with customers of each Company in the Business (or if all such contracts are substantially similar, the form of such contract and a list of persons or entities party to such an agreement).
4. Agreements of each Company in the Business for research and/or design and development.
5. Any agreement which prohibits each Company in the Business from freely engaging in any business anywhere in the world.
6. Any tax sharing or tax indemnification agreements involving each Company involved in the Business.

C.   LABOR

1. Employment agreements with any officer, individual employee or other person on a full-time or consulting basis.
2. Non-disclosure agreements and non-compete agreements binding any present or former employees.
3. Management, consulting or advisory agreements with any third party.
4. Collective bargaining agreements with any labor union.
5. Files relating to any outstanding orders, decrees or judgments and files with respect to pending or threatened labor disputes (including strikes, grievances and arbitration proceedings).

D.   EMPLOYEE BENEFITS

1. Bonus, pension, profit sharing, retirement and other forms of deferred compensation plans together with all actuarial reports and last agreements, evidence of any qualification under the Internal Revenue Code and ERISA (or similar Canadian or other foreign statues and regulations), correspondence with respect to such qualification

and the last three annual reports on Form 5500 (or the Canadian equivalent), severance plans, employee handbooks or pamphlets.

2. Stock purchase plans, stock option plans, health and welfare, insurance and other employee benefits plans.

3. Agreements with any person or organization affiliated with the Company providing for the payment of any cash or other compensation upon the change in control of the Company or any of its subsidiaries or prohibiting competition or the disclosure of secrets or confidential information.

E.   LITIGATION

1. Copies of all counsel letters received by the Company in response to audit inquiries for the past 5 years.

2. List of, and files concerning, any pending or threatened litigation, any material claims settled or adjudicated within the past 5 years, and any past or current investigations or proceedings (pending or threatened) by any third party or governmental agencies (including environmental, tax, employee safety matters and EEOC (or pay-equity or other similar Canadian) matters).

3. Information regarding any material contingent liabilities and material unasserted claims and information regarding any unasserted violation of any employee safety and environmental laws and any asserted or unasserted pollution clean up liability.

F.   REAL ESTATE

1. Description of any real estate owned by the Company and copies of related deeds, surveys, title insurance policies, title opinions, certificates of occupancy, easements, condemnation orders, zoning variances and recent appraisals.

2. Copies of all leases whereby the Company leases (as lessee or lessor) any real estate, facility or office space.

G.   PERSONAL PROPERTY

1. Copies of all leases, whereby the Company leases (as lessee or lessor) any machinery, vehicles or other equipment (both operating and capitalized) with annual payments in excess of $____.

H.   INTELLECTUAL PROPERTY

1. List of registered and unregistered proprietary rights (patents, trademarks, service marks, trade names, corporate names, copyrights, and applications therefore) of the Company.

2. Agreements and files relating to proprietary rights (patents, trade-marks, service marks trade names, corporate names, copyrights, etc.) of the Company, including registrations and royalty agreements and licenses held or granted with respect thereto (including without limitation foreign manufacturing and/or technology licenses), and any pending or threatened infringement actions by or against the Company related to such rights.
3. Agreements and files to any other proprietary rights of the Company.

I.   INSURANCE MATTERS

1. Summary description of insurance coverage, including but not lim-ited to the name of the insurer, insured party, insurance agent, policyholder and period and scope of coverage (including whether the coverage is claims made or occurrence or other basis and a de-scription of the method of calculation of deductibles and ceilings); copies of policies and agreements.
2. Information on claims history, methods of reserving for uninsured portion of claims and methods of self insurance.

J.   ENVIRONMENTAL

1. A list of facilities or other properties formerly owned, leased or op-erated by the Company and reports of environmental audits or site assessments in the possession of the Company, including any Phase I or Phase II assessments or asbestos surveys, relating to any such fa-cilities or properties;
2. Copies of environmental permits for facilities or properties currently owned or operated by Company;
3. Copies of all environmental notices of violations, complaints, consent decrees, and other documents indicating noncompliance with envi-ronmental laws or regulations or guidelines, received by the Com-pany from local, state, provincial or federal governmental authorities, together with documentation indicating how such situations were resolved;
4. Copies of any private party complaints, claims, lawsuits or other documents relating to potential environmental liability of the Com-pany or any of its subsidiaries to private parties;
5. Listing of underground storage tanks currently or previously present at the properties and facilities listed in response to Item 1, copies of per-mits, licenses or registrations relating to such tanks, and documentation of underground storage tank removals and any corrective action or re-medial work; documentation of "sign-offs," "no further action letters," "clean closure letters" and information submitted to or received from regulatory agencies regarding underground storage tank matters;
6. Description of any release of hazardous substances or petroleum known by the Company to have occurred at the properties and

facilities listed in response to Item 1; descriptions of any corrective or remedial action relating to any such releases;

7. Copies of any information request, PRP notices, "106 orders," or other notices received by the Company pursuant to CERCLA or similar state or Canadian federal or provincial laws relating to liability for hazardous substance releases at offsite facilities or facilities described in response to Item 1, together with material correspondence and documents (including any relating to the Company's share of liability) with respect to any such matters; and

8. Copies of any written analyses conducted by the Company or any outside consultant relating to future environmental activities (e.g, upgrades to equipment, improvements in practices, etc.) of the Company for which expenditure of more than $_____ is certain or reasonably anticipated within the next five years and an estimate of the costs of such activities.

K.   FINANCIAL STATEMENTS

1. All audited financial statements for the Company for the most recent five (5) years and fiscal year and unaudited financial statements for each fiscal quarter since the most recent audited statement.

2. Any notes from conferences with accountants or financial officer for the Company to review information provided pursuant to Item L.1 and accounting problems.

3. Auditors' reports to management and attorneys' letters to auditors of the Company applicable to each period covered by the audited financial statements provided.

L.   TAXES

1. Federal, state and local income tax returns for the five most recent fiscal years of the Company.

2. Property and other tax returns, reports and forms, if any, for the five most recent fiscal years.

3. List of audits or examination of returns, reports or forms described pursuant to Items M.1 and M.2 and of all deficiencies, proposed and assessed as a result of such examinations, if any; evidence of satisfaction of same.

M.   FINANCIAL AGREEMENTS

1. Indentures and loan agreements, to which the Company is a party if any.

2. Guarantee agreements to which the Company is a party.

3. Credit agreements for the Company including lines of credit and a description of banking relationships.

N. INSURANCE

1. List and description of all insurance policies.

O. REGISTRATION, FILINGS, LICENSES AND PERMITS

1. Copies of all filings of the Company with the Securities and Exchange Commission (including registration orders).
2. Copies of all state Blue Sky filings.
3. Copies of all filings with the National Association of Securities Dealers (including CRD Report).
4. Copies of all other government licenses or permits.
5. Copies of government licenses or permits of employees or agents.
6. Copies of any documents relating to or investigations or audit of the Company, agency governmental agency or authority.

P. LIENS AND ENCUMBRANCES

1. List and description of all material liens (including tax liens), charges, security interests, pledges, easements, covenants, agreements, restrictions and encumbrances.
2. All decrees, awards, orders or judgments applicable to the business or operations of the Company, with out limitation, any relating to wages, hours and working conditions, advertising and sale of services, trade regulation, license, patent or copyright infringement, and antitrust.

Closing Checklist

ACQUISITION OF TREKKER MARKETING, INC.
BY
GALAXY INTERNATIONAL CORPORATION
JUNE _____, 2004

I. PRINCIPAL AGREEMENTS AND RELATED DOCUMENTS

1. Stock Purchase Agreement by and among the Stockholders named therein, Trekker Marketing, Inc. and Galaxy International Corporation, or its Nominee for all of the outstanding capital stock of Trekker Marketing, Inc. dated as of April _____ 2004, including Annex I and the following Schedules and Exhibits attached thereto ("Stock Purchase Agreement"):

   a. Schedule 1.2(a)   Purchase Price
   b. Schedule 1.3   Delivery of Shares and Purchase Price
   c. Schedule 9.2(f)   Indemnification and Reimbursement by Stockholders and Optionholders
   d. Exhibit 1.3(c)   Form of Stock Issuance Agreement
   e. Exhibit 1.3(g)   Form of Deferred Note
   f. Exhibit 2.3(g)   Form of Guaranty
   g. Exhibit 7.1(k)   Form of Subordinated Note Exchange Agreement and Subordinated Note
   h. Exhibit 7.1(n)   Form of Employment Agreement
   i. Exhibit 7.1(o)   Form of Stockholder Release
   j. Exhibit 7.1(p)   Form of Non-Competition Agreement

2. Trekker Marketing, Inc. Disclosure Schedules to the Stock Purchase Agreement
3. Stockholders Disclosure Schedules to the Stock Purchase Agreement

4. Stockholders' Representative Request and Authorization dated as of ____, 2004 authorizing the execution and delivery of Amendment Number One to the Stock Purchase Agreement.

5. Stock Issuance Agreement by and between Galaxy International Corporation and Stanley Rockledge dated as of June ____, 2004, including Investor Certification attached thereto as Exhibit A.

6. Stock Issuance Agreement by and between Galaxy International Corporation and Fred Merlin dated as of June ____, 2004, including Investor Certification attached thereto as Exhibit A.

7. Stock Issuance Agreement by and between Galaxy International Corporation and Randy Moses dated as of June ____, 2004, including Investor Certification attached thereto as Exhibit A.

8. Stock Issuance Agreement by and between Galaxy International Corporation and Charles Tealeaf dated as of June ____, 2004, including Investor Certification attached thereto as Exhibit A.

9. Copy of Galaxy International Corporation-Annual Report for the year ended December 31, 2003, and the Quarterly Report filed on March ____, 2004, delivered to each of the Stockholders who were party to the Stock-Issuance Agreement pursuant to paragraph 6 thereof.

10. Amended and Restated Employment Agreement dated as of June ____, 2004 by and among Trekker Marketing, Inc., Galaxy International Corporation and Fred Merlin with Exhibits attached thereto, including Trade Secret and Confidentiality Agreement and Invention Agreement.

11. Employment Agreement dated as of June ____, 2004 by and among Dwindle, Inc., Trekker Marketing. Inc., Galaxy International Corporation and Randy Moses with Exhibits attached thereto, including Trade Secret and Confidentiality Agreement and Invention Agreement.

12. Employment Agreement dated as of June ____, 2004 by and among Trekker Marketing, Inc., Galaxy International Corporation and Melvin Kirkpatrick with Exhibits attached thereto, including Trade Secret and Confidentiality Agreement and Invention Agreement.

13. General Release dated as of July ____, 2004 from each Stockholder of Trekker Marketing, Inc. to and in favor of, and for the benefit of Trekker Marketing, Inc. and Galaxy International Corporation.

14. Spousal Consents of Stockholders of Trekker Marketing, Inc.

15. NonCompetition Agreement dated as of June ____, 2004 by and among Trekker Marketing, Inc., Galaxy International Corporation, and its nominee and Fred Merlin.

16. NonCompetition Agreement dated as of June ____, 2004 by and among Trekker Marketing, Inc., Galaxy International Corporation, and its nominee and Randy Moses.

17. NonCompetition Agreement dated as of June ____, 2004 by and among Trekker Marketing, Inc., Galaxy International Corporation, and its nominee and Stanley Rockledge.

18. Consulting Agreement dated as of June ____, 2004 by and among Trekker Marketing, Inc. and Stanley Rockledge.

II. DOCUMENTS DELIVERED BY TREKKER MARKETING, INC. AND ITS SHAREHOLDERS

1. Termination of Stockholders Agreement dated as of June ____, 2004 executed by all the Stockholders of Trekker Marketing Inc.
2. Termination of Amended and Restated Management Agreement dated as of June _____, 2004 by and among Swift Rohn, L.L.C. and Trekker Marketing, Inc.
3. Trekker Marketing, Inc. Officer's Certificate dated as of July____, 2004 delivered in accordance with Section 7.1(c) of the Stock Purchase Agreement.
4. Trekker Marketing Inc. Secretary's Certificate dated as of July ____, 2004 delivered in accordance with Section 7.1(f) of the Stock Purchase Agreement, including Exhibit A attached thereto.
5. Trekker Marketing, Inc. Written Consent in Lieu of Meeting of the majority holders of Common Stock, Series A Preferred Stock and Series B Preferred Stock dated June ____, 2004 approving the Stock Purchase Agreement and related transactions and copy of the notice dated June _____, 2004 to remaining shareholders pursuant to Section 603(b) of the California Corporations Code as to action taken by majority holders.
6. Consent to Assignment Agreement dated as of June ____, 2004 by and between Trekker Marketing Inc. and Lois Merlin Trust for the lease premises located at 333 Surfside Road, San Diego, California.
7. Officer's Certificate for Trekker Marketing Inc. dated as of June ____, 2004 as to the repayment of all option loans pursuant to Section 7(j)(ii) of the Stock Purchase Agreement.
8. Letter dated June ____, 2004 from Trekker Marketing Inc. and acknowledged and agreed to by each of Option Holders of Trekker Marketing, Inc. as to the cancellation of their stock options under the terms of the Stock Purchase Agreement.
9. Copies of the stock certificates representing 100% of the capital stock of Trekker, including stock powers executed by the stockholders transferring the shares to Galaxy International Corp. on ____, 2004 under the terms of the Stock Purchase Agreement.
10. Letter dated July ____, 2004 from Trekker Marketing Inc. to Galaxy International Corp. waiving the requirement of the receipt of an opinion of counsel as a condition to the transfer or assignment of the shares of Common Stock, Series A Preferred Stock and Series B Preferred Stock.
11. Wire Transfer Instructions for cash portion of Initial Purchase Price pursuant to Section 1.3(d) of the Stock Purchase Agreement dated June ____, 2004.

III. DOCUMENTS DELIVERED BY GALAXY INTERNATIONAL CORPORATION

1. Evidence of notification of issuance of shares of common stock of Galaxy International Corporation to Charles Tealeaf, Randy Moses, Melvin Kirkpatrick, Merlin Family Trust, and Stanley Rockledge.

2. Copies of the Deferred Notes issued on June _____, 2004 to the following Stockholders in the amounts indicated:

    [List Omitted]

3. Copies of the Deferred Notes issued on June_____, 2004 to the following Option Holders in the amounts indicated:

    [List Omitted]

4. Guaranty of Galaxy International Corporation to each of the holders of the Deferred Notes dated June _____, 2004.

5. Galaxy International Corporation Officer's Certificate dated of June _____, 2004 delivered, in accordance with Section 7.2(c) of the Stock Purchase Agreement

6. Galaxy International Corporation Secretary's Certificate dated as of June_____, 2004 delivered in accordance with Section 7.2(d) of the Stock Purchase Agreement, including Exhibit A attached thereto.

IV. CORPORATE DOCUMENTS DELIVERED BY TREKKER MARKETING, INC. AND ITS SUBSIDIARIES

1. Trekker Marketing, Inc. certified Articles of Incorporation and Good Standing, Certificate both issued by the California Secretary of State on June _____, 2004 and Tax Status Letter issued by the California Franchise Tax Board on June _____, 2004.

2. El Segundo Rat, Inc. certified Articles of Incorporation and Good Standing Certificate both issued by the California Secretary of State on June _____, 2004 and Tax Status letter issued by the California Franchise Tax Board on June _____, 2004.

3. Skateboard World Industries Inc. certified Articles of Incorporation and Good Standing Certificate both issued by the California Secretary of State on June _____, 2004 and Tax Status Letter issued by the California Franchise Tax Board on June_____, 2004.

4. Trekker Asia Limited Memorandum of Articles of Association and Certificate of Continuing Registration issued by the Register of Companies of Hong Kong on June _____, 2004.

5. Resignations of J.B. Hubble, Stanley Rockledge, Fred Merlin, Andrew Norton and Linda Swine as Directors of Trekker Marketing, Inc. effective as of June _____, 2004.

6. Resignations of Fred Merlin, Stanley Rockledge, Linda Swine, J.B. Hubble and Andrew Norton as Directors of El Segando Hat, Inc. effective as of June _____, 2004.

7. Resignations of Fred Merlin and Stanley Rockledge as Directors of Skateboard World Industries, Inc. effective as of June _____, 2004.

V. LEGAL OPINIONS

1. Opinion letter of Klever & Coolidge dated June _____, 2004, including Trekker Marketing, Inc Support Certificate, with exhibits attached thereto.

2. Opinion letter of Bigar, Strong & Wise, P.C., dated June _____, 2004.

VI. DOCUMENTS DELIVERED IN CONNECTION WITH THE SUBORDINATED NOTE EXCHANGE AGREEMENT

1. Subordinated Note Exchange Agreement dated as of June _____, 2004 by and among the Note Holders named therein and Trekker Marketing, Inc.
2. Consent and Amendment No. 1 to the Loan. Guaranty and Security Agreement dated as of June _____, 2004 by and among Comenca Bank-California, Trekker Marketing, Inc. and its subsidiaries named therein.
3. Amendment No. 1 to Intercreditor and Subordination Agreement dated as of July 2, 2002 by and among Trekker Marketing, Inc. and its subsidiaries named therein, Comerica Bank-California and the holders of the Subordinated Notes.
4. Wire Transfer instructions for Sub Note Holders payout of $XX pursuant to Section 1.3(e) of the Stock Purchase Agreement.
5. Copies of the "canceled" Senior Subordinated Notes issued to the following individuals in the amounts indicated:

[List Omitted]

6. Guaranty of Galaxy International Corporation to each of the holders of the Subordinated Notes dated June _____, 2004.

VII. SECURITIES FILINGS OF GALAXY INTERNATIONAL CORPORATION AND GALAXY INTERNATIONAL CORP.

1. Form D — Notice of Sale of Securities Pursuant to Regulation D, Section 4(6) and or the Uniform Limited Offering Exemption filed by Galaxy International Corporation with the Securities and Exchange Commission and the California Commissioner of Corporations on June _____, 2004 in connection with the issuance of the Common Stock.

|G|
Fairness Opinions

- Lazard's Fairness Opinion – Annex B to Pfizer/Pharmacia Form S-4
- Bear Stearns Fairness Opinion – Annex C to Pfizer/Pharmacia Form S-4
- Goldman Sachs Fairness Opinion – Annex D to Pfizer/Pharmacia Form S-4

Lazard's Fairness Opinion

LAZARD

July 13, 2002

The Board of Directors
Pfizer Inc.
235 East 42nd Street
New York, N.Y. 10017

Dear Members of the Board:

We understand that Pfizer Inc. ("Pfizer") and Pharmacia Corporation (the "Subject Company") propose to enter into an Agreement and Plan of Merger, dated as of July 13, 2002 (the "Agreement"), pursuant to which Pfizer will acquire the Subject Company in a transaction (the "Merger") in which each issued and outstanding share of the Subject Company's common stock will be converted into the right to receive 1.40 shares (the "Exchange Ratio") of Pfizer's common stock. In addition, each issued and outstanding share of the Subject Company's Series B Convertible Perpetual Preferred Stock will be converted into the right to receive one share of Series A Convertible Perpetual Preferred Stock of Pfizer. We also understand that the Subject Company intends to dispose of its interests in Monsanto Company ("Monsanto") and that the consummation of the Merger is conditioned on the completion of such disposition (the "Monsanto Disposition"). The terms and conditions of the Merger are more fully set forth in the Agreement.

You have requested our opinion as to the fairness to Pfizer, from a financial point of view, of the Exchange Ratio as of the date hereof. In connection with this opinion, we have:

 (i) Reviewed the financial terms and conditions of the Agreement and the Certificate of Designations for Series A Convertible Perpetual Preferred Stock of Pfizer;

 (ii) Analyzed certain historical publicly available business and financial information relating to Pfizer and the Subject Company;

 (iii) Reviewed various financial forecasts and other data provided to us by Pfizer and the Subject Company relating to their respective businesses;

 (iv) Reviewed the synergistic savings and benefits and the timing of their occurrence as projected by Pfizer to be realized by the combined entity in connection with the Merger;

 (v) Held discussions with members of the senior managements of Pfizer and the Subject Company with respect to the business and prospects of Pfizer and the Subject Company, respectively, the strategic objectives of each and the possible benefits that might be realized following the Merger as projected by Pfizer;

(vi)   Reviewed public information with respect to certain other companies in lines of businesses we believe to be generally comparable to the businesses of Pfizer and the Subject Company;

(vii)   Reviewed the financial terms of certain significant business combinations involving companies in lines of businesses we believe to be generally comparable to those of Pfizer and the Subject Company;

(viii)   Reviewed the historical trading prices and trading volumes of Pfizer's, the Subject Company's and Monsanto's common stock;

(ix)   Reviewed the pro forma financial results, financial condition and capitalization of Pfizer giving effect to the Merger provided to us by the management of Pfizer, and

(x)   Conducted such other financial studies, analyses and investigations as we deemed appropriate.

We have relied upon the accuracy and completeness of the foregoing information. We have not assumed any responsibility for any independent verification of such information or any independent valuation or appraisal of any of the assets and liabilities of Pfizer or the Subject Company, or concerning the solvency of or issues relating to solvency concerning either of the foregoing entities. With respect to financial forecasts, including the synergistic savings and benefits projected by Pfizer to be realized following the Merger, and the timing thereof, we have assumed that they have been reasonably prepared on bases reflecting the best currently available estimates and judgments of the managements of Pfizer and of the Subject Company as to the future financial performance of Pfizer and the Subject Company, respectively, and of Pfizer with respect to the combined entity. We assume no responsibility for and express no view as to such forecasts or the assumptions on which they are based.

Further, our opinion is necessarily based on economic, monetary, market and other conditions as in effect on, and the information made available to us as of, the date hereof. We assume no responsibility for updating or revising our opinion based on circumstances or events occurring after the date hereof.

In rendering our opinion, we have assumed that the Merger will be consummated on the terms and subject to the conditions described in the Agreement without any waiver or modification of any material terms or conditions by Pfizer, that obtaining the necessary regulatory approvals for the Merger will not have an adverse effect on Pfizer or the Subject Company and that the synergistic savings and benefits of the Merger projected by the management of Pfizer will be substantially realized both in scope and timing. In addition, we have assumed that (i) the Merger will be accounted for as a tax-free "reorganization" within the meaning of Section 368(a) of the Internal Revenue Code, (ii) the number of outstanding shares of common stock of the Subject Company on a fully diluted basis will not be materially different than as represented in the Agreement and (iii) the other representations and warranties of the Subject Company and Pfizer contained in the Agreement are true and complete.

We do not express any opinion as to the price at which the common stock of Pfizer or the Subject Company may trade subsequent to the announcement of the Merger or as to the price at which the common stock of Pfizer may trade subsequent to the consummation of the Merger. We are also not expressing any opinion as to any aspect of the Monsanto Disposition.

Lazard Fréres & Co. LLC is acting as an investment banker to Pfizer in connection with the Merger and will receive a fee for our services, a substantial portion of which is payable upon the closing of the Merger. We have in the past provided investment banking services to Pfizer for which we have received customary fees. In addition, in the ordinary course of our business, we may actively trade shares of Pfizer's, the Subject Company's and Monsanto's common stock and other securities of Pfizer, the Subject Company and Monsanto for our own account and for the accounts of our customers and, accordingly, may at any time hold a long or short position in such securities.

Our engagement and the opinion expressed herein are for the benefit and use of Pfizer's board of directors. Our opinion does not address the merits of the underlying decision by Pfizer to engage in the Merger and does not constitute a recommendation to any stockholder of Pfizer as to how such stockholder should vote on, or take any other action with respect to, the Merger. It is understood that this letter may not be disclosed or otherwise referred to without our prior consent, except as may otherwise be required by law or by a court of competent jurisdiction.

Based on and subject to the foregoing, we are of the opinion that, as of the date hereof, the Exchange Ratio is fair to Pfizer from a financial point of view.

Very truly yours,

LAZARD FRÈRES & CO. LLC

By:

Steven J. Golub
Managing Director

Bear Stearns Fairness Opinion

ANNEX C

**BEAR
STEARNS**

Bear, Stearns & Co. Inc.
383 Madison Avenue
New York, New York 10179
Tel.212.272.2000
www.bearstearns.com

July 13, 2002

The Board of Directors
Pfizer Inc.
235 East 42nd Street
New York, NY 10017

Ladies and Gentlemen:

We understand that Pfizer Inc. ("Pfizer") and Pharmacia Corporation ("Pharmacia") intend to enter into an Agreement and Plan of Merger, dated as of July 13, 2002 (the "Agreement"), among Pfizer, Pilsner Acquisition Sub Corp., a wholly-owned subsidiary of Pfizer ("Merger Sub"), and Pharmacia pursuant to which Merger Sub will be merged with and into Pharmacia (the "Merger"). We further understand that, at the effective time of the Merger, each issued and outstanding share of common stock, par value $2.00 per share, of Pharmacia ("Pharmacia Common Stock") will be converted into the right to receive 1.4 shares (the "Exchange Ratio") of common stock, par value $0.05 per share, of Pfizer ("Pfizer Common Stock"). In addition, each issued and outstanding share of Series B Convertible Perpetual Preferred Stock, par value $0.01 per share, of Pharmacia will be converted into the right to receive one share of Series A Convertible Perpetual Preferred Stock of Pfizer. We also understand that Pharmacia intends to dispose of its interest in Monsanto Company ("Monsanto") and that the consummation of the Merger is conditioned on the completion of such disposition (the "Monsanto Disposition").

You have asked us to render our opinion as to whether the Exchange Ratio is fair, from a financial point of view, to Pfizer.

In the course of performing our review and analyses for rendering this opinion, we have:

- reviewed the Agreement and the Certificate of Designations for Series A Convertible Perpetual Preferred Stock of Pfizer Inc.;
- reviewed each of Pfizer's and Pharmacia's Annual Reports to Shareholders and Annual Reports on Form 10-K for the years ended

December 31, 1999 through 2001, their respective Quarterly Reports on Form 10-Q for the period ended March 31, 2002 and their Reports on Form 8-K for the three years ended the date hereof;

- reviewed certain operating and financial information provided to us by the senior managements of Pfizer and of Pharmacia relating to Pfizer's and Pharmacia's respective businesses and prospects, including financial projections for Pfizer for the years ending December 31, 2002 through 2004 prepared by the management of Pfizer (the "Pfizer Projections") and for Pharmacia for the years ending December 31, 2002 through 2004 prepared by the management of Pharmacia, assuming the completion of the Monsanto Disposition (the "Pharmacia Projections") (the Pfizer Projections and the Pharmacia Projections collectively referred to herein as the "Projections") and certain other forward-looking information;

- reviewed certain estimates of cost savings and other combination benefits expected to result from the Merger prepared and provided to us by the management of Pfizer (collectively, the "Projected Benefits");

- met with certain members of the senior managements of Pfizer and of Pharmacia and Pharmacia's advisors to discuss (i) the current business landscape and competitive dynamics related to the markets in which Pfizer and Pharmacia operate; (ii) each company's business, operations, historical and projected financial results, future prospects and financial condition; (iii) each company's views of the strategic, business, operational and financial rationale for, and expected strategic benefits and other implications of, the Merger; (iv) the Projections and Projected Benefits and (v) certain other assumptions and judgments underlying certain estimates which we deemed relevant to our analysis;

- reviewed the historical prices, valuation parameters and trading volumes of Pfizer Common Stock, Pharmacia Common Stock and the common stock, par value $0.01 per share, of Monsanto;

- reviewed publicly available financial data, stock market performance data and valuation parameters of companies which we deemed generally comparable to Pfizer and Pharmacia or otherwise relevant to our analysis;

- reviewed the terms, to the extent publicly available, of recent mergers and acquisitions of companies which we deemed generally comparable to the Merger or otherwise relevant to our analysis;

- performed discounted cash flow analyses based on the Projections and the Projected Benefits furnished to us;

- reviewed the pro forma financial results, financial condition and capitalization of Pfizer giving effect to the Merger provided to us by the management of Pfizer; and

- conducted such other studies, analyses, inquiries and investigations as we deemed appropriate.

We have relied upon and assumed, without independent verification, the accuracy and completeness of the financial and other information, including, without limitation, the Projections and the Projected Benefits, provided to us by Pfizer and Pharmacia. With respect to the Projections and the Projected

Benefits, we have relied on representations that they have been reasonably prepared on bases reflecting the best currently available estimates and judgments of the senior managements of Pfizer and of Pharmacia as to the expected future performance of Pfizer and Pharmacia, respectively. We have not assumed any responsibility for the independent verification of any such information or of the Projections and the Projected Benefits provided to us, and we have further relied upon the assurances of the senior managements of Pfizer and of Pharmacia that they are unaware of any facts that would make the information, the Projections or the Projected Benefits provided to us incomplete or misleading.

In arriving at our opinion, we have not performed or obtained any independent appraisal of the assets or liabilities (contingent or otherwise) of Pfizer or Pharmacia, nor have we been furnished with any such appraisals. We have assumed that the Merger will qualify as a tax-free "reorganization" within the meaning of Section 368(a) of the Internal Revenue Code. We have assumed that the Merger will be consummated in a timely manner and in accordance with the terms and conditions of the Agreement without any limitations, restrictions, conditions, waivers, amendments or modifications, regulatory or otherwise, that collectively would have a material effect on Pfizer or Pharmacia.

We do not express any opinion as to the price or range of prices at which Pfizer Common Stock or Pharmacia Common Stock may trade subsequent to the announcement of the Merger or as to the price or range of prices at which Pfizer Common Stock may trade subsequent to the consummation of the Merger. We are also not expressing any opinion as to any aspect of the Monsanto Disposition.

We have acted as a financial advisor to Pfizer in connection with the Merger and will receive a customary fee for such services, a substantial portion of which is contingent on successful consummation of the Merger. Bear Stearns has been previously engaged by Pharmacia to provide certain investment banking and financial advisory services in connection with actual and prospective merger, acquisition and divestiture transactions as well as certain capital raising transactions, for which we received customary compensation. In the ordinary course of business, Bear Stearns and its affiliates may actively trade the equity and debt securities and/or bank debt of Pfizer, Pharmacia and/or Monsanto for our own account and for the account of our customers and, accordingly, may at any time hold a long or short position in such securities or bank debt.

It is understood that this letter is intended for the benefit and use of the Board of Directors of Pfizer and does not constitute a recommendation to the Board of Directors of Pfizer or any holders of Pfizer Common Stock as to how to vote in connection with the Merger. This opinion does not address Pfizer's underlying business decision to pursue the Merger, the relative merits of the Merger as compared to any alternative business strategies that might exist for Pfizer or the effects of any other transaction in which Pfizer might engage. This letter is not to be used for any other purpose, or be reproduced, disseminated, quoted from or referred to at any time, in whole or in part, without our prior written consent; provided, however, that this letter may be included in its entirety in any joint proxy statement/prospectus to be distributed to the holders of Pfizer Common Stock in connection with the Merger. Our opinion is subject to the assumptions and conditions contained herein and is necessarily based on economic, market and other conditions, and the information made available to us, as of the date hereof. We assume no responsibility for updating or revising our opinion based on circumstances or events occurring after the date hereof.

Based on and subject to the foregoing, it is our opinion that, as of the date hereof, the Exchange Ratio is fair, from a financial point of view, to Pfizer.

Very truly yours,

BEAR, STEARNS & CO. INC.

By: _____
President

Goldman Sachs Fairness Opinion

Goldman, Sachs & Co.
85 Broad Street, New York, New York 10004
Tel: 212-902-1000

Goldman
Sachs

July 13, 2002

Board of Directors
Pharmacia Corporation
100 Route 206 North
Pcapack, NJ 07977

Ladies and Gentlemen:

You have requested our opinion as to the fairness from a financial point of view to the holders of the outstanding shares of common stock, par value $2.00 per share ("Company Common Stock"), of Pharmacia Corporation (the "Company") of the exchange ratio of 1.40 shares of common stock, par value $0.05 per share ("Pfizer Common Stock"), of Pfizer Inc. ("Pfizer") to be received for each share of Company Common Stock (the "Exchange Ratio") pursuant to the Agreement and Plan of Merger, dated as of July 13, 2002 (the "Agreement"), among Pfizer, Pilsner Acquisition Sub Corp. and the Company.

Goldman, Sachs & Co., as part of its investment banking business, is continually engaged in performing financial analyses with respect to businesses and their securities in conncction with mergers and acquisitions, negotiated underwritings, competitive biddings, secondary distributions of listed and unlisted securities and private placements and for estate, corporate and other purposes. We are familiar with the Company, having provided certain investment banking services to the Company from time to time, including having acted as its financial advisor in connection with the sale of its 45% stake in Amersham Biosciences to Amersham plc in March 2002 for one billion dollars, having acted as lead manager of the initial public offering of 35,000,000 shares of the common stock of its then wholly-owned subsidiary, Monsanto Company, in October, 2000, and having acted as its financial advisor in connection with, and having participated in certain of the negotiations leading to, the

Agreement. We also are currently advising the Company on the proposed spin-off of its approximate 85% interest in Monsanto Company to its shareholders (the "Spin-off"). We may also provide investment banking services to Pfizer and its subsidiaries in the future. Goldman, Sachs & Co. provides a full range of financial advisory and securities services and, in the course of normal trading activities, may from time to time effect transactions and hold securities, including derivative securities, of the Company or Pfizer for its own account and for the account of its customers.

In connection with this opinion, we have reviewed, among other things, the Agreement; Annual Reports to Stockholders and Annual Reports on Form 10-K of the Company and Pfizer for each of the five years ended December 31, 2001; certain interim reports to stockholders and Quarterly Reports on Form 10-Q of the Company and Pfizer; certain other communications from the Company and Pfizer to their respective stockholders; and certain internal financial analyses and forecasts for the Company and Pfizer prepared by their respective managements, including certain cost savings and operating synergies expected to result from the transaction contemplated by the Agreement (the "Synergies"). We also have held discussions with members of the senior management of the Company and Pfizer regarding their assessments of the strategic rationale for, and the potential benefits of, the transaction contemplated by the Agreement and the past and current business operations, financial condition and future prospects of their respective companies. In addition, we have reviewed the reported price and trading activity for the Company Common Stock and the Pfizer Common Stock, compared certain financial and stock market information for the Company and Pfizer with similar information for certain other companies the securities of which are publicly traded, reviewed the financial terms of certain recent business combinations in the pharmaceutical industry specifically and in other industries generally and performed such other studies and analyses as we considered appropriate.

We have relied upon the accuracy and completeness of all of the financial, accounting and other information discussed with or reviewed by us and have assumed such accuracy and completeness for purposes of rendering this opinion. In that regard, we have assumed with your consent that the internal financial forecasts prepared by the respective managements of the Company and Pfizer, including the Synergies, have been reasonably prepared on a basis reflecting the best currently available estimates and judgments of the Company and Pfizer. In addition, we have not made an independent evaluation or appraisal of the assets and liabilities of the Company or Pfizer or any of their respective subsidiaries and we have not been furnished with any such evaluation or appraisal. We also have assumed that all material governmental, regulatory or other consents and approvals necessary for the consummation of the transaction contemplated by the Agreement will be obtained without any meaningful adverse effect on the Company or Pfizer or on the expected benefits of the transaction contemplated by the Agreement. In addition, we have assumed that the Spin-off will be completed prior to the closing of the merger contemplated by the Agreement. Our advisory services and the opinion expressed herein are provided for the information and assistance of the Board of Directors of the Company in connection with its consideration of the transaction contemplated by the Agreement and such opinion does not constitute a recommendation as to how any holder of Company Common Stock should vote with respect to such transaction.

Based upon and subject to the foregoing and based upon such other matters as we consider relevant, it is our opinion that, as of the date hereof, the Exchange Ratio pursuant to the Agreement is fair from a financial point of view to the holders of Company Common Stock.

Very truly yours,

(GOLDMAN, SACHS & CO.)

Table of Cases

Principal cases are indicated by italics.

Index